JUSTICE STATISTICS

JUSTICE STATISTICS

AN EXTENDED LOOK AT CRIME IN THE UNITED STATES

Sixth Edition
2021

Edited by
Shana Hertz Hattis

Lanham • Boulder • New York • London

Published by Bernan Press
An imprint of The Rowman & Littlefield Publishing Group, Inc.
4501 Forbes Boulevard, Suite 200, Lanham, Maryland 20706
www.rowman.com
800-462-6420

86-90 Paul Street, London, EC2A 4NE

ISBN: 978-1-63671-040-2
eISBN: 978-1-63671-041-9

∞™ The paper used in this publication meets the minimum requirements of American National Standard for Information Sciences—Permanence of Paper for Printed Library Materials, ANSI/NISO Z39.48-1992.

Printed in the United States of America

Contents

Contents

v

Part 4. Federal Justice Statistics, 2017–2018

Part 5. Hate Crime Statistics, 2019

Part 6. Indicators of School Crime and Safety, 2019

INTRODUCTION

Bernan Press is pleased to present the sixth edition of its comprehensive collection of justice statistics in the United States. This volume provides a fresh look at the valuable information compiled by the Department of Justice, including its subsidiaries, the Bureau of Justice Statistics (BJS) and the Federal Bureau of Investigation (FBI).

The book brings together 12 key reports that fall under the general topic of "justice". Topics covered include criminal victimization, identity theft, crime in the United States, hate crimes, probation, parole, school violence, and law enforcement officers killed and assaulted. Tables in this volume provide a comprehensive account of each of these subjects; for more information, including full-scope methodologies and information about standard errors for each table, please see the full reports at the URLs listed below.

Each section contains statistical tables and figures highlighting the data, as well as a brief summary of the report's methodology and at-a-glance highlights of the most compelling information.

The reports:

Capital Punishment, 2019 discusses both prisoners on Death Row in the United States and prisoners executed in the applicable year. It can be found at https://bjs.ojp.gov/sites/g/files/xyckuh236/files/media/document/cp19st.pdf.

Crime in the United States, 2019, provides an introduction to overall crime trends. This report is more fully presented in Bernan Press's companion volume, *Crime in the United States.* However, given the importance of this data in the understanding of justice and crime trends in the United States, its most relevant tables have been included in this volume. Also appearing in this book, and not contained in the complementary *Crime* volume, is the full rang of the UCR's expanded offense tables. Additional material is provided from three supplementary reports: *Federal Crime Data, Human Trafficking,* and *Cargo Theft.* The full report can be accessed at https://ucr.fbi.gov/crime-in-the-u.s/2019/crime-in-the-u.s.-2019.

Criminal Victimization, 2019, takes a close look at the victims of violent and property crime in the United States. The full report is accessible at https://bjs.ojp.gov/content/pub/pdf/cv19.pdf.

Federal Justice Statistics, 2017–2018, returns with an updated report to this volume. It describes the activities, workloads, and outcomes of the federal judicial system from arrest to conviction and imprisonment. It can be found at https://bjs.ojp.gov/library/publications/federal-justice-statistics-2017-2018.

Hate Crime Statistics, 2019, details the hate crimes committed in the United States throughout the year. It can be accessed at https://ucr.fbi.gov/hate-crime/2019.

Indicators of School Crime and Safety, 2019 is an annual report that presents data on crime and safety at school from the perspectives of students, teachers, and principals. Conducted jointly by the Bureau of Justice Statistics and the National Center for Education Statistics, the report's data sources include the National Crime Victimization Survey (NCVS), the School Crime Supplement to the NCVS, the Youth Risk Behavior Survey, and the School Survey on Crime and Safety. The full report can be accessed at https://nces.ed.gov/pubsearch/pubsinfo.asp?pubid=2020063.

Jail Inmates in 2019, presents estimates of the inmate populations of jails based on various demographic characteristics. The full report can be accessed at https://bjs.ojp.gov/content/pub/pdf/ji19.pdf.

Law Enforcement Officers Killed and Assaulted, 2019 (LEOKA), is the primary resource for data about harm done to law enforcement officers. This volume provides a comprehensive sample of the report; further information can be obtained at https://ucr.fbi.gov/leoka/2019.

Probation and Parole in the United States, 2017–2018, details data about post-release inmates still in the legal system. The report can be accessed at https://bjs.ojp.gov/content/pub/pdf/ppus1718.pdf.

Update on Prisoner Recidivism: A 9-Year Follow-up Period (2005-2014) is expanded in this edition. It examines the rate, number, and percentage of prisoners who were arrested at least once during the nine years following their release. It can be found at https://www.bjs.gov/content/pub/pdf/18upr9yfup0514.pdf.

Victims of Identity Theft, 2018, analyses the ramifications of identity theft from judicial, financial, and relational persepctives. The full report can be found at https://bjs.ojp.gov/library/publications/victims-identity-theft-2018.

Preliminary data regarding the impact of the COVID-19 pandemic on prisoners can be found in Appendix B. This data is derived from a March 2021 report from the Bureau of Justice Statistics and can be found at https://bjs.ojp.gov/content/pub/pdf/icljpjj20.pdf.

ABOUT THE EDITOR

Shana Hertz Hattis is an editor with over a decade of experience in statistical and government research publications. Past titles include *State Profiles: The Population and Economy of Each U.S. State, Crime in the United States,* and *The Almanac of American Education.* She earned her bachelor of science in journalism and master of science in education degrees from Northwestern University.

PART 1

Capital Punishment, 2019

HIGHLIGHTS

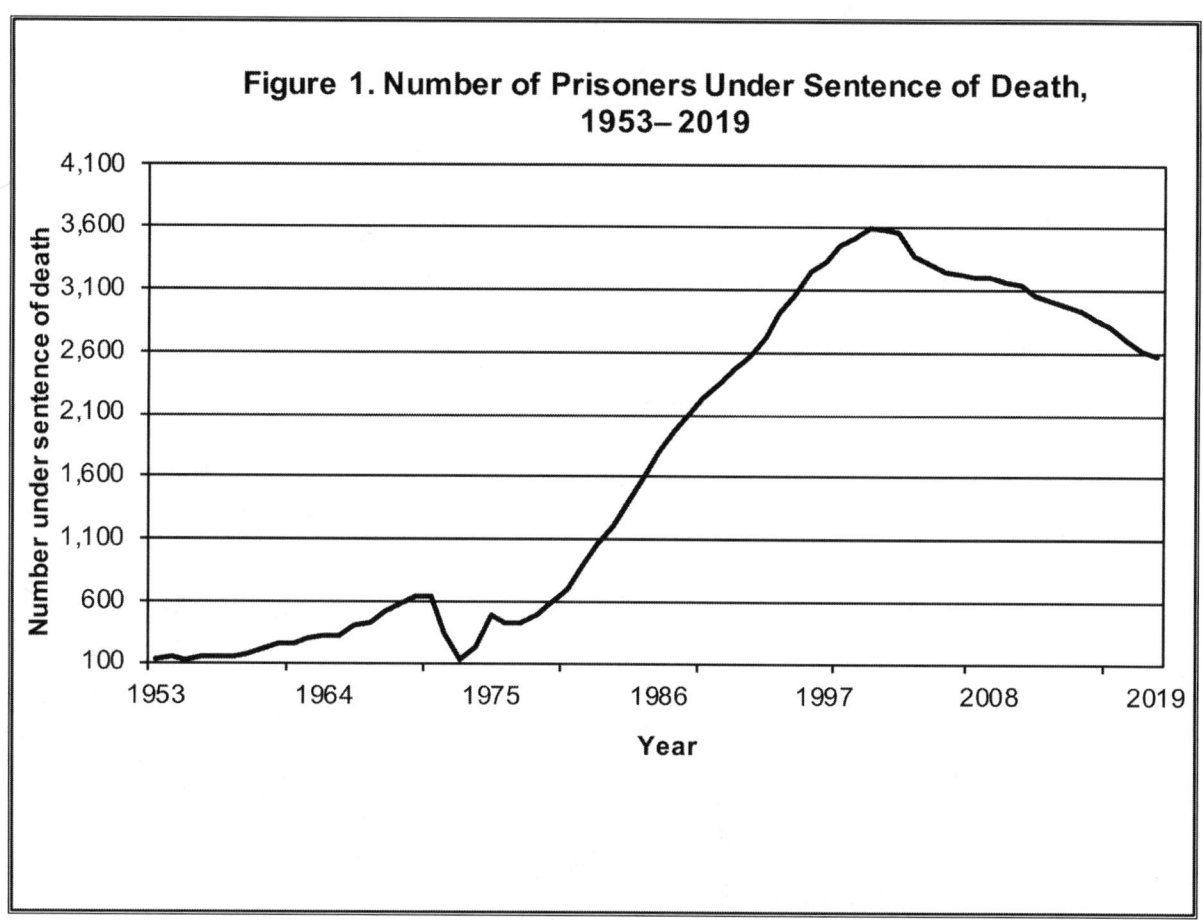

Figure 1. Number of Prisoners Under Sentence of Death, 1953–2019

- At yearend 2019, 32 states and Federal Bureau of Prisons (BOP) held 2,570 prisoners under sentence of death, 56 persons (2 percent) fewer than at yearend 2018. This was the 19th consecutive year in which this number has decreased.

- Twenty-two prisoners were executed in the United States in 2019; 14 were White and 7 were Black. One prisoner was of Hispanic/Latino origin. These prisoners had been on death row for an average of 22 years.

- The number of prisoners executed in 2019 represented the smallest number of executions since 1991, when 14 prisoners were executed.

- The largest decline in the number of prisoners under sentence of death in 2019 occurred in California (down 11 prisoners), followed by Pennsylvania (down 8 prisoners), Texas (down 7 prisoners), and Tennessee (down 6 prisoners), while 3 states held more prisoners (North Carolina [up

3 prisoners], Ohio [up 2 prisoners], and South Carolina [up 1 prisoner]).

- Approximately 56 percent of prisoners under sentence of death at yearend 2019 were White, while approximately 41 percent were Black and approximately 15 percent of were of Hispanic or Latino origin (in cases in which origin was known).

- Approximately 98 percent of prisoners under sentence of death were male.

- Nearly half of prisoners held under sentence of death were located in California (28.1 percent), Florida (13.2 percent), and Texas (8.4 percent). In 2019, Texas executed 9 prisoners; Florida, 2 prisoners; and California, no prisoners.

- Eleven states and the BOP received a total of 31 prisoners under sentence of death in 2019; 21 states and the BOP removed 65 prisoners from under sentence of death by means other than execution.

Table 1. Status of the Death Penalty, December 31, 2019

(Number.)

State	Executions in 2019	Number of prisoners under sentence of death
Total	22	2,570
Alabama...	3	175
Arizona..	0	116
Arkansas..	0	30
California...	0	724
Colorado	0	3
Delaware..	0	0
Federal Bureau of Prisons..	0	61
Florida	2	340
Georgia	3	46
Idaho...	0	9
Indiana..	0	8
Kansas...	0	10
Kentucky	0	27
Louisiana	0	68
Mississippi...	0	40
Missouri...	1	22
Montana..	0	2
Nebraska...	0	12
Nevada	0	71
New Hampshire	0	1
New York	0	0
North Carolina...	0	143
Ohio..	0	139
Oklahoma..	0	46
Oregon..	0	29
Pennsylvania	0	134
South Carolina...	0	36
South Dakota...	1	1
Tennessee..	3	52
Texas...	9	216
Utah..	0	7
Virginia..	0	2
Washington..	0	0
Wyoming...	0	0

NOTE: Jurisdictions without the death penalty in 2019 include Alaska, Connecticut, District of Columbia, Hawaii, Illinois, Iowa, Maine, Maryland, Massachusetts, Michigan, Minnesota, New Hampshire, New Jersey, New Mexico, North Dakota, Rhode Island, Vermont, West Virginia, and Wisconsin. While the Washington Supreme Court has declared the state's death penalty statute unconstitutional as applied (State v. Gregory, 192 Wash. 2d 1, 427 P.3d 621 (2018)), no legislative action has been taken to revise or repeal the statute. The state continues to report that the death penalty is authorized. New Hampshire repealed its death penalty statute, efective May 30, 2019. As of December 31, 2019, one male prisoner remained under a previously imposed sentence of death. New York, Delaware, Washington, and Wyoming held no inmates under sentence of death on December 31, 2019.

Table 2. Prisoners Under Sentence of Death, by Region, Jurisdiction, and Race, 2018 and 2019

(Number.)

Region and jurisdiction	Prisoners under sentence of death, 12/31/18			Received under sentence of death, 2019			Removed from death row (excluding executions), 2019[1]			Executed, 2019			Prisoners under sentence of death, 12/31/19		
	Total[2]	White[3]	Black[3]	Total[2]	White[3]	Black[3]	Total[2]	White[3]	Black[3]	Total[2]	White[3]	Black[3]	Total[2]	White[3]	Black[3]
U.S. Total............................	2,626	1,470	1,091	31	20	11	65	32	31	22	15	7	2,570	1,443	1,064
Federal[4]	61	35	25	1	0	1	1	0	1	0	0	0	61	35	25
State....................................	2,565	1,435	1,066	30	20	10	64	32	30	22	15	7	2,509	1,408	1,039
Northeast............................	143	65	75	1	1	0	9	2	6	0	0	0	135	64	69
New Hampshire	1	0	1	0	0	0	0	0	0	0	0	0	1	0	1
New York	0	0	0	0	0	0	0	0	0	0	0	0	0	0	0
Pennsylvania	142	65	74	1	1	0	9	2	6	0	0	0	134	64	68
Midwest..............................	195	101	93	6	3	3	7	5	2	2	2	0	192	97	94
Indiana	9	7	2	0	0	0	1	1	0	0	0	0	8	6	2
Kansas..................................	10	7	3	0	0	0	0	0	0	0	0	0	10	7	3
Missouri................................	25	18	7	0	0	0	2	2	0	1	1	0	22	15	7
Nebraska...............................	12	9	3	0	0	0	0	0	0	0	0	0	12	9	3
Ohio.....................................	137	58	78	6	3	3	4	2	2	0	0	0	139	59	79
South Dakota........................	2	2	0	0	0	0	0	0	0	1	1	0	1	1	0
South..................................	1,248	652	578	21	14	7	28	10	17	20	13	7	1,221	643	561
Alabama................................	176	88	88	3	2	1	1	0	1	3	2	1	175	88	87
Arkansas...............................	31	16	15	0	0	0	1	1	0	0	0	0	30	15	15
Delaware...............................	0	0	0	0	0	0	0	0	0	0	0	0	0	0	0
Florida	344	215	128	6	5	1	8	5	2	2	2	0	340	213	127
Georgia	50	23	27	1	0	1	2	0	2	3	0	3	46	23	23
Kentucky	30	25	5	0	0	0	3	1	2	0	0	0	27	24	3
Louisiana	69	23	46	0	0	0	1	0	1	0	0	0	68	23	45
Mississippi.............................	43	18	24	0	0	0	3	1	2	0	0	0	40	17	22
North Carolina.......................	140	56	77	3	2	1	0	0	0	0	0	0	143	58	78
Oklahoma..............................	47	22	21	1	0	1	2	0	2	0	0	0	46	22	20
South Carolina.......................	35	16	19	2	1	1	1	0	1	0	0	0	36	17	19
Tennessee..............................	58	29	28	0	0	0	3	1	2	3	3	0	52	25	26
Texas	223	121	98	5	4	1	3	1	2	9	6	3	216	118	94
Virginia	2	0	2	0	0	0	0	0	0	0	0	0	2	0	2
West....................................	979	617	320	2	2	0	20	15	5	0	0	0	961	604	315
Arizona.................................	116	89	20	1	1	0	1	1	0	0	0	0	116	89	20
California...............................	735	436	268	1	1	0	12	8	4	0	0	0	724	429	264
Colorado	3	0	3	0	0	0	0	0	0	0	0	0	3	0	3
Idaho....................................	9	9	0	0	0	0	0	0	0	0	0	0	9	9	0
Montana................................	2	2	0	0	0	0	0	0	0	0	0	0	2	2	0
Nevada	74	46	26	0	0	0	3	2	1	0	0	0	71	44	25
New Mexico...........................	2	2	0	0	0	0	2	2	0	0	0	0	0	0	0
Oregon..................................	30	27	2	0	0	0	1	1	0	0	0	0	29	26	2
Utah.....................................	8	6	1	0	0	0	1	1	0	0	0	0	7	5	1
Washington	0	0	0	0	0	0	0	0	0	0	0	0	0	0	0
Wyoming...............................	0	0	0	0	0	0	0	0	0	0	0	0	0	0	0

NOTE: Some counts for year-end 2018 are revised from those reported in Capital Punishment, 2018 ñ Statistical Tables (NCJ 254786, BJS, September 2020). The revised counts include 3 prisoners who were either reported late to the National Prisoner Statistics program or were not in the custody of state correctional authorities on December 31, 2018 (1 each in the Nebraska, Tennessee, and Nevada). The revised counts exclude 5 prisoners who were relieved of a death sentence before December 31, 2018 (2 in Nevada and 1 each in Pennsylvania, Indiana, and California).
[1]Includes 15 deaths from natural causes (6 in California, 2 in Mississippi, and 1 each in Ohio, Florida, Oklahoma, Tennessee, Texas, Arizona, and Utah), 2†deaths by suicide (1 each in California and Nevada), and 3 deaths resulting from acute drug toxicity (2 in California and 1 in Oklahoma).
[2]Includes American Indians or Alaska Natives and Asians, Native Hawaiians, or Other Pacific Islanders.
[3]Includes persons of Hispanic origin.
[4]Excludes persons held under the jurisdiction of the U.S. Armed Forces with a military death sentence for murder.

Table 3. Prisoners Removed from Under Sentence of Death, by Region, Jurisdiction, and Method of Removal, 2019

(Number.)

Region and jurisdiction	Not overturned by appeals court or higher court				Overturned by appeals court or higher court		
	Total	Execution	Other death¹	Sentence commuted	Capital statute	Capital conviction	Death sentence
U.S. Total	87	22	20	2	2	19	22
Federal	1	0	0	0	0	0	1
State	86	22	20	2	2	19	21
Northeast	9	0	0	0	0	1	8
Pennsylvania	9	0	0	0	0	1	8
Midwest	9	2	1	0	0	1	5
Indiana	1	0	0	0	0	0	1
Missouri	3	1	0	0	0	0	2
Ohio	4	0	1	0	0	1	2
South Dakota	1	1	0	0	0	0	0
South	48	20	7	2	0	14	5
Alabama	4	3	0	0	0	1	0
Arkansas	1	0	0	0	0	1	0
Florida	10	2	1	0	0	7	0
Georgia	5	3	0	0	0	0	2
Kentucky	3	0	0	2	0	1	0
Louisiana	1	0	0	0	0	0	1
Mississippi	3	0	2	0	0	1	0
Oklahoma	2	0	2	0	0	0	0
South Carolina	1	0	0	0	0	1	0
Tennessee	6	3	1	0	0	1	1
Texas	12	9	1	0	0	1	1
West	20	0	12	0	2	3	3
Arizona	1	0	1	0	0	0	0
California	12	0	9	0	0	1	2
Nevada	3	0	1	0	0	1	1
New Mexico	2	0	0	0	2	0	0
Oregon	1	0	0	0	0	1	0
Utah	1	0	1	0	0	0	0

¹In 2019, other deaths were due to natural causes, suicide, and acute drug toxicity.

Table 4. Demographic Characteristics for Prisoners Under Sentence of Death, 2019

(Number; percent; years; grade level.)

Characteristic	Total yearend	Admissions	Removals
Total (number)..	2,570	31	87
Sex (percent)			
Male...	98.0	96.8	98.9
Female...	2.0	3.2	1.1
Race (percent)			
White[1]	56.1	64.5	54.0
Black[1]	41.4	35.5	43.7
American Indian/Alaska Native[1]	0.8	0.0	0.0
Asian/Native Hawaiian/Other Pacific Islander[1,2]	1.6	0.0	2.3
Ethnicity (percent)[3]			
Hispanic/Latino	15.1	11.1	10.3
Non-Hispanic/Latino...................................	84.9	88.9	89.7
Age (percent)			
18 to 19 years..	0.0	0.0	0.0
20 to 24 years..	0.1	0.0	0.0
25 to 29 years..	1.4	19.4	0.0
30 to 34 years..	4.7	22.6	1.1
35 to 39 years..	8.4	32.3	8.0
40 to 44 years..	13.7	9.7	10.3
45 to 49 years..	16.8	9.7	25.3
50 to 54 years..	16.5	3.2	12.6
55 to 59 years..	15.9	3.2	12.6
60 to 64 years..	11.3	0.0	9.2
65 years and older......................................	11.1	0.0	20.7
Average Age (years)			
Mean..	51	36	54
Median..	51	36	52
Education (percent)[4]			
8th grade or less...	11.8	31.3	17.1
9th to 11th grade	34.8	18.8	27.6
High school graduate/GED	44.3	37.5	43.4
Any college...	9.1	12.5	11.8
Median Education Level			
Grade..	12th	12th	12th
Marital Status (percent)[5]			
Married	21.3	22.2	22.5
Divorced/separated......................................	19.6	27.8	17.5
Widowed	3.6	0	3.8
Never married	55.5	50	56.3

NOTE: Percentages are based on prisoners for whom data were reported. Details may not sum to totals due to rounding.
[1]Includes persons of Hispanic origin.
[2]Includes 36 Asians and 6 Native Hawaiians or Other Pacific Islanders at year-end 2019. Two Asian prisoners were removed during 2019.
[3]Excludes 232 prisoners from total year-end, 4 admissions, and 9 removals because ethnicity was unknown.
[4]Excludes 547 prisoners from total year-end, 15 admissions, and 11 removals because education level was unknown.
[5]Excludes 376 prisoners from total year-end, 13 admissions, and 7 removals because marital status was unknown.

Table 5. Advance Count of Executions, January 1, 2020–December 31, 2020

(Number.)

Year	Number of executions
Total	17
Federal...	10
Texas...	3
Alabama..	1
Georgia	1
Missouri..	1
Tennessee..	1

Table 6. Authorized Method of Execution, by State, 2019

(Percent; number.)

State	Lethal injection[1]	Electrocution	Lethal gas	Hanging[1]	Firing squad	Nitrogen hypoxia
Total	32	9	3	2	3	3
Alabama...	√	√				√
Arizona[2]...	√		√			
Arkansas[3]...	√	√				
California[4]..	√					
Colorado	√					
Delaware[5]...	√			√		
Florida	√	√				
Georgia	√					
Idaho..	√					
Indiana	√					
Kansas	√					
Kentucky[6]	√	√				
Louisiana	√					
Mississippi[7]	√	√			√	√
Missouri...	√		√			
Montana...	√					
Nebraska	√					
Nevada	√					
New York	√					
North Carolina	√					
Ohio	√					
Oklahoma[7]..	√	√			√	√
Oregon	√					
Pennsylvania	√					
South Carolina	√	√				
South Dakota[8]	√					
Tennessee[9]..	√	√				
Texas..	√					
Utah[10]..	√				√	
Virginia	√	√				
Washington	√			√		
Wyoming[11]	√		√			

NOTE: The method of execution of federal prisoners is lethal injection, pursuant to 28 C.F.R. Part 26. For ofenses prosecuted under the Violent Crime Control and Law Enforcement Act of 1994, the execution method is that of the state in which the conviction took place (18 U.S.C. § 3596).
[1] Counts exclude New Hampshire, which repealed the death penalty efective May 30, 2019. The one male prisoner remaining under sentence of death is subject to execution by lethal injection or by hanging if lethal injection cannot be given.
[2] Authorizes lethal injection for persons sentenced after November 23, 1992. Prisoners sentenced before that date may select lethal injection or gas.
[3] Authorizes lethal injection for persons whose offense occurred on or after July 4, 1983. Prisoners whose ofense occurred before that date may select lethal injection or electrocution. Electrocution is the authorized method if lethal injection is invalidated by an unappealable court order.
[4] Both lethal injection and lethal gas are authorized by statute (Cal. Pen. Code 3604). However, use of lethal gas was invalided by a federal court (Fierro v. Terhune, 147 F.3d 1158, 1160 (9th Cir. 1998)).
[5] Authorizes hanging if lethal injection is held to be unconstitutional by a court of competent jurisdiction.
[6] Authorizes lethal injection for persons sentenced on or after March 31, 1998. Prisoners sentenced before that date may select lethal injection or electrocution.
[7] Authorizes nitrogen hypoxia if lethal injection is held to be unconstitutional, electrocution if both lethal injection and nitrogen hypoxia are held to be unconstitutional, and fring squad if all other methods are held to be unconstitutional.
[8] Any person sentenced to death prior to July 1, 2017, may choose to be executed in the manner provided by South Dakota law at the time of the person's conviction or sentence.
[9] Authorizes lethal injection for persons whose capital ofense occurred after December 31, 1998. Prisoners whose ofense occurred before that date may select electrocution by written waiver. Electrocution is the authorized method if a court or the commissioner of corrections determines that lethal injection cannot be given. If both methods are ruled unconstitutional, state law allows for the use of any method that is constitutional.
[10] Authorizes fring squad if lethal injection is held unconstitutional. Prisoners who selected execution by fring squad prior to May 3, 2004, may still be entitled to execution by that method.
[11] Authorizes lethal gas if lethal injection is held to be unconstitutional.

Table 7. Number of Persons Executed Under Civil Authority in the United States, 1930–2019

(Number.)

Year	Executions
1930	155
1931	153
1932	140
1933	160
1934	168
1935	199
1936	195
1937	147
1938	190
1939	160
1940	124
1941	123
1942	147
1943	131
1944	120
1945	117
1946	131
1947	153
1948	119
1949	119
1950	82
1951	105
1952	83
1953	62
1954	81
1955	76
1956	65
1957	65
1958	49
1959	49
1960	56
1961	42
1962	47
1963	21
1964	15
1965	7
1966	1
1967	2
1968	0
1969	0
1970	0
1971	0
1972	0
1973	0
1974	0

(Number.)

Year	Executions
1975	0
1976	0
1977	1
1978	0
1979	2
1980	0
1981	1
1982	2
1983	5
1984	21
1985	18
1986	18
1987	25
1988	11
1989	16
1990	23
1991	14
1992	31
1993	38
1994	31
1995	56
1996	45
1997	74
1998	68
1999	98
2000	85
2001	66
2002	71
2003	65
2004	59
2005	60
2006	53
2007	42
2008	37
2009	52
2010	46
2011	43
2012	43
2013	39
2014	35
2015	28
2016	20
2017	23
2018	25
2019	22

NOTE: Excludes 160 executions carried out by military authorities from 1930 to 1961.

Table 8. Number of Persons Under Sentence of Death, 1953–2019

(Number.)

Year	Number of prisoners under sentence of death	Year	Number of prisoners under sentence of death
1953	131	1988	2,117
1954	147	1989	2,243
1955	125	1990	2,346
1956	146	1991	2,465
1957	151	1992	2,580
1958	147	1993	2,727
1959	164	1994	2,905
1960	212	1995	3,064
1961	257	1996	3,242
1962	267	1997	3,328
1963	297	1998	3,465
1964	315	1999	3,527
1965	331	2000	3,601
1966	406	2001	3,577
1967	435	2002	3,562
1968	517	2003	3,377
1969	575	2004	3,320
1970	631	2005	3,245
1971	642	2006	3,228
1972	334	2007	3,215
1973	134	2008	3,210
1974	244	2009	3,173
1975	488	2010	3,139
1976	420	2011	3,065
1977	423	2012	3,011
1978	482	2013	2,983
1979	593	2014	2,942
1980	692	2015	2,872
1981	860	2016	2,797
1982	1,066	2017	2,703
1983	1,209	2018	2,626
1984	1,420	2019	2,570
1985	1,575		
1986	1,800		
1987	1,967		

Table 9. Admissions to and Removal from Under Sentence of Death, 1973–2019

(Number.)

Year	Admissions	Removals
1973	44	240
1974	161	55
1975	318	67
1976	249	317
1977	159	156
1978	211	150
1979	172	61
1980	202	101
1981	249	84
1982	287	79
1983	266	123
1984	305	90
1985	291	130
1986	320	109
1987	311	142
1988	317	165
1989	275	149
1990	270	152
1991	285	159
1992	300	173
1993	299	162
1994	330	153
1995	325	171
1996	323	155
1997	283	187
1998	310	174
1999	287	221
2000	235	173
2001	164	194
2002	172	191
2003	156	346
2004	140	198
2005	143	216
2006	125	145
2007	129	140
2008	122	136
2009	118	166
2010	116	143
2011	84	155
2012	85	124
2013	85	118
2014	70	116
2015	54	122
2016	33	99
2017	37	133
2018	41	117
2019	31	87

Table 10. Number of Prisoners Under Sentence of Death, by Race, 1968–2019

(Number.)

Year	White[1]	Black[1]	Other[1,2]
1968	243	271	3
1969	263	310	2
1970	293	335	3
1971	306	332	4
1972	167	166	1
1973	64	68	2
1974	110	128	6
1975	218	262	8
1976	225	195	0
1977	229	192	2
1978	281	197	4
1979	354	236	3
1980	424	264	4
1981	499	353	8
1982	613	441	12
1983	692	505	12
1984	806	598	16
1985	896	664	15
1986	1,013	762	25
1987	1,128	813	26
1988	1,235	848	34
1989	1,308	898	37
1990	1,368	940	38
1991	1,449	979	37
1992	1,511	1,031	38
1993	1,575	1,111	41
1994	1,653	1,203	49
1995	1,732	1,284	48
1996	1,833	1,358	51
1997	1,864	1,408	56
1998	1,917	1,489	59
1999	1,960	1,515	65
2000	1,989	1,541	71
2001	1,968	1,538	71
2002	1,939	1,551	72
2003	1,882	1,417	78
2004	1,856	1,390	74
2005	1,802	1,366	77
2006	1,806	1,353	74
2007	1,806	1,338	71
2008	1,795	1,343	72
2009	1,779	1,318	76
2010	1,743	1,309	87
2011	1,721	1,274	70
2012	1,684	1,258	69
2013	1,670	1,251	62
2014	1,647	1,233	62
2015	1,606	1,202	64
2016	1,553	1,179	65
2017	1,508	1,129	66
2018	1,470	1,091	65
2019	1,443	1,064	63

NOTE: Data on Hispanic origin was not collected prior to 1977.
[1]Includes persons of Hispanic origin.
[2]Includes American Indians or Alaska Natives; Asians, Native Hawaiians, or Other Pacific Islanders; and persons for whom only ethnicity was identified.

Table 11. Female Prisoners Under Sentence of Death, by Region, Jurisdiction, and Race, 2018 and 2019

(Number.)

Region and jurisdiction	Female prisoners under sentence of death, 12/31/18			Received under sentence of death, 2019			Removed from death row, 2019			Female prisoners under sentence of death, 12/31/19		
	Total[1]	White[2]	Black[2]	Total[1]	White[2]	Black[2]	Total[1]	White[2]	Black[2]	Total[1]	White[2]	Black[2]
U.S. Total..........................	52	39	10	1	0	1	1	1	0	52	38	11
Federal.............................	1	1	0	0	0	0	0	0	0	1	1	0
State.................................	51	38	10	1	0	1	1	1	0	51	37	11
Midwest..........................	1	1	0	0	0	0	0	0	0	1	1	0
Ohio..................................	1	1	0	0	0	0	0	0	0	1	1	0
South..............................	22	14	7	1	0	1	0	0	0	23	14	8
Alabama............................	5	4	1	0	0	0	0	0	0	5	4	1
Florida	3	1	2	0	0	0	0	0	0	3	1	2
Georgia	0	0	0	1	0	1	0	0	0	1	0	1
Kentucky	1	1	0	0	0	0	0	0	0	1	1	0
Louisiana	1	0	1	0	0	0	0	0	0	1	0	1
Mississippi........................	1	1	0	0	0	0	0	0	0	1	1	0
North Carolina..................	3	1	1	0	0	0	0	0	0	3	1	1
Oklahoma.........................	1	1	0	0	0	0	0	0	0	1	1	0
Tennessee.........................	1	1	0	0	0	0	0	0	0	1	1	0
Texas	6	4	2	0	0	0	0	0	0	6	4	2
West	28	23	3	0	0	0	1	1	0	27	22	3
Arizona.............................	3	3	0	0	0	0	0	0	0	3	3	0
California..........................	23	18	3	0	0	0	1	1	0	22	17	3
Idaho................................	1	1	0	0	0	0	0	0	0	1	1	0
Oregon	1	1	0	0	0	0	0	0	0	1	1	0

NOTE: Counts of female prisoners under sentence of death at year-end 2018 have been revised from those reported in Capital Punishment, 2018 (NCJ 254786, BJS, September 2020). The revised counts exclude one female prisoner in Indiana who was relieved of a death sentence before December 31, 2018.
[1]Includes American Indians or Alaska Natives and Asians, Native Hawaiians, or Other Pacific Islanders.
[2]Includes persons of Hispanic origin.

Table 12. Hispanic Prisoners Under Sentence of Death, by Region and Jurisdiction, 2018 and 2019

(Number.)

Region and jurisdiction	Hispanic prisoners under sentence of death, 12/31/18	Received under sentence of death, 2019	Removed from death row (excluding executions), 2019	Executed, 2019	Hispanic prisoners under sentence of death, 12/31/19
U.S. Total.............................	359	3	7	1	354
Federal..................................	7	0	0	0	7
State....................................	352	3	7	1	347
Northeast.............................	16	0	2	0	14
Pennsylvania	16	0	2	0	14
Midwest..............................	10	0	0	0	10
Nebraska	6	0	0	0	6
Ohio	4	0	0	0	4
South..................................	96	2	2	1	95
Alabama................................	1	0	0	0	1
Arkansas...............................	1	0	1	0	0
Florida	22	0	0	0	22
Georgia	2	0	0	0	2
Louisiana	2	0	0	0	2
Mississippi.............................	1	0	0	0	1
North Carolina	3	0	0	0	3
Oklahoma..............................	1	0	0	0	1
South Carolina	1	0	0	0	1
Tennessee..............................	1	0	0	0	1
Texas	61	2	1	1	61
West...................................	230	1	3	0	228
Arizona.................................	24	0	0	0	24
California...............................	193	1	2	0	192
Idaho	1	0	0	0	1
Nevada	7	0	1	0	6
Oregon	3	0	0	0	3
Utah	2	0	0	0	2

Table 13. Criminal History of Prisoners Under Sentence of Death, by Race or Ethnicity, 2019

(Percent.)

Characteristic	All prisoners[1]	White[2]	Black[2]	Hispanic
U.S. Total.............................	100.0	100.0	100.0	100.0
Prior Felony Convictions[3].................				
Yes	67.8	64.0	73.1	65.4
No	32.2	36.0	26.9	34.6
Prior Homicide Convictions[4]............				
Yes	9.5	9.4	10.1	9.1
No	90.5	90.6	89.9	90.9
Legal Status at Time of Capital Offense[5].............................				
Charges pending	8.3	9.9	7.6	5.9
Probation..............................	11.3	10.0	11.4	14.2
Parole	16.0	13.7	17.8	17.6
On escape.............................	1.2	1.6	0.9	0.9
Incarcerated..........................	4.4	5.8	3.5	3.4
Other status..........................	0.1	0.0	0.1	0.3
None	58.8	59.0	58.8	57.6

NOTE: Percentages are based on prisoners for whom data were reported. Details may not sum to totals due to rounding.
[1]Includes American Indians or Alaska Natives and Asians, Native Hawaiians, or Other Pacific Islanders.
[2]Excludes persons of Hispanic origin (e.g., White refers to non-Hispanic Whites and Black refers to non-Hispanic Blacks).
[3]Excludes 202 prisoners because data were not reported.
[4]Excludes 33 prisoners because data were not reported.
[5]Excludes 296 prisoners because data were not reported.

Table 14. Prisoners Under Sentence of Death on December 31, 2019, by Year of Sentencing

(Number; years.)

Region and jurisdiction	1976 to 1980	1980 to 1984	1985 to 1988	1989 to 1992	1993 to 1996	1997 to 2000	2001 to 2004	2005 to 2008	2009 to 2012	2013 to 2016	2017	2018	2019	Under sentence of death, 12/31/19	Average years under sentence of death, 12/31/19
U.S. Total........................	21	85	151	244	397	419	288	342	308	208	36	40	31	2,570	18.7
Federal.............................	0	0	0	0	3	5	17	18	7	6	2	2	1	61	13.3
Alabama...........................	0	2	4	10	24	31	19	36	24	17	2	3	3	175	16.2
Arizona............................	1	3	4	12	16	6	10	18	32	7	4	2	1	116	16.4
Arkansas..........................	1	0	0	2	7	3	3	5	2	4	1	2	0	30	16.5
California.........................	5	39	59	94	115	126	59	71	81	61	9	4	1	724	20.4
Colorado	0	0	0	0	1	0	0	1	1	0	0	0	0	3	:
Florida	8	17	20	45	48	51	22	40	44	29	3	7	6	340	19.5
Georgia	0	0	3	3	7	11	4	10	5	2	0	0	1	46	18.4
Idaho...............................	0	0	1	2	3	0	2	1	0	0	0	0	0	9	:
Indiana	0	0	0	0	1	2	1	0	1	3	0	0	0	8	:
Kansas.............................	0	0	0	0	0	0	3	3	2	2	0	0	0	10	11.4
Kentucky	1	4	4	1	3	7	2	3	1	1	0	0	0	27	24.4
Louisiana	0	0	4	4	12	22	8	6	8	3	0	1	0	68	19.2
Mississippi........................	0	1	0	4	6	5	8	3	7	3	1	2	0	40	16.8
Missouri...........................	0	1	2	0	0	0	2	11	2	3	0	1	0	22	14.4
Montana..........................	0	1	0	1	0	0	0	0	0	0	0	0	0	2	:
Nebraska	0	0	0	0	1	0	2	4	2	0	1	2	0	12	11.5
Nevada	1	7	8	3	17	10	3	6	6	5	4	1	0	71	21
New Hampshire	0	0	0	0	0	0	0	1	0	0	0	0	0	1	:
North Carolina	0	0	1	7	51	39	19	13	7	3	0	0	3	143	20.4
Ohio	0	3	14	14	19	19	19	13	13	14	1	4	6	139	18.2
Oklahoma........................	0	0	1	1	3	5	10	14	3	5	2	1	1	46	13.8
Oregon	0	0	0	2	6	7	3	4	7	0	0	0	0	29	17.8
Pennsylvania	0	2	11	15	23	19	15	17	17	11	2	1	1	134	18.9
South Carolina.................	0	2	0	1	2	6	9	11	2	1	0	0	2	36	16.6
South Dakota...................	0	0	0	0	0	0	0	0	1	0	0	0	0	1	:
Tennessee........................	0	2	5	9	8	9	7	3	6	2	0	1	0	52	21.4
Texas	4	1	8	12	20	35	41	28	27	25	4	6	5	216	16
Utah	0	0	2	2	1	1	0	0	0	1	0	0	0	7	:
Virginia............................	0	0	0	0	0	0	0	2	0	0	0	0	0	2	:

NOTE: For persons sentenced to death more than once, counts are based on the year of the most recent death sentence.
: = Not calculated. A reliable average cannot be calculated from fewer than 10 cases.

METHODOLOGY

Capital punishment information is collected annually as part of the Bureau of Justice Statistics' (BJS) National Prisoner Statistics program (NPS-8). This data series is collected in two parts:

- Data on persons under sentence of death are obtained from the department of corrections in each jurisdiction currently authorizing capital punishment.

- The status of death penalty statutes is obtained from the Office of the Attorney General in each of the 50 states, the U.S. Attorney's Office in the District of Columbia, and Federal Bureau of Prisons for the federal government.

Data collection forms are available on the BJS website at www.bjs.gov.

The NPS-8 covers all persons under a state or federal civil sentence of death at any time during the year. This incudes capital offenders transferred from prison to mental hospitals and those who may have escaped from custody. It excludes persons sentenced to death under the Uniform Code of Military Justice and those whose death sentences have been overturned by a court or executive action, regardless of their current incarceration status.

Statistics in this report may differ from data collected by other organizations for various reasons:

- The NPS-8 adds prisoners to the population under sentence of death not at sentencing, but at the time they are admitted to a state or federal correctional facility.

- If prisoners entered prison under a death sentence or were reported as being relieved of a death sentence in one year but the admission or removal had occurred in a previous year, counts are adjusted to reflect the actual dates of sentence or removal.

- NPS-8 counts are for the last day of the calendar year and will differ from counts for more recent periods.

DEFINITIONS

Aggravating factor—Specific elements of a crime defined by statute. When present, these factors may allow a jury to impose a death sentence for a person convicted of a capital offense. Sometimes these are also called aggravating circumstances.

Capital conviction—A formal declaration that a defendant is guilty of a capital offense, made by the verdict of a jury, the decision of a judge, or a guilty plea by the defendant in a court of law.

Capital offense—A criminal offense punishable by death. Offenses that are eligible for a death sentence are defined by statute in each jurisdiction that authorizes capital punishment. The most common is first-degree murder accompanied by at least one aggravating factor.

Lists of capital offenses by state and by federal can be found at the end of this section.

Capital punishment—The process of sentencing convicted offenders to death for the most serious crimes and carrying out that sentence. The specific offenses and circumstances which determine if a crime is eligible for a death sentence are defined by statute and are prescribed by Congress or a state legislature.

Capital statute—State or federal laws dictating specific crimes that are eligible for a death sentence and specific procedures to be followed in carrying out such sentences.

Civil authority—For the purposes of this report, the state or federal entities responsible for implementation and enforcement of capital punishment laws, excluding military authorities.

Commutation—Reduction of a death sentence by a governor or a board of advisors empaneled to review sentences. Criteria for granting a commutation vary by state. The new sentence can be to life or a term of years.

Death row—A slang term referring to the area of a prison in which prisoners under sentence of death are housed. Usage of the term "death row" continues despite the fact that many states do not maintain a separate unit or facility for prisoners under sentence of death.

Received under sentence of death—Persons admitted to prison after being sentenced to death by a court.

Removal from under sentence of death—A prisoner who was previously under sentence of death and is no longer included in the count of persons under sentence of death. An inmate can be relieved of a death sentence by several methods: execution, death by causes other than execution, commutation, or an overturned capital conviction or sentence.

Sentence of death—A sentence imposed by a court for a capital offense which authorizes the state to execute a convicted offender.

Yearend—As of December 31 of the calendar year.

Capital Offenses, by State, 2019

State	Offenses
Alabama	Intentional murder (Ala. Stat. Ann. § 13A-5-40(a)(1)-(21)) with 14 aggravating factors (Ala. Stat. Ann. § 13A-5-49).
Arizona	First-degree murder, including premeditated murder and felony murder, accompanied by at least 1 of 10 aggravating factors (A.R.S. § 13-703(F)).
Arkansas	Capital murder (Ark. Code Ann. § 5-10-101) with a finding of at least 1 of 10 aggravating circumstances; and treason (Ark. Code Ann. § 5-51-201).
California	First-degree murder with special circumstances; military sabotage; train wreck causing death; treason; perjury resulting in the execution of an innocent person; and fatal assault by a prisoner serving a life sentence.
Colorado	First-degree murder with at least 1 of 17 aggravating factors; first-degree kidnapping resulting in death; and treason.
Delaware	First-degree murder (11 Del. C. § 636) with at least 1 statutory aggravating circumstance (11 Del. C. § 4209). The Delaware Supreme Court held that a portion of Delaware's death penalty sentencing statute (11 Del. C. § 4209) was unconstitutional (*Rauf v. State*, 145 A.3d 430 (Del. 2016)). No legislative action has been taken to amend the statute. As a result, capital cases are no longer pursued in Delaware.
Florida	First-degree murder with aggravating factors; felony murder; and capital drug-trafficking felonies.
Georgia	Murder with aggravating circumstances; rape, armed robbery, or kidnapping with bodily injury or ransom when the victim dies; aircraft hijacking; and treason (O.C.G.A. § 17-10-30).
Idaho	First-degree murder with aggravating factors; first-degree kidnapping; and perjury resulting in the execution of an innocent person.
Indiana	Murder with 1 or more of 18 aggravating circumstances (I.C. 35-50-2-9).
Kansas	Intentional and premeditated killing of a person in 1 or more of 7 different circumstances (K.S.A. 21-5401).
Kentucky	Capital murder with the presence of at least 1 statutory aggravating circumstance; and capital kidnapping (K.R.S. 532.025).
Louisiana	First-degree murder with aggravating circumstances (La. R.S. 14:30); and treason (La. R.S. 14:113).
Mississippi	Capital murder with aggravating circumstances (Miss. Code Ann. § 97-3-19(2)); and aircraft piracy (Miss. Code Ann. § 97-25-55(1)).
Missouri	First-degree murder with at least 1 statutory aggravating circumstance (565.020 R.S.M.O. 2000).
Montana	Deliberate homicide, including felony murder, with 1 of 9 aggravating circumstances (Mont. Code Ann. § 46-18-303); aggravated kidnapping resulting in death of victim or rescuer; attempted deliberate homicide; aggravated assault or kidnapping while in detention; and capital sexual intercourse without consent (Mont. Code Ann. § 45-5-503).
Nebraska	First-degree murder with a finding of 1 or more statutory aggravating circumstances.
Nevada	First-degree murder with at least 1 of 15 aggravating circumstances (N.R.S. 200.030, 200.033, 200.035).
New York	First-degree murder with 1 of 13 aggravating factors (NY Penal Law § 125.27). The New York Court of Appeals held that a portion of New York's death penalty sentencing statute (C.P.L. 400.27) was unconstitutional (People v. Taylor, 9 N.Y.3d 129 (2007)). No legislative action has been taken to amend the statute. As a result, capital cases are no longer pursued in New York.
North Carolina	First-degree murder (N.C. Gen. Stat. § 14-17) with the finding of at least 1 of 11 statutory aggravating circumstances (N.C. Gen. Stat. § 15A-2000).
Ohio	Aggravated murder with at least 1 of 10 aggravating circumstances (O.R.C. 2903.01, 2929.02, 2929.04).

State	Offenses
Oklahoma	First-degree murder (21 O.S. § 701.7) in conjunction with a finding of at least 1 of 8 statutorily defined aggravating circumstances (21 O.S. § 701.12).
Oregon	Aggravated murder (O.R.S. 163.095).
Pennsylvania	First-degree murder (18 Pa.C.S.A § 2502(a)) with 18 aggravating circumstances (42 Pa.C.S.A § 9711).
South Carolina	Murder with at least 1 of 12 aggravating circumstances (S.C. Code § 16-3-20(C)(a)).
South Dakota	First-degree murder (S.D.C.L. 22-16-4) with 1 of 10 aggravating circumstances (S.D.C.L. 23A-27A-1).
Tennessee	First-degree murder (Tenn. Code Ann. § 39-13-202) with 1 of 18 aggravating circumstances (Tenn. Code Ann. § 39-13-204).
Texas	Capital murder, defined as criminal homicide with 1 of 9 statutory aggravators (Tex. Penal Code § 19.03).
Utah	Aggravated murder (Utah Code Ann. § 76-5-202).
Virginia	Capital murder, defined as premeditated murder accompanied by 1 of 15 aggravating circumstances (VA Code § 18.2-31(A)(1-15)).
Washington	Aggravated first-degree murder. The Washington Supreme Court has declared the state's death penalty statute unconstitutional as applied (*State v. Gregory*, 192 Wash. 2d 1, 427 P.3d 621 (2018)). No legislative action has been taken to revise or repeal the statute.
Wyoming	First-degree murder; including premeditated murder and murder during the commission of sexual assault, sexual abuse of a minor, arson, robbery, burglary, escape, resisting arrest, kidnapping, or abuse of a minor younger than age 16 (W.S.A. § 6-2-101(a)).

NOTE: New Hampshire repealed its death penalty effective May 30, 2019. One male prisoner remains under a previously imposed sentence of death.

Federal Capital Offenses, 2019

Statute	Description
8 U.S.C. 1342	Murder related to the smuggling of aliens.
18 U.S.C. 32-34	Destruction of aircraft, motor vehicles, or related facilities resulting in death.
18 U.S.C. 36	Murder committed during a drug-related drive-by shooting.
18 U.S.C. 37	Murder committed at an airport serving international civil aviation.
18 U.S.C. 115(b)(3) [by cross-reference to 18 U.S.C. 1111]	Retaliatory murder of a member of the immediate family of law enforcement officials.
18 U.S.C. 241, 242, 245, 247	Civil rights offenses resulting in death.
18 U.S.C. 351 [by cross-reference to 18 U.S.C. 1111]	Murder of a member of Congress, an important executive official, or a Supreme Court Justice.
18 U.S.C. 794	Espionage.
18 U.S.C. 844(d), (f), (i)	Death resulting from offenses involving transportation of explosives, destruction of government property, or destruction of property related to foreign or interstate commerce.
18 U.S.C. 924(i)	Murder committed by the use of a firearm during a crime of violence or a drug-trafficking crime.
18 U.S.C. 930	Murder committed in a federal government facility.
18 U.S.C. 1091	Genocide.
18 U.S.C. 1111	First-degree murder.

Statute	Description
18 U.S.C. 1114	Murder of a federal judge or law enforcement official.
18 U.S.C. 1116	Murder of a foreign official.
18 U.S.C. 1118	Murder by a federal prisoner.
18 U.S.C. 1119	Murder of a U.S. national in a foreign country.
18 U.S.C. 1120	Murder by an escaped federal prisoner already sentenced to life imprisonment.
18 U.S.C. 1121	Murder of a state or local law enforcement official or other person aiding in a federal investigation; murder of a state correctional officer.
18 U.S.C. 1201	Murder during a kidnapping.
18 U.S.C. 1203	Murder during a hostage taking.
18 U.S.C. 1503	Murder of a court officer or juror.
18 U.S.C. 1512	Murder with the intent of preventing testimony by a witness, victim, or informant.
18 U.S.C. 1513	Retaliatory murder of a witness, victim, or informant.
18 U.S.C. 1716	Mailing of injurious articles with intent to kill or resulting in death.
18 U.S.C. 1751 [by cross-reference to 18 U.S.C. 1111]	Assassination or kidnapping resulting in the death of the President or Vice President.
18 U.S.C. 1958	Murder for hire.
18 U.S.C. 1959	Murder involved in a racketeering offense.
18 U.S.C. 1992	Willful wrecking of a train resulting in death.
18 U.S.C. 2113	Bank robbery-related murder or kidnapping.
18 U.S.C. 2119	Murder related to a carjacking.
18 U.S.C. 2245	Murder related to rape or child molestation.
18 U.S.C. 2251	Murder related to sexual exploitation of children.
18 U.S.C. 2280	Murder committed during an offense against maritime navigation.
18 U.S.C. 2281	Murder committed during an offense against a maritime fixed platform.
18 U.S.C. 2332	Terrorist murder of a U.S. national in another country.
18 U.S.C. 2332a	Murder by the use of a weapon of mass destruction.
18 U.S.C. 2340	Murder involving torture.
18 U.S.C. 2381	Treason.
21 U.S.C. 848(e)	Murder related to a continuing criminal enterprise or related murder of a federal, state, or local law enforcement officer.
49 U.S.C. 1472-1473	Death resulting from aircraft hijacking.

PART 2

Crime in the United States, 2019

HIGHLIGHTS

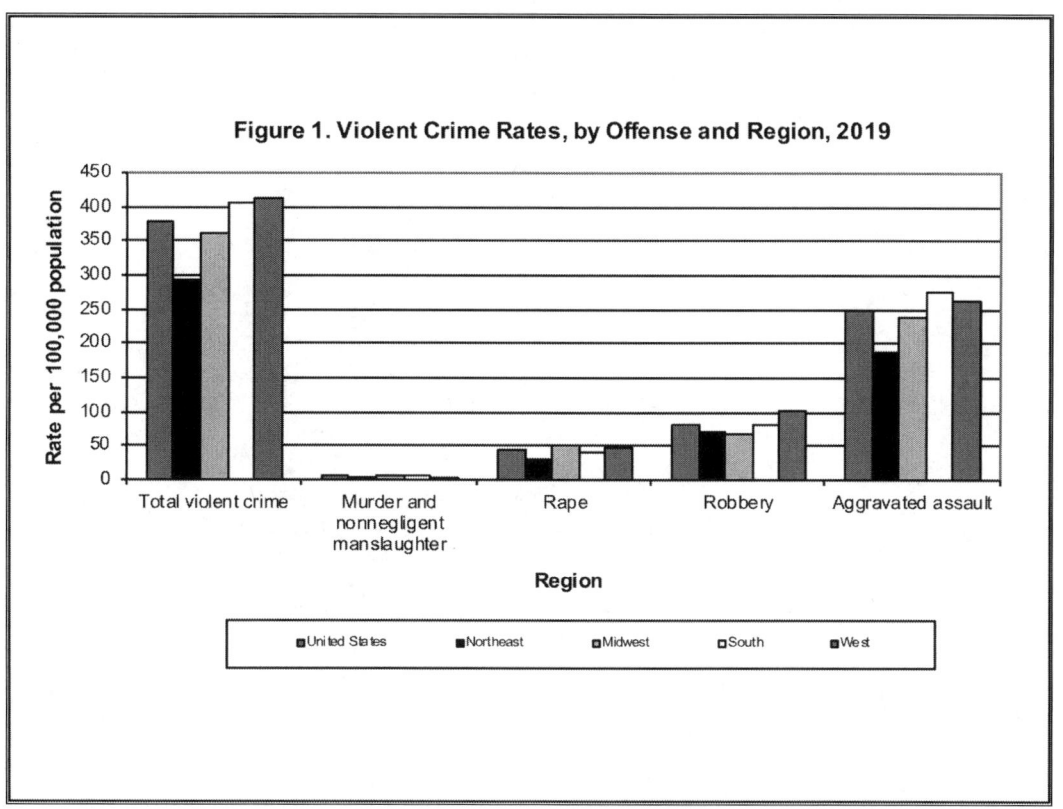

Figure 1. Violent Crime Rates, by Offense and Region, 2019

- An estimated 1,203,808 violent crimes occurred nation-wide, a decrease of 0.5 percent from the 2018 estimate. Aggravated assaults accounted for 68.2 percent of violent crimes reported to law enforcement in 2019.

- The 2-year trend showed that property crime offenses (an estimated total of 6,925,677) declined 4.1 percent in 2019 when compared with the 2018 estimate. Larceny-theft accounted for 73.4 percent of all property crimes in 2018.

- In 2019, 45.5 percent of violent crimes (almost unchanged from 2018) and 17.2 percent of property crimes (a decrease of 0.4 percent from 2018) were cleared by arrest or exceptional mean.

- Law enforcement made an estimated 10,085,287 arrests nationwide in 2019. Of these arrests, 495,871 were for violent crimes, and 1,074,367 were for property crimes. The highest number of arrests were for drug abuse violations (estimated at 1,558,862 arrests), driving under the influence (estimated at 1,024,508), and larceny-thefts (estimated at 813,073).

- Nationwide, the rate of sworn officers was 2.4 per 1,000 inhabitants. The rate of full-time law enforcement employees (civilian and sworn) per 1,000 inhabitants was 3.5.

- There were 293 violent crimes and 3,981 property crimes known to law enforcement at federal agencies in 2019.

- Of participating states, Texas had the most human trafficking violations in 2019, with 450.

- In 2019, 721 cargo theft incidents were reported among participating states, and 2.8 percent of these thefts were recovered.

Table 1. Crime in the United States, by Volume and Rate Per 100,000 Inhabitants, 2000–2019

(Number, rate per 100,000 population.)

Year	Population[1]	Violent crime[2] Number	Rate	Murder and nonnegligent manslaughter Number	Rate	Rape (revised definition)[3] Number	Rate	Rape (legacy definition)[4] Number	Rate	Robbery Number	Rate	Aggravated assault Number	Rate
2000	281,421,906	1,425,486	506.5	15,586	5.5	X	X	90,178	32.0	408,016	145.0	911,706	324.0
2001[5]	285,317,559	1,439,480	504.5	16,037	5.6	X	X	90,863	31.8	423,557	148.5	909,023	318.6
2002	287,973,924	1,423,677	494.4	16,229	5.6	X	X	95,235	33.1	420,806	146.1	891,407	309.5
2003	290,788,976	1,383,676	475.8	16,528	5.7	X	X	93,883	32.3	414,235	142.5	859,030	295.4
2004	293,656,842	1,360,088	463.2	16,148	5.5	X	X	95,089	32.4	401,470	136.7	847,381	288.6
2005	296,507,061	1,390,745	469.0	16,740	5.6	X	X	94,347	31.8	417,438	140.8	862,220	290.8
2006	299,398,484	1,435,123	479.3	17,309	5.8	X	X	94,472	31.6	449,246	150.0	874,096	292.0
2007	301,621,157	1,422,970	471.8	17,128	5.7	X	X	92,160	30.6	447,324	148.3	866,358	287.2
2008	304,059,724	1,394,461	458.6	16,465	5.4	X	X	90,750	29.8	443,563	145.9	843,683	277.5
2009	307,006,550	1,325,896	431.9	15,399	5.0	X	X	89,241	29.1	408,742	133.1	812,514	264.7
2010	309,330,219	1,251,248	404.5	14,722	4.8	X	X	85,593	27.7	369,089	119.3	781,844	252.8
2011	311,587,816	1,206,005	387.1	14,661	4.7	X	X	84,175	27.0	354,746	113.9	752,423	241.5
2012	313,873,685	1,217,057	387.8	14,856	4.7	X	X	85,141	27.1	355,051	113.1	762,009	242.8
2013	316,497,531	1,168,298	369.1	14,319	4.5	113,695	35.9	82,109	25.9	345,093	109.0	726,777	229.6
2014	318,907,401	1,153,022	361.6	14,164	4.4	118,027	37.0	84,864	26.6	322,905	101.3	731,089	229.2
2015	320,896,618	1,199,310	373.7	15,883	4.9	126,134	39.3	91,261	28.4	328,109	102.2	764,057	238.1
2016	323,405,935	1,250,162	386.6	17,413	5.4	132,414	40.9	96,970	30.0	332,797	102.9	802,982	248.3
2017	325,147,121	1,247,917	383.8	17,294	5.3	135,666	41.7	99,708	30.7	320,596	98.6	810,319	249.2
2018[6]	326,687,501	1,209,997	370.4	16,374	5.0	143,765	44.0	101,363	31.0	281,278	86.1	810,982	248.2
2019	328,239,523	1,203,808	366.7	16,425	5.0	139,815	42.6	98,213	29.9	267,988	81.6	821,182	250.2

Year	Property crime Number	Rate	Burglary Number	Rate	Larceny-theft Number	Rate	Motor vehicle theft Number	Rate
2000	10,182,584	3,618.3	2,050,992	728.8	6,971,590	2,477.3	1,160,002	412.2
2001[5]	10,437,189	3,658.1	2,116,531	741.8	7,092,267	2,485.7	1,228,391	430.5
2002	10,455,277	3,630.6	2,151,252	747.0	7,057,379	2,450.7	1,246,646	432.9
2003	10,442,862	3,591.2	2,154,834	741.0	7,026,802	2,416.5	1,261,226	433.7
2004	10,319,386	3,514.1	2,144,446	730.3	6,937,089	2,362.3	1,237,851	421.5
2005	10,174,754	3,431.5	2,155,448	726.9	6,783,447	2,287.8	1,235,859	416.8
2006	10,019,601	3,346.6	2,194,993	733.1	6,626,363	2,213.2	1,198,245	400.2
2007	9,882,212	3,276.4	2,190,198	726.1	6,591,542	2,185.4	1,100,472	364.9
2008	9,774,152	3,214.6	2,228,887	733.0	6,586,206	2,166.1	959,059	315.4
2009	9,337,060	3,041.3	2,203,313	717.7	6,338,095	2,064.5	795,652	259.2
2010	9,112,625	2,945.9	2,168,459	701.0	6,204,601	2,005.8	739,565	239.1
2011	9,052,743	2,905.4	2,185,140	701.3	6,151,095	1,974.1	716,508	230.0
2012	9,001,992	2,868.0	2,109,932	672.2	6,168,874	1,965.4	723,186	230.4
2013	8,651,892	2,733.6	1,932,139	610.5	6,019,465	1,901.9	700,288	221.3
2014	8,209,010	2,574.1	1,713,153	537.2	5,809,054	1,821.5	686,803	215.4
2015	8,024,115	2,500.5	1,587,564	494.7	5,723,488	1,783.6	713,063	222.2
2016	7,928,530	2,451.6	1,516,405	468.9	5,644,835	1,745.4	767,290	237.3
2017	7,682,988	2,362.9	1,397,045	429.7	5,513,000	1,695.5	772,943	237.7
2018[6]	7,219,084	2,209.8	1,235,013	378.0	5,232,167	1,601.6	751,904	230.2
2019	6,925,677	2,109.9	1,117,696	340.5	5,086,096	1,549.5	721,885	219.9

Note: Although arson data are included in the trend and clearance tables, sufficient data are not available to estimate totals for this offense. Therefore, no arson data are published in this table.
X = Not applicable.
[1] Populations are U.S. Census Bureau provisional estimates as of July 1 for each year except 2000 and 2010, which are decennial census counts.
[2] The violent crime figures include the offenses of murder, rape (legacy definition), robbery, and aggravated assault.
[3] The figures shown in this column for the offense of rape were estimated using the revised UCR definition of rape.
[4] The figures shown in this column for the offense of rape were estimated using the legacy UCR definition of rape.
[5] The murder and nonnegligent homicides that occurred as a result of the events of September 11, 2001, are not included in this table.
[6] The crime figures have been adjusted.

Table 1A. Crime in the United States, Percent Change in Volume and Rate Per 100,000 Inhabitants for 2 Years, 5 Years, and 10 Years, 2010–2019

(Percent change.)

Year	Violent crime[1] Number	Violent crime[1] Rate	Murder and nonnegligent manslaughter Number	Murder and nonnegligent manslaughter Rate	Rape (revised definition)[2] Number	Rape (revised definition)[2] Rate	Rape (legacy definition)[3] Number	Rape (legacy definition)[3] Rate	Robbery Number	Robbery Rate
2010–2019........................	-3.8	-9.3	+11.6	+5.1	X	X	+14.7	+8.1	-27.4	-31.6
2015–2019........................	+0.4	-1.9	+3.4	+1.1	+10.8	+8.4	+7.6	+5.2	-18.3	-20.2
2018–2019........................	-0.5	-1.0	+0.3	-0.2	-2.7	-3.2	-3.1	-3.6	-4.7	-5.2

X = Not applicable.
[1]The violent crime figures include the offenses of murder, rape (legacy definition), robbery, and aggravated assault.
[2]The figures shown in this column for the offense of rape were estimated using the revised UCR definition of rape.
[3]The figures shown in this column for the offense of rape were estimated using the legacy UCR definition of rape.

Table 2. Crime in the United States,[1] by Region, Geographic Division, and State, 2018–2019

(Number, rate per 100,000 population, percent.)

Area	Population[2]	Violent crime[3] Number	Violent crime[3] Rate	Murder and nonnegligent manslaughter Number	Murder and nonnegligent manslaughter Rate	Rape[4] Number	Rape[4] Rate	Robbery Number	Robbery Rate
UNITED STATES[5,6,7]									
2018..................................	326,687,501	1,252,399	383.4	16,374	5.0	143,765	44.0	281,278	86.1
2019..................................	328,239,523	1,245,410	379.4	16,425	5.0	139,815	42.6	267,988	81.6
Percent change		-0.6	-1.0	+0.3	-0.2	-2.7	-3.2	-4.7	-5.2
NORTHEAST									
2018..................................	56,046,620	164,441	293.4	1,926	3.4	17,674	31.5	41,794	74.6
2019..................................	55,982,803	163,717	292.4	1,834	3.3	17,315	30.9	40,073	71.6
Percent change		-0.4	-0.3	-4.8	-4.7	-2.0	-1.9	-4.1	-4.0
New England									
2018..................................	14,802,967	40,316	272.4	351	2.4	4,846	32.7	8,951	60.5
2019..................................	14,853,290	37,992	255.8	290	2.0	4,998	33.6	7,448	50.1
Percent change		-5.8	-6.1	-17.4	-17.7	+3.1	+2.8	-16.8	-17.1
Connecticut									
2018	3,571,520	7,485	209.6	86	2.4	873	24.4	2,205	61.7
2019	3,565,287	6,546	183.6	104	2.9	771	21.6	1,929	54.1
Percent change		-12.5	-12.4	+20.9	+21.1	-11.7	-11.5	-12.5	-12.4
Maine									
2018	1,339,057	1,500	112.0	23	1.7	447	33.4	228	17.0
2019	1,344,212	1,548	115.2	20	1.5	516	38.4	188	14.0
Percent change		+3.2	+2.8	-13.0	-13.4	+15.4	+15.0	-17.5	-17.9
Massachusetts..................									
2018	6,882,635	23,424	340.3	138	2.0	2,465	35.8	4,084	59.3
2019	6,892,503	22,578	327.6	152	2.2	2,204	32.0	3,613	52.4
Percent change		-3.6	-3.7	+10.1	+10.0	-10.6	-10.7	-11.5	-11.7
New Hampshire................									
2018	1,353,465	2,404	177.6	21	1.6	578	42.7	342	25.3
2019	1,359,711	2,074	152.5	33	2.4	590	43.4	313	23.0
Percent change		-13.7	-14.1	+57.1	+56.4	+2.1	+1.6	-8.5	-8.9
Rhode Island									
2018	1,058,287	2,326	219.8	16	1.5	494	46.7	453	42.8
2019	1,059,361	2,342	221.1	25	2.4	491	46.3	418	39.5
Percent change		+0.7	+0.6	+56.3	+56.1	-0.6	-0.7	-7.7	-7.8
Vermont............................									
2018	624,358	1,155	185.0	11	1.8	326	52.2	73	11.7
2019	623,989	1,262	202.2	11	1.8	278	44.6	71	11.4
Percent change		+9.3	+9.3	0.0	+0.1	-14.7	-14.7	-2.7	-2.7
Middle Atlantic..................									
2018..................................	41,217,298	126,147	306.1	1,631	4.0	12,491	30.3	34,409	83.5
2019..................................	41,137,740	127,367	309.6	1,489	3.6	12,465	30.3	33,541	81.5
Percent change		+1.0	+1.2	-8.7	-8.5	-0.2	*	-2.5	-2.3
New Jersey									
2018	8,886,025	18,536	208.6	285	3.2	1,424	16.0	6,364	71.6
2019	8,882,190	18,375	206.9	262	2.9	1,531	17.2	5,730	64.5
Percent change		-0.9	-0.8	-8.1	-8.0	+7.5	+7.6	-10.0	-9.9

Table 1A. Crime in the United States, Percent Change in Volume and Rate Per 100,000 Inhabitants for 2 Years, 5 Years, and 10 Years, 2010–2019—*Continued*

(Percent change.)

Year	Aggravated assault		Property crime		Burglary		Larceny-theft		Motor vehicle theft	
	Number	Rate	Number	Rate	Number	Rate	Number	Rate	Number	Rate
2010–2019	+5.0	-1.0	-24.0	-28.4	-48.5	-51.4	-18.0	-22.7	-2.4	-8.0
2015–2019	+7.5	+5.1	-13.7	-15.6	-29.6	-31.2	-11.1	-13.1	+1.2	-1.0
2018–2019	+1.3	+0.8	-4.1	-4.5	-9.5	-9.9	-2.8	-3.3	-4.0	-4.4

Table 2. Crime in the United States,[1] by Region, Geographic Division, and State, 2018–2019—*Continued*

(Number, rate per 100,000 population, percent.)

Area	Population[2]	Aggravated assault		Property crime		Burglary		Larceny-theft		Motor vehicle theft	
		Number	Rate	Number	Rate	Number	Rate	Number	Rate	Number	Rate
UNITED STATES5[6,7]											
2018	326,687,501	810,982	248.2	7,219,084	2,209.8	1,235,013	378.0	5,232,167	1,601.6	751,904	230.2
2019	328,239,523	821,182	250.2	6,925,677	2,109.9	1,117,696	340.5	5,086,096	1,549.5	721,885	219.9
Percent change		+1.3	+0.8	-4.1	-4.5	-9.5	-9.9	-2.8	-3.3	-4.0	-4.4
NORTHEAST											
2018	56,046,620	103,047	183.9	805,583	1,437.3	108,455	193.5	642,548	1,146.5	54,580	97.4
2019	55,982,803	104,495	186.7	755,968	1,350.4	93,798	167.5	611,369	1,092.1	50,801	90.7
Percent change		+1.4	+1.5	-6.2	-6.1	-13.5	-13.4	-4.9	-4.7	-6.9	-6.8
New England											
2018	14,802,967	26,168	176.8	228,239	1,541.8	36,877	249.1	173,141	1,169.6	18,221	123.1
2019	14,853,290	25,256	170.0	207,956	1,400.1	30,647	206.3	159,890	1,076.5	17,419	117.3
Percent change		-3.5	-3.8	-8.9	-9.2	-16.9	-17.2	-7.7	-8.0	-4.4	-4.7
Connecticut											
2018	3,571,520	4,321	121.0	59,356	1,661.9	7,983	223.5	44,181	1,237.0	7,192	201.4
2019	3,565,287	3,742	105.0	50,862	1,426.6	6,441	180.7	38,457	1,078.7	5,964	167.3
Percent change		-13.4	-13.2	-14.3	-14.2	-19.3	-19.2	-13.0	-12.8	-17.1	-16.9
Maine											
2018	1,339,057	802	59.9	18,201	1,359.2	2,712	202.5	14,712	1,098.7	777	58.0
2019	1,344,212	824	61.3	16,743	1,245.6	2,350	174.8	13,667	1,016.7	726	54.0
Percent change		+2.7	+2.3	-8.0	-8.4	-13.3	-13.7	-7.1	-7.5	-6.6	-6.9
Massachusetts											
2018	6,882,635	16,737	243.2	87,658	1,273.6	14,095	204.8	66,968	973.0	6,595	95.8
2019	6,892,503	16,609	241.0	81,317	1,179.8	12,341	179.0	62,844	911.8	6,132	89.0
Percent change		-0.8	-0.9	-7.2	-7.4	-12.4	-12.6	-6.2	-6.3	-7.0	-7.2
New Hampshire											
2018	1,353,465	1,463	108.1	17,201	1,270.9	1,908	141.0	14,396	1,063.6	897	66.3
2019	1,359,711	1,138	83.7	16,442	1,209.2	1,717	126.3	13,832	1,017.3	893	65.7
Percent change		-22.2	-22.6	-4.4	-4.9	-10.0	-10.4	-3.9	-4.4	-0.4	-0.9
Rhode Island											
2018	1,058,287	1,363	128.8	17,625	1,665.4	2,817	266.2	13,270	1,253.9	1,538	145.3
2019	1,059,361	1,408	132.9	16,259	1,534.8	2,321	219.1	12,580	1,187.5	1,358	128.2
Percent change		+3.3	+3.2	-7.8	-7.8	-17.6	-17.7	-5.2	-5.3	-11.7	-11.8
Vermont											
2018	624,358	745	119.3	8,211	1,315.1	1,496	239.6	6,451	1,033.2	264	42.3
2019	623,989	902	144.6	8,888	1,424.4	1,275	204.3	7,315	1,172.3	298	47.8
Percent change		+21.1	+21.1	+8.2	+8.3	-14.8	-14.7	+13.4	+13.5	+12.9	+12.9
Middle Atlantic											
2010	41,217,298	77,616	188.3	597,331	1,449.2	77,444	187.9	482,570	1,170.8	37,317	90.5
2019	41,137,740	79,872	194.2	565,457	1,374.5	67,353	163.7	462,674	1,124.7	35,430	86.1
Percent change		+2.9	+3.1	-5.3	-5.2	-13.0	-12.9	-4.1	-3.9	-5.1	-4.9
New Jersey											
2018	8,886,025	10,463	117.7	125,155	1,408.4	19,232	216.4	94,886	1,067.8	11,037	124.2
2019	8,882,190	10,852	122.2	118,637	1,335.7	16,399	184.6	91,902	1,034.7	10,336	116.4
Percent change		+3.7	+3.8	-5.2	-5.2	-14.7	-14.7	-3.1	-3.1	-6.4	-6.3

Table 2. Crime in the United States,[1] by Region, Geographic Division, and State, 2018–2019—*Continued*

(Number, rate per 100,000 population, percent.)

Area	Population[2]	Violent crime[3] Number	Violent crime[3] Rate	Murder and nonnegligent manslaughter Number	Murder and nonnegligent manslaughter Rate	Rape[4] Number	Rape[4] Rate	Robbery Number	Robbery Rate
New York.............									
2018	19,530,351	68,512	350.8	562	2.9	6,577	33.7	18,191	93.1
2019	19,453,561	69,764	358.6	558	2.9	6,583	33.8	18,068	92.9
Percent change		+1.8	+2.2	-0.7	-0.3	+0.1	+0.5	-0.7	-0.3
Pennsylvania....................									
2018	12,800,922	39,099	305.4	784	6.1	4,490	35.1	9,854	77.0
2019	12,801,989	39,228	306.4	669	5.2	4,351	34.0	9,743	76.1
Percent change		+0.3	+0.3	-14.7	-14.7	-3.1	-3.1	-1.1	-1.1
MIDWEST[5]									
2018..................	68,236,628	249,802	366.1	3,618	5.3	35,194	51.6	50,404	73.9
2019..................	68,329,004	247,162	361.7	3,414	5.0	34,057	49.8	46,412	67.9
Percent change		-1.1	-1.2	-5.6	-5.8	-3.2	-3.4	-7.9	-8.0
East North Central.............									
2018..................	46,886,387	174,319	371.8	2,646	5.6	24,678	52.6	38,727	82.6
2019..................	46,902,431	171,552	365.8	2,478	5.3	23,780	50.7	34,982	74.6
Percent change		-1.6	-1.6	-6.3	-6.4	-3.6	-3.7	-9.7	-9.7
Illinois....................									
2018	12,723,071	52,343	411.4	902	7.1	6,106	48.0	14,251	112.0
2019	12,671,821	51,561	406.9	832	6.6	6,078	48.0	12,464	98.4
Percent change		-1.5	-1.1	-7.8	-7.4	-0.5	-0.1	-12.5	-12.2
Indiana....................									
2018	6,695,497	25,009	373.5	418	6.2	2,486	37.1	5,737	85.7
2019	6,732,219	24,966	370.8	377	5.6	2,475	36.8	5,331	79.2
Percent change		-0.2	-0.7	-9.8	-10.3	-0.4	-1.0	-7.1	-7.6
Michigan....................									
2018	9,984,072	45,176	452.5	555	5.6	7,901	79.1	5,638	56.5
2019	9,986,857	43,686	437.4	556	5.6	7,235	72.4	5,350	53.6
Percent change		-3.3	-3.3	+0.2	+0.2	-8.4	-8.5	-5.1	-5.1
Ohio....................									
2018	11,676,341	34,426	294.8	596	5.1	5,852	50.1	9,608	82.3
2019	11,689,100	34,269	293.2	538	4.6	5,731	49.0	8,846	75.7
Percent change		-0.5	-0.6	-9.7	-9.8	-2.1	-2.2	-7.9	-8.0
Wisconsin....................									
2018....................	5,807,406	17,365	299.0	175	3.0	2,333	40.2	3,493	60.1
2019	5,822,434	17,070	293.2	175	3.0	2,261	38.8	2,991	51.4
Percent change		-1.7	-2.0	0.0	-0.3	-3.1	-3.3	-14.4	-14.6
West North Central[5]									
2018..................	21,350,241	75,483	353.5	972	4.6	10,516	49.3	11,677	54.7
2019..................	21,426,573	75,610	352.9	936	4.4	10,277	48.0	11,430	53.3
Percent change		+0.2	-0.2	-3.7	-4.0	-2.3	-2.6	-2.1	-2.5
Iowa[5]....................									
2018	3,148,618	8,303	263.7	70	2.2	1,126	35.8	989	31.4
2019	3,155,070	8,410	266.6	60	1.9	1,164	36.9	863	27.4
Percent change		+1.3	+1.1	-14.3	-14.5	+3.4	+3.2	-12.7	-12.9
Kansas									
2018	2,911,359	12,861	441.8	122	4.2	1,664	57.2	1,420	48.8
2019	2,913,314	11,968	410.8	105	3.6	1,416	48.6	1,293	44.4
Percent change		-6.9	-7.0	-13.9	-14.0	-14.9	-15.0	-8.9	-9.0
Minnesota....................									
2018	5,606,249	12,403	221.2	107	1.9	2,475	44.1	2,946	52.5
2019	5,639,632	13,332	236.4	117	2.1	2,448	43.4	3,149	55.8
Percent change		+7.5	+6.9	+9.3	+8.7	-1.1	-1.7	+6.9	+6.3
Missouri									
2018	6,121,623	30,696	501.4	599	9.8	2,935	47.9	5,206	85.0
2019	6,137,428	30,380	495.0	568	9.3	2,917	47.5	4,959	80.8
Percent change		-1.0	-1.3	-5.2	-5.4	-0.6	-0.9	-4.7	-5.0
Nebraska....................									
2018	1,925,614	5,583	289.9	44	2.3	1,290	67.0	736	38.2
2019	1,934,408	5,821	300.9	45	2.3	1,253	64.8	792	40.9
Percent change		+4.3	+3.8	+2.3	+1.8	-2.9	-3.3	+7.6	+7.1
North Dakota									
2018	758,080	2,154	284.1	18	2.4	409	54.0	158	20.8
2019	762,062	2,169	284.6	24	3.1	437	57.3	179	23.5
Percent change		+0.7	+0.2	+33.3	+32.6	+6.8	+6.3	+13.3	+12.7
South Dakota									
2018	878,698	3,483	396.4	12	1.4	617	70.2	222	25.3
2019	884,659	3,530	399.0	17	1.9	642	72.6	195	22.0
Percent change		+1.3	+0.7	+41.7	+40.7	+4.1	+3.4	-12.2	-12.8

Table 2. Crime in the United States,[1] by Region, Geographic Division, and State, 2018–2019—*Continued*

(Number, rate per 100,000 population, percent.)

Area	Population[2]	Aggravated assault		Property crime		Burglary		Larceny-theft		Motor vehicle theft	
		Number	Rate	Number	Rate	Number	Rate	Number	Rate	Number	Rate
New York											
2018	19,530,351	43,182	221.1	281,543	1,441.6	31,158	159.5	237,243	1,214.7	13,142	67.3
2019	19,453,561	44,555	229.0	267,155	1,373.3	27,600	141.9	226,851	1,166.1	12,704	65.3
Percent change		+3.2	+3.6	-5.1	-4.7	-11.4	-11.1	-4.4	-4.0	-3.3	-3.0
Pennsylvania											
2018	12,800,922	23,971	187.3	190,633	1,489.2	27,054	211.3	150,441	1,175.2	13,138	102.6
2019	12,801,989	24,465	191.1	179,665	1,403.4	23,354	182.4	143,921	1,124.2	12,390	96.8
Percent change		+2.1	+2.1	-5.8	-5.8	-13.7	-13.7	-4.3	-4.3	-5.7	-5.7
MIDWEST[5]											
2018	68,236,628	160,586	235.3	1,389,261	2,035.9	240,009	351.7	1,016,958	1,490.3	132,294	193.9
2019	68,329,004	163,279	239.0	1,322,428	1,935.4	215,395	315.2	977,491	1,430.6	129,542	189.6
Percent change		+1.7	+1.5	-4.8	-4.9	-10.3	-10.4	-3.9	-4.0	-2.1	-2.2
East North Central											
2018	46,886,387	108,268	230.9	908,899	1,938.5	160,681	342.7	667,067	1,422.7	81,151	173.1
2019	46,902,431	110,312	235.2	850,937	1,814.3	141,361	301.4	633,277	1,350.2	76,299	162.7
Percent change		+1.9	+1.9	-6.4	-6.4	-12.0	-12.1	-5.1	-5.1	-6.0	-6.0
Illinois											
2018	12,723,071	31,084	244.3	246,679	1,938.8	39,317	309.0	187,517	1,473.8	19,845	156.0
2019	12,671,821	32,187	254.0	233,984	1,846.5	34,433	271.7	180,776	1,426.6	18,775	148.2
Percent change		+3.5	+4.0	-5.1	-4.8	-12.4	-12.1	-3.6	-3.2	-5.4	-5.0
Indiana											
2018	6,695,497	16,368	244.5	146,948	2,194.7	25,894	386.7	105,861	1,581.1	15,193	226.9
2019	6,732,219	16,783	249.3	132,694	1,971.0	21,795	323.7	97,176	1,443.4	13,723	203.8
Percent change		+2.5	+2.0	-9.7	-10.2	-15.8	-16.3	-8.2	-8.7	-9.7	-10.2
Michigan											
2018	9,984,072	31,082	311.3	166,186	1,664.5	31,834	318.8	116,876	1,170.6	17,476	175.0
2019	9,986,857	30,545	305.9	158,296	1,585.0	28,572	286.1	111,980	1,121.3	17,744	177.7
Percent change		-1.7	-1.8	-4.7	-4.8	-10.2	-10.3	-4.2	-4.2	+1.5	+1.5
Ohio											
2018	11,676,341	18,370	157.3	257,848	2,208.3	49,456	423.6	188,433	1,613.8	19,959	170.9
2019	11,689,100	19,154	163.9	240,291	2,055.7	43,894	375.5	177,725	1,520.4	18,672	159.7
Percent change		+4.3	+4.2	-6.8	-6.9	-11.2	-11.3	-5.7	-5.8	-6.4	-6.6
Wisconsin											
2018	5,807,406	11,364	195.7	91,238	1,571.1	14,180	244.2	68,380	1,177.5	8,678	149.4
2019	5,822,434	11,643	200.0	85,672	1,471.4	12,667	217.6	65,620	1,127.0	7,385	126.8
Percent change		+2.5	+2.2	-6.1	-6.3	-10.7	-10.9	-4.0	-4.3	-14.9	-15.1
West North Central[5]											
2018	21,350,241	52,318	245.0	480,362	2,249.9	79,328	371.6	349,891	1,638.8	51,143	239.5
2019	21,426,573	52,967	247.2	471,491	2,200.5	74,034	345.5	344,214	1,606.5	53,243	248.5
Percent change		+1.2	+0.9	-1.8	-2.2	-6.7	-7.0	-1.6	-2.0	+4.1	+3.7
Iowa[5]											
2018	3,148,618	6,118	194.3	57,024	1,811.1	12,433	394.9	39,498	1,254.5	5,093	161.8
2019	3,155,070	6,323	200.4	54,699	1,733.7	11,710	371.1	37,847	1,199.6	5,142	163.0
Percent change		+3.4	+3.1	-4.1	-4.3	-5.8	-6.0	-4.2	-4.4	+1.0	+0.8
Kansas											
2018	2,911,359	9,655	331.6	77,449	2,660.2	12,792	439.4	56,726	1,948.4	7,931	272.4
2019	2,913,314	9,154	314.2	67,428	2,314.5	9,984	342.7	50,165	1,721.9	7,279	249.9
Percent change		-5.2	-5.3	-12.9	-13.0	-22.0	-22.0	-11.6	-11.6	-8.2	-8.3
Minnesota											
2018	5,606,249	6,875	122.6	112,186	2,001.1	16,206	289.1	85,849	1,531.3	10,131	180.7
2019	5,639,632	7,618	135.1	117,236	2,078.8	15,927	282.4	90,092	1,597.5	11,217	198.9
Percent change		+10.8	+10.2	+4.5	+3.9	-1.7	-2.3	+4.9	+4.3	+10.7	+10.1
Missouri											
2018	6,121,623	21,956	358.7	162,698	2,657.8	27,345	446.7	115,506	1,886.9	19,847	324.2
2019	6,137,428	21,936	357.4	161,946	2,638.7	26,414	430.4	114,460	1,865.0	21,072	343.3
Percent change		-0.1	-0.3	-0.5	-0.7	-3.4	-3.7	-0.9	-1.2	+6.2	+5.9
Nebraska											
2018	1,925,614	3,513	182.4	40,193	2,087.3	5,308	275.7	29,987	1,557.3	4,898	254.4
2019	1,934,408	3,731	192.9	39,449	2,039.3	4,745	245.3	29,719	1,536.3	4,985	257.7
Percent change		+6.2	+5.7	-1.9	-2.3	-10.6	-11.0	-0.9	-1.3	+1.8	+1.3
North Dakota											
2018	758,080	1,569	207.0	15,621	2,060.6	2,742	361.7	11,088	1,462.6	1,791	236.3
2019	762,062	1,529	200.6	15,066	1,977.0	2,608	342.2	10,666	1,399.6	1,792	235.2
Percent change		-2.5	-3.1	-3.6	-4.1	-4.9	-5.4	-3.8	-4.3	+0.1	-0.5
South Dakota											
2018	878,698	2,632	299.5	15,191	1,728.8	2,502	284.7	11,237	1,278.8	1,452	165.2
2019	884,659	2,676	302.5	15,667	1,771.0	2,646	299.1	11,265	1,273.4	1,756	198.5
Percent change		+1.7	+1.0	+3.1	+2.4	+5.8	+5.0	+0.2	-0.4	+20.9	+20.1

Table 2. Crime in the United States,[1] by Region, Geographic Division, and State, 2018–2019—*Continued*

(Number, rate per 100,000 population, percent.)

Area	Population[2]	Violent crime[3] Number	Rate	Murder and nonnegligent manslaughter Number	Rate	Rape[4] Number	Rate	Robbery Number	Rate
SOUTH[6,7]									
2018..................................	124,569,433	507,232	407.2	7,581	6.1	52,571	42.2	106,258	85.3
2019..................................	125,580,448	510,565	406.6	8,002	6.4	52,119	41.5	102,570	81.7
Percent change		+0.7	-0.2	+5.6	+4.7	-0.9	-1.7	-3.5	-4.2
South Atlantic[6,7]									
2018..................................	65,229,624	242,214	371.3	3,929	6.0	23,082	35.4	53,483	82.0
2019..................................	65,784,817	245,159	372.7	4,132	6.3	23,223	35.3	51,679	78.6
Percent change		+1.2	+0.4	+5.2	+4.3	+0.6	-0.2	-3.4	-4.2
Delaware..........................									
2018	965,479	4,079	422.5	46	4.8	334	34.6	861	89.2
2019	973,764	4,115	422.6	48	4.9	310	31.8	790	81.1
Percent change		+0.9	*	+4.3	+3.5	-7.2	-8.0	-8.2	-9.0
District of Columbia[6]									
2018	701,547	6,995	997.1	160	22.8	450	64.1	2,415	344.2
2019	705,749	7,403	1,049.0	166	23.5	345	48.9	2,713	384.4
Percent change		+5.8	+5.2	+3.8	+3.1	-23.3	-23.8	+12.3	+11.7
Florida............................									
2018	21,244,317	81,980	385.9	1,107	5.2	8,438	39.7	16,884	79.5
2019	21,477,737	81,270	378.4	1,122	5.2	8,456	39.4	16,217	75.5
Percent change		-0.9	-1.9	+1.4	+0.3	+0.2	-0.9	-4.0	-5.0
Georgia............................									
2018	10,511,131	35,619	338.9	647	6.2	2,798	26.6	8,499	80.9
2019	10,617,423	36,170	340.7	654	6.2	2,922	27.5	7,961	75.0
Percent change		+1.5	+0.5	+1.1	+0.1	+4.4	+3.4	-6.3	-7.3
Maryland..........................									
2018	6,035,802	28,330	469.4	491	8.1	1,991	33.0	9,716	161.0
2019	6,045,680	27,456	454.1	542	9.0	1,913	31.6	9,203	152.2
Percent change		-3.1	-3.2	+10.4	+10.2	-3.9	-4.1	-5.3	-5.4
North Carolina[7]									
2018	10,381,615	36,980	356.2	574	5.5	2,633	25.4	7,573	72.9
2019	10,488,084	38,995	371.8	632	6.0	3,247	31.0	7,599	72.5
Percent change		+5.4	+4.4	+10.1	+9.0	+23.3	+22.1	+0.3	-0.7
South Carolina									
2018	5,084,156	25,463	500.8	411	8.1	2,650	52.1	3,592	70.7
2019	5,148,714	26,323	511.3	464	9.0	2,460	47.8	3,294	64.0
Percent change		+3.4	+2.1	+12.9	+11.5	-7.2	-8.3	-8.3	-9.4
Virginia									
2018	8,501,286	17,357	204.2	417	4.9	3,072	36.1	3,610	42.5
2019	8,535,519	17,753	208.0	426	5.0	2,816	33.0	3,524	41.3
Percent change		+2.3	+1.9	+2.2	+1.7	-8.3	-8.7	-2.4	-2.8
West Virginia...................									
2018	1,804,291	5,411	299.9	76	4.2	716	39.7	333	18.5
2019	1,792,147	5,674	316.6	78	4.4	754	42.1	378	21.1
Percent change		+4.9	+5.6	+2.6	+3.3	+5.3	+6.0	+13.5	+14.3
East South Central									
2018..................................	19,101,485	85,902	449.7	1,355	7.1	7,514	39.3	15,438	80.8
2019..................................	19,176,181	83,666	436.3	1,409	7.3	7,200	37.5	13,952	72.8
Percent change		-2.6	-3.0	+4.0	+3.6	-4.2	-4.6	-9.6	-10.0
Alabama									
2018	4,887,681	25,567	523.1	383	7.8	2,032	41.6	4,047	82.8
2019	4,903,185	25,046	510.8	358	7.3	2,068	42.2	3,941	80.4
Percent change		-2.0	-2.3	-6.5	-6.8	+1.8	+1.4	-2.6	-2.9
Kentucky..........................									
2018	4,461,153	9,719	217.9	250	5.6	1,875	42.0	2,469	55.3
2019	4,467,673	9,701	217.1	221	4.9	1,572	35.2	2,161	48.4
Percent change		-0.2	-0.3	-11.6	-11.7	-16.2	-16.3	-12.5	-12.6
Mississippi									
2018	2,981,020	7,929	266.0	214	7.2	596	20.0	1,700	57.0
2019	2,976,149	8,272	277.9	332	11.2	747	25.1	1,700	57.1
Percent change		+4.3	+4.5	+55.1	+55.4	+25.3	+25.5	0.0	+0.2
Tennessee									
2018	6,771,631	42,687	630.4	508	7.5	3,011	44.5	7,222	106.7
2019	6,829,174	40,647	595.2	498	7.3	2,813	41.2	6,150	90.1
Percent change		-4.8	-5.6	-2.0	-2.8	-6.6	-7.4	-14.8	-15.6
West South Central									
2018..................................	40,238,324	179,116	445.1	2,297	5.7	21,975	54.6	37,337	92.8
2019..................................	40,619,450	181,740	447.4	2,461	6.1	21,696	53.4	36,939	90.9
Percent change		+1.5	+0.5	+7.1	+6.1	-1.3	-2.2	-1.1	-2.0

Table 2. Crime in the United States,[1] by Region, Geographic Division, and State, 2018–2019—*Continued*

(Number, rate per 100,000 population, percent.)

Area	Population[2]	Aggravated assault		Property crime		Burglary		Larceny-theft		Motor vehicle theft	
		Number	Rate	Number	Rate	Number	Rate	Number	Rate	Number	Rate
SOUTH[6,7]											
2018................................	124,569,433	340,822	273.6	3,040,614	2,440.9	547,925	439.9	2,213,649	1,777.0	279,040	224.0
2019................................	125,580,448	347,874	277.0	2,957,758	2,355.3	501,817	399.6	2,175,494	1,732.4	280,447	223.3
Percent change		+2.1	+1.2	-2.7	-3.5	-8.4	-9.2	-1.7	-2.5	+0.5	-0.3
South Atlantic[6,7]											
2018................................	65,229,624	161,720	247.9	1,510,368	2,315.5	251,583	385.7	1,131,644	1,734.9	127,141	194.9
2019................................	65,784,817	166,125	252.5	1,450,962	2,205.6	226,274	344.0	1,100,944	1,673.6	123,744	188.1
Percent change		+2.7	+1.9	-3.9	-4.7	-10.1	-10.8	-2.7	-3.5	-2.7	-3.5
Delaware..........................											
2018	965,479	2,838	293.9	22,405	2,320.6	3,154	326.7	17,780	1,841.6	1,471	152.4
2019	973,764	2,967	304.7	21,931	2,252.2	2,968	304.8	17,359	1,782.7	1,604	164.7
Percent change		+4.5	+3.7	-2.1	-2.9	-5.9	-6.7	-2.4	-3.2	+9.0	+8.1
District of Columbia[6]											
2018	701,547	3,970	565.9	30,726	4,379.7	1,788	254.9	26,345	3,755.3	2,593	369.6
2019	705,749	4,179	592.1	30,821	4,367.1	1,843	261.1	26,645	3,775.4	2,333	330.6
Percent change		+5.3	+4.6	+0.3	-0.3	+3.1	+2.5	+1.1	+0.5	-10.0	-10.6
Florida.............................											
2018	21,244,317	55,551	261.5	486,017	2,287.8	71,933	338.6	372,919	1,755.4	41,165	193.8
2019	21,477,737	55,475	258.3	460,846	2,145.7	63,396	295.2	358,402	1,668.7	39,048	181.8
Percent change		-0.1	-1.2	-5.2	-6.2	-11.9	-12.8	-3.9	-4.9	-5.1	-6.2
Georgia............................											
2018	10,511,131	23,675	225.2	277,803	2,642.9	46,816	445.4	205,631	1,956.3	25,356	241.2
2019	10,617,423	24,633	232.0	252,249	2,375.8	39,506	372.1	188,967	1,779.8	23,776	223.9
Percent change		+4.0	+3.0	-9.2	-10.1	-15.6	-16.5	-8.1	-9.0	-6.2	-7.2
Maryland..........................											
2018	6,035,802	16,132	267.3	122,945	2,036.9	18,910	313.3	91,887	1,522.4	12,148	201.3
2019	6,045,680	15,798	261.3	117,901	1,950.2	16,862	278.9	89,780	1,485.0	11,259	186.2
Percent change		-2.1	-2.2	-4.1	-4.3	-10.8	-11.0	-2.3	-2.5	-7.3	-7.5
North Carolina[7]											
2018	10,381,615	26,200	252.4	243,323	2,343.8	57,450	553.4	169,376	1,631.5	16,497	158.9
2019	10,488,084	27,517	262.4	247,236	2,357.3	54,447	519.1	174,728	1,666.0	18,061	172.2
Percent change		+5.0	+4.0	+1.6	+0.6	-5.2	-6.2	+3.2	+2.1	+9.5	+8.4
South Carolina											
2018	5,084,156	18,810	370.0	156,330	3,074.8	29,957	589.2	111,427	2,191.7	14,946	294.0
2019	5,148,714	20,105	390.5	151,389	2,940.3	27,461	533.4	108,953	2,116.1	14,975	290.8
Percent change		+6.9	+5.5	-3.2	-4.4	-8.3	-9.5	-2.2	-3.4	+0.2	-1.1
Virginia											
2018	8,501,286	10,258	120.7	142,931	1,681.3	15,659	184.2	116,496	1,370.3	10,776	126.8
2019	8,535,519	10,987	128.7	140,213	1,642.7	13,900	162.8	116,044	1,359.5	10,269	120.3
Percent change		+7.1	+6.7	-1.9	-2.3	-11.2	-11.6	-0.4	-0.8	-4.7	-5.1
West Virginia...................											
2018	1,804,291	4,286	237.5	27,888	1,545.6	5,916	327.9	19,783	1,096.4	2,189	121.3
2019	1,792,147	4,464	249.1	28,376	1,583.4	5,891	328.7	20,066	1,119.7	2,419	135.0
Percent change		+4.2	+4.9	+1.7	+2.4	-0.4	+0.3	+1.4	+2.1	+10.5	+11.3
East South Central											
2018................................	19,101,485	61,595	322.5	492,535	2,578.5	100,456	525.9	342,552	1,793.3	49,527	259.3
2019................................	19,176,181	61,105	318.7	467,762	2,439.3	90,051	469.6	330,011	1,720.9	47,700	248.7
Percent change		-0.8	-1.2	-5.0	-5.4	-10.4	-10.7	-3.7	-4.0	-3.7	-4.1
Alabama											
2018	4,887,681	19,105	390.9	138,702	2,837.8	29,101	595.4	96,328	1,970.8	13,273	271.6
2019	4,903,185	18,679	381.0	131,133	2,674.4	26,079	531.9	92,477	1,886.1	12,577	256.5
Percent change		-2.2	-2.5	-5.5	-5.8	-10.4	-10.7	-4.0	-4.3	-5.2	-5.5
Kentucky..........................											
2018	4,461,153	5,125	114.9	89,235	2,000.3	17,462	391.4	61,313	1,374.4	10,460	234.5
2019	4,467,673	5,747	128.6	84,769	1,897.4	15,443	345.7	59,130	1,323.5	10,196	228.2
Percent change		+12.1	+12.0	-5.0	-5.1	-11.6	-11.7	-3.6	-3.7	-2.5	-2.7
Mississippi........................											
2018	2,981,020	5,419	181.8	71,701	2,405.3	20,355	682.8	46,201	1,549.8	5,145	172.6
2019	2,976,149	5,493	184.6	70,707	2,375.8	18,660	627.0	46,300	1,555.7	5,747	193.1
Percent change		+1.4	+1.5	-1.4	-1.2	-8.3	-8.2	+0.2	+0.4	+11.7	+11.9
Tennessee											
2018	6,771,631	31,946	471.8	192,897	2,848.6	33,538	495.3	138,710	2,048.4	20,649	304.9
2019	6,829,174	31,186	456.7	181,153	2,652.6	29,869	437.4	132,104	1,934.4	19,180	280.9
Percent change		-2.4	-3.2	-6.1	-6.9	-10.9	-11.7	-4.8	-5.6	-7.1	-7.9
West South Central											
2018................................	40,238,324	117,507	292.0	1,037,711	2,578.9	195,886	486.8	739,453	1,837.7	102,372	254.4
2019................................	40,619,450	120,644	297.0	1,039,034	2,558.0	185,492	456.7	744,539	1,833.0	109,003	268.4
Percent change		+2.7	+1.7	+0.1	-0.8	-5.3	-6.2	+0.7	-0.3	+6.5	+5.5

Table 2. Crime in the United States,[1] by Region, Geographic Division, and State, 2018–2019—*Continued*

(Number, rate per 100,000 population, percent.)

Area	Population[2]	Violent crime[3] Number	Violent crime[3] Rate	Murder and nonnegligent manslaughter Number	Murder and nonnegligent manslaughter Rate	Rape[4] Number	Rape[4] Rate	Robbery Number	Robbery Rate
Arkansas									
2018	3,009,733	16,904	561.6	222	7.4	2,341	77.8	1,593	52.9
2019	3,017,804	17,643	584.6	242	8.0	2,331	77.2	1,557	51.6
Percent change		+4.4	+4.1	+9.0	+8.7	-0.4	-0.7	-2.3	-2.5
Louisiana									
2018	4,659,690	25,314	543.3	533	11.4	2,105	45.2	4,600	98.7
2019	4,648,794	25,537	549.3	544	11.7	2,273	48.9	4,025	86.6
Percent change		+0.9	+1.1	+2.1	+2.3	+8.0	+8.2	-12.5	-12.3
Oklahoma									
2018	3,940,235	18,701	474.6	215	5.5	2,431	61.7	2,805	71.2
2019	3,956,971	17,086	431.8	266	6.7	2,268	57.3	2,369	59.9
Percent change		-8.6	-9.0	+23.7	+23.2	-6.7	-7.1	-15.5	-15.9
Texas									
2018	28,628,666	118,197	412.9	1,327	4.6	15,098	52.7	28,339	99.0
2019	28,995,881	121,474	418.9	1,409	4.9	14,824	51.1	28,988	100.0
Percent change		+2.8	+1.5	+6.2	+4.8	-1.8	-3.1	+2.3	+1.0
WEST									
2018	77,834,820	330,924	425.2	3,249	4.2	38,326	49.2	82,822	106.4
2019	78,347,268	323,966	413.5	3,175	4.1	36,324	46.4	78,933	100.7
Percent change		-2.1	-2.7	-2.3	-2.9	-5.2	-5.8	-4.7	-5.3
Mountain									
2018	24,511,745	108,278	441.7	1,101	4.5	15,175	61.9	18,575	75.8
2019	24,854,998	104,878	422.0	1,054	4.2	14,562	58.6	17,252	69.4
Percent change		-3.1	-4.5	-4.3	-5.6	-4.0	-5.4	-7.1	-8.4
Arizona									
2018	7,158,024	34,053	475.7	383	5.4	3,605	50.4	6,509	90.9
2019	7,278,717	33,141	455.3	365	5.0	3,662	50.3	6,410	88.1
Percent change		-2.7	-4.3	-4.7	-6.3	+1.6	-0.1	-1.5	-3.2
Colorado									
2018	5,691,287	22,851	401.5	215	3.8	4,328	76.0	3,781	66.4
2019	5,758,736	21,938	381.0	218	3.8	3,872	67.2	3,663	63.6
Percent change		-4.0	-5.1	+1.4	+0.2	-10.5	-11.6	-3.1	-4.3
Idaho									
2018	1,750,536	4,196	239.7	34	1.9	927	53.0	195	11.1
2019	1,787,065	4,000	223.8	35	2.0	809	45.3	155	8.7
Percent change		-4.7	-6.6	+2.9	+0.8	-12.7	-14.5	-20.5	-22.1
Montana									
2018	1,060,665	4,040	380.9	37	3.5	569	53.6	270	25.5
2019	1,068,778	4,328	404.9	27	2.5	624	58.4	205	19.2
Percent change		+7.1	+6.3	-27.0	-27.6	+9.7	+8.8	-24.1	-24.7
Nevada									
2018	3,027,341	16,715	552.1	202	6.7	2,329	76.9	3,862	127.6
2019	3,080,156	15,210	493.8	143	4.6	2,161	70.2	3,286	106.7
Percent change		-9.0	-10.6	-29.2	-30.4	-7.2	-8.8	-14.9	-16.4
New Mexico									
2018	2,092,741	17,637	842.8	153	7.3	1,302	62.2	2,646	126.4
2019	2,096,829	17,450	832.2	181	8.6	1,288	61.4	2,341	111.6
Percent change		-1.1	-1.3	+18.3	+18.1	-1.1	-1.3	-11.5	-11.7
Utah									
2018	3,153,550	7,551	239.4	63	2.0	1,854	58.8	1,237	39.2
2019	3,205,958	7,553	235.6	72	2.2	1,822	56.8	1,125	35.1
Percent change		*	-1.6	+14.3	+12.4	-1.7	-3.3	-9.1	-10.5
Wyoming									
2018	577,601	1,235	213.8	14	2.4	261	45.2	75	13.0
2019	578,759	1,258	217.4	13	2.2	324	56.0	67	11.6
Percent change		+1.9	+1.7	-7.1	-7.3	+24.1	+23.9	-10.7	-10.8
Pacific									
2018	53,323,075	222,646	417.5	2,148	4.0	23,151	43.4	64,247	120.5
2019	53,492,270	219,088	409.6	2,121	4.0	21,762	40.7	61,681	115.3
Percent change		-1.6	-1.9	-1.3	-1.6	-6.0	-6.3	-4.0	-4.3
Alaska									
2018	735,139	6,555	891.7	47	6.4	1,212	164.9	896	121.9
2019	731,545	6,343	867.1	69	9.4	1,088	148.7	826	112.9
Percent change		-3.2	-2.8	+46.8	+47.5	-10.2	-9.8	-7.8	-7.4
California									
2018	39,461,588	176,604	447.5	1,739	4.4	15,506	39.3	54,328	137.7
2019	39,512,223	174,331	441.2	1,690	4.3	14,799	37.5	52,301	132.4
Percent change		-1.3	-1.4	-2.8	-2.9	-4.6	-4.7	-3.7	-3.9

(Number, rate per 100,000 population, percent.)

Area	Population[2]	Aggravated assault Number	Aggravated assault Rate	Property crime Number	Property crime Rate	Burglary Number	Burglary Rate	Larceny-theft Number	Larceny-theft Rate	Motor vehicle theft Number	Motor vehicle theft Rate
Arkansas											
2018	3,009,733	12,748	423.6	89,177	2,963.0	19,520	648.6	62,350	2,071.6	7,307	242.8
2019	3,017,804	13,513	447.8	86,250	2,858.0	18,095	599.6	60,735	2,012.6	7,420	245.9
Percent change		+6.0	+5.7	-3.3	-3.5	-7.3	-7.5	-2.6	-2.9	+1.5	+1.3
Louisiana											
2018	4,659,690	18,076	387.9	152,996	3,283.4	31,291	671.5	110,066	2,362.1	11,639	249.8
2019	4,648,794	18,695	402.1	146,993	3,162.0	26,918	579.0	109,359	2,352.4	10,716	230.5
Percent change		+3.4	+3.7	-3.9	-3.7	-14.0	-13.8	-0.6	-0.4	-7.9	-7.7
Oklahoma											
2018	3,940,235	13,250	336.3	114,395	2,903.3	27,178	689.8	73,799	1,873.0	13,418	340.5
2019	3,956,971	12,183	307.9	112,587	2,845.3	26,577	671.7	72,632	1,835.5	13,378	338.1
Percent change		-8.1	-8.4	-1.6	-2.0	-2.2	-2.6	-1.6	-2.0	-0.3	-0.7
Texas											
2018	28,628,666	73,433	256.5	681,143	2,379.2	117,897	411.8	493,238	1,722.9	70,008	244.5
2019	28,995,881	76,253	263.0	693,204	2,390.7	113,902	392.8	501,813	1,730.6	77,489	267.2
Percent change		+3.8	+2.5	+1.8	+0.5	-3.4	-4.6	+1.7	+0.5	+10.7	+9.3
WEST											
2018	77,834,820	206,527	265.3	1,983,626	2,548.5	338,624	435.1	1,359,012	1,746.0	285,990	367.4
2019	78,347,268	205,534	262.3	1,889,523	2,411.7	306,686	391.4	1,321,742	1,687.0	261,095	333.3
Percent change		-0.5	-1.1	-4.7	-5.4	-9.4	-10.0	-2.7	-3.4	-8.7	-9.3
Mountain											
2018	24,511,745	73,427	299.6	630,953	2,574.1	107,336	437.9	447,137	1,824.2	76,480	312.0
2019	24,854,998	72,010	289.7	587,493	2,363.7	95,964	386.1	419,649	1,688.4	71,880	289.2
Percent change		-1.9	-3.3	-6.9	-8.2	-10.6	-11.8	-6.1	-7.4	-6.0	-7.3
Arizona											
2018	7,158,024	23,556	329.1	192,730	2,692.5	31,787	444.1	141,789	1,980.8	19,154	267.6
2019	7,278,717	22,704	311.9	177,638	2,440.5	28,699	394.3	130,788	1,796.9	18,151	249.4
Percent change		-3.6	-5.2	-7.8	-9.4	-9.7	-11.2	-7.8	-9.3	-5.2	-6.8
Colorado											
2018	5,691,287	14,527	255.2	154,292	2,711.0	21,757	382.3	110,518	1,941.9	22,017	386.9
2019	5,758,736	14,185	246.3	149,189	2,590.7	20,064	348.4	107,012	1,858.3	22,113	384.0
Percent change		-2.4	-3.5	-3.3	-4.4	-7.8	-8.9	-3.2	-4.3	+0.4	-0.7
Idaho											
2018	1,750,536	3,040	173.7	25,822	1,475.1	4,990	285.1	18,876	1,078.3	1,956	111.7
2019	1,787,065	3,001	167.9	21,793	1,219.5	3,927	219.7	16,295	911.8	1,571	87.9
Percent change		-1.3	-3.3	-15.6	-17.3	-21.3	-22.9	-13.7	-15.4	-19.7	-21.3
Montana											
2018	1,060,665	3,164	298.3	26,787	2,525.5	3,329	313.9	20,641	1,946.0	2,817	265.6
2019	1,068,778	3,472	324.9	23,440	2,193.2	2,887	270.1	18,176	1,700.6	2,377	222.4
Percent change		+9.7	+8.9	-12.5	-13.2	-13.3	-13.9	-11.9	-12.6	-15.6	-16.3
Nevada											
2018	3,027,341	10,322	341.0	73,998	2,444.3	17,741	586.0	44,341	1,464.7	11,916	393.6
2019	3,080,156	9,620	312.3	71,525	2,322.1	15,510	503.5	44,755	1,453.0	11,260	365.6
Percent change		-6.8	-8.4	-3.3	-5.0	-12.6	-14.1	+0.9	-0.8	-5.5	-7.1
New Mexico											
2018	2,092,741	13,536	646.8	70,722	3,379.4	16,102	769.4	44,592	2,130.8	10,028	479.2
2019	2,096,829	13,640	650.5	65,269	3,112.7	14,610	696.8	41,702	1,988.8	8,957	427.2
Percent change		+0.8	+0.6	-7.7	-7.9	-9.3	-9.4	-6.5	-6.7	-10.7	-10.9
Utah											
2018	3,153,550	4,397	139.4	76,294	2,419.3	10,079	319.6	58,406	1,852.1	7,809	247.6
2019	3,205,958	4,534	141.4	69,546	2,169.3	8,871	276.7	53,937	1,682.4	6,738	210.2
Percent change		+3.1	+1.4	-8.8	-10.3	-12.0	-13.4	-7.7	-9.2	-13.7	-15.1
Wyoming											
2018	577,601	885	153.2	10,308	1,784.6	1,551	268.5	7,974	1,380.5	783	135.6
2019	578,759	854	147.6	9,093	1,571.1	1,396	241.2	6,984	1,206.7	713	123.2
Percent change		-3.5	-3.7	-11.8	-12.0	-10.0	-10.2	-12.4	-12.6	-8.9	-9.1
Pacific											
2018	53,323,075	133,100	249.6	1,352,673	2,536.7	231,288	433.7	911,875	1,710.1	209,510	392.9
2019	53,492,270	133,524	249.6	1,302,030	2,434.1	210,722	393.9	902,093	1,686.4	189,215	353.7
Percent change		+0.3	*	-3.7	-4.0	-8.9	-9.2	-1.1	-1.4	-9.7	-10.0
Alaska											
2018	735,139	4,400	598.5	24,345	3,311.6	3,985	542.1	16,364	2,226.0	3,996	543.6
2019	731,545	4,360	596.0	21,294	2,910.8	3,563	487.1	15,114	2,066.0	2,617	357.7
Percent change		-0.9	-0.4	-12.5	-12.1	-10.6	-10.2	-7.6	-7.2	-34.5	-34.2
California											
2018	39,461,588	105,031	266.2	941,644	2,386.2	164,645	417.2	621,779	1,575.7	155,220	393.3
2019	39,512,223	105,541	267.1	921,114	2,331.2	152,555	386.1	626,802	1,586.3	141,757	358.8
Percent change		+0.5	+0.4	-2.2	-2.3	-7.3	-7.5	+0.8	+0.7	-8.7	-8.8

Table 2. Crime in the United States,[1] by Region, Geographic Division, and State, 2018–2019—*Continued*

(Number, rate per 100,000 population, percent.)

Area	Population[2]	Violent crime[3]		Murder and nonnegligent manslaughter		Rape[4]		Robbery	
		Number	Rate	Number	Rate	Number	Rate	Number	Rate
Hawaii............................									
2018	1,420,593	3,622	255.0	40	2.8	709	49.9	951	66.9
2019	1,415,872	4,042	285.5	48	3.4	765	54.0	1,131	79.9
Percent change		+11.6	+12.0	+20.0	+20.4	+7.9	+8.3	+18.9	+19.3
Oregon									
2018	4,181,886	12,146	290.4	86	2.1	2,114	50.6	2,515	60.1
2019	4,217,737	11,995	284.4	116	2.8	1,778	42.2	2,276	54.0
Percent change		-1.2	-2.1	+34.9	+33.7	-15.9	-16.6	-9.5	-10.3
Washington									
2018	7,523,869	23,719	315.3	236	3.1	3,610	48.0	5,557	73.9
2019	7,614,893	22,377	293.9	198	2.6	3,332	43.8	5,147	67.6
Percent change		-5.7	-6.8	-16.1	-17.1	-7.7	-8.8	-7.4	-8.5
Puerto Rico									
2018..................................	3,193,354	6,417	200.9	639	20.0	198	6.2	2,271	71.1
2019..................................	3,193,694	6,479	202.9	606	19.0	215	6.7	2,121	66.4
Percent change		+1.0	+1.0	-5.2	-5.2	+8.6	+8.6	-6.6	-6.6

(Number, rate per 100,000 population, percent.)

Area	Population[2]	Aggravated assault		Property crime		Burglary		Larceny-theft		Motor vehicle theft	
		Number	Rate	Number	Rate	Number	Rate	Number	Rate	Number	Rate
Hawaii............................											
2018	1,420,593	1,922	135.3	41,027	2,888.0	5,709	401.9	29,600	2,083.6	5,718	402.5
2019	1,415,872	2,098	148.2	40,228	2,841.2	5,340	377.2	29,634	2,093.0	5,254	371.1
Percent change		+9.2	+9.5	-1.9	-1.6	-6.5	-6.2	+0.1	+0.4	-8.1	-7.8
Oregon											
2018	4,181,886	7,431	177.7	122,401	2,926.9	16,515	394.9	89,191	2,132.8	16,695	399.2
2019	4,217,737	7,825	185.5	115,170	2,730.6	14,724	349.1	85,261	2,021.5	15,185	360.0
Percent change		+5.3	+4.4	-5.9	-6.7	-10.8	-11.6	-4.4	-5.2	-9.0	-9.8
Washington											
2018	7,523,869	14,316	190.3	223,256	2,967.3	40,434	537.4	154,941	2,059.3	27,881	370.6
2019	7,614,893	13,700	179.9	204,224	2,681.9	34,540	453.6	145,282	1,907.9	24,402	320.5
Percent change		-4.3	-5.4	-8.5	-9.6	-14.6	-15.6	-6.2	-7.4	-12.5	-13.5
Puerto Rico											
2018...............................	3,193,354	3,309	103.6	24,851	778.2	5,486	171.8	15,658	490.3	3,707	116.1
2019...............................	3,193,694	3,537	110.7	22,441	702.7	4,291	134.4	14,483	453.5	3,667	114.8
Percent change		+6.9	+6.9	-9.7	-9.7	-21.8	-21.8	-7.5	-7.5	-1.1	-1.1

Note: Although arson data are included in the trend and clearance tables, sufficient data are not available to estimate totals for this offense. Therefore, no arson data are published in this table.

* = Less than one-tenth of 1 percent.

[1]The previous year's crime figures have been adjusted.

[2]Population figures are U.S. Census Bureau provisional estimates as of July 1, 2019.

[3]The violent crime figures include the offenses of murder, rape (revised definition), robbery, and aggravated assault.

[4]The figures shown in this column for the offense of rape were estimated using the revised Uniform Crime Reporting (UCR) definition of rape. See chapter notes for more detail.

[5]Limited data for 2018 were available for Iowa.

[6]Includes offenses reported by the Metro Transit Police and the District of Columbia Fire and Emergency Medical Services: Arson Investigation Unit.

[7]This state's agencies submitted rape data according to the legacy UCR definition of rape.

Table 3. Crime in the United States, by State and Area, 2019

(Number, percent, rate per 100,000 population.)

Area	Population	Violent crime[1]	Murder and nonnegligent manslaughter	Rape[2]	Robbery	Aggravated assault	Property crime	Burglary	Larceny-theft	Motor vehicle theft
Alabama										
Metropolitan statistical area	3,728,978									
Area actually reporting	76.6%	12,880	182	1,141	1,706	9,851	65,789	12,388	47,299	6,102
Estimated total	100.0%	19,951	300	1,542	3,432	14,677	104,658	20,728	73,857	10,073
Cities outside metropolitan areas	528,518									
Area actually reporting	89.3%	3,327	36	297	266	2,728	17,915	3,140	13,382	1,393
Estimated total	100.0%	3,541	37	310	301	2,893	19,177	3,364	14,305	1,508
Nonmetropolitan counties	645,689									
Area actually reporting	72.4%	874	13	148	55	658	4,927	1,387	2,887	653
Estimated total	100.0%	1,554	21	216	208	1,109	7,298	1,987	4,315	996
State total	4,903,185	25,046	358	2,068	3,941	18,679	131,133	26,079	92,477	12,577
Rate per 100,000 inhabitants		510.8	7.3	42.2	80.4	381.0	2,674.4	531.9	1,886.1	256.5
Alaska										
Metropolitan statistical area	339,740									
Area actually reporting	100.0%	3,924	37	585	690	2,612	14,713	2,015	10,883	1,815
Cities outside metropolitan areas	127,436									
Area actually reporting	97.1%	1,032	9	225	71	727	3,555	467	2,760	328
Estimated total	100.0%	1,050	9	225	71	745	3,596	475	2,785	336
Nonmetropolitan counties	264,369									
Area actually reporting	100.0%	1,369	23	278	65	1,003	2,985	1,073	1,446	466
State total	731,545	6,343	69	1,088	826	4,360	21,294	3,563	15,114	2,617
Rate per 100,000 inhabitants		867.1	9.4	148.7	112.9	596.0	2,910.8	487.1	2,066.0	357.7
Arizona										
Metropolitan statistical area	6,926,575									
Area actually reporting	93.6%	26,975	314	3,203	6,171	17,287	163,728	25,572	121,711	16,445
Estimated total	100.0%	28,465	332	3,360	6,316	18,457	169,802	26,720	125,905	17,177
Cities outside metropolitan areas	126,113									
Area actually reporting	93.3%	4,280	26	294	75	3,885	6,061	1,419	3,868	774
Estimated total	100.0%	4,341	26	296	80	3,939	6,385	1,477	4,115	793
Nonmetropolitan counties	226,029									
Area actually reporting	100.0%	335	7	6	14	308	1,451	502	768	181
State total	7,278,717	33,141	365	3,662	6,410	22,704	177,638	28,699	130,788	18,151
Rate per 100,000 inhabitants		455.3	5.0	50.3	88.1	311.9	2,440.5	394.3	1,796.9	249.4
Arkansas										
Metropolitan statistical area	1,912,942									
Area actually reporting	95.3%	11,787	166	1,373	1,214	9,034	58,348	11,579	41,508	5,261
Estimated total	100.0%	12,317	172	1,444	1,277	9,424	61,525	12,103	43,905	5,517
Cities outside metropolitan areas	500,348									
Area actually reporting	93.8%	3,107	51	472	221	2,363	15,641	3,554	11,193	894
Estimated total	100.0%	3,268	53	497	233	2,485	16,457	3,748	11,767	942
Nonmetropolitan counties	604,514									
Area actually reporting	81.5%	1,703	15	334	37	1,317	6,709	1,825	4,081	803
Estimated total	100.0%	2,058	17	390	47	1,604	8,268	2,244	5,063	961
State total	3,017,804	17,643	242	2,331	1,557	13,513	86,250	18,095	60,735	7,420
Rate per 100,000 inhabitants		584.6	8.0	77.2	51.6	447.8	2,858.0	599.6	2,012.6	245.9
California										
Metropolitan statistical area	38,682,717									
Area actually reporting	99.9%	170,767	1,652	14,334	51,859	102,922	904,772	148,097	616,986	139,689
Estimated total	100.0%	170,793	1,652	14,336	51,862	102,943	904,915	148,134	617,075	139,706
Cities outside metropolitan areas	267,543									
Area actually reporting	100.0%	1,542	12	192	254	1,084	7,837	1,649	5,254	934
Nonmetropolitan counties	561,963									
Area actually reporting	100.0%	1,996	26	271	185	1,514	8,362	2,772	4,473	1,117
State total	39,512,223	174,331	1,690	14,799	52,301	105,541	921,114	152,555	626,802	141,757
Rate per 100,000 inhabitants		441.2	4.3	37.5	132.4	267.1	2,331.2	386.1	1,586.3	358.8
Colorado										
Metropolitan statistical area	5,045,741									
Area actually reporting	97.5%	19,666	187	3,326	3,505	12,648	133,050	17,395	95,114	20,541
Estimated total	100.0%	20,284	193	3,456	3,579	13,056	137,155	17,937	97,993	21,225
Cities outside metropolitan areas	343,675									
Area actually reporting	95.1%	1,000	8	258	69	665	8,475	1,152	6,813	510
Estimated total	100.0%	1,037	8	262	70	697	8,772	1,202	7,040	530
Nonmetropolitan counties	369,320									
Area actually reporting	95.1%	582	14	149	14	405	3,024	849	1,844	331
Estimated total	100.0%	617	17	154	14	432	3,262	925	1,979	358

Table 3. Crime in the United States, by State and Area, 2019—Continued

(Number, percent, rate per 100,000 population.)

Area	Population	Violent crime[1]	Murder and nonnegligent manslaughter	Rape[2]	Robbery	Aggravated assault	Property crime	Burglary	Larceny-theft	Motor vehicle theft
State total............	5,758,736	21,938	218	3,872	3,663	14,185	149,189	20,064	107,012	22,113
Rate per 100,000 inhabitants		381.0	3.8	67.2	63.6	246.3	2,590.7	348.4	1,858.3	384.0
Connecticut										
Metropolitan statistical area..................................	2,964,813									
Area actually reporting..........................	100.0%	6,227	92	675	1,883	3,577	48,028	5,955	36,501	5,572
Cities outside metropolitan areas.........................	112,020									
Area actually reporting	100.0%	82	3	29	12	38	1,117	121	896	100
Nonmetropolitan counties	488,454									
Area actually reporting	100.0%	237	9	67	34	127	1,717	365	1,060	292
State total........................	3,565,287	6,546	104	771	1,929	3,742	50,862	6,441	38,457	5,964
Rate per 100,000 inhabitants		183.6	2.9	21.6	54.1	105.0	1,426.6	180.7	1,078.7	167.3
Delaware										
Metropolitan statistical area..................................	973,764									
Area actually reporting	100.0%	4,115	48	310	790	2,967	21,931	2,968	17,359	1,604
Cities outside metropolitan areas.........................	None									
Nonmetropolitan counties	None									
State total........................	973,764	4,115	48	310	790	2,967	21,931	2,968	17,359	1,604
Rate per 100,000 inhabitants		422.6	4.9	31.8	81.1	304.7	2,252.2	304.8	1,782.7	164.7
District of Columbia[3]										
Metropolitan statistical area..................................	705,749									
Area actually reporting	100.0%	7,403	166	345	2,713	4,179	30,821	1,843	26,645	2,333
Cities outside metropolitan areas.........................	None									
Nonmetropolitan counties	None									
District total........................	705,749	7,403	166	345	2,713	4,179	30,821	1,843	26,645	2,333
Rate per 100,000 inhabitants		1,049.0	23.5	48.9	384.4	592.1	4,367.1	261.1	3,775.4	330.6
Florida										
Metropolitan statistical area..................................	20,789,824									
Area actually reporting	99.9%	78,493	1,088	8,189	15,976	53,240	448,932	60,219	350,521	38,192
Estimated total...................	100.0%	78,513	1,088	8,191	15,979	53,255	449,076	60,247	350,626	38,203
Cities outside metropolitan areas.........................	141,342									
Area actually reporting	92.9%	763	8	37	98	620	3,994	818	2,933	243
Estimated total...................	100.0%	804	8	37	102	657	4,169	876	3,035	258
Nonmetropolitan counties	546,571									
Area actually reporting	93.4%	1,839	24	217	125	1,473	7,040	2,112	4,381	547
Estimated total...................	100.0%	1,953	26	228	136	1,563	7,601	2,273	4,741	587
State total........................	21,477,737	81,270	1,122	8,456	16,217	55,475	460,846	63,396	358,402	39,048
Rate per 100,000 inhabitants		378.4	5.2	39.4	75.5	258.3	2,145.7	295.2	1,668.7	181.8
Georgia										
Metropolitan statistical area..................................	8,820,462									
Area actually reporting	93.8%	28,497	542	2,310	6,964	18,681	200,844	30,111	150,187	20,546
Estimated total...................	100.0%	30,614	558	2,478	7,336	20,242	214,626	32,162	160,880	21,584
Cities outside metropolitan areas.........................	638,977									
Area actually reporting	81.2%	2,485	51	175	420	1,839	18,897	2,988	15,125	784
Estimated total	100.0%	2,861	54	197	472	2,138	21,735	3,504	17,334	897
Nonmetropolitan counties	1,157,984									
Area actually reporting	90.3%	2,405	40	213	144	2,008	14,622	3,465	9,986	1,171
Estimated total...................	100.0%	2,695	42	247	153	2,253	15,888	3,840	10,753	1,295
State total........................	10,617,423	36,170	654	2,922	7,961	24,633	252,249	39,506	188,967	23,776
Rate per 100,000 inhabitants		340.7	6.2	27.5	75.0	232.0	2,375.8	372.1	1,779.8	223.9
Hawaii										
Metropolitan statistical area..................................	1,142,377									
Area actually reporting	100.0%	3,087	28	450	1,021	1,588	34,247	4,441	25,308	4,498
Cities outside metropolitan areas.........................	None									
Nonmetropolitan counties	273,495									
Area actually reporting	73.6%	680	16	288	48	328	4,444	656	3,196	592
State total........................	100.0%	955	20	315	110	510	5,981	899	4,326	756
Rate per 100,000 inhabitants	1,415,872	4,042	48	765	1,131	2,098	40,228	5,340	29,634	5,254
		285.5	3.4	54.0	79.9	148.2	2,841.2	377.2	2,093.0	371.1
Idaho										
Metropolitan statistical area..................................	1,328,563									
Area actually reporting	99.8%	3,217	18	685	140	2,374	17,685	3,077	13,378	1,230
Cities outside metropolitan areas.........................	100.0%	3,223	18	686	140	2,379	17,720	3,083	13,404	1,233
Area actually reporting	184,404									
Estimated total	97.5%	352	1	59	11	281	2,204	397	1,667	140

Table 3. Crime in the United States, by State and Area, 2019—*Continued*

(Number, percent, rate per 100,000 population.)

Area	Population	Violent crime[1]	Murder and nonnegligent manslaughter	Rape[2]	Robbery	Aggravated assault	Property crime	Burglary	Larceny-theft	Motor vehicle theft
Nonmetropolitan counties	100.0%	362	1	61	11	289	2,274	410	1,719	145
Area actually reporting	274,098									
Estimated total	100.0%	415	16	62	4	333	1,799	434	1,172	193
State total..	1,787,065	4,000	35	809	155	3,001	21,793	3,927	16,295	1,571
Rate per 100,000 inhabitants		223.8	2.0	45.3	8.7	167.9	1,219.5	219.7	911.8	87.9
Illinois										
Metropolitan statistical area................................	11,250,485									
Area actually reporting	97.4%	47,147	772	5,159	12,142	29,074	209,020	29,308	162,231	17,481
Estimated total	100.0%	47,898	777	5,288	12,266	29,567	214,444	30,102	166,463	17,879
Cities outside metropolitan areas........................	806,403									
Area actually reporting	84.3%	2,349	26	506	164	1,653	13,515	2,498	10,534	483
Estimated total	100.0%	2,571	26	533	172	1,840	15,028	2,834	11,639	555
Nonmetropolitan counties	614,933									
Area actually reporting	90.0%	1,016	29	244	26	717	4,108	1,360	2,436	312
Estimated total	100.0%	1,092	29	257	26	780	4,512	1,497	2,674	341
State total..	12,671,821	51,561	832	6,078	12,464	32,187	233,984	34,433	180,776	18,775
Rate per 100,000 inhabitants		406.9	6.6	48.0	98.4	254.0	1,846.5	271.7	1,426.6	148.2
Indiana										
Metropolitan statistical area................................	5,267,529									
Area actually reporting...........................	83.6%	20,739	314	1,922	4,908	13,595	102,535	16,775	74,430	11,330
Estimated total..	100.0%	22,290	329	2,083	5,126	14,752	113,852	18,419	83,178	12,255
Cities outside metropolitan areas........................	550,564									
Area actually reporting............................	63.9%	939	9	110	92	728	7,715	902	6,315	498
Estimated total	100.0%	1,562	19	227	145	1,171	11,471	1,348	9,377	746
Nonmetropolitan counties	914,126									
Area actually reporting	54.1%	672	15	99	41	517	3,938	1,062	2,427	449
Estimated total	100.0%	1,114	29	165	60	860	7,371	2,028	4,621	722
State total..	6,732,219	24,966	377	2,475	5,331	16,783	132,694	21,795	97,176	13,723
Rate per 100,000 inhabitants		370.8	5.6	36.8	79.2	249.3	1,971.0	323.7	1,443.4	203.8
Iowa										
Metropolitan statistical area................................	1,936,796									
Area actually reporting	99.7%	5,897	47	767	785	4,298	40,335	8,397	27,930	4,008
Estimated total	100.0%	5,916	47	769	788	4,312	40,467	8,424	28,021	4,022
Cities outside metropolitan areas........................	571,915									
Area actually reporting	92.5%	1,680	8	250	67	1,355	10,388	2,050	7,640	698
Estimated total	100.0%	1,781	8	269	69	1,435	11,120	2,181	8,199	740
Nonmetropolitan counties	646,359									
Area actually reporting	97.7%	690	5	123	6	556	3,004	1,068	1,569	367
Estimated total	100.0%	713	5	126	6	576	3,112	1,105	1,627	380
State total..	3,155,070	8,410	60	1,164	863	6,323	54,699	11,710	37,847	5,142
Rate per 100,000 inhabitants		266.6	1.9	36.9	27.4	200.4	1,733.7	371.1	1,199.6	163.0
Kansas										
Metropolitan statistical area................................	2,025,373									
Area actually reporting	95.0%	8,394	72	931	969	6,422	45,635	6,174	34,260	5,201
Estimated total	100.0%	9,339	83	1,033	1,151	7,072	51,894	6,979	38,847	6,068
Cities outside metropolitan areas........................	565,513									
Area actually reporting	96.5%	1,818	12	287	124	1,395	12,031	1,972	9,259	800
Estimated total	100.0%	1,865	12	297	124	1,432	12,329	2,050	9,457	822
Nonmetropolitan counties	322,428									
Area actually reporting	97.1%	743	10	83	18	632	3,103	926	1,800	377
Estimated total	100.0%	764	10	86	18	650	3,205	955	1,861	389
State total..	2,913,314	11,968	105	1,416	1,293	9,154	67,428	9,984	50,165	7,279
Rate per 100,000 inhabitants		410.8	3.6	48.6	44.4	314.2	2,314.5	342.7	1,721.9	249.9
Kentucky										
Metropolitan statistical area................................	2,664,226									
Area actually reporting	99.9%	7,572	164	879	1,892	4,637	64,472	10,604	46,165	7,703
Estimated total	100.0%	7,572	164	879	1,892	4,637	64,511	10,610	46,193	7,708
Cities outside metropolitan areas........................	529,864									
Area actually reporting	98.0%	829	13	207	170	439	11,654	2,015	8,709	930
Estimated total	100.0%	833	13	207	172	441	11,784	2,041	8,804	939
Nonmetropolitan counties	1,273,583									
Area actually reporting	100.0%	1,296	44	486	97	669	8,474	2,792	4,133	1,549
State total..	4,467,673	9,701	221	1,572	2,161	5,747	84,769	15,443	59,130	10,196
Rate per 100,000 inhabitants		217.1	4.9	35.2	48.4	128.6	1,897.4	345.7	1,323.5	228.2

Table 3. Crime in the United States, by State and Area, 2019—Continued

(Number, percent, rate per 100,000 population.)

Area	Population	Violent crime[1]	Murder and nonnegligent manslaughter	Rape[2]	Robbery	Aggravated assault	Property crime	Burglary	Larceny-theft	Motor vehicle theft
Louisiana										
Metropolitan statistical area	3,915,216									
Area actually reporting	94.7%	21,056	475	1,939	3,632	15,010	125,043	21,718	93,822	9,503
Estimated total	100.0%	22,165	493	1,992	3,746	15,934	131,212	23,018	98,327	9,867
Cities outside metropolitan areas	267,576									
Area actually reporting	75.2%	1,588	23	117	174	1,274	8,226	2,008	5,939	279
Estimated total	100.0%	1,817	23	131	199	1,464	9,500	2,254	6,906	340
Nonmetropolitan counties	466,002									
Area actually reporting	96.7%	1,508	27	145	77	1,259	6,084	1,600	3,990	494
Estimated total	100.0%	1,555	28	150	80	1,297	6,281	1,646	4,126	509
State total	4,648,794	25,537	544	2,273	4,025	18,695	146,993	26,918	109,359	10,716
Rate per 100,000 inhabitants		549.3	11.7	48.9	86.6	402.1	3,162.0	579.0	2,352.4	230.5
Maine										
Metropolitan statistical area	799,195									
Area actually reporting	100.0%	872	8	247	138	479	10,593	1,277	8,929	387
Cities outside metropolitan areas	258,428									
Area actually reporting	100.0%	356	5	132	33	186	3,950	528	3,259	163
Nonmetropolitan counties	286,589									
Area actually reporting	100.0%	320	7	137	17	159	2,200	545	1,479	176
State total	1,344,212	1,548	20	516	188	824	16,743	2,350	13,667	726
Rate per 100,000 inhabitants		115.2	1.5	38.4	14.0	61.3	1,245.6	174.8	1,016.7	54.0
Maryland										
Metropolitan statistical area	5,895,999									
Area actually reporting	100.0%	27,100	538	1,861	9,150	15,551	115,527	16,382	87,952	11,193
Cities outside metropolitan areas	51,212									
Area actually reporting	100.0%	225	4	23	45	153	1,596	249	1,310	37
Nonmetropolitan counties	98,469									
Area actually reporting	100.0%	131	0	29	8	94	778	231	518	29
State total	6,045,680	27,456	542	1,913	9,203	15,798	117,901	16,862	89,780	11,259
Rate per 100,000 inhabitants		454.1	9.0	31.6	152.2	261.3	1,950.2	278.9	1,485.0	186.2
Massachusetts										
Metropolitan statistical area	6,863,792									
Area actually reporting	98.2%	22,199	152	2,159	3,588	16,300	79,955	12,124	61,784	6,047
Estimated total	100.0%	22,463	152	2,194	3,611	16,506	80,985	12,296	62,575	6,114
Cities outside metropolitan areas	28,711									
Area actually reporting	100.0%	115	0	10	2	103	332	45	269	18
Nonmetropolitan counties										
Area actually reporting	100.0%	0	0	0	0	0	0	0	0	0
State total	6,892,503	22,578	152	2,204	3,613	16,609	81,317	12,341	62,844	6,132
Rate per 100,000 inhabitants		327.6	2.2	32.0	52.4	241.0	1,179.8	179.0	911.8	89.0
Michigan										
Metropolitan statistical area	8,189,617									
Area actually reporting	99.3%	38,719	510	5,465	5,247	27,497	138,960	24,755	97,615	16,590
Estimated total	100.0%	38,826	510	5,490	5,253	27,573	139,444	24,835	97,990	16,619
Cities outside metropolitan areas	578,010									
Area actually reporting	97.6%	1,684	12	541	67	1,064	9,096	1,025	7,676	395
Estimated total	100.0%	1,704	12	546	67	1,079	9,205	1,039	7,766	400
Nonmetropolitan counties	1,218,430									
Area actually reporting	96.2%	3,097	34	1,180	30	1,853	9,378	2,626	6,039	713
Estimated total	100.0%	3,156	34	1,199	30	1,893	9,647	2,698	6,224	725
State total	9,986,857	43,686	556	7,235	5,350	30,545	158,296	28,572	111,980	17,744
Rate per 100,000 inhabitants		437.4	5.6	72.4	53.6	305.9	1,585.0	286.1	1,121.3	177.7
Minnesota										
Metropolitan statistical area	4,394,131									
Area actually reporting	100.0%	11,396	105	1,973	3,047	6,271	100,569	13,139	77,450	9,980
Estimated total	568,835									
Cities outside metropolitan areas	95.7%	1,232	5	281	84	862	11,729	1,461	9,542	726
Area actually reporting	100.0%	1,233	5	281	84	863	11,754	1,464	9,563	727
Estimated total	676,666									
Nonmetropolitan counties	98.6%	695	7	192	18	478	4,862	1,310	3,048	504
Area actually reporting	100.0%	703	7	194	18	484	4,913	1,324	3,079	510
State total	5,639,632	13,332	117	2,448	3,149	7,618	117,236	15,927	90,092	11,217
Rate per 100,000 inhabitants		236.4	2.1	43.4	55.8	135.1	2,078.8	282.4	1,597.5	198.9

Table 3. Crime in the United States, by State and Area, 2019—*Continued*

(Number, percent, rate per 100,000 population.)

Area	Population	Violent crime[1]	Murder and nonnegligent manslaughter	Rape[2]	Robbery	Aggravated assault	Property crime	Burglary	Larceny-theft	Motor vehicle theft
Mississippi[4]										
Metropolitan statistical area	1,439,666									
Area actually reporting	78.4%	3,235	141	432	883	1,779	30,660	5,668	22,012	2,980
Estimated total	100.0%	4,273	158	452	960	2,703	37,017	6,985	26,536	3,496
Cities outside metropolitan areas	554,808									
Area actually reporting	31.9%	931	38	112	144	637	7,037	1,698	4,967	372
Estimated total	100.0%	2,394	107	162	481	1,644	21,069	5,969	13,941	1,159
Nonmetropolitan counties	981,675									
Area actually reporting	28.2%	516	13	95	84	324	3,410	1,448	1,649	313
Estimated total	100.0%	1,605	67	133	259	1,146	12,621	5,706	5,823	1,092
State total	2,976,149	8,272	332	747	1,700	5,493	70,707	18,660	46,300	5,747
Rate per 100,000 inhabitants		277.9	11.2	25.1	57.1	184.6	2,375.8	627.0	1,555.7	193.1
Missouri										
Metropolitan statistical area	4,606,823									
Area actually reporting	99.5%	25,504	519	2,375	4,733	17,877	129,712	19,711	91,741	18,260
Estimated total	100.0%	25,679	520	2,381	4,740	18,038	130,293	19,864	92,117	18,312
Cities outside metropolitan areas	649,460									
Area actually reporting	96.4%	2,295	20	337	158	1,780	20,987	3,251	16,399	1,337
Estimated total	100.0%	2,394	20	338	159	1,877	21,518	3,317	16,845	1,356
Nonmetropolitan counties	881,145									
Area actually reporting	96.9%	2,245	28	193	59	1,965	9,852	3,139	5,351	1,362
Estimated total	100.0%	2,307	28	198	60	2,021	10,135	3,233	5,498	1,404
State total	6,137,428	30,380	568	2,917	4,959	21,936	161,946	26,414	114,460	21,072
Rate per 100,000 inhabitants		495.0	9.3	47.5	80.8	357.4	2,638.7	430.4	1,865.0	343.3
Montana										
Metropolitan statistical area	382,587									
Area actually reporting	100.0%	1,689	8	234	155	1,292	12,476	1,506	9,731	1,239
Cities outside metropolitan areas	230,654									
Area actually reporting	98.0%	1,500	9	226	30	1,235	5,995	625	4,838	532
Nonmetropolitan counties	455,537	1,522	9	227	30	1,256	6,063	632	4,892	539
Area actually reporting	97.7%	1,087	10	159	20	898	4,796	731	3,481	584
State total	100.0%	1,117	10	163	20	924	4,901	749	3,553	599
Rate per 100,000 inhabitants	1,068,778	4,328	27	624	205	3,472	23,440	2,887	18,176	2,377
		404.9	2.5	58.4	19.2	324.9	2,193.2	270.1	1,700.6	222.4
Nebraska										
Metropolitan statistical area	1,264,647									
Area actually reporting	99.6%	4,720	33	919	748	3,020	31,084	3,433	23,355	4,296
Estimated total	100.0%	4,766	33	950	748	3,035	31,147	3,433	23,418	4,296
Cities outside metropolitan areas	342,937									
Area actually reporting	94.1%	716	5	222	37	452	6,295	888	4,957	450
Estimated total	100.0%	727	5	226	37	459	6,523	918	5,142	463
Nonmetropolitan counties	326,824									
Area actually reporting	87.4%	289	7	69	7	206	1,512	334	985	193
Estimated total	100.0%	328	7	77	7	237	1,779	394	1,159	226
State total	1,934,408	5,821	45	1,253	792	3,731	39,449	4,745	29,719	4,985
Rate per 100,000 inhabitants		300.9	2.3	64.8	40.9	192.9	2,039.3	245.3	1,536.3	257.7
Nevada										
Metropolitan statistical area	2,801,329									
Area actually reporting	100.0%	14,359	127	2,008	3,232	8,992	67,801	14,711	42,280	10,810
Cities outside metropolitan areas	48,376									
Area actually reporting	100.0%	211	5	40	16	150	1,179	237	825	117
Nonmetropolitan counties	230,451									
Area actually reporting	95.9%	593	10	102	37	444	2,456	529	1,604	323
Estimated total	100.0%	640	11	113	38	478	2,545	562	1,650	333
State total	3,080,156	15,210	143	2,161	3,286	9,620	71,525	15,510	44,755	11,260
Rate per 100,000 inhabitants		493.8	4.6	70.2	106.7	312.3	2,322.1	503.5	1,453.0	365.6
New Hampshire										
Metropolitan statistical area	857,832									
Area actually reporting	99.2%	1,376	16	329	221	810	9,917	1,019	8,389	509
Estimated total	100.0%	1,391	16	333	223	819	10,205	1,028	8,666	511
Cities outside metropolitan areas	465,800									
Area actually reporting	92.2%	581	17	214	79	271	5,373	562	4,488	323
Estimated total	100.0%	632	17	236	84	295	5,903	631	4,923	349
Nonmetropolitan counties	36,079									
Area actually reporting	92.3%	35	0	14	4	17	243	46	171	26
Estimated total	100.0%	51	0	21	6	24	334	58	243	33

Table 3. Crime in the United States, by State and Area, 2019—*Continued*

(Number, percent, rate per 100,000 population.)

Area	Population	Violent crime[1]	Murder and nonnegligent manslaughter	Rape[2]	Robbery	Aggravated assault	Property crime	Burglary	Larceny-theft	Motor vehicle theft
State total	1,359,711	2,074	33	590	313	1,138	16,442	1,717	13,832	893
Rate per 100,000 inhabitants		152.5	2.4	43.4	23.0	83.7	1,209.2	126.3	1,017.3	65.7
New Jersey										
Metropolitan statistical area	8,882,190									
Area actually reporting	100.0%	18,375	262	1,531	5,730	10,852	118,637	16,399	91,902	10,336
Cities outside metropolitan areas	None									
Nonmetropolitan counties	None									
State total	8,882,190	18,375	262	1,531	5,730	10,852	118,637	16,399	91,902	10,336
Rate per 100,000 inhabitants		206.9	2.9	17.2	64.5	122.2	1,335.7	184.6	1,034.7	116.4
New Mexico										
Metropolitan statistical area	1,411,105									
Area actually reporting	91.4%	12,163	115	878	1,994	9,176	47,641	10,066	30,689	6,886
Estimated total	100.0%	12,859	117	903	2,022	9,817	49,041	10,693	31,294	7,054
Cities outside metropolitan areas	395,686									
Area actually reporting	94.4%	2,674	40	248	249	2,137	12,074	2,467	8,413	1,194
Estimated total	100.0%	2,963	41	251	280	2,391	12,630	2,688	8,716	1,226
Nonmetropolitan counties	290,038									
Area actually reporting	97.4%	1,598	23	133	38	1,404	3,503	1,191	1,645	667
Estimated total	100.0%	1,628	23	134	39	1,432	3,598	1,229	1,692	677
State total	2,096,829	17,450	181	1,288	2,341	13,640	65,269	14,610	41,702	8,957
Rate per 100,000 inhabitants		832.2	8.6	61.4	111.6	650.5	3,112.7	696.8	1,988.8	427.2
New York										
Metropolitan statistical area	18,100,822									
Area actually reporting	99.1%	67,175	546	5,653	17,891	43,085	250,291	24,744	213,411	12,136
Estimated total	100.0%	67,287	546	5,661	17,918	43,162	251,205	24,854	214,182	12,169
Cities outside metropolitan areas	499,079									
Area actually reporting	95.1%	1,113	4	287	110	712	8,359	1,255	6,895	209
Estimated total	100.0%	1,132	4	290	111	727	8,553	1,283	7,058	212
Nonmetropolitan counties	853,660									
Area actually reporting	94.6%	1,326	8	627	38	653	7,234	1,429	5,488	317
Estimated total	100.0%	1,345	8	632	39	666	7,397	1,463	5,611	323
State total	19,453,561	69,764	558	6,583	18,068	44,555	267,155	27,600	226,851	12,704
Rate per 100,000 inhabitants		358.6	2.9	33.8	92.9	229.0	1,373.3	141.9	1,166.1	65.3
North Carolina[5]										
Metropolitan statistical area	8,503,759									
Area actually reporting	82.6%	27,331	421	2,093	5,952	18,865	171,283	32,606	125,793	12,884
Estimated total	100.0%	31,802	483	2,497	6,622	22,200	200,678	39,627	146,034	15,017
Cities outside metropolitan areas	588,106									
Area actually reporting	63.1%	2,256	37	203	382	1,634	15,667	3,686	11,181	800
Estimated total	100.0%	3,513	50	297	611	2,555	24,323	5,855	17,281	1,187
Nonmetropolitan counties	1,396,219									
Area actually reporting	73.5%	2,632	70	335	260	1,967	16,227	6,532	8,313	1,382
Estimated total	100.0%	3,680	99	453	366	2,762	22,235	8,965	11,413	1,857
State total	10,488,084	38,995	632	3,247	7,599	27,517	247,236	54,447	174,728	18,061
Rate per 100,000 inhabitants		371.8	6.0	31.0	72.5	262.4	2,357.3	519.1	1,666.0	172.2
North Dakota										
Metropolitan statistical area	382,454									
Area actually reporting	100.0%	1,230	10	261	151	808	9,400	1,585	6,873	942
Cities outside metropolitan areas	190,013									
Area actually reporting	99.9%	747	10	124	26	587	4,138	630	2,910	598
Estimated total	100.0%	747	10	124	26	587	4,139	630	2,911	598
Nonmetropolitan counties	189,595									
Area actually reporting	100.0%	192	4	52	2	134	1,527	393	882	252
State total	762,062	2,169	24	437	179	1,529	15,066	2,608	10,666	1,792
Rate per 100,000 inhabitants		284.6	3.1	57.3	23.5	200.6	1,977.0	342.2	1,399.6	235.2
Ohio[4]										
Metropolitan statistical area	9,386,086									
Area actually reporting	91.0%	29,614	489	4,445	8,287	16,393	189,426	35,722	137,623	16,081
Estimated total	100.0%	30,840	495	4,736	8,520	17,089	203,961	37,714	149,512	16,735
Cities outside metropolitan areas	1,016,283									
Area actually reporting	78.2%	1,499	8	459	191	841	18,427	2,481	15,210	736
Estimated total	100.0%	2,001	8	611	263	1,119	24,942	3,337	20,641	964
Nonmetropolitan counties	1,286,731									
Area actually reporting	84.2%	1,225	29	325	52	819	9,442	2,349	6,280	813
Estimated total	100.0%	1,428	35	384	63	946	11,388	2,843	7,572	973

Table 3. Crime in the United States, by State and Area, 2019—*Continued*

(Number, percent, rate per 100,000 population.)

Area	Population	Violent crime[1]	Murder and nonnegligent manslaughter	Rape[2]	Robbery	Aggravated assault	Property crime	Burglary	Larceny-theft	Motor vehicle theft
State total............	11,689,100	34,269	538	5,731	8,846	19,154	240,291	43,894	177,725	18,672
Rate per 100,000 inhabitants		293.2	4.6	49.0	75.7	163.9	2,055.7	375.5	1,520.4	159.7
Oklahoma										
Metropolitan statistical area............	2,636,166									
Area actually reporting	100.0%	13,071	209	1,637	2,070	9,155	81,441	18,566	52,513	10,362
Cities outside metropolitan areas............	734,808									
Area actually reporting............	96.9%	2,924	35	427	262	2,200	23,565	5,284	16,352	1,929
Estimated total............	100.0%	2,925	35	427	262	2,201	23,572	5,286	16,356	1,930
Nonmetropolitan counties	585,997									
Area actually reporting	98.1%	1,070	22	200	36	812	7,415	2,666	3,685	1,064
Estimated total	100.0%	1,090	22	204	37	827	7,574	2,725	3,763	1,086
State total............	3,956,971	17,086	266	2,268	2,369	12,183	112,587	26,577	72,632	13,378
Rate per 100,000 inhabitants		431.8	6.7	57.3	59.9	307.9	2,845.3	671.7	1,835.5	338.1
Oregon[4]										
Metropolitan statistical area............	3,542,422									
Area actually reporting	99.4%	10,120	93	1,484	2,096	6,447	99,327	11,989	73,638	13,700
Estimated total	100.0%	10,176	93	1,494	2,098	6,491	99,681	12,034	73,924	13,723
Cities outside metropolitan areas............	312,995									
Area actually reporting	97.2%	1,046	15	178	150	703	10,316	1,384	8,144	788
Estimated total	100.0%	1,064	15	182	151	716	10,490	1,411	8,279	800
Nonmetropolitan counties	362,320									
Area actually reporting	79.1%	618	7	82	21	508	3,965	1,009	2,438	518
Estimated total	100.0%	755	8	102	27	618	4,999	1,279	3,058	662
State total............	4,217,737	11,995	116	1,778	2,276	7,825	115,170	14,724	85,261	15,185
Rate per 100,000 inhabitants		284.4	2.8	42.2	54.0	185.5	2,730.6	349.1	2,021.5	360.0
Pennsylvania										
Metropolitan statistical area............	11,356,999									
Area actually reporting	99.2%	36,227	631	3,656	9,536	22,404	164,977	20,488	132,755	11,734
Estimated total	100.0%	36,357	631	3,662	9,548	22,516	165,748	20,577	133,398	11,773
Cities outside metropolitan areas............	641,738									
Area actually reporting	94.8%	1,415	7	135	108	1,165	6,410	879	5,353	178
Estimated total	100.0%	1,439	7	136	108	1,188	6,554	898	5,476	180
Nonmetropolitan counties	803,252									
Area actually reporting	100.0%	1,432	31	553	87	761	7,363	1,879	5,047	437
State total............	12,801,989	39,228	669	4,351	9,743	24,465	179,665	23,354	143,921	12,390
Rate per 100,000 inhabitants		306.4	5.2	34.0	76.1	191.1	1,403.4	182.4	1,124.2	96.8
Puerto Rico										
Metropolitan statistical area............	3,193,694									
Area actually reporting	100.0%	6,180	572	205	2,086	3,317	21,967	4,115	14,227	3,625
Cities outside metropolitan areas............										
Area actually reporting............	100.0%	299	34	10	35	220	474	176	256	42
Total	3,193,694	6,479	606	215	2,121	3,537	22,441	4,291	14,483	3,667
Rate per 100,000 inhabitants		202.9	19.0	6.7	66.4	110.7	702.7	134.4	453.5	114.8
Rhode Island										
Metropolitan statistical area............	1,059,361									
Area actually reporting	100.0%	2,342	25	491	418	1,408	16,259	2,321	12,580	1,358
Cities outside metropolitan areas............	None									
Nonmetropolitan counties	None									
State total............	1,059,361	2,342	25	491	418	1,408	16,259	2,321	12,580	1,358
Rate per 100,000 inhabitants		221.1	2.4	46.3	39.5	132.9	1,534.8	219.1	1,187.5	128.2
South Carolina										
Metropolitan statistical area............	4,412,435									
Area actually reporting	99.0%	21,045	340	2,111	2,816	15,778	126,047	21,448	91,850	12,749
Estimated total............	100.0%	21,415	345	2,140	2,844	16,086	127,857	21,830	93,137	12,890
Cities outside metropolitan areas............	202,637									
Area actually reporting............	97.2%	2,045	43	111	239	1,652	10,095	1,976	7,458	661
Estimated total............	100.0%	2,114	46	113	246	1,709	10,430	2,055	7,696	679
Nonmetropolitan counties	533,642									
Area actually reporting	97.0%	2,717	72	201	197	2,247	12,737	3,462	7,904	1,371
Estimated total............	100.0%	2,794	73	207	204	2,310	13,102	3,576	8,120	1,406
State total............	5,148,714	26,323	464	2,460	3,294	20,105	151,389	27,461	108,953	14,975
Rate per 100,000 inhabitants		511.3	9.0	47.8	64.0	390.5	2,940.3	533.4	2,116.1	290.8

Table 3. Crime in the United States, by State and Area, 2019—*Continued*

(Number, percent, rate per 100,000 population.)

Area	Population	Violent crime[1]	Murder and nonnegligent manslaughter	Rape[2]	Robbery	Aggravated assault	Property crime	Burglary	Larceny-theft	Motor vehicle theft
South Dakota										
Metropolitan statistical area	425,108									
Area actually reporting	99.5%	1,806	10	335	140	1,321	10,022	1,707	7,141	1,174
Estimated total	100.0%	1,809	10	335	140	1,324	10,031	1,711	7,144	1,176
Cities outside metropolitan areas	222,043									
Area actually reporting	97.1%	1,459	4	270	26	1,159	4,457	586	3,430	441
Estimated total	100.0%	1,481	4	273	26	1,178	4,553	604	3,501	448
Nonmetropolitan counties	237,508									
Area actually reporting	85.8%	176	2	28	0	146	887	271	500	116
Estimated total	100.0%	240	3	34	29	174	1,083	331	620	132
State total	884,659	3,530	17	642	195	2,676	15,667	2,646	11,265	1,756
Rate per 100,000 inhabitants		399.0	1.9	72.6	22.0	302.5	1,771.0	299.1	1,273.4	198.5
Tennessee										
Metropolitan statistical area	5,346,297									
Area actually reporting	100.0%	35,287	449	2,360	5,894	26,584	152,843	23,900	112,931	16,012
Cities outside metropolitan areas	484,538									
Area actually reporting	100.0%	2,668	21	232	177	2,238	15,786	2,393	12,153	1,240
Nonmetropolitan counties	998,339									
Area actually reporting	100.0%	2,692	28	221	79	2,364	12,524	3,576	7,020	1,928
State total	6,829,174	40,647	498	2,813	6,150	31,186	181,153	29,869	132,104	19,180
Rate per 100,000 inhabitants		595.2	7.3	41.2	90.1	456.7	2,652.6	437.4	1,934.4	280.9
Texas										
Metropolitan statistical area	25,893,314									
Area actually reporting	99.6%	112,832	1,308	13,380	28,389	69,755	644,773	101,161	470,229	73,383
Estimated total	100.0%	113,040	1,309	13,400	28,406	69,925	646,291	101,452	471,296	73,543
Cities outside metropolitan areas	1,451,495									
Area actually reporting	96.5%	5,283	45	765	444	4,029	30,263	6,749	21,413	2,101
Estimated total	100.0%	5,400	45	787	446	4,122	30,904	6,940	21,807	2,157
Nonmetropolitan counties	1,651,072									
Area actually reporting	96.8%	3,010	55	633	136	2,186	15,847	5,458	8,618	1,771
Estimated total	100.0%	3,034	55	637	136	2,206	16,009	5,510	8,710	1,789
State total	28,995,881	121,474	1,409	14,824	28,988	76,253	693,204	113,902	501,813	77,489
Rate per 100,000 inhabitants		418.9	4.9	51.1	100.0	263.0	2,390.7	392.8	1,730.6	267.2
Utah										
Metropolitan statistical area	2,871,718									
Area actually reporting	99.8%	6,730	60	1,593	1,099	3,978	64,459	8,117	49,983	6,359
Estimated total	100.0%	6,755	60	1,601	1,102	3,992	64,792	8,162	50,248	6,382
Cities outside metropolitan areas	153,031									
Area actually reporting	86.2%	349	0	113	11	225	2,455	304	2,014	137
Estimated total	100.0%	414	0	134	11	269	2,797	360	2,281	156
Nonmetropolitan counties	181,209									
Area actually reporting	91.0%	338	12	77	11	238	1,768	307	1,279	182
Estimated total	100.0%	384	12	87	12	273	1,957	349	1,408	200
State total	3,205,958	7,553	72	1,822	1,125	4,534	69,546	8,871	53,937	6,738
Rate per 100,000 inhabitants		235.6	2.2	56.8	35.1	141.4	2,169.3	276.7	1,682.4	210.2
Vermont										
Metropolitan statistical area	221,448									
Area actually reporting	100.0%	444	5	114	32	293	3,786	406	3,284	96
Cities outside metropolitan areas	190,677									
Area actually reporting	100.0%	505	0	108	32	365	3,646	446	3,101	99
Nonmetropolitan counties	211,864									
Area actually reporting	100.0%	313	6	56	7	244	1,456	423	930	103
State total	623,989	1,262	11	278	71	902	8,888	1,275	7,315	298
Rate per 100,000 inhabitants		202.2	1.8	44.6	11.4	144.6	1,424.4	204.3	1,172.3	47.8
Virginia										
Metropolitan statistical area	7,489,609									
Area actually reporting	99.9%	15,713	344	2,340	3,338	9,691	126,904	11,783	105,821	9,300
Estimated total	100.0%	15,713	344	2,340	3,338	9,691	126,941	11,786	105,851	9,304
Cities outside metropolitan areas	243,163									
Area actually reporting	98.5%	572	15	114	75	368	5,840	655	4,903	282
Estimated total	100.0%	575	15	114	75	371	5,867	659	4,925	283
Nonmetropolitan counties	802,747									
Area actually reporting	100.0%	1,465	67	362	111	925	7,405	1,455	5,268	682

Table 3. Crime in the United States, by State and Area, 2019—*Continued*

(Number, percent, rate per 100,000 population.)

Area	Population	Violent crime[1]	Murder and nonnegligent manslaughter	Rape[2]	Robbery	Aggravated assault	Property crime	Burglary	Larceny-theft	Motor vehicle theft
State total..........	8,535,519	17,753	426	2,816	3,524	10,987	140,213	13,900	116,044	10,269
Rate per 100,000 inhabitants		208.0	5.0	33.0	41.3	128.7	1,642.7	162.8	1,359.5	120.3
Washington										
Metropolitan statistical area..........	6,838,838									
Area actually reporting	99.8%	20,734	182	2,937	5,002	12,613	189,481	31,171	135,283	23,027
Estimated total	100.0%	20,805	183	2,961	5,008	12,653	190,177	31,342	135,759	23,076
Cities outside metropolitan areas..........	313,850									
Area actually reporting..........	94.7%	924	7	224	108	585	8,892	1,633	6,427	832
Estimated total	100.0%	961	7	232	110	612	9,360	1,729	6,767	864
Nonmetropolitan counties	462,205									
Area actually reporting..........	100.0%	611	8	139	29	435	4,687	1,469	2,756	462
State total..........	7,614,893	22,377	198	3,332	5,147	13,700	204,224	34,540	145,282	24,402
Rate per 100,000 inhabitants		293.9	2.6	43.8	67.6	179.9	2,681.9	453.6	1,907.9	320.5
West Virginia										
Metropolitan statistical area..........	1,156,599									
Area actually reporting	84.7%	3,621	51	514	299	2,757	20,104	4,344	13,957	1,803
Estimated total..........	100.0%	3,939	55	547	324	3,013	21,838	4,730	15,162	1,946
Cities outside metropolitan areas..........	174,190									
Area actually reporting..........	82.7%	391	7	50	13	321	1,652	209	1,370	73
Estimated total..........	100.0%	708	8	82	33	585	3,754	303	3,332	119
Nonmetropolitan counties	461,358									
Area actually reporting..........	83.1%	908	15	119	21	753	2,628	792	1,495	341
Estimated total..........	100.0%	1,027	15	125	21	866	2,784	858	1,572	354
State total..........	1,792,147	5,674	78	754	378	4,464	28,376	5,891	20,066	2,419
Rate per 100,000 inhabitants		316.6	4.4	42.1	21.1	249.1	1,583.4	328.7	1,119.7	135.0
Wisconsin..........	4,350,936									
Metropolitan statistical area..........	98.8%	14,828	149	1,731	2,913	10,035	69,373	10,258	52,575	6,540
Area actually reporting..........	100.0%	14,878	149	1,748	2,915	10,066	70,020	10,365	53,091	6,564
Estimated total..........	642,215									
Cities outside metropolitan areas..........	93.7%	1,249	16	309	53	871	9,875	849	8,589	437
Area actually reporting	100.0%	1,287	16	313	54	904	10,579	902	9,220	457
Estimated total..........	829,283									
Nonmetropolitan counties	98.6%	893	10	198	22	663	4,992	1,376	3,257	359
Area actually reporting	100.0%	905	10	200	22	673	5,073	1,400	3,309	364
State total..........	5,822,434	17,070	175	2,261	2,991	11,643	85,672	12,667	65,620	7,385
Rate per 100,000 inhabitants		293.2	3.0	38.8	51.4	200.0	1,471.4	217.6	1,127.0	126.8
Wyoming										
Metropolitan statistical area..........	179,210									
Area actually reporting..........	81.0%	449	7	112	53	277	3,970	583	3,057	330
Estimated total	100.0%	553	7	128	58	360	4,304	698	3,239	367
Cities outside metropolitan areas..........	238,934									
Area actually reporting..........	91.9%	468	6	146	9	307	3,496	478	2,784	234
Estimated total..........	100.0%	492	6	154	9	323	3,724	510	2,964	250
Nonmetropolitan counties	160,615									
Area actually reporting	92.1%	194	0	39	0	155	973	170	716	87
Estimated total..........	100.0%	213	0	42	0	171	1,065	188	781	96
State total..........	578,759	1,258	13	324	67	854	9,093	1,396	6,984	713
Rate per 100,000 inhabitants		217.4	2.2	56.0	11.6	147.6	1,571.1	241.2	1,206.7	123.2

Note: Although arson data are included in the trend and clearance tables, sufficient data are not available to estimate totals for this offense. Therefore, no arson data are published in this table.
[1]The violent crime figures include the offenses of murder, rape (revised definition), robbery, and aggravated assault.
[2]The figures shown in this column for the offense of rape were estimated using the revised Uniform Crime Reporting (UCR) definition of rape. See chapter notes for further explanation.
[3]Includes offenses reported by the Metro Transit Police and the Arson Investigation Unit of the District of Columbia Fire and Emergency Medical Services.
[4]Agencies within this state submitted rape data according to the legacy UCR definition of rape.

Table 4. Crime in the United States, by Selected Metropolitan Statistical Area, 2019

(Number, percent, rate per 100,000 population.)

Area	Population	Violent crime	Murder and nonnegligent manslaughter	Rape[1]	Robbery	Aggravated assault	Property crime	Burglary	Larceny-theft	Motor vehicle theft
Abilene, TX M.S.A.	171,125									
Includes Callahan, Jones, and Taylor Counties........................										
City of Abilene..	123,665	458	6	87	68	297	3,112	576	2,330	206
Total area actually reporting....................................	100.0%	543	6	105	72	360	3,603	765	2,596	242
Rate per 100,000 inhabitants....................................		317.3	3.5	61.4	42.1	210.4	2,105.5	447.0	1,517.0	141.4
Akron, OH M.S.A.[2]...	703,784									
Includes Portage[2] and Summit Counties........................										
City of Akron..	197,882	1,782	27	181	328	1,246	6,568	1,686	4,305	577
Total area actually reporting....................................	94.5%	2,540	33	285	443	1,779	13,746	2,687	10,196	863
Estimated total..	100.0%	2,616	33	318	455	1,810	14,445	2,770	10,781	894
Rate per 100,000 inhabitants....................................		371.7	4.7	45.2	64.7	257.2	2,052.5	393.6	1,531.9	127.0
Albany, GA M.S.A.[3]...	149,257									
Includes Dougherty, Lee, Terrell, and Worth Counties[3]..........										
City of Albany[3]..	74,989	790	12	32	165	581	3,452	729	2,489	234
Total area actually reporting....................................	97.4%	1,057	12	65	199	781	4,951	1,062	3,565	324
Estimated total..	100.0%	1,071	12	66	202	791	5,057	1,074	3,650	333
Rate per 100,000 inhabitants....................................		717.6	8.0	44.2	135.3	530.0	3,388.1	719.6	2,445.4	223.1
Albany-Lebanon, OR M.S.A..............................	128,105									
Includes Linn County...										
City of Albany..	54,993	70	1	10	16	43	1,467	128	1,242	97
City of Lebanon...	17,304	29	0	11	0	18	372	22	323	27
Total area actually reporting....................................	100.0%	175	6	35	24	110	2,743	342	2,162	239
Rate per 100,000 inhabitants....................................		136.6	4.7	27.3	18.7	85.9	2,141.2	267.0	1,687.7	186.6
Albany-Schenectady-Troy, NY M.S.A.	879,862									
Includes Albany, Rensselaer, Saratoga, Schenectady, and										
Schoharie Counties...										
City of Albany..	97,221	736	4	60	189	483	2,919	445	2,315	159
City of Schenectady..	65,504	528	3	56	133	336	1,770	248	1,392	130
City of Troy..	49,286	296	3	25	73	195	1,365	225	1,035	105
Total area actually reporting....................................	100.0%	2,266	14	350	483	1,419	15,367	1,743	12,988	636
Rate per 100,000 inhabitants....................................		257.5	1.6	39.8	54.9	161.3	1,746.5	198.1	1,476.1	72.3
Albuquerque, NM M.S.A.[4]	918,114	.								
Includes Bernalillo, Sandoval, Torrance, and Valencia										
Counties...										
City of Albuquerque[4]	561,920	7,596	84	486	1,699	5,327			20,634	5,425
Total area actually reporting....................................	87.2%	9,004	91	564	1,768	6,581			23,626	6,025
Estimated total..	100.0%	9,580	93	588	1,781	7,118			24,180	6,188
Rate per 100,000 inhabitants....................................		1,043.4	10.1	64.0	194.0	775.3			2,633.7	674.0
Alexandria, LA M.S.A...	152,025									
Includes Grant and Rapides Parishes............................										
City of Alexandria..	46,630	732	9	16	132	575	4,180	892	3,056	232
Total area actually reporting....................................	82.5%	1,172	14	67	159	932	6,428	1,584	4,460	384
Estimated total..	100.0%	1,291	16	71	165	1,039	6,900	1,682	4,805	413
Rate per 100,000 inhabitants....................................		849.2	10.5	46.7	108.5	683.4	4,538.7	1,106.4	3,160.7	271.7
Altoona, PA M.S.A...	121,762									
Includes Blair County..										
City of Altoona...	43,429	264	0	83	22	159	675	142	481	52
Total area actually reporting....................................	100.0%	406	1	111	33	261	1,510	271	1,163	76
Rate per 100,000 inhabitants....................................		333.4	0.8	91.2	27.1	214.4	1,240.1	222.6	955.1	62.4
Amarillo, TX M.S.A....	266,054									
Includes Armstrong, Carson, Oldham, Potter, and Randall										
Counties...										
City of Amarillo..	201,036	1,447	15	161	246	1,025	7,835	1,439	5,425	971
Total area actually reporting....................................	99.9%	1,584	16	194	257	1,117	8,578	1,650	5,862	1,066
Estimated total..	100.0%	1,584	16	194	257	1,117	8,579	1,650	5,863	1,066
Rate per 100,000 inhabitants....................................		595.4	6.0	72.9	96.6	419.8	3,224.5	620.2	2,203.7	400.7
Ames, IA M.S.A....	124,947									
Includes Boone and Story Counties.............................										
City of Ames..	68,237	135	1	44	21	69	1,171	138	975	58
Total area actually reporting....................................	100.0%	249	2	64	22	161	1,745	256	1,381	108
Rate per 100,000 inhabitants....................................		199.3	1.6	51.2	17.6	128.9	1,396.6	204.9	1,105.3	86.4

Table 4. Crime in the United States, by Selected Metropolitan Statistical Area, 2019—*Continued*

(Number, percent, rate per 100,000 population.)

Area	Population	Violent crime	Murder and nonnegligent manslaughter	Rape[1]	Robbery	Aggravated assault	Property crime	Burglary	Larceny-theft	Motor vehicle theft
Anchorage, AK M.S.A.	306,136									
Includes Anchorage Municipality and Matanuska-Susitna Borough										
City of Anchorage.........	287,731	3,581	32	540	621	2,388	12,261	1,692	9,038	1,531
Total area actually reporting.........	100.0%	3,657	34	546	638	2,439	13,222	1,837	9,766	1,619
Rate per 100,000 inhabitants.........		1,194.6	11.1	178.4	208.4	796.7	4,319.0	600.1	3,190.1	528.8
Ann Arbor, MI M.S.A.............................	373,308									
Includes Washtenaw County.........										
City of Ann Arbor.........	122,893	309	2	77	46	184	2,124	197	1,789	138
Total area actually reporting.........	100.0%	1,327	8	250	143	926	6,159	743	4,940	476
Rate per 100,000 inhabitants.........		355.5	2.1	67.0	38.3	248.1	1,649.8	199.0	1,323.3	127.5
Appleton, WI M.S.A.[3]	238,721									
Includes Calumet and Outagamie Counties.........										
City of Appleton	74,757	206	2	32	23	149	1,073	107	910	56
Total area actually reporting.........	97.4%	384	4	80	26	274	2,497	259	2,104	134
Estimated total.........	100.0%	392	4	82	27	279	2,599	266	2,195	138
Rate per 100,000 inhabitants.........		164.2	1.7	34.3	11.3	116.9	1,088.7	111.4	919.5	57.8
Asheville, NC M.S.A.[3]	463,796									
Includes Buncombe, Haywood, Henderson, and Madison Counties[3].........										
City of Asheville[3].........	93,641	695	6	59	163	467	5,923	833	4,552	538
Total area actually reporting.........	76.8%	1,221	12	116	215	878	11,093	2,373	7,709	1,011
Estimated total.........	100.0%	1,466	15	144	241	1,066	12,815	2,898	8,760	1,157
Rate per 100,000 inhabitants.........		316.1	3.2	31.0	52.0	229.8	2,763.1	624.8	1,888.8	249.5
Atlantic City-Hammonton, NJ M.S.A.	263,100									
Includes Atlantic County.........										
City of Atlantic City.........	37,593	323	11	29	182	101	1,738	130	1,519	89
City of Hammonton.........	14,003	25	0	1	4	20	115	25	78	12
Total area actually reporting.........	100.0%	672	13	49	272	338	6,314	857	5,174	283
Rate per 100,000 inhabitants.........		255.4	4.9	18.6	103.4	128.5	2,399.8	325.7	1,966.6	107.6
Augusta-Richmond County, GA-SC M.S.A.[3]	609,036									
Includes Burke, Columbia, Lincoln, McDuffie, and Richmond Counties, GA[3] and Aiken and Edgefield Counties, SC										
Total area actually reporting.........	96.5%	2,085	47	177	404	1,457	14,629	2,456	10,994	1,179
Estimated total.........	100.0%	2,199	49	186	411	1,553	15,097	2,580	11,292	1,225
Rate per 100,000 inhabitants.........		361.1	8.0	30.5	67.5	255.0	2,478.8	423.6	1,854.1	201.1
Austin-Round Rock-Georgetown, TX M.S.A.[3]	2,217,312									
Includes Bastrop, Caldwell,[3] Hays, Travis,[3] and Williamson Counties.........										
City of Austin[3].........	986,062	3,953	32	534	971	2,416	36,588	4,344	29,216	3,028
City of Round Rock.........	132,747	165	3	21	51	90	2,235	165	2,017	53
City of Georgetown.........	78,332	81	0	25	8	48	730	103	586	41
City of San Marcos.........	66,279	241	8	78	26	129	1,530	228	1,176	126
Total area actually reporting.........	99.9%	6,359	56	1,071	1,261	3,971	53,424	6,954	42,248	4,222
Estimated total.........	100.0%	6,361	56	1,071	1,261	3,973	53,442	6,958	42,260	4,224
Rate per 100,000 inhabitants.........		286.9	2.5	48.3	56.9	179.2	2,410.2	313.8	1,905.9	190.5
Bakersfield, CA M.S.A.	896,356									
Includes Kern County.........										
City of Bakersfield.........	388,080	1,766	34	116	701	915	16,074	3,888	9,277	2,909
Total area actually reporting.........	100.0%	5,567	84	455	1,238	3,790	29,604	7,595	16,126	5,883
Rate per 100,000 inhabitants.........		621.1	9.4	50.8	138.1	422.8	3,302.7	847.3	1,799.1	656.3
Baltimore-Columbia-Towson, MD M.S.A.	2,800,231									
Includes Anne Arundel, Baltimore, Carroll, Harford, Howard, and Queen Anne's Counties and Baltimore City.........										
City of Baltimore.........	597,239	11,101	348	324	4,856	5,573	25,748	5,414	16,395	3,939
Total area actually reporting.........	100.0%	19,564	434	1,025	6,797	11,308	66,044	10,213	49,114	6,717
Rate per 100,000 inhabitants.........		698.7	15.5	36.6	242.7	403.8	2,358.5	364.7	1,753.9	239.9
Bangor, ME M.S.A.	151,245									
Includes Penobscot County										
City of Bangor	31,872	35	1	1	15	18	1,168	64	1,076	28
Total area actually reporting.........	100.0%	67	1	7	20	39	2,355	221	2,060	74
Rate per 100,000 inhabitants.........		44.3	0.7	4.6	13.2	25.8	1,557.1	146.1	1,362.0	48.9

Table 4. Crime in the United States, by Selected Metropolitan Statistical Area, 2019—*Continued*

(Number, percent, rate per 100,000 population.)

Area	Population	Violent crime	Murder and nonnegligent manslaughter	Rape[1]	Robbery	Aggravated assault	Property crime	Burglary	Larceny-theft	Motor vehicle theft
Barnstable Town, MA M.S.A.	211,470									
Includes Barnstable County										
City of Barnstable	44,032	178	2	22	14	140	425	61	350	14
Total area actually reporting	100.0%	691	2	113	29	547	2,017	401	1,542	74
Rate per 100,000 inhabitants		326.8	0.9	53.4	13.7	258.7	953.8	189.6	729.2	35.0
Baton Rouge, LA M.S.A.	852,152									
Includes Ascension, Assumption, East Baton Rouge, East Feliciana, Iberville, Livingston, Pointe Coupee, St. Helena, West Baton Rouge, and West Feliciana Parishes										
City of Baton Rouge	220,648	2,066	70	52	645	1,299	11,673	2,258	8,616	799
Total area actually reporting	98.8%	4,679	120	240	912	3,407	27,976	4,599	21,713	1,664
Estimated total	100.0%	4,721	120	241	915	3,445	28,266	4,661	21,926	1,679
Rate per 100,000 inhabitants		554.0	14.1	28.3	107.4	404.3	3,317.0	547.0	2,573.0	197.0
Battle Creek, MI M.S.A.[4]	133,965									
Includes Calhoun County										
City of Battle Creek	60,607	568	5	60	67	436	1,969	460	1,377	132
Total area actually reporting	99.9%	836	6	108	91	631			2,733	227
Estimated total	100.0%	836	6	108	91	631			2,733	227
Rate per 100,000 inhabitants		624.0	4.5	80.6	67.9	471.0			2,040.1	169.4
Bay City, MI M.S.A.	103,201									
Includes Bay County										
City of Bay City	32,793	271	2	35	20	214	654	135	476	43
Total area actually reporting	100.0%	396	3	78	29	286	1,295	266	944	85
Rate per 100,000 inhabitants		383.7	2.9	75.6	28.1	277.1	1,254.8	257.7	914.7	82.4
Beaumont-Port Arthur, TX M.S.A.[3]	394,118									
Includes Hardin, Jefferson, and Orange Counties										
City of Beaumont	118,562	1,241	19	97	323	802	4,287	950	2,999	338
City of Port Arthur[3]	55,084	344	9	29	84	222	1,203	326	757	120
Total area actually reporting	99.9%	2,132	34	186	465	1,447	8,637	2,006	5,794	837
Estimated total	100.0%	2,133	34	186	465	1,448	8,644	2,007	5,799	838
Rate per 100,000 inhabitants		541.2	8.6	47.2	118.0	367.4	2,193.3	509.2	1,471.4	212.6
Bellingham, WA M.S.A.	228,098									
Includes Whatcom County										
City of Bellingham	91,906	251	4	28	61	158	2,689	323	2,251	115
Total area actually reporting	100.0%	502	9	100	78	315	4,792	821	3,744	227
Rate per 100,000 inhabitants		220.1	3.9	43.8	34.2	138.1	2,100.9	359.9	1,641.4	99.5
Bend, OR M.S.A.	195,856									
Includes Deschutes County										
City of Bend	100,588	154	0	30	21	103	1,919	135	1,678	106
Total area actually reporting	100.0%	324	1	57	31	235	3,763	341	3,169	253
Rate per 100,000 inhabitants		165.4	0.5	29.1	15.8	120.0	1,921.3	174.1	1,618.0	129.2
Billings, MT M.S.A.[4]	181,514									
Includes Carbon, Stillwater, and Yellowstone Counties										
City of Billings[4]	110,198			75	98	499	4,499	608	3,266	625
Total area actually reporting	100.0%			103	106	679	5,468	721	4,008	739
Rate per 100,000 inhabitants				56.7	58.4	374.1	3,012.4	397.2	2,208.1	407.1
Binghamton, NY M.S.A.	237,535									
Includes Broome and Tioga Counties										
City of Binghamton	44,475	355	2	42	66	245	1,907	417	1,429	61
Total area actually reporting	99.4%	678	6	171	108	393	4,762	801	3,809	152
Estimated total	100.0%	678	6	171	108	393	4,773	802	3,819	152
Rate per 100,000 inhabitants		285.4	2.5	72.0	45.5	165.4	2,009.4	337.6	1,607.8	64.0
Bismarck, ND M.S.A.	128,869									
Includes Burleigh, Morton, and Oliver Counties										
City of Bismarck	74,705	228	1	64	36	127	2,079	225	1,647	207
Total area actually reporting	100.0%	394	5	104	44	241	2,983	340	2,295	348
Rate per 100,000 inhabitants		305.7	3.9	80.7	34.1	187.0	2,314.8	263.8	1,780.9	270.0
Blacksburg-Christiansburg, VA M.S.A.	167,936									
Includes Giles, Montgomery, and Pulaski Counties and Radford City										

(Number, percent, rate per 100,000 population.)

Area	Population	Violent crime	Murder and nonnegligent manslaughter	Rape[1]	Robbery	Aggravated assault	Property crime	Burglary	Larceny-theft	Motor vehicle theft
City of Blacksburg	44,948	50	0	26	1	23	275	38	228	9
City of Christiansburg	22,700	31	0	7	4	20	466	28	424	14
Total area actually reporting	100.0%	323	2	106	20	195	2,781	332	2,311	138
Rate per 100,000 inhabitants		192.3	1.2	63.1	11.9	116.1	1,656.0	197.7	1,376.1	82.2
Bloomington, IL M.S.A.	172,429									
Includes McLean County										
City of Bloomington	78,107	387	1	49	57	280	1,096	171	851	74
Total area actually reporting	97.1%	601	3	115	82	401	2,312	324	1,851	137
Estimated total	100.0%	610	3	117	83	407	2,385	334	1,909	142
Rate per 100,000 inhabitants		353.8	1.7	67.9	48.1	236.0	1,383.2	193.7	1,107.1	82.4
Boise City, ID M.S.A.	749,238									
Includes Ada, Boise, Canyon, Gem, and Owyhee Counties										
City of Boise	231,314	649	4	164	44	437	3,653	470	2,952	231
Total area actually reporting	99.6%	1,874	10	436	83	1,345	9,275	1,507	7,063	705
Estimated total	100.0%	1,880	10	437	83	1,350	9,310	1,513	7,089	708
Rate per 100,000 inhabitants		250.9	1.3	58.3	11.1	180.2	1,242.6	201.9	946.2	94.5
Boston-Cambridge-Newton, MA-NH M.S.A.[3,5]	4,880,689									
Includes the Metropolitan Divisions of Boston, MA; Cambridge-Newton-Framingham, MA; and Rockingham County-Strafford County, NH										
City of Boston, MA[3,5]	698,941	4,244	42	231	1,039	2,932		1,703	10,590	
City of Cambridge, MA	119,908	334	1	26	67	240	1,983	161	1,724	98
City of Newton, MA	88,658	49	0	4	10	35	510	75	424	11
City of Framingham, MA	73,127	297	1	20	29	247	800	158	609	33
City of Waltham, MA	62,737	102	0	13	7	82	512	70	420	22
Total area actually reporting	98.8%	13,450	93	1,253	2,328	9,776		6,767	43,000	
Estimated total	100.0%	13,556	93	1,270	2,333	9,860		6,840	43,333	
Rate per 100,000 inhabitants		277.7	1.9	26.0	47.8	202.0		140.1	887.8	
Boston, MA M.D.[3,5]	2,032,861									
Includes Norfolk, Plymouth, and Suffolk Counties										
Total area actually reporting	98.7%	8,008	61	625	1,595	5,727		3,351	21,175	
Estimated total	100.0%	8,057	61	633	1,598	5,765		3,384	21,322	
Rate per 100,000 inhabitants		396.3	3.0	31.1	78.6	283.6		166.5	1,048.9	
Cambridge-Newton-Framingham, MA M.D.[3]	2,406,489									
Includes Essex and Middlesex Counties										
Total area actually reporting	98.6%	5,008	27	485	680	3,816	22,303	2,934	17,780	1,589
Estimated total	100.0%	5,065	27	494	682	3,862	22,543	2,974	17,966	1,603
Rate per 100,000 inhabitants		210.5	1.1	20.5	28.3	160.5	936.8	123.6	746.6	66.6
Rockingham County-Strafford County, NH M.D.	441,339									
Includes Rockingham and Strafford Counties										
Total area actually reporting	100.0%	434	5	143	53	233	4,770	482	4,045	243
Rate per 100,000 inhabitants		98.3	1.1	32.4	12.0	52.8	1,080.8	109.2	916.5	55.1
Boulder, CO M.S.A.	328,673									
Includes Boulder County										
City of Boulder	108,519	278	1	41	37	199	3,284	405	2,628	251
Total area actually reporting	100.0%	895	3	224	83	585	8,038	999	6,341	698
Rate per 100,000 inhabitants		272.3	0.9	68.2	25.3	178.0	2,445.6	303.9	1,929.3	212.4
Bowling Green, KY M.S.A.	179,183									
Includes Allen, Butler, Edmonson, and Warren Counties										
City of Bowling Green	69,627	203	4	63	55	81	3,250	386	2,610	254
Total area actually reporting	100.0%	275	6	85	62	122	4,188	645	3,184	359
Rate per 100,000 inhabitants		153.5	3.3	47.4	34.6	68.1	2,337.3	360.0	1,777.0	200.4
Bremerton-Silverdale-Port Orchard, WA M.S.A.	271,215									
Includes Kitsap County										
City of Bremerton	41,675	168	1	26	34	107	1,358	234	984	140
City of Port Orchard	14,684	66	0	7	14	45	492	74	376	42
Total area actually reporting	100.0%	709	4	157	81	467	5,392	989	3,944	459
Rate per 100,000 inhabitants		261.4	1.5	57.9	29.9	172.2	1,988.1	364.7	1,454.2	169.2
Bridgeport-Stamford-Norwalk, CT M.S.A.	929,479									
Includes Fairfield County										

Table 4. Crime in the United States, by Selected Metropolitan Statistical Area, 2019—*Continued*

(Number, percent, rate per 100,000 population.)

Area	Population	Violent crime	Murder and nonnegligent manslaughter	Rape[1]	Robbery	Aggravated assault	Property crime	Burglary	Larceny-theft	Motor vehicle theft
City of Bridgeport	144,908	843	17	71	392	363	2,465	555	1,292	618
City of Stamford	130,678	264	5	27	87	145	1,803	196	1,446	161
City of Norwalk	89,440	183	1	8	29	145	1,247	133	989	125
City of Danbury	85,167	97	1	15	28	53	1,045	132	827	86
City of Stratford	52,034	71	1	13	25	32	859	97	654	108
Total area actually reporting	100.0%	1,619	28	162	609	820	11,232	1,542	8,325	1,365
Rate per 100,000 inhabitants		174.2	3.0	17.4	65.5	88.2	1,208.4	165.9	895.7	146.9
Brownsville-Harlingen, TX M.S.A.[3]	423,309									
Includes Cameron County										
City of Brownsville	184,418	776	0	82	143	551	4,553	631	3,801	121
City of Harlingen	65,481	273	0	54	54	165	3,152	443	2,613	96
Total area actually reporting	100.0%	1,588	4	233	236	1,115	10,705	1,670	8,682	353
Rate per 100,000 inhabitants		375.1	0.9	55.0	55.8	263.4	2,528.9	394.5	2,051.0	83.4
Buffalo-Cheektowaga, NY M.S.A.	1,123,277									
Includes Erie and Niagara Counties										
City of Buffalo	255,686	2,533	47	121	802	1,563	8,298	1,610	6,009	679
City of Cheektowaga Town	76,821	187	2	15	57	113	2,153	208	1,856	89
Total area actually reporting	98.2%	3,962	60	329	1,130	2,443	20,762	3,051	16,504	1,207
Estimated total	100.0%	3,980	60	332	1,133	2,455	20,987	3,073	16,699	1,215
Rate per 100,000 inhabitants		354.3	5.3	29.6	100.9	218.6	1,868.4	273.6	1,486.6	108.2
Burlington, NC M.S.A.[3]	168,317									
Includes Alamance County[3]										
City of Burlington[3]	54,108	460	10	42	66	342	2,490	534	1,815	141
Total area actually reporting	91.0%	631	13	60	88	470	3,926	895	2,804	227
Estimated total	100.0%	686	14	66	98	508	4,443	993	3,196	254
Rate per 100,000 inhabitants		407.6	8.3	39.2	58.2	301.8	2,639.7	590.0	1,898.8	150.9
Burlington-South Burlington, VT M.S.A.	221,448									
Includes Chittenden, Franklin, and Grand Isle Counties										
City of Burlington	42,958	174	2	41	13	118	1,110	109	976	25
City of South Burlington	19,687	22	0	6	4	12	687	32	647	8
Total area actually reporting	100.0%	444	5	114	32	293	3,786	406	3,284	96
Rate per 100,000 inhabitants		200.5	2.3	51.5	14.5	132.3	1,709.7	183.3	1,483.0	43.4
California-Lexington Park, MD M.S.A.	112,993									
Includes St. Mary's County										
Total area actually reporting	100.0%	231	1	29	46	155	1,880	333	1,476	71
Rate per 100,000 inhabitants		204.4	0.9	25.7	40.7	137.2	1,663.8	294.7	1,306.3	62.8
Canton-Massillon, OH M.S.A.	397,244									
Includes Carroll and Stark Counties										
City of Canton	70,139	981	6	135	188	652	3,712	962	2,429	321
City of Massillon	32,433	72	1	26	14	31	743	116	610	17
Total area actually reporting	96.9%	1,328	9	239	236	844	8,608	1,918	6,128	562
Estimated total	100.0%	1,345	9	242	239	855	8,832	1,946	6,313	573
Rate per 100,000 inhabitants		338.6	2.3	60.9	60.2	215.2	2,223.3	489.9	1,589.2	144.2
Cape Coral-Fort Myers, FL M.S.A.	767,771									
Includes Lee County										
City of Cape Coral	194,183	226	5	16	36	169	2,176	274	1,739	163
City of Fort Myers	85,127	486	9	34	94	349	1,952	245	1,553	154
Total area actually reporting	100.0%	1,979	23	246	386	1,324	8,890	1,343	6,792	755
Rate per 100,000 inhabitants		257.8	3.0	32.0	50.3	172.4	1,157.9	174.9	884.6	98.3
Cape Girardeau, MO-IL M.S.A.	96,976									
Includes Alexander County, IL and Bollinger and Cape Girardeau Counties, MO										
City of Cape Girardeau, MO	40,077	233	6	24	46	157	1,432	215	1,145	72
Total area actually reporting	97.8%	370	7	32	46	285	2,027	378	1,540	109
Estimated total	100.0%	373	7	33	46	287	2,060	383	1,566	111
Rate per 100,000 inhabitants		384.6	7.2	34.0	47.4	295.9	2,124.2	394.9	1,614.8	114.5
Carson City, NV M.S.A.	55,491									
Includes Carson City										
Total area actually reporting	100.0%	193	0	47	11	135	711	152	487	72
Rate per 100,000 inhabitants		347.8	0.0	84.7	19.8	243.3	1,281.3	273.9	877.6	129.8

Table 4. Crime in the United States, by Selected Metropolitan Statistical Area, 2019—*Continued*

(Number, percent, rate per 100,000 population.)

Area	Population	Violent crime	Murder and nonnegligent manslaughter	Rape[1]	Robbery	Aggravated assault	Property crime	Burglary	Larceny-theft	Motor vehicle theft
Casper, WY M.S.A.................................	79,489									
Includes Natrona County................................										
City of Casper..	57,752	169	2	58	18	91	1,677	285	1,271	121
Total area actually reporting............................	100.0%	227	2	68	25	132	1,966	370	1,441	155
Rate per 100,000 inhabitants...........................		285.6	2.5	85.5	31.5	166.1	2,473.3	465.5	1,812.8	195.0
Cedar Rapids, IA M.S.A............................	272,728									
Includes Benton, Jones, and Linn Counties.............										
City of Cedar Rapids....................................	134,007	345	2	27	83	233	4,470	837	3,268	365
Total area actually reporting............................	99.1%	505	2	56	89	358	5,498	1,077	3,947	474
Estimated total..	100.0%	514	2	57	90	365	5,566	1,091	3,994	481
Rate per 100,000 inhabitants...........................		188.5	0.7	20.9	33.0	133.8	2,040.9	400.0	1,464.5	176.4
Champaign-Urbana, IL M.S.A.......................	226,393									
Includes Champaign and Piatt Counties................										
City of Champaign......................................	88,891	827	2	73	94	658	2,203	300	1,777	126
City of Urbana..	42,080	124	1	30	36	57	1,090	161	890	39
Total area actually reporting............................	99.2%	1,098	3	158	156	781	4,482	735	3,533	214
Estimated total..	100.0%	1,099	3	158	156	782	4,507	739	3,553	215
Rate per 100,000 inhabitants...........................		485.4	1.3	69.8	68.9	345.4	1,990.8	326.4	1,569.4	95.0
Charleston-North Charleston, SC M.S.A...........	804,618									
Includes Berkeley, Charleston, and Dorchester Counties......										
City of Charleston.......................................	138,254	516	8	51	95	362	3,124	292	2,335	497
City of North Charleston.................................	115,312	1,114	26	103	229	756	6,941	853	5,123	965
Total area actually reporting............................	99.0%	3,148	72	328	497	2,251	21,218	3,031	15,573	2,614
Estimated total..	100.0%	3,202	72	333	502	2,295	21,554	3,084	15,835	2,635
Rate per 100,000 inhabitants...........................		398.0	8.9	41.4	62.4	285.2	2,678.8	383.3	1,968.0	327.5
Charlottesville, VA M.S.A..........................	219,120									
Includes Albemarle, Buckingham, Fluvanna, Greene, and										
Nelson Counties and Charlottesville City................										
City of Charlottesville...................................	48,453	157	0	32	22	103	1,124	122	924	78
Total area actually reporting............................	100.0%	385	5	102	38	240	3,104	314	2,617	173
Rate per 100,000 inhabitants...........................		175.7	2.3	46.5	17.3	109.5	1,416.6	143.3	1,194.3	79.0
Chattanooga, TN-GA M.S.A.[3].....................	564,924									
Includes Catoosa, Dade, and Walker Counties, GA[3] and										
Hamilton, Marion, and Sequatchie Counties, TN..........										
City of Chattanooga, TN.................................	181,848	1,946	33	161	196	1,556	10,106	1,098	7,694	1,314
Total area actually reporting............................	97.1%	2,914	36	237	250	2,391	16,071	2,098	12,059	1,914
Estimated total..	100.0%	2,969	36	242	255	2,436	16,332	2,150	12,244	1,938
Rate per 100,000 inhabitants...........................		525.6	6.4	42.8	45.1	431.2	2,891.0	380.6	2,167.4	343.1
Chico, CA M.S.A....................................	230,749									
Includes Butte County..................................										
City of Chico..	95,826	557	0	100	104	353	2,406	272	1,753	381
Total area actually reporting............................	100.0%	1,024	7	180	167	670	5,322	1,111	3,343	868
Rate per 100,000 inhabitants...........................		443.8	3.0	78.0	72.4	290.4	2,306.4	481.5	1,448.8	376.2
Cincinnati, OH-KY-IN M.S.A.......................	2,217,647									
Includes Dearborn, Franklin, Ohio, and Union Counties,										
IN; Boone, Bracken, Campbell, Gallatin, Grant, Kenton,										
and Pendleton Counties, KY; and Brown, Butler, Clermont,										
Hamilton, and Warren Counties, OH....................										
City of Cincinnati, OH...................................	303,335	2,562	64	280	872	1,346	13,051	2,765	8,935	1,351
Total area actually reporting............................	89.8%	4,923	90	872	1,438	2,523	40,924	6,551	31,014	3,359
Estimated total..	100.0%	5,264	92	931	1,486	2,755	43,841	7,067	33,240	3,534
Rate per 100,000 inhabitants...........................		237.4	4.1	42.0	67.0	124.2	1,976.9	318.7	1,498.9	159.4
Clarksville, TN-KY M.S.A..........................	309,897									
Includes Christian and Trigg Counties, KY and Montgomery										
and Stewart Counties, TN...............................										
City of Clarksville, TN...................................	159,996	926	14	103	116	693	4,467	543	3,457	467
Total area actually reporting............................	100.0%	1,201	21	150	151	879	7,005	1,145	5,176	684
Rate per 100,000 inhabitants...........................		387.5	6.8	48.4	48.7	283.6	2,260.4	369.5	1,670.2	220.7
Cleveland, TN M.S.A...............................	124,685									
Includes Bradley and Polk Counties.....................										
City of Cleveland..	45,453	464	2	35	42	385	2,403	371	1,845	187

(Number, percent, rate per 100,000 population.)

Area	Population	Violent crime	Murder and nonnegligent manslaughter	Rape[1]	Robbery	Aggravated assault	Property crime	Burglary	Larceny-theft	Motor vehicle theft
Total area actually reporting..................................	100.0%	698	3	52	57	586	3,564	626	2,577	361
Rate per 100,000 inhabitants..............................		559.8	2.4	41.7	45.7	470.0	2,858.4	502.1	2,066.8	289.5
Cleveland-Elyria, OH M.S.A.[2, 3]	2,051,044									
Includes Cuyahoga, Geauga, Lake, Lorain, and Medina Counties..................................										
City of Cleveland	381,829	5,791	92	479	1,895	3,325	17,057	4,311	9,968	2,778
City of Elyria	53,806	137	4	35	37	61	921	207	665	49
Total area actually reporting..................	86.8%	7,897	119	748	2,387	4,643	33,474	6,909	22,694	3,871
Estimated total..................................	100.0%	8,271	122	841	2,472	4,836	37,974	7,473	26,422	4,079
Rate per 100,000 inhabitants..............................		403.3	5.9	41.0	120.5	235.8	1,851.4	364.4	1,288.2	198.9
Coeur d'Alene, ID M.S.A.	165,319									
Includes Kootenai County										
City of Coeur d'Alene	52,256	132	0	38	8	86	712	83	579	50
Total area actually reporting..................	100.0%	362	1	68	16	277	2,099	338	1,627	134
Rate per 100,000 inhabitants..............................		219.0	0.6	41.1	9.7	167.6	1,269.7	204.5	984.2	81.1
College Station-Bryan, TX M.S.A.[3]	265,223									
Includes Brazos, Burleson, and Robertson Counties................										
City of College Station[3]..................................	119,246	225	1	48	43	133	2,098	391	1,529	178
City of Bryan..................................	86,632	370	2	90	57	221	1,928	336	1,444	148
Total area actually reporting..................	99.4%	693	5	164	111	413	5,204	999	3,798	407
Estimated total..................................	100.0%	696	5	164	111	416	5,228	1,004	3,814	410
Rate per 100,000 inhabitants..............................		262.4	1.9	61.8	41.9	156.8	1,971.2	378.5	1,438.0	154.6
Colorado Springs, CO M.S.A...........................	747,633									
Includes El Paso and Teller Counties										
City of Colorado Springs..................................	479,648	2,806	23	431	485	1,867	17,587	2,400	12,095	3,092
Total area actually reporting..................	98.5%	3,464	33	579	550	2,302	20,970	2,945	14,380	3,645
Estimated total..................................	100.0%	3,482	33	582	554	2,313	21,290	2,972	14,645	3,673
Rate per 100,000 inhabitants..............................		465.7	4.4	77.8	74.1	309.4	2,847.7	397.5	1,958.8	491.3
Columbia, MO M.S.A.[3]	209,738									
Includes Boone, Cooper, and Howard[3] Counties										
City of Columbia[3]..................................	125,017	401	11	69	74	247	3,243	499	2,431	313
Total area actually reporting..................	99.2%	566	14	100	85	367	4,552	708	3,390	454
Estimated total..................................	100.0%	570	14	101	85	370	4,577	714	3,406	457
Rate per 100,000 inhabitants..............................		271.8	6.7	48.2	40.5	176.4	2,182.2	340.4	1,623.9	217.9
Columbia, SC M.S.A.	841,451									
Includes Calhoun, Fairfield, Kershaw, Lexington, Richland, and Saluda Counties..................................										
City of Columbia..................................	133,790	1,037	29	88	220	700	7,027	916	5,216	895
Total area actually reporting..................	100.0%	4,909	71	412	696	3,730	28,376	4,480	20,448	3,448
Rate per 100,000 inhabitants..............................		583.4	8.4	49.0	82.7	443.3	3,372.3	532.4	2,430.1	409.8
Columbus, IN M.S.A.[3]	83,691									
Includes Bartholomew County										
City of Columbus..................................	47,991	67	0	40	17	10	1,439	130	1,254	55
Total area actually reporting..................	100.0%	122	0	58	19	45	1,864	208	1,559	97
Rate per 100,000 inhabitants..............................		145.8	0.0	69.3	22.7	53.8	2,227.2	248.5	1,862.8	115.9
Columbus, OH M.S.A.	2,129,346									
Includes Delaware, Fairfield, Franklin, Hocking, Licking, Madison, Morrow, Perry, Pickaway, and Union Counties........										
City of Columbus..................................	906,120	4,561	81	882	1,810	1,788	29,974	5,809	20,606	3,559
Total area actually reporting..................	93.5%	5,889	112	1,284	2,088	2,405	48,501	8,551	35,380	4,570
Estimated total..................................	100.0%	6,100	113	1,327	2,127	2,533	50,897	8,890	37,326	4,681
Rate per 100,000 inhabitants..............................		286.5	5.3	62.3	99.9	119.0	2,390.3	417.5	1,752.9	219.8
Corpus Christi, TX M.S.A.[3]	429,610									
Includes Nueces and San Patricio Counties										
City of Corpus Christi[3]..................................	320,320	2,616	31	266	498	1,823	11,347	1,961	8,494	892
Total area actually reporting..................	99.9%	3,165	35	313	536	2,281	13,605	2,443	10,112	1,050
Estimated total..................................	100.0%	3,166	35	313	536	2,282	13,613	2,445	10,117	1,051
Rate per 100,000 inhabitants..............................		736.9	8.1	72.9	124.8	531.2	3,168.7	569.1	2,354.9	244.6
Crestview-Fort Walton Beach-Destin, FL M.S.A.	282,526									
Includes Okaloosa and Walton Counties										

(Number, percent, rate per 100,000 population.)

Area	Population	Violent crime	Murder and nonnegligent manslaughter	Rape[1]	Robbery	Aggravated assault	Property crime	Burglary	Larceny-theft	Motor vehicle theft
City of Crestview	25,152	96	3	11	20	62	644	107	478	59
City of Fort Walton Beach	22,645	68	2	18	1	47	475	59	372	44
Total area actually reporting	99.7%	882	13	131	64	674	4,699	631	3,680	388
Estimated total	100.0%	885	13	131	65	676	4,718	635	3,694	389
Rate per 100,000 inhabitants		313.2	4.6	46.4	23.0	239.3	1,669.9	224.8	1,307.5	137.7
Cumberland, MD-WV M.S.A.	96,806									
Includes Allegany County, MD and Mineral County, WV										
City of Cumberland, MD	19,321	151	0	9	33	109	869	216	627	26
Total area actually reporting	98.5%	262	0	27	44	191	1,729	374	1,284	71
Estimated total	100.0%	266	0	27	44	195	1,762	381	1,307	74
Rate per 100,000 inhabitants		274.8	0.0	27.9	45.5	201.4	1,820.1	393.6	1,350.1	76.4
Danville, IL M.S.A.	75,878									
Includes Vermilion County										
City of Danville	30,642	536	7	50	65	414	1,370	341	957	72
Total area actually reporting	100.0%	710	7	92	74	537	2,161	602	1,453	106
Rate per 100,000 inhabitants		935.7	9.2	121.2	97.5	707.7	2,848.0	793.4	1,914.9	139.7
Davenport-Moline-Rock Island, IA-IL M.S.A.	379,899									
Includes Henry, Mercer, and Rock Island Counties, IL and Scott County, IA										
City of Davenport, IA	102,392	609	2	84	124	399	3,918	745	2,830	343
City of Moline, IL	41,701	219	1	36	26	156	978	190	727	61
City of Rock Island, IL	37,517	139	1	14	29	95	878	166	599	113
Total area actually reporting	96.7%	1,367	8	208	208	943	8,152	1,566	5,919	667
Estimated total	100.0%	1,392	8	212	211	961	8,353	1,596	6,074	683
Rate per 100,000 inhabitants		366.4	2.1	55.8	55.5	253.0	2,198.7	420.1	1,598.8	179.8
Dayton-Kettering, OH M.S.A.[3]	805,963									
Includes Greene, Miami, and Montgomery Counties										
City of Dayton	140,427	1,351	48	200	347	756	5,673	1,533	3,393	747
City of Kettering	54,974	56	1	27	13	15	794	139	604	51
Total area actually reporting	93.7%	2,551	60	487	623	1,381	16,890	3,287	12,128	1,475
Estimated total	100.0%	2,647	60	530	641	1,416	18,206	3,477	13,211	1,518
Rate per 100,000 inhabitants		328.4	7.4	65.8	79.5	175.7	2,258.9	431.4	1,639.2	188.3
Decatur, IL M.S.A.	103,506									
Includes Macon County										
City of Decatur	70,710	375	11	52	65	247	1,954	442	1,339	173
Total area actually reporting	100.0%	434	11	64	71	288	2,382	520	1,671	191
Rate per 100,000 inhabitants		419.3	10.6	61.8	68.6	278.2	2,301.3	502.4	1,614.4	184.5
Deltona-Daytona Beach-Ormond Beach, FL M.S.A.	664,033									
Includes Flagler and Volusia Counties										
City of Daytona Beach	69,834	794	13	18	109	654	2,833	380	2,213	240
City of Ormond Beach	44,005	133	1	13	15	104	1,119	158	894	67
City of DeLand	34,468	198	4	1	26	167	1,126	182	873	71
Total area actually reporting	100.0%	2,120	28	136	289	1,667	11,988	1,879	9,180	929
Rate per 100,000 inhabitants		319.3	4.2	20.5	43.5	251.0	1,805.3	283.0	1,382.5	139.9
Detroit-Warren-Dearborn, MI M.S.A.	4,320,314									
Includes the Metropolitan Divisions of Detroit-Dearborn-Livonia and Warren-Troy-Farmington Hills										
City of Detroit	663,502	13,040	275	952	2,346	9,467	28,550	6,820	14,844	6,886
City of Warren	134,653	648	8	89	83	468	2,465	569	1,540	356
City of Dearborn	93,902	305	4	36	56	209	2,104	201	1,637	266
City of Livonia	93,644	167	0	22	18	127	1,411	126	1,173	112
City of Troy	84,688	67	2	10	8	47	1,042	70	918	54
City of Farmington Hills	81,262	87	0	17	7	63	759	145	547	67
City of Southfield	73,335	200	1	33	45	121	1,508	358	898	252
City of Taylor	60,923	378	1	35	41	301	1,386	242	998	146
City of Pontiac	59,791	769	10	66	108	585	1,300	315	875	110
City of Novi	61,699	48	1	8	2	37	514	21	466	27
Total area actually reporting	100.0%	22,332	363	2,443	3,481	16,045	72,684	13,451	47,916	11,317
Rate per 100,000 inhabitants		516.9	8.4	56.5	80.6	371.4	1,682.4	311.3	1,109.1	261.9
Detroit-Dearborn-Livonia, MI M.D.	1,741,965									
Includes Wayne County										
Total area actually reporting	100.0%	17,147	313	1,499	2,891	12,444	46,878	9,438	28,410	9,030
Rate per 100,000 inhabitants		984.3	18.0	86.1	166.0	714.4	2,691.1	541.8	1,630.9	518.4

Table 4. Crime in the United States, by Selected Metropolitan Statistical Area, 2019—*Continued*

(Number, percent, rate per 100,000 population.)

Area	Population	Violent crime	Murder and nonnegligent manslaughter	Rape[1]	Robbery	Aggravated assault	Property crime	Burglary	Larceny-theft	Motor vehicle theft
Warren-Troy-Farmington Hills, MI M.D.	2,578,349									
Includes Lapeer, Livingston, Macomb, Oakland, and St. Clair Counties										
Total area actually reporting	100.0%	5,185	50	944	590	3,601	25,806	4,013	19,506	2,287
Rate per 100,000 inhabitants		201.1	1.9	36.6	22.9	139.7	1,000.9	155.6	756.5	88.7
Dover, DE M.S.A.	180,168									
Includes Kent County										
City of Dover	38,361	334	4	13	49	268	2,057	82	1,886	89
Total area actually reporting	100.0%	770	6	71	97	596	4,019	430	3,380	209
Rate per 100,000 inhabitants		427.4	3.3	39.4	53.8	330.8	2,230.7	238.7	1,876.0	116.0
Dubuque, IA M.S.A.	96,742									
Includes Dubuque County										
City of Dubuque	57,973	110	0	34	9	67	949	138	747	64
Total area actually reporting	100.0%	130	1	42	9	78	1,103	180	842	81
Rate per 100,000 inhabitants		134.4	1.0	43.4	9.3	80.6	1,140.1	186.1	870.4	83.7
Duluth, MN-WI M.S.A.[3]	288,792									
Includes Carlton, Lake, and St. Louis[3] Counties, MN and Douglas County, WI										
City of Duluth, MN	85,846	292	2	37	69	184	3,670	481	2,977	212
Total area actually reporting	100.0%	604	4	126	80	394	7,697	1,100	6,131	466
Rate per 100,000 inhabitants		209.1	1.4	43.6	27.7	136.4	2,665.2	380.9	2,123.0	161.4
Durham-Chapel Hill, NC M.S.A.[3]	644,500									
Includes Chatham, Durham, Granville, Orange and Person Counties[3]										
City of Durham[3]	280,282	2,046	37	121	626	1,262	10,672	1,972	7,942	758
City of Chapel Hill[3]	61,457	58	0	10	17	31	926	184	706	36
Total area actually reporting	96.7%	2,752	46	194	730	1,782	15,906	3,044	11,836	1,026
Estimated total	100.0%	2,830	47	203	744	1,836	16,639	3,183	12,392	1,064
Rate per 100,000 inhabitants		439.1	7.3	31.5	115.4	284.9	2,581.7	493.9	1,922.7	165.1
East Stroudsburg, PA M.S.A.	169,228									
Includes Monroe County										
Total area actually reporting	100.0%	400	4	64	28	304	2,551	379	2,089	83
Rate per 100,000 inhabitants		236.4	2.4	37.8	16.5	179.6	1,507.4	224.0	1,234.4	49.0
Eau Claire, WI M.S.A.[3]	169,360									
Includes Chippewa and Eau Claire Counties										
City of Eau Claire	69,195	191	0	58	22	111	1,634	252	1,317	65
Total area actually reporting	100.0%	363	5	118	26	214	2,600	423	2,046	131
Rate per 100,000 inhabitants		214.3	3.0	69.7	15.4	126.4	1,535.2	249.8	1,208.1	77.4
El Centro, CA M.S.A.	181,194									
Includes Imperial County										
City of El Centro	44,303	143	3	9	41	90	1,184	228	861	95
Total area actually reporting	94.7%	589	7	28	80	474	3,476	769	2,236	471
Estimated total	100.0%	615	7	30	83	495	3,619	806	2,325	488
Rate per 100,000 inhabitants		339.4	3.9	16.6	45.8	273.2	1,997.3	444.8	1,283.2	269.3
Elizabethtown-Fort Knox, KY M.S.A.	153,255									
Includes Hardin, Larue, and Meade Counties										
City of Elizabethtown	30,383	49	3	13	15	18	452	140	239	73
Total area actually reporting	100.0%	153	6	33	39	75	1,738	472	1,045	221
Rate per 100,000 inhabitants		99.8	3.9	21.5	25.4	48.9	1,134.1	308.0	681.9	144.2
Elmira, NY M.S.A.	83,232									
Includes Chemung County										
City of Elmira	26,958	83	1	0	40	42	831	172	643	16
Total area actually reporting	100.0%	178	1	19	45	113	1,445	238	1,174	33
Rate per 100,000 inhabitants		213.9	1.2	22.8	54.1	135.8	1,736.1	285.9	1,410.5	39.6
El Paso, TX M.S.A.[3]	845,194									
Includes El Paso3 and Hudspeth Counties										
City of El Paso[3]	686,793	2,422	40	310	338	1,734	10,378	1,048	8,479	851
Total area actually reporting	100.0%	2,816	41	369	363	2,043	11,967	1,296	9,661	1,010
Rate per 100,000 inhabitants		333.2	4.9	43.7	42.9	241.7	1,415.9	153.3	1,143.1	119.5

Table 4. Crime in the United States, by Selected Metropolitan Statistical Area, 2019—*Continued*

(Number, percent, rate per 100,000 population.)

Area	Population	Violent crime	Murder and nonnegligent manslaughter	Rape[1]	Robbery	Aggravated assault	Property crime	Burglary	Larceny-theft	Motor vehicle theft
Enid, OK M.S.A.	60,773									
Includes Garfield County										
City of Enid	49,598	204	1	44	9	150	1,625	364	1,148	113
Total area actually reporting	100.0%	225	1	47	9	168	1,812	411	1,275	126
Rate per 100,000 inhabitants		370.2	1.6	77.3	14.8	276.4	2,981.6	676.3	2,098.0	207.3
Erie, PA M.S.A.	270,606									
Includes Erie County										
City of Erie	95,834	476	9	54	93	320	1,817	342	1,379	96
Total area actually reporting	99.5%	807	9	118	115	565	4,311	644	3,518	149
Estimated total	100.0%	809	9	118	115	567	4,322	645	3,527	150
Rate per 100,000 inhabitants		299.0	3.3	43.6	42.5	209.5	1,597.2	238.4	1,303.4	55.4
Eugene-Springfield, OR M.S.A.[4]	381,434									
Includes Lane County										
City of Eugene	173,183	675	2	123	180	370	6,184	964	4,614	606
City of Springfield	63,438	190	1	34	32	123	1,978	169	1,640	169
Total area actually reporting	99.1%			180	225	773	10,372	1,493	7,880	999
Estimated total	100.0%			181	225	777	10,440	1,499	7,938	1,003
Rate per 100,000 inhabitants				47.5	59.0	203.7	2,737.0	393.0	2,081.1	263.0
Evansville, IN-KY M.S.A.	315,399									
Includes Posey, Vanderburgh, and Warrick Counties, IN and Henderson County, KY										
City of Evansville	117,700	721	11	90	153	467	4,917	588	3,926	403
Total area actually reporting	91.9%	990	17	130	172	671	6,954	912	5,455	587
Estimated total	100.0%	1,032	17	133	176	706	7,199	953	5,639	607
Rate per 100,000 inhabitants		327.2	5.4	42.2	55.8	223.8	2,282.5	302.2	1,787.9	192.5
Fairbanks, AK M.S.A.	33,604									
Includes Fairbanks North Star Borough										
City of Fairbanks	31,493	247	3	33	52	159	1,353	163	1,006	184
Total area actually reporting	100.0%	267	3	39	52	173	1,491	178	1,117	196
Rate per 100,000 inhabitants		794.5	8.9	116.1	154.7	514.8	4,437.0	529.7	3,324.0	583.3
Fargo, ND-MN M.S.A.	247,762									
Includes Clay County, MN and Cass County, ND										
City of Fargo, ND	127,423	574	5	111	78	380	3,978	830	2,757	391
Total area actually reporting	100.0%	735	5	153	105	472	5,794	1,164	4,066	564
Rate per 100,000 inhabitants		296.7	2.0	61.8	42.4	190.5	2,338.5	469.8	1,641.1	227.6
Flagstaff, AZ M.S.A.	144,001									
Includes Coconino County										
City of Flagstaff	75,013	367	1	42	43	281	2,371	140	2,169	62
Total area actually reporting	100.0%	664	8	78	55	523	3,527	284	3,118	125
Rate per 100,000 inhabitants		461.1	5.6	54.2	38.2	363.2	2,449.3	197.2	2,165.3	86.8
Flint, MI M.S.A.[4]	403,666									
Includes Genesee County[4]										
City of Flint	95,212	1,284	23	64	78	1,119	1,986	559	1,220	207
Total area actually reporting	100.0%	2,340	30	259	177	1,874			4,624	600
Rate per 100,000 inhabitants		579.7	7.4	64.2	43.8	464.2			1,145.5	148.6
Florence, SC M.S.A.	204,992									
Includes Darlington and Florence Counties										
City of Florence	37,640	447	7	29	58	353	2,496	388	1,909	199
Total area actually reporting	98.8%	1,678	34	140	220	1,284	8,235	1,927	5,665	643
Estimated total	100.0%	1,688	34	141	221	1,292	8,321	1,945	5,728	648
Rate per 100,000 inhabitants		823.4	16.6	68.8	107.8	630.3	4,059.2	948.8	2,794.3	316.1
Fond du Lac, WI M.S.A.	103,125									
Includes Fond du Lac County										
City of Fond du Lac	42,954	134	0	28	14	92	797	59	697	41
Total area actually reporting	100.0%	182	0	50	15	117	1,131	178	898	55
Rate per 100,000 inhabitants		176.5	0.0	48.5	14.5	113.5	1,096.7	172.6	870.8	53.3
Fort Collins, CO M.S.A.	355,815									
Includes Larimer County										
City of Fort Collins	170,889	371	1	41	36	293	3,713	350	3,135	228
Total area actually reporting	100.0%	833	3	124	63	643	6,683	691	5,533	459
Rate per 100,000 inhabitants		234.1	0.8	34.8	17.7	180.7	1,878.2	194.2	1,555.0	129.0

Table 4. Crime in the United States, by Selected Metropolitan Statistical Area, 2019—*Continued*

(Number, percent, rate per 100,000 population.)

Area	Population	Violent crime	Murder and nonnegligent manslaughter	Rape[1]	Robbery	Aggravated assault	Property crime	Burglary	Larceny-theft	Motor vehicle theft
Fort Smith, AR-OK M.S.A....	249,623									
Includes Crawford, Franklin, and Sebastian Counties, AR and										
Sequoyah County, OK..										
City of Fort Smith, AR	88,041	863	4	97	90	672	5,127	812	3,929	386
Total area actually reporting......................................	99.6%	1,457	8	206	106	1,137	7,925	1,501	5,815	609
Estimated total..	100.0%	1,462	8	207	106	1,141	7,944	1,506	5,828	610
Rate per 100,000 inhabitants.....................................		585.7	3.2	82.9	42.5	457.1	3,182.4	603.3	2,334.7	244.4
Fort Wayne, IN M.S.A...	412,827									
Includes Allen and Whitley Counties										
City of Fort Wayne..	269,366	974	26	145	357	446	7,437	990	5,879	568
Total area actually reporting......................................	94.4%	1,227	30	195	401	601	8,580	1,167	6,714	699
Estimated total..	100.0%	1,259	30	196	403	630	8,726	1,200	6,811	715
Rate per 100,000 inhabitants.....................................		305.0	7.3	47.5	97.6	152.6	2,113.7	290.7	1,649.8	173.2
Gainesville, FL M.S.A....	329,709									
Includes Alachua, Gilchrist, and Levy Counties										
City of Gainesville	135,085	928	2	153	185	588	4,712	501	3,803	408
Total area actually reporting......................................	100.0%	2,282	7	309	297	1,669	8,091	1,345	6,054	692
Rate per 100,000 inhabitants.....................................		692.1	2.1	93.7	90.1	506.2	2,454.0	407.9	1,836.2	209.9
Glens Falls, NY M.S.A....	124,339									
Includes Warren and Washington Counties................										
City of Glens Falls	14,306	28	0	8	1	19	100	18	80	2
Total area actually reporting......................................	98.0%	156	0	94	6	56	885	123	728	34
Estimated total..	100.0%	158	0	94	6	58	906	126	745	35
Rate per 100,000 inhabitants.....................................		127.1	0.0	75.6	4.8	46.6	728.7	101.3	599.2	28.1
Goldsboro, NC M.S.A.[3]...	123,222									
Includes Wayne County[3]										
City of Goldsboro[3]...	34,085	267	2	7	50	208	1,985	380	1,506	99
Total area actually reporting......................................	97.7%	501	4	10	82	405	3,298	865	2,180	253
Estimated total..	100.0%	511	4	11	82	414	3,376	887	2,229	260
Rate per 100,000 inhabitants.....................................		414.7	3.2	8.9	66.5	336.0	2,739.8	719.8	1,808.9	211.0
Grand Forks, ND-MN M.S.A.[3].................................	101,736									
Includes Polk County,[3] MN and Grand Forks County, ND										
City of Grand Forks, ND	57,459	166	0	25	23	118	1,422	218	1,101	103
Total area actually reporting......................................	100.0%	255	1	42	24	188	2,080	336	1,594	150
Rate per 100,000 inhabitants.....................................		250.6	1.0	41.3	23.6	184.8	2,044.5	330.3	1,566.8	147.4
Grand Island, NE M.S.A....	75,855									
Includes Hall, Howard, and Merrick Counties..........										
City of Grand Island	51,821	236	1	55	14	166	1,323	189	1,034	100
Total area actually reporting......................................	100.0%	285	1	60	15	209	1,456	224	1,118	114
Rate per 100,000 inhabitants.....................................		375.7	1.3	79.1	19.8	275.5	1,919.5	295.3	1,473.9	150.3
Grand Junction, CO M.S.A.	153,429									
Includes Mesa County...										
City of Grand Junction...	63,949	235	3	43	30	159	2,463	278	2,034	151
Total area actually reporting......................................	99.2%	427	9	85	49	284	3,764	555	2,932	277
Estimated total..	100.0%	435	9	85	50	291	3,893	562	3,049	282
Rate per 100,000 inhabitants.....................................		283.5	5.9	55.4	32.6	189.7	2,537.3	366.3	1,987.2	183.8
Grand Rapids-Kentwood, MI M.S.A.[4]	1,079,969									
Includes Ionia, Kent, Montcalm, and Ottawa Counties										
City of Grand Rapids..	201,799	1,286	8	144	274	860	3,850	595	2,754	501
City of Kentwood	52,274	162	0	23	20	119	1,111	170	850	91
Total area actually reporting......................................	99.9%	3,469	24	857	446	2,142			10,937	1,248
Estimated total..	100.0%	3,472	24	857	446	2,145			10,952	1,249
Rate per 100,000 inhabitants.....................................		321.5	2.2	79.4	41.3	198.6			1,014.1	115.7
Grants Pass, OR M.S.A.	87,564									
Includes Josephine County..										
City of Grants Pass...	38,475	121	0	24	21	76	1,235	151	958	126
Total area actually reporting......................................	100.0%	209	0	37	24	148	1,643	229	1,114	300
Rate per 100,000 inhabitants.....................................		238.7	0.0	42.3	27.4	169.0	1,876.3	261.5	1,272.2	342.6
Great Falls, MT M.S.A.[4]	81,418									
Includes Cascade County[4]										
City of Great Falls	58,637	302	0	39	18	245	3,405	318	2,826	261

Table 4. Crime in the United States, by Selected Metropolitan Statistical Area, 2019—*Continued*

(Number, percent, rate per 100,000 population.)

Area	Population	Violent crime	Murder and nonnegligent manslaughter	Rape[1]	Robbery	Aggravated assault	Property crime	Burglary	Larceny-theft	Motor vehicle theft
Total area actually reporting	100.0%			43	21	314	3,653	375	2,983	295
Rate per 100,000 inhabitants				52.8	25.8	385.7	4,486.7	460.6	3,663.8	362.3
Greeley, CO M.S.A.[3]	321,385									
Includes Weld County										
City of Greeley	109,255	386	2	71	67	246	2,542	338	1,898	306
Total area actually reporting	94.7%	660	5	154	87	414	4,767	654	3,509	604
Estimated total	100.0%	694	5	158	93	438	5,246	701	3,894	651
Rate per 100,000 inhabitants		215.9	1.6	49.2	28.9	136.3	1,632.3	218.1	1,211.6	202.6
Green Bay, WI M.S.A.	323,107									
Includes Brown, Kewaunee, and Oconto Counties										
City of Green Bay	104,992	529	3	78	49	399	1,724	245	1,355	124
Total area actually reporting	100.0%	730	5	135	56	534	3,549	423	2,938	188
Rate per 100,000 inhabitants		225.9	1.5	41.8	17.3	165.3	1,098.4	130.9	909.3	58.2
Greensboro-High Point, NC M.S.A.[3]	772,854									
Includes Guilford, Randolph, and Rockingham Counties[3]										
City of Greensboro[3]	298,025	2,440	43	113	621	1,663	10,994	2,215	7,792	987
City of High Point[3]	113,307	828	19	44	133	632	3,726	621	2,705	400
Total area actually reporting	81.4%	3,738	69	216	825	2,628	18,073	3,793	12,660	1,620
Estimated total	100.0%	4,098	75	255	876	2,892	20,835	4,473	14,540	1,822
Rate per 100,000 inhabitants		530.2	9.7	33.0	113.3	374.2	2,695.9	578.8	1,881.3	235.7
Greenville, NC M.S.A.[3]	181,242									
Includes Pitt County[3]										
City of Greenville[3]	94,193	437	5	17	94	321	2,837	415	2,308	114
Total area actually reporting	96.3%	630	8	34	131	457	4,165	806	3,176	183
Estimated total	100.0%	657	8	37	135	477	4,383	852	3,335	196
Rate per 100,000 inhabitants		362.5	4.4	20.4	74.5	263.2	2,418.3	470.1	1,840.1	108.1
Gulfport-Biloxi, MS M.S.A.[3]	417,585									
Includes Hancock, Harrison, Jackson, and Stone Counties										
City of Gulfport	72,383	236	12	25	65	134	3,492	419	2,805	268
City of Biloxi	46,185	188	3	35	65	85	2,663	619	1,877	167
Total area actually reporting	95.3%	888	26	152	220	490	13,273	2,225	9,887	1,161
Estimated total	100.0%	924	27	158	228	511	13,849	2,300	10,356	1,193
Rate per 100,000 inhabitants		221.3	6.5	37.8	54.6	122.4	3,316.5	550.8	2,480.0	285.7
Hanford-Corcoran, CA M.S.A.	149,966									
Includes Kings County										
City of Hanford	57,232	257	0	18	40	199	1,242	131	900	211
City of Corcoran	21,353	118	1	8	12	97	272	65	157	50
Total area actually reporting	100.0%	757	4	71	88	594	2,466	410	1,662	394
Rate per 100,000 inhabitants		504.8	2.7	47.3	58.7	396.1	1,644.4	273.4	1,108.3	262.7
Harrisonburg, VA M.S.A.	135,787									
Includes Rockingham County and Harrisonburg City										
City of Harrisonburg	54,387	112	0	32	17	63	924	68	813	43
Total area actually reporting	100.0%	172	0	62	19	91	1,583	208	1,296	79
Rate per 100,000 inhabitants		126.7	0.0	45.7	14.0	67.0	1,165.8	153.2	954.4	58.2
Hartford-East Hartford-Middletown, CT M.S.A.[3, 5]	1,015,769									
Includes Hartford, Middlesex, and Tolland Counties										
City of Hartford	122,245	1,049	21	31	271	726	3,424	427	2,464	533
City of East Hartford	49,842	76	1	18	31	26	775	109	525	141
City of Middletown	45,963	38	0	5	10	23	613	62	474	77
Total area actually reporting	100.0%	2,021	32	197	565	1,227		1,999	13,411	
Rate per 100,000 inhabitants		199.0	3.2	19.4	55.6	120.8		196.8	1,320.3	
Hilton Head Island-Bluffton, SC M.S.A.	221,873									
Includes Beaufort and Jasper Counties										
City of Bluffton	24,812	46	1	9	10	26	220	35	175	10
Total area actually reporting	91.6%	784	11	69	138	566	3,085	499	2,374	212
Estimated total	100.0%	882	13	77	143	649	3,476	610	2,615	251
Rate per 100,000 inhabitants		397.5	5.9	34.7	64.5	292.5	1,566.7	274.9	1,178.6	113.1
Homosassa Springs, FL M.S.A.	147,739									
Includes Citrus County										
Total area actually reporting	100.0%	373	4	29	40	300	2,055	394	1,466	195
Rate per 100,000 inhabitants		252.5	2.7	19.6	27.1	203.1	1,391.0	266.7	992.3	132.0

Table 4. Crime in the United States, by Selected Metropolitan Statistical Area, 2019—*Continued*

(Number, percent, rate per 100,000 population.)

Area	Population	Violent crime	Murder and nonnegligent manslaughter	Rape[1]	Robbery	Aggravated assault	Property crime	Burglary	Larceny-theft	Motor vehicle theft
Hot Springs, AR M.S.A.[4]	99,238									
Includes Garland County[4]										
City of Hot Springs	37,263	241	10	38	42	151	2,674	755	1,710	209
Total area actually reporting	100.0%	520	10	63	50	397			2,385	354
Rate per 100,000 inhabitants		524.0	10.1	63.5	50.4	400.0			2,403.3	356.7
Houma-Thibodaux, LA M.S.A.	208,034									
Includes Lafourche and Terrebonne Parishes										
City of Houma	32,771	209	4	17	22	166	1,489	169	1,260	60
City of Thibodaux	14,587	81	4	5	0	72	515	63	432	20
Total area actually reporting	97.9%	761	20	70	38	633	6,005	874	4,866	265
Estimated total	100.0%	779	20	70	38	651	6,097	899	4,928	270
Rate per 100,000 inhabitants		374.5	9.6	33.6	18.3	312.9	2,930.8	432.1	2,368.8	129.8
Huntington-Ashland, WV-KY-OH M.S.A.	356,404									
Includes Boyd, Carter, and Greenup Counties, KY; Lawrence County OH; and Cabell, Putnam, and Wayne Counties, WV										
City of Huntington, WV	45,675	330	4	56	59	211	1,792	456	1,147	189
City of Ashland, KY	20,222	59	3	11	14	31	740	96	608	36
Total area actually reporting	86.7%	826	12	145	91	578	5,254	1,164	3,588	502
Estimated total	100.0%	945	14	158	101	672	5,969	1,317	4,094	558
Rate per 100,000 inhabitants		265.1	3.9	44.3	28.3	188.6	1,674.8	369.5	1,148.7	156.6
Idaho Falls, ID M.S.A.	151,591									
Includes Bonneville, Butte, and Jefferson Counties										
City of Idaho Falls	62,088	172	1	37	11	123	940	264	608	68
Total area actually reporting	100.0%	310	2	54	14	240	1,651	443	1,092	116
Rate per 100,000 inhabitants		204.5	1.3	35.6	9.2	158.3	1,089.1	292.2	720.4	76.5
Iowa City, IA M.S.A.	175,274									
Includes Johnson and Washington Counties										
City of Iowa City	77,390	167	1	40	25	101	1,252	314	867	71
Total area actually reporting	99.4%	480	4	95	43	338	2,629	505	1,985	139
Estimated total	100.0%	485	4	96	44	341	2,658	511	2,005	142
Rate per 100,000 inhabitants		276.7	2.3	54.8	25.1	194.6	1,516.5	291.5	1,143.9	81.0
Ithaca, NY M.S.A	102,363									
Includes Tompkins County										
City of Ithaca	31,122	41	1	5	9	26	840	56	768	16
Total area actually reporting	100.0%	127	1	53	19	54	1,707	197	1,478	32
Rate per 100,000 inhabitants		124.1	1.0	51.8	18.6	52.8	1,667.6	192.5	1,443.9	31.3
Jackson, MI M.S.A.	158,260									
Includes Jackson County										
City of Jackson	32,503	360	4	51	37	268	1,344	206	1,025	113
Total area actually reporting	100.0%	814	5	162	50	597	3,173	420	2,528	225
Rate per 100,000 inhabitants		514.3	3.2	102.4	31.6	377.2	2,004.9	265.4	1,597.4	142.2
Jackson, TN M.S.A.	178,143									
Includes Chester, Crockett, Gibson, and Madison Counties										
City of Jackson	66,915	650	17	30	97	506	2,473	374	1,904	195
Total area actually reporting	100.0%	1,093	21	66	129	877	4,179	751	3,062	366
Rate per 100,000 inhabitants		613.6	11.8	37.0	72.4	492.3	2,345.9	421.6	1,718.8	205.5
Jacksonville, FL M.S.A.	1,549,030									
Includes Baker, Clay, Duval, Nassau, and St. Johns Counties										
City of Jacksonville	909,142	5,886	129	554	1,294	3,909	30,088	4,906	22,373	2,809
Total area actually reporting	100.0%	7,353	143	779	1,456	4,975	38,810	6,410	28,976	3,424
Rate per 100,000 inhabitants		474.7	9.2	50.3	94.0	321.2	2,505.4	413.8	1,870.6	221.0
Janesville-Beloit, WI M.S.A.[3]	163,288									
Includes Rock County										
City of Janesville	64,687	148	1	38	28	81	1,577	137	1,397	43
City of Beloit[3]	37,025	154	4	19	31	100	1,114	122	921	71
Total area actually reporting	100.0%	380	5	75	69	231	3,247	356	2,738	153
Rate per 100,000 inhabitants		232.7	3.1	45.9	42.3	141.5	1,988.5	218.0	1,676.8	93.7
Jefferson City, MO M.S.A.	151,555									
Includes Callaway, Cole, Moniteau, and Osage Counties										
City of Jefferson City	42,793	119	2	30	23	64	1,101	125	910	66

Table 4. Crime in the United States, by Selected Metropolitan Statistical Area, 2019—*Continued*

(Number, percent, rate per 100,000 population.)

Area	Population	Violent crime	Murder and nonnegligent manslaughter	Rape[1]	Robbery	Aggravated assault	Property crime	Burglary	Larceny-theft	Motor vehicle theft
Total area actually reporting..............................	100.0%	334	7	58	29	240	2,826	490	2,127	209
Rate per 100,000 inhabitants.................................		220.4	4.6	38.3	19.1	158.4	1,864.7	323.3	1,403.5	137.9
Johnson City, TN M.S.A.....................................	203,289									
Includes Carter, Unicoi, and Washington Counties.................										
City of Johnson City..	67,197	286	1	28	38	219	2,390	301	1,904	185
Total area actually reporting...............................	100.0%	668	3	59	47	559	4,498	712	3,330	456
Rate per 100,000 inhabitants................................		328.6	1.5	29.0	23.1	275.0	2,212.6	350.2	1,638.1	224.3
Jonesboro, AR M.S.A.	133,624									
Includes Craighead and Poinsett Counties.........................										
City of Jonesboro...	78,261	537	13	74	58	392	2,982	1,092	1,758	132
Total area actually reporting...............................	98.7%	733	15	131	65	522	4,077	1,405	2,440	232
Estimated total..	100.0%	743	15	133	66	529	4,116	1,414	2,467	235
Rate per 100,000 inhabitants................................		556.0	11.2	99.5	49.4	395.9	3,080.3	1,058.2	1,846.2	175.9
Joplin, MO M.S.A.	179,103									
Includes Jasper and Newton Counties										
City of Joplin..	50,635	307	2	63	63	179	3,677	521	2,815	341
Total area actually reporting...............................	100.0%	593	3	107	83	400	6,555	1,028	4,863	664
Rate per 100,000 inhabitants................................		331.1	1.7	59.7	46.3	223.3	3,659.9	574.0	2,715.2	370.7
Kahului-Wailuku-Lahaina, HI M.S.A.................	167,475									
Includes Maui County										
Total area actually reporting...............................	100.0%	449	1	110	67	271	4,984	577	3,746	661
Rate per 100,000 inhabitants................................		268.1	0.6	65.7	40.0	161.8	2,976.0	344.5	2,236.8	394.7
Kalamazoo-Portage, MI M.S.A.	266,016									
Includes Kalamazoo County										
City of Kalamazoo	76,827	949	9	110	182	648	3,578	703	2,546	329
City of Portage	49,583	136	0	30	14	92	1,549	204	1,279	66
Total area actually reporting...............................	99.2%	1,518	12	225	259	1,022	8,555	1,556	6,288	711
Estimated total..	100.0%	1,523	12	226	259	1,026	8,583	1,560	6,311	712
Rate per 100,000 inhabitants................................		572.5	4.5	85.0	97.4	385.7	3,226.5	586.4	2,372.4	267.7
Kankakee, IL M.S.A.	109,111									
Includes Kankakee County										
City of Kankakee	25,872	236	4	29	53	150	873	156	675	42
Total area actually reporting...............................	98.6%	423	5	58	90	270	2,072	297	1,690	85
Estimated total..	100.0%	424	5	58	90	271	2,096	301	1,709	86
Rate per 100,000 inhabitants................................		388.6	4.6	53.2	82.5	248.4	1,921.0	275.9	1,566.3	78.8
Kennewick-Richland, WA M.S.A.	300,701									
Includes Benton and Franklin Counties...........................										
City of Kennewick..	84,072	253	2	54	49	148	2,487	378	1,907	202
City of Richland	58,514	100	2	24	9	65	1,199	195	949	55
Total area actually reporting...............................	100.0%	660	8	136	111	405	5,851	945	4,391	515
Rate per 100,000 inhabitants................................		219.5	2.7	45.2	36.9	134.7	1,945.8	314.3	1,460.3	171.3
Killeen-Temple, TX M.S.A.[3]	454,647									
Includes Bell, Coryell, and Lampasas[3] Counties.....................										
City of Killeen	151,832	583	14	105	124	340	3,432	818	2,296	318
City of Temple	77,558	217	4	61	39	113	1,718	244	1,276	198
Total area actually reporting...............................	99.3%	1,196	19	259	201	717	8,187	1,615	5,916	656
Estimated total..	100.0%	1,202	19	259	201	723	8,231	1,624	5,946	661
Rate per 100,000 inhabitants................................		264.4	4.2	57.0	44.2	159.0	1,810.4	357.2	1,307.8	145.4
Kingsport-Bristol, TN-VA M.S.A.	305,838									
Includes Hawkins and Sullivan Counties, TN and Scott and Washington Counties and Bristol City, VA...........................										
City of Kingsport, TN	54,218	332	3	22	35	272	2,829	324	2,232	273
City of Bristol, TN..	26,900	135	1	15	12	107	813	138	604	71
Total area actually reporting...............................	100.0%	920	14	107	74	725	7,019	1,097	5,154	768
Rate per 100,000 inhabitants................................		300.8	4.6	35.0	24.2	237.1	2,295.0	358.7	1,685.2	251.1
Kingston, NY M.S.A.	177,151									
Includes Ulster County										
City of Kingston..	22,844	68	2	13	10	43	498	59	419	20
Total area actually reporting...............................	89.6%	249	4	72	19	154	1,740	234	1,439	67

Table 4. Crime in the United States, by Selected Metropolitan Statistical Area, 2019—*Continued*

(Number, percent, rate per 100,000 population.)

Area	Population	Violent crime	Murder and nonnegligent manslaughter	Rape[1]	Robbery	Aggravated assault	Property crime	Burglary	Larceny-theft	Motor vehicle theft
Estimated total...	100.0%	266	4	75	22	165	1,932	253	1,604	75
Rate per 100,000 inhabitants................................		150.2	2.3	42.3	12.4	93.1	1,090.6	142.8	905.4	42.3
Knoxville, TN M.S.A.	866,295									
Includes Anderson, Blount, Campbell, Knox, Loudon, Morgan, Roane, and Union Counties										
City of Knoxville	188,666	1,259	22	146	232	859	8,207	1,157	6,067	983
Total area actually reporting...............................	100.0%	3,064	35	370	322	2,337	18,423	3,036	13,115	2,272
Rate per 100,000 inhabitants................................		353.7	4.0	42.7	37.2	269.8	2,126.6	350.5	1,513.9	262.3
Kokomo, IN M.S.A.	82,480									
Includes Howard County.......................................										
City of Kokomo	57,845	392	5	25	48	314	1,493	312	1,081	100
Total area actually reporting...............................	98.7%	455	5	31	53	366	1,625	342	1,172	111
Estimated total..	100.0%	458	5	31	54	368	1,651	345	1,193	113
Rate per 100,000 inhabitants................................		555.3	6.1	37.6	65.5	446.2	2,001.7	418.3	1,446.4	137.0
La Crosse-Onalaska, WI-MN M.S.A.[3]	136,997									
Includes Houston County,[3] MN and La Crosse County, WI										
City of La Crosse, WI..	51,591	122	2	27	26	67	1,850	226	1,561	63
City of Onalaska, WI	18,825	10	0	2	2	6	522	24	491	7
Total area actually reporting...............................	100.0%	169	2	31	28	108	2,820	337	2,391	92
Rate per 100,000 inhabitants................................		123.4	1.5	22.6	20.4	78.8	2,058.4	246.0	1,745.3	67.2
Lafayette, LA M.S.A.	489,368									
Includes Acadia, Iberia, Lafayette, St. Martin, and Vermilion Parishes...										
City of Lafayette	126,694	664	14	16	148	486	5,454	1,032	4,101	321
Total area actually reporting...............................	83.3%	1,726	31	98	257	1,340	11,013	2,399	7,963	651
Estimated total..	100.0%	2,283	38	124	335	1,786	14,108	3,031	10,246	831
Rate per 100,000 inhabitants................................		466.5	7.8	25.3	68.5	365.0	2,882.9	619.4	2,093.7	169.8
Lafayette-West Lafayette, IN M.S.A.	233,135									
Includes Benton, Carroll, Tippecanoe, and Warren Counties...										
City of Lafayette	72,585	352	5	38	55	254	2,388	387	1,844	157
City of West Lafayette..	49,154	32	0	5	3	24	357	42	304	11
Total area actually reporting...............................	83.1%	451	8	67	69	307	3,573	580	2,778	215
Estimated total..	100.0%	520	8	73	78	361	3,960	649	3,059	252
Rate per 100,000 inhabitants................................		223.0	3.4	31.3	33.5	154.8	1,698.6	278.4	1,312.1	108.1
Lake Charles, LA M.S.A.	210,155									
Includes Calcasieu and Cameron Parishes.................										
City of Lake Charles	78,733	413	11	52	83	267	2,907	1,212	1,467	228
Total area actually reporting...............................	95.2%	1,099	15	144	128	812	7,991	2,311	5,073	607
Estimated total..	100.0%	1,151	19	145	130	857	8,189	2,349	5,222	618
Rate per 100,000 inhabitants................................		547.7	9.0	69.0	61.9	407.8	3,896.6	1,117.7	2,484.8	294.1
Lake Havasu City-Kingman, AZ M.S.A.	210,855									
Includes Mohave County.......................................										
City of Lake Havasu City	55,413	87	1	29	3	54	670	108	519	43
City of Kingman...	30,600	100	0	9	12	79	1,342	208	1,039	95
Total area actually reporting...............................	97.7%	452	6	67	59	320	5,347	1,124	3,736	487
Estimated total..	100.0%	485	6	69	63	347	5,564	1,171	3,887	506
Rate per 100,000 inhabitants................................		230.0	2.8	32.7	29.9	164.6	2,638.8	555.4	1,843.4	240.0
Lakeland-Winter Haven, FL M.S.A.	717,190									
Includes Polk County..										
City of Lakeland	112,237	350	7	63	97	183	3,230	438	2,589	203
City of Winter Haven	44,211	187	3	22	25	137	1,126	181	884	61
Total area actually reporting...............................	100.0%	1,990	23	166	300	1,501	11,797	1,947	8,914	936
Rate per 100,000 inhabitants................................		277.5	3.2	23.1	41.8	209.3	1,644.9	271.5	1,242.9	130.5
Lansing-East Lansing, MI M.S.A.[4]	550,643									
Includes Clinton, Eaton, Ingham, and Shiawassee Counties....										
City of Lansing...	118,953	1,313	12	140	178	983	3,355	763	2,225	367
City of East Lansing	47,913	88	0	40	11	37	840	113	563	164
Total area actually reporting...............................	100.0%	2,367	19	489	268	1,591			6,637	864
Rate per 100,000 inhabitants................................		429.9	3.5	88.8	48.7	288.9			1,205.3	156.9

Table 4. Crime in the United States, by Selected Metropolitan Statistical Area, 2019—*Continued*

(Number, percent, rate per 100,000 population.)

Area	Population	Violent crime	Murder and nonnegligent manslaughter	Rape[1]	Robbery	Aggravated assault	Property crime	Burglary	Larceny-theft	Motor vehicle theft
Laredo, TX M.S.A.[3]	277,386									
Includes Webb County										
City of Laredo[3]	264,916	836	4	104	164	564	4,692	708	3,726	258
Total area actually reporting	98.3%	882	6	108	167	601	4,944	767	3,862	315
Estimated total	100.0%	893	6	110	168	609	5,037	782	3,932	323
Rate per 100,000 inhabitants		321.9	2.2	39.7	60.6	219.5	1,815.9	281.9	1,417.5	116.4
Las Cruces, NM M.S.A.	218,180									
Includes Dona Ana County										
City of Las Cruces	103,520	514	10	64	57	383	3,707	654	2,746	307
Estimated total	100.0%	1,215	12	124	69	1,010	5,049	1,070	3,548	431
Rate per 100,000 inhabitants		556.9	5.5	56.8	31.6	462.9	2,314.1	490.4	1,626.2	197.5
Las Vegas-Henderson-Paradise, NV M.S.A.	2,270,103									
Includes Clark County										
City of Las Vegas Metropolitan Police Department	1,666,803	8,854	84	1,439	2,118	5,213	46,197	10,646	28,240	7,311
City of Henderson	317,732	543	9	75	191	268	5,554	907	4,093	554
Total area actually reporting	100.0%	11,935	112	1,661	2,808	7,354	58,207	13,003	36,145	9,059
Rate per 100,000 inhabitants		525.7	4.9	73.2	123.7	324.0	2,564.1	572.8	1,592.2	399.1
Lawton, OK M.S.A.[3]	125,205									
Includes Comanche and Cotton Counties										
City of Lawton	92,256	854	15	97	91	651	2,972	877	1,836	259
Total area actually reporting	100.0%	897	16	105	96	680	3,338	1,010	2,016	312
Rate per 100,000 inhabitants		716.4	12.8	83.9	76.7	543.1	2,666.0	806.7	1,610.2	249.2
Lebanon, PA M.S.A.	142,102									
Includes Lebanon County										
City of Lebanon	25,959	65	1	5	21	38	528	77	430	21
Total area actually reporting	97.9%	233	1	35	22	175	1,653	189	1,420	44
Estimated total	100.0%	237	1	35	22	179	1,683	192	1,445	46
Rate per 100,000 inhabitants		166.8	0.7	24.6	15.5	126.0	1,184.4	135.1	1,016.9	32.4
Lewiston, ID-WA M.S.A.	63,370									
Includes Nez Perce County, ID and Asotin County, WA										
City of Lewiston, ID	32,931	42	0	15	2	25	955	145	755	55
Total area actually reporting	100.0%	88	1	30	6	51	1,525	239	1,207	79
Rate per 100,000 inhabitants		138.9	1.6	47.3	9.5	80.5	2,406.5	377.2	1,904.7	124.7
Lewiston-Auburn, ME M.S.A.	108,026									
Includes Androscoggin County										
City of Lewiston	35,865	107	0	31	18	58	716	122	555	39
City of Auburn	23,214	34	1	13	5	15	511	56	445	10
Total area actually reporting	100.0%	186	1	65	25	95	1,454	219	1,170	65
Rate per 100,000 inhabitants		172.2	0.9	60.2	23.1	87.9	1,346.0	202.7	1,083.1	60.2
Lexington-Fayette, KY M.S.A.	520,442									
Includes Bourbon, Clark, Fayette, Jessamine, Scott, and Woodford Counties										
City of Lexington	326,070	967	26	175	362	404	9,776	1,537	7,333	906
Total area actually reporting	100.0%	1,200	27	235	417	521	14,148	2,156	10,732	1,260
Rate per 100,000 inhabitants		230.6	5.2	45.2	80.1	100.1	2,718.5	414.3	2,062.1	242.1
Lima, OH M.S.A.[2]	102,023									
Includes Allen County										
City of Lima	36,653	259	4	59	64	132	1,493	392	1,037	64
Total area actually reporting	93.8%	311	5	76	80	150	2,374	543	1,724	107
Estimated total	100.0%	322	5	79	82	156	2,480	558	1,810	112
Rate per 100,000 inhabitants		315.6	4.9	77.4	80.4	152.9	2,430.8	546.9	1,774.1	109.8
Lincoln, NE M.S.A.	337,340									
Includes Lancaster and Seward Counties										
City of Lincoln	291,128	1,115	5	323	166	621	8,008	988	6,566	454
Total area actually reporting	99.4%	1,149	5	345	166	633	8,394	1,043	6,863	488
Estimated total	100.0%	1,170	5	359	166	640	8,423	1,043	6,892	488
Rate per 100,000 inhabitants		346.8	1.5	106.4	49.2	189.7	2,496.9	309.2	2,043.0	144.7
Little Rock-North Little Rock-Conway, AR M.S.A.[4]	743,875									
Includes Faulkner, Grant, Lonoke, Perry, Pulaski, and Saline[4] Counties										

(Number, percent, rate per 100,000 population.)

Area	Population	Violent crime	Murder and nonnegligent manslaughter	Rape[1]	Robbery	Aggravated assault	Property crime	Burglary	Larceny-theft	Motor vehicle theft
City of Little Rock..............................	198,382	3,009	38	209	391	2,371	12,145	1,760	9,316	1,069
City of North Little Rock......................	66,604	562	12	23	106	421	2,479	380	1,723	376
City of Conway..................................	67,336	324	2	49	51	222	1,842	177	1,567	98
Total area actually reporting................	99.9%	5,815	75	539	689	4,512				2,586
Estimated total...................................	100.0%	5,819	75	540	689	4,515				2,587
Rate per 100,000 inhabitants...............		782.3	10.1	72.6	92.6	607.0				347.8
Logan, UT-ID M.S.A.	142,499									
Includes Franklin County, ID and Cache County, UT..............										
City of Logan, UT...............................	52,029	113	3	35	5	70	691	105	549	37
Total area actually reporting................	91.5%	169	6	70	6	87	1,163	173	899	91
Estimated total...................................	100.0%	183	6	75	7	95	1,313	195	1,014	104
Rate per 100,000 inhabitants...............		128.4	4.2	52.6	4.9	66.7	921.4	136.8	711.6	73.0
Longview, TX M.S.A.[3,4]............................	285,060									
Includes Gregg, Harrison, Rusk, and Upshur Counties............										
City of Longview................................	81,783	374	4	62	63	245	2,410	411	1,809	190
Total area actually reporting................	99.7%	922	20	128	113	661		1,362		529
Estimated total...................................	100.0%	924	20	128	113	663		1,365		530
Rate per 100,000 inhabitants...............		324.1	7.0	44.9	39.6	232.6		478.8		185.9
Longview, WA M.S.A...............................	109,465									
Includes Cowlitz County										
City of Longview................................	38,282	101	1	30	19	51	1,102	159	841	102
Total area actually reporting................	100.0%	213	5	71	26	111	2,054	343	1,521	190
Rate per 100,000 inhabitants...............		194.6	4.6	64.9	23.8	101.4	1,876.4	313.3	1,389.5	173.6
Los Angeles-Long Beach-Anaheim, CA M.S.A...................	13,236,726									
Includes the Metropolitan Divisions of Anaheim-Santa Ana-Irvine and Los Angeles-Long Beach-Glendale										
City of Los Angeles	4,015,546	29,400	258	2,274	9,652	17,216	95,704	13,809	66,253	15,642
City of Long Beach..............................	467,974	2,369	34	249	958	1,128	11,297	2,185	6,754	2,358
City of Anaheim..................................	353,915	1,120	8	141	396	575	8,258	1,123	5,904	1,231
City of Santa Ana................................	333,664	1,453	13	207	472	761	6,808	854	4,611	1,343
City of Irvine	292,673	188	1	52	66	69	3,823	574	3,086	163
City of Glendale..................................	202,601	231	5	16	93	117	3,305	480	2,562	263
City of Torrance..................................	145,183	280	3	26	114	137	2,853	399	2,161	293
City of Pasadena.................................	141,913	613	4	46	147	416	2,866	570	2,036	260
City of Orange....................................	139,830	180	3	18	76	83	2,184	387	1,546	251
City of Costa Mesa	114,047	312	0	52	104	156	3,739	450	2,934	355
City of Burbank	103,738	189	1	11	54	123	2,617	299	2,107	211
City of Carson.....................................	91,947	444	5	31	122	286	2,004	328	1,277	399
City of Santa Monica	91,621	664	3	40	247	374	3,964	577	3,143	244
City of Newport Beach.........................	85,325	135	5	29	32	69	1,764	273	1,344	147
City of Tustin	80,356	141	1	16	61	63	2,118	241	1,694	183
City of Gardena..................................	59,833	324	3	20	131	170	1,202	236	658	308
City of Arcadia....................................	58,899	84	1	10	35	38	1,348	301	973	74
City of Fountain Valley.........................	55,858	53	0	5	23	25	1,163	163	914	86
Total area actually reporting................	100.0%	63,201	565	5,063	20,816	36,757	283,364	46,511	192,723	44,130
Rate per 100,000 inhabitants...............		477.5	4.3	38.2	157.3	277.7	2,140.7	351.4	1,456.0	333.4
Anaheim-Santa Ana-Irvine, CA M.D...............................	3,180,759									
Includes Orange County......................										
Total area actually reporting................	100.0%	6,797	57	894	2,209	3,637	59,186	8,529	43,956	6,701
Rate per 100,000 inhabitants...............		213.7	1.8	28.1	69.4	114.3	1,860.8	268.1	1,381.9	210.7
Los Angeles-Long Beach-Glendale, CA M.D.	10,055,967									
Includes Los Angeles County										
Total area actually reporting................	100.0%	56,404	508	4,169	18,607	33,120	224,178	37,982	148,767	37,429
Rate per 100,000 inhabitants...............		560.9	5.1	41.5	185.0	329.4	2,229.3	377.7	1,479.4	372.2
Louisville/Jefferson County, KY-IN M.S.A..........................	1,269,402									
Includes Clark, Floyd, Harrison, and Washington Counties, IN and Bullitt, Henry, Jefferson, Oldham, Shelby, and Spencer Counties, KY...............										
City of Louisville Metro, KY	675,501	4,640	94	201	1,008	3,337	26,287	4,316	18,037	3,934
Total area actually reporting................	90.7%	5,345	103	306	1,159	3,777	34,835	5,482	24,355	4,998
Estimated total...................................	100.0%	5,545	105	330	1,191	3,919	36,356	5,686	25,538	5,132
Rate per 100,000 inhabitants...............		436.8	8.3	26.0	93.8	308.7	2,864.0	447.9	2,011.8	404.3

Table 4. Crime in the United States, by Selected Metropolitan Statistical Area, 2019—*Continued*

(Number, percent, rate per 100,000 population.)

Area	Population	Violent crime	Murder and nonnegligent manslaughter	Rape[1]	Robbery	Aggravated assault	Property crime	Burglary	Larceny-theft	Motor vehicle theft
Lubbock, TX M.S.A.[3]	320,574									
Includes Crosby, Lubbock, and Lynn[3] Counties										
City of Lubbock	259,208	2,613	10	268	468	1,867	11,940	2,391	8,324	1,225
Total area actually reporting	99.0%	2,682	11	285	472	1,914	12,898	2,601	8,971	1,326
Estimated total	100.0%	2,688	11	285	472	1,920	12,941	2,609	9,001	1,331
Rate per 100,000 inhabitants		838.5	3.4	88.9	147.2	598.9	4,036.8	813.9	2,807.8	415.2
Lynchburg, VA M.S.A.	263,190									
Includes Amherst, Appomattox, Bedford, and Campbell Counties and Lynchburg City										
City of Lynchburg	82,512	316	2	35	60	219	1,802	261	1,382	159
Total area actually reporting	100.0%	607	10	80	80	437	3,832	541	3,010	281
Rate per 100,000 inhabitants		230.6	3.8	30.4	30.4	166.0	1,456.0	205.6	1,143.7	106.8
Macon-Bibb County, GA M.S.A.[3]	229,193									
Includes Bibb, Crawford, Jones, Monroe, and Twiggs Counties[3]										
Total area actually reporting	100.0%	1,042	21	56	298	667	7,931	1,645	5,589	697
Rate per 100,000 inhabitants		454.6	9.2	24.4	130.0	291.0	3,460.4	717.7	2,438.6	304.1
Madera, CA M.S.A.	157,191									
Includes Madera County										
City of Madera	66,250	334	2	32	77	223	1,301	235	824	242
Total area actually reporting	100.0%	830	3	68	94	665	2,693	682	1,595	416
Rate per 100,000 inhabitants		528.0	1.9	43.3	59.8	423.1	1,713.2	433.9	1,014.7	264.6
Madison, WI M.S.A.[3]	666,719									
Includes Columbia, Dane, Green,[3] and Iowa Counties										
City of Madison	261,270	940	4	107	217	612	6,464	1,046	4,873	545
Total area actually reporting	99.9%	1,445	8	201	291	945	11,164	1,686	8,594	884
Estimated total	100.0%	1,452	8	207	291	946	11,432	1,733	8,811	888
Rate per 100,000 inhabitants		217.8	1.2	31.0	43.6	141.9	1,714.7	259.9	1,321.5	133.2
Manchester-Nashua, NH M.S.A.	416,493									
Includes Hillsborough County										
City of Manchester	112,895	678	6	62	133	477	2,678	299	2,225	154
City of Nashua	89,586	129	1	69	20	39	1,151	81	1,016	54
Total area actually reporting	98.3%	942	11	186	168	577	5,147	537	4,344	266
Estimated total	100.0%	957	11	190	170	586	5,435	546	4,621	268
Rate per 100,000 inhabitants		229.8	2.6	45.6	40.8	140.7	1,304.9	131.1	1,109.5	64.3
Manhattan, KS M.S.A.[4]	130,661									
Includes Geary, Pottawatomie, and Riley[4] Counties										
Total area actually reporting	100.0%	563	4	67	41	451			1,701	170
Rate per 100,000 inhabitants		430.9	3.1	51.3	31.4	345.2			1,301.8	130.1
Mankato, MN M.S.A.[3]	102,065									
Includes Blue Earth and Nicollet Counties										
City of Mankato	42,955	110	0	29	12	69	1,462	186	1,217	59
Total area actually reporting	100.0%	182	0	58	15	109	1,938	267	1,579	92
Rate per 100,000 inhabitants		178.3	0.0	56.8	14.7	106.8	1,898.8	261.6	1,547.1	90.1
Mansfield, OH M.S.A.	120,502									
Includes Richland County										
City of Mansfield	46,418	187	3	48	38	98	1,996	396	1,523	77
Total area actually reporting	98.5%	272	4	90	46	132	3,250	618	2,514	118
Estimated total	100.0%	276	4	91	47	134	3,309	622	2,567	120
Rate per 100,000 inhabitants		229.0	3.3	75.5	39.0	111.2	2,746.0	516.2	2,130.3	99.6
McAllen-Edinburg-Mission, TX M.S.A.[3]	871,926									
Includes Hidalgo County[3]										
City of McAllen	144,915	140	1	33	39	67	3,595	152	3,415	28
City of Edinburg	100,896	281	6	53	40	182	2,959	335	2,577	47
City of Mission	85,705	105	1	37	23	44	1,618	161	1,387	70
Total area actually reporting	99.0%	2,324	19	433	334	1,538	19,108	2,505	15,830	773
Estimated total	100.0%	2,345	19	436	337	1,553	19,284	2,533	15,963	788
Rate per 100,000 inhabitants		268.9	2.2	50.0	38.7	178.1	2,211.7	290.5	1,830.8	90.4

Table 4. Crime in the United States, by Selected Metropolitan Statistical Area, 2019—*Continued*

(Number, percent, rate per 100,000 population.)

Area	Population	Violent crime	Murder and nonnegligent manslaughter	Rape[1]	Robbery	Aggravated assault	Property crime	Burglary	Larceny-theft	Motor vehicle theft
Memphis, TN-MS-AR M.S.A.[2, 3]	1,344,796									
Includes Crittenden County, AR; DeSoto, Marshall, Tate, and Tunica[2] Counties, MS; and Fayette, Shelby, and Tipton Counties, TN....										
City of Memphis, TN....	650,410	12,367	190	468	2,432	9,277	39,860	7,833	27,981	4,046
Total area actually reporting....	95.8%	14,888	235	668	2,777	11,208	53,652	10,136	37,935	5,581
Estimated total....	100.0%	15,068	237	706	2,785	11,340	54,510	10,341	38,501	5,668
Rate per 100,000 inhabitants....		1,120.5	17.6	52.5	207.1	843.3	4,053.4	769.0	2,863.0	421.5
Merced, CA M.S.A.	274,771									
Includes Merced County										
City of Merced....	83,854	540	5	34	103	398	2,342	396	1,439	507
Total area actually reporting....	100.0%	1,520	12	82	202	1,224	6,898	1,418	4,089	1,391
Rate per 100,000 inhabitants....		553.2	4.4	29.8	73.5	445.5	2,510.5	516.1	1,488.1	506.2
Miami-Fort Lauderdale-Pompano Beach, FL M.S.A.	6,235,390									
Includes the Metropolitan Divisions of Fort Lauderdale-Pompano Beach-Sunrise, Miami-Miami Beach-Kendall, and West Palm Beach-Boca Raton-Boynton Beach										
City of Miami....	480,505	2,850	43	152	769	1,886	17,624	1,771	14,219	1,634
City of Fort Lauderdale....	184,765	1,098	21	93	408	576	9,082	1,275	6,945	862
City of Pompano Beach....	113,536	900	8	73	317	502	4,277	661	3,058	558
City of West Palm Beach....	112,798	859	17	79	304	459	4,231	464	3,314	453
City of Boca Raton....	101,163	186	3	36	63	84	2,183	244	1,769	170
City of Sunrise....	96,919	191	4	17	63	107	2,014	157	1,673	184
City of Miami Beach....	92,185	852	6	92	284	470	6,977	717	5,894	366
City of Deerfield Beach....	81,602	351	6	31	99	215	2,161	211	1,703	247
City of Boynton Beach	79,360	566	4	30	120	412	2,618	254	2,147	217
City of Delray Beach....	70,509	336	5	33	87	211	2,418	299	1,914	205
City of Jupiter	66,906	118	2	17	22	77	1,035	79	895	61
City of Doral....	64,168	62	1	9	13	39	1,475	66	1,287	122
City of Palm Beach Gardens....	57,236	78	1	9	22	46	1,295	71	1,173	51
City of Coral Gables....	51,530	50	0	4	17	29	1,343	157	1,103	83
Total area actually reporting....	100.0%	26,314	399	2,208	7,107	16,600	167,498	16,910	135,086	15,502
Rate per 100,000 inhabitants....		422.0	6.4	35.4	114.0	266.2	2,686.2	271.2	2,166.4	248.6
Fort Lauderdale-Pompano Beach-Deerfield Beach, FL M.D.	1,963,433									
Includes Broward County										
Total area actually reporting....	100.0%	7,332	110	692	2,134	4,396	50,026	5,481	39,400	5,145
Rate per 100,000 inhabitants		373.4	5.6	35.2	108.7	223.9	2,547.9	279.2	2,006.7	262.0
Miami-Miami Beach-Kendall, FL M.D.	2,775,173									
Includes Miami-Dade County....										
Total area actually reporting....	100.0%	13,339	202	955	3,649	8,533	85,544	7,936	69,952	7,656
Rate per 100,000 inhabitants		480.7	7.3	34.4	131.5	307.5	3,082.5	286.0	2,520.6	275.9
West Palm Beach-Boca Raton-Boynton Beach, FL M.D.	1,496,784									
Includes Palm Beach County....										
Total area actually reporting....	100.0%	5,643	87	561	1,324	3,671	31,928	3,493	25,734	2,701
Rate per 100,000 inhabitants		377.0	5.8	37.5	88.5	245.3	2,133.1	233.4	1,719.3	180.5
Midland, MI M.S.A.	82,943									
Includes Midland County										
City of Midland....	41,791	56	1	21	4	30	392	36	344	12
Total area actually reporting....	100.0%	118	1	58	4	55	660	92	545	23
Rate per 100,000 inhabitants....		142.3	1.2	69.9	4.8	66.3	795.7	110.9	657.1	27.7
Milwaukee-Waukesha, WI M.S.A.[3]	1,576,634									
Includes Milwaukee, Ozaukee, Washington, and Waukesha Counties....										
City of Milwaukee....	590,923	7,874	97	427	1,911	5,439	15,097	3,594	8,053	3,450
City of Waukesha	72,718	67	1	25	8	33	690	77	575	38
Total area actually reporting....	100.0%	9,111	111	631	2,151	6,218	30,333	4,820	21,346	4,167
Rate per 100,000 inhabitants....		577.9	7.0	40.0	136.4	394.4	1,923.9	305.7	1,353.9	264.3
Minneapolis-St. Paul-Bloomington, MN-WI M.S.A.[3]	3,643,083									
Includes Anoka,[3] Carver, Chisago, Dakota, Hennepin, Isanti, Le Sueur, Mille Lacs, Ramsey, Scott, Sherburne, Washington, and Wright Counties, MN and Pierce and St. Croix Counties, WI......										

Table 4. Crime in the United States, by Selected Metropolitan Statistical Area, 2019—*Continued*

(Number, percent, rate per 100,000 population.)

Area	Population	Violent crime	Murder and nonnegligent manslaughter	Rape[1]	Robbery	Aggravated assault	Property crime	Burglary	Larceny-theft	Motor vehicle theft
City of Minneapolis, MN[3]	431,016	3,990	46	459	1,289	2,196	19,469	3,397	13,172	2,900
City of St. Paul, MN	310,263	1,752	28	236	542	946	11,208	2,038	6,751	2,419
City of Bloomington, MN	85,902	203	3	54	61	85	3,079	183	2,731	165
City of Plymouth, MN	80,616	37	0	8	5	24	938	152	742	44
City of Eagan, MN	66,824	39	0	12	12	15	1,294	93	1,129	72
City of Eden Prairie, MN	64,777	52	0	13	14	25	700	68	610	22
City of Minnetonka, MN	54,497	30	0	8	7	15	772	91	643	38
City of Edina, MN	53,076	47	0	15	15	17	983	140	794	49
Total area actually reporting	99.9%	9,923	97	1,626	2,851	5,349	84,941	11,059	64,891	8,991
Estimated total	100.0%	9,926	97	1,627	2,851	5,351	84,987	11,062	64,932	8,993
Rate per 100,000 inhabitants		272.5	2.7	44.7	78.3	146.9	2,332.8	303.6	1,782.3	246.9
Missoula, MT M.S.A.	119,655									
Includes Missoula County										
City of Missoula	75,422	310	3	75	27	205	3,082	342	2,565	175
Total area actually reporting	100.0%	418	3	88	28	299	3,355	410	2,740	205
Rate per 100,000 inhabitants		349.3	2.5	73.5	23.4	249.9	2,803.9	342.7	2,289.9	171.3
Modesto, CA M.S.A.	549,632									
Includes Stanislaus County										
City of Modesto	216,542	1,758	13	94	399	1,252	7,183	1,149	4,849	1,185
Total area actually reporting	100.0%	2,908	25	170	724	1,989	14,274	2,628	9,155	2,491
Rate per 100,000 inhabitants		529.1	4.5	30.9	131.7	361.9	2,597.0	478.1	1,665.7	453.2
Monroe, LA M.S.A.	200,739									
Includes Morehouse, Ouachita, and Union Parishes										
City of Monroe	47,746	843	9	37	171	626	3,141	623	2,339	179
Total area actually reporting	96.5%	1,606	23	102	251	1,230	8,142	1,862	5,788	492
Estimated total	100.0%	1,631	23	102	253	1,253	8,353	1,903	5,948	502
Rate per 100,000 inhabitants		812.5	11.5	50.8	126.0	624.2	4,161.1	948.0	2,963.1	250.1
Morgantown, WV M.S.A.	140,923									
Includes Monongalia and Preston Counties										
City of Morgantown	31,281	67	0	9	5	53	489	71	383	35
Total area actually reporting	88.8%	244	1	41	11	191	1,515	309	1,098	108
Estimated total	100.0%	288	1	46	16	225	1,862	370	1,363	129
Rate per 100,000 inhabitants		204.4	0.7	32.6	11.4	159.7	1,321.3	262.6	967.2	91.5
Morristown, TN M.S.A.	142,399									
Includes Grainger, Hamblen, and Jefferson Counties										
City of Morristown	30,044	255	2	16	18	219	1,423	169	1,140	114
Total area actually reporting	100.0%	552	4	47	29	472	2,919	506	2,114	299
Rate per 100,000 inhabitants		387.6	2.8	33.0	20.4	331.5	2,049.9	355.3	1,484.6	210.0
Mount Vernon-Anacortes, WA M.S.A.	129,233									
Includes Skagit County										
City of Mount Vernon	36,274	55	0	13	17	25	1,140	126	899	115
City of Anacortes	17,483	20	1	2	6	11	387	67	306	14
Total area actually reporting	100.0%	201	2	40	42	117	3,178	506	2,433	239
Rate per 100,000 inhabitants		155.5	1.5	31.0	32.5	90.5	2,459.1	391.5	1,882.6	184.9
Muskegon, MI M.S.A.[4]	173,362									
Includes Muskegon County										
City of Muskegon	37,178	308	8	27	46	227	1,293	252	911	130
Total area actually reporting	100.0%	786	17	127	103	539			3,434	264
Rate per 100,000 inhabitants		453.4	9.8	73.3	59.4	310.9			1,980.8	152.3
Myrtle Beach-Conway-North Myrtle Beach, SC-NC M.S.A.[3]	495,661									
Includes Brunswick County, NC[3] and Horry County, SC										
City of Myrtle Beach, SC	34,860	415	3	52	98	262	3,916	304	3,384	228
City of Conway, SC	26,127	111	1	14	11	85	884	90	739	55
City of North Myrtle Beach, SC	16,942	71	1	15	10	45	1,115	108	910	97
Total area actually reporting	82.0%	1,586	19	253	223	1,091	13,645	1,862	10,789	994
Estimated total	100.0%	1,772	22	274	241	1,235	14,926	2,275	11,542	1,109
Rate per 100,000 inhabitants		357.5	4.4	55.3	48.6	249.2	3,011.3	459.0	2,328.6	223.7
Napa, CA M.S.A.	138,570									
Includes Napa County										
City of Napa	79,526	280	1	66	55	158	1,232	248	847	137

Table 4. Crime in the United States, by Selected Metropolitan Statistical Area, 2019—Continued

(Number, percent, rate per 100,000 population.)

Area	Population	Violent crime	Murder and nonnegligent manslaughter	Rape[1]	Robbery	Aggravated assault	Property crime	Burglary	Larceny-theft	Motor vehicle theft
Total area actually reporting..................................	100.0%	753	1	90	70	592	2,162	395	1,578	189
Rate per 100,000 inhabitants..............................		543.4	0.7	64.9	50.5	427.2	1,560.2	285.1	1,138.8	136.4
Naples-Marco Island, FL M.S.A.	383,360									
Includes Collier County										
City of Naples..	22,369	11	1	2	1	7	323	29	275	19
City of Marco Island..	18,124	7	0	1	2	4	83	7	74	2
Total area actually reporting.................................	100.0%	896	9	127	147	613	4,308	469	3,530	309
Rate per 100,000 inhabitants..............................		233.7	2.3	33.1	38.3	159.9	1,123.7	122.3	920.8	80.6
Nashville-Davidson–Murfreesboro–Franklin, TN M.S.A. ...	1,941,822									
Includes Cannon, Cheatham, Davidson, Dickson, Macon, Maury, Robertson, Rutherford, Smith, Sumner, Trousdale, Williamson, and Wilson Counties										
City of Metropolitan Nashville Police Department....................	687,361	7,376	83	438	1,978	4,877	27,777	3,374	21,655	2,748
City of Murfreesboro	145,929	611	4	96	106	405	4,228	510	3,454	264
City of Franklin	83,517	138	0	15	10	113	926	58	814	54
Total area actually reporting.................................	100.0%	11,078	118	804	2,313	7,843	47,565	5,896	37,196	4,473
Rate per 100,000 inhabitants..............................		570.5	6.1	41.4	119.1	403.9	2,449.5	303.6	1,915.5	230.4
New Bern, NC M.S.A.[3]	124,876									
Includes Craven, Jones, and Pamlico Counties[3].......................										
City of New Bern[3]	30,187	125	0	5	21	99	999	195	787	17
Total area actually reporting.................................	88.9%	321	4	29	38	250	2,683	810	1,738	135
Estimated total...	100.0%	355	4	32	42	277	2,954	881	1,919	154
Rate per 100,000 inhabitants..............................		284.3	3.2	25.6	33.6	221.8	2,365.5	705.5	1,536.7	123.3
New Haven-Milford, CT M.S.A.	802,507									
Includes New Haven County										
City of New Haven...	130,494	1,168	13	45	321	789	4,958	659	3,580	719
City of Milford..	54,898	29	1	0	16	12	1,028	95	853	80
Total area actually reporting.................................	100.0%	2,189	28	208	643	1,310	16,938	2,046	12,729	2,163
Rate per 100,000 inhabitants..............................		272.8	3.5	25.9	80.1	163.2	2,110.6	255.0	1,586.2	269.5
New Orleans-Metairie, LA M.S.A.	1,273,092									
Includes Jefferson, Orleans, Plaquemines, St. Bernard, St. Charles, St. James, St. John the Baptist, and St. Tammany Parishes										
City of New Orleans..	394,498	4,516	121	774	1,013	2,608	20,879	2,143	15,785	2,951
Total area actually reporting.................................	95.4%	6,765	198	955	1,377	4,235	38,541	4,351	30,206	3,984
Estimated total...	100.0%	7,021	203	975	1,398	4,445	40,101	4,699	31,317	4,085
Rate per 100,000 inhabitants..............................		551.5	15.9	76.6	109.8	349.1	3,149.9	369.1	2,459.9	320.9
Niles, MI M.S.A.	153,430									
Includes Berrien County										
City of Niles..	11,106	86	0	20	17	49	366	49	274	43
Total area actually reporting.................................	100.0%	845	5	168	79	593	3,340	503	2,540	297
Rate per 100,000 inhabitants..............................		550.7	3.3	109.5	51.5	386.5	2,176.9	327.8	1,655.5	193.6
North Port-Sarasota-Bradenton, FL M.S.A.	831,795									
Includes Manatee and Sarasota Counties										
City of North Port	70,181	95	1	22	8	64	967	89	847	31
City of Sarasota	58,470	319	4	28	66	221	1,857	264	1,462	131
City of Bradenton	58,782	360	6	22	57	275	1,474	204	1,191	79
City of Venice	23,726	20	1	1	3	15	283	30	242	11
Total area actually reporting.................................	100.0%	2,732	26	286	380	2,040	13,924	1,872	11,213	839
Rate per 100,000 inhabitants..............................		328.4	3.1	34.4	45.7	245.3	1,674.0	225.1	1,348.0	100.9
Norwich-New London, CT M.S.A.	174,879									
Includes New London County										
City of Norwich...	38,964	149	0	26	22	101	533	112	368	53
City of New London..	26,856	79	0	19	32	28	461	90	329	42
Total area actually reporting.................................	100.0%	339	3	82	59	195	2,322	338	1,835	149
Rate per 100,000 inhabitants..............................		193.8	1.7	46.9	33.7	111.5	1,327.8	193.3	1,049.3	85.2
Ocala, FL M.S.A...	361,126									
Includes Marion County										
City of Ocala...	60,932	493	7	52	108	326	2,548	252	2,131	165
Total area actually reporting.................................	100.0%	1,556	31	227	211	1,087	6,841	1,198	4,947	696
Rate per 100,000 inhabitants..............................		430.9	8.6	62.9	58.4	301.0	1,894.4	331.7	1,369.9	192.7

(Number, percent, rate per 100,000 population.)

Area	Population	Violent crime	Murder and nonnegligent manslaughter	Rape[1]	Robbery	Aggravated assault	Property crime	Burglary	Larceny-theft	Motor vehicle theft
Ocean City, NJ M.S.A.............................	91,575									
Includes Cape May County										
City of Ocean City..................................	10,962	6	0	0	2	4	323	37	285	1
Total area actually reporting......................	100.0%	161	0	24	23	114	1,909	291	1,573	45
Rate per 100,000 inhabitants......................		175.8	0.0	26.2	25.1	124.5	2,084.6	317.8	1,717.7	49.1
Odessa, TX M.S.A................................	164,546									
Includes Ector County										
City of Odessa..	123,468	1,282	13	141	128	1,000	3,624	469	2,656	499
Total area actually reporting......................	100.0%	1,451	17	152	147	1,135	5,205	707	3,641	857
Rate per 100,000 inhabitants......................		881.8	10.3	92.4	89.3	689.8	3,163.2	429.7	2,212.8	520.8
Ogden-Clearfield, UT M.S.A.[3,4]...............	683,537									
Includes Box Elder,[3] Davis, Morgan,[4] and Weber Counties......										
City of Ogden..	87,875	384	6	84	63	231	3,211	484	2,382	345
City of Clearfield...................................	32,217	56	0	12	5	39	369	38	292	39
Total area actually reporting......................	99.5%	1,162	9	360	121	672			8,619	978
Estimated total......................................	100.0%	1,167	9	361	122	675			8,703	984
Rate per 100,000 inhabitants......................		170.7	1.3	52.8	17.8	98.8			1,273.2	144.0
Oklahoma City, OK M.S.A.[3]......................	1,411,162									
Includes Canadian, Cleveland, Grady, Lincoln, Logan, McClain, and Oklahoma Counties....................										
City of Oklahoma City[3]	657,819	4,751	75	539	888	3,249	26,918	6,206	16,922	3,790
Total area actually reporting......................	100.0%	6,506	108	886	1,133	4,379	43,321	9,577	28,189	5,555
Rate per 100,000 inhabitants......................		461.0	7.7	62.8	80.3	310.3	3,069.9	678.7	1,997.6	393.6
Olympia-Lacey-Tumwater, WA M.S.A...............	289,877									
Includes Thurston County										
City of Olympia......................................	53,286	254	2	25	70	157	1,854	244	1,409	201
City of Lacey..	51,816	105	0	29	17	59	1,436	180	1,136	120
City of Tumwater....................................	24,167	73	0	14	18	41	648	99	483	66
Total area actually reporting......................	100.0%	715	5	99	129	482	6,005	1,108	4,274	623
Rate per 100,000 inhabitants......................		246.7	1.7	34.2	44.5	166.3	2,071.6	382.2	1,474.4	214.9
Omaha-Council Bluffs, NE-IA M.S.A...............	947,962									
Includes Harrison, Mills, and Pottawattamie Counties, IA and Cass, Douglas, Sarpy, Saunders, and Washington Counties, NE										
City of Omaha, NE..................................	470,481	2,883	23	379	519	1,962	17,144	1,684	12,307	3,153
City of Council Bluffs, IA	62,427	493	6	39	57	391	3,649	529	2,629	491
Total area actually reporting......................	99.7%	3,891	34	571	629	2,657	25,055	2,792	18,061	4,202
Estimated total......................................	100.0%	3,916	34	588	629	2,665	25,089	2,792	18,095	4,202
Rate per 100,000 inhabitants......................		413.1	3.6	62.0	66.4	281.1	2,646.6	294.5	1,908.8	443.3
Orlando-Kissimmee-Sanford, FL M.S.A.	2,614,835									
Includes Lake, Orange, Osceola, and Seminole Counties										
City of Orlando......................................	292,120	2,157	25	204	536	1,392	14,100	1,464	11,362	1,274
City of Kissimmee..................................	75,544	368	3	42	54	269	1,899	257	1,504	138
City of Sanford	60,844	497	2	62	116	317	2,127	315	1,689	123
Total area actually reporting......................	100.0%	11,242	120	1,179	2,298	7,645	62,756	9,389	47,901	5,466
Rate per 100,000 inhabitants......................		429.9	4.6	45.1	87.9	292.4	2,400.0	359.1	1,831.9	209.0
Oshkosh-Neenah, WI M.S.A.[3]......................	171,309									
Includes Winnebago County										
City of Oshkosh[3]....................................	66,797	190	0	50	16	124	1,067	213	794	60
City of Neenah[3].....................................	26,133	45	1	10	0	34	330	28	288	14
Total area actually reporting......................	100.0%	338	1	86	21	230	2,008	339	1,563	106
Rate per 100,000 inhabitants......................		197.3	0.6	50.2	12.3	134.3	1,172.2	197.9	912.4	61.9
Owensboro, KY M.S.A.	119,217									
Includes Daviess, Hancock, and McLean Counties										
City of Owensboro..................................	60,107	135	6	30	33	66	2,432	358	1,874	200
Total area actually reporting......................	100.0%	159	8	41	34	76	2,896	490	2,152	254
Rate per 100,000 inhabitants......................		133.4	6.7	34.4	28.5	63.7	2,429.2	411.0	1,805.1	213.1
Oxnard-Thousand Oaks-Ventura, CA M.S.A.	847,049									
Includes Ventura County............................										
City of Oxnard	211,349	724	13	62	275	374	4,242	670	2,987	585
City of Thousand Oaks.............................	127,811	88	0	27	23	38	1,392	244	1,084	64

Table 4. Crime in the United States, by Selected Metropolitan Statistical Area, 2019—*Continued*

(Number, percent, rate per 100,000 population.)

Area	Population	Violent crime	Murder and nonnegligent manslaughter	Rape[1]	Robbery	Aggravated assault	Property crime	Burglary	Larceny-theft	Motor vehicle theft
City of Ventura	111,596	458	3	56	106	293	2,969	353	2,362	254
City of Camarillo	69,628	58	0	22	16	20	817	100	676	41
Total area actually reporting	100.0%	1,830	24	232	527	1,047	12,634	1,946	9,454	1,234
Rate per 100,000 inhabitants		216.0	2.8	27.4	62.2	123.6	1,491.5	229.7	1,116.1	145.7
Palm Bay-Melbourne-Titusville, FL M.S.A.	599,498									
Includes Brevard County										
City of Palm Bay	115,520	396	8	71	59	258	1,981	334	1,499	148
City of Melbourne	83,668	579	1	80	87	411	2,802	439	2,219	144
City of Titusville	46,866	377	2	37	52	286	1,492	289	1,031	172
Total area actually reporting	100.0%	2,224	23	262	332	1,607	12,269	2,019	9,322	928
Rate per 100,000 inhabitants		371.0	3.8	43.7	55.4	268.1	2,046.5	336.8	1,555.0	154.8
Panama City, FL M.S.A.	186,063									
Includes Bay County										
City of Panama City	37,199	228	2	5	42	179	1,914	384	1,308	222
Total area actually reporting	100.0%	826	8	91	103	624	5,707	1,097	4,139	471
Rate per 100,000 inhabitants		443.9	4.3	48.9	55.4	335.4	3,067.2	589.6	2,224.5	253.1
Pensacola-Ferry Pass-Brent, FL M.S.A.	497,168									
Includes Escambia and Santa Rosa Counties										
City of Pensacola	52,801	312	3	35	38	236	1,888	287	1,508	93
Total area actually reporting	100.0%	2,037	32	247	355	1,403	10,827	2,189	7,862	776
Rate per 100,000 inhabitants		409.7	6.4	49.7	71.4	282.2	2,177.7	440.3	1,581.4	156.1
Peoria, IL M.S.A.	399,839									
Includes Fulton, Marshall, Peoria, Stark, Tazewell, and Woodford Counties										
City of Peoria	110,955	1,158	25	65	268	800	4,160	758	2,959	443
Total area actually reporting	94.9%	1,775	30	193	309	1,243	7,432	1,481	5,290	661
Estimated total	100.0%	1,807	30	198	312	1,267	7,735	1,524	5,530	681
Rate per 100,000 inhabitants		451.9	7.5	49.5	78.0	316.9	1,934.5	381.2	1,383.1	170.3
Phoenix-Mesa-Chandler, AZ M.S.A.[3,4]	4,949,304									
Includes Maricopa and Pinal Counties										
City of Phoenix	1,688,722	11,803	131	1,139	3,197	7,336	55,974	9,471	39,427	7,076
City of Mesa	518,160	1,953	11	286	390	1,266	9,683	1,518	7,326	839
City of Chandler	259,881	593	4	134	102	353	5,382	547	4,458	377
City of Scottsdale	260,464	415	3	136	110	166	5,099	662	4,173	264
City of Tempe	196,499	889	8	141	209	531	7,420	922	5,891	607
City of Casa Grande[3]	58,366	274	2	27	33	212	1,336	149	1,071	116
Total area actually reporting	91.3%	19,721	208	2,313	4,672	12,528			85,599	11,791
Estimated total	100.0%	21,110	226	2,464	4,805	13,615			89,332	12,465
Rate per 100,000 inhabitants		426.5	4.6	49.8	97.1	275.1			1,804.9	251.9
Pine Bluff, AR M.S.A.[4]	88,005									
Includes Cleveland, Jefferson, and Lincoln Counties										
City of Pine Bluff[4]	41,505	644	23	23	96	502			1,448	271
Total area actually reporting	98.6%	782	28	50	102	602			1,906	366
Estimated total	100.0%	788	28	51	102	607			1,924	368
Rate per 100,000 inhabitants		895.4	31.8	58.0	115.9	689.7			2,186.2	418.2
Pittsfield, MA M.S.A.[3]	124,775									
Includes Berkshire County										
City of Pittsfield	42,268	300	2	36	31	231	796	263	490	43
Total area actually reporting	90.2%	446	2	73	43	328	1,617	431	1,119	67
Estimated total	100.0%	475	2	76	46	351	1,730	450	1,205	75
Rate per 100,000 inhabitants		380.7	1.6	60.9	36.9	281.3	1,386.5	360.6	965.7	60.1
Pocatello, ID M.S.A.	95,848									
Includes Bannock and Power Counties										
City of Pocatello	56,514	233	1	30	9	193	1,326	226	1,012	88
Total area actually reporting	100.0%	287	1	42	15	229	2,018	288	1,614	116
Rate per 100,000 inhabitants		299.4	1.0	43.8	15.6	238.9	2,105.4	300.5	1,683.9	121.0
Portland-South Portland, ME M.S.A.[3]	539,924									
Includes Cumberland, Sagadahoc,[3] and York Counties										
City of Portland	66,458	161	3	29	43	86	1,715	181	1,460	74
City of South Portland	25,686	48	0	17	8	23	563	39	505	19
Total area actually reporting	100.0%	619	6	175	93	345	6,784	837	5,699	248
Rate per 100,000 inhabitants		114.6	1.1	32.4	17.2	63.9	1,256.5	155.0	1,055.5	45.9

Table 4. Crime in the United States, by Selected Metropolitan Statistical Area, 2019—*Continued*

(Number, percent, rate per 100,000 population.)

Area	Population	Violent crime	Murder and nonnegligent manslaughter	Rape[1]	Robbery	Aggravated assault	Property crime	Burglary	Larceny-theft	Motor vehicle theft
Portland-Vancouver-Hillsboro, OR-WA M.S.A.	2,500,376									
Includes Clackamas, Columbia, Multnomah, Washington, and Yamhill Counties, OR and Clark and Skamania Counties, WA										
City of Portland, OR	662,114	3,606	29	368	979	2,230	34,452	4,200	23,820	6,432
City of Vancouver, WA	185,034	889	3	206	185	495	5,998	888	4,302	808
City of Hillsboro, OR	110,549	274	0	77	56	141	2,164	175	1,779	210
City of Beaverton, OR	100,130	217	1	53	49	114	1,988	185	1,601	202
City of Tigard, OR	55,621	119	0	13	29	77	1,410	137	1,158	115
Total area actually reporting	98.5%	7,514	59	1,246	1,666	4,543	68,398	8,444	48,993	10,961
Estimated total	100.0%	7,565	59	1,255	1,668	4,583	68,684	8,483	49,221	10,980
Rate per 100,000 inhabitants		302.6	2.4	50.2	66.7	183.3	2,746.9	339.3	1,968.5	439.1
Port St. Lucie, FL M.S.A.	486,186									
Includes Martin and St. Lucie Counties										
City of Port St. Lucie	199,433	293	7	43	47	196	1,696	177	1,438	81
Total area actually reporting	100.0%	1,161	24	200	194	743	6,184	764	4,991	429
Rate per 100,000 inhabitants		238.8	4.9	41.1	39.9	152.8	1,271.9	157.1	1,026.6	88.2
Poughkeepsie-Newburg-Middletown, NY M.S.A.	672,535									
Includes Dutchess and Orange Counties										
City of Poughkeepsie	30,422	235	3	26	63	143	513	73	402	38
City of Newburgh	28,070	317	3	19	82	213	640	137	484	19
City of Middletown	27,801	87	3	16	16	52	308	45	249	14
City of Woodbury Town	11,006	3	0	0	1	2	460	5	450	5
Total area actually reporting	89.7%	1,263	16	245	234	768	7,372	690	6,449	233
Estimated total	100.0%	1,286	16	246	235	789	7,443	696	6,512	235
Rate per 100,000 inhabitants		191.2	2.4	36.6	34.9	117.3	1,106.7	103.5	968.3	34.9
Prescott Valley-Prescott, AZ M.S.A.	234,899									
Includes Yavapai County										
City of Prescott Valley	46,700	93	3	11	6	73	474	51	404	19
City of Prescott	43,781	214	1	20	11	182	684	134	518	32
Total area actually reporting	100.0%	651	9	35	28	579	3,143	520	2,413	210
Rate per 100,000 inhabitants		277.1	3.8	14.9	11.9	246.5	1,338.0	221.4	1,027.3	89.4
Providence-Warwick, RI-MA M.S.A.	1,620,927									
Includes Bristol County, MA and Bristol, Kent, Newport, Providence, and Washington Counties, RI										
City of Providence, RI	179,762	892	13	106	241	532	5,413	715	4,224	474
City of Warwick, RI	80,749	76	2	29	8	37	1,239	108	1,073	58
Total area actually reporting	99.5%	4,566	38	724	779	3,025	22,801	3,637	17,335	1,829
Estimated total	100.0%	4,580	38	726	780	3,036	22,854	3,647	17,375	1,832
Rate per 100,000 inhabitants		282.6	2.3	44.8	48.1	187.3	1,409.9	225.0	1,071.9	113.0
Provo-Orem, UT M.S.A.[3]	646,530									
Includes Juab and Utah Counties										
City of Provo	117,189	135	1	44	13	77	1,767	163	1,476	128
City of Orem	98,686	89	2	37	11	39	1,970	156	1,673	141
Total area actually reporting	100.0%	583	7	204	51	321	8,264	859	6,865	540
Rate per 100,000 inhabitants		90.2	1.1	31.6	7.9	49.6	1,278.2	132.9	1,061.8	83.5
Pueblo, CO M.S.A.[5]	167,847									
Includes Pueblo County										
City of Pueblo[5]	112,381		5	110		481	4,801	894	3,208	699
Total area actually reporting	100.0%		7	110		519	5,859	1,077	3,928	854
Rate per 100,000 inhabitants			4.2	65.5		309.2	3,490.7	641.7	2,340.2	508.8
Punta Gorda, FL M.S.A.	187,062									
Includes Charlotte County										
City of Punta Gorda	20,458	18	0	0	4	14	278	11	260	7
Total area actually reporting	100.0%	367	2	41	20	304	2,114	273	1,708	133
Rate per 100,000 inhabitants		196.2	1.1	21.9	10.7	162.5	1,130.1	145.9	913.1	71.1
Racine, WI M.S.A.[3]	196,488									
Includes Racine County										
City of Racine	77,269	291	4	45	53	189	990	212	682	96
Total area actually reporting	79.1%	364	4	53	61	246	1,798	291	1,366	141
Estimated total	100.0%	625	1	77	131	416	2,801	546	2,067	188
Rate per 100,000 inhabitants		318.1	0.5	39.2	66.7	211.7	1,425.5	277.9	1,052.0	95.7

(Number, percent, rate per 100,000 population.)

Area	Population	Violent crime	Murder and nonnegligent manslaughter	Rape[1]	Robbery	Aggravated assault	Property crime	Burglary	Larceny-theft	Motor vehicle theft
Raleigh-Cary, NC M.S.A.[3]	1,392,882									
Includes Franklin, Johnston, and Wake Counties[3]										
City of Raleigh[3]	477,828	1,222	5	164	322	731	8,520	1,200	6,572	748
City of Cary[3]	172,525	114	1	12	34	67	1,560	185	1,298	77
Total area actually reporting	99.3%	2,366	24	295	516	1,531	19,161	3,046	14,705	1,410
Estimated total	100.0%	2,404	24	299	521	1,560	19,469	3,117	14,921	1,431
Rate per 100,000 inhabitants		172.6	1.7	21.5	37.4	112.0	1,397.7	223.8	1,071.2	102.7
Rapid City, SD M.S.A.	140,743									
Includes Meade and Pennington Counties										
City of Rapid City	76,343	540	4	114	64	358	2,454	488	1,646	320
Total area actually reporting	100.0%	749	5	182	69	493	3,382	693	2,282	407
Rate per 100,000 inhabitants		532.2	3.6	129.3	49.0	350.3	2,403.0	492.4	1,621.4	289.2
Reno, NV M.S.A.[3]	475,735									
Includes Storey and Washoe[3] Counties										
City of Reno[3]	254,349	1,419	12	178	308	921	5,344	822	3,343	1,179
Total area actually reporting	100.0%	2,231	15	300	413	1,503	8,883	1,556	5,648	1,679
Rate per 100,000 inhabitants		469.0	3.2	63.1	86.8	315.9	1,867.2	327.1	1,187.2	352.9
Richmond, VA M.S.A.	1,287,449									
Includes Amelia, Charles City, Chesterfield, Dinwiddie, Goochland, Hanover, Henrico, King and Queen, King William, New Kent, Powhatan, Prince George, and Sussex Counties and Colonial Heights, Hopewell, Petersburg, and Richmond Cities										
City of Richmond	230,721	1,068	55	45	385	583	8,074	986	6,234	854
Total area actually reporting	100.0%	2,932	107	344	776	1,705	27,824	2,788	22,939	2,097
Rate per 100,000 inhabitants		227.7	8.3	26.7	60.3	132.4	2,161.2	216.6	1,781.7	162.9
Riverside-San Bernardino-Ontario, CA M.S.A.	4,632,925									
Includes Riverside and San Bernardino Counties										
City of Riverside	333,260	1,686	17	139	476	1,054	9,790	1,302	6,997	1,491
City of San Bernardino	216,715	2,858	46	140	906	1,766	9,081	2,029	4,974	2,078
City of Ontario	183,322	659	10	85	223	341	4,290	710	2,652	928
City of Corona	170,875	291	4	43	103	141	3,482	646	2,251	585
City of Temecula	116,630	166	1	8	72	85	2,626	318	2,018	290
City of Chino	93,348	329	3	35	96	195	2,224	376	1,649	199
City of Redlands	71,941	257	1	40	70	146	2,108	330	1,534	244
City of Palm Desert	53,776	136	3	7	24	102	1,848	338	1,382	128
Total area actually reporting	100.0%	19,730	265	1,386	5,252	12,827	105,402	20,268	65,805	19,329
Rate per 100,000 inhabitants		425.9	5.7	29.9	113.4	276.9	2,275.1	437.5	1,420.4	417.2
Roanoke, VA M.S.A.	313,075									
Includes Botetourt, Craig, Franklin, and Roanoke Counties and Roanoke and Salem Cities										
City of Roanoke	99,752	386	13	41	106	226	4,402	519	3,585	298
Total area actually reporting	100.0%	748	18	101	144	485	7,487	887	6,051	549
Rate per 100,000 inhabitants		238.9	5.7	32.3	46.0	154.9	2,391.4	283.3	1,932.8	175.4
Rochester, MN M.S.A.[3]	221,013									
Includes Dodge,[3] Fillmore, Olmsted,[3] and Wabasha Counties										
City of Rochester[3]	118,267	254	1	62	34	157	2,225	282	1,816	127
Total area actually reporting	100.0%	337	2	72	37	226	2,813	408	2,235	170
Rate per 100,000 inhabitants		152.5	0.9	32.6	16.7	102.3	1,272.8	184.6	1,011.3	76.9
Rochester, NY M.S.A.	1,064,123									
Includes Livingston, Monroe, Ontario, Orleans, Wayne, and Yates Counties										
City of Rochester	205,769	1,540	33	102	429	976	7,142	1,269	5,222	651
Total area actually reporting	99.2%	2,642	38	465	607	1,532	17,751	2,625	14,060	1,066
Estimated total	100.0%	2,647	38	465	607	1,537	17,819	2,633	14,118	1,068
Rate per 100,000 inhabitants		248.7	3.6	43.7	57.0	144.4	1,674.5	247.4	1,326.7	100.4
Rockford, IL M.S.A.	334,726									
Includes Boone and Winnebago Counties										
City of Rockford	145,717	1,711	14	125	282	1,290	4,848	1,001	3,458	389
Total area actually reporting	99.4%	2,121	20	224	315	1,562	7,201	1,419	5,237	545
Estimated total	100.0%	2,124	20	225	315	1,564	7,233	1,424	5,262	547
Rate per 100,000 inhabitants		634.5	6.0	67.2	94.1	467.2	2,160.9	425.4	1,572.0	163.4

Table 4. Crime in the United States, by Selected Metropolitan Statistical Area, 2019—*Continued*

(Number, percent, rate per 100,000 population.)

Area	Population	Violent crime	Murder and nonnegligent manslaughter	Rape[1]	Robbery	Aggravated assault	Property crime	Burglary	Larceny-theft	Motor vehicle theft
Sacramento-Roseville-Folsom, CA M.S.A.	2,350,381									
Includes El Dorado, Placer, Sacramento, and Yolo Counties....										
City of Sacramento..	513,934	3,223	34	127	1,039	2,023	16,354	2,993	10,644	2,717
City of Roseville..	141,744	259	4	32	96	127	3,154	389	2,518	247
City of Folsom..	79,927	82	0	12	29	41	1,484	278	1,127	79
City of Rancho Cordova...	75,869	225	5	12	56	152	1,422	233	1,004	185
City of West Sacramento..	54,372	212	1	34	79	98	1,603	236	1,158	209
Total area actually reporting..................................	100.0%	8,322	96	647	2,397	5,182	51,565	9,157	35,737	6,671
Rate per 100,000 inhabitants................................		354.1	4.1	27.5	102.0	220.5	2,193.9	389.6	1,520.5	283.8
Saginaw, MI M.S.A...	189,217									
Includes Saginaw County.......................................										
City of Saginaw..	47,954	707	9	34	51	613	743	245	421	77
Total area actually reporting..................................	100.0%	1,180	17	127	86	950	2,731	578	1,990	163
Rate per 100,000 inhabitants................................		623.6	9.0	67.1	45.5	502.1	1,443.3	305.5	1,051.7	86.1
Salem, OR M.S.A.[2]	435,428									
Includes Marion2 and Polk Counties										
City of Salem	175,867	670	0	35	152	483	6,488	680	4,966	842
Total area actually reporting..................................	99.9%	1,152	6	90	232	824	12,057	1,454	9,017	1,586
Estimated total...	100.0%	1,176	6	114	232	824	12,057	1,454	9,017	1,586
Rate per 100,000 inhabitants................................		270.1	1.4	26.2	53.3	189.2	2,769.0	333.9	2,070.8	364.2
Salinas, CA M.S.A.	434,363									
Includes Monterey County										
City of Salinas..	156,943	782	8	66	241	467	3,532	742	1,709	1,081
Total area actually reporting..................................	100.0%	1,433	15	139	368	911	7,735	1,524	4,562	1,649
Rate per 100,000 inhabitants................................		329.9	3.5	32.0	84.7	209.7	1,780.8	350.9	1,050.3	379.6
Salisbury, MD-DE M.S.A.....................................	413,262									
Includes Sussex County, DE and Somerset, Wicomico, and										
Worcester Counties, MD..										
City of Salisbury, MD..	33,132	294	0	19	58	217	1,422	207	1,170	45
Total area actually reporting..................................	100.0%	1,370	5	124	193	1,048	8,572	1,491	6,817	264
Rate per 100,000 inhabitants................................		331.5	1.2	30.0	46.7	253.6	2,074.2	360.8	1,649.6	63.9
Salt Lake City, UT M.S.A.[3]	1,237,086									
Includes Salt Lake and Tooele Counties...................										
City of Salt Lake City...	202,426	1,442	13	234	403	792	11,452	1,290	8,902	1,260
Total area actually reporting..................................	100.0%	4,536	37	882	901	2,716	41,240	4,904	31,788	4,548
Rate per 100,000 inhabitants................................		366.7	3.0	71.3	72.8	219.5	3,333.6	396.4	2,569.6	367.6
San Angelo, TX M.S.A........................................	121,245									
Includes Irion, Sterling, and Tom Green Counties										
City of San Angelo..	101,072	357	5	56	32	264	3,173	512	2,437	224
Total area actually reporting..................................	100.0%	398	6	82	34	276	3,491	607	2,632	252
Rate per 100,000 inhabitants................................		328.3	4.9	67.6	28.0	227.6	2,879.3	500.6	2,170.8	207.8
San Antonio-New Braunfels, TX M.S.A.[3]	2,552,063									
Includes Atascosa, Bandera,[3] Bexar, Comal, Guadalupe,										
Kendall, Medina, and Wilson[3] Counties...................										
City of San Antonio..	1,559,166	11,046	105	1,630	1,965	7,346	67,422	8,172	51,469	7,781
City of New Braunfels..	88,706	219	2	21	25	171	1,120	209	805	106
Total area actually reporting..................................	99.8%	13,155	130	2,003	2,213	8,809	83,646	11,079	63,323	9,244
Estimated total...	100.0%	13,166	130	2,004	2,213	8,819	83,725	11,096	63,376	9,253
Rate per 100,000 inhabitants................................		515.9	5.1	78.5	86.7	345.6	3,280.7	434.8	2,483.3	362.6
San Diego-Chula Vista-Carlsbad, CA M.S.A........	3,346,196									
Includes San Diego County										
City of San Diego..	1,441,737	5,215	50	561	1,346	3,258	27,141	3,543	18,426	5,172
City of Chula Vista...	275,230	904	3	61	265	575	3,816	486	2,503	827
City of Carlsbad..	117,220	240	3	40	39	158	2,135	297	1,671	167
City of Poway...	49,928	51	2	2	12	35	490	91	354	45
Total area actually reporting..................................	100.0%	11,417	86	1,106	2,892	7,333	55,242	7,696	37,865	9,681
Rate per 100,000 inhabitants................................		341.2	2.6	33.1	86.4	219.1	1,650.9	230.0	1,131.6	289.3
San Francisco-Oakland-Berkeley, CA M.S.A.	4,739,872									
Includes the Metropolitan Divisions of Oakland-Berkeley-										
Livermore, San Francisco-San Mateo-Redwood City, and San										
Rafael										

Table 4. Crime in the United States, by Selected Metropolitan Statistical Area, 2019—*Continued*

(Number, percent, rate per 100,000 population.)

Area	Population	Violent crime	Murder and nonnegligent manslaughter	Rape[1]	Robbery	Aggravated assault	Property crime	Burglary	Larceny-theft	Motor vehicle theft
City of San Francisco	886,007	5,933	40	324	3,055	2,514	48,780	4,644	39,887	4,249
City of Oakland	434,036	5,520	78	372	2,859	2,211	27,868	2,599	20,228	5,041
City of Berkeley	122,788	618	0	74	369	175	6,256	771	4,993	492
City of San Mateo	106,020	266	2	45	68	151	2,217	516	1,523	178
City of Livermore	91,418	193	2	30	39	122	1,554	139	1,279	136
City of Redwood City	87,427	189	0	32	70	87	1,343	165	1,014	164
City of Pleasanton	84,017	112	0	12	56	44	1,632	149	1,386	97
City of San Ramon	76,387	58	0	4	21	33	1,099	179	869	51
City of Walnut Creek	70,546	120	0	6	40	74	2,496	307	2,034	155
City of South San Francisco	68,251	166	2	19	64	81	1,484	230	1,074	180
City of San Rafael	58,819	230	0	23	87	120	1,686	299	1,173	214
Total area actually reporting	100.0%	22,317	201	1,718	10,305	10,093	167,013	18,004	127,917	21,092
Rate per 100,000 inhabitants		470.8	4.2	36.2	217.4	212.9	3,523.6	379.8	2,698.7	445.0
Oakland-Berkeley-Livermore, CA M.D.	2,826,061									
Includes Alameda and Contra Costa Counties										
Total area actually reporting	100.0%	13,872	150	1,022	6,435	6,265	95,286	10,096	70,324	14,866
Rate per 100,000 inhabitants		490.9	5.3	36.2	227.7	221.7	3,371.7	357.2	2,488.4	526.0
San Francisco-San Mateo-Redwood City, CA M.D.	1,655,482									
Includes San Francisco and San Mateo Counties										
Total area actually reporting	100.0%	7,929	50	652	3,725	3,502	66,284	6,907	53,571	5,806
Rate per 100,000 inhabitants		479.0	3.0	39.4	225.0	211.5	4,003.9	417.2	3,236.0	350.7
San Rafael, CA M.D.	258,329									
Includes Marin County										
Total area actually reporting	100.0%	516	1	44	145	326	5,443	1,001	4,022	420
Rate per 100,000 inhabitants		199.7	0.4	17.0	56.1	126.2	2,107.0	387.5	1,556.9	162.6
San Jose-Sunnyvale-Santa Clara, CA M.S.A.	2,002,715									
Includes San Benito and Santa Clara Counties										
City of San Jose	1,040,008	4,559	32	671	1,339	2,517	25,164	4,114	14,924	6,126
City of Sunnyvale	154,859	259	0	37	84	138	3,380	458	2,598	324
City of Santa Clara	131,173	214	0	35	73	106	4,748	363	4,013	372
City of Mountain View	84,599	165	0	20	49	96	2,463	321	2,030	112
City of Milpitas	82,344	102	2	15	48	37	2,193	201	1,791	201
City of Palo Alto	66,938	86	1	10	46	29	1,983	179	1,722	82
City of Cupertino	60,357	55	1	6	14	34	1,018	175	803	40
Total area actually reporting	100.0%	6,508	46	940	1,865	3,657	48,078	6,923	32,978	8,177
Rate per 100,000 inhabitants		325.0	2.3	46.9	93.1	182.6	2,400.6	345.7	1,646.7	408.3
San Luis Obispo-Paso Robles, CA M.S.A.	283,427									
Includes San Luis Obispo County										
City of San Luis Obispo	47,735	192	0	44	34	114	1,738	277	1,387	74
City of Paso Robles	32,528	53	0	9	13	31	646	78	523	45
Total area actually reporting	100.0%	630	5	95	77	453	5,119	995	3,800	324
Rate per 100,000 inhabitants		222.3	1.8	33.5	27.2	159.8	1,806.1	351.1	1,340.7	114.3
Santa Cruz-Watsonville, CA M.S.A.	273,351									
Includes Santa Cruz County										
City of Santa Cruz	65,263	389	0	29	88	272	2,932	348	2,363	221
City of Watsonville	54,261	328	1	37	53	237	971	148	589	234
Total area actually reporting	100.0%	1,106	6	137	182	781	7,005	1,039	5,138	828
Rate per 100,000 inhabitants		404.6	2.2	50.1	66.6	285.7	2,562.6	380.1	1,879.6	302.9
Santa Rosa-Petaluma, CA M.S.A.	497,643									
Includes Sonoma County										
City of Santa Rosa	177,884	857	3	146	126	582	2,874	486	2,077	311
City of Petaluma	62,425	190	3	22	28	137	789	109	626	54
Total area actually reporting	100.0%	2,016	9	277	243	1,487	6,760	1,228	4,966	566
Rate per 100,000 inhabitants		405.1	1.8	55.7	48.8	298.8	1,358.4	246.8	997.9	113.7
Scranton–Wilkes-Barre, PA M.S.A.	553,678									
Includes Lackawanna, Luzerne, and Wyoming Counties										
City of Scranton	77,323	1,199	0	45	66	1,088	1,347	239	1,026	82
City of Wilkes-Barre	40,722	242	3	24	68	147	852	194	616	42
Total area actually reporting	95.4%	2,180	7	157	207	1,809	6,729	1,104	5,283	342
Estimated total	100.0%	2,220	7	160	210	1,843	6,974	1,133	5,488	353
Rate per 100,000 inhabitants		401.0	1.3	28.9	37.9	332.9	1,259.6	204.6	991.2	63.8

Table 4. Crime in the United States, by Selected Metropolitan Statistical Area, 2019—*Continued*

(Number, percent, rate per 100,000 population.)

Area	Population	Violent crime	Murder and nonnegligent manslaughter	Rape[1]	Robbery	Aggravated assault	Property crime	Burglary	Larceny-theft	Motor vehicle theft
Sebastian-Vero Beach, FL M.S.A.	158,842									
Includes Indian River County										
City of Sebastian	26,232	19	0	6	4	9	297	20	262	15
City of Vero Beach	17,503	54	0	6	8	40	343	46	275	22
Total area actually reporting	100.0%	352	6	36	31	279	2,095	248	1,708	139
Rate per 100,000 inhabitants		221.6	3.8	22.7	19.5	175.6	1,318.9	156.1	1,075.3	87.5
Sebring-Avon Park, FL M.S.A.	105,547									
Includes Highlands County										
City of Sebring	11,008	57	6	9	13	29	481	131	339	11
Total area actually reporting	100.0%	280	11	30	58	181	2,341	546	1,709	86
Rate per 100,000 inhabitants		265.3	10.4	28.4	55.0	171.5	2,218.0	517.3	1,619.2	81.5
Sheboygan, WI M.S.A.[3]	115,305									
Includes Sheboygan County										
City of Sheboygan	48,035	172	0	48	10	114	783	88	676	19
Total area actually reporting	100.0%	207	0	59	11	137	1,272	125	1,103	44
Rate per 100,000 inhabitants		179.5	0.0	51.2	9.5	118.8	1,103.2	108.4	956.6	38.2
Sherman-Denison, TX M.S.A.[3]	134,857									
Includes Grayson County										
City of Sherman[3]	43,002	179	3	32	27	117	1,122	241	790	91
City of Denison[3]	25,432	106	1	22	5	78	464	103	304	57
Total area actually reporting	98.4%	338	5	71	40	222	2,162	494	1,454	214
Estimated total	100.0%	342	5	71	40	226	2,194	500	1,476	218
Rate per 100,000 inhabitants		253.6	3.7	52.6	29.7	167.6	1,626.9	370.8	1,094.5	161.7
Shreveport-Bossier City, LA M.S.A.	395,040									
Includes Bossier, Caddo, and De Soto Parishes										
City of Shreveport	187,556	1,462	35	133	294	1,000	9,189	1,626	6,915	648
City of Bossier City	69,044	546	2	52	72	420	3,225	461	2,382	382
Total area actually reporting	100.0%	2,225	41	201	371	1,612	13,978	2,403	10,451	1,124
Rate per 100,000 inhabitants		563.2	10.4	50.9	93.9	408.1	3,538.4	608.3	2,645.6	284.5
Sierra Vista-Douglas, AZ M.S.A.	126,231									
Includes Cochise County										
City of Sierra Vista	44,310	116	2	7	16	91	987	124	800	63
City of Douglas	15,786	10	0	0	0	10	594	88	486	20
Total area actually reporting	92.1%	207	3	11	19	174	2,283	448	1,678	157
Estimated total	100.0%	275	3	15	27	230	2,729	545	1,988	196
Rate per 100,000 inhabitants		217.9	2.4	11.9	21.4	182.2	2,161.9	431.7	1,574.9	155.3
Sioux City, IA-NE-SD M.S.A.	143,233									
Includes Woodbury County, IA; Dakota and Dixon Counties, NE; and Union County, SD										
City of Sioux City, IA	82,333	366	2	50	57	257	3,203	645	2,310	248
Total area actually reporting	100.0%	452	2	58	61	331	4,013	816	2,871	326
Rate per 100,000 inhabitants		315.6	1.4	40.5	42.6	231.1	2,801.7	569.7	2,004.4	227.6
Sioux Falls, SD M.S.A.	268,714									
Includes Lincoln, McCook, Minnehaha, and Turner Counties										
City of Sioux Falls	185,628	897	4	116	68	709	5,653	695	4,300	658
Total area actually reporting	99.3%	1,040	5	151	71	813	6,513	989	4,769	755
Estimated total	100.0%	1,043	5	151	71	816	6,522	993	4,772	757
Rate per 100,000 inhabitants		388.1	1.9	56.2	26.4	303.7	2,427.1	369.5	1,775.9	281.7
Spartanburg, SC M.S.A.	317,919									
Includes Spartanburg and Union Counties										
City of Spartanburg	37,754	448	6	24	77	341	2,450	440	1,839	171
Total area actually reporting	99.8%	1,597	23	104	175	1,295	8,708	1,937	5,949	822
Estimated total	100.0%	1,599	23	104	175	1,297	8,729	1,941	5,965	823
Rate per 100,000 inhabitants		503.0	7.2	32.7	55.0	408.0	2,745.7	610.5	1,876.3	258.9
Spokane-Spokane Valley, WA M.S.A.	563,721									
Includes Spokane and Stevens Counties										
City of Spokane	220,432	1,520	6	230	311	973	13,048	1,743	10,026	1,279
City of Spokane Valley	100,983	311	1	38	82	190	4,465	483	3,626	356
Total area actually reporting	99.1%	2,140	13	351	428	1,348	21,565	3,048	16,540	1,977
Estimated total	100.0%	2,148	13	352	429	1,354	21,682	3,066	16,628	1,988
Rate per 100,000 inhabitants		381.0	2.3	62.4	76.1	240.2	3,846.2	543.9	2,949.7	352.7

Table 4. Crime in the United States, by Selected Metropolitan Statistical Area, 2019—*Continued*

(Number, percent, rate per 100,000 population.)

Area	Population	Violent crime	Murder and nonnegligent manslaughter	Rape[1]	Robbery	Aggravated assault	Property crime	Burglary	Larceny-theft	Motor vehicle theft
Springfield, IL M.S.A.	206,349									
Includes Menard and Sangamon Counties										
City of Springfield	114,393	889	9	108	208	564	5,080	1,039	3,776	265
Total area actually reporting	97.9%	1,200	10	145	238	807	5,979	1,341	4,281	357
Estimated total	100.0%	1,205	10	145	238	812	6,047	1,352	4,333	362
Rate per 100,000 inhabitants		584.0	4.8	70.3	115.3	393.5	2,930.5	655.2	2,099.8	175.4
Springfield, MA M.S.A.	698,309									
Includes Franklin, Hampden and Hampshire Counties										
City of Springfield	154,306	1,397	20	81	358	938	4,005	746	2,766	493
Total area actually reporting	96.6%	3,222	31	354	551	2,286	11,950	2,131	8,836	983
Estimated total	100.0%	3,294	31	361	562	2,340	12,211	2,171	9,037	1,003
Rate per 100,000 inhabitants		471.7	4.4	51.7	80.5	335.1	1,748.7	310.9	1,294.1	143.6
Springfield, MO M.S.A.[3]	470,347									
Includes Christian, Dallas, Greene, Polk, and Webster Counties										
City of Springfield	169,235	2,571	11	356	319	1,885	13,188	2,068	9,436	1,684
Total area actually reporting	99.8%	2,974	17	435	348	2,174	17,244	2,885	12,285	2,074
Estimated total	100.0%	2,976	17	435	348	2,176	17,261	2,889	12,296	2,076
Rate per 100,000 inhabitants		632.7	3.6	92.5	74.0	462.6	3,669.8	614.2	2,614.2	441.4
Springfield, OH M.S.A.	133,886									
Includes Clark County										
City of Springfield	59,128	292	3	14	124	151	2,992	763	1,978	251
Total area actually reporting	92.6%	315	3	14	124	174	3,341	847	2,231	263
Estimated total	100.0%	330	3	17	127	183	3,554	871	2,413	270
Rate per 100,000 inhabitants		246.5	2.2	12.7	94.9	136.7	2,654.5	650.6	1,802.3	201.7
State College, PA M.S.A.	163,681									
Includes Centre County										
City of State College	58,633	54	3	11	8	32	548	36	497	15
Total area actually reporting	100.0%	200	3	99	20	78	1,466	177	1,255	34
Rate per 100,000 inhabitants		122.2	1.8	60.5	12.2	47.7	895.6	108.1	766.7	20.8
Staunton, VA M.S.A.	122,903									
Includes Augusta County and Staunton and Waynesboro Cities										
City of Staunton	24,931	51	0	18	5	28	473	35	419	19
Total area actually reporting	100.0%	210	2	46	13	149	1,756	255	1,360	141
Rate per 100,000 inhabitants		170.9	1.6	37.4	10.6	121.2	1,428.8	207.5	1,106.6	114.7
St. Cloud, MN M.S.A.[3]	200,776									
Includes Benton and Stearns Counties										
City of St. Cloud	68,311	298	0	73	50	175	2,443	225	2,044	174
Total area actually reporting	100.0%	371	1	88	57	225	4,102	393	3,444	265
Rate per 100,000 inhabitants		184.8	0.5	43.8	28.4	112.1	2,043.1	195.7	1,715.3	132.0
St. George, UT M.S.A.	175,978									
Includes Washington County										
City of St. George	89,160	181	2	48	13	118	1,397	229	1,023	145
Total area actually reporting	98.3%	293	3	81	20	189	2,455	397	1,856	202
Estimated total	100.0%	299	3	83	21	192	2,536	408	1,922	206
Rate per 100,000 inhabitants		169.9	1.7	47.2	11.9	109.1	1,441.1	231.8	1,092.2	117.1
St. Joseph, MO-KS M.S.A.	126,250									
Includes Doniphan County, KS and Andrew, Buchanan, and DeKalb Counties, MO										
City of St. Joseph, MO	75,872	431	2	124	54	251	4,355	584	3,132	639
Total area actually reporting	99.0%	505	3	146	56	300	4,868	680	3,453	735
Estimated total	100.0%	511	3	146	57	305	4,889	685	3,468	736
Rate per 100,000 inhabitants		404.8	2.4	115.6	45.1	241.6	3,872.5	542.6	2,746.9	583.0
Stockton, CA M.S.A.	754,858									
Includes San Joaquin County										
City of Stockton	313,604	4,380	34	181	1,158	3,007	12,367	2,209	8,480	1,678
Total area actually reporting	100.0%	5,952	50	301	1,560	4,041	21,409	3,771	14,560	3,078
Rate per 100,000 inhabitants		788.5	6.6	39.9	206.7	535.3	2,836.2	499.6	1,928.8	407.8

Table 4. Crime in the United States, by Selected Metropolitan Statistical Area, 2019—*Continued*

(Number, percent, rate per 100,000 population.)

Area	Population	Violent crime	Murder and nonnegligent manslaughter	Rape[1]	Robbery	Aggravated assault	Property crime	Burglary	Larceny-theft	Motor vehicle theft
Sumter, SC M.S.A...	140,002									
Includes Clarendon and Sumter Counties.............................										
City of Sumter	39,546	418	8	11	48	351	1,796	397	1,291	108
Total area actually reporting..	100.0%	1,006	17	52	96	841	4,411	1,093	2,989	329
Rate per 100,000 inhabitants..		718.6	12.1	37.1	68.6	600.7	3,150.7	780.7	2,135.0	235.0
Syracuse, NY M.S.A......................................	645,385									
Includes Madison, Onondaga, and Oswego Counties.............										
City of Syracuse	142,438	1,129	19	105	246	759	4,464	850	3,051	563
Total area actually reporting..	100.0%	1,807	20	370	330	1,087	10,822	1,626	8,318	878
Rate per 100,000 inhabitants..		280.0	3.1	57.3	51.1	168.4	1,676.8	251.9	1,288.8	136.0
Tallahassee, FL M.S.A.	384,437									
Includes Gadsden, Jefferson, Leon, and Wakulla Counties......										
City of Tallahassee	195,104	1,359	20	197	252	890	7,763	1,187	5,897	679
Total area actually reporting..	99.2%	2,019	25	272	311	1,411	11,200	2,141	8,119	940
Estimated total...	100.0%	2,028	25	273	312	1,418	11,266	2,154	8,167	945
Rate per 100,000 inhabitants..		527.5	6.5	71.0	81.2	368.9	2,930.5	560.3	2,124.4	245.8
Tampa-St. Petersburg-Clearwater, FL M.S.A......................	3,167,603									
Includes Hernando, Hillsborough, Pasco, and Pinellas										
Counties...										
City of Tampa	400,501	1,622	31	120	285	1,186	6,523	1,022	4,978	523
City of St. Petersburg...	267,696	1,594	17	125	297	1,155	8,592	1,044	6,765	783
City of Clearwater...	117,458	469	2	80	98	289	2,810	268	2,370	172
City of Largo...	85,740	329	5	71	74	179	2,348	202	1,991	155
City of Pinellas Park...	53,589	206	3	40	52	111	2,038	192	1,753	93
Total area actually reporting..	99.9%	9,246	126	1,169	1,575	6,376	53,335	6,834	42,460	4,041
Estimated total...	100.0%	9,254	126	1,170	1,576	6,382	53,394	6,845	42,503	4,046
Rate per 100,000 inhabitants..		292.1	4.0	36.9	49.8	201.5	1,685.6	216.1	1,341.8	127.7
Texarkana, TX-AR M.S.A.[3]..	149,595									
Includes Little River and Miller Counties, AR and Bowie										
County, TX										
City of Texarkana, TX	37,401	157	3	33	43	78	1,710	280	1,347	83
Total area actually reporting..	100.0%	676	8	90	77	501	3,968	836	2,902	230
Rate per 100,000 inhabitants..		451.9	5.3	60.2	51.5	334.9	2,652.5	558.8	1,939.9	153.7
The Villages, FL M.S.A..................................	132,914									
Includes Sumter County...										
Total area actually reporting..	100.0%	249	5	18	20	206	1,139	318	703	118
Rate per 100,000 inhabitants..		187.3	3.8	13.5	15.0	155.0	856.9	239.3	528.9	88.8
Toledo, OH M.S.A.......................................	641,535									
Includes Fulton, Lucas, Ottawa, and Wood Counties.............										
City of Toledo	273,505	2,604	34	205	655	1,710	9,470	2,362	6,314	794
Total area actually reporting..	91.1%	2,960	35	298	707	1,920	14,757	2,880	10,879	998
Estimated total...	100.0%	3,026	36	311	717	1,962	15,736	3,011	11,685	1,040
Rate per 100,000 inhabitants..		471.7	5.6	48.5	111.8	305.8	2,452.9	469.3	1,821.4	162.1
Topeka, KS M.S.A.[4]......................................	231,941									
Includes Jackson, Jefferson, Osage,4 Shawnee, and										
Wabaunsee Counties...										
City of Topeka	125,655	895	13	74	243	565	6,271	905	4,404	962
Total area actually reporting..	97.9%	1,122	16	106	250	750			5,533	1,155
Estimated total...	100.0%	1,143	16	106	254	767			5,588	1,159
Rate per 100,000 inhabitants..		492.8	6.9	45.7	109.5	330.7			2,409.2	499.7
Trenton-Princeton, NJ M.S.A.	368,390									
Includes Mercer County...										
City of Trenton	83,457	937	15	70	300	552	1,748	360	1,142	246
City of Princeton...	31,610	10	0	1	0	9	238	45	190	3
Total area actually reporting..	100.0%	1,277	17	118	389	753	5,571	931	4,139	501
Rate per 100,000 inhabitants..		346.6	4.6	32.0	105.6	204.4	1,512.3	252.7	1,123.5	136.0
Tucson, AZ M.S.A........................................	1,047,076									
Includes Pima County..										
City of Tucson	548,374	3,775	40	527	1,105	2,103	17,943	2,497	13,196	2,250
Total area actually reporting..	100.0%	4,685	56	653	1,297	2,679	30,170	4,242	22,701	3,227
Rate per 100,000 inhabitants..		447.4	5.3	62.4	123.9	255.9	2,881.4	405.1	2,168.0	308.2

Table 4. Crime in the United States, by Selected Metropolitan Statistical Area, 2019—*Continued*

(Number, percent, rate per 100,000 population.)

Area	Population	Violent crime	Murder and nonnegligent manslaughter	Rape[1]	Robbery	Aggravated assault	Property crime	Burglary	Larceny-theft	Motor vehicle theft
Tulsa, OK M.S.A.....................	998,117									
Includes Creek, Okmulgee, Osage, Pawnee, Rogers, Tulsa, and Wagoner Counties....................										
City of Tulsa....................	401,700	3,964	55	341	718	2,850	21,336	4,846	13,457	3,033
Total area actually reporting....................	100.0%	5,286	82	573	828	3,803	32,217	7,356	20,556	4,305
Rate per 100,000 inhabitants....................		529.6	8.2	57.4	83.0	381.0	3,227.8	737.0	2,059.5	431.3
Twin Falls, ID M.S.A.....................	111,928									
Includes Jerome and Twin Falls Counties....................										
City of Twin Falls....................	50,463	201	1	27	10	163	1,034	152	827	55
Total area actually reporting....................	100.0%	321	2	62	10	247	1,519	304	1,116	99
Rate per 100,000 inhabitants....................		286.8	1.8	55.4	8.9	220.7	1,357.1	271.6	997.1	88.4
Tyler, TX M.S.A.	231,362									
Includes Smith County										
City of Tyler	106,851	401	0	72	58	271	3,206	439	2,597	170
Total area actually reporting....................	100.0%	773	7	133	83	550	5,034	926	3,680	428
Rate per 100,000 inhabitants....................		334.1	3.0	57.5	35.9	237.7	2,175.8	400.2	1,590.6	185.0
Urban Honolulu, HI M.S.A.	974,902									
Includes Honolulu County										
Total area actually reporting....................	100.0%	2,638	27	340	954	1,317	29,263	3,864	21,562	3,837
Rate per 100,000 inhabitants....................		270.6	2.8	34.9	97.9	135.1	3,001.6	396.3	2,211.7	393.6
Utica-Rome, NY M.S.A.	288,854									
Includes Herkimer and Oneida Counties....................										
City of Utica....................	59,842	374	6	31	143	194	1,986	261	1,635	90
City of Rome....................	32,019	54	1	8	11	34	524	84	416	24
Total area actually reporting....................	100.0%	784	8	177	177	422	4,544	597	3,756	191
Rate per 100,000 inhabitants....................		271.4	2.8	61.3	61.3	146.1	1,573.1	206.7	1,300.3	66.1
Vallejo, CA M.S.A.	447,069									
Includes Solano County....................										
City of Vallejo	122,657	1,037	12	138	336	551	4,941	2,888	1,148	905
Total area actually reporting....................	100.0%	2,114	21	264	661	1,168	13,161	3,727	7,369	2,065
Rate per 100,000 inhabitants....................		472.9	4.7	59.1	147.9	261.3	2,943.8	833.7	1,648.3	461.9
Victoria, TX M.S.A.	99,703									
Includes Goliad and Victoria Counties										
City of Victoria....................	67,581	347	3	66	52	226	1,974	382	1,474	118
Total area actually reporting....................	100.0%	463	7	88	60	308	2,452	529	1,747	176
Rate per 100,000 inhabitants....................		464.4	7.0	88.3	60.2	308.9	2,459.3	530.6	1,752.2	176.5
Vineland-Bridgeton, NJ M.S.A.....................	149,590									
Includes Cumberland County										
City of Vineland....................	59,860	211	1	32	55	123	1,686	269	1,375	42
City of Bridgeton....................	24,331	223	2	17	114	90	848	261	549	38
Total area actually reporting....................	100.0%	631	7	72	235	317	4,047	816	3,103	128
Rate per 100,000 inhabitants....................		421.8	4.7	48.1	157.1	211.9	2,705.4	545.5	2,074.3	85.6
Virginia Beach-Norfolk-Newport News, VA-NC M.S.A.[3] ...	1,761,473									
Includes Camden, Currituck and Gates Counties, NC[3] and Gloucester, Isle of Wight, James City, Mathews, Southampton, and York Counties and Chesapeake, Franklin, Hampton, Newport News, Norfolk, Poquoson, Portsmouth, Suffolk, Virginia Beach, and Williamsburg Cities, VA										
City of Virginia Beach....................	449,038	581	30	79	196	276	7,906	530	6,797	579
City of Norfolk, VA....................	242,813	1,325	36	134	311	844	8,405	841	6,765	799
City of Newport News, VA....................	177,319	1,056	24	64	164	804	4,484	503	3,641	340
City of Hampton, VA....................	133,173	393	15	42	122	214	3,994	347	3,397	250
City of Portsmouth, VA....................	93,991	889	16	37	230	606	5,509	846	4,189	474
Total area actually reporting....................	99.3%	6,141	140	596	1,285	4,120	42,321	4,179	34,941	3,201
Estimated total....................	100.0%	6,157	141	598	1,286	4,132	42,452	4,232	35,008	3,212
Rate per 100,000 inhabitants....................		349.5	8.0	33.9	73.0	234.6	2,410.0	240.3	1,987.4	182.3
Visalia, CA M.S.A.	464,847									
Includes Tulare County....................										
City of Visalia	134,961	586	4	111	159	312	3,900	747	2,627	526
Total area actually reporting....................	100.0%	1,692	20	194	389	1,089	10,625	2,025	6,755	1,845
Rate per 100,000 inhabitants....................		364.0	4.3	41.7	83.7	234.3	2,285.7	435.6	1,453.2	396.9

Table 4. Crime in the United States, by Selected Metropolitan Statistical Area, 2019—*Continued*

(Number, percent, rate per 100,000 population.)

Area	Population	Violent crime	Murder and nonnegligent manslaughter	Rape[1]	Robbery	Aggravated assault	Property crime	Burglary	Larceny-theft	Motor vehicle theft
Waco, TX M.S.A.[3].....................	272,588									
Includes Falls and McLennan Counties										
City of Waco..........................	139,870	799	10	88	133	568	4,599	784	3,492	323
Total area actually reporting..................	95.0%	1,129	12	161	170	786	6,767	1,183	5,006	578
Estimated total..........................	100.0%	1,166	13	164	172	817	6,976	1,234	5,136	606
Rate per 100,000 inhabitants..................		427.8	4.8	60.2	63.1	299.7	2,559.2	452.7	1,884.2	222.3
Walla Walla, WA M.S.A.......................	60,962									
Includes Walla Walla County....................										
City of Walla Walla	33,047	114	2	29	16	67	1,052	161	814	77
Total area actually reporting..................	100.0%	145	3	34	18	90	1,479	276	1,095	108
Rate per 100,000 inhabitants..................		237.9	4.9	55.8	29.5	147.6	2,426.1	452.7	1,796.2	177.2
Warner Robins, GA M.S.A.[3]......................	184,460									
Includes Houston and Peach Counties[3]...................										
City of Warner Robins[3]......................	76,623	420	3	44	104	269	3,609	626	2,744	239
Total area actually reporting..................	90.3%	709	3	86	143	477	5,278	924	4,011	343
Estimated total..........................	100.0%	765	4	90	160	511	5,732	974	4,365	393
Rate per 100,000 inhabitants..................		414.7	2.2	48.8	86.7	277.0	3,107.4	528.0	2,366.4	213.1
Washington-Arlington-Alexandria, DC-VA-MD-WV M.S.A.[3, 4]......................	6,301,628									
Includes the Metropolitan Divisions of Frederick-Gaithersburg-Rockville, MD and Washington-Arlington-Alexandria, DC-VA-MD-WV										
City of Washington, D.C.	705,749	6,896	166	342	2,359	4,029	29,965	1,840	25,827	2,298
City of Alexandria, VA..................	162,258	288	2	19	80	187	2,517	117	2,005	395
City of Frederick, MD	73,030	296	2	37	54	203	1,364	199	1,112	53
Total area actually reporting..................	99.9%			1,839	5,623	9,306	102,402	7,856	85,833	8,713
Estimated total..........................	100.0%			1,840	5,624	9,309	102,470	7,865	85,885	8,720
Rate per 100,000 inhabitants..................				29.2	89.2	147.7	1,626.1	124.8	1,362.9	138.4
Frederick-Gaithersburg-Rockville, MD M.D...................	1,314,401									
Includes Frederick and Montgomery Counties										
Total area actually reporting......................	100.0%	2,167	18	355	644	1,150	17,671	1,812	14,848	1,011
Rate per 100,000 inhabitants		164.9	1.4	27.0	49.0	87.5	1,344.4	137.9	1,129.6	76.9
Washington-Arlington-Alexandria, DC-VA-MD-WV M.D.[3, 4]	4,987,227									
Includes District of Columbia; Calvert, Charles, and Prince George's[3] Counties, MD; Arlington, Clarke, Culpeper, Fairfax, Fauquier, Loudoun, Madison, Prince William, Rappahannock, Spotsylvania, Stafford, and Warren Counties and Alexandria, Fairfax, Falls Church, Fredericksburg, Manassas, and Manassas Park Cities, VA; and Jefferson County, WV......................										
Total area actually reporting..................	99.9%			1,484	4,979	8,156	84,731	6,044	70,985	7,702
Estimated total..........................	100.0%			1,485	4,980	8,159	84,799	6,053	71,037	7,709
Rate per 100,000 inhabitants..................				29.8	99.9	163.6	1,700.3	121.4	1,424.4	154.6
Watertown-Fort Drum, NY M.S.A.	110,566									
Includes Jefferson County										
City of Watertown........................	25,102	154	0	57	14	83	887	108	743	36
Total area actually reporting..................	100.0%	243	0	96	20	127	1,615	187	1,375	53
Rate per 100,000 inhabitants..................		219.8	0.0	86.8	18.1	114.9	1,460.7	169.1	1,243.6	47.9
Wausau-Weston, WI M.S.A.[3]	162,956									
Includes Lincoln and Marathon[3] Counties...........................										
City of Wausau[3]......................	38,507	156	1	42	5	108	521	81	396	44
Total area actually reporting..................	100.0%	360	1	88	12	259	1,499	233	1,182	84
Rate per 100,000 inhabitants..................		220.9	0.6	54.0	7.4	158.9	919.9	143.0	725.3	51.5
Weirton-Steubenville, WV-OH M.S.A.	115,836									
Includes Jefferson County, OH and Brooke and Hancock Counties, WV										
City of Weirton, WV	18,296	11	0	1	0	10	88	2	84	2
City of Steubenville, OH......................	17,768	33	3	6	9	15	803	55	735	13
Total area actually reporting......................	81.9%	136	3	20	10	103	1,085	86	968	31
Estimated total......................	100.0%	179	3	26	15	135	1,566	151	1,363	52
Rate per 100,000 inhabitants......................		154.5	2.6	22.4	12.9	116.5	1,351.9	130.4	1,176.7	44.9

Table 4. Crime in the United States, by Selected Metropolitan Statistical Area, 2019—*Continued*

(Number, percent, rate per 100,000 population.)

Area	Population	Violent crime	Murder and nonnegligent manslaughter	Rape[1]	Robbery	Aggravated assault	Property crime	Burglary	Larceny-theft	Motor vehicle theft
Wenatchee, WA M.S.A.................................	120,654									
Includes Chelan and Douglas Counties..............................										
City of Wenatchee....................................	34,513	62	1	16	10	35	638	66	532	40
Total area actually reporting.............................	100.0%	128	2	28	12	86	1,380	229	1,065	86
Rate per 100,000 inhabitants............................		106.1	1.7	23.2	9.9	71.3	1,143.8	189.8	882.7	71.3
Wichita, KS M.S.A.[5]	638,097									
Includes Butler, Harvey, Sedgwick, and Sumner Counties.......										
City of Wichita......................................	390,080	4,451	35	367	461	3,588	20,759	2,677	15,777	2,305
Total area actually reporting.............................	99.2%	4,962	39	472	493	3,958		3,330		2,623
Estimated total......................................	100.0%	4,985	39	472	497	3,977		3,351		2,627
Rate per 100,000 inhabitants............................		781.2	6.1	74.0	77.9	623.3		525.2		411.7
Wichita Falls, TX M.S.A.	150,317									
Includes Archer, Clay, and Wichita Counties										
City of Wichita Falls	104,551	364	4	103	85	172	3,183	557	2,394	232
Total area actually reporting.............................	95.4%	461	4	127	92	238	3,747	711	2,737	299
Estimated total......................................	100.0%	479	4	128	93	254	3,856	738	2,804	314
Rate per 100,000 inhabitants............................		318.7	2.7	85.2	61.9	169.0	2,565.2	491.0	1,865.4	208.9
Wilmington, NC M.S.A.[3]............................	299,507									
Includes New Hanover and Pender Counties[3]										
City of Wilmington[3]...................................	124,750	759	7	74	127	551	3,593	771	2,564	258
Total area actually reporting.............................	80.2%	1,015	7	118	159	731	5,686	1,105	4,249	332
Estimated total......................................	100.0%	1,138	9	132	171	826	6,534	1,380	4,746	408
Rate per 100,000 inhabitants............................		380.0	3.0	44.1	57.1	275.8	2,181.6	460.8	1,584.6	136.2
Winchester, VA-WV M.S.A.	140,516									
Includes Frederick County and Winchester City, VA and										
Hampshire County, WV										
City of Winchester, VA.................................	28,201	80	1	39	6	34	657	76	559	22
Total area actually reporting.............................	99.7%	225	1	66	20	138	1,794	244	1,440	110
Estimated total......................................	100.0%	226	1	66	20	139	1,803	246	1,446	111
Rate per 100,000 inhabitants............................		160.8	0.7	47.0	14.2	98.9	1,283.1	175.1	1,029.1	79.0
Worcester, MA-CT M.S.A.[3]	870,501									
Includes Windham County, CT and Worcester County, MA....										
City of Worcester, MA.................................	184,945	1,165	13	40	229	883	3,792	786	2,637	369
Total area actually reporting.............................	97.4%	2,659	17	302	336	2,004	9,100	1,590	6,778	732
Estimated total......................................	100.0%	2,702	17	308	339	2,038	9,273	1,620	6,909	744
Rate per 100,000 inhabitants............................		310.4	2.0	35.4	38.9	234.1	1,065.2	186.1	793.7	85.5
Yakima, WA M.S.A.	251,470									
Includes Yakima County....................................										
City of Yakima	94,168	420	9	44	91	276	2,723	439	1,866	418
Total area actually reporting.............................	95.6%	684	19	89*	140	436	6,281	1,098	4,100	1,083
Estimated total......................................	100.0%	703	19	93	142	449	6,536	1,140	4,289	1,107
Rate per 100,000 inhabitants............................		279.6	7.6	37.0	56.5	178.6	2,599.1	453.3	1,705.6	440.2
Yuba City, CA M.S.A.	174,368									
Includes Sutter and Yuba Counties............................										
City of Yuba City.....................................	67,164	241	3	28	52	158	1,823	230	1,334	259
Total area actually reporting.............................	100.0%	644	11	73	126	434	4,291	803	2,661	827
Rate per 100,000 inhabitants............................		369.3	6.3	41.9	72.3	248.9	2,460.9	460.5	1,526.1	474.3
Yuma, AZ M.S.A.[3]	214,209									
Includes Yuma County										
City of Yuma	98,769	376	11	27	29	309	2,302	483	1,586	233
Total area actually reporting.............................	100.0%	595	24	46	41	484	3,707	793	2,466	448
Rate per 100,000 inhabitants............................		277.8	11.2	21.5	19.1	225.9	1,730.6	370.2	1,151.2	209.1
Aguadilla-Isabela, Puerto Rico M.S.A.	289,289									
Includes Aguada, Aguadilla, Anasco, Isabela, Lares, Moca,										
Rincon, San Sebastian, and Utuado Municipios......................										
Total area actually reporting.............................	100.0%	430	14	21	51	344	1,434	412	965	57
Rate per 100,000 inhabitants............................		148.6	4.8	7.3	17.6	118.9	495.7	142.4	333.6	19.7
Arecibo, Puerto Rico M.S.A.	174,606									
Includes Arecibo, Camuy, Hatillo, and Quebradillas										
Municipios............................										

Table 4. Crime in the United States, by Selected Metropolitan Statistical Area, 2019—*Continued*

(Number, percent, rate per 100,000 population.)

Area	Population	Violent crime	Murder and nonnegligent manslaughter	Rape[1]	Robbery	Aggravated assault	Property crime	Burglary	Larceny-theft	Motor vehicle theft
Total area actually reporting....................................	100.0%	286	18	13	74	181	799	229	485	85
Rate per 100,000 inhabitants...................................		163.8	10.3	7.4	42.4	103.7	457.6	131.2	277.8	48.7
Guayama, Puerto Rico M.S.A.	72,914									
Includes Arroyo, Guayama, and Patillas Municipios										
Total area actually reporting....................................	100.0%	153	10	4	22	117	354	104	234	16
Rate per 100,000 inhabitants...................................		209.8	13.7	5.5	30.2	160.5	485.5	142.6	320.9	21.9
Mayaguez, Puerto Rico M.S.A..............................	94,975									
Includes Hormigueros, Las Marias, and Mayaguez										
Municipios										
Total area actually reporting....................................	100.0%	107	4	7	25	71	378	71	278	29
Rate per 100,000 inhabitants...................................		112.7	4.2	7.4	26.3	74.8	398.0	74.8	292.7	30.5
Ponce, Puerto Rico M.S.A.	215,295									
Includes Adjuntas, Juana Diaz, Ponce, and Villalba Municipios										
Total area actually reporting....................................	100.0%	356	26	8	134	188	1,235	242	825	168
Rate per 100,000 inhabitants...................................		165.4	12.1	3.7	62.2	87.3	573.6	112.4	383.2	78.0
San German, Puerto Rico M.S.A............................	121,464									
Includes Cabo Rojo, Lajas, Sabana Grande, and San German										
Municipios										
Total area actually reporting....................................	100.0%	101	13	3	7	78	403	95	290	18
Rate per 100,000 inhabitants...................................		83.2	10.7	2.5	5.8	64.2	331.8	78.2	238.8	14.8
San Juan-Bayamon-Caguas, Puerto Rico M.S.A.	2,023,227									
Includes Aguas Buenas, Aibonito, Barceloneta, Barranquitas,										
Bayamon, Caguas, Canovanas, Carolina, Catano, Cayey,										
Ceiba, Ciales, Cidra, Comerio, Corozal, Dorado, Fajardo,										
Florida, Guaynabo, Gurabo, Humacao, Juncos, Las Piedras,										
Loiza, Luquillo, Manati, Maunabo, Morovis, Naguabo,										
Naranjito, Orocovis, Rio Grande, San Juan, San Lorenzo,										
Toa Alta, Toa Baja, Trujillo Alto, Vega Alta, Vega Baja, and										
Yabucoa Municipios..										
Total area actually reporting....................................	100.0%	4,599	477	138	1,754	2,230	17,097	2,896	10,966	3,235
Rate per 100,000 inhabitants...................................		227.3	23.6	6.8	86.7	110.2	845.0	143.1	542.0	159.9
Yauco, Puerto Rico M.S.A.	85,830									
Includes Guanica, Guayanilla, Penuelas, and Yauco										
Municipios										
Total area actually reporting....................................	100.0%	148	10	11	19	108	267	66	184	17
Rate per 100,000 inhabitants...................................		172.4	11.7	12.8	22.1	125.8	311.1	76.9	214.4	19.8

[1]The figures shown in this column for the offense of rape were reported using only the revised Uniform Crime Reporting (UCR) definition of rape. See the chapter notes for further explanation.
[2]One or more agency(s) wihin this Metropolitan Statistical Area submitted rape data classified according to the legacy UCR definition. See the chapter notes for further explanation.
[3]Because of changes in the state/local agency's reporting practices, figures are not comparable to previous years' data.
[4]The FBI determined that the agency's data were overreported. Consequently, those data are not included in this table.
[5]The FBI determined that the agency's data were underreported. Consequently, those data are not included in this table.

Table 5. Offense Analysis, United States, 2015–2019

(Number.)

Classification	2015	2016	2017	2018[1]	2019
Murder	15,883	17,413	17,294	16,374	16,425
Rape[2]	126,134	132,414	135,666	143,765	139,815
Robbery[3]	328,109	332,797	320,596	281,278	267,988
By location					
Street/highway	130,724	129,337	119,180	102,149	94,090
Commercial house	47,229	50,785	49,654	45,148	44,128
Gas or service station	8,916	9,708	9,603	8,863	8,555
Convenience store	18,661	20,656	21,048	19,647	18,312
Residence	54,142	55,102	51,260	45,408	42,806
Bank	5,691	5,914	5,441	4,461	3,834
Miscellaneous	62,747	61,296	64,410	55,602	56,264
Burglary[3]	1,587,564	1,516,405	1,397,045	1,235,013	1,117,696
By location					
Residence (dwelling)	1,136,664	1,054,470	939,509	808,611	702,449
Residence, night	328,736	311,805	285,358	257,085	238,635
Residence, day	594,668	543,930	474,495	408,349	354,398
Residence, unknown	213,260	198,735	179,656	143,178	109,415
Nonresidence (store, office, etc.)	450,900	461,935	457,536	426,402	415,247
Nonresidence, night	189,167	199,741	200,859	190,817	191,663
Nonresidence, day	159,177	159,630	157,375	151,091	152,956
Nonresidence, unknown	102,556	102,564	99,302	84,493	70,629
Larceny-theft (except motor vehicle theft)[3]	5,723,488	5,644,835	5,513,000	5,232,167	5,086,096
By type					
Pocket-picking	31,208	27,648	31,026	27,326	29,481
Purse-snatching	23,144	22,671	21,961	20,113	18,568
Shoplifting	1,276,575	1,179,137	1,144,948	1,116,664	1,113,785
From motor vehicles (except accessories)	1,373,720	1,477,587	1,477,684	1,410,567	1,379,757
Motor vehicle accessories	399,452	415,590	407,017	324,298	325,800
Bicycles	205,600	184,546	174,803	157,042	154,009
From buildings	664,381	605,765	586,612	534,418	498,121
From coin-operated machines	13,020	12,349	12,014	11,511	11,328
All others	1,736,388	1,719,542	1,656,937	1,630,232	1,555,247
By value					
Over $200	2,613,333	2,561,619	2,529,654	2,445,915	2,407,972
$50 to $200	1,278,027	1,221,246	1,169,612	1,120,011	1,079,509
Under $50	1,832,128	1,861,970	1,813,734	1,666,185	1,598,615
Motor vehicle theft	713,063	767,290	772,943	751,904	721,885

[1] The crime figures have been adjusted.

[2] The figures shown for this offense of rape were estimated using the revised Uniform Crime Reporting (UCR) definition of rape. See chapter notes for more detail.

[3] Because of rounding, the number of offenses may not add to the total.

Table 6. Crime Trends, by Population Group, 2018–2019

(Number, percent change.)

Population group	Violent crime	Murder and nonnegligent manslaughter	Rape[1]	Robbery	Aggravated assault	Property crime	Burglary	Larceny-theft	Motor vehicle theft	Arson	Number of agencies	Estimated population, 2019
Total, All Agencies												
2018	1,142,958	14,915	131,959	261,241	734,843	6,621,258	1,104,712	4,785,340	696,099	35,107		
2019	1,135,093	15,020	126,958	248,681	744,434	6,358,176	998,474	4,659,007	667,300	33,395	15,261	307,140,768
Percent change	-0.7	+0.7	-3.8	-4.8	+1.3	-4.0	-9.6	-2.6	-4.1	-4.9		
Total, Cities												
2018	916,541	11,646	98,794	230,353	575,748	5,322,104	829,649	3,904,823	560,635	26,997		
2019	911,416	11,762	94,778	219,080	585,796	5,133,915	751,526	3,819,909	536,344	26,136	11,023	210,976,208
Percent change	-0.6	+1.0	-4.1	-4.9	+1.7	-3.5	-9.4	-2.2	-4.3	-3.2		
Group I (250,000 and over)												
2018	445,300	6,067	38,088	131,006	270,139	1,965,032	312,400	1,381,781	259,944	10,907		
2019	444,396	6,185	36,109	125,730	276,372	1,934,133	289,121	1,382,779	251,510	10,723	86	62,641,973
Percent change	-0.2	+1.9	-5.2	-4.0	+2.3	-1.6	-7.5	+0.1	-3.2	-1.7		
1,000,000 and over (Group I subset)												
2018	190,674	2,224	15,452	60,259	112,739	713,836	108,420	508,266	93,478	3,672		
2019	192,648	2,209	15,071	58,737	116,631	707,846	99,871	513,190	91,185	3,600	11	27,806,004
Percent change	+1.0	-0.7	-2.5	-2.5	+3.5	-0.8	-7.9	+1.0	-2.5	-2.0		
500,000 to 999,999 (Group I subset)												
2018	145,955	2,141	11,403	42,090	90,321	707,239	113,298	497,820	92,324	3,797		
2019	143,997	2,289	10,505	39,402	91,801	684,426	105,433	487,358	88,038	3,597	26	18,474,842
Percent change	-1.3	+6.9	-7.9	-6.4	+1.6	-3.2	-6.9	-2.1	-4.6	-5.3		
250,000 to 499,999 (Group I subset)												
2018	108,671	1,702	11,233	28,657	67,079	543,957	90,682	375,695	74,142	3,438		
2019	107,751	1,687	10,533	27,591	67,940	541,861	83,817	382,231	72,287	3,526	49	16,361,127
Percent change	-0.8	-0.9	-6.2	-3.7	+1.3	-0.4	-7.6	+1.7	-2.5	+2.6		
Group II (100,000 to 249,999)												
2018	139,303	1,833	15,785	35,875	85,810	885,077	138,400	637,127	105,333	4,217		
2019	140,053	1,841	14,772	33,871	89,569	844,779	124,271	618,458	98,007	4,043	220	31,945,830
Percent change	+0.5	+0.4	-6.4	-5.6	+4.4	-4.6	-10.2	-2.9	-7.0	-4.1		
Group III (50,000 to 99,999)												
2018	112,336	1,282	13,372	26,923	70,759	778,839	120,597	579,227	75,119	3,896		
2019	110,416	1,254	13,028	25,385	70,749	748,189	107,498	566,010	71,055	3,626	492	34,283,540
Percent change	-1.7	-2.2	-2.6	-5.7	*	-3.9	-10.9	-2.3	-5.4	-6.9		
Group IV (25,000 to 49,999)												
2018	81,996	1,004	11,829	17,120	52,043	633,847	94,717	486,908	49,495	2,727		
2019	80,560	1,016	11,167	15,829	52,548	605,639	84,376	470,766	47,792	2,705	888	30,781,974
Percent change	-1.8	+1.2	-5.6	-7.5	+1.0	-4.5	-10.9	-3.3	-3.4	-0.8		
Group V (10,000 to 24,999)												
2018	72,343	809	10,304	11,906	49,324	578,557	90,127	445,525	40,532	2,373		
2019	70,475	838	10,112	11,004	48,521	544,868	79,393	424,801	38,339	2,335	1,799	28,730,692
Percent change	-2.6	+3.6	-1.9	-7.6	-1.6	-5.8	-11.9	-4.7	-5.4	-1.6		
Group VI (under 10,000)												
2018	65,263	651	9,416	7,523	47,673	480,752	73,408	374,255	30,212	2,877		
2019	65,516	628	9,590	7,261	48,037	456,307	66,867	357,095	29,641	2,704	7,538	22,592,199
Percent change	+0.4	-3.5	+1.8	-3.5	+0.8	-5.1	-8.9	-4.6	-1.9	-6.0		
Metropolitan Counties												
2018	180,792	2,457	24,343	28,695	125,297	1,060,896	205,351	737,843	111,565	6,137		
2019	177,882	2,442	23,472	27,477	124,491	1,002,794	183,458	706,947	106,956	5,433	1,922	73,179,304
Percent change	-1.6	-0.6	-3.6	-4.2	-0.6	-5.5	-10.7	-4.2	-4.1	-11.5		
Nonmetropolitan Counties[2]												
2018	45,625	812	8,822	2,193	33,798	238,258	69,712	142,674	23,899	1,973		
2019	45,795	816	8,708	2,124	34,147	221,467	63,490	132,151	24,000	1,826	2,316	22,985,256
Percent change	+0.4	+0.5	-1.3	-3.1	+1.0	-7.0	-8.9	-7.4	+0.4	-7.5		
Suburban Areas[3]												
2018	314,980	3,972	43,742	54,668	212,598	2,179,059	361,192	1,611,305	195,519	11,043		
2019	309,842	3,917	42,129	52,030	211,766	2,069,523	322,835	1,548,496	188,088	10,104	8,421	133,848,983
Percent change	-1.6	-1.4	-3.7	-4.8	-0.4	-5.0	-10.6	-3.9	-3.8	-8.5		

* = Less than one-tenth of one percent.
[1] The figures shown in the rape (revised definition) column include only those reported by law enforcement agencies that used the revised Uniform Crime Reporting (UCR) definition of rape. See chapter notes for more detail.
[2] Includes state police agencies that report aggregately for the entire state.
[3] Suburban areas include law enforcement agencies in cities with less than 50,000 inhabitants and county law enforcement agencies that are within a Metropolitan Statistical Area. Suburban areas exclude all metropolitan agencies associated with a principal city. The agencies associated with suburban areas also appear in other groups within this table.

Table 7. Rate: Number of Crimes Per 100,000 Population, by Population Group, 2019

(Number, rate.)

Population group	Violent crime		Murder and nonnegligent manslaughter		Rape[1]		Robbery		Aggravated assault	
	Number of offenses known	Rate	Number of offenses known	Rate	Number of offenses known	Rate	Number of offenses known	Rate	Number of offenses known	Rate
Total, All Agencies........................	1,081,697	387.0	14,014	5.0	122,822	44.0	237,873	85.1	706,988	253.0
Total, Cities................................	873,689	449.2	11,039	5.7	92,472	47.6	210,769	108.4	559,409	287.7
Group I (250,000 and over)........................	430,847	715.8	5,794	9.6	35,621	59.2	121,748	202.3	267,684	444.7
1,000,000 and over (Group I subset)........	181,251	691.3	1,944	7.4	14,291	54.5	54,543	208.0	110,473	421.4
500,000 to 999,999 (Group I subset).......	138,815	796.3	2,184	12.5	10,518	60.3	37,942	217.6	88,171	505.8
250,000 to 499,999 (Group I subset).......	110,781	669.8	1,666	10.1	10,812	65.4	29,263	176.9	69,040	417.5
Group II (100,000 to 249,999).....................	139,414	451.9	1,817	5.9	14,924	48.6	33,469	108.9	89,204	289.1
Group III (50,000 to 99,999)	106,412	333.2	1,196	3.8	12,654	39.6	24,217	75.8	68,345	214.0
Group IV (25,000 to 49,999)........................	75,729	270.5	933	3.3	10,763	38.4	14,944	53.4	49,089	175.3
Group V (10,000 to 24,999)	63,994	254.8	753	3.0	9,636	38.5	10,057	40.0	43,548	173.6
Group VI (under 10,000).............................	57,293	310.9	546	3.0	8,874	48.3	6,334	34.4	41,539	225.4
Metropolitan Counties	166,611	255.7	2,224	3.4	22,200	34.2	25,201	38.7	116,986	179.5
Nonmetropolitan Counties[2]	41,397	208.4	751	3.8	8,150	41.1	1,903	9.6	30,593	154.0
Suburban Areas[3]	287,940	243.3	3,569	3.0	40,024	33.9	48,063	40.6	196,284	165.9

NOTE: Due to a system upgrade, the rates in this table are now caculated using aggregate popualtion for each individual offense. The agency counts and population are provided for each individual offense. See Appendix V for further explanations of these changes.

[1]The figures shown in this column for the offense of rape were reported using only the revised Uniform Crime Reporting definition of rape. See the chapter notes for further explanation.

[2]Includes state police agencies that report aggregately for the entire state.

[3]Suburban areas include law enforcement agencies in cities with less than 50,000 inhabitants and county law enforcement agencies that are within a Metropolitan Statistical Area. Suburban areas exclude all metropolitan agencies associated with a principal city. The agencies associated with suburban areas also appear in other groups within this table.

Table 7. Rate: Number of Crimes Per 100,000 Population, by Population Group, 2019—*Continued*

(Number, rate.)

Population group	Property crime Number of offenses known	Property crime Rate	Burglary Number of offenses known	Burglary Rate	Larceny-theft Number of offenses known	Larceny-theft Rate	Motor vehicle theft Number of offenses known	Motor vehicle theft Rate
Total, All Agencies.................................	5,954,888	2,130.3	937,367	336.7	4,383,165	1,569.2	634,356	227.6
Total, Cities..	4,847,733	2,492.2	713,134	368.1	3,620,225	1,862.7	514,374	265.5
Group I (250,000 and over).........................	1,853,455	3,079.4	276,877	464.4	1,334,313	2,216.9	242,265	407.2
1,000,000 and over (Group I subset)...................	667,672	2,546.7	95,427	364.0	485,179	1,850.6	87,066	332.1
500,000 to 999,999 (Group I subset)..................	645,353	3,701.9	97,495	577.9	465,157	2,668.2	82,701	494.2
250,000 to 499,999 (Group I subset)..................	540,430	3,267.7	83,955	507.6	383,977	2,321.7	72,498	438.4
Group II (100,000 to 249,999)...............................	834,255	2,704.2	124,515	403.6	612,218	1,984.5	97,522	316.1
Group III (50,000 to 99,999)..............................	706,211	2,211.6	101,485	317.8	537,090	1,685.5	67,636	212.3
Group IV (25,000 to 49,999)...............................	562,852	2,010.4	79,048	284.1	438,758	1,568.6	45,046	160.9
Group V (10,000 to 24,999)	489,238	1,947.6	71,688	285.7	382,237	1,525.0	35,313	140.7
Group VI (under 10,000)..	401,722	2,180.2	59,521	323.4	315,609	1,713.9	26,592	144.3
Metropolitan Counties	910,152	1,396.9	166,581	257.1	645,121	990.8	98,450	151.1
Nonmetropolitan Counties[2]	197,003	991.6	57,652	290.3	117,819	593.4	21,532	108.4
Suburban Areas[3]	1,885,710	1,593.5	295,785	251.0	1,415,616	1,197.3	174,309	147.3

NOTE: Due to a system upgrade, the rates in this table are now caculated using aggregate popualtion for each individual offense. The agency counts and population are provided for each individual offense. See Appendix V for further explanations of these changes.

[1]The figures shown in this column for the offense of rape were reported using only the revised Uniform Crime Reporting definition of rape. See the chapter notes for further explanation.

[2]Includes state police agencies that report aggregately for the entire state.

[3]Suburban areas include law enforcement agencies in cities with less than 50,000 inhabitants and county law enforcement agencies that are within a Metropolitan Statistical Area. Suburban areas exclude all metropolitan agencies associated with a principal city. The agencies associated with suburban areas also appear in other groups within this table.

Table 8. Offense Analysis, Number and Percent Change, 2018–2019

(Number, percent, dollars; 13,848 agencies; 2019 estimated population 273,654,275.)

Classification	Number of offenses, 2019	Percent change from 2018	Percent distribution[1]	Average value (dollars)
Murder..	13,002	+1.5	NA	X
Rape[2]..	114,810	-3.0	NA	X
Robbery	211,113	-4.4	100.0	$1,797
By location				
Street/highway..	74,121	-6.3	35.1	1,529
Commercial house..	34,763	-3.6	16.5	1,772
Gas or service station	6,739	-3.1	3.2	1,248
Convenience store..	14,426	-6.9	6.8	1,006
Residence...	33,721	-5.0	16.0	2,560
Bank	3,020	-15.2	1.4	4,213
Miscellaneous...	44,323	+0.3	21.0	1,864
Burglary	917,464	-8.6	100.0	2,661
By location				
Residence (dwelling)...	576,607	-40.7	62.8	8,290
Residence, night	195,884	-5.9	21.4	2,345
Residence, day	290,909	-12.0	31.7	2,507
Residence, unknown..	89,814	-22.8	9.8	3,439
Nonresidence (store, office, etc.)	340,857	-13.1	37.2	8,781
Nonresidence, night..	157,327	+0.8	17.1	2,667
Nonresidence, day	125,554	+1.5	13.7	2,510
Nonresidence, unknown..	57,976	-15.4	6.3	3,604
Larceny-theft (except motor vehicle theft).........................	4,132,566	-1.8	100.0	1,162
By type				
Pocket-picking..	23,954	+10.3	0.6	1,235
Purse-snatching..	15,087	-6.2	0.4	651
Shoplifting	904,975	+1.2	21.9	338
From motor vehicles (except accessories)	1,121,083	-1.6	27.1	1,012
Motor vehicle accessories	264,720	+1.0	6.4	690
Bicycles	125,136	-2.9	3.0	569
From buildings	404,734	-6.1	9.8	1,663
From coin-operated machines	9,204	-0.8	0.2	829
All others	1,263,673	-3.3	30.6	1,888
By value				
Over $200..	1,956,531	-0.7	47.3	2,395
$50 to $200...	877,125	-2.4	21.2	107
Under $50..	1,298,910	-3.0	31.4	14
Motor Vehicle Theft..	612,187	-3.8	NA	8,886

NA = Not available.
X = Not applicable.
* = Less than one-tenth of one percent.
[1]Because of rounding, the percentages may not add to 100.0.
[2]The rape figure in this table is an aggregate total of the data submitted using both the revised and legacy Uniform Crime Reporting definitions. See the chapter notes for further explanation.

Table 9. Property Stolen and Recovered, by Type and Value, 2019

(Dollars, percent; 14,165 agencies; 2019 estimated population 285,731,352.)

Type of property	Value of property (dollars)		Percent recovered
	Stolen	Recovered	
Total	$13,339,804,036	$3,861,187,443	28.9
Currency, notes, etc.	1,423,559,757	36,980,933	2.6
Jewelry and precious metals.................................	1,057,763,740	36,890,088	3.5
Clothing and furs..	383,191,187	31,171,004	8.1
Locally stolen motor vehicles...............................	5,752,240,315	3,228,870,193	56.1
Office equipment..	420,417,080	23,237,884	5.5
Televisions, radios, stereos, etc............................	323,393,740	14,009,033	4.3
Firearms..	116,159,390	13,495,262	11.6
Household goods...	186,264,170	8,179,579	4.4
Consumable goods..	160,368,125	13,380,144	8.3
Livestock...	14,350,714	1,570,468	10.9
Miscellaneous	3,502,095,818	453,402,855	12.9

Table 10. Number and Percent of Offenses Cleared by Arrest or Exceptional Means, by Population Group, 2019

(Number, percent.)

Population group	Violent crime	Murder and nonnegligent manslaughter	Rape[1]	Robbery	Aggravated assault	Property crime	Burglary	Larceny-theft	Motor vehicle theft	Arson[2]	Number of agencies	Estimated population, 2019
Total, All Agencies												
Offenses known	1,105,563	14,325	124,817	239,643	726,778	6,203,201	981,264	4,533,178	655,778	32,981	15,008	297,524,524
Percent cleared by arrest..............	45.5	61.4	32.9	30.5	52.3	17.2	14.1	18.4	13.8	23.8		
Total Cities												
Offenses known	878,923	11,020	92,241	209,959	565,703	4,976,072	733,199	3,693,498	523,739	25,636	10,779	201,853,210
Percent cleared by arrest..............	43.5	59.2	30.8	29.7	50.4	17.0	13.6	18.3	12.6	22.6		
Group I (250,000 and over)												
Offenses known	422,438	5,693	34,899	119,642	262,204	1,853,997	280,302	1,320,696	242,429	10,570	85	59,934,909
Percent cleared by arrest..............	38.2	57.6	29.5	27.1	44.0	11.4	11.2	11.7	9.8	16.5		
1,000,000 and over (Group I subset)												
Offenses known	167,116	1,717	13,310	50,754	101,335	626,897	90,293	451,107	82,104	3,393	10	25,098,940
Percent cleared by arrest..............	42.5	67.3	33.8	31.0	49.0	11.6	11.7	12.0	9.4	12.7		
500,000 to 999,999 (Group I subset)												
Offenses known	144,314	2,289	10,822	39,402	91,801	685,236	106,192	487,358	88,038	3,648	26	18,474,842
Percent cleared by arrest..............	35.6	54.7	28.0	24.4	40.8	10.2	10.7	10.2	9.5	19.1		
250,000 to 499,999 (Group I subset)												
Offenses known	111,008	1,687	10,767	29,486	69,068	541,864	83,817	382,231	72,287	3,529	49	16,361,127
Percent cleared by arrest..............	35.1	51.5	25.6	23.8	41.0	12.8	11.2	13.5	10.7	17.3		
Group II (100,000 to 249,999)												
Offenses known	140,059	1,817	14,997	33,820	89,425	848,193	125,498	619,505	99,211	3,979	217	31,723,575
Percent cleared by arrest..............	43.3	60.9	30.6	29.9	50.2	15.4	12.8	16.4	12.1	25.9		
Group III (50,000 to 99,999)												
Offenses known	107,657	1,155	12,721	24,308	69,473	725,084	104,499	547,385	69,667	3,533	467	32,634,179
Percent cleared by arrest..............	48.8	60.7	34.0	33.9	56.5	18.9	14.2	20.5	13.7	24.3		
Group IV (25,000 to 49,999)												
Offenses known	75,927	937	10,486	14,925	49,579	575,373	80,395	446,492	45,900	2,586	827	28,786,886
Percent cleared by arrest..............	48.7	58.2	30.2	34.5	56.7	22.2	15.0	24.1	15.6	25.7		
Group V (10,000 to 24,999)												
Offenses known	66,748	783	9,561	10,148	46,256	521,268	76,010	406,489	36,529	2,240	1,689	26,893,861
Percent cleared by arrest..............	52.7	64.0	33.0	36.7	60.1	25.3	16.8	27.5	19.0	30.4		
Group VI (under 10,000)												
Offenses known	66,094	635	9,577	7,116	48,766	452,157	66,495	352,931	30,003	2,728	7,494	21,879,800
Percent cleared by arrest..............	53.8	62.0	30.0	40.1	60.3	23.9	18.8	25.0	22.3	29.9		
Metropolitan Counties												
Offenses known	180,344	2,475	23,744	27,531	126,594	1,003,685	183,893	706,656	107,686	5,450	1,905	72,761,754
Percent cleared by arrest..............	52.9	69.4	39.4	35.1	59.0	17.9	15.4	18.6	17.5	27.8		
Nonmetropolitan Counties												
Offenses known	46,296	830	8,832	2,153	34,481	223,444	64,172	133,024	24,353	1,895	2,324	22,909,560
Percent cleared by arrest..............	54.6	66.9	36.9	40.3	59.8	18.1	15.7	18.2	22.6	29.0		
Suburban Areas[3]												
Offenses known	305,904	3,834	41,324	50,446	210,300	2,020,200	317,024	1,507,725	185,517	9,934	8,144	129,507,894
Percent cleared by arrest..............	52.7	66.6	36.6	35.9	59.7	20.5	15.9	21.8	17.2	28.2		

[1]The figures shown in the rape column include only those reported by law enforcement agencies that used the revised Uniform Crime Reporting definition of rape.
[2]Not all agencies submit reports for arson to the FBI. As a result, the number of reports the FBI uses to compute the percent of offenses cleared for arson is less than the number it uses to compute the percent of offenses cleared for all other offenses.
[3]Suburban area includes law enforcement agencies in cities with less than 50,000 inhabitants and county law enforcement agencies that are within a Metropolitan Statistical Area. Suburban area excludes all metropolitan agencies associated with a principal city. The agencies associated with suburban areas also appear in other groups within this table.

Table 11. Estimated Number of Arrests, 2019

(Number.)

Offense	Arrests
Total[1]	10,085,207
Violent crime[2]	495,871
Murder and nonnegligent manslaughter	11,060
Rape[3]	24,986
Robbery	74,547
Aggravated assault	385,278
Property crime[2]	1,074,367
Burglary	171,590
Larceny-theft	813,073
Motor vehicle theft	80,636
Arson	9,068
Other assaults	1,025,711
Forgery and counterfeiting	45,183
Fraud	112,707
Embezzlement	13,497
Stolen property; buying, receiving, possessing	88,272
Vandalism	180,501
Weapons; carrying, possessing, etc.	153,161
Prostitution and commercialized vice	26,713
Sex offenses (except forcible rape and prostitution)	40,796
Drug abuse violations	1,558,862
Gambling	2,458
Offenses against the family and children	85,687
Driving under the influence	1,024,508
Liquor laws	175,548
Drunkenness	316,032
Disorderly conduct	310,331
Vagrancy	21,896
All other offenses (except traffic)	3,318,453
Suspicion	579
Curfew and loitering law violations	14,653

[1]Does not include suspicion.
[2]Violent crimes are offenses of murder and nonnegligent manslaughter, rape, robbery, and aggravated assault. Property crimes are offenses of burglary, larceny-theft, motor vehicle theft, and arson.
[3]The rape figures in this table are an aggregate total of the data submitted using both the revised and legacy Uniform Crime Reporting definitions.

Table 12. Number and Rate of Arrests, by Geographic Region, 2019

(Number, rate per 100,000 inhabitants.)

Offense charged	United States total (10,831 agencies; population 229,735,355) Total	Rate	Northeast (2,330 agencies; population 35,810,078) Total	Rate	Midwest (2,883 agencies; population 43,951,001) Total	Rate	South (3,792 agencies; population 78,293,710) Total	Rate	West (1,826 agencies; population 71,680,566) Total	Rate
Total[1]	6,917,223	3,011.0	886,938	2,476.8	1,306,691	2,973.1	2,519,358	3,217.8	2,204,236	3,075.1
Violent crime[2]	359,092	156.3	37,356	104.3	56,258	128.0	109,807	140.3	155,671	217.2
Murder and nonnegligent manslaughter	7,711	3.4	652	1.8	1,394	3.2	3,353	4.3	2,312	3.2
Rape[3]	16,966	7.4	2,449	6.8	3,967	9.0	5,484	7.0	5,066	7.1
Robbery	56,854	24.7	6,690	18.7	7,749	17.6	18,874	24.1	23,541	32.8
Aggravated assault	277,561	120.8	27,565	77.0	43,148	98.2	82,096	104.9	124,752	174.0
Property crime[2]	788,636	343.3	106,085	296.2	156,168	355.3	293,751	375.2	232,632	324.5
Burglary	120,242	52.3	12,755	35.6	15,954	36.3	40,230	51.4	51,303	71.6
Larceny-theft	604,287	263.0	88,121	246.1	129,859	295.5	232,526	297.0	153,781	214.5
Motor vehicle theft	57,738	25.1	4,538	12.7	9,259	21.1	19,126	24.4	24,815	34.6
Arson	6,369	2.8	671	1.9	1,096	2.5	1,869	2.4	2,733	3.8
Other assaults	717,793	312.4	104,755	292.5	146,069	332.3	260,246	332.4	206,723	288.4
Forgery and counterfeiting	32,495	14.1	4,861	13.6	5,783	13.2	13,653	17.4	8,198	11.4
Fraud	79,954	34.8	13,032	36.4	17,856	40.6	30,457	38.9	18,609	26.0
Embezzlement	10,003	4.4	866	2.4	1,986	4.5	4,934	6.3	2,217	3.1
Stolen property; buying, receiving, possessing	64,027	27.9	7,367	20.6	12,807	29.1	19,801	25.3	24,052	33.6
Vandalism	128,474	55.9	23,884	66.7	24,702	56.2	31,930	40.8	47,958	66.9
Weapons; carrying, possessing, etc.	110,130	47.9	10,397	29.0	22,185	50.5	37,071	47.3	40,477	56.5
Prostitution and commercialized vice	20,015	8.7	2,021	5.6	1,822	4.1	6,006	7.7	10,166	14.2
Sex offenses (except forcible rape and prostitution)	28,973	12.6	4,248	11.9	4,916	11.2	5,855	7.5	13,954	19.5
Drug abuse violations	1,067,764	464.8	152,508	425.9	176,747	402.1	406,667	519.4	331,842	462.9
Gambling	1,909	0.8	273	0.8	182	0.4	726	0.9	728	1.0
Offenses against the family and children	58,720	25.6	11,747	32.8	10,902	24.8	24,606	31.4	11,465	16.0
Driving under the influence	658,902	286.8	91,365	255.1	136,193	309.9	191,198	244.2	240,146	335.0
Liquor laws	112,467	49.0	8,809	24.6	40,395	91.9	30,286	38.7	32,977	46.0
Drunkenness	219,696	95.6	15,235	42.5	12,284	27.9	118,132	150.9	74,045	103.3
Disorderly conduct	211,960	92.3	42,778	119.5	71,290	162.2	53,522	68.4	44,370	61.9
Vagrancy	16,104	7.0	1,209	3.4	2,323	5.3	3,113	4.0	9,459	13.2
All other offenses (except traffic)	2,219,328	966.0	247,423	690.9	402,626	916.1	873,940	1,116.2	695,339	970.1
Suspicion	329	0.1	100	0.3	32	0.1	80	0.1	117	0.2
Curfew and loitering law violations	10,781	4.7	719	2.0	3,197	7.3	3,657	4.7	3,208	4.5

[1] Does not include suspicion.
[2] Violent crimes are offenses of murder and nonnegligent manslaughter, rape, robbery, and aggravated assault. Property crimes are offenses of burglary, larceny-theft, motor vehicle theft, and arson.
[3] The rape figures in this table are aggregate totals of the data submitted based on both the legacy and revised Uniform Crime Reporting definitions.

Table 13. Number and Rate of Arrests, by Population Group, 2019

(Number, rate per 100,000 inhabitants.)

Offense charged	Total (10,831 agencies; population 229,735,355)		Total cities (7,979 cities; population 159,706,353)		Group I (70 cities, 250,000 and over; population 43,703,387)		Group II (182 cities, 100,000 to 249,999; population 26,636,848)		Group III (389 cities, 50,000 to 99,999; population 27,232,262)		Group IV (689 cities, 25,000 to 49,999; population 24,056,009)	
	Total	Rate	Total	Rate	Total	Rate	Total	Rate	Total	Rate	Total	Rate
Total[2]	6,917,223	3,011.0	5,004,922	3,133.8	1,172,912	2,683.8	830,531	3,118.0	799,672	2,936.5	714,256	2,969.1
Violent crime[3]	359,092	156.3	280,634	175.7	103,922	237.8	54,801	205.7	42,967	157.8	29,934	124.4
Murder and nonnegligent manslaughter.................................	7,711	3.4	5,693	3.6	2,516	5.8	1,139	4.3	666	2.4	555	2.3
Rape[4]	16,966	7.4	12,070	7.6	3,590	8.2	2,041	7.7	1,907	7.0	1,557	6.5
Robbery.............................	56,854	24.7	48,151	30.1	20,899	47.8	9,256	34.7	7,215	26.5	4,903	20.4
Aggravated assault	277,561	120.8	214,720	134.4	76,917	176.0	42,365	159.0	33,179	121.8	22,919	95.3
Property crime[3]	788,636	343.3	646,218	404.6	143,531	328.4	108,980	409.1	109,650	402.6	104,300	433.6
Burglary.............................	120,242	52.3	92,073	57.7	26,367	60.3	17,610	66.1	15,599	57.3	12,246	50.9
Larceny-theft	604,287	263.0	505,838	316.7	100,466	229.9	81,614	306.4	87,196	320.2	86,640	360.2
Motor vehicle theft	57,738	25.1	43,390	27.2	15,290	35.0	8,913	33.5	6,109	22.4	4,741	19.7
Arson.............................	6,369	2.8	4,917	3.1	1,408	3.2	843	3.2	746	2.7	673	2.8
Other assaults.............................	717,793	312.4	552,879	346.2	153,670	351.6	96,157	361.0	88,852	326.3	77,162	320.8
Forgery and counterfeiting.............	32,495	14.1	24,813	15.5	4,404	10.1	4,083	15.3	4,178	15.3	4,108	17.1
Fraud.............................	79,954	34.8	59,417	37.2	11,158	25.5	8,860	33.3	9,718	35.7	9,285	38.6
Embezzlement	10,003	4.4	8,061	5.0	2,017	4.6	1,148	4.3	1,557	5.7	1,377	5.7
Stolen property; buying, receiving, possessing	64,027	27.9	48,895	30.6	15,399	35.2	8,781	33.0	8,591	31.5	6,574	27.3
Vandalism.............................	128,474	55.9	101,046	63.3	27,696	63.4	16,791	63.0	15,987	58.7	14,504	60.3
Weapons; carrying, possessing, etc.	110,130	47.9	82,918	51.9	30,274	69.3	15,026	56.4	11,841	43.5	9,302	38.7
Prostitution and commercialized vice.............................	20,015	8.7	17,588	11.0	12,054	27.6	2,645	9.9	1,241	4.6	850	3.5
Sex offenses (except forcible rape and prostitution).............................	28,973	12.6	21,212	13.3	6,079	13.9	3,701	13.9	3,621	13.3	2,817	11.7
Drug abuse violations...................	1,067,764	464.8	752,471	471.2	156,387	357.8	131,398	493.3	131,982	484.7	107,686	447.6
Gambling.............................	1,909	0.8	1,205	0.8	445	1.0	204	0.8	225	0.8	100	0.4
Offenses against the family and children	58,720	25.6	32,341	20.3	6,596	15.1	5,696	21.4	4,217	15.5	4,547	18.9
Driving under the influence............	658,902	286.8	389,429	243.8	81,407	186.3	55,323	207.7	59,300	217.8	59,372	246.8
Liquor laws	112,467	49.0	88,737	55.6	13,155	30.1	11,405	42.8	11,485	42.2	11,282	46.9
Drunkenness.............................	219,696	95.6	188,238	117.9	28,838	66.0	34,315	128.8	32,197	118.2	27,115	112.7
Disorderly conduct.......................	211,960	92.3	175,498	109.9	24,400	55.8	25,957	97.4	27,164	99.7	28,176	117.1
Vagrancy	16,104	7.0	14,326	9.0	7,098	16.2	2,979	11.2	1,290	4.7	1,295	5.4
All other offenses (except traffic)....	2,219,328	966.0	1,509,280	945.0	342,321	783.3	240,796	904.0	231,946	851.7	212,992	885.4
Suspicion	329	0.1	211	0.1	0	0.0	2	*	11	*	37	0.2
Curfew and loitering law violations	10,781	4.7	9,716	6.1	2,061	4.7	1,485	5.6	1,663	6.1	1,478	6.1

Table 13. Number and Rate of Arrests, by Population Group, 2019—*Continued*

(Number, rate per 100,000 inhabitants.)

Offense charged	Group V (1,355 cities, 10,000 to 24,999; population 21,714,346)		Group VI (5,294 cities, under 10,000; population 16,363,501)		Metropolitan counties (1,230 agencies; population 51,841,134)		Nonmetropolitan counties (1,622 agencies; population 18,187,868)		Suburban areas[1] (5,820 agencies; population 97,421,942)	
	Total	Rate	Total	Rate	Total	Rate	Total	Rate	Total	Rate
Total[2]	708,338	3,262.1	779,213	4,761.9	1,370,463	2,643.6	541,838	2,979.1	2,713,085	2,784.9
Violent crime[3]	25,759	118.6	23,251	142.1	61,801	119.2	16,657	91.6	110,435	113.4
Murder and nonnegligent manslaughter...................................	490	2.3	327	2.0	1,496	2.9	522	2.9	2,251	2.3
Rape[4]...	1,570	7.2	1,405	8.6	3,446	6.6	1,450	8.0	6,183	6.3
Robbery..	3,368	15.5	2,510	15.3	7,929	15.3	774	4.3	15,584	16.0
Aggravated assault	20,331	93.6	19,009	116.2	48,930	94.4	13,911	76.5	86,417	88.7
Property crime[3]...............................	101,498	467.4	78,259	478.3	116,025	223.8	26,393	145.1	297,738	305.6
Burglary..	10,505	48.4	9,746	59.6	20,629	39.8	7,540	41.5	40,785	41.9
Larceny-theft	86,200	397.0	63,722	389.4	83,278	160.6	15,171	83.4	235,319	241.5
Motor vehicle theft	4,184	19.3	4,153	25.4	11,057	21.3	3,291	18.1	19,436	20.0
Arson..	609	2.8	638	3.9	1,061	2.0	391	2.1	2,198	2.3
Other assaults..................................	70,595	325.1	66,443	406.0	121,001	233.4	43,913	241.4	251,819	258.5
Forgery and counterfeiting...............	3,949	18.2	4,091	25.0	5,998	11.6	1,684	9.3	13,438	13.8
Fraud..	8,371	38.6	12,025	73.5	15,770	30.4	4,767	26.2	33,686	34.6
Embezzlement	1,177	5.4	785	4.8	1,589	3.1	353	1.9	3,697	3.8
Stolen property; buying, receiving, possessing	5,116	23.6	4,434	27.1	11,868	22.9	3,264	17.9	23,275	23.9
Vandalism...	13,250	61.0	12,818	.78.3	20,924	40.4	6,504	35.8	44,333	45.5
Weapons; carrying, possessing, etc. .	7,942	36.6	8,533	52.1	21,245	41.0	5,967	32.8	38,587	39.6
Prostitution and commercialized vice	506	2.3	292	1.8	2,308	4.5	119	0.7	3,510	3.6
Sex offenses (except forcible rape and prostitution).............................	2,496	11.5	2,498	15.3	5,879	11.3	1,882	10.3	10,967	11.3
Drug abuse violations.......................	102,599	472.5	122,419	748.1	225,843	435.6	89,450	491.8	443,360	455.1
Gambling..	114	0.5	117	0.7	603	1.2	101	0.6	822	0.8
Offenses against the family and children	4,882	22.5	6,403	39.1	19,510	37.6	6,869	37.8	27,274	28.0
Driving under the influence..............	65,394	301.2	68,633	419.4	181,678	350.5	87,795	482.7	310,392	318.6
Liquor laws	14,743	67.9	26,667	163.0	14,407	27.8	9,323	51.3	44,448	45.6
Drunkenness....................................	26,501	122.0	39,272	240.0	22,232	42.9	9,226	50.7	66,799	68.6
Disorderly conduct	31,277	144.0	38,524	235.4	25,038	48.3	11,424	62.8	80,244	82.4
Vagrancy	930	4.3	734	4.5	1,543	3.0	235	1.3	3,214	3.3
All other offenses (except traffic)......	219,316	1,010.0	261,909	1,600.6	494,274	953.4	215,774	1,186.4	901,402	925.3
Suspicion	64	0.3	97	0.6	71	0.1	47	0.3	196	0.2
Curfew and loitering law violations ..	1,923	8.9	1,106	6.8	927	1.8	138	0.8	3,645	3.7

* = Less than one-tenth of one percent.
[1]Suburban areas include law enforcement agencies in cities with less than 50,000 inhabitants and county law enforcement agencies that are within a Metropolitan Statistical Area. Suburban areas exclude all metropolitan agencies associated with a principal city. The agencies associated with suburban areas also appear in other groups within this table.
[2]Does not include suspicion.
[3]Violent crimes are offenses of murder and nonnegligent manslaughter, forcible rape, robbery, and aggravated assault. Property crimes are offenses of burglary, larceny-theft, motor vehicle theft, and arson.
[4]The rape figures in this table are aggregate totals of the data submitted based on both the legacy and revised Uniform Crime Reporting definitions.

Table 14. Ten-Year Arrest Trends, 2010 and 2019

(Number, percent change; 8,891 agencies; 2019 estimated population 196,355,871; 2010 estimated population 185,356,420.)

Offense charged	Number of persons arrested								
	Total, all ages			Under 18 years of age			18 years of age and over		
	2010	2019	Percent change	2010	2019	Percent change	2010	2019	Percent change
Total[1]	7,595,396	6,000,327	-21.0	960,881	428,053	-55.5	6,634,515	5,572,274	-16.0
Violent crime[2]	320,464	295,421	-7.8	42,211	28,999	-31.3	278,253	266,422	-4.3
Murder and nonnegligent manslaughter	6,019	6,232	+3.5	555	468	-15.7	5,464	5,764	+5.5
Rape[3]	11,999	14,374		1,754	2,494		10,245	11,880	
Robbery	61,150	45,615	-25.4	14,338	9,635	-32.8	46,812	35,980	-23.1
Aggravated assault	241,296	229,200	-5.0	25,564	16,402	-35.8	215,732	212,798	-1.4
Property crime[2]	982,799	691,921	-29.6	227,247	77,161	-66.0	755,552	614,760	-18.6
Burglary	174,468	103,290	-40.8	39,296	12,517	-68.1	135,172	90,773	-32.8
Larceny-theft	761,675	534,836	-29.8	176,335	55,581	-68.5	585,340	479,255	-18.1
Motor vehicle theft	39,709	48,329	+21.7	8,596	7,974	-7.2	31,113	40,355	+29.7
Arson	6,947	5,466	-21.3	3,020	1,089	-63.9	3,927	4,377	+11.5
Other assaults	748,116	616,083	-17.6	121,461	77,359	-36.3	626,655	538,724	-14.0
Forgery and counterfeiting	44,102	28,678	-35.0	1,003	528	-47.4	43,099	28,150	-34.7
Fraud	107,992	71,125	-34.1	3,463	2,369	-31.6	104,529	68,756	-34.2
Embezzlement	10,800	9,153	-15.3	263	374	+42.2	10,537	8,779	-16.7
Stolen property; buying, receiving, possessing	59,261	56,957	-3.9	9,459	5,730	-39.4	49,802	51,227	+2.9
Vandalism	152,085	111,524	-26.7	47,671	20,131	-57.8	104,414	91,393	-12.5
Weapons; carrying, possessing, etc.	89,968	91,440	+1.6	18,181	9,769	-46.3	71,787	81,671	+13.8
Prostitution and commercialized vice	27,780	13,496	-51.4	543	196	-63.9	27,237	13,300	-51.2
Sex offenses (except forcible rape and prostitution)	41,298	25,684	-37.8	7,813	4,237	-45.8	33,485	21,447	-36.0
Drug abuse violations	935,117	927,704	-0.8	100,611	49,841	-50.5	834,506	877,863	+5.2
Gambling	2,402	1,514	-37.0	142	117	-17.6	2,260	1,397	-38.2
Offenses against the family and children	69,657	50,957	-26.8	2,421	1,877	-22.5	67,236	49,080	-27.0
Driving under the influence	786,469	546,213	-30.5	7,131	3,092	-56.6	779,338	543,121	-30.3
Liquor laws	312,762	98,455	-68.5	61,565	15,508	-74.8	251,197	82,947	-67.0
Drunkenness	340,974	186,298	-45.4	8,484	2,076	-75.5	332,490	184,222	-44.6
Disorderly conduct	335,720	186,342	-44.5	82,555	32,962	-60.1	253,165	153,380	-39.4
Vagrancy	16,898	15,000	-11.2	824	227	-72.5	16,074	14,773	-8.1
All other offenses (except traffic)	2,169,047	1,966,945	-9.3	176,148	86,083	-51.1	1,992,899	1,880,862	-5.6
Suspicion	634	224	-64.7	80	14	-82.5	554	210	-62.1
Curfew and loitering law violations	41,685	9,417	-77.4	41,685	9,417	-77.4	NA	NA	NA

NA = Not available.

[1] Does not include suspicion.

[2] Violent crimes are offenses of murder and nonnegligent manslaughter, rape, robbery, and aggravated assault. Property crimes are offenses of burglary, larceny-theft, motor vehicle theft, and arson.

[3] The 2010 rape figures are based on the legacy definition, and the 2019 rape figures are aggregate totals based on both the legacy and revised Uniform Crime Reporting definitions. For this reason, a percent change is not provided.

Table 15. Five-Year Arrest Trends, by Age, 2015 and 2019

(Number, percent change; 9,656 agencies; 2019 estimated population 201,599,471; 2015 estimated population 197,695,401.)

Offense charged	Number of persons arrested								
	Total, all ages			Under 18 years of age			18 years of age and over		
	2015	2019	Percent change	2015	2019	Percent change	2015	2019	Percent change
Total[1]	6,611,598	6,146,623	-7.0	562,729	431,375	-23.3	6,048,869	5,715,248	-5.5
Violent crime[2]	301,429	303,801	+0.8	29,987	29,496	-1.6	271,442	274,305	+1.1
Murder and nonnegligent manslaughter ...	6,254	6,620	+5.9	437	518	+18.5	5,817	6,102	+4.9
Rape[3]	13,794	14,816	+7.4	2,229	2,544	+14.1	11,565	12,272	+6.1
Robbery	53,591	46,537	-13.2	9,936	9,914	-0.2	43,655	36,623	-16.1
Aggravated assault	227,790	235,828	+3.5	17,385	16,520	-5.0	210,405	219,308	+4.2
Property crime[2]	912,536	705,257	-22.7	131,612	78,229	-40.6	780,924	627,028	-19.7
Burglary	134,310	105,699	-21.3	22,307	13,064	-41.4	112,003	92,635	-17.3
Larceny-theft	726,267	542,323	-25.3	99,528	55,457	-44.3	626,739	486,866	-22.3
Motor vehicle theft	46,430	51,698	+11.3	8,007	8,634	+7.8	38,423	43,064	+12.1
Arson	5,529	5,537	+0.1	1,770	1,074	-39.3	3,759	4,463	+18.7
Other assaults	658,483	627,873	-4.6	82,257	76,546	-6.9	576,226	551,327	-4.3
Forgery and counterfeiting	33,036	29,569	-10.5	635	552	-13.1	32,401	29,017	-10.4
Fraud	80,686	71,636	-11.2	2,546	2,260	-11.2	78,140	69,376	-11.2
Embezzlement	10,269	8,967	-12.7	373	375	+0.5	9,896	8,592	-13.2
Stolen property; buying, receiving, possessing	55,332	57,620	+4.1	6,419	5,724	-10.8	48,913	51,896	+6.1
Vandalism	120,552	113,162	-6.1	26,823	20,263	-24.5	93,729	92,899	-0.9
Weapons; carrying, possessing, etc.	85,497	93,928	+9.9	11,551	9,779	-15.3	73,946	84,149	+13.8
Prostitution and commercialized vice	18,502	11,600	-37.3	268	101	-62.3	18,234	11,499	-36.9
Sex offenses (except forcible rape and prostitution)	29,855	25,261	-15.4	5,308	4,188	-21.1	24,547	21,073	-14.2
Drug abuse violations	901,591	953,535	+5.8	61,084	49,305	-19.3	840,507	904,230	+7.6
Gambling	2,058	1,576	-23.4	189	138	-27.0	1,869	1,438	-23.1
Offenses against the family and children ...	61,356	53,467	-12.9	1,997	1,982	-0.8	59,359	51,485	-13.3
Driving under the influence	639,378	583,840	-8.7	4,032	3,260	-19.1	635,346	580,580	-8.6
Liquor laws	166,853	102,327	-38.7	27,353	15,904	-41.9	139,500	86,423	-38.0
Drunkenness	269,816	209,130	-22.5	3,712	2,117	-43.0	266,104	207,013	-22.2
Disorderly conduct	227,862	193,178	-15.2	41,421	33,277	-19.7	186,441	159,901	-14.2
Vagrancy	14,837	12,102	-18.4	590	236	-60.0	14,247	11,866	-16.7
All other offenses (except traffic)	2,002,856	1,979,056	-1.2	105,758	87,905	-16.9	1,897,098	1,891,151	-0.3
Suspicion	926	216	-76.7	65	11	-83.1	861	205	-76.2
Curfew and loitering law violations	18,814	9,738	-48.2	18,814	9,738	-48.2	NA	NA	NA

NA = Not available.
[1]Does not include suspicion.
[2]Violent crimes are offenses of murder and nonnegligent manslaughter, rape, robbery, and aggravated assault. Property crimes are offenses of burglary, larceny-theft, motor vehicle theft, and arson.
[3]The rape figures in this table are aggregate totals of the data submitted based on both the legacy and revised Uniform Crime Reporting definitions.

Table 16. Current Year Over Previous Year Arrest Trends, 2018–2019

(Number, percent change; 9,752 agencies; 2019 estimated population 208,476,526; 2018 estimated population 207,708,086.)

	Number of persons arrested											
	Total, all ages			Under 15 years of age			Under 18 years of age			18 years of age and over		
Offense charged	2018	2019	Percent change	2018	2019	Percent change	2018	2019	Percent change	2018	2019	Percent change
Total[1]	6,507,396	6,266,826	-3.7	137,873	144,430	+4.8	462,625	447,119	-3.4	6,044,771	5,819,707	-3.7
Violent crime[2]	333,280	330,199	-0.9	9,624	9,999	+3.9	32,060	32,439	+1.2	301,220	297,760	-1.1
Murder and nonnegligent manslaughter ...	6,966	6,942	-0.3	59	69	+16.9	560	547	-2.3	6,406	6,395	-0.2
Rape[3]	15,943	15,550	-2.5	1,146	1,180	+3.0	2,730	2,686	-1.6	13,213	12,864	-2.6
Robbery	54,841	52,388	-4.5	2,159	2,488	+15.2	10,859	11,408	+5.1	43,982	40,980	-6.8
Aggravated assault	255,530	255,319	-0.1	6,260	6,262	*	17,911	17,798	-0.6	237,619	237,521	*
Property crime[2]	751,830	725,934	-3.4	24,827	24,341	-2.0	86,530	80,588	-6.9	665,300	645,346	-3.0
Burglary	115,538	109,691	-5.1	4,347	4,345	*	14,412	13,161	-8.7	101,126	96,530	-4.5
Larceny-theft	572,801	556,357	-2.9	17,488	16,954	-3.1	61,757	57,391	-7.1	511,044	498,966	-2.4
Motor vehicle theft	57,392	53,995	-5.9	2,280	2,388	+4.7	9,141	8,885	-2.8	48,251	45,110	-6.5
Arson	6,099	5,891	-3.4	712	654	-8.1	1,220	1,151	-5.7	4,879	4,740	-2.8
Other assaults	652,952	644,473	-1.3	32,478	34,904	+7.5	78,790	79,903	+1.4	574,162	564,570	-1.7
Forgery and counterfeiting.........	32,269	29,905	-7.3	137	89	-35.0	704	566	-19.6	31,565	29,339	-7.1
Fraud	74,544	73,124	-1.9	530	578	+9.1	2,392	2,415	+1.0	72,152	70,709	-2.0
Embezzlement	9,642	9,292	-3.6	16	23	+43.8	396	380	-4.0	9,246	8,912	-3.6
Stolen property; buying, receiving, possessing	61,966	58,578	-5.5	1,341	1,288	-4.0	6,309	6,012	-4.7	55,657	52,566	-5.6
Vandalism	116,231	117,479	+1.1	7,753	9,093	+17.3	20,113	20,860	+3.7	96,118	96,619	+0.5
Weapons; carrying, possessing, etc.	101,562	100,805	-0.7	3,072	3,139	+2.2	10,462	10,737	+2.6	91,100	90,068	-1.1
Prostitution and commercialized vice.........	17,031	15,828	-7.1	29	22	-24.1	129	105	-18.6	16,902	15,723	-7.0
Sex offenses (except forcible rape and prostitution)............	28,057	26,533	-5.4	2,230	2,196	-1.5	4,737	4,495	-5.1	23,320	22,038	-5.5
Drug abuse violations.................	1,044,876	969,293	-7.2	9,971	10,037	+0.7	57,734	51,048	-11.6	987,142	918,245	-7.0
Gambling.......................................	1,431	1,637	+14.4	15	9	-40.0	68	80	+17.6	1,363	1,557	+14.2
Offenses against the family and children ...	55,647	51,192	-8.0	713	742	+4.1	2,031	1,972	-2.9	53,616	49,220	-8.2
Driving under the influence........	610,062	602,319	-1.3	71	79	+11.3	3,281	3,288	+0.2	606,781	599,031	-1.3
Liquor laws	113,734	103,181	-9.3	2,392	2,454	+2.6	17,170	15,711	-8.5	96,564	87,470	-9.4
Drunkenness.................................	216,510	203,319	-6.1	351	313	-10.8	2,266	2,133	-5.9	214,244	201,186	-6.1
Disorderly conduct	198,993	196,190	-1.4	14,060	14,991	+6.6	34,060	34,425	+1.1	164,933	161,765	-1.9
Vagrancy	14,321	12,743	-11.0	103	77	-25.2	392	250	-36.2	13,929	12,493	-10.3
All other offenses (except traffic)...............	2,061,684	1,984,816	-3.7	24,956	26,695	+7.0	92,227	89,726	-2.7	1,969,457	1,895,090	-3.8
Suspicion	400	292	-27.0	10	7	-30.0	32	15	-53.1	368	277	-24.7
Curfew and loitering law violations...........	10,774	9,986	-7.3	3,204	3,361	+4.9	10,774	9,986	-7.3	NA	NA	NA

NA = Not available.
* = Less than one-tenth of one percent.
[1]Does not include suspicion.
[2]Violent crimes are offenses of murder and nonnegligent manslaughter, rape, robbery, and aggravated assault. Property crimes are offenses of burglary, larceny-theft, motor vehicle theft, and arson.
[3]The rape figures in this table are aggregate totals of the data submitted based on both the legacy and revised Uniform Crime Reporting definitions.

Table 17. Full-Time Law Enforcement Employees,[1] by Region and Geographic Division and Population Group, 2019

(Number, rate per 1,000 inhabitants.)

Region/geographic division	Total (10,247 cities; population 196,900,226)	Group I (85 cities, 250,000 and over; population 62,520,440)	Group II (207 cities, 100,000 to 249,999; population 30,396,345)	Group III (427 cities, 50,000 to 99,999; population 29,799,314)	Group IV (788 cities, 25,000 to 49,999; population 27,147,744)	Group V (1,644 cities, 10,000 to 24,999; population 26,146,921)
Total						
Number of employees	569,819	209,882	64,904	61,893	57,795	61,106
Average number of employees per 1,000 inhabitants	2.9	3.4	2.1	2.1	2.1	2.3
Northeast						
Number of employees	158,999	67,819	8,052	15,640	18,733	18,713
Average number of employees per 1,000 inhabitants	3.6	5.8	2.9	2.4	2.2	2.2
New England						
Number of employees	33,586	2,922	4,020	6,216	7,322	7,054
Average number of employees per 1,000 inhabitants	2.6	4.2	2.9	2.3	2.3	2.3
Middle Atlantic						
Number of employees	125,413	64,897	4,032	9,424	11,411	11,659
Average number of employees per 1,000 inhabitants	4.0	5.9	2.9	2.5	2.2	2.1
Midwest						
Number of employees	103,578	34,720	8,237	12,874	12,126	14,394
Average number of employees per 1,000 inhabitants	2.6	3.8	2.0	1.8	1.9	2.1
East North Central						
Number of employees	68,219	27,075	4,453	8,186	8,705	8,711
Average number of employees per 1,000 inhabitants	2.7	4.3	2.0	1.9	1.9	2.0
West North Central						
Number of employees	35,359	7,645	3,784	4,688	3,421	5,683
Average number of employees per 1,000 inhabitants	2.5	2.8	2.0	1.7	1.9	2.1
South						
Number of employees	190,329	55,052	28,746	18,297	18,389	21,229
Average number of employees per 1,000 inhabitants	3.2	2.8	2.5	2.5	2.6	2.9
South Atlantic						
Number of employees	88,165	22,582	13,187	10,967	9,166	9,598
Average number of employees per 1,000 inhabitants	3.5	3.4	2.6	2.6	2.7	3.1
East South Central						
Number of employees	33,367	6,548	4,931	2,110	4,167	4,335
Average number of employees per 1,000 inhabitants	3.6	2.8	3.0	2.6	2.7	3.0
West South Central						
Number of employees	68,797	25,922	10,628	5,220	5,056	7,296
Average number of employees per 1,000 inhabitants	2.8	2.4	2.1	2.3	2.3	2.7
West						
Number of employees	116,913	52,291	19,869	15,082	8,547	6,770
Average number of employees per 1,000 inhabitants	2.2	2.4	1.7	1.7	1.7	2.0
Mountain						
Number of employees	41,859	18,575	5,762	4,594	3,171	2,391
Average number of employees per 1,000 inhabitants	2.4	2.4	2.0	1.9	1.7	2.2
Pacific						
Number of employees	75,054	33,716	14,107	10,488	5,376	4,379
Average number of employees per 1,000 inhabitants	2.1	2.4	1.6	1.6	1.7	1.9

(Number, rate per 1,000 inhabitants.)

Region/geographic division	Group VI (7,096 cities, under 10,000; population 20,889,462)	Total city agencies	2019 estimated city population	County[2] (3,000 agencies; population 91,457,371)	Total city and county agencies	2019 estimated total agency population	Suburban areas[3] (7,079 agencies; population 123,692,820)
Total							
Number of employees	114,239	10,247	196,900,226	433,451	13,247	288,357,597	468,532
Average number of employees per 1,000 inhabitants	5.5			4.7			3.8
Northeast							
Number of employees	30,042	2,526	44,387,838				
Average number of employees per 1,000 inhabitants	4.8						
New England							
Number of employees	6,052	781	12,741,851				
Average number of employees per 1,000 inhabitants	3.5						
Middle Atlantic							
Number of employees	23,990	1,745	31,645,987				
Average number of employees per 1,000 inhabitants	5.3						
Midwest							
Number of employees	21,227	2,679	39,233,426				
Average number of employees per 1,000 inhabitants	3.7						
East North Central							
Number of employees	11,089	1,446	24,836,151				
Average number of employees per 1,000 inhabitants	3.5						
West North Central							
Number of employees	10,138	1,233	14,397,275				
Average number of employees per 1,000 inhabitants	3.9						
South							
Number of employees	48,616	3,659	59,614,470				
Average number of employees per 1,000 inhabitants	7.3						
South Atlantic							
Number of employees	22,665	1,582	25,223,887				
Average number of employees per 1,000 inhabitants	8.2						
East South Central							
Number of employees	11,276	852	9,391,674				
Average number of employees per 1,000 inhabitants	6.9						
West South Central							
Number of employees	14,675	1,225	24,998,909				
Average number of employees per 1,000 inhabitants	6.4						
West							
Number of employees	14,354	1,383	53,664,492				
Average number of employees per 1,000 inhabitants	6.5						
Mountain							
Number of employees	7,366	612	17,181,579				
Average number of employees per 1,000 inhabitants	6.6						
Pacific							
Number of employees	6,988	771	36,482,913				
Average number of employees per 1,000 inhabitants	6.3						

[1] Full-time law enforcement employees include civilians.
[2] The designation county is a combination of both metropolitan and nonmetropolitan counties.
[3] Suburban areas include law enforcement agencies in cities with less than 50,000 inhabitants and county law enforcement agencies that are within a Metropolitan Statistical Area. Suburban areas exclude all metropolitan agencies associated with a principal city. The agencies associated with suburban areas also appear in other groups within this table.

Table 18. Full-Time Law Enforcement Officers, by Region, Geographic Division, and Population Group, 2019

(Number, rate per 1,000 inhabitants.)

Region/geographic division	Total (10,247 cities; population 196,900,226)	Group I (85 cities, 250,000 and over; population 62,520,440)	Group II (207 cities, 100,000 to 249,999; population 30,396,345)	Group III (427 cities, 50,000 to 99,999; population 29,799,314)	Group IV (788 cities, 25,000 to 49,999; population 27,147,744)	Group V (1,644 cities, 10,000 to 24,999; population 26,146,921)
Total						
Number of officers	443,173	160,606	49,987	48,113	46,485	49,861
Average number of officers per 1,000 inhabitants	2.3	2.6	1.6	1.6	1.7	1.9
Northeast						
Number of officers	125,176	49,224	6,853	12,975	15,848	16,006
Average number of officers per 1,000 inhabitants	2.8	4.2	2.5	2.0	1.9	1.8
New England						
Number of officers	27,416	2,143	3,488	5,210	6,089	5,708
Average number of officers per 1,000 inhabitants	2.2	3.1	2.5	2.0	1.9	1.9
Middle Atlantic						
Number of officers	97,760	47,081	3,365	7,765	9,759	10,298
Average number of officers per 1,000 inhabitants	3.1	4.3	2.5	2.1	1.8	1.8
Midwest						
Number of officers	86,159	29,721	6,763	10,395	9,843	11,972
Average number of officers per 1,000 inhabitants	2.2	3.3	1.6	1.5	1.5	1.7
East North Central						
Number of officers	57,919	23,850	3,713	6,642	7,108	7,335
Average number of officers per 1,000 inhabitants	2.3	3.8	1.7	1.6	1.6	1.7
West North Central						
Number of officers	28,240	5,871	3,050	3,753	2,735	4,637
Average number of officers per 1,000 inhabitants	2.0	2.2	1.6	1.4	1.5	1.7
South						
Number of officers	147,357	43,069	22,183	14,216	14,559	16,816
Average number of officers per 1,000 inhabitants	2.5	2.2	1.9	1.9	2.0	2.3
South Atlantic						
Number of officers	68,818	17,371	10,275	8,529	7,370	7,712
Average number of officers per 1,000 inhabitants	2.7	2.6	2.0	2.0	2.1	2.5
East South Central						
Number of officers	26,143	5,263	3,897	1,730	3,341	3,517
Average number of officers per 1,000 inhabitants	2.8	2.2	2.4	2.1	2.2	2.5
West South Central						
Number of officers	52,396	20,435	8,011	3,957	3,848	5,587
Average number of officers per 1,000 inhabitants	2.1	1.9	1.6	1.7	1.8	2.1
West						
Number of officers	84,481	38,592	14,188	10,527	6,235	5,067
Average number of officers per 1,000 inhabitants	1.6	1.7	1.2	1.2	1.2	1.5
Mountain						
Number of officers	30,238	13,341	4,272	3,245	2,414	1,843
Average number of officers per 1,000 inhabitants	1.8	1.7	1.5	1.3	1.3	1.7
Pacific						
Number of officers	54,243	25,251	9,916	7,282	3,821	3,224
Average number of officers per 1,000 inhabitants	1.5	1.8	1.1	1.1	1.2	1.4

Table 18. Full-Time Law Enforcement Officers, by Region, Geographic Division, and Population Group, 2019—*Continued*

(Number, rate per 1,000 inhabitants.)

Region/geographic division	Group VI (7,096 cities, under 10,000; population 20,889,462)	Total city agencies	2019 estimated city population	County[1] (3,000 agencies; population 91,457,371)	Total city and county agencies	2019 estimated total agency population	Suburban areas[2] (7,079 agencies; population 123,692,820)
Total							
Number of officers	88,121	10,247	196,900,226	254,022	13,247	288,357,597	307,028
Average number of officers per 1,000 inhabitants	4.2			2.8			2.5
Northeast							
Number of officers	24,270	2,526	44,387,838				
Average number of officers per 1,000 inhabitants	3.9						
New England							
Number of officers	4,778	781	12,741,851				
Average number of officers per 1,000 inhabitants	2.8						
Middle Atlantic							
Number of officers	19,492	1,745	31,645,987				
Average number of officers per 1,000 inhabitants	4.3						
Midwest							
Number of officers	17,465	2,679	39,233,426				
Average number of officers per 1,000 inhabitants	3.0						
East North Central							
Number of officers	9,271	1,446	24,836,151				
Average number of officers per 1,000 inhabitants	2.9						
West North Central							
Number of officers	8,194	1,233	14,397,275				
Average number of officers per 1,000 inhabitants	3.2						
South							
Number of officers	36,514	3,659	59,614,470				
Average number of officers per 1,000 inhabitants	5.5						
South Atlantic							
Number of officers	17,561	1,582	25,223,887				
Average number of officers per 1,000 inhabitants	6.3						
East South Central							
Number of officers	8,395	852	9,391,674				
Average number of officers per 1,000 inhabitants	5.1						
West South Central							
Number of officers	10,558	1,225	24,998,909				
Average number of officers per 1,000 inhabitants	4.6						
West							
Number of officers	9,872	1,383	53,664,492				
Average number of officers per 1,000 inhabitants	4.5						
Mountain							
Number of officers	5,123	612	17,181,579				
Average number of officers per 1,000 inhabitants	4.6						
Pacific							
Number of officers	4,749	771	36,482,913				
Average number of officers per 1,000 inhabitants	4.3						

[1]The designation county is a combination of both metropolitan and nonmetropolitan counties.
[2]Suburban areas include law enforcement agencies in cities with less than 50,000 inhabitants and county law enforcement agencies that are within a Metropolitan Statistical Area. Suburban areas exclude all metropolitan agencies associated with a principal city. The agencies associated with suburban areas also appear in other groups within this table.

Table 19. Full-Time Law Enforcement Employees, by Selected State and City, 2019

(Number.)

State/city	Population	Total law enforcement employees	Total officers	Total civilians
ALABAMA				
Abbeville	2,548	14	9	5
Adamsville	4,302	28	15	13
Addison	721	4	4	0
Alabaster	33,620	89	72	17
Albertville	21,611	69	45	24
Alexander City	14,410	67	51	16
Aliceville	2,280	6	5	1
Andalusia	8,699	35	25	10
Anniston	21,391	96	89	7
Arab	8,350	37	27	10
Ardmore	1,450	11	7	4
Argo	4,335	7	6	1
Arley	345	2	2	0
Ashford	2,154	5	4	1
Ashland	1,900	16	11	5
Ashville	2,332	4	4	0
Athens	26,833	56	45	11
Atmore	9,255	36	28	8
Attalla	5,769	28	22	6
Auburn	67,407	150	130	20
Baker Hill	249	4	4	0
Bay Minette	9,427	31	24	7
Bayou La Batre	2,492	18	13	5
Bear Creek	1,038	2	2	0
Berry	1,093	3	3	0
Bessemer	26,402	149	107	42
Birmingham	209,649	1,023	851	172
Boaz	9,680	33	23	10
Brent	4,751	7	7	0
Brighton	2,766	1	1	0
Brilliant	866	1	1	0
Brookside	1,318	8	5	3
Brookwood	1,861	6	6	0
Brundidge	1,923	17	9	8
Calera	14,750	41	32	9
Camden	1,797	10	8	2
Camp Hill	948	5	5	0
Carbon Hill	1,903	9	3	6
Carrollton	950	3	3	0
Cedar Bluff	1,817	5	5	0
Centre	3,517	12	11	1
Centreville	2,623	7	7	0
Chatom	1,185	4	4	0
Cherokee	999	6	6	0
Chickasaw	5,704	23	20	3
Childersburg	4,846	20	18	2
Citronelle	3,887	17	11	6
Clayton	2,839	4	4	0
Clio	1,259	3	3	0
Coaling	1,660	4	4	0
Collinsville	1,959	10	4	6
Columbia	734	2	2	0
Columbiana	4,644	15	11	4
Coosada	1,311	8	5	3
Cordova	1,917	6	4	2
Cottonwood	1,240	3	3	0
Courtland	584	1	1	0
Creola	2,028	31	14	17
Cullman	15,956	71	50	21
Dadeville	3,063	15	14	1
Daphne	27,157	104	69	35
Dauphin Island	1,306	28	12	16
Decatur	54,074	151	139	12
Demopolis	6,639	24	20	4
Dora	1,881	11	7	4
Double Springs	1,024	8	7	1
Douglas	775	5	5	0
Eclectic	1,026	8	7	1
Elba	3,820	23	12	11
Elberta	1,751	11	10	1

Table 19. Full-Time Law Enforcement Employees, by Selected State and City, 2019—*Continued*

(Number.)

State/city	Population	Total law enforcement employees	Total officers	Total civilians
Enterprise	28,463	72	54	18
Eufaula	11,758	59	38	21
Eutaw	2,621	10	9	1
Evergreen	3,572	25	19	6
Excel	637	2	2	0
Fairhope	22,932	64	40	24
Falkville	1,244	6	5	1
Fayette	4,292	12	12	0
Florala	1,894	7	7	0
Florence	40,543	132	106	26
Foley	19,419	94	64	30
Fort Deposit	1,149	5	5	0
Frisco City	1,156	2	2	0
Fultondale	9,344	34	27	7
Gardendale	14,036	41	31	10
Geneva	4,321	13	9	4
Georgiana	1,601	9	6	3
Glencoe	5,133	10	9	1
Gordo	1,609	4	4	0
Grant	915	2	2	0
Greenville	7,485	30	25	5
Guin	2,251	6	6	0
Gulf Shores	12,739	69	48	21
Guntersville	8,517	47	36	11
Gurley	812	6	6	0
Haleyville	3,927	16	11	5
Hamilton	6,547	15	13	2
Harpersville	1,725	8	8	0
Hartford	2,586	15	11	4
Hartselle	14,442	31	30	1
Hayneville	796	4	3	1
Headland	4,738	20	12	8
Heflin	3,427	12	11	1
Helena	19,870	30	25	5
Hillsboro	512	2	2	0
Hokes Bluff	4,248	9	7	2
Hollywood	955	5	4	1
Homewood	25,428	117	81	36
Hoover	85,670	225	188	37
Hueytown	15,290	44	35	9
Huntsville	199,465	648	442	206
Irondale	12,582	41	34	7
Jacksons Gap	813	3	3	0
Jacksonville	12,453	38	30	8
Jasper	13,393	70	50	20
Kimberly	3,383	7	7	0
Kinsey	2,221	2	2	0
LaFayette	2,926	14	13	1
Lake View	2,520	4	3	1
Lanett	6,208	31	29	2
Leeds	12,086	27	26	1
Leesburg	1,017	3	3	0
Leighton	706	9	9	0
Level Plains	2,016	3	3	0
Lexington	705	4	4	0
Lincoln	6,763	21	19	2
Linden	1,873	6	6	0
Lineville	2,247	11	7	4
Lipscomb	2,142	8	3	5
Livingston	3,354	8	4	4
Louisville	456	3	3	0
Loxley	2,695	21	15	6
Lynn	640	2	1	1
Madison	51,375	111	82	29
Margaret	5,105	2	2	0
Marion	3,203	7	6	1
McIntosh	218	8	8	0
Mentone	369	3	2	1
Midfield	5,031	23	17	6
Midland City	2,371	8	4	4
Millport	976	1	1	0

Table 19. Full-Time Law Enforcement Employees, by Selected State and City, 2019—*Continued*

(Number.)

State/city	Population	Total law enforcement employees	Total officers	Total civilians
Millry	500	2	2	0
Mobile	244,775	635	482	153
Monroeville	5,774	33	26	7
Montevallo	6,720	20	16	4
Montgomery	197,315	563	467	96
Moody	13,240	22	21	1
Morris	2,156	6	6	0
Moulton	3,206	11	11	0
Moundville	2,460	10	9	1
Mountain Brook	20,292	74	59	15
Mount Vernon	1,490	5	4	1
Munford	1,360	1	1	0
New Hope	2,912	6	6	0
New Site	754	2	2	0
North Courtland	608	4	4	0
Northport	26,043	67	48	19
Notasulga	814	16	9	7
Oakman	718	1	1	0
Odenville	3,816	9	9	0
Ohatchee	1,151	6	6	0
Oneonta	6,619	21	20	1
Opelika	31,109	99	78	21
Opp	6,403	29	20	9
Orange Beach	6,202	78	53	25
Owens Crossroads	2,082	5	5	0
Oxford	21,131	78	64	14
Parrish	931	3	3	0
Pelham	24,033	85	69	16
Pell City	13,936	42	40	2
Phenix City	36,874	94	71	23
Piedmont	4,555	18	13	5
Pine Hill	862	2	2	0
Pisgah	695	1	1	0
Pleasant Grove	10,101	22	17	5
Prattville	35,857	89	81	8
Priceville	3,761	5	5	0
Prichard	21,405	54	36	18
Ragland	1,700	3	3	0
Rainbow City	9,558	45	29	16
Red Bay	3,051	13	9	4
Red Level	476	2	2	0
Reform	1,550	5	5	0
Riverside	2,325	3	3	0
Roanoke	5,914	28	22	6
Robertsdale	6,978	28	17	11
Rogersville	1,228	5	5	0
Samson	1,865	7	7	0
Saraland	14,763	56	43	13
Sardis City	1,797	5	5	0
Satsuma	6,159	18	14	4
Scottsboro	14,360	74	46	28
Sheffield	8,876	36	27	9
Shorter	396	12	5	7
Silverhill	1,040	7	6	1
Skyline	815	2	1	1
Snead	842	13	13	0
Somerville	769	2	2	0
Southside	8,868	19	14	5
Spanish Fort	9,282	26	22	4
Springville	4,290	11	11	0
Steele	1,077	4	4	0
St. Florian	677	5	5	0
Stevenson	1,941	7	5	2
Sumiton	2,335	18	9	9
Summerdale	1,614	12	11	1
Sylacauga	12,108	39	37	2
Talladega	15,201	45	41	4
Tallassee	4,560	8	8	0
Tarrant	6,131	25	19	6
Thomaston	380	1	1	0
Thomasville	3,879	26	21	5

Table 19. Full-Time Law Enforcement Employees, by Selected State and City, 2019—*Continued*

(Number.)

State/city	Population	Total law enforcement employees	Total officers	Total civilians
Trafford	624	7	7	0
Triana	634	1	1	0
Trinity	2,449	8	8	0
Troy	19,245	80	60	20
Trussville	22,609	77	65	12
Tuscaloosa	102,518	356	279	77
Tuskegee	8,250	32	20	12
Union Springs	3,421	19	12	7
Uniontown	2,211	7	6	1
Valley	9,168	29	26	3
Vance	1,678	5	5	0
Vernon	1,839	8	8	0
Vestavia Hills	34,538	99	96	3
Wadley	725	4	4	0
Wedowee	794	9	8	1
West Blocton	1,233	2	2	0
White Hall	754	7	6	1
Winfield	4,451	14	13	1
York	2,235	4	4	0
ALASKA				
Anchorage	287,731	574	427	147
Bethel	6,544	25	13	12
Bristol Bay Borough	852	9	4	5
Cordova	2,150	9	3	6
Craig	1,313	9	4	5
Dillingham	2,405	17	7	10
Fairbanks	31,493	44	39	5
Haines	2,441	8	3	5
Homer	5,913	20	11	9
Hoonah	792	8	4	4
Juneau	31,810	81	48	33
Kenai	7,862	24	16	8
Ketchikan	8,316	34	23	11
Klawock	822	4	4	0
Kodiak	5,947	43	18	25
Kotzebue	3,272	13	6	7
Nome	3,899	12	10	2
North Pole	2,111	11	9	2
North Slope Borough	9,801	76	45	31
Palmer	7,490	25	15	10
Petersburg	3,181	10	7	3
Sand Point	1,161	6	5	1
Seward	2,732	22	10	12
Sitka	8,512	22	10	12
Skagway	1,159	11	4	7
Soldotna	4,756	17	14	3
St. Paul	498	8	3	5
Unalaska	4,513	21	11	10
Valdez	3,816	12	12	0
Wasilla	10,915	58	24	34
Whittier	203	7	7	0
Wrangell	2,489	12	5	7
ARIZONA				
Apache Junction	42,531	95	61	34
Avondale	87,117	191	134	57
Benson	4,843	21	13	8
Bisbee	5,161	15	11	4
Buckeye	77,904	129	91	38
Bullhead City	40,532	107	68	39
Camp Verde	11,286	35	22	13
Casa Grande	58,366	99	72	27
Chandler	259,881	484	328	156
Chino Valley	12,162	27	22	5
Clarkdale	4,434	11	10	1
Clifton	3,758	13	6	7
Colorado City	4,862	18	10	8
Coolidge	13,138	43	32	11
Cottonwood	12,331	52	29	23
Douglas	15,786	42	30	12

(Number.)

State/city	Population	Total law enforcement employees	Total officers	Total civilians
Eagar	4,897	8	6	2
El Mirage	36,185	68	47	21
Eloy	19,758	38	28	10
Flagstaff	75,013	159	110	49
Florence	26,385	37	29	8
Fredonia	1,296	3	3	0
Gilbert	253,619	409	281	128
Glendale	253,951	550	410	140
Globe	7,323	21	18	3
Goodyear	85,305	154	113	41
Hayden	979	6	6	0
Holbrook	5,098	13	11	2
Huachuca City	1,723	7	5	2
Jerome	459	5	5	0
Kearny	2,170	10	5	5
Kingman	30,600	60	45	15
Lake Havasu City	55,413	109	70	39
Mammoth	1,669	4	3	1
Marana	48,816	125	94	31
Maricopa	50,881	91	67	24
Mesa	518,160	1,202	797	405
Miami	1,768	15	8	7
Nogales	20,112	63	46	17
Oro Valley	45,970	126	98	28
Page	7,588	29	19	10
Paradise Valley	14,733	50	34	16
Parker	3,219	14	11	3
Patagonia	877	4	4	0
Payson	15,760	42	25	17
Peoria	174,571	286	201	85
Phoenix	1,688,722	3,919	2,928	991
Pima	2,530	6	6	0
Pinetop-Lakeside	4,452	17	14	3
Prescott	43,781	91	74	17
Prescott Valley	46,700	92	68	24
Quartzsite	3,776	11	8	3
Safford	9,916	25	22	3
Sahuarita	30,928	55	42	13
San Luis	34,192	59	39	20
Scottsdale	260,464	616	385	231
Sedona	10,373	39	24	15
Show Low	11,401	49	31	18
Sierra Vista	44,310	76	59	17
Snowflake-Taylor	10,173	18	12	6
Somerton	16,771	20	13	7
South Tucson	5,704	17	15	2
Springerville	1,984	8	6	2
St. Johns	3,520	9	6	3
Superior	3,175	15	14	1
Surprise	140,962	198	143	55
Tempe	196,499	480	338	142
Thatcher	5,177	12	11	1
Tolleson	7,399	49	31	18
Tombstone	1,289	9	7	2
Tucson	548,374	1,129	901	228
Wellton	3,048	7	6	1
Wickenburg	7,054	27	21	6
Willcox	3,507	19	11	8
Williams	3,251	23	13	10
Winslow	9,393	34	24	10
Yuma	98,769	256	153	103
ARKANSAS				
Alexander	3,315	8	8	0
Alma	5,888	21	14	7
Altus	729	2	2	0
Amity	675	1	1	0
Arkadelphia	10,451	29	23	6
Ashdown	4,370	14	12	2
Ash Flat	1,095	4	4	0
Atkins	3,037	9	8	1

(Number.)

State/city	Population	Total law enforcement employees	Total officers	Total civilians
Augusta	1,939	7	6	1
Austin	3,973	4	4	0
Bald Knob	2,872	13	8	5
Barling	5,010	11	11	0
Batesville	10,889	25	24	1
Bay	1,805	4	4	0
Bearden	859	1	1	0
Beebe	8,242	21	15	6
Bella Vista	28,931	49	34	15
Benton	37,161	90	68	22
Bentonville	53,434	115	81	34
Berryville	5,547	16	14	2
Bethel Heights	2,810	7	6	1
Black Rock	605	1	1	0
Blytheville	13,468	50	34	16
Bono	2,444	4	4	0
Booneville	3,829	12	8	4
Bradford	732	3	3	0
Brinkley	2,623	18	11	7
Brookland	3,759	6	6	0
Bryant	21,214	54	43	11
Bull Shoals	1,971	4	4	0
Cabot	26,875	54	44	10
Caddo Valley	588	7	4	3
Camden	10,742	40	22	18
Cammack Village	720	4	3	1
Caraway	1,266	3	3	0
Carlisle	2,184	9	5	4
Cave Springs	5,580	7	7	0
Cedarville	1,413	2	2	0
Centerton	16,542	24	22	2
Charleston	2,454	5	5	0
Cherokee Village	4,634	9	8	1
Cherry Valley	583	1	1	0
Clarendon	1,373	4	4	0
Clarksville	9,813	23	19	4
Clinton	2,489	8	7	1
Concord	233	1	1	0
Conway	67,336	172	127	45
Corning	3,093	12	8	4
Cotter	940	2	2	0
Crossett	4,846	27	17	10
Damascus	377	1	1	0
Danville	2,414	7	6	1
Dardanelle	4,555	17	11	6
Decatur	1,813	6	6	0
De Queen	6,593	16	14	2
Dermott	2,517	10	6	4
Des Arc	1,580	6	6	0
DeWitt	3,019	11	7	4
Diamond City	798	1	1	0
Diaz	1,197	3	3	0
Dierks	1,089	4	4	0
Dover	1,434	5	5	0
Dumas	4,084	24	12	12
Dyer	897	2	2	0
Earle	2,201	6	5	1
El Dorado	17,820	67	51	16
Elkins	3,246	8	8	0
England	2,723	11	7	4
Etowah	317	1	1	0
Eudora	1,930	7	5	2
Eureka Springs	2,092	17	12	5
Fairfield Bay	2,202	16	7	9
Farmington	7,387	17	17	0
Fayetteville	88,500	174	126	48
Flippin	1,340	7	7	0
Fordyce	3,745	14	9	5
Forrest City	13,887	40	28	12
Fort Smith	88,041	192	151	41
Gassville	2,156	4	4	0

(Number.)

State/city	Population	Total law enforcement employees	Total officers	Total civilians
Gentry	3,924	11	9	2
Glenwood	2,095	2	2	0
Gosnell	3,148	7	7	0
Gravette	3,443	12	11	1
Greenbrier	5,660	15	10	5
Green Forest	2,763	13	12	1
Greenland	1,450	4	4	0
Greenwood	9,436	23	21	2
Greers Ferry	851	5	4	1
Gurdon	2,069	5	4	1
Guy	782	2	2	0
Hamburg	2,636	7	6	1
Hampton	1,281	3	3	0
Hardy	761	4	4	0
Harrisburg	2,368	7	5	2
Harrison	13,107	43	32	11
Haskell	4,715	8	8	0
Hazen	1,336	7	6	1
Heber Springs	6,912	26	16	10
Helena-West Helena	10,187	24	13	11
Higginson	684	1	1	0
Highfill	656	3	3	0
Highland	1,100	3	3	0
Hope	9,666	36	25	11
Hot Springs	37,263	137	102	35
Hoxie	2,588	4	4	0
Huntington	616	1	1	0
Jacksonville	28,273	62	52	10
Johnson	3,781	8	8	0
Jonesboro	78,261	174	158	16
Judsonia	1,981	4	3	1
Kensett	1,618	3	3	0
Lake City	2,598	4	4	0
Lakeview	715	2	2	0
Lake Village	2,241	16	10	6
Lamar	1,740	3	3	0
Lavaca	2,440	3	3	0
Leachville	1,714	5	4	1
Lepanto	1,803	7	3	4
Lewisville	1,105	2	2	0
Lincoln	2,500	6	6	0
Little Flock	2,791	7	7	0
Little Rock	198,382	713	581	132
Lonoke	4,261	16	12	4
Lowell	9,723	24	19	5
Luxora	1,016	1	1	0
Madison	685	6	3	3
Magnolia	11,440	25	23	2
Malvern	10,946	23	21	2
Mammoth Spring	942	2	2	0
Mansfield	1,101	4	4	0
Marianna	3,398	20	13	7
Marion	12,344	35	31	4
Marked Tree	2,462	12	8	4
Marmaduke	1,264	4	4	0
Marvell	920	7	4	3
Maumelle	18,223	50	38	12
Mayflower	2,489	9	9	0
McCrory	1,513	6	5	1
McGehee	3,681	27	10	17
McRae	661	1	1	0
Mena	5,508	13	12	1
Mineral Springs	1,148	3	2	1
Monette	1,603	4	4	0
Monticello	9,438	29	21	8
Morrilton	6,631	27	24	3
Mountainburg	608	3	3	0
Mountain Home	12,458	37	29	8
Mountain View	2,850	11	10	1
Mulberry	1,644	4	4	0
Murfreesboro	1,533	3	3	0

Table 19. Full-Time Law Enforcement Employees, by Selected State and City, 2019—*Continued*

(Number.)

State/city	Population	Total law enforcement employees	Total officers	Total civilians
Nashville	4,403	17	16	1
Newport	7,485	25	18	7
North Little Rock	66,604	207	175	32
Ola	1,217	4	3	1
Osceola	6,653	35	25	10
Ozark	3,573	13	11	2
Pangburn	580	2	2	0
Paragould	29,245	75	54	21
Paris	3,392	14	9	5
Parkin	991	2	2	0
Pea Ridge	6,230	16	15	1
Perryville	1,454	6	6	0
Piggott	3,569	7	7	0
Pine Bluff	41,505	140	118	22
Plainview	581	1	1	0
Plumerville	773	4	3	1
Pocahontas	6,647	16	15	1
Pottsville	3,332	9	7	2
Prairie Grove	6,595	14	14	0
Prescott	2,985	10	9	1
Quitman	711	4	4	0
Ravenden	443	1	1	0
Redfield	1,564	6	5	1
Rogers	69,168	155	111	44
Rose Bud	483	4	3	1
Russellville	29,446	59	53	6
Salem	1,637	4	4	0
Searcy	23,873	70	51	19
Shannon Hills	4,017	6	6	0
Sheridan	4,954	30	15	15
Sherwood	31,435	97	74	23
Siloam Springs	17,235	53	38	15
Springdale	82,358	204	145	59
Stamps	1,444	4	3	1
Star City	2,058	6	5	1
St. Charles	208	1	1	0
Stuttgart	8,589	33	24	9
Sulphur Springs	534	3	3	0
Swifton	727	2	2	0
Texarkana	29,971	90	79	11
Trumann	7,043	22	16	6
Tuckerman	1,671	4	4	0
Tyronza	734	3	2	1
Van Buren	23,800	64	53	11
Vilonia	4,762	9	9	0
Waldron	3,332	10	9	1
Walnut Ridge	5,019	8	8	0
Ward	5,454	12	10	2
Warren	5,634	19	11	8
Weiner	679	1	1	0
West Fork	2,672	7	6	1
West Memphis	24,442	111	89	22
White Hall	5,014	17	15	2
Wilson	819	1	1	0
Wynne	7,812	21	19	2
CALIFORNIA				
Alameda	78,907	108	74	34
Albany	20,083	31	22	9
Alhambra	84,837	118	76	42
Alturas	2,471	8	7	1
Anaheim	353,915	592	418	174
Anderson	10,545	28	20	8
Angels Camp	3,909	8	7	1
Antioch	112,641	149	106	43
Arcadia	58,899	92	66	26
Arcata	18,332	43	29	14
Arroyo Grande	18,188	30	26	4
Arvin	21,811	26	18	8
Atascadero	30,579	39	28	11
Atherton	7,222	26	17	9

Table 19. Full-Time Law Enforcement Employees, by Selected State and City, 2019—*Continued*

(Number.)

State/city	Population	Total law enforcement employees	Total officers	Total civilians
Atwater	29,632	34	25	9
Auburn	14,201	28	20	8
Avenal	12,991	18	17	1
Azusa	50,405	89	56	33
Bakersfield	388,080	559	380	179
Baldwin Park	75,862	93	70	23
Banning	31,450	44	26	18
Barstow	24,121	57	39	18
Bear Valley	5,507	6	5	1
Beaumont	50,990	59	43	16
Bell	35,759	40	29	11
Bell Gardens	42,366	69	46	23
Belmont	27,272	42	30	12
Belvedere	2,114	7	7	0
Benicia	28,471	47	28	19
Berkeley	122,788	253	159	94
Beverly Hills	34,211	217	131	86
Bishop	3,731	19	12	7
Blythe	19,889	28	18	10
Brawley	26,379	39	26	13
Brea	44,155	86	56	30
Brentwood	65,483	90	60	30
Brisbane	4,746	17	13	4
Broadmoor	4,446	11	10	1
Buena Park	82,627	131	89	42
Burbank	103,738	215	139	76
Burlingame	30,677	57	38	19
Calexico	40,327	34	20	14
California City	14,319	23	14	9
Calipatria	7,387	5	5	0
Calistoga	5,341	13	8	5
Campbell	42,697	70	44	26
Capitola	10,101	27	20	7
Carlsbad	117,220	182	126	56
Carmel	3,877	22	14	8
Cathedral City	55,346	72	50	22
Central Marin	34,793	46	42	4
Ceres	49,134	68	49	19
Chico	95,826	146	95	51
Chino	93,348	160	109	51
Chowchilla	18,792	27	18	9
Chula Vista	275,230	315	232	83
Citrus Heights	88,496	134	84	50
Claremont	36,681	63	39	24
Clayton	12,356	12	10	2
Clearlake	15,400	37	23	14
Cloverdale	8,910	21	13	8
Clovis	114,170	160	100	60
Coalinga	16,356	22	14	8
Colma	1,512	25	19	6
Colton	55,059	80	52	28
Colusa	5,903	7	6	1
Concord	130,615	200	146	54
Corcoran	21,353	32	19	13
Corning	7,537	21	13	8
Corona	170,875	209	143	66
Coronado	21,115	67	47	20
Costa Mesa	114,047	192	127	65
Cotati	7,641	18	12	6
Covina	47,985	78	52	26
Crescent City	6,716	12	11	1
Culver City	39,252	155	111	44
Cypress	49,085	65	51	14
Daly City	107,748	127	101	26
Davis	69,767	92	57	35
Delano	53,002	72	51	21
Del Rey Oaks	1,674	10	10	0
Desert Hot Springs	29,107	32	23	9
Dinuba	24,685	44	34	10
Dixon	20,775	30	25	5
Dos Palos	5,594	13	9	4

(Number.)

State/city	Population	Total law enforcement employees	Total officers	Total civilians
Downey	112,330	161	117	44
East Palo Alto	29,686	42	34	8
El Cajon	103,686	183	120	63
El Centro	44,303	68	44	24
El Cerrito	25,857	45	37	8
Elk Grove	175,492	238	140	98
El Monte	115,830	160	118	42
El Segundo	16,727	79	61	18
Emeryville	12,380	53	39	14
Escalon	7,644	12	11	1
Escondido	153,215	211	154	57
Etna	716	3	3	0
Eureka	26,973	70	47	23
Exeter	10,557	19	17	2
Fairfax	7,569	16	11	5
Fairfield	118,383	183	116	67
Farmersville	10,781	15	14	1
Ferndale	1,363	5	5	0
Firebaugh	8,433	16	11	5
Folsom	79,927	102	74	28
Fontana	215,883	285	188	97
Fort Bragg	7,366	22	15	7
Fortuna	12,317	24	16	8
Foster City	34,624	50	35	15
Fountain Valley	55,858	79	59	20
Fowler	6,904	12	12	0
Fremont	240,887	281	181	100
Fresno	534,285	1,077	806	271
Fullerton	140,194	193	134	59
Galt	26,796	48	33	15
Gardena	59,833	116	89	27
Garden Grove	172,832	239	163	76
Gilroy	60,106	97	64	33
Glendale	202,601	335	231	104
Glendora	52,211	79	50	29
Gonzales	8,408	15	12	3
Grass Valley	12,919	36	29	7
Greenfield	17,809	28	22	6
Gridley	6,618	18	12	6
Grover Beach	13,574	25	17	8
Guadalupe	7,696	13	11	2
Gustine	5,896	7	6	1
Hanford	57,232	87	58	29
Hawthorne	87,305	133	88	45
Hayward	161,588	294	180	114
Healdsburg	12,208	25	17	8
Hemet	86,082	128	90	38
Hercules	25,789	27	24	3
Hermosa Beach	19,460	62	32	30
Hillsborough	11,521	34	24	10
Hollister	40,399	40	33	7
Huntington Beach	201,843	303	196	107
Huntington Park	58,181	85	56	29
Huron	7,359	17	13	4
Imperial	18,090	23	19	4
Indio	92,803	108	68	40
Inglewood	109,386	247	192	55
Ione	8,454	9	9	0
Irvine	292,673	325	224	101
Irwindale	1,469	33	27	6
Jackson	4,797	10	9	1
Kensington	5,407	7	7	0
Kerman	15,223	20	17	3
King City	14,170	22	17	5
Kingsburg	12,123	20	17	3
Laguna Beach	23,020	98	54	44
La Habra	62,416	101	69	32
Lakeport	4,959	12	11	1
Lake Shastina	2,566	2	2	0
La Mesa	59,865	92	62	30
La Palma	15,571	27	20	7

Table 19. Full-Time Law Enforcement Employees, by Selected State and City, 2019—*Continued*

(Number.)

State/city	Population	Total law enforcement employees	Total officers	Total civilians
La Verne	32,344	55	37	18
Lemoore	26,728	41	33	8
Lincoln	48,625	29	21	8
Lindsay	13,708	18	15	3
Livermore	91,418	144	95	49
Livingston	14,607	30	20	10
Lodi	67,612	105	74	31
Lompoc	42,818	56	37	19
Long Beach	467,974	1,203	817	386
Los Alamitos	11,541	21	17	4
Los Altos	30,716	43	30	13
Los Angeles	4,015,546	12,954	10,002	2,952
Los Banos	40,607	62	36	26
Los Gatos	30,793	60	37	23
Madera	66,250	92	66	26
Mammoth Lakes	8,114	15	12	3
Manhattan Beach	35,583	100	62	38
Manteca	83,523	106	74	32
Marina	22,911	34	27	7
Martinez	38,692	43	32	11
Marysville	12,572	26	18	8
McFarland	15,529	14	8	6
Mendota	11,433	16	14	2
Menlo Park	34,871	71	48	23
Merced	83,854	133	93	40
Mill Valley	14,343	27	21	6
Milpitas	82,344	114	88	26
Modesto	216,542	309	205	104
Monrovia	36,730	74	46	28
Montclair	39,787	64	44	20
Montebello	62,650	97	72	25
Monterey	28,337	65	49	16
Monterey Park	60,424	99	69	30
Moraga	17,908	13	11	2
Morgan Hill	46,118	61	41	20
Morro Bay	10,624	17	15	2
Mountain View	84,599	135	96	39
Mount Shasta	3,274	12	8	4
Murrieta	116,413	138	99	39
Napa	79,526	120	72	48
National City	61,791	124	84	40
Nevada City	3,150	12	10	2
Newark	48,945	75	53	22
Newman	11,844	16	13	3
Newport Beach	85,325	225	142	83
Novato	56,134	77	58	19
Oakdale	23,808	32	22	10
Oakland	434,036	1,023	740	283
Oceanside	177,129	288	203	85
Ontario	183,322	388	283	105
Orange	139,830	216	143	73
Orange Cove	9,635	12	11	1
Orland	7,679	13	11	2
Oroville	19,268	39	21	18
Oxnard	211,349	324	230	94
Pacifica	38,938	35	32	3
Pacific Grove	15,605	30	21	9
Palm Springs	48,846	149	101	48
Palo Alto	66,938	137	77	60
Palos Verdes Estates	13,400	32	20	12
Paradise	26,879	19	11	8
Parlier	15,384	22	17	5
Pasadena	141,913	343	222	121
Paso Robles	32,528	50	36	14
Petaluma	62,425	94	63	31
Piedmont	11,307	27	17	10
Pinole	19,439	42	26	16
Pismo Beach	8,285	33	21	12
Pittsburg	73,637	105	82	23
Placentia	51,756	67	43	24
Placerville	11,123	25	18	7

Table 19. Full-Time Law Enforcement Employees, by Selected State and City, 2019—*Continued*

(Number.)

State/city	Population	Total law enforcement employees	Total officers	Total civilians
Pleasant Hill	35,125	56	44	12
Pleasanton	84,017	110	77	33
Pomona	152,776	252	147	105
Porterville	60,209	102	65	37
Port Hueneme	22,232	27	19	8
Red Bluff	14,308	40	25	15
Redding	92,009	140	101	39
Redlands	71,941	124	85	39
Redondo Beach	67,473	142	91	51
Redwood City	87,427	111	84	27
Reedley	25,740	43	28	15
Rialto	103,965	134	102	32
Richmond	110,988	227	163	64
Ridgecrest	29,101	49	31	18
Rio Dell	3,392	6	6	0
Rio Vista	9,502	12	10	2
Ripon	16,103	30	21	9
Riverside	333,260	512	366	146
Rocklin	68,554	84	58	26
Rohnert Park	44,131	101	75	26
Roseville	141,744	191	130	61
Ross	2,470	8	8	0
Sacramento	513,934	993	678	315
Salinas	156,943	192	146	46
San Bernardino	216,715	368	244	124
San Bruno	43,297	61	45	16
Sand City	407	11	10	1
San Diego	1,441,737	2,387	1,764	623
San Fernando	24,621	44	31	13
San Francisco	886,007	2,907	2,279	628
San Gabriel	40,422	66	51	15
Sanger	25,443	43	39	4
San Jose	1,040,008	1,607	1,150	457
San Leandro	90,297	129	87	42
San Luis Obispo	47,735	89	61	28
San Marino	13,196	34	26	8
San Mateo	106,020	142	103	39
San Pablo	31,336	82	57	25
San Rafael	58,819	82	60	22
San Ramon	76,387	85	66	19
Santa Ana	333,664	558	340	218
Santa Barbara	91,717	206	132	74
Santa Clara	131,173	222	150	72
Santa Cruz	65,263	122	81	41
Santa Maria	108,414	184	135	49
Santa Monica	91,621	394	219	175
Santa Paula	30,098	45	32	13
Santa Rosa	177,884	243	166	77
Sausalito	7,118	23	17	6
Scotts Valley	11,875	24	17	7
Seal Beach	24,120	53	38	15
Seaside	34,036	45	33	12
Sebastopol	7,815	21	14	7
Selma	24,983	48	36	12
Shafter	20,456	35	26	9
Sierra Madre	10,917	18	15	3
Signal Hill	11,624	44	32	12
Simi Valley	126,025	165	119	46
Soledad	26,015	21	16	5
Sonora	4,867	17	10	7
South Gate	94,445	114	72	42
South Lake Tahoe	22,116	59	38	21
South Pasadena	25,612	51	33	18
South San Francisco	68,251	111	80	31
Stallion Springs	2,648	2	2	0
St. Helena	6,195	16	11	5
Stockton	313,604	664	459	205
Suisun City	29,922	32	20	12
Sunnyvale	154,859	292	217	75
Susanville	14,878	19	16	3
Sutter Creek	2,624	4	4	0

(Number.)

State/city	Population	Total law enforcement employees	Total officers	Total civilians
Taft.	9,413	24	14	10
Tehachapi	12,211	26	17	9
Tiburon	9,135	17	13	4
Torrance	145,183	311	206	105
Tracy	92,895	135	86	49
Truckee	16,611	38	24	14
Tulare	65,134	105	67	38
Tulelake	985	3	3	0
Turlock	74,120	111	75	36
Tustin	80,356	141	90	51
Ukiah	16,197	45	26	19
Union City	75,202	88	71	17
Upland	77,398	106	71	35
Vacaville	101,147	167	110	57
Vallejo	122,657	148	101	47
Ventura	111,596	183	135	48
Vernon	112	55	41	14
Visalia	134,961	219	147	72
Walnut Creek	70,546	121	82	39
Watsonville	54,261	94	75	19
Weed	2,673	14	9	5
West Covina	106,335	141	88	53
Westminster	91,086	120	81	39
Westmorland	2,275	5	5	0
West Sacramento	54,372	96	69	27
Wheatland	3,940	9	8	1
Whittier	86,158	167	118	49
Williams	5,348	13	11	2
Willits	4,937	13	8	5
Winters	7,374	13	11	2
Woodlake	7,682	12	11	1
Woodland	61,176	80	65	15
Yreka	7,527	22	14	8
Yuba City	67,164	88	59	29
COLORADO				
Alamosa	10,086	28	24	4
Arvada	122,312	200	157	43
Aspen	7,461	37	27	10
Ault	1,885	6	5	1
Aurora	380,600	911	688	223
Avon	6,496	19	17	2
Basalt	4,209	10	9	1
Bayfield	2,754	9	8	1
Black Hawk	128	33	21	12
Blue River	937	2	2	0
Boulder	108,519	271	177	94
Breckenridge	5,079	24	20	4
Brighton	42,267	101	75	26
Broomfield	70,708	223	117	106
Brush	5,372	15	12	3
Buena Vista	2,857	9	8	1
Burlington	3,072	8	5	3
Calhan	840	4	4	0
Canon City	16,793	44	34	10
Carbondale	6,941	14	11	3
Castle Rock	67,208	99	71	28
Cedaredge	2,269	7	6	1
Centennial	112,129	179	133	46
Center	2,312	20	5	15
Cherry Hills Village	6,734	29	25	4
Collbran	699	2	2	0
Colorado Springs	479,648	1,028	725	303
Columbine Valley	1,519	5	5	0
Commerce City	60,198	136	110	26
Cortez	8,748	48	29	19
Craig	8,886	26	21	5
Crested Butte	1,708	9	8	1
Cripple Creek	1,271	19	12	7
Dacono	6,074	16	13	3
De Beque	504	4	4	0

(Number.)

State/city	Population	Total law enforcement employees	Total officers	Total civilians
Del Norte	1,548	3	2	1
Delta	8,929	22	18	4
Denver	728,941	1,859	1,551	308
Dillon	981	11	10	1
Dinosaur	328	2	2	0
Durango	19,271	63	51	12
Eagle	7,021	10	9	1
Eaton	5,690	12	10	2
Edgewater	5,363	15	15	0
Elizabeth	1,424	10	8	2
Empire	306	1	1	0
Englewood	35,273	107	76	31
Erie	26,523	40	34	6
Estes Park	6,406	33	19	14
Evans	21,585	37	33	4
Fairplay	773	4	4	0
Federal Heights	13,021	38	25	13
Firestone	15,558	34	27	7
Florence	3,965	14	13	1
Fort Collins	170,889	317	214	103
Fort Lupton	8,388	22	19	3
Fort Morgan	11,355	29	22	7
Fountain	31,041	59	52	7
Fowler	1,139	3	3	0
Fraser/Winter Park	2,371	11	9	2
Frederick	14,238	25	21	4
Frisco	3,220	13	10	3
Fruita	13,504	18	15	3
Garden City	267	4	4	0
Georgetown	1,095	3	3	0
Glendale	5,289	40	29	11
Glenwood Springs	10,027	31	24	7
Golden	21,522	67	50	17
Granby	2,133	10	8	2
Grand Junction	63,949	193	110	83
Greeley	109,255	209	152	57
Green Mountain Falls	714	1	1	0
Greenwood Village	16,046	78	59	19
Gunnison	6,689	31	16	15
Gypsum	7,467	4	4	0
Haxtun	902	3	3	0
Hayden	1,992	8	6	2
Holyoke	2,204	4	4	0
Hotchkiss	932	4	4	0
Hudson	1,806	5	4	1
Idaho Springs	1,803	12	9	3
Ignacio	892	7	7	0
Johnstown	15,547	24	21	3
Keenesburg	1,242	11	10	1
Kersey	1,679	5	4	1
Kremmling	1,511	5	4	1
Lafayette	29,522	50	41	9
La Junta	6,983	18	12	6
Lakeside	8	5	4	1
Lakewood	158,645	437	311	126
Lamar	7,619	31	16	15
La Salle	2,400	8	8	0
La Veta	812	2	2	0
Leadville	2,785	9	7	2
Limon	1,929	7	6	1
Littleton	48,831	102	78	24
Lochbuie	7,265	12	10	2
Log Lane Village	874	2	2	0
Lone Tree	15,129	63	55	8
Longmont	97,928	227	150	77
Louisville	21,532	36	31	5
Loveland	78,856	161	113	48
Mancos	1,429	4	4	0
Manitou Springs	5,388	15	13	2
Manzanola	417	2	2	0
Mead	4,924	10	8	2

(Number.)

State/city	Population	Total law enforcement employees	Total officers	Total civilians
Meeker	2,238	4	4	0
Milliken	7,978	14	11	3
Monte Vista	4,084	16	13	3
Montrose	19,564	56	37	19
Monument	8,298	22	18	4
Morrison	425	10	9	1
Mountain View	541	10	9	1
Mountain Village	1,450	10	7	3
Mount Crested Butte	859	9	8	1
Nederland	1,560	5	4	1
New Castle	5,095	10	9	1
Northglenn	39,420	77	58	19
Oak Creek	975	3	3	0
Olathe	1,824	4	4	0
Ouray	1,011	5	5	0
Pagosa Springs	2,044	8	7	1
Palisade	2,723	11	10	1
Palmer Lake	2,819	2	2	0
Paonia	1,463	4	4	0
Parachute	1,125	6	5	1
Parker	57,050	113	74	39
Platteville	3,922	10	9	1
Pueblo	112,381	269	218	51
Rangely	2,278	9	4	5
Ridgway	1,032	3	3	0
Rifle	9,782	25	20	5
Rocky Ford	3,811	13	8	5
Salida	6,061	20	18	2
Sanford	880	1	1	0
Severance	5,362	9	7	2
Sheridan	6,233	35	34	1
Silt	3,215	7	6	1
Silverthorne	4,948	20	16	4
Simla	642	3	3	0
Snowmass Village	2,767	12	9	3
South Fork	348	3	3	0
Springfield	1,369	2	2	0
Steamboat Springs	13,365	38	27	11
Sterling	13,573	29	23	6
Telluride	2,518	13	8	5
Thornton	142,168	319	242	77
Timnath	5,027	9	8	1
Trinidad	8,116	35	21	14
Walsh	513	1	1	0
Westminster	114,392	271	195	76
Wheat Ridge	31,553	101	83	18
Wiggins	1,010	2	2	0
Windsor	30,587	48	41	7
Woodland Park	7,863	26	18	8
Wray	2,331	6	5	1
Yuma	3,452	8	6	2
CONNECTICUT				
Ansonia	18,656	50	43	7
Avon	18,320	41	32	9
Berlin	20,500	54	41	13
Bethel	19,855	51	38	13
Bloomfield	21,406	61	48	13
Branford	28,002	66	53	13
Bridgeport	144,908	411	365	46
Bristol	59,977	142	117	25
Brookfield	17,071	44	34	10
Canton	10,267	21	16	5
Cheshire	29,167	62	48	14
Clinton	12,914	35	27	8
Coventry	12,411	21	16	5
Cromwell	13,894	35	26	9
Danbury	85,167	153	148	5
Darien	21,880	64	51	13
Derby	12,468	36	34	2
East Hampton	12,842	18	16	2

Table 19. Full-Time Law Enforcement Employees, by Selected State and City, 2019—*Continued*

(Number.)

State/city	Population	Total law enforcement employees	Total officers	Total civilians
East Hartford	49,842	145	111	34
East Haven	28,635	54	50	4
East Lyme	18,588	32	24	8
Easton	7,519	20	15	5
East Windsor	11,399	34	25	9
Enfield	44,443	115	93	22
Fairfield	62,239	127	106	21
Farmington	25,525	61	46	15
Glastonbury	34,497	74	56	18
Granby	11,386	21	16	5
Greenwich	62,905	182	155	27
Groton	8,967	34	27	7
Groton Long Point	509	5	5	0
Groton Town	29,046	83	65	18
Guilford	22,194	44	37	7
Hamden	60,855	129	102	27
Hartford	122,245	483	447	36
Ledyard	14,698	32	23	9
Madison	18,087	42	30	12
Manchester	57,630	152	112	40
Meriden	59,378	131	120	11
Middlebury	7,750	12	10	2
Middletown	45,963	125	112	13
Milford	54,898	136	112	24
Monroe	19,466	56	43	13
Naugatuck	31,214	67	56	11
New Britain	72,354	166	158	8
New Canaan	20,268	52	46	6
Newington	30,060	65	52	13
New London	26,856	85	69	16
New Milford	26,835	57	45	12
Newtown	27,795	48	45	3
North Branford	14,127	28	23	5
North Haven	23,642	59	50	9
Norwalk	89,440	214	176	38
Norwich	38,964	101	85	16
Old Saybrook	10,069	32	24	8
Orange	13,948	56	45	11
Plainfield	15,145	21	16	5
Plainville	17,610	46	38	8
Plymouth	11,573	26	21	5
Portland	9,281	13	12	1
Putnam	9,374	23	15	8
Redding	9,120	22	16	6
Ridgefield	25,050	46	41	5
Rocky Hill	20,199	48	37	11
Seymour	16,505	43	41	2
Shelton	41,287	58	50	8
Simsbury	25,169	49	38	11
Southington	43,886	87	68	19
South Windsor	26,097	55	41	14
Stamford	130,678	285	266	19
Stonington	18,439	51	39	12
Stratford	52,034	108	103	5
Suffield	15,740	26	19	7
Thomaston	7,521	16	13	3
Torrington	33,972	86	76	10
Trumbull	35,772	86	76	10
Vernon	29,318	61	47	14
Wallingford	44,457	98	72	26
Waterbury	107,812	335	293	42
Waterford	18,812	55	49	6
Watertown	21,534	49	40	9
West Hartford	62,875	141	122	19
Weston	10,254	18	17	1
Westport	28,332	70	64	6
Wethersfield	26,009	63	48	15
Willimantic	17,660	49	44	5
Wilton	18,439	42	39	3
Winchester	10,585	27	22	5
Windsor	28,717	64	51	13

(Number.)

State/city	Population	Total law enforcement employees	Total officers	Total civilians
Windsor Locks	12,924	36	28	8
Wolcott	16,642	37	26	11
Woodbridge	8,782	31	24	7
DELAWARE				
Bethany Beach	1,244	11	10	1
Blades	1,469	3	3	0
Bridgeville	2,407	7	7	0
Camden	3,507	9	9	0
Cheswold	1,639	5	5	0
Dagsboro	916	4	4	0
Delaware City	1,830	5	4	1
Delmar	1,822	14	13	1
Dewey Beach	394	10	8	2
Dover	38,361	130	99	31
Ellendale	444	1	1	0
Elsmere	5,963	13	12	1
Felton	1,420	4	4	0
Fenwick Island	445	8	7	1
Georgetown	7,558	23	19	4
Greenwood	1,138	4	3	1
Harrington	3,652	14	13	1
Laurel	4,469	20	19	1
Lewes	3,286	14	13	1
Middletown	23,079	42	34	8
Milford	11,592	48	36	12
Millsboro	4,524	18	16	2
Milton	3,017	8	7	1
Newark	33,957	89	71	18
New Castle	5,558	16	15	1
Newport	1,026	7	7	0
Ocean View	2,180	12	11	1
Rehoboth Beach	1,546	29	17	12
Seaford	7,987	33	26	7
Selbyville	2,540	10	9	1
Smyrna	11,768	32	25	7
South Bethany	528	5	5	0
Wilmington	70,624	360	306	54
Wyoming	1,565	3	3	0
DISTRICT OF COLUMBIA				
Washington	705,749	4,524	3,809	715
FLORIDA				
Altamonte Springs	44,582	115	95	20
Apopka	55,072	139	100	39
Arcadia	8,274	23	19	4
Astatula	2,091	7	7	0
Atlantic Beach	13,983	41	28	13
Atlantis	2,126	16	11	5
Auburndale	16,679	43	35	8
Aventura	38,259	126	89	37
Bal Harbour Village	3,086	37	24	13
Bartow	20,296	55	37	18
Bay Harbor Islands	6,018	27	21	6
Belleair	4,253	14	12	2
Belle Isle	7,326	21	19	2
Belleview	5,086	17	15	2
Blountstown	2,473	18	12	6
Boca Raton	101,163	304	209	95
Bonifay	2,683	6	6	0
Bowling Green	2,899	7	7	0
Boynton Beach	79,360	184	139	45
Bradenton	58,782	148	116	32
Bradenton Beach	1,292	10	10	0
Bunnell	2,865	14	12	2
Carrabelle	2,488	4	4	0
Casselberry	29,244	60	50	10
Cedar Key	685	4	4	0
Center Hill	1,472	2	2	0
Chattahoochee	3,004	10	10	0

Table 19. Full-Time Law Enforcement Employees, by Selected State and City, 2019—*Continued*

(Number.)

State/city	Population	Total law enforcement employees	Total officers	Total civilians
Clearwater	117,458	330	245	85
Clermont	37,818	82	75	7
Clewiston	8,098	22	16	6
Cocoa	18,807	92	64	28
Cocoa Beach	11,806	57	37	20
Coconut Creek	62,471	144	106	38
Cooper City	36,890	70	53	17
Coral Gables	51,530	240	169	71
Coral Springs	134,967	308	218	90
Cottondale	902	3	3	0
Crescent City	1,540	7	6	1
Crestview	25,152	55	38	17
Cross City	1,710	5	5	0
Dade City	7,337	30	23	7
Dania Beach	32,593	81	74	7
Davenport	5,814	15	14	1
Daytona Beach	69,834	293	244	49
Daytona Beach Shores	4,579	41	31	10
Deerfield Beach	81,602	128	120	8
DeFuniak Springs	6,940	25	19	6
DeLand	34,468	79	61	18
Delray Beach	70,509	228	162	66
Doral	64,168	180	136	44
Dunnellon	1,830	8	7	1
Eatonville	2,317	14	12	2
Edgewater	22,926	34	29	5
Edgewood	3,044	16	13	3
El Portal	2,479	9	9	0
Eustis	21,432	53	40	13
Fellsmere	5,830	10	9	1
Fernandina Beach	12,710	41	36	5
Fort Lauderdale	184,765	690	525	165
Fort Myers	85,127	314	225	89
Fort Pierce	46,597	138	113	25
Fort Walton Beach	22,645	61	44	17
Gainesville	135,085	343	253	90
Graceville	2,191	8	7	1
Green Cove Springs	8,505	27	21	6
Groveland	15,667	44	31	13
Gulfport	12,449	35	31	4
Gulf Stream	891	12	12	0
Haines City	25,746	65	52	13
Hallandale Beach	40,297	118	87	31
Havana	1,701	15	10	5
Hialeah	240,688	344	272	72
Hialeah Gardens	24,337	66	48	18
Hillsboro Beach	2,038	19	15	4
Holly Hill	12,403	29	25	4
Holmes Beach	4,355	26	17	9
Homestead	71,757	147	113	34
Howey-in-the-Hills	1,185	6	6	0
Indialantic	2,937	15	10	5
Indian Harbour Beach	8,616	29	21	8
Indian Shores	3,816	14	12	2
Interlachen	1,461	4	4	0
Jacksonville	909,142	3,050	1,731	1,319
Jacksonville Beach	23,974	81	62	19
Jasper	4,057	8	7	1
Jennings	862	3	3	0
Juno Beach	3,709	17	15	2
Jupiter	66,906	145	116	29
Jupiter Inlet Colony	459	4	4	0
Jupiter Island	934	23	18	5
Kenneth City	5,074	14	13	1
Kissimmee	75,544	218	141	77
Lake Alfred	6,123	17	12	5
Lake City	12,141	54	38	16
Lake Clarke Shores	3,657	10	9	1
Lake Hamilton	1,472	7	6	1
Lake Helen	2,837	7	6	1
Lakeland	112,237	336	236	100

(Number.)

State/city	Population	Total law enforcement employees	Total officers	Total civilians
Lake Mary	17,778	54	45	9
Lake Placid	2,459	10	8	2
Lake Wales	16,901	48	43	5
Largo	85,740	179	139	40
Lauderdale-by-the-Sea	6,745	25	23	2
Lauderdale Lakes	36,784	42	40	2
Lawtey	722	3	3	0
Leesburg	23,527	88	67	21
Lighthouse Point	11,403	38	30	8
Live Oak	6,988	36	17	19
Longboat Key	7,379	22	19	3
Longwood	15,320	48	43	5
Madison	2,769	15	14	1
Maitland	18,222	61	53	8
Manalapan	474	16	14	2
Marco Island	18,124	34	31	3
Margate	59,371	149	114	35
Marianna	7,034	22	17	5
Mascotte	5,977	13	12	1
Medley	896	48	40	8
Melbourne	83,668	215	145	70
Melbourne Beach	3,313	11	10	1
Miami	480,505	1,760	1,298	462
Miami Beach	92,185	491	410	81
Miami Gardens	113,786	265	203	62
Miami Shores	10,572	47	40	7
Miami Springs	14,374	55	44	11
Milton	10,460	24	18	6
Miramar	143,334	300	219	81
Monticello	2,413	13	9	4
Mount Dora	14,491	59	40	19
Naples	22,369	103	71	32
Neptune Beach	7,332	29	20	9
New Port Richey	16,703	60	43	17
New Smyrna Beach	27,743	66	47	19
Niceville	15,947	36	25	11
North Bay Village	8,425	37	30	7
North Lauderdale	44,808	57	52	5
North Miami	63,547	145	111	34
North Miami Beach	46,307	133	98	35
North Palm Beach	13,273	35	30	5
North Port	70,181	148	113	35
Oakland	3,160	15	13	2
Oakland Park	45,857	92	81	11
Ocala	60,932	270	178	92
Ocean Ridge	1,978	22	17	5
Ocoee	49,451	99	85	14
Opa Locka	16,501	49	42	7
Orange City	11,920	29	25	4
Orange Park	8,852	34	26	8
Orlando	292,120	962	745	217
Ormond Beach	44,005	92	71	21
Oviedo	42,684	76	68	8
Palatka	10,450	39	32	7
Palm Bay	115,520	219	156	63
Palm Beach	8,884	92	62	30
Palm Beach Gardens	57,236	178	122	56
Palmetto	13,855	50	35	15
Palm Springs	25,303	59	39	20
Panama City	37,199	119	89	30
Panama City Beach	13,266	87	70	17
Parker	4,616	11	10	1
Parkland	35,244	46	41	5
Pembroke Pines	174,641	332	240	92
Pensacola	52,801	200	148	52
Perry	6,918	23	21	2
Pinellas Park	53,589	126	107	19
Plantation	95,474	262	165	97
Plant City	39,725	87	70	17
Pompano Beach	113,536	252	224	28
Ponce Inlet	3,315	13	11	2

State/city	Population	Total law enforcement employees	Total officers	Total civilians
Port Richey	2,894	21	15	6
Port St. Joe	3,579	9	9	0
Port St. Lucie	199,433	300	232	68
Punta Gorda	20,458	52	36	16
Quincy	7,143	34	26	8
Riviera Beach	35,130	161	117	44
Rockledge	28,078	66	50	16
Sanford	60,844	154	131	23
Sanibel	7,525	51	25	26
Sarasota	58,470	235	175	60
Satellite Beach	11,219	36	25	11
Sea Ranch Lakes	626	11	7	4
Sebastian	26,232	60	41	19
Sebring	11,008	39	34	5
Sewall's Point	2,244	10	9	1
South Daytona	13,159	34	28	6
South Miami	12,284	56	47	9
Starke	5,402	18	16	2
St. Augustine	14,778	66	53	13
St. Petersburg	267,696	757	552	205
Stuart	16,424	61	43	18
Sunny Isles Beach	22,476	63	51	12
Sunrise	96,919	249	187	62
Surfside	5,829	42	31	11
Tallahassee	195,104	434	369	65
Tamarac	66,799	97	80	17
Tampa	400,501	1,215	936	279
Tavares	17,962	30	27	3
Temple Terrace	26,725	61	46	15
Tequesta	6,195	24	19	5
Titusville	46,866	124	79	45
Treasure Island	6,978	23	19	4
Trenton	2,141	3	2	1
Umatilla	3,852	11	10	1
Valparaiso	5,218	16	11	5
Venice	23,726	63	50	13
Vero Beach	17,503	73	52	21
Village of Pinecrest	19,760	70	43	27
Virginia Gardens	2,460	8	7	1
Wauchula	4,890	16	13	3
Welaka	712	1	1	0
West Melbourne	24,077	55	46	9
West Miami	8,362	23	19	4
Weston	71,946	105	87	18
West Palm Beach	112,798	377	285	92
West Park	15,246	43	39	4
White Springs	766	4	4	0
Wildwood	7,310	37	33	4
Wilton Manors	12,948	47	34	13
Winter Garden	46,750	106	79	27
Winter Haven	44,211	117	87	30
Winter Park	31,494	102	74	28
Winter Springs	37,854	54	41	13
Zephyrhills	15,836	48	33	15
GEORGIA				
Abbeville	2,784	6	5	1
Adairsville	4,953	18	16	2
Alamo	3,348	4	4	0
Alapaha	671	3	1	2
Albany	74,989	185	154	31
Alma	3,438	12	10	2
Alpharetta	67,411	152	108	44
Americus	15,110	44	34	10
Arcade	1,946	4	4	0
Athens-Clarke County	127,246	280	215	65
Atlanta	507,369	2,090	1,600	490
Auburn	7,687	22	17	5
Austell	7,287	29	22	7
Avondale Estates	3,179	13	13	0
Bainbridge	11,986	43	34	9

Table 19. Full-Time Law Enforcement Employees, by Selected State and City, 2019—*Continued*

(Number.)

State/city	Population	Total law enforcement employees	Total officers	Total civilians
Ball Ground	2,225	4	4	0
Barnesville	6,714	21	19	2
Bartow	253	2	2	0
Baxley	4,697	10	9	1
Blairsville	621	8	7	1
Blakely	4,573	17	15	2
Bloomingdale	2,732	18	15	3
Blue Ridge	1,458	10	9	1
Blythe	697	3	3	0
Boston	1,314	4	4	0
Bowdon	2,110	10	8	2
Braselton	12,297	20	19	1
Braswell	382	3	1	2
Bremen	6,575	21	19	2
Brookhaven	54,734	83	71	12
Brooklet	1,751	6	5	1
Brunswick	16,493	56	52	4
Buchanan	1,167	12	10	2
Buena Vista	2,054	3	3	0
Byron	5,269	24	19	5
Cairo	9,381	29	26	3
Calhoun	17,069	56	48	8
Camilla	4,893	21	18	3
Canon	837	1	1	0
Canton	30,109	55	48	7
Carrollton	26,724	84	70	14
Cartersville	21,322	69	60	9
Cecil	277	3	2	1
Cedartown	10,270	33	29	4
Centerville	7,854	24	19	5
Chatsworth	4,321	19	18	1
Chattahoochee Hills	3,285	11	11	0
Clarkston	12,840	19	16	3
Claxton	2,218	11	10	1
Cleveland	4,042	16	15	1
Cochran	4,851	14	11	3
College Park	15,278	128	89	39
Commerce	6,980	26	20	6
Conyers	16,115	88	65	23
Cordele	10,578	37	27	10
Cornelia	4,554	19	17	2
Covington	14,128	69	58	11
Cumming	6,501	20	18	2
Dallas	13,888	37	27	10
Dalton	33,544	101	89	12
Danielsville	592	2	2	0
Darien	1,891	12	11	1
Dawson	4,049	18	13	5
Decatur	26,612	58	44	14
Dillard	370	4	3	1
Doerun	744	5	4	1
Donalsonville	2,539	14	13	1
Doraville	10,600	58	42	16
Douglas	11,608	41	36	5
Douglasville	34,609	110	92	18
Dublin	15,756	74	60	14
Duluth	29,893	88	69	19
Dunwoody	49,868	78	64	14
Eastman	5,127	14	12	2
Eatonton	6,625	28	20	8
Edison	1,430	6	5	1
Elberton	4,321	23	20	3
Ellijay	1,722	12	11	1
Emerson	1,603	9	8	1
Enigma	1,339	3	3	0
Eton	917	4	4	0
Euharlee	4,372	11	10	1
Fairburn	16,264	52	41	11
Fairmount	743	5	5	0
Fayetteville	18,041	62	53	9
Fitzgerald	8,661	33	28	5

Table 19. Full-Time Law Enforcement Employees, by Selected State and City, 2019—*Continued*

(Number.)

State/city	Population	Total law enforcement employees	Total officers	Total civilians
Flowery Branch	8,256	19	17	2
Folkston	4,662	7	7	0
Forest Park	20,273	83	64	19
Forsyth	4,150	14	12	2
Fort Oglethorpe	10,126	30	28	2
Fort Valley	8,866	29	25	4
Franklin	916	8	8	0
Franklin Springs	1,232	3	3	0
Gainesville	42,500	113	98	15
Garden City	8,854	44	36	8
Glennville	5,084	11	9	2
Gordon	1,867	11	6	5
Grantville	3,295	14	13	1
Greensboro	3,365	20	17	3
Greenville	837	7	6	1
Griffin	22,840	83	74	9
Grovetown	14,918	31	24	7
Guyton	2,142	2	1	1
Hahira	3,021	11	9	2
Hampton	8,044	20	18	2
Harlem	3,358	9	7	2
Hartwell	4,447	26	21	5
Helen	555	9	8	1
Hephzibah	3,930	4	4	0
Hiawassee	902	5	5	0
Hinesville	32,871	99	83	16
Hiram	4,173	19	16	3
Hogansville	3,113	19	13	6
Holly Springs	13,458	36	35	1
Homerville	2,348	8	7	1
Jackson	5,086	14	13	1
Jasper	3,975	19	17	2
Jesup	9,779	33	31	2
Johns Creek	85,258	87	78	9
Jonesboro	4,927	36	28	8
Kennesaw	34,641	74	67	7
Kingston	656	2	1	1
LaGrange	30,398	96	79	17
Lake City	2,858	19	17	2
Lavonia	2,162	15	14	1
Lawrenceville	30,120	94	69	25
Leslie	369	5	4	1
Lilburn	12,769	36	31	5
Lithonia	2,404	8	7	1
Locust Grove	7,409	28	25	3
Loganville	12,822	31	29	2
Louisville	2,142	6	6	0
Lyons	4,258	17	14	3
Madison	4,177	15	13	2
Manchester	3,958	17	12	5
Marietta	61,324	180	135	45
Marshallville	1,237	4	3	1
McDonough	26,277	54	47	7
McIntyre	602	5	5	0
McRae-Helena	8,352	12	11	1
Metter	3,949	12	11	1
Midville	256	1	1	0
Midway	2,020	6	4	2
Milledgeville	18,655	52	34	18
Milton	40,067	47	38	9
Monroe	13,662	48	44	4
Montezuma	2,969	12	10	2
Morrow	7,636	30	27	3
Moultrie	14,126	37	33	4
Newnan	40,720	104	90	14
Norcross	16,769	59	38	21
Norman Park	966	3	1	2
Ocilla	3,606	14	14	0
Omega	1,222	7	5	2
Oxford	2,337	3	3	0
Palmetto	4,743	15	12	3

Table 19. Full-Time Law Enforcement Employees, by Selected State and City, 2019—*Continued*

(Number.)

State/city	Population	Total law enforcement employees	Total officers	Total civilians
Peachtree City	35,929	65	60	5
Pelham	3,474	14	12	2
Pembroke	2,623	9	9	0
Pooler	24,917	67	60	7
Port Wentworth	9,015	36	30	6
Remerton	1,083	9	8	1
Rincon	10,260	15	12	3
Ringgold	3,625	10	10	0
Riverdale	16,950	40	33	7
Rockmart	4,320	22	20	2
Sandersville	5,420	21	17	4
Sandy Springs	110,760	151	134	17
Savannah	240,631	572	493	79
Shiloh	485	1	1	0
Smyrna	57,423	138	86	52
Snellville	20,113	59	47	12
Social Circle	4,592	16	15	1
Sparta	1,209	13	7	6
Springfield	4,260	10	9	1
Statham	2,775	5	4	1
Stone Mountain	6,388	17	16	1
Sylvania	2,427	10	8	2
Sylvester	5,704	20	16	4
Tallapoosa	3,154	11	10	1
Thomasville	18,533	65	59	6
Thunderbolt	2,677	11	9	2
Union City	22,200	70	61	9
Vidalia	10,397	35	24	11
Warm Springs	402	2	2	0
Warner Robins	76,623	151	108	43
Waynesboro	5,387	28	22	6
Winder	17,385	47	39	8
Woodstock	33,470	59	54	5
Wrens	1,942	12	11	1
Wrightsville	3,617	7	6	1
HAWAII				
Honolulu	974,902	2,349	1,864	485
IDAHO				
Aberdeen	1,946	5	5	0
American Falls	4,354	7	5	2
Ashton	1,052	2	2	0
Bellevue	2,441	4	4	0
Blackfoot	11,938	30	27	3
Boise	231,314	385	298	87
Bonners Ferry	2,606	7	7	0
Buhl	4,440	10	9	1
Caldwell	57,940	92	76	16
Chubbuck	15,490	36	22	14
Coeur d'Alene	52,256	112	90	22
Cottonwood	935	1	1	0
Emmett	6,950	16	13	3
Filer	2,894	5	5	0
Fruitland	5,472	16	12	4
Garden City	12,033	34	27	7
Gooding	3,457	9	7	2
Grangeville	3,205	4	4	0
Hagerman	883	1	1	0
Hailey	8,575	15	14	1
Heyburn	3,460	8	7	1
Homedale	2,681	6	5	1
Idaho City	468	1	1	0
Idaho Falls	62,088	137	90	47
Jerome	11,921	21	18	3
Kellogg	2,117	9	8	1
Ketchum	2,843	12	11	1
Kimberly	4,052	9	8	1
Lewiston	32,931	68	43	25
McCall	3,541	12	10	2
Meridian	111,196	145	112	33

(Number.)

State/city	Population	Total law enforcement employees	Total officers	Total civilians
Middleton	8,395	10	9	1
Montpelier	2,514	6	5	1
Moscow	26,018	45	37	8
Mountain Home	14,476	34	30	4
Nampa	98,208	176	125	51
Orofino	3,115	6	5	1
Osburn	1,549	2	2	0
Parma	2,152	5	5	0
Payette	7,535	15	13	2
Pinehurst	1,616	2	2	0
Pocatello	56,514	131	89	42
Ponderay	1,145	7	6	1
Post Falls	35,649	74	46	28
Preston	5,533	9	8	1
Priest River	1,868	6	5	1
Rathdrum	8,968	18	15	3
Rexburg	29,109	41	32	9
Rigby	4,225	8	7	1
Rupert	5,791	13	12	1
Salmon	3,141	8	8	0
Sandpoint	8,873	24	20	4
Shelley	4,423	8	8	0
Shoshone	1,514	6	6	0
Soda Springs	3,029	7	7	0
Spirit Lake	2,596	9	7	2
St. Anthony	3,572	6	6	0
Sun Valley	1,482	13	12	1
Twin Falls	50,463	95	75	20
Weiser	5,369	13	10	3
Wendell	2,707	4	4	0
Wilder	1,827	5	5	0
ILLINOIS				
Albany	868	1	1	0
Aledo	3,448	8	7	1
Algonquin	31,016	54	47	7
Alsip	18,830	43	40	3
Altamont	2,278	6	6	0
Alton	26,360	83	61	22
Amboy	2,301	3	3	0
Anna	4,110	7	7	0
Arlington Heights	75,249	133	106	27
Arthur	2,220	4	4	0
Ashland	1,181	1	1	0
Assumption	1,071	2	2	0
Athens	1,913	5	5	0
Auburn	4,664	6	6	0
Aurora	199,784	362	298	64
Aviston	2,128	1	1	0
Barrington Hills	4,205	20	16	4
Bartonville	6,137	15	10	5
Beardstown	5,425	10	9	1
Bedford Park	602	46	36	10
Berkeley	5,056	19	15	4
Berwyn	54,702	166	114	52
Bethalto	9,270	18	13	5
Bethany	1,258	2	2	0
Bloomington	78,107	157	124	33
Blue Island	23,037	42	32	10
Blue Mound	1,073	1	1	0
Bolingbrook	75,394	123	110	13
Bourbonnais	19,588	28	26	2
Bradley	15,205	44	33	11
Braidwood	6,199	16	13	3
Breese	4,498	8	7	1
Bridgeview	16,153	30	30	0
Brighton	2,137	4	4	0
Buffalo Grove	40,768	75	62	13
Burbank	28,483	52	44	8
Burr Ridge	10,828	31	27	4
Byron	3,585	7	6	1

Table 19. Full-Time Law Enforcement Employees, by Selected State and City, 2019—*Continued*

(Number.)

State/city	Population	Total law enforcement employees	Total officers	Total civilians
Cahokia	13,864	39	31	8
Calumet City	36,128	97	73	24
Cambridge	2,078	1	1	0
Campton Hills	11,202	5	5	0
Carbondale	25,242	81	64	17
Carlinville	5,498	17	12	5
Carol Stream	39,599	92	74	18
Carrollton	2,404	6	6	0
Carthage	2,448	4	4	0
Cary	17,728	25	24	1
Caseyville	4,088	14	13	1
Centreville	4,922	9	8	1
Champaign	88,891	140	117	23
Charleston	19,987	34	31	3
Chatham	12,809	20	14	6
Chenoa	3,143	4	4	0
Cherry Valley	2,877	15	14	1
Chicago	2,707,064	14,015	13,160	855
Chicago Heights	29,471	93	78	15
Chicago Ridge	14,017	35	31	4
Chillicothe	6,071	12	12	0
Cicero	81,270	180	156	24
Coal City	5,340	14	13	1
Coal Valley	3,760	9	8	1
Colfax	1,017	1	1	0
Cortland	4,369	6	6	0
Countryside	5,957	27	24	3
Crest Hill	20,534	32	30	2
Crete	8,096	20	18	2
Crystal Lake	39,944	68	59	9
Dallas City	870	3	3	0
Dana	152	1	1	0
Danville	30,642	64	55	9
Darien	21,935	37	32	5
Decatur	70,710	149	141	8
Deer Creek	661	1	1	0
Deerfield	18,848	54	40	14
DeKalb	42,428	76	61	15
Delavan	1,605	4	4	0
De Soto	1,510	4	3	1
Des Plaines	59,023	117	100	17
Dupo	3,810	8	8	0
Du Quoin	5,705	13	9	4
Dwight	3,962	10	9	1
East Dubuque	1,571	6	6	0
Edwardsville	25,047	60	45	15
Effingham	12,662	38	24	14
Elburn	5,967	8	7	1
Elgin	112,112	243	180	63
Elizabeth	721	1	1	0
Elk Grove Village	32,371	100	86	14
Elmhurst	46,857	85	67	18
Elmwood	2,021	2	2	0
Elmwood Park	24,185	43	36	7
Elwood	2,257	12	11	1
Essex	759	1	1	0
Eureka	5,276	6	6	0
Evanston	74,047	212	157	55
Evergreen Park	19,260	77	58	19
Fairbury	3,602	6	6	0
Fairfield	4,961	14	10	4
Fairmount	602	1	1	0
Farmington	2,236	6	6	0
Fisher	1,966	2	2	0
Flossmoor	9,211	24	19	5
Fox Lake	10,457	29	23	6
Fox River Grove	4,610	8	8	0
Frankfort	19,352	36	32	4
Freeburg	4,240	11	10	1
Freeport	23,721	63	47	16
Fulton	3,330	10	9	1

Table 19. Full-Time Law Enforcement Employees, by Selected State and City, 2019—*Continued*

(Number.)

State/city	Population	Total law enforcement employees	Total officers	Total civilians
Galena	3,155	11	10	1
Genoa	5,211	7	6	1
Georgetown	3,205	4	4	0
Gibson City	3,283	8	7	1
Gifford	1,100	1	1	0
Gillespie	3,097	11	8	3
Glencoe	8,887	39	34	5
Glendale Heights	33,878	70	54	16
Glenview	47,581	72	67	5
Glenwood	8,767	25	22	3
Goodfield	998	1	1	0
Grafton	632	3	3	0
Granite City	28,315	68	56	12
Greenfield	981	2	2	0
Greenup	1,486	4	4	0
Gurnee	30,493	97	62	35
Hampshire	6,425	10	10	0
Hampton	1,757	4	4	0
Hanover Park	37,699	83	57	26
Hartford	1,344	5	4	1
Harvard	9,092	20	18	2
Harwood Heights	8,388	27	24	3
Hawthorn Woods	8,651	13	12	1
Henry	2,205	5	4	1
Herrin	12,878	27	18	9
Hickory Hills	13,806	34	27	7
Highland	9,836	27	20	7
Highwood	5,250	12	11	1
Hillsboro	5,972	10	10	0
Hinckley	2,033	3	3	0
Hodgkins	1,883	24	22	2
Hoffman Estates	51,105	103	86	17
Homer	1,165	1	1	0
Homewood	18,831	45	40	5
Hoopeston	5,046	20	11	9
Hudson	1,816	3	3	0
Indian Head Park	3,742	8	7	1
Inverness	7,442	14	12	2
Itasca	10,032	25	22	3
Jacksonville	18,667	43	39	4
Jerseyville	8,208	21	15	6
Joliet	148,155	339	270	69
Kankakee	25,872	72	68	4
Kansas	721	1	1	0
Kildeer	4,033	9	8	1
Kingston	1,159	2	2	0
Kirkland	1,715	2	2	0
Ladd	1,199	1	1	0
La Grange	15,424	28	24	4
La Grange Park	13,260	23	21	2
Lake Bluff	5,606	17	15	2
Lake Forest	19,564	40	35	5
Lake in the Hills	28,811	48	40	8
Lakemoor	6,008	15	14	1
Lake Villa	8,625	18	17	1
Lakewood	4,006	9	8	1
Lake Zurich	20,060	50	33	17
Lemont	17,297	27	22	5
Le Roy	3,542	8	8	0
Lincoln	13,584	26	26	0
Lindenhurst	14,296	15	13	2
Litchfield	6,708	15	14	1
Lockport	25,587	45	39	6
Lombard	44,672	74	62	12
Lovington	1,044	2	2	0
Lyons	10,436	14	12	2
Machesney Park	22,594	23	22	1
Mackinaw	1,901	2	2	0
Manhattan	8,121	11	10	1
Maple Park	1,341	1	1	0
Marissa	1,807	3	3	0

Table 19. Full-Time Law Enforcement Employees, by Selected State and City, 2019—*Continued*

(Number.)

State/city	Population	Total law enforcement employees	Total officers	Total civilians
Marquette Heights	2,644	5	5	0
Marseilles	4,844	10	9	1
Maryville	8,033	14	13	1
Mason City	2,133	3	3	0
Mattoon	17,629	40	36	4
Mazon	972	2	1	1
McLean	797	1	1	0
Melrose Park	24,863	89	72	17
Metropolis	5,986	19	13	6
Midlothian	14,433	32	29	3
Milan	5,012	16	15	1
Milledgeville	945	2	2	0
Millstadt	3,869	8	8	0
Minier	1,188	2	2	0
Mokena	20,573	34	31	3
Momence	3,089	8	8	0
Monmouth	8,944	31	20	11
Montgomery	19,927	36	32	4
Morris	15,083	29	25	4
Morrison	4,026	7	7	0
Morrisonville	1,003	2	1	1
Morton	16,209	24	22	2
Morton Grove	22,904	57	46	11
Mount Carmel	6,988	15	10	5
Mount Morris	2,786	5	4	1
Mount Olive	1,941	5	4	1
Mount Prospect	54,089	102	83	19
Mount Pulaski	1,471	2	2	0
Mount Vernon	14,802	52	40	12
Mount Zion	5,799	12	10	2
Moweaqua	1,715	3	3	0
Mundelein	31,260	74	53	21
Naperville	149,061	251	166	85
New Athens	1,885	4	4	0
New Lenox	27,103	41	36	5
Newton	2,855	7	6	1
Niles	29,104	69	55	14
Nokomis	2,110	5	4	1
Normal	55,013	90	82	8
Northfield	5,418	21	19	2
North Pekin	1,526	7	7	0
Oak Brook	8,096	46	39	7
Oak Lawn	55,361	128	113	15
Oak Park	52,311	137	109	28
Oakwood	1,496	3	3	0
Oblong	1,368	1	1	0
O'Fallon	29,686	66	48	18
Okawville	1,362	4	4	0
Olney	8,800	13	12	1
Oregon	3,471	9	8	1
Orion	1,790	2	2	0
Orland Hills	7,066	10	10	0
Orland Park	58,519	127	99	28
Ottawa	18,047	50	35	15
Palatine	67,984	131	107	24
Palestine	1,272	1	1	0
Palos Hills	17,158	34	31	3
Palos Park	4,768	11	10	1
Paris	8,288	21	15	6
Park City	7,442	13	11	2
Paxton	4,196	7	7	0
Pecatonica	2,081	3	3	0
Pekin	32,033	61	54	7
Peoria	110,955	225	203	22
Peotone	4,135	11	10	1
Peru	9,738	26	24	2
Petersburg	2,214	6	6	0
Pittsfield	4,228	9	9	0
Plainfield	44,691	70	57	13
Pontiac	11,211	20	18	2
Princeton	7,500	18	17	1

Table 19. Full-Time Law Enforcement Employees, by Selected State and City, 2019—*Continued*

(Number.)

State/city	Population	Total law enforcement employees	Total officers	Total civilians
Rantoul	12,657	38	31	7
Raymond	941	1	1	0
Richmond	1,921	7	7	0
Ridge Farm	817	1	1	0
Riverdale	13,161	36	30	6
River Forest	10,869	29	27	2
Riverton	3,398	9	9	0
Riverwoods	3,585	7	7	0
Rockdale	1,924	5	5	0
Rockford	145,719	338	298	40
Rock Island	37,517	105	78	27
Rolling Meadows	23,703	56	49	7
Romeoville	39,616	75	62	13
Roscoe	10,492	14	13	1
Rossville	1,223	3	3	0
Round Lake	18,266	29	26	3
Roxana	1,439	7	6	1
Royalton	1,116	3	3	0
Rushville	2,867	5	5	0
Salem	7,053	26	18	8
Sandwich	7,364	20	16	4
San Jose	602	2	2	0
Sauget	164	10	10	0
Savanna	2,767	6	6	0
Schaumburg	73,412	140	109	31
Shorewood	17,606	33	29	4
Silvis	7,538	20	17	3
Skokie	63,082	159	114	45
Smithton	3,836	6	6	0
South Barrington	5,047	22	19	3
South Beloit	7,636	13	12	1
South Chicago Heights	4,029	10	9	1
South Elgin	23,634	36	32	4
South Holland	21,438	45	42	3
South Pekin	1,088	2	2	0
South Roxana	1,991	5	5	0
Springfield	114,393	269	241	28
Spring Valley	5,156	12	11	1
St. Charles	33,118	64	54	10
Steger	9,301	16	15	1
St. Elmo	1,389	3	3	0
Sterling	14,510	38	29	9
Stockton	1,707	6	5	1
Streamwood	39,529	66	57	9
Sullivan	4,487	11	9	2
Summit	11,205	32	30	2
Swansea	13,432	23	21	2
Thayer	658	2	2	0
Thornton	2,423	12	11	1
Tilton	2,638	4	4	0
Tinley Park	56,119	93	80	13
Tolono	3,447	2	2	0
Trenton	2,593	5	5	0
Tuscola	4,336	8	7	1
Urbana	42,080	72	58	14
Vandalia	6,664	12	12	0
Vernon Hills	26,847	66	43	23
Vienna	1,443	3	3	0
Villa Park	21,651	48	39	9
Virden	3,333	10	6	4
Warren	1,301	4	3	1
Warrensburg	1,124	2	2	0
Warrenville	13,268	39	31	8
Watseka	4,809	12	11	1
Waukegan	86,505	189	146	43
Waverly	1,200	1	1	0
Wayne	2,426	2	2	0
Westchester	16,224	37	33	4
West City	640	11	7	4
West Dundee	8,388	21	19	2
Western Springs	13,460	24	21	3

(Number.)

State/city	Population	Total law enforcement employees	Total officers	Total civilians
Westmont	24,642	43	37	6
Westville	2,964	4	4	0
Wheaton	53,160	79	64	15
Wheeling	39,028	91	59	32
Willowbrook	8,486	25	22	3
Willow Springs	5,658	11	10	1
Wilmette	27,289	64	44	20
Winfield	9,758	17	16	1
Winnebago	2,963	6	6	0
Wood River	10,108	26	18	8
Woodstock	25,324	41	37	4
Worth	10,534	28	26	2
Yorkville	20,541	33	30	3
Zion	23,617	48	44	4
INDIANA				
Albion	2,337	6	6	0
Anderson	54,899	122	101	21
Angola	8,715	23	18	5
Auburn	13,464	24	23	1
Bargersville	7,973	13	12	1
Batesville	6,704	18	13	5
Bedford	13,271	42	33	9
Bloomington	85,542	157	97	60
Bluffton	10,134	34	21	13
Bremen	4,472	17	12	5
Brownsburg	27,005	49	43	6
Butler	2,712	8	7	1
Cannelton	1,479	3	3	0
Carmel	95,388	144	119	25
Cedar Lake	12,896	22	19	3
Chesterton	13,929	26	22	4
Clarksville	21,630	60	54	6
Clinton	4,701	10	8	2
Columbia City	9,203	22	21	1
Crawfordsville	16,136	44	39	5
Crown Point	30,341	53	48	5
Cumberland	5,894	16	14	2
Dyer	15,939	34	31	3
East Chicago	27,717	88	82	6
Ellettsville	6,731	12	11	1
Fairmount	2,754	7	6	1
Fort Wayne	269,366	542	480	62
Franklin	25,443	57	52	5
Greenfield	22,800	44	42	2
Greenwood	59,797	69	62	7
Hammond	75,201	244	210	34
Hartford City	5,716	12	10	2
Highland	22,220	46	39	7
Hobart	27,880	78	67	11
Huntingburg	6,133	13	12	1
Indianapolis	883,699	2,803	2,121	682
Jasper	15,629	30	22	8
Jeffersonville	47,723	88	84	4
Knox	3,515	8	8	0
Kokomo	57,845	99	81	18
Logansport	17,660	41	40	1
Markle	1,085	5	5	0
Merrillville	34,724	67	60	7
Mooresville	9,747	26	20	6
Munster	22,412	44	40	4
Nappanee	6,853	17	15	2
New Whiteland	6,242	9	8	1
Noblesville	64,567	103	92	11
North Webster	1,164	5	5	0
Plainfield	35,317	64	58	6
Plymouth	9,872	26	24	2
Portage	36,800	74	67	7
Rensselaer	5,820	17	10	7
Roseland	633	13	4	9
Rushville	6,012	16	11	5

(Number.)

State/city	Population	Total law enforcement employees	Total officers	Total civilians
Schererville	28,412	62	48	14
Sellersburg	8,949	18	16	2
Shelbyville	19,362	58	43	15
Shirley	862	2	2	0
Silver Lake	924	3	3	0
South Bend	101,944	278	234	44
Speedway	12,202	50	35	15
St. John	18,478	25	22	3
Terre Haute	60,749	140	131	9
Valparaiso	33,980	63	57	6
Walkerton	2,274	10	6	4
Warsaw	15,120	43	36	7
Westfield	43,212	59	55	4
West Lafayette	49,154	66	47	19
Whitestown	9,810	31	30	1
Whiting	4,757	20	18	2
Winchester	4,676	13	12	1
Zionsville	27,630	40	38	2
IOWA				
Ackley	1,495	3	3	0
Adel	5,136	10	9	1
Albia	3,725	7	6	1
Algona	5,413	14	10	4
Altoona	19,441	33	31	2
Ames	68,237	80	57	23
Anamosa	5,502	9	8	1
Ankeny	68,238	72	62	10
Asbury	5,834	5	5	0
Atlantic	6,514	13	12	1
Audubon	1,883	4	4	0
Belle Plaine	2,432	5	5	0
Belmond	2,287	5	5	0
Bettendorf	36,972	51	45	6
Blue Grass	1,704	3	3	0
Boone	12,448	18	17	1
Burlington	24,751	49	44	5
Camanche	4,341	9	9	0
Carlisle	4,334	9	8	1
Carroll	9,775	16	15	1
Carter Lake	3,783	11	10	1
Cedar Falls	41,269	61	60	1
Cedar Rapids	134,007	284	220	64
Centerville	5,459	18	11	7
Charles City	7,334	20	13	7
Cherokee	4,855	9	8	1
Clarinda	5,352	11	10	1
Clarion	2,729	8	7	1
Clear Lake	7,555	20	16	4
Clinton	24,982	52	46	6
Clive	17,305	30	27	3
Colfax	2,066	4	4	0
Coralville	22,035	39	34	5
Council Bluffs	62,427	134	113	21
Creston	7,784	16	12	4
Davenport	102,392	192	169	23
Dayton	782	1	1	0
Decorah	7,529	19	11	8
Denison	8,415	18	13	5
Des Moines	218,384	450	351	99
DeWitt	5,153	11	10	1
Dubuque	57,973	112	105	7
Dyersville	4,245	7	7	0
Eldora	2,608	4	4	0
Eldridge	6,972	10	9	1
Emmetsburg	3,691	7	6	1
Estherville	5,609	13	13	0
Evansdale	4,758	9	8	1
Fairfield	10,539	20	13	7
Forest City	4,036	9	8	1
Fort Dodge	23,973	43	40	3

(Number.)

State/city	Population	Total law enforcement employees	Total officers	Total civilians
Fort Madison	10,392	21	19	2
Glenwood	5,321	12	10	2
Gowrie	959	1	1	0
Grinnell	9,333	16	14	2
Grundy Center	2,679	5	5	0
Hampton	4,207	8	7	1
Harlan	4,796	9	8	1
Hawarden	2,479	4	4	0
Hiawatha	7,441	14	14	0
Humboldt	4,578	6	6	0
Independence	6,086	12	11	1
Indianola	16,235	22	19	3
Iowa City	77,390	108	85	23
Iowa Falls	5,006	14	10	4
Jefferson	4,123	8	8	0
Johnston	22,708	35	31	4
Keokuk	10,214	25	21	4
Knoxville	7,193	15	14	1
Lansing	941	3	3	0
Le Claire	4,000	8	7	1
Le Mars	10,018	16	14	2
Leon	1,815	3	3	0
Lisbon	2,260	3	3	0
Manchester	4,958	15	10	5
Maquoketa	5,972	18	11	7
Marengo	2,447	3	3	0
Marion	40,612	57	43	14
Marshalltown	27,002	47	42	5
Mason City	26,976	58	52	6
Missouri Valley	2,609	6	6	0
Monticello	3,898	8	7	1
Mount Pleasant	8,749	16	14	2
Mount Vernon	4,449	6	6	0
Muscatine	23,823	41	37	4
Nevada	6,744	12	10	2
New Hampton	3,374	6	6	0
Newton	15,205	28	23	5
North Liberty	20,086	24	22	2
Norwalk	11,871	20	19	1
Oelwein	5,886	14	10	4
Ogden	1,988	2	2	0
Onawa	2,762	5	5	0
Orange City	6,112	7	7	0
Osage	3,538	7	6	1
Osceola	5,224	12	11	1
Oskaloosa	11,415	19	17	2
Ottumwa	24,488	51	41	10
Pella	10,334	24	18	6
Perry	7,421	20	13	7
Pleasant Hill	10,228	22	20	2
Polk City	5,013	7	7	0
Postville	2,065	4	4	0
Prairie City	1,736	3	3	0
Princeton	953	1	1	0
Red Oak	5,287	12	10	2
Rock Valley	3,824	6	6	0
Sac City	2,056	4	4	0
Sergeant Bluff	4,993	9	8	1
Sheldon	5,099	6	6	0
Shenandoah	4,859	13	10	3
Sigourney	2,010	4	3	1
Sioux Center	7,688	7	7	0
Sioux City	82,339	149	126	23
Spencer	11,008	29	20	9
Spirit Lake	5,097	10	9	1
Storm Lake	10,430	23	19	4
Story City	3,362	6	6	0
Tama	2,730	6	6	0
Tipton	3,224	7	6	1
University Heights	1,051	4	4	0
Urbandale	44,541	60	52	8

(Number.)

State/city	Population	Total law enforcement employees	Total officers	Total civilians
Van Meter	1,202	2	2	0
Vinton	5,074	9	8	1
Washington	7,315	11	10	1
Waterloo	67,723	130	121	9
Waukee	24,255	29	26	3
Waukon	3,654	4	4	0
Waverly	10,187	16	15	1
Webster City	7,684	15	9	6
West Branch	2,439	4	4	0
West Burlington	2,882	7	7	0
West Des Moines	67,978	98	86	12
Williamsburg	3,159	7	7	0
Windsor Heights	4,896	14	13	1
Winterset	5,332	8	8	0
KANSAS				
Abilene	6,235	16	13	3
Alma	773	1	1	0
Altamont	1,024	3	3	0
Andale	995	3	3	0
Andover	13,472	31	24	7
Arkansas City	11,718	30	26	4
Arma	1,427	4	4	0
Atchison	10,509	24	24	0
Attica	556	1	1	0
Atwood	1,204	3	3	0
Augusta	9,334	26	19	7
Baldwin City	4,713	13	11	2
Basehor	6,418	16	14	2
Baxter Springs	3,907	14	11	3
Bel Aire	8,252	11	10	1
Belle Plaine	1,555	6	6	0
Belleville	1,877	5	5	0
Benton	868	2	2	0
Blue Rapids	956	2	2	0
Bonner Springs	7,850	27	24	3
Buhler	1,280	3	3	0
Burlingame	885	1	1	0
Burlington	2,545	9	7	2
Burrton	850	2	2	0
Caldwell	990	3	3	0
Caney	1,966	9	5	4
Canton	693	1	1	0
Carbondale	1,371	3	3	0
Cedar Vale	510	1	1	0
Chanute	9,006	18	16	2
Chapman	1,350	2	2	0
Cheney	2,181	5	5	0
Cherokee	710	1	1	0
Cherryvale	2,127	7	6	1
Claflin	608	1	1	0
Clay Center	3,946	7	6	1
Clearwater	2,550	5	4	1
Coffeyville	9,260	32	24	8
Colby	5,305	14	13	1
Columbus	3,042	10	8	2
Colwich	1,419	3	3	0
Concordia	4,904	13	8	5
Council Grove	2,064	8	7	1
Derby	25,012	53	43	10
Dodge City	27,314	55	40	15
Eastborough	732	8	7	1
Edwardsville	4,505	18	17	1
El Dorado	12,899	26	23	3
Elkhart	1,775	2	2	0
Ellinwood	1,950	5	5	0
Ellis	2,024	5	5	0
Ellsworth	2,983	7	6	1
Emporia	24,747	48	41	7
Erie	1,077	4	3	1
Eudora	6,414	12	12	0

State/city	Population	Total law enforcement employees	Total officers	Total civilians
Fairway	3,978	8	8	0
Fort Scott	7,729	22	21	1
Fredonia	2,239	7	6	1
Frontenac	3,406	8	7	1
Galena	2,848	12	11	1
Galva	866	1	1	0
Garden City	26,509	83	57	26
Gardner	22,229	38	33	5
Garnett	3,244	8	8	0
Girard	2,692	7	6	1
Goddard	4,764	14	13	1
Goodland	4,374	10	9	1
Grandview Plaza	1,563	8	7	1
Great Bend	15,069	35	31	4
Halstead	2,018	6	5	1
Haven	1,189	3	3	0
Havensville	157	1	1	0
Hays	20,894	40	35	5
Haysville	11,319	31	24	7
Herington	2,277	8	7	1
Hesston	3,736	8	7	1
Hiawatha	3,119	10	9	1
Highland	999	2	2	0
Hill City	1,408	4	4	0
Hoisington	2,486	7	6	1
Holcomb	2,082	3	2	1
Holton	3,239	7	7	0
Holyrood	419	1	1	0
Horton	1,679	9	5	4
Howard	593	1	1	0
Hoxie	1,198	2	2	0
Hugoton	3,777	8	6	2
Hutchinson	40,431	104	68	36
Independence	8,497	28	20	8
Inman	1,327	4	4	0
Iola	5,265	16	15	1
Junction City	21,921	67	47	20
Kansas City	153,601	423	324	99
Kechi	2,006	5	4	1
Kingman	2,874	7	7	0
Kiowa	931	2	2	0
La Cygne	1,117	2	2	0
La Harpe	523	1	1	0
Lake Quivira	942	1	1	0
Lansing	12,051	19	18	1
Larned	3,739	6	6	0
Lawrence	98,505	168	143	25
Leavenworth	36,149	74	54	20
Leawood	35,052	76	55	21
Lebo	889	1	1	0
Lenexa	56,240	135	85	50
Liberal	19,368	51	35	16
Lindsborg	3,269	8	7	1
Little River	518	2	2	0
Louisburg	4,532	12	11	1
Lyndon	1,016	1	1	0
Lyons	3,483	6	5	1
Macksville	530	1	1	0
Maize	4,836	14	13	1
Marion	1,770	5	5	0
Marysville	3,264	9	8	1
McLouth	839	2	2	0
McPherson	13,070	43	35	8
Meade	1,546	4	3	1
Merriam	11,197	34	29	5
Minneapolis	1,920	5	5	0
Mission	9,379	35	31	4
Mission Hills	3,588	3	3	0
Moran	508	1	1	0
Mound City	685	1	1	0
Moundridge	1,864	5	5	0

(Number.)

State/city	Population	Total law enforcement employees	Total officers	Total civilians
Mount Hope	798	2	2	0
Mulvane	6,451	21	15	6
Neodesha	2,289	8	7	1
Newton	18,697	39	35	4
North Newton	1,752	4	4	0
Oberlin	1,718	4	4	0
Olathe	141,371	215	187	28
Onaga	689	1	1	0
Osage City	2,807	7	7	0
Osborne	1,274	3	3	0
Oswego	1,682	4	4	0
Ottawa	12,221	32	27	5
Overbrook	1,018	2	2	0
Overland Park	194,983	310	246	64
Oxford	1,000	3	3	0
Paola	5,676	22	16	6
Park City	7,779	17	15	2
Parsons	9,569	27	21	6
Peabody	1,098	3	3	0
Pittsburg	20,168	75	48	27
Plainville	1,829	5	5	0
Pleasanton	1,170	2	2	0
Prairie Village	22,508	56	42	14
Pratt	6,606	23	15	8
Roeland Park	6,761	16	14	2
Rose Hill	3,969	9	8	1
Rossville	1,130	2	2	0
Russell	4,455	9	8	1
Sabetha	2,569	10	6	4
Salina	46,567	107	78	29
Scranton	685	1	1	0
Sedan	1,004	1	1	0
Sedgwick	1,635	1	1	0
Seneca	2,058	4	4	0
Shawnee	66,300	113	93	20
South Hutchinson	2,509	6	6	0
Spearville	795	1	1	0
Spring Hill	7,186	13	12	1
Sterling	2,194	5	5	0
St. George	1,046	2	1	1
St. John	1,176	2	2	0
St. Marys	2,636	5	5	0
Tonganoxie	5,591	13	12	1
Topeka	125,655	328	278	50
Troy	969	1	1	0
Udall	709	2	2	0
Ulysses	5,709	11	10	1
Valley Center	7,376	19	17	2
Victoria	1,221	2	2	0
Wamego	4,808	12	8	4
Wellington	7,698	17	15	2
Wellsville	1,795	6	5	1
Westwood	1,674	9	8	1
Wichita	390,080	844	649	195
Wilson	731	1	1	0
Winfield	12,023	28	23	5
Yates Center	1,337	4	4	0
KENTUCKY				
Albany	2,001	7	7	0
Alexandria	9,692	20	16	4
Anchorage	2,443	14	10	4
Ashland	20,222	51	48	3
Auburn	1,376	2	2	0
Augusta	1,135	3	3	0
Bancroft	515	1	1	0
Bardstown	13,239	30	28	2
Beattyville	1,194	6	6	0
Beaver Dam	3,600	5	5	0
Bellefonte	827	4	4	0
Benham	426	1	1	0

Table 19. Full-Time Law Enforcement Employees, by Selected State and City, 2019—*Continued*

(Number.)

State/city	Population	Total law enforcement employees	Total officers	Total civilians
Benton	4,461	8	8	0
Berea	16,074	36	33	3
Bloomfield	1,063	1	1	0
Booneville	126	1	1	0
Brandenburg	2,902	5	5	0
Brodhead	1,182	2	2	0
Brownsville	835	3	3	0
Burgin	981	1	1	0
Burkesville	1,459	10	6	4
Burnside	905	6	5	1
Cadiz	2,673	8	7	1
Calvert City	2,492	8	7	1
Campbellsville	11,488	12	11	1
Carlisle	1,954	9	5	4
Carrollton	3,817	16	15	1
Catlettsburg	1,746	8	8	0
Cave City	2,451	9	9	0
Central City	5,726	16	14	2
Clinton	1,249	3	3	0
Cloverport	1,160	1	1	0
Coal Run Village	1,486	4	4	0
Cold Spring	6,509	12	12	0
Columbia	4,645	42	37	5
Covington	40,350	121	110	11
Cumberland	1,936	6	6	0
Cynthiana	6,354	17	15	2
Danville	16,873	36	34	2
Dayton	5,527	14	13	1
Dry Ridge	2,229	2	2	0
Eddyville	2,525	6	6	0
Edgewood	8,749	12	12	0
Edmonton	1,567	7	7	0
Elizabethtown	30,383	75	56	19
Elkton	2,115	6	5	1
Elsmere	8,673	16	16	0
Eminence	2,594	6	6	0
Erlanger	23,116	44	41	3
Eubank	331	1	1	0
Evarts	808	3	3	0
Falmouth	2,089	7	6	1
Flatwoods	7,041	13	13	0
Flemingsburg	2,801	8	8	0
Florence	32,848	67	64	3
Fort Mitchell	8,252	15	15	0
Fort Thomas	16,386	24	23	1
Fort Wright	5,744	14	14	0
Frankfort	27,723	70	56	14
Franklin	9,036	24	23	1
Fulton	2,145	12	11	1
Georgetown	35,106	81	57	24
Grayson	3,923	12	11	1
Greensburg	2,087	10	6	4
Greenup	1,107	4	4	0
Greenville	4,224	11	11	0
Guthrie	1,398	5	5	0
Hardinsburg	2,346	5	5	0
Harlan	1,507	13	10	3
Harrodsburg	8,509	19	16	3
Hartford	2,749	5	5	0
Hazard	4,938	25	19	6
Heritage Creek	1,148	11	11	0
Highland Heights	7,114	12	11	1
Hillview	9,235	18	17	1
Hodgenville	3,239	7	7	0
Hopkinsville	30,895	111	77	34
Horse Cave	2,402	7	7	0
Hustonville	369	1	1	0
Independence	28,541	38	36	2
Indian Hills	2,998	7	7	0
Irvine	2,307	5	5	0
Irvington	1,187	4	4	0

Table 19. Full-Time Law Enforcement Employees, by Selected State and City, 2019—*Continued*

(Number.)

State/city	Population	Total law enforcement employees	Total officers	Total civilians
Jackson	1,954	13	8	5
Jamestown	1,787	5	5	0
Jeffersontown	28,015	62	51	11
Jenkins	1,930	4	4	0
Junction City	2,315	2	2	0
La Grange	9,080	19	17	2
Lakeside Park-Crestview Hills	6,046	13	12	1
Lancaster	3,862	14	14	0
Lawrenceburg	11,538	23	15	8
Lebanon	5,716	26	17	9
Lebanon Junction	1,973	2	2	0
Leitchfield	6,852	20	19	1
Lewisburg	802	1	1	0
Lexington	326,070	692	602	90
Louisa	2,365	6	6	0
Louisville Metro	675,501	1,446	1,191	255
Loyall	606	1	1	0
Ludlow	4,495	12	11	1
Madisonville	18,711	61	47	14
Marion	2,853	10	5	5
Mayfield	9,851	30	28	2
Maysville	8,750	34	24	10
McKee	785	1	1	0
Middlesboro	9,223	27	24	3
Middletown	7,957	11	10	1
Millersburg	799	1	1	0
Monticello	6,015	10	10	0
Morehead	7,736	29	20	9
Morganfield	3,387	7	7	0
Mount Sterling	7,326	24	22	2
Mount Vernon	2,442	8	8	0
Mount Washington	14,855	24	22	2
Muldraugh	1,000	3	3	0
Murray	19,545	44	37	7
New Haven	894	1	1	0
Newport	14,965	39	36	3
Nicholasville	31,188	76	68	8
Oak Grove	7,359	23	17	6
Olive Hill	1,560	7	7	0
Owingsville	1,566	6	6	0
Paducah	24,832	77	71	6
Paintsville	4,013	10	9	1
Paris	9,879	25	23	2
Park Hills	2,980	7	7	0
Pembroke	893	1	1	0
Pewee Valley	1,576	1	1	0
Pikeville	6,592	30	20	10
Pineville	1,763	7	7	0
Pippa Passes	677	9	1	8
Prestonsburg	3,550	22	15	7
Princeton	6,105	15	14	1
Prospect	4,954	7	6	1
Raceland	2,337	7	7	0
Radcliff	22,998	50	36	14
Ravenna	562	1	1	0
Richmond	36,458	66	57	9
Russell	3,221	13	13	0
Russell Springs	2,632	11	10	1
Russellville	7,068	24	23	1
Sadieville	364	1	1	0
Salyersville	1,712	4	4	0
Science Hill	697	3	3	0
Scottsville	4,520	28	16	12
Shelbyville	16,531	30	29	1
Shepherdsville	12,515	39	37	2
Shively	15,845	36	30	6
Simpsonville	2,945	9	9	0
Smiths Grove	803	1	1	0
Somerset	11,519	43	38	5
Southgate	3,962	8	8	0
Springfield	2,965	15	8	7

Table 19. Full-Time Law Enforcement Employees, by Selected State and City, 2019—*Continued*

(Number.)

State/city	Population	Total law enforcement employees	Total officers	Total civilians
Stamping Ground	802	2	2	0
Stanford	3,679	14	10	4
Stanton	2,651	9	9	0
St. Matthews	18,275	45	39	6
Taylor Mill	6,810	12	11	1
Taylorsville	1,286	5	5	0
Trenton	375	1	1	0
Uniontown	930	1	1	0
Vanceburg	1,387	6	6	0
Versailles	26,625	35	34	1
Villa Hills	7,465	14	14	0
Vine Grove	6,468	7	7	0
Warsaw	1,699	2	2	0
West Buechel	1,285	8	8	0
West Point	870	3	3	0
Whitesburg	1,845	6	5	1
Wilder	3,074	8	8	0
Williamsburg	5,298	19	18	1
Williamstown	3,946	8	7	1
Wilmore	6,489	9	8	1
Winchester	18,605	46	32	14
Woodlawn Park	978	1	1	0
Worthington	1,505	4	4	0
LOUISIANA				
Abbeville	12,142	31	28	3
Addis	5,747	12	11	1
Alexandria	46,630	170	137	33
Arnaudville	1,054	9	5	4
Baker	13,240	36	27	9
Basile	1,799	9	8	1
Bastrop	10,156	25	25	0
Baton Rouge	220,648	770	616	154
Bernice	1,611	2	2	0
Berwick	4,416	14	13	1
Blanchard	3,147	7	6	1
Bogalusa	11,681	48	29	19
Bossier City	69,044	198	162	36
Breaux Bridge	8,237	21	19	2
Broussard	12,985	36	32	4
Carencro	9,387	31	29	2
Church Point	4,424	17	17	0
Clinton	1,500	6	6	0
Crowley	12,621	51	49	2
Cullen	1,069	1	1	0
Denham Springs	9,713	37	29	8
De Ridder	10,765	30	25	5
Epps	819	2	1	1
Erath	2,059	11	7	4
Eunice	9,939	36	22	14
Farmerville	3,725	13	13	0
Fisher	219	1	1	0
Florien	601	3	3	0
Folsom	873	5	4	1
Franklinton	3,761	23	17	6
French Settlement	1,182	5	5	0
Georgetown	326	4	3	1
Golden Meadow	1,969	7	5	2
Gonzales	10,940	45	40	5
Gramercy	3,307	8	8	0
Greensburg	653	5	5	0
Greenwood	3,141	11	10	1
Gretna	17,729	146	103	43
Hammond	20,887	106	79	27
Harahan	9,298	28	21	7
Haughton	3,372	14	13	1
Houma	32,771	89	73	16
Ida	205	1	1	0
Independence	1,921	9	9	0
Iowa	3,262	18	13	5
Jena	3,370	7	6	1

State/city	Population	Total law enforcement employees	Total officers	Total civilians
Jennings	9,886	28	22	6
Kaplan	4,465	21	15	6
Kinder	2,388	15	12	3
Krotz Springs	1,208	6	5	1
Lafayette	126,694	334	280	54
Lake Arthur	2,778	9	9	0
Lake Charles	78,733	174	141	33
Lake Providence	3,496	11	6	5
Leesville	5,617	26	18	8
Lutcher	3,192	2	2	0
Mamou	3,151	13	13	0
Mandeville	12,331	46	36	10
Mansfield	4,695	20	14	6
Many	2,704	11	11	0
Marion	741	1	1	0
Minden	11,984	29	28	1
Monroe	47,746	169	130	39
Morgan City	10,749	53	47	6
Natchitoches	17,747	65	52	13
New Orleans	394,498	1,448	1,154	294
Oil City	980	4	4	0
Olla	1,349	3	3	0
Opelousas	16,049	58	45	13
Patterson	5,806	25	25	0
Pineville	14,261	75	67	8
Plaquemine	6,562	28	22	6
Pollock	479	5	4	1
Ponchatoula	7,478	32	26	6
Port Allen	4,940	17	16	1
Port Vincent	751	3	3	0
Rayne	8,088	22	21	1
Ruston	22,148	46	34	12
Scott	8,725	31	29	2
Shreveport	187,556	709	536	173
Sibley	1,144	2	2	0
Springhill	4,792	17	15	2
Sterlington	2,912	3	3	0
St. Gabriel	7,458	22	14	8
Sulphur	20,200	68	47	21
Tallulah	6,701	13	9	4
Thibodaux	14,587	65	53	12
Tickfaw	787	5	5	0
Vidalia	3,871	35	29	6
Walker	6,296	23	19	4
Welsh	3,254	16	15	1
Westlake	4,959	20	17	3
West Monroe	12,350	67	46	21
Westwego	8,415	38	38	0
White Castle	1,711	9	7	2
Winnfield	4,307	16	10	6
Youngsville	15,020	33	28	5
Zachary	18,009	45	42	3
MAINE				
Ashland	1,206	3	3	0
Auburn	23,214	60	53	7
Augusta	18,629	59	46	13
Baileyville	1,442	5	5	0
Bangor	31,872	94	78	16
Bar Harbor	7,682	28	20	8
Bath	8,309	23	19	4
Belfast	6,720	16	15	1
Berwick	7,860	13	12	1
Biddeford	21,545	78	55	23
Boothbay Harbor	2,204	8	7	1
Brewer	9,000	22	20	2
Bridgton	5,388	8	7	1
Brunswick	20,510	46	32	14
Bucksport	4,926	12	8	4
Buxton	8,345	14	7	7
Calais	2,973	8	8	0

Table 19. Full-Time Law Enforcement Employees, by Selected State and City, 2019—*Continued*

(Number.)

State/city	Population	Total law enforcement employees	Total officers	Total civilians
Camden	4,823	13	11	2
Cape Elizabeth	9,352	15	14	1
Caribou	7,548	17	16	1
Carrabassett Valley	777	1	1	0
Clinton	3,329	4	4	0
Cumberland	8,295	13	11	2
Damariscotta	2,151	6	5	1
Dexter	3,671	6	6	0
Dixfield	2,465	4	4	0
Dover-Foxcroft	4,033	6	6	0
East Millinocket	2,919	3	3	0
Eastport	1,251	3	3	0
Eliot	6,817	9	8	1
Ellsworth	8,088	19	16	3
Fairfield	6,534	10	10	0
Falmouth	12,378	29	20	9
Farmington	7,603	11	10	1
Fort Fairfield	3,256	5	5	0
Fort Kent	3,816	8	4	4
Freeport	8,593	17	15	2
Fryeburg	3,398	5	5	0
Gardiner	5,645	12	12	0
Gorham	17,818	25	23	2
Gouldsboro	1,745	2	2	0
Greenville	1,595	3	3	0
Hallowell	2,371	5	5	0
Hampden	7,352	12	11	1
Holden	3,081	4	4	0
Houlton	5,720	17	12	5
Islesboro	565	1	1	0
Jay	4,586	9	8	1
Kennebunk	11,622	27	24	3
Kennebunkport	3,660	19	14	5
Kittery	9,890	27	21	6
Lewiston	35,865	92	80	12
Limestone	2,200	3	3	0
Lincoln	4,886	9	8	1
Lisbon	8,975	20	14	6
Livermore Falls	3,134	6	6	0
Machias	2,055	3	3	0
Madawaska	3,662	7	6	1
Mechanic Falls	2,973	5	5	0
Mexico	2,605	5	5	0
Milbridge	1,255	2	2	0
Millinocket	4,241	7	7	0
Milo	2,270	3	3	0
Monmouth	4,131	4	4	0
Newport	3,269	6	6	0
North Berwick	4,731	9	8	1
Norway	4,979	9	8	1
Oakland	6,296	11	10	1
Ogunquit	931	12	11	1
Old Orchard Beach	8,946	24	22	2
Old Town	7,413	17	16	1
Orono	10,722	16	15	1
Oxford	4,100	8	7	1
Paris	5,112	8	7	1
Phippsburg	2,259	1	1	0
Pittsfield	3,999	7	6	1
Portland	66,458	207	150	57
Presque Isle	8,918	19	14	5
Rangeley	1,143	3	3	0
Richmond	3,440	4	4	0
Rockland	7,128	19	17	2
Rockport	3,378	6	6	0
Rumford	5,670	13	13	0
Sabattus	5,064	9	8	1
Saco	19,908	46	33	13
Sanford	21,233	44	40	4
Scarborough	20,542	61	40	21
Searsport	2,648	3	3	0

(Number.)

State/city	Population	Total law enforcement employees	Total officers	Total civilians
Skowhegan........	8,214	16	15	1
South Berwick........	7,564	9	8	1
South Portland........	25,686	58	52	6
Southwest Harbor........	1,795	9	5	4
Thomaston	2,767	2	2	0
Topsham........	8,863	16	15	1
Van Buren........	1,972	3	3	0
Veazie........	1,814	4	4	0
Waldoboro	5,041	9	8	1
Washburn........	1,533	2	2	0
Waterville........	16,765	37	29	8
Wells	10,670	32	23	9
Westbrook........	19,166	43	37	6
Wilton	3,924	6	6	0
Windham........	18,627	30	27	3
Winslow	7,598	12	11	1
Winthrop	5,979	12	8	4
Wiscasset........	3,697	5	4	1
Yarmouth	8,540	15	14	1
York	13,231	38	27	11
MARYLAND				
Aberdeen........	16,194	51	39	12
Annapolis	39,277	148	118	30
Baltimore........	597,239	2,940	2,465	475
Baltimore City Sheriff........		187	122	65
Bel Air........	10,031	39	29	10
Berlin	4,862	16	13	3
Berwyn Heights........	3,278	10	9	1
Bladensburg........	9,476	35	24	11
Boonsboro	3,596	4	3	1
Bowie	59,093	81	61	20
Brentwood........	3,494	5	4	1
Brunswick........	6,426	16	16	0
Cambridge........	12,264	42	38	4
Capitol Heights........	4,551	15	13	2
Centreville	4,882	13	13	0
Chestertown........	5,027	13	12	1
Cheverly	6,482	12	10	2
Chevy Chase Village........	2,073	16	10	6
Colmar Manor........	1,468	3	2	1
Cottage City	1,363	4	4	0
Crisfield	2,554	12	9	3
Cumberland........	19,321	56	49	7
Delmar........	3,248	14	13	1
Denton	4,504	15	14	1
District Heights	6,015	8	7	1
Easton	16,523	51	43	8
Edmonston	1,499	4	3	1
Elkton	15,662	46	40	6
Fairmount Heights	1,533	2	2	0
Federalsburg	2,652	9	8	1
Forest Heights	2,583	8	7	1
Frederick........	73,030	189	140	49
Frostburg........	8,510	20	17	3
Fruitland	5,346	22	20	2
Glenarden	6,234	19	17	2
Greenbelt	23,417	63	43	20
Greensboro........	1,874	4	4	0
Hagerstown........	40,258	101	81	20
Hampstead	6,397	10	9	1
Hancock........	1,539	3	2	1
Havre de Grace........	13,890	44	34	10
Hurlock........	2,013	8	7	1
Hyattsville........	18,331	53	38	15
Landover Hills	1,656	4	3	1
La Plata........	9,538	20	18	2
Laurel	25,814	83	62	21
Luke	61	1	1	0
Manchester........	4,858	6	6	0
Morningside	1,296	8	7	1

(Number.)

State/city	Population	Total law enforcement employees	Total officers	Total civilians
Mount Airy	9,472	12	10	2
Mount Rainier	8,143	18	16	2
New Carrollton	13,036	29	22	7
North East	3,639	11	10	1
Oakland	1,816	2	2	0
Ocean City	6,905	137	105	32
Ocean Pines	12,264	16	12	4
Oxford	598	3	3	0
Perryville	4,431	14	12	2
Pocomoke City	4,025	24	17	7
Princess Anne	3,549	14	12	2
Ridgely	1,652	5	5	0
Rising Sun	2,799	6	6	0
Riverdale Park	7,258	27	20	7
Rock Hall	1,264	3	3	0
Salisbury	33,132	108	85	23
Seat Pleasant	4,803	24	20	4
Smithsburg	2,967	5	4	1
Snow Hill	2,029	6	6	0
St. Michaels	1,025	10	9	1
Sykesville	3,959	7	6	1
Takoma Park	17,893	46	34	12
Taneytown	6,824	22	12	10
Thurmont	6,824	14	11	3
University Park	2,651	9	8	1
Upper Marlboro	675	3	3	0
Westminster	18,664	55	42	13
MASSACHUSETTS				
Abington	16,448	29	27	2
Acton	23,780	54	43	11
Acushnet	10,533	24	21	3
Agawam	28,736	67	54	13
Amesbury	17,595	37	30	7
Amherst	39,603	64	46	18
Andover	36,547	73	54	19
Aquinnah	328	4	4	0
Arlington	45,614	78	64	14
Ashburnham	6,330	17	12	5
Ashby	3,228	11	6	5
Ashfield	1,734	1	1	0
Ashland	17,742	34	27	7
Attleboro	44,959	86	73	13
Auburn	16,724	47	36	11
Avon	4,504	19	15	4
Ayer	8,192	32	20	12
Barnstable	44,032	132	106	26
Barre	5,573	10	9	1
Becket	1,724	4	4	0
Bedford	14,193	37	29	8
Belchertown	15,195	26	20	6
Bellingham	17,143	37	30	7
Berkley	6,799	13	13	0
Berlin	3,241	11	10	1
Bernardston	2,113	3	3	0
Beverly	42,317	69	66	3
Billerica	43,882	70	65	5
Blackstone	9,294	20	16	4
Bolton	5,393	13	12	1
Boston	698,941	2,922	2,143	779
Bourne	19,734	50	41	9
Boxborough	6,540	19	12	7
Boxford	8,352	13	13	0
Boylston	4,694	14	10	4
Braintree	37,145	100	84	16
Brewster	9,725	29	24	5
Brockton	95,287	218	195	23
Brookfield	3,440	5	5	0
Brookline	58,928	158	128	30
Buckland	1,872	2	2	0
Burlington	29,082	71	64	7

Table 19. Full-Time Law Enforcement Employees, by Selected State and City, 2019—*Continued*

(Number.)

State/city	Population	Total law enforcement employees	Total officers	Total civilians
Cambridge	119,908	301	267	34
Canton	23,706	44	44	0
Carlisle	5,255	15	10	5
Carver	11,721	22	17	5
Chatham	6,117	27	21	6
Chelmsford	35,218	67	53	14
Chelsea	40,496	115	107	8
Cheshire	3,133	1	1	0
Chicopee	55,293	157	130	27
Clinton	13,964	38	28	10
Cohasset	8,609	20	19	1
Concord	19,253	46	36	10
Dalton	6,546	12	10	2
Danvers	27,664	56	44	12
Dartmouth	34,035	83	68	15
Dedham	25,203	59	56	3
Deerfield	5,032	11	10	1
Dennis	13,738	55	45	10
Dighton	7,935	18	13	5
Douglas	8,946	19	15	4
Dover	6,118	17	16	1
Dracut	31,786	46	41	5
Dudley	11,754	14	13	1
Dunstable	3,405	9	8	1
East Bridgewater	14,472	28	22	6
Eastham	4,823	23	17	6
Easthampton	15,979	34	28	6
East Longmeadow	16,269	29	27	2
Easton	25,079	46	37	9
Edgartown	4,362	21	19	2
Egremont	1,206	4	4	0
Erving	1,771	6	6	0
Essex	3,795	9	8	1
Everett	47,195	139	123	16
Fairhaven	15,996	38	32	6
Fall River	89,066	286	227	59
Falmouth	30,717	58	54	4
Fitchburg	40,621	95	77	18
Foxborough	17,631	39	36	3
Framingham	73,127	143	125	18
Franklin	33,149	54	52	2
Freetown	9,388	24	19	5
Gardner	20,628	46	33	13
Georgetown	8,777	18	13	5
Gill	1,490	2	2	0
Gloucester	30,362	66	60	6
Goshen	1,065	2	2	0
Grafton	18,880	24	20	4
Granby	6,360	15	11	4
Great Barrington	6,822	18	17	1
Greenfield	17,464	46	33	13
Groton	11,388	27	20	7
Groveland	6,846	13	11	2
Hadley	5,358	20	16	4
Halifax	7,874	13	12	1
Hamilton	8,075	18	13	5
Hampden	5,199	16	11	5
Hanson	10,876	25	20	5
Hardwick	3,039	5	5	0
Harwich	12,028	42	35	7
Haverhill	63,935	108	90	18
Hingham	23,960	49	47	2
Holbrook	10,990	22	21	1
Holland	2,484	2	2	0
Holliston	14,996	29	23	6
Holyoke	40,178	130	112	18
Hopedale	5,929	16	12	4
Hopkinton	18,585	34	24	10
Hudson	19,910	42	32	10
Hull	10,402	29	27	2
Ipswich	14,095	29	25	4

Table 19. Full-Time Law Enforcement Employees, by Selected State and City, 2019—*Continued*

(Number.)

State/city	Population	Total law enforcement employees	Total officers	Total civilians
Kingston	13,758	33	25	8
Lakeville	11,419	22	19	3
Lancaster	8,136	12	11	1
Lanesboro	2,950	6	6	0
Lawrence	80,243	162	141	21
Leicester	11,368	21	20	1
Lenox	4,951	9	9	0
Leominster	41,631	92	75	17
Lexington	33,824	63	46	17
Lincoln	6,798	18	13	5
Littleton	10,334	28	20	8
Longmeadow	15,737	33	27	6
Lowell	111,423	342	244	98
Ludlow	21,395	49	38	11
Lunenburg	11,781	17	16	1
Lynn	94,449	187	168	19
Lynnfield	13,130	26	21	5
Malden	60,746	111	100	11
Mansfield	23,987	48	38	10
Marblehead	20,574	42	31	11
Marion	5,132	15	15	0
Marlborough	39,673	75	66	9
Marshfield	25,794	43	40	3
Mashpee	14,094	44	35	9
Mattapoisett	6,372	20	20	0
Maynard	10,654	27	21	6
Medfield	12,913	20	14	6
Medford	57,484	122	102	20
Medway	13,405	24	23	1
Melrose	28,120	49	48	1
Mendon	6,176	19	14	5
Methuen	50,727	116	96	20
Middleboro	25,183	49	42	7
Middleton	10,113	18	16	2
Millbury	13,837	25	21	4
Millis	8,252	18	16	2
Millville	3,249	7	6	1
Montague	8,298	21	17	4
Nahant	3,511	13	12	1
Natick	36,358	72	54	18
Needham	31,275	56	49	7
New Bedford	94,613	301	243	58
Newton	88,658	194	149	45
Norfolk	11,992	23	21	2
Northampton	28,735	70	63	7
North Andover	31,428	49	37	12
North Attleboro	29,202	63	48	15
Northborough	15,075	29	22	7
Northbridge	16,732	27	20	7
North Reading	15,687	34	31	3
Norton	19,894	35	34	1
Norwell	11,105	25	22	3
Norwood	29,185	72	61	11
Orange	7,643	14	13	1
Orleans	5,742	27	21	6
Oxford	13,973	27	21	6
Palmer	12,258	25	21	4
Paxton	4,944	19	15	4
Peabody	53,104	112	92	20
Pelham	1,322	2	2	0
Pembroke	18,378	34	32	2
Pepperell	12,146	17	16	1
Pittsfield	42,268	110	88	22
Plymouth	60,870	144	128	16
Plympton	2,980	8	8	0
Princeton	3,459	7	6	1
Provincetown	2,939	27	19	8
Quincy	94,113	240	209	31
Randolph	34,385	64	58	6
Raynham	14,322	36	29	7
Reading	25,305	62	45	17

Table 19. Full-Time Law Enforcement Employees, by Selected State and City, 2019—*Continued*

(Number.)

State/city	Population	Total law enforcement employees	Total officers	Total civilians
Rehoboth	12,252	33	27	6
Revere	53,654	113	106	7
Rockport	7,280	21	17	4
Salem	43,443	104	94	10
Sandwich	20,016	35	35	0
Saugus	28,378	72	59	13
Scituate	18,774	38	35	3
Sharon	18,973	36	31	5
Sherborn	4,334	13	12	1
Somerset	18,036	36	31	5
Somerville	81,668	159	127	32
Southborough	10,140	24	19	5
Southbridge	16,826	45	34	11
Southwick	9,772	23	18	5
Spencer	11,911	23	18	5
Springfield	154,306	552	489	63
Stockbridge	1,898	8	7	1
Stoneham	22,732	45	39	6
Stoughton	28,961	72	60	12
Stow	7,234	15	11	4
Sturbridge	9,611	26	19	7
Sudbury	19,727	41	30	11
Sunderland	3,656	6	5	1
Sutton	9,551	19	14	5
Swampscott	15,296	31	30	1
Swansea	16,681	40	34	6
Taunton	57,028	121	115	6
Templeton	8,109	13	8	5
Tewksbury	31,424	75	62	13
Topsfield	6,644	14	13	1
Townsend	9,546	15	14	1
Truro	1,984	18	13	5
Uxbridge	14,066	23	18	5
Wakefield	27,178	44	43	1
Walpole	25,150	54	43	11
Waltham	62,737	176	144	32
Wareham	22,592	56	45	11
Watertown	36,189	83	70	13
Wayland	13,891	31	24	7
Wellesley	29,651	55	41	14
Wellfleet	2,705	20	15	5
Wenham	5,295	11	10	1
Westborough	19,155	35	33	2
West Brookfield	3,767	6	6	0
Westfield	41,507	94	88	6
Westford	24,403	50	46	4
Westminster	7,902	15	13	2
West Newbury	4,712	15	10	5
Weston	12,138	35	25	10
Westport	15,920	33	30	3
West Springfield	28,628	95	85	10
West Tisbury	2,911	10	9	1
Westwood	16,199	43	33	10
Weymouth	57,776	119	99	20
Whitman	15,134	27	26	1
Wilbraham	14,730	28	27	1
Williamsburg	2,489	1	1	0
Williamstown	8,021	13	12	1
Wilmington	23,915	51	48	3
Winchendon	10,897	20	15	5
Winchester	22,850	46	36	10
Winthrop	18,692	35	34	1
Woburn	40,251	84	80	4
Worcester	184,945	506	456	50
Wrentham	11,989	22	21	1
Yarmouth	23,076	74	60	14
MICHIGAN				
Adrian	20,334	33	31	2
Adrian Township	6,239	2	2	0
Akron	374	1	1	0

(Number.)

State/city	Population	Total law enforcement employees	Total officers	Total civilians
Albion	8,462	17	16	1
Allegan	5,038	9	8	1
Allen Park	26,945	45	42	3
Alma	8,866	14	13	1
Almont	2,814	7	7	0
Alpena	9,901	20	18	2
Ann Arbor	122,893	153	124	29
Argentine Township	6,506	4	4	0
Armada	1,730	2	2	0
Auburn Hills	24,393	54	49	5
Au Gres	834	1	1	0
Bad Axe	2,923	8	7	1
Bangor	1,823	5	5	0
Baraga	1,949	2	2	0
Baroda-Lake Township	3,859	4	4	0
Barry Township	3,510	3	3	0
Bath Township	13,131	13	12	1
Battle Creek	60,607	132	111	21
Bay City	32,793	56	51	5
Beaverton	1,176	3	3	0
Belding	5,747	8	8	0
Bellaire	1,067	2	2	0
Belleville	3,873	10	8	2
Bellevue	1,291	2	2	0
Benton Harbor	9,801	25	20	5
Benton Township	14,372	26	22	4
Berkley	15,482	35	28	7
Berrien Springs-Oronoko Township	8,940	9	8	1
Beverly Hills	10,429	29	25	4
Big Rapids	10,389	17	17	0
Birch Run	1,462	6	5	1
Birmingham	21,479	43	32	11
Blackman Township	37,002	41	39	2
Blissfield	3,250	6	6	0
Bloomfield Hills	4,027	26	23	3
Bloomfield Township	42,326	86	68	18
Boyne City	3,752	7	6	1
Breckenridge	1,261	1	1	0
Bridgeport Township	9,778	9	8	1
Bridgman	2,224	5	5	0
Brighton	7,684	18	15	3
Bronson	2,308	4	4	0
Brown City	1,240	2	2	0
Brownstown Township	32,083	39	31	8
Buchanan	4,274	10	9	1
Buena Vista Township	8,095	14	13	1
Burton	28,496	38	36	2
Cadillac	10,466	17	15	2
Calumet	691	1	1	0
Cambridge Township	5,657	4	4	0
Canton Township	93,406	131	91	40
Capac	1,822	2	2	0
Carleton	2,356	4	3	1
Caro	3,969	7	7	0
Carrollton Township	5,626	6	6	0
Carson City	1,117	2	2	0
Caseville	731	2	2	0
Caspian-Gaastra	1,165	1	1	0
Cass City	2,268	4	4	0
Cassopolis	1,695	5	5	0
Center Line	8,232	22	18	4
Central Lake	938	1	1	0
Charlevoix	2,498	8	7	1
Charlotte	9,088	15	14	1
Cheboygan	4,695	9	9	0
Chelsea	5,543	14	10	4
Chesterfield Township	46,774	56	42	14
Chikaming Township	3,108	6	5	1
Chocolay Township	5,931	5	4	1
Clare	3,061	8	8	0
Clawson	11,948	18	17	1

Table 19. Full-Time Law Enforcement Employees, by Selected State and City, 2019—*Continued*

(Number.)

State/city	Population	Total law enforcement employees	Total officers	Total civilians
Clayton Township	7,110	7	6	1
Clay Township	8,844	23	18	5
Clinton	2,274	4	4	0
Clinton Township	101,308	104	95	9
Clio	2,483	4	4	0
Coldwater	12,098	20	18	2
Coleman	1,188	2	2	0
Coloma Township	6,362	11	8	3
Colon	1,159	3	3	0
Columbia Township	7,359	7	7	0
Constantine	2,105	6	5	1
Corunna	3,337	3	3	0
Covert Township	2,853	7	7	0
Croswell	2,262	6	6	0
Crystal Falls	1,359	2	2	0
Davison	4,874	7	6	1
Davison Township	19,207	21	19	2
Dearborn	93,902	234	187	47
Dearborn Heights	55,368	98	79	19
Decatur	1,731	5	5	0
Denton Township	5,379	4	4	0
Detroit	663,502	3,126	2,517	609
DeWitt	4,790	7	6	1
DeWitt Township	15,613	16	15	1
Dowagiac	5,719	15	14	1
Dryden Township	4,734	4	4	0
Dundee	4,486	3	3	0
Durand	3,825	29	12	17
East Grand Rapids	12,040	29	27	2
East Jordan	2,351	4	4	0
East Lansing	47,913	64	52	12
Eastpointe	32,340	46	42	4
Eaton Rapids	5,216	10	9	1
Eau Claire	599	1	1	0
Ecorse	9,601	18	16	2
Elk Rapids	1,618	5	5	0
Emmett Township	11,668	16	14	2
Erie Township	4,342	3	3	0
Escanaba	12,129	46	32	14
Essexville	3,296	4	3	1
Evart	1,865	4	3	1
Fair Haven Township	1,038	1	1	0
Farmington	10,587	24	23	1
Farmington Hills	81,262	138	106	32
Fennville	1,421	1	1	0
Fenton	11,281	22	13	9
Ferndale	20,097	50	42	8
Flat Rock	10,024	18	18	0
Flint	95,212	117	94	23
Flint Township	30,319	51	43	8
Flushing	7,860	9	9	0
Flushing Township	10,174	6	6	0
Forsyth Township	6,197	10	8	2
Fowlerville	2,869	7	6	1
Frankenmuth	5,458	7	7	0
Frankfort	1,289	4	4	0
Franklin	3,268	10	10	0
Fraser	14,578	44	34	10
Fremont	4,103	8	7	1
Fruitport Township	14,346	10	10	0
Gaines Township	6,080	1	1	0
Galesburg	2,082	4	4	0
Garden City	26,420	37	34	3
Garfield Township	838	1	1	0
Gaylord	3,709	10	9	1
Genesee Township	20,410	18	16	2
Gerrish Township	2,922	5	5	0
Gibraltar	4,467	10	9	1
Gladstone	4,699	11	10	1
Gladwin	2,880	5	5	0
Grand Beach	281	2	2	0

State/city	Population	Total law enforcement employees	Total officers	Total civilians
Grand Blanc	7,865	18	15	3
Grand Blanc Township	36,523	49	42	7
Grand Haven	11,155	36	33	3
Grand Ledge	7,862	14	14	0
Grand Rapids	201,799	368	299	69
Grandville	16,021	27	25	2
Grant	892	1	1	0
Grayling	1,833	8	8	0
Green Oak Township	19,075	17	15	2
Greenville	8,447	19	17	2
Grosse Ile Township	10,135	24	17	7
Grosse Pointe	5,141	27	22	5
Grosse Pointe Farms	9,108	37	32	5
Grosse Pointe Park	11,041	37	32	5
Grosse Pointe Shores	2,836	17	17	0
Grosse Pointe Woods	15,350	33	27	6
Hamburg Township	21,755	21	18	3
Hampton Township	9,428	9	9	0
Hamtramck	21,633	35	30	5
Hancock	4,533	8	8	0
Harbor Beach	1,584	4	4	0
Harbor Springs	1,208	9	9	0
Harper Woods	13,746	33	30	3
Hart	2,089	5	5	0
Hartford	2,589	5	5	0
Hastings	7,313	17	15	2
Hazel Park	16,478	39	34	5
Hesperia	941	2	2	0
Highland Park	10,703	8	6	2
Hillsdale	8,020	15	13	2
Holland	33,356	66	57	9
Holly	6,185	8	8	0
Home Township	1,373	1	1	0
Hopkins	611	1	1	0
Houghton	8,029	11	10	1
Howell	9,637	20	18	2
Hudson	2,207	2	2	0
Huntington Woods	6,321	18	17	1
Huron Township	16,089	26	20	6
Imlay City	3,575	11	8	3
Inkster	24,268	37	25	12
Ionia	10,907	17	15	2
Iron Mountain	7,320	12	12	0
Iron River	2,816	4	4	0
Ironwood	4,883	10	10	0
Ishpeming	6,426	12	11	1
Ishpeming Township	3,528	1	1	0
Jackson	32,503	56	44	12
Jonesville	2,204	3	3	0
Kalamazoo	76,827	262	240	22
Kalamazoo Township	24,613	40	33	7
Kalkaska	2,086	3	3	0
Keego Harbor	3,462	9	9	0
Kentwood	52,274	79	68	11
Kingsford	4,950	19	19	0
Kingston	409	1	1	0
Kinross Township	7,288	2	2	0
Laingsburg	1,281	1	1	0
Lake Angelus	309	1	1	0
Lake Linden	962	1	1	0
Lake Odessa	2,036	4	4	0
Lake Orion	3,177	5	4	1
Lakeview	1,007	2	2	0
L'Anse	1,855	4	4	0
Lansing	118,953	246	200	46
Lansing Township	8,294	15	14	1
Lapeer	8,597	20	19	1
Lathrup Village	4,124	11	10	1
Laurium	1,912	4	4	0
Lawton	1,799	5	5	0
Lennon	482	1	1	0

Table 19. Full-Time Law Enforcement Employees, by Selected State and City, 2019—*Continued*

(Number.)

State/city	Population	Total law enforcement employees	Total officers	Total civilians
Leslie	1,909	3	3	0
Lexington	1,099	3	3	0
Lincoln Park	36,336	54	47	7
Lincoln Township	14,615	11	10	1
Linden	3,908	5	5	0
Litchfield	1,333	2	2	0
Livonia	93,644	160	124	36
Lowell	4,198	6	5	1
Ludington	8,144	15	14	1
Luna Pier	1,407	2	2	0
Mackinac Island	468	5	5	0
Mackinaw City	797	7	7	0
Madison Heights	30,081	56	45	11
Madison Township	8,287	5	5	0
Mancelona	1,364	1	1	0
Manistee	6,103	39	17	22
Manistique	2,915	8	8	0
Manton	1,544	1	1	0
Marenisco Township	1,434	1	1	0
Marine City	4,061	5	4	1
Marlette	1,756	4	4	0
Marquette	20,599	39	34	5
Marshall	6,997	14	14	0
Marysville	9,656	16	14	2
Mason	8,483	13	12	1
Mattawan	1,970	7	7	0
Mayville	882	1	1	0
Melvindale	10,264	24	22	2
Memphis	1,184	1	1	0
Mendon	854	2	2	0
Menominee	8,052	17	16	1
Meridian Township	43,790	42	38	4
Metamora Township	4,287	4	4	0
Metro Police Authority of Genesee County	19,931	27	24	3
Michiana	181	3	3	0
Midland	41,791	52	50	2
Milan	6,106	9	9	0
Milford	16,984	21	19	2
Millington	995	2	2	0
Monroe	19,600	43	38	5
Montague	2,359	5	5	0
Montrose Township	7,447	9	8	1
Morenci	2,146	2	2	0
Morrice	894	2	2	0
Mount Morris	2,834	4	4	0
Mount Morris Township	20,274	31	28	3
Mount Pleasant	25,315	34	28	6
Munising	2,177	4	4	0
Muskegon	37,178	76	68	8
Muskegon Heights	10,717	25	22	3
Muskegon Township	17,937	15	14	1
Napoleon Township	6,757	5	5	0
Nashville	1,678	4	4	0
Negaunee	4,544	9	9	0
Newaygo	2,068	7	7	0
New Baltimore	12,444	18	17	1
New Buffalo	1,877	5	5	0
New Era	446	1	1	0
Niles	11,106	26	17	9
Northfield Township	8,788	12	10	2
North Muskegon	3,797	9	8	1
Northville	5,971	13	12	1
Northville Township	29,170	45	33	12
Norton Shores	24,702	33	31	2
Norway	2,756	6	6	0
Novi	61,699	93	70	23
Oak Park	29,654	61	49	12
Olivet	1,857	2	2	0
Ontwa Township-Edwardsburg	6,553	7	7	0
Orchard Lake	2,483	9	8	1
Oscoda Township	6,746	12	11	1

(Number.)

State/city	Population	Total law enforcement employees	Total officers	Total civilians
Otsego	4,007	7	6	1
Ovid	1,611	2	2	0
Owosso	14,399	18	17	1
Oxford	3,574	5	5	0
Paw Paw	3,370	9	8	1
Pentwater	853	3	3	0
Perry	2,075	4	4	0
Petoskey	5,747	19	19	0
Pigeon	1,123	1	1	0
Pinckney	2,410	6	6	0
Pinconning	1,238	1	1	0
Pittsfield Township	39,417	41	40	1
Plainwell	3,804	9	8	1
Pleasant Ridge	2,465	6	6	0
Plymouth	9,175	17	16	1
Plymouth Township	27,020	43	28	15
Portage	49,583	70	57	13
Port Austin	620	1	1	0
Port Huron	28,783	69	53	16
Portland	3,932	6	6	0
Potterville	2,712	2	2	0
Prairieville Township	3,525	2	2	0
Quincy	1,616	3	3	0
Raisin Township	7,760	5	5	0
Reading	1,042	1	1	0
Redford Township	46,742	68	60	8
Reed City	2,377	4	4	0
Reese	1,364	2	2	0
Richfield Township, Genesee County	8,358	11	9	2
Richfield Township, Roscommon County	3,630	6	5	1
Richland	806	3	3	0
Richland Township, Saginaw County	3,925	3	3	0
Richmond	5,904	11	9	2
River Rouge	7,404	20	18	2
Riverview	12,027	25	24	1
Rochester	13,429	30	22	8
Rockford	6,377	10	9	1
Rockwood	3,165	6	6	0
Rogers City	2,663	6	6	0
Romeo	3,608	11	8	3
Romulus	23,507	51	39	12
Roosevelt Park	3,793	5	5	0
Roseville	47,381	72	69	3
Royal Oak	59,742	111	78	33
Saginaw	47,954	61	53	8
Saginaw Township	39,022	48	43	5
Saline	9,431	18	14	4
Sandusky	2,508	6	5	1
Sault Ste. Marie	13,478	28	24	4
Schoolcraft	1,559	3	3	0
Scottville	1,210	2	2	0
Sebewaing	1,629	2	2	0
Shelby	2,032	2	2	0
Shelby Township	80,806	92	73	19
Shepherd	1,489	2	2	0
Somerset Township	4,541	3	3	0
Southfield	73,335	148	123	25
Southgate	28,979	45	40	5
South Haven	4,326	26	20	6
South Lyon	11,896	16	15	1
South Rockwood	1,670	2	2	0
Sparta	4,391	5	5	0
Spring Arbor Township	8,009	2	2	0
Springport Township	2,148	2	2	0
Stanton	1,435	1	1	0
St. Charles	1,891	2	2	0
St. Clair	5,286	7	7	0
St. Clair Shores	59,365	87	82	5
Sterling Heights	133,377	174	152	22
St. Ignace	2,309	4	4	0
St. Johns	7,938	11	10	1

(Number.)

State/city	Population	Total law enforcement employees	Total officers	Total civilians
St. Joseph	8,355	23	22	1
St. Joseph Township	9,738	12	11	1
St. Louis	7,104	8	6	2
Stockbridge	1,257	3	3	0
Sturgis	10,779	24	19	5
Sumpter Township	9,407	18	16	2
Sylvan Lake	1,864	5	5	0
Tawas	4,471	5	4	1
Taylor	60,923	90	74	16
Tecumseh	8,382	15	14	1
Thomas Township	11,438	9	8	1
Three Rivers	7,643	16	15	1
Tittabawassee Township	9,863	7	6	1
Traverse City	15,772	31	29	2
Trenton	18,147	35	34	1
Troy	84,688	154	107	47
Tuscarora Township	2,934	9	8	1
Ubly	785	1	1	0
Unadilla Township	3,425	3	3	0
Union City	1,566	5	5	0
Utica	5,195	18	14	4
Van Buren Township	28,294	55	40	15
Vassar	2,534	5	5	0
Vernon	770	1	1	0
Vicksburg	3,490	6	6	0
Walker	25,051	42	38	4
Walled Lake	7,184	8	8	0
Warren	134,653	241	203	38
Waterford Township	73,105	74	58	16
Watersmeet Township	1,359	1	1	0
Watervliet	1,652	3	3	0
Wayland	4,272	7	6	1
Wayne	16,816	22	21	1
West Bloomfield Township	66,067	107	78	29
West Branch	2,048	6	5	1
Westland	81,444	105	81	24
White Cloud	1,395	2	2	0
Whitehall	2,785	8	8	0
White Lake Township	31,556	38	28	10
White Pigeon	1,521	4	4	0
Williamston	3,972	7	6	1
Wixom	14,074	24	21	3
Wolverine Lake	4,825	7	7	0
Woodhaven	12,438	31	30	1
Wyandotte	24,829	46	35	11
Wyoming	76,295	101	87	14
Yale	1,875	3	3	0
Ypsilanti	21,178	33	28	5
Zeeland	5,572	13	12	1
Zilwaukee	1,523	1	1	0
MINNESOTA				
Adrian	1,220	2	2	0
Aitkin	1,985	7	6	1
Akeley	442	1	1	0
Albany	2,752	5	4	1
Albert Lea	17,597	31	28	3
Alexandria	13,914	29	25	4
Annandale	3,415	6	5	1
Anoka	17,591	39	29	10
Appleton	1,322	3	3	0
Apple Valley	54,779	61	53	8
Arlington	2,163	4	4	0
Atwater	1,110	1	1	0
Audubon	527	1	1	0
Austin	25,224	37	34	3
Avon	1,597	4	3	1
Babbitt	1,498	5	5	0
Bagley	1,405	3	3	0
Barnesville	2,608	5	5	0
Battle Lake	938	2	2	0

(Number.)

State/city	Population	Total law enforcement employees	Total officers	Total civilians
Baxter	8,401	16	15	1
Bayport	3,834	5	5	0
Becker	4,957	8	7	1
Belgrade/Brooten	1,524	3	3	0
Belle Plaine	7,232	12	10	2
Bemidji	15,550	35	32	3
Benson	3,050	8	7	1
Big Lake	11,236	15	13	2
Blackduck	838	2	2	0
Blaine	66,260	84	67	17
Blooming Prairie	1,956	3	3	0
Bloomington	85,902	151	119	32
Blue Earth	3,113	5	5	0
Bovey	785	2	2	0
Braham	1,791	5	5	0
Brainerd	13,449	31	25	6
Breckenridge	3,175	8	8	0
Breezy Point	2,418	7	6	1
Breitung Township	612	2	2	0
Brooklyn Center	31,000	61	49	12
Brooklyn Park	81,211	140	106	34
Brownton	723	1	1	0
Buffalo	16,421	21	17	4
Buffalo Lake	680	2	2	0
Burnsville	61,306	81	71	10
Caledonia	2,718	7	6	1
Callaway	231	1	1	0
Cambridge	9,008	16	15	1
Canby	1,674	3	3	0
Cannon Falls	4,063	10	8	2
Centennial Lakes	11,025	18	16	2
Champlin	25,636	31	26	5
Chaska	27,143	29	23	6
Chisholm	4,875	11	10	1
Clara City	1,282	2	2	0
Clearbrook	520	1	1	0
Cloquet	12,009	23	21	2
Cold Spring/Richmond	5,656	11	10	1
Coleraine	1,973	2	2	0
Columbia Heights	20,632	31	25	6
Coon Rapids	62,652	76	66	10
Corcoran	6,195	10	9	1
Cottage Grove	37,534	48	42	6
Crookston	7,794	18	16	2
Crosby	2,335	7	7	0
Crosslake	2,294	5	5	0
Crystal	23,184	40	34	6
Danube	457	1	1	0
Dawson/Boyd	1,547	3	3	0
Dayton	6,542	9	8	1
Deephaven	3,980	8	7	1
Deer River	933	4	4	0
Detroit Lakes	9,362	19	17	2
Dilworth	4,491	6	5	1
Duluth	85,846	180	148	32
Dundas	1,623	2	2	0
Eagan	66,824	87	72	15
Eagle Lake	3,195	3	3	0
East Grand Forks	8,597	25	23	2
East Range	3,590	8	8	0
Eden Prairie	64,777	91	68	23
Eden Valley	1,035	1	1	0
Edina	53,076	79	55	24
Elko New Market	4,783	5	5	0
Elk River	25,081	42	34	8
Elmore	617	1	1	0
Ely	3,344	8	7	1
Eveleth	3,582	12	11	1
Fairfax	1,127	2	2	0
Fairmont	10,023	20	18	2
Faribault	23,913	41	33	8

(Number.)

State/city	Population	Total law enforcement employees	Total officers	Total civilians
Farmington	23,335	27	24	3
Fergus Falls	13,900	29	24	5
Floodwood	523	3	2	1
Foley	2,671	4	4	0
Forest Lake	20,457	28	25	3
Frazee	1,397	3	3	0
Fridley	27,805	49	44	5
Fulda	1,209	2	2	0
Gaylord	2,236	4	4	0
Gilbert	1,788	7	6	1
Glencoe	5,444	9	8	1
Glenwood	2,593	6	5	1
Golden Valley	21,934	41	31	10
Goodhue	1,178	2	2	0
Goodview	4,149	5	4	1
Grand Rapids	11,267	23	20	3
Granite Falls	2,700	7	6	1
Hallock	899	1	1	0
Hastings	22,774	31	27	4
Hawley	2,223	5	5	0
Hector	1,045	2	2	0
Henning	814	2	2	0
Hermantown	9,770	18	15	3
Heron Lake	647	1	1	0
Hibbing	15,895	30	27	3
Hill City	585	1	1	0
Hokah	543	1	1	0
Hopkins	18,735	37	29	8
Houston	963	2	2	0
Howard Lake	2,091	3	3	0
Hutchinson	13,960	36	23	13
International Falls	5,871	12	12	0
Inver Grove Heights	35,668	46	41	5
Isanti	5,985	8	7	1
Isle	803	4	4	0
Janesville	2,261	4	4	0
Jordan	6,384	13	11	2
Kasson	6,514	10	9	1
Keewatin	1,008	3	3	0
Kenyon	1,805	3	3	0
Kimball	797	1	1	0
La Crescent	4,981	9	8	1
Lake City	5,140	11	10	1
Lake Crystal	2,496	3	3	0
Lakefield	1,610	3	3	0
Lake Park	801	2	2	0
Lakes Area	9,833	15	13	2
Lake Shore	1,056	2	2	0
Lakeville	67,206	68	58	10
Lamberton	766	1	1	0
Le Center	2,482	3	3	0
Lester Prairie	1,722	3	3	0
Le Sueur	4,016	8	7	1
Lewiston	1,558	2	2	0
Lino Lakes	21,925	30	27	3
Litchfield	6,632	12	11	1
Little Falls	8,669	16	14	2
Long Prairie	3,297	6	6	0
Lonsdale	4,141	8	7	1
Madelia	2,266	4	4	0
Madison Lake	1,198	2	2	0
Mankato	42,955	61	53	8
Maple Grove	73,170	83	68	15
Mapleton	2,203	3	3	0
Maplewood	41,341	58	53	5
Marshall	13,511	25	22	3
Medina	6,852	11	10	1
Melrose	3,642	6	5	1
Menahga	1,326	3	3	0
Mendota Heights	11,373	22	21	1
Milaca	2,909	7	6	1

(Number.)

State/city	Population	Total law enforcement employees	Total officers	Total civilians
Minneapolis	431,016	1,041	861	180
Minneota	1,360	1	1	0
Minnesota Lake	640	1	1	0
Minnetonka	54,497	65	57	8
Minnetrista	10,527	17	13	4
Montevideo	5,071	12	11	1
Montgomery	2,995	8	7	1
Moorhead	43,847	73	58	15
Moose Lake	2,821	6	5	1
Morris	5,360	10	8	2
Motley	650	2	2	0
Mounds View	13,307	24	22	2
Mountain Lake	2,047	4	4	0
Nashwauk	947	4	4	0
New Brighton	23,058	36	30	6
New Hope	21,147	43	34	9
New Prague	8,326	12	10	2
New Richland	1,188	2	2	0
New Ulm	13,205	23	21	2
New York Mills	1,228	3	3	0
Nisswa	2,066	6	6	0
North Branch	10,641	13	11	2
Northfield	20,707	29	24	5
North Mankato	13,977	14	13	1
North St. Paul	12,595	18	16	2
Oakdale	28,097	40	33	7
Oak Park Heights	4,972	11	10	1
Olivia	2,328	5	5	0
Onamia	861	3	3	0
Orono	20,349	31	27	4
Ortonville	1,774	4	4	0
Osakis	1,750	3	3	0
Osseo	2,801	7	6	1
Owatonna	25,792	39	35	4
Parkers Prairie	1,002	2	2	0
Park Rapids	4,262	12	11	1
Paynesville	2,510	5	5	0
Pelican Rapids	2,507	5	5	0
Pequot Lakes	2,328	7	6	1
Perham	3,625	7	6	1
Pierz	1,364	2	2	0
Pike Bay	1,681	2	2	0
Pillager	482	1	1	0
Pine River	925	4	4	0
Plainview	3,295	8	7	1
Plymouth	80,616	95	79	16
Preston	1,290	3	3	0
Princeton	4,711	14	12	2
Prior Lake	27,362	31	27	4
Proctor	3,038	8	7	1
Ramsey	27,358	29	26	3
Red Wing	16,408	32	28	4
Redwood Falls	4,951	13	11	2
Renville	1,177	3	3	0
Rice	1,389	2	2	0
Richfield	36,100	54	45	9
Robbinsdale	14,555	28	24	4
Rochester	118,267	203	138	65
Rogers	13,417	21	18	3
Roseau	2,665	6	5	1
Rosemount	24,961	29	24	5
Roseville	36,750	58	48	10
Rushford	1,703	3	3	0
Sartell	18,754	23	20	3
Sauk Centre	4,492	8	7	1
Sauk Rapids	14,015	18	17	1
Savage	32,336	44	34	10
Sebeka	674	2	2	0
Shakopee	41,892	60	48	12
Sherburn	1,088	4	4	0
Silver Bay	1,764	5	5	0

Table 19. Full-Time Law Enforcement Employees, by Selected State and City, 2019—*Continued*

(Number.)

State/city	Population	Total law enforcement employees	Total officers	Total civilians
Silver Lake	813	1	1	0
Slayton	1,979	5	4	1
Sleepy Eye	3,347	7	7	0
South Lake Minnetonka	12,762	16	14	2
South St. Paul	20,148	35	30	5
Springfield	1,999	5	5	0
Spring Grove	1,264	2	2	0
Spring Lake Park	6,994	14	11	3
St. Anthony	9,172	23	20	3
Staples	2,945	7	6	1
Starbuck	1,255	4	4	0
St. Charles	3,773	7	7	0
St. Cloud	68,311	140	113	27
St. Francis	7,894	15	12	3
Stillwater	19,496	27	22	5
St. James	4,426	8	7	1
St. Joseph	7,227	10	9	1
St. Louis Park	49,535	70	56	14
St. Paul	310,263	832	649	183
St. Paul Park	5,410	9	9	0
St. Peter	12,032	19	14	5
Thief River Falls	8,825	19	17	2
Tracy	2,094	3	3	0
Trimont	699	1	1	0
Truman	1,045	2	2	0
Twin Valley	761	2	2	0
Two Harbors	3,523	9	8	1
Tyler	1,071	2	2	0
Verndale	573	2	2	0
Virginia	8,398	23	23	0
Wabasha	2,471	8	7	1
Wadena	4,097	10	9	1
Waite Park	7,764	21	18	3
Walker	930	3	3	0
Warroad	1,796	6	5	1
Waseca	8,841	19	17	2
Waterville	1,874	4	4	0
Wayzata	6,560	15	13	2
Wells	2,170	5	5	0
Westbrook	706	1	1	0
West Concord	768	1	1	0
West Hennepin	5,670	12	10	2
West St. Paul	19,694	35	31	4
Wheaton	1,295	3	3	0
White Bear Lake	26,176	34	30	4
Willmar	19,684	38	34	4
Windom	4,393	10	9	1
Winnebago	1,341	3	3	0
Winona	26,720	43	39	4
Winsted	2,247	4	4	0
Woodbury	72,527	89	77	12
Worthington	13,329	34	23	11
Wyoming	7,993	11	10	1
Zumbrota	3,477	6	6	0
MISSISSIPPI				
Ackerman	1,443	5	5	0
Amory	6,819	27	20	7
Batesville	7,234	53	41	12
Biloxi	46,185	187	131	56
Booneville	8,742	25	20	5
Brandon	24,426	49	36	13
Brookhaven	12,037	46	36	10
Byram	11,672	39	26	13
Clinton	25,167	74	55	19
D'Iberville	14,125	40	37	3
Edwards	991	1	1	0
Florence	4,500	23	18	5
Flowood	9,401	67	51	16
Fulton	4,044	10	10	0
Gautier	18,563	45	34	11

(Number.)

State/city	Population	Total law enforcement employees	Total officers	Total civilians
Gulfport	72,383	204	152	52
Hattiesburg	45,971	157	106	51
Hernando	16,613	51	42	9
Horn Lake	27,256	61	47	14
Iuka	2,945	12	9	3
Leakesville	896	1	1	0
Madison	25,862	88	68	20
Magee	4,184	27	17	10
Meridian	36,878	94	74	20
Natchez	14,917	44	36	8
New Albany	8,858	28	26	2
Ocean Springs	17,864	45	35	10
Olive Branch	38,761	91	83	8
Oxford	25,306	100	85	15
Pascagoula	21,610	77	55	22
Pass Christian	6,285	25	20	5
Petal	10,702	31	26	5
Philadelphia	7,135	29	22	7
Ridgeland	24,171	88	59	29
Starkville	25,485	80	58	22
Summit	1,577	8	7	1
Vicksburg	21,928	81	65	16
West Point	10,430	31	27	4
Yazoo City	10,757	21	15	6
MISSOURI				
Adrian	1,599	3	3	0
Advance	1,337	3	3	0
Anderson	2,000	6	6	0
Annapolis	338	1	1	0
Appleton City	1,068	1	1	0
Archie	1,210	4	4	0
Arnold	21,102	61	54	7
Ash Grove	1,447	11	5	6
Ashland	3,975	9	8	1
Aurora	7,455	22	16	6
Ava	2,902	12	7	5
Ballwin	30,158	53	44	9
Battlefield	6,348	9	9	0
Bella Villa	726	5	5	0
Bellefontaine Neighbors	10,416	28	26	2
Bel-Nor	1,398	6	6	0
Bel-Ridge	2,681	15	15	0
Belton	23,657	57	36	21
Berkeley	8,868	31	24	7
Bernie	1,884	9	5	4
Bertrand	745	1	1	0
Bethany	3,065	4	4	0
Billings	1,114	3	3	0
Bloomfield	1,835	5	4	1
Blue Springs	55,415	142	96	46
Bolivar	11,129	26	18	8
Bonne Terre	7,081	11	11	0
Boonville	8,410	28	21	7
Bourbon	1,596	3	3	0
Bowling Green	5,662	12	10	2
Branson	11,688	69	46	23
Branson West	449	8	7	1
Breckenridge Hills	4,590	17	15	2
Brentwood	7,992	27	26	1
Bridgeton	11,608	63	53	10
Brookfield	4,232	10	8	2
Buckner	3,025	8	7	1
Buffalo	3,073	6	5	1
Butler	4,017	15	9	6
Byrnes Mill	3,024	6	6	0
Cabool	2,103	12	8	4
California	4,438	8	7	1
Calverton Park	1,269	8	8	0
Camdenton	4,138	20	17	3
Cameron	9,674	24	16	8

Table 19. Full-Time Law Enforcement Employees, by Selected State and City, 2019—*Continued*

(Number.)

State/city	Population	Total law enforcement employees	Total officers	Total civilians
Campbell	1,812	4	4	0
Canalou	301	1	1	0
Canton	2,314	6	5	1
Cape Girardeau	40,077	118	82	36
Carl Junction	8,242	15	10	5
Carrollton	3,477	8	7	1
Carterville	1,971	5	5	0
Carthage	14,808	37	28	9
Caruthersville	5,451	19	17	2
Cassville	3,327	12	12	0
Charleston	5,490	19	13	6
Chesterfield	47,663	104	92	12
Chillicothe	9,700	27	19	8
Clarkson Valley	2,614	6	6	0
Clarkton	1,156	2	2	0
Claycomo	1,501	11	11	0
Clayton	16,936	56	48	8
Cleveland	663	2	2	0
Clever	2,787	6	5	1
Clinton	8,939	23	22	1
Cole Camp	1,120	2	2	0
Columbia	125,017	195	158	37
Concordia	2,354	5	5	0
Cottleville	5,849	12	12	0
Country Club Hills	1,265	7	7	0
Country Club Village	2,485	1	1	0
Crestwood	11,845	33	27	6
Creve Coeur	18,829	52	47	5
Crocker	1,016	4	4	0
Crystal City	4,698	22	15	7
Cuba	3,293	16	15	1
Delta	438	1	1	0
Desloge	4,841	12	11	1
De Soto	6,355	24	17	7
Des Peres	8,697	49	41	8
Dexter	7,861	23	18	5
Diamond	923	2	2	0
Dixon	1,421	5	4	1
Doolittle	600	1	1	0
Duenweg	1,378	4	4	0
Duquesne	1,577	9	8	1
Edgar Springs	193	1	1	0
Edina	1,111	2	2	0
Edmundson	830	11	10	1
Eldon	4,649	18	17	1
El Dorado Springs	3,594	10	6	4
Ellisville	9,946	25	24	1
Eminence	578	1	1	0
Eureka	10,834	29	26	3
Excelsior Springs	11,715	34	24	10
Exeter	773	1	1	0
Fair Grove	1,520	6	6	0
Farmington	19,178	38	29	9
Fayette	2,719	7	7	0
Ferrelview	866	1	1	0
Festus	12,098	39	29	10
Flordell Hills	776	5	5	0
Florissant	51,148	120	94	26
Fordland	850	2	2	0
Foristell	589	6	6	0
Forsyth	2,582	7	6	1
Fredericktown	3,999	14	13	1
Frontenac	3,851	21	20	1
Fulton	12,620	32	26	6
Gallatin	1,750	1	1	0
Gideon	967	2	2	0
Gladstone	27,553	61	45	16
Glasgow	1,095	3	3	0
Glendale	5,873	14	11	3
Goodman	1,257	2	2	0
Gower	1,461	1	1	0

State/city	Population	Total law enforcement employees	Total officers	Total civilians
Grain Valley	14,464	28	23	5
Grandview	25,022	71	56	15
Greenfield	1,309	3	3	0
Greenwood	5,854	11	11	0
Hamilton	1,694	5	5	0
Hannibal	17,487	48	37	11
Hardin	533	1	1	0
Harrisonville	10,095	31	23	8
Hartville	605	2	2	0
Hayti	2,548	6	6	0
Hazelwood	25,146	76	60	16
Henrietta	354	1	1	0
Herculaneum	4,149	9	8	1
Hermann	2,325	13	7	6
Higginsville	4,588	23	10	13
Highlandville	1,052	1	1	0
Hillsboro	3,231	11	11	0
Hillsdale	1,568	9	8	1
Holden	2,220	7	7	0
Hollister	4,608	21	13	8
Holts Summit	4,697	11	10	1
Hornersville	596	1	1	0
Houston	2,091	8	8	0
Howardville	339	2	1	1
Humansville	1,059	1	1	0
Huntsville	1,513	3	3	0
Iberia	749	1	1	0
Independence	116,931	272	199	73
Ironton	1,380	7	7	0
Jackson	15,151	36	29	7
Jasper	969	2	2	0
Jefferson City	42,793	123	88	35
Jonesburg	709	1	1	0
Joplin	50,635	134	100	34
Kansas City	495,964	1,819	1,299	520
Kearney	10,736	18	17	1
Kennett	10,093	27	20	7
Kimberling City	2,286	6	6	0
Kirksville	17,572	33	30	3
Kirkwood	27,785	79	60	19
Knob Noster	2,753	7	6	1
Laddonia	494	1	1	0
Ladue	8,650	32	26	6
La Grange	902	5	5	0
Lake Lotawana	2,126	4	4	0
Lake Ozark	1,832	16	10	6
Lakeshire	1,393	3	3	0
Lake St. Louis	16,444	42	33	9
Lake Tapawingo	720	4	3	1
Lake Winnebago	1,194	5	5	0
Lamar	4,279	15	13	2
Lanagan	410	2	2	0
La Plata	1,312	4	4	0
Lathrop	2,009	5	5	0
Laurie	947	6	6	0
Lawson	2,389	10	9	1
Leadington	613	4	4	0
Leadwood	1,153	4	4	0
Lebanon	14,841	40	28	12
Lee's Summit	99,365	203	145	58
Leeton	547	1	1	0
Lexington	4,514	9	7	2
Liberty	32,109	56	39	17
Licking	3,087	5	5	0
Lincoln	1,191	3	3	0
Linn	1,627	4	4	0
Linn Creek	252	3	3	0
Lone Jack	1,342	9	8	1
Louisiana	3,241	8	5	3
Macon	5,339	14	12	2
Manchester	18,176	37	33	4

Table 19. Full-Time Law Enforcement Employees, by Selected State and City, 2019—*Continued*

(Number.)

State/city	Population	Total law enforcement employees	Total officers	Total civilians
Mansfield	1,250	4	4	0
Maplewood	8,108	35	33	2
Marble Hill	1,463	3	3	0
Marceline	2,092	10	10	0
Marionville	2,177	3	3	0
Marshall	12,915	29	24	5
Marshfield	7,566	13	12	1
Maryland Heights	26,964	96	77	19
Maryville	11,643	26	19	7
Matthews	597	3	3	0
Memphis	1,866	3	3	0
Merriam Woods	1,870	3	3	0
Mexico	11,529	28	27	1
Milan	1,796	5	5	0
Miner	943	10	6	4
Moberly	13,559	36	24	12
Moline Acres	2,352	11	10	1
Monett	9,148	23	21	2
Monroe City	2,439	10	9	1
Montgomery City	2,647	6	6	0
Morehouse	865	1	1	0
Moscow Mills	3,298	6	6	0
Mound City	1,025	2	2	0
Mountain Grove	4,681	16	14	2
Mountain View	2,643	9	8	1
Mount Vernon	4,504	11	11	0
Neosho	12,076	28	26	2
Nevada	8,237	25	21	4
Newburg	437	1	1	0
New Franklin	1,072	1	1	0
New Haven	2,071	11	11	0
New London	970	2	2	0
New Madrid	2,825	22	14	8
Niangua	426	2	2	0
Nixa	22,235	41	35	6
Noel	1,833	1	1	0
Normandy	7,489	28	27	1
North Kansas City	4,573	50	39	11
Northwoods	4,386	18	17	1
Oak Grove	8,226	15	14	1
Oakland	1,378	79	60	19
Odessa	5,190	10	9	1
O'Fallon	89,611	145	112	33
Olivette	7,842	24	23	1
Oregon	755	1	1	0
Oronogo	2,694	5	5	0
Orrick	799	2	2	0
Osage Beach	4,598	24	20	4
Osceola	900	3	3	0
Overland	15,587	55	44	11
Owensville	2,574	9	8	1
Ozark	20,490	35	32	3
Pacific	7,265	23	18	5
Pagedale	3,293	17	17	0
Palmyra	3,606	9	8	1
Park Hills	8,484	18	17	1
Parkville	7,143	18	17	1
Peculiar	5,417	11	10	1
Perry	694	1	1	0
Perryville	8,466	30	24	6
Pevely	5,917	20	14	6
Piedmont	1,915	6	6	0
Pierce City	1,305	3	3	0
Pilot Grove	758	1	1	0
Pilot Knob	719	2	2	0
Pineville	801	12	12	0
Platte City	5,002	11	11	0
Platte Woods	409	2	2	0
Plattsburg	2,245	5	5	0
Pleasant Hill	8,705	17	13	4
Pleasant Valley	3,073	13	8	5

(Number.)

State/city	Population	Total law enforcement employees	Total officers	Total civilians
Polo	532	1	1	0
Poplar Bluff	17,044	57	44	13
Portageville	2,964	15	11	4
Potosi	2,609	11	10	1
Purdy	1,099	2	2	0
Queen City	619	1	1	0
Qulin	456	1	1	0
Raymore	22,121	37	28	9
Raytown	28,932	46	32	14
Republic	16,715	25	21	4
Rich Hill	1,323	1	1	0
Richland	1,757	4	4	0
Richmond	5,615	14	12	2
Richmond Heights	8,550	41	40	1
Riverside	3,522	35	26	9
Riverview	2,836	12	12	0
Rockaway Beach	880	2	1	1
Rock Hill	4,620	12	11	1
Rock Port	1,188	3	3	0
Rogersville	3,888	8	8	0
Rolla	20,482	53	31	22
Salem	4,895	18	13	5
Salisbury	1,520	4	3	1
Sarcoxie	1,321	3	3	0
Savannah	5,212	8	7	1
Scott City	4,493	18	13	5
Sedalia	21,742	57	41	16
Seligman	848	1	1	0
Senath	1,611	2	2	0
Seneca	2,392	6	6	0
Seymour	2,016	7	7	0
Shelbina	1,612	6	5	1
Shrewsbury	6,098	22	20	2
Sikeston	16,079	73	58	15
Smithville	10,503	19	19	0
Southwest City	962	3	3	0
Sparta	1,937	4	4	0
Springfield	169,235	421	347	74
St. Ann	12,670	78	49	29
St. Charles	71,341	149	109	40
St. Clair	4,695	16	14	2
Steele	1,921	5	5	0
Steelville	1,664	7	7	0
Ste. Genevieve	4,445	11	11	0
Stewartsville	739	1	1	0
St. James	4,048	13	12	1
St. John	6,354	22	21	1
St. Joseph	75,872	173	130	43
St. Louis	300,521	1,609	1,201	408
Stover	1,073	2	2	0
St. Peters	57,697	120	92	28
Strafford	2,477	6	6	0
St. Robert	6,034	24	16	8
Sugar Creek	3,269	21	16	5
Sullivan	7,111	26	19	7
Summersville	487	2	2	0
Sunrise Beach	500	3	3	0
Sunset Hills	8,480	32	25	7
Sweet Springs	1,414	3	3	0
Tarkio	1,422	4	2	2
Terre du Lac	2,382	6	6	0
Thayer	2,132	10	6	4
Town and Country	11,177	30	29	1
Trenton	5,779	19	12	7
Troy	12,705	25	23	2
Truesdale	870	1	1	0
Union	11,905	27	25	2
University City	34,211	91	68	23
Urbana	411	1	1	0
Van Buren	800	5	5	0
Vandalia	4,072	6	5	1

(Number.)

State/city	Population	Total law enforcement employees	Total officers	Total civilians
Velda City	1,373	5	5	0
Verona	606	4	2	2
Versailles	2,450	11	10	1
Vienna	582	2	2	0
Vinita Park	10,979	44	40	4
Walnut Grove	803	1	1	0
Warrensburg	20,435	41	36	5
Warrenton	8,247	24	20	4
Warsaw	2,206	7	7	0
Warson Woods	1,925	6	6	0
Washington	14,064	33	30	3
Waverly	836	2	1	1
Waynesville	5,265	13	12	1
Weatherby Lake	2,079	5	5	0
Webb City	11,999	27	23	4
Webster Groves	22,876	47	45	2
Wellsville	1,144	3	3	0
Wentzville	42,892	93	72	21
Weston	1,829	5	5	0
West Plains	12,284	33	26	7
Wheaton	693	2	2	0
Willard	5,616	10	9	1
Willow Springs	2,103	7	6	1
Winfield	1,492	5	5	0
Winona	1,290	1	1	0
Woodson Terrace	4,043	19	17	2
Wright City	4,052	16	15	1
MONTANA				
Baker	1,928	5	5	0
Belgrade	9,204	20	16	4
Billings	110,198	177	151	26
Boulder	1,278	3	3	0
Bozeman	50,152	72	62	10
Bridger	760	3	3	0
Chinook	1,282	4	4	0
Colstrip	2,271	11	7	4
Columbia Falls	5,695	11	10	1
Columbus	2,069	5	5	0
Cut Bank	3,038	7	7	0
Deer Lodge	2,888	5	5	0
Dillon	4,276	11	10	1
East Helena	2,098	3	3	0
Ennis	1,019	1	1	0
Eureka	1,125	4	4	0
Fairview	884	3	3	0
Fort Benton	1,441	4	4	0
Glasgow	3,334	10	6	4
Glendive	4,964	12	8	4
Great Falls	58,637	129	88	41
Hamilton	4,879	16	14	2
Havre	9,738	24	18	6
Helena	32,806	78	53	25
Hot Springs	570	2	2	0
Kalispell	24,473	48	39	9
Laurel	6,768	19	13	6
Lewistown	5,790	13	13	0
Libby	2,750	6	6	0
Livingston	7,884	22	15	7
Manhattan	1,865	4	4	0
Miles City	8,393	18	18	0
Missoula	75,422	133	106	27
Plains	1,116	3	3	0
Polson	5,075	17	16	1
Red Lodge	2,316	7	7	0
Ronan City	2,113	6	6	0
Sidney	6,376	13	12	1
Stevensville	2,051	3	2	1
Thompson Falls	1,403	5	5	0
Troy	936	3	3	0
West Yellowstone	1,396	14	7	7

Table 19. Full-Time Law Enforcement Employees, by Selected State and City, 2019—*Continued*

(Number.)

State/city	Population	Total law enforcement employees	Total officers	Total civilians
Whitefish	8,079	18	16	2
Wolf Point	2,761	9	7	2
NEBRASKA				
Albion	1,584	3	3	0
Alliance	8,022	21	15	6
Ashland	2,604	5	4	1
Aurora	4,539	10	9	1
Bayard	1,090	4	4	0
Beatrice	12,227	36	22	14
Bellevue	53,880	106	90	16
Bennington	1,529	1	1	0
Blair	7,836	18	16	2
Boys Town	579	14	14	0
Broken Bow	3,532	8	7	1
Burwell	1,175	2	2	0
Central City	2,868	6	5	1
Chadron	5,446	20	13	7
Columbus	23,406	43	36	7
Cozad	3,757	8	8	0
Crete	7,094	13	12	1
Emerson	796	2	2	0
Falls City	4,130	12	8	4
Fremont	26,523	38	33	5
Gering	8,189	19	17	2
Gordon	1,497	6	4	2
Gothenburg	3,433	6	5	1
Grand Island	51,821	100	83	17
Harvard	963	2	2	0
Hastings	24,778	53	38	15
Holdrege	5,394	17	10	7
Imperial	2,074	4	4	0
Kearney	34,124	70	56	14
Kimball	2,343	6	5	1
Laurel	916	1	1	0
La Vista	17,223	45	39	6
Lexington	10,108	22	20	2
Lincoln	291,128	480	344	136
Madison	2,378	3	3	0
McCook	7,533	20	16	4
Milford	2,095	3	3	0
Minden	2,985	5	5	0
Mitchell	1,633	2	2	0
Morrill	892	2	2	0
Nebraska City	7,273	14	13	1
Neligh	1,503	3	3	0
Norfolk	24,698	56	39	17
North Platte	23,705	65	41	24
Ogallala	4,476	10	9	1
Omaha	470,481	1,020	868	152
O'Neill	3,615	9	8	1
Ord	2,087	4	3	1
Papillion	20,580	48	44	4
Pierce	1,721	3	3	0
Plattsmouth	6,478	17	14	3
Ralston	7,468	15	14	1
Randolph	888	1	1	0
Ravenna	1,369	2	2	0
Schuyler	6,396	10	9	1
Scottsbluff	15,862	37	31	6
Scribner	800	1	1	0
Seward	7,250	13	12	1
Sidney	6,331	15	13	2
South Sioux City	12,771	28	27	1
St. Paul	2,354	4	4	0
Superior	1,812	4	4	0
Tekamah	1,692	4	4	0
Tilden	934	1	1	0
Valentine	2,751	7	6	1
Valley	2,904	6	6	0
Wahoo	4,513	7	7	0

Table 19. Full-Time Law Enforcement Employees, by Selected State and City, 2019—*Continued*

(Number.)

State/city	Population	Total law enforcement employees	Total officers	Total civilians
Waterloo	923	4	4	0
Wayne	5,615	13	8	5
West Point	3,307	7	6	1
Wymore	1,329	2	2	0
York	7,877	17	14	3
NEVADA				
Boulder City	16,102	52	36	16
Carlin	2,259	8	6	2
Elko	20,601	44	37	7
Fallon	8,478	33	24	9
Las Vegas Metropolitan Police Department	1,666,803	4,562	3,115	1,447
Lovelock	1,806	5	3	2
Mesquite	19,612	53	41	12
Reno	254,349	442	324	118
Sparks	106,010	156	111	45
West Wendover	4,247	23	13	10
Winnemucca	7,800	26	23	3
Yerington	3,185	6	5	1
NEW HAMPSHIRE				
Alexandria	1,620	2	2	0
Allenstown	4,435	12	10	2
Alstead	1,931	2	2	0
Alton	5,339	14	12	2
Amherst	11,344	20	19	1
Antrim	2,702	6	5	1
Ashland	2,053	5	5	0
Atkinson	7,037	9	8	1
Auburn	5,608	11	9	2
Barnstead	4,668	5	5	0
Barrington	9,263	12	11	1
Bartlett	2,809	4	2	2
Bedford	22,887	49	36	13
Belmont	7,293	18	15	3
Bennington	1,512	2	2	0
Berlin	10,230	31	23	8
Bethlehem	2,569	6	6	0
Boscawen	4,095	8	7	1
Bow	8,004	14	13	1
Bradford	1,710	3	3	0
Brentwood	4,730	6	6	0
Bristol	3,057	9	8	1
Brookline	5,461	9	8	1
Campton	3,305	9	7	2
Canaan	3,896	7	6	1
Candia	3,945	7	6	1
Canterbury	2,468	3	3	0
Carroll	740	4	4	0
Center Harbor	1,099	3	3	0
Charlestown	4,998	10	6	4
Chester	5,295	8	7	1
Chesterfield	3,602	7	6	1
Chichester	2,709	5	5	0
Claremont	12,920	30	24	6
Colebrook	2,114	5	5	0
Concord	43,509	93	82	11
Conway	10,287	33	24	9
Danville	4,584	5	5	0
Deerfield	4,562	9	8	1
Deering	1,967	2	2	0
Derry	33,672	67	54	13
Dover	31,950	73	52	21
Dublin	1,538	4	3	1
Dunbarton	2,870	5	5	0
Durham	16,810	24	21	3
East Kingston	2,430	5	5	0
Effingham	1,480	1	1	0
Enfield	4,563	8	7	1
Epping	7,117	16	15	1
Epsom	4,777	6	5	1

Table 19. Full-Time Law Enforcement Employees, by Selected State and City, 2019—*Continued*

(Number.)

State/city	Population	Total law enforcement employees	Total officers	Total civilians
Exeter	15,425	33	24	9
Farmington	6,932	15	14	1
Fitzwilliam	2,373	4	3	1
Franconia	1,111	3	3	0
Franklin	8,743	24	16	8
Freedom	1,562	2	2	0
Fremont	4,803	6	5	1
Gilford	7,197	21	16	5
Gilmanton	3,754	4	3	1
Goffstown	18,163	43	28	15
Gorham	2,579	9	5	4
Grantham	2,946	5	4	1
Greenland	4,195	9	8	1
Hampstead	8,662	9	9	0
Hampton	15,616	45	36	9
Hampton Falls	2,385	4	4	0
Hancock	1,658	3	3	0
Hanover	11,531	33	19	14
Haverhill	4,568	9	8	1
Henniker	5,009	10	9	1
Hillsborough	5,990	23	15	8
Hinsdale	3,888	7	6	1
Holderness	2,109	6	6	0
Hollis	7,976	18	13	5
Hooksett	14,554	38	28	10
Hopkinton	5,759	7	6	1
Hudson	25,695	62	46	16
Jackson	856	2	2	0
Jaffrey	5,278	12	11	1
Keene	22,999	49	38	11
Kensington	2,118	5	4	1
Kingston	6,362	8	7	1
Laconia	16,534	49	40	9
Lancaster	3,219	8	7	1
Lebanon	13,661	46	33	13
Lee	4,494	9	8	1
Lincoln	1,775	14	9	5
Lisbon	1,583	3	3	0
Litchfield	8,660	15	13	2
Littleton	5,889	14	11	3
Londonderry	26,567	75	60	15
Loudon	5,660	7	6	1
Lyme	1,675	2	2	0
Lyndeborough	1,740	1	1	0
Madison	2,613	4	4	0
Manchester	112,895	279	225	54
Marlborough	2,068	3	3	0
Mason	1,441	2	2	0
Meredith	6,424	17	13	4
Merrimack	26,028	53	41	12
Middleton	1,827	3	3	0
Milford	16,121	32	27	5
Milton	4,652	9	8	1
Mont Vernon	2,603	3	3	0
Moultonborough	4,174	11	10	1
Nashua	89,586	223	167	56
New Boston	5,856	9	8	1
Newbury	2,245	4	4	0
New Castle	982	4	4	0
New Durham	2,704	4	4	0
Newfields	1,735	3	3	0
New Hampton	2,216	7	6	1
Newington	810	11	10	1
New Ipswich	5,408	7	6	1
New London	4,470	14	9	5
Newmarket	9,161	21	14	7
Newport	6,348	17	12	5
Newton	4,972	9	7	2
Northfield	4,940	7	6	1
North Hampton	4,512	13	12	1
Northwood	4,302	7	6	1

(Number.)

State/city	Population	Total law enforcement employees	Total officers	Total civilians
Nottingham	5,149	7	6	1
Orford	1,302	1	1	0
Ossipee	4,401	10	9	1
Pelham	14,198	31	24	7
Pembroke	7,240	14	12	2
Peterborough	6,669	13	11	2
Pittsburg	807	1	1	0
Pittsfield	4,142	7	7	0
Plainfield	2,381	2	2	0
Plaistow	7,734	22	15	7
Plymouth	6,755	19	12	7
Portsmouth	21,951	89	66	23
Raymond	10,475	25	17	8
Rindge	6,308	9	8	1
Rochester	31,527	70	55	15
Rollinsford	2,591	5	5	0
Rye	5,464	11	10	1
Salem	29,612	79	63	16
Sanbornton	2,975	6	5	1
Sandown	6,501	7	6	1
Sandwich	1,358	2	2	0
Seabrook	8,880	31	24	7
Somersworth	11,979	33	26	7
South Hampton	829	2	2	0
Springfield	1,342	2	2	0
Strafford	4,205	6	5	1
Stratham	7,479	12	11	1
Sugar Hill	579	2	2	0
Sunapee	3,489	6	5	1
Tamworth	3,077	3	3	0
Thornton	2,513	6	5	1
Tilton	3,557	21	16	5
Troy	2,091	2	2	0
Tuftonboro	2,414	4	4	0
Wakefield	5,789	12	11	1
Warner	2,953	4	3	1
Washington	1,104	1	1	0
Waterville Valley	243	7	6	1
Weare	9,111	12	11	1
Webster	1,962	2	2	0
Whitefield	2,201	7	6	1
Wilton	3,768	6	6	0
Winchester	4,192	8	7	1
Windham	14,876	27	20	7
Wolfeboro	6,403	19	13	6
Woodstock	1,369	6	6	0
NEW JERSEY				
Aberdeen Township	18,700	47	40	7
Absecon	8,436	31	25	6
Allendale	6,795	20	15	5
Allenhurst	484	13	9	4
Allentown	1,784	6	5	1
Alpine	1,856	12	12	0
Andover Township	5,870	17	12	5
Asbury Park	15,437	94	90	4
Atlantic City	37,593	224	190	34
Atlantic Highlands	4,308	19	14	5
Audubon	8,601	19	18	1
Avalon	1,236	31	21	10
Avon-by-the-Sea	1,766	12	12	0
Barnegat Township	23,399	51	49	2
Barrington	6,620	16	15	1
Bay Head	976	11	10	1
Bayonne	65,032	247	184	63
Beach Haven	1,191	14	13	1
Beachwood	11,275	22	20	2
Bedminster Township	8,043	18	16	2
Belleville	36,531	110	102	8
Bellmawr	11,294	24	23	1
Belmar	5,562	30	25	5

Table 19. Full-Time Law Enforcement Employees, by Selected State and City, 2019—*Continued*

(Number.)

State/city	Population	Total law enforcement employees	Total officers	Total civilians
Belvidere	2,564	7	6	1
Bergenfield	27,432	56	45	11
Berkeley Heights Township	13,592	33	27	6
Berkeley Township	41,738	92	72	20
Berlin	7,510	19	18	1
Berlin Township	5,651	18	17	1
Bernards Township	27,228	42	38	4
Bernardsville	7,670	26	20	6
Beverly	2,476	8	8	0
Blairstown Township	5,703	9	8	1
Bloomfield	50,307	152	125	27
Bloomingdale	8,089	18	17	1
Bogota	8,403	20	15	5
Boonton	8,157	29	23	6
Boonton Township	4,279	13	13	0
Bordentown City	3,786	14	14	0
Bordentown Township	12,018	24	23	1
Bound Brook	10,257	31	26	5
Bradley Beach	4,158	22	18	4
Branchburg Township	14,551	25	23	2
Brick Township	75,592	210	141	69
Bridgeton	24,331	73	61	12
Bridgewater Township	44,610	86	79	7
Brielle	4,683	17	16	1
Brigantine	8,684	44	34	10
Brooklawn	1,899	7	7	0
Burlington City	9,877	37	33	4
Burlington Township	22,516	58	49	9
Butler	7,613	18	16	2
Byram Township	7,875	14	14	0
Caldwell	7,943	23	22	1
Camden County Police Department	73,270	390	350	40
Cape May	3,428	28	23	5
Carlstadt	6,170	31	26	5
Carney's Point Township	7,664	20	19	1
Carteret	23,645	74	64	10
Cedar Grove Township	12,508	31	30	1
Chatham	8,696	25	21	4
Chatham Township	10,219	24	22	2
Cherry Hill Township	70,716	169	139	30
Chesilhurst	1,616	10	9	1
Chesterfield Township	7,474	11	10	1
Chester Township	7,731	24	23	1
Cinnaminson Township	16,477	27	27	0
Clark Township	16,022	51	40	11
Clayton	8,709	16	15	1
Clementon	4,919	13	12	1
Cliffside Park	26,115	49	47	2
Clifton	85,021	186	153	33
Clinton	2,679	10	10	0
Clinton Township	12,801	23	22	1
Closter	8,562	21	20	1
Collingswood	13,850	31	27	4
Colts Neck Township	9,846	28	27	1
Cranbury Township	4,013	20	19	1
Cranford Township	24,251	68	54	14
Cresskill	8,761	27	22	5
Deal	719	21	17	4
Delanco Township	4,463	13	12	1
Delaware Township	4,419	8	7	1
Delran Township	16,473	34	30	4
Demarest	4,912	13	13	0
Denville Township	16,590	42	33	9
Deptford Township	30,258	71	65	6
Dover	17,852	43	38	5
Dumont	17,649	40	32	8
Dunellen	7,244	19	19	0
Eastampton Township	5,938	18	17	1
East Brunswick Township	47,857	108	83	25
East Greenwich Township	10,658	21	19	2
East Hanover Township	10,990	38	34	4

(Number.)

State/city	Population	Total law enforcement employees	Total officers	Total civilians
East Newark	2,661	7	7	0
East Orange	64,200	267	215	52
East Rutherford	9,831	40	37	3
East Windsor Township	27,343	52	46	6
Eatontown	12,215	49	37	12
Edgewater	12,821	37	31	6
Edgewater Park Township	8,644	15	15	0
Edison Township	100,282	223	173	50
Egg Harbor City	4,085	15	14	1
Egg Harbor Township	42,475	117	86	31
Elizabeth	128,753	411	313	98
Elk Township	4,154	12	11	1
Elmer	1,300	2	2	0
Elmwood Park	20,104	52	47	5
Emerson	7,640	25	22	3
Englewood	28,683	101	77	24
Englewood Cliffs	5,368	22	21	1
Englishtown	1,937	7	7	0
Essex Fells	2,072	13	13	0
Evesham Township	44,999	102	92	10
Ewing Township	36,338	103	83	20
Fairfield Township, Essex County	7,472	46	42	4
Fair Haven	5,784	13	13	0
Fair Lawn	33,064	69	60	9
Fairview	14,285	36	32	4
Fanwood	7,718	18	17	1
Far Hills	909	6	6	0
Flemington	4,590	14	14	0
Florence Township	12,593	31	29	2
Florham Park	11,522	40	34	6
Fort Lee	38,062	113	92	21
Franklin	4,699	17	16	1
Franklin Lakes	11,109	30	23	7
Franklin Township, Gloucester County	16,264	45	41	4
Franklin Township, Hunterdon County	3,560	6	6	0
Franklin Township, Somerset County	66,173	132	111	21
Freehold Borough	11,733	34	30	4
Freehold Township	34,560	70	66	4
Frenchtown	1,348	3	2	1
Galloway Township	35,813	79	59	20
Garfield	31,888	73	63	10
Garwood	4,361	20	16	4
Gibbsboro	2,212	8	8	0
Glassboro	20,082	54	49	5
Glen Ridge	7,574	26	22	4
Glen Rock	11,803	25	23	2
Gloucester City	11,168	34	32	2
Gloucester Township	63,500	162	130	32
Green Brook Township	7,071	24	23	1
Greenwich Township, Gloucester County	4,777	18	17	1
Greenwich Township, Warren County	5,447	12	12	0
Guttenberg	11,289	27	26	1
Hackensack	44,505	120	98	22
Hackettstown	9,431	20	19	1
Haddonfield	11,261	23	21	2
Haddon Heights	7,515	16	15	1
Haddon Township	14,489	27	26	1
Haledon	8,277	18	18	0
Hamburg	3,102	10	9	1
Hamilton Township, Atlantic County	25,667	80	56	24
Hamilton Township, Mercer County	87,027	204	170	34
Hammonton	14,003	35	29	6
Hanover Township	14,447	38	31	7
Harding Township	3,805	14	13	1
Hardyston Township	7,760	24	18	6
Harrington Park	4,751	11	11	0
Harrison	18,374	56	43	13
Harrison Township	13,125	24	23	1
Harvey Cedars	339	10	9	1
Hasbrouck Heights	12,049	31	29	2
Haworth	3,420	13	12	1

(Number.)

State/city	Population	Total law enforcement employees	Total officers	Total civilians
Hawthorne	18,699	38	32	6
Hazlet Township	19,739	51	45	6
High Bridge	3,427	7	7	0
Highland Park	13,791	36	28	8
Highlands	4,739	17	14	3
Hightstown	5,264	13	12	1
Hillsborough Township	39,813	62	53	9
Hillsdale	10,382	23	19	4
Hillside Township	22,024	79	67	12
Hi-Nella	855	12	12	0
Hoboken	53,641	156	140	16
Ho-Ho-Kus	4,091	20	16	4
Holland Township	5,081	8	7	1
Holmdel Township	16,648	49	42	7
Hopatcong	14,091	32	24	8
Hopewell Township	17,854	38	30	8
Howell Township	52,242	104	88	16
Independence Township	5,420	10	9	1
Irvington	54,034	234	172	62
Island Heights	1,675	7	7	0
Jackson Township	57,380	116	96	20
Jamesburg	5,931	20	16	4
Jefferson Township	20,877	42	34	8
Jersey City	266,508	1,284	1,005	279
Keansburg	9,674	42	33	9
Kearny	41,314	151	113	38
Kenilworth	8,218	31	26	5
Keyport	7,032	22	20	2
Kinnelon	9,984	17	16	1
Lacey Township	29,247	60	46	14
Lakehurst	2,701	14	12	2
Lakewood Township	105,403	182	149	33
Lambertville	3,782	12	10	2
Laurel Springs	1,860	7	7	0
Lavallette	1,846	14	12	2
Lawnside	2,874	8	8	0
Lawrence Township, Mercer County	32,415	62	58	4
Lebanon Township	6,061	11	10	1
Leonia	9,088	22	19	3
Lincoln Park	10,162	30	25	5
Linden	42,592	171	140	31
Lindenwold	17,197	47	44	3
Linwood	6,697	19	18	1
Little Egg Harbor Township	21,508	55	44	11
Little Falls Township	14,513	36	30	6
Little Ferry	10,794	33	28	5
Little Silver	5,793	21	16	5
Livingston Township	29,998	81	71	10
Lodi	24,488	50	47	3
Logan Township	5,854	21	20	1
Long Beach Township	3,060	49	36	13
Long Branch	30,352	110	87	23
Long Hill Township	8,500	25	23	2
Longport	854	13	13	0
Lopatcong Township	8,350	17	16	1
Lower Alloways Creek Township	1,663	11	11	0
Lower Township	21,325	55	49	6
Lumberton Township	12,162	24	22	2
Lyndhurst Township	22,741	56	53	3
Madison	16,533	39	31	8
Magnolia	4,247	12	12	0
Mahwah Township	26,317	62	53	9
Manalapan Township	39,662	59	56	3
Manasquan	5,839	22	16	6
Manchester Township	43,369	93	73	20
Mansfield Township, Burlington County	8,520	16	15	1
Mansfield Township, Warren County	7,347	16	15	1
Mantoloking	252	11	10	1
Mantua Township	14,779	30	28	2
Manville	10,205	27	24	3
Maple Shade Township	18,451	38	34	4

(Number.)

State/city	Population	Total law enforcement employees	Total officers	Total civilians
Maplewood Township	25,297	77	65	12
Margate City	5,912	36	28	8
Marlboro Township	39,850	115	89	26
Matawan	8,716	23	22	1
Maywood	9,667	29	25	4
Medford Lakes	3,922	12	11	1
Medford Township	23,393	41	37	4
Mendham	4,876	13	12	1
Mendham Township	5,700	16	15	1
Merchantville	3,687	15	14	1
Metuchen	14,423	35	29	6
Middlesex Borough	13,659	34	31	3
Middle Township	18,225	66	53	13
Middletown Township	65,361	125	113	12
Midland Park	7,246	19	18	1
Millburn Township	20,085	61	55	6
Milltown	7,020	19	16	3
Millville	27,528	84	74	10
Monmouth Beach	3,222	10	9	1
Monroe Township, Gloucester County	36,884	66	60	6
Monroe Township, Middlesex County	45,342	80	61	19
Montclair	38,625	124	109	15
Montgomery Township	23,364	40	34	6
Montvale	8,657	27	25	2
Montville Township	21,208	46	40	6
Moonachie	2,736	24	21	3
Moorestown Township	20,307	38	33	5
Morris Plains	5,935	18	16	2
Morristown	19,153	60	56	4
Morris Township	22,080	44	41	3
Mountain Lakes	4,269	14	13	1
Mountainside	6,888	29	23	6
Mount Arlington	5,964	16	15	1
Mount Ephraim	4,567	14	13	1
Mount Holly Township	9,568	28	25	3
Mount Laurel Township	41,109	79	72	7
Mount Olive Township	29,025	59	49	10
Mullica Township	5,897	13	12	1
Neptune City	4,625	20	19	1
Neptune Township	27,549	91	79	12
Netcong	3,151	10	10	0
Newark	281,422	1,533	1,187	346
New Brunswick	55,995	173	150	23
New Hanover Township	8,123	3	3	0
New Milford	16,506	42	36	6
New Providence	13,592	28	26	2
Newton	7,916	30	25	5
North Arlington	15,710	39	32	7
North Bergen Township	61,447	134	116	18
North Brunswick Township	41,706	99	83	16
North Caldwell	6,645	18	14	4
Northfield	8,163	23	22	1
North Haledon	8,379	24	19	5
North Hanover Township	7,476	11	10	1
North Plainfield	21,474	55	47	8
Northvale	4,937	12	12	0
North Wildwood	3,763	35	27	8
Norwood	5,816	17	16	1
Nutley Township	28,384	85	72	13
Oakland	12,992	32	27	5
Oaklyn	3,936	17	16	1
Ocean City	10,962	70	61	9
Ocean Gate	2,025	10	9	1
Oceanport	5,739	15	14	1
Ocean Township, Monmouth County	26,638	75	62	13
Ocean Township, Ocean County	9,134	32	23	9
Ogdensburg	2,247	6	6	0
Old Bridge Township	65,659	121	100	21
Old Tappan	5,944	14	13	1
Oradell	8,181	24	23	1
Orange City	30,558	144	122	22

Table 19. Full-Time Law Enforcement Employees, by Selected State and City, 2019—*Continued*

(Number.)

State/city	Population	Total law enforcement employees	Total officers	Total civilians
Palisades Park	20,877	39	34	5
Palmyra	7,134	19	18	1
Paramus	26,460	110	91	19
Park Ridge	8,761	20	19	1
Parsippany-Troy Hills Township	51,907	126	103	23
Passaic	69,639	194	160	34
Paterson	144,866	526	419	107
Paulsboro	5,828	22	20	2
Peapack-Gladstone	2,591	9	8	1
Pemberton Borough	1,321	6	6	0
Pemberton Township	26,966	46	42	4
Pennington	2,516	6	5	1
Pennsauken Township	35,506	80	73	7
Penns Grove	4,746	17	16	1
Pennsville Township	12,345	23	21	2
Pequannock Township	15,045	37	32	5
Perth Amboy	51,816	149	119	30
Phillipsburg	14,228	40	39	1
Pine Beach	2,173	7	6	1
Pine Hill	10,419	24	22	2
Pine Valley	12	6	6	0
Piscataway Township	56,783	103	82	21
Pitman	8,709	18	17	1
Plainfield	50,576	142	121	21
Plainsboro Township	22,976	48	36	12
Pleasantville	20,388	71	65	6
Plumsted Township	8,545	15	14	1
Pohatcong Township	3,181	16	15	1
Point Pleasant	18,684	43	33	10
Point Pleasant Beach	4,516	29	23	6
Pompton Lakes	10,953	29	25	4
Princeton	31,610	64	56	8
Prospect Park	5,831	19	18	1
Rahway	30,072	93	76	17
Ramsey	14,978	39	33	6
Randolph Township	25,490	41	35	6
Raritan	7,999	22	21	1
Raritan Township	22,220	34	31	3
Readington Township	15,805	25	23	2
Red Bank	12,016	45	39	6
Ridgefield	11,240	31	29	2
Ridgefield Park	12,983	41	34	7
Ridgewood	25,192	52	47	5
Ringwood	12,165	26	21	5
Riverdale	4,255	22	17	5
River Edge	11,500	28	25	3
Riverside Township	7,806	16	16	0
Riverton	2,675	6	6	0
River Vale Township	10,063	23	22	1
Robbinsville Township	14,635	37	29	8
Rochelle Park Township	5,598	24	20	4
Rockaway	6,325	16	15	1
Rockaway Township	25,756	63	52	11
Roseland	5,826	24	23	1
Roselle	21,903	66	54	12
Roselle Park	13,630	36	34	2
Roxbury Township	22,755	45	42	3
Rumson	6,740	21	17	4
Runnemede	8,262	16	15	1
Rutherford	18,423	42	40	2
Saddle Brook Township	13,897	39	34	5
Saddle River	3,186	24	19	5
Salem	4,702	20	18	2
Sayreville	44,581	100	85	15
Scotch Plains Township	24,383	52	49	3
Sea Bright	1,352	20	11	9
Sea Girt	1,764	13	12	1
Sea Isle City	2,035	30	23	7
Seaside Heights	2,902	28	25	3
Seaside Park	1,538	13	12	1
Secaucus	21,217	88	73	15

Table 19. Full-Time Law Enforcement Employees, by Selected State and City, 2019—*Continued*

(Number.)

State/city	Population	Total law enforcement employees	Total officers	Total civilians
Ship Bottom	1,144	12	11	1
Shrewsbury	4,122	20	15	5
Somerdale	5,492	18	17	1
Somers Point	10,224	31	24	7
Somerville	12,198	34	32	2
South Amboy	8,922	33	28	5
South Bound Brook	4,570	13	13	0
South Brunswick Township	46,038	115	83	32
South Hackensack Township	2,465	24	21	3
South Orange Village	16,740	52	45	7
South Plainfield	24,114	73	59	14
South River	15,945	42	32	10
South Toms River	3,780	12	11	1
Sparta Township	18,532	43	31	12
Spotswood	8,276	28	24	4
Springfield Township, Burlington County	3,252	11	10	1
Springfield Township, Union County	17,661	46	42	4
Spring Lake	2,917	13	13	0
Spring Lake Heights	4,538	15	15	0
Stafford Township	27,609	79	55	24
Stanhope	3,281	10	9	1
Stone Harbor	804	19	17	2
Stratford	6,926	15	15	0
Summit	21,980	50	46	4
Surf City	1,193	10	10	0
Teaneck Township	40,533	108	91	17
Tenafly	14,586	40	34	6
Teterboro	68	24	21	3
Tewksbury Township	5,765	12	11	1
Tinton Falls	17,506	43	41	2
Toms River Township	93,836	192	163	29
Totowa	10,754	32	28	4
Trenton	83,457	347	279	68
Tuckerton	3,370	13	12	1
Union Beach	5,396	20	16	4
Union City	68,459	210	172	38
Union Township	58,736	181	130	51
Upper Saddle River	8,245	20	16	4
Ventnor City	9,966	46	33	13
Vernon Township	21,912	42	33	9
Verona	13,355	36	30	6
Vineland	59,860	173	146	27
Voorhees Township	29,099	64	55	9
Waldwick	10,240	26	21	5
Wallington	11,568	24	23	1
Wall Township	25,648	84	67	17
Wanaque	11,772	29	24	5
Warren Township	15,772	38	31	7
Washington Township, Bergen County	9,219	25	20	5
Washington Township, Gloucester County	47,126	87	79	8
Washington Township, Morris County	18,296	30	29	1
Washington Township, Warren County	6,391	27	26	1
Watchung	6,054	37	31	6
Waterford Township	10,664	29	28	1
Wayne Township	53,279	145	117	28
Weehawken Township	15,115	72	54	18
Westampton Township	8,666	27	24	3
West Amwell Township	2,727	6	6	0
West Caldwell Township	10,840	29	25	4
West Deptford Township	20,902	46	43	3
Westfield	29,688	74	61	13
West Long Branch	7,889	22	21	1
West Milford Township	26,287	50	43	7
West New York	53,145	125	112	13
West Orange	47,696	108	95	13
Westville	4,128	14	13	1
West Wildwood	553	6	6	0
West Windsor Township	28,026	60	48	12
Westwood	11,129	36	30	6
Wharton	6,417	23	21	2
Wildwood	4,959	54	44	10

Table 19. Full-Time Law Enforcement Employees, by Selected State and City, 2019—*Continued*

(Number.)

State/city	Population	Total law enforcement employees	Total officers	Total civilians
Wildwood Crest	3,051	26	23	3
Willingboro Township	31,920	76	67	9
Winfield Township	1,507	10	10	0
Winslow Township	38,390	80	74	6
Woodbridge Township	100,125	272	206	66
Woodbury	9,768	28	26	2
Woodbury Heights	2,949	8	7	1
Woodcliff Lake	5,853	20	19	1
Woodland Park	12,657	34	30	4
Woodlynne	2,901	8	6	2
Wood-Ridge	9,328	28	24	4
Woodstown	3,440	10	9	1
Woolwich Township	13,075	29	27	2
Wyckoff Township	17,030	26	26	0
NEW MEXICO				
Albuquerque	561,920	1,464	908	556
Anthony	9,284	11	9	2
Capitan	1,417	3	3	0
Clayton	2,691	13	7	6
Corrales	8,715	14	11	3
Deming	14,011	39	35	4
Dexter	1,236	6	5	1
Edgewood	6,161	14	10	4
Hatch	1,605	8	7	1
Hobbs	38,835	114	81	33
Las Cruces	103,520	259	187	72
Las Vegas	12,994	47	34	13
Lovington	11,322	34	25	9
Magdalena	873	3	3	0
Milan	3,632	9	7	2
Portales	11,675	33	23	10
Raton	5,939	22	14	8
Ruidoso	7,826	32	22	10
Santa Clara	1,765	4	3	1
San Ysidro	199	2	2	0
Springer	898	2	2	0
Sunland Park	18,103	22	20	2
Taos	5,963	27	22	5
Texico	1,078	2	2	0
NEW YORK				
Addison Town and Village	2,471	3	3	0
Akron Village	2,851	2	2	0
Albany	97,221	382	293	89
Albion Village	5,802	13	13	0
Alfred Village	3,988	5	5	0
Altamont Village	1,679	1	1	0
Amherst Town	120,864	180	152	28
Amityville Village	9,430	25	24	1
Amsterdam	17,773	44	40	4
Arcade Village	1,933	5	5	0
Ardsley Village	4,538	19	19	0
Asharoken Village	644	3	3	0
Attica Village	2,411	4	4	0
Auburn	26,307	61	56	5
Avon Village	3,201	5	5	0
Baldwinsville Village	7,931	14	13	1
Ballston Spa Village	5,257	4	4	0
Bath Village	5,446	11	10	1
Beacon	14,510	37	35	2
Bedford Town	17,791	45	40	5
Belmont Village	904	1	1	0
Bethlehem Town	35,275	53	38	15
Binghamton	44,475	144	131	13
Blooming Grove Town	11,816	17	15	2
Bolivar Village	976	1	1	0
Briarcliff Manor Village	8,267	21	21	0
Brighton Town	36,036	44	38	6
Brockport Village	8,241	16	15	1
Bronxville Village	6,459	23	21	2

(Number.)

State/city	Population	Total law enforcement employees	Total officers	Total civilians
Buffalo..	255,686	908	729	179
Cairo Town..	6,413	2	2	0
Cambridge Village	1,794	3	3	0
Camillus Town and Village	24,160	27	24	3
Canajoharie Village..	2,136	5	5	0
Canandaigua	10,217	26	24	2
Canisteo Village...	2,131	2	2	0
Canton Village	6,407	12	11	1
Carmel Town	34,251	39	32	7
Carthage Village	3,336	3	3	0
Catskill Village	3,797	15	13	2
Cayuga Heights Village	3,666	7	6	1
Cazenovia Village...	2,842	6	5	1
Cheektowaga Town..	76,821	154	117	37
Chester Town	8,043	15	15	0
Chester Village...	4,120	14	13	1
Chittenango Village	4,835	3	2	1
Clarkstown Town..	80,599	188	164	24
Clayton Village	1,828	3	3	0
Cobleskill Village	4,329	11	11	0
Coeymans Town	7,297	4	3	1
Cohoes...	16,717	35	33	2
Colchester Town..	1,965	2	2	0
Colonie Town	79,509	152	118	34
Corning	10,533	24	20	4
Cornwall-on-Hudson Village	2,914	3	3	0
Cornwall Town...	9,502	12	9	3
Cortland	18,655	45	42	3
Crawford Town	9,171	12	11	1
Croton-on-Hudson Village	8,131	22	20	2
Cuba Town...	3,083	5	5	0
Deerpark Town	7,714	4	4	0
Delhi Village...	3,094	5	5	0
Depew Village..	15,008	35	29	6
DeWitt Town	25,000	46	43	3
Dobbs Ferry Village	10,990	28	26	2
Dryden Village	2,121	4	4	0
Dunkirk..	11,712	37	36	1
East Aurora-Aurora Town	13,785	21	16	5
Eastchester Town...	20,073	48	46	2
East Greenbush Town	16,324	33	25	8
East Hampton Town...	19,901	89	66	23
East Hampton Village...	1,129	29	24	5
East Rochester Village..	6,522	9	8	1
Eden Town	7,621	4	3	1
Ellenville Village	3,980	10	10	0
Ellicott Town..	5,014	13	13	0
Ellicottville..	1,575	4	4	0
Elmira	26,958	82	72	10
Elmira Heights Village	3,819	9	9	0
Elmira Town...	5,589	3	3	0
Elmsford Village	5,295	25	22	3
Evans Town	16,118	29	22	7
Fairport Village..	5,334	11	10	1
Floral Park Village..	15,927	46	34	12
Florida Village	2,851	1	1	0
Fort Edward Village..	3,253	5	5	0
Fort Plain Village	2,224	3	3	0
Frankfort Town	4,817	3	3	0
Frankfort Village	2,432	4	4	0
Freeport Village..	43,064	111	99	12
Fulton City...	11,163	36	35	1
Garden City Village	22,514	65	51	14
Gates Town	28,366	35	31	4
Geddes Town	10,038	19	17	2
Geneseo Village	8,158	8	8	0
Geneva...	12,708	35	33	2
Glen Cove..	27,228	57	52	5
Glens Falls...	14,306	32	30	2
Glenville Town	21,634	25	24	1
Gloversville	14,738	38	35	3

(Number.)

State/city	Population	Total law enforcement employees	Total officers	Total civilians
Goshen Town	8,798	6	6	0
Goshen Village	5,337	21	18	3
Gouverneur Village	3,660	9	6	3
Granville Village	2,422	5	5	0
Great Neck Estates Village	2,884	17	14	3
Greece Town	95,777	107	99	8
Greenburgh Town	45,040	144	112	32
Greenwood Lake Village	3,074	4	3	1
Guilderland Town	34,133	55	39	16
Hamburg Town	46,445	62	62	0
Hamburg Village	9,725	15	14	1
Hamilton Village	4,081	4	4	0
Harriman Village	2,439	7	7	0
Harrison Town	27,946	78	67	11
Hastings-on-Hudson Village	7,916	19	19	0
Hempstead Village	55,404	139	110	29
Highland Falls Village	3,816	10	7	3
Homer Village	3,100	5	4	1
Hoosick Falls Village	3,359	3	3	0
Horseheads Village	6,390	9	9	0
Hudson	6,076	30	25	5
Hudson Falls Village	7,023	12	12	0
Hunter Town	2,628	3	3	0
Huntington Bay Village	1,434	4	4	0
Hyde Park Town	20,808	18	15	3
Ilion Village	7,685	19	18	1
Inlet Town	302	2	2	0
Irondequoit Town	49,729	59	50	9
Irvington Village	6,506	22	22	0
Ithaca	31,122	72	63	9
Jamestown	29,102	72	62	10
Johnson City Village	14,196	43	38	5
Johnstown	8,198	25	24	1
Kenmore Village	15,025	30	26	4
Kensington Village	1,189	6	6	0
Kent Town	13,235	23	18	5
Kingston	22,844	76	71	5
Lackawanna	17,724	53	46	7
Lake Placid Village	2,369	16	13	3
Lake Success Village	3,153	28	24	4
Lakewood-Busti	7,193	11	10	1
Lancaster Town	37,571	67	52	15
Larchmont Village	6,096	26	24	2
Le Roy Village	4,146	7	7	0
Lewisboro Town	12,582	3	3	0
Lewiston Town and Village	15,763	12	11	1
Liberty Village	4,083	20	18	2
Little Falls	4,642	12	11	1
Liverpool Village	2,202	4	4	0
Lloyd Harbor Village	3,667	14	12	2
Lloyd Town	10,463	13	11	2
Lockport	20,345	51	49	2
Long Beach	33,552	84	66	18
Lowville Village	3,315	6	6	0
Lynbrook Village	19,492	49	49	0
Macedon Town and Village	8,877	7	6	1
Malone Village	5,581	13	13	0
Malverne Village	8,514	24	24	0
Mamaroneck Town	12,088	37	36	1
Mamaroneck Village	19,183	57	50	7
Manlius Town	24,168	42	37	5
Marlborough Town	8,601	9	7	2
Massena Village	10,177	26	20	6
Medina Village	5,631	13	12	1
Menands Village	3,885	14	11	3
Middleport Village	1,745	4	4	0
Middletown	27,801	81	68	13
Mohawk Village	2,533	4	4	0
Monroe Village	8,593	23	19	4
Montgomery Town	9,168	17	13	4
Montgomery Village	4,621	4	4	0

(Number.)

State/city	Population	Total law enforcement employees	Total officers	Total civilians
Moriah Town	4,557	2	2	0
Mount Pleasant Town	27,044	51	45	6
Mount Vernon	67,619	270	208	62
Newark Village	8,799	17	16	1
New Berlin Town	1,510	1	1	0
Newburgh	28,070	92	80	12
Newburgh Town	31,128	46	35	11
New Castle Town	17,896	39	37	2
New Hartford Town and Village	20,294	23	20	3
New Paltz Town and Village	14,212	23	20	3
New Rochelle	78,936	222	164	58
New Windsor Town	27,971	62	50	12
New York	8,379,043	52,696	36,563	16,133
New York Mills Village	3,217	5	5	0
Niagara Falls	47,900	164	146	18
Niagara Town	7,958	7	6	1
Niskayuna Town	22,407	29	27	2
Nissequogue Village	1,731	1	1	0
North Castle Town	12,248	34	32	2
North Greenbush Town	12,274	20	18	2
Northport Village	7,288	21	17	4
North Syracuse Village	6,637	12	11	1
North Tonawanda	30,228	53	49	4
Norwich	6,581	14	14	0
Ogdensburg	10,484	30	25	5
Ogden Town	20,144	15	12	3
Old Brookville Village	2,202	34	26	8
Old Westbury Village	4,752	30	25	5
Olean	13,499	40	34	6
Oneida	10,864	29	25	4
Oneonta City	13,915	27	22	5
Orangetown Town	37,371	89	82	7
Orchard Park Town	29,599	46	35	11
Ossining Village	24,991	68	60	8
Oswego City	17,239	53	46	7
Owego Village	3,887	3	2	1
Peekskill	24,243	62	53	9
Pelham Manor Village	5,567	27	26	1
Pelham Village	6,911	29	26	3
Penn Yan Village	4,910	13	12	1
Perry Village	3,442	4	4	0
Plattsburgh City	19,367	51	45	6
Pleasantville Village	7,261	23	21	2
Port Chester Village	29,317	64	62	2
Port Dickinson Village	1,527	5	4	1
Port Jervis	8,523	32	31	1
Port Washington	19,396	69	61	8
Potsdam Village	8,917	18	15	3
Poughkeepsie	30,422	116	89	27
Pound Ridge Town	5,159	2	1	1
Quogue Village	1,015	15	14	1
Ramapo Town	94,633	126	105	21
Rensselaer City	9,193	35	28	7
Riverhead Town	33,536	102	87	15
Rochester	205,769	850	738	112
Rockville Centre Village	24,669	64	55	9
Rome	32,019	74	72	2
Rosendale Town	5,826	1	1	0
Rotterdam Town	29,855	45	42	3
Rye	15,756	40	36	4
Rye Brook Village	9,530	26	25	1
Sag Harbor Village	2,298	12	11	1
Salamanca	5,439	15	15	0
Saranac Lake Village	5,221	12	12	0
Saratoga Springs	28,186	86	72	14
Saugerties Town	19,095	27	23	4
Scarsdale Village	17,954	46	41	5
Schenectady	65,504	187	161	26
Schodack Town	11,722	12	11	1
Scotia Village	7,641	13	12	1
Seneca Falls Town	8,632	19	17	2

Table 19. Full-Time Law Enforcement Employees, by Selected State and City, 2019—*Continued*

(Number.)

State/city	Population	Total law enforcement employees	Total officers	Total civilians
Shawangunk Town	13,853	4	4	0
Shelter Island Town	2,413	10	9	1
Sherrill	2,991	3	3	0
Sidney Village	3,573	8	8	0
Skaneateles Village	2,464	3	2	1
Solvay Village	6,227	14	13	1
Southampton Town	51,090	139	98	41
Southampton Village	3,326	46	32	14
South Glens Falls Village	3,677	6	6	0
South Nyack Village	3,500	6	6	0
Southold Town	19,915	69	49	20
Spring Valley Village	32,367	64	55	9
Stony Point Town	15,413	26	25	1
Suffern Village	11,063	25	21	4
Syracuse	142,438	471	403	68
Tarrytown Village	11,416	35	32	3
Ticonderoga Town	4,790	7	7	0
Tonawanda	14,754	34	28	6
Tonawanda Town	56,717	146	100	46
Troy	49,286	138	128	10
Trumansburg Village	1,757	2	2	0
Tuckahoe Village	6,584	26	23	3
Tupper Lake Village	3,466	8	8	0
Ulster Town	12,625	27	23	4
Utica	59,842	173	162	11
Vernon Village	1,156	1	1	0
Walden Village	6,670	16	13	3
Wallkill Town	29,236	50	49	1
Warsaw Village	3,251	5	5	0
Warwick Town	18,372	38	33	5
Washingtonville Village	5,740	17	15	2
Waterloo Village	4,885	9	8	1
Watertown	25,102	70	67	3
Watervliet	9,954	24	23	1
Waverly Village	4,119	10	9	1
Webb Town	1,790	6	6	0
Webster Town and Village	45,163	38	34	4
Weedsport Village	1,711	1	1	0
Wellsville Village	4,366	12	11	1
Westfield Village	2,981	6	6	0
Westhampton Beach Village	1,811	16	14	2
West Seneca Town	45,399	80	66	14
White Plains	58,259	190	181	9
Woodbury Town	11,006	25	21	4
Woodstock Town	5,781	10	10	0
Yonkers	200,075	681	598	83
Yorktown Town	36,426	68	59	9
NORTH CAROLINA				
Aberdeen	7,892	30	28	2
Ahoskie	4,772	17	15	2
Albemarle	16,134	49	42	7
Andrews	1,839	5	5	0
Angier	5,363	16	16	0
Apex	56,276	108	88	20
Archdale	11,509	32	26	6
Asheboro	25,894	81	73	8
Asheville	93,641	286	232	54
Atlantic Beach	1,506	16	15	1
Ayden	5,128	22	18	4
Badin	1,968	2	2	0
Bailey	560	2	2	0
Bakersville	450	1	1	0
Bald Head Island	182	27	24	3
Banner Elk	1,101	9	8	1
Beaufort	4,417	18	17	1
Beech Mountain	324	13	9	4
Belhaven	1,567	7	6	1
Belmont	12,812	42	35	7
Benson	3,901	15	14	1
Bessemer City	5,552	15	14	1

Table 19. Full-Time Law Enforcement Employees, by Selected State and City, 2019—*Continued*

(Number.)

State/city	Population	Total law enforcement employees	Total officers	Total civilians
Bethel	1,610	4	4	0
Beulaville	1,306	4	4	0
Biltmore Forest	1,410	14	11	3
Biscoe	1,724	8	7	1
Black Creek	766	3	3	0
Black Mountain	8,187	24	20	4
Bladenboro	1,627	6	6	0
Blowing Rock	1,316	12	10	2
Boiling Spring Lakes	6,238	12	10	2
Boiling Springs	4,551	10	10	0
Boone	19,893	45	32	13
Boonville	1,152	4	4	0
Brevard	7,928	32	25	7
Bridgeton	441	1	1	0
Broadway	1,290	4	4	0
Bryson City	1,453	6	5	1
Bunn	377	3	2	1
Burgaw	4,176	12	11	1
Burlington	54,108	170	132	38
Burnsville	1,641	8	8	0
Butner	7,847	40	34	6
Candor	815	4	4	0
Canton	4,349	21	16	5
Cape Carteret	2,076	7	7	0
Carolina Beach	6,437	29	26	3
Carrboro	21,542	39	35	4
Carthage	2,524	12	11	1
Cary	172,525	227	186	41
Caswell Beach	428	4	4	0
Chadbourn	1,711	9	8	1
Chapel Hill	61,457	96	82	14
Charlotte-Mecklenburg1	944,260	2,295	1,823	472
Cherryville	6,062	19	14	5
China Grove	4,220	13	13	0
Chocowinity	794	3	3	0
Claremont	1,407	9	9	0
Clayton	23,842	49	46	3
Cleveland	882	3	3	0
Clinton	8,512	31	27	4
Clyde	1,311	4	4	0
Coats	2,510	7	7	0
Columbus	995	9	8	1
Concord	96,138	201	171	30
Conover	8,426	27	24	3
Conway	729	1	1	0
Cooleemee	969	1	1	0
Cornelius	30,407	78	60	18
Cramerton	4,454	16	16	0
Creedmoor	4,636	19	15	4
Dallas	4,787	15	13	2
Davidson	13,193	22	20	2
Dobson	1,543	8	8	0
Drexel	1,849	5	5	0
Duck	390	13	12	1
Dunn	9,768	44	38	6
Durham	280,282	638	471	167
East Bend	593	2	2	0
East Spencer	1,550	7	7	0
Eden	14,773	47	43	4
Edenton	4,631	47	43	4
Elizabeth City	17,424	66	55	11
Elizabethtown	3,447	16	15	1
Elkin	4,038	21	17	4
Elon	12,214	20	19	1
Emerald Isle	3,706	19	18	1
Enfield	2,288	10	9	1
Erwin	5,148	12	11	1
Fair Bluff	882	3	3	0
Fairmont	2,601	8	7	1
Farmville	4,679	23	18	5
Fayetteville	209,614	560	396	164

Table 19. Full-Time Law Enforcement Employees, by Selected State and City, 2019—*Continued*

(Number.)

State/city	Population	Total law enforcement employees	Total officers	Total civilians
Fletcher	8,485	17	16	1
Forest City	7,116	30	28	2
Four Oaks	2,224	8	8	0
Foxfire Village	1,031	3	3	0
Franklin	4,062	18	17	1
Franklinton	2,195	7	7	0
Fremont	1,264	4	4	0
Fuquay-Varina	30,977	57	49	8
Garner	31,137	74	65	9
Garysburg	918	2	2	0
Gaston	1,016	3	3	0
Gastonia	77,716	192	170	22
Gibsonville	7,356	19	18	1
Glen Alpine	1,480	5	5	0
Goldsboro	34,085	114	98	16
Graham	15,185	41	38	3
Granite Falls	4,629	17	13	4
Granite Quarry	2,999	8	8	0
Greensboro	298,025	767	637	130
Greenville	94,193	244	194	50
Grifton	2,658	7	7	0
Hamlet	6,312	19	18	1
Havelock	20,128	37	28	9
Haw River	2,525	9	9	0
Henderson	14,883	57	42	15
Hendersonville	14,234	57	40	17
Hertford	2,109	9	7	2
Hickory	41,040	147	110	37
Highlands	974	14	13	1
High Point	113,307	284	231	53
Hillsborough	7,321	30	28	2
Holden Beach	656	8	8	0
Holly Ridge	2,829	10	9	1
Holly Springs	38,577	74	57	17
Hope Mills	15,878	41	37	4
Hot Springs	578	1	1	0
Hudson	3,704	14	13	1
Huntersville	58,512	101	91	10
Indian Beach	119	5	5	0
Jackson	455	2	2	0
Jacksonville	72,300	144	113	31
Jefferson	1,534	5	5	0
Jonesville	2,200	10	9	1
Kannapolis	50,725	101	72	29
Kenansville	855	3	3	0
Kenly	1,574	8	8	0
Kernersville	24,980	86	67	19
Kill Devil Hills	7,268	34	28	6
King	6,878	24	21	3
Kings Mountain	10,965	43	33	10
Kinston	19,886	67	56	11
Kitty Hawk	3,563	18	15	3
Knightdale	18,351	35	32	3
Kure Beach	2,113	13	12	1
Lake Lure	1,150	10	9	1
Lake Royale	2,758	7	7	0
Lake Waccamaw	1,395	4	4	0
Landis	3,133	12	12	0
Laurel Park	2,342	7	7	0
Laurinburg	14,928	43	41	2
Leland	23,360	38	35	3
Lenoir	17,904	68	51	17
Lexington	18,917	66	55	11
Liberty	2,656	11	10	1
Lilesville	485	2	2	0
Lillington	3,658	15	14	1
Lincolnton	11,022	36	32	4
Littleton	589	3	3	0
Locust	3,246	13	13	0
Long View	4,921	14	13	1
Louisburg	3,549	17	16	1

(Number.)

State/city	Population	Total law enforcement employees	Total officers	Total civilians
Lowell	3,709	9	9	0
Lumberton	20,754	97	87	10
Madison	2,103	18	18	0
Maggie Valley	1,230	10	9	1
Magnolia	954	2	2	0
Maiden	3,439	19	18	1
Manteo	1,453	7	6	1
Marion	7,837	27	25	2
Marshall	911	3	3	0
Mars Hill	2,054	5	5	0
Marshville	2,748	8	8	0
Matthews	33,372	69	58	11
Maxton	2,359	9	5	4
Mayodan	2,358	14	14	0
Maysville	955	3	3	0
Mebane	16,203	39	35	4
Micro	530	1	1	0
Middlesex	824	5	5	0
Mint Hill	27,776	37	33	4
Misenheimer	692	5	5	0
Mocksville	5,322	21	20	1
Monroe	35,630	99	88	11
Montreat	852	5	5	0
Mooresville	38,967	102	81	21
Morehead City	9,721	43	39	4
Morganton	16,524	97	61	36
Morrisville	28,796	40	38	2
Mount Airy	10,242	46	32	14
Mount Gilead	1,144	7	7	0
Mount Holly	16,475	40	32	8
Mount Olive	4,652	16	15	1
Murfreesboro	3,072	9	8	1
Murphy	1,657	10	9	1
Nags Head	2,963	25	23	2
Nashville	5,523	14	13	1
Navassa	2,217	3	3	0
New Bern	30,187	111	86	25
Newland	684	5	5	0
Newport	4,666	8	8	0
Newton	13,153	40	31	9
Newton Grove	564	3	3	0
Norlina	1,050	5	5	0
North Topsail Beach	738	12	11	1
Northwest	782	2	2	0
North Wilkesboro	4,220	26	25	1
Norwood	2,438	9	9	0
Oakboro	1,899	8	8	0
Oak Island	8,244	25	23	2
Ocean Isle Beach	644	13	12	1
Old Fort	921	4	4	0
Oriental	852	2	2	0
Oxford	8,851	32	30	2
Parkton	414	2	2	0
Pembroke	2,994	17	13	4
Pikeville	678	4	4	0
Pilot Mountain	1,416	9	8	1
Pinebluff	1,582	3	3	0
Pinehurst	16,522	30	25	5
Pine Knoll Shores	1,331	8	8	0
Pine Level	2,016	5	5	0
Pinetops	1,240	9	7	2
Pineville	9,088	47	36	11
Pink Hill	507	2	2	0
Pittsboro	4,359	13	13	0
Plymouth	3,400	11	10	1
Polkton	2,880	3	3	0
Princeton	1,402	4	4	0
Raeford	5,001	19	17	2
Raleigh	477,828	646	544	102
Ramseur	1,689	6	6	0
Randleman	4,119	16	16	0

(Number.)

State/city	Population	Total law enforcement employees	Total officers	Total civilians
Ranlo	3,661	11	10	1
Red Springs	3,341	13	12	1
Reidsville	13,959	54	49	5
Richlands	1,698	8	8	0
Rich Square	837	1	1	0
River Bend	3,033	6	6	0
Roanoke Rapids	14,354	40	34	6
Robbins	1,215	4	4	0
Robersonville	1,348	7	7	0
Rockingham	8,687	38	36	2
Rockwell	2,151	7	7	0
Rocky Mount	53,827	182	144	38
Rolesville	8,924	21	20	1
Rose Hill	1,623	6	6	0
Rowland	1,002	7	6	1
Roxboro	8,299	35	30	5
Rutherfordton	4,047	15	14	1
Salisbury	33,877	93	79	14
Saluda	690	4	4	0
Sanford	30,135	99	75	24
Scotland Neck	1,852	8	7	1
Seagrove	228	1	1	0
Selma	7,018	23	22	1
Seven Devils	217	6	6	0
Shallotte	4,396	15	14	1
Sharpsburg	2,013	7	6	1
Shelby	20,004	85	72	13
Siler City	8,237	24	18	6
Smithfield	12,882	39	35	4
Snow Hill	1,513	7	7	0
Southern Pines	14,524	48	40	8
Southern Shores	2,940	12	11	1
Southport	3,961	9	9	0
Sparta	1,758	6	6	0
Spencer	3,238	11	11	0
Spindale	4,215	11	11	0
Spring Hope	1,305	7	7	0
Spring Lake	12,069	30	27	3
Spruce Pine	2,138	10	10	0
Stallings	16,173	25	22	3
Stanfield	1,536	5	5	0
Stanley	3,769	11	10	1
Stantonsburg	777	4	4	0
Star	845	4	4	0
Statesville	27,372	93	71	22
Stoneville	1,237	5	5	0
St. Pauls	2,323	16	12	4
Sugar Mountain	197	5	5	0
Sunset Beach	4,002	15	15	0
Surf City	2,487	22	21	1
Swansboro	3,354	14	13	1
Sylva	2,742	12	12	0
Tabor City	4,136	11	10	1
Tarboro	10,765	36	30	6
Taylorsville	2,185	13	13	0
Taylortown	847	4	3	1
Thomasville	26,617	72	66	6
Topsail Beach	435	10	9	1
Trent Woods	4,030	5	5	0
Troutman	2,755	13	13	0
Troy	3,326	10	9	1
Tryon	1,609	9	7	2
Valdese	4,435	12	11	1
Vanceboro	966	3	3	0
Vass	792	4	4	0
Wadesboro	5,228	28	23	5
Wagram	770	1	1	0
Wake Forest	46,145	100	78	22
Wallace	3,894	20	16	4
Walnut Creek	863	3	3	0
Warrenton	837	5	4	1

(Number.)

State/city	Population	Total law enforcement employees	Total officers	Total civilians
Warsaw	3,115	16	14	2
Washington	9,497	40	31	9
Waxhaw	17,203	28	26	2
Waynesville	10,146	43	33	10
Weaverville	4,013	17	16	1
Weldon	1,472	8	8	0
Wendell	8,096	18	17	1
West Jefferson	1,311	8	8	0
Whispering Pines	3,385	9	8	1
Whitakers	701	2	2	0
White Lake	776	6	6	0
Whiteville	5,338	25	21	4
Wilkesboro	3,491	24	22	2
Williamston	5,217	23	20	3
Wilmington	124,750	336	267	69
Wilson	49,344	131	116	15
Wilson's Mills	2,744	6	6	0
Windsor	3,310	8	8	0
Wingate	4,557	7	7	0
Winston-Salem	248,445	674	518	156
Winterville	9,922	23	22	1
Woodfin	6,634	14	13	1
Woodland	701	1	1	0
Wrightsville Beach	2,550	26	24	2
Yadkinville	2,890	14	13	1
Youngsville	1,365	12	11	1
Zebulon	5,814	22	21	1
NORTH DAKOTA				
Belfield	1,028	3	2	1
Berthold	497	1	1	0
Beulah	3,200	6	5	1
Bismarck	74,705	154	125	29
Bowman	1,604	4	4	0
Burlington	1,233	2	2	0
Carrington	1,980	3	3	0
Cavalier	1,253	3	3	0
Devils Lake	7,294	21	19	2
Dickinson	23,428	59	40	19
Ellendale	1,223	2	2	0
Emerado	456	1	1	0
Fargo	127,423	201	178	23
Fessenden	442	1	1	0
Grafton	4,144	10	9	1
Grand Forks	57,459	105	90	15
Harvey	1,683	4	4	0
Hazen	2,321	4	4	0
Jamestown	15,198	31	27	4
Kenmare	1,010	2	2	0
Killdeer	1,213	5	5	0
Lamoure	898	1	1	0
Lincoln	3,986	5	5	0
Lisbon	2,036	4	4	0
Mandan	23,012	44	37	7
Medora	130	2	2	0
Minot	48,185	109	83	26
Napoleon	763	1	1	0
New Town	2,621	6	5	1
Northwood	904	2	2	0
Oakes	1,694	3	3	0
Powers Lake	279	2	2	0
Ray	866	1	1	0
Rolette	599	1	1	0
Rolla	1,278	4	4	0
Rugby	2,661	5	5	0
Stanley	2,813	5	5	0
Steele	709	1	1	0
Surrey	1,445	4	4	0
Thompson	1,021	1	1	0
Tioga	1,639	7	5	2
Valley City	6,351	16	14	2

(Number.)

State/city	Population	Total law enforcement employees	Total officers	Total civilians
Wahpeton	7,752	16	14	2
Watford City	8,488	27	22	5
West Fargo	38,171	76	63	13
Williston	28,966	81	70	11
Wishek	921	2	2	0
OHIO				
Ada	5,509	7	7	0
Addyston	943	1	1	0
American Township	12,050	1	1	0
Amherst	12,166	29	21	8
Arcanum	2,006	4	4	0
Archbold	4,320	11	10	1
Ashland	20,410	34	27	7
Aurora	16,319	36	27	9
Barberton	26,015	39	38	1
Bath Township, Summit County	9,659	28	21	7
Bay Village	15,235	27	23	4
Beavercreek	47,672	67	50	17
Beaver Township	6,415	14	10	4
Bedford	12,485	39	34	5
Bellefontaine	13,145	37	30	7
Bellville	1,895	6	6	0
Belpre	6,386	16	11	5
Berea	18,573	31	29	2
Bexley	13,956	37	31	6
Blue Ash	12,307	40	33	7
Bluffton	4,049	9	9	0
Bowling Green	31,719	54	40	14
Brunswick	34,977	51	39	12
Butler Township	7,819	18	17	1
Cambridge	10,318	32	26	6
Canal Fulton	5,450	11	10	1
Canfield	7,199	26	19	7
Canton	70,139	201	167	34
Carlisle	5,457	8	7	1
Catawba Island Township	3,556	5	5	0
Centerville	23,744	55	40	15
Chagrin Falls	3,941	14	13	1
Cheviot	8,269	11	11	0
Chillicothe	21,670	58	47	11
Cincinnati	303,335	1,157	1,024	133
Circleville	14,025	20	13	7
Clayton	13,221	19	18	1
Clearcreek Township	16,070	17	16	1
Cleveland	381,829	1,785	1,560	225
Cleveland Heights	44,098	100	96	4
Clyde	6,147	19	15	4
Colerain Township	59,479	61	53	8
Columbiana	6,209	18	14	4
Copley Township	17,309	22	21	1
Covington	2,694	7	6	1
Cridersville	1,793	4	4	0
Dayton	140,427	426	363	63
Deer Park	5,654	14	10	4
Defiance	16,601	34	30	4
Delaware	40,616	63	56	7
Dublin	49,626	109	68	41
East Cleveland	17,001	42	41	1
Eastlake	18,074	35	24	11
Eaton	8,136	17	16	1
Elida	1,801	2	2	0
Elmore	1,373	5	5	0
Englewood	13,478	27	20	7
Evendale	2,839	22	20	2
Fairfield Township	22,956	25	23	2
Forest Park	18,673	43	36	7
Fort Loramie	1,521	2	2	0
Fort Recovery	1,456	3	3	0
Fostoria	13,230	26	22	4
Frazeysburg	1,309	2	2	0

(Number.)

State/city	Population	Total law enforcement employees	Total officers	Total civilians
Genoa	2,284	4	4	0
German Township, Montgomery County	2,897	6	6	0
Glenwillow	932	4	4	0
Grandview Heights	8,581	25	20	5
Greenhills	3,591	11	10	1
Harrison	11,837	25	22	3
Heath	10,933	28	20	8
Hinckley Township	8,076	12	11	1
Hiram	1,128	3	3	0
Holland	1,642	9	9	0
Hubbard Township	5,306	10	9	1
Huber Heights	38,183	74	52	22
Indian Hill	5,897	26	21	5
Ironton	10,576	16	15	1
Kalida	1,586	1	1	0
Kenton	8,198	15	15	0
Kettering	54,974	118	80	38
Kirtland	6,823	14	9	5
Lakewood	49,802	113	94	19
Lancaster	40,622	82	65	17
Lexington	4,666	15	11	4
Liberty Township	11,420	18	18	0
Lockland	3,455	16	15	1
Lordstown	3,248	13	9	4
Lyndhurst	13,407	37	29	8
Macedonia	12,028	24	23	1
Madison Township, Franklin County	19,682	18	17	1
Mansfield	46,418	113	77	36
Mariemont	3,473	11	10	1
Mason	33,939	54	50	4
Maumee	13,656	57	43	14
Mayfield Heights	18,519	50	39	11
Miamisburg	19,913	39	37	2
Miami Township, Montgomery County	29,188	44	41	3
Middlefield	2,713	9	9	0
Middletown	48,878	108	67	41
Mifflin Township	2,632	10	10	0
Milan	1,331	3	3	0
Milford	6,880	21	19	2
Milton Township	2,439	4	4	0
Minerva Park	1,334	10	9	1
Mogadore	3,832	8	8	0
Monroe	16,531	42	32	10
Montgomery	10,867	22	20	2
Moraine	6,455	30	22	8
Mount Vernon	16,663	34	31	3
Navarre	1,846	6	6	0
New Albany	11,332	32	23	9
Newark	50,340	75	64	11
New Boston	2,093	13	9	4
New Bremen	2,977	7	7	0
Newcomerstown	3,743	8	5	3
New Franklin	14,162	22	14	8
New London	2,368	5	5	0
New Philadelphia	17,434	26	22	4
Newton Falls	4,481	5	5	0
Newtown	2,666	9	8	1
Niles	18,222	42	36	6
North Ridgeville	34,469	46	39	7
North Royalton	30,177	50	36	14
Northwood	5,445	22	17	5
Norton	12,007	24	23	1
Norwalk	16,903	31	24	7
Oberlin	8,302	22	17	5
Olmsted Falls	8,861	10	10	0
Orrville	8,461	17	16	1
Ottawa	4,317	8	8	0
Oxford Township	2,224	3	3	0
Pandora	1,107	2	2	0
Peninsula	558	3	3	0
Pepper Pike	6,371	17	17	0

(Number.)

State/city	Population	Total law enforcement employees	Total officers	Total civilians
Perkins Township	11,687	23	22	1
Perrysburg Township	13,013	31	24	7
Perry Township, Franklin County	3,788	12	11	1
Plain City	4,452	10	9	1
Poland Township	11,859	11	11	0
Port Clinton	5,914	20	15	5
Powell	13,545	21	19	2
Reading	10,995	26	22	4
Reynoldsburg	38,578	79	60	19
Roaming Shores Village	1,451	4	4	0
Rossford	6,575	16	15	1
Russell Township	5,219	11	10	1
Sagamore Hills	10,934	22	21	1
Salem	11,644	23	23	0
Salineville	1,219	2	2	0
Seaman	896	2	2	0
Seven Hills	11,621	17	16	1
Shaker Heights	27,127	78	61	17
Sharonville	13,873	50	39	11
Shawnee Hills	822	6	6	0
Shawnee Township	12,056	20	14	6
Sidney	20,437	47	37	10
Silver Lake	2,498	9	8	1
Solon	22,830	65	47	18
South Charleston	1,613	3	3	0
South Russell	3,767	9	9	0
Springboro	18,975	33	29	4
Springfield	59,128	127	116	11
Springfield Township, Mahoning County	6,415	10	10	0
St. Clairsville	4,991	10	9	1
Steubenville	17,768	43	38	5
St. Henry	2,554	3	3	0
Stow	34,862	50	41	9
Streetsboro	16,561	35	29	6
Sugarcreek	2,220	6	6	0
Sugarcreek Township	8,494	17	15	2
Sylvania	19,046	40	33	7
Sylvania Township	29,754	60	43	17
Tallmadge	17,583	29	25	4
Tiffin	17,498	39	29	10
Toledo	273,505	695	637	58
Trenton	13,154	21	16	5
Trotwood	24,435	35	33	2
Troy	26,250	44	41	3
Uhrichsville	5,317	9	9	0
Uniontown	3,353	12	10	2
University Heights	12,852	30	28	2
Upper Sandusky	6,467	17	13	4
Urbana	11,309	19	19	0
Valley View, Cuyahoga County	1,999	20	18	2
Vandalia	15,018	40	30	10
Van Wert	10,662	32	23	9
Wadsworth	24,058	40	31	9
Walton Hills	2,283	15	11	4
Warren	38,012	72	68	4
Washington Court House	14,150	27	22	5
West Liberty	1,787	4	4	0
West Salem	1,475	1	1	0
West Union	3,153	5	4	1
Whitehouse	4,887	11	11	0
Wickliffe	12,758	40	30	10
Wooster	26,615	50	43	7
Wyoming	8,596	22	19	3
Xenia	26,926	68	43	25
Zanesville	25,346	99	59	40
OKLAHOMA				
Achille	541	3	2	1
Ada	17,321	40	36	4
Adair	817	11	9	2
Allen	930	3	2	1

Table 19. Full-Time Law Enforcement Employees, by Selected State and City, 2019—*Continued*

(Number.)

State/city	Population	Total law enforcement employees	Total officers	Total civilians
Altus	18,572	50	38	12
Alva	5,022	10	10	0
Amber	467	1	1	0
Anadarko	6,540	19	17	2
Antlers	2,296	11	6	5
Apache	1,399	4	4	0
Arcadia	276	1	1	0
Ardmore	24,830	50	45	5
Arkoma	1,907	4	2	2
Atoka	3,131	15	15	0
Barnsdall	1,143	3	3	0
Bartlesville	36,502	86	63	23
Beaver	1,390	1	1	0
Beggs	1,227	7	3	4
Bennington	366	1	1	0
Bernice	579	2	2	0
Bethany	19,346	38	30	8
Big Cabin	252	4	3	1
Binger	636	1	1	0
Bixby	28,383	44	35	9
Blackwell	6,610	20	14	6
Blanchard	9,028	15	11	4
Boise City	1,077	2	2	0
Bokchito	688	6	5	1
Bokoshe	493	2	2	0
Boley	1,175	2	2	0
Boswell	679	3	2	1
Bristow	4,195	13	9	4
Broken Arrow	110,480	205	152	53
Broken Bow	4,053	17	12	5
Burns Flat	1,920	5	4	1
Cache	2,814	6	5	1
Caddo	1,091	4	4	0
Calera	2,375	11	10	1
Calvin	273	1	1	0
Caney	196	4	3	1
Canton	592	2	2	0
Carnegie	1,651	8	4	4
Carney	656	1	1	0
Cashion	883	1	1	0
Catoosa	6,975	16	15	1
Cement	481	1	1	0
Chandler	3,094	11	7	4
Chattanooga	441	2	1	1
Checotah	3,143	13	10	3
Chelsea	1,902	4	4	0
Cherokee	1,509	3	3	0
Chickasha	16,395	38	27	11
Choctaw	12,812	21	17	4
Chouteau	2,086	10	9	1
Claremore	18,786	47	39	8
Clayton	794	4	4	0
Cleveland	3,136	8	8	0
Clinton	9,179	25	17	8
Coalgate	1,779	5	5	0
Colbert	1,250	3	2	1
Colcord	838	4	4	0
Collinsville	7,271	19	12	7
Commerce	2,392	5	5	0
Cordell	2,753	4	4	0
Covington	533	1	1	0
Coweta	10,016	20	14	6
Crescent	1,547	7	5	2
Cushing	7,639	21	15	6
Cyril	1,022	2	2	0
Davenport	816	1	1	0
Davis	2,911	10	8	2
Del City	21,794	45	35	10
Depew	479	1	1	0
Dewar	847	2	2	0
Dewey	3,405	12	10	2

Table 19. Full-Time Law Enforcement Employees, by Selected State and City, 2019—*Continued*

(Number.)

State/city	Population	Total law enforcement employees	Total officers	Total civilians
Dibble	871	5	4	1
Dickson	1,251	3	2	1
Disney	307	2	2	0
Drumright	2,816	5	5	0
Duncan	22,296	66	49	17
Durant	18,478	44	39	5
Earlsboro	652	1	1	0
Edmond	94,699	157	122	35
Eldorado	410	1	1	0
Elgin	3,294	5	5	0
Elk City	11,509	40	26	14
Elmore City	706	5	4	1
El Reno	19,830	55	35	20
Enid	49,598	123	95	28
Erick	988	2	2	0
Eufaula	2,907	9	9	0
Fairfax	1,268	3	1	2
Fairland	1,031	2	2	0
Fairview	2,601	8	4	4
Fletcher	1,128	1	1	0
Forest Park	1,075	3	1	2
Fort Cobb	613	1	1	0
Fort Gibson	3,972	13	12	1
Fort Towson	486	1	1	0
Frederick	3,558	9	6	3
Gans	298	1	1	0
Geary	1,276	10	5	5
Glenpool	14,356	31	24	7
Goodwell	1,289	4	4	0
Gore	939	4	3	1
Grandfield	938	1	1	0
Granite	1,968	3	3	0
Grove	7,129	31	21	10
Guthrie	11,597	32	22	10
Guymon	11,247	24	16	8
Haileyville	753	4	4	0
Harrah	6,602	11	10	1
Hartshorne	1,930	5	3	2
Haskell	1,913	6	6	0
Healdton	2,688	4	4	0
Heavener	3,285	14	13	1
Hennessey	2,241	9	5	4
Henryetta	5,517	18	13	5
Hinton	3,228	6	6	0
Hobart	3,403	12	6	6
Holdenville	5,518	10	9	1
Hollis	1,856	9	5	4
Hominy	3,381	9	4	5
Hooker	1,882	3	3	0
Howe	786	3	3	0
Hugo	5,081	22	16	6
Hulbert	584	7	5	2
Hydro	937	4	3	1
Idabel	6,816	25	20	5
Inola	1,820	6	5	1
Jay	2,532	15	9	6
Jenks	24,264	34	25	9
Jennings	357	1	1	0
Jones	3,196	7	7	0
Kansas	802	4	4	0
Kellyville	1,155	2	2	0
Keota	544	1	1	0
Kiefer	2,039	5	5	0
Kingfisher	4,962	15	12	3
Kingston	1,676	7	7	0
Kiowa	668	7	5	2
Konawa	1,211	3	2	1
Krebs	1,922	8	6	2
Lahoma	621	1	1	0
Langley	823	3	3	0
Langston	1,842	3	2	1

(Number.)

State/city	Population	Total law enforcement employees	Total officers	Total civilians
Laverne	1,374	2	1	1
Lawton	92,256	222	190	32
Lexington	2,152	11	6	5
Lindsay	2,798	16	10	6
Locust Grove	1,401	10	6	4
Lone Grove	5,111	10	7	3
Luther	1,834	4	4	0
Madill	4,056	12	11	1
Mangum	2,735	10	6	4
Mannford	3,210	11	8	3
Marietta	2,771	7	6	1
Marlow	4,398	10	10	0
Maud	1,060	4	4	0
Maysville	1,208	4	3	1
McAlester	17,840	48	45	3
McCurtain	503	2	1	1
McLoud	4,746	11	10	1
Medford	936	3	3	0
Medicine Park	450	2	2	0
Meeker	1,149	5	5	0
Miami	13,078	31	30	1
Midwest City	57,678	126	100	26
Minco	1,641	5	5	0
Moore	62,998	93	87	6
Mooreland	1,176	4	3	1
Morris	1,416	3	3	0
Mounds	1,253	2	2	0
Mountain View	726	2	2	0
Muldrow	3,226	13	8	5
Muskogee	37,174	91	83	8
Mustang	22,630	38	26	12
Nash	194	1	1	0
Newcastle	10,649	21	20	1
Newkirk	2,181	5	4	1
Nichols Hills	3,945	23	16	7
Nicoma Park	2,481	6	6	0
Ninnekah	1,041	4	3	1
Noble	6,922	19	13	6
Norman	125,076	242	179	63
North Enid	932	4	4	0
Nowata	3,598	8	6	2
Oilton	1,012	2	2	0
Okarche	1,351	6	5	1
Okeene	1,142	2	2	0
Okemah	3,168	14	9	5
Oklahoma City	657,890	1,455	1,173	282
Okmulgee	11,702	26	24	2
Olustee	563	1	1	0
Oologah	1,176	5	5	0
Owasso	37,654	79	58	21
Paoli	613	3	2	1
Pauls Valley	6,157	20	15	5
Pawhuska	3,410	15	10	5
Pawnee	2,107	5	5	0
Perkins	2,833	8	8	0
Perry	4,905	20	13	7
Piedmont	8,553	10	9	1
Pocola	4,124	12	8	4
Ponca City	23,876	72	50	22
Pond Creek	822	2	2	0
Porum	702	3	3	0
Poteau	8,961	33	26	7
Prague	2,385	13	8	5
Pryor Creek	9,395	38	29	9
Purcell	6,481	23	20	3
Quinton	980	4	4	0
Ramona	543	2	1	1
Rattan	297	3	3	0
Ringling	966	1	1	0
Roland	3,894	11	8	3
Rush Springs	1,262	5	5	0

State/city	Population	Total law enforcement employees	Total officers	Total civilians
Salina	1,396	6	6	0
Sallisaw	8,391	30	22	8
Sand Springs	20,024	43	33	10
Sapulpa	20,888	56	45	11
Savanna	649	8	6	2
Sawyer	311	4	3	1
Sayre	4,476	12	7	5
Seminole	7,134	17	14	3
Shady Point	998	2	2	0
Shattuck	1,280	1	1	0
Shawnee	31,627	84	67	17
Skiatook	8,041	19	15	4
Snyder	1,271	2	2	0
South Coffeyville	740	5	5	0
Spencer	3,989	5	3	2
Sperry	1,329	5	5	0
Spiro	2,171	5	4	1
Sportsmen Acres	307	1	1	0
Stigler	2,719	13	9	4
Stillwater	51,008	127	80	47
Stilwell	4,054	20	13	7
Stratford	1,535	6	3	3
Stringtown	397	3	3	0
Stroud	2,713	12	7	5
Sulphur	5,028	12	10	2
Tahlequah	16,861	45	38	7
Talala	278	1	1	0
Talihina	1,086	8	4	4
Tecumseh	6,667	14	13	1
Texhoma	917	2	2	0
Thackerville	488	2	1	1
The Village	9,535	29	23	6
Thomas	1,205	1	1	0
Tipton	762	1	1	0
Tishomingo	3,040	8	7	1
Tonkawa	3,006	12	8	4
Tryon	499	1	1	0
Tulsa	401,700	1,037	842	195
Tupelo	303	2	2	0
Tushka	303	3	3	0
Tuttle	7,553	16	11	5
Tyrone	760	2	1	1
Union City	2,193	11	10	1
Valley Brook	776	6	5	1
Valliant	731	4	4	0
Velma	595	1	1	0
Verden	535	1	1	0
Verdigris	4,603	7	6	1
Vian	1,351	6	6	0
Vici	708	1	1	0
Vinita	5,343	22	15	7
Wagoner	9,154	22	17	5
Walters	2,379	5	4	1
Warner	1,588	4	4	0
Warr Acres	10,331	33	26	7
Washington	664	2	1	1
Watonga	2,837	11	9	2
Watts	310	2	1	1
Waukomis	1,290	2	2	0
Waurika	1,919	3	3	0
Waynoka	913	3	3	0
Weatherford	12,186	37	23	14
Webbers Falls	593	4	4	0
Weleetka	964	8	5	3
Wellston	783	3	3	0
West Siloam Springs	870	11	10	1
Westville	1,543	9	5	4
Wetumka	1,198	3	3	0
Wewoka	3,252	8	7	1
Wilburton	2,560	7	6	1
Wilson	1,697	4	4	0

Table 19. Full-Time Law Enforcement Employees, by Selected State and City, 2019—*Continued*

(Number.)

State/city	Population	Total law enforcement employees	Total officers	Total civilians
Wister	1,063	3	3	0
Woodward	12,195	27	23	4
Wright City	733	1	1	0
Wyandotte	330	5	4	1
Wynnewood	2,207	6	5	1
Yale	1,192	7	4	3
Yukon	28,184	67	46	21
OREGON				
Albany	54,993	95	63	32
Amity	1,729	9	2	7
Ashland	21,415	36	29	7
Astoria	10,040	28	16	12
Aumsville	4,241	7	6	1
Baker City	9,750	17	15	2
Bandon	3,139	8	8	0
Beaverton	100,130	183	142	41
Bend	100,588	133	101	32
Black Butte		8	7	1
Boardman	3,425	12	11	1
Brookings	6,480	21	14	7
Burns	2,781	4	4	0
Canby	17,962	29	25	4
Cannon Beach	1,756	10	8	2
Carlton	2,206	5	3	2
Central Point	18,753	34	27	7
Coburg	1,156	4	3	1
Columbia City	2,048	8	5	3
Coos Bay	16,471	35	23	12
Coquille	3,933	8	7	1
Corvallis	59,196	96	62	34
Cottage Grove	10,437	30	17	13
Dallas	16,983	24	19	5
Eagle Point	9,530	12	11	1
Enterprise	1,966	4	4	0
Eugene	173,183	306	181	125
Florence	9,183	20	13	7
Forest Grove	25,063	35	29	6
Gearhart	1,612	3	3	0
Gervais	2,783	6	5	1
Gladstone	12,340	18	15	3
Gold Beach	2,298	9	6	3
Grants Pass	38,475	91	57	34
Gresham	110,692	161	130	31
Hermiston	17,780	32	27	5
Hillsboro	110,549	182	134	48
Hood River	7,876	15	14	1
Hubbard	3,598	6	5	1
Independence	10,367	20	15	5
Jacksonville	2,919	6	5	1
John Day	1,654	6	5	1
Junction City	6,292	9	7	2
Keizer	40,109	47	39	8
King City	4,072	8	7	1
Klamath Falls	22,447	41	34	7
La Grande	13,294	31	18	13
Lake Oswego	39,888	65	42	23
Lebanon	17,304	40	28	12
Lincoln City	9,115	35	25	10
Madras	7,028	11	10	1
Malin	821	7	7	0
Manzanita	664	4	4	0
McMinnville	34,935	49	43	6
Medford	83,316	150	104	46
Milton-Freewater	7,051	15	10	5
Milwaukie	21,075	42	37	5
Molalla	9,328	17	15	2
Monmouth	10,630	14	13	1
Mount Angel	3,621	8	6	2
Myrtle Creek	3,508	9	7	2
Myrtle Point	2,556	6	5	1

Table 19. Full-Time Law Enforcement Employees, by Selected State and City, 2019—*Continued*

(Number.)

State/city	Population	Total law enforcement employees	Total officers	Total civilians
Newberg-Dundee	27,378	48	35	13
Newport	10,772	29	21	8
North Bend	9,775	31	24	7
North Plains	2,226	3	3	0
Nyssa	3,191	8	7	1
Oakridge	3,351	7	5	2
Ontario	11,044	27	23	4
Oregon City	37,723	54	46	8
Pendleton	16,796	28	24	4
Philomath	4,871	9	8	1
Phoenix	4,627	11	9	2
Pilot Rock	1,510	3	3	0
Portland	662,114	1,157	889	268
Port Orford	1,150	5	5	0
Prineville	10,479	32	19	13
Rainier	2,017	6	5	1
Redmond	31,558	48	39	9
Reedsport	4,123	12	7	5
Rockaway Beach	1,415	3	3	0
Rogue River	2,365	8	5	3
Roseburg	23,447	41	35	6
Salem	175,867	322	183	139
Sandy	11,555	18	15	3
Scappoose	7,592	11	10	1
Seaside	6,833	26	18	8
Sherwood	19,865	25	22	3
Silverton	10,831	19	16	3
Springfield	63,438	95	65	30
Stayton	8,318	11	10	1
St. Helens	13,900	22	19	3
Sunriver		13	12	1
Sutherlin	8,136	18	14	4
Sweet Home	9,931	22	15	7
Talent	6,604	10	8	2
The Dalles	15,752	26	23	3
Tigard	55,621	84	68	16
Tillamook	5,347	11	10	1
Toledo	3,648	13	7	6
Tualatin	27,788	47	40	7
Turner	2,151	2	2	0
Umatilla	7,202	11	9	2
Vernonia	2,288	4	3	1
Warrenton	5,772	13	12	1
West Linn	26,962	31	28	3
Winston	5,515	11	9	2
Woodburn	26,338	40	32	8
Yamhill	1,192	8	3	5
PENNSYLVANIA				
Ahington Township, Montgomery County	55,476	109	91	18
Adams Township, Butler County	14,330	17	17	0
Adams Township, Cambria County	5,533	12	5	7
Akron	4,033	7	7	0
Albion	1,457	1	1	0
Alburtis	2,658	4	4	0
Aldan	4,149	5	5	0
Aleppo Township	1,867	17	14	3
Aliquippa	8,844	18	17	1
Allegheny Township, Blair County	6,512	8	7	1
Allegheny Township, Westmoreland County	8,053	11	10	1
Allegheny Valley Regional	3,262	2	2	0
Allentown	121,855	236	214	22
Altoona	43,429	67	59	8
Ambler	6,505	14	13	1
Ambridge	6,601	11	11	0
Amity Township	13,243	14	13	1
Annville Township	5,017	10	8	2
Archbald	7,021	18	18	0
Armagh Township	3,794	1	1	0
Arnold	4,826	9	9	0
Ashland	2,670	2	2	0

Table 19. Full-Time Law Enforcement Employees, by Selected State and City, 2019—*Continued*

(Number.)

State/city	Population	Total law enforcement employees	Total officers	Total civilians
Ashley	2,715	4	4	0
Aspinwall	2,701	5	5	0
Aston Township	16,699	18	16	2
Athens	3,191	4	4	0
Athens Township	5,077	10	9	1
Avalon	4,539	6	5	1
Avis	1,489	2	2	0
Avoca	2,617	2	2	0
Baden	3,880	3	3	0
Baldwin Borough	19,426	22	21	1
Baldwin Township	1,926	5	5	0
Bally	1,281	2	2	0
Bangor	5,234	11	10	1
Beaver	4,271	11	10	1
Beaver Falls	9,473	19	18	1
Beaver Meadows	838	1	1	0
Bell Acres	1,380	3	3	0
Bellefonte	6,293	13	10	3
Bellevue	8,064	16	13	3
Bellwood	1,741	3	3	0
Ben Avon	1,738	17	14	3
Ben Avon Heights	362	17	14	3
Bensalem Township	60,647	130	100	30
Bentleyville	2,488	1	1	0
Berlin	1,947	2	2	0
Bern Township	7,033	12	12	0
Berwick	9,943	18	16	2
Bethel Park	32,523	44	38	6
Bethel Township, Berks County	4,178	3	3	0
Bethlehem	75,895	161	146	15
Bethlehem Township	24,088	36	35	1
Biglerville	1,220	2	2	0
Birdsboro	5,167	8	7	1
Birmingham Township	4,210	3	3	0
Blairsville	3,224	5	5	0
Blair Township	4,500	5	5	0
Blakely	6,201	6	6	0
Blawnox	1,379	3	3	0
Bloomsburg Town	13,806	23	18	5
Bonneauville	1,838	1	1	0
Boyertown	4,077	8	7	1
Brackenridge	3,140	4	4	0
Braddock Hills	1,813	2	2	0
Bradford	8,220	18	18	0
Bradford Township	4,597	5	5	0
Branch Township	1,735	2	2	0
Brecknock Township, Berks County	4,669	5	5	0
Brentwood	9,291	14	13	1
Briar Creek Township	2,965	4	4	0
Bridgeport	4,582	10	9	1
Bridgeville	4,970	9	8	1
Bridgewater	847	2	2	0
Brighton Township	8,260	12	12	0
Bristol	9,583	16	14	2
Bristol Township	53,508	67	58	9
Brockway	2,038	3	2	1
Brookhaven	8,026	9	8	1
Brookville	3,793	7	6	1
Bryn Athyn	1,410	4	4	0
Buckingham Township	20,279	26	24	2
Buffalo Township	7,334	5	5	0
Buffalo Valley Regional	12,741	15	14	1
Bushkill Township	8,624	16	15	1
Butler	12,901	24	23	1
Butler Township, Butler County	16,447	23	21	2
Butler Township, Luzerne County	9,885	12	11	1
Butler Township, Schuylkill County	5,636	5	5	0
Caernarvon Township, Berks County	4,174	8	7	1
California	6,701	7	6	1
Caln Township	14,363	23	22	1
Cambria Township	5,697	3	3	0

Table 19. Full-Time Law Enforcement Employees, by Selected State and City, 2019—*Continued*

(Number.)

State/city	Population	Total law enforcement employees	Total officers	Total civilians
Cambridge Springs	2,648	3	3	0
Camp Hill	7,922	13	12	1
Canonsburg	8,789	18	16	2
Canton	1,878	1	1	0
Carbondale	8,387	10	10	0
Carnegie	7,828	14	13	1
Carrolltown	789	6	6	0
Carroll Township, Washington County	5,459	3	3	0
Carroll Valley	3,944	5	4	1
Castle Shannon	8,249	15	14	1
Catasauqua	6,619	10	9	1
Catawissa	1,471	3	3	0
Cecil Township	12,883	21	20	1
Center Township	11,313	20	19	1
Centerville	3,148	2	2	0
Central Berks Regional	13,528	20	19	1
Central Bucks Regional	15,494	29	26	3
Chambersburg	21,131	35	32	3
Charleroi Regional	6,500	9	8	1
Chartiers Township	8,031	13	13	0
Cheltenham Township	37,274	77	69	8
Chester	33,905	96	85	11
Chippewa Township	7,943	8	7	1
Christiana	1,173	9	9	0
Churchill	2,905	8	8	0
Clairton	6,539	12	12	0
Clarion	5,896	9	8	1
Clarks Summit	6,214	5	5	0
Clearfield	5,844	11	7	4
Cleona	2,221	4	4	0
Clifton Heights	6,685	11	10	1
Clymer	1,265	1	1	0
Coaldale	2,138	3	3	0
Coal Township	10,242	12	11	1
Coatesville	13,118	30	26	4
Cochranton	1,077	2	2	0
Colebrookdale District	6,062	11	9	2
Collegeville	5,115	8	8	0
Collier Township	8,346	17	16	1
Collingdale	8,771	9	8	1
Colonial Regional	18,218	25	23	2
Columbia	10,366	21	19	2
Conemaugh Township, Cambria County	1,838	1	1	0
Conemaugh Township, Somerset County	6,831	6	6	0
Conewago Township, Adams County	7,233	10	9	1
Conneaut Lake Regional	3,436	4	3	1
Connellsville	7,276	16	15	1
Conoy Township	3,465	19	17	2
Conshohocken	8,091	21	19	2
Conway	2,070	4	4	0
Conyngham	1,862	3	3	0
Coopersburg	2,531	7	7	0
Coraopolis	5,482	13	9	4
Cornwall	4,383	7	6	1
Corry	6,249	11	10	1
Coudersport	2,406	4	4	0
Covington Township	2,255	3	3	0
Crafton	6,178	10	9	1
Cranberry Township	32,022	34	31	3
Crescent Township	2,553	5	5	0
Cresson	1,556	10	10	0
Cresson Township	2,492	5	5	0
Croyle Township	2,213	1	1	0
Cumberland Township, Adams County	6,265	6	6	0
Cumberland Township, Greene County	6,180	6	6	0
Cumru Township	15,496	26	25	1
Curwensville	2,382	4	3	1
Dallas	2,765	4	4	0
Dallas Township	9,354	12	11	1
Dalton	1,191	3	3	0
Danville	4,613	9	7	2

(Number.)

State/city	Population	Total law enforcement employees	Total officers	Total civilians
Darby	10,677	18	17	1
Darby Township	9,256	15	14	1
Delmont	2,545	4	4	0
Derry	2,512	1	1	0
Derry Township, Dauphin County	25,273	59	40	19
Dickson City	5,772	8	7	1
Donegal Township	3,243	2	2	0
Donora	4,574	6	6	0
Dormont	8,286	14	13	1
Douglass Township, Berks County	3,616	6	6	0
Douglass Township, Montgomery County	10,636	13	12	1
Downingtown	7,932	19	16	3
Doylestown Township	17,397	23	21	2
Dublin Borough	2,140	3	2	1
DuBois	7,371	14	13	1
Duncansville	1,162	1	1	0
Dunmore	12,996	17	17	0
Dunnstable Township	1,010	2	2	0
Dupont	2,676	2	2	0
Duquesne	5,546	15	15	0
Duryea	4,855	2	2	0
East Bangor	1,699	1	1	0
East Brandywine Township	9,123	17	15	2
East Cocalico Township	10,568	17	17	0
East Coventry Township	6,771	8	7	1
East Earl Township	6,935	8	8	0
Eastern Adams Regional	7,413	6	6	0
Eastern Pike Regional	4,625	11	10	1
East Fallowfield Township	7,588	7	7	0
East Franklin Township	3,849	1	1	0
East Greenville	2,962	3	3	0
East Hempfield Township	24,750	37	33	4
East Lampeter Township	17,072	41	38	3
East Lansdowne	2,662	5	3	2
East Marlborough Township	7,520	1	1	0
East McKeesport	2,617	3	3	0
East Norriton Township	14,059	28	27	1
Easton	27,268	66	61	5
East Pennsboro Township	21,549	23	22	1
East Pikeland Township	7,356	10	10	0
Easttown Township	10,668	13	12	1
East Union Township	1,592	2	2	0
East Vincent Township	7,392	7	7	0
East Whiteland Township	12,646	22	20	2
Ebensburg	3,060	5	5	0
Economy	9,129	13	12	1
Eddystone	2,404	10	9	1
Edgewood	2,999	9	9	0
Edgeworth	1,647	13	4	9
Edinboro	5,460	8	8	0
Edwardsville	4,697	5	5	0
Elder Township	969	2	2	0
Elizabeth	1,966	1	1	0
Elizabethtown	11,440	19	17	2
Elizabeth Township	12,991	12	12	0
Ellwood City	7,342	12	10	2
Emmaus	11,479	22	20	2
Emporium	1,806	2	2	0
Emsworth	2,358	17	14	3
Erie	95,834	193	172	21
Etna	3,324	8	7	1
Evans City-Seven Fields Regional	4,445	3	3	0
Everett	1,719	3	3	0
Exeter	5,584	2	2	0
Exeter Township, Berks County	26,029	31	29	2
Exeter Township, Luzerne County	2,357	1	1	0
Fairview Township, Luzerne County	4,515	7	7	0
Fairview Township, York County	17,664	21	18	3
Falls Township, Bucks County	33,707	58	50	8
Farrell	4,603	14	13	1
Fawn Township	2,304	2	2	0

(Number.)

State/city	Population	Total law enforcement employees	Total officers	Total civilians
Ferguson Township	19,734	24	22	2
Ferndale	1,485	1	1	0
Findlay Township	5,981	18	17	1
Fleetwood	4,123	6	6	0
Folcroft	6,615	12	11	1
Ford City	2,770	3	3	0
Forest City	1,741	2	2	0
Forest Hills	6,284	9	9	0
Forks Township	15,741	22	21	1
Forty Fort	4,087	5	5	0
Forward Township	3,270	1	1	0
Foster Township, McKean County	4,047	5	5	0
Fox Chapel	5,261	11	11	0
Frackville	3,609	5	5	0
Franconia Township	13,355	11	10	1
Franklin	6,022	23	17	6
Franklin Park	14,910	15	14	1
Franklin Township, Beaver County	3,858	2	2	0
Franklin Township, Carbon County	4,156	4	4	0
Franklin Township, Columbia County	583	5	5	0
Frazer Township	1,122	2	2	0
Freedom Township	3,324	3	3	0
Freeland	3,428	4	4	0
Freemansburg	2,631	3	3	0
Freeport	1,682	2	2	0
Galeton	1,080	1	1	0
Gallitzin	1,759	6	6	0
Geistown	2,257	3	3	0
German Township	4,801	2	2	0
Gettysburg	7,732	12	11	1
Girard	2,927	4	4	0
Glassport	4,318	8	8	0
Glenolden	7,140	11	10	1
Granville Township	4,971	10	8	2
Greene County Regional Police Department	5,250	3	2	1
Greenfield Township, Blair County	3,944	2	2	0
Greensburg	14,108	38	28	10
Green Tree	4,914	11	10	1
Greenville	5,308	9	8	1
Grove City	7,840	12	11	1
Hamburg	4,398	7	6	1
Hampden Township	30,861	27	26	1
Hampton Township	18,218	19	18	1
Hanover	15,707	28	25	3
Hanover Township, Luzerne County	10,842	17	16	1
Harmar Township	3,019	8	7	1
Harmony Township	2,999	5	5	0
Harrisburg	49,195	165	141	24
Harrison Township	10,271	14	13	1
Harveys Lake	2,768	2	2	0
Hastings	1,171	2	2	0
Hatboro	7,446	21	17	4
Hatfield Township	21,151	30	28	2
Haverford Township	49,370	82	70	12
Hegins Township	3,371	2	2	0
Heidelberg	1,211	3	3	0
Heidelberg Township, Berks County	1,749	1	1	0
Hellam Township	8,632	11	9	2
Hellertown	5,852	11	10	1
Hemlock Township	2,229	9	9	0
Hempfield Township, Mercer County	3,596	7	6	1
Hermitage	15,428	33	30	3
Highspire	2,371	15	15	0
Hilltown Township	15,589	20	17	3
Hollidaysburg	5,701	10	8	2
Homer City	1,591	2	2	0
Honesdale	4,248	5	5	0
Honey Brook	1,765	1	1	0
Hooversville	597	1	1	0
Hopewell Township	12,618	16	15	1
Horsham Township	26,580	48	39	9

Table 19. Full-Time Law Enforcement Employees, by Selected State and City, 2019—*Continued*

(Number.)

State/city	Population	Total law enforcement employees	Total officers	Total civilians
Houston	1,237	1	1	0
Hughestown	1,375	1	1	0
Hughesville	2,029	3	3	0
Hummelstown	4,879	7	6	1
Huntingdon	6,943	12	12	0
Independence Township, Beaver County	2,342	2	2	0
Indiana	12,974	22	20	2
Indiana Township	7,157	10	10	0
Indian Lake	380	2	2	0
Ingram	3,212	4	4	0
Irwin	3,742	4	4	0
Jackson Township, Butler County	4,145	10	8	2
Jackson Township, Cambria County	4,041	2	2	0
Jackson Township, Luzerne County	4,638	2	2	0
Jeannette	9,069	14	13	1
Jefferson Hills Borough	11,211	21	20	1
Jefferson Township, Mercer County	1,814	2	2	0
Jenkins Township	4,547	4	4	0
Jenkintown	4,431	16	14	2
Jermyn	2,060	2	2	0
Jim Thorpe	4,645	8	7	1
Johnsonburg	2,287	3	3	0
Johnstown	20,663	43	38	5
Kane	3,450	3	3	0
Kennedy Township	8,181	10	8	2
Kennett Square	6,213	15	12	3
Kidder Township	1,931	5	5	0
Kilbuck Township	722	17	14	3
Kingston	12,824	21	19	2
Kingston Township	6,882	13	13	0
Kiskiminetas Township	4,474	9	9	0
Kittanning	3,743	8	7	1
Kline Township	1,360	2	1	1
Knox	1,065	2	2	0
Koppel	713	2	2	0
Kulpmont	2,751	1	1	0
Kutztown	5,099	14	12	2
Lake City	2,877	3	3	0
Lancaster Township, Butler County	2,683	4	4	0
Langhorne Borough	1,580	1	1	0
Lansdale	16,759	36	35	1
Lansdowne	10,621	18	15	3
Lansford	3,800	6	6	0
Larksville	4,394	7	7	0
Latrobe	7,831	14	13	1
Laureldale	3,925	5	5	0
Lawrence Park Township	3,755	9	8	1
Lawrence Township, Clearfield County	7,547	9	8	1
Lebanon	25,959	44	41	3
Leechburg	1,989	3	3	0
Leetsdale	1,173	5	5	0
Lehighton	5,309	12	11	1
Lehigh Township, Northampton County	10,488	13	12	1
Lehman Township	3,499	6	6	0
Lewistown	8,135	13	12	1
Liberty Township, Adams County	1,264	1	1	0
Limerick Township	19,180	32	30	2
Lincoln	1,030	2	2	0
Linesville	978	7	7	0
Lititz	9,496	17	15	2
Littlestown	4,507	9	8	1
Lock Haven	9,030	16	14	2
Locust Township	1,394	5	5	0
Logan Township	12,209	18	16	2
Lower Allen Township	19,650	25	22	3
Lower Burrell	11,077	18	17	1
Lower Chichester Township	3,461	5	5	0
Lower Frederick Township	4,888	3	3	0
Lower Gwynedd Township	11,533	19	18	1
Lower Heidelberg Township	6,192	10	9	1
Lower Makefield Township	32,787	42	38	4

Table 19. Full-Time Law Enforcement Employees, by Selected State and City, 2019—*Continued*

(Number.)

State/city	Population	Total law enforcement employees	Total officers	Total civilians
Lower Merion Township	59,796	152	135	17
Lower Moreland Township	13,163	34	30	4
Lower Paxton Township	49,795	65	58	7
Lower Pottsgrove Township	12,115	19	17	2
Lower Providence Township	26,980	32	30	2
Lower Salford Township	15,534	21	19	2
Lower Saucon Township	10,867	17	15	2
Lower Southampton Township	19,225	36	32	4
Lower Swatara Township	8,913	14	13	1
Lower Windsor Township	7,604	10	9	1
Luzerne Township	5,896	1	1	0
Macungie	3,182	5	5	0
Mahanoy Township	3,194	1	1	0
Mahoning Township, Carbon County	4,232	6	6	0
Mahoning Township, Lawrence County	2,875	1	1	0
Mahoning Township, Montour County	4,151	8	7	1
Malvern	3,506	8	7	1
Manheim	4,859	18	17	1
Manheim Township	40,486	78	65	13
Manor	3,378	3	3	0
Manor Township, Armstrong County	4,053	3	3	0
Manor Township, Lancaster County	21,059	21	19	2
Mansfield	2,940	5	5	0
Marcus Hook	2,397	5	4	1
Marietta	2,609	19	17	2
Marion Township, Beaver County	872	2	2	0
Marion Township, Berks County	1,952	3	3	0
Marlborough Township	3,397	4	4	0
Marple Township	23,859	34	31	3
Mars	1,616	1	1	0
Martinsburg	1,837	2	2	0
Marysville	2,556	2	2	0
Masontown	3,287	4	4	0
Mayfield	1,695	2	2	0
McAdoo	2,154	4	4	0
McCandless	28,281	30	28	2
McDonald Borough	2,058	6	5	1
McKeesport	20,765	48	45	3
McKees Rocks	5,861	9	8	1
McSherrystown	3,091	4	4	0
Meadville	12,642	28	22	6
Mechanicsburg	8,994	16	14	2
Media	5,713	22	14	8
Mercer	1,851	5	5	0
Mercersburg	1,541	2	2	0
Meshoppen	1,422	2	2	0
Middleburg	1,289	4	3	1
Middlesex Township, Butler County	5,608	4	4	0
Middlesex Township, Cumberland County	7,502	14	13	1
Middletown	9,327	13	12	1
Middletown Township	45,013	61	55	6
Midland	2,469	3	3	0
Mifflinburg	3,512	10	9	1
Mifflin County Regional	16,923	15	14	1
Milford	980	2	2	0
Millbourne	1,157	1	1	0
Millcreek Township, Erie County	52,965	81	64	17
Millcreek Township, Lebanon County	5,783	2	2	0
Millersburg	2,544	3	2	1
Millersville	8,416	15	13	2
Millvale	3,578	6	6	0
Milton	6,711	9	8	1
Minersville	4,150	6	6	0
Mohnton	3,043	4	4	0
Monaca	5,427	9	9	0
Monessen	7,225	12	11	1
Monongahela	9,795	7	6	1
Monroeville	27,429	55	44	11
Montgomery	1,509	1	1	0
Montgomery Township	26,317	45	43	2
Montour Township	1,289	3	3	0

(Number.)

State/city	Population	Total law enforcement employees	Total officers	Total civilians
Moon Township	25,647	38	31	7
Moore Township	9,415	11	10	1
Morrisville	8,522	13	11	2
Morton	2,663	5	4	1
Moscow	2,061	2	2	0
Mount Carmel	5,537	8	8	0
Mount Carmel Township	2,970	6	6	0
Mount Gretna Borough	208	7	6	1
Mount Holly Springs	2,047	3	3	0
Mount Joy	8,303	13	12	1
Mount Lebanon	32,001	54	45	9
Mount Pleasant	4,213	3	3	0
Mount Pleasant Township	3,529	5	5	0
Mount Union	2,343	4	4	0
Muhlenberg Township	20,392	31	29	2
Muncy	2,420	3	3	0
Muncy Township	1,207	2	2	0
Munhall	11,041	26	24	2
Murrysville	19,655	23	21	2
Nanticoke	10,318	14	13	1
Nanty Glo	2,487	1	1	0
Narberth	4,356	7	6	1
Neshannock Township	9,230	8	8	0
Nesquehoning	3,248	5	5	0
Nether Providence Township	13,747	16	15	1
Neville Township	1,047	17	14	3
Newberry Township	15,885	18	16	2
New Bethlehem	2,701	3	3	0
New Brighton	8,708	9	7	2
New Britain Township	11,444	15	14	1
New Castle	21,624	38	37	1
New Cumberland	7,304	10	9	1
New Florence	648	1	1	0
New Hanover Township	13,314	12	11	1
New Holland	5,485	16	15	1
New Hope	2,527	11	9	2
New Kensington	12,273	22	22	0
Newport Township	5,386	3	3	0
New Sewickley Township	7,175	11	10	1
Newtown	2,239	6	6	0
Newtown Township, Bucks County	22,796	32	28	4
Newtown Township, Delaware County	13,928	20	18	2
Newville	1,350	2	2	0
New Wilmington	2,178	5	5	0
Norristown	34,430	81	68	13
Northampton	9,921	14	12	2
Northampton Township	39,171	49	43	6
North Belle Vernon	1,858	2	2	0
North Catasauqua	2,839	5	5	0
North Cornwall Township	7,976	9	9	0
North Coventry Township	8,004	12	11	1
North East, Erie County	4,051	7	7	0
Northeastern Regional	11,938	13	12	1
Northern Berks Regional	13,475	17	16	1
Northern Cambria Borough	3,510	2	2	0
Northern Lancaster County Regional	36,506	26	24	2
Northern Regional	35,875	31	29	2
Northern York County Regional	70,378	55	51	4
North Hopewell Township	2,807	1	1	0
North Huntingdon Township	30,387	34	28	6
North Londonderry Township	8,632	10	9	1
North Middleton Township	11,713	11	10	1
North Strabane Township	14,751	24	23	1
Northumberland	3,605	5	5	0
North Versailles Township	12,034	24	19	5
North Wales	3,270	5	5	0
Northwest Lancaster County Regional	20,480	21	19	2
Norwood	5,881	7	6	1
Oakmont	6,566	7	7	0
O'Hara Township	8,671	17	16	1
Ohio Township	7,067	17	14	3

Table 19. Full-Time Law Enforcement Employees, by Selected State and City, 2019—*Continued*

(Number.)

State/city	Population	Total law enforcement employees	Total officers	Total civilians
Ohioville	3,284	2	2	0
Oil City	9,654	22	16	6
Old Forge	7,891	5	5	0
Old Lycoming Township	4,913	9	9	0
Olyphant	5,032	6	6	0
Orangeville Area	1,728	1	1	0
Orwigsburg	2,952	6	6	0
Oxford	5,637	11	10	1
Palmerton	5,334	9	8	1
Palmer Township	21,558	37	35	2
Palmyra	7,609	9	8	1
Parkesburg	3,963	9	8	1
Parkside	2,322	3	3	0
Parks Township	2,554	2	2	0
Patterson Township	4,161	4	4	0
Patton	1,609	2	2	0
Patton Township	16,075	21	19	2
Penbrook	2,977	6	6	0
Penndel	2,140	1	1	0
Penn Hills	40,809	53	50	3
Pennridge Regional	10,977	15	13	2
Penn Township, Butler County	4,887	5	4	1
Penn Township, Westmoreland County	19,308	23	21	2
Penn Township, York County	16,669	25	23	2
Perkasie	8,621	19	17	2
Perryopolis	1,671	2	2	0
Peters Township	22,163	23	21	2
Philadelphia	1,589,014	7,412	6,584	828
Phoenixville	17,019	32	31	1
Pine Creek Township	3,242	2	2	0
Pitcairn	3,173	3	3	0
Pittsburgh	300,548	1,064	1,013	51
Pittston	7,758	9	9	0
Pittston Township	3,384	6	5	1
Plains Township	9,689	19	18	1
Pleasant Hills	8,061	20	18	2
Plum	27,134	30	24	6
Plumstead Township	14,588	18	16	2
Plymouth	5,780	4	4	0
Plymouth Township, Montgomery County	17,704	51	44	7
Pocono Mountain Regional	43,086	48	43	5
Pocono Township	10,949	20	20	0
Point Township	3,598	6	6	0
Polk	775	2	2	0
Portage	2,391	2	2	0
Port Allegany	2,001	3	3	0
Port Carbon	1,772	2	2	0
Port Vue	3,658	2	2	0
Pottstown	22,705	57	46	11
Pottsville	13,463	23	22	1
Pringle	957	21	19	2
Prospect Park	6,480	9	9	0
Pulaski Township, Lawrence County	3,248	2	2	0
Punxsutawney	5,734	9	8	1
Pymatuning Township	3,057	7	6	1
Quakertown	8,793	20	18	2
Quarryville	2,769	4	4	0
Raccoon Township	2,905	4	4	0
Radnor Township	31,796	46	42	4
Ralpho Township	4,214	6	6	0
Rankin	2,033	1	1	0
Reading	88,549	176	154	22
Reading Township	5,859	2	2	0
Redstone Township	4,173	3	3	0
Reilly Township	688	2	2	0
Renovo	1,210	1	1	0
Reserve Township	3,221	4	4	0
Reynoldsville	2,648	1	1	0
Rice Township	3,585	6	6	0
Richland Township, Bucks County	13,411	17	15	2
Richland Township, Cambria County	11,865	21	20	1

(Number.)

State/city	Population	Total law enforcement employees	Total officers	Total civilians
Ridgway	3,756	7	6	1
Ridley Park	7,046	13	10	3
Ridley Township	31,154	37	32	5
Riverside	1,850	3	3	0
Roaring Brook Township	1,970	2	2	0
Roaring Creek Township	532	5	5	0
Roaring Spring	2,448	3	3	0
Robeson Township	7,491	5	5	0
Robinson Township, Allegheny County	13,711	31	29	2
Rochester Township	2,638	4	4	0
Rockledge	2,533	5	5	0
Ross Township	30,410	46	44	2
Rostraver Township	11,005	17	16	1
Royalton	1,040	5	5	0
Royersford	4,770	9	9	0
Rural Valley	815	1	1	0
Rush Township	3,254	1	1	0
Sadsbury Township, Chester County	4,117	4	4	0
Salem Township, Luzerne County	4,189	7	7	0
Salisbury Township	13,991	21	19	2
Sandy Lake	629	1	1	0
Sandy Township	10,445	11	10	1
Saxonburg	1,445	2	2	0
Saxton	686	3	3	0
Sayre	6,402	13	10	3
Schuylkill Haven	5,100	8	8	0
Schuylkill Township, Chester County	8,655	13	11	2
Scottdale	4,093	6	6	0
Scott Township, Allegheny County	16,456	23	22	1
Scott Township, Columbia County	5,092	6	6	0
Scott Township, Lackawanna County	4,772	4	4	0
Scranton	77,323	161	146	15
Selinsgrove	5,962	7	6	1
Seward	464	1	1	0
Sewickley Heights	803	3	3	0
Shaler Township	27,860	28	26	2
Shamokin	6,938	11	10	1
Shamokin Dam	1,723	3	3	0
Sharon Hill	5,674	10	9	1
Sharpsburg	3,324	6	6	0
Shenandoah	4,755	5	5	0
Shenango Township, Lawrence County	7,182	7	7	0
Shenango Township, Mercer County	3,675	10	10	0
Shillington	5,338	8	7	1
Shinglehouse	1,054	1	1	0
Shippensburg	5,586	10	9	1
Shippingport	190	1	1	0
Shiremanstown	1,621	2	2	0
Silver Lake Township	1,587	1	1	0
Silver Spring Township	18,580	24	23	1
Sinking Spring	4,132	6	5	1
Slate Belt Regional	12,506	24	23	1
Slatington	4,317	5	5	0
Slippery Rock	3,517	4	4	0
Smethport	1,530	2	2	0
Smith Township	4,362	4	4	0
Solebury Township	8,542	16	14	2
Somerset	5,856	7	6	1
Souderton	7,164	6	5	1
South Abington Township	8,960	12	11	1
South Beaver Township	2,648	4	4	0
South Buffalo Township	2,520	2	2	0
South Centre Township	4,169	7	7	0
South Coatesville	1,461	2	2	0
South Connellsville Borough	1,865	1	1	0
Southern Chester County Regional	16,428	19	17	2
Southern Regional York County	11,568	16	14	2
South Fayette Township	15,928	18	17	1
South Fork	842	1	1	0
South Greensburg	1,988	2	2	0
South Heidelberg Township	7,436	10	10	0

State/city	Population	Total law enforcement employees	Total officers	Total civilians
South Lebanon Township	10,043	9	8	1
South Londonderry Township	8,679	8	8	0
South Park Township	13,257	16	15	1
South Pymatuning Township	2,526	4	4	0
Southwestern Regional	17,870	15	14	1
Southwest Greensburg	2,016	2	2	0
Southwest Regional, Washington County	131	5	2	3
South Whitehall Township	19,994	42	40	2
South Williamsport	6,071	10	9	1
Spring City	3,316	2	2	0
Springdale	3,294	4	4	0
Springettsbury Township	26,888	35	32	3
Springfield Township, Bucks County	5,044	4	4	0
Springfield Township, Delaware County	24,208	37	32	5
Springfield Township, Montgomery County	19,971	30	29	1
Spring Garden Township	13,237	23	20	3
Spring Township, Berks County	27,681	29	28	1
Spring Township, Centre County	7,944	8	7	1
St. Clair Boro	2,821	9	9	0
Steelton	5,945	14	12	2
St. Marys City	12,277	16	15	1
Stoneboro	984	1	1	0
Stonycreek Township	2,583	5	5	0
Stowe Township	6,141	10	9	1
Strasburg	3,005	5	5	0
Stroud Area Regional	35,351	59	52	7
Sugarcreek	4,924	3	3	0
Sugarloaf Township, Luzerne County	3,920	5	5	0
Sugar Notch	960	1	1	0
Summerhill Township	2,260	2	2	0
Summit Hill	2,950	7	5	2
Sunbury	9,352	19	15	4
Susquehanna Regional	8,436	19	17	2
Susquehanna Township	1,841	2	2	0
Susquehanna Township, Dauphin County	25,238	43	41	2
Swarthmore	6,428	9	9	0
Swatara Township	26,643	52	49	3
Sweden Township	817	1	1	0
Swissvale	8,652	15	15	0
Swoyersville	4,942	5	5	0
Sykesville	1,117	1	1	0
Tamaqua	6,657	9	8	1
Tarentum	4,373	8	7	1
Tatamy	1,141	1	1	0
Taylor	5,886	7	7	0
Throop	3,902	7	7	0
Tiadaghton Valley Regional	7,578	11	10	1
Tilden Township	3,616	4	4	0
Tinicum Township, Bucks County	3,956	5	5	0
Tinicum Township, Delaware County	4,097	18	16	2
Tioga	646	1	1	0
Titusville	5,194	9	9	0
Towamencin Township	18,604	28	28	0
Towanda	2,832	7	7	0
Trafford	3,038	5	5	0
Trainer	1,843	4	4	0
Tredyffrin Township	29,523	47	41	6
Tremont	1,665	2	2	0
Troy	1,244	2	2	0
Tullytown	1,919	6	5	1
Tulpehocken Township	3,412	3	3	0
Tunkhannock Township, Wyoming County	6,068	9	8	1
Turtle Creek	5,155	5	5	0
Tyrone	5,160	14	11	3
Union City	3,126	5	4	1
Uniontown	9,774	27	20	7
Union Township, Lawrence County	4,863	7	7	0
Upland	3,303	8	7	1
Upper Allen Township	20,432	24	23	1
Upper Burrell Township	2,220	2	2	0
Upper Chichester Township	16,925	24	23	1

Table 19. Full-Time Law Enforcement Employees, by Selected State and City, 2019—*Continued*

(Number.)

State/city	Population	Total law enforcement employees	Total officers	Total civilians
Upper Darby Township	82,708	145	126	19
Upper Dublin Township	26,624	50	40	10
Upper Gwynedd Township	15,891	26	26	0
Upper Macungie Township	25,384	31	29	2
Upper Makefield Township	8,560	17	16	1
Upper Merion Township	31,410	90	71	19
Upper Moreland Township	24,109	42	36	6
Upper Nazareth Township	7,072	9	8	1
Upper Perkiomen	3,876	4	4	0
Upper Pottsgrove Township	5,785	10	9	1
Upper Providence Township, Delaware County	10,437	16	15	1
Upper Providence Township, Montgomery County	24,674	31	29	2
Upper Saucon Township	17,451	22	21	1
Upper Southampton Township	14,987	25	22	3
Upper St. Clair Township	19,741	37	30	7
Upper Uwchlan Township	11,653	11	11	0
Upper Yoder Township	5,047	13	13	0
Uwchlan Township	19,011	23	22	1
Valley Township	7,934	6	6	0
Vandergrift	4,873	9	8	1
Vernon Township	5,371	4	4	0
Verona	2,407	4	3	1
Versailles	1,459	2	2	0
Walnutport	2,090	4	4	0
Warminster Township	32,293	48	44	4
Warren	9,054	20	16	4
Warrington Township	24,607	35	32	3
Warwick Township, Bucks County	14,646	18	17	1
Washington Township, Fayette County	3,619	4	4	0
Washington Township, Northampton County	5,259	6	5	1
Washington Township, Westmoreland County	7,062	9	9	0
Washington, Washington County	13,448	33	31	2
Watsontown	2,247	6	6	0
Waverly Township	1,679	4	4	0
Waynesburg	3,996	8	8	0
Weatherly	2,458	4	4	0
Wellsboro	3,236	7	7	0
Wesleyville	3,120	8	7	1
West Brandywine Township	7,508	7	6	1
West Brownsville	962	1	1	0
West Caln Township	9,113	4	4	0
West Carroll Township	1,203	2	2	0
West Chester	20,255	64	47	17
West Conshohocken	1,435	13	12	1
West Cornwall Township	2,058	7	6	1
West Deer Township	11,996	12	11	1
West Earl Township	8,484	6	6	0
Western Berks Regional	4,847	3	3	0
West Fallowfield Township	2,596	2	2	0
Westfield	1,034	2	2	0
West Goshen Township	23,157	36	31	5
West Hazleton	4,463	7	5	2
West Hempfield Township	16,603	23	21	2
West Hills Regional	9,925	12	11	1
West Homestead	1,875	7	6	1
West Lampeter Township	16,039	17	16	1
West Mahanoy Township	2,708	3	3	0
West Manchester Township	18,860	30	27	3
West Manheim Township	8,663	10	9	1
West Mead Township	5,008	4	2	2
West Mifflin	19,628	41	34	7
West Newton	2,478	2	2	0
West Norriton Township	15,650	31	29	2
West Penn Township	4,246	2	2	0
West Pike Run	1,541	1	1	0
West Pittston	4,737	3	3	0
West Pottsgrove Township	3,876	7	7	0
West Reading	4,224	15	13	2
West Sadsbury Township	2,487	4	4	0
West Salem Township	3,369	9	8	1
West Shore Regional	7,732	13	12	1

Table 19. Full-Time Law Enforcement Employees, by Selected State and City, 2019—*Continued*

(Number.)

State/city	Population	Total law enforcement employees	Total officers	Total civilians
Westtown-East Goshen Regional	32,366	33	30	3
West View	6,528	13	11	2
West Vincent Township	5,887	7	6	1
West Whiteland Township	18,389	26	24	2
West York	4,581	12	12	0
Whitehall	13,611	25	20	5
Whitehall Township	27,829	51	46	5
White Haven Borough	1,103	3	3	0
Whitemarsh Township	18,213	41	36	5
White Oak	7,456	12	11	1
Whitpain Township	19,294	38	32	6
Wiconisco Township	1,201	1	1	0
Wilkes-Barre	40,722	80	76	4
Wilkes-Barre Township	2,886	13	12	1
Wilkinsburg	15,389	25	23	2
Wilkins Township	6,137	13	12	1
Williamsburg	1,174	2	2	0
Williamsport	28,220	52	48	4
Willistown Township	11,052	20	18	2
Wilson	7,822	15	14	1
Windber	3,825	3	2	1
Womelsdorf	2,899	1	1	0
Woodward Township	2,356	2	2	0
Wyoming	3,011	4	4	0
Wyomissing	10,504	25	23	2
Yardley	2,517	5	5	0
Yeadon	11,474	14	13	1
York	44,150	120	105	15
York Area Regional	54,192	50	45	5
Youngsville	1,611	2	2	0
Zelienople	3,614	10	9	1
Zerbe Township	1,761	1	1	0
RHODE ISLAND				
Barrington	16,090	33	26	7
Bristol	22,070	50	40	10
Burrillville	16,859	32	25	7
Central Falls	19,423	42	35	7
Charlestown	7,819	25	20	5
Coventry	34,751	72	57	15
Cranston	81,471	180	149	31
Cumberland	35,206	57	46	11
East Greenwich	13,119	37	30	7
East Providence	47,590	103	86	17
Foster	4,730	13	9	4
Glocester	10,281	20	15	5
Hopkinton	8,110	19	14	5
Jamestown	5,508	19	14	5
Johnston	29,424	79	66	13
Lincoln	21,891	44	36	8
Little Compton	3,488	14	10	4
Middletown	15,934	41	37	4
Narragansett	15,411	53	40	13
Newport	24,584	97	81	16
New Shoreham	1,032	8	4	4
North Kingstown	26,286	62	51	11
North Providence	32,655	81	63	18
North Smithfield	12,568	27	26	1
Pawtucket	72,030	171	137	34
Portsmouth	17,330	38	36	2
Providence	179,762	526	436	90
Richmond	7,701	18	13	5
Scituate	10,707	28	17	11
Smithfield	21,790	54	41	13
South Kingstown	30,656	70	53	17
Tiverton	15,745	41	29	12
Warren	10,419	30	25	5
Warwick	80,749	207	162	45
Westerly	22,475	63	49	14
West Greenwich	6,375	19	13	6
West Warwick	28,847	60	48	12

Table 19. Full-Time Law Enforcement Employees, by Selected State and City, 2019—*Continued*

(Number.)

State/city	Population	Total law enforcement employees	Total officers	Total civilians
Woonsocket	41,709	113	100	13
SOUTH CAROLINA				
Abbeville	5,017	22	19	3
Aiken	30,922	144	90	54
Allendale	2,924	6	6	0
Anderson	27,498	120	107	13
Andrews	2,851	7	6	1
Atlantic Beach	440	5	4	1
Bamberg	3,195	11	9	2
Barnwell	4,321	17	15	2
Batesburg-Leesville	5,389	28	22	6
Beaufort	13,485	49	44	5
Belton	4,434	1	1	0
Bennettsville	7,726	33	31	2
Bishopville	2,927	14	12	2
Blacksburg	1,883	9	8	1
Blackville	2,194	7	6	1
Bluffton	24,812	57	51	6
Bonneau	483	2	2	0
Bowman	904	3	3	0
Branchville	952	3	2	1
Briarcliffe Acres	593	1	1	0
Burnettown	2,751	1	1	0
Calhoun Falls	1,912	3	3	0
Camden	7,242	36	32	4
Cameron	396	1	1	0
Campobello	588	9	8	1
Cayce	14,211	76	64	12
Central	5,380	10	9	1
Chapin	1,653	6	6	0
Charleston	138,254	510	403	107
Cheraw	5,589	30	23	7
Chester	5,368	29	19	10
Chesterfield	1,415	6	5	1
Clemson	17,547	43	32	11
Clinton	8,412	27	21	6
Clio	660	4	4	0
Clover	6,575	26	21	5
Columbia	133,790	442	349	93
Conway	26,127	58	50	8
Coward	767	1	1	0
Cowpens	2,408	10	8	2
Darlington	5,886	31	28	3
Denmark	2,924	11	10	1
Dillon	6,318	27	26	1
Due West	1,240	5	5	0
Duncan	3,573	19	18	1
Easley	21,390	62	51	11
Edgefield	4,771	11	11	0
Edisto Beach	406	7	7	0
Ehrhardt	481	3	1	2
Elgin	1,612	7	6	1
Elloree	642	3	3	0
Estill	1,855	10	8	2
Eutawville	292	2	2	0
Florence	37,640	106	83	23
Folly Beach	2,657	23	17	6
Forest Acres	10,320	34	27	7
Fort Lawn	879	3	2	1
Fort Mill	21,219	64	54	10
Fountain Inn	10,375	31	25	6
Gaffney	12,528	42	37	5
Gaston	1,692	4	4	0
Georgetown	8,733	41	34	7
Gifford	261	3	2	1
Goose Creek	43,683	95	70	25
Great Falls	1,875	4	4	0
Greenville	69,830	249	202	47
Greenwood	23,427	55	50	5
Greer	32,976	82	59	23

State/city	Population	Total law enforcement employees	Total officers	Total civilians
Hampton	2,499	12	12	0
Hanahan	26,941	30	28	2
Hardeeville	7,075	23	21	2
Hartsville	7,524	40	38	2
Hemingway	400	4	3	1
Holly Hill	1,181	6	6	0
Honea Path	3,810	13	13	0
Irmo	12,516	28	25	3
Isle of Palms	4,366	22	16	6
Jackson	1,792	5	4	1
Jamestown	83	5	4	1
Johnsonville	1,494	7	6	1
Johnston	2,353	8	8	0
Jonesville	834	4	4	0
Lake City	6,541	25	21	4
Lake View	755	4	4	0
Landrum	2,658	18	17	1
Lane	452	3	1	2
Latta	1,288	6	6	0
Laurens	8,823	28	23	5
Lexington	22,160	61	58	3
Liberty	3,152	16	12	4
Loris	2,740	15	12	3
Lyman	3,661	13	12	1
Marion	6,373	21	18	3
Mauldin	25,453	57	46	11
McCormick	2,298	6	6	0
Moncks Corner	11,986	32	29	3
Mount Pleasant	92,448	171	148	23
Mullins	4,290	19	18	1
Myrtle Beach	34,860	308	229	79
Newberry	10,333	30	26	4
New Ellenton	2,145	2	2	0
Ninety Six	2,039	6	6	0
North	716	5	5	0
North Augusta	23,875	89	64	25
North Charleston	115,312	413	332	81
North Myrtle Beach	16,942	154	84	70
Norway	308	1	1	0
Pamplico	1,221	3	3	0
Pelion	704	3	2	1
Pickens	3,171	15	15	0
Port Royal	13,368	25	24	1
Quinby	927	1	1	0
Ridgeland	3,807	13	12	1
Ridge Spring	758	1	1	0
Ridgeville	1,750	2	2	0
Rock Hill	75,342	195	149	46
Salley	416	1	1	0
Saluda	3,641	11	10	1
Simpsonville	23,682	53	43	10
Society Hill	533	3	3	0
South Congaree	2,483	7	6	1
Spartanburg	37,754	143	124	19
Springdale	2,753	9	9	0
Springfield	486	2	2	0
St. George	2,197	11	10	1
Summerton	939	5	5	0
Sumter	39,546	154	109	45
Surfside Beach	4,553	23	19	4
Swansea	959	4	3	1
Tega Cay	11,322	27	25	2
Travelers Rest	5,339	21	15	6
Trenton	260	1	1	0
Union	7,694	32	29	3
Wagener	838	2	2	0
Walhalla	4,384	14	13	1
Walterboro	5,429	30	28	2
Ware Shoals	2,156	7	7	0
Wellford	2,697	11	9	2
West Columbia	17,986	57	51	6

Table 19. Full-Time Law Enforcement Employees, by Selected State and City, 2019—*Continued*

(Number.)

State/city	Population	Total law enforcement employees	Total officers	Total civilians
Westminster	2,570	5	5	0
West Pelzer	948	3	3	0
West Union	325	2	2	0
Whitmire	1,469	4	3	1
Williamston	4,249	18	17	1
Winnsboro	3,165	19	18	1
Woodruff	4,356	12	11	1
Yemassee	954	8	8	0
York	8,294	41	35	6
SOUTH DAKOTA				
Aberdeen	28,870	57	48	9
Alcester	744	2	2	0
Avon	597	1	1	0
Belle Fourche	5,600	13	11	2
Beresford	1,989	4	4	0
Box Elder	10,077	16	14	2
Brandon	10,244	14	13	1
Brookings	24,823	53	37	16
Burke	586	1	1	0
Canton	3,521	6	6	0
Centerville	879	2	2	0
Chamberlain	2,345	6	6	0
Clark	1,056	2	2	0
Deadwood	1,307	18	15	3
Eagle Butte	1,350	1	1	0
Elk Point	1,857	4	4	0
Faith	413	2	2	0
Flandreau	2,323	8	7	1
Freeman	1,290	2	2	0
Gettysburg	1,110	2	2	0
Gregory	1,244	3	3	0
Groton	1,506	4	4	0
Hot Springs	3,485	8	7	1
Huron	13,840	26	25	1
Jefferson	507	2	2	0
Kadoka	714	1	1	0
Lake Norden	506	2	2	0
Lead	2,958	7	6	1
Lennox	2,476	4	4	0
Madison	7,558	14	13	1
Martin	1,071	4	4	0
Menno	622	1	1	0
Milbank	3,131	7	7	0
Miller	1,353	4	4	0
Mitchell	15,733	41	27	14
Mobridge	3,550	14	7	7
Murdo	442	2	2	0
North Sioux City	2,932	8	8	0
Parkston	1,497	2	2	0
Philip	773	2	2	0
Pierre	14,018	41	24	17
Platte	1,263	2	2	0
Rapid City	76,343	168	134	34
Scotland	814	1	1	0
Sioux Falls	185,628	290	255	35
Sisseton	2,423	7	7	0
Spearfish	11,842	31	23	8
Springfield	1,935	2	2	0
Sturgis	6,983	18	15	3
Summerset	2,796	5	4	1
Tea	5,898	7	7	0
Tripp	630	3	3	0
Tyndall	1,036	2	2	0
Vermillion	10,833	21	19	2
Wagner	1,561	4	4	0
Watertown	22,233	52	36	16
Webster	1,746	5	5	0
Whitewood	969	3	3	0
Winner	2,843	10	10	0
Yankton	14,730	31	30	1

Table 19. Full-Time Law Enforcement Employees, by Selected State and City, 2019—*Continued*

(Number.)

State/city	Population	Total law enforcement employees	Total officers	Total civilians
TENNESSEE				
Adamsville	2,171	7	6	1
Alamo	2,294	3	3	0
Alcoa	10,798	51	43	8
Alexandria	1,006	4	3	1
Algood	4,549	15	15	0
Ardmore	1,229	11	7	4
Ashland City	4,708	17	15	2
Athens	13,879	34	32	2
Atoka	9,510	23	22	1
Baileyton	445	3	3	0
Bartlett	59,610	159	123	36
Baxter	1,514	6	6	0
Bean Station	3,085	7	7	0
Belle Meade	2,879	23	15	8
Bells	2,455	5	5	0
Benton	1,258	7	6	1
Berry Hill	515	18	14	4
Big Sandy	522	1	1	0
Blaine	1,871	3	3	0
Bluff City	1,661	8	8	0
Bolivar	4,888	24	22	2
Bradford	983	4	4	0
Brentwood	43,217	80	63	17
Brighton	2,926	8	8	0
Bristol	26,900	85	67	18
Brownsville	9,336	40	36	4
Bruceton	1,400	5	3	2
Burns	1,456	2	2	0
Calhoun	498	4	3	1
Camden	3,573	20	12	8
Carthage	2,276	12	8	4
Caryville	2,146	6	6	0
Celina	1,453	8	5	3
Centerville	3,564	17	15	2
Chapel Hill	1,532	7	6	1
Charleston	695	3	3	0
Chattanooga	181,848	563	469	94
Church Hill	6,671	11	9	2
Clarksville	159,996	353	289	64
Cleveland	45,453	112	100	12
Clifton	2,665	5	5	0
Clinton	10,062	44	34	10
Collegedale	11,929	20	20	0
Collierville	51,273	127	93	34
Collinwood	939	4	4	0
Columbia	40,001	99	88	11
Cookeville	34,373	93	71	22
Coopertown	4,590	5	4	1
Cornersville	1,271	2	2	0
Covington	8,755	31	30	1
Cowan	1,657	3	3	0
Crossville	11,643	46	43	3
Cumberland City	308	2	2	0
Dandridge	3,168	12	11	1
Dayton	7,408	19	19	0
Decatur	1,646	6	6	0
Decaturville	860	1	1	0
Decherd	2,386	12	11	1
Dickson	15,703	66	59	7
Dover	1,489	3	3	0
Dresden	2,908	9	8	1
Dunlap	5,155	12	12	0
Dyer	2,204	7	6	1
Dyersburg	16,300	65	57	8
Eagleville	714	2	2	0
East Ridge	21,027	49	44	5
Elizabethton	13,409	42	38	4
Elkton	528	2	2	0
Englewood	1,524	7	6	1

Table 19. Full-Time Law Enforcement Employees, by Selected State and City, 2019—*Continued*

(Number.)

State/city	Population	Total law enforcement employees	Total officers	Total civilians
Erin	1,287	6	5	1
Erwin	5,826	16	16	0
Estill Springs	2,030	7	7	0
Ethridge	489	4	3	1
Etowah	3,482	12	11	1
Fairview	9,153	22	22	0
Fayetteville	7,047	28	27	1
Franklin	83,517	144	132	12
Friendship	670	1	1	0
Gainesboro	944	4	4	0
Gallatin	41,918	98	84	14
Gallaway	644	4	4	0
Gatlinburg	4,163	55	45	10
Germantown	39,127	127	105	22
Gibson	394	4	3	1
Gleason	1,364	5	5	0
Goodlettsville	16,976	57	42	15
Gordonsville	1,239	6	6	0
Grand Junction	266	3	3	0
Graysville	1,564	5	5	0
Greenbrier	6,887	15	14	1
Greeneville	14,881	55	53	2
Greenfield	2,063	6	5	1
Halls	2,079	7	7	0
Harriman	6,121	22	21	1
Henderson	6,314	16	16	0
Hendersonville	58,388	144	128	16
Henry	466	1	1	0
Hohenwald	3,680	14	14	0
Hollow Rock	675	1	1	0
Hornbeak	394	1	1	0
Humboldt	8,165	31	25	6
Huntingdon	3,805	18	14	4
Huntland	839	2	2	0
Jacksboro	1,919	6	5	1
Jackson	66,915	257	217	40
Jamestown	1,960	9	9	0
Jasper	3,361	8	8	0
Jefferson City	8,193	30	28	2
Jellico	2,161	5	4	1
Johnson City	67,197	170	141	29
Jonesborough	5,487	21	16	5
Kenton	1,195	3	3	0
Kimball	1,421	9	9	0
Kingsport	54,218	158	118	40
Kingston	5,809	13	12	1
Kingston Springs	2,750	7	5	2
Knoxville	188,666	490	370	120
Lafayette	5,309	24	16	8
La Follette	6,651	31	22	9
La Vergne	36,227	71	55	16
Lawrenceburg	10,877	39	34	5
Lebanon	36,337	129	101	28
Lenoir City	9,392	27	25	2
Lewisburg	12,245	31	30	1
Lexington	7,723	34	28	6
Livingston	4,014	22	17	5
Lookout Mountain	1,866	20	15	5
Loretto	1,789	5	5	0
Loudon	5,869	17	16	1
Madisonville	4,949	20	17	3
Manchester	11,020	38	34	4
Martin	10,488	40	30	10
Maryville	29,415	64	58	6
Mason	1,549	4	4	0
Maynardville	2,397	4	4	0
McEwen	1,733	5	5	0
McKenzie	5,509	22	17	5
McMinnville	13,696	36	32	4
Medina	4,334	8	8	0
Memphis	650,410	2,635	2,058	577

Table 19. Full-Time Law Enforcement Employees, by Selected State and City, 2019—*Continued*

(Number.)

State/city	Population	Total law enforcement employees	Total officers	Total civilians
Metropolitan Nashville Police Department	687,361	1,775	1,412	363
Middleton	637	3	3	0
Milan	7,613	32	25	7
Millersville	6,829	16	15	1
Millington	10,669	44	32	12
Minor Hill	532	2	2	0
Monteagle	1,225	7	6	1
Monterey	2,888	10	9	1
Morristown	30,044	87	82	5
Moscow	559	3	3	0
Mountain City	2,407	9	9	0
Mount Carmel	5,295	7	6	1
Mount Juliet	37,359	77	62	15
Mount Pleasant	4,934	20	14	6
Munford	6,083	18	18	0
Murfreesboro	145,929	300	248	52
Newbern	3,312	12	12	0
New Johnsonville	1,900	5	5	0
New Market	1,372	5	2	3
Newport	6,786	31	27	4
New Tazewell	2,702	10	10	0
Niota	727	4	3	1
Nolensville	9,488	13	12	1
Norris	1,609	5	5	0
Oakland	8,323	19	17	2
Oak Ridge	29,084	79	63	16
Obion	1,042	2	2	0
Oliver Springs	3,419	14	10	4
Oneida	3,704	16	11	5
Paris	10,047	37	26	11
Parsons	2,304	8	8	0
Petersburg	564	1	1	0
Pigeon Forge	6,383	74	59	15
Piperton	1,887	8	8	0
Pittman Center	581	4	4	0
Plainview	2,126	2	2	0
Pleasant View	4,686	6	6	0
Portland	12,995	33	29	4
Pulaski	7,628	27	24	3
Puryear	666	1	1	0
Red Bank	11,779	25	23	2
Red Boiling Springs	1,140	5	5	0
Ridgely	1,641	5	5	0
Ripley	7,818	29	23	6
Rockwood	5,439	17	16	1
Rocky Top	1,766	9	6	3
Rogersville	4,277	14	13	1
Rossville	950	7	7	0
Rutherford	1,066	4	3	1
Rutledge	1,352	3	3	0
Savannah	6,941	23	21	2
Scotts Hill	977	3	3	0
Selmer	4,401	17	15	2
Sevierville	16,760	72	56	16
Sharon	911	2	2	0
Shelbyville	22,062	51	41	10
Signal Mountain	8,605	17	15	2
Smithville	4,828	15	14	1
Smyrna	52,225	110	87	23
Soddy-Daisy	13,818	37	30	7
Somerville	3,213	10	9	1
South Carthage	1,386	4	4	0
South Fulton	2,214	8	7	1
South Pittsburg	3,008	9	9	0
Sparta	4,957	17	14	3
Spencer	1,646	2	2	0
Spring City	1,865	10	10	0
Springfield	17,022	42	37	5
Spring Hill	43,303	65	61	4
St. Joseph	814	1	1	0
Surgoinsville	1,772	1	1	0

State/city	Population	Total law enforcement employees	Total officers	Total civilians
Sweetwater	5,875	20	19	1
Tazewell	2,273	7	7	0
Tellico Plains	921	6	5	1
Tiptonville	4,286	7	7	0
Townsend	446	4	4	0
Tracy City	1,389	5	5	0
Trenton	4,022	22	16	6
Trezevant	842	2	2	0
Trimble	613	1	1	0
Troy	1,317	5	5	0
Tullahoma	19,468	38	33	5
Tusculum	2,805	2	2	0
Union City	10,340	40	31	9
Vonore	1,539	9	9	0
Wartburg	896	6	6	0
Wartrace	692	2	1	1
Watertown	1,519	4	4	0
Waverly	4,081	14	13	1
Waynesboro	2,307	6	6	0
Westmoreland	2,431	11	10	1
White Bluff	3,659	5	5	0
White House	12,822	25	22	3
White Pine	2,356	11	10	1
Whiteville	4,466	6	6	0
Whitwell	1,723	5	4	1
Winchester	8,733	26	24	2
Woodbury	2,878	10	9	1
TEXAS				
Abernathy	2,713	5	5	0
Abilene	123,665	274	213	61
Addison	16,339	71	60	11
Alamo	19,903	41	34	7
Alamo Heights	8,808	33	21	12
Alice	18,858	41	32	9
Allen	105,961	197	138	59
Alton	18,096	25	20	5
Alvarado	4,468	20	18	2
Alvin	27,159	77	48	29
Amarillo	201,036	413	333	80
Andrews	14,133	21	20	1
Angleton	19,660	60	36	24
Anson	2,275	6	5	1
Aransas Pass	8,118	40	27	13
Archer City	1,732	2	2	0
Arcola	2,627	6	6	0
Argyle	4,339	11	9	2
Arlington	402,304	882	680	202
Arp	1,016	8	7	1
Athens	12,807	31	24	7
Atlanta	5,497	17	12	5
Austin	986,062	2,469	1,802	667
Azle	13,691	34	24	10
Baird	1,508	2	2	0
Balch Springs	25,511	60	41	19
Balcones Heights	3,366	24	19	5
Ballinger	3,615	8	6	2
Bangs	1,540	2	2	0
Bastrop	9,714	28	24	4
Bay City	17,501	59	38	21
Baytown	77,707	220	170	50
Beaumont	118,562	318	248	70
Bedford	49,771	129	81	48
Beeville	12,866	28	20	8
Bellaire	19,233	56	41	15
Bellmead	10,817	29	20	9
Bells	1,506	4	4	0
Bellville	4,288	12	11	1
Belton	22,741	48	36	12
Benbrook	23,872	50	41	9
Beverly Hills	1,989	12	6	6

(Number.)

State/city	Population	Total law enforcement employees	Total officers	Total civilians
Big Spring	28,278	47	33	14
Blanco	2,040	11	10	1
Blue Mound	2,485	10	6	4
Boerne	18,135	62	41	21
Bogata	1,060	5	5	0
Borger	12,536	30	28	2
Bovina	1,807	2	2	0
Brady	5,288	15	9	6
Brazoria	3,123	12	7	5
Breckenridge	5,453	16	11	5
Bremond	962	3	3	0
Brenham	17,375	38	35	3
Bridge City	7,998	18	13	5
Bridgeport	6,670	23	16	7
Brookshire	5,592	22	17	5
Brookside Village	1,603	4	4	0
Brownfield	9,270	24	19	5
Brownsboro	1,283	4	4	0
Brownsville	184,418	317	234	83
Brownwood	18,646	60	38	22
Bryan	86,632	181	149	32
Bullard	3,722	11	10	1
Burkburnett	11,305	24	17	7
Burleson	48,743	93	67	26
Cactus	3,194	10	7	3
Caddo Mills	1,656	7	7	0
Caldwell	4,433	10	9	1
Cameron	5,530	14	10	4
Canyon	16,312	29	26	3
Carrollton	139,179	207	162	45
Carthage	6,491	21	16	5
Castle Hills	4,515	28	22	6
Castroville	3,144	9	8	1
Cedar Hill	48,866	92	70	22
Celina	13,977	26	25	1
Center	5,271	23	16	7
Chandler	3,142	8	8	0
Chillicothe	668	2	2	0
Cibolo	32,112	42	38	4
Cisco	3,735	13	11	2
Cleburne	30,860	64	49	15
Cleveland	8,284	30	18	12
Clifton	3,454	8	7	1
Clute	11,740	36	24	12
Clyde	3,868	11	10	1
Coleman	4,341	7	7	0
College Station	119,246	204	141	63
Collinsville	1,951	3	3	0
Colorado City	3,831	15	8	7
Combes	3,064	7	7	0
Commerce	9,467	19	14	5
Converse	28,598	53	48	5
Coppell	42,181	68	59	9
Copperas Cove	32,693	64	46	18
Corinth	22,090	37	31	6
Corpus Christi	329,320	660	426	234
Corrigan	1,605	15	9	6
Corsicana	23,823	56	42	14
Crane	3,725	15	9	6
Crockett	6,484	18	15	3
Crosbyton	1,602	1	1	0
Crowley	16,027	39	26	13
Crystal City	7,283	16	10	6
Cuero	8,259	16	15	1
Daingerfield	2,360	6	5	1
Dalhart	8,338	16	12	4
Dallas	1,363,295	3,624	3,075	549
Dalworthington Gardens	2,403	16	11	5
Dayton	8,464	31	21	10
Decatur	7,116	34	28	6
Deer Park	34,167	90	63	27

(Number.)

State/city	Population	Total law enforcement employees	Total officers	Total civilians
Del Rio	35,947	87	61	26
Denison	25,432	58	44	14
Denton	141,492	224	181	43
Denver City	4,933	16	10	6
Devine	4,931	14	11	3
Diboll	5,228	20	15	5
Dickinson	21,101	46	30	16
Dimmitt	4,146	7	5	2
Donna	16,715	47	35	12
Double Oak	3,073	8	8	0
Driscoll	752	5	3	2
Dumas	14,290	28	23	5
Duncanville	39,430	64	50	14
Early	3,105	11	9	2
Eastland	3,913	13	11	2
Edinburg	100,896	220	160	60
Edna	5,924	10	8	2
El Campo	11,615	43	30	13
Electra	2,696	12	7	5
Elgin	10,475	34	25	9
El Paso	686,793	1,412	1,171	241
Emory	1,353	6	5	1
Falfurrias	4,819	12	10	2
Farmers Branch	41,932	96	72	24
Farwell	1,314	3	3	0
Fate	15,378	19	18	1
Ferris	2,876	17	12	5
Florence	1,288	2	2	0
Floresville	7,970	21	19	2
Flower Mound	79,052	134	89	45
Floydada	2,711	6	6	0
Forney	25,374	43	29	14
Fort Stockton	8,402	30	20	10
Fort Worth	915,237	2,075	1,650	425
Freeport	12,213	46	32	14
Friendswood	40,735	77	58	19
Friona	3,888	9	5	4
Frisco	199,445	299	199	100
Fulshear	13,967	25	23	2
Fulton	1,559	1	1	0
Gainesville	16,688	53	39	14
Galena Park	10,934	22	17	5
Galveston	50,801	193	146	47
Garland	244,277	477	355	122
Garrison	894	2	2	0
Gatesville	12,311	27	18	9
George West	2,586	10	8	2
Gilmer	5,164	19	15	4
Gladewater	6,349	19	14	5
Glenn Heights	13,520	28	20	8
Gorman	1,034	4	2	2
Graham	8,670	22	21	1
Granbury	10,752	44	38	6
Grand Prairie	196,971	422	279	143
Grand Saline	3,171	10	9	1
Grapevine	54,979	150	98	52
Greenville	28,613	75	54	21
Gregory	1,917	5	5	0
Groesbeck	4,302	8	8	0
Groves	15,601	26	22	4
Gun Barrel City	6,273	19	14	5
Hamilton	3,008	10	8	2
Hamlin	1,982	9	5	4
Harker Heights	32,527	56	47	9
Harlingen	65,481	173	133	40
Haskell	3,234	6	5	1
Hawkins	1,331	3	3	0
Hawley	616	1	1	0
Hearne	4,510	16	10	6
Heath	9,179	23	22	1
Hedwig Village	2,684	22	16	6

Table 19. Full-Time Law Enforcement Employees, by Selected State and City, 2019—*Continued*

(Number.)

State/city	Population	Total law enforcement employees	Total officers	Total civilians
Henderson	13,226	43	33	10
Hewitt	15,019	36	26	10
Hidalgo	14,281	38	29	9
Highland Park	9,251	72	58	14
Highland Village	16,721	42	32	10
Hill Country Village	1,109	14	10	4
Hillsboro	8,476	37	28	9
Hitchcock	8,023	21	15	6
Hollywood Park	3,406	15	14	1
Honey Grove	1,718	4	4	0
Horizon City	20,131	45	26	19
Horseshoe Bay	4,030	20	17	3
Houston	2,355,606	6,337	5,264	1,073
Howe	3,432	6	5	1
Hudson	4,909	4	4	0
Humble	16,157	83	64	19
Huntsville	41,881	67	59	8
Hutto	27,993	52	46	6
Idalou	2,289	4	4	0
Indian Lake	858	2	2	0
Ingleside	10,366	23	16	7
Iowa Colony	2,024	7	7	0
Iowa Park	6,369	17	11	6
Irving	245,423	525	364	161
Italy	1,945	6	5	1
Jacksboro	4,353	10	9	1
Jacksonville	14,969	42	30	12
Jarrell	1,800	7	7	0
Jasper	7,647	29	22	7
Jersey Village	8,006	28	26	2
Jonestown	2,118	9	8	1
Josephine	1,739	4	3	1
Jourdanton	4,537	11	10	1
Katy	19,966	86	66	20
Keene	6,584	13	12	1
Keller	48,387	88	48	40
Kemah	2,056	24	18	6
Kemp	1,219	7	7	0
Kerens	1,532	5	5	0
Kerrville	23,902	62	47	15
Kilgore	15,047	49	36	13
Killeen	151,832	285	235	50
Kingsville	25,401	63	38	25
Kirby	8,841	19	16	3
Knox City	1,110	2	2	0
Kress	684	1	1	0
Lacy-Lakeview	6,720	27	17	10
La Feria	7,341	19	18	1
Lago Vista	7,255	25	18	7
La Grange	4,630	13	12	1
Laguna Vista	3,163	9	9	0
Lake Dallas	8,052	18	15	3
Lake Jackson	27,624	69	49	20
Lakeside	1,614	7	7	0
Lakeview, Harrison County	6,361	14	13	1
Lake Worth	4,993	33	24	9
La Marque	17,088	44	33	11
Lampasas	8,067	32	21	11
Lancaster	39,795	64	58	6
La Porte	35,622	101	77	24
Laredo	264,916	576	498	78
League City	109,401	168	120	48
Leander	61,314	81	61	20
Levelland	13,530	35	24	11
Lewisville	108,000	218	148	70
Liberty	9,471	27	17	10
Lindale	6,338	24	17	7
Littlefield	5,911	20	13	7
Live Oak	16,280	51	37	14
Livingston	5,112	28	21	7
Longview	81,783	214	169	45

Table 19. Full-Time Law Enforcement Employees, by Selected State and City, 2019—*Continued*

(Number.)

State/city	Population	Total law enforcement employees	Total officers	Total civilians
Lorena	1,776	10	8	2
Lufkin	35,555	102	77	25
Madisonville	4,776	14	11	3
Magnolia	2,218	16	13	3
Mansfield	72,979	211	111	100
Manvel	12,721	28	22	6
Marble Falls	7,047	36	23	13
Marshall	23,036	56	39	17
Mathis	4,768	14	10	4
McKinney	200,615	277	210	67
Meadows Place	4,616	16	15	1
Melissa	11,195	14	14	0
Memorial Villages	12,472	44	31	13
Mercedes	16,882	39	32	7
Merkel	2,623	5	5	0
Mesquite	143,078	311	231	80
Midland	146,806	207	160	47
Midlothian	28,313	90	59	31
Miles	862	1	1	0
Mineola	4,804	19	12	7
Missouri City	75,747	146	104	42
Monahans	7,770	20	14	6
Mont Belvieu	6,647	21	15	6
Morgans Point Resort	4,637	9	9	0
Moulton	910	4	4	0
Mount Pleasant	16,307	46	33	13
Muleshoe	5,029	14	7	7
Murphy	20,962	31	20	11
Mustang Ridge	1,001	5	5	0
Nacogdoches	33,613	86	60	26
Naples	1,302	4	4	0
Nash	3,783	9	9	0
Nassau Bay	4,040	13	12	1
Natalia	1,602	4	4	0
Navasota	7,795	23	18	5
Nederland	17,557	39	23	16
Needville	3,094	7	7	0
New Boston	4,663	20	16	4
Newton	2,346	4	4	0
Nocona	2,975	6	5	1
Northeast	3,404	13	12	1
Northlake	3,341	15	14	1
North Richland Hills	71,816	189	113	76
Oak Ridge North	3,174	16	16	0
Odessa	123,468	197	137	60
O'Donnell	825	1	1	0
Olmos Park	2,478	14	13	1
Olney	3,091	6	5	1
Olton	2,090	2	2	0
Onalaska	2,852	8	8	0
Orange	18,468	58	43	15
Overton	2,510	9	6	3
Palmer	2,079	11	10	1
Palmhurst	2,771	15	11	4
Palm Valley	1,249	5	5	0
Panhandle	2,322	4	4	0
Pantego	2,556	16	11	5
Paris	24,787	82	57	25
Parker	4,951	10	9	1
Pasadena	153,689	369	291	78
Pearland	126,206	227	161	66
Pearsall	10,604	19	15	4
Penitas	4,915	17	15	2
Perryton	8,577	22	13	9
Petersburg	1,133	3	3	0
Pharr	80,896	154	124	30
Pinehurst	2,006	8	6	2
Pittsburg	4,720	13	11	2
Plainview	20,231	38	31	7
Plano	291,611	585	403	182
Pleasanton	10,911	30	24	6

Table 19. Full-Time Law Enforcement Employees, by Selected State and City, 2019—*Continued*

(Number.)

State/city	Population	Total law enforcement employees	Total officers	Total civilians
Port Aransas	4,260	29	20	9
Port Arthur	55,084	151	117	34
Port Isabel	5,058	19	15	4
Portland	17,604	47	32	15
Port Lavaca	12,072	23	17	6
Poteet	3,524	11	10	1
Pottsboro	2,488	10	8	2
Prairie View	6,543	11	10	1
Primera	5,103	9	8	1
Princeton	12,569	25	23	2
Prosper	24,814	41	29	12
Queen City	1,450	6	6	0
Quitman	1,855	7	7	0
Ralls	1,814	3	3	0
Rancho Viejo	2,480	8	8	0
Ranger	2,413	6	5	1
Raymondville	10,894	25	16	9
Red Oak	13,429	31	28	3
Reno, Lamar County	3,333	6	5	1
Richardson	123,893	255	168	87
Richmond	12,086	42	30	12
Richwood	4,007	10	10	0
Riesel	1,036	3	3	0
River Oaks	7,738	23	17	6
Roanoke	9,563	43	33	10
Robinson	11,945	33	22	11
Robstown	11,347	33	24	9
Rockdale	5,665	11	11	0
Rockport	10,854	31	27	4
Roma	11,527	36	28	8
Rosenberg	38,936	104	80	24
Rowlett	67,604	117	86	31
Royse City	13,539	26	22	4
Rusk	5,582	13	12	1
Sabinal	1,675	5	4	1
Sachse	26,926	45	33	12
Saginaw	24,382	49	38	11
Salado	2,375	5	5	0
San Antonio	1,559,166	3,362	2,297	1,065
San Benito	24,394	46	39	7
San Diego	4,226	6	5	1
San Juan	37,542	60	39	21
San Saba	3,152	5	5	0
Santa Anna	1,032	3	3	0
Santa Fe	13,657	26	20	6
Schertz	42,337	90	59	31
Seabrook	14,611	40	30	10
Seagoville	17,120	32	22	10
Seagraves	2,904	7	5	2
Sealy	6,593	23	21	2
Selma	12,054	32	28	4
Seymour	2,600	7	4	3
Shallowater	2,547	5	5	0
Shavano Park	4,052	19	18	1
Shenandoah	3,077	26	25	1
Sherman	43,002	91	68	23
Slaton	5,877	18	13	5
Snyder	11,161	24	21	3
Sour Lake	1,887	8	7	1
South Houston	17,655	43	30	13
Southlake	33,049	66	60	6
South Padre Island	2,805	37	27	10
Spearman	3,275	4	4	0
Spring Valley	4,414	24	18	6
Stafford	18,380	78	61	17
Stamford	2,898	7	6	1
Stratford	2,103	4	3	1
Sudan	904	2	2	0
Sugar Land	119,944	190	168	22
Sullivan City	4,152	15	9	6
Sulphur Springs	16,220	39	28	11

(Number.)

State/city	Population	Total law enforcement employees	Total officers	Total civilians
Sunset Valley	683	14	13	1
Sweetwater	10,467	31	25	6
Taft	2,904	6	6	0
Tahoka	2,624	4	4	0
Tatum	1,394	5	5	0
Taylor	17,405	40	29	11
Temple	77,558	196	157	39
Terrell	18,395	59	40	19
Terrell Hills	5,496	14	14	0
Texarkana	37,401	97	85	12
Texas City	49,659	111	85	26
Three Rivers	1,945	11	10	1
Tioga	1,035	4	4	0
Tomball	11,897	58	42	16
Tool	2,337	10	6	4
Trophy Club	13,031	24	20	4
Tulia	4,644	14	6	8
Tye	1,318	6	5	1
Tyler	106,851	238	193	45
Universal City	21,062	43	32	11
University Park	25,434	56	39	17
Uvalde	16,233	55	40	15
Van	2,713	9	9	0
Van Alstyne	4,437	15	10	5
Venus	3,986	12	12	0
Vernon	10,312	26	19	7
Victoria	67,581	150	112	38
Vidor	10,499	31	24	7
Waco	139,870	334	241	93
Waller	3,611	13	12	1
Watauga	24,685	45	34	11
Waxahachie	37,805	89	69	20
Weatherford	32,656	78	60	18
Webster	11,273	65	48	17
Weimar	2,180	8	7	1
Weslaco	41,729	97	77	20
West Columbia	3,881	17	12	5
West Orange	3,299	11	9	2
Westover Hills	685	16	11	5
West University Place	15,818	30	23	7
Westworth	2,720	18	13	5
Wharton	8,627	32	24	8
White Oak	6,345	20	16	4
White Settlement	18,127	45	37	8
Whitney	2,188	7	7	0
Wichita Falls	104,551	282	197	85
Willis	6,587	19	17	2
Wills Point	3,684	11	10	1
Winters	2,448	7	6	1
Wolfforth	5,445	13	12	1
Woodway	9,033	42	30	12
Wylie	52,921	70	62	8
Yoakum	5,962	18	11	7
UTAH				
Alta	383	8	4	4
American Fork/Cedar Hills	43,610	52	44	8
Big Water	506	1	1	0
Blanding	3,738	5	5	0
Bluffdale	15,976	13	13	0
Bountiful	44,280	57	38	19
Brian Head	92	5	5	0
Brigham City	19,592	31	26	5
Cedar City	33,614	44	39	5
Centerville	18,018	23	20	3
Clearfield	32,217	38	30	8
Clinton	22,544	22	19	3
Cottonwood Heights	34,183	47	38	9
Draper	49,112	54	44	10
East Carbon	1,561	4	4	0
Enoch	7,199	8	6	2

(Number.)

State/city	Population	Total law enforcement employees	Total officers	Total civilians
Ephraim	7,449	8	7	1
Fairview	1,352	1	1	0
Farmington	25,409	25	21	4
Grantsville	11,942	17	15	2
Gunnison	3,564	6	4	2
Harrisville	6,845	11	10	1
Heber	17,142	28	22	6
Helper	2,077	5	5	0
Herriman	48,948	46	37	9
Hildale	2,928	15	9	6
Hurricane	18,850	31	28	3
Kanab	4,850	8	7	1
Kaysville	32,691	31	28	3
La Verkin	4,442	5	5	0
Layton	78,585	110	78	32
Lehi	68,697	58	52	6
Lindon	11,085	17	15	2
Logan	52,029	83	53	30
Lone Peak	30,273	27	22	5
Mantua	905	1	1	0
Mapleton	10,463	11	8	3
Moab	5,349	25	16	9
Monticello	1,998	3	3	0
Mount Pleasant	3,517	4	4	0
Murray	49,642	88	75	13
Naples	2,113	7	6	1
Nephi	6,207	13	10	3
North Ogden	20,352	21	18	3
North Park	16,411	11	9	2
North Salt Lake	21,501	29	23	6
Ogden	87,875	169	137	32
Orem	98,686	115	85	30
Park City	8,620	38	32	6
Parowan	3,139	5	5	0
Payson	19,981	24	23	1
Perry	5,171	8	7	1
Pleasant Grove	39,066	37	28	9
Pleasant View	11,137	11	10	1
Price	8,174	17	15	2
Provo	117,189	158	109	49
Richfield	7,952	16	15	1
Riverdale	8,821	22	19	3
Riverton	45,153	39	35	4
Roosevelt	7,189	14	12	2
Roy	39,001	45	38	7
Salem	8,760	11	10	1
Salina	2,573	4	4	0
Salt Lake City	202,426	647	503	144
Sandy	97,797	147	109	38
Santa Clara/Ivins	17,346	18	14	4
Santaquin/Genola	14,288	14	13	1
Saratoga Springs	33,647	27	24	3
Smithfield	12,107	11	10	1
South Jordan	77,645	65	60	5
South Ogden	17,215	24	21	3
South Salt Lake	25,599	79	64	15
Spanish Fork	40,604	43	39	4
Spring City	1,077	1	1	0
Springdale	620	9	8	1
Springville	33,542	38	28	10
St. George	89,160	160	113	47
Sunset	5,364	8	8	0
Syracuse	31,230	25	23	2
Tooele	35,719	46	38	8
Tremonton	9,038	13	11	2
Washington	29,047	32	28	4
West Bountiful	5,790	11	10	1
West Jordan	117,644	153	117	36
West Valley	137,269	246	203	43
Willard	1,932	2	2	0
Woods Cross	11,531	19	17	2

(Number.)

State/city	Population	Total law enforcement employees	Total officers	Total civilians
VERMONT				
Barre	8,551	21	20	1
Barre Town	7,679	8	7	1
Bellows Falls	2,988	8	7	1
Bennington	14,912	33	25	8
Berlin	2,789	11	9	2
Bradford	2,701	2	2	0
Brandon	3,744	8	7	1
Brattleboro	11,401	36	24	12
Brighton	1,184	1	1	0
Bristol	3,883	3	3	0
Burlington	42,958	133	93	40
Canaan	926	1	1	0
Castleton	4,507	4	4	0
Chester	3,018	6	5	1
Colchester	17,548	34	26	8
Dover	1,057	7	6	1
Essex	22,213	31	25	6
Fair Haven	2,554	4	4	0
Hardwick	2,852	8	7	1
Hartford	9,654	28	19	9
Hinesburg	4,601	4	4	0
Killington	757	3	3	0
Ludlow	1,876	11	6	5
Lyndonville	1,160	3	3	0
Manchester	4,242	13	9	4
Middlebury	8,776	17	15	2
Milton	11,064	18	17	1
Montpelier	7,386	27	17	10
Morristown	5,465	11	11	0
Newport	4,216	18	14	4
Northfield	5,990	8	7	1
Norwich	3,307	5	4	1
Pittsford	2,786	1	1	0
Richmond	4,178	5	5	0
Royalton	2,864	1	1	0
Rutland	15,191	51	38	13
Rutland Town	4,096	5	5	0
Shelburne	7,857	16	10	6
South Burlington	19,687	49	40	9
Springfield	8,900	19	13	6
St. Albans	6,800	32	21	11
St. Johnsbury	7,158	16	10	6
Stowe	4,452	12	12	0
Swanton	6,595	7	6	1
Thetford	2,545	3	3	0
Vergennes	2,596	8	8	0
Weathersfield	2,753	2	2	0
Williston	10,026	17	14	3
Wilmington	1,801	7	5	2
Windsor	3,324	11	10	1
Winhall	731	9	8	1
Winooski	7,346	20	16	4
Woodstock	2,925	6	5	1
VIRGINIA				
Abingdon	7,933	27	24	3
Alexandria	162,258	413	322	91
Altavista	3,409	15	14	1
Amherst	2,179	6	6	0
Appalachia	1,544	3	3	0
Ashland	7,916	28	25	3
Bedford	6,588	26	22	4
Berryville	4,363	10	9	1
Big Stone Gap	5,170	13	12	1
Blacksburg	44,948	72	62	10
Blackstone	3,360	14	11	3
Bluefield	4,822	20	15	5
Bowling Green	1,187	1	1	0
Bridgewater	6,167	9	9	0

(Number.)

State/city	Population	Total law enforcement employees	Total officers	Total civilians
Bristol	16,234	73	52	21
Broadway	3,973	5	5	0
Brookneal	1,098	2	2	0
Buena Vista	6,156	17	16	1
Burkeville	402	1	1	0
Cape Charles	1,002	6	6	0
Cedar Bluff	1,003	3	3	0
Charlottesville	48,453	136	110	26
Chase City	2,212	10	9	1
Chatham	1,433	3	3	0
Chesapeake	243,726	577	388	189
Chilhowie	1,710	6	6	0
Chincoteague	2,872	14	10	4
Christiansburg	22,700	67	62	5
Clarksville	1,170	8	7	1
Clifton Forge	3,465	11	10	1
Clintwood	1,287	2	2	0
Coeburn	1,857	7	6	1
Colonial Beach	3,593	10	9	1
Colonial Heights	17,793	58	54	4
Covington	5,372	26	17	9
Crewe	2,148	7	6	1
Culpeper	18,873	52	45	7
Damascus	787	4	4	0
Danville	40,191	131	120	11
Dayton	1,636	4	4	0
Dublin	2,604	8	7	1
Dumfries	5,265	12	11	1
Elkton	2,900	6	5	1
Emporia	5,000	36	25	11
Exmore	1,368	7	7	0
Fairfax City	24,689	79	60	19
Falls Church	15,008	44	31	13
Farmville	7,830	29	27	2
Franklin	7,899	34	24	10
Fredericksburg	29,641	96	73	23
Front Royal	15,336	52	38	14
Galax	6,320	39	23	16
Gate City	1,857	5	5	0
Glade Spring	1,426	2	2	0
Glasgow	1,111	1	1	0
Gordonsville	1,621	7	7	0
Gretna	1,197	3	3	0
Grottoes	2,860	7	6	1
Grundy	900	6	6	0
Halifax	1,217	5	5	0
Hampton	133,173	377	285	92
Harrisonburg	54,387	127	109	18
Haymarket	1,740	6	6	0
Haysi	472	3	2	1
Herndon	24,693	71	56	15
Hillsville	2,644	12	11	1
Honaker	1,330	4	4	0
Hopewell	22,461	86	66	20
Hurt	1,226	2	2	0
Independence	896	2	2	0
Jonesville	931	3	3	0
Kenbridge	1,180	5	5	0
Kilmarnock	1,410	5	5	0
La Crosse	573	1	1	0
Lawrenceville	993	6	6	0
Lebanon	3,148	15	14	1
Leesburg	55,461	96	80	16
Lexington	7,107	21	18	3
Louisa	1,721	4	4	0
Luray	4,853	13	12	1
Lynchburg	82,512	189	165	24
Manassas	41,850	118	85	33
Manassas Park	17,602	37	30	7
Marion	5,593	19	18	1
Martinsville	12,726	48	43	5

Table 19. Full-Time Law Enforcement Employees, by Selected State and City, 2019—*Continued*

(Number.)

State/city	Population	Total law enforcement employees	Total officers	Total civilians
Middleburg	864	7	6	1
Middletown	1,396	4	3	1
Mount Jackson	2,115	6	6	0
Narrows	1,955	5	5	0
New Market	2,256	6	6	0
Newport News	177,319	603	445	158
Norfolk	242,813	783	691	92
Norton	3,940	22	14	8
Occoquan	1,109	1	1	0
Onancock	1,210	5	5	0
Onley	500	5	5	0
Orange	5,092	17	15	2
Parksley	810	2	2	0
Pearisburg	2,639	7	7	0
Pembroke	1,085	3	3	0
Pennington Gap	1,716	6	6	0
Petersburg	31,273	112	91	21
Pocahontas	354	1	1	0
Poquoson	12,126	27	26	1
Portsmouth	93,991	274	220	54
Pound	927	4	4	0
Pulaski	8,683	32	28	4
Purcellville	10,346	20	18	2
Radford	18,487	48	35	13
Remington	659	1	1	0
Rich Creek	743	1	1	0
Richlands	5,198	24	19	5
Richmond	230,721	851	734	117
Roanoke	99,752	291	248	43
Rocky Mount	4,744	26	24	2
Rural Retreat	1,453	1	1	0
Salem	25,590	87	65	22
Saltville	1,910	5	5	0
Shenandoah	2,335	5	5	0
Smithfield	8,485	26	22	4
South Boston	7,601	31	29	2
South Hill	4,335	23	21	2
Stanley	1,670	5	5	0
Staunton	24,931	64	48	16
Stephens City	2,069	2	2	0
St. Paul	862	6	6	0
Strasburg	6,686	18	17	1
Suffolk	91,486	233	173	60
Tangier	704	1	1	0
Tappahannock	2,391	9	8	1
Tazewell	4,140	16	15	1
Timberville	2,697	6	6	0
Victoria	1,603	4	4	0
Vienna	16,660	50	40	10
Vinton	8,110	25	23	2
Virginia Beach	449,038	938	760	178
Warrenton	9,977	25	23	2
Warsaw	1,488	4	4	0
Waverly	1,949	14	8	6
Waynesboro	22,711	59	48	11
Weber City	1,204	3	3	0
West Point	3,254	10	9	1
Williamsburg	14,965	43	41	2
Winchester	28,201	86	76	10
Windsor	2,763	7	7	0
Wise	2,926	13	12	1
Woodstock	5,267	19	17	2
Wytheville	7,909	28	25	3
WASHINGTON				
Aberdeen	16,627	51	36	15
Airway Heights	9,545	21	20	1
Algona	3,247	10	8	2
Anacortes	17,483	30	24	6
Arlington	20,043	33	28	5
Asotin	1,299	1	1	0

Table 19. Full-Time Law Enforcement Employees, by Selected State and City, 2019—*Continued*

(Number.)

State/city	Population	Total law enforcement employees	Total officers	Total civilians
Auburn	83,468	133	113	20
Bainbridge Island	25,080	29	23	6
Battle Ground	21,375	28	24	4
Bellevue	150,200	221	185	36
Bellingham	91,906	173	117	56
Black Diamond	4,518	11	9	2
Blaine	5,534	16	14	2
Bonney Lake	21,574	37	30	7
Bothell	47,565	97	67	30
Bremerton	41,675	72	59	13
Brewster	2,363	6	5	1
Brier	7,070	8	7	1
Buckley	5,534	12	10	2
Burien	52,388	74	52	22
Burlington	9,219	31	25	6
Camas	24,388	32	28	4
Carnation	2,297	3	2	1
Castle Rock	2,291	5	4	1
Centralia	17,603	37	29	8
Chehalis	7,682	22	17	5
Cheney	12,632	23	17	6
Chewelah	2,673	6	5	1
Clarkston	7,426	16	14	2
Cle Elum	2,989	6	6	0
Clyde Hill	3,436	10	9	1
Colfax	2,926	4	4	0
College Place	9,428	17	14	3
Colville	4,845	12	10	2
Connell	5,772	8	7	1
Cosmopolis	1,646	6	5	1
Coulee Dam	1,082	2	2	0
Covington	21,698	25	19	6
Des Moines	32,708	49	38	11
Dupont	9,672	14	10	4
Duvall	8,244	14	13	1
East Wenatchee	14,293	24	21	3
Eatonville	3,061	6	5	1
Edgewood	11,981	12	11	1
Edmonds	43,152	66	51	15
Ellensburg	21,324	32	26	6
Elma	3,323	10	7	3
Enumclaw	11,975	32	19	13
Ephrata	8,253	17	15	2
Everett	112,302	239	199	40
Everson	4,428	7	6	1
Federal Way	98,025	155	128	27
Ferndale	15,007	23	20	3
Fife	10,324	40	30	10
Fircrest	6,852	9	9	0
Forks	3,903	10	4	6
Gig Harbor	10,931	21	19	2
Goldendale	3,508	11	9	2
Grand Coulee	2,079	7	7	0
Grandview	11,179	22	18	4
Granger	3,863	8	8	0
Hoquiam	8,580	26	24	2
Issaquah	40,651	62	36	26
Kalama	2,766	7	6	1
Kelso	12,354	30	26	4
Kenmore	23,430	20	15	5
Kennewick	84,072	118	102	16
Kent	131,003	207	152	55
Kettle Falls	1,636	4	3	1
Kirkland	90,708	147	108	39
Kittitas	1,511	3	3	0
La Center	3,324	9	8	1
Lacey	51,816	65	55	10
Lake Forest Park	13,690	23	20	3
Lake Stevens	34,081	39	32	7
Lakewood	60,916	111	97	14
Langley	1,152	3	3	0

(Number.)

State/city	Population	Total law enforcement employees	Total officers	Total civilians
Liberty Lake	11,043	14	13	1
Long Beach	1,441	9	8	1
Longview	38,282	71	59	12
Lynden	15,116	19	15	4
Lynnwood	38,847	101	67	34
Mabton	2,281	3	3	0
Maple Valley	27,705	25	20	5
Marysville	71,081	92	65	27
Mattawa	4,641	6	5	1
McCleary	1,743	4	4	0
Medina	3,337	11	9	2
Mercer Island	26,408	36	31	5
Mill Creek	21,360	29	24	5
Milton	8,381	14	14	0
Monroe	19,630	42	32	10
Montesano	4,033	9	8	1
Morton	1,185	3	3	0
Moses Lake	24,490	46	38	8
Mountlake Terrace	21,617	36	28	8
Mount Vernon	36,274	58	45	13
Moxee	4,151	7	6	1
Mukilteo	21,704	35	29	6
Napavine	1,973	4	3	1
Newcastle	12,015	14	11	3
Newport	2,156	5	4	1
Normandy Park	6,699	10	9	1
Oak Harbor	23,554	38	26	12
Ocean Shores	6,181	10	9	1
Odessa	879	2	2	0
Olympia	53,286	105	72	33
Omak	4,806	12	11	1
Oroville	1,678	4	3	1
Orting	8,629	10	8	2
Othello	8,388	24	17	7
Pacific	7,297	12	11	1
Palouse	1,084	4	2	2
Pasco	76,412	91	82	9
Pe Ell	672	1	1	0
Port Angeles	20,207	63	32	31
Port Orchard	14,684	25	22	3
Port Townsend	9,780	19	15	4
Poulsbo	11,154	25	18	7
Prosser	6,388	15	14	1
Pullman	34,585	43	28	15
Puyallup	42,509	90	68	22
Quincy	7,977	30	22	8
Raymond	2,976	6	5	1
Reardan	596	1	1	0
Redmond	69,501	123	84	39
Renton	103,452	157	125	32
Republic	1,071	2	2	0
Richland	58,514	79	62	17
Ridgefield	8,955	12	11	1
Ritzville	1,645	4	4	0
Roy	828	2	2	0
Royal City	2,240	3	3	0
Ruston	855	5	5	0
Sammamish	66,820	37	29	8
SeaTac	29,533	67	49	18
Seattle	763,706	1,960	1,416	544
Sedro Woolley	12,184	19	16	3
Selah	8,110	18	15	3
Sequim	7,599	24	20	4
Shelton	10,432	21	18	3
Shoreline	57,216	69	49	20
Snohomish	10,319	19	17	2
Snoqualmie	14,183	29	25	4
Soap Lake	1,613	5	4	1
South Bend	1,680	6	4	2
Spokane	220,432	412	332	80
Spokane Valley	100,983	132	109	23

(Number.)

State/city	Population	Total law enforcement employees	Total officers	Total civilians
Stanwood	7,330	13	11	2
Steilacoom	6,423	11	10	1
Sumas	1,529	7	6	1
Sumner	10,270	23	19	4
Sunnyside	16,839	45	26	19
Tacoma	218,650	400	359	41
Tenino	1,873	5	4	1
Tieton	1,318	2	2	0
Toledo	765	3	2	1
Toppenish	8,886	16	11	5
Tukwila	20,439	94	74	20
Tumwater	24,167	36	28	8
Twisp	964	3	3	0
Union Gap	6,162	20	17	3
University Place	34,085	18	17	1
Vancouver	185,034	265	213	52
Walla Walla	33,047	72	43	29
Wapato	5,045	9	7	2
Warden	2,784	5	3	2
Washougal	16,305	23	20	3
Wenatchee	34,513	50	39	11
Westport	2,080	7	6	1
West Richland	15,343	24	20	4
White Salmon	2,655	7	6	1
Winlock	1,392	1	1	0
Winthrop	457	3	2	1
Woodinville	13,068	21	16	5
Woodland	6,469	12	10	2
Yakima	94,168	171	131	40
Yelm	9,741	17	15	2
Zillah	3,164	9	8	1
WEST VIRGINIA				
Alderson	1,130	4	4	0
Anmoore	739	2	2	0
Ansted	1,321	2	2	0
Athens	896	1	1	0
Barboursville	4,215	24	22	2
Barrackville	1,289	1	1	0
Beckley	16,010	68	52	16
Belington	1,859	3	3	0
Belle	1,128	4	4	0
Benwood	1,268	6	6	0
Berkeley Springs	599	2	2	0
Bethlehem	2,321	5	5	0
Bluefield	9,644	33	27	6
Bradshaw	277	1	1	0
Bramwell	339	2	2	0
Bridgeport	8,751	35	31	4
Buckhannon	5,479	12	11	1
Burnsville	481	1	1	0
Cameron	846	2	2	0
Cedar Grove	918	1	1	0
Ceredo	1,299	8	4	4
Chapmanville	1,104	6	6	0
Charleston	46,732	183	159	24
Charles Town	6,171	19	16	3
Chesapeake	1,415	2	2	0
Chester	2,393	6	5	1
Clarksburg	15,349	42	39	3
Clendenin	1,109	5	5	0
Danville	611	2	2	0
Davy	343	1	1	0
Delbarton	498	2	2	0
Dunbar	7,123	14	13	1
Eleanor	1,606	2	2	0
Elkins	7,008	12	11	1
Fairmont	18,372	38	33	5
Fairview	403	1	1	0
Farmington	364	1	1	0
Fayetteville	2,738	13	12	1

Table 19. Full-Time Law Enforcement Employees, by Selected State and City, 2019—*Continued*

(Number.)

State/city	Population	Total law enforcement employees	Total officers	Total civilians
Follansbee	2,706	7	7	0
Fort Gay	669	3	3	0
Gary	798	1	1	0
Gassaway	853	1	1	0
Gauley Bridge	554	1	1	0
Gilbert	392	2	2	0
Glasgow	839	1	1	0
Glen Dale	1,375	6	6	0
Glenville	1,454	3	3	0
Grafton	5,025	9	8	1
Grantsville	523	1	1	0
Grant Town	594	1	1	0
Granville	3,105	16	16	0
Hamlin	1,049	3	2	1
Harpers Ferry/Bolivar	1,304	4	3	1
Harrisville	1,699	1	1	0
Hartford City	597	1	1	0
Hinton	2,362	7	6	1
Hundred	264	1	1	0
Huntington	45,675	94	92	2
Hurricane	6,534	21	19	2
Iaeger	246	1	1	0
Kenova	3,010	14	10	4
Kermit	353	1	1	0
Keyser	4,933	15	10	5
Kimball	155	1	1	0
Kingwood	2,939	1	1	0
Lewisburg	3,830	14	12	2
Logan	1,481	11	8	3
Lumberport	839	1	1	0
Mabscott	1,267	2	2	0
Madison	2,720	8	7	1
Man	640	2	2	0
Mannington	2,027	4	4	0
Marmet	1,372	5	5	0
Martinsburg	17,494	57	47	10
Mason	934	5	4	1
Masontown	546	2	1	1
Matewan	428	1	1	0
McMechen	1,722	4	4	0
Milton	2,588	11	10	1
Monongah	1,154	1	1	0
Montgomery	1,516	8	7	1
Moorefield	2,418	10	9	1
Morgantown	31,281	83	71	12
Moundsville	8,323	20	16	4
Mount Hope	1,278	6	5	1
Mullens	1,311	3	3	0
New Cumberland	1,028	2	1	1
New Haven	1,477	3	3	0
New Martinsville	5,114	14	11	3
Nitro	6,406	19	18	1
Nutter Fort	1,522	5	5	0
Oak Hill	8,140	21	17	4
Oceana	1,204	4	4	0
Paden City	2,361	4	3	1
Parkersburg	29,482	80	66	14
Parsons	1,406	1	1	0
Pennsboro	1,023	1	1	0
Petersburg	2,649	1	1	0
Philippi	3,406	6	6	0
Piedmont	796	1	1	0
Pineville	578	3	3	0
Point Pleasant	4,094	8	7	1
Pratt	562	2	2	0
Princeton	5,695	24	22	2
Rainelle	1,490	5	4	1
Ranson	5,288	16	15	1
Ravenswood	3,646	11	10	1
Reedsville	611	1	1	0
Rhodell	158	2	1	1

State/city	Population	Total law enforcement employees	Total officers	Total civilians
Richwood	1,868	3	3	0
Ridgeley	617	1	1	0
Ripley	3,179	11	10	1
Rivesville	907	1	1	0
Romney	1,702	5	4	1
Ronceverte	1,674	6	6	0
Rupert	895	1	1	0
Salem	1,558	5	4	1
Shepherdstown	1,827	6	5	1
Shinnston	2,108	7	6	1
Sistersville	1,291	3	3	0
Smithers	735	4	3	1
Sophia	1,251	5	5	0
South Charleston	12,094	49	46	3
Spencer	2,063	5	5	0
St. Albans	9,956	26	23	3
Star City	2,003	5	4	1
St. Marys	1,782	5	4	1
Stonewood	1,717	3	3	0
Summersville	3,292	15	14	1
Sutton	1,014	1	1	0
Sylvester	137	1	1	0
Terra Alta	1,507	2	2	0
Triadelphia	749	1	1	0
Vienna	10,157	23	19	4
War	688	2	2	0
Wayne	1,382	1	1	0
Webster Springs	671	5	4	1
Weirton	18,296	42	38	4
Welch	1,645	6	5	1
Wellsburg	2,531	6	5	1
West Logan	361	1	1	0
West Milford	603	2	2	0
Weston	3,887	8	6	2
Westover	4,244	13	12	1
West Union	815	2	1	1
Wheeling	26,562	74	65	9
White Hall	658	5	5	0
White Sulphur Springs	2,395	8	7	1
Whitesville	433	2	2	0
Williamson	2,694	7	6	1
Williamstown	2,879	8	7	1
Winfield	2,378	6	6	0
WISCONSIN				
Adams	1,886	3	3	0
Albany	994	3	3	0
Algoma	3,030	10	5	5
Altoona	7,939	14	13	1
Amery	2,792	6	6	0
Antigo	7,771	17	15	2
Appleton	74,757	137	110	27
Argyle	819	1	1	0
Ashland	7,859	20	18	2
Ashwaubenon	17,311	59	52	7
Athens	1,078	1	1	0
Bangor	1,468	3	3	0
Baraboo	12,151	35	29	6
Barneveld	1,256	1	1	0
Barron	3,306	6	6	0
Bayfield	476	3	3	0
Bayside	4,342	12	12	0
Beaver Dam	16,375	36	32	4
Belleville	2,459	6	5	1
Beloit Town	7,707	14	12	2
Berlin	5,401	13	12	1
Big Bend	1,460	3	3	0
Birchwood	433	2	1	1
Black River Falls	3,454	6	5	1
Blair	1,345	3	3	0
Bloomer	3,499	8	7	1

Table 19. Full-Time Law Enforcement Employees, by Selected State and City, 2019—*Continued*

(Number.)

State/city	Population	Total law enforcement employees	Total officers	Total civilians
Bloomfield	6,342	8	8	0
Blue Mounds	1,000	2	1	1
Boscobel	3,129	12	6	6
Boyceville	1,130	2	2	0
Brillion	3,100	8	8	0
Brodhead	3,240	12	8	4
Brookfield	38,879	93	76	17
Brookfield Township	6,281	16	15	1
Brown Deer	11,869	34	31	3
Brownsville	573	1	1	0
Burlington	11,057	23	22	1
Butler	1,807	8	7	1
Caledonia	25,123	34	32	2
Campbellsport	1,969	1	1	0
Campbell Township	4,337	5	5	0
Cashton	1,111	1	1	0
Cedarburg	11,548	29	21	8
Chenequa	604	8	8	0
Chetek	2,097	5	4	1
Chilton	3,774	7	7	0
Chippewa Falls	14,237	26	23	3
Cleveland	1,450	3	2	1
Clintonville	4,307	15	11	4
Colby-Abbotsford	4,152	9	8	1
Colfax	1,154	2	2	0
Columbus	5,090	11	9	2
Cornell	1,396	3	3	0
Cottage Grove	7,203	28	13	15
Crandon	1,826	5	4	1
Cross Plains	4,346	7	6	1
Cuba City	2,034	4	4	0
Cudahy	18,164	41	31	10
Cumberland	2,099	6	6	0
Darlington	2,324	5	5	0
Deforest	10,766	22	19	3
Delafield	7,610	18	16	2
Delavan	9,889	28	23	5
Delavan Town	5,339	12	11	1
De Pere	25,163	39	35	4
Dodgeville	4,713	10	10	0
Durand	1,810	4	4	0
Eagle Village	2,112	2	2	0
East Troy	4,327	8	8	0
Eau Claire	69,195	132	96	36
Edgar	1,439	1	1	0
Edgerton	5,646	11	10	1
Eleva	664	1	1	0
Elkhart Lake	1,018	3	3	0
Elkhorn	9,989	16	14	2
Elk Mound	878	1	1	0
Ellsworth	3,306	5	5	0
Elm Grove	6,195	25	17	8
Elroy	1,300	3	3	0
Evansville	5,424	9	8	1
Everest Metropolitan	17,340	30	27	3
Fall Creek	1,308	2	2	0
Fennimore	2,465	5	5	0
Fitchburg	30,854	62	51	11
Fond du Lac	42,954	76	68	8
Fontana	1,729	8	7	1
Fort Atkinson	12,519	28	20	8
Fox Lake	1,445	3	3	0
Fox Point	6,599	16	15	1
Fox Valley Metro	22,190	27	25	2
Franklin	35,875	76	60	16
Frederic	1,086	12	12	0
Galesville	1,571	4	4	0
Geneva Town	5,045	8	7	1
Genoa City	2,992	7	6	1
Germantown	19,983	71	60	11
Gillett	1,295	3	3	0

(Number.)

State/city	Population	Total law enforcement employees	Total officers	Total civilians
Gilman	393	2	1	1
Glendale	12,792	48	42	6
Grafton	11,798	26	20	6
Grand Chute	23,450	40	35	5
Grand Rapids	7,405	6	6	0
Grantsburg	1,283	3	3	0
Green Bay	104,992	218	181	37
Greendale	14,057	39	29	10
Greenfield	37,387	79	60	19
Green Lake	961	3	3	0
Hales Corners	7,578	19	17	2
Hartford	15,460	32	28	4
Hartford Township	3,570	3	1	2
Hartland	9,366	19	17	2
Hayward	2,296	14	7	7
Hazel Green	1,225	2	2	0
Highland	833	1	1	0
Hillsboro	1,398	4	2	2
Hobart-Lawrence	15,460	11	10	1
Holmen	10,217	14	13	1
Horicon	3,587	8	7	1
Hortonville	2,805	7	6	1
Hudson	14,074	31	28	3
Hurley	1,426	7	6	1
Independence	1,295	3	3	0
Iron Ridge	891	1	1	0
Iron River	1,135	3	3	0
Jackson	7,218	12	11	1
Janesville	64,687	117	104	13
Jefferson	8,042	17	14	3
Juneau	2,639	5	4	1
Kaukauna	16,341	26	25	1
Kenosha	100,255	218	206	12
Kewaskum	4,244	8	8	0
Kewaunee	2,836	6	6	0
Kiel	3,808	8	7	1
Kohler	2,063	8	7	1
Kronenwetter	8,095	9	8	1
La Crosse	51,591	114	94	20
Ladysmith	3,111	8	7	1
La Farge	760	2	1	1
Lake Delton	3,005	24	21	3
Lake Geneva	8,001	32	24	8
Lake Hallie	6,724	10	9	1
Lake Mills	5,949	12	10	2
Lancaster	3,716	7	7	0
Lena	538	2	1	1
Linn Township	2,406	6	6	0
Lodi	3,070	11	5	6
Lomira	2,469	4	3	1
Luxemburg	2,557	1	1	0
Madison	261,270	687	501	186
Manawa	1,286	3	3	0
Manitowoc	32,497	74	64	10
Maple Bluff	1,319	4	3	1
Marathon City	1,500	3	3	0
Marinette	10,569	25	21	4
Marion	1,183	4	4	0
Markesan	1,395	4	4	0
Marshall Village	3,967	10	9	1
Marshfield	18,216	48	41	7
Mauston	4,364	10	9	1
Mayville	4,859	9	8	1
McFarland	8,961	19	17	2
Medford	4,313	10	9	1
Menasha	17,809	38	31	7
Menomonee Falls	37,936	73	58	15
Menomonie	16,573	31	25	6
Mequon	24,548	49	39	10
Merrill	9,017	24	21	3
Middleton	20,072	46	38	8

Table 19. Full-Time Law Enforcement Employees, by Selected State and City, 2019—*Continued*

(Number.)

State/city	Population	Total law enforcement employees	Total officers	Total civilians
Milton	5,621	12	11	1
Milwaukee	590,923	2,265	1,850	415
Mineral Point	2,477	6	6	0
Minocqua	4,409	15	10	5
Mishicot	1,382	3	3	0
Mondovi	2,563	4	4	0
Monona	8,106	26	21	5
Monroe	10,537	32	25	7
Montello	1,461	3	2	1
Monticello	1,197	3	3	0
Mosinee	4,072	8	7	1
Mount Horeb	7,481	13	13	0
Mount Pleasant	27,070	62	56	6
Mukwonago	8,144	22	15	7
Muscoda	1,252	3	3	0
Muskego	25,224	48	39	9
Neenah	26,133	50	38	12
Neillsville	2,388	6	5	1
Nekoosa	2,432	7	7	0
New Berlin	39,752	83	69	14
New Glarus	2,187	3	3	0
New Holstein	3,056	7	6	1
New Lisbon	2,513	4	4	0
New London	7,118	18	17	1
New Richmond	9,268	19	18	1
Niagara	1,545	3	3	0
North Fond du Lac	5,098	11	9	2
North Hudson	3,813	4	3	1
Oak Creek	36,679	86	62	24
Oconomowoc	16,980	30	23	7
Oconomowoc Lake	604	7	6	1
Oconomowoc Town	8,741	12	11	1
Oconto	4,517	9	9	0
Oconto Falls	2,793	6	6	0
Omro	3,587	8	7	1
Onalaska	18,825	29	26	3
Oregon	10,677	21	18	3
Osceola	2,511	6	5	1
Oshkosh	66,797	113	96	17
Osseo	1,672	4	4	0
Palmyra	1,767	6	6	0
Park Falls	2,212	7	7	0
Pepin	758	1	1	0
Peshtigo	3,333	6	6	0
Pewaukee Village	8,190	18	17	1
Phillips	1,339	5	5	0
Pittsville	829	2	2	0
Plainfield	824	2	1	1
Platteville	12,115	25	18	7
Pleasant Prairie	21,074	45	34	11
Plover	13,164	22	19	3
Plymouth	8,765	15	15	0
Portage	10,452	28	24	4
Port Edwards	1,772	2	2	0
Port Washington	11,908	24	19	5
Poynette	2,499	6	5	1
Prairie du Chien	5,636	13	12	1
Prescott	4,278	11	10	1
Princeton	1,167	4	4	0
Pulaski	3,598	9	8	1
Racine	77,269	229	196	33
Reedsburg	9,554	28	21	7
Rhinelander	7,615	19	17	2
Rice Lake	8,369	18	18	0
Richland Center	4,923	22	10	12
Rio	1,033	2	2	0
Ripon	7,820	18	13	5
Ripon Town	1,374	1	1	0
River Falls	16,069	28	25	3
River Hills	1,579	12	11	1
Rome Town	2,727	6	6	0

(Number.)

State/city	Population	Total law enforcement employees	Total officers	Total civilians
Rosendale	1,029	1	1	0
Rothschild	5,266	14	12	2
Sauk Prairie	4,633	16	14	2
Saukville	4,428	24	11	13
Seymour	3,474	6	6	0
Shawano	8,876	22	20	2
Sheboygan	48,035	100	81	19
Sheboygan Falls	7,947	17	15	2
Shiocton	919	2	2	0
Shorewood	13,217	28	24	4
Shorewood Hills	2,079	9	7	2
Shullsburg	1,189	1	1	0
Siren	770	7	3	4
Slinger	5,527	12	11	1
South Milwaukee	20,731	41	35	6
Sparta	9,823	24	22	2
Spencer	1,883	4	4	0
Spooner	2,598	9	7	2
Spring Green	1,644	3	2	1
Stanley	3,710	5	5	0
St. Croix Falls	2,032	11	5	6
Stevens Point	26,095	49	45	4
St. Francis	9,526	22	21	1
Stoughton	13,110	28	22	6
Sturgeon Bay	8,937	23	21	2
Sturtevant	6,645	14	13	1
Summit	4,944	10	10	0
Sun Prairie	34,562	74	53	21
Superior	25,967	65	60	5
Theresa	1,204	2	2	0
Thiensville	3,139	8	7	1
Thorp	1,618	3	3	0
Three Lakes	2,101	4	4	0
Tomah	9,406	22	20	2
Tomahawk	3,130	9	8	1
Town of East Troy	4,064	13	6	7
Town of Madison	6,934	13	12	1
Trempealeau	1,652	3	3	0
Twin Lakes	6,157	17	12	5
Two Rivers	11,027	29	26	3
Verona	13,510	26	24	2
Viroqua	4,412	11	9	2
Walworth	2,837	8	7	1
Washburn	2,039	5	5	0
Waterford Town	6,505	9	8	1
Waterloo	3,350	7	6	1
Watertown	23,596	54	40	14
Waukesha	72,718	159	122	37
Waunakee	14,163	24	22	2
Waupaca	5,874	16	15	1
Waupun	11,315	18	17	1
Wausau	38,507	84	76	8
Wautoma	2,118	5	4	1
Wauwatosa	48,562	117	93	24
Webster	616	3	3	0
West Allis	59,302	157	123	34
West Bend	31,638	70	53	17
Westby	2,238	4	4	0
West Milwaukee	4,107	24	19	5
West Salem	5,087	8	7	1
Whitefish Bay	13,816	25	24	1
Whitehall	1,569	4	4	0
Whitewater	14,997	31	22	9
Wild Rose	691	2	2	0
Williams Bay	2,638	17	8	9
Wilton	500	1	1	0
Winneconne	2,506	6	5	1
Wisconsin Dells	3,033	20	15	5
Wisconsin Rapids	17,613	51	47	4
Woodruff	1,962	6	5	1

Table 19. Full-Time Law Enforcement Employees, by Selected State and City, 2019—*Continued*

(Number.)

State/city	Population	Total law enforcement employees	Total officers	Total civilians
WYOMING				
Afton	2,017	4	4	0
Casper	57,752	144	97	47
Cheyenne	64,501	126	105	21
Cody	9,865	23	20	3
Diamondville	756	4	4	0
Douglas	6,294	16	13	3
Evanston	11,624	31	26	5
Evansville	2,977	13	11	2
Gillette	31,960	80	53	27
Glenrock	2,544	14	7	7
Green River	11,927	31	25	6
Greybull	1,857	6	5	1
Hanna	766	3	3	0
Jackson	10,534	39	32	7
Kemmerer	2,745	6	6	0
Lander	7,489	19	18	1
Laramie	32,669	75	46	29
Lusk	1,537	6	6	0
Mills	3,975	20	14	6
Moorcroft	1,068	4	3	1
Newcastle	3,386	15	8	7
Pine Bluffs	1,170	3	3	0
Powell	6,310	25	18	7
Rawlins	8,589	27	16	11
Riverton	11,004	41	27	14
Rock Springs	23,092	48	41	7
Saratoga	1,615	8	4	4
Sheridan	17,895	43	27	16
Sundance	1,285	3	3	0
Thermopolis	2,830	13	7	6
Torrington	6,709	25	18	7
Wheatland	3,544	9	8	1
Worland	5,026	12	11	1

[1]The employee data presented in this table for Charlotte-Mecklenburg represent only Charlotte-Mecklenburg Police Department and exclude Mecklenburg County Sheriff's Office.

Table 20. Murder Victims, by Race, Ethnicity, and Sex, 2019

(Number.)

Race	Total	Sex		
		Male	Female	Unknown
Total	13,927	10,908	2,991	28
White	5,787	4,026	1,759	2
Black	7,484	6,446	1,035	3
Other race	422	280	140	2
Unknown race	234	156	57	21
Hispanic or Latino[1]	2,193	1,768	425	0
Not Hispanic or Latino[1]	8,881	6,975	1,900	6
Unknown[1]	1,808	1,373	425	10

[1]Not all agencies provide ethnicity data, therefore the race and ethnicity totals will not equal.

Table 20A. Murder Victims, by Age, Sex, Race, and Ethnicity, 2019

(Number; percent; single victim/single offender.)

Age	Total	Sex				Race				Ethnicity		
		Male	Female	Unknown		White	Black or African American	Other[1]	Unknown	Hispanic/ Latino	Not Hispanic/ Latino	Unknown
Total	13,927	10,908	2,991	28		5,787	7,484	422	234	2,193	8,881	1,808
Percent distribution[2]	100.0	78.3	21.5	0.2		41.6	53.7	3.0	1.7	17.0	68.9	14.0
Under 18[3]	1,146	828	314	4		473	610	38	25	218	676	170
Under 22[3]	2,859	2,270	584	5		1,028	1,711	71	49	524	1,789	353
18 and over[3]	12,697	10,031	2,653	13		5,279	6,847	384	187	1,966	8,176	1,608
Infant (under 1)	154	80	71	3		88	53	4	9	31	92	21
1 to 4	210	128	82	0		98	97	9	6	35	114	45
5 to 8	116	73	43	0		53	52	9	2	12	81	11
9 to 12	87	48	39	0		51	34	2	0	16	53	8
13 to 16	307	257	49	1		110	181	12	4	73	177	43
17 to 19	1,136	969	166	1		364	733	20	19	222	702	145
20 to 24	2,149	1,799	349	1		672	1,401	51	25	355	1,383	266
25 to 29	2,161	1,829	330	2		675	1,423	42	21	340	1,394	251
30 to 34	1,753	1,453	300	0		625	1,042	54	32	295	1,117	212
35 to 39	1,370	1,082	287	1		562	741	42	25	242	891	159
40 to 44	1,103	845	256	2		513	541	36	13	168	700	149
45 to 49	797	598	195	4		398	354	36	9	112	506	101
50 to 54	630	449	180	1		338	251	28	13	87	393	98
55 to 59	640	480	160	0		378	233	19	10	88	425	83
60 to 64	463	327	135	1		268	161	26	8	42	294	76
65 to 69	282	183	99	0		178	86	12	6	29	185	44
70 to 74	207	125	82	0		159	38	5	5	13	145	34
75 and over	278	134	144	0		222	36	15	5	24	200	32
Unknown	84	49	24	11		35	27	0	22	9	29	30

[1]Includes American Indian or Alaska Native, Asian, Native Hawaiian or Other Pacific Islander.
[2]Because of rounding, the percentages may not add to 100.0.
[3]Does not include unknown ages.

Table 21. Murder Offenders, by Age, Sex, Race, and Ethnicity, 2019

(Number; percent; single victim/single offender.)

Age	Total	Sex			Race				Ethnicity[1]		
		Male	Female	Unknown	White	Black or African American	Other[2]	Unknown	Hispanic/ Latino	Not Hispanic/ Latino	Unknown
Total	16,245	10,335	1,408	4,502	4,728	6,425	340	4,752	1,531	6,102	8,555
Percent distribution[3]	100.0	63.6	8.7	27.7	29.1	39.6	2.1	29.3	9.5	37.7	52.8
Under 18[4]	829	745	77	7	309	476	17	27	154	378	293
Under 22[4]	2,936	2,636	283	17	1,008	1,796	65	67	472	1,486	970
18 and over[4]	10,436	9,027	1,311	98	4,339	5,541	317	239	1,331	5,514	3,557
Infant (under 1).............................	0	0	0	0	0	0	0	0	0	0	0
1 to 4	4	1	0	3	1	0	0	3	1	1	2
5 to 8	1	1	0	0	0	1	0	0	0	0	1
9 to 12	16	12	4	0	6	8	1	1	0	10	6
13 to 16	450	399	50	1	165	260	11	14	83	202	163
17 to 19	1,441	1,311	125	5	492	891	32	26	241	735	462
20 to 24	2,345	2,086	249	10	790	1,441	64	50	356	1,223	761
25 to 29	2,065	1,768	288	9	729	1,246	62	28	277	1,099	680
30 to 34	1,389	1,204	180	5	585	733	49	22	175	728	481
35 to 39	1,073	900	166	7	510	509	34	20	138	551	378
40 to 44	746	644	99	3	356	352	24	14	73	414	256
45 to 49	535	442	86	7	294	206	20	15	67	267	199
50 to 54	403	333	47	23	208	145	20	30	32	216	154
55 to 59	341	262	49	30	181	115	8	37	18	170	152
60 to 64	198	173	25	0	135	61	1	1	13	120	64
65 to 69	107	101	6	0	76	27	2	2	5	62	40
70 to 74	60	55	5	0	48	11	1	0	3	37	20
75 and over	91	80	9	2	72	11	5	3	3	57	31
Unknown......................................	4,980	563	20	4,397	80	408	6	4,486	46	210	4,705

[1]Not all agencies provide ethnicity data, therefore the race and ethnicity totals will not equal.
[2]Includes American Indian or Alaska Native, Asian, Native Hawaiian or Other Pacific Islander.
[3]Because of rounding, the percentages may not add to 100.0.
[4]Does not include unknown ages.

Table 22. Murder, by Victim/Offender Situations, 2019

(Number; percent.)

Situation	Total	Percent distribution (may not add to 100.0 due to rounding)
Total	13,927	100.0
Single victim/single offender	7,047	50.6
Single victim/unknown offender or offenders............................	3,533	25.4
Single victim/multiple offenders	1,782	12.8
Multiple victims/single offender...............................	960	6.9
Multiple victims/multiple offenders...........................	268	1.9
Multiple victims/unknown offender or offenders.......................	337	2.4

Table 23. Murder Age of Victim, by Age of Offender, 2019

(Number; single victim/single offender.)

| Age of victim | Total | Age of offender | | |
		Under 18 years	18 years and over	Unknown
Total	6,578	281	6,051	246
Under 18	464	86	382	16
18 and over	6,066	195	5,643	228
Unknown............................	28	0	26	2

Note: This table is based on incidents where some information about the offender is known by law enforcement; therefore, when the offender age, sex, and race are all reported as unknown, these data are excluded from the table.

Table 24. Murder, Race, Ethnicity, and Sex of Victim by Race, Ethnicity, and Sex of Offender, 2019

(Number; single victim/single offender.)

| Victim characteristic | Total | Sex | | | Race | | | | Ethnicity | | |
		Male	Female	Unknown	White	Black or African American	Other[1]	Unknown	Hispanic/ Latino	Not Hispanic/ Latino	Unknown
Race											
White	3,299	2,594	566	56	83	2,915	359	25	738	1,542	1,019
Black or African American.......................	2,906	246	2,574	23	63	2,606	273	27	95	1,841	970
Other race[1]	247	57	40	138	12	211	34	2	18	144	85
Unknown	126	51	38	8	29	107	17	2	23	47	56
Sex											
Male	4,716	1,892	2,524	153	147	4,191	477	48	652	2,536	1,528
Female.............................	1,857	1,054	694	72	37	1,647	203	7	221	1,038	598
Unknown..........................	5	2	0	0	3	1	3	1	1	0	4
Ethnicity											
Hispanic or Latino	987	759	177	14	37	894	78	15	595	241	151
Not Hispanic or Latino.............	4,205	1,681	2,298	142	84	3,731	448	26	220	3,170	815
Unknown..........................	1,386	508	743	69	66	1,214	157	15	59	163	1,164

NOTE: This table is based on incidents where some information about the offender is known by law enforcement; therefore, when the offender age, sex, and race are all reported as unknown, these data are excluded from the table.
[1] Includes American Indian or Alaska Native, Asian, Native Hawaiian or Other Pacific Islander.

Table 25. Murder Victims, by Weapons, 2015–2019

(Number.)

Weapons	2015	2016	2017	2018	2019
Total	13,847	15,355	15,206	14,446	13,927
Total firearms...	9,143	10,398	11,014	10,445	10,258
Handguns	6,194	6,778	7,052	6,683	6,368
Rifles	215	300	389	305	364
Shotguns..	248	247	263	237	200
Other guns...	152	172	178	164	45
Firearms, type not stated...........................	2,334	2,901	3,132	3,056	3,281
Knives or cutting instruments........................	1,533	1,562	1,608	1,542	1,476
Blunt objects (clubs, hammers, etc.)	438	466	474	455	397
Personal weapons (hands, fists, feet, etc.)[1]	651	668	715	712	600
Poison...	8	12	15	6	16
Explosives	1	1	0	4	3
Fire...	63	78	93	76	81
Narcotics..	70	119	112	102	93
Drowning...	12	9	8	9	7
Strangulation...	96	97	90	75	64
Asphyxiation..	105	93	112	92	92
Other weapons or weapons not stated	1,727	1,852	965	928	840

NOTE: The Uniform Crime Reporting Technical Refresh enables updating of prior years' crime data; therefore, data presented in this table may not match previously published data.
1 Pushed is included in personal weapons.

Table 26. Murder, Types of Weapon, by Region, 2019[1]

(Number.)

State	All weapons[2]	Firearms	Knives or cutting instruments	Unknown or other dangerous weapons	Personal weapons (hands, feet, fists, etc.)[3]
Total	100.0	73.7	10.6	11.4	4.3
Northeast	100.0	64.5	16.2	13.4	5.9
Midwest	100.0	76.0	8.2	11.9	3.9
South	100.0	79.0	8.2	9.6	3.2
West	100.0	65.9	14.6	13.5	6.0

[1]Guam and U.S. Virgin Islands totals are not included in this table.
[2]Because of rounding, the percentages may not add to 100.0.
[3]Pushed is included in personal weapons.

Table 27. Justifiable Homicide by Weapon, Law Enforcement,[1] 2015–2019

(Number.)

Year	Total	Total firearms	Handguns	Rifles	Shotguns	Firearms, type not stated	Knives or cutting instruments	Other dangerous weapons	Personal weapons
2015	457	456	316	40	7	93	0	1	0
2016	440	432	313	51	5	63	2	5	1
2017	444	436	284	57	2	93	3	4	1
2018	435	431	292	56	4	79	1	2	1
2019	340	334	248	32	2	52	2	2	2

NOTE: The Uniform Crime Reporting Technical Refresh enables updating of prior years' crime data; therefore, data presented in this table may not match previously published data.
[1]The killing of a felon by a law enforcement officer in the line of duty.

Table 28. Justifiable Homicide by Weapon, Private Citizen,[1] 2015–2019

(Number.)

Year	Total	Total firearms	Handguns	Rifles	Shotguns	Firearms, type not stated	Knives or cutting instruments	Other dangerous weapons	Personal weapons
2015	333	268	216	6	13	33	40	10	15
2016	334	278	201	11	9	57	34	8	14
2017	368	313	238	7	8	60	35	8	12
2018	375	317	229	6	10	72	33	13	12
2019	386	334	237	16	8	73	32	8	12

NOTE: The Uniform Crime Reporting Technical Refresh enables updating of prior years' crime data; therefore, data presented in this table may not match previously published data.
[1]The killing of a felon, during the commission of a felony, by a private citizen.

Table 29. Robbery, Types of Weapons Used, Percent Distribution by Region, 2019

(Percent.)

Region	Total all weapons[1]	Armed			Strong-arm
		Firearms	Knives or cutting instruments	Other weapons	
Total	100.0	36.4	8.5	10.3	44.4
Northeast	100.0	21.6	12.5	10.2	55.7
Midwest	100.0	40.8	5.4	10.2	43.6
South	100.0	48.9	7.1	8.8	35.2
West	100.0	26.4	9.6	12.0	52.0

[1]Because of rounding, the percentages may not add to 100.0.

Table 30. Aggravated Assault, Types of Weapons Used, Percent Distribution by Region, 2019

(Percent.)

Region	Total all weapons[1]	Firearms	Knives or cutting instruments	Other weapons (clubs, blunt objects, etc.)	Personal weapons (hands, fists, feet, etc.)
Total	100.0	27.6	17.5	29.8	25.2
Northeast	100.0	12.0	23.0	31.7	33.3
Midwest	100.0	31.1	15.7	28.1	25.2
South	100.0	35.9	17.2	29.1	17.8
West	100.0	19.9	16.3	31.0	32.8

1 Because of rounding, the percentages may not add to 100.0.

Table 31. Larceny-Theft, Percent Distribution by Region, 2019

(Percent.)

Region	Larceny-theft									
	Total (may not sum to 100.0 due to rounding)	Pocket-picking	Purse-snatching	Shoplifting	From motor vehicles (except accessories)	Motor vehicle accessories	Bicycles	From buildings	From coin-operated machines	All others
Total	100.0	0.6	0.4	22.2	27.0	6.5	3.1	10.0	0.2	29.9
Northeast	100.0	1.0	0.4	27.3	18.4	4.4	4.4	16.0	0.1	28.2
Midwest	100.0	0.4	0.4	23.6	19.9	6.0	2.8	11.8	0.2	35.0
South	100.0	0.6	0.3	22.8	27.3	6.5	2.3	8.4	0.3	31.5
West	100.0	0.7	0.4	18.9	33.3	7.6	4.0	9.2	0.2	25.6

Table 32. Motor Vehicle Theft, Percent Distribution by Region, 2019

(Percent.)

Region	Motor vehicle theft			
	Total (may not sum to 100.0 due to rounding)	Autos	Trucks and buses	Other vehicles
Total	100.0	74.5	16.2	9.3
Northeast	100.0	86.1	3.8	10.0
Midwest	100.0	83.5	8.6	8.0
South	100.0	70.1	19.2	10.8
West	100.0	73.4	18.3	8.3

Table 33. Arson Rate, by Population Group, 2019

(Number; rate; 12,375 agencies; 2019 estimated population 263,837,337; rate per 100,000 inhabitants.)

Population group	Rate
Total, All Agencies	12.1
Total, cities	13.9
Group I (250,000 and over)	21.8
1,000,000 and over	19.5
500,000 to 999,999	23.1
250,000 to 499,999	23.4
Group II (100,000 to 249,999)	13.2
Group III (50,000 to 99,999)	10.9
Group IV (25,000 to 49,999)	9.4
Group V (10,000 to 24,999)	8.8
Group VI (Under 10,000)	13.8
Metropolitan counties	7.7
Nonmetropolitan counties	8.9
Suburban areas[1]	8.0

1 Suburban areas include law enforcement agencies in cities with less than 50,000 inhabitants and county law enforcement agencies that are within a Metropolitan Statistical Area. Suburban areas exclude all metropolitan agencies associated with a principal city. The agencies associated with suburban areas also appear in other groups within this table.

Table 34. Arson, by Type of Property, 2019

(Number; percent, dollars; 15,234 agencies; 2019 estimated population 294,402,737.)

Property classification	Number of arson offenses	Percent distribution[1]	Percent not in use	Average damage	Total clearances	Percent of arsons cleared[2]	Percent of clearances under 18
Total	32,358	100.0	NA	$16,371	7,568	23.4	17.0
Total structure	13,969	43.2	12.7	$29,568	3,919	28.1	16.5
Single occupancy residential	6,251	19.3	11.9	$30,308	1,660	26.6	12.2
Other residential.............................	2,400	7.4	7.4	$31,776	751	31.3	9.5
Storage...	713	2.2	17.5	$18,281	195	27.3	20.5
Industrial/manufacturing	137	0.4	21.9	$190,336	33	24.1	15.2
Other commercial............................	1,572	4.9	17.0	$36,402	442	28.1	13.3
Community/public............................	1,229	3.8	20.2	$15,751	458	37.3	42.4
Other structure...............................	1,667	5.2	11.0	$18,972	380	22.8	20.3
Total mobile....................................	7,522	23.2	NA	$8,526	893	11.9	8.6
Motor vehicles................................	7,068	21.8	NA	$8,057	805	11.4	8.1
Other mobile...................................	454	1.4	NA	$15,827	88	19.4	13.6
Other...	10,867	33.6	NA	$4,836	2,756	25.4	20.2

NA = Not available.
[1]Because of rounding, the percentages may not add to 100.0.
[2]Includes arsons cleared by arrest or exceptional means.

Table 35. Offenses Known to Law Enforcement, by Selected Federal Agency, 2019

(Number.)

Agency and unit/office	Violent crime	Murder and nonnegligent manslaughter	Rape	Robbery	Aggravated assault	Property crime	Burglary	Larceny-theft	Motor vehicle theft	Arson
National Institutes of Health..............	0	0	0	0	0	80	5	75	0	0
United States Dept. of Defense										
United States Marine Corps Law Enforcement............	0	0	0	0	0	124	11	113	0	0
United States Army	0	0	0	0	0	370	3	367	0	16
United States Navy Law Enforcement	2	0	0	0	2	86	4	81	1	1
United States Dept. of the Interior										
Bureau of Indian Affairs[1]										
Bureau of Land Management......................	7	0	0	0	7	568	14	524	30	44
Bureau of Reclamation	0	0	0	0	0	2	1	1	0	2
Fish and Wildlife Service	25	1	1	3	20	175	20	127	28	7
National Park Service..........................	293	9	32	91	161	3,981	296	3,603	82	42

[1]The Bureau of Indian Affairs submits these statistics to the FBI Uniform Crime Reporting Program on a monthly basis throughout the calendar year and can be found in Table 11 of Crime in the United States, 2019.

Table 36. Full-Time Law Enforcement Employees, by Selected Federal Agency, 2019

(Number.)

Agency and unit/office	Total law enforcement employees	Total officers	Total civilians
National Institutes of Health.................................	98	76	22
United States Dept. of the Interior			
Bureau of Land Management..............................	277	260	17
National Park Service..	2,278	1,986	292

Table 37. Number of Arrestees by NIBRS Offense Code, by Selected FBI Field Office, 2019

(Number.)

NIBRS Offense Code	09A - 09C	11A - 11D	13A - 13C	23A - 23H	26A - 26G	35A - 35B	39A - 39D	40A - 40C	64A - 64B	100	120	200	210	240
NIBRS Offense Description	Homicide offenses	Sex offenses	Assault offenses	Larceny/ theft offenses	Fraud offenses	Drug/ narcotic offenses	Gambling offenses	Prostitution offenses	Human trafficking	Kidnapping/ abduction	Robbery	Arson	Extortion/ blackmail	Motor Vehicle Theft
	# Arrested	# Arrested	# Arrested	# Arrested	# Arrested	# Arrested	# Arrested	# Arrested	# Arrested	# Arrested	# Arrested	# Arrested	# Arrested	# Arrested
Grand Total, All Field Offices.	154	285	853	47	2,582	5,350	15	73	997	195	810	6	4	2
Albany	0	0	3	1	19	109	0	0	17	2	4	0	0	0
Albuquerque	11	25	60	0	31	143	0	0	2	5	17	0	1	0
Anchorage	0	0	1	0	12	18	0	0	7	1	3	0	0	0
Atlanta	1	5	10	0	55	126	0	0	24	0	16	0	0	0
Baltimore	7	2	3	0	40	39	0	0	8	1	32	0	0	0
Birmingham	2	0	3	0	14	30	0	0	6	4	6	0	0	0
Boston	0	0	10	1	77	134	0	0	16	5	33	0	0	0
Buffalo	0	0	0	0	4	11	0	0	0	0	0	0	0	0
Charlotte	1	2	5	0	18	65	0	0	11	1	17	0	0	0
Chicago	2	0	8	0	53	75	0	0	8	2	42	0	0	0
Cincinnati	4	4	6	4	25	73	0	0	14	0	0	0	0	0
Cleveland	0	0	3	1	69	187	0	0	9	1	22	0	0	0
Columbia	0	1	8	2	17	133	0	0	3	2	7	0	0	0
Dallas	1	1	8	2	56	79	0	0	26	12	37	0	0	0
Denver	3	20	26	1	33	47	0	0	12	6	30	1	0	0
Detroit	1	8	33	0	74	88	0	45	31	3	28	0	0	0
El Paso	3	3	6	0	7	49	0	0	10	5	4	0	0	0
Honolulu	0	1	7	0	8	28	0	0	10	0	7	0	0	0
Houston	1	0	5	0	38	72	0	1	15	8	11	0	0	0
Indianapolis	0	0	2	1	69	163	0	0	44	4	24	0	0	1
Jackson	7	7	6	1	36	55	0	0	11	2	7	0	0	0
Jacksonville	0	0	9	1	24	12	0	0	19	0	4	0	0	0
Kansas City	0	1	7	1	31	102	0	0	29	1	7	0	0	0
Knoxville	0	1	1	1	12	126	0	0	6	0	2	0	0	0
Las Vegas	2	0	2	0	15	74	0	0	5	1	4	0	0	0
Little Rock	1	0	3	0	2	103	0	8	15	0	7	0	0	0
Los Angeles	12	0	17	0	174	146	0	0	4	0	12	0	0	0
Louisville	3	0	5	0	45	59	0	0	26	2	4	0	0	0
Memphis	0	1	5	0	33	34	0	0	15	3	16	0	0	0
Miami	1	1	17	2	194	90	0	0	24	17	21	0	0	0
Milwaukee	2	0	2	0	8	30	0	0	32	0	20	0	0	0
Minneapolis	9	91	88	0	17	185	0	0	23	5	27	0	0	0
Mobile	0	0	4	0	10	9	0	0	2	0	12	0	0	0
New Haven	0	1	2	0	27	105	0	0	9	3	2	0	0	0
New Orleans	0	1	2	11	46	44	0	0	12	3	6	0	0	0
New York	13	4	21	0	288	102	8	0	57	16	15	0	0	0
Newark	1	1	3	0	89	114	0	0	6	1	23	0	0	0
Norfolk	1	1	5	0	41	25	0	0	6	0	0	0	0	0
Oklahoma City	2	3	7	2	20	86	0	0	24	0	12	0	0	0
Omaha	3	18	43	1	38	95	0	6	18	4	16	0	0	0
Philadelphia	1	5	11	3	169	169	0	0	39	20	57	0	2	1
Phoenix	22	29	149	3	31	121	0	0	6	25	17	4	0	0
Pittsburgh	0	0	0	0	19	188	0	12	16	0	61	0	0	0
Portland	0	2	14	0	14	51	0	0	22	1	17	0	0	0
Richmond	1	3	9	0	16	7	0	0	9	1	4	0	0	0
Sacramento	0	1	1	0	31	93	2	0	16	1	7	0	0	0
Salt Lake City	6	18	89	1	23	123	5	0	23	2	17	0	0	0
St. Louis	2	0	2	1	30	88	0	0	19	0	6	0	0	0
San Antonio	0	3	34	0	51	92	0	0	20	8	12	0	0	0
San Diego	2	0	5	0	41	102	0	0	50	0	13	0	0	0
San Francisco	2	0	4	3	78	42	0	0	3	0	7	0	0	0
San Juan[1]	13	3	8	0	53	299	0	1	17	9	12	0	0	0
Seattle	7	12	32	2	20	37	0	0	8	1	7	0	0	0
Springfield	0	0	10	0	3	45	0	0	30	0	4	0	0	0
Tampa	1	1	16	0	45	522	0	0	19	4	6	0	1	0
Washington, Dc	3	5	13	1	89	106	0	0	54	3	6	1	0	0

Table 37. Number of Arrestees by NIBRS Offense Code, by Selected FBI Field Office, 2019—*Continued*

(Number.)

NIBRS Offense Code	250	270	280	290	370	510	520	720		90J	90Z			
NIBRS Offense Description	Counter-feiting/ forgery # Arrested	Embezzle-ment # Arrested	Stolen property offenses # Arrested	Destruction/ damage/ vandalism of property # Arrested	Pornography/ obscene material # Arrested	Bribery # Arrested	Weapon law violations # Arrested	Animal cruelty # Arrested	Count of arrestees for Group A Offenses	Trespass of real property # Arrested	All other offenses # Arrested	Count of arrestees for Group B Offenses	Total number of arrestees	Population per Field Office
Grand Total, All Field Offices.	92	113	97	39	1,115	56	2,982	7	15,874	2	7,280	7,282	23,156	33,16,83,105
Albany	0	0	0	0	17	0	14	0	186	0	27	27	213	39,76,491
Albuquerque	0	0	3	0	4	0	131	1	434	0	113	113	547	20,96,829
Anchorage	0	0	0	0	5	2	22	0	71	0	10	10	81	7,31,545
Atlanta	0	0	0	1	16	1	71	0	326	0	161	161	487	1,06,17,423
Baltimore	3	1	6	0	18	5	52	0	217	0	146	146	363	70,19,444
Birmingham	0	1	0	0	9	2	31	0	108	0	61	61	169	28,96,978
Boston	3	0	0	0	19	0	44	0	342	0	237	237	579	1,06,55,787
Buffalo	0	0	0	0	0	0	0	0	15	0	15	15	30	27,62,081
Charlotte	0	0	0	0	13	2	74	0	209	0	77	77	286	1,04,88,084
Chicago	0	3	0	2	9	1	57	0	262	0	104	104	366	92,55,097
Cincinnati	4	0	1	0	34	0	42	0	211	0	94	94	305	59,93,903
Cleveland	0	1	6	0	25	0	103	0	427	0	190	190	617	56,95,197
Columbia	6	0	0	0	4	0	39	0	222	0	105	105	327	51,48,714
Dallas	4	2	5	1	40	0	41	0	315	0	185	185	500	1,10,60,577
Denver	0	1	0	0	16	2	20	0	218	0	83	83	301	63,37,495
Detroit	2	1	7	1	40	0	72	0	434	0	171	171	605	99,86,857
El Paso	0	4	5	2	8	3	7	0	116	0	66	66	182	12,90,663
Honolulu	0	4	0	0	3	0	12	0	80	0	39	39	119	14,15,872
Houston	3	1	2	1	33	0	27	0	218	0	105	105	323	88,10,016
Indianapolis	2	0	3	2	59	0	84	0	458	0	123	123	581	67,32,219
Jackson	0	8	6	0	12	0	83	0	241	0	49	49	290	29,76,149
Jacksonville	0	0	1	0	9	0	15	1	95	0	37	37	132	53,48,652
Kansas City	0	0	3	0	41	0	68	0	291	0	119	119	410	61,24,353
Knoxville	0	0	0	0	13	0	30	0	192	0	77	77	269	26,53,711
Las Vegas	0	0	0	0	19	0	27	0	149	0	51	51	200	30,80,156
Little Rock	0	1	2	0	21	0	40	0	203	0	49	49	252	30,17,804
Los Angeles	1	2	0	1	25	3	78	0	475	0	534	534	1,009	1,94,45,734
Louisville	1	3	0	0	16	0	26	0	190	0	113	113	303	44,67,673
Memphis	0	4	3	0	18	0	20	0	152	0	104	104	256	41,75,463
Miami	1	15	10	1	24	2	46	0	466	0	447	447	913	71,02,118
Milwaukee	1	0	2	0	7	0	25	0	129	0	83	83	212	58,22,434
Minneapolis	0	10	5	3	37	0	45	0	545	0	142	142	687	72,86,353
Mobile	0	4	0	0	5	0	55	0	101	0	28	28	129	20,06,207
New Haven	0	0	1	0	13	0	45	0	208	0	76	76	284	35,65,287
New Orleans	0	0	0	1	14	0	50	0	190	0	66	66	256	46,48,794
New York	22	5	4	7	32	6	117	3	720	0	742	742	1,462	1,33,38,978
Newark	1	5	0	0	12	1	80	0	337	0	261	261	598	80,25,896
Norfolk	1	0	3	0	17	0	9	0	109	0	84	84	193	17,55,393
Oklahoma City	2	0	0	1	12	0	40	0	211	0	113	113	324	39,56,971
Omaha	1	3	0	4	28	0	89	0	367	0	67	67	434	50,89,478
Philadelphia	14	5	6	0	37	0	75	0	614	1	222	223	837	99,68,430
Phoenix	0	0	0	0	14	0	27	0	448	0	108	108	556	72,78,717
Pittsburgh	0	1	5	0	31	0	57	0	420	0	216	216	636	54,82,000
Portland	0	1	0	0	18	0	28	0	168	0	56	56	224	42,17,737
Richmond	0	1	0	0	3	0	12	0	66	0	37	37	103	41,64,091
Sacramento	0	0	0	1	28	0	65	0	246	0	93	93	339	81,39,046
Salt Lake City	1	0	0	1	18	6	107	0	440	1	109	110	550	60,61,801
St. Louis	0	0	1	1	36	0	145	0	331	0	50	50	381	29,26,389
San Antonio	0	7	1	0	33	5	34	0	300	0	178	178	478	78,34,625
San Diego	12	0	0	1	9	0	31	0	266	0	90	90	356	35,27,390
San Francisco	1	2	0	0	2	0	70	0	214	0	52	52	266	84,00,053
San Juan[1]	0	8	1	4	14	4	106	0	552	0	225	225	777	34,43,582
Seattle	0	2	0	0	15	0	34	0	177	0	40	40	217	76,14,893
Springfield	0	0	1	0	29	0	38	0	160	0	53	53	213	34,16,724
Tampa	0	7	0	1	36	0	50	2	711	0	87	87	798	90,26,967
Washington, Dc	6	0	4	2	45	11	172	0	521	0	310	310	831	33,21,784

[1]Population for the San Juan Field Office is a combination of the U.S. Census Bureau's 2010 decennial population for the U.S. Virgin Islands and population estimation for Puerto Rico.

Table 38. Number of Arrestees for Child Exploitation, by Selected FBI Field Office, 2019

(Number.)

Field office	Arrests	Population per field office
Albany	34	3,976,491
Albuquerque	23	2,096,829
Anchorage	12	731,545
Atlanta	40	10,617,423
Baltimore	25	7,019,444
Birmingham	15	2,896,978
Boston	26	10,655,787
Buffalo	65	2,762,081
Charlotte	53	10,488,084
Chicago	13	9,255,097
Cincinnati	48	5,993,903
Cleveland	32	5,695,197
Columbia	8	5,148,714
Dallas	65	11,060,577
Denver	38	6,337,495
Detroit	69	9,986,857
El Paso	19	1,290,663
Honolulu	13	1,415,872
Houston	43	8,810,016
Indianapolis	102	6,732,219
Jackson	24	2,976,149
Jacksonville	16	5,348,652
Kansas City	64	6,124,353
Knoxville	20	2,653,711
Las Vegas	24	3,080,156
Little Rock	31	3,017,804
Los Angeles	29	19,445,734
Louisville	37	4,467,673
Memphis	32	4,175,463
Miami	41	7,102,118
Milwaukee	12	5,822,434
Minneapolis	108	7,286,353
Mobile	7	2,006,207
New Haven	23	3,565,287
New Orleans	23	4,648,794
New York	56	13,338,978
Newark	15	8,025,896
Norfolk	24	1,755,393
Oklahoma City	31	3,956,971
Omaha	58	5,089,478
Philadelphia	64	9,968,430
Phoenix	28	7,278,717
Pittsburgh	73	5,482,000
Portland	36	4,217,737
Richmond	9	4,164,091
Sacramento	37	8,139,046
Salt Lake City	52	6,061,801
St. Louis	53	2,926,389
San Antonio	50	7,834,625
San Diego	20	3,527,390
San Francisco	2	8,400,053
San Juan[1]	27	3,443,582
Seattle	27	7,614,893
Springfield	58	3,416,724
Tampa	52	9,026,967
Washington, DC	72	3,321,784

[1]Population for the San Juan Field Office is a combination of the U.S. Census Bureau's 2010 decennial population for the U.S. Virgin Islands and population estimation for Puerto Rico.

Table 39. Number of Arrestees by NIBRS Offense Code, by Selected ATF Judicial District, 2019

(Number.)

NIBRS Offense Code	09A - 09C	11A - 11D	13A - 13C	23A - 23H	26A - 26G	35A - 35B	36A - 36B	39A - 39 D	64A - 64B	100	120
NIBRS Offense Description	Homicide offenses	Sex offenses	Assault offenses	Larceny/ theft offenses	Fraud offenses	Drug/ narcotic offenses	Sex offenses, nonforcible	Gambling offenses	Human trafficking	Kidnapping/ abduction	Robbery
	# Arrested	# Arrested	# Arrested	# Arrested	# Arrested	# Arrested	# Arrested	# Arrested	# Arrested	# Arrested	# Arrested
Grand Total, All Judicial Districts	90	36	127	47	352	3,118	44	12	29	10	102
Alabama, Middle District....................................	0	0	0	1	2	10	0	0	0	0	2
Alabama, Northern District.................................	0	0	0	1	1	12	3	0	0	0	1
Alabama, Southern District	0	0	0	0	0	9	0	0	0	0	0
Alaska...	0	0	0	0	1	2	0	0	0	0	0
Arizona...	0	1	3	1	11	52	4	0	0	1	0
Arkansas, Eastern District..................................	0	0	0	0	0	7	0	0	0	0	0
Arkansas, Western District	0	0	0	0	1	10	0	0	0	0	0
California, Central District..................................	2	2	2	0	4	26	1	0	0	1	2
California, Eastern District..................................	1	0	0	0	6	47	0	0	0	0	0
California, Northern District	0	1	0	0	8	8	3	0	0	0	0
California, Southern District	0	2	1	1	2	113	1	0	1	1	1
Colorado..	0	0	0	1	2	41	0	0	0	0	1
Connecticut..	1	0	2	0	1	62	0	0	0	0	0
Delaware..	0	0	0	0	2	3	0	0	0	0	0
District of Columbia...	62	11	60	3	16	22	7	0	4	3	21
Florida, Middle District	1	0	1	1	1	21	0	0	0	0	1
Florida, Northern District...................................	0	0	2	0	0	9	0	0	1	0	0
Florida, Southern District...................................	2	0	0	3	17	66	0	0	0	0	3
Georgia, Middle District	0	0	1	0	3	66	1	0	1	0	0
Georgia, Northern District..................................	1	0	3	0	2	47	0	0	0	0	1
Georgia, Southern District..................................	0	0	0	0	0	17	0	0	0	0	0
Guam[1]...	0	0	0	0	0	2	0	0	0	0	0
Hawaii..	0	0	4	0	7	35	1	12	1	0	2
Idaho...	0	0	1	0	2	12	4	0	0	0	1
Illinois, Central District	0	1	0	0	0	18	1	0	0	0	0
Illinois, Northern District...................................	0	0	0	0	5	18	0	0	0	0	0
Illinois, Southern District...................................	0	0	0	0	0	17	0	0	0	0	2
Indiana, Northern District..................................	0	0	0	0	0	3	0	0	0	0	0
Indiana, Southern District..................................	0	1	0	0	2	6	0	0	1	0	0
Iowa, Northern District......................................	0	1	0	0	1	73	3	0	4	1	1
Iowa, Southern District......................................	0	0	0	0	1	18	1	0	0	0	0
Kansas..	1	0	1	1	0	36	1	0	0	0	2
Kentucky, Eastern District..................................	0	0	0	0	0	18	0	0	0	0	1
Kentucky, Western District.................................	0	0	0	0	1	14	0	0	1	0	0
Louisiana, Eastern District..................................	1	0	0	1	0	6	0	0	0	0	1
Louisiana, Middle District	0	0	0	0	5	8	0	0	0	0	0
Louisiana, Western District	1	0	0	0	0	4	0	0	0	0	0
Maine...	0	0	0	0	0	6	0	0	0	0	3
Maryland..	0	0	0	0	1	10	0	0	0	0	0
Massachusetts..	0	0	0	0	1	6	0	0	0	0	0
Michigan, Eastern District..................................	0	1	1	0	4	13	0	0	0	0	2
Michigan, Western District	0	0	0	0	0	11	0	0	0	0	0
Minnesota..	0	0	0	0	0	14	0	0	1	0	1
Mississippi, Northern District.............................	0	0	0	0	0	43	2	0	0	0	0
Mississippi, Southern District.............................	0	0	0	2	1	20	0	0	0	0	1
Missouri, Eastern District...................................	0	0	0	4	32	166	1	0	0	0	14
Missouri, Western District	0	0	0	2	5	57	1	0	0	0	0
Montana...	1	0	1	0	2	16	0	0	0	0	0
Nebraska..	0	0	0	1	7	36	1	0	0	0	2
Nevada...	0	0	1	1	1	9	0	0	1	0	1
New Hampshire	0	0	0	0	1	67	0	0	1	0	0
New Jersey..	1	0	1	1	11	57	0	0	0	0	0
New Mexico..	1	0	3	0	3	54	3	0	0	0	0
New York, Eastern District..................................	2	3	1	0	31	34	2	0	1	1	1
New York, Northern District...............................	0	0	2	0	4	5	0	0	3	0	0
New York, Southern District...............................	3	0	2	0	15	42	0	0	0	0	3
New York, Western District................................	0	0	0	0	0	7	0	0	0	0	0
North Carolina, Eastern District	0	1	2	1	5	32	0	0	0	0	1
North Carolina, Middle District..........................	2	0	0	0	1	13	0	0	0	0	1
North Carolina, Western District........................	0	1	1	0	3	20	0	0	1	0	0
North Dakota...	0	0	0	0	2	18	0	0	0	0	0
Northern Mariana Islands[1]................................	0	0	0	0	0	0	0	0	0	0	0
Ohio, Northern District......................................	0	0	2	0	1	114	1	0	0	0	0
Ohio, Southern District......................................	0	0	0	3	14	76	0	0	0	0	8
Oklahoma, Eastern District................................	0	0	3	0	0	3	0	0	0	0	0
Oklahoma, Northern District	0	1	0	0	1	17	0	0	1	0	0

Table 39. Number of Arrestees by NIBRS Offense Code, by Selected ATF Judicial District, 2019—*Continued*

(Number.)

NIBRS Offense Code	200	210	220	240	250	270	280	290	370	510	520
NIBRS Offense Description	Arson	Extortion/ blackmail	Burglary/ breaking & entering	Motor vehicle theft	Counterfeiting/ forgery	Embezzlement	Stolen property offenses	Destruction/ damage/ vandalism of property	Pornography/ obscene material	Bribery	Weapon law violations
	# Arrested	# Arrested	# Arrested	# Arrested	# Arrested	# Arrested	# Arrested	# Arrested	# Arrested	# Arrested	# Arrested
Grand Total, All Judicial Districts	7	18	16	1	28	5	14	3	97	2	1,696
Alabama, Middle District	1	0	0	0	0	0	0	0	4	0	54
Alabama, Northern District	0	0	0	0	0	0	0	0	0	0	69
Alabama, Southern District	0	0	0	0	0	0	0	0	0	0	13
Alaska	0	0	0	0	0	0	0	0	0	0	1
Arizona	0	0	0	0	0	0	0	0	1	0	3
Arkansas, Eastern District	0	0	0	0	0	0	0	0	0	0	3
Arkansas, Western District	0	0	0	0	0	0	0	0	1	0	1
California, Central District	0	0	0	0	0	0	0	0	1	0	0
California, Eastern District	0	0	0	0	0	0	1	0	0	0	5
California, Northern District	0	0	0	0	1	0	0	0	1	0	5
California, Southern District	0	0	0	0	0	0	1	0	7	0	6
Colorado	0	0	0	0	0	0	0	0	1	0	5
Connecticut	0	0	0	0	0	0	0	0	0	0	2
Delaware	0	0	0	0	0	0	0	0	0	0	2
District of Columbia	0	7	12	1	0	0	2	1	8	2	35
Florida, Middle District	0	0	0	0	0	0	0	0	0	0	3
Florida, Northern District	0	0	0	0	1	0	0	0	0	0	2
Florida, Southern District	0	0	0	0	0	0	0	0	1	0	9
Georgia, Middle District	0	0	0	0	2	0	0	0	0	0	30
Georgia, Northern District	0	0	0	0	0	0	0	0	0	0	13
Georgia, Southern District	0	0	0	0	0	0	0	0	1	0	6
Guam[1]	0	0	0	0	0	0	0	0	0	0	3
Hawaii	1	0	0	0	0	1	0	0	1	0	14
Idaho	0	0	0	0	0	0	0	0	1	0	8
Illinois, Central District	0	0	0	0	0	0	0	0	1	0	4
Illinois, Northern District	0	0	1	0	0	0	0	0	0	0	8
Illinois, Southern District	0	0	0	0	0	0	0	0	1	0	9
Indiana, Northern District	0	0	0	0	0	0	0	0	0	0	2
Indiana, Southern District	0	0	0	0	1	0	0	0	1	0	8
Iowa, Northern District	0	4	0	0	0	0	0	0	7	0	80
Iowa, Southern District	0	0	0	0	4	0	0	0	11	0	8
Kansas	0	0	0	0	0	0	0	0	3	0	19
Kentucky, Eastern District	0	0	0	0	0	0	0	0	0	0	7
Kentucky, Western District	0	0	0	0	0	0	0	0	0	0	17
Louisiana, Eastern District	0	0	0	0	0	0	0	0	0	0	2
Louisiana, Middle District	0	0	0	0	0	0	0	0	0	0	22
Louisiana, Western District	0	0	0	0	0	0	0	0	0	0	4
Maine	0	0	0	0	1	0	0	0	0	0	1
Maryland	0	0	0	0	0	0	0	0	0	0	1
Massachusetts	0	0	0	0	0	0	0	0	0	0	0
Michigan, Eastern District	0	2	1	0	0	0	0	0	0	0	7
Michigan, Western District	0	0	0	0	0	0	0	0	0	0	1
Minnesota	0	0	0	0	0	0	0	0	2	0	4
Mississippi, Northern District	0	0	0	0	3	0	0	0	3	0	33
Mississippi, Southern District	0	0	0	0	0	0	0	0	0	0	24
Missouri, Eastern District	0	0	0	0	3	0	0	0	3	0	449
Missouri, Western District	0	0	0	0	0	0	0	0	4	0	54
Montana	0	0	0	0	0	0	0	0	0	0	8
Nebraska	0	0	0	0	0	0	0	0	9	0	19
Nevada	0	0	0	0	0	0	0	0	0	0	4
New Hampshire	0	0	0	0	0	0	2	0	1	0	5
New Jersey	0	0	0	0	0	0	0	0	0	0	36
New Mexico	0	0	0	0	0	0	0	0	0	0	13
New York, Eastern District	0	1	0	0	1	0	0	0	0	0	12
New York, Northern District	0	0	0	0	0	0	0	0	0	0	2
New York, Southern District	0	2	0	0	0	1	5	0	0	0	10
New York, Western District	0	0	0	0	0	0	0	0	0	0	0
North Carolina, Eastern District	0	0	0	0	0	0	1	0	0	0	31
North Carolina, Middle District	0	0	0	0	0	0	0	0	0	0	7
North Carolina, Western District	0	0	0	0	0	0	0	0	2	0	10
North Dakota	0	0	0	0	0	0	0	0	0	0	0
Northern Mariana Islands[1]	0	0	0	0	0	0	0	0	0	0	0
Ohio, Northern District	0	0	1	0	4	1	0	0	1	0	20
Ohio, Southern District	2	0	0	0	2	0	0	0	1	0	17
Oklahoma, Eastern District	0	0	0	0	0	0	0	0	0	0	4
Oklahoma, Northern District	0	0	0	0	0	0	0	0	0	0	10

Table 39. Number of Arrestees by NIBRS Offense Code, by Selected ATF Judicial District, 2019—*Continued*

(Number.)

NIBRS Offense Code	09A - 09C	11A - 11D	13A - 13C	23A - 23H	26A - 26G	35A - 35B	36A - 36B	39A - 39 D	64A - 64B	100	120
NIBRS Offense Description	Homicide offenses	Sex offenses	Assault offenses	Larceny/ theft offenses	Fraud offenses	Drug/ narcotic offenses	Sex offenses, nonforcible	Gambling offenses	Human trafficking	Kidnapping/ abduction	Robbery
	# Arrested	# Arrested	# Arrested	# Arrested	# Arrested	# Arrested	# Arrested	# Arrested	# Arrested	# Arrested	# Arrested
Oklahoma, Western District	0	0	0	0	2	15	0	0	0	1	1
Oregon	1	1	2	0	4	33	0	0	0	0	0
Pennsylvania, Eastern District	0	0	1	0	5	16	0	0	0	0	0
Pennsylvania, Middle District	0	0	0	0	0	10	0	0	0	0	0
Pennsylvania, Western District	0	0	0	0	3	24	0	0	0	0	0
Puerto Rico	0	0	0	0	2	34	0	0	0	0	2
Rhode Island	0	0	1	0	2	3	0	0	0	0	1
South Carolina	0	0	0	4	3	27	0	0	0	0	0
South Dakota	0	2	4	4	3	53	0	0	0	1	0
Tennessee, Eastern District	0	0	0	0	1	189	0	0	0	0	0
Tennessee, Middle District	1	0	1	0	1	8	0	0	0	0	3
Tennessee, Western District	0	0	0	0	9	9	0	0	0	0	0
Texas, Eastern District	0	3	1	0	1	81	0	0	0	0	0
Texas, Northern District	0	1	5	0	7	94	0	0	4	0	1
Texas, Southern District	1	0	2	3	12	110	0	0	0	0	5
Texas, Western District	1	1	3	2	9	103	0	0	0	0	3
U.S. Virgin Islands[1]	0	0	0	0	0	0	1	0	0	0	0
Utah	0	0	1	0	0	41	0	0	0	0	0
Vermont	0	0	0	0	4	23	0	0	0	0	1
Virginia, Eastern District	0	0	1	1	2	21	1	0	0	0	3
Virginia, Western District	1	1	1	0	17	74	0	0	0	0	0
Washington, Eastern District	2	0	2	2	3	20	0	0	0	0	0
Washington, Western District	0	0	0	0	0	11	0	0	0	0	0
West Virginia, Northern District	0	0	0	1	5	98	0	0	0	0	0
West Virginia, Southern District	0	0	1	0	3	78	0	0	0	0	0
Wisconsin, Eastern District	0	0	0	1	4	12	0	0	0	0	1
Wisconsin, Western District	0	0	0	0	0	3	0	0	0	0	0
Wyoming	0	0	0	0	0	24	0	0	2	0	0

Table 39. Number of Arrestees by NIBRS Offense Code, by Selected ATF Judicial District, 2019—*Continued*

(Number.)

NIBRS Offense Code	200	210	220	240	250	270	280	290	370	510	520
NIBRS Offense Description	Arson	Extortion/ blackmail	Burglary/ breaking & entering	Motor vehicle theft	Counterfeiting/ forgery	Embezzlement	Stolen property offenses	Destruction/ damage/ vandalism of property	Pornography/ obscene material	Bribery	Weapon law violations
	# Arrested	# Arrested	# Arrested	# Arrested	# Arrested	# Arrested	# Arrested	# Arrested	# Arrested	# Arrested	# Arrested
Oklahoma, Western District	0	0	0	0	0	0	0	0	0	0	21
Oregon..	1	0	0	0	0	0	0	2	0	0	7
Pennsylvania, Eastern District	0	0	0	0	0	0	0	0	0	0	2
Pennsylvania, Middle District	0	0	0	0	0	0	0	0	0	0	1
Pennsylvania, Western District...............................	0	0	0	0	0	0	0	0	0	0	6
Puerto Rico	0	0	0	0	0	0	0	0	0	0	8
Rhode Island..	1	0	0	0	0	0	0	0	0	0	2
South Carolina..	0	0	0	0	0	0	0	0	1	0	4
South Dakota..	0	0	1	0	0	0	0	0	4	0	13
Tennessee, Eastern District....................................	0	0	0	0	0	0	0	0	1	0	28
Tennessee, Middle District.....................................	0	0	0	0	0	0	0	0	1	0	69
Tennessee, Western District	0	1	0	0	0	0	0	0	0	0	33
Texas, Eastern District	0	0	0	0	0	0	0	0	0	0	11
Texas, Northern District...	0	0	0	0	3	0	1	0	0	0	34
Texas, Southern District...	0	0	0	0	0	0	0	0	1	0	23
Texas, Western District..	0	0	0	0	2	1	2	0	4	0	71
U.S. Virgin Islands[1]	0	0	0	0	0	0	0	0	0	0	0
Utah	0	0	0	0	0	0	0	0	0	0	8
Vermont...	0	0	0	0	0	0	0	0	0	0	8
Virginia, Eastern District	0	0	0	0	0	0	0	0	2	0	5
Virginia, Western District.......................................	0	0	0	0	0	0	0	0	0	0	20
Washington, Eastern District	0	1	0	0	0	0	0	0	0	0	8
Washington, Western District.................................	0	0	0	0	0	0	0	0	0	0	2
West Virginia, Northern District.............................	0	0	0	0	0	0	0	0	3	0	11
West Virginia, Southern District.............................	0	0	0	0	0	0	0	0	2	0	23
Wisconsin, Eastern District	1	0	0	0	0	0	0	0	0	0	7
Wisconsin, Western District....................................	0	0	0	0	0	0	0	0	0	0	5
Wyoming..	0	0	0	0	0	0	0	0	0	0	2

[1]The population figures for Guam, Northern Mariana Island, and U.S. Virgin Islands were gathered from the 2010 U.S. Census.

Table 39. Number of Arrestees by NIBRS Offense Code, by Selected ATF Judicial District, 2019—*Continued*

(Number.)

NIBRS Offense Code / NIBRS Offense Description	Count of arrestees for Group A Offenses	90C Disorderly conduct # Arrested	90D Driving under the influence # Arrested	90F Family offenses, nonviolent # Arrested	90H Peeping tom # Arrested	90J Trespass of real property # Arrested	90Z All other offenses # Arrested	Count of arrestees for Group B Offenses	Total number of arrestees	Population per Judicial District
Grand Total, All Judicial Districts	5,854	1	4	1	1	1	32,392	32,400	38,254	331,754,322
Alabama, Middle District	74	0	0	0	0	0	100	100	174	1,155,815
Alabama, Northern District	87	0	0	0	0	0	237	237	324	2,896,978
Alabama, Southern District	22	0	0	0	0	0	283	283	305	850,392
Alaska	4	0	0	0	0	0	122	122	126	731,545
Arizona	77	0	0	0	0	0	2,064	2,064	2,141	7,278,717
Arkansas, Eastern District	10	0	0	0	0	0	176	176	186	1,637,576
Arkansas, Western District	13	0	0	0	0	0	42	42	55	1,380,228
California, Central District	41	0	0	0	0	0	530	530	571	19,445,734
California, Eastern District	60	0	0	0	0	0	261	261	321	8,139,046
California, Northern District	27	0	0	0	0	0	335	335	362	8,400,053
California, Southern District	137	0	0	1	0	0	1,264	1,265	1,402	3,527,390
Colorado	51	0	0	0	0	0	213	213	264	5,758,736
Connecticut	68	0	0	0	0	0	113	113	181	3,565,287
Delaware	7	0	0	0	0	0	20	20	27	973,764
District of Columbia	277	1	0	0	1	1	3,257	3,260	3,537	705,749
Florida, Middle District	29	0	0	0	0	0	521	521	550	12,488,308
Florida, Northern District	15	0	1	0	0	0	135	136	151	1,887,311
Florida, Southern District	101	0	0	0	0	0	561	561	662	7,102,118
Georgia, Middle District	104	0	0	0	0	0	96	96	200	2,025,219
Georgia, Northern District	67	0	0	0	0	0	221	221	288	6,989,789
Georgia, Southern District	24	0	0	0	0	0	157	157	181	1,602,415
Guam[1]	5	0	0	0	0	0	35	35	40	159,358
Hawaii	79	0	0	0	0	0	126	126	205	1,415,872
Idaho	29	0	0	0	0	0	167	167	196	1,787,065
Illinois, Central District	25	0	0	0	0	0	222	222	247	2,177,477
Illinois, Northern District	32	0	0	0	0	0	164	164	196	9,255,097
Illinois, Southern District	29	0	0	0	0	0	199	199	228	1,239,247
Indiana, Northern District	5	0	0	0	0	0	143	143	148	2,610,821
Indiana, Southern District	20	0	0	0	0	0	175	175	195	4,121,398
Iowa, Northern District	175	0	0	0	0	0	207	207	382	1,317,377
Iowa, Southern District	43	0	0	0	0	0	321	321	364	1,837,693
Kansas	64	0	0	0	0	0	369	369	433	2,913,314
Kentucky, Eastern District	26	0	0	0	0	0	258	258	284	2,213,795
Kentucky, Western District	33	0	0	0	0	0	117	117	150	2,253,878
Louisiana, Eastern District	11	0	0	0	0	0	124	124	135	1,684,031
Louisiana, Middle District	35	0	0	0	0	0	59	59	94	830,107
Louisiana, Western District	9	0	0	0	0	0	79	79	88	2,134,656
Maine	11	0	0	0	0	0	99	99	110	1,344,212
Maryland	12	0	0	0	0	0	368	368	380	6,045,680
Massachusetts	7	0	0	0	0	0	259	259	266	6,892,503
Michigan, Eastern District	31	0	0	0	0	0	225	225	256	6,452,970
Michigan, Western District	12	0	0	0	0	0	148	148	160	3,533,887
Minnesota	22	0	0	0	0	0	238	238	260	5,639,632
Mississippi, Northern District	84	0	0	0	0	0	139	139	223	1,107,636
Mississippi, Southern District	48	0	0	0	0	0	155	155	203	1,868,513
Missouri, Eastern District	672	0	0	0	0	0	536	536	1,208	2,926,389
Missouri, Western District	123	0	0	0	0	0	388	388	511	3,211,039
Montana	28	0	0	0	0	0	401	401	429	1,068,778
Nebraska	75	0	0	0	0	0	396	396	471	1,934,408
Nevada	18	0	0	0	0	0	303	303	321	3,080,156
New Hampshire	77	0	0	0	0	0	94	94	171	1,359,711
New Jersey	107	0	0	0	0	0	206	206	313	8,882,190
New Mexico	77	0	0	0	0	0	801	801	878	2,096,829
New York, Eastern District	90	0	0	0	0	0	202	202	292	11,203,328
New York, Northern District	16	0	0	0	0	0	170	170	186	3,352,502
New York, Southern District	83	0	0	0	0	0	338	338	421	2,135,650
New York, Western District	7	0	0	0	0	0	244	244	251	2,762,081
North Carolina, Eastern District	74	0	0	0	0	0	311	311	385	4,129,850
North Carolina, Middle District	24	0	0	0	0	0	290	290	314	3,034,317
North Carolina, Western District	38	0	0	0	0	0	384	384	422	3,323,917
North Dakota	20	0	0	0	0	0	275	275	295	762,062
Northern Mariana Islands[1]	0	0	0	0	0	0	2	2	2	53,883
Ohio, Northern District	145	0	0	0	0	0	314	314	459	5,695,197
Ohio, Southern District	123	0	0	0	0	0	257	257	380	5,993,903
Oklahoma, Eastern District	10	0	0	0	0	0	45	45	55	724,312
Oklahoma, Northern District	30	0	0	0	0	0	145	145	175	1,092,593

(Number.)

NIBRS Offense Code / NIBRS Offense Description	Count of arrestees for Group A Offenses	90C Disorderly conduct # Arrested	90D Driving under the influence # Arrested	90F Family offenses, nonviolent # Arrested	90H Peeping tom # Arrested	90J Trespass of real property # Arrested	90Z All other offenses # Arrested	Count of arrestees for Group B Offenses	Total number of arrestees	Population per Judicial District
Oklahoma, Western District	40	0	0	0	0	0	168	168	208	2,140,066
Oregon	51	0	0	0	0	0	498	498	549	4,217,737
Pennsylvania, Eastern District	24	0	0	0	0	0	202	202	226	5,777,910
Pennsylvania, Middle District	11	0	0	0	0	0	146	146	157	3,334,226
Pennsylvania, Western District	33	0	0	0	0	0	230	230	263	3,689,853
Puerto Rico	46	0	0	0	0	0	422	422	468	3,195,153
Rhode Island	10	0	0	0	0	0	39	39	49	1,059,361
South Carolina	39	0	0	0	0	0	517	517	556	5,148,714
South Dakota	85	0	0	0	0	0	610	610	695	884,659
Tennessee, Eastern District	219	0	0	0	0	0	500	500	719	2,653,711
Tennessee, Middle District	84	0	0	0	0	0	137	137	221	2,606,370
Tennessee, Western District	52	0	0	0	0	0	309	309	361	1,569,093
Texas, Eastern District	97	0	0	0	0	0	243	243	340	4,043,987
Texas, Northern District	150	0	0	0	0	0	535	535	685	7,547,162
Texas, Southern District	157	0	0	0	0	0	2,006	2,006	2,163	9,965,548
Texas, Western District	202	0	3	0	0	0	2,327	2,330	2,532	7,439,184
U.S. Virgin Islands[1]	1	0	0	0	0	0	16	16	17	106,405
Utah	50	0	0	0	0	0	370	370	420	3,205,958
Vermont	36	0	0	0	0	0	96	96	132	623,989
Virginia, Eastern District	36	0	0	0	0	0	291	291	327	6,223,634
Virginia, Western District	114	0	0	0	0	0	183	183	297	2,311,885
Washington, Eastern District	38	0	0	0	0	0	249	249	287	1,638,935
Washington, Western District	13	0	0	0	0	0	288	288	301	5,975,958
West Virginia, Northern District	118	0	0	0	0	0	277	277	395	864,566
West Virginia, Southern District	107	0	0	0	0	0	171	171	278	927,581
Wisconsin, Eastern District	26	0	0	0	0	0	169	169	195	3,413,224
Wisconsin, Western District	8	0	0	0	0	0	62	62	70	2,409,210
Wyoming	28	0	0	0	0	0	125	125	153	578,759

[1] The population figures for Guam, Northern Mariana Island, and U.S. Virgin Islands were gathered from the 2010 U.S. Census.

Table 40. Number of Arrestees from Federally Issued Warrants by NIBRS Offense Code, by Selected U.S. Marshals Service Judicial District, 2019

(Number.)

NIBRS Offense Code / Description	09A-09C Homicide offenses # Arrested	11A-11D Sex offenses # Arrested	13A-13C Assault offenses # Arrested	23A-23H Larceny/theft offenses # Arrested	26A-26G Fraud offenses # Arrested	35A-35B Drug/narcotic offenses # Arrested	36A-36B Sex offenses, nonforcible # Arrested	39A-39D Gambling offenses # Arrested	64A-64B Human trafficking # Arrested	100 Kidnapping/abduction # Arrested	120 Robbery # Arrested	200 Arson # Arrested	210 Extortion/blackmail # Arrested	220 Burglary/breaking & entering # Arrested	240 Motor vehicle theft # Arrested	250 Counterfeiting/forgery # Arrested
Grand Total, All Judicial Districts....	90	36	127	47	352	3,118	44	12	29	10	102	7	18	16	1	28
Alabama, Middle District	0	0	0	1	2	10	0	0	0	0	2	1	0	0	0	0
Alabama, Northern District	0	0	0	1	1	12	3	0	0	0	1	0	0	0	0	0
Alabama, Southern District	0	0	0	0	0	9	0	0	0	0	0	0	0	0	0	0
Alaska	0	0	0	0	1	2	0	0	0	0	0	0	0	0	0	0
Arizona	0	1	3	1	11	52	4	0	0	1	0	0	0	0	0	0
Arkansas, Eastern District	0	0	0	0	0	7	0	0	0	0	0	0	0	0	0	0
Arkansas, Western District	0	0	0	0	1	10	0	0	0	0	0	0	0	0	0	0
California, Central District	2	2	2	0	4	26	1	0	0	1	2	0	0	0	0	0
California, Eastern District	1	0	0	0	6	47	0	0	0	0	0	0	0	0	0	0
California, Northern District	0	1	0	0	8	8	3	0	0	0	0	0	0	0	0	1
California, Southern District	0	2	1	1	2	113	1	0	1	1	1	0	0	0	0	0
Colorado	0	0	0	1	2	41	0	0	0	0	1	0	0	0	0	0
Connecticut	1	0	2	0	1	62	0	0	0	0	0	0	0	0	0	0
Delaware	0	0	0	0	2	3	0	0	0	0	0	0	0	0	0	0
District of Columbia	62	11	60	3	16	22	7	0	4	3	21	0	7	12	1	0
Florida, Middle District	1	0	1	1	1	21	0	0	0	0	1	0	0	0	0	0
Florida, Northern District	0	0	2	0	0	9	0	0	1	0	0	0	0	0	0	1
Florida, Southern District	2	0	0	3	17	66	0	0	0	0	3	0	0	0	0	0
Georgia, Middle District	0	0	1	0	3	66	1	0	1	0	0	0	0	0	0	2
Georgia, Northern District	1	0	3	0	2	47	0	0	0	0	1	0	0	0	0	0
Georgia, Southern District	0	0	0	0	0	17	0	0	0	0	0	0	0	0	0	0
Guam[1]	0	0	0	0	0	2	0	0	0	0	0	0	0	0	0	0
Hawaii	0	0	4	0	7	35	1	12	1	0	2	1	0	0	0	0
Idaho	0	0	1	0	2	12	4	0	0	0	1	0	0	0	0	0
Illinois, Central District	0	1	0	0	0	18	1	0	0	0	0	0	0	0	0	0
Illinois, Northern District	0	0	0	0	5	18	0	0	0	0	0	0	0	1	0	0
Illinois, Southern District	0	0	0	0	0	17	0	0	0	0	2	0	0	0	0	0
Indiana, Northern District	0	0	0	0	0	3	0	0	0	0	0	0	0	0	0	0
Indiana, Southern District	0	1	0	0	2	6	0	0	1	0	0	0	0	0	0	1
Iowa, Northern District	0	1	0	0	1	73	3	0	4	1	1	0	4	0	0	0
Iowa, Southern District	0	0	0	0	1	18	1	0	0	0	0	0	0	0	0	4
Kansas	1	0	1	1	0	36	1	0	0	0	2	0	0	0	0	0
Kentucky, Eastern District	0	0	0	0	0	18	0	0	0	0	1	0	0	0	0	0
Kentucky, Western District	0	0	0	0	1	14	0	0	1	0	0	0	0	0	0	0
Louisiana, Eastern District	1	0	0	1	0	6	0	0	0	0	1	0	0	0	0	0

Table 40. Number of Arrestees from Federally Issued Warrants by NIBRS Offense Code, by Selected U.S. Marshals Service Judicial District, 2019—*Continued*

(Number.)

NIBRS Offense Code	270	280	290	370	510	520		90C	90D	90F	90H	90J	90Z			
NIBRS Offense Description	Embezz-lement	Stolen property offenses	Destruction/ damage/ vandalism of property	Porno-graphy/ obscene material	Bribery	Weapon law violations	Count of arrestees for Group A Offenses	Disorderly conduct	Driving under the influence	Family offenses, nonviolent	Peeping tom	Trespass of real property	All other offenses	Count of arrestees for Group B Offenses	Total number of arrestees	Population per Judicial District
	# Arrested	# Arrested	# Arrested	# Arrested	# Arrested	# Arrested		# Arrested	# Arrested	# Arrested	# Arrested	# Arrested	# Arrested			
Grand Total, All Judicial Districts....	5	14	3	97	2	1,696	5,854	1	4	1	1	1	32,392	32,400	38,254	331,754,322
Alabama, Middle District..................	0	0	0	4	0	54	74	0	0	0	0	0	100	100	174	1,155,815
Alabama, Northern District..................	0	0	0	0	0	69	87	0	0	0	0	0	237	237	324	2,896,978
Alabama, Southern District..................	0	0	0	0	0	13	22	0	0	0	0	0	283	283	305	850,392
Alaska..................	0	0	0	0	0	1	4	0	0	0	0	0	122	122	126	731,545
Arizona..................	0	0	0	1	0	3	77	0	0	0	0	0	2,064	2,064	2,141	7,278,717
Arkansas, Eastern District..................	0	0	0	0	0	3	10	0	0	0	0	0	176	176	186	1,637,576
Arkansas, Western District..................	0	0	0	1	0	1	13	0	0	0	0	0	42	42	55	1,380,228
California, Central District..................	0	0	0	1	0	0	41	0	0	0	0	0	530	530	571	19,445,734
California, Eastern District..................	0	1	0	0	0	5	60	0	0	0	0	0	261	261	321	8,139,046
California, Northern District..................	0	0	0	1	0	5	27	0	0	0	0	0	335	335	362	8,400,053
California, Southern District..................	1	0	0	7	0	6	137	0	0	1	0	0	1,264	1,265	1,402	3,527,390
Colorado..............	0	0	0	1	0	5	51	0	0	0	0	0	213	213	264	5,758,736
Connecticut...........	0	0	0	0	0	2	68	0	0	0	0	0	113	113	181	3,565,287
Delaware..............	0	0	0	0	0	2	7	0	0	0	0	0	20	20	27	973,764
District of Columbia	0	2	1	8	2	35	277	1	0	0	1	1	3,257	3,260	3,537	705,749
Florida, Middle District..................	0	0	0	0	0	3	29	0	0	0	0	0	521	521	550	12,488,308
Florida, Northern District..................	0	0	0	0	0	2	15	0	1	0	0	0	135	136	151	1,887,311
Florida, Southern District..................	0	0	0	1	0	9	101	0	0	0	0	0	561	561	662	7,102,118
Georgia, Middle District..................	0	0	0	0	0	30	104	0	0	0	0	0	96	96	200	2,025,219
Georgia, Northern District..................	0	0	0	0	0	13	67	0	0	0	0	0	221	221	288	6,989,789
Georgia, Southern District..................	0	0	0	1	0	6	24	0	0	0	0	0	157	157	181	1,602,415
Guam 1..................	0	0	0	0	0	3	5	0	0	0	0	0	35	35	40	159,358
Hawaii..................	1	0	0	1	0	14	79	0	0	0	0	0	126	126	205	1,415,872
Idaho..................	0	0	0	1	0	8	29	0	0	0	0	0	167	167	196	1,787,065
Illinois, Central District..................	0	0	0	1	0	4	25	0	0	0	0	0	222	222	247	2,177,477
Illinois, Northern District..................	0	0	0	0	0	8	32	0	0	0	0	0	164	164	196	9,255,097
Illinois, Southern District..................	0	0	0	1	0	9	29	0	0	0	0	0	199	199	228	1,239,247
Indiana, Northern District..................	0	0	0	0	0	2	5	0	0	0	0	0	143	143	148	2,610,821
Indiana, Southern District..................	0	0	0	1	0	8	20	0	0	0	0	0	175	175	195	4,121,398
Iowa, Northern District..................	0	0	0	7	0	80	175	0	0	0	0	0	207	207	382	1,317,377
Iowa, Southern District..................	0	0	0	11	0	8	43	0	0	0	0	0	321	321	364	1,837,693
Kansas..................	0	0	0	3	0	19	64	0	0	0	0	0	369	369	433	2,913,314
Kentucky, Eastern District..................	0	0	0	0	0	7	26	0	0	0	0	0	258	258	284	2,213,795
Kentucky, Western District..................	0	0	0	0	0	17	33	0	0	0	0	0	117	117	150	2,253,878
Louisiana, Eastern District..................	0	0	0	0	0	2	11	0	0	0	0	0	124	124	135	1,684,031

Table 40. Number of Arrestees from Federally Issued Warrants by NIBRS Offense Code, by Selected U.S. Marshals Service Judicial District, 2019—*Continued*

(Number.)

NIBRS Offense Code / NIBRS Offense Description	09A - 09C Homicide offenses # Arrested	11A - 11D Sex offenses # Arrested	13A - 13C Assault offenses # Arrested	23A - 23H Larceny/ theft offenses # Arrested	26A - 26G Fraud offenses # Arrested	35A - 35B Drug/ narcotic offenses # Arrested	36A - 36B Sex offenses, nonforcible # Arrested	39A - 39 D Gambling offenses # Arrested	64A - 64B Human trafficking # Arrested	100 Kidnapping/ abduction # Arrested	120 Robbery # Arrested	200 Arson # Arrested	210 Extortion/ blackmail # Arrested	220 Burglary/ breaking & entering # Arrested	240 Motor vehicle theft # Arrested	250 Counter- feiting/ forgery # Arrested
Louisiana, Middle District	0	0	0	0	5	8	0	0	0	0	0	0	0	0	0	0
Louisiana, Western District	1	0	0	0	0	4	0	0	0	0	0	0	0	0	0	0
Maine	0	0	0	0	0	6	0	0	0	0	3	0	0	0	0	1
Maryland	0	0	0	0	1	10	0	0	0	0	0	0	0	0	0	0
Massachusetts	0	0	0	0	1	6	0	0	0	0	0	0	0	0	0	0
Michigan, Eastern District	0	1	1	0	4	13	0	0	0	0	2	0	2	1	0	0
Michigan, Western District	0	0	0	0	0	11	0	0	0	0	0	0	0	0	0	0
Minnesota	0	0	0	0	0	14	0	0	1	0	1	0	0	0	0	0
Mississippi, Northern District	0	0	0	0	0	43	2	0	0	0	0	0	0	0	0	3
Mississippi, Southern District	0	0	0	2	1	20	0	0	0	0	1	0	0	0	0	0
Missouri, Eastern District	0	0	0	4	32	166	1	0	0	0	14	0	0	0	0	3
Missouri, Western District	0	0	0	2	5	57	1	0	0	0	0	0	0	0	0	0
Montana	1	0	1	0	2	16	0	0	0	0	0	0	0	0	0	0
Nebraska	0	0	0	1	7	36	1	0	0	0	2	0	0	0	0	0
Nevada	0	0	1	1	1	9	0	0	1	0	1	0	0	0	0	0
New Hampshire	0	0	0	0	1	67	0	0	1	0	0	0	0	0	0	0
New Jersey	1	0	1	1	11	57	0	0	0	0	0	0	0	0	0	0
New Mexico	1	0	3	0	3	54	3	0	0	0	0	0	0	0	0	0
New York, Eastern District	2	3	1	0	31	34	2	0	1	1	1	0	1	0	0	1
New York, Northern District	0	0	2	0	4	5	0	0	3	0	0	0	0	0	0	0
New York, Southern District	3	0	2	0	15	42	0	0	0	0	3	0	2	0	0	0
New York, Western District	0	0	0	0	0	7	0	0	0	0	0	0	0	0	0	0
North Carolina, Eastern District	0	1	2	1	5	32	0	0	0	0	1	0	0	0	0	0
North Carolina, Middle District	2	0	0	0	1	13	0	0	0	0	1	0	0	0	0	0
North Carolina, Western District	0	1	1	0	3	20	0	0	1	0	0	0	0	0	0	0
North Dakota	0	0	0	0	2	18	0	0	0	0	0	0	0	0	0	0
Northern Mariana Islands[1]	0	0	0	0	0	0	0	0	0	0	0	0	0	0	0	0
Ohio, Northern District	0	0	2	0	1	114	1	0	0	0	0	0	0	1	0	4
Ohio, Southern District	0	0	0	3	14	76	0	0	0	0	8	2	0	0	0	2
Oklahoma, Eastern District	0	0	3	0	0	3	0	0	0	0	0	0	0	0	0	0
Oklahoma, Northern District	0	1	0	0	1	17	0	0	1	0	0	0	0	0	0	0
Oklahoma, Western District	0	0	0	0	2	15	0	0	0	1	1	0	0	0	0	0
Oregon	1	1	2	0	4	33	0	0	0	0	0	1	0	0	0	0
Pennsylvania, Eastern District	0	0	1	0	5	16	0	0	0	0	0	0	0	0	0	0
Pennsylvania, Middle District	0	0	0	0	0	10	0	0	0	0	0	0	0	0	0	0
Pennsylvania, Western District	0	0	0	0	3	24	0	0	0	0	0	0	0	0	0	0
Puerto Rico	0	0	0	0	2	34	0	0	0	0	2	0	0	0	0	0
Rhode Island	0	0	1	0	2	3	0	0	0	0	1	1	0	0	0	0
South Carolina	0	0	0	4	3	27	0	0	0	0	0	0	0	0	0	0

Table 40. Number of Arrestees from Federally Issued Warrants by NIBRS Offense Code, by Selected U.S. Marshals Service Judicial District, 2019—*Continued*

(Number.)

NIBRS Offense Code	270	280	290	370	510	520		90C	90D	90F	90H	90J	90Z			
NIBRS Offense Description	Embezzlement	Stolen property offenses	Destruction/ damage/ vandalism of property	Pornography/ obscene material	Bribery	Weapon law violations	Count of arrestees for Group A Offenses	Disorderly conduct	Driving under the influence	Family offenses, nonviolent	Peeping tom	Trespass of real property	All other offenses	Count of arrestees for Group B Offenses	Total number of arrestees	Population per Judicial District
	# Arrested	# Arrested	# Arrested	# Arrested	# Arrested	# Arrested		# Arrested	# Arrested	# Arrested	# Arrested	# Arrested	# Arrested			
Louisiana, Middle District	0	0	0	0	0	22	35	0	0	0	0	0	59	59	94	830,107
Louisiana, Western District	0	0	0	0	0	4	9	0	0	0	0	0	79	79	88	2,134,656
Maine	0	0	0	0	0	1	11	0	0	0	0	0	99	99	110	1,344,212
Maryland	0	0	0	0	0	1	12	0	0	0	0	0	368	368	380	6,045,680
Massachusetts	0	0	0	0	0	0	7	0	0	0	0	0	259	259	266	6,892,503
Michigan, Eastern District	0	0	0	0	0	7	31	0	0	0	0	0	225	225	256	6,452,970
Michigan, Western District	0	0	0	0	0	1	12	0	0	0	0	0	148	148	160	3,533,887
Minnesota	0	0	0	2	0	4	22	0	0	0	0	0	238	238	260	5,639,632
Mississippi, Northern District	0	0	0	3	0	33	84	0	0	0	0	0	139	139	223	1,107,636
Mississippi, Southern District	0	0	0	0	0	24	48	0	0	0	0	0	155	155	203	1,868,513
Missouri, Eastern District	0	0	0	3	0	449	672	0	0	0	0	0	536	536	1,208	2,926,389
Missouri, Western District	0	0	0	4	0	54	123	0	0	0	0	0	388	388	511	3,211,039
Montana	0	0	0	0	0	8	28	0	0	0	0	0	401	401	429	1,068,778
Nebraska	0	0	0	9	0	19	75	0	0	0	0	0	396	396	471	1,934,408
Nevada	0	0	0	0	0	4	18	0	0	0	0	0	303	303	321	3,080,156
New Hampshire	0	2	0	1	0	5	77	0	0	0	0	0	94	94	171	1,359,711
New Jersey	0	0	0	0	0	36	107	0	0	0	0	0	206	206	313	8,882,190
New Mexico	0	0	0	0	0	13	77	0	0	0	0	0	801	801	878	2,096,829
New York, Eastern District	0	0	0	0	0	12	90	0	0	0	0	0	202	202	292	11,203,328
New York, Northern District	0	0	0	0	0	2	16	0	0	0	0	0	170	170	186	3,352,502
New York, Southern District	1	5	0	0	0	10	83	0	0	0	0	0	338	338	421	2,135,650
New York, Western District	0	0	0	0	0	0	7	0	0	0	0	0	244	244	251	2,762,081
North Carolina, Eastern District	0	1	0	0	0	31	74	0	0	0	0	0	311	311	385	4,129,850
North Carolina, Middle District	0	0	0	0	0	7	24	0	0	0	0	0	290	290	314	3,034,317
North Carolina, Western District	0	0	0	2	0	10	38	0	0	0	0	0	384	384	422	3,323,917
North Dakota	0	0	0	0	0	0	20	0	0	0	0	0	275	275	295	762,062
Northern Mariana Islands[1]	0	0	0	0	0	0	0	0	0	0	0	0	2	2	2	53,883
Ohio, Northern District	1	0	0	1	0	20	145	0	0	0	0	0	314	314	459	5,695,197
Ohio, Southern District	0	0	0	1	0	17	123	0	0	0	0	0	257	257	380	5,993,903
Oklahoma, Eastern District	0	0	0	0	0	4	10	0	0	0	0	0	45	45	55	724,312
Oklahoma, Northern District	0	0	0	0	0	10	30	0	0	0	0	0	145	145	175	1,092,593
Oklahoma, Western District	0	0	0	0	0	21	40	0	0	0	0	0	168	168	208	2,140,066
Oregon	0	0	2	0	0	7	51	0	0	0	0	0	498	498	549	4,217,737
Pennsylvania, Eastern District	0	0	0	0	0	2	24	0	0	0	0	0	202	202	226	5,777,910
Pennsylvania, Middle District	0	0	0	0	0	1	11	0	0	0	0	0	146	146	157	3,334,226
Pennsylvania, Western District	0	0	0	0	0	6	33	0	0	0	0	0	230	230	263	3,689,853
Puerto Rico	0	0	0	0	0	8	46	0	0	0	0	0	422	422	468	3,195,153
Rhode Island	0	0	0	0	0	2	10	0	0	0	0	0	39	39	49	1,059,361
South Carolina	0	0	0	1	0	4	39	0	0	0	0	0	517	517	556	5,148,714

Table 40. Number of Arrestees from Federally Issued Warrants by NIBRS Offense Code, by Selected U.S. Marshals Service Judicial District, 2019—*Continued*

(Number.)

NIBRS Offense Code NIBRS Offense Description	09A - 09C Homicide offenses # Arrested	11A - 11D Sex offenses # Arrested	13A - 13C Assault offenses # Arrested	23A - 23H Larceny/ theft offenses # Arrested	26A - 26G Fraud offenses # Arrested	35A - 35B Drug/ narcotic offenses # Arrested	36A - 36B Sex offenses, nonforcible # Arrested	39A - 39 D Gambling offenses # Arrested	64A - 64B Human trafficking # Arrested	100 Kidnapping/ abduction # Arrested	120 Robbery # Arrested	200 Arson # Arrested	210 Extortion/ blackmail # Arrested	220 Burglary/ breaking & entering # Arrested	240 Motor vehicle theft # Arrested	250 Counter- feiting/ forgery # Arrested
South Dakota	0	2	4	4	3	53	0	0	0	1	0	0	0	1	0	0
Tennessee, Eastern District	0	0	0	0	1	189	0	0	0	0	0	0	0	0	0	0
Tennessee, Middle District	1	0	1	0	1	8	0	0	0	0	3	0	0	0	0	0
Tennessee, Western District	0	0	0	0	9	9	0	0	0	0	0	0	1	0	0	0
Texas, Eastern District	0	3	1	0	1	81	0	0	0	0	0	0	0	0	0	0
Texas, Northern District	0	1	5	0	7	94	0	0	4	0	1	0	0	0	0	3
Texas, Southern District	1	0	2	3	12	110	0	0	0	0	5	0	0	0	0	0
Texas, Western District	1	1	3	2	9	103	0	0	0	0	3	0	0	0	0	2
U.S. Virgin Islands[1]	0	0	0	0	0	0	1	0	0	0	0	0	0	0	0	0
Utah	0	0	1	0	0	41	0	0	0	0	0	0	0	0	0	0
Vermont	0	0	0	0	4	23	0	0	0	0	1	0	0	0	0	0
Virginia, Eastern District	0	0	1	1	2	21	1	0	0	0	3	0	0	0	0	0
Virginia, Western District	1	1	1	0	17	74	0	0	0	0	0	0	0	0	0	0
Washington, Eastern District	2	0	2	2	3	20	0	0	0	0	0	0	1	0	0	0
Washington, Western District	0	0	0	0	0	11	0	0	0	0	0	0	0	0	0	0
West Virginia, Northern District	0	0	0	1	5	98	0	0	0	0	0	0	0	0	0	0
West Virginia, Southern District	0	0	1	0	3	78	0	0	0	0	0	0	0	0	0	0
Wisconsin, Eastern District	0	0	0	1	4	12	0	0	0	0	1	1	0	0	0	0
Wisconsin, Western District	0	0	0	0	0	3	0	0	0	0	0	0	0	0	0	0
Wyoming	0	0	0	0	0	24	0	0	2	0	0	0	0	0	0	0

Table 40. Number of Arrestees from Federally Issued Warrants by NIBRS Offense Code, by Selected U.S. Marshals Service Judicial District, 2019—*Continued*

(Number.)

NIBRS Offense Code	270	280	290	370	510	520		90C	90D	90F	90H	90J	90Z			
NIBRS Offense Description	Embezzlement	Stolen property offenses	Destruction/ damage/ vandalism of property	Pornography/ obscene material	Bribery	Weapon law violations	Count of arrestees for Group A Offenses	Disorderly conduct	Driving under the influence	Family offenses, nonviolent	Peeping tom	Trespass of real property	All other offenses	Count of arrestees for Group B Offenses	Total number of arrestees	Population per Judicial District
	# Arrested	# Arrested	# Arrested	# Arrested	# Arrested	# Arrested		# Arrested	# Arrested	# Arrested	# Arrested	# Arrested	# Arrested			
South Dakota..........	0	0	0	4	0	13	85	0	0	0	0	0	610	610	695	884,659
Tennessee, Eastern District....................	0	0	0	1	0	28	219	0	0	0	0	0	500	500	719	2,653,711
Tennessee, Middle District....................	0	0	0	1	0	69	84	0	0	0	0	0	137	137	221	2,606,370
Tennessee, Western District....................	0	0	0	0	0	33	52	0	0	0	0	0	309	309	361	1,569,093
Texas, Eastern District....................	0	0	0	0	0	11	97	0	0	0	0	0	243	243	340	4,043,987
Texas, Northern District....................	0	1	0	0	0	34	150	0	0	0	0	0	535	535	685	7,547,162
Texas, Southern District....................	0	0	0	1	0	23	157	0	0	0	0	0	2,006	2,006	2,163	9,965,548
Texas, Western District....................	1	2	0	4	0	71	202	0	3	0	0	0	2,327	2,330	2,532	7,439,184
U.S. Virgin Islands[1]	0	0	0	0	0	0	1	0	0	0	0	0	16	16	17	106,405
Utah	0	0	0	0	0	8	50	0	0	0	0	0	370	370	420	3,205,958
Vermont	0	0	0	0	0	8	36	0	0	0	0	0	96	96	132	623,989
Virginia, Eastern District....................	0	0	0	2	0	5	36	0	0	0	0	0	291	291	327	6,223,634
Virginia, Western District....................	0	0	0	0	0	20	114	0	0	0	0	0	183	183	297	2,311,885
Washington, Eastern District..............	0	0	0	0	0	8	38	0	0	0	0	0	249	249	287	1,638,935
Washington, Western District..............	0	0	0	0	0	2	13	0	0	0	0	0	288	288	301	5,975,958
West Virginia, Northern District	0	0	0	3	0	11	118	0	0	0	0	0	277	277	395	864,566
West Virginia, Southern District.....	0	0	0	2	0	23	107	0	0	0	0	0	171	171	278	927,581
Wisconsin, Eastern District....................	0	0	0	0	0	7	26	0	0	0	0	0	169	169	195	3,413,224
Wisconsin, Western District....................	0	0	0	0	0	5	8	0	0	0	0	0	62	62	70	2,409,210
Wyoming................	0	0	0	0	0	2	28	0	0	0	0	0	125	125	153	578,759

[1]Population for Guam, Northern Mariana Island, and U.S. Virgin Islands was gathered from the 2010 U.S. Census.

Table 41. Number of Arrestees from State-Issued Warrants by NIBRS Offense Code, by Selected U.S. Marshals Service Judicial District, 2019

(Number.)

NIBRS Offense Code / NIBRS Offense Description	09A-09C Homicide offenses	11A-11D Sex offenses	13A-13C Assault offenses	23A-23H Larceny/theft offenses	26A-26G Fraud offenses	35A-35B Drug/narcotic offenses	36A-36B Sex offenses, nonforcible	39A-39D Gambling offenses	40A-40C Prostitution offenses	64A-64B Human trafficking	100 Kidnapping/abduction	120 Robbery	200 Arson
	# Arrested	# Arrested	# Arrested	# Arrested	# Arrested	# Arrested	# Arrested	# Arrested	# Arrested	# Arrested	# Arrested	# Arrested	# Arrested
Grand Total All Judicial Districts ...	4,883	5,109	14,391	1,163	695	13,060	983	9	49	217	1,218	5,990	244
Alabama, Middle District	69	86	186	0	0	107	1	0	0	1	18	185	2
Alabama, Northern District	73	81	135	8	2	93	12	0	0	1	13	85	5
Alabama, Southern District	36	41	35	2	4	103	12	0	0	0	6	37	0
Alaska	1	7	12	8	3	1	1	0	0	1	0	2	0
Arizona	70	46	160	7	13	124	15	0	0	30	23	104	3
Arkansas, Eastern District	48	26	55	20	0	15	4	0	0	1	3	30	1
Arkansas, Western District	5	6	15	0	0	7	0	0	0	0	0	9	0
California, Central District	273	131	247	25	18	97	22	0	2	5	36	144	6
California, Eastern District	75	35	88	2	5	31	4	0	2	1	16	52	1
California, Northern District	54	17	35	6	9	30	3	2	0	0	5	32	0
California, Southern District	52	104	269	28	50	205	18	0	3	0	16	127	2
Colorado	46	52	136	7	6	70	2	0	2	0	18	39	1
Connecticut	20	52	66	0	2	22	0	0	0	0	3	19	0
Delaware	14	12	49	2	4	27	2	0	0	0	1	36	2
District of Columbia	2	1	2	7	0	3	0	0	0	0	2	1	0
Florida, Middle District	140	145	377	9	15	215	19	0	0	2	37	132	5
Florida, Northern District	46	60	188	49	15	196	6	0	0	0	24	55	2
Florida, Southern District	162	87	293	9	17	134	29	0	1	1	33	227	1
Georgia, Middle District	46	45	298	11	5	291	6	2	0	0	26	69	6
Georgia, Northern District	128	132	445	2	1	102	16	0	0	18	42	162	1
Georgia, Southern District	52	38	234	18	0	46	3	0	0	0	20	36	0
Guam[1]	1	0	0	1	0	0	0	0	0	0	0	0	0
Hawaii	2	7	6	2	0	5	0	0	1	0	2	14	0
Idaho	1	73	77	0	1	17	7	0	0	2	2	9	3
Illinois, Central District	53	30	149	3	5	332	7	0	0	1	3	38	2
Illinois, Northern District	143	388	318	28	16	96	16	0	0	3	10	147	9
Illinois, Southern District	17	12	49	4	3	60	1	0	0	0	2	14	0
Indiana, Northern District	32	29	46	6	3	71	11	0	0	0	6	34	1
Indiana, Southern District	43	65	64	1	7	185	1	0	1	1	7	78	3
Iowa, Northern District	8	8	18	0	1	24	1	0	0	0	1	2	1
Iowa, Southern District	1	7	16	4	1	20	1	0	0	1	2	4	0
Kansas	27	35	141	3	1	286	3	3	1	3	7	38	2
Kentucky, Eastern District	12	8	14	0	1	79	2	0	0	0	2	9	0
Kentucky, Western District	15	4	27	0	1	19	1	0	0	2	6	17	0
Louisiana, Eastern District	104	58	169	6	2	33	16	0	0	1	12	95	1
Louisiana, Middle District	25	15	49	3	3	10	1	0	0	0	3	23	1
Louisiana, Western District	173	48	117	16	4	112	23	0	0	2	13	62	4
Maine	0	5	16	0	0	14	1	0	0	0	2	5	0
Maryland	111	52	393	9	6	119	21	0	4	1	8	134	6
Massachusetts	58	96	475	21	2	264	17	0	5	0	33	117	3
Michigan, Eastern District	84	113	351	58	76	214	7	0	2	2	4	82	9
Michigan, Western District	16	95	163	9	5	179	9	0	4	0	4	21	1
Minnesota	19	25	82	2	4	29	11	0	3	0	1	30	3
Mississippi, Northern District	49	25	114	15	5	207	10	0	0	2	6	27	4
Mississippi, Southern District	95	36	163	23	10	226	13	0	1	0	20	101	4
Missouri, Eastern District	31	26	53	3	3	125	7	0	0	0	5	23	0
Missouri, Western District	20	20	44	15	5	90	9	0	0	0	7	15	1
Montana	18	21	76	29	4	214	5	0	0	0	9	16	0
Nebraska	21	40	333	70	13	287	7	0	0	2	5	65	9
Nevada	17	24	69	12	16	137	15	1	0	0	11	19	0
New Hampshire	3	7	15	15	0	51	0	0	0	0	1	2	0
New Jersey	67	72	299	6	18	209	24	0	1	0	12	114	3
New Mexico	41	32	138	9	18	192	7	0	0	3	14	27	2
New York, Eastern District	89	22	76	17	1	93	7	0	0	0	1	59	1
New York, Northern District	39	16	67	3	1	129	16	0	0	1	1	56	1
New York, Southern District	29	5	52	4	0	29	1	0	0	0	2	20	0
New York, Western District	23	17	82	5	1	108	9	0	0	0	3	56	3
North Carolina, Eastern District	77	38	123	21	11	123	15	0	0	3	30	85	4
North Carolina, Middle District	42	28	56	0	0	34	13	0	1	0	16	63	3
North Carolina, Western District	20	12	54	6	2	227	8	0	0	1	18	44	4
North Dakota	5	19	58	5	3	104	4	0	0	4	0	24	0
Northern Mariana Islands[1]	0	0	2	0	0	0	0	0	0	0	0	0	0
Ohio, Northern District	124	156	551	65	19	574	27	0	2	8	37	189	21

Table 41. Number of Arrestees from State-Issued Warrants by NIBRS Offense Code, by Selected U.S. Marshals Service Judicial District, 2019—Continued

(Number.)

NIBRS Offense Code	210	220	240	250	270	280	290	370	510	520	720	
NIBRS Offense Description	Extortion/ blackmail	Burglary/ breaking & entering	Motor vehicle theft	Counter- feiting/ forgery	Embezzle- ment	Stolen property offenses	Destruction/ damage/ vandalism of property	Pornography/ obscene material	Bribery	Weapon law violations	Animal cruelty	Count of arrestees for Group A Offenses
	# Arrested	# Arrested	# Arrested	# Arrested	# Arrested	# Arrested	# Arrested	# Arrested	# Arrested	# Arrested	# Arrested	
Grand Total All Judicial Districts ...	61	3,779	703	258	40	374	119	499	14	5,614	2	59,474
Alabama, Middle District..................	2	24	0	0	0	0	0	1	0	73	0	755
Alabama, Northern District...............	0	47	3	0	0	4	1	8	0	39	0	610
Alabama, Southern District	0	32	5	1	0	12	2	3	0	24	0	355
Alaska..................................	0	4	4	2	0	0	0	0	0	0	0	46
Arizona.................................	2	45	58	4	0	2	1	7	0	65	0	779
Arkansas, Eastern District...............	0	7	0	10	0	0	2	1	0	31	0	254
Arkansas, Western District	0	0	0	0	0	0	0	0	0	5	0	47
California, Central District	10	61	29	5	0	16	0	16	0	127	0	1,270
California, Eastern District................	5	14	10	0	0	3	0	0	0	89	0	433
California, Northern District	1	23	5	2	2	5	1	2	0	34	0	268
California, Southern District	2	45	43	9	2	10	14	7	0	76	0	1,082
Colorado...............................	0	27	12	3	0	0	2	2	1	20	0	446
Connecticut............................	0	6	0	1	0	0	0	1	0	43	0	235
Delaware	0	20	2	5	0	0	0	1	0	42	0	219
District of Columbia	0	0	3	1	0	0	0	0	0	1	0	23
Florida, Middle District	3	109	8	2	0	2	1	19	4	112	0	1,356
Florida, Northern District.................	1	42	9	1	1	2	3	9	0	61	0	770
Florida, Southern District................	0	95	6	1	0	4	0	3	0	61	0	1,164
Georgia, Middle District	0	54	16	2	0	2	2	3	0	131	0	1,015
Georgia, Northern District.................	0	40	4	2	0	0	2	3	0	150	0	1,250
Georgia, Southern District...............	0	18	3	0	0	0	0	3	0	107	0	578
Guam[1].................................	0	2	0	0	0	0	0	0	0	0	0	4
Hawaii	0	1	1	1	0	2	1	0	0	2	0	47
Idaho..................................	0	8	0	0	0	0	0	2	0	10	0	212
Illinois, Central District	0	43	2	2	0	2	0	2	0	113	0	787
Illinois, Northern District..................	0	83	3	18	0	8	2	13	0	49	0	1,350
Illinois, Southern District.................	0	18	1	1	0	2	0	2	0	101	0	287
Indiana, Northern District.................	0	32	5	1	0	0	0	2	0	17	0	296
Indiana, Southern District.................	0	42	4	1	2	6	1	1	0	64	1	578
Iowa, Northern District....................	0	6	0	0	0	0	1	0	0	9	0	80
Iowa, Southern District...................	0	5	3	1	0	0	0	0	0	11	0	77
Kansas.................................	2	15	4	1	0	9	4	8	0	119	0	712
Kentucky, Eastern District................	0	11	0	0	0	0	1	1	0	11	0	151
Kentucky, Western District	0	8	2	0	0	4	0	0	0	19	0	125
Louisiana, Eastern District.................	0	61	6	1	1	0	14	3	0	44	0	627
Louisiana, Middle District	0	43	3	0	0	1	1	3	0	10	0	194
Louisiana, Western District	0	67	1	2	0	4	3	17	0	130	0	798
Maine	0	2	0	0	0	0	0	1	0	4	0	50
Maryland...............................	0	104	20	1	1	0	2	5	0	47	0	1,044
Massachusetts	4	28	3	4	0	6	2	7	0	116	0	1,261
Michigan, Eastern District.................	1	86	9	10	10	14	4	8	2	90	0	1,236
Michigan, Western District..........	1	45	3	1	0	3	0	4	0	43	0	606
Minnesota..............................	0	11	2	0	0	2	0	4	0	36	0	264
Mississippi, Northern District	1	41	2	3	2	6	1	3	0	62	0	583
Mississippi, Southern District	1	74	20	4	2	8	1	2	0	82	0	886
Missouri, Eastern District..................	0	23	0	1	0	3	1	0	0	65	0	369
Missouri, Western District	0	19	8	1	0	10	3	2	0	37	0	306
Montana................................	0	29	7	3	1	1	0	1	0	1	0	435
Nebraska...............................	0	31	31	4	0	2	0	5	0	63	0	988
Nevada.................................	0	31	5	4	6	9	3	0	0	14	0	393
New Hampshire	0	4	0	0	0	4	0	0	0	4	0	106
New Jersey..............................	2	61	11	2	0	15	2	7	0	159	0	1,084
New Mexico.............................	5	33	68	6	2	8	2	5	0	27	0	639
New York, Eastern District................	0	30	0	3	0	1	0	0	0	43	0	443
New York, Northern District...............	0	54	0	1	0	0	0	2	0	46	1	434
New York, Southern District..............	0	16	0	0	0	1	0	0	0	24	0	183
New York, Western District...............	0	77	1	2	0	0	0	1	0	50	0	438
North Carolina, Eastern District	1	47	2	1	0	2	8	13	0	84	0	688
North Carolina, Middle District..........	0	4	0	0	0	0	0	0	0	50	0	310
North Carolina, Western District........	0	21	4	0	0	3	1	0	0	91	0	516
North Dakota............................	0	42	2	0	0	2	0	4	0	14	0	290
Northern Mariana Islands[1].................	0	0	0	0	0	0	0	0	0	0	0	2
Ohio, Northern District....................	3	235	22	16	0	16	3	12	0	177	0	2,257

Table 41. Number of Arrestees from State-Issued Warrants by NIBRS Offense Code, by Selected U.S. Marshals Service Judicial District, 2019—*Continued*

(Number.)

NIBRS Offense Code	09A - 09C	11A - 11D	13A - 13C	23A - 23H	26A - 26G	35A - 35B	36A - 36B	39A - 39D	40A - 40C	64A - 64B	100	120	200
NIBRS Offense Description	Homicide offenses	Sex offenses	Assault offenses	Larceny/ theft offenses	Fraud offenses	Drug/ narcotic offenses	Sex offenses, nonforcible	Gambling offenses	Prostitution offenses	Human trafficking	Kidnapping/ abduction	Robbery	Arson
	# Arrested	# Arrested	# Arrested	# Arrested	# Arrested	# Arrested	# Arrested	# Arrested	# Arrested	# Arrested	# Arrested	# Arrested	# Arrested
Ohio, Southern District	45	72	311	76	18	858	20	0	0	2	27	112	12
Oklahoma, Eastern District	9	18	39	0	1	22	1	0	0	0	8	10	1
Oklahoma, Northern District	23	26	69	5	4	41	8	0	1	0	5	18	2
Oklahoma, Western District	33	22	52	0	3	28	2	0	0	0	7	35	2
Oregon	22	69	59	3	0	76	17	0	1	5	9	26	1
Pennsylvania, Eastern District	84	24	170	9	15	88	4	0	0	1	9	65	4
Pennsylvania, Middle District	47	51	108	12	13	282	7	0	0	1	3	44	8
Pennsylvania, Western District	39	36	109	11	7	134	3	0	0	0	9	54	2
Puerto Rico	28	0	4	1	2	25	2	0	0	0	0	11	1
Rhode Island	7	20	53	11	10	45	0	0	0	1	3	15	1
South Carolina	402	169	535	54	26	588	43	0	0	33	147	302	6
South Dakota	4	34	122	4	1	87	0	0	0	2	8	5	2
Tennessee, Eastern District	46	15	81	2	5	285	4	0	0	0	11	30	1
Tennessee, Middle District	27	23	45	4	2	42	4	0	0	0	6	23	0
Tennessee, Western District	164	75	211	35	5	224	16	0	0	22	20	103	2
Texas, Eastern District	18	104	138	16	3	197	12	1	0	1	5	90	3
Texas, Northern District	166	565	1,049	21	33	369	141	0	3	9	35	319	19
Texas, Southern District	185	230	1,418	44	36	476	59	0	7	15	72	622	9
Texas, Western District	86	210	371	19	28	234	10	0	0	7	24	153	7
U.S. Virgin Islands[1]	1	0	2	0	0	1	0	0	0	0	0	1	0
Utah	10	65	158	9	9	132	26	0	0	7	8	58	1
Vermont	2	3	12	0	0	20	3	0	0	1	0	2	0
Virginia, Eastern District	102	84	200	14	10	138	33	0	1	0	42	112	1
Virginia, Western District	30	59	133	47	9	988	20	0	0	4	44	75	6
Washington, Eastern District	34	29	141	7	4	43	1	0	0	0	18	46	1
Washington, Western District	44	55	102	4	1	138	13	0	0	1	12	33	2
West Virginia, Northern District	8	3	5	3	0	18	1	0	0	0	1	7	0
West Virginia, Southern District	7	11	45	26	8	162	3	0	0	0	7	6	2
Wisconsin, Eastern District	34	17	48	3	1	53	0	0	0	0	0	28	1
Wisconsin, Western District	9	27	110	2	0	20	1	0	0	1	8	24	2
Wyoming	0	0	1	2	0	0	0	0	0	0	0	0	0

Table 41. Number of Arrestees from State-Issued Warrants by NIBRS Offense Code, by Selected U.S. Marshals Service Judicial District, 2019—*Continued*

(Number.)

NIBRS Offense Code	210	220	240	250	270	280	290	370	510	520	720	
NIBRS Offense Description	Extortion/ blackmail	Burglary/ breaking & entering	Motor vehicle theft	Counter-feiting/ forgery	Embezzle-ment	Stolen property offenses	Destruction/ damage/ vandalism of property	Pornography/ obscene material	Bribery	Weapon law violations	Animal cruelty	Count of arrestees for Group A Offenses
	# Arrested	# Arrested	# Arrested	# Arrested	# Arrested	# Arrested	# Arrested	# Arrested	# Arrested	# Arrested	# Arrested	
Ohio, Southern District......................	3	164	13	12	0	46	4	8	2	167	0	1,972
Oklahoma, Eastern District...............	0	6	2	0	0	0	0	2	0	42	0	161
Oklahoma, Northern District.............	1	3	5	2	1	6	0	1	0	38	0	259
Oklahoma, Western District	0	10	2	2	0	2	1	3	0	35	0	239
Oregon..	0	12	3	0	1	0	0	0	0	28	0	332
Pennsylvania, Eastern District	1	19	1	7	0	7	0	4	0	48	0	560
Pennsylvania, Middle District.............	0	55	0	3	0	1	0	1	0	45	0	681
Pennsylvania, Western District...........	0	40	4	3	0	5	0	0	0	28	0	484
Puerto Rico...	0	2	1	0	0	0	0	0	0	39	0	116
Rhode Island..	0	13	3	3	1	1	0	0	0	21	0	208
South Carolina.....................................	0	272	2	7	1	4	6	65	0	467	0	3,129
South Dakota.......................................	0	53	1	0	0	6	1	5	0	12	0	347
Tennessee, Eastern District...............	0	20	2	0	0	0	0	0	0	30	0	532
Tennessee, Middle District.................	0	12	1	0	0	0	0	2	0	8	0	199
Tennessee, Western District	0	46	9	13	0	16	4	39	0	192	0	1,196
Texas, Eastern District	0	67	4	5	0	1	0	17	3	46	0	731
Texas, Northern District.....................	0	120	8	11	0	7	1	45	0	104	0	3,025
Texas, Southern District.....................	3	207	53	14	0	3	3	25	1	155	0	3,637
Texas, Western District.......................	0	67	19	8	0	22	0	18	1	65	0	1,349
U.S. Virgin Islands[1]	0	0	0	0	0	1	0	0	0	1	0	7
Utah..	0	45	7	3	0	12	0	2	0	61	0	613
Vermont..	0	3	0	0	0	0	0	0	0	0	0	46
Virginia, Eastern District....................	2	31	14	0	1	1	1	1	0	198	0	986
Virginia, Western District...................	0	72	22	8	1	1	3	16	0	175	0	1,713
Washington, Eastern District.............	3	52	6	4	0	6	1	4	0	45	0	445
Washington, Western District...........	1	30	4	2	0	2	1	3	0	54	0	502
West Virginia, Northern District........	0	3	0	0	0	0	0	2	0	3	0	54
West Virginia, Southern District........	0	35	33	2	2	7	0	1	0	15	0	372
Wisconsin, Eastern District	0	13	5	2	0	0	1	4	0	20	0	230
Wisconsin, Western District...............	0	1	3	0	0	0	1	2	0	42	0	253
Wyoming..	0	0	1	0	0	0	0	0	0	1	0	5

1 Population for Guam, Northern Mariana Island, and U.S. Virgin Islands was gathered from the 2010 U.S. Census.

Table 41. Number of Arrestees from State-Issued Warrants by NIBRS Offense Code, by Selected U.S. Marshals Service Judicial District, 2019—*Continued*

(Number.)

NIBRS Offense Code	90B	90C	90D	90F	90G	90H	90J	90Z	Count of arrestees for Group B Offenses	Total number of arrestees	Population per Judicial District
NIBRS Offense Description	Curfew/ loitering/ vagrancy violations	Disorderly conduct	Driving under the influence	Family offenses, nonviolent	Liquor law violations	Peeping tom	Trespass of real property	All other offenses			
	# Arrested	# Arrested	# Arrested	# Arrested	# Arrested	# Arrested	# Arrested	# Arrested			
Grand Total All Judicial Districts ...	13	109	173	1,182	5	16	44	34,671	36,213	95,687	331,754,322
Alabama, Middle District..................	0	1	0	22	0	0	0	127	150	905	1,155,815
Alabama, Northern District..............	0	0	0	24	0	0	0	443	467	1,077	2,896,978
Alabama, Southern District	0	1	0	14	0	0	0	162	177	532	850,392
Alaska..	0	1	0	0	2	0	1	73	77	123	731,545
Arizona.......................................	0	1	1	5	0	0	1	736	744	1,523	7,278,717
Arkansas, Eastern District................	0	0	0	3	0	0	0	170	173	427	1,637,576
Arkansas, Western District	0	0	0	0	0	0	0	41	41	88	1,380,228
California, Central District...............	0	3	6	55	0	0	0	827	891	2,161	19,445,734
California, Eastern District...............	0	1	0	7	0	0	0	535	543	976	8,139,046
California, Northern District	0	1	0	3	0	0	0	311	315	583	8,400,053
California, Southern District	0	0	30	53	0	0	0	2,111	2,194	3,276	3,527,390
Colorado	0	0	1	3	0	1	0	695	700	1,146	5,758,736
Connecticut................................	0	0	0	2	0	0	0	190	192	427	3,565,287
Delaware....................................	0	0	0	2	0	0	0	134	136	355	973,764
District of Columbia......................	0	0	0	0	0	0	0	20	20	43	705,749
Florida, Middle District	0	0	1	33	0	2	1	244	281	1,637	12,488,308
Florida, Northern District	0	1	1	20	0	0	5	431	458	1,228	1,887,311
Florida, Southern District................	0	0	0	8	0	0	1	251	260	1,424	7,102,118
Georgia, Middle District	0	0	0	18	0	0	0	729	747	1,762	2,025,219
Georgia, Northern District	0	0	0	11	0	0	0	393	404	1,654	6,989,789
Georgia, Southern District...............	0	1	0	18	0	0	0	312	331	909	1,602,415
Guam[1].......................................	0	0	0	0	0	0	0	92	92	96	159,358
Hawaii..	0	0	0	0	0	0	0	79	79	126	1,415,872
Idaho...	0	0	0	16	0	6	0	60	82	294	1,787,065
Illinois, Central District	0	0	1	7	0	0	1	437	446	1,233	2,177,477
Illinois, Northern District................	0	2	8	2	0	0	0	723	735	2,085	9,255,097
Illinois, Southern District................	0	1	0	1	0	0	0	355	357	644	1,239,247
Indiana, Northern District................	0	0	2	13	0	0	0	106	121	417	2,610,821
Indiana, Southern District...............	0	0	1	7	0	0	2	271	281	859	4,121,398
Iowa, Northern District..................	0	0	0	0	0	0	0	98	98	178	1,317,377
Iowa, Southern District...................	0	0	0	3	0	0	0	223	226	303	1,837,693
Kansas.......................................	0	2	2	3	0	0	4	1,539	1,550	2,262	2,913,314
Kentucky, Eastern District...............	0	0	0	0	0	0	0	156	156	307	2,213,795
Kentucky, Western District..............	0	0	0	1	0	0	0	222	223	348	2,253,878
Louisiana, Eastern District...............	0	2	0	6	0	0	0	189	197	824	1,684,031
Louisiana, Middle District................	0	0	0	1	0	0	0	137	138	332	830,107
Louisiana, Western District..............	1	0	0	11	0	0	1	215	228	1,026	2,134,656
Maine..	0	0	0	0	0	0	0	15	15	65	1,344,212
Maryland	0	0	0	9	0	0	0	312	321	1,365	6,045,680
Massachusetts.............................	0	0	2	6	0	0	0	219	227	1,488	6,892,503
Michigan, Eastern District...............	0	0	13	12	0	0	0	958	983	2,219	6,452,970
Michigan, Western District..............	0	4	0	2	0	0	0	864	870	1,476	3,533,887
Minnesota..................................	0	0	2	1	0	0	0	392	395	659	5,639,632
Mississippi, Northern District	0	1	4	2	0	0	0	200	207	790	1,107,636
Mississippi, Southern District............	0	0	1	8	0	0	0	294	303	1,189	1,868,513
Missouri, Eastern District................	0	0	1	3	0	0	0	155	159	528	2,926,389
Missouri, Western District	0	0	4	6	0	0	1	190	201	507	3,211,039
Montana....................................	0	1	3	5	0	1	0	1,174	1,184	1,619	1,068,778
Nebraska....................................	0	1	17	13	0	0	0	168	199	1,187	1,934,408
Nevada......................................	0	1	3	17	0	0	0	151	172	565	3,080,156
New Hampshire	0	0	0	2	0	0	1	192	195	301	1,359,711
New Jersey..................................	1	1	0	19	0	0	0	1,021	1,042	2,126	8,882,190
New Mexico.................................	0	0	3	25	0	0	0	400	428	1,067	2,096,829
New York, Eastern District...............	0	0	1	0	0	0	0	222	223	666	11,203,328
New York, Northern District	1	0	0	0	0	0	0	313	314	748	3,352,502
New York, Southern District..............	0	1	0	1	0	0	0	113	115	298	2,135,650
New York, Western District..............	0	0	0	0	0	0	0	212	212	650	2,762,081
North Carolina, Eastern District	0	0	0	1	0	0	0	365	366	1,054	4,129,850
North Carolina, Middle District..........	0	0	0	0	0	0	1	95	96	406	3,034,317
North Carolina, Western District........	0	0	0	1	0	0	0	241	242	758	3,323,917
North Dakota...............................	0	2	0	24	0	0	0	526	552	842	762,062
Northern Mariana Islands[1].................	0	0	0	0	0	0	0	1	1	3	53,883
Ohio, Northern District....................	1	3	8	52	1	0	3	990	1,058	3,315	5,695,197

Table 41. Number of Arrestees from State-Issued Warrants by NIBRS Offense Code, by Selected U.S. Marshals Service Judicial District, 2019—*Continued*

(Number.)

NIBRS Offense Code / NIBRS Offense Description	90B Curfew/loitering/vagrancy violations # Arrested	90C Disorderly conduct # Arrested	90D Driving under the influence # Arrested	90F Family offenses, nonviolent # Arrested	90G Liquor law violations # Arrested	90H Peeping tom # Arrested	90J Trespass of real property # Arrested	90Z All other offenses # Arrested	Count of arrestees for Group B Offenses	Total number of arrestees	Population per Judicial District
Ohio, Southern District	0	2	1	69	0	0	1	1,164	1,237	3,209	5,993,903
Oklahoma, Eastern District	0	0	0	4	0	0	0	93	97	258	724,312
Oklahoma, Northern District	0	0	2	20	0	0	0	116	138	397	1,092,593
Oklahoma, Western District	0	1	0	11	0	0	0	113	125	364	2,140,066
Oregon	5	0	1	0	0	0	0	280	286	618	4,217,737
Pennsylvania, Eastern District	1	1	0	1	0	0	1	548	552	1,112	5,777,910
Pennsylvania, Middle District	0	5	4	11	0	0	0	504	524	1,205	3,334,226
Pennsylvania, Western District	0	1	1	4	0	0	0	534	540	1,024	3,689,853
Puerto Rico	0	0	0	0	0	0	0	8	8	124	3,195,153
Rhode Island	0	0	0	3	0	1	0	177	181	389	1,059,361
South Carolina	0	8	0	70	0	0	1	472	551	3,680	5,148,714
South Dakota	1	2	2	5	0	0	0	60	70	417	884,659
Tennessee, Eastern District	0	1	0	9	0	0	0	251	261	793	2,653,711
Tennessee, Middle District	0	0	0	1	0	0	0	190	191	390	2,606,370
Tennessee, Western District	0	0	0	28	0	0	0	534	562	1,758	1,569,093
Texas, Eastern District	0	1	9	33	0	0	1	363	407	1,138	4,043,987
Texas, Northern District	0	15	5	91	0	1	2	678	792	3,817	7,547,162
Texas, Southern District	2	31	25	117	0	1	8	1,280	1,464	5,101	9,965,548
Texas, Western District	0	4	4	51	2	2	0	718	781	2,130	7,439,184
U.S. Virgin Islands[1]	0	0	0	0	0	0	0	5	5	12	106,405
Utah	0	0	1	5	0	0	2	56	64	677	3,205,958
Vermont	0	0	0	0	0	0	0	17	17	63	623,989
Virginia, Eastern District	0	1	0	12	0	0	2	304	319	1,305	6,223,634
Virginia, Western District	0	0	0	20	0	0	0	498	518	2,231	2,311,885
Washington, Eastern District	0	2	0	0	0	0	2	721	725	1,170	1,638,935
Washington, Western District	0	0	0	5	0	0	0	636	641	1,143	5,975,958
West Virginia, Northern District	0	0	0	0	0	0	1	81	82	136	864,566
West Virginia, Southern District	0	0	1	11	0	0	0	253	265	637	927,581
Wisconsin, Eastern District	0	1	1	4	0	0	0	178	184	414	3,413,224
Wisconsin, Western District	0	0	0	16	0	1	0	212	229	482	2,409,210
Wyoming	0	0	0	0	0	0	0	7	7	12	578,759

[1]Population for Guam, Northern Mariana Island, and U.S. Virgin Islands was gathered from the 2010 U.S. Census.

Table 41A. Number of Arrestees from State-Issued Warrants by NIBRS Offense Code, by Department of Justice Office of the Inspector General Judicial District, 2019

(Number.)

NIBRS Offense Code NIBRS Offense Description	Population per Judicial District	Crimes Against Person		Count of arrestees for Crimes Against Person	Crimes Against Property			
		11A - 11D	36A - 36B		26A - 26E	270	280	290
		Sex offenses	Sex offenses, nonforcible		Fraud offenses	Embezzlement	Stolen property offenses	Destruction/ damage/ vandalism of property
		# Arrested	# Arrested	# Arrested	# Arrested	# Arrested	# Arrested	# Arrested
Grand Total, All Judicial Districts	331,754,322	3	1	4	13	2	2	1
Alabama, Middle District	1,155,815	0	0	0	0	0	0	0
Alabama, Northern District	2,896,978	0	0	0	0	0	0	1
Alabama, Southern District	850,392	0	0	0	0	0	0	0
Alaska	731,545	0	0	0	0	0	0	0
Arizona	7,278,717	0	0	0	0	0	0	0
Arkansas, Eastern District	1,637,576	1	0	1	0	0	0	0
Arkansas, Western District	1,380,228	0	0	0	0	0	0	0
California, Central District	19,445,734	0	0	0	1	0	0	0
California, Eastern District	8,139,046	0	0	0	0	0	0	0
California, Northern District	8,400,053	0	0	0	0	0	0	0
California, Southern District	3,527,390	0	0	0	1	0	0	0
Colorado	5,758,736	0	0	0	1	0	0	0
Connecticut	3,565,287	0	0	0	0	0	0	0
Delaware	973,764	0	0	0	0	0	0	0
District of Columbia	705,749	0	0	0	0	0	0	0
Florida, Middle District	12,488,308	0	0	0	0	0	0	0
Florida, Northern District	1,887,311	0	0	0	0	0	0	0
Florida, Southern District	7,102,118	0	0	0	0	0	0	0
Georgia, Middle District	2,025,219	0	0	0	0	0	0	0
Georgia, Northern District	6,989,789	0	0	0	0	0	0	0
Georgia, Southern District	1,602,415	0	1	1	0	0	0	0
Guam[1]	159,358	0	0	0	0	0	0	0
Hawaii	1,415,872	0	0	0	0	0	0	0
Idaho	1,787,065	0	0	0	0	0	0	0
Illinois, Central District	2,177,477	0	0	0	0	0	0	0
Illinois, Northern District	9,255,097	0	0	0	0	0	0	0
Illinois, Southern District	1,239,247	0	0	0	0	0	0	0
Indiana, Northern District	2,610,821	0	0	0	0	0	0	0
Indiana, Southern District	4,121,398	0	0	0	0	0	0	0
Iowa, Northern District	1,317,377	0	0	0	0	0	0	0
Iowa, Southern District	1,837,693	0	0	0	0	0	0	0
Kansas	2,913,314	0	0	0	0	0	0	0
Kentucky, Eastern District	2,213,795	0	0	0	0	0	0	0
Kentucky, Western District	2,253,878	0	0	0	0	0	0	0
Louisiana, Eastern District	1,684,031	0	0	0	0	0	0	0
Louisiana, Middle District	830,107	0	0	0	0	0	0	0
Louisiana, Western District	2,134,656	0	0	0	0	0	0	0
Maine	1,344,212	0	0	0	0	0	0	0
Maryland	6,045,680	0	0	0	0	0	0	0
Massachusetts	6,892,503	0	0	0	0	0	0	0
Michigan, Eastern District	6,452,970	0	0	0	0	0	0	0
Michigan, Western District	3,533,887	0	0	0	0	0	0	0
Minnesota	5,639,632	0	0	0	0	0	0	0
Mississippi, Northern District	1,107,636	0	0	0	0	0	0	0
Mississippi, Southern District	1,868,513	0	0	0	0	0	0	0
Missouri, Eastern District	2,926,389	0	0	0	0	1	0	0
Missouri, Western District	3,211,039	0	0	0	2	0	0	0
Montana	1,068,778	0	0	0	2	0	0	0
Nebraska	1,934,408	0	0	0	0	0	0	0
Nevada	3,080,156	0	0	0	0	0	0	0
New Hampshire	1,359,711	0	0	0	0	0	0	0
New Jersey	8,882,190	0	0	0	0	0	0	0
New Mexico	2,096,829	0	0	0	0	0	0	0
New York, Eastern District	11,203,328	1	0	1	0	0	0	0
New York, Northern District	3,352,502	0	0	0	0	0	0	0
New York, Southern District	2,135,650	1	0	1	0	0	0	0
New York, Western District	2,762,081	0	0	0	0	0	0	0
North Carolina, Eastern District	4,129,850	0	0	0	0	0	0	0
North Carolina, Middle District	3,034,317	0	0	0	0	0	0	0
North Carolina, Western District	3,323,917	0	0	0	0	0	0	0
North Dakota	762,062	0	0	0	0	0	0	0

Table 41A. Number of Arrestees from State-Issued Warrants by NIBRS Offense Code, by Department of Justice Office of the Inspector General Judicial District, 2019—*Continued*

(Number.)

NIBRS Offense Code	Crimes Against Property 510	Counts arrestees for Crimes Against Property	Crimes Against Society 35A - 35B	Counts of arrestees for Crimes Against Society	Count of arrestees for Group A Offenses	Group B 90Z All other offenses (Includes all alcohol & tobacco offenses)	Count of arrestees for Group B Offenses	Total number of arrestees
NIBRS Offense Description	Bribery		Drug/narcotic offenses					
	# Arrested		# Arrested			# Arrested		
Grand Total, All Judicial Districts	14	32	9	9	45	8	8	53
Alabama, Middle District...	0	0	0	0	0	0	0	0
Alabama, Northern District...	0	1	0	0	1	0	0	1
Alabama, Southern District	0	0	0	0	0	0	0	0
Alaska..	0	0	0	0	0	0	0	0
Arizona..	1	1	0	0	1	1	1	2
Arkansas, Eastern District	1	1	0	0	2	0	0	2
Arkansas, Western District	0	0	0	0	0	0	0	0
California, Central District	0	1	2	2	3	0	0	3
California, Eastern District	0	0	0	0	0	0	0	0
California, Northern District	0	0	0	0	0	0	0	0
California, Southern District	0	1	0	0	1	0	0	1
Colorado	0	1	0	0	1	0	0	1
Connecticut	0	0	0	0	0	0	0	0
Delaware	0	0	0	0	0	0	0	0
District of Columbia	0	0	0	0	0	0	0	0
Florida, Middle District	0	0	0	0	0	0	0	0
Florida, Northern District	0	0	0	0	0	0	0	0
Florida, Southern District	1	1	0	0	1	0	0	1
Georgia, Middle District	0	0	0	0	0	0	0	0
Georgia, Northern District...	0	0	0	0	0	0	0	0
Georgia, Southern District...	1	1	0	0	2	2	2	4
Guam[1]	0	0	0	0	0	0	0	0
Hawaii	0	0	0	0	0	0	0	0
Idaho...	0	0	0	0	0	0	0	0
Illinois, Central District	0	0	0	0	0	0	0	0
Illinois, Northern District...	0	0	0	0	0	0	0	0
Illinois, Southern District...	0	0	0	0	0	0	0	0
Indiana, Northern District	0	0	0	0	0	0	0	0
Indiana, Southern District	0	0	0	0	0	0	0	0
Iowa, Northern District..	0	0	0	0	0	0	0	0
Iowa, Southern District..	0	0	0	0	0	0	0	0
Kansas	0	0	0	0	0	0	0	0
Kentucky, Eastern District..	0	0	1	1	1	0	0	1
Kentucky, Western District...	0	0	0	0	0	0	0	0
Louisiana, Eastern District	0	0	0	0	0	0	0	0
Louisiana, Middle District	0	0	0	0	0	0	0	0
Louisiana, Western District...	0	0	0	0	0	0	0	0
Maine..	0	0	0	0	0	0	0	0
Maryland	0	0	0	0	0	0	0	0
Massachusetts	0	0	0	0	0	0	0	0
Michigan, Eastern District..	0	0	0	0	0	0	0	0
Michigan, Western District...	0	0	0	0	0	0	0	0
Minnesota	0	0	0	0	0	0	0	0
Mississippi, Northern District	0	0	0	0	0	0	0	0
Mississippi, Southern District.....................................	1	1	0	0	1	0	0	1
Missouri, Eastern District...	0	1	0	0	1	0	0	1
Missouri, Western District	0	2	0	0	2	0	0	2
Montana..	0	2	0	0	2	0	0	2
Nebraska..	0	0	0	0	0	0	0	0
Nevada	0	0	0	0	0	0	0	0
New Hampshire	0	0	0	0	0	0	0	0
New Jersey...	0	0	0	0	0	0	0	0
New Mexico...	0	0	2	2	2	0	0	2
New York, Eastern District..	0	0	0	0	1	0	0	1
New York, Northern District.......................................	0	0	0	0	0	0	0	0
New York, Southern District.......................................	0	0	0	0	1	0	0	1
New York, Western District..	0	0	1	1	1	0	0	1
North Carolina, Eastern District	0	0	0	0	0	1	1	1
North Carolina, Middle District..................................	0	0	0	0	0	0	0	0
North Carolina, Western District................................	0	0	0	0	0	0	0	0
North Dakota...	0	0	0	0	0	0	0	0

Table 41A. Number of Arrestees from State-Issued Warrants by NIBRS Offense Code, by Department of Justice Office of the Inspector General Judicial District, 2019—*Continued*

(Number.)

NIBRS Offense Code		Crimes Against Person			Crimes Against Property			
		11A - 11D	36A - 36B		26A - 26E	270	280	290
NIBRS Offense Description	Population per Judicial District	Sex offenses	Sex offenses, nonforcible	Count of arrestees for Crimes Against Person	Fraud offenses	Embezzlement	Stolen property offenses	Destruction/ damage/ vandalism of property
		# Arrested	# Arrested		# Arrested	# Arrested	# Arrested	# Arrested
Northern Mariana Islands[1]	53,883	0	0	0	0	0	0	0
Ohio, Northern District	5,695,197	0	0	0	0	0	0	0
Ohio, Southern District	5,993,903	0	0	0	0	0	0	0
Oklahoma, Eastern District	724,312	0	0	0	0	0	0	0
Oklahoma, Northern District	1,092,593	0	0	0	0	0	0	0
Oklahoma, Western District	2,140,066	0	0	0	0	0	0	0
Oregon	4,217,737	0	0	0	0	0	0	0
Pennsylvania, Eastern District	5,777,910	0	0	0	0	0	0	0
Pennsylvania, Middle District	3,334,226	0	0	0	1	0	0	0
Pennsylvania, Western District	3,689,853	0	0	0	0	0	0	0
Puerto Rico	3,195,153	0	0	0	0	0	0	0
Rhode Island	1,059,361	0	0	0	0	0	0	0
South Carolina	5,148,714	0	0	0	1	0	0	0
South Dakota	884,659	0	0	0	0	0	0	0
Tennessee, Eastern District	2,653,711	0	0	0	0	0	0	0
Tennessee, Middle District	2,606,370	0	0	0	0	0	0	0
Tennessee, Western District	1,569,093	0	0	0	0	0	0	0
Texas, Eastern District	4,043,987	0	0	0	0	0	0	0
Texas, Northern District	7,547,162	0	0	0	2	1	2	0
Texas, Southern District	9,965,548	0	0	0	0	0	0	0
Texas, Western District	7,439,184	0	0	0	1	0	0	0
U. S. Virgin Islands[1]	106,405	0	0	0	0	0	0	0
Utah	3,205,958	0	0	0	1	0	0	0
Vermont	623,989	0	0	0	0	0	0	0
Virginia, Eastern District	6,223,634	0	0	0	0	0	0	0
Virginia, Western District	2,311,885	0	0	0	0	0	0	0
Washington, Eastern District	1,638,935	0	0	0	0	0	0	0
Washington, Western District	5,975,958	0	0	0	0	0	0	0
West Virginia, Northern District	864,566	0	0	0	0	0	0	0
West Virginia, Southern District	927,581	0	0	0	0	0	0	0
Wisconsin, Eastern District	3,413,224	0	0	0	0	0	0	0
Wisconsin, Western District	2,409,210	0	0	0	0	0	0	0
Wyoming	578,759	0	0	0	0	0	0	0

Table 41A. Number of Arrestees from State-Issued Warrants by NIBRS Offense Code, by Department of Justice Office of the Inspector General Judicial District, 2019—*Continued*

(Number.)

NIBRS Offense Code	Crimes Against Property 510	Counts arrestees for Crimes Against Property	Crimes Against Society 35A - 35B	Counts of arrestees for Crimes Against Society	Count of arrestees for Group A Offenses	Group B 90Z All other offenses (Includes all alcohol & tobacco offenses)	Count of arrestees for Group B Offenses	Total number of arrestees
NIBRS Offense Description	Bribery # Arrested		Drug/narcotic offenses # Arrested			# Arrested		
Northern Mariana Islands[1]	0	0	0	0	0	0	0	0
Ohio, Northern District	0	0	0	0	0	0	0	0
Ohio, Southern District	0	0	0	0	0	0	0	0
Oklahoma, Eastern District	0	0	0	0	0	0	0	0
Oklahoma, Northern District	0	0	0	0	0	0	0	0
Oklahoma, Western District	0	0	1	1	1	0	0	1
Oregon	0	0	0	0	0	0	0	0
Pennsylvania, Eastern District	0	0	0	0	0	0	0	0
Pennsylvania, Middle District	0	1	0	0	1	0	0	1
Pennsylvania, Western District	0	0	0	0	0	0	0	0
Puerto Rico	0	0	0	0	0	0	0	0
Rhode Island	0	0	0	0	0	0	0	0
South Carolina	0	1	0	0	1	1	1	2
South Dakota	0	0	0	0	0	0	0	0
Tennessee, Eastern District	0	0	0	0	0	0	0	0
Tennessee, Middle District	0	0	0	0	0	0	0	0
Tennessee, Western District	0	0	0	0	0	0	0	0
Texas, Eastern District	0	0	0	0	0	1	1	1
Texas, Northern District	1	6	0	0	6	1	1	7
Texas, Southern District	5	5	1	1	6	0	0	6
Texas, Western District	3	4	0	0	4	1	1	5
U. S. Virgin Islands[1]	0	0	0	0	0	0	0	0
Utah	0	1	0	0	1	0	0	1
Vermont	0	0	0	0	0	0	0	0
Virginia, Eastern District	0	0	1	1	1	0	0	1
Virginia, Western District	0	0	0	0	0	0	0	0
Washington, Eastern District	0	0	0	0	0	0	0	0
Washington, Western District	0	0	0	0	0	0	0	0
West Virginia, Northern District	0	0	0	0	0	0	0	0
West Virginia, Southern District	0	0	0	0	0	0	0	0
Wisconsin, Eastern District	0	0	0	0	0	0	0	0
Wisconsin, Western District	0	0	0	0	0	0	0	0
Wyoming	0	0	0	0	0	0	0	0

[1]The population figures for Guam, Northern Mariana Island, and U.S. Virgin Islands were gathered from the 2010 U.S. Census

Table 42. Number of Arrestees, United States Environmental Protection Agency Office of the Inspector General, by NIBRS Offense Code and Selected Judicial District, 2019

(Number.)

NIBRS Offense Code / NIBRS Offense Description	Population per Judicial District	Crimes Against Property 26A - 26E Fraud offenses # Arrested	Count of arrestees for crimes against property
Grand Total, All Judicial Districts	331,754,322	2	2
Alabama, Middle District............................	1,155,815	0	0
Alabama, Northern District.................................	2,896,978	0	0
Alabama, Southern District	850,392	0	0
Alaska...	731,545	0	0
Arizona..	7,278,717	0	0
Arkansas, Eastern District..................................	1,637,576	0	0
Arkansas, Western District	1,380,228	0	0
California, Central District.................................	19,445,734	0	0
California, Eastern District.................................	8,139,046	0	0
California, Northern District	8,400,053	1	1
California, Southern District	3,527,390	0	0
Colorado	5,758,736	0	0
Connecticut..	3,565,287	0	0
Delaware	973,764	0	0
District of Columbia..	705,749	0	0
Florida, Middle District	12,488,308	0	0
Florida, Northern District...................................	1,887,311	0	0
Florida, Southern District...................................	7,102,118	0	0
Georgia, Middle District	2,025,219	0	0
Georgia, Northern District..................................	6,989,789	0	0
Georgia, Southern District..................................	1,602,415	0	0
Guam[1]	159,358	0	0
Hawaii	1,415,872	0	0
Idaho	1,787,065	0	0
Illinois, Central District	2,177,477	0	0
Illinois, Northern District...................................	9,255,097	0	0
Illinois, Southern District...................................	1,239,247	0	0
Indiana, Northern District..................................	2,610,821	0	0
Indiana, Southern District..................................	4,121,398	0	0
Iowa, Northern District......................................	1,317,377	0	0
Iowa, Southern District......................................	1,837,693	0	0
Kansas..	2,913,314	0	0
Kentucky, Eastern District..................................	2,213,795	0	0
Kentucky, Western District.................................	2,253,878	0	0
Louisiana, Eastern District.................................	1,684,031	0	0
Louisiana, Middle District	830,107	0	0
Louisiana, Western District................................	2,134,656	0	0
Maine...	1,344,212	0	0
Maryland	6,045,680	0	0
Massachusetts	6,892,503	0	0
Michigan, Eastern District..................................	6,452,970	0	0
Michigan, Western District.................................	3,533,887	0	0
Minnesota	5,639,632	0	0
Mississippi, Northern District	1,107,636	0	0
Mississippi, Southern District............................	1,868,513	0	0
Missouri, Eastern District...................................	2,926,389	0	0
Missouri, Western District	3,211,039	0	0
Montana...	1,068,778	0	0
Nebraska	1,934,408	0	0
Nevada	3,080,156	0	0
New Hampshire	1,359,711	0	0
New Jersey..	8,882,190	1	1
New Mexico..	2,096,829	0	0
New York, Eastern District.................................	11,203,328	0	0
New York, Northern District...............................	3,352,502	0	0
New York, Southern District...............................	2,135,650	0	0
New York, Western District................................	2,762,081	0	0
North Carolina, Eastern District	4,129,850	0	0
North Carolina, Middle District..........................	3,034,317	0	0
North Carolina, Western District........................	3,323,917	0	0
North Dakota..	762,062	0	0
Northern Mariana Islands[1]................................	53,883	0	0
Ohio, Northern District......................................	5,695,197	0	0
Ohio, Southern District......................................	5,993,903	0	0

Table 42. Number of Arrestees, United States Environmental Protection Agency Office of the Inspector General, by NIBRS Offense Code and Selected Judicial District, 2019—*Continued*

(Number.)

NIBRS Offense Code NIBRS Offense Description	Population per Judicial District	Crimes Against Property 26A - 26E Fraud offenses # Arrested	Count of arrestees for crimes against property
Oklahoma, Eastern District	724,312	0	0
Oklahoma, Northern District	1,092,593	0	0
Oklahoma, Western District	2,140,066	0	0
Oregon	4,217,737	0	0
Pennsylvania, Eastern District	5,777,910	0	0
Pennsylvania, Middle District	3,334,226	0	0
Pennsylvania, Western District	3,689,853	0	0
Puerto Rico	3,195,153	0	0
Rhode Island	1,059,361	0	0
South Carolina	5,148,714	0	0
South Dakota	884,659	0	0
Tennessee, Eastern District	2,653,711	0	0
Tennessee, Middle District	2,606,370	0	0
Tennessee, Western District	1,569,093	0	0
Texas, Eastern District	4,043,987	0	0
Texas, Northern District	7,547,162	0	0
Texas, Southern District	9,965,548	0	0
Texas, Western District	7,439,184	0	0
U. S. Virgin Islands[1]	106,405	0	0
Utah	3,205,958	0	0
Vermont	623,989	0	0
Virginia, Eastern District	6,223,634	0	0
Virginia, Western District	2,311,885	0	0
Washington, Eastern District	1,638,935	0	0
Washington, Western District	5,975,958	0	0
West Virginia, Northern District	864,566	0	0
West Virginia, Southern District	927,581	0	0
Wisconsin, Eastern District	3,413,224	0	0
Wisconsin, Western District	2,409,210	0	0
Wyoming	578,759	0	0

[1]The population figures for Guam, Northern Mariana Island, and U.S. Virgin Islands were gathered from the 2010 U.S. Census

Table 43. FBI Employment, by Gender, 2019

(Number.)

Employee	Male	Female	Total
Total	21,215	16,770	37,985
Special agents...............................	10,900	2,726	13,626
Professional staff...........................	10,105	13,998	24,103
Police officers................................	210	46	256

Table 44. ATF Employment, by Gender, 2019

(Number.)

Employee	Male	Female	Total
Total	3,446	1,617	5,063
Special agents...............................	2,226	382	2,608
Professional staff...........................	1,220	1,235	2,455
Police officers................................	0	0	0

Table 45. USMS Employment, by Gender, 2019

(Number.)

Employee	Male	Female	Total
Total	3,961	1,256	5,217
Special agents...............................	3,320	333	3,653
Professional staff...........................	548	909	1,457
Police officers................................	93	14	107

Table 46. DOJ OIG Employment, by Gender, 2019

(Number.)

Employee	Male	Female	Total
Total	267	244	511
Special agents...............................	90	23	113
Professional staff...........................	177	221	398
Police officers................................	0	0	0

Table 47. EPA OIG Employment, by Gender, 2019

(Number.)

Employee	Male	Female	Total
Total	35	12	47
Special agents...............................	33	10	43
Professional staff...........................	2	2	4
Police officers................................	0	0	0

Table 48. Human Trafficking, Offenses and Clearances by Participating State, 2019

(Number.)

State	Commercial sex acts			Involuntary servitude			Total		
	Offenses	Total cleared	Clearances under 18	Offenses	Total cleared	Clearances under 18	Offenses	Total cleared	Clearances under 18
Alabama	0	0	0	0	0	0	0	0	0
Alaska	7	2	0	0	0	0	7	2	0
Arizona	52	9	0	1	1	0	53	10	0
Arkansas	1	0	0	0	0	0	1	0	0
California[1]	0	0	0	0	0	0	0	0	0
Colorado	44	13	0	4	2	0	48	15	0
Connecticut	5	1	0	3	1	0	8	2	0
Delaware	15	4	0	10	2	0	25	6	0
Florida	106	64	0	11	8	0	117	72	0
Georgia	48	6	2	6	0	0	54	6	2
Hawaii	5	2	0	0	0	0	5	2	0
Idaho	2	0	0	0	0	0	2	0	0
Illinois	29	0	0	8	1	0	37	1	0
Indiana	6	1	0	4	0	0	10	1	0
Kansas	2	2	0	0	0	0	2	2	0
Kentucky	21	5	0	7	0	0	28	5	0
Louisiana	7	6	0	3	3	0	10	9	0
Maine	4	1	0	1	0	0	5	1	0
Maryland	29	15	0	8	3	1	37	18	1
Massachusetts	23	8	0	12	4	0	35	12	0
Michigan	4	3	0	0	0	0	4	3	0
Minnesota	175	134	1	13	0	0	188	134	1
Mississippi	2	1	0	0	0	0	2	1	0
Missouri	21	9	0	6	2	0	27	11	0
Montana	3	0	0	0	0	0	3	0	0
Nebraska[1]	0	0	0	0	0	0	0	0	0
Nevada	182	64	1	0	0	0	182	64	1
New Hampshire	5	0	0	0	0	0	5	0	0
New Jersey	2	0	0	2	2	0	4	2	0
New Mexico	3	0	0	3	1	0	6	1	0
New York[1]	0	0	0	0	0	0	0	0	0
North Carolina	33	12	0	23	8	0	56	20	0
North Dakota	4	0	0	0	0	0	4	0	0
Ohio	7	1	0	1	0	0	8	1	0
Oklahoma	5	2	0	0	0	0	5	2	0
Oregon	28	10	0	9	9	0	37	19	0
Puerto Rico	0	0	0	0	0	0	2	0	0
Rhode Island	8	7	0	4	4	0	12	11	0
South Carolina	19	8	0	3	1	0	22	9	0
South Dakota	2	0	0	0	0	0	2	0	0
Tennessee	42	20	0	4	1	0	46	21	0
Texas	337	124	5	113	89	5	450	213	10
Utah	75	64	0	0	0	0	75	64	0
Vermont	6	1	0	0	0	0	6	1	0
Virginia	37	28	1	4	1	0	41	29	1
Washington	53	26	0	3	0	0	56	26	0
West Virginia	49	19	0	1	0	0	50	19	0
Wisconsin	99	53	2	7	7	0	106	60	2
Wyoming	0	0	0	0	0	0	0	0	0

[1] Data submitted through the Bureau of Indian Affairs.

Table 49. Human Trafficking Arrests, by Age and Participating State, 2019

(Number.)

State	Juvenile		Adult	
	Male	Female	Male	Female
Arizona				
Commercial sex acts	0	0	0	0
Involuntary servitude..........................	0	0	1	0
Colorado				
Commercial sex acts	0	0	0	1
Involuntary servitude..........................	0	0	0	0
Connecticut				
Commercial sex acts	0	0	2	0
Involuntary servitude..........................	0	0	0	0
Delaware				
Commercial sex acts	0	0	1	0
Involuntary servitude..........................	0	0	0	0
Georgia				
Commercial sex acts	0	0	5	1
Involuntary servitude..........................	0	0	0	0
Hawaii				
Commercial sex acts	0	0	1	0
Involuntary servitude..........................	0	0	0	0
Indiana				
Commercial sex acts	1	0	1	0
Involuntary servitude..........................	2	0	0	0
Kentucky				
Commercial sex acts	0	0	0	0
Involuntary servitude..........................	0	0	1	0
Louisiana				
Commercial sex acts	1	0	5	1
Involuntary servitude..........................	0	0	2	1
Maryland				
Commercial sex acts	0	0	9	1
Involuntary servitude..........................	0	0	2	0
Massachusetts				
Commercial sex acts	0	0	3	1
Involuntary servitude..........................	0	0	2	1
Michigan				
Commercial sex acts	0	0	36	0
Involuntary servitude..........................	0	0	0	0
Minnesota				
Commercial sex acts	1	0	106	14
Involuntary servitude..........................	0	0	0	0
Mississippi				
Commercial sex acts	0	0	1	1
Involuntary servitude..........................	0	0	0	0
Missouri				
Commercial sex acts	0	0	6	1
Involuntary servitude..........................	0	0	1	0
Nevada				
Commercial sex acts	0	0	17	5
Involuntary servitude..........................	1	0	4	5
New Jersey				
Commercial sex acts	0	0	3	2
Involuntary servitude..........................	0	0	9	10
New Mexico				
Commercial sex acts	0	0	0	0
Involuntary servitude..........................	0	0	1	0

Table 49. Human Trafficking Arrests, by Age and Participating State, 2019—*Continued*

(Number.)

State	Juvenile		Adult	
	Male	Female	Male	Female
Ohio				
Commercial sex acts	0	0	3	0
Involuntary servitude............................	0	0	0	0
Oklahoma				
Commercial sex acts	2	2	20	16
Involuntary servitude............................	1	0	0	3
Oregon				
Commercial sex acts	0	0	3	0
Involuntary servitude............................	0	0	2	2
Rhode Island				
Commercial sex acts	0	0	2	4
Involuntary servitude............................	0	0	0	1
South Carolina				
Commercial sex acts	0	0	2	2
Involuntary servitude............................	0	0	1	0
Tennessee				
Commercial sex acts	0	0	13	4
Involuntary servitude............................	0	0	4	1
Texas				
Commercial sex acts	0	0	40	11
Involuntary servitude............................	5	1	13	6
Utah				
Commercial sex acts	0	0	38	0
Involuntary servitude............................	0	0	0	0
Vermont				
Commercial sex acts	0	0	1	0
Involuntary servitude............................	0	0	0	0
Virginia				
Commercial sex acts	0	1	4	1
Involuntary servitude............................	0	0	0	0
Washington				
Commercial sex acts	0	0	28	0
Involuntary servitude............................	0	0	16	7
West Virginia				
Commercial sex acts	0	0	10	0
Involuntary servitude............................	0	0	0	0
Wisconsin				
Commercial sex acts	1	4	88	35
Involuntary servitude............................	0	1	28	11

Table 50. Human Trafficking Arrests, by Race and Participating State, 2019

(Number.)

State	Juvenile						Adult					
	White	Black or African American	American Indian/ Alaska Native	Asian	Native Hawaiian/ Other Pacific Islander	Total	White	Black or African American	American Indian/ Alaska Native	Asian	Native Hawaiian/ Other Pacific Islander	Total
Colorado												
Commercial sex acts	0	0	0	0	0	0	0	0	0	1	0	1
Involuntary servitude	0	0	0	0	0	0	0	0	0	0	0	0
Connecticut												
Commercial sex acts	0	0	0	0	0	0	1	1	0	0	0	2
Involuntary servitude	0	0	0	0	0	0	0	0	0	0	0	0
Delaware												
Commercial sex acts	0	0	0	0	0	0	0	1	0	0	0	1
Involuntary servitude	0	0	0	0	0	0	0	0	0	0	0	0
Georgia												
Commercial sex acts	0	0	0	0	0	0	5	1	0	0	0	6
Involuntary servitude	0	0	0	0	0	0	0	0	0	0	0	0
Indiana												
Commercial sex acts	1	0	0	0	0	1	1	0	0	0	0	1
Involuntary servitude	3	0	0	0	0	3	0	0	0	0	0	0
Kentucky												
Commercial sex acts	0	0	0	0	0	0	0	0	0	0	0	0
Involuntary servitude	0	0	0	0	0	0	1	0	0	0	0	1
Louisiana												
Commercial sex acts	0	1	0	0	0	1	3	3	0	0	0	6
Involuntary servitude	0	0	0	0	0	0	2	1	0	0	0	3
Maryland												
Commercial sex acts	0	0	0	0	0	0	3	6	0	1	0	10
Involuntary servitude	0	0	0	0	0	0	0	2	0	0	0	2
Massachusetts												
Commercial sex acts	0	0	0	0	0	0	3	1	0	0	0	4
Involuntary servitude	0	0	0	0	0	0	2	0	0	1	0	3
Michigan												
Commercial sex acts	0	0	0	0	0	0	28	7	0	0	0	35
Involuntary servitude	0	0	0	0	0	0	0	0	0	0	0	0
Minnesota												
Commercial sex acts	1	0	0	0	0	1	66	39	3	12	0	120
Involuntary servitude	0	0	0	0	0	0	0	0	0	0	0	0
Mississippi												
Commercial sex acts	0	0	0	0	0	0	0	2	0	0	0	2
Involuntary servitude	0	0	0	0	0	0	0	0	0	0	0	0
Missouri												
Commercial sex acts	0	0	0	0	0	0	3	6	0	0	0	9
Involuntary servitude	0	0	0	0	0	0	2	0	0	0	0	2
Nevada												
Commercial sex acts	0	0	0	0	0	0	6	16	0	0	0	22
Involuntary servitude	0	0	0	0	0	0	5	4	0	0	0	9
New Jersey												
Commercial sex acts	0	0	0	0	0	0	2	3	0	0	0	5
Involuntary servitude	0	0	0	0	0	0	14	5	0	0	0	19
New Mexico												
Commercial sex acts	0	0	0	0	0	0	0	0	0	0	0	0
Involuntary servitude	0	0	0	0	0	0	0	1	0	0	0	1
Ohio												
Commercial sex acts	0	0	0	0	0	0	1	2	0	0	0	3
Involuntary servitude	0	0	0	0	0	0	0	0	0	0	0	0

Table 50. Human Trafficking Arrests, by Race and Participating State, 2019—*Continued*

(Number.)

State	Juvenile						Adult					
	White	Black or African American	American Indian/ Alaska Native	Asian	Native Hawaiian/ Other Pacific Islander	Total	White	Black or African American	American Indian/ Alaska Native	Asian	Native Hawaiian/ Other Pacific Islander	Total
Oklahoma												
Commercial sex acts	2	1	1	0	0	4	28	5	3	0	0	36
Involuntary servitude	0	1	0	0	0	1	2	1	0	0	0	3
Oregon												
Commercial sex acts	0	0	0	0	0	0	2	1	0	0	0	3
Involuntary servitude	0	0	0	0	0	0	4	0	0	0	0	4
Rhode Island												
Commercial sex acts	0	0	0	0	0	0	3	0	0	3	0	6
Involuntary servitude	0	0	0	0	0	0	0	1	0	0	0	1
South Carolina												
Commercial sex acts	0	0	0	0	0	0	3	1	0	0	0	4
Involuntary servitude	0	0	0	0	0	0	0	1	0	0	0	1
Tennessee												
Commercial sex acts	0	0	0	0	0	0	10	5	0	2	0	17
Involuntary servitude	0	0	0	0	0	0	3	0	0	1	0	4
Texas												
Commercial sex acts	0	0	0	0	0	0	31	19	0	0	0	50
Involuntary servitude	6	0	0	0	0	6	13	5	0	0	0	18
Utah												
Commercial sex acts	0	0	0	0	0	0	30	1	0	2	0	33
Involuntary servitude	0	0	0	0	0	0	0	0	0	0	0	0
Vermont												
Commercial sex acts	0	0	0	0	0	0	1	0	0	0	0	1
Involuntary servitude	0	0	0	0	0	0	0	0	0	0	0	0
Virginia												
Commercial sex acts	0	1	0	0	0	1	1	4	0	0	0	5
Involuntary servitude	0	0	0	0	0	0	0	0	0	0	0	0
Washington												
Commercial sex acts	0	0	0	0	0	0	14	3	0	2	0	19
Involuntary servitude	0	0	0	0	0	0	7	3	9	4	0	23
West Virginia												
Commercial sex acts	0	0	0	0	0	0	10	0	0	0	0	10
Involuntary servitude	0	0	0	0	0	0	0	0	0	0	0	0
Wisconsin												
Commercial sex acts	3	2	0	0	0	5	82	35	5	0	0	122
Involuntary servitude	1	0	0	0	0	1	32	6	1	0	0	39

Table 51. Human Trafficking Arrests, by Ethnicity and Participating State, 2019

(Number.)

State	Juvenile			Adult		
	Hispanic or Latino	Not Hispanic or Latino	Total	Hispanic or Latino	Not Hispanic or Latino	Total
Arizona						
Commercial sex acts	0	0	0	0	0	0
Involuntary servitude	0	0	0	1	0	1
Colorado						
Commercial sex acts	0	0	0	0	1	1
Involuntary servitude	0	0	0	0	0	0
Connecticut						
Commercial sex acts	0	0	0	1	0	1
Involuntary servitude	0	0	0	0	0	0
Delaware						
Commercial sex acts	0	0	0	0	1	1
Involuntary servitude	0	0	0	0	0	0
Georgia						
Commercial sex acts	0	0	0	0	5	5
Involuntary servitude	0	0	0	0	0	0
Indiana						
Commercial sex acts	0	0	0	1	0	1
Involuntary servitude	0	0	0	0	0	0
Kentucky						
Commercial sex acts	0	1	1	0	0	0
Involuntary servitude	0	3	3	0	0	0
Louisiana						
Commercial sex acts	0	0	0	0	0	0
Involuntary servitude	0	0	0	1	0	1
Maryland						
Commercial sex acts	0	0	0	0	10	10
Involuntary servitude	0	0	0	0	2	2
Massachusetts						
Commercial sex acts	0	0	0	1	3	4
Involuntary servitude	0	0	0	1	2	3
Michigan						
Commercial sex acts	0	0	0	1	1	2
Involuntary servitude	0	0	0	0	0	0
Minnesota						
Commercial sex acts	0	1	1	35	85	120
Involuntary servitude	0	0	0	0	0	0
Mississippi						
Commercial sex acts	0	0	0	0	2	2
Involuntary servitude	0	0	0	0	0	0
Missouri						
Commercial sex acts	0	0	0	0	9	9
Involuntary servitude	0	0	0	1	1	2
Nevada						
Commercial sex acts	0	0	0	0	22	22
Involuntary servitude	0	0	0	2	7	9
New Jersey						
Commercial sex acts	0	0	0	0	5	5
Involuntary servitude	0	0	0	3	16	19
New Mexico						
Commercial sex acts	0	0	0	0	0	0
Involuntary servitude	0	0	0	0	1	1
Ohio						
Commercial sex acts	0	0	0	0	3	3
Involuntary servitude	0	0	0	0	0	0

Table 51. Human Trafficking Arrests, by Ethnicity and Participating State, 2019—*Continued*

(Number.)

State	Juvenile			Adult		
	Hispanic or Latino	Not Hispanic or Latino	Total	Hispanic or Latino	Not Hispanic or Latino	Total
Oklahoma						
Commercial sex acts	0	4	4	1	35	36
Involuntary servitude...................	0	1	1	0	3	3
Oregon						
Commercial sex acts	0	0	0	1	1	2
Involuntary servitude...................	0	0	0	0	4	4
Rhode Island						
Commercial sex acts	0	0	0	0	6	6
Involuntary servitude...................	0	0	0	1	0	1
South Carolina						
Commercial sex acts	0	0	0	0	4	4
Involuntary servitude...................	0	0	0	0	1	1
Tennessee						
Commercial sex acts	0	0	0	2	15	17
Involuntary servitude...................	0	0	0	2	3	5
Texas						
Commercial sex acts	0	0	0	13	38	51
Involuntary servitude...................	6	0	6	10	9	19
Utah						
Commercial sex acts	0	0	0	1	3	4
Involuntary servitude...................	0	0	0	0	0	0
Vermont						
Commercial sex acts	0	0	0	0	1	1
Involuntary servitude...................	0	0	0	0	0	0
Virginia						
Commercial sex acts	0	0	0	0	5	5
Involuntary servitude...................	0	0	0	0	0	0
Washington						
Commercial sex acts	0	0	0	2	3	5
Involuntary servitude...................	0	0	0	0	0	0
West Virginia						
Commercial sex acts	0	0	0	0	10	10
Involuntary servitude...................	0	0	0	0	0	0
Wisconsin						
Commercial sex acts	0	2	2	1	24	25
Involuntary servitude...................	0	0	0	0	1	1

Note: Not all agencies provide ethnicity data; therefore, the race and ethnicity totals will not equal.

Table 52. Cargo Theft by Participating State, by Incidents and Stolen/Recovered Values, 2019

(Number; dollars; percent.)

State	Number of agencies reporting an incident	Number of incidents reported	Value of property		Percent recovered
			Stolen	Recovered	
Total	184	721	$139,677,562	$3,848,816	2.8
Alaska...........................	2	6	4,741	0	0.0
Arkansas.........................	1	1	20	0	0.0
Colorado.........................	6	14	543,115	55,000	10.1
Delaware	5	12	577,534	285,000	49.3
Florida	19	102	125,809,354	680,322	0.5
Georgia	9	14	288,745	0	0.0
Hawaii	1	2	3,440	0	0.0
Idaho............................	3	4	115	1	0.9
Indiana	3	4	117,256	70,000	59.7
Kentucky	20	34	2,731,532	36,289	1.3
Maine............................	2	2	10	0	0.0
Maryland	1	11	72,155	6,563	9.1
Michigan	14	50	600,295	150,102	25.0
Minnesota	1	1	8,000	0	0.0
Mississippi.......................	3	5	14,680	0	0.0
Missouri.........................	3	4	61,855	1	*
Nebraska	3	4	8,596	7,306	85.0
New Jersey.......................	3	3	392,451	0	0.0
Ohio	8	24	443,691	242,670	54.7
Oregon..........................	3	8	93,146	92,946	99.8
Rhode Island.....................	1	1	23,362	0	0.0
South Dakota.....................	1	1	80,000	80,000	100.0
Tennessee........................	21	238	1,918,160	500,015	26.1
Texas	23	128	4,881,599	1,186,081	24.3
Utah	1	1	1	0	0.0
Virginia..........................	21	27	765,084	406,019	53.1
Washington.......................	6	20	238,625	50,501	21.2

* = Less than one-tenth of 1 percent.

Table 53. Cargo Theft Property Stolen and Recovered, by Type of Value, 2019

(Dollars; percent.)

Type of property	Value of property		Percent recovered
	Stolen	Recovered	
Total	$139,677,562	$3,848,816	2.8
Aircraft parts, accessories....................................	530,000	500,000	94.3
Alcohol..	224,308	25,429	11.3
Automobile...	1,160,703	557,240	48.0
Bicycles...	19,600	0	0.0
Building materials	377,531	0	0.0
Camping, hunting, fishing equipment, supplies....	300	0	0.0
Chemicals..	626	320	51.1
Clothes, furs	1,975,649	3,201	0.2
Collections, collectibles	2	1	50.0
Computer hardware, software	2,534,133	83,280	3.3
Consumable goods...	2,924,734	39,252	1.3
Credit, debit cards[1]	0	0	
Crops...	7	0	0.0
Documents, personal or business[1]	0	0	
Drugs, narcotics...	14,701	1	*
Explosives	5,774	5,000	86.6
Farm equipment	1,210	0	0.0
Firearm accessories	400	0	0.0
Firearms..	16,744	0	0.0
Fuel	24,604	0	0.0
Household goods..	449,574	56,564	12.6
Identity documents[1]	0	0	
Identity intangibles[1]	0	0	
Industrial equipment...	136,061	0	0.0
Jewelry, precious metals......................................	119,845	1	*
Lawn, yard, garden equipment	1,000,100	0	0.0
Logging equipment..	400	0	0.0
Medical, medical lab equipment..........................	10,450	0	0.0
Merchandise...	1,018,619	356,308	35.0
Metals, non-precious	226,900	0	0.0
Money..	90,104	0	0.0
Musical instruments...	50	0	0.0
Nonnegotiable instrument[1]	0	0	
Office equipment...	2,630	0	0.0
Other...	2,076,500	184,326	8.9
Other motor vehicles..	269,001	100,002	37.2
Pending inventory..	10	1	10.0
Portable electronic communications.....................	474,858	6,563	1.4
Purse, wallet	6,917	502	7.3
Radio, TV, VCR	108,378	500	0.5
Recordings	120,033,130	0	0.0
Recreational vehicles..	2	1	50.0
Structure, other	10,000	0	0.0
Structure, storage	1	0	0.0
Tools..	263,023	218	0.1
Trailers...	903,592	435,001	48.1
Trucks..	2,143,103	1,493,104	69.7
Vehicle parts...	523,288	2,001	0.4

* = Less than one-tenth of 1 percent.
[1]According to Uniform Crime Reporting guidelines, the value of property stolen and/or recovered must be zero for this property description.

Table 54. Cargo Theft, by Location, 2019

(Number.)

Type of property	Total at location
Air, bus, train terminal	71
Auto dealership new, used	2
Commercial, office building	65
Construction site	4
Convenience store	38
Cyberspace	1
Department, discount store	13
Dock, wharf, freight, modal terminal	51
Drug store, doctor's office, hospital	5
Farm facility	3
Field, woods	14
Government, public building	5
Grocery, supermarket	10
Highway, road, alley, street, sidewalk	89
Hotel, motel, etc.	5
Industrial site	17
Liquor store	4
Parking, drop lot, garage	236
Park, playground	4
Rental storage facility	5
Residence, home	33
Rest area	2
Restaurant	6
School, college	1
Service, gas station	46
Specialty store (TV, fur, etc.)	5
Other, unknown	37

Table 55. Cargo Theft, by Victim Type, 2019

(Number.)

Victim type	Total victims
Business	562
Financial institution	1
Government	3
Individual	159
Other	5
Society, public	4
Unknown	24

Table 56. Cargo Theft, by Offense, 2019

(Number.)

Type of property	Total at location
Grand total of offenses	785
Cargo theft applicable offenses	
All other larceny	251
Burglary	48
Embezzlement	12
False pretenses, swindle, confidence game	7
Impersonation	2
Motor vehicle theft	92
Robbery	3
Theft from building	15
Theft from motor vehicle	322
Total cargo theft applicable offenses	752
Other offenses occurring with cargo offenses	
Counterfeiting, forgery	1
Destruction of property	23
Drug equipment violations	2
Drug, narcotic violations	3
Simple assault	1
Stolen property offense	2
Weapon law	1
Total other offenses occurring with cargo offense	33

METHODOLOGY

Submitting Uniform Crime Reporting (UCR) program data to the Federal Bureau of Investigation (FBI) is a collective effort on the part of city, county, state, tribal, and federal law enforcement agencies to present a nationwide view of crime. Law enforcement agencies in 46 states and the District of Columbia voluntarily contribute crime data to the UCR program through their respective state UCR programs. For those states that do not have a state program, local agencies submit crime statistics directly to the FBI. The state UCR programs function as liaisons between local agencies and the FBI. Many states have mandatory reporting requirements, and many state programs collect data beyond the scope of the UCR program to address crime problems specific to their particular jurisdictions. In most cases, state programs also provide direct and frequent service to participating law enforcement agencies, make information readily available for statewide use, and help streamline the national program's operations.

A Note Regarding Rape

In 2013, the FBI UCR Program initiated collection of rape data under a revised definition within the Summary Reporting System. Previously, offense data for forcible rape was collected under the legacy UCR definition: the carnal knowledge of a female forcibly and against her will. Beginning with the 2013 data year, the term "forcible" was removed from the offense title, and the definition was changed. The revised UCR definition of rape is: Penetration, no matter how slight, of the vagina or anus with any body part or object, or oral penetration by a sex organ of another person, without the consent of the victim. Attempts or assaults to commit rape are also included; however, statutory rape and incest are excluded. For more information, please see https://www.fbi.gov/about-us/cjis/ucr/crime-in-the-u.s/2013/crime-in-the-u.s.-2013/rape-addendum/rape_addendum_final.

Criteria for State UCR programs

The criteria established for state programs ensure consistency and comparability in the data submitted to the national program, as well as regular and timely reporting. These criteria are:

1. A UCR Program must conform to the FBI UCR Program's submission standards, definitions, specifications, and required deadlines.

2. A UCR Program must establish data integrity procedures and have personnel assigned to assist contributing agencies in quality assurance practices and crime reporting procedures. Data integrity procedures should include crime trend assessments, offense classification verification, and technical specification validation.

3. A UCR Program's submissions must cover more than 50 percent of the law enforcement agencies within its established reporting domain and be willing to cover any and all UCR-contributing agencies that wish to use the UCR Program from within its domain. (An agency wishing to become a UCR Program must be willing to report for all of the agencies within the state.)

4. A UCR Program must furnish the FBI UCR Program with all of the UCR data collected by the law enforcement agencies within its domain.

These requirements do not prohibit the state from gathering other statistical data beyond the national collection.

Data Completeness and Quality

National program staff members contact the state UCR program in connection with crime-reporting matters and, when necessary and approved by the state, they contact individual contributors within the state. To fulfill its responsibilities in connection with the UCR program, the FBI reviews and edits individual agency reports for completeness and quality. Upon request, they conduct training programs within the state on law enforcement record-keeping and crime-reporting procedures. The FBI conducts an audit of each state's UCR data collection procedures once every three years, in accordance with audit standards established by the federal government. Should circumstances develop in which the state program does not comply with the aforementioned requirements, the national program may institute a direct collection of data from law enforcement agencies within the state.

Reporting Procedures

Offenses known and value of property–Law enforcement agencies tabulate the number of Part I offenses reported based on records of all reports of crime received from victims, officers who discover infractions, or other sources, and submit these reports each month to the FBI directly or through their state UCR programs. Part I offenses include murder and non-negligent manslaughter, forcible rape, robbery, aggravated assault, burglary, larceny-theft, motor vehicle theft, and arson.

Each month, law enforcement agencies also submit to the FBI the value of property stolen and recovered in connection with the offenses and detailed information pertaining to criminal homicide.

Unfounded offenses and clearances—When, through investigation, an agency determines that complaints of crimes are unfounded or false, the agency eliminates that offense from its crime tally through an entry on the monthly report. The report also provides the total number of actual Part I offenses, the number of offenses cleared, and the number of clearances that involve only offenders under the age of 18. (Law enforcement can clear crimes in one of two ways: by the arrest of at least one person who is charged and turned over to the court for prosecution or by exceptional means—when some element beyond law enforcement's control precludes the arrest of a known offender.)

Persons arrested—In addition to reporting Part I offenses each month, law enforcement agencies also provide data on the age, sex, and race of persons arrested for Part I and Part II offenses. Part II offenses encompass all crimes, except traffic violations, that are not classified as Part I offenses.

Officers killed or assaulted—Each month, law enforcement agencies also report information to the UCR program regarding law enforcement officers killed or assaulted, and each year they report the number of full-time sworn and civilian law enforcement personnel employed as of October 31.

Editing Procedures

The UCR program thoroughly examines each report it receives for arithmetical accuracy and for deviations in crime data from month to month and from present to past years that may indicate errors. UCR staff members compare an agency's monthly reports with its previous submissions and with reports from similar agencies to identify any unusual fluctuations in the agency's crime count. Considerable variations in crime levels may indicate modified records procedures, incomplete reporting, or changes in the jurisdiction's geopolitical structure.

Evaluation of trends—Data reliability is a high priority of the FBI, which brings any deviations or arithmetical adjustments to the attention of state UCR programs or the submitting agencies. Typically, FBI staff members study the monthly reports to evaluate periodic trends prepared for individual reporting units. Any significant increase or decrease becomes the subject of a special inquiry. Changes in crime reporting procedures or annexations that affect an agency's jurisdiction can influence the level of reported crime. When this occurs, the FBI excludes the figures for specific crime categories or totals, if necessary, from the trend tabulations.

Training for contributors—In addition to the evaluation of trends, the FBI provides training seminars and instructional materials on crime reporting procedures to assist contributors in complying with UCR standards. Throughout the country, representatives from the national program coordinate with representatives of state programs and law enforcement personnel and hold training sessions to explain the purpose of the program, the rules of uniform classification and scoring, and the methods of assembling the information for reporting. When an individual agency has specific problems with compiling its crime statistics and its remedial efforts are unsuccessful, personnel from the FBI's Criminal Justice Information Services Division may visit the contributor to aid in resolving the problems.

UCR Handbook—The national UCR program publishes the *Uniform Crime Reporting (UCR) Handbook* (revised 2004), which details procedures for classifying and scoring offenses and serves as the contributing agencies' basic resource for preparing reports. The national staff also produces letters to UCR contributors, state program bulletins, and UCR newsletters as needed. These publications provide policy updates and new information, as well as clarification of reporting issues.

The final responsibility for data submissions rests with the individual contributing law enforcement agency. Although the FBI makes every effort through its editing procedures, training practices, and correspondence to ensure the validity of the data it receives, the accuracy of the statistics depends primarily on the adherence of each contributor to the established standards of reporting. Deviations from these established standards that cannot be resolved by the national UCR program may be brought to the attention of the Criminal Justice Information Systems Committees of the International Association of Chiefs of Police and the National Sheriffs' Association.

NIBRS Conversion

Thirty-three state programs are certified to provide their UCR data in the expanded National Incident-Based Reporting System (NIBRS) format. For presentation in this book, the NIBRS data were converted to the historical Summary Reporting System data. The UCR program staff constructed the NIBRS database to allow for such conversion so that UCR's long-running time series could continue.

Crime Trends

By showing fluctuations from year to year, trend statistics offer the data user an added perspective from which to study crime. Percent change tabulations in this publication are computed only for reporting agencies that provided comparable data for the periods under consideration. The FBI excludes from the trend calculations all figures except those received for common months from common agencies. Also excluded are unusual fluctuations of data that the FBI determines are the result of such variables as improved records procedures, annexations, and so on.

Caution to Users

Data users should exercise care in making any direct comparison between data in this publication and those in prior issues of *Crime in the United States*. Because of differing levels of participation from year to year and reporting problems that require the FBI to estimate crime counts for certain contributors, some data may not be comparable. In addition, this publication may contain updates to data provided in prior years' publications.

For information about the FBI's caution against ranking, including warnings about variables affecting crime and characteristics of jurisdictions, please see http://www.fbi.gov/about-us/cjis/ucr/ucr-statistics-their-proper-use.

Offense Estimation

Some tables in this publication contain statistics for the entire United States. Because not all law enforcement agencies provide data for complete reporting periods, the FBI includes estimated crime numbers in these presentations. The FBI estimates data for three areas: Metropolitan Statistical Areas (MSAs), cities outside MSAs, and nonmetropolitan counties; and computes estimates for participating agencies that do not provide 12 months of complete data. For agencies supplying 3 to 11 months of data, the national UCR program estimates for the missing data by following a standard estimation procedure using the data provided by the agency. If an agency has supplied less than 3 months of data, the FBI computes estimates by using the known crime figures of similar areas within a state and assigning the same proportion of crime volumes to nonreporting agencies. The estimation process considers the following: population size covered by the agency; type of jurisdiction; for example, police department versus sheriff's office; and geographic location.

Estimation of State-Level Data

In response to various circumstances, the FBI calculates estimated offense totals for certain states. For example, some states do not provide forcible rape figures in accordance with UCR guidelines. In addition, problems at the state level have, at times, resulted in no useable data. Also, the conversion of the National Incident-Based Reporting System (NIBRS) data to summary data has contributed to the need for unique estimation procedures.

Expanded Offense Tables

Expanded offense data are the details of the various offenses that the Uniform Crime Reporting Program collects beyond the count of how many crimes law enforcement agencies report. These details may include the type of weapon used in a crime, the type or value of items stolen, and so forth. Expanded homicide data provide supplemental details about murders such as the age, sex, and race of both the victim and the offender, the weapon used in the homicide, the circumstances surrounding the offense, and the relationship of the victim to the offender. In addition, expanded data includes trends (for example, 2-year comparisons) and rates per 100,000 inhabitants.

Expanded offense data, including expanded homicide data, are information collected in addition to the reports of the number of crimes known. As a result, law enforcement agencies can report an offense without providing the supplemental data about that offense.

Federal Crime Data

In past years, these agencies' data were included in various tables in *Crime in the United States*. *Federal Crime Data* signals the move to presenting federal data in a way more attuned with local, state, and tribal UCR data. Included are the federal agencies that have submitted traditional UCR data for some time.

A few agencies, such as the National Institutes of Health (NIH) and several agencies within the U.S. Department of the Interior (DOI), investigate and police in ways similar to local or state authorities. These federal agencies have long reported data to the UCR Program. However, other federal agencies, the FBI included, found it more difficult to fit into the UCR model. This annual report was originally designed as a stepping stone to finding ways to provide a similar transparency and access to federal crime data that the UCR Program has brought to local, state, and tribal crime data for nearly 90 years. The arrest data from the FBI, ATF, and USMS have all been mapped to correspond to the UCR's National Incident-Based Reporting System (NIBRS) offense codes. This makes the overlay of federal data with local and state data much easier.

Comparability of federal data to state and local data

The best approach to viewing the federal data offered is to use it to gain an overall impression of the intensity of certain types of offenses within a specific area by overlaying the federal arrests in conjunction with the local and state information. As developments in the data collection continue to occur, more details will become available from federal agencies, and these impressions will become more sharply focused.

Federal crime data are often different from local and state data, not only in their collection, but also in their generation. The UCR Program has built its traditional data collection on three triggering events that are common to local and state agencies. Offense information begins with either, first, a complaint of a victim/citizen or, second, the observation of a crime in progress by a law enforcement officer. A third trigger for data is when an arrest is made and information related to that occurrence is reported.

For federal agencies, the initiation of investigation may be prompted in different ways. Many crimes, such as human trafficking and hate crime and their associated data, are brought to the attention of the FBI in much the same fashion:

- Reports from victims
- Liaison with other law enforcement agencies
- Information about victims (e.g., human trafficking, hate crime) brought to the FBI by nongovernmental organizations
- Reports from the media

The decision to handle a crime as a federal investigation or as a local investigation is determined on a case-by-case basis. Some of the factors that enter into the decision for federal agencies to pursue an investigation are the available evidence, the availability of resources at the local level, and, in the case of hate crime, statutory provisions that determine whether the U.S. Attorney will accept the case as a federal one. In addition, some states do not have a hate crime statute under which to pursue a case.

Why federal numbers are smaller than those of other UCR agencies

As mentioned previously, federal investigations, by nature, often begin under different circumstances and proceed and conclude on different timeframes than investigations conducted by local and state agencies. Just as federal agencies often do not have traditional offenses known to report, they also typically do not have a number of offenses to report until a case has been built and an arrest or indictment has occurred. Perhaps most impactful on the federal numbers is the fact that federal agencies often play a collaborative role with local and state agencies in crime investigations. Because the UCR Program has the "most local reporting" rule, which specifies that the agency involved that is the most local jurisdiction should report the incident to the UCR Program, investigations and arrests that federal authorities have worked on often are reported by city, county, state, or tribal agencies.

The UCR Program defines law enforcement officers as individuals who ordinarily carry a firearm and a badge, have full arrest powers, and are paid from governmental funds set aside specifically to pay sworn law enforcement.

Civilian employees include full-time agency personnel such as clerks, radio dispatchers, meter attendants, stenographers, jailers, correctional officers, and mechanics.

Data were not included for arrests made in joint investigations with other agencies when local or state codes were used nor for Human Trafficking cases when different provisions of the U.S. Code were used for the basis of arrest.

These data include arrests by the FBI or task forces for the following:

09A – 09C Homicide Arrests

Section
1111 – Murder
1112 – Manslaughter
1114 – Protection of officers and employees of the United States 3592(c) – Aggravating factors for homicide

11A – 11D Sex Offense Arrests

Title 18 USC

13A – 13C Assault Arrests

Section
2241 – Aggravated sexual abuse
2242 – Sexual abuse
2243 – Sexual abuse of a minor or ward 2244C – Abusive sexual contact
2251 – Sexual exploitation of children

Section
111 – Assaulting, resisting, or impeding certain officers or employees
113 – Assaults within maritime and territorial jurisdiction
844(e) – Whoever, through the use of mail, telephone, telegraph, or other instrument of interstate or foreign commerce willfully makes any threat
871 – Threats against President and successors to the President
875 – Interstate communications
876 – Mailing threatening communications
879 – Threats against former Presidents and certain other persons
1389 – Prohibition on attacks on United States servicemen on account of service
1501 – Assault on process server
1503 – Influencing or injuring officer or juror generally
1512 – Tampering with a witness, victim, or an informant
1841 – Protection of unborn children
2231 – Assault or resistance
2237 – Criminal sanctions for failure to heave to, obstruction of boarding, or providing false information
7212 – Attempts to interfere with administration of internal revenue laws
46504 – Interference with flight crew members and attendants

23A – 23H Larceny and Theft Arrests

26A – 26E Fraud Arrests

Section
1167 – Theft from gaming establishments on Indian lands
1708 – Theft or receipt of stolen mail matter generally

35A – 35 B Drug and Narcotics Arrests

862 – Denial of federal benefits to drug traffickers and possessors

864 – Anhydrous ammonia

881 – Forfeitures drug abuse prevention and control

952 – Importation of controlled substances

959 – Possession, manufacture, or distribution of controlled substance

960 – Unlawful for any person to knowingly or intentionally import or export a controlled substance

70503 – While on board a covered vessel, an individual my not knowingly or intentionally manufacture or distribute, or possess with intent to manufacture or distribute, a controlled substance

70506 – A person shall be punished under the Comprehensive Drug Abuse Prevention and Control Act of 1970

70507 – Seizure of property described in the Drug Abuse Prevention and Control Act

39A – 39D Gambling Offenses Arrests

Section

1084 – Transmission of wagering information

64A – 64B Human Trafficking Arrests

Section

1324 – Bringing in and harboring certain aliens

1351 – Fraud in foreign labor contracting

1581 – Peonage; obstructing enforcement

1583 – Enticement into slavery

1584 – Sale into involuntary servitude

1589 – Forced labor

1591 – Sex trafficking of children or by force, fraud, or coercion

1592 – Unlawful conduct with respect to documents in furtherance of trafficking, peonage, slavery, involuntary servitude, or forced labor

1593A – Benefitting financially from peonage, slavery, and trafficking in persons 1594 – General provisions

1596 – Additional jurisdiction in certain trafficking offenses

1597 – Unlawful conduct with respect to immigration documents

2251A – Selling or buying children

2421 – Transportation generally

2422 – Coercion and enticement

2423 – Transportation of minors

2425 – Use of interstate facilities to transmit information about a minor

3271 – Trafficking in persons offenses committed by persons employed by or accompanying the federal government outside the United States

100 Kidnapping and Abduction Arrests

120 Robbery Arrests

200 Arson Arrests

Section

1201 – Kidnapping

1202 – Ransom money

1203 – Hostage taking

1204 – International parental kidnapping

Section

2113 – Bank robbery and incidental crimes

Section

81 – Arson within special maritime and territorial jurisdiction

210 Extortion and Blackmail Arrests

Section

875 – Interstate communications

892 – Making extortionate extensions of credit

893 – Financing extortionate extensions of credit

894 – Collection of extensions of credit by extortionate means

250 Counterfeiting and Forgery Arrests

Section

21 – Stolen or counterfeit nature of property for certain crimes

473 – Dealing in counterfeit obligations or securities

499 – Military, naval, or official passes

505 – Seals of courts; signatures of judges or court officers

514 – Fictitious obligations

642 – Tools and materials for counterfeiting purposes

1010 – Department of Housing and Urban Development and Federal Housing Administration transactions

1546 – Fraud and misuse of visas, permits, and other documents

2320 – Trafficking in counterfeit goods or services

270 Embezzlement Arrests

Section

153 – Embezzlement against estate

641 – Public money, property or records

654 – Officer or employee of United States converting property of another

656 – Theft, embezzlement, or misapplication by bank officer or employee

657 – Lending, credit and insurance institutions

659 – Interstate of foreign shipments by carrier; state prosecutions

664 – Theft or embezzlement from employee benefit plan

1163 – Embezzlement and theft from Indian tribal organizations

1168 – Theft by officers or employees of gaming establishments on Indian lands

280 Stolen Property Arrests

Section
2312 – Transportation of stolen vehicles
2314 – Transportation of stolen goods, securities, moneys, fraudulent state tax stamps, or articles used in counterfeiting
2315 – Sale or receipt of stolen goods, securities, moneys, or fraudulent state tax stamps
2321 – Trafficking in certain motor vehicles or motor vehicle parts

290 Destruction, Damage, and Vandalism of Property Arrests

Section
248 – Freedom of access to clinic entrances
1366 – Destruction of energy facility
1512(c) – Whoever corruptly alters, destroys, mutilates, or conceals a record, document, or other object, or attempts to do so, with the intent to impair the object's integrity or availability for use in an official proceeding
1703 – Delay or destruction of mail or newspapers
1705 – Destruction of letter boxes or mail

370 Pornography and Obscene Material Arrests

Section
1462 – Importation or transportation of obscene material
1465 – Production and transportation of obscene matters for sale or distribution
1466 – Engaging in the business of selling or transferring obscene matter
1470 – Transfer of obscene material to minors
2252 – Certain activities relating to material involving the sexual exploitation of minors 2252A – Activities relating to material constituting or containing child pornography 2260 – Production of sexually explicit depictions of a minor for importation into the United States
223 – Obscene or harassing telephone calls in the District of Columbia or in interstate or foreign communications

Section
201 – Bribery of public officials and witnesses
212 – Offer of loan or gratuity to financial institution examiner
215 – Receipt of commissions or gifts for procuring loans
224 – Bribery in sporting events
1510 – Obstruction of criminal investigation

Section
841 – "Person" means any individual, corporation, company, association, firm, partnership, society, or joint stock company
842 – Unlawful acts in explosive materials
843 – Licenses and user permits in explosive materials
844 – Penalties in explosive materials

846 – Additional powers of the Attorney General in explosive materials
847 – Rules and regulations in explosive materials
848 – Effect on State Law in explosive materials
921 – The term "firearm" means (A) any weapon (including a starter gun) which will or is designed to or may readily be converted to expel a projectile by the action of an

510 Bribery Arrests

4520 Weapon Law Arrests

explosive; (B) the frame or receiver of any such weapon; (C) any firearm muffler or firearm silencer; or (D) any destructive device
922(a) – Unlawful for any person, other than a licensed importer, licensed manufacturer, licensed dealer, or licensed collector to transport into or receive in the state where he resides
922(c) – A licensed importer, licensed manufacturer, or licensed dealer may sell a firearm to a person who does not appear in person at the license's business premise' only if transferee submits a sworn statement
922(d) – Unlawful for any person to sell or otherwise dispose of a firearm or ammunition to any person knowing or having reasonable cause to believe that a person under indictment, a fugitive from justice, unlawful user of or addicted to a controlled substance, has been adjudicated as a mental defective or committed to a mental institution, is illegally in the United States, discharged from the Armed Forces under dishonorable conditions, has renounced his citizenship, subject to a court order that restrains such person from harassing, stalking or threatening an intimate partner, and has been convicted in any court of a misdemeanor crime of domestic violence.
922(e) – It shall be unlawful for any person knowingly to deliver or cause to be delivered to any common or contract carrier for transportation or shipment in interstate or foreign commerce, to person other than licensed importers, licensed manufacturers, license dealers, or licensed collectors, any package or other container in which there is any firearm
922(g) – Unlawful for any person who has been convicted in any court of, a crime punishable by imprisonment for a term exceeding one year
922(j) – It shall be unlawful for any person to receive, possess, conceal, store, barter, sell, or dispose of any stolen firearm or stolen ammunition, or pledge or accept as security for a loan any stolen firearm or stolen ammunition
922(k) – It shall be unlawful for any person knowingly to transport, ship, or receive, in interstate or foreign commerce, any firearm which has had the importer's or manufacturer's serial number removed, obliterated, altered
922(n) – It shall be unlawful for any person who is under indictment for a crime punishable by imprisonment for a term exceeding one year to ship or transport in interstate or foreign commerce

922(o) – It shall be unlawful for any person to transfer or possess a machinegun 923 – Licensing

924 - Penalties

928 – Separability

930 – Possession of firearms and dangerous weapons in federal facilities 3665 – Firearms possessed by convicted felons

5841 – Registration of firearms

5842 – Identification of firearms

5861 – Prohibited acts under machine guns, etc.

5861(c) – To receive or possess a firearm made in violation of the provisions of machine guns, etc.

5861(d) – To receive or possess a firearm which is not registered to him in the National Firearms Registration and Transfer Record

5861(f) – To make a firearm in violation of the provisions

5861(i) – To receive or possess a firearm which is not identified by a serial number as required

5861(l) – To make, or cause making of, a false entry on any application, return, or record required by this chapter, knowing such entry to be false

46505 – Carrying a weapon or explosive on an aircraft

720 Animal Cruelty Arrests

Section

2156 – Animal fighting venture prohibition

41 – Hunting, fishing, trapping; disturbance or injury on wildlife refuges

90G Liquor Law Arrests

47 – Use of aircraft or motor vehicles to hunt certain wild horses or burros; pollution of watering holes

49 – Enforcement of animal fighting prohibitions

Section

1156 – Intoxicants possessed unlawfully 3113 – Liquor law violations in Indian country

90Z All Other Offenses Arrests

Section

1229 – Initiation of removal proceedings

1325 – Improper entry by alien

1325(a) – Improper time or place; avoidance of examination or inspection; misrepresentation and concealment of facts

1326 – Reentry of removed aliens

84 – Interference with aids to navigation; penalty

506(a) – Any person who willfully infringes a copyright shall be punished

4 – Misprision of felony

13 – Laws of States adopted for areas within federal jurisdiction

39(a) – Aiming a laser pointer at an aircraft

42 – Importation or shipment or injurious mammals, birds, fish (including mollusks and crustacea), amphibia, and reptiles; permits, specimens for museums; regulations

219 – Officers and employees acting as agents of foreign principals

228 – Failure to pay legal child support obligations

243(b) – Exclusion of jurors on account of race or color

371 – Conspiracy to commit offense or to defraud United States

372 – Conspiracy to impede or injure officer

373 – Solicitation to commit a crime of violence

402 – Contempts constituting crimes

513 – Securities of the states and private entities

545 – Smuggling goods into the United States

554 – Smuggling goods from the United States

751 – Prisoners in custody of institution or officer

793(e) – Gathering, transmitting or losing defense information

831 – Prohibited transactions involving nuclear material

842(p) – Distribution of Information Relating to Explosives, Destructive Devices, and Weapons of Mass Destruction

931 – Prohibition on purchase, ownership, or possession of body armor by violent felons

951 – Agents of foreign governments

951(a) – Whoever, other than a diplomatic or consular officer or attaché, acts in the United States as an agent of a foreign government without prior notification to the Attorney General if required

952 – Diplomatic codes and correspondence

955 – Financial transactions with foreign governments

956 – Conspiracy to kill, kidnap, main, or injure persons or damage property in a foreign country

960 – Expedition against friendly nation

981 – Civil forfeiture

1030 – Fraud and related activity in connection with computers

1071 – Concealing person from arrest

1073 – Flight to avoid prosecution or giving testimony

1083 – Transportation between shore and ship; penalties

1117 – Conspiracy to murder

1349 – Attempt and conspiracy

1365 – Tampering with consumer products

1425 – Procurement of citizenship or naturalization unlawfully

1511 – Obstruction of state or local law enforcement

1512 – Tampering with a witness, victim, or an informant

1519 – Destruction, alteration, or falsification of records in federal investigations and bankruptcy

1621 – Perjury generally

1622 – Subornation of perjury

1623 – False declarations before grand jury or court

1651 – Piracy under law of nations

1692 – Foreign mail as United States mail

1791 – Providing or possessing contraband in prison

1801 – Video voyeurism

1831 – Economic espionage

1924 – Unauthorized removal and retention of classified documents or material

1960 – Prohibition of unlicensed money transmitting businesses

1992 – Terrorist attaches and other violence against railroad carriers and against mass transportation systems on land, on water, or through the air

2156 – Production of defective national-defense material, national-defense premises, or national defense utilities

2250 – Failure to register as a sex offender

2332 – Criminal penalties for terrorism

2332A – Use of weapons of mass destruction

2332B – Acts of terrorism transcending national boundaries

2332F – Bombings of places of public use, government facilities, public transportation systems and infrastructure facilities

2339 – Harboring or concealing terrorists

2339A – Providing material support to terrorists

2339B – Providing material support or resources to designated foreign terrorist organizations

2341 – Definitions for trafficking in contraband cigarettes and smokeless tobacco 2342 – Unlawful acts for trafficking in contraband cigarettes and smokeless tobacco 2342(a) – It shall be unlawful for any person knowingly to ship, transport, receive, possess, sell, distribute, or purchase contraband cigarettes or contraband smokeless tobacco

2344 – Penalties for trafficking in contraband cigarettes and smokeless tobacco

2401 – Renumbered 2441

2441 – War crimes

2442 – Recruitment or use of child soldiers

3062 – General arrest authority for violation of release conditions

3103 – Grounds for issuing search warrant

3122 – Application for an order for a pen register or a trap and trace device

3146 – Penalty for failure to appear

3184 – Fugitives from foreign country to United States

3290 – Fugitives from justice

3606 – Arrest and return of a probationer

3615 – Criminal default

7201 – Attempt to evade or defeat tax

7202 – Willful failure to collect or pay over tax

7203 – Willful failure to file return, supply information, or pay tax

5324 – Structuring transactions to evade reporting requirement prohibited

5332 – Bulk cash smuggling into or out of the United States

1311 – Effluent limitations

1319(c) – Enforcement of criminal penalties

2077 – Unauthorized dealings in special nuclear material

46312 – Transportation hazardous material

Child Exploitation Arrests

Section

1204 – International parental kidnapping

1462 – Importation or transportation of obscene matters

1466 – Engaging in the business of selling or transferring obscene matter

1470 – Transfer of obscene material to minors

2241 – Aggravated sexual abuse

2242 – Sexual abuse

2243 – Sexual abuse of a minor or ward

2244c – Sexual abuse offenses involving your children

2251 – Sexual exploitation of children

2252 – Certain activities relating to material involving the sexual exploitation of minors 2260 – Production of sexually explicit depictions of a minor for importation into the United States

2421 – Transportation generally

2422 – Coercion and enticement

2423 – Transportation of minors

Employee counts were as of December 2016 for both FBI and ATF.

Population estimation

Population estimates used in this table are the U.S. Census Bureau's published resident population estimates for counties for 2015. The U.S. Census Bureau calculates estimates based on the decennial census of 2010 and by applying measures of population changes. See https://factfinder.census.gov/faces/tableservices/jsf/pages/productview.xhtml?pid=PEP_2016_PEPANNRES&src=pt for further information on county breakdowns for each state.

Human Trafficking

As state participation has grown, the UCR Program has seen an increase in human trafficking data submissions. The program will continue efforts to expand, gather, and make available information regarding human trafficking incidents.

Trafficking Victims Protection Act

In January 2013, the national UCR Program began collecting offense and arrest data regarding human trafficking as authorized by the William Wilberforce Trafficking Victims Protection Reauthorization Act of 2008. The act requires the FBI to collect human trafficking offense data and to make distinctions between prostitution, assisting or promoting prostitution, and purchasing prostitution.

To comply with the Wilberforce Act, the national UCR Program created two additional offenses in the Summary Reporting System (SRS) and the National Incident-Based Reporting System (NIBRS) through which the UCR Program collects both offense and arrest data. The definitions for these offenses are:

Human Trafficking/Commercial Sex Acts: inducing a person by force, fraud, or coercion to participate in commercial sex acts, or in which the person induced to perform such act(s) has not attained 18 years of age.

Human Trafficking/Involuntary Servitude: obtaining of a person(s) through recruitment, harboring, transportation, or provision, and subjecting such persons by force, fraud, or coercion into involuntary servitude, peonage, debt bondage, or slavery (not to include commercial sex acts).

The data in the tables included in this report reflect the offenses and arrests recorded by state and local law enforcement agencies (LEAs) that currently have the ability to report the data to the national UCR Program. As such, they should not be interpreted as a definitive statement of the level or characteristics of human trafficking as a whole. The data declaration pages, which will help the user better understand the data, and the methodology used for the four following tables are located in the Data Declarations and Methodology section near the end of this report. In addition, a Question and Answer section about human trafficking data is provided as a supplement to this report.

Note: Regarding the data reported to the UCR Program, it is important to note that these data represent only one view of a complex issue—the law enforcement perspective. However, due to the nature of human trafficking, many of these crimes are never reported to the local, state, tribal, and federal LEAs that investigate them. In addition to the law enforcement facet in fighting these crimes, there are victim service organizations whose mission it is to serve the needs of the victims of human trafficking. In order to have the complete picture of human trafficking, it would be necessary to gather information from all of these sources.

Tables include the states that have added human trafficking offenses to their data collection and the number of agencies per state participating in the UCR Program. Even though a state program included human trafficking, the individual agencies in that state may or may not have added it to their collections. Indiana, Mississippi, and portions of Ohio have no UCR state program to manage the collection of UCR data within the state. Each law enforcement agency is responsible for reporting its crime data directly to the FBI.

For UCR purposes, juveniles are individuals under the age of 18 years. Adults are 18 years of age or older.

The data used in creating these tables were from law enforcement agencies submitting one or more human trafficking incidents for at least 1 month of the calendar year. Also included are zero data for states which have incorporated human trafficking offenses in their data collection where no 2016 human trafficking incidents were reported to the FBI UCR Program.

The published data, therefore, do not necessarily represent reports from each participating agency for all 12 months of the calendar year. When the FBI determines that an agency's data collection methodology does not comply with national UCR guidelines, the figure(s) for that agency's offense(s) will not be included in the table, and the discrepancy will be explained in a footnote.

Cargo Theft

The FBI's Uniform Crime Reporting (UCR) Program collects cargo theft data to inform the law enforcement community, state and federal legislators, academia, and the public at large about this particular crime. The data can be used to create awareness and to measure the impact cargo theft has on the economy and potential threats to national security. Often cargo theft offenses are part of larger criminal schemes and have been found to be components of organized crime rings, drug trafficking, and funding for terrorism. The UCR collection of cargo theft data is new with only 4 years of data published, but the number of agencies reporting cargo theft incidents has increased each year. As more agencies participate, future versions of this cargo theft report will depict a more complete account of the occurrences of cargo theft in the United States.

Due to the significant economic impact cargo theft has on the United States economy, and the potential for use by terrorist organizations, Congress mandated H.R. 3199, the USA Patriot Improvement and Reauthorization Act of 2005 on March 9, 2006. It required the Attorney General to "take the steps necessary to ensure that reports of cargo theft collected by Federal, State, and local officials are reflected as a separate category in the Uniform Crime Reporting System, or any successor system, by no later than December 31, 2006." In response to this mandate, the Criminal Justice Information Services (CJIS) Advisory Policy Board approved a definition for collecting cargo theft in December 2006. Creation of the data specifications required to capture cargo theft data in the UCR's Summary Reporting System as well as the National Incident-Based Reporting System were finalized in 2010 with the first publication of cargo theft data in 2013.

Cargo theft is defined as "The criminal taking of any cargo including, but not limited to, goods, chattels, money, or baggage that constitutes, in whole or in part, a commercial shipment of freight moving in commerce, from any pipeline system, railroad car, motor truck, or other vehicle, or from any tank or storage facility, station house, platform, or depot, or from any vessel or wharf, or from any aircraft, air terminal, airport, aircraft terminal or air navigation facility, or from any intermodal container, intermodal chassis, trailer, container freight station, warehouse, freight distribution facility, or freight consolidation facility. For purposes of this definition, cargo shall be deemed as moving in commerce at all points between the point of origin and the final destination, regardless of any temporary stop while awaiting transshipment or otherwise."

This definition was developed, not as a legal description for prosecutorial purposes, but to capture the essence of the national cargo theft problem in the United States. The legal elements of knowledge and intent were intentionally omitted.

Participation in the UCR Program is voluntary, and agencies or states may choose not to participate. Participation in the cargo theft data has remained steady; however, several factors have been identified having a direct impact on this important data collection:

- States may not have the resources required to make the necessary technical changes or to align their local and state statutes with federal requirements.
- States may not have the necessary resources to conduct data quality checks on reported incidents associated with cargo theft, which could result in inaccurate data.
- States may not have adequate resources to train participants on how to recognize and properly record cargo theft incidents.
- States may not perceive cargo theft as a priority or a significant problem within their states and make decisions based on their immediate needs regarding resource allocation.

Quality data concerning cargo theft can help us better understand this crime and the threats associated with it. As more agencies choose to report their incidents, the FBI's UCR Program will be able to provide more information about cargo theft on a national scale. For additional information on the UCR Program's collection of cargo theft incidents, visit https://www.fbi.gov/about-us/cjis/ucr/ucr-program-data-collections.

Tables present by state the total number of agencies that submitted data about cargo theft incidents, the number of incidents reported, the reported value of stolen property, the value and percentage of recovered property for each submitting state.

Data used were from all law enforcement agencies submitting one or more cargo theft incidents for at least 1 month of the calendar year. The published data, therefore, do not necessarily represent reports from each participating agency for all 12 months of the calendar year. Based on UCR guidelines, the property descriptions of credit/debit cards, nonnegotiable instruments, documents/personal or business, and identity-intangible, must be submitted with zero value for stolen and/or recovered. In the Cargo Theft Program, the victim of a cargo theft may be an individual, a business, an institution, or society as a whole. The UCR Program counted one for each victim type reported in an incident.

Because cargo theft has been defined as "the criminal **taking of** any cargo . . .," there are specific crimes against property that apply to cargo theft. The applicable crimes against property include:

120 = Robbery
23D = Theft from building
23F = Theft from motor vehicle
23H = All other larceny
26A = False pretenses, swindle, confidence game
26B = Credit card, automatic teller machine fraud
26C = Impersonation
26E = Wire fraud
210 = Extortion, blackmail
220 = Burglary, breaking & entering
240 = Motor vehicle theft
270 = Embezzlement
510 = Bribery

In addition, cargo theft is not considered an offense by itself; all offenses that happen within a cargo theft incident are to be reported. Cargo theft data are derived by capturing the additional element of "theft of cargo" in incidents that contain any of the applicable offenses.

PART 3

Criminal Victimization, 2019

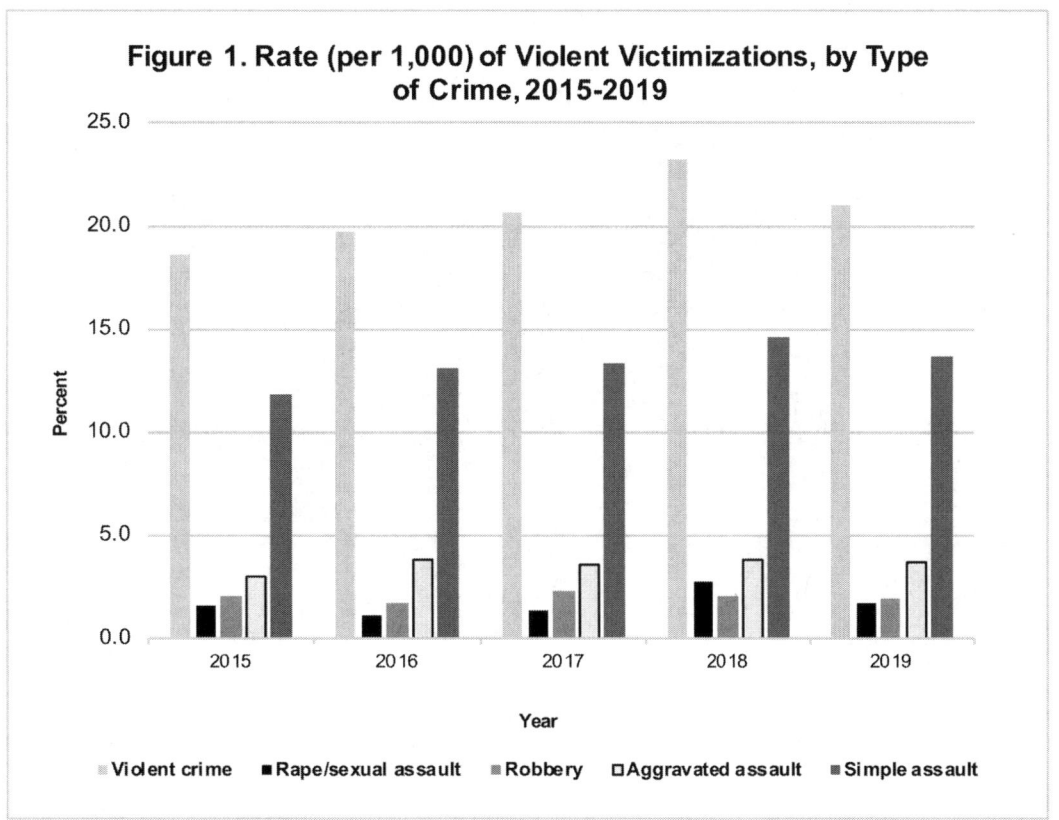

Figure 1. Rate (per 1,000) of Violent Victimizations, by Type of Crime, 2015-2019

- Between. 2018 and 2019, there was a decline of approximately 15 percent in the rate of violent crime (excluding simple assault); the total for persons age 12 and older fell from 8.6 to 7.3 victimizations per 1,000 persons.

- Among females, the rate of violent victimization excluding simple assault fell 27 percent from 2018 to 2019.

- From 2018 to 2019, 29 percent fewer Black persons and 22 percent fewer White persons were victims of serious crimes.

- The rate of violent victimization in urban areas—based on the NCVS's new classifications of urban, suburban, and rural areas—declined 20 percent from 2018 to 2019.

- There were 880,000 fewer victims of serious crimes (generally felonies) in 2019 than in 2018, a drop of 19 percent.

Table 1. Number and Rate of Violent Victimizations, by Type of Crime, 2015-2019

(Number; percent.)

Type of violent crime	2015 Number	2015 Rate per 1,000[1]	2016 Number	2016 Rate per 1,000[1]	2017 Number	2017 Rate per 1,000[1]	2018 Number	2018 Rate per 1,000[1]	2019* Number	2019* Rate per 1,000[1]
Violent Crime[2]	5,006,620[A]	18.6	5,353,820	19.7	5,612,670	20.6	6,385,520	23.2	5,813,410	21.0
Rape/sexual assault[3]	431,840	1.6	298,410[A]	1.1[A]	393,980	1.4	734,630[B]	2.7[B]	459,310	1.7
Robbery	578,580	2.1	458,810	1.7	613,840	2.3	573,100	2.1	534,420	1.9
Assault	3,996,200[B]	14.8[A]	4,596,600	16.9	4,604,850	16.9	5,077,790	18.4	4,819,680	17.4
Aggravated assault	816,760[A]	3.0	1,040,580	3.8	993,170	3.6	1,058,040	3.8	1,019,490	3.7
Simple assault	3,179,440[A]	11.8	3,556,020	13.1	3,611,680	13.3	4,019,750	14.6	3,800,190	13.7
Violent crime excluding simple assault[4]	1,827,170	6.8	1,797,790	6.6	2,000,990	7.3	2,365,770[B]	8.6[B]	2,013,220	7.3

NOTE: Details may not sum to totals due to rounding. Violent-crime categories include rape or sexual assault, robbery, aggravated assault, and simple assault, and they include threatened, attempted, and completed occurrences of those crimes. Year-to-year statistically significant differences may vary from those previously reported. Previously, BJS created standard errors and presented testing for statistically significant differences among National Crime Victimization Survey (NCVS) estimates in this table using generalized variance function parameters, while this table uses the Balanced Repeated Replication method.
* = Comparison year.
A = Significant difference from comparison year at the 90% confidence level.
B = Significant difference from comparison year at the 96% confidence level.
[1]Rate is per 1,000 persons age 12 years or older.
[2]Excludes homicide because the NCVS is based on interviews with victims.
[3]See Methodology for details on the measurement of rape or sexual assault in the NCVS.
[4]Includes rape or sexual assault, robbery, and aggravated assault; this category was called serious violent crime prior to *Criminal Victimization, 2018*.

Table 2. Number and Rate of Property Victimizations, by Type of Crime, 2015–2019

(Number; rate.)

Type of property crime	2015 Number	2015 Rate per 1,000[1]	2016 Number	2016 Rate per 1,000[1]	2017 Number	2017 Rate per 1,000[1]	2018 Number	2018 Rate per 1,000[1]	2019* Number	2019* Rate per 1,000[1]
Total	14,611,040	110.7[B]	15,815,310	118.6[B]	13,340,220	108.4[B]	13,502,840[B]	108.2[B]	12,818,000	101.4
Burglary/trespassing[2]	2,904,570	22.0[B]	3,160,450	23.7[B]	2,538,170[B]	20.6[B]	2,639,620[B]	21.1[B]	2,178,400	17.2
Burglary[3]	2,020,730	15.3[B]	2,205,180	16.5[B]	1,688,890	13.7[B]	1,867,620[B]	15.0[B]	1,484,730	11.7
Trespassing[4]	883,850	6.7[A]	955,270	7.2[B]	849,280[A]	6.9[B]	772,000	6.2	693,670	5.5
Motor vehicle theft	564,160	4.3	618,330	4.6	516,810	4.2	534,010	4.3	495,670	3.9
Other theft[5]	11,142,310	84.4	12,036,530	90.3[B]	10,285,240	83.6	10,329,210	82.7	10,143,930	80.2

NOTE: Details may not sum to totals due to rounding. Categories include threatened, attempted, and completed crimes. The number of property crimes should not be compared from 2017, 2018, or 2019 to 2016 or 2015, as the National Crime Victimization Survey (NCVS) household weighting adjustment was updated for 2017 onward, which decreased the number of estimated households by about 8%. Property crime rates are unaffected by this change. See Methodology for details. Year-to-year statistically significant differences may vary from those previously reported. Previously, BJS created standard errors and presented testing for statistically significant differences among NCVS estimates in this table using generalized variance function parameters, while this table uses the Balanced Repeated Replication method. See Methodology for more information.
* = Comparison year.
A = Significant difference from comparison year at the 90% confidence level.
B = Significant difference from comparison year at the 95% confidence level.
[1]Rate is per 1,000 households. See appendix table 35 for number of households.
[2]Called household burglary prior to Criminal Victimization, 2018. Includes unlawful or forcible entry or attempted entry of places, including a permanent residence, other residence (e.g., a hotel room or vacation residence), or other structure (e.g., a garage or shed), but does not include trespassing on land.
[3]Includes only crimes where the offender committed or attempted a theft. Estimates differ from those previously published in the Criminal Victimization, 2018 report because a coding error that affected the generation of those earlier estimates has been corrected.
[4]Includes crimes where the offender did not commit or attempt a theft. Does not include trespassing on land. Estimates differ from those previously published in the Criminal Victimization, 2018 report because a coding error that affected the generation of those earlier estimates has been corrected.
[5]Includes other unlawful taking or attempted unlawful taking of property or cash without personal contact with the victim. Incidents involving theft of property from within the same household would classify as theft if the offender has a legal right to be in the house (such as a maid, delivery person, or guest). If the offender has no legal right to be in the house, the incident would classify as a burglary.

Table 3. Number and Rate of Violent Victimizations, by Selected Characteristics of Violent Crime, 2018 and 2019

(Number; rate per 1,000 persons age 12 years or older.)

Selected characteristics of violent crime	2018 Number	2018 Rate per 1,000[1]	2019* Number	2019* Rate per 1,000[1]
Domestic violence[2]	1,333,050	4.8	1,164,540	4.2
Intimate partnet violence[3]	847,230	3.1	695,060	2.5
Stranger violence[4]	2,493,750	9.1	2,254,740	8.1
Violent crime involving injury	1,449,530	5.3	1,265,680	4.6
Violent crime involving a weapon	1,329,700	4.8	1,119,060	4.0

Note: Details may not sum to totals due to rounding. Violent-crime categories include rape or sexual assault, robbery, aggravated assault, and simple assault. They also include threatened, attempted, and completed occurrences of those crimes. Other violent-crime categories in this table, including domestic violence and violent crime involving injury, are not mutually exclusive from these categories or from each other.
* = Comparison year.
[1]Rate is per 1,000 persons age 12 or older.
[2]Includes the subset of violent victimizations that were committed by intimate partners or family members.
[3]Includes the subset of domestic-violence victimizations that were committed by intimate partners, which include current or former spouses, boyfriends, or girlfriends.
[4]Includes the subset of violent victimizations that were committed by someone unknown to the victim.

Table 4. Rate of Completed, Attempted, and Threatened Violent Victimizations, 2015–2019

(Rate per 1,000 persons age 12 years or older.)

Violent victimizations	2015	2016	2017	2018	2019*
Total[1]	18.6	19.7	20.6	23.2	21.0
Completed	6.0	5.1	5.6	6.9[A]	5.5
Attempted	6.4	6.0	6.8	7.2	7.0
Threatened	6.1[B]	8.5	8.2	9.2	8.5

NOTE: Details may not sum to totals due to rounding. Violent-victimization categories include rape or sexual assault, robbery, aggravated assault, and simple assault.
* = Comparison year.
A = Significant difference from comparison year at the 90% confidence level.
B = Significant difference from comparison year at the 95% confidence level.
[1]Statistically significant differences for the total victimization rates are presented using the Balanced Repeated Replication method. Generalized variance function parameters were used to calculate statistically significant differences for the rest of the table.

Table 5. Rates of Crime Reported to Police in the Uniform Crime Reporting Program and in the National Crime Victimization Survey, 2018 and 2019

(Rate.)

Type of crime	2018 UCR rate per 1,000 residents[1]	Rate per 1,000 persons age 12 years or older 2018 NCVS	Rate per 1,000 persons age 12 years or older 2019 NCVS
Violent crime excluding simple assault	3.7	4.3	3.4
Murder	0.1	X	X
Rape/sexual assault[2]	0.4	0.7	0.6
Robbery	0.9	1.3	0.9
Aggravated assault	2.5	2.3	1.9

Type of crime	2018 UCR rate per 1,000 residents[1]	Rate per 1,000 households 2018 NCVS	Rate per 1,000 households 2019 NCVS
Property crime	22.0	36.9	33.0
Burglary[3]	3.8	7.1	6.0
Motor vehicle theft	2.3	3.4	3.1

NOTE: National Crime Victimization Survey (NCVS) and Uniform Crime Reporting (UCR) program crime rates are calculated differently. UCR crime rates are normally reported per 100,000 persons but were recalculated for this report to align with the reporting of NCVS crime rates.
X = Not applicable.
[1]Includes crimes against populations not included in the NCVS: persons age 11 or younger, persons who are homeless, persons who are institutionalized, and crimes against commercial establishments.
[2]The NCVS estimate includes sexual assault; the UCR does not. The UCR estimate is based on its revised definition of rape.
[3]The UCR defines burglary as forcible entry, unlawful entry where no force is used, or attempted forcible entry of a structure to commit a felony or theft. The NCVS defines burglary as the unlawful or forcible entry or attempted entry of places, including a permanent residence, other residence (e.g., a hotel room or vacation residence), or other structure (e.g., a garage or shed), where there was a completed or attempted theft. NCVS estimates differ from those previously published in the Criminal Victimization, 2018 report because a coding error that affected the generation of those earlier estimates has been corrected.

Table 6. Percent and Rate of Victimizations Reported to the Police, by Type of Crime, 2018 and 2019

(Percent; rate per 1,000 persons age 12 or older for violent crime and per 1,000 households for property crime.)

Type of crime	Percent of victimizations reported to police		Rate of victimizations reported to police per 1,000[1]	
	2018	2019*	2018	2019*
Violent Crime[2]	42.6	40.9	9.9	8.6
Rape/sexual assault[3]	24.9	33.9	0.7	0.6
Robbery	62.6[B]	46.6	1.3	0.9
Assault	43.0	40.9	7.9	7.1
Aggravated assault	60.5	52.1	2.3	1.9
Simple assault	38.4	37.9	5.6	5.2
Violent crime excluding simple assault[4]	49.9	46.5	4.3	3.4
Selected Characteristics of Violent Crime				
Domestic violence[5]	47.0	52.2	2.3	2.2
Intimate partner violence[6]	45.0[B]	58.4	1.4	1.5
Stranger violence[7]	44.5	39.9	4.0	3.3
Violent crime involving injury	54.3	49.5	2.9	2.3
Violent crime involving a weapon	60.3	52.4	2.9[A]	2.1
Property Crime	34.1	32.5	36.9[B]	33.0
Burglary/trespassing[8]	46.6	48.5	9.9[B]	8.3
Burglary[9]	47.5	51.4	7.1[A]	6.0
Trespassing[10]	44.5	42.2	2.8	2.3
Motor vehicle theft	78.6	79.5	3.4	3.1
Other theft[11]	28.6[A]	26.8	23.7[B]	21.5

NOTE: Violent-crime categories include rape or sexual assault, robbery, aggravated assault, and simple assault, and they include threatened, attempted, and completed occurrences of those crimes. Other violent-crime categories in this table, including domestic violence and violent crime involving injury, are not mutually exclusive from these categories or from each other.
* = Comparison year.
A = Significant difference from comparison year at the 90% confidence level.
B = Significant difference from comparison year at the 95% confidence level.
[1]Rates are per 1,000 persons age 12 or older for violent crime reported to police and per 1,000 households for property crime reported to police.
[2]Excludes homicide because the National Crime Victimization Survey (NCVS) is based on interviews with victims.
[3]See Methodology for details on the measurement of rape or sexual assault in the NCVS.
[4]Includes rape or sexual assault, robbery, and aggravated assault; this category was called serious violent crime prior to Criminal Victimization, 2018.
[5]Includes the subset of violent victimizations that were committed by intimate partners or family members.
[6]Includes the subset of domestic-violence victimizations that were committed by intimate partners, which include current or former spouses, boyfriends, or girlfriends.
[7]Includes the subset of violent victimizations that were committed by someone unknown to the victim.
[8]Called household burglary prior to Criminal Victimization, 2018. Includes unlawful or forcible entry or attempted entry of places, including a permanent residence, other residence (e.g., a hotel room or vacation residence), or other structure (e.g., a garage or shed), but does not include trespassing on land.
[9]Includes only crimes where the offender committed or attempted a theft. Estimates differ from those previously published in the Criminal Victimization, 2018 report because a coding error that affected the generation of those earlier estimates has been corrected.
[10]Includes crimes where the offender did not commit or attempt a theft. Does not include trespassing on land. Estimates differ from those previously published in the Criminal Victimization, 2018 report because a coding error that affected the generation of those earlier estimates has been corrected.
[11]Includes the taking or attempted unlawful taking of property or cash without personal contact with the victim. Incidents involving theft of property from within the same household would classify as theft if the offender has a legal right to be in the house (such as a maid, delivery person, or guest). If the offender has no legal right to be in the house, the incident would classify as a burglary.

Table 7. Rate of Violent Victimization Reported and Not Reported to Police, by Completed, Attempted, and Threatened Crimes, 2015–2019

(Rate.)

Violent crime	Rate of reported crime per 1,000[1]					Rate of unreported crime per 1,000[1]				
	2015	2016	2017	2018	2019*	2015	2016	2017	2018	2019*
Total	8.6	8.6	9.2	9.9	8.6	9.5 [B]	10.8	10.9	12.9	12.1
Completed...............................	3.3	2.5	2.8	3.3	2.5	2.6	2.6	2.6	3.5	2.8
Attempted...............................	3.1	2.6	2.9	3.2	2.9	3.3	3.3	3.8	3.8	4.0
Threatened	2.2 [A]	3.6	3.5	3.4	3.1	3.6 [B]	4.9	4.5	5.6	5.3

NOTE: Details may not sum to totals due to rounding and missing data. Violent-crime categories include rape or sexual assault, robbery, aggravated assault, and simple assault. Each year between 2015 and 2019, whether the crime was reported to police or not was unknown at a rate of 0.3 to 0.5 victimizations per 1,000 persons age 12 or older.
* = Comparison year.
A = Difference with comparison year is significant at the 90% confidence level.
B = Difference with comparison year is significant at the 95% confidence level.
[1]Rate is per 1,000 persons age 12 or older.

Table 8. Percent of Violent Victimizations for Which Victims Received Assistance from a Victim-Service Agency, by Type of Crime, 2018 and 2019

(Percent.)

Type of crime	2018	2019*
Violent Crime[1]	10.6 [B]	7.7
Violent crime excluding simple assault[2]	12.8	10.8
Simple assault...	9.4 [B]	6.0
Intimate partner violence[3]	18.1 [A]	26.1
Violent crime involving injury	14.7	17.9
Violent crime involving a weapon...	11.2	7.1

* = Comparison year.
A = Significant difference from comparison year at the 95% confidence level.
B = Significant difference from comparison year at the 90% confidence level.
[1]Includes rape or sexual assault, robbery, aggravated assault, and simple assault. Includes threatened, attempted, and completed occurrences of those crimes. Excludes homicide because the National Crime Victimization Survey is based on interviews with victims.
[2]Includes rape or sexual assault, robbery, and aggravated assault; this category was called serious violent crime prior to Criminal Victimization, 2018.
[3]Includes the subset of domestic-violence victimizations that were committed by intimate partners, which include current or former spouses, boyfriends, or girlfriends.

Table 9. Rate of Violent Victimization, by Type of Crime and Demographic Characteristics of Victims, 2018 and 2019

(Rate per 1,000 persons age 12 years or older for violent crime; rate per 1,000 households for property crime.)

Victim demographic characteristic	Total violent victimization[1]		Violent victimization excluding simple assault[2]	
	2018	2019*	2018	2019*
Total[3]	23.2	21.0	8.6 B	7.3
Sex				
Male...	22.1	21.2	7.5	7.5
Female..	24.3	20.8	9.6 B	7.0
Race/Ethnicity				
White[4]	24.7 A	21.0	8.2	6.5
Black[4]	20.4	18.7	10.0	7.0
Hispanic..	18.6	21.3	8.5	10.2
Asian[4]	16.2 B	7.5	5.6 B	1.9 !
Other[4,5]	49.2	66.3	20.5	20.9
Age				
12 to 17 years..................................	34.2	35.2	10.1	11.0
18 to 24 years..................................	35.9	37.2	16.3	16.0
25 to 34 years..................................	31.8 A	25.0	11.3	8.9
35 to 49 years..................................	25.2 A	19.5	9.8 A	6.7
50 to 64 years..................................	18.3	18.9	6.4	5.6
65 years and over	6.5	6.0	2.3	1.9
Martial Status				
Never married..................................	33.5	31.2	12.9	11.9
Married..	12.1	11.5	4.1	3.0
Widow/widower	12.5	10.7	4.3	4.9
Divorced	39.1 B	28.5	14.8	10.7
Separated	58.2	64.1	20.8	19.5
Household Income				
Less than $25,000	40.8	37.8	19.0 A	14.2
$25,000 to $49,999	23.5	19.7	9.3	7.5
$50,000 to $99,999	16.5	16.6	4.7	5.5
$100,000 to $199,999	19.2	16.2	5.8	3.9
$200,000 or more	16.3	18.0	3.0 B	7.0

NOTE: Rates are per 1,000 persons age 12 or older. Includes threatened, attempted, and completed occurrences of those crimes.
* = Comparison group.
A = Significant difference from comparison group at the 90% confidence level.
B = Significant difference from comparison group at the 95% confidence level.
! = Interpret estimate with caution. Estimate is based on 10 or fewer sample cases or coefficient of variation is greater than 50%.
[1]Includes rape or sexual assault, robbery, aggravated assault, and simple assault. Excludes homicide because the National Crime Victimization Survey is based on interviews with victims.
[2]Includes rape or sexual assault, robbery, and aggravated assault; this category was called serious violent crime prior to Criminal Victimization, 2018.
[3]Statistically significant differences for the total victimization rates are presented using the Balanced Repeated Replication method. Generalized variance function parameters were used to calculate statistically significant differences for the rest of the table.
[4]Excludes persons of Hispanic origin (e.g., White refers to non-Hispanic Whites and Black refers to non-Hispanic Blacks).
[5]Includes Native Hawaiians and Other Pacific Islanders, American Indians and Alaska Natives, and persons of two or more races.

Table 10. Percent and Rate of Violent Victimizations Reported to Police, by Type of Crime and Demographic Characteristics of Victims, 2019

(Percent; rate.)

Victim demographic characteristic	Total violent victimization[1]		Violent victimization excluding simple assault[1]	
	Percent	Rate per 1,000[2]	Percent	Rate per 1,000[2]
Total	40.9	8.6	46.5	3.4
Sex				
Male*	35.7	7.5	46.4	3.5
Female	45.9[B]	9.6	46.6	3.3
Race/Ethnicity				
White[3]*	37	7.8	46.9	3
Black[3]	45.2[B]	9.2	52.1	3.7
Hispanic	48.8[B]	10.4	48.7	5.0[B]
Asian[3]	47.9	3.6[B]	42.9 !	0.8 B !
Other[2,3]	39.8	26.4[B]	27.3[B]	5.7
Age				
12 to 17 years	24.0[B]	8.4[B]	37.4	4.1
18 to 24 years*	37.9	14.1	36.4	5.8
25 to 34 years	46.4	11.6	60.2[B]	5.3
35 to 49 years	44.4	8.6[B]	42.2	2.8[B]
50 to 64 years	47.1[A]	8.9[B]	52.5[B]	2.9[B]
65 years and over	41.9	2.5[B]	61.0[B]	1.1[B]
Martial Status				
Never married*	34.8	10.9	42.3	5
Married	45.4[B]	5.2[B]	49.8	1.5[B]
Widow/widower	47.3	5.0[B]	63.9[A]	3.1
Divorced	46.2[B]	13.2	49.7	5.3
Separated	61.7[B]	39.6[B]	60.9[A]	11.9[A]
Household Income				
Less than $25,000	41.8	15.8[B]	46.8	6.6[B]
$25,000 to $49,999	44.7	8.8	57.4[A]	4.3[B]
$50,000 to $99,999*	43.1	7.2	44.5	2.4
$100,000 to $199,999	33.0[A]	5.3	43.1	1.7
$200,000 or more	29.5[B]	5.3	13.4[B]	0.9[B]

NOTE: Violent-crime categories include rape or sexual assault, robbery, aggravated assault, and simple assault, and they include threatened, attempted, and completed occurrences of those crimes.
* = Comparison group.
A = Significant difference from comparison group at the 90% confidence level.
B = Significant difference from comparison group at the 95% confidence level.
! = Interpret estimate with caution. Estimate is based on 10 or fewer sample cases or coefficient of variation is greater than 50%.
[1]Rates are per 1,000 persons age 12 or older.
[2]Includes Native Hawaiians and Other Pacific Islanders, American Indians and Alaska Natives, and persons of two or more races.
[3]Excludes persons of Hispanic origin (e.g., White refers to non-Hispanic Whites and Black refers to non-Hispanic Blacks).

Table 11. Rate of Victimization, by Type of Crime and Location of Residence, 2018 and 2019

(Rate.[1])

Location of residence[5]	Violent crime[2]		Violent crime excluding simple assault[3]		Property crime[4]	
	2018	2019*	2018	2019*	2018	2019*
New Definition						
Urban[6]	26.5 A	21.1	12.2 B	8.0	146.9	153.0
Suburban[7]	23.8	22.3	8.6	7.6	108.6 B	100.8
Rural[8]	18.9	16.3	6.3	5.6	80.3 B	68.1
Old Definition						
Urban[9]	28.9	26.0	12.2	9.5	142.9	144.4
Suburban[10]	18.6	16.5	6.1	5.7	86.7 B	74.9
Rural[11]	26.9	26.3	9.6	7.7	101.7 A	92.1

NOTE: Statistically significant differences for the new definition rates are presented using the Balanced Repeated Replication method of direct estimation. Statistically significant differences for the old definition rates are presented using generalized variance function parameters.
* = Comparison year.
A = Significant difference from comparison year at the 90% confidence level.
B = Significant difference from comparison year at the 95% confidence level.
[1]Rate is per 1,000 persons age 12 or older for violent crime and per 1,000 households for property crime.
[2]Includes rape or sexual assault, robbery, aggravated assault, and simple assault. Excludes homicide because the National Crime Victimization Survey (NCVS) is based on interviews with victims.
[3]Includes rape or sexual assault, robbery, and aggravated assault; this category was called serious violent crime prior to Criminal Victimization, 2018.
[4]Includes burglary, residential trespassing, motor-vehicle theft, and other theft.
[5]See Classification of urban, suburban, and rural areas in the National Crime Victimization Survey and Methodology for details on the measurement of location of residence in the NCVS.
[6]All census blocks within cities or Census-designated places that meet certain criteria based on their population and density. See Classification of urban, suburban, and rural areas in the National Crime Victimization Survey.
[7]All other census blocks not classified as urban or rural.
[8]All census blocks not in Census Bureau-defined urbanized areas or urban clusters.
[9]Within the principal city of a Metropolitan Statistical Area (MSA).
[10]Within an MSA but not in a principal city of the MSA.
[11]Not within an MSA.

Table 12. Percent and Number of Violent Incidents, by Total Population and Victim and Offender Demographic Characteristics, 2019

(Number; percent; ratio.)

Demographic characteristic	Number of violent incidents			Percent of violent incidents			Ratio of percentages		
	Population[1]	Offender[2]	Victim	Percent of population[1]*	Offender[2]	Victim	Offender to victim	Offender to population	Victim to population
Total	276,872,470	5,440,680	5,440,680	100.0	100.0	100.0	1.0	1.0	1.0
Sex									
Male.........................	134,693,660	3,806,570	2,668,600	48.6	75.0[B]	49.0	1.5	1.5	1.0
Female.......................	142,178,810	1,085,550	2,772,070	51.4	21.4[B]	51.0	0.4	0.4	1.0
Both male and female offenders.............................	X	182,030	X	X	3.6	X	X	X	X
Race/Ethnicity									
White[3]	171,423,480	2,289,390	3,379,920	61.9	50.2[B]	62.1	0.8	0.8	1.0
Black[3]	33,397,100	1,140,470	582,650	12.1	25.0[B]	10.7	2.3	2.1	0.9
Hispanic[4]......................	47,890,870	853,990	926,650	17.3	18.7	17.0	1.1	1.1	1.0
Asian[3]	17,401,410	44,520	123,400	6.3	1.0[B]	2.3[B]	0.4	0.2	0.4
Other[3,5].......................	6,759,600	208,170	428,050	2.4	4.6[B]	7.9[B]	0.6	1.9	3.2
Multiple offenders of various races[3]...........................	X	27,720 !	X	X	0.6 !	X	X	X	X
Age									
11 years or younger................	X	94,230	X	X	2.0	X	X	X	X
12 to 17 years.........................	24,941,440	723,630	800,300	9.0	15.6[B]	14.7[B]	1.1	1.7	1.6
18 to 29 years.........................	52,798,870	1,348,610	1,617,860	19.1	29.0[B]	29.7[B]	1.0	1.5	1.6
30 years or older....................	199,132,160	2,323,940	3,022,520	71.9	50.0[B]	55.6[B]	0.9	0.7	0.8
Multiple offenders of various ages...........................	X	157,390	X	X	3.4	X	X	X	X

NOTE: Details may not sum to totals due to rounding and missing data for offender characteristics. An incident is a specific criminal act involving one or more victims. Offender characteristics are based on victims' perceptions of offenders.
* = Comparison year.
! = Interpret estimate with caution. Estimate is based on 10 or fewer sample cases or coefficient of variation is greater than 50%.
A = Significant difference from comparison year at the 90% confidence level.
B = Significant difference from comparison year at the 95% confidence level.
[1]The National Crime Victimization Survey (NCVS) population represents persons age 12 or older living in non-institutionalized residential settings in the U.S.
[2]Includes those incidents in which the perceived offender characteristics were reported. The sex of the offender was unknown in 7% of incidents, the race or ethnicity of the offender was unknown in 16% of incidents, and the age of the offender was unknown in 15% of incidents.
[3]Excludes persons of Hispanic origin (e.g., White refers to non-Hispanic Whites and Black refers to non-Hispanic Blacks).
[4]If the victim perceived any of the offenders in a multiple offender incident to be of Hispanic origin, they are classified as Hispanic.
[5]Includes Native Hawaiians and Other Pacific Islanders, American Indians and Alaska Natives, and persons of two or more races.
[6]While the NCVS does not survey victims age 11 or younger, victims may report the offender to be age 11 or younger.

METHODOLOGY

Data are from the Bureau of Justice Statistics' (BJS) National Crime Victimization Survey (NCVS), which collects information on nonfatal crimes against persons age 12 or older from a nationally representative sample of U.S. households. The NCVS measures violent crimes, which include rape or sexual assault, robbery, aggravated assault, and simple assault. Property crimes include household burglary, motor vehicle theft, and theft. The survey also measures personal larceny, which includes pickpocketing and purse snatching. Unless otherwise noted, findings in this report are significant at the 95 percent confidence level. For additional estimates excluded from this report, see the NCVS Victimization Analysis Tool (NVAT) on the BJS Web site.

The NCVS is a self-reported survey administered annually from January 1 to December 31. Annual NCVS estimates are based on the number and characteristics of crimes respondents experienced during the prior 6 months, not including the month in which they were interviewed. Therefore, the 2019 survey covers crimes experienced from July 1, 2018, to November 30, 2019, and March 15, 2019 is the middle of the reference period. Crimes are classified by the year of the survey and not by the year of the crime.

NCVS data can be used to produce—

Prevalence estimates: The number or percentage of unique persons who were crime victims, or of unique households that experienced crime.

Victimization estimates: The total number of times that people or households were victimized by crime. For personal crimes, the number of victimizations is the number of victims of that crime. Each crime against a household is counted as having a single victim—the affected household.

Incident estimates: The number of specific criminal acts involving one or more victims.

NCVS methods of variance estimation

For surveys with complex sample designs, such as the NCVS, several methods can be used to estimate the magnitude of sampling error associated with an estimate. In previous reports, BJS has used both generalized variance function (GVF) parameters and direct-variance estimation for generating standard errors and testing statistically significant differences between NCVS estimates. Compared to GVFs, direct-variance estimation is generally considered more accurate in approximating the true variance.

This year's bulletin presents tables 1 and 2 using the Balanced Repeated Replication (BRR) method, a form of direct-variance estimation, and continues to present other victimization and incidence estimates using GVFs (except for totals in tables 4, 9, 24, and 25 that are also presented in tables 1 and 2, and statistics in table 12 that are based on the new classification of urban, suburban, and rural areas). The Taylor Series Linearization (TSL) method, another form of direct-variance estimation, continues to be used to generate standard errors for prevalence estimates. BJS has an active research program on direct-variance estimation that seeks to improve the quality and accuracy of NCVS estimates.

NCVS and UCR

The Bureau of Justice Statistics' National Crime Victimization Survey (NCVS) measures crime reported and not reported to police. The Uniform Crime Reporting (UCR) program, administered by the Federal Bureau of Investigation (FBI), measures only crime recorded by police.

In 2018, the UCR reported that 3.7 total violent crimes (including murder and non-negligent manslaughter, rape, robbery, and aggravated assault) per 1,000 residents and 22.0 property crimes (including burglary and motor-vehicle theft) per 1,000 residents were known to law enforcement. The 2018 NCVS estimated that 4.3 violent crimes excluding simple assault per 1,000 persons age 12 or older, and 36.9 property crimes per 1,000 households, were reported to law enforcement. The 2019 NCVS estimated that 3.4 violent crimes excluding simple assault per 1,000 persons age 12 or older, and 33.0 property crimes per 1,000 households, were reported to law enforcement.

Because the NCVS and the UCR measure an overlapping, but not identical, set of offenses and use different approaches in measuring them, complete congruity should not be expected between estimates from these two sources. Restricting the NCVS to violent crime reported to police, and excluding simple assault, keeps the measures as similar as possible. However, significant methodological and definitional differences remain between how these violent crimes are measured in the NCVS and the UCR:

The UCR includes murder, non-negligent manslaughter, and commercial crimes (including burglary of commercial establishments), while the NCVS excludes those crime types.

The UCR excludes sexual assault, which the NCVS includes.

The UCR property-crime rates are per person, while the NCVS's are per household. (There were 2.2 persons age 12 or older per household in 2019.) Moreover, because the number of households may not grow at the same rate each year as the total population, trend data for rates of property crimes measured by the two programs may not be entirely comparable.

NCVS estimates are based on interviews with a nationally representative sample of persons in U.S. households. UCR estimates are based on counts of crimes recorded by law enforcement agencies and are weighted to compensate for incomplete reporting.

The NCVS does not measure crimes against persons who are homeless or who live in institutions (e.g., nursing homes and correctional institutions) or on military bases. Also, it does not measure crimes against children age 11 or younger. The UCR measures crimes against all U.S. residents, including crimes against children age 11 or younger. In some states mandatory reporting laws require that persons report certain crimes against youth. Due to these factors, the age distribution of crimes measured in the UCR differs from that of the NCVS.

Taken together, these two measures of crime provide a more comprehensive picture of crime in the U.S. For additional information about the differences between the NCVS and UCR, see *The Nation's Two Crime Measures* (NCJ 246832, BJS, September 2014).

Classification of urban, suburban, and rural areas in the National Crime Victimization Survey

This year, the Bureau of Justice Statistics (BJS) provides new classifications of urban, suburban, and rural areas for the National Crime Victimization Survey (NCVS), with the goal of presenting a more accurate picture of where criminal victimizations occur.

Historically, the NCVS has classified areas as urban, suburban, or rural based on the following definitions:

Urban: within a principal city of a Metropolitan Statistical Area (MSA)

Suburban: within an MSA but not within a principal city of the MSA

Rural: outside of an MSA

These definitions are straightforward, but they suffer from two main shortcomings:

1. Metropolitan statistical areas are based on entire counties, and counties almost always contain both rural and non-rural areas. Yet the NCVS's historical definitions classify each county as being either entirely rural (if not part of an MSA) or entirely non-rural (if part of an MSA).

For example, California's San Bernardino County, which includes much of the Mojave Desert and covers more than twice as much land as the state of Maryland, is classified as containing no rural areas under the NCVS's historical definitions. This is because San Bernardino County is part of the Riverside-San Bernardino-Ontario MSA, and the NCVS's historical definitions do not classify any part of an MSA as being rural. On the other hand, Colorado's La Plata County, home of Durango, is classified under the historical definitions as being entirely rural, because it is not part of an MSA. This is true even though the Census Bureau says that, as of 2010, 40 percent of La Plata County's population lived in non-rural areas.

Similarly, Casmalia, Calif. had a 2010 population of 138 people and is surrounded by undeveloped land. Because it is located within a county (Santa Barbara) that is designated as an MSA (the Santa Maria-Santa Barbara MSA), the NCVS's historical definitions classify Casmalia as suburban. Meanwhile, Bozeman, Mont., with a 2010 population of 37,280—270 times that of Casmalia—is classified by the NCVS's historical definitions as rural, because it is located in a county that is not part of an MSA.

2. The Office of Management and Budget (OMB) designates principal cities (of which there are anywhere from 1 to nearly 20 in a given MSA) as being among "the more significant places in each Metropolitan and Micropolitan Statistical Area…in terms of population and employment." The principal city designation is not necessarily indicative of urban status, nor is it intended to be. Yet the NCVS's historical definitions classify all principal cities of MSAs as urban, and all other places as not urban.

As a result, Union City, N.J., located just across the Hudson River from Midtown Manhattan, is classified by the NCVS's historical definitions as suburban, due to its not being defined as a principal city. Union City had a 2010 population density of 51,918 people per square mile, more than three times the population density of San Francisco (17,180). Meanwhile, Rome, N.Y., which had a 2010 population density of 451 people per square mile—less than 1 percent that of Union City—is classified by the historical definitions as urban. The same is true for Yuma, Ariz., Hilton Head Island, S.C., and Foley, Ala. None of these had a population density in 2010 that was even 2 percent that of Union City, yet all are classified as urban under the NCVS's historical definitions, while Union City is classified as suburban.

These are not isolated examples. Weighted housing-unit density (discussed more below) is essentially a measure of how closely people live to one another. Based on the 2010 Census of Population and Housing and 2013 OMB principal-city designations, 506 of the 674 principal cities in the United States (75 percent) had weighted housing-unit densities below that of the U.S. as a whole. In other words, three-quarters of the places classified by the historical definitions as urban were *less* densely developed than the areas where most U.S. residents lived.

A new definition:

BJS's new NCVS definition of urban is based on the notion that urban places are those that are densely populated, are at the center of a major metropolitan area, or some combination of these. BJS's specific criteria is that a place is urban if it is—

The main city or Census-designated place (i.e., the first place listed) in a 500,000-person (Census-designated) "urbanized area," with a weighted housing-unit density within its city limits of at least 3,000 housing units per square mile. In other words, the primary city in a large "urbanized area" qualifies as urban if it meets the weighted-housing-unit-density threshold of 3,000 housing units per square mile. (The overall weighted housing-unit density for the U.S. is 2,396, based on the 2010 Census.)

A named city or Census-designated place in a 500,000-person (Census-designated) "urbanized area," with a weighted housing-unit density of at least 4,000 housing units per square mile within its city limits. In other words, a city that is prominent enough to be included by the Census Bureau in the name of a large "urbanized area" (for example, Long Beach in the Los Angeles-Long Beach-Anaheim urbanized area) qualifies as urban if it meets the weighted-housing-unit-density threshold of 4,000 housing units per square mile.

Any city or Census-designated place with a population of at least 50,000 and a weighted housing-unit density of at least 5,000 housing units per square mile.

Any city or Census-designated place with a population of at least 10,000 and a weighted housing-unit density of at least 10,000 housing units per square mile.

The Census Bureau's "urbanized areas" referenced in this definition are similar to OMB's metropolitan areas, but they delineate areas of substantial population rather than utilizing entire counties. The weighted housing-unit density referenced in this definition is discussed in greater detail below.

In addition to developing this definition of urban, BJS has adopted the Census Bureau's definition of rural to replace the historical NCVS definition of rural. The Census Bureau provides specific, carefully drawn boundaries around "urban areas" (both larger "urbanized areas" and smaller "urban clusters") using set criteria, classifying everything outside of those boundaries as rural.

BJS classifies areas that are neither urban nor rural as suburban. In comparison to places that are urban, suburban areas are characterized by lower density, a larger ratio of single-family homes to apartments, and layouts based principally on automobile transportation. Some suburban areas, those that might be thought of as "suburbia proper," do not have their own urban centers but are located near a separate urban city. Other suburban areas are cities or towns that have urban centers, but those centers have smaller populations than their surrounding suburban areas, so the bulk of the city's population lives in suburban areas. (Cities are the smallest geographical designations that can realistically be used in classifying areas as urban.) In short, suburban areas are a mix of "suburbia proper," towns, and some generally smaller cities that are more suburban than urban.

BJS uses weighted housing-unit density in its new NCVS definitions because that measure provides a better indication of the degree of urban density than conventional population density does. Conventional population density is derived by dividing population by land area, and it measures how densely populated a given area of land is. As of the 2010 Census, the U.S. as a whole had a conventional population density of 87 people per square mile; however, most U.S. residents do not live in areas where there are only 87 people per square mile. The experience of most U.S. residents is more fully captured by weighted population density, which is essentially a measure of how densely populated an area is from the perspective of those who live in it.

Weighted housing-unit density is similar to weighted population density, with the difference being that the latter focuses on population and the former on housing units. In comparing weighted housing-unit density to weighted population density, John R. Ottensmann writes, "Housing units better represent the physical pattern of urban development, as they are relatively fixed."

Housing-unit density is the number of housing units per square mile in a given area. Weighted housing-unit density, under BJS's approach, is the weighted average of the housing densities for all census tracts in an area, with the tracts weighted by their number of housing units.

For ease of explanation, imagine an area with only two census tracts. One tract has 2,000 housing units, covers 2 square miles, and thus has a housing-unit density of 1,000 housing units per square mile. The other tract has 6,000 housing units, covers 1 square mile, and thus has a housing-unit density of 6,000 housing units per square mile. The area's weighted housing-unit density is the weighted average of these two tract-level housing-unit densities, or $(1{,}000*2{,}000+6{,}000*6{,}000)/8{,}000 = 4{,}750$. Otherwise put, the weighted housing-unit density is based one-quarter on the first tract's density (because it contains one-quarter of the housing units) and three-quarters on the second tract's density.

Weighted housing-unit density identifies urban places much more clearly than conventional population density does. Among places with populations of at least 10,000 people in 2010, Chicago rises from #71 in conventional population density to #16 in weighted housing-unit density, New Orleans from #2,212 to #190, and Urban Honolulu from #474 to #13. Meanwhile,

Passaic, N.J. falls from #7 in conventional population density to #45 in weighted housing-unit density, while Santa Ana, Calif. falls from #67 to #237 (moving from 4 places above Chicago to 221 places below).

Comparing the old and new definitions:

Both the old and new NCVS definitions, as would be expected, classify New York's five boroughs as urban (New York City's weighted housing-unit density is a nation-leading 29,345 housing units per square mile), and they both add Jersey City, N.J. (weighted housing-unit density of 13,837 housing units per square mile), Newark, N.J. (8,788), and White Plains, N.Y. (5,671). The old definition also includes New Brunswick, N.J. (4,908) and Lakewood, N.J. (2,106).

The new definition reclassifies Lakewood and New Brunswick as suburban (although just a 2 percent increase in New Brunswick's weighted housing-unit density would qualify it as urban) and adds the following places as urban: Guttenberg, N.J. (weighted housing-unit density of 29,171 housing units per square mile); Hoboken, N.J. (25,870); West New York (21,763); Union City, N.J. (20,477); Cliffside Park, N.J. (12,001); Mount Vernon, N.Y. (8,811); East Orange, N.J. (8,763); Bayonne, N.J. (8,263); Yonkers, N.Y. (7,930); Elizabeth, N.J. (7,468); Passaic, N.J. (7,424); and Paterson, N.J. (6,739).

As the accompanying map of the Washington, D.C. area shows, both the old and new definitions include Washington, D.C. (weighted housing-unit density of 10,115 housing units per square mile), Arlington, Va. (10,485), Alexandria, Va. (7,714), and Silver Spring, Md. (6,135), as urban places. The new definitions do not classify anywhere else in the D.C. area as urban. The old definitions added as urban Bethesda, Md. (4,325), Gaithersburg, Md. (2,836), Reston, Va. (2,543), Rockville, Md. (2,534), and Frederick, Md. (2,235), all of which the new definitions classify as suburban.

The new definitions more closely fit U.S. residents' own sense of where they live, as reflected in the American Housing Survey (AHS). For each of five metropolitan or micropolitan area designations, the following table and figure show how most AHS respondents in 2017 classified where they lived (and what percentage of respondents gave that classification), what percentage of people would be classified that same way by the new and old NCVS definitions, and the difference between the AHS result and the new and old NCVS results.

As table 11 shows, 58 percent of AHS respondents who lived in the biggest principal city of an MSA said that they lived in an urban place. Forty-three percent of them would be classified as living in an urban place by the new NCVS definitions, a difference of 15 percentage points (58 percent versus 43 percent) from the portion of AHS respondents who gave that answer. In

comparison, 100 percent of those respondents would be classified as living in an urban place by the old NCVS definitions, a difference of 42 percentage points (58 percent vs. 100 percent) from the portion of AHS respondents who gave that answer. While AHS respondents' answers about where they live are not necessarily dispositive, the new NCVS definitions fare far better than the old ones versus the AHS in every category, by a margin of at least 21 percentage points per category and an average margin of 33 points per category.

Under the new definitions, 12 percent of the population lives in urban areas, 69 percent in suburban areas, and 19 percent in rural areas, compared to 33 percent in urban areas, 53 percent in suburban areas, and 14 percent in rural areas under the old definitions. Of the main cities in the 15 largest MSAs in the U.S., the new definitions classify 13 as urban. The two classified as suburban—Phoenix, Ariz. and Riverside, Calif.—had 2010 weighted housing-unit densities below that of the U.S. as a whole.

According to the historical NCVS definitions, by far the most urban region in the country is the West, followed by the South (using the Census Bureau's regional classifications). Under the new definitions, the Northeast is by far the most urban region, followed in order by the West, Midwest, and South. The most suburban region according to the old definitions is the Northeast. Under the new definitions, the West is the most suburban region, with the Northeast being the least suburban region.

2016 NCVS Sample Redesign

To produce estimates on criminal victimization, the Bureau of Justice Statistics' (BJS) National Crime Victimization Survey (NCVS) collects information from a sample of U.S. households that represents the nation. The sample design is periodically changed to maintain the representativeness of the survey. In 2016, the NCVS sample was redesigned for two reasons:

1. To reflect changes in the U.S. population based on the 2010 Decennial Census

2. To make it possible to produce state- and local-level victimization estimates for the largest 22 states and specific metropolitan areas within those states

Every 10 years, the U.S. Census Bureau conducts the official population count of the United States. In 2016, a redesign of the NCVS sample was necessary to account for shifts in the population identified through the 2010 Decennial Census. From 2000 to 2010, the number of people residing in individual U.S. counties changed. Almost two-thirds of the nation's 3,143 counties gained population. Most counties along coastlines experienced population growth during this period, while others that lost population were clustered by region and were found in areas such as the Great Plains and Mississippi Delta.

The NCVS sampling process involves selecting primary sampling units (PSUs), which are counties, groups of counties, or large metropolitan areas identified through the Decennial Census and the U.S. Census Bureau's American Community Survey.[7] Within the PSUs selected, the sampling process identifies addresses to be included in the sample and interviews are conducted with persons and households at those addresses. Sampled households remain in the NCVS sample for seven waves (each wave is a 6-month period). The decennial sample update ensures that the sample reflects current population distributions. This process requires a phased shift of counties included in the 2000 sample design to those selected for the 2010 sample design, resulting in three types of counties in 2016: 1) continuing counties—those in both the 2000 and 2010 sample designs; 2) outgoing counties—those that were in the 2000 sample design, but not the 2010 sample design; and 3) new counties—those that were selected into the 2010 sample design, but were not in the 2000 sample design.

As part of ongoing efforts to enhance the usefulness and relevance of the NCVS, the sample also was expanded and redistributed to produce state and local estimates of victimization. Because the primary purpose of the NCVS has been to generate national estimates, the sample was initially designed to be representative of the United States as a whole and not individual states and local areas. To produce reliable estimates for the 22 most populous states and specific metropolitan areas within those states, it was necessary to change the NCVS sample design.

Implications of the 2016 Sample Redesign

When the 2016 NCVS data collection was complete, a comparison of the 2015 and 2016 victimization estimates showed that the violent and property crime rates had increased. Given recent patterns in NCVS data, these increases seemed too large to be a result of actual growth in crime, suggesting that the sample redesign may have affected the victimization rates. To better understand these results, the 2015 and 2016 victimization rates for new and continuing sample counties were examined separately. These comparisons showed that from 2015 to 2016 there were no statistically significant differences for continuing sample counties in the rates of total property crime, total violent crime, and total serious violent crime. In comparison, rates of total violent crime and total serious violent crime were higher in the new sample counties than in the outgoing sample counties.

Differences in Rates of Reporting to Police in the UCR and NCVS

For 2016, the Federal Bureau of Investigation's (FBI) Uniform Crime Reporting (UCR) program showed that 3.9 serious violent crimes per 1,000 persons and 24.5 property crimes per 1,000 persons were known to law enforcement. According to the Bureau of Justice Statistics' (BJS) National Crime Victimization Survey (NCVS), 3.6 serious violent crimes per 1,000 persons age 12 or older and 42.6 property crimes per 1,000 households were reported to law enforcement during this same year.

Because the NCVS and UCR measure an overlapping, but not identical, set of offenses and use different methodologies, congruity is not expected between estimates from these two data sources. Restricting the NCVS to serious violence reported to police keeps the measures as similar as possible. However, significant methodological and definitional differences remain between serious violent crimes in the NCVS and the UCR:

- The UCR includes homicide and commercial crimes, while the NCVS excludes these crime types.

- The UCR excludes sexual assault, which the NCVS includes.

- NCVS estimates are based on interviews with a nationally representative sample of persons in U.S. households. UCR estimates are based on counts of crimes reported by an incomplete census of law enforcement agencies and are weighted to compensate for the incomplete reporting.

- The NCVS excludes crimes against children age 11 or younger and persons in institutions (e.g., nursing homes and correctional institutions). It may also exclude highly mobile populations and persons who are homeless. Victimizations against these persons are included in the UCR.

Given these differences, the two measures of crime should not be compared but should be viewed as complementary sources, which together provide a more comprehensive picture of crime in the United States. For additional information about the differences between the two programs, see *The Nation's Two Crime Measures* (NCJ 246832, BJS web, September 2014).

Prevalence of Crime

Annual estimates of a population's risk for criminal victimization may be examined using victimization or prevalence rates. Historically, Bureau of Justice Statistics (BJS) reports based on National Crime Victimization Survey (NCVS) data rely on victimization rates, which measure the extent to which victimizations occur in a specified population during a specific time. For crimes affecting persons, NCVS victimization rates are estimated by dividing the number of victimizations that occur during a specified time (T) by the population at risk for those victimizations and multiplying the rate by 1,000.

Prevalence rates also describe the level of victimization but are based on the number of unique persons (or households) in the population experiencing at least one victimization during a specified time. The key distinction between a victimization and prevalence rate is whether the numerator consists of the number of victimizations or victims. For example, a person who experienced two robberies on separate occasions within the past year would be counted twice in the victimization rate but once in the prevalence rate. Prevalence rates are estimated by dividing the number of victims in the specified population by the total number of persons in the population and multiplying the rate by 100. This is the percentage of the population victimized at least once in a given period.

Victimization and prevalence rates may also be produced for household crimes, such as burglary. In these instances, numerators and denominators are adjusted to reflect households rather than persons. To better understand the percentage of the population that is victimized at least once in a given period, prevalence rates are presented by type of crime and certain demographic characteristics. (For further information about measuring prevalence in the NCVS, see *Measuring the Prevalence of Crime with the National Crime Victimization Survey*, NCJ 241656, BJS web, September 2013.)

Survey Methodology

The Bureau of Justice Statistics' National Crime Victimization Survey (NCVS) is an annual data collection carried out by the U.S. Census Bureau. The NCVS is a self-reported survey that is administered annually from January 1 to December 31. Annual NCVS estimates are based on the number and characteristics of crimes respondents experienced during the prior 6 months, not including the month in which they were interviewed. Therefore, the 2019 survey covers crimes experienced from July 1, 2018 to November 30, 2019, and March 15, 2019 is the middle of the reference period. Crimes are classified by the year of the survey and not by the year of the crime.

The NCVS is administered to persons age 12 or older from a nationally representative sample of U.S. households. It collects information on nonfatal personal crimes (rape or sexual assault, robbery, aggravated and simple assault, and personal larceny (purse-snatching and pick-pocketing) and household property crimes (burglary/trespassing, motor-vehicle theft, and other types of theft). The survey collects information on threatened, attempted, and completed crimes. It collects data both on crimes reported and not reported to police. Unless specified otherwise, estimates in this report include threatened, attempted, and completed crimes. In addition to providing annual level and change estimates on criminal victimization, the NCVS is the primary source of information on the nature of criminal victimization incidents.

Survey respondents provide information about themselves (including age, sex, race, ethnicity, marital status, educational level, and income) and whether they experienced a victimization. For each victimization incident, respondents report information about the offender (including age, sex, race, ethnicity,

and victim-offender relationship), characteristics of the crime (including time and place of occurrence, use of weapons, nature of injury, and economic consequences), whether the crime was reported to police, reasons the crime was or was not reported, and experiences with the criminal justice system.

Household information, including household-level demographics (e.g., income) and property victimizations committed against the household (e.g., burglary/trespassing), is typically collected from the reference person. The reference person is any responsible adult member of the household who is not likely to permanently leave the household. Because an owner or renter of the sampled housing unit is normally the most responsible and knowledgeable household member, this person is generally designated as the reference person and household respondent. However, a household respondent does not have to be one of the household members who owns or rents the unit.

In the NCVS, a household is defined as a group of persons who all reside at a sampled address. Persons are considered household members when the sampled address is their usual place of residence at the time of the interview and when they have no primary place of residence elsewhere. Once selected, households remain in the sample for 3½ years, and eligible persons in these households are interviewed every 6 months, either in person or over the phone, for a total of seven interviews.

First interviews are typically conducted in person, with subsequent interviews conducted either in person or by phone. New households rotate into the sample on an ongoing basis to replace outgoing households that have been in the sample for the full 3½-year period. The sample includes persons living in group quarters, such as dormitories, rooming houses, and religious-group dwellings, and excludes persons living on military bases or in institutional settings such as correctional or hospital facilities, and persons who are homeless.

Measurement of crime in the National Crime Victimization Survey

BJS presents data from the NCVS on victimization, incident, and prevalence rates. Victimization rates measure the extent to which violent and property victimizations occur in a specified population during a specified time. Victimization numbers show the total number of times that people or households are victimized by crime. For crimes affecting persons, NCVS victimization rates are estimated by dividing the number of victimizations that occur during a specified time by the population at risk for those victimizations and multiplying the rate by 1,000.

For victimization rates, each victimization represents one person (for personal crimes) or one household (for property crimes) affected by a crime. Every victimization experienced by a person or household during the year is counted. For example, if one person experiences two violent crimes during the year, both are counted in the victimization rate. If one household experiences two property crimes, both are counted in the victimization rate. Victimization estimates are presented in figure 3, tables 1 through 10, table 12, and tables 23 through 25 in this report.

Incident rates are another measure of crime. The number of incidents is the number of specific criminal acts involving one or more victims. If every victimization had one victim, the number of incidents would be the same as the number of victimizations. If there was more than one victim, the incident estimate is adjusted to compensate for the possibility that the incident could be reported several times by multiple victims and thus be over-counted. For example, if two people were robbed during the same incident, this crime would be counted as one incident and two victimizations. Incident estimates are presented in tables 13 through 17, and tables 25 through 30 in this report.

A third measure, reflecting a population's risk of experiencing one or more criminal victimizations, is prevalence rates. Like victimization rates, prevalence rates describe the level of victimization, but the latter are based on the number of unique persons or households in the population experiencing at least one victimization during a specified time. The key distinction between a victimization and prevalence rate is whether the numerator consists of the number of victimizations or the number of unique victims. For example, a person who experienced two robberies within the past year would be counted twice in the victimization rate but only once in the prevalence rate. Prevalence rates are estimated by dividing the number of unique victims or victimized households in the specified population by the total number of persons or households in the population and multiplying the rate by 100, yielding the percentage of the population victimized at least once in a period.

Prevalence rates are presented in figures 1 and 2, and tables 18 through 22 in this report. Prevalence rates for property crimes can be produced at the household or person levels by adjusting the numerators and denominators to reflect households or persons. Table 20 presents property-crime prevalence rates at the household level, and table 21 presents serious property-crime prevalence rates at the personal level.

For more information about measuring prevalence in the NCVS, see *Measuring the Prevalence of Crime with the National Crime Victimization Survey* (NCJ 241656, BJS, September 2013).

Nonresponse and Weighting Adjustments

The 2019 NCVS data file includes 155,076 household interviews. Overall, 71 percent of eligible households completed interviews. Within participating households, interviews with 249,008 persons were completed in 2019, representing an 83 percent response rate among eligible persons from responding households.

Victimizations that occurred outside of the U.S. were excluded from this report. In 2019, about 1 percent of the unweighted victimizations occurred outside of the U.S.

NCVS data are weighted to produce annual estimates of victimization for persons age 12 or older living in U.S. households. Because the NCVS relies on a sample rather than a census of the entire U.S. population, weights are designed to adjust to known population totals and to compensate for survey nonresponse and other aspects of the complex sample design.

NCVS data files include person, household, victimization, and incident weights. Person weights provide an estimate of the population represented by each person in the sample. Household weights provide an estimate of the household population represented by each household in the sample. After proper adjustment, both person and household weights are also typically used to form the denominator in calculations of crime rates. For personal crimes, the incident weight is derived by dividing the person weight of a victim by the total number of persons victimized during an incident, as reported by the respondent. For property crimes measured at the household level, the incident weight and the household weight are the same, because the victim of a property crime is considered to be the household as a whole. The incident weight is most frequently used to calculate estimates of offenders' and victims' demographics.

Victimization weights used in this report account for the number of persons victimized during an incident and for high-frequency repeat-victimizations (i.e., series victimizations). Series victimizations are similar in type to one another but occur with such frequency that a victim is unable to recall each individual event or describe each event in detail. Survey procedures allow NCVS interviewers to identify and classify these similar victimizations as series victimizations and to collect detailed information on only the most recent incident in the series.

The weighting counts series victimizations as the actual number of victimizations reported by the victim, up to a maximum of 10. Doing so produces more reliable estimates of crime levels than counting such victimizations only once, while the cap at 10 minimizes the effect of extreme outliers on rates. According to the 2019 data, series victimizations accounted for 1.4 percent of all victimizations and 3.1 percent of all violent victimizations. Additional information on the enumeration of series victimizations is detailed in the report *Methods for Counting High-Frequency Repeat Victimizations in the National Crime Victimization Survey* (NCJ 237308, BJS, April 2012).

Changes to the household weighting adjustment in 2017

The 2017 NCVS weights included a new adjustment that modified household weights to reflect independent housing-unit totals available internally at the U.S. Census Bureau. This new adjustment was applied only to household weights for housing units and does not affect person weights. Historically, the household weights were adjusted to reflect independent totals for the person population. This new weighting adjustment improves on the prior one and better aligns the number of estimated households in the NCVS with other Census household-survey estimates. Due to this new adjustment, the 2017 NCVS estimate for the number of households was about 8 percent lower than the 2016 NCVS estimate. As a result, the estimate of the number of households affected by property crime was also about 8 percent lower. When making comparisons of property crime at the household level between 2017 and prior years, compare victimization or prevalence *rates*. Rates are unaffected by this change in weighting methodology because both the numerator and denominator are equally affected. Comparisons of the number of households that were victimized between 2017 and prior years are inappropriate due to this change in weighting methodology. Property crime measured at the person level is unaffected by the change (as presented in measures of serious crime). For more information on weighting in the NCVS, see the *Non-response and weighting adjustments* section in this methodology and *National Crime Victimization Survey, 2016 Technical Documentation* (NCJ 251442, BJS, December 2017).

Changes to the classification of urban, suburban, and rural areas

Beginning in 2019, the NCVS employed a new method for classifying geographical areas (see *Classification of urban, suburban, and rural areas in the National Crime Victimization Survey* on pp. 12-15). All census blocks not in urbanized areas or urbanized clusters, as defined by the Census Bureau, are classified as rural, consistent with the Census Bureau's definition of rural. Census blocks within cities or Census-designated places that meet certain criteria based on population and density are classified as urban (see appendix table 36), while all other census blocks in urbanized areas or urban clusters are classified as suburban.

Classifications of urban places are based on population size, weighted housing-unit density, and the Census Bureau's designations of urbanized areas and urban clusters, using data from the 2010 Census. Housing-unit density is the number of housing units per square mile in a given area. Weighted housing-unit density, under BJS's approach, is the weighted average of the housing-unit densities for all census tracts in an area, with the tracts weighted by their number of housing units. Housing-unit addresses are converted into geographical coordinates through a process called geocoding. Housing units that cannot be geocoded are imputed. For more information on imputation procedures, see *National Crime Victimization Survey, 2016 Technical Documentation* (NCJ 251442, BJS, December 2017).

Table 31 shows the 2019 U.S. resident population for those age 12 or older and the number of households in each category (urban, suburban, rural) under both the new and historical classifications. About one-third of the U.S. resident population age 12 or older were classified as residing in an urban area under the historical definition, compared to about one-eighth under the new definition. The percentage of the resident population classified as residing in a suburban area shifted from 53 percent to 69 percent, while the percentage classified as rural shifted from 14 percent to 19 percent. Similar shifts in the number of households were observed under the new classification.

Standard Error Computations

When national estimates are derived from a sample, as with the NCVS, caution must be used when comparing one estimate to another or when comparing estimates over time. Although one estimate may be larger than another, estimates based on a sample have some degree of sampling error. The sampling error of an estimate depends on several factors, including the amount of variation in the responses and the size of the sample. When the sampling error around an estimate is taken into account, estimates that appear different may not be statistically significant.

One measure of the sampling error associated with an estimate is the standard error. The standard error may vary from one estimate to the next. Generally, an estimate with a smaller standard error provides a more reliable approximation of the true value than an estimate with a larger standard error. Estimates with relatively large standard errors have less precision and reliability and should be interpreted with caution.

NCVS Measurement of Rape and Sexual Assault

Thee NCVS uses a two-stage measurement approach in the screening and classification of criminal victimization, including rape and sexual assault. In the first stage of screening, survey respondents are administered a series of "short-cue" screening questions designed to help respondents think about different experiences they may have had during the reference period (see NCVS-1 at https://www.bjs.gov/ content/pub/pdf/ncvs15_bsq. pdf).

This design improves respondent recall of events, particularly for incidents that may not immediately come to mind as crimes, such as those committed by family members and acquaintances. Respondents who answer affirmatively to any of the short-cue screening items are subsequently administered a crime incident report (CIR) designed to classify incidents into specific crime types (see NCVS-2 at https://www.bjs.gov/content/pub/pdf/ ncvs15_cir.pdf).

First stage of measurement. Two short-cue screening questions are specifically designed to target sexual violence:

1. Other than any incidents already mentioned, has anyone attacked or threatened you in any of these ways: (a) with any weapon, such as a gun or knife; (b) with anything like a baseball bat, frying pan, scissors, or stick; (c) by something thrown, such as a rock or bottle; (d) by grabbing, punching, or choking; (e) any rape, attempted rape, or other types of sexual attack; (f) any face-to-face threats; **or** (g) any attack or threat or use of force by anyone at all? Please mention it even if you are not certain it was a crime.

2. Incidents involving forced or unwanted sexual acts are often difficult to talk about. Other than any incidents already mentioned, have you been forced or coerced to engage in unwanted sexual activity by (a) someone you did not know; (b) a casual acquaintance; or (c) someone you knew well?

Respondents may screen into a CIR if they respond affirmatively to another short-cue screening question. For instance, a separate screening question cues respondents to think of attacks or threats that took place in specific locations, such as at home, work, or school. A respondent who recalled a sexual victimization that occurred at home, work, or school and answered affirmatively would be administered a CIR even if they did not respond affirmatively to the screening question targeting sexual violence.

Second stage of measurement. The CIR is used to collect information on the attributes of each incident. The key attributes of sexual violence that are used to classify a victimization as a rape or sexual assault are the type of attack and physical injury suffered. Victims are asked if "the offender hit you, knock[ed] you down, or actually attack[ed] you in any way;" if "the offender TR[IED] to attack you;" or if "the offender THREATEN[ED] you with harm in any way?" The survey participant is classified as a victim of rape or sexual assault if he or she responds affirmatively to one of these three questions and then responds that the completed, attempted, or threatened attack was (a) rape; (b) attempted rape; (c) sexual assault; (d) verbal threat of rape; (e) verbal threat of sexual assault other than rape; (f) unwanted sexual contact with force (e.g., grabbing, fondling); or (g) unwanted sexual contact without force (e.g., grabbing, fondling).

Whether the victim selects one of these response options to describe the attack, he or she is also classified as a victim of rape or sexual assault if the injuries suffered as a result of the incident are described as: (a) rape; (b) attempted rape; or (c) sexual assault other than rape or attempted rape.

Coercion. Although the CIR does not ask respondents if psychological coercion was used, one screening question targeted to rape and sexual violence asks respondents if force or coercion was used to initiate unwanted sexual activity.

The final classification of incidents by the CIR results in the following definitions of rape and sexual assault used in the NCVS:

Rape. Coerced or forced sexual intercourse. Forced sexual intercourse means vaginal, anal, or oral penetration by the offender(s). This category could include incidents where the penetration was from a foreign object such as a bottle. Includes attempted rapes, male and female victims, and both heterosexual and same-sex rape. Attempted rape includes verbal threats of rape.

Sexual assault. A wide range of victimizations, separate from rape or attempted rape. ese crimes include attacks or attempted attacks generally involving unwanted sexual contact between victim and offender. Sexual assaults may or may not involve force and include such things as grabbing or fondling. Sexual assault also includes verbal threats.

Comparison of NCVS Estimates to Other Survey Estimates

During the past several decades, a number of other surveys have also been used to study rape and sexual assault in the general population. BJS estimates of rape and sexual assault from the NCVS have typically been lower than estimates derived from other federal and private surveys. However, the NCVS methodology and definitions of rape and sexual assault differ from many of these surveys in important ways that contribute to the variation in estimates of the prevalence and incidence of these victimizations. Additional information about differences in self-report estimates of rape and sexual assault is available on the BJS website. BJS continues an active research program on the collection of rape and sexual assault data in an effort to improve the quality and accuracy of these estimates.

Despite the current differences in methods and estimates that exist between the NCVS and other surveys measuring rape and sexual assault, a strength of the NCVS is its capacity to be used to make comparisons between population subgroups and over time. Methodological differences that exist between the NCVS and the other surveys should not impact NCVS comparisons between groups or in trends over time.

PART 4

Federal Justice Statistics, 2017–2018

HIGHLIGHTS

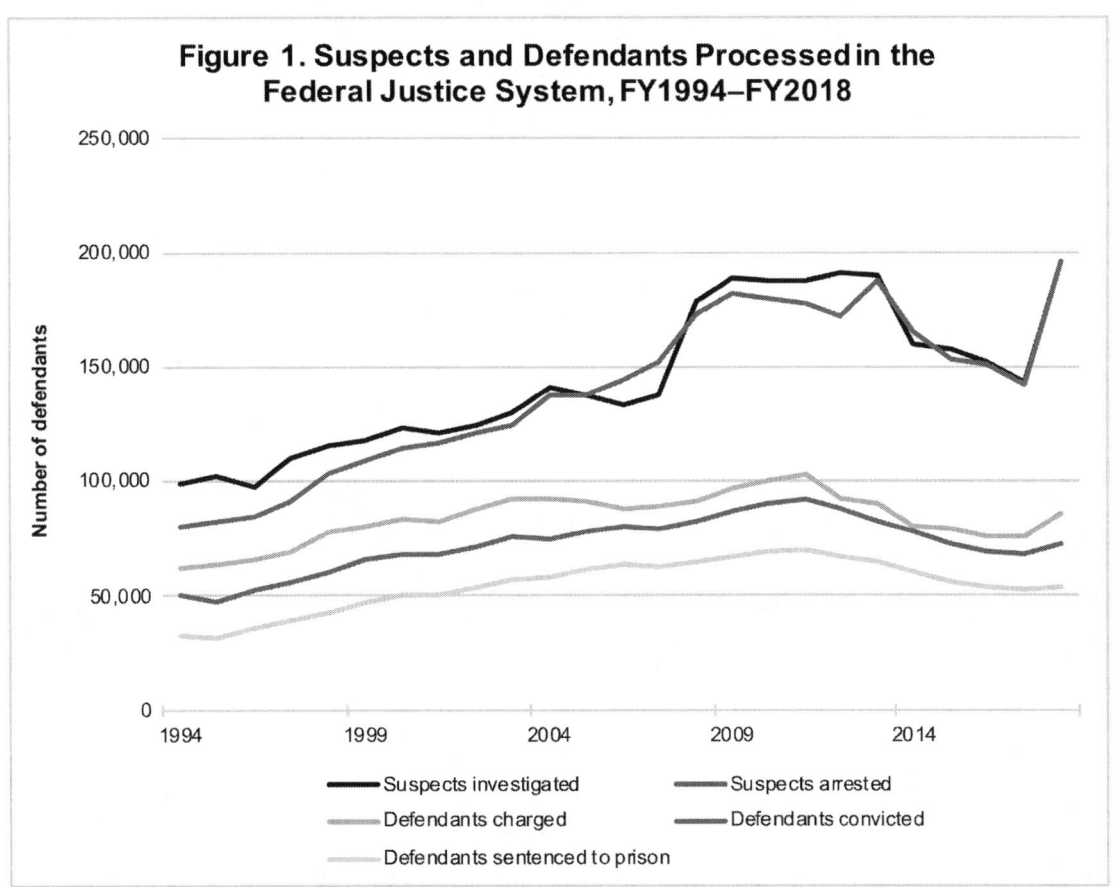

Figure 1. Suspects and Defendants Processed in the Federal Justice System, FY1994–FY2018

- Federal law enforcement agencies made a total of 195,771 arrests in fiscal year (FY) 2018, a 38 percent increase from FY2017 (142,008 arrests).

- Nearly two-thirds (65 percent) of all federal arrests in FY2018 took place in the five federal judicial districts along the U.S.-Mexico border. These districts are listed individually in the tables in this section.

- Fifty-six percent of federal arrests in FY2018 involved an immigration offense as the most serious arrest offense.

- In FY2018, Drug Enforcement Administration (DEA) arrests occurred most frequently for methamphetamine (8,088 arrests) and for heroin and opioids (7,098 arrests).

- Approximately 31 percent of defendants charged in U.S. district court in FY2018 were from Mexico, while 8 percent were from Central America and 2 percent were from the Caribbean; non-U.S. citizens made up 43 percent of defendants charged in FY2018.

Table 1. Offenders in Federal Confinement or under Federal Supervision in the Community, FY 2008, FY 2017, and FY 2018 (Yearend)

(Number; percent.)

Characteristic	FY 2008 Number	FY 2008 Percent	FY 2017 Number	FY 2017 Percent	FY 2018 Number	FY 2018 Percent
Total	381,723	100.0	372,531	100.0	372,354	100.0
Secure confinement...	234,629	61.4	218,222	58.6	222,315	59.7
Pre-trial detention	56,745	14.8	53,579	14.4	60,430	16.2
Federal Bureau of Prisons (post-sentencing)[1]	177,884	46.6	164,643	44.2	161,885	43.5
Community supervision...	147,094	38.6	154,309	41.4	150,039	40.3
Pre-trial release supervision..............................	27,041	7.1	21,848	5.9	22,597	6.1
Post-sentencing supervision..............................	120,053	31.5	132,461	35.6	127,442	34.2
Supervised release	94,703	24.8	114,537	30.7	111,024	29.8
Probation..	23,054	6.0	16,895	4.5	15,465	4.2
Parole...	2,296	0.6	1,029	0.3	953	0.3

Note: Details may not sum to totals due to rounding. Federal offender populations are shown as of September 30, 2008, 2017, and 2018.
[1]Counts include federally sentenced prisoners in the custody of the Federal Bureau of Prisons (BOP). Counts exclude persons in federal prison for District of Columbia code offenses, military code offenses, treaty transfer cases, and as state boarders. Unsentenced federal offenders in the BOP are counted in pre-trial detention counts.

Table 2. Federal Arrests, by Most Serious Offense and Federal District, FY 2017 and FY 2018

(Number; percent.)

Characteristic	FY 2017 Number	FY 2017 Percent	FY 2018 Number	FY 2018 Percent	Percent change, 2017–2018
Total arrests	142,008	100.0	195,771	100.0	37.9
Most serious offense at arrest					
Violent...	3,679	2.6	3,811	1.9	3.6
Property...	10,246	7.2	10,395	5.3	1.5
Fraud..	8,672	6.1	8,966	4.6	3.4
Other..	1,574	1.1	1,429	0.7	-9.2
Drug..	22,611	15.9	22,387	11.4	
Public order...	7,775	5.5	7,428	3.8	-4.5
Regulatory..	252	0.2	234	0.1	-7.1
Other...	7,523	5.3	7,194	3.7	-4.4
Weapons..	9,091	6.4	10,562	5.4	16.2
Immigration..	58,031	40.9	108,667	55.5	87.3
Material witness......................................	5,684	4.0	7,472	3.8	31.5
Supervision violations	24,890	17.5	25,049	12.8	0.6
Federal judicial district					
U.S./Mexico border district	76,171	53.6	126,293	64.5	65.8
Arizona..	20,664	14.6	28,934	14.8	40.0
California Southern...............................	8,003	5.6	13,710	7.0	71.3
New Mexico	5,989	4.2	9,641	4.9	61.0
Texas Southern	21,405	15.1	45,740	23.4	113.7
Texas Western	20,110	14.2	28,268	14.4	40.6
Other..	65,837	46.4	69,478	35.5	5.5

Note: Suspects with more than one arrest are counted separately. The most serious offense at arrest is determined by the deputy U.S. marshal at booking. The federal judicial district is the location of the federal court where booking takes place. Data were missing for offense in 2017 (1).

Table 3. Suspects in Matters Opened by U.S. Attorneys, by Referring Authority, FY 2008, FY 2016, FY 2017, and FY 2018

(Percent; number.)

Department or authority	FY 2008	FY 2016	FY 2017	FY 2018
Defense..	2.4	2.0	2.2	1.4
Homeland Security...	60.1	52.6	47.6	59.1
Interior..	1.5	2.0	2.0	1.0
Justice...	22.7	29.7	33.2	26.1
Treasury...	1.4	1.3	1.2	0.7
Federal/state task forces................................	2.1	2.0	2.8	2.9
Other[1]..	9.8	10.4	11.0	8.8
Number of suspects......................................	178,570	151,994	143,684	195,842

Note: Details may not sum to totals due to rounding. The department or authority is the entity making the referral for criminal action to the U.S. attorneys offices. Percentages are based on records with non-missing referring-authority data. Data were missing for referring authority in 2008 (276), in 2016 (41), and in 2018 (1). The unit of count is a suspect in a matter referred to U.S. attorneys. Suspects in more than one matter are counted separately. A matter is opened when a federal prosecutor spends one hour or more investigating.
[1]Includes departments of Agriculture, Commerce, Education, Energy, Health and Human Services, Labor, State, and Transportation; and state and local authorities.

Table 4. Outcome and Case Processing Time of Suspects in Matters Concluded, FY 2018

(Number; percent; days.)

Characteristic	Outcome[1]				Prosecutor decision/case-processing time (median days)[2]			
	Number of suspects in matters concluded	Prosecuted in U.S. district court	Disposed of by U.S. magistrate	Declined to prosecute	Total	Decision to prosecute in U.S. district court	Decision to dispose of by U.S. magistrate	Decision to decline matter
Total	195,757	42.5	44.7	12.8	12	24	1	516
Lead charge[2]								
Violent.......................................	5,081	54.0	9.5	36.6	89	27	114	307
Property	19,020	51.2	7.4	41.5	302	97	128	663
Fraud..	16,700	50.3	6.8	43.0	333	123	114	679
Other...	2,320	57.7	11.6	30.7	112	31	232	481
Drug...	31,919	73.3	9.0	17.8	39	26	73	576
Public order..................................	18,228	45.9	18.3	35.9	152	40	84	520
Regulatory	3,192	37.7	15.6	46.7	225	37	57	559
Other...	15,036	47.6	18.9	33.6	140	41	90	509
Weapons......................................	13,672	76.2	4.6	19.3	35	26	78	246
Immigration	107,794	26.4	73.1	0.5	2	22	1	379
Federal judicial district								
U.S./Mexico border	114,557	27.7	70.1	2.2	2	23	1	509
Arizona.....................................	26,630	19.8	76.7	3.5	0	26	0	534
California Southern.................	11,297	56.3	42.8	0.9	15	25	7	513
New Mexico	9,859	42.7	53.2	4.1	8	11	5	419
Texas Southern	40,678	16.6	82.2	1.2	1	20	0	675
Texas Western	26,093	34.9	62.9	2.2	7	23	2	464
Other.......................................	81,200	63.3	8.9	27.8	87	28	105	517

[1]Details may not sum to totals due to rounding. The unit of count is a suspect in a matter referred to U.S. attorneys. Suspects investigated in more than one matter are counted separately. Data were missing for lead charge (43).
[2]Case-processing time reflects the time from receipt of a matter to the U.S. attorneys decision to prosecute the matter as a case in U.S. district court, refer the matter for disposal by a U.S. magistrate, or decline the matter, resulting in no further action in U.S. district court. The median is the midpoint of processing time. A median of one day means that at least half of the suspects received a disposition within a day of when the matter was referred.
[3]The lead charge is the substantive statute that is the primary basis for referral. It is most often, but not always, the charge with the greatest potential sentence.

Table 5. Demographic Characteristics of Defendants Charged in U.S. Federal District Court, by Sex of Defendant, FY 2018

(Number; percent; years.)

Demographic characteristic	All defendants		Male		Female	
	Number	Percent	Number	Percent	Number	Percent
Total	73,110	100.0	63,654	100.0	9,278	100.0
Race/Ethnicity						
White[1]	13,448	19.1	10,677	17.3	2,768	31.3
Black[1]	14,239	20.2	12,621	20.5	1,611	18.2
Hispanic...	40,510	57.4	36,556	59.2	3,941	44.6
Asian/Native Hawaiian/Other Pacific Islander[1]	967	1.4	737	1.2	228	2.6
American Indian/Alaska Native[1]	1,422	2.0	1,137	1.8	284	3.2
Age						
17 years or younger	25	<0.1	25	<0.1	0	0.0
18 to 19 years...............................	764	1.1	642	1.0	122	1.3
20 to 24 years...............................	8,018	11.0	6,875	10.8	1,140	12.3
25 to 29 years...............................	12,579	17.2	10,955	17.2	1,617	17.4
30 to 34 years...............................	13,402	18.4	11,840	18.6	1,557	16.8
35 to 39 years...............................	12,565	17.2	11,107	17.5	1,451	15.6
40 to 44 years...............................	9,526	13.1	8,404	13.2	1,119	12.1
45 to 49 years...............................	6,534	9.0	5,637	8.9	895	9.7
50 to 54 years...............................	4,271	5.9	3,683	5.8	584	6.3
55 to 59 years...............................	2,609	3.6	2,237	3.5	370	4.0
60 to 64 years...............................	1,480	2.0	1,258	2.0	218	2.4
65 years or older............................	1,188	1.6	982	1.5	203	2.2
Median age (years).........................	35 yrs.	X	35 yrs.	X	35 yrs.	X
Citizenship						
U.S. citizen......................................	41,338	57.0	34,068	53.8	7,248	79.0
Non-U.S. citizen	31,204	43.0	29,258	46.2	1,931	21.0
Country/Region of Citizenship						
North America	70,868	97.7	61,866	97.7	8,966	97.7
United States................................	41,338	57.0	34,068	53.8	7,248	79.0
Mexico..	22,364	30.8	21,078	33.3	1,273	13.9
Canada	91	0.1	69	0.1	22	0.2
Caribbean Islands[2].......................	1,210	1.7	1,102	1.7	108	1.2
Central America[2].........................	5,865	8.1	5,549	8.8	315	3.4
South America[2]...............................	858	1.2	783	1.2	75	0.8
Asia and Oceania[2]...........................	389	0.5	317	0.5	71	0.8
Europe[2]...	235	0.3	192	0.3	43	0.5
Africa[2]...	192	0.3	168	0.3	24	0.3

NOTE: Details may not sum to totals due to rounding. The unit of count is a defendant in a case filed in U.S. district court. Defendants charged in more than one case are counted separately. Includes defendants charged in U.S. district court with a felony or a Class A or B misdemeanor as the most serious charge. Data were missing for sex (178), race or ethnicity (2,524), age (149), and citizenship (568).
X = Not applicable.
[1]Excludes persons of Hispanic origin (e.g., White refers to non-Hispanic Whites and Black refers to non-Hispanic Blacks). The defendant self-reported race and ethnicity during the pre-trial interview. Information was collected for one race and one ethnicity category.
[2]Countries aggregated by region.

Table 6. Disposition and Case-Processing Time of Defendants in Cases Terminated in U.S. District Court, FY 2018

(Number; percent; days.)

Most serious offense at termination	Total cases terminated	Convicted			Not convicted		
		Total	Guilty plea	Bench/jury trial	Total	Bench/jury trial	Dismissed
All offenses..	78,996	91.9	89.9	2.0	8.1	0.4	7.7
Type of charge							
Felony..	71,138	94.2	92.1	2.1	5.8	0.5	5.3
Violent	2,634	91.5	85.5	6.0	8.5	1.8	6.8
Property	8,624	91.8	87.9	4.0	8.2	0.7	7.4
Fraud....................................	7,512	92.0	88.0	4.0	8.0	0.6	7.4
Other....................................	1,112	91.0	87.2	3.8	9.0	1.3	7.7
Drug	20,991	92.8	90.6	2.2	7.2	0.3	6.8
Public order..............................	6,673	92.3	88.4	3.9	7.7	0.8	6.9
Regulatory...........................	721	87.9	82.3	5.7	12.1	2.4	9.7
Other...................................	5,952	92.8	89.2	3.7	7.2	0.6	6.5
Weapons...................................	8,498	94.3	91.7	2.6	5.7	0.9	4.8
Immigration	23,718	97.2	96.9	0.3	2.8	0.1	2.7
Misdemeanor...................................	7,858	70.7	70.1	0.6	29.3	0.3	29.1
Federal judicial district							
U.S./Mexico border	29,815	95.9	95.3	0.6	4.1	0.3	3.8
Arizona..	4,843	95.9	94.9	1.0	4.1	0.3	3.9
California Southern.........................	6,126	92.8	92.0	0.8	7.2	0.4	6.8
New Mexico	4,043	98.5	98.4	0.1	1.5	<0.1	1.5
Texas Southern	6,371	96.3	95.7	0.6	3.7	0.2	3.4
Texas Western	8,432	96.6	96.1	0.5	3.4	0.2	3.1
Other...	49,181	89.4	86.6	2.8	10.6	0.6	10.0
Median days from filing to disposition[1] ...	201 days	198 days	195 days	549 days	258 days	266 days	258 days

NOTE: Details may not sum to totals due to rounding. Includes information on felony defendants; Class A misdemeanants, whether handled by U.S. district judges or U.S. magistrates; and other misdemeanants, provided they were handled by U.S. district judges. Court personnel determine the most serious offense at termination as the offense with the greatest statutory-maximum sentence. The unit of count is a defendant in a case terminated in U.S. district court. Defendants in more than one case are counted separately. The median is the midpoint between the slowest and fastest processing times. A median of 201 days means that half of the defendants received a disposition in less than 201 days and half received a disposition in more than 201 days.
[1]Includes the interval from the time a case is filed in U.S. district court to sentencing for defendants who were convicted, and the interval from case filing to disposition for defendants who were not convicted or whose cases were dismissed.

Table 7. Type and Length of Sentence Imposed for Convicted Offenders, by Offense and District, FY 2018

(Number; percent; months.)

Most serious offense at case termination	Number convicted	Type of sentence				Median sentence length (months)	
		Prison[1]	Probation only	Fine only	Suspended sentence	Prison	Probation
All offenses..................................	72,588	74.8	8.5	2.1	14.5	30	36
Type of Offense							
Felony...	67,035	78.2	7.2	0.3	14.4	34	36
Violent	2,410	93.1	2.6	0.1	4.2	77	36
Property	7,920	65.3	21.7	0.6	12.3	24	36
Fraud.......................................	6,908	67.3	19.4	0.7	12.7	24	36
Other.......................................	1,012	52.0	38.1	0.2	9.7	21	36
Drug	19,489	91.0	3.7	0.3	5.0	63	36
Public order...............................	6,159	80.2	13.3	0.8	5.7	48	36
Regulatory	634	59.6	30.0	2.9	7.6	24	36
Other.......................................	5,525	82.6	11.4	0.6	5.5	51	36
Weapons....................................	8,014	91.5	4.1	0.3	4.1	48	36
Immigration	23,043	64.9	5.0	0.2	29.9	12	36
Misdemeanor..................................	5,553	34.3	24.9	24.2	16.6	4	12
Federal Judicial District							
U.S./Mexico border	28,598	73.3	6.5	0.2	20.0	14	36
Arizona..................................	4,643	75.0	7.6	<0.1	17.4	14	36
California Southern................	5,685	69.2	4.4	0.2	26.2	14	60
New Mexico	3,983	98.5	1.5	<0.1	<0.1	2	24
Texas Southern	6,138	87.4	2.8	0.2	9.6	21	36
Texas Western	8,149	52.3	12.5	0.4	34.8	18	36
Other	43,990	75.8	9.9	3.4	11.0	51	36

NOTE: Details may not sum to totals due to rounding. The unit of count is a defendant in a case terminated with a conviction and sentence in U.S. district court. Defendants convicted and sentenced in more than one case are counted separately. The most serious offense is determined by court personnel as the offense with the greatest statutory-maximum sentence. The median prison term is the midpoint of prison terms imposed. A median of 30 months means that half of the defendants received a prison term of less than 30 months and half received a prison term of more than 30 months. Data were missing for type of sentence (240).
[1]Includes sentences to incarceration, such as mixed (a prison term followed by a probation term) and life sentences.

Table 8. Admissions and Releases of Federal Prisoners, by Offense, FY 2018

(Number.)

Most serious commitment offense[1]	Population at start of the year[2]	Prisoners admitted			Prisoners released			Population at end of year[7]	Net population change
		District court[3]			First release[4]				
		Sentence of 1 year or less	Sentence of more than 1 year	All other[5]	Time served 1 year or less	Time served more than 1 year	All other[6]		
Total	167,034	7,824	39,796	11,628	9,679	42,725	11,993	161,885	-5,149
Violent......................................	10,023	76	1,409	957	98	1,538	1,071	9,758	-265
Property....................................	10,125	705	3,298	1,251	848	3,827	1,327	9,377	-748
Fraud	8,575	554	2,826	921	672	3,313	956	7,935	-640
Other	1,550	151	472	330	176	514	371	1,442	-108
Drug...	79,058	689	15,660	4,731	864	17,690	4,849	76,735	-2,323
Public order	24,679	504	5,513	1,332	571	4,477	1,348	25,632	953
Regulatory.............................	3,027	170	1,074	162	186	974	162	3,111	84
Other	21,652	334	4,439	1,170	385	3,503	1,186	22,521	869
Weapons	28,397	175	6,980	2,505	188	6,472	2,523	28,874	477
Immigration..............................	14,024	5,618	6,804	780	7,040	8,535	807	10,844	-3,180

NOTE: The unit of count is a person admitted to or released from the Federal Bureau of Prisons. Offenders who are admitted and released in the same year are counted separately. Excludes District of Columbia Superior Court offenders, military code offenders, state boarders, and foreign treaty transfers. Offenders who entered or left a prison temporarily (such as for transit to another location, for health care, or to serve a weekend sentence) are not counted as admitted or released. Data were missing for offense at the start of the year (728) and at the end of the year (665).
-- = Less than 0.05 percent.
[1]The offense with the longest sentence imposed at conviction.
[2]The population as of October 1, 2017.
[3]Prisoners who were committed by a U.S. district court for U.S. Code violations.
[4]Prisoners who were released after being committed by a U.S. district court.
[5]Prisoners who were committed following a return to prison for violating conditions of their supervised release or who were received for examination, treatment, or transfer to another jurisdiction.
[6]Prisoners who were released from prison without a new court commitment after they were committed for violating conditions of their supervised release.
[7]The population as of September 30, 2018.

Table 9. Demographic Characteristics of Federally Sentenced Offenders in the Custody of the Federal Bureau of Prisons, Fiscal Year-End 2008 and 2018

(Number; percent.)

Offender characteristic	2008 Number	2008 Percent	2018 Number	2018 Percent	Average annual growth, 2008–2018[1]
All prisoners	177,884	100.0	161,885	100.0	-0.9
Sex					
Male..	165,916	93.3	150,465	92.9	-0.9
Female...	11,968	6.7	11,420	7.1	-0.4
Race/Ethnicity					
White[2]	49,963	28.1	46,512	28.7	-0.7
Black[2]	65,672	36.9	57,132	35.3	-1.4
Hispanic..	56,445	31.7	52,372	32.4	-0.6
Asian/Native Hawaiian/Other Pacific Islander[2]	2,679	1.5	2,237	1.4	-1.7
American Indian/Alaska Native[2]	3,125	1.8	3,632	2.2	1.5
Age					
17 years or younger	30	<0.1	4	<0.1	<0.1
18 to 19 years...	401	0.2	184	0.1	-6.3
20 to 24 years...	10,613	6.0	6,055	3.7	-5.3
25 to 29 years...	28,317	15.9	18,110	11.2	-4.3
30 to 34 years...	35,601	20.0	25,553	15.8	-3.1
35 to 39 years...	33,237	18.7	30,352	18.7	-0.8
40 to 44 years...	24,544	13.8	26,475	16.4	0.8
45 to 49 years...	18,816	10.6	20,742	12.8	1.0
50 to 54 years...	12,105	6.8	14,067	8.7	1.6
55 to 59 years...	7,161	4.0	9,639	6.0	3.1
60 to 64 years...	4,031	2.3	5,600	3.5	3.4
65 years or older..	3,028	1.7	5,104	3.2	5.5
Median age (years)..	37 yrs.	X	40 yrs.	X	X
Citizenship					
U.S. citizen...	131,215	73.9	131,035	80.9	0.0
Non-U.S. citizen..	46,444	26.1	30,848	19.1	-3.8
Country/region of citizenship					
North America	172,120	96.9	157,680	97.4	-0.8
United States..	131,215	73.9	131,035	80.9	0.0
Mexico...	31,898	18.0	20,584	12.7	-4.0
Canada...	372	0.2	184	0.1	-6.4
Caribbean Islands[3]..	5,547	3.1	3,127	1.9	-5.5
Central America[3]	3,088	1.7	2,750	1.7	-0.8
South America[3]..	3,127	1.8	2,358	1.5	-2.6
Asia and Oceania[3]..	1,394	0.8	858	0.5	-4.7
Europe[3]...	509	0.3	524	0.3	0.3
Africa[3]	509	0.3	463	0.3	-0.7

NOTE: Details may not sum to totals due to rounding. Federal prisoner populations are shown as of September 30, 2008 and 2018. Includes prisoners sentenced in U.S. district court. Excludes District of Columbia code offenders, military code offenders, foreign treaty transfers, state boarders, and pre-sentenced offenders. Data were missing for citizenship in 2008 (225) and in 2018 (2).
X = Not applicable.
[1] Calculated using each fiscal-year-end count from 2008 to 2018.
[2] Excludes persons of Hispanic origin (e.g., White refers to non-Hispanic whites and Black refers to non-Hispanic Blacks). The prisoner self-reported race and ethnicity during the pre-sentence interview. Information was collected for one race and one ethnicity category.
[3] Countries aggregated by region.

Table 10. Demographic Characteristics of Offenders Under Post-Sentencing Federal Supervision, FY 2018

(Number; percent.)

Demographic characteristic	All offenders Number	All offenders Percent	Probation Number	Probation Percent	Supervised release Number	Supervised release Percent	Parole Number	Parole Percent
All prisoners	127,478	100.0	15,468	12.1	111,055	87.1	955	0.8
Sex								
Male..................................	106,151	83.4	9,508	62.3	95,711	86.2	932	97.6
Female...............................	21,109	16.6	5,746	37.7	15,340	13.8	23	2.4
Race/ethnicity								
White[1]	42,366	34.1	6,398	43.8	35,656	32.8	312	34.9
Black[1]	44,114	35.5	3,901	26.7	39,771	36.5	442	49.4
Hispanic...........................	32,139	25.8	3,286	22.5	28,743	26.4	110	12.3
Asian/Native Hawaiian/Other Pacific Islander[1]	2,867	2.3	575	3.9	2,274	2.1	18	2.0
American Indian/Alaska Native[1]	2,887	2.3	449	3.1	2,425	2.2	13	1.5
Age								
17 years or younger	11	<0.1	10	0.1	1	<0.1	0	<0.1
18 to 19 years............................	92	0.1	75	0.5	17	<0.1	0	<0.1
20 to 24 years............................	3,489	2.7	1,245	8.2	2,233	2.0	11	1.2
25 to 29 years............................	11,259	8.9	1,982	13.0	9,224	8.3	53	5.6
30 to 34 years............................	17,022	13.4	1,908	12.5	15,051	13.6	63	6.6
35 to 39 years............................	21,568	17.0	1,955	12.8	19,558	17.6	55	5.8
40 to 44 years............................	20,276	15.9	1,702	11.2	18,500	16.7	74	7.8
45 to 49 years............................	17,064	13.4	1,614	10.6	15,339	13.8	111	11.6
50 to 54 years............................	12,735	10.0	1,364	8.9	11,263	10.1	108	11.3
55 to 59 years............................	9,897	7.8	1,237	8.1	8,547	7.7	113	11.8
60 to 64 years............................	6,427	5.1	935	6.1	5,368	4.8	124	13.0
65 years or older.........................	7,425	5.8	1,231	8.1	5,951	5.4	243	25.5
Median age (years).....................	42 yrs.	X	41 yrs.	X	42 yrs.	X	55 yrs.	X
Citizenship								
U.S. citizen..............................	123,163	97.0	14,417	94.7	107,843	97.3	903	95.4
Non-U.S. citizen	3,816	3.0	811	5.3	2,961	2.7	44	4.7
Country/region of citizenship								
North America	125,804	99.1	14,903	97.9	109,971	99.2	930	98.2
United States............................	123,163	97.0	14,417	94.7	107,843	97.3	903	95.4
Mexico..................................	860	0.7	192	1.3	660	0.6	8	0.8
Canada..................................	45	<0.1	21	0.1	24	<0.1	0	<0.1
Caribbean Islands[2]	1,457	1.2	174	1.1	1,266	1.1	17	1.8
Central America[2]	279	0.2	99	0.7	178	0.2	2	0.2
South America[2]	198	0.2	57	0.4	130	0.1	11	1.2
Asia and Oceania[2]	577	0.5	139	0.9	434	0.4	4	0.4
Europe[2]...................................	229	0.2	70	0.5	157	0.1	2	0.2
Africa[2]	171	0.1	59	0.4	112	0.1	0	<0.1

NOTE: Details may not sum to totals due to rounding. Total includes offenders for whom characteristics were unknown. The unit of count is an individual offender under federal supervision on September 30, 2018. Percentages are based on non-missing cases. Data were missing for type of supervised release (105), sex (218), race or ethnicity (3,105), age (213), and citizenship (499).
X = Not applicable
[1]Excludes persons of Hispanic origin (e.g., ìwhiteî refers to non-Hispanic whites and ìblackî refers to non-Hispanic blacks). The offender self-reported race and ethnicity during the pre-trial interview. Information was collected for one race and one ethnicity category.
[2]Countries aggregated by region.

METHODOLOGY

Federal Justice Statistics describes persons processed by the federal criminal justice system. Data are from the Federal Justice Statistics Program (FJSP). The FJSP collects, standardizes, and reports on administrative data received from six federal justice agencies: the U.S. Marshals Service, Drug Enforcement Administration, Executive Office for U.S. Attorneys, Administrative Office of the U.S. Courts, U.S. Sentencing Commission, and Federal Bureau of Prisons.

This report describes the annual activity, workloads, and outcomes of the federal criminal justice system from arrest to imprisonment. Findings are based on data from the U.S. Marshals Service, Drug Enforcement Administration (DEA), Executive Office for U.S. Attorneys, Administrative Office of the U.S. Courts, and Federal Bureau of Prisons. This report presents data on arrests and investigations by law enforcement agency and growth rates by type of offense and federal judicial district. It also examines trends on drug arrests by the DEA, and it includes the most recent available data on sentences imposed and their lengths by type of offense.

Definitions of Major Offense Categories

Violent—Includes murder, non-negligent or negligent manslaughter, aggravated or simple assault, sex abuse, robbery, kidnapping, and threats against the president.

Property—Includes fraudulent and other types of property offenses.

Fraudulent property—Includes embezzlement, fraud (including tax fraud), forgery, and counterfeiting.

Other property—Includes burglary, larceny, motor-vehicle theft, arson, transportation of stolen property, and other property offenses, such as destruction of property and trespassing.

Drug—Includes the manufacture, import, export, distribution, or dispensing of a controlled substance (or a counterfeit substance), or the possession of a controlled substance (or a counterfeit substance) with intent to manufacture or distribute.

Public order—Includes regulatory and other types of offenses.

Regulatory public order—Includes violation of agriculture, antitrust, labor, food and drug, motor carrier, and other federal regulations.

Other public order—Includes non-regulatory violations concerning tax law (tax fraud), bribery, perjury, national defense, escape, racketeering and extortion, gambling, liquor, mailing or transporting obscene materials, traffic, migratory birds, conspiracy, aiding and abetting, jurisdiction, and other offenses.

Weapons—Includes violations of any of the provisions of 18 U.S.C. §§ 922-923 concerning the manufacturing, importing, possessing, receiving, and licensing of firearms and ammunition.

Immigration—Includes offenses involving illegal entrance into the United States, illegally reentering after being deported, willfully failing to leave when so ordered, or bringing in or harboring any aliens not admitted by an immigration officer.

Supervision violations—Includes violation of bail, violation of pre-trial or post-sentencing supervision in the community (probation), and failure to appear.

Report Methodology

This report uses data from the Federal Justice Statistics Program (FJSP), a collection from the Bureau of Justice Statistics (BJS). The FJSP receives administrative data files from six federal criminal justice agencies. Data represent the federal criminal case processing stages from arrest to imprisonment. BJS standardizes this information to maximize comparability across and within agencies over time. This includes—

- counting each appearance of an individual in the data during a fiscal year (October 1 through September 30), whether it be for a criminal arrest, matter, case, or imprisonment stay

- delineating fiscal year as the period for reported events

- applying a uniform offense classification across agencies

- classifying disposition and sentences imposed

FJSP Data Sources

U.S. Marshals Service: The Justice Detainee Information System provides information on suspects arrested for federal offenses. Suspects may be counted more than once in a fiscal year if they are arrested multiple times during the period. This report uses most serious arrest offense as classified by the deputy U.S. Marshal at the time of booking. Each of the 94 federal judicial districts in the United States have a U.S. Marshal. Deputy U.S. Marshals take federal suspects who have been charged with a crime into custody, which includes booking, processing, and detaining suspects. They also oversee court security and coordinate prisoner transportation, among other duties.

Drug Enforcement Administration (DEA): The Defendant Statistical System contains data on suspects arrested by DEA agents within the U.S. The data include information on characteristics of arrestees and the type of drug for which they were arrested. Suspects may be counted more than once in a fiscal year if they are arrested multiple times by the DEA during this period.

Executive Office for U.S. Attorneys: The Legal Information Office Network System database contains information on the investigation and prosecution of suspects in criminal matters received and concluded and criminal cases filed and terminated by U.S. attorneys. Suspects may be counted more than once in a fiscal year if they are involved in multiple matters received and concluded during the period. A matter is defined as a referral in which an attorney spends one hour or more investigating. The lead charge is used to classify the most serious offense at referral and is defined as the substantive statute that is the primary basis of referral.

Administrative Office of the U.S. Courts (AOUSC): The Criminal Master File contains information about the criminal proceedings against defendants whose cases were filed and terminated in U.S. district courts. It includes information on felony defendants, Class A misdemeanants—whether handled by U.S. district court judges or U.S. magistrates—and other misdemeanants provided they were handled by U.S. district court judges. A felony is classified as an offense for which the maximum term of imprisonment is more than one year in prison. Offenses classified as misdemeanors include those for which the maximum term of imprisonment is less than one year in prison. Class A misdemeanors include offenses for which the maximum term of imprisonment is one year or less but more than 6 months in prison. Class B misdemeanors include offenses for which the maximum term of imprisonment is 6 months or less but more than 30 days in prison.

Offenses are based on the most serious charged offense, as determined by the probation officer responsible for interviewing the defendant. The probation officer classifies the offense charged into AOUSC four-digit offense codes, which are maintained and updated by the AOUSC. For defendants charged with more than one offense on an indictment, the probation officer chooses as the charged offense the one carrying the most severe penalty or, in the case of two or more charges carrying the same penalty, the one with the highest offense severity. The offense severity level is determined by the AOUSC, which ranks offenses according to the maximum sentence, type of crime, and maximum fine amount. These four-digit codes are then aggregated into the primary offense charges used for this report.

This report also uses AOUSC data from the Probation and Pretrial Services Automated Case Tracking System (PACTS), which contains information on defendants interviewed and supervised by pre-trial services. These data are used to describe background characteristics of defendants arraigned. Post-sentencing data from PACTS are used to describe persons under post-sentencing supervision in the community.

U.S. Sentencing Commission: The Monitoring Database contains information on criminal defendants sentenced pursuant to the provisions of the Sentencing Reform Act of 1984. Data files are limited to those defendants whose court records have been obtained by the U.S. Sentencing Commission. These data do not appear in this report.

Federal Bureau of Prisons (BOP): The SENTRY database contains information on all federally sentenced offenders admitted into or released from federal prison during a fiscal year and offenders in federal prison at the end of each fiscal year (September 30). The prisoner count reported by the FJSP differs from what is reported by the BOP although data are from the same source (SENTRY). For example, the BOP reports 181,698 prisoners as of September 30, 2018. The FJSP starts with data extracted from SENTRY that differs slightly (down 396) from this total (181,302). Of the 181,302 records, 13,882 records were dropped because the prisoner was not designated at an assigned BOP custodial facility. The excluded records included designations to community confinement, home confinement, hospital, Immigration and Customs Enforcement detention, material witness, and pre-sentence admission. Next, 902 records were excluded due to missing commitment offense, and 4,113 prisoners were dropped as they were sentenced by the District of Columbia Superior Court. Finally, 520 prisoner records were dropped because the prisoner was a state boarder, a treaty transfer, or serving a sentence from a military court commitment. Of the 181,302 prisoners reported by the BOP in custody on September 30, 2018, a total of 161,885 (89 percent of the total population) met the criteria as federally sentenced prisoners.

Other Resources

FJSP data are available in the Federal Criminal Case Processing Statistics Tool, an interactive BJS. tool that permits users to query the federal data and download the results as a spreadsheet. This tool is available on the BJS Web site. It provides statistics by the stage of the federal criminal-case process, including law enforcement, prosecution and courts, and incarceration. Users can generate queries for up to three variables using data for the years 1998 to 2016. Users can also generate queries by the title and section of the U.S. criminal code.

PART 5

Hate Crime Statistics, 2019

HIGHLIGHTS

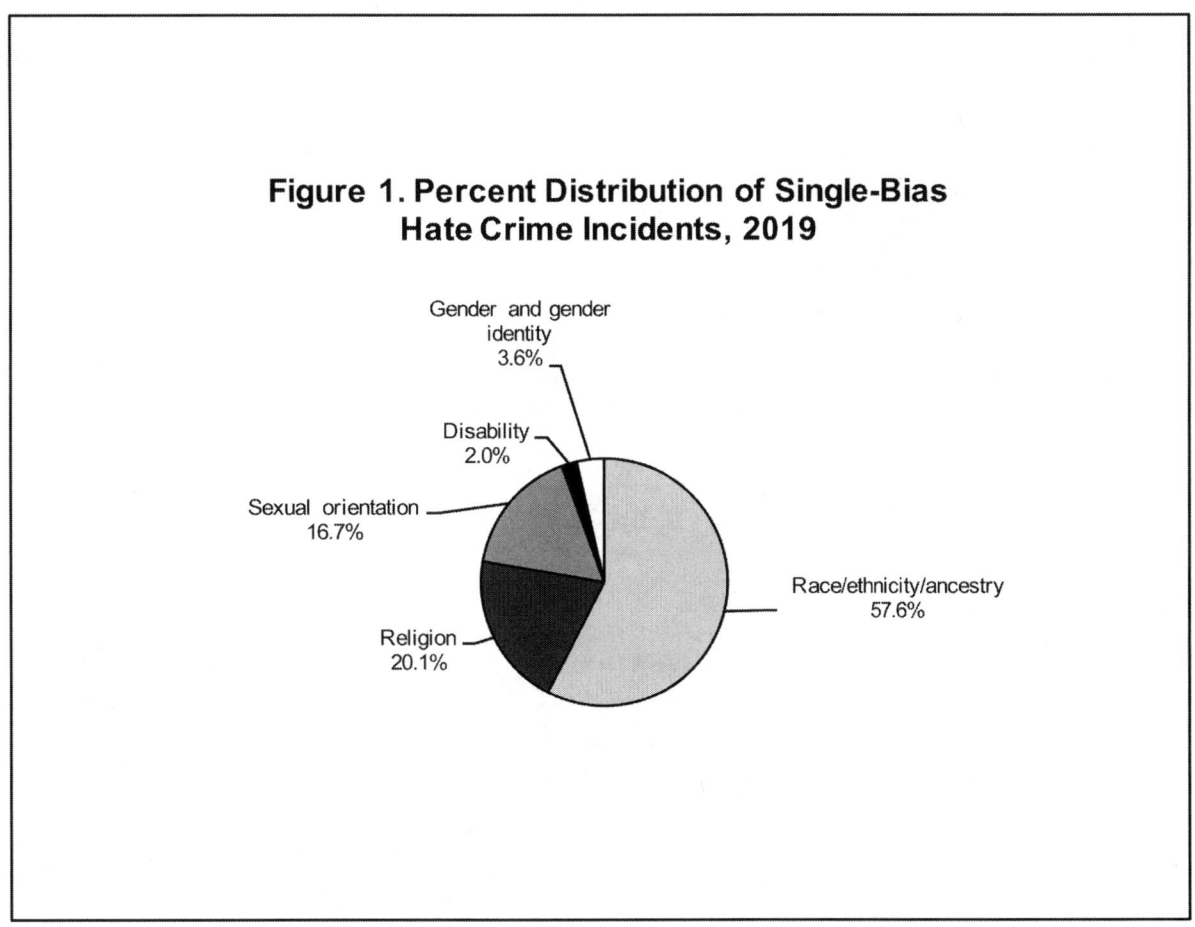

Figure 1. Percent Distribution of Single-Bias Hate Crime Incidents, 2019

Gender and gender identity 3.6%

Disability 2.0%

Sexual orientation 16.7%

Race/ethnicity/ancestry 57.6%

Religion 20.1%

- In 2019, there were 7,103 single-bias incidents that involved 8,302 offenses, 8,552 victims, and 6,268 known offenders; the 211 multiple-bias incidents reported in 2019 involved 257 offenses, 260 victims, and 138 known offenders.

- An analysis of data for victims of single-bias hate crime incidents in 2019 showed that 57.6 percent of the victims were targeted because of the offenders' bias against race/ethnicity/ancestry, 20.1 percent were victimized because of bias against religion, and 16.7 percent were targeted because of bias against sexual orientation.

- In 2019, race was reported for 6,406 known hate crime offenders; of these offenders: 52.5 percent were White,

23.9 percent were Black or African American, 6.6 percent were groups made up of individuals of various races (group of multiple races), 1.1 percent were American Indian or Alaska Native, 0.9 percent (58 offenders) were Asian, and 0.3 percent (22 offenders) were Native Hawaiian or Other Pacific Islander.

- Of the 5,512 hate crime offenses classified as crimes against persons in 2019, 40.0 percent were for intimidation, 36.7 percent were for simple assault, and 21.0 percent were for aggravated assault. Fifty-one (51) murders; 30 rapes; and 3 offenses of human trafficking, commercial sex acts were reported as hate crimes. The remaining 41 hate crime offenses were reported in the category of other.

Table 1. Incidents, Offenses, Victims, and Known Offenders, by Bias Motivation, 2019

(Number.)

Bias motivation	Incidents	Offenses	Victims[1]	Known offenders[2]
Total	7,314	8,559	8,812	6,406
Single-Bias Incidents	7,103	8,302	8,552	6,268
Race/Ethnicity/Ancestry	3,963	4,784	4,930	3,550
Anti-White	666	755	775	645
Anti-Black or African American	1,930	2,314	2,391	1,682
Anti-American Indian or Alaska Native	119	126	135	101
Anti-Asian	158	205	215	153
Anti-Native Hawaiian or Other Pacific Islander	21	25	26	26
Anti-Multiple Races, Group	134	171	173	82
Anti-Arab	95	122	126	86
Anti-Hispanic or Latino	527	676	693	547
Anti-Other Race/Ethnicity/Ancestry	313	390	396	228
Religion	1,521	1,650	1,715	1,012
Anti-Jewish	953	995	1,032	602
Anti-Catholic	64	66	66	42
Anti-Protestant	24	24	24	19
Anti-Islamic (Muslim)	176	219	227	145
Anti-Other Religion	88	108	108	56
Anti-Multiple Religions, Group	37	42	44	26
Anti-Mormon	12	14	15	8
Anti-Jehovah's Witness	7	7	7	7
Anti-Eastern Orthodox (Russian, Greek, Other)	44	47	49	34
Anti-Other Christian	49	60	65	23
Anti-Buddhist	5	5	5	5
Anti-Hindu	7	7	7	4
Anti-Sikh	49	50	60	36
Anti-Atheism/Agnosticism/etc.	6	6	6	5
Sexual Orientation	1,195	1,395	1,429	1,250
Anti-Gay (Male)	746	867	883	828
Anti-Lesbian	115	142	143	107
Anti-Lesbian, Gay, Bisexual, or Transgender (Mixed Group)	291	342	357	279
Anti-Heterosexual	17	17	19	14
Anti-Bisexual	26	27	27	22
Disability	157	169	170	156
Anti-Physical	49	53	53	33
Anti-Mental	108	116	117	123
Gender	69	80	81	67
Anti-Male	17	18	18	17
Anti-Female	52	62	63	50
Gender Identity	198	224	227	233
Anti-Transgender	151	173	175	190
Anti-Gender Non-Conforming	47	51	52	43
Multiple-Bias Incidents[3]	211	257	260	138

[1] The term victim may refer to an individual, business/financial institution, government entity, religious organization, or society/public as a whole.
[2] The term known offender does not imply the suspect's identity is known; rather, the term indicates some aspect of the suspect was identified, thus distinguishing the suspect from an unknown offender.
[3] A multiple-bias incident is an incident in which one or more offense types are motivated by two or more biases.

Table 2. Incidents, Offenses, Victims, and Known Offenders, by Offense Type, 2019

(Number.)

Offense type	Incidents[1]	Offenses	Victims[2]	Known offenders[3]
Total	7,314	8,559	8,812	6,406
Crimes Against Persons	4,526	5,512	5,512	4,857
Murder and nonnegligent manslaughter ...	18	51	51	19
Rape[4]	30	30	30	36
Aggravated assault	866	1,158	1,158	1,094
Simple assault	1,730	2,023	2,023	2,030
Intimidation	1,849	2,206	2,206	1,640
Human trafficking, commercial sex acts	2	3	3	3
Other[5]	31	41	41	35
Crimes Against Property	2,811	2,811	3,064	1,598
Robbery	125	125	149	227
Burglary	114	114	129	64
Larceny-theft	284	284	297	179
Motor vehicle theft	19	19	19	9
Arson	60	60	78	40
Destruction/damage/vandalism	2,152	2,152	2,316	1,045
Other[5]	57	57	76	34
Crimes Against Society[5]	236	236	236	279

[1]The actual number of incidents is 7,314. However, the column figures will not add to the total because incidents may include more than one offense type, and these are counted in each appropriate offense type category.
[2]The term victim may refer to an individual, business/financial institution, government entity, religious organization, or society/public as a whole.
[3]The term known offender does not imply the suspect's identity is known; rather, the term indicates some aspect of the suspect was identified, thus distinguishing the suspect from an unknown offender. The actual number of known offenders is 6,406. However, the column figures will not add to the total because some offenders are responsible for more than one offense type, and are, therefore, counted more than once in this table.
[4]Only the revised Uniform Crime Reporting definition of rape was used for the figures reported in this row.
[5]The figures shown include additional offenses collected in the National Incident-Based Reporting System.

Table 3. Offenses, Known Offender's Race and Ethnicity, by Offense Type, 2019

(Number.)

Bias motivation	Total offenses	Known offender's race							Known offender's ethnicity[1]				Unknown offender
		White	Black or African American	American Indian or Alaska Native	Asian	Native Hawaiian or Other Pacific Islander	Group of multiple races	Unknown race	Hispanic or Latino	Not Hispanic or Latino	Group of multiple ethnicities	Unknown ethnicity	
Total	8,559	3,564	1,385	76	57	19	268	784	504	1,862	71	2,775	2,406
Crimes Against Persons	5,512	2,865	1,171	59	40	18	218	342	412	1,531	60	2,209	799
Murder and nonnegligent manslaughter	51	40	5	0	0	0	0	5	0	10	0	34	1
Rape[2]	30	12	13	0	0	0	1	1	2	7	1	15	3
Aggravated assault	1,158	631	295	15	5	7	55	65	135	372	13	418	85
Simple assault	2,023	1,023	505	27	15	7	109	146	171	543	32	831	191
Intimidation	2,206	1,132	343	17	20	4	52	122	99	587	14	887	516
Human trafficking, commercial sex acts	3	3	0	0	0	0	0	0	2	1	0	0	0
Other[3]	41	24	10	0	0	0	1	3	3	11	0	24	3
Crimes Against Property	2,811	532	173	10	13	1	48	441	80	246	8	444	1,593
Robbery	125	26	48	1	2	1	15	12	19	15	2	56	20
Burglary	114	31	6	1	1	0	2	5	5	14	0	24	68
Larceny-theft	284	83	36	2	0	0	4	12	8	27	0	92	147
Motor vehicle theft	19	6	1	0	0	0	0	0	2	2	0	3	12
Arson	60	20	4	0	0	0	1	6	1	17	0	7	29
Destruction/damage/ vandalism	2,152	345	74	6	9	0	26	404	42	166	6	242	1,288
Other[3]	57	21	4	0	1	0	0	2	3	5	0	20	29
Crimes Against Society[3]	236	167	41	7	4	0	2	1	12	85	3	122	14

[1]The sum of offenses by the known offender's ethnicity does not equal the sum of offenses by the known offender's race because not all law enforcement agencies that report offender race data also report offender ethnicity data.
[2]Only the revised Uniform Crime Reporting definition of rape was used for the figures reported in this row.
[3]Includes additional offenses collected in the National Incident-Based Reporting System.

Table 4. Offenses, Offense Type, by Bias Motivation, 2019

(Number.)

Bias motivation	Total offenses	Crimes against persons						
		Murder and nonnegligent manslaughter	Rape[1]	Aggravated assault	Simple assault	Intimidation	Human trafficking, commercial sex acts	Other[2]
Total	8,559	51	30	1,158	2,023	2,206	3	41
Single-Bias Incidents	8,302	51	30	1,139	1,976	2,134	3	41
Race/Ethnicity/Ancestry	4,784	31	12	726	1,225	1,385	0	13
Anti-White	755	0	6	108	240	143	0	3
Anti-Black or African American	2,314	1	2	344	546	797	0	8
Anti-American Indian or Alaska Native	126	0	1	5	26	11	0	1
Anti-Asian	205	4	1	30	78	50	0	0
Anti-Native Hawaiian or Other Pacific Islander	25	0	0	4	4	1	0	0
Anti-Multiple Races, Group	171	3	0	17	27	57	0	0
Anti-Arab	122	0	0	20	36	37	0	0
Anti-Hispanic or Latino	676	1	1	141	195	213	0	0
Anti-Other Race/Ethnicity/Ancestry	390	22	1	57	73	76	0	1
Religion	1,650	12	3	89	159	320	0	9
Anti-Jewish	995	6	1	23	82	164	0	0
Anti-Catholic	66	1	2	1	1	8	0	1
Anti-Protestant	24	0	0	1	1	2	0	0
Anti-Islamic (Muslim)	219	1	0	42	41	92	0	0
Anti-Other Religion	108	1	0	9	8	20	0	6
Anti-Multiple Religions, Group	42	3	0	1	3	8	0	0
Anti-Mormon	14	0	0	3	0	2	0	0
Anti-Jehovah's Witness	7	0	0	2	2	1	0	0
Anti-Eastern Orthodox (Russian, Greek, Other)	47	0	0	2	8	2	0	2
Anti-Other Christian	60	0	0	1	3	20	0	0
Anti-Buddhist	5	0	0	0	1	0	0	0
Anti-Hindu	7	0	0	0	2	0	0	0
Anti-Sikh	50	0	0	4	7	1	0	0
Anti-Atheism/Agnosticism/etc.	6	0	0	0	0	0	0	0
Sexual Orientation	1,395	7	6	246	438	359	1	4
Anti-Gay (Male)	867	2	4	170	292	216	0	3
Anti-Lesbian	142	0	0	33	39	43	0	0
Anti-Lesbian, Gay, Bisexual, or Transgender (Mixed Group)	342	5	1	38	95	92	1	1
Anti-Heterosexual	17	0	0	1	3	3	0	0
Anti-Bisexual	27	0	1	4	9	5	0	0
Disability	169	0	1	20	47	15	2	7
Anti-Physical	53	0	0	4	10	3	2	3
Anti-Mental	116	0	1	16	37	12	0	4
Gender	80	0	3	7	27	18	0	4
Anti-Male	18	0	1	1	8	2	0	0
Anti-Female	62	0	2	6	19	16	0	4
Gender Identity	224	1	5	51	80	37	0	4
Anti-Transgender	173	1	3	48	64	32	0	2
Anti-Gender Non-Conforming	51	0	2	3	16	5	0	2
Multiple-Bias Incidents[3]	257	0	0	19	47	72	0	0

Table 4. Offenses, Offense Type, by Bias Motivation, 2019—*Continued*

(Number.)

Bias motivation	Crimes against property							Crimes against society[2]
	Robbery	Burglary	Larceny- theft	Motor vehicle theft	Arson	Destruction/ damage/ vandalism	Other[2]	
Total	125	114	284	19	60	2,152	57	236
Single-Bias Incidents.............................	125	109	282	19	55	2,050	57	231
Race/Ethnicity/Ancestry	62	46	149	13	16	901	35	170
Anti-White	16	10	56	4	1	72	15	81
Anti-Black or African American..........................	13	17	19	3	9	516	5	34
Anti-American Indian or Alaska Native..............	4	5	32	4	1	15	3	18
Anti-Asian	4	3	3	1	2	25	0	4
Anti-Native Hawaiian or Other Pacific Islander ...	0	0	4	0	0	1	2	9
Anti-Multiple Races, Group	1	0	6	0	0	53	4	3
Anti-Arab	1	1	3	0	0	21	0	3
Anti-Hispanic or Latino.................................	16	4	12	0	1	81	4	7
Anti-Other Race/Ethnicity/Ancestry	7	6	14	1	2	117	2	11
Religion..	8	38	57	3	34	877	7	34
Anti-Jewish	2	9	12	0	10	684	0	2
Anti-Catholic...	0	5	4	1	5	37	0	0
Anti-Protestant...	0	2	6	0	1	10	0	1
Anti-Islamic (Muslim).....................................	2	3	1	0	4	31	2	0
Anti-Other Religion	0	6	7	0	9	38	1	3
Anti-Multiple Religions, Group	1	0	2	0	0	21	0	3
Anti-Mormon	1	0	0	0	0	8	0	0
Anti-Jehovah's Witness..................................	0	0	0	0	0	2	0	0
Anti-Eastern Orthodox (Russian, Greek, Other) ..	0	5	9	1	0	7	1	10
Anti-Other Christian.....................................	0	3	0	0	3	27	1	2
Anti-Buddhist...	0	0	2	0	0	2	0	0
Anti-Hindu	0	1	1	0	1	1	0	1
Anti-Sikh..	2	4	11	0	1	8	2	10
Anti-Atheism/Agnosticism/etc..........................	0	0	2	1	0	1	0	2
Sexual Orientation...	47	12	25	1	4	233	2	10
Anti-Gay (Male)...	33	4	6	1	2	128	1	5
Anti-Lesbian...	2	1	5	0	0	18	0	1
Anti-Lesbian, Gay, Bisexual, or Transgender (Mixed Group)	10	4	12	0	2	79	1	1
Anti-Heterosexual...	1	2	1	0	0	4	0	2
Anti-Bisexual	1	1	1	0	0	4	0	1
Disability...	4	5	37	2	0	12	7	10
Anti-Physical...	4	1	14	2	0	5	3	2
Anti-Mental...	0	4	23	0	0	7	4	8
Gender...	1	3	1	0	1	12	0	3
Anti-Male...	1	2	1	0	0	1	0	1
Anti-Female	0	1	0	0	1	11	0	2
Gender Identity...	3	5	13	0	0	15	6	4
Anti-Transgender	3	3	5	0	0	9	2	1
Anti-Gender Non-Conforming..........................	0	2	8	0	0	6	4	3
Multiple-Bias Incidents[3]..................................	0	5	2	0	5	102	0	5

[1]Only the revised Uniform Crime Reporting definition of rape was used for the figures reported in this column.
[2]Includes additional offenses collected in the National Incident-Based Reporting System.
[3]A multiple-bias incident is an incident in which one or more offense types are motivated by two or more biases.

Table 5. Offenses, Known Offender's Race, by Bias Motivation, 2019

(Number.)

Bias motivation	Total offenses	White	Black or African American	American Indian or Alaska Native	Asian	Native Hawaiian or Other Pacific Islander	Group of multiple races	Unknown race
Total	8,496	3,511	1,605	64	95	19	285	718
Single-Bias Incidents	8,327	3,462	1,536	64	93	19	282	714
Race/Ethnicity/Ancestry	4,954	2,309	907	46	62	9	185	276
Anti-White	1,001	252	492	20	6	1	23	36
Anti-Black or African American	2,325	1,330	115	16	34	3	100	149
Anti-American Indian or Alaska Native	204	106	27	1	2	0	7	2
Anti-Asian	171	70	33	0	14	2	4	6
Anti-Native Hawaiian or Other Pacific Islander	26	8	11	0	0	2	0	0
Anti-Multiple Races, Group	166	45	8	0	2	0	15	11
Anti-Arab	100	62	17	0	1	0	1	4
Anti-Hispanic or Latino	644	322	152	8	2	1	24	47
Anti-Other Race/Ethnicity/Ancestry	317	114	52	1	1	0	11	21
Religion	1,550	439	122	6	16	6	30	306
Anti-Jewish	896	179	41	1	7	0	14	258
Anti-Catholic	59	26	3	1	1	0	0	5
Anti-Protestant	38	13	3	0	0	0	2	1
Anti-Islamic (Muslim)	225	98	32	0	5	0	6	22
Anti-Other Religion	96	31	12	0	1	5	2	8
Anti-Multiple Religions, Group	50	12	6	0	0	0	0	3
Anti-Mormon	9	4	0	0	0	1	0	0
Anti-Jehovah's Witness	9	3	0	1	0	0	0	0
Anti-Eastern Orthodox (Russian, Greek, Other)	32	19	4	1	0	0	0	1
Anti-Other Christian	42	11	5	0	1	0	5	5
Anti-Buddhist	10	4	3	0	1	0	0	0
Anti-Hindu	14	8	1	0	0	0	0	3
Anti-Sikh	64	30	10	2	0	0	1	0
Anti-Atheism/Agnosticism/etc.	6	1	2	0	0	0	0	0
Sexual Orientation	1,404	535	380	11	12	4	56	110
Anti-Gay (Male)	839	307	245	6	6	3	39	83
Anti-Lesbian	171	80	36	0	2	0	5	7
Anti-Lesbian, Gay, Bisexual, or Transgender (Mixed Group)	353	128	92	5	4	1	12	19
Anti-Heterosexual	20	14	1	0	0	0	0	0
Anti-Bisexual	21	6	6	0	0	0	0	1
Disability	177	92	37	1	3	0	3	4
Anti-Physical	67	30	15	0	2	0	1	1
Anti-Mental	110	62	22	1	1	0	2	3
Gender	58	30	14	0	0	0	1	0
Anti-Male	26	13	8	0	0	0	1	0
Anti-Female	32	17	6	0	0	0	0	0
Gender Identity	184	57	76	0	0	0	7	18
Anti-Transgender	157	50	65				7	16
Anti-Gender Non-Conforming	27	7	11	0	0	0	0	2
Multiple-Bias Incidents[2]	169	49	69	0	2	0	3	4

Table 5. Offenses, Known Offender's Race, by Bias Motivation, 2019—*Continued*

(Number.)

Bias motivation	Known offender's ethnicity[1]				Unknown offender
	Hispanic or Latino	Not Hispanic or Latino	Group of multiple ethnicities	Unknown ethnicity	
Total	412	1,847	51	3,065	2,199
Single-Bias Incidents	402	1,765	49	3,032	2,157
Race/Ethnicity/Ancestry	218	1,180	27	1,939	1,160
Anti-White	40	287	12	431	171
Anti-Black or African American.............	106	491	7	918	578
Anti-American Indian or Alaska Native......	8	39	0	97	59
Anti-Asian	8	42	0	59	42
Anti-Native Hawaiian or Other Pacific Islander ...	0	13	0	7	5
Anti-Multiple Races, Group	2	22	3	42	85
Anti-Arab	3	29	0	40	15
Anti-Hispanic or Latino	41	212	1	240	88
Anti-Other Race/Ethnicity/Ancestry	10	45	4	105	117
Religion	28	193	10	360	625
Anti-Jewish	7	82	3	143	396
Anti-Catholic.............................	3	10	0	16	23
Anti-Protestant...........................	2	3	0	14	19
Anti-Islamic (Muslim)......................	7	31	4	88	62
Anti-Other Religion	2	11	0	33	37
Anti-Multiple Religions, Group	0	2	0	15	29
Anti-Mormon	0	1	0	2	4
Anti-Jehovah's Witness....................	1	2	0	1	5
Anti-Eastern Orthodox (Russian, Greek, Other) ...	1	12	0	12	7
Anti-Other Christian	2	8	0	8	15
Anti-Buddhist.............................	0	7	0	1	2
Anti-Hindu	1	2	0	8	2
Anti-Sikh	2	21	3	17	21
Anti-Atheism/Agnosticism/etc.............	0	1	0	2	3
Sexual Orientation.........................	130	299	11	531	296
Anti-Gay (Male)...........................	94	205	9	284	150
Anti-Lesbian..............................	18	35	1	60	41
Anti-Lesbian, Gay, Bisexual, or Transgender (Mixed Group) ...	18	53	1	167	92
Anti-Heterosexual.........................	0	2	0	12	5
Anti-Bisexual	0	4	0	8	8
Disability.................................	8	37	1	92	37
Anti-Physical.............................	4	9	1	33	18
Anti-Mental...............................	4	28	0	59	19
Gender	1	9	0	32	13
Anti-Male.................................	1	8	0	13	4
Anti-Female...............................	0	1	0	19	9
Gender Identity	17	47	0	78	26
Anti-Transgender	17	36	0	72	19
Anti-Gender Non-Conforming...............	0	11	0	6	7
Multiple-Bias Incidents[2]	10	82	2	33	42

[1] The aggregate of offenses by the known offender's ethnicity does not equal the aggregate of offenses by the known offender's race because not all law enforcement agencies that report offender race data also report offender ethnicity data.
[2] A multiple-bias incident is an incident in which one or more offense types are motivated by two or more biases.

Table 6. Offenses, Victim Type, by Offense Type, 2019

(Number.)

Offense type	Total offenses	Victim type					
		Individual	Business/ financial institution	Government	Religious organization	Society/ public[1]	Other/ unknown/ multiple
Total	8,559	6,731	501	265	216	236	610
Crimes against persons[2]	5,512	5,512	NA	NA	NA	NA	NA
Crimes against property	2,811	1,219	501	265	216	0	610
Robbery	125	109	3	0	0	0	13
Burglary	114	74	20	2	12	0	6
Larceny-theft...................................	284	184	79	5	2	0	14
Motor vehicle theft................................	19	19	0	0	0	0	0
Arson...	60	27	5	0	25	0	3
Destruction/damage/vandalism................	2,512	760	385	258	177	0	572
Other[2]	57	46	9	0	0	0	2
Crimes against society[2]	236	NA	NA	NA	NA	289	NA

NA = Not available.
[1]The victim type society/public is collected only in the National Incident-Based Reporting System (NIBRS).
[2]Includes additional offenses collected in the NIBRS.

Table 7. Victims, Offense Type, by Bias Motivation, 2019

(Number.)

Bias motivation	Total victims[1]	Total number of adult victims[2]	Total number of juvenile victims[2]	Murder and nonnegligent manslaughter	Rape[3]	Aggravated assault	Simple assault	Intimidation	Human trafficking, commercial sex acts	Other[4]
Total	8,812	5,909	719	51	30	1,158	2,023	2,206	3	41
Single-Bias Incidents	8,552	5,770	693	51	30	1,139	1,976	2,134	3	41
Race/Ethnicity/Ancestry	4,930	3,625	435	31	12	726	1,225	1,385	0	13
Anti-White	775	566	41	0	6	108	240	143	0	3
Anti-Black or African American....	2,391	1,747	256	1	2	344	546	797	0	8
Anti-American Indian or Alaska Native...	135	85	6	0	1	5	26	11	0	1
Anti-Asian	215	172	10	4	1	30	78	50	0	0
Anti-Native Hawaiian or Other Pacific Islander	26	14	3	0	0	4	4	1	0	0
Anti-Multiple Races, Group	173	106	9	3	0	17	27	57	0	0
Anti-Arab........................	126	93	8	0	0	20	36	37	0	0
Anti-Hispanic or Latino	693	569	75	1	1	141	195	213	0	0
Anti-Other Race/Ethnicity/Ancestry	396	273	27	22	1	57	73	76	0	1
Religion.........................	1,715	699	80	12	3	89	159	320	0	9
Anti-Jewish	1,032	328	33	6	1	23	82	164	0	0
Anti-Catholic....................	66	19	3	1	2	1	1	8	0	1
Anti-Protestant..................	24	13	0	0	0	1	1	2	0	0
Anti-Islamic (Muslim)............	227	151	30	1	0	42	41	92	0	0
Anti-Other Religion	108	49	2	1	0	9	8	20	0	6
Anti-Multiple Religions, Group ...	44	16	1	3	0	1	3	8	0	0
Anti-Mormon	15	9	0	0	0	3	0	2	0	0
Anti-Jehovah's Witness...........	7	5	0	0	0	2	2	1	0	0
Anti-Eastern Orthodox (Russian, Greek, Other)	49	28	6	0	0	2	8	2	0	2
Anti-Other Christian	65	27	2	0	0	1	3	20	0	0
Anti-Buddhist...................	5	2	0	0	0	0	1	0	0	0
Anti-Hindu......................	7	4	0	0	0	0	2	0	0	0
Anti-Sikh.......................	60	47	3	0	0	4	7	1	0	0
Anti-Atheism/Agnosticism/etc....	6	1	0	0	0	0	0	0	0	0
Sexual Orientation...............	1,429	1,106	121	7	6	246	438	359	1	4
Anti-Gay (Male).................	883	699	66	2	4	170	292	216	0	3
Anti-Lesbian....................	143	110	18	0	0	33	39	43	0	0
Anti-Lesbian, Gay, Bisexual, or Transgender (Mixed Group)......................	357	266	27	5	1	38	95	92	1	1
Anti-Heterosexual...............	19	11	4	0	0	1	3	3	0	0
Anti-Bisexual	27	20	6	0	1	4	9	5	0	0
Disability........................	170	115	29	0	1	20	47	15	2	7
Anti-Physical....................	53	38	8	0	0	4	10	3	2	3
Anti-Mental.....................	117	77	21	0	1	16	37	12	0	4
Gender..........................	81	65	4	0	3	7	27	18	0	4
Anti-Male.......................	18	17	0	0	1	1	8	2	0	0
Anti-Female.....................	63	48	4	0	2	6	19	16	0	4
Gender Identity..................	227	160	24	1	5	51	80	37	0	4
Anti-Transgender	175	124	20	1	3	48	64	32	0	2
Anti-Gender Non-Conforming.....	52	36	4	0	2	3	16	5	0	2
Multiple-Bias Incidents[5]...........	260	139	26	0	0	19	47	72	0	0

Table 7. Victims, Offense Type, by Bias Motivation, 2019—*Continued*

(Number.)

Bias motivation	Crimes against property							Crimes against society[4]
	Robbery	Burglary	Larceny- theft	Motor vehicle theft	Arson	Destruction/ damage/ vandalism	Other[4]	
Total	149	129	297	19	78	2,316	76	236
Single-Bias Incidents	149	123	294	19	73	2,213	76	231
Race/Ethnicity/Ancestry	75	54	156	13	22	995	53	170
Anti-White	17	13	60	4	3	82	15	81
Anti-Black or African American	17	19	19	3	11	568	22	34
Anti-American Indian or Alaska Native	5	7	34	4	3	16	4	18
Anti-Asian	6	4	3	1	2	32	0	4
Anti-Native Hawaiian or Other Pacific Islander	0	0	4	0	0	2	2	9
Anti-Multiple Races, Group	1	0	7	0	0	54	4	3
Anti-Arab	2	1	3	0	0	24	0	3
Anti-Hispanic or Latino	19	4	12	0	1	95	4	7
Anti-Other Race/Ethnicity/Ancestry	8	6	14	1	2	122	2	11
Religion	11	42	58	3	43	925	7	34
Anti-Jewish	2	9	12	0	19	712	0	2
Anti-Catholic	0	5	4	1	5	37	0	0
Anti-Protestant	0	2	6	0	1	10	0	1
Anti-Islamic (Muslim)	2	4	1	0	4	38	2	0
Anti-Other Religion	0	6	7	0	9	38	1	3
Anti-Multiple Religions, Group	2	0	2	0	0	22	0	3
Anti-Mormon	2	0	0	0	0	8	0	0
Anti-Jehovah's Witness	0	0	0	0	0	2	0	0
Anti-Eastern Orthodox (Russian, Greek, Other)	0	6	9	1	0	8	1	10
Anti-Other Christian	0	5	0	0	3	30	1	2
Anti-Buddhist	0	0	2	0	0	2	0	0
Anti-Hindu	0	1	1	0	1	1	0	1
Anti-Sikh	3	4	12	0	1	16	2	10
Anti-Atheism/Agnosticism/etc.	0	0	2	1	0	1	0	2
Sexual Orientation	53	14	28	1	6	254	2	10
Anti-Gay (Male)	37	6	7	1	2	137	1	5
Anti-Lesbian	2	1	5	0	0	19	0	1
Anti-Lesbian, Gay, Bisexual, or Transgender (Mixed Group)	11	4	13	0	4	90	1	1
Anti-Heterosexual	2	2	2	0	0	4	0	2
Anti-Bisexual	1	1	1	0	0	4	0	1
Disability	4	5	38	2	0	12	7	10
Anti-Physical	4	1	14	2	0	5	3	2
Anti-Mental	0	4	24	0	0	7	4	8
Gender	1	3	1	0	2	12	0	3
Anti-Male	1	2	1	0	0	1	0	1
Anti-Female	0	1	0	0	2	11	0	2
Gender Identity	5	5	13	0	0	15	7	4
Anti-Transgender	5	3	5	0	0	9	2	1
Anti-Gender Non-Conforming	0	2	8	0	0	6	5	3
Multiple-Bias Incidents[5]	0	6	3	0	5	103	0	5

NOTE: The aggregate of adult and juvenile individual victims does not equal the total number of victims because total victims include individuals, businesses/financial institutions, government entities, religious organizations, and society/public as a whole. In addition, the aggregate of adult and juvenile individual victims does not equal the aggregate of victims of crimes against persons because not all law enforcement agencies report the ages of individual victims.
[1]The term victim may refer to an individual, business/financial institution, government entity, religious organization, or society/public as a whole.
[2]The figures shown are individual victims only.
[3]Only the revised Uniform Crime Reporting definition of rape is used for the figures reported in this column.
[4]The figures shown include additional offenses collected in the National Incident-Based Reporting System.
[5]A multiple-bias incident is an incident in which one or more offense types are motivated by two or more biases.

Table 8. Incidents, Victim Type, by Bias Motivation, 2019

(Number.)

Bias motivation	Total incidents	Victim type					
		Individual	Business/ financial institution	Government	Religious organization	Society/ public[1]	Other/ unknown/ multiple
Total	7,314	5,524	478	263	208	194	647
Single-Bias Incidents..	7,103	5,410	466	240	194	191	602
Race/Ethnicity/Ancestry.................................	3,963	3,269	218	120	12	136	208
Religion..	1,521	701	182	103	170	29	336
Sexual Orientation.......................................	1,195	1,068	42	14	12	9	50
Disability	157	137	8	1	0	10	1
Gender..	69	60	2	1	0	3	3
Gender Identity	198	175	14	1	0	4	4
Multiple-Bias Incidents[2]......................................	211	114	12	23	14	3	45

[1]The victim type society/public is collected only in the National Incident-Based Reporting System.
[2]A multiple-bias incident is an incident in which one or more offense types are motivated by two or more biases.

Table 9. Known Offenders,[1] by Known Offender's Race, Ethnicity, and Age, 2019

(Number.)

Race/ethnicity/age	Total
Race..	6,406
White	3,365
Black or African American..	1,532
American Indian or Alaska Native..	68
Asian	58
Native Hawaiian or Other Pacific Islander	22
Group of multiple races[2]	425
Unknown race	936
Ethnicity[3]	5,443
Hispanic or Latino...	547
Not Hispanic or Latino...	1,801
Group of multiple ethnicities[4]	103
Unknown ethnicity..	2,992
Age[3]..	5,599
Total known offenders 18 and over	4,734
Total known offenders under 18..	865

[1]The term known offender does not imply the suspect's identity is known; rather, the term indicates some aspect of the suspect was identified, thus distinguishing the suspect from an unknown offender.
[2]The term group of multiple races is used to describe a group of offenders of varying races.
[3]The total number of known offenders by age and the total number of known offenders by ethnicity do not equal the total number of known offenders by race because not all law enforcement agencies report the age and/or ethnicity of the known offenders.
[4]The term group of multiple ethnicities is used to describe a group of offenders of varying ethnicities.

Table 10. Incidents, Bias Motivation, by Location, 2019

(Number.)

Location	Total incidents	Bias motivation						Multiple- bias incidents[1]
		Race/ethnicity/ ancestry	Religion	Sexual orientation	Disability	Gender	Gender identity	
Total	7,314	3,963	1,521	1,195	157	69	198	211
Abandoned/condemned structure............................	11	4	5	0	0	0	0	2
Air/bus/train terminal	113	69	11	23	1	2	1	6
Amusement park	5	2	0	3	0	0	0	0
Arena/stadium/fairgrounds/coliseum	9	3	1	4	0	0	0	1
Auto dealership new/used.......................................	6	3	2	0	0	0	1	0
Bank/savings and loan..	21	16	3	1	0	0	1	0
Bar/nightclub	124	66	11	41	0	1	2	3
Camp/campground..	8	6	2	0	0	0	0	0
Church/synagogue/temple/mosque	322	34	255	19	0	0	0	14
Commercial office building	161	92	28	26	1	1	6	7
Community center	21	8	2	9	0	0	2	0
Construction site..	23	14	6	1	1	0	0	1
Convenience store	127	82	16	19	2	1	4	3
Cyberspace	36	21	10	2	0	0	1	2
Daycare facility..	4	3	1	0	0	0	0	0
Department/discount store......................................	101	67	14	12	0	2	3	3
Dock/wharf/freight/modal terminal	2	1	1	0	0	0	0	0
Drug store/doctor's office/hospital	94	56	15	8	4	6	4	1
Farm facility	3	2	0	0	0	0	1	0
Field/woods	61	30	19	8	0	0	1	3
Gambling facility/casino/race track	2	1	0	1	0	0	0	0
Government/public building.....................................	132	86	24	15	2	1	3	1
Grocery/supermarket..	99	65	9	10	7	0	7	1
Highway/road/alley/street/sidewalk.........................	1,329	814	142	268	23	6	50	26
Hotel/motel/etc..	55	33	8	10	1	0	2	1
Industrial site	18	13	2	3	0	0	0	0
Jail/prison/penitentiary/corrections facility..............	90	64	1	18	1	2	3	1
Lake/waterway/beach..	16	9	1	6	0	0	0	0
Liquor store	26	13	7	3	2	0	0	1
Park/playground...	196	98	50	26	1	0	3	18
Parking/drop lot/garage	341	245	27	52	4	2	6	5
Rental storage facility...	14	10	3	0	0	1	0	0
Residence/home..	1,800	1,004	272	336	76	29	51	32
Rest area..	4	3	0	1	0	0	0	0
Restaurant	214	138	15	45	3	0	5	8
School/college[2]	50	28	11	9	1	0	1	0
School—college/university.......................................	195	93	52	31	2	5	2	10
School—elementary/secondary	458	232	115	47	12	2	9	41
Service/gas station	76	53	9	7	3	0	2	2
Shelter—mission/homeless......................................	32	17	0	10	1	0	3	1
Shopping mall..	17	8	0	5	0	0	1	3
Specialty store (TV, fur, etc.)..................................	63	36	15	6	1	0	3	2
Tribal Lands	1	0	0	0	0	0	0	1
Other/unknown	822	311	356	109	7	8	20	11
Multiple locations	12	10	0	1	1	0	0	0

[1]A multiple-bias incident is an incident in which one or more offense types are motivated by two or more biases.
[2]The location designation School/college has been retained for agencies that have not updated their records management systems to include the new location designations of School—college/university and School—elementary/secondary, which allow for more specificity in reporting.

Table 11. Offenses, Offense Type, by Participating State/Federal, 2019

(Number.)

State	Total offenses	Crimes against persons						
		Murder and nonnegligent manslaughter	Rape[1]	Aggravated assault	Simple assault	Intimidation	Human trafficking, commercial sex acts	Other[2]
Total	8,559	51	30	1,158	2,023	2,206	3	41
Alabama[3]	0	0	0	0	0	0	0	0
Alaska	17	0	0	6	6	2	0	0
Arizona	254	0	0	20	67	110	0	0
Arkansas	10	0	0	4	0	2	0	0
California	1,221	1	3	290	272	264	0	0
Colorado	257	0	1	46	69	70	2	0
Connecticut	86	0	0	3	22	37	0	0
Delaware	27	0	0	2	3	12	0	0
District of Columbia	247	0	0	43	113	45	0	0
Florida	131	0	1	23	43	20	0	0
Georgia	123	0	0	11	47	23	0	3
Hawaii	51	0	0	7	23	16	0	0
Idaho	38	0	0	4	12	14	0	0
Illinois	95	0	0	22	39	24	0	0
Indiana	87	2	0	6	18	36	1	0
Iowa	13	0	0	2	4	3	0	0
Kansas	99	0	0	8	15	26	0	2
Kentucky	179	0	0	9	40	66	0	0
Louisiana	33	0	0	5	9	5	0	0
Maine	24	0	0	0	3	17	0	0
Maryland	18	0	0	0	2	2	0	0
Massachusetts	441	0	0	54	84	169	0	0
Michigan	495	0	4	65	135	152	0	6
Minnesota	123	0	0	17	28	35	0	1
Mississippi	15	0	0	0	2	2	0	1
Missouri	106	0	1	27	33	29	0	0
Montana	35	0	0	10	8	0	0	0
Nebraska	57	0	0	3	16	9	0	0
Nevada	53	0	0	13	14	6	0	0
New Hampshire	17	0	0	0	4	5	0	0
New Jersey	478	1	0	11	40	152	0	0
New Mexico	63	1	0	15	22	4	0	1
New York	618	5	1	35	166	12	0	0
North Carolina	248	0	1	22	62	91	0	0
North Dakota	20	0	0	1	6	8	0	0
Ohio	428	0	4	26	67	107	0	4
Oklahoma	30	0	0	4	6	8	0	0
Oregon	205	0	0	30	53	39	0	0
Pennsylvania	50	0	0	6	6	18	0	0
Rhode Island	21	0	0	2	6	2	0	0
South Carolina	82	0	0	10	15	18	0	4
South Dakota	21	0	0	2	9	3	0	0
Tennessee	152	0	0	20	37	33	0	0
Texas	560	22	8	108	127	92	0	4
Utah	34	0	0	9	4	0	0	7
Vermont	37	0	0	2	7	1	0	0
Virginia	185	0	0	12	55	55	0	3
Washington	664	1	3	82	164	259	0	2
West Virginia	36	0	0	3	7	8	0	0
Wisconsin	83	0	3	5	25	15	0	3
Wyoming	6	0	0	0	2	1	0	0
Federal								
Federal Bureau of Investigation, Field Offices	180	18	0	53	6	75	0	0
Pentagon Force Protection Agency	1	0	0	0	0	0	0	0
United States Army	1	0	0	0	0	0	0	0
United States Navy Law Enforcement	4	0	0	0	0	4	0	0

(Number.)

State	Crimes against property							Crimes against society[2]
	Robbery	Burglary	Larceny- theft	Motor vehicle theft	Arson	Destruction/ damage/ vandalism	Other[2]	
Total	125	114	284	19	60	2,152	57	236
Alabama[3]......................................	0	0	0	0	0	0	0	0
Alaska...	1	0	0	0	0	2	0	0
Arizona...	0	1	2	0	0	48	2	4
Arkansas.......................................	0	0	2	0	0	2	0	0
California......................................	35	11	5	1	9	330	0	0
Colorado	2	5	1	0	0	60	0	1
Connecticut..................................	2	0	1	0	0	18	1	2
Delaware.......................................	0	0	0	0	0	10	0	0
District of Columbia.....................	11	0	0	0	0	35	0	0
Florida	0	2	0	0	2	40	0	0
Georgia	0	3	8	0	1	24	2	1
Hawaii	2	0	0	0	0	2	0	1
Idaho..	0	1	1	0	0	4	1	1
Illinois	4	0	0	0	1	5	0	0
Indiana	0	1	2	0	0	19	1	1
Iowa	0	0	1	0	0	3	0	0
Kansas..	0	5	9	0	1	22	3	8
Kentucky.......................................	2	7	5	1	3	34	2	10
Louisiana......................................	0	2	4	1	0	2	0	5
Maine	0	0	0	0	0	4	0	0
Maryland.......................................	2	0	0	0	0	12	0	0
Massachusetts	1	2	2	0	3	124	1	1
Michigan.......................................	3	5	24	5	2	64	9	21
Minnesota.....................................	3	0	2	0	2	35	0	0
Mississippi....................................	1	1	2	1	0	3	1	1
Missouri..	1	0	2	0	1	10	0	2
Montana.......................................	0	0	3	0	0	14	0	0
Nebraska.......................................	0	2	9	0	0	8	0	10
Nevada	1	0	2	0	2	15	0	0
New Hampshire	0	0	1	0	0	7	0	0
New Jersey....................................	4	1	1	0	1	267	0	0
New Mexico...................................	1	1	2	1	0	12	2	1
New York	7	3	9	0	1	379	0	0
North Carolina..............................	3	6	4	0	2	54	0	3
North Dakota................................	0	0	0	0	0	5	0	0
Ohio..	9	20	80	7	1	52	8	43
Oklahoma......................................	0	0	0	0	1	11	0	0
Oregon..	1	1	9	0	4	60	1	7
Pennsylvania.................................	0	1	0	0	6	13	0	0
Rhode Island.................................	0	0	0	0	0	11	0	0
South Carolina..............................	0	4	8	0	0	14	1	8
South Dakota................................	0	0	0	0	0	7	0	0
Tennessee.....................................	1	1	1	1	1	19	0	38
Texas	8	17	45	1	0	84	11	33
Utah..	0	0	4	0	0	7	0	3
Vermont..	0	0	2	0	1	23	0	1
Virginia...	2	0	4	0	0	47	1	6
Washington...................................	16	6	16	0	1	97	7	10
West Virginia	1	3	2	0	0	4	1	7
Wisconsin......................................	1	2	6	0	0	14	2	7
Wyoming.......................................	0	0	1	0	0	2	0	0
Federal								
Federal Bureau of Investigation, Field Offices.....	0	0	1	0	14	13	0	0
Pentagon Force Protection Agency....................	0	0	0	0	0	1	0	0
United States Army.........................	0	0	1	0	0	0	0	0
United States Navy Law Enforcement...............	0	0	0	0	0	0	0	0

[1] Only the revised Uniform Crime Reporting definition of rape was used for the figures shown in this column.
[2] The figures shown include additional offenses collected in the National Incident-Based Reporting System.
[3] Limited data for 2019 were available for Alabama.

Table 12. Agency Hate Crime Reporting, by Participating State/Territory and Federal, 2019

(Number.)

State	Number of participating agencies	Population covered	Agencies submitting incident reports	Total number of incidents reported
Total	15,588	305,284,239	2,172	7,314
Alabama[1]..	2	85,670	0	0
Alaska...	33	727,792	5	11
Arizona...	92	6,395,924	17	209
Arkansas...	278	2,813,597	6	9
California...	737	39,502,561	195	1,015
Colorado	221	5,705,335	50	210
Connecticut......................................	102	3,373,874	40	76
Delaware...	63	973,764	10	22
District of Columbia	2	705,749	2	222
Florida..	638	20,901,840	51	111
Georgia	495	9,290,789	50	102
Hawaii	1	974,902	1	41
Idaho...	106	1,782,402	9	24
Illinois...	728	12,125,954	23	65
Indiana	214	3,643,904	23	75
Iowa..	246	3,135,918	8	10
Kansas...	377	2,610,898	53	78
Kentucky	410	4,460,061	67	146
Louisiana	137	3,536,544	11	26
Maine..	134	1,344,212	10	19
Maryland	153	6,045,680	9	18
Massachusetts..................................	360	6,772,985	83	388
Michigan...	638	9,969,410	188	434
Minnesota	379	5,533,121	35	104
Mississippi.......................................	42	882,028	5	14
Missouri..	571	6,077,911	28	83
Montana..	103	1,055,460	16	32
Nebraska	130	1,813,150	23	46
Nevada	48	3,070,743	5	44
New Hampshire	188	1,313,554	14	16
New Jersey.......................................	556	8,638,072	208	472
New Mexico......................................	23	819,112	6	50
New York	558	18,949,575	65	611
North Carolina	332	8,740,258	80	210
North Dakota....................................	109	762,062	12	18
Ohio..	551	9,730,885	134	391
Oklahoma..	438	3,946,211	22	28
Oregon...	204	4,056,079	46	175
Pennsylvania	1,424	12,585,495	15	41
Rhode Island....................................	48	1,058,329	10	17
South Carolina..................................	405	5,081,688	36	68
South Dakota....................................	128	848,738	13	20
Tennessee..	465	6,830,634	42	117
Texas	1,059	28,885,669	167	456
Utah..	121	3,077,345	14	18
Vermont..	89	628,664	17	33
Virginia...	415	8,533,624	57	163
Washington......................................	253	7,587,677	77	542
West Virginia	240	1,574,978	18	31
Wisconsin..	437	5,810,699	43	74
Wyoming...	55	512,713	5	5
Federal[2]				
Federal Bureau of Investigation, Field Offices............................	45	0	45	118
Pentagon Force Protection Agency...	1	0	1	1
United States Air Force, Office of Special Investigations...........	1	0	0	0
United States Army............................	1	0	1	1
United States Marine Corps Law Enforcement........................	1	0	0	0
United States Navy Law Enforcement....................................	1	0	1	4

[1]Limited data for 2019 were available for Alabama.
[2]Population estimates are not attributed to the federal agencies.

Table 13. Hate Crime Incidents Per Bias Motivation and Quarter, by Selected State and Agency and Federal, 2019

(Number.)

State/agency	Race/ Ethnicity/ Ancestry	Religion	Sexual orientation	Disability	Gender	Gender Identity	1st quarter	2nd quarter	3rd quarter	4th quarter	Population[1]
ALASKA											
Total	7	0	4	0	0	0					
Cities	7	0	4	0	0	0					
Anchorage..............................	4	0	2	0	0	0	1	2	3	0	287,731
Fairbanks................................	1	0	0	0	0	0	0	1	0	0	31,493
Kotzebue................................	1	0	0	0	0	0	0	0	1	0	3,272
North Pole..............................	1	0	0	0	0	0	0	1	0		2,111
Soldotna................................	0	0	2	0	0	0	0	0	0	2	4,756
ARIZONA											
Total	143	36	30	3	2	3					
Cities	143	32	30	3	2	3					
Apache Junction	2	1	1	1	0	0	1	3	0	1	42,531
Casa Grande...........................	1	0	0	0	0	0	0	0	1	0	58,366
Coolidge................................	4	0	0	0	0	0	2	2	0	0	13,138
Flagstaff.................................	0	1	0	0	0	0	1	0	0	0	75,013
Gilbert...................................	0	2	0	0	0	0	1	0	1	0	253,619
Glendale................................	9	0	0	0	0	0	2	2	4	1	253,951
Mesa.....................................	2	0	1	0	0	0	0	0	1	2	518,160
Page......................................	1	0	0	0	0	0	0	1			7,588
Phoenix[2]..............................	111	20	23	0	2	3	31	43	33	44	1,688,722
San Luis.................................	1	0	0	0	0	0	0	0	0	1	34,192
Scottsdale..............................	1	1	1	0	0	0	1	2	0	0	260,464
Somerton...............................	1	0	0	0	0	0	0	0	0	1	16,771
Surprise.................................	2	1	0	0	0	0	0	2	0	1	140,962
Tempe...................................	1	0	0	0	0	0	0	1	0	0	196,499
Tucson...................................	6	6	4	0	0	0	4	5	5	2	548,374
Yuma.....................................	1	0	0	2	0	0	1	0	0	2	98,769
Universities and Colleges	0	4	0	0	0	0					
University of Arizona...............	0	4	0	0	0	0	1	0	1	2	48,318
ARKANSAS											
Total	8	0	1	0	0	0					
Cities	7	0	0	0	0	0					
Benton...................................	1	0	0	0	0	0	0	0	0	1	37,161
Conway..................................	1	0	0	0	0	0	0	0	1	0	67,336
Fort Smith..............................	4	0	0	0	0	0	0	0	2	2	88,041
Searcy....................................	1	0	0	0	0	0	0	0	0	1	23,873
Nonmetropolitan Counties....................................	1	0	1	0	0	0					
Logan	1	0	0	0	0	0	0	0	0	1	
Pope......................................	0	0	1	0	0	0	0	1	0	0	
CALIFORNIA											
Total	524	208	235	10	7	33					
Cities	447	193	212	8	5	30					
Alameda................................	2	0	0	0	0	0	0	1	0	1	78,907
Antioch..................................	2	1	1	0	0	0	0	2	1	1	112,641
Apple Valley...........................	0	0	2	0	0	0	0	2	0	0	74,051
Arvin.....................................	0	1	0	0	0	0	0	1	0	0	21,811
Azusa	2	0	1	0	0	0	0	2	1	0	50,405
Bakersfield..............................	1	0	1	1	0	0	1	0	1	1	388,080
Beaumont...............................	1	0	0	0	0	0	0	0	1	0	50,990
Bell.......................................	0	0	1	0	1	0	1	1	0	0	35,759
Bellflower	1	0	0	0	0	0	0	1	0	0	77,196
Bell Gardens	0	0	1	0	0	0	0	1	0	0	42,366
Belmont.................................	0	0	1	0	0	1	0	0	0	2	27,272
Berkeley.................................	4	2	2	0	0	0	0	2	0	6	122,788
Beverly Hills...........................	1	6	2	0	0	0	2	2	2	3	34,211
Big Bear.................................	1	0	0	0	0	0	0	1	0	0	5,311
Brea......................................	0	1	4	0	0	0	0	4	0	1	44,155
Brentwood..............................	0	4	0	0	0	0	1	0	2	1	65,483

Table 13. Hate Crime Incidents Per Bias Motivation and Quarter, by Selected State and Agency and Federal, 2019—Continued

(Number.)

State/agency	Race/ Ethnicity/ Ancestry	Religion	Sexual orientation	Disability	Gender	Gender Identity	1st quarter	2nd quarter	3rd quarter	4th quarter	Population[1]
Brisbane	1	0	0	0	0	0	1	0	0	0	4,746
Buena Park	1	0	0	0	0	0	0	1	0	0	82,627
Burbank	7	0	0	0	0	0	2	4	1	0	103,738
Camarillo	1	0	0	0	0	0	0	1	0	0	69,628
Capitola	0	1	0	0	0	0	0	1	0	0	10,101
Carlsbad	5	0	0	0	0	0	0	2	0	3	117,220
Cathedral City	1	0	0	0	0	0	0	0	0	1	55,346
Central Marin	0	1	0	0	0	0	0	0	1	0	34,793
Chico	2	0	0	0	0	0	0	2	0	0	95,826
Chino	2	1	0	0	0	0	0	0	1	2	93,348
Chula Vista	6	2	0	0	1	0	4	1	2	2	275,230
Citrus Heights	1	0	1	0	0	0	0	1	0	1	88,496
Claremont	1	0	1	0	0	0	0	0	1	1	36,681
Clearlake	2	1	0	0	0	0	2	0	1	0	15,400
Clovis	1	0	0	0	0	0	0	0	0	1	114,170
Coachella	0	0	1	0	0	0	0	1	0	0	46,485
Compton	1	0	0	0	0	0	1	0	0	0	96,638
Concord	2	0	0	0	0	0	1	0	1	0	130,615
Coronado	0	0	1	0	0	1	0	0	2	0	21,115
Costa Mesa	3	0	0	0	0	0	1	0	2	0	114,047
Cupertino	1	0	0	0	0	0	0	0	0	1	60,357
Cypress	1	0	0	0	0	0	0	0	0	1	49,085
Davis	0	1	0	0	0	0	0	1	0	0	69,767
Delano	2	0	0	0	0	0	1	0	1	0	53,002
Dublin	1	0	0	0	0	0	0	0	1	0	66,072
El Cajon	1	0	0	0	0	0	0	1	0	0	103,686
El Cerrito	1	0	0	0	0	0	0	0	0	1	25,857
Elk Grove	0	1	0	0	0	0	0	0	0	1	175,492
El Monte	3	0	0	0	0	0	2	1	0	0	115,830
El Segundo	1	0	0	0	0	0	0	0	0	1	16,727
Emeryville	1	0	0	0	0	0	0	1	0	0	12,380
Escondido	3	1	0	0	0	0	2	0	0	2	153,215
Eureka	1	0	1	0	0	0	1	1	0	0	26,973
Fairfield	1	0	1	0	0	0	2	0	0	0	118,383
Folsom	0	0	1	0	0	0	0	0	0	1	79,927
Fontana	1	0	0	0	0	0	0	0	1	0	215,883
Fountain Valley	1	0	0	0	0	0	0	1	0	0	55,858
Fremont	2	2	0	0	0	0	0	1	1	2	240,887
Fresno	8	2	2	0	0	2	10	2	2		534,285
Fullerton	1	0	1	0	0	0	1	0	1	0	140,194
Galt	0	0	1	0	0	0	1	0	0	0	26,796
Garden Grove	1	0	1	0	0	1	0	2	0	1	172,832
Greenfield	1	0	0	0	0	0	0	0	1	0	17,809
Hawthorne	2	0	2	0	1	1	0	2	2	2	87,305
Hayward	4	0	0	0	0	0	1	1	1	1	161,588
Huntington Beach	4	3	1	0	0	0	1	1	2	4	201,843
Huntington Park	1	0	1	0	0	0	1	1	0	0	58,181
Imperial	0	1	0	0	0	0	0	0	0	1	18,090
Imperial Beach	2	2	0	0	0	0	1	0	1	2	27,583
Irvine	4	1	2	0	0	0	0	2	4	1	292,673
Laguna Woods	0	1	0	0	0	0	0	0	0	1	16,043
Lake Forest	0	1	0	0	0	0	0	0	1	0	86,691
Lancaster	7	1	1	0	0	0	1	2	5	1	159,335
Lemon Grove	1	0	0	0	0	0	1	0	0	0	27,175
Livermore	1	0	1	0	0	0	1	0	1	0	91,418
Long Beach	18	1	4	0	0	0	6	4	7	6	467,974
Los Angeles[2]	118	81	70	2	0	14	58	77	85	64	4,015,546
Malibu	1	0	0	0	0	0	0	0	1	0	12,794
Marina	1	0	0	0	0	0	0	0	0	1	22,911
Martinez	0	1	1	0	0	0	0	1	1	0	38,692
Marysville	0	1	0	0	0	0	1	0		0	12,572
Mission Viejo	0	2	0	0	0	0	1	0	1	0	95,453
Modesto	3	0	0	0	0	0	1	2	0	0	216,542
Montebello	0	1	0	0	0	0	0	1	0	0	62,650
Monterey	0	0	1	0	0	0	0	0	0	1	28,337
Monterey Park	1	0	0	0	0	0	0	0	1	0	60,424
Moreno Valley	1	0	0	0	0	0	1	0	0	0	210,979

(Number.)

State/agency	Race/Ethnicity/Ancestry	Religion	Sexual orientation	Disability	Gender	Gender Identity	1st quarter	2nd quarter	3rd quarter	4th quarter	Population[1]
National City	1	0	0	0	0	0	0	0	0	1	61,791
Novato	2	0	0	0	0	0	0	0	2	0	56,134
Oakdale	1	0	0	0	0	0	0	0	0	1	23,808
Oakland	5	3	5	0	0	0	2	3	5	3	434,036
Oceanside	3	1	4	0	0	0	1	4	3	0	177,129
Ontario	1	0	0	0	0	0	0	0	1	0	183,322
Orange	3	0	0	0	0	0	0	0	1	2	139,830
Oroville	2	0	0	0	0	0	1	1	0	0	19,268
Oxnard	1	0	0	0	0	0	0	0	1	0	211,349
Pacifica	1	0	0	0	0	0	0	0	1	0	38,938
Palmdale	3	0	0	0	0	0	0	0	2	1	157,138
Palm Springs	4	2	5	0	0	0	3	4	1	3	48,846
Palo Alto[2]	1	2	2	0	0	0	1	0	1	2	66,938
Parlier	0	0	1	0	0	0	0	0	1	0	15,384
Pasadena	2	2	0	0	0	0	0	1	2	1	141,913
Paso Robles	1	0	0	0	0	0	1	0	0	0	32,528
Petaluma	3	0	1	0	0	0	0	1	3	0	62,425
Pico Rivera	0	0	1	0	0	0	0	0	1	0	62,880
Pittsburg	0	1	1	1	0	0	0	1	0	2	73,637
Placentia	0	1	0	0	0	0	1	0	0	0	51,756
Pleasant Hill	1	0	0	0	0	0	0	0	0	1	35,125
Pomona	4	0	1	0	0	0	1	3	1	0	152,776
Poway	1	1	0	0	0	0	0	1	0	1	49,928
Rancho Cordova	1	0	0	0	0	0	1	0	0	0	75,869
Rancho Cucamonga	1	0	0	0	0	0	1		0	0	179,247
Rancho Santa Margarita	1	0	0	0	1	0	0	0	0	2	48,377
Red Bluff	2	0	0	0	0	0	0	1	1	0	14,308
Redding	1	0	0	0	0	0	1				92,009
Redlands	0	0	2	0	0	0	0	0	2	0	71,941
Redondo Beach	0	1	0	0	0	0	0	0	1	0	67,473
Redwood City	0	0	0	0	0	1	0	0	1	0	87,427
Rialto	1	0	0	0	0	0	0	0	0	1	103,965
Richmond	7	0	2	0	0	0	3	2	0	4	110,988
Ridgecrest	0	0	1	0	0	0	0	0	0	1	29,101
Riverside	10	1	4	0	0	0	8	3	4	0	333,260
Rohnert Park	1	0	0	0	0	0	0	0	1	0	44,131
Rosemead	1	0	0	0	0	0	1	0	0	0	54,489
Roseville	5	0	0	1	0	0	1	3	1	1	141,744
Sacramento	1	1	1	1	0	2	1	0	4	1	513,934
Salinas	0	0	1	0	0	0	0	1	0	0	156,943
San Bernardino	4	0	4	0	0	0	1	0	2	5	216,715
San Bruno	1	0	0	0	0	0	0	0	1	0	43,297
San Clemente	1	2	2	0	0	0	1	0	3	1	65,018
San Diego	8	11	9	1	0	1	9	8	9	4	1,441,737
San Francisco	35	5	22	0	0	2	17	17	24	6	886,007
San Gabriel	2	0	0	0	0	0	0	1	1	0	40,422
San Jose	13	7	10	1	0	2	9	8	7	9	1,040,008
San Leandro	0	0	2	0	0	0	1	1	0	0	90,297
San Luis Obispo	6	2	1	0	0	1	1	2	2	5	47,735
San Marcos	1	1	0	0	0	0	1	0	0	1	98,598
San Mateo	7	0	0	0	0	0	1	0	1	5	106,020
San Rafael	5	0	1	0	0	0	1	1	2	2	58,819
San Ramon	2	0	1	0	0	0	1	1	1	0	76,387
Santa Ana	3	6	2	0	0	0	2	4	3	2	333,664
Santa Clarita	1	1	0	0	0	0	0	1	1	0	218,103
Santa Cruz	1	0	1	0	0	0	1	1	0	0	65,263
Santa Monica	1	2	1	0	0	0	1	0	2	1	91,621
Santa Rosa	2	0	2	0	1	0	2	1	2	0	177,884
Seaside	1	1	0	0	0	0	1	1	0	0	34,036
South El Monte	1	0	1	0	0	0	1	1	0	0	20,852
South Lake Tahoe	0	1	0	0	0	0	0	1	0	0	22,116
Stockton	1	2	1	0	0	0	0	1	1	2	313,604
Sunnyvale	2	4	0	0	0	0	1	2	0	3	154,859
Temecula	1	0	0	0	0	0	0	0	0	1	116,630
Thousand Oaks	0	0	1	0	0	0	0	1	0	0	127,811
Torrance	1	0	1	0	0	0	0	0	2	0	145,183
Tracy	0	1	0	0	0	0	1	0	0	0	92,895

Table 13. Hate Crime Incidents Per Bias Motivation and Quarter, by Selected State and Agency and Federal, 2019—Continued

(Number.)

State/agency	Race/ Ethnicity/ Ancestry	Religion	Sexual orientation	Disability	Gender	Gender Identity	1st quarter	2nd quarter	3rd quarter	4th quarter	Population[1]
Turlock	1	1	1	0	0	0	2	0	0	1	74,120
Union City	6	0	0	0	0	0	5	1	0	0	75,202
Upland	2	0	0	0	0	0	0	0	0	2	77,398
Vacaville	5	0	0	0	0	0	0	3	0	2	101,147
Ventura	2	1	1	0	0	0	1	1	1	1	111,596
Walnut Creek	2	2	1	0	0	0	1	2	1	1	70,546
West Hollywood	0	1	0	0	0	0	1	0	0	0	37,173
Westminster	2	1	0	0	0	0	2		0	1	91,086
Whittier	0	0	1	0	0	0	0		0	1	86,158
Windsor	1	0	0	0	0	0	1	0	0	0	27,981
Yorba Linda	1	0	1	0	0	0	0	0	2	0	68,225
Yuba City	0	0	0	0	0	1	0	0	1	0	67,164
Yucca Valley	0	0	1	0	0	0	1	0	0	0	21,858
Universities and Colleges	17	2	1	0	0	0					
California State University											
Chico	1	0	0	0	0	0	0	1	0	0	19,754
East Bay	1	0	0	0	0	0	1	0	0	0	19,613
Northridge	1	0	0	0	0	0	0	0	0	1	44,639
Humboldt State University	7	1	0	0	0	0	1	4	0	3	9,262
San Diego State University	1	0	0	0	0	0	0	1	0	0	37,748
San Francisco State University	1	0	0	0	0	0	0	0	1	0	33,506
University of California											
Davis	4	0	0	0	0	0	0	2	1	1	39,783
Irvine	1	0	0	0	0	0	0	0	0	1	37,170
San Diego	0	1	1	0	0	0	1	1	0	0	37,744
Metropolitan Counties	52	12	17	2	1	3					
Los Angeles	10	1	3	0	1	0	5	5	3	2	
Marin	2	2	0	0	0	0	0	2	2	0	
Merced	1	0	0	0	0	0	1	0	0	0	
Monterey	1	0	0	0	0	0	0	0	1	0	
Napa	1	0	1	0	0	0	0	0	2	0	
Orange	6	1	1	1	0	0	1	4	2	2	
Riverside	3	1	1	0	0	0	2	1	1	1	
Sacramento	2	0	0	0	0	2	0	1	1	2	
San Bernardino	0	0	2	0	0	0	2	0	0	0	
San Diego	12	4	6	1	0	1	6	7	8	3	
San Luis Obispo	0	1	1	0	0	0	0	0	1	1	
San Mateo	3	0	1	0	0	0	0	0	3	1	
Santa Barbara	0	1	0	0	0	0	0	0	1	0	
Santa Clara	4	1	0	0	0	0	1	1	2	1	
Santa Cruz	6	0	1	0	0	0	2	2	1	2	
Tulare	1	0	0	0	0	0	0	0	0	1	
Nonmetropolitan Counties	2	1	2	0	0	0					
Glenn	0	0	1	0	0	0		1	0	0	
Mendocino	1	1	0	0	0	0	1	1	0	0	
Nevada	1	0	0	0	0	0	0	0	1	0	
Tuolumne	0	0	1	0	0	0	0	0	1	0	
Other Agencies	6	0	3	0	1	0					
Los Angeles Transportation Services Bureau	0	0	3	0	1	0	3	0	0	1	
Port of San Diego Harbor	5	0	0	0	0	0	1		3	1	
Santa Clara Transit District	1	0	0	0	0	0	0	1	0	0	
COLORADO											
Total	117	36	47	7	0	5					
Cities	96	30	40	3	0	2					
Aurora	2	0	0	0	0	0	0	1	1	0	380,600
Boulder	4	1	3	0	0	0	2	2	0	4	108,519
Brighton	1	1	0	0	0	0	0	0	0	2	42,267
Broomfield	1	0	0	0	0	0	0	0	1	0	70,798
Canon City	1	1	0	0	0	0	1	1	0	0	16,793
Carbondale	1	0	0	0	0	0	0	0	0	1	6,941
Castle Rock	1	0	0	0	0	0	0	0	0	1	67,208

Table 13. Hate Crime Incidents Per Bias Motivation and Quarter, by Selected State and Agency and Federal, 2019—*Continued*

(Number.)

State/agency	Number of incidents per bias motivation						Number of incidents per quarter				
	Race/ Ethnicity/ Ancestry	Religion	Sexual orientation	Disability	Gender	Gender Identity	1st quarter	2nd quarter	3rd quarter	4th quarter	Population[1]
Centennial................................	0	2	0	0	0	0	0	1	0	1	112,129
Colorado Springs........................	6	2	4	0	0	0	1	3	5	3	479,648
Commerce City...........................	2	0	0	0	0	0	1	0	1	0	60,198
Denver.......................................	40	15	26	2	0	2	11	39	25	10	728,941
Durango.....................................	1	1	0	0	0	0	0	1	0	1	19,271
Edgewater..................................	1	0	0	0	0	0	1	0	0	0	5,363
Englewood..................................	2	0	0	0	0	0	1	1	0	0	35,273
Evans...	3	0	0	0	0	0	1	0	2	0	21,585
Fort Collins[2].............................	4	2	1	0	0	0	2	2	0	2	170,889
Frisco..	1	0	0	0	0	0	0	1	0	0	3,220
Glenwood Springs.......................	4	0	0	0	0	0	2	0	1	1	10,027
Grand Junction...........................	2	1	0	0	0	0	1	1	1	0	63,949
Greenwood Village......................	1	0	1	0	0	0	1	1	0	0	16,046
Hudson......................................	0	0	1	0	0	0	1	0	0	0	1,806
Lone Tree...................................	1	0	0	0	0	0	0	0	1	0	15,129
Longmont...................................	2	0	1	1	0	0	2	1	1	0	97,928
Loveland.....................................	1	0	0	0	0	0	1	0	0	0	78,856
Manitou Springs..........................	0	1	0	0	0	0	0	0	1	0	5,388
Parker..	2	1	0	0	0	0	2	1	0	0	57,050
Pueblo..	1	1	0	0	0	0	1	0	0	1	112,381
Rifle..	2	0	0	0	0	0	0	1	1	0	9,782
Silt..	1	0	0	0	0	0	1	0	0	0	3,215
Sterling......................................	1	0	0	0	0	0	0	0	1	0	13,573
Thornton[2].................................	3	1	2	0	0	0	0	2	1	2	142,168
Timnath......................................	1	0	0	0	0	0	0	1	0	0	5,027
Westminster................................	3	0	1	0	0	0	0	0	3	1	114,392
Universities and Colleges..........	10	1	1	0	0	0					
Colorado State University, Fort Collins..........	2	1	0	0	0	0	1	0	1	1	37,676
Fort Lewis College.......................	1	0	0	0	0	0	0	1	0	0	3,730
University of Colorado, Boulder......	7	0	0	0	0	0	2	0	3	2	39,302
University of Northern Colorado......	0	0	1	0	0	0	0	0	1	0	15,825
Metropolitan Counties..............	4	4	3	4	0	1					
Adams.......................................	1	0	0	1	0	0	1	0	1	0	
Douglas......................................	2	2	0	2	0	0	1	1	2	2	
Jefferson....................................	1	0	0	1	0	0	1	1	0	0	
Larimer......................................	0	1	0	0	0	1	2	0	0	0	
Mesa...	0	0	2	0	0	0	0	1	1	0	
Park..	0	1	1	0	0	0	0	1	1	0	
Nonmetropolitan Counties........	7	1	3	0	0	2					
Bent...	0	1	0	0	0	0	0	1	0	0	
Custer..	1	0	0	0	0	0	1	0	0	0	
Fremont......................................	1	0	1	0	0	0	0	1	1	0	
Garfield......................................	1	0	0	0	0	2	1	1	1	0	
Huerfano....................................	2	0	1	0	0	0	1	1	1	0	
San Miguel.................................	1	0	0	0	0	0	0	0	1	0	
Summit.......................................	1	0	1	0	0	0	1	0	1	0	
CONNECTICUT											
Total.....................................	48	16	11	0	1	0					
Cities....................................	45	12	11	0	1	0					
Bloomfield..................................	0	1	0	0	0	0	0	0	1	0	21,406
Bridgeport..................................	1	1	1	0	0	0	1	2	0	0	144,908
Bristol..	1	0	0	0	0	0	1	0	0	0	59,977
Cheshire.....................................	0	1	0	0	0	0	0	1	0	0	29,167
Danbury......................................	3	0	0	0	0	0	1	1	1	0	85,167
Derby...	1	0	0	0	0	0	0	0	1	0	12,468
East Hartford..............................	1	1	1	0	0	0	0	1	1	1	49,842
East Lyme...................................	1	0	0	0	0	0	0	0	0	1	18,588
Enfield.......................................	2	0	0	0	0	0	0	0	1	1	44,443
Farmington.................................	1	0	0	0	0	0	1	0	0	0	25,525
Glastonbury................................	2	0	1	0	0	0	2	1	0	0	34,497
Madison.....................................	1	0	0	0	0	0	0	0	0	1	18,087
Manchester.................................	4	0	1	0	0	0	1	1	2	1	57,630

Table 13. Hate Crime Incidents Per Bias Motivation and Quarter, by Selected State and Agency and Federal, 2019—*Continued*

(Number.)

State/agency	Number of incidents per bias motivation						Number of incidents per quarter				Population[1]
	Race/ Ethnicity/ Ancestry	Religion	Sexual orientation	Disability	Gender	Gender Identity	1st quarter	2nd quarter	3rd quarter	4th quarter	
Middletown	1	0	0	0	0	0	0	0	1	0	45,963
Milford	1	0	1	0	0	0		1	0	1	54,898
New Britain	2	1	0	0	0	0		1	1	1	72,354
New Haven	5	2	2	0	0	0	2	5	1	1	130,494
New London	1	0	0	0	0	0	0	1	0	0	26,856
New Milford	1	0	0	0	0	0	0	1	0	0	26,835
Norwalk	1	0	0	0	0	0	0	0	0	1	89,440
Norwich	0	0	1	0	0	0	0	0	1	0	38,964
Old Saybrook	2	0	0	0	0	0	0	0	2	0	10,069
Orange	1	0	0	0	0	0	0	0	1	0	13,948
Plainville	1	0	0	0	0	0	0	0	1	0	17,610
Plymouth	1	0	0	0	0	0	0	0	0	1	11,573
Ridgefield	1	0	0	0	0	0	0	0	0	1	25,050
Seymour	0	1	0	0	0	0	1	0	0	0	16,505
Stamford	3	3	2	0	0	0	0	1	3	4	130,678
Torrington	1	0	0	0	1	0	1	0	0	1	33,972
Wallingford	1	0	0	0	0	0	1	0	0	0	44,457
West Hartford	1	0	0	0	0	0	1	0	0	0	62,875
West Haven	1	0	0	0	0	0	0	0	1	0	54,794
Westport	0	1	0	0	0	0	0	0	1	0	28,332
Wethersfield	1	0	0	0	0	0	1	0	0	0	26,009
Willimantic	0	0	1	0	0	0	0	1	0	0	17,660
Wilton	1	0	0	0	0	0	1	0	0	0	18,439
Universities and Colleges	2	1	0	0	0	0					
Southern Connecticut State University	1	0	0	0	0	0	0	0	1	0	11,642
University of Connecticut, Storrs, Avery Point, and Hartford[3]	1	0	0	0	0	0	0	0	0	1	
Yale University	0	1	0	0	0	0				1	13,972
State Police Agencies	1	3	0	0	0	0					
Connecticut State Police	1	3	0	0	0	0	0	1	2	1	
DELAWARE											
Total	10	4	7	0	0	1					
Cities	4	2	3	0	0	1					
Bethany Beach	1	0	0	0	0	0	0	0	1	0	1,244
Dover	0	1	2	0	0	0	1	0	1	1	38,361
Milford	2	0	0	0	0	0	0	1	0	1	11,592
Seaford	1	1	0	0	0	0	1	0	1	0	7,987
Wilmington	0	0	1	0	0	1	0	2	0	0	70,624
Universities and Colleges	3	0	2	0	0	0					
Delaware State University	0	0	1	0	0	0	1	0	0	0	4,633
University of Delaware	3	0	1	0	0	0	1	1	1	1	25,534
Metropolitan Counties	1	1	1	0	0	0					
New Castle County Police Department	1	1	1	0	0	0	1	2	0	0	
State Police Agencies	2	1	1	0	0	0					
State Police											
New Castle County	2	1	0	0	0	0	1	0	1	1	
Sussex County	0	0	1	0	0	0	0	0	1	0	
DISTRICT OF COLUMBIA											
Total	119	8	65	1	2	27					
Cities	107	5	60	1	2	27					
Washington	107	5	60	1	2	27	53	57	55	37	705,749
Other Agencies	12	3	5	0	0	0					
Metro Transit Police	12	3	5	0	0	0	8	3	6	3	
FLORIDA											
Total	48	36	27	0	0	0					

(Number.)

State/agency	Number of incidents per bias motivation						Number of incidents per quarter				Population[1]
	Race/ Ethnicity/ Ancestry	Religion	Sexual orientation	Disability	Gender	Gender Identity	1st quarter	2nd quarter	3rd quarter	4th quarter	
Cities	32	32	19	0	0	0					
Bal Harbour Village	0	1	0	0	0	0	1				3,086
Boca Raton	1	1	0	0	0	0	0	0	1	1	101,163
Cape Coral	1	0	1	0	0	0	0	1	0	1	194,183
Davie	3	0	0	0	0	0	2	1	0	0	108,486
DeLand	1	0	0	0	0	0	1	0	0	0	34,468
Deerfield Beach	0	0	1	0	0	0	0	0	0	1	81,602
Fort Lauderdale	2	0	1	0	0	0	0	3	0	0	184,765
Fort Myers	1	0	0	0	0	0	1	0	0	0	85,127
Gainesville	2	1	1	0	0	0	1	1	1	1	135,085
Jacksonville	4	0	0	0	0	0	0	1	2	1	909,142
Largo	2	0	0	0	0	0	0	0	0	2	85,740
Miami	0	2	0	0	0	0	1	0	1	0	480,505
Miami Beach	0	16	4	0	0	0	8	4	4	4	92,185
Miami Gardens	0	1	0	0	0	0	0	1	0	0	113,786
Miami Shores	0	0	1	0	0	0	0	1	0	0	10,572
Miramar	0	0	2	0	0	0	2	0	0	0	143,334
New Port Richey	1	0	0	0	0	0	0	0	0	1	16,703
North Miami	1	0	0	0	0	0	1	0	0	0	63,547
North Miami Beach	2	1	0	0	0	0		1	1	1	46,307
North Port	1	0	0	0	0	0	1	0	0	0	70,181
Oakland Park	0	0	1	0	0	0	0	0	1	0	45,857
Ocala	1	0	1	0	0	0	0	0	0	2	60,932
Orlando	1	1	2	0	0	0	2	1	0	1	292,120
Palm Bay	0	0	1	0	0	0	0	0	0	1	115,520
Palm Beach Gardens	1	1	0	0	0	0	0	0	2	0	57,236
Pompano Beach	1	0	1	0	0	0	0	0	2	0	113,536
Port St. Lucie	1	1	1	0	0	0		1	1	1	199,433
Royal Palm Beach	1	0	0	0	0	0		1	0	0	40,802
Sarasota	1	0	0	0	0	0	0	0	0	1	58,470
St. Augustine	0	1	0	0	0	0	1	0	0	0	14,778
Sunny Isles Beach	0	0	1	0	0	0	0	1	0	0	22,476
Sunrise	0	1	0	0	0	0	1	0	0	0	96,919
Tampa	0	2	0	0	0	0	1	1	0	0	400,501
Temple Terrace	1	0	0	0	0	0	0	0	0	1	26,725
Titusville	0	1	0	0	0	0	0	0	0	1	46,866
Weston	0	1	0	0	0	0	0	0	0	1	71,946
Winter Garden	2	0	0	0	0	0	0	2	0	0	46,750
Metropolitan Counties	15	4	8	0	0	0					
Alachua	0	0	1	0	0	0	0	0	1	0	
Bay	1	0	0	0	0	0	1	0	0	0	
Lake	2	0	0	0	0	0	2	0	0	0	
Lee	5	0	0	0	0	0	1	0	2	2	
Miami-Dade	0	3	2	0	0	0	1	2		2	
Orange	1	1	1	0	0	0	0	2	0	1	
Osceola	1	0	1	0	0	0	1	0	1	0	
Pasco	1	0	1	0	0	0	1	1	0	0	
Santa Rosa	0	0	1	0	0	0	0	0	0	1	
Sarasota	1	0	0	0	0	0	0	0	0	1	
St. Johns	1	0	0	0	0	0	0	0	0	1	
Sumter	1	0	1	0	0	0	2	0	0	0	
Volusia	1	0	0	0	0	0	1	0	0	0	
Other Agencies	1	0	0	0	0	0					
Fort Lauderdale Airport	1	0	0	0	0	0	0	0	1	0	
GEORGIA											
Total	77	9	6	4	3	3					
Cities	48	5	3	1	1	1					
Albany	1	0	0	0	0	0	0	0	1	0	74,989
Atlanta	0	1	0	0	0	0	1	0	0		507,369
Brookhaven	1	0	1	0	0	0	0	0	0	2	54,734
Cartersville	1	0	0	0	0	0	1	0	0	0	21,322
College Park	1	0	0	0	0	0	0	0	0	1	15,278
Columbus	1	1	0	0	0	0			1	1	194,356

Table 13. Hate Crime Incidents Per Bias Motivation and Quarter, by Selected State and Agency and Federal, 2019—*Continued*

(Number.)

State/agency	Number of incidents per bias motivation						Number of incidents per quarter				Population[1]
	Race/ Ethnicity/ Ancestry	Religion	Sexual orientation	Disability	Gender	Gender Identity	1st quarter	2nd quarter	3rd quarter	4th quarter	
Douglasville	2	0	0	0	0	0	0	0	0	2	34,609
Dunwoody	3	0	1	0	0	0	2	1	0	1	49,868
Emerson	0	1	0	0	0	0	0	0	1	0	1,603
Fayetteville	0	0	0	0	1	0	0	0	0	1	18,041
Garden City	1	0	0	0	0	0	1	0	0	0	8,854
Glennville	0	0	1	0	0	0	0	0	0	1	5,084
Griffin	3	0	0	0	0	0	0	0	0	3	22,840
Johns Creek	2	0	0	0	0	0	0	0	0	2	85,258
Kennesaw	3	1	0	0	0	0	0	0	0	4	34,641
Lilburn	1	0	0	0	0	0	0	0	0	1	12,769
Manchester	2	0	0	0	0	0	0	1	1	0	3,958
Marietta	1	0	0	0	0	0	0	0	0	1	61,324
Milledgeville	4	0	0	0	0	0	0	0	0	4	18,655
Monroe	1	0	0	0	0	0	0	0	0	1	13,662
Newnan	1	0	0	0	0	0	0	0	0	1	40,720
Omega	0	0	0	0	0	1				1	1,222
Sandy Springs	4	1	0	1	0	0	0	1	1	4	110,760
Smyrna	2	0	0	0	0	0	0	0	0	2	57,423
Snellville	1	0	0	0	0	0	0	0	0	1	20,113
Sparta	4	0	0	0	0	0	0	0	0	4	1,209
Suwanee	1	0	0	0	0	0	0	1	0	0	21,331
Warner Robins	7	0	0	0	0	0	0	0	0	7	76,623
Universities and Colleges	4	0	0	0	0	0					
Fort Valley State University	4	0	0	0	0	0	0	0	0	4	3,044
Metropolitan Counties	19	3	3	1	1	2					
Cherokee	0	1	0	0	0	0	0	0	0	1	
Cobb County Police Department	11	1	2	0	0	0	3	4	2	5	
Coweta	0	0	1	0	0	0	0	0	1	0	
Douglas	1	0	0	0	0	1	0	0	0	2	
Fayette	1	0	0	0	0	0	0	0	0	1	
Forsyth	2	0	0	0	0	0	0	0	0	2	
Hall	1	0	0	1	0	0	0	1	1	0	
Haralson	1	0	0	0	0	0			0	1	
Lee	0	0	0	0	1	0	0	0	1	0	
Murray	0	1	0	0	0	0			0	1	
Newton	0	0	0	0	0	1	0	0	1	0	
Paulding	1	0	0	0	0	0	0	0	0	1	
Whitfield	1	0	0	0	0	0	0	0	1		
Nonmetropolitan Counties	4	0	0	1	1	0					
Banks	0	0	0	1	0	0	1	0	0		
Decatur	1	0	0	0	0	0	0	0	0	1	
Fannin	1	0	0	0	0	0	0	0	0	1	
Montgomery	1	0	0	0	0	0			1	0	
Pierce	1	0	0	0	1	0	2	0	0	0	
Other Agencies	2	1	0	1	0	0					
Atlanta Public Schools	1	0	0	0	0	0	0	0	0	1	
Fulton County School System	0	1	0	1	0	0	0	0	0	2	
Gwinnett County Public Schools	1	0	0	0	0	0	0	0	1	0	
HAWAII											
Total	30	2	9	0	0	0					
Cities	30	2	9	0	0	0					
Honolulu	30	2	9	0	0	0	15	7	12	7	974,902
IDAHO											
Total	18	1	4	1	0	0					
Cities	12	0	4	0	0	0					
Boise	6	0	2	0	0	0	3	2	1	2	231,314
Chubbuck	1	0	0	0	0	0	1	0	0	0	15,490
Coeur d'Alene	3	0	0	0	0	0	0	0	0	3	52,256
Jerome	1	0	0	0	0	0	1	0	0	0	11,921

Table 13. Hate Crime Incidents Per Bias Motivation and Quarter, by Selected State and Agency and Federal, 2019—*Continued*

(Number.)

State/agency	Race/Ethnicity/Ancestry	Religion	Sexual orientation	Disability	Gender	Gender Identity	1st quarter	2nd quarter	3rd quarter	4th quarter	Population[1]
Pocatello	0	0	1	0	0	0	0	1	0	0	56,514
Post Falls	1	0	1	0	0	0	1	0	1	0	35,649
Nonmetropolitan Counties	3	0	0	1	0	0					95,386
Bonneville	3	0	0	1	0	0	0	3	0	1	55,304
											49,908
Nonmetropolitan Counties	3	1	0	0	0	0					
Cassia	3	0	0	0	0	0	0	1	2	0	
Idaho	0	1	0	0	0	0	1	0	0	0	
ILLINOIS											
Total	34	9	17	0	0	6					
Cities	30	9	17	0	0	6					
Aurora	0	1	0	0	0	0	0	0	0	1	199,784
Bartonville	0	0	1	0	0	0	1	0	0	0	6,137
Bloomingdale	0	1	0	0	0	0	1	0		0	21,872
Bolingbrook	0	0	2	0	0	0	0	1		1	75,394
Chicago[2]	18	5	11	0	0	6	13	17	9	0	2,707,064
DeKalb	1	0	0	0	0	0	0	1	0	0	42,428
Elk Grove Village	1	0	0	0	0	0	0	1	0	0	32,371
Fairview Heights	1	0	0	0	0	0	0	0	0	1	16,368
Farmington	1	0	0	0	0	0	0	1	0	0	2,236
Galesburg	0	1	0	0	0	0	1	0	0	0	30,220
Genoa	0	1	0	0	0	0	0	1	0		5,211
Hoopeston	1	0	0	0	0	0	1	0	0	0	5,046
Joliet	0	0	1	0	0	0	1	0	0	0	148,155
Montgomery	1	0	0	0	0	0	0	0	1	0	19,927
Pingree Grove	1	0	0	0	0	0	0	0	1	0	9,765
Pontiac	1	0	0	0	0	0	1	0	0	0	11,211
Rockford	1	0	2	0	0	0	1	1	1	0	145,719
Springfield	1	0	0	0	0	0	0	0	0	1	114,393
Steger	1	0	0	0	0	0	0	1	0	0	9,301
Streamwood	1	0	0	0	0	0	0	0	1	0	39,529
Metropolitan Counties	4	0	0	0	0	0					
Lake	1	0	0	0	0	0	0			1	
Peoria	2	0	0	0	0	0	0	1	1	0	
Sangamon	1	0	0	0	0	0	0	1	0	0	
INDIANA											
Total	47	13	14	0	0	2					
Cities	43	11	10	0	0	2					
Bloomington	1	0	0	0	0	0	1	0	0	0	85,542
Columbus	7	0	1	0	0	0	0	1	0	2	47,991
Evansville	1	0	0	0	0	0			1		117,700
Fort Wayne	1	1	1	0	0	0	1	1	1	0	269,366
Frankfort	1	0	0	0	0	0			1		15,759
Hammond	5	0	1	0	0	0	2	1	3		75,201
Hobart	2	0	0	0	0	0	0	0	1	1	27,880
Indianapolis	13	5	3	0	0	1	5	3	8	6	883,699
Lafayette	6	2	2	0	0	0		4	4	2	72,585
Leavenworth	0	0	1	0	0	0		0		1	232
Linton	1	1	0	0	0	0		0	2		5,185
Plainfield[2]	3	0	1	0	0	0			2	1	35,317
Schererville	0	1	0	0	0	0		1	0	0	28,412
South Bend	4	1	0	0	0	1	2	1	2	1	101,944
Terre Haute	3	0	0	0	0	0	1	0	2	0	60,749
Universities and Colleges	0	1	1	0	0	0					
Butler University	0	0	1	0	0	0	1				5,306
University of Indianapolis[3]	0	1	0	0	0	0			1	0	
Metropolitan Counties	4	1	2	0	0	0					
La Porte	1	0	0	0	0	0	0	0	1	0	
Madison	1	0	0	0	0	0	0	0	0	1	

(Number.)

State/agency	Number of incidents per bias motivation						Number of incidents per quarter				Population[1]
	Race/ Ethnicity/ Ancestry	Religion	Sexual orientation	Disability	Gender	Gender Identity	1st quarter	2nd quarter	3rd quarter	4th quarter	
Porter	0	1	0	0	0	0	0	0	1	0	
St. Joseph	1	0	0	0	0	0	0	0	0	1	
Vigo	1	0	2	0	0	0	0	0	2	1	
State Police Agencies	0	0	1	0	0	0					
State Police, Greene County	0	0	1	0	0	0	0	0	1	0	
IOWA											
Total	6	0	4	0	0	0					
Cities	5	0	4	0	0	0					
Ames	0	0	2	0	0	0	0	1	1	0	68,237
Clive	0	0	1	0	0	0	0	0	0	1	17,305
Davenport	1	0	0	0	0	0	0	0	0	1	102,392
Dubuque	1	0	0	0	0	0	0	0	1	0	57,973
Iowa City	2	0	0	0	0	0	0	2	0	0	77,390
Sioux City	0	0	1	0	0	0	1	0	0	0	82,339
Waterloo	1	0	0	0	0	0	0	0	1	0	67,723
Universities and Colleges	1	0	0	0	0	0					
Iowa State University	1	0	0	0	0	0	0	0	0	1	39,108
Metropolitan Counties	1	1	0	0	0	0					
Dubuque	1	1	0	0	0	0	1	0	1	0	
KANSAS											
Total	38	27	7	3	1	2					
Cities	32	12	5	3	0	2					
Atchison	1	0	0	0	0	0	0	1	0	0	10,509
Basehor	0	1	0	0	0	0	0	0	0	1	6,418
Bel Aire	0	1	0	0	0	0	1	0	0	0	8,252
Bonner Springs	1	0	0	0	0	0	0	1	0	0	7,850
Cherryvale	0	1	0	0	0	0	0	1	0	0	2,127
Clay Center	0	0	0	1	0	0	0	0	1	0	3,946
Coffeyville	0	1	0	0	0	0	0	0	0	1	9,260
Columbus	1	0	0	0	0	0	0	0	0	1	3,042
Concordia	1	0	1	0	0	0	0	0	0	2	4,904
Dodge City	2	0	0	0	0	0	0	1	0	1	27,314
El Dorado	1	0	0	0	0	0	0	0	1	0	12,899
Garden City	1	0	1	0	0	0	2	0	0	0	26,509
Gardner	1	0	0	0	0	0	0	0	1	0	22,229
Garnett	1	0	0	0	0	0	0	0	0	1	3,244
Goodland	0	1	0	0	0	0	1	0	0	0	4,374
Hays	1	0	0	0	0	0	0	0	1	0	20,894
Haysville	0	1	0	0	0	0	1	0	0	0	11,319
Hiawatha	1	1	0	0	0	0	0	1	1	0	3,119
Hillsboro	1	0	0	1	0	0	2	0	0	0	2,814
Hoisington	1	0	0	0	0	0	0	1	0	0	2,486
Hutchinson	2	0	0	0	0	0	1	0	1	0	40,431
Independence	0	0	1	0	0	0	0	0	1	0	8,497
Larned	1	0	0	0	0	0	0	1	0	0	3,739
Leavenworth	2	0	0	0	0	0	0	0	2	0	36,149
Leawood	0	0	0	1	0	0	1	0	0	0	35,052
Lindsborg	0	1	0	0	0	0	0	1	0	0	3,269
Maize	0	1	0	0	0	0	1	0	0	0	4,836
Paola	1	0	0	0	0	0	0	1	0	0	5,676
Salina	6	0	0	0	0	2	1	6	0	1	46,567
Shawnee	2	0	0	0	0	0	0	1	1	0	66,300
Tonganoxie	1	1	0	0	0	0	1	0	0	1	5,591
Topeka	1	0	0	0	0	0	1	0	0	0	125,655
Valley Center	0	1	0	0	0	0	0	0	1	0	7,376
Wichita	2	0	2	0	0	0	1	0	2	1	390,080
Winfield	0	1	0	0	0	0	0	0	0	1	12,023
Universities and Colleges	2	0	0	0	0	0					
University of Kansas											

Table 13. Hate Crime Incidents Per Bias Motivation and Quarter, by Selected State and Agency and Federal, 2019—*Continued*

(Number.)

State/agency	Number of incidents per bias motivation						Number of incidents per quarter				
	Race/ Ethnicity/ Ancestry	Religion	Sexual orientation	Disability	Gender	Gender Identity	1st quarter	2nd quarter	3rd quarter	4th quarter	Population[1]
Main Campus	1	0	0	0	0	0	1	0	0	0	31,136
Medical Center[3]	1	0	0	0	0	0	1	0	0	0	
Metropolitan Counties	1	6	1	0	1	0					
Doniphan	0	1	0	0	0	0	0	0	1	0	
Jefferson	0	2	0	0	1	0	0	2	1	0	
Johnson	1	0	0	0	0	0	0	1	0	0	
Pottawatomie	0	1	0	0	0	0	0	1	0	0	
Riley County Police Department	0	0	1	0	0	0	0	0	1	0	
Sedgwick	0	2	0	0	0	0	0	2	0	0	
Nonmetropolitan Counties	2	7	1	0	0	0					
Barton	0	1	0	0	0	0	0	1	0	0	
Edwards	0	1	0	0	0	0	1	0	0	0	
Labette	0	3	0	0	0	0	1	1	0	1	
McPherson	0	1	0	0	0	0	1	0	0	0	
Nemaha	0	1	1	0	0	0	0	1	1	0	
Saline	1	0	0	0	0	0	0	0	0	1	
Thomas	1	0	0	0	0	0	0	1	0	0	
State Police Agencies	1	1	0	0	0	0					
Highway Patrol											
Troop B	1	0	0	0	0	0	1	0	0	0	
Troop C	0	1	0	0	0	0	0	1	0	0	
Other Agencies	0	1	0	0	0	0					
Kansas Department of Wildlife and Parks	0	1	0	0	0	0	1	0	0	0	
KENTUCKY											
Total	114	12	19	1	2	4					
Cities	78	7	10	1	1	3					
Ashland	3	0	0	0	0	0	2	1	0	0	20,222
Audubon Park	1	0	0	0	0	0	0	1	0	0	1,504
Berea	2	0	0	0	0	0	1	1	0	0	16,074
Bowling Green	3	0	1	0	0	0	0	2	0	2	69,627
Campbellsville	2	0	0	0	0	0	0	0	1	1	11,488
Covington	8	0	0	0	0	0	6	0	0	2	40,350
Edgewood	1	0	0	0	0	0	0	0	0	1	8,749
Erlanger	1	0	0	0	0	0	1	0	0	0	23,116
Florence	2	0	0	1	0	0	1	1	0	1	32,848
Frankfort	3	0	0	0	0	0	2	0	1	0	27,723
Georgetown	3	0	0	0	0	0	2	1	0	0	35,106
Glasgow	1	0	0	0	0	0	1	0	0	0	14,475
Hodgenville	1	0	0	0	0	0	1	0	0	0	3,239
Hopkinsville	2	0	0	0	0	0	1	1	0	0	30,895
Jeffersontown	1	0	1	0	0	0	1	1	0	0	28,015
La Grange	1	0	0	0	0	0	1	0	0	0	9,080
Leitchfield	1	0	1	0	0	0	2	0	0	0	6,852
Lexington[2]	15	1	2	0	0	0	4	5	5	3	326,070
Louisville Metro	4	4	2	0	0	1	2	3	2	4	675,501
Mayfield	1	0	0	0	0	0	0	0	1	0	9,851
Maysville	2	0	0	0	0	0	0	2	0	0	8,750
Morehead	1	0	0	0	0	0	0	0	0	1	7,736
Newport	1	0	1	0	0	0	1	0	0	1	14,965
Nicholasville	1	0	0	0	0	0	1	0	0	0	31,188
Owensboro	5	0	0	0	0	0	0	0	4	1	60,107
Paducah	3	2	1	0	0	0	1	2	2	1	24,832
Radcliff	2	0	0	0	0	0	0	0	2	0	22,998
Richmond	1	0	0	0	0	0	1	0	0	0	36,458
Russell Springs	1	0	0	0	0	0	0	1	0	0	2,632
Shively	2	0	0	0	0	0	0	1	1	0	15,845
Simpsonville	0	0	1	0	0	0	1	0	0	0	2,945
Stanton	1	0	0	0	0	0	0	1	0	0	2,651
St. Matthews	0	0	0	0	1	0	0	0	0	1	18,275
Versailles	1	0	0	0	0	1	1	0	0	1	26,625
West Buechel	1	0	0	0	0	0	1	0	0	0	1,285
Winchester	0	0	0	0	0	1	0	1	0	0	18,605

(Number.)

State/agency	Race/Ethnicity/Ancestry	Religion	Sexual orientation	Disability	Gender	Gender Identity	1st quarter	2nd quarter	3rd quarter	4th quarter	Population[1]
Universities and Colleges	3	0	1	0	0	0					
University of Kentucky	1	0	0	0	0	0	1	0	0	0	31,102
University of Louisville	1	0	1	0	0	0	1	0	0	1	24,828
Western Kentucky University	1	0	0	0	0	0	0	0	0	1	24,560
Metropolitan Counties	9	2	5	0	1	0					
Boone[2]	4	1	3	0	1	0	1	2	3	1	
Bourbon	0	0	1	0	0	0	0	0	1	0	
Campbell County Police Department	1	0	0	0	0	0	0	0	1	0	
Christian	1	0	0	0	0	0	1	0	0	0	
Daviess	1	0	0	0	0	0	0	1	0	0	
Grant	1	0	0	0	0	0	1	0	0	0	
Hardin	1	0	0	0	0	0	0	1	0	0	
Warren	0	1	1	0	0	0	1	0	1	0	
Nonmetropolitan Counties	13	1	2	0	0	0					
Boyle	2	0	0	0	0	0	2	0	0	0	
Franklin	1	0	0	0	0	0	1	0	0	0	
Fulton	0	0	1	0	0	0	0	0	0	1	
Harrison	1	0	0	0	0	0	0	1	0	0	
Hopkins	2	0	0	0	0	0	1	0	0	1	
Knox[2]	1	1	0	0	0	0	0	0	0	1	
Logan	0	0	1	0	0	0	1	0	0	0	
Madison	1	0	0	0	0	0	0	0	0	1	
Marshall	1	0	0	0	0	0	1	0	0	0	
McCracken	2	0	0	0	0	0	0	0	1	1	
Pulaski	1	0	0	0	0	0	1	0	0	0	
Todd	1	0	0	0	0	0	0	0	0	1	
State Police Agencies	6	2	1	0	0	0					
State Police											
Bowling Green	2	0	0	0	0	0	1	0	1	0	
Elizabethtown[2]	2	2	0	0	0	0	0	0	1	2	
Mayfield[2]	1	0	1	0	0	0	0	1	0	0	
Richmond	1	0	0	0	0	0	0	1	0	0	
Other Agencies	5	0	0	0	0	1					
Fayette County Schools	1	0	0	0	0	0	0	1	0	0	
Greater Hardin County Narcotics Task Force	1	0	0	0	0	0	1	0	0	0	
Jefferson County School District	2	0	0	0	0	1	0	1	1	1	
Metcalfe County Schools	1	0	0	0	0	0	0	0	0	1	
LOUISIANA											
Total	9	8	7	2	0	0					
Cities	3	3	4	1	0	0					
Baton Rouge	0	0	1	0	0	0	0	1	0	0	220,648
New Orleans	2	0	3	0	0	0	2	1	1	1	394,498
Thibodaux	1	1	0	1	0	0	0	1	1	1	14,587
West Monroe	0	2	0	0	0	0	1	0	1	0	12,350
Metropolitan Counties	4	4	3	1	0	0					
Ascension	0	1	0	0	0	0	0	0	1	0	
Bossier	1	0	1	1	0	0	1	2	0	0	
Calcasieu	2	2	2	0	0	0	1	1	2	2	
Lafourche	0	1	0	0	0	0	0	0	1	0	
St. James	1	0	0	0	0	0	0	0	0	1	
Nonmetropolitan Counties	2	1	0	0	0	0					
Evangeline	0	1	0	0	0	0	0	1	0	0	
Madison	2	0	0	0	0	0	2	0	0	0	
MAINE											
Total	10	2	7	0	0	0					
Cities	8	2	7	0	0	0					
Augusta	0	1	1	0	0	0	0	1	0	1	18,629

Table 13. Hate Crime Incidents Per Bias Motivation and Quarter, by Selected State and Agency and Federal, 2019—*Continued*

(Number.)

State/agency	Race/ Ethnicity/ Ancestry	Religion	Sexual orientation	Disability	Gender	Gender Identity	1st quarter	2nd quarter	3rd quarter	4th quarter	Population[1]
Biddeford	0	0	1	0	0	0	0	0	1	0	21,545
Lewiston	2	0	0	0	0	0	0	0	0	2	35,865
Portland	4	0	1	0	0	0	1	1	2	1	66,458
Rockland	1	0	0	0	0	0	0	0	1	0	7,128
Saco	1	0	3	0	0	0	1	2	1	0	19,908
Sanford	0	0	1	0	0	0	0	1	0	0	21,233
South Portland	0	1	0	0	0	0	0	0	0	1	25,686
Nonmetropolitan Counties	1	0	0	0	0	0					
Franklin	1	0	0	0	0	0	0	0	0	1	
State Police Agencies	1	0	0	0	0	0					
Maine State Police	1	0	0	0	0	0	1	0	0	0	
MARYLAND											
Total	7	4	7	1	0	0					
Cities	1	0	1	0	0	0					
Takoma Park	0	0	1	0	0	0	0	0	1	0	17,893
Westminster	1	0	0	0	0	0	1	0	0	0	18,664
Universities and Colleges	1	0	0	1	0	0					
University of Maryland											
Baltimore County	0	0	0	1	0	0	1	0	0	0	15,681
College Park	1	0	0	0	0	0	0	0	1	0	44,052
Metropolitan Counties	4	4	6	0	0	0					
Carroll	1	0	0	0	0	0	1	0	0	0	
Harford	1	0	0	0	0	0	0		1	0	
Montgomery County Police Department	0	3	1	0	0	0	2	2	0	0	
Prince George's County Police Department[2]	2	1	5	0	0	0	1	0	2	4	
Other Agencies	1	0	0	0	0	0					
Natural Resources Police	1	0	0	0	0	0	1	0	0	0	
MASSACHUSETTS											
Total	213	101	92	1	2	7					
Cities	202	88	86	1	2	7					
Acton	4	2	0	0	0	0	2	1	2	1	23,780
Amherst	0	0	0	0	1	0	0	1	0	0	39,603
Andover	0	2	0	0	0	0	0	0	1	1	36,547
Arlington[2]	3	3	2	0	0	1	1	3	1	2	45,614
Ashburnham	0	0	1	0	0	0	0	1	0	0	6,330
Attleboro	0	0	1	0	0	0	0	1	0	0	44,959
Barnstable[2]	3	3	0	0	0	0	2	0	3	0	44,032
Belmont	1	0	0	0	0	0	0	0	0	1	26,331
Boston[2]	113	26	47	0	1	1	39	57	39	42	698,941
Braintree	1	1	0	0	0	0	0	0	2	0	37,145
Brewster	0	0	1	0	0	0	0	0	1	0	9,725
Brockton	2	0	0	0	0	0	2	0	0	0	95,287
Brookline	4	2	0	0	0	0	1	1	1	3	58,928
Cambridge[2]	9	6	3	0	0	2	4	4	5	5	119,908
Chilmark	1	0	0	0	0	0	0	1	0	0	920
Concord	1	0	0	0	0	0	1	0	0	0	19,253
Danvers[2]	2	2	0	0	0	0	0	1	0	2	27,664
Dracut	1	0	0	0	0	0	0	0	1	0	31,786
Easthampton	0	0	1	0	0	0	0	1	0	0	15,979
Edgartown	1	0	0	0	0	0	0	0	1	0	4,362
Everett	1	0	0	0	0	0	0	0	1	0	47,195
Fall River	0	1	0	0	0	0	1	0	0	0	89,066
Framingham	0	1	0	0	0	0	0	1	0	0	73,127
Gloucester	1	0	0	0	0	0	0	0	1	0	30,362
Greenfield	1	1	1	0	0	0	1	1	1	0	17,464
Hamilton[2]	1	1	0	0	0	0	0	0	1	0	8,075
Haverhill[2]	4	2	1	0	0	0	0	3	2	1	63,935
Hingham	1	0	0	0	0	0	0	1	0	0	23,960

Table 13. Hate Crime Incidents Per Bias Motivation and Quarter, by Selected State and Agency and Federal, 2019—Continued

(Number.)

State/agency	Number of incidents per bias motivation						Number of incidents per quarter				
	Race/ Ethnicity/ Ancestry	Religion	Sexual orientation	Disability	Gender	Gender Identity	1st quarter	2nd quarter	3rd quarter	4th quarter	Population[1]
Hull[2]	1	1	0	0	0	0	0	0	1	0	10,402
Kingston	0	1	0	0	0	0	0	0	1	0	13,758
Leominster	1	0	0	0	0	0	0	0	0	1	41,631
Lynn	2	4	1	0	0	0	0	2	5	0	94,449
Malden	2	1	0	0	0	0	0	1	0	2	60,746
Manchester-by-the-Sea	0	3	0	0	0	0	3	0	0	0	5,423
Medford	1	3	0	0	0	0	0	1	1	2	57,484
Medway	0	1	0	0	0	0	1	0	0	0	13,405
Methuen	0	1	0	0	0	0	0	1	0	0	50,727
Milton	1	0	1	0	0	0	1	1	0	0	27,471
Montague	0	1	0	0	0	0	0	0	0	1	8,298
Natick	1	0	1	0	0	0	1	0	1	0	36,358
Needham	0	1	0	0	0	0	0	1	0	0	31,275
Newburyport	1	0	1	0	0	0	0	2	0	0	18,158
Newton[2]	2	1	2	0	0	1	3	0	0	2	88,658
North Andover	0	1	0	0	0	0	0	1	0	0	31,428
Northampton	1	0	2	0	0	0	0	2	0	1	28,735
Oak Bluffs	2	0	0	0	0	0	1	0	1	0	4,681
Pepperell	0	1	0	0	0	0	0	1	0	0	12,146
Pittsfield	0	0	1	0	0	0	0	0	1	0	42,268
Provincetown	4	0	1	0	0	0	1	2	1	1	2,939
Quincy	3	2	2	0	0	0	2	2	2	1	94,113
Randolph	1	0	0	0	0	0	0	0	0	1	34,385
Revere	1	0	0	0	0	0	0	0	0	1	53,654
Salem[2]	1	3	5	0	0	1	1	4	1	2	43,443
Sharon	0	1	0	0	0	0	0	1	0	0	18,973
Somerville	3	2	0	0	0	0	1	1	1	2	81,668
Spencer	1	1	0	0	0	0	0	0	2	0	11,911
Springfield[2]	7	0	1	1	0	0	1	2	2	3	154,306
Sturbridge	1	0	0	0	0	0	0	1	0	0	9,611
Sunderland[2]	1	1	0	0	0	0	0	0	1	0	3,656
Swampscott	1	1	1	0	0	0	1	0	1	1	15,296
Tewksbury	0	0	1	0	0	0	0	1	0	0	31,424
Tisbury	0	0	1	0	0	0	0	1	0	0	4,116
Waltham	2	0	0	0	0	0	0	1	1	0	62,737
Webster[2]	0	0	1	0	0	1	0	0	1	0	16,925
Wilbraham[2]	1	1	0	0	0	0	0	0	1	0	14,730
Winchester	1	0	2	0	0	0	1	0	0	2	22,850
Winthrop	0	1	0	0	0	0	0	1	0	0	18,692
Worcester	4	2	4	0	0	0	1	5	1	3	184,945
Universities and Colleges	10	13	5	0	0	0					
Boston University	1	0	1	0	0	0	0	0	0	2	41,418
Fitchburg State University	0	0	1	0	0	0	0	0	0	1	11,496
Framingham State University	1	0	0	0	0	0	1		0	0	9,007
Harvard University	2	1	0	0	0	0	0	0	3	0	40,803
Massachusetts College of Liberal Arts	0	1	0	0	0	0	0	1	0	0	2,157
Massasoit Community College	0	1	0	0	0	0	0	1	0	0	10,323
Northeastern University	3	1	0	0	0	0	3	0	0	1	27,795
Salem State University	0	0	1	0	0	0	1	0	0	0	10,556
Smith College	0	1	0	0	0	0	0	0	0	1	3,259
Tufts University, Medford	0	1	1	0	0	0	0	0	1	1	12,492
Westfield State University	1	0	0	0	0	0	0	0	1	0	7,598
Wheaton College	1	6	1	0	0	0	1	0	0	7	1,715
Worcester Polytechnic Institute[2]	1	1	0	0	0	0	0	0	1	0	7,338
Other Agencies	1	0	1	0	0	0					
Massachusetts Bay Transportation Authority											
Middlesex County	0	0	1	0	0	0	1				
Norfolk County	1	0	0	0	0	0	1				
MICHIGAN											
Total	313	51	44	9	15	2					
Cities	208	33	35	9	12	0					
Adrian	2	0	0	0	0	0	0	0	1	1	20,334
Albion	2	0	0	1	0	0	1	1	0	1	8,462

(Number.)

State/agency	Number of incidents per bias motivation						Number of incidents per quarter				
	Race/ Ethnicity/ Ancestry	Religion	Sexual orientation	Disability	Gender	Gender Identity	1st quarter	2nd quarter	3rd quarter	4th quarter	Population[1]
Allen Park	1	0	0	0	0	0	1	0	0	0	26,945
Almont	1	0	0	0	0	0	0	0	0	1	2,814
Ann Arbor	3	0	0	0	0	0	0	0	3	0	122,893
Auburn Hills	1	0	0	0	0	0	0	0	0	1	24,393
Baroda-Lake Township	0	1	0	0	0	0	1	0	0	0	3,859
Bay City	0	1	0	0	0	0	0	1	0	0	32,793
Benton Harbor	0	1	0	0	0	0	0	0	0	1	9,801
Benton Township	1	0	0	0	0	0	0	1	0	0	14,372
Berkley	1	0	0	0	0	0	0	1	0	0	15,482
Bloomfield Township	1	0	0	0	0	0	0	1	0	0	42,326
Bridgeport Township	1	0	0	0	0	0	0	0	0	1	9,778
Buchanan	0	0	0	1	1	0	0	0	1	1	4,274
Burton	5	0	0	0	0	0	0	1	3	1	28,496
Cadillac	3	0	0	0	0	0	0	2	0	1	10,466
Cambridge Township	1	0	0	0	0	0	0	0	0	1	5,657
Canton Township	4	1	0	0	0	0	2	2	0	1	93,406
Capac	1	0	1	0	0	0	0	0	0	2	1,822
Caro	1	0	0	0	0	0	1	0	0	0	3,969
Carrollton Township	0	0	1	0	0	0	1	0	0	0	5,626
Cassopolis	2	0	0	0	1	0	0	0	3	0	1,695
Clinton Township	1	1	0	0	0	0	0	0	1	1	101,308
Coloma Township	1	0	0	0	0	0	0	1	0	0	6,362
Crystal Falls	4	0	0	0	0	0	1	3	0	0	1,359
Dearborn	1	3	0	0	0	0	2	0	1	1	93,902
Dearborn Heights	2	1	0	0	0	0	0	1	2	0	55,368
Detroit	30	1	18	2	1	0	8	16	16	12	663,502
DeWitt Township	1	0	0	0	0	0	1	0	0	0	15,613
East Grand Rapids	2	0	0	0	0	0	0	2	0	0	12,040
East Lansing	0	2	0	0	0	0	0	2	0	0	47,913
Eastpointe	0	0	1	0	0	0	0	0	0	1	32,340
Ecorse	1	0	0	0	0	0	0	1	0	0	9,601
Escanaba	1	0	0	0	0	0	0	1	0	0	12,129
Farmington	0	2	0	0	0	0	1	1	0	0	10,587
Ferndale	1	0	1	0	0	0	0	2	0	0	20,097
Flint	2	0	0	0	0	0	0	2	0	0	95,212
Flushing	1	0	0	0	0	0	0	1	0	0	7,860
Fowlerville	0	0	0	0	3	0	1	1	0	1	2,869
Frankenmuth	2	0	0	0	0	0	0	1	0	1	5,458
Fraser	2	0	0	0	0	0	1	0	0	1	14,578
Fremont	1	0	0	0	0	0	0	1	0	0	4,103
Garden City	2	0	0	0	0	0	0	0	1	1	26,420
Genesee Township	1	0	0	0	0	0	0	0	1	0	20,410
Grand Blanc Township	1	0	0	0	0	0	0	0	0	1	36,523
Grand Haven	1	2	0	0	0	0	0	2	1	0	11,155
Grand Rapids	5	0	0	0	0	0	0	0	2	3	201,799
Grandville	3	0	0	1	0	0	0	0	7	2	16,021
Grosse Pointe Park	1	0	0	0	0	0	0	0	0	1	11,041
Grosse Pointe Woods	1	0	0	0	0	0	1	0	0	0	15,350
Hartford	1	0	0	0	0	0	0	0	0	1	2,589
Hazel Park	0	1	0	0	0	0	0	0	1	0	16,478
Highland Park	11	0	1	0	4	0	1	10	4	1	10,703
Holly	1	0	0	0	0	0	0	1	0	0	6,185
Huron Township	2	0	0	0	0	0	0	0	2	0	16,089
Imlay City	1	0	0	0	0	0	1	0	0	0	3,575
Inkster	1	0	0	0	0	0	1	0	0	0	24,268
Jackson	0	0	1	0	0	0	0	0	1	0	32,503
Jonesville	0	0	0	1	0	0	0	0	1	0	2,204
Kalamazoo	3	0	0	0	0	0	1	0	2	0	76,827
Lansing	4	0	1	0	0	0	1	1	2	1	118,953
Lincoln Park	1	0	0	0	0	0	0	1	0	0	36,336
Lincoln Township	0	1	0	0	0	0	0	0	0	1	14,615
Livonia	2	0	0	0	0	0	0	0	1	1	93,644
Lowell	1	0	0	0	0	0	0	1	0	0	4,198
Madison Heights	2	1	0	0	0	0	0	2	0	1	30,081
Manistee	0	1	0	0	0	0	0	0	0	1	6,103
Marquette	0	3	0	0	0	0	0	0	1	2	20,599
Melvindale	2	0	0	0	0	0	1	0	0	1	10,264

Table 13. Hate Crime Incidents Per Bias Motivation and Quarter, by Selected State and Agency and Federal, 2019—*Continued*

(Number.)

State/agency	Number of incidents per bias motivation						Number of incidents per quarter				Population[1]
	Race/ Ethnicity/ Ancestry	Religion	Sexual orientation	Disability	Gender	Gender Identity	1st quarter	2nd quarter	3rd quarter	4th quarter	
Menominee	1	0	0	0	0	0	0	0	1	0	8,052
Meridian Township	3	0	0	0	0	0	0	0	1	2	43,790
Metro Police Authority of Genesee County	1	0	0	0	0	0	0	1	0	0	19,931
Midland	2	0	0	0	0	0	1	0	0	1	41,791
Milford	1	0	1	0	0	0	0	1	1	0	16,984
Morenci	1	0	0	0	0	0	1	0	0	0	2,146
Mount Pleasant	1	0	1	0	0	0	0	1	1	0	25,315
Muskegon Heights	0	0	1	0	0	0	0	1	0	0	10,717
Muskegon Township	1	0	0	0	0	0	0	0	1	0	17,937
Newaygo	1	0	0	0	0	0	0	0	0	1	2,068
Northville Township	2	0	0	0	0	0	0	0	0	2	29,170
Norton Shores	1	0	0	0	0	0	0	0	1	0	24,702
Ontwa Township-Edwardsburg	1	0	0	0	0	0	0	1	0	0	6,553
Orion Township	1	0	0	0	0	0	0	0	0	1	36,878
Owosso	0	1	0	0	0	0	1	0	0	0	14,399
Pittsfield Township	1	1	0	0	0	0	2	0	0	0	39,417
Pontiac	1	0	0	0	0	0	0	0	1	0	59,791
Port Huron	1	0	0	0	0	0	0	0	1	0	28,783
Portage	1	0	0	0	0	0	0	0	1	0	49,583
Redford Township	1	0	0	0	0	0	0	0	1	0	46,742
Rochester	0	0	1	0	0	0	0	0	0	1	13,429
Romeo	1	0	0	0	0	0	0	0	1	0	3,608
Romulus	1	0	0	0	0	0	0	0	0	1	23,507
Roseville	2	0	1	0	0	0	0	1	2	0	47,381
Royal Oak	1	1	0	0	0	0	1	0	0	1	59,742
Saginaw Township	1	0	0	0	0	0	0	0	1	0	39,022
Saline	2	0	0	0	0	0	1	0	1	0	9,431
Shelby Township	1	0	0	0	0	0	1	0	0	0	80,806
South Haven	2	0	1	0	1	0	1	0	3	0	4,326
Southfield	2	1	1	0	0	0	1	1	0	2	73,335
Southgate	1	0	0	0	0	0	0	1	0	0	28,979
St. Johns	0	0	1	0	0	0	0	1	0	0	7,938
St. Joseph	0	0	1	1	0	0	0	0	1	1	8,355
Sterling Heights	2	0	0	0	0	0	0	0	0	2	133,377
Sylvan Lake	2	0	0	0	0	0	0	2	0	0	1,864
Taylor	1	1	0	0	0	0	0	1	1	0	60,923
Tecumseh	2	0	0	0	0	0	2	0	0	0	8,382
Thomas Township	1	0	0	0	0	0	1	0	0	0	11,438
Three Oaks	0	0	0	1	0	0	0	0	1	0	1,549
Tittabawassee Township	1	0	0	0	0	0	0	1	0	0	9,863
Traverse City	2	1	0	0	0	0	0	0	0	3	15,772
Troy	2	0	0	0	0	0	0	0	1	1	84,688
Utica	0	1	0	0	1	0	0	1	1	0	5,195
Van Buren Township	4	0	0	0	0	0	1	1	1	1	28,294
Warren	5	0	1	0	0	0	1	2	2	1	134,653
Waterford Township	3	1	0	0	0	0	1	0	1	2	73,105
West Bloomfield Township	5	2	0	0	0	0	0	2	2	3	66,067
White Lake Township	1	0	0	0	0	0	0	0	1	0	31,556
Wixom	1	0	0	0	0	0	0	0	1	0	14,074
Wyoming	7	0	0	1	0	0	1	2	3	2	76,295
Ypsilanti	2	0	0	0	0	0	0	0	1	1	21,178
Universities and Colleges	7	1	3	0	0	2					
Eastern Michigan University	0	0	1	0	0	1	1	1	0	0	23,715
Oakland University	0	0	0	0	0	1	0	0	1	0	22,694
University of Michigan											
Ann Arbor	6	1	1	0	0	0	2	1	3	2	47,543
Flint	0	0	1	0	0	0	0	0	1	0	9,138
Washtenaw Community College	1	0	0	0	0	0	0	1	0	0	21,041
Metropolitan Counties	30	5	2	0	1	0					
Bay	1	0	0	0	0	0	0	0	1	0	
Berrien	0	2	0	0	0	0	0	0	0	2	
Calhoun	1	0	0	0	0	0	0	0	0	1	
Eaton	3	0	0	0	0	0	1	2	0	0	
Genesee	3	1	0	0	0	0	0	3	0	1	
Ingham	1	0	0	0	0	0	0	0	1	0	
Ionia	6	0	0	0	0	0	1	1	2	2	
Jackson	0	0	1	0	0	0	0	0	1	0	

(Number.)

State/agency	Number of incidents per bias motivation						Number of incidents per quarter				Population[1]
	Race/ Ethnicity/ Ancestry	Religion	Sexual orientation	Disability	Gender	Gender Identity	1st quarter	2nd quarter	3rd quarter	4th quarter	
Kalamazoo	4	0	0	0	0	0	0	1	2	1	
Kent	1	0	0	0	0	0	0	0	0	1	
Lapeer	1	0	0	0	0	0	0	0	0	1	
Livingston	2	0	0	0	0	0	1	0	1	0	
Ottawa	2	1	1	0	0	0	1	2	0	1	
Saginaw	2	0	0	0	1	0	2	0	0	1	
Washtenaw	3	1	0	0	0	0	2	1	0	1	
Nonmetropolitan Counties	17	3	2	0	1	0					
Alcona	1	0	0	0	0	0	0	1	0	0	
Alpena	1	0	0	0	0	0	1	0	0	0	
Baraga	0	1	0	0	0	0	0	0	1	0	
Barry	1	0	1	0	0	0	1	0	0	1	
Benzie	2	0	0	0	0	0	1	0	1	0	
Hillsdale	1	0	0	0	0	0	0	1	0	0	
Isabella	0	0	1	0	0	0	0	0	0	1	
Leelanau	1	0	0	0	0	0	0	0	1	0	
Luce	1	0	0	0	0	0	0	0	1	0	
Mackinac	1	0	0	0	0	0	0	1	0	0	
Mason	2	0	0	0	0	0	0	2	0	0	
Oceana	0	1	0	0	0	0	0	0	1	0	
Ontonagon	0	0	0	0	1	0	0	0	1	0	
Van Buren	3	1	0	0	0	0	0	0	3	1	
Wexford	3	0	0	0	0	0	0	1	1	1	
State Police Agencies	50	9	2	0	1	0					
State Police											
Alger County	0	1	0	0	0	0	0	0	1	0	
Allegan County	1	0	0	0	0	0	0	0	1	0	
Alpena County	4	1	0	0	0	0	0	2	0	3	
Calhoun County	1	0	0	0	0	0	0	1	0	0	
Cass County	1	0	0	0	0	0	0	1	0	0	
Chippewa County	1	0	0	0	0	0	0	0	0	1	
Grand Traverse County	2	0	0	0	0	0	1	1	0	0	
Gratiot County	1	0	0	0	0	0	0	1	0	0	
Hillsdale County	2	0	0	0	0	0	1	0	1	0	
Houghton County	4	2	0	0	0	0	0	1	3	2	
Ingham County	2	1	0	0	0	0	0	3	0	0	
Ionia County	1	0	0	0	0	0	1	0	0	0	
Iosco County	0	1	0	0	0	0	0	0	0	1	
Jackson County	1	1	0	0	0	0	0	1	1	0	
Kalamazoo County	1	0	0	0	0	0	0	0	1	0	
Kent County	0	1	0	0	0	0	0	0	1	0	
Lapeer County	1	0	0	0	0	0	0	0	1	0	
Livingston County	3	0	0	0	0	0	0	1	1	1	
Mackinac County	1	0	0	0	0	0	1	0	0	0	
Manistee County	1	0	0	0	0	0	0	1	0	0	
Mecosta County	2	0	0	0	0	0	1	0	1	0	
Montcalm County	2	0	0	0	0	0	0	1	1	0	
Muskegon County	1	0	0	0	0	0	0	1	0	0	
Oakland County	3	1	0	0	0	0	0	2	2	0	
Oceana County	2	0	0	0	0	0	1	1	0	0	
Ogemaw County	0	0	1	0	0	0	0	1	0	0	
Ontonagon County	1	0	0	0	0	0	0	0	1	0	
Sanilac County	1	0	0	0	0	0	0	1	0	0	
St. Clair County	1	0	0	0	0	0	0	1	0	0	
St. Joseph County	2	0	0	0	0	0	0	1	0	1	
Washtenaw County	2	0	1	0	1	0	0	2	0	2	
Wayne County	5	0	0	0	0	0	0	1	3	1	
Other Agencies	1	0	0	0	0	0					
Huron-Clinton Metropolitan Authority, Stony Creek Metropark	1	0	0	0	0	0	0	0	1	0	
MINNESOTA											
Total	59	20	17	1	3	4					
Cities	52	17	16	0	1	3					
Alexandria	0	1	0	0	0	0	0	1	0	0	13,914

Table 13. Hate Crime Incidents Per Bias Motivation and Quarter, by Selected State and Agency and Federal, 2019—*Continued*

(Number.)

State/agency	Number of incidents per bias motivation						Number of incidents per quarter				
	Race/ Ethnicity/ Ancestry	Religion	Sexual orientation	Disability	Gender	Gender Identity	1st quarter	2nd quarter	3rd quarter	4th quarter	Population[1]
Coon Rapids	0	0	1	0	0	0	1	0	0	0	62,652
Cottage Grove	1	0	0	0	0	0	1	0			37,534
East Grand Forks	0	0	1	0	0	0	1	0	0	0	8,597
Eden Prairie	2	0	0	0	0	0	0	2			64,777
Edina	0	1	0	0	0	0	1	0			53,076
Fairmont	1	0	0	0	0	0	0	0	0	1	10,023
Faribault	0	1	0	0	0	0	0	1			23,913
Fergus Falls	1	0	0	0	0	0	0	0	0	1	13,900
Hastings	1	0	0	0	0	0	0	1			22,774
Jordan	0	0	1	0	0	0		1			6,384
Mankato	9	1	3	0	0	0	2	0	7	4	42,955
Maple Grove	1	0	0	0	0	0	0	1			73,170
Maplewood	1	0	0	0	0	0	1	0	0	0	41,341
Minneapolis	17	5	6	0	1	3	4	7	16	5	431,016
Minnetonka	1	1	0	0	0	0	1	1			54,497
New Brighton	0	2	0	0	0	0	0	1	0	1	23,058
New Ulm	1	0	0	0	0	0	0	0	1	0	13,205
Plymouth	1	0	0	0	0	0	1	0			80,616
Red Wing	0	0	1	0	0	0	0	1	0	0	16,408
Rochester	3	1	0	0	0	0	1	2	1	0	118,267
Savage	1	0	0	0	0	0	1	0			32,336
St. Louis Park	2	3	0	0	0	0	0	1	3	1	49,535
St. Paul	8	1	2	0	0	0	0	11			310,263
Wabasha	1	0	0	0	0	0	0	0	1	0	2,471
Waseca	0	0	1	0	0	0	0	0	1	0	8,841
Universities and Colleges	0	2	0	0	2	0					
University of Minnesota, Twin Cities	0	2	0	0	2	0	0	1	2	1	64,115
Metropolitan Counties	4	0	1	1	0	1					
Blue Earth	1	0	0	0	0	0	1	0	0	0	
Carver	2	0	0	0	0	0	0	0	1	1	
Olmsted	0	0	1	0	0	0	0	0	1	0	
Ramsey	1	0	0	1	0	1	0	1	0	2	
Nonmetropolitan Counties	2	1	0	0	0	0					
Hubbard	1	0	0	0	0	0	0	1			
Kandiyohi	1	0	0	0	0	0	0	1			
Lac qui Parle	0	1	0	0	0	0	0	0	0	1	
Other Agencies	1	0	0	0	0	0					
Capitol Security, St. Paul	1	0	0	0	0	0	0	1		0	
MISSISSIPPI											
Total	6	1	1	6	0	0					
Cities	2	1	1	6	0	0					
Byram	0	0	0	6	0	0	2	0	2	2	11,672
Hernando	0	1	0	0	0	0	0	1	0	0	16,613
Kosciusko	2	0	0	0	0	0	0	0	2	0	6,774
Ridgeland	0	0	1	0	0	0	0	1	0	0	24,171
Nonmetropolitan Counties	4	0	0	0	0	0					
George	4	0	0	0	0	0	0	2	0	2	
MISSOURI											
Total	52	13	16	1	0	1					
Cities	43	9	10	1	0	1					
Belton	1	0	2	0	0	1	0	1	1	2	23,657
Blue Springs	0	1	1	0	0	0	1	0	0	1	55,415
Boonville	1	0	0	0	0	0	0	1	0	0	8,410
Cape Girardeau	0	0	1	0	0	0	0	0	1	0	40,077
Carthage	0	1	0	0	0	0	0	0	0	1	14,808
Fulton	1	0	0	0	0	0	0	0	1	0	12,620
Gladstone	3	0	0	0	0	0	0	1	0	2	27,553
Grain Valley	2	0	0	0	0	0	1	0	1	0	14,464

(Number.)

State/agency	Number of incidents per bias motivation						Number of incidents per quarter				Population[1]
	Race/ Ethnicity/ Ancestry	Religion	Sexual orientation	Disability	Gender	Gender Identity	1st quarter	2nd quarter	3rd quarter	4th quarter	
Independence	3	0	0	0	0	0	0	1	0	2	116,931
Jefferson City	2	0	0	0	0	0	1	0	0	1	42,793
Kansas City	25	6	2	1	0	0	7	3	13	11	495,964
Lawson	0	0	1	0	0	0	0	0	0	1	2,389
Lee's Summit	1	0	0	0	0	0	0	0	1	0	99,365
Springfield	0	0	1	0	0	0	0	0	1	0	169,235
St. Louis	1	1	2	0	0	0	0	2	1	1	300,521
St. Peters	2	0	0	0	0	0	0	1	1	0	57,697
Sunset Hills	1	0	0	0	0	0	0	0	1	0	8,480
Universities and Colleges	2	1	1	0	0	0					
Missouri University of Science and Technology	0	0	1	0	0	0	0	0	1	0	9,466
Missouri Western State University	0	1	0	0	0	0	1	0	0	0	6,302
University of Missouri, Columbia	2	0	0	0	0	0	1	0	1	0	34,329
Metropolitan Counties	3	3	4	0	0	0					
Greene	1	0	0	0	0	0	0	0	0	1	
Howard	0	0	1	0	0	0	0	0	0	1	
St. Charles County Police Department	2	3	1	0	0	0	0	0	3	3	
St. Louis County Police Department	0	0	2	0	0	0	1	1	0	0	
Nonmetropolitan Counties	3	0	1	0	0	0					
Camden	1	0	1	0	0	0	0	1	1	0	
Henry	1	0	0	0	0	0	0	1	0	0	
Johnson	1	0	0	0	0	0	0	0	0	1	
State Police Agencies	1	0	0	0	0	0					
Missouri State Highway Patrol	1	0	0	0	0	0	0	0	1	0	
MONTANA											
Total	16	9	2	1	1	3					
Cities	9	4	2	1	0	3					
Billings	2	1	1	0	0	0	0	0	3	1	110,198
Bozeman	1	0	0	0	0	0	1	0	0	0	50,152
Great Falls	2	1	0	1	0	0	0	0	0	4	58,637
Helena	1	1	0	0	0	0	1	0	0	1	32,806
Kalispell	0	1	0	0	0	2	2	0	0	1	24,473
Livingston	1	0	0	0	0	0	1	0	0	0	7,884
Missoula	1	0	0	0	0	0	0	1	0	0	75,422
Polson	0	0	1	0	0	0	0	0	1	0	5,075
Whitefish	1	0	0	0	0	1	1	1	0	0	8,079
Universities and Colleges	1	1	0	0	1	0					
Montana State University	1	1	0	0	1	0	2	0	0	1	18,722
Metropolitan Counties	2	1	0	0	0	0					
Cascade	1	1	0	0	0	0	1	0	1	0	
Missoula	1	0	0	0	0	0	1	0	0	0	
Nonmetropolitan Counties	4	3	0	0	0	0					
Big Horn	3	0	0	0	0	0	0	2	0	1	
Flathead	0	1	0	0	0	0	0	0	1	0	
Liberty	0	1	0	0	0	0	0	1	0		
Ravalli	1	1	0	0	0	0	0	0	1	1	
NEBRASKA											
Total	38	3	3	2	0	0					
Cities	24	3	3	1	0	0					
Broken Bow	5	0	0	0	0	0	0	0	1	4	3,532
Crete	1	0	0	0	0	0	0	0	0	1	7,094
Fremont	1	0	0	1	0	0	0	0	0	2	26,523
Gordon	1	0	0	0	0	0	0	0	1	0	1,497
Grand Island	1	0	0	0	0	0	0	0	1	0	51,821
Kearney	1	0	0	0	0	0	1	0	0	0	34,124
Lincoln	5	2	2	0	0	0	4	2	3	0	291,128

(Number.)

State/agency	Number of incidents per bias motivation						Number of incidents per quarter				
	Race/ Ethnicity/ Ancestry	Religion	Sexual orientation	Disability	Gender	Gender Identity	1st quarter	2nd quarter	3rd quarter	4th quarter	Population[1]
McCook	1	0	0	0	0	0	0	0	0	1	7,533
Mitchell	1	0	0	0	0	0	0	1	0	0	1,633
Norfolk	1	0	1	0	0	0	0	1	0	1	24,698
North Platte	3	0	0	0	0	0	0	0	3	0	23,705
Omaha	0	1	0	0	0	0	1	0	0	0	470,481
Schuyler	2	0	0	0	0	0	0	0	0	2	6,396
Valentine	1	0	0	0	0	0	0	0	1	0	2,751
Universities and Colleges	3	0	0	0	0	0					
University of Nebraska, Lincoln	3	0	0	0	0	0	0	1	2	0	28,642
Metropolitan Counties	3	0	0	1	0	0					
Douglas	2	0	0	0	0	0	0	1	1	0	
Howard	1	0	0	0	0	0	0	0	1	0	
Sarpy	0	0	0	1	0	0	0	0	0	1	
Nonmetropolitan Counties	8	0	0	0	0	0					
Custer	4	0	0	0	0	0	0	0	0	4	
Hamilton	1	0	0	0	0	0	0	0	0	1	
Jefferson	1	0	0	0	0	0	0	0	0	1	
Keith	1	0	0	0	0	0	0	0	0	1	
Lincoln	1	0	0	0	0	0	0	0	0	1	
NEVADA											
Total	27	10	4	1	0	2					
Cities	22	10	4	1	0	2					
Henderson	2	2	0	0	0	1	1	2	0	2	317,732
Las Vegas Metropolitan Police Department	11	5	4	1	0	1	4	7	8	3	1,666,803
North Las Vegas	6	2	0	0	0	0	2	2	2	2	249,854
Reno	3	1	0	0	0	0	1	0	3	0	254,349
Other Agencies	5	0	0	0	0	0					
Clark County School District	5	0	0	0	0	0	1		1	3	
NEW HAMPSHIRE											
Total	8	5	3	0	0	0					
Cities	7	5	3	0	0	0					
Auburn	0	1	0	0	0	0	0	1	0	0	5,608
Concord	1	1	0	0	0	0	0	1	0	1	43,509
Conway	0	0	1	0	0	0	0	0	1	0	10,287
Hanover	1	0	0	0	0	0	1	0	0	0	11,531
Henniker	1	0	0	0	0	0	1	0	0	0	5,009
Hooksett	1	0	0	0	0	0	0	0	0	1	14,554
Jaffrey	0	1	0	0	0	0	0	1	0	0	5,278
Keene	1	0	1	0	0	0	1	1	0	0	22,999
Milton	1	0	0	0	0	0	0	0	0	1	4,652
Pelham	0	1	0	0	0	0	0	1	0	0	14,198
Portsmouth	0	0	1	0	0	0	1	0	0	0	21,951
Somersworth	1	0	0	0	0	0	0	1	0	0	11,979
Tilton	0	1	0	0	0	0	0	1	0	0	3,557
Universities and Colleges	1	0	0	0	0	0					
University of New Hampshire	1	0	0	0	0	0	0	0	0	1	16,859
NEW JERSEY											
Total	252	250	65	1	5	8					
Cities	224	228	56	1	5	6					
Aberdeen Township	3	3	0	0	0	0	1	3	0	2	18,700
Barnegat Township	2	0	0	0	0	0	1	0	0	1	23,399
Barrington	0	0	1	0	0	0	0	1	0	0	6,620
Bayonne[2]	2	4	1	0	0	0	0	0	4	0	65,032
Bedminster Township	1	0	0	0	0	0	1	0	0	0	8,043
Berkeley Heights Township[2]	2	1	0	0	0	0	0	0	1	1	13,592
Berkeley Township[2]	2	1	0	0	0	0	1	1	0	0	41,738

Table 13. Hate Crime Incidents Per Bias Motivation and Quarter, by Selected State and Agency and Federal, 2019—*Continued*

(Number.)

State/agency	Number of incidents per bias motivation						Number of incidents per quarter				Population[1]
	Race/ Ethnicity/ Ancestry	Religion	Sexual orientation	Disability	Gender	Gender Identity	1st quarter	2nd quarter	3rd quarter	4th quarter	
Berlin[2]	1	1	0	0	0	0	0	0	1	0	7,510
Blairstown Township	1	1	0	0	0	0	0	0	0	2	5,703
Bogota	0	0	1	0	0	0	1	0	0	0	8,403
Boonton[2]	1	1	0	0	0	0	0	0	1	0	8,157
Bordentown Township	1	0	0	0	0	0	0	0	1	0	12,018
Brick Township	1	1	0	0	0	0	1	1	0	0	75,592
Bridgeton	3	0	1	0	0	0	3	1	0	0	24,331
Bridgewater Township	1	2	1	0	0	0	0	2	0	2	44,610
Brigantine	1	0	1	0	0	0	0	0	0	2	8,684
Burlington Township	1	0	0	0	0	0	0	0	1	0	22,516
Camden County Police Department	3	0	1	0	0	0	3	0	0	1	73,270
Cape May	1	0	0	0	0	0	1	0	0	0	3,428
Carteret[2]	1	1	0	0	0	0	0	0	0	1	23,645
Chatham Township	0	1	0	0	0	0	0	0	0	1	10,219
Cherry Hill Township[2]	2	2	1	0	0	0	1	1	1	1	70,716
Cinnaminson Township	0	2	0	0	0	0	1	0	0	1	16,477
Clifton	3	1	0	0	0	0	0	2	0	2	85,021
Clinton Township	0	1	0	0	0	0	0	0	0	1	12,801
Collingswood[2]	1	1	0	0	0	0	1	0	0	0	13,850
Colts Neck Township	0	1	0	0	0	0	0	1	0	0	9,846
Cranbury Township	1	0	0	0	0	0	0	1	0	0	4,013
Cranford Township[2]	2	1	0	0	0	0	0	1	0	1	24,251
Dover	1	0	0	0	0	0	1	0	0	0	17,852
Dumont	0	3	0	0	0	0	1	0	2	0	17,649
Dunellen	1	0	0	0	0	0	0	0	1	0	7,244
Eastampton Township	1	0	0	0	0	0	0	1	0	0	5,938
East Brunswick Township	1	2	0	0	0	0	1	1	1	0	47,857
East Windsor Township	0	2	0	0	0	0	0	0	1	1	27,343
Edgewater[2]	1	1	0	0	0	0	0	1	0	0	12,821
Edison Township[2]	2	3	0	1	0	0	1	0	2	2	100,282
Egg Harbor Township	1	1	0	0	0	0	0	1	1	0	42,475
Elizabeth[2]	1	1	1	0	0	0	0	1	1	0	128,753
Elmwood Park[2]	1	1	0	0	0	0	0	0	0	1	20,104
Emerson[2]	1	1	0	0	0	0	0	1	0	0	7,640
Englewood[2]	4	2	0	0	0	0	2	1	1	1	28,683
Evesham Township[2]	1	1	1	0	0	0	0	0	1	1	44,999
Ewing Township	1	1	0	0	0	0	1	0	1	0	36,338
Fair Lawn	0	6	0	0	0	0	0	0	2	4	33,064
Fairview	1	0	0	0	0	0	0	0	0	1	14,285
Fanwood[2]	1	1	0	0	0	0	0	0	1	0	7,718
Florham Park	2	0	0	0	0	0	0	0	1	1	11,522
Franklin	0	1	0	0	0	0	0	0	0	1	4,699
Franklin Township, Gloucester County	1	0	0	0	0	0	0	0	0	1	16,264
Freehold Township	1	0	0	0	0	0	1	0	0	0	34,560
Garfield	1	0	0	0	0	0	0	0	0	1	31,888
Glen Rock	0	5	0	0	0	0	0	2	3	0	11,803
Gloucester City	2	0	0	0	0	0	0	1	1	0	11,168
Hackensack[2]	4	3	0	0	0	0	1	0	3	1	44,505
Haddon Heights	0	0	1	0	0	0	0	0	0	1	7,515
Haddon Township	1	0	0	0	0	0	1	0	0	0	14,489
Hamilton Township, Atlantic County	1	1	0	0	0	0	1	1	0	0	25,667
Hamilton Township, Mercer County[2]	3	1	1	0	0	0	0	0	1	3	87,027
Hardyston Township	0	0	1	0	0	0	0	1	0	0	7,760
Harrison	2	0	0	0	0	0	0	1	1	0	18,374
Harrison Township[2]	1	0	1	0	0	0	0	0	1	0	13,125
Hawthorne	1	0	0	0	0	0	0	0	0	1	18,699
Hazlet Township	0	1	0	0	0	1	0	2	0	0	19,739
Highland Park	1	0	1	0	0	0	0	0	0	2	13,791
Hightstown	0	0	1	0	0	0	0	0	0	1	5,264
Hillsborough Township	0	0	1	0	0	0	0	0	1	0	39,813
Hillsdale[2]	4	2	1	0	0	0	2	1	0	2	10,382
Hoboken[2]	3	2	0	0	0	0	1	1	2	0	53,641
Holmdel Township	3	2	0	0	0	0	3	1	1	0	16,648
Hopewell Township	1	0	0	0	0	0	0	0	0	1	17,854
Howell Township[2]	4	6	1	0	0	0	0	3	1	3	52,242
Jackson Township	0	2	0	0	0	0	0	1	1	0	57,380
Jefferson Township[2]	1	3	0	0	0	0	0	1	0	2	20,877

Table 13. Hate Crime Incidents Per Bias Motivation and Quarter, by Selected State and Agency and Federal, 2019—*Continued*

(Number.)

State/agency	Number of incidents per bias motivation						Number of incidents per quarter				
	Race/ Ethnicity/ Ancestry	Religion	Sexual orientation	Disability	Gender	Gender Identity	1st quarter	2nd quarter	3rd quarter	4th quarter	Population[1]
Jersey City[2]	4	4	1	0	1	0	0	3	2	2	266,508
Keansburg	1	1	0	0	0	0	0	0	0	2	9,674
Lacey Township	0	1	0	0	0	0	0	1	0	0	29,247
Lakewood Township	1	24	0	0	0	0	3	15	3	4	105,403
Lawrence Township, Mercer County[2]	3	1	0	0	0	0	0	1	1	1	32,415
Linden	1	0	0	0	0	0	0	0	1	0	42,592
Lindenwold	1	0	0	0	0	0	0	0	0	1	17,197
Livingston Township[2]	2	2	0	0	0	0	1	2	0	0	29,998
Lodi	1	0	0	0	0	0	1	0	0	0	24,488
Long Beach Township	0	1	0	0	0	0	0	0	1	0	3,060
Long Branch[2]	3	2	3	0	0	1	0	2	2	0	30,352
Lower Township	1	0	0	0	0	0	0	0	1	0	21,325
Madison	1	0	0	0	0	0	1	0	0	0	16,533
Mahwah Township	1	0	0	0	0	0	0	0	0	1	26,317
Manalapan Township	1	1	0	0	0	0	1	0	1	0	39,662
Manchester Township[2]	6	1	0	0	0	0	2	2	2	0	43,369
Maple Shade Township	1	0	0	0	0	0	0	1	0	0	18,451
Marlboro Township[2]	1	3	2	0	1	0	1	4	0	0	39,850
Maywood	1	0	0	0	0	0	0	0	1	0	9,667
Medford Township	1	0	0	0	0	0	0	0	0	1	23,393
Mendham	0	1	0	0	0	0	0	0	0	1	4,876
Metuchen[2]	1	1	1	0	0	0	0	0	0	1	14,423
Middlesex Borough	1	0	0	0	0	0	1	0	0	0	13,659
Middle Township	1	0	0	0	0	0	1	0	0	0	18,225
Middletown Township[2]	2	1	1	0	0	0	0	0	1	2	65,361
Midland Park	0	1	0	0	0	0	0	0	0	1	7,246
Millville	2	0	0	0	0	0	0	1	0	1	27,528
Montclair[2]	2	4	0	0	0	0	2	0	0	3	38,625
Montvale	0	1	0	0	0	0	1	0	0	0	8,657
Moorestown Township	0	1	0	0	0	0	0	1	0	0	20,307
Morristown	0	1	0	0	0	0	1	0	0	0	19,153
Morris Township	1	0	0	0	0	0	0	0	1	0	22,080
Mountain Lakes	0	1	0	0	0	0	1	0	0	0	4,269
Mountainside	0	1	0	0	0	0	0	0	0	1	6,888
Mount Holly Township	0	0	1	0	0	0	0	0	0	1	9,568
Mount Laurel Township	1	0	0	0	0	0	1	0	0	0	41,109
Mount Olive Township[2]	2	1	1	0	0	0	0	0	2	0	29,025
Neptune Township	1	4	0	0	0	0	1	0	0	4	27,549
Newark[2]	1	1	0	0	0	0	0	0	0	1	281,422
New Brunswick[2]	0	0	1	0	0	1	0	1	0	0	55,995
New Milford	1	0	0	0	0	0	0	0	1	0	16,506
Newton	1	1	0	0	0	0	0	0	0	2	7,916
North Arlington	0	1	0	0	0	0	1	0	0	0	15,710
North Bergen Township[2]	3	1	1	0	1	0	1	1	1	0	61,447
North Caldwell	0	1	0	0	0	0	1	0	0	0	6,645
Norwood	1	0	0	0	0	0	0	0	0	1	5,816
Oakland	1	1	1	0	0	0	0	0	2	1	12,992
Oceanport	1	0	0	0	0	0	1	0	0	0	5,739
Ocean Township, Monmouth County	0	1	0	0	0	0	1	0	0	0	26,638
Old Bridge Township	0	1	0	0	0	0	0	0	1	0	65,659
Oradell[2]	2	0	1	0	0	0	1	0	0	1	8,181
Paramus[2]	1	2	0	0	0	0	0	2	0	0	26,460
Parsippany-Troy Hills Township[2]	3	1	1	0	0	0	1	2	0	1	51,907
Passaic[2]	2	3	1	0	1	0	0	3	3	0	69,639
Paterson	0	1	0	0	0	0	0	0	0	1	144,866
Pequannock Township	0	1	0	0	0	0	1	0	0	0	15,045
Phillipsburg	2	0	0	0	0	0	0	1	0	0	14,228
Piscataway Township	2	1	1	0	0	0	0	4	0	0	56,783
Pitman	1	0	0	0	0	0	0	0	1	0	8,709
Plainfield	1	0	0	0	0	0	0	0	1	0	50,576
Pleasantville	0	1	1	0	0	0	0	2	0	0	20,388
Plumsted Township	0	1	0	0	0	0	0	0	0	1	8,545
Point Pleasant	1	0	0	0	0	0	0	0	0	1	18,684
Princeton	0	0	1	0	0	0	1	0	0	0	31,610
Rahway[2]	1	1	0	0	0	0	0	0	0	1	30,072
Ramsey[2]	1	1	1	0	0	0	0	2	0	0	14,978
Randolph Township	1	2	0	0	0	0	0	1	0	2	25,490

(Number.)

State/agency	Number of incidents per bias motivation						Number of incidents per quarter				Population[1]
	Race/ Ethnicity/ Ancestry	Religion	Sexual orientation	Disability	Gender	Gender Identity	1st quarter	2nd quarter	3rd quarter	4th quarter	
Raritan Township[2]	1	1	0	0	0	0	0	0	0	1	22,220
Ridgefield Park	1	1	1	0	0	0	0	2	1	0	12,983
Ridgewood[2]	3	6	0	0	0	0	3	1	2	1	25,192
Riverdale	0	1	0	0	0	0	0	0	1	0	4,255
River Edge[2]	1	1	1	0	0	0	0	0	0	1	11,500
Riverside Township	1	0	1	0	0	0	1	1	0	0	7,806
Riverton	1	0	0	0	0	0	0	0	0	1	2,675
Rockaway Township[2]	2	4	0	0	0	0	0	2	0	2	25,756
Roselle	0	0	1	0	0	0	0	0	0	1	21,903
Roselle Park	1	0	0	0	0	0	0	1	0	0	13,630
Roxbury Township	0	3	0	0	0	0	1	0	0	2	22,755
Runnemede[2]	1	2	0	0	0	0	1	1	0	0	8,262
Rutherford	1	0	0	0	0	0	1	0	0	0	18,423
Secaucus[2]	1	1	0	0	0	0	1	0	0	0	21,217
South Brunswick Township[2]	1	1	0	0	0	0	0	0	0	1	46,038
South Orange Village	1	1	0	0	0	0	2	0	0	0	16,740
South Plainfield	1	2	0	0	0	0	0	1	2	0	24,114
South River	1	0	0	0	0	0	0	0	1	0	15,945
Sparta Township[2]	1	1	0	0	0	0	0	0	0	1	18,532
Spotswood	0	1	0	0	0	0	0	0	1	0	8,276
Springfield Township, Union County	0	1	0	0	0	0	0	0	0	1	17,661
Stratford	0	0	1	0	0	0	0	1	0	0	6,926
Summit	0	2	0	0	0	0	0	1	0	1	21,980
Teaneck Township[2]	1	4	0	0	0	0	0	3	0	1	40,533
Tenafly	0	1	0	0	0	0	0	1	0	0	14,586
Tewksbury Township[2]	1	1	0	0	0	0	0	0	1	0	5,765
Tinton Falls	1	1	0	0	0	0	1	1	0	0	17,506
Toms River Township	0	2	0	0	0	0	1	1	0	0	93,836
Trenton[2]	0	1	2	0	0	0	0	0	0	2	83,457
Union City[2]	2	2	0	0	0	0	1	1	0	1	68,459
Union Township	0	2	0	0	0	0	0	2	0	0	58,736
Ventnor City	0	0	1	0	0	0	0	0	0	1	9,966
Verona[2]	1	2	0	0	0	0	1	0	1	0	13,355
Vineland	3	0	0	0	0	1	0	2	1	1	59,860
Voorhees Township	3	5	0	0	0	0	1	0	3	4	29,099
Washington Township, Bergen County	0	0	1	0	0	0	1	0	0	0	9,219
Washington Township, Gloucester County	4	0	0	0	0	0	0	2	1	1	47,126
Wayne Township[2]	3	5	3	0	1	1	0	2	3	2	53,279
Weehawken Township[2]	1	0	2	0	0	0	0	0	0	2	15,115
Westampton Township	1	1	0	0	0	0	0	1	1	0	8,666
West Caldwell Township	1	0	0	0	0	0	0	1	0	0	10,840
Westfield[2]	5	5	0	0	0	0	1	2	1	3	29,688
West Milford Township	1	0	1	0	0	0	0	1	1	0	26,287
Westwood	2	0	0	0	0	0	0	1	0	1	11,129
Wildwood	1	0	0	0	0	0	1	0	0	0	4,959
Willingboro Township[2]	3	1	1	0	0	1	0	0	1	2	31,920
Winslow Township	1	0	0	0	0	0	0	0	0	1	38,390
Woodbridge Township	2	1	0	0	0	0	0	0	2	1	100,125
Woodbury	1	0	0	0	0	0	0	1	0	0	9,768
Woodland Park	1	0	0	0	0	0	0	1	0	0	12,657
Wyckoff Township[2]	1	2	1	0	0	0	0	0	1	1	17,030
Universities and Colleges	13	9	3	0	0	0					
Monmouth University	0	1	0	0	0	0	1	0	0	0	6,936
Montclair State University[2]	1	1	0	0	0	0	1		0	0	24,022
Princeton University[2]	2	2	0	0	0	0	1	0	1	1	8,593
Rutgers University											
Camden[2]	1	1	0	0	0	0	0	1			7,904
Newark	1	1	0	0	0	0	1	0	0	1	15,220
New Brunswick[2]	7	2	3	0	0	0	2	5	1	2	55,698
The College of New Jersey[2]	1	1	0	0	0	0	1	0	0	0	8,630
Metropolitan Counties	4	1	1	0	0	0					
Bergen	1	0	0	0	0	0	0	1	0	0	
Essex[2]	2	1	1	0	0	0	0	2	1	0	
Hudson	1	0	0	0	0	0	0	0	0	1	

Table 13. Hate Crime Incidents Per Bias Motivation and Quarter, by Selected State and Agency and Federal, 2019—Continued

(Number.)

State/agency	Number of incidents per bias motivation						Number of incidents per quarter				
	Race/ Ethnicity/ Ancestry	Religion	Sexual orientation	Disability	Gender	Gender Identity	1st quarter	2nd quarter	3rd quarter	4th quarter	Population[1]
State Police Agencies..	5	4	4	0	0	2					
New Jersey State Police[2]...	5	4	4	0	0	2	1	1	3	4	
Other Agencies..	6	8	1	0	0	0					
New Jersey Transit Police[2]	4	3	0	0	0	0	1	3	1	0	
Park Police											
Morris County..	1	0	0	0	0	0	0	0	0	1	
Union County...	0	1	0	0	0	0	0	0	1	0	
Prosecutor, Cape May County2	1	1	1	0	0	0		1			
State Park Police	0	3	0	0	0	0	1	0	2	0	
NEW MEXICO											
Total	30	8	8	1	0	3					
Cities	28	8	8	1	0	3					
Albuquerque...	25	7	6	1	0	0	7	9	17	6	561,920
Belen...	2	0	0	0	0	0		1	1		7,094
Farmington..	0	1	0	0	0	0		1			44,633
Las Cruces...	1	0	2	0	0	0	0	0	2	1	103,520
Sunland Park..	0	0	0	0	0	3	1	0	1	1	18,103
Metropolitan Counties	2	0	0	0	0	0					
Dona Ana	2	0	0	0	0	0	0	0	1	1	
NEW YORK											
Total	164	357	73	1	0	16					
Cities	125	297	60	1	0	13					
Albany...	5	1	3	0	0	0	4	1	3	1	97,221
Amherst Town..	0	1	0	0	0	0	0	0	1	0	120,864
Bedford Town...	0	1	0	0	0	0	0	0	0	1	17,791
Brighton Town..	2	1	0	0	0	0	0	1	1	1	36,036
Buffalo...	5	0	0	0	0	0	3	1	1	0	255,686
Canandaigua..	0	1	0	0	0	0	0	0	1	0	10,217
Clarkstown Town..	0	2	0	0	0	0	1	0	1	0	80,599
Cobleskill Village..	0	0	1	0	0	0	0	0	1	0	4,329
Colonie Town...	1	0	0	0	0	0	0	1	0	0	79,509
Cortland...	1	1	0	0	0	0	0	0	1	1	18,655
Freeport Village..	1	0	0	0	0	0	0	1	0	0	43,064
Geneva...	0	3	0	0	0	0	0	0	3	0	12,708
Glen Cove...	0	1	0	0	0	0	0	0	0	1	27,228
Greece Town...	0	1	0	0	0	0	0	1			95,777
Hastings-on-Hudson Village	0	1	0	0	0	0	0	1	0	0	7,916
Lloyd Harbor Village...	0	1	0	0	0	0	0	0	1	0	3,667
Middletown..	1	0	0	0	0	0	0	1	0	0	27,801
Mount Vernon..	1	1	0	0	0	0	1	1	0	0	67,619
New Castle Town..	1	0	0	0	0	0	0	1	0	0	17,896
New York...	90	266	53	1	0	13	115	97	94	117	8,379,043
Newburgh...	1	0	1	0	0	0	0	1	1	0	28,070
Pelham Village..	0	1	0	0	0	0	0	0	1	0	6,911
Port Washington...	0	1	0	0	0	0	0	0	1	0	19,396
Poughkeepsie..	2	0	0	0	0	0	0	2	0	0	30,422
Poughkeepsie Town...	1	0	0	0	0	0	0	0	1	0	38,889
Ramapo Town...	0	2	0	0	0	0	0	0	1	1	94,633
Rochester..	3	1	1	0	0	0	2	1	1	1	205,769
Rockville Centre Village..	0	1	0	0	0	0	0	0	0	1	24,669
Scarsdale Village...	0	2	0	0	0	0	0	0	2	0	17,954
Southampton Town...	0	3	0	0	0	0	1	0	0	2	51,090
Syracuse...	0	1	0	0	0	0	1	0	0	0	142,438
Tonawanda...	1	0	0	0	0	0	0	1	0	0	14,754
Utica...	2	1	0	0	0	0	1	1	1	0	59,842
White Plains..	2	0	0	0	0	0	2	0	0		58,259
Yonkers...	4	2	1	0	0	0	3	2	0	2	200,075
Yorktown Town...	1	0	0	0	0	0	1	0	0	0	36,426
Universities and Colleges	6	0	0	0	0	0					
State University of New York Police											

Table 13. Hate Crime Incidents Per Bias Motivation and Quarter, by Selected State and Agency and Federal, 2019—*Continued*

(Number.)

State/agency	Race/Ethnicity/Ancestry	Religion	Sexual orientation	Disability	Gender	Gender Identity	1st quarter	2nd quarter	3rd quarter	4th quarter	Population[1]
Buffalo	1	0	0	0	0	0	0	0	0	1	34,183
New Paltz	1	0	0	0	0	0	0	0	1	0	9,669
Plattsburgh	2	0	0	0	0	0	0	0	1	1	6,558
Stony Brook	2	0	0	0	0	0	1	1	0	0	30,012
Metropolitan Counties	14	27	8	0	0	1					
Dutchess	1	0	4	0	0	0	3	0	1	1	
Madison	0	0	0	0	0	1	0	0	1	0	
Nassau	6	22	1	0	0	0	4	11	8	6	
Suffolk County Police Department	7	4	3	0	0	0	3	6	4	1	
Westchester Public Safety	0	1	0	0	0	0	0	0	0	1	
State Police Agencies	9	18	3	0	0	2					
State Police											
Albany County	0	2	0	0	0	0	0	0	0	2	
Cattaraugus County	1	0	0	0	0	0	0	0	1	0	
Clinton County	0	1	0	0	0	0	0	1	0	0	
Dutchess County	1	0	0	0	0	1	1	0	0	1	
Livingston County	0	1	0	0	0	0	0	0	1	0	
Montgomery County	0	1	0	0	0	0	0	0	1	0	
Niagara County	1	0	0	0	0	0	0	1	0	0	
Onondaga County	0	0	1	0	0	0	0	0	1	0	
Ontario County	1	0	0	0	0	0	1	0	0	0	
Orange County	1	6	0	0	0	0	1	5	1		
Oswego County	0	1	0	0	0	0	0	0	1	0	
Schenectady County	1	0	0	0	0	0	0	1	0	0	
St. Lawrence County	2	0	0	0	0	0	0	0	1	1	
Sullivan County	0	3	0	0	0	0	1	0	2	0	
Tioga County	1	0	0	0	0	0	0	1	0	0	
Ulster County	0	2	0	0	0	1	1	0	1	1	
Wayne County	0	0	1	0	0	0	0	0	1	0	
Westchester County	0	1	1	0	0	0	1	0	1		
Other Agencies	10	15	2	0	0	0					
New York City Department of Environmental Protection Police, Eastview Precinct	1	0	0	0	0	0	1	0	0	0	
New York City Metropolitan Transportation Authority	9	15	2	0	0	0	5	10	7	4	
NORTH CAROLINA											
Total	132	42	30	7	0	0					
Cities	84	31	22	1	0	0					
Aberdeen	0	1	0	0	0	0	0	0	0	1	7,892
Apex	1	0	0	0	0	0	1	0	0	0	56,276
Asheville	3	3	1	0	0	0	2	2	1	2	93,641
Beaufort	3	0	0	0	0	0	1	2	0	0	4,417
Biltmore Forest	0	1	0	0	0	0	1	0	0	0	1,410
Burlington	0	0	1	0	0	0	0	0	1	0	54,108
Canton	1	0	0	0	0	0	1	0	0	0	4,349
Cary	1	0	0	0	0	0	0	0	0	1	172,525
Chapel Hill	1	0	1	0	0	0	0	1	1	0	61,457
Charlotte-Mecklenburg	10	7	1	0	0	0	2	3	4	9	944,260
Clayton	2	0	0	0	0	0	1	0	1	0	23,842
Cleveland	0	1	0	0	0	0	0	0	0	1	882
Dallas	1	0	0	0	0	0	0	0	1	0	4,787
Dunn	0	1	0	0	0	0	0	1	0	0	9,768
Durham	3	0	0	0	0	0	0	2	1	0	280,282
Elon	1	2	0	0	0	0	1	0	1	1	12,214
Fayetteville	8	1	2	0	0	0	1	3	5	2	209,614
Greensboro	8	1	0	1	0	0	0	4	4	2	298,025
Greenville	3	0	2	0	0	0	1	1	0	3	94,193
Hickory	1	0	2	0	0	0	0	1	2	0	41,040
High Point	2	0	0	0	0	0	1	1	0	0	113,307
Hope Mills	1	0	0	0	0	0	0	1	0	0	15,878
Jacksonville	2	0	0	0	0	0	1	1			72,300
Kernersville	0	0	1	0	0	0	0	0	0	1	24,980

Table 13. Hate Crime Incidents Per Bias Motivation and Quarter, by Selected State and Agency and Federal, 2019—*Continued*

(Number.)

State/agency	Number of incidents per bias motivation						Number of incidents per quarter				Population[1]
	Race/ Ethnicity/ Ancestry	Religion	Sexual orientation	Disability	Gender	Gender Identity	1st quarter	2nd quarter	3rd quarter	4th quarter	
Knightdale	1	0	0	0	0	0	0	1	0	0	18,351
Leland	4	0	0	0	0	0		3	1	0	23,360
Lenoir	1	0	0	0	0	0	0	0	1	0	17,904
Marion	1	0	0	0	0	0	0	0	0	1	7,837
Matthews[2]	0	2	2	0	0	0	0	1	1	1	33,372
Mebane	3	0	0	0	0	0	0	1	0	2	16,203
Mooresville	1	0	0	0	0	0	0	1	0	0	38,967
Morganton	0	1	0	0	0	0	0	1	0	0	16,524
New Bern	0	0	1	0	0	0	0	0	0	1	30,187
Newton	1	0	0	0	0	0	0	0	0	1	13,153
Pineville	0	0	1	0	0	0	1	0	0	0	9,088
Raleigh	7	2	5	0	0	0	4	3	3	4	477,828
Red Springs	0	2	0	0	0	0	0	0	0	2	3,341
Salisbury	1	0	0	0	0	0	1	0	0	0	33,877
Troutman	1	0	0	0	0	0	0	0	0	1	2,755
Wake Forest	2	0	0	0	0	0	0	0	1	1	46,145
Washington	1	0	0	0	0	0	0	0	0	1	9,497
Wilmington	7	6	2	0	0	0	2	3	7	3	124,750
Wilson	1	0	0	0	0	0	1	0	0	0	49,344
Universities and Colleges	1	0	2	0	0	0					
North Carolina State University, Raleigh	0	0	1	0	0	0	1	0	0	0	39,136
University of North Carolina											
Chapel Hill	1	0	0	0	0	0	1	0	0	0	32,180
Greensboro	0	0	1	0	0	0			0	1	22,419
Metropolitan Counties	32	4	6	5	0	0					
Alamance	4	0	0	0	0	0	1	0	1	2	
Buncombe	1	1	2	0	0	0	0	2	1	1	
Burke	3	0	0	0	0	0	1	0	1	1	
Cabarrus	0	1	0	0	0	0	1	0	0	0	
Caldwell	1	0	0	1	0	0	1	0	0	1	
Craven	2	0	1	0	0	0	1	1	0	1	
Cumberland	1	0	1	0	0	0	1	1	0	0	
Currituck	2	0	1	0	0	0	1	1	0	1	
Durham	0	0	1	0	0	0	0	1			
Forsyth	1	0	0	0	0	0			1	0	
Franklin	2	0	0	0	0	0	0	1	1	0	
Granville	1	1	0	0	0	0	1	0	0	1	
New Hanover	1	0	0	0	0	0	0	1	0	0	
Onslow	2	0	0	3	0	0	3	1	0	1	
Pamlico	1	0	0	0	0	0	1	0	0	0	
Person	2	0	0	0	0	0	0	0	0	2	
Pitt	5	0	0	0	0	0	1	3	1	0	
Union	2	1	0	1	0	0	2	1	1	0	
Wake	1	0	0	0	0	0	0	0	0	1	
Nonmetropolitan Counties	12	7	0	1	0	0					
Ashe	0	1	0	0	0	0	0	1	0	0	
Avery	0	2	0	0	0	0	0	1	1	0	
Bertie	0	1	0	0	0	0	1	0			
Carteret	1	0	0	0	0	0	0	1	0	0	
Caswell	4	0	0	0	0	0	0	2	2	0	
Dare	1	0	0	0	0	0	1	0	0	0	
Duplin	0	1	0	0	0	0	0	1			
Jackson	2	0	0	0	0	0	0	1	1		
Macon	1	1	0	0	0	0	1	0	0	1	
McDowell	0	0	0	1	0	0	0	0	0	1	
Moore	1	0	0	0	0	0	0	0	0	1	
Robeson	2	0	0	0	0	0	0	0	1	1	
Watauga	0	1	0	0	0	0	0	0	1	0	
Other Agencies	3	0	0	0	0	0					
State Capitol Police	1	0	0	0	0	0	1	0	0	0	
WakeMed Campus Police	2	0	0	0	0	0	1	1	0	0	
NORTH DAKOTA											
Total	14	1	3	0	0	0					

Table 13. Hate Crime Incidents Per Bias Motivation and Quarter, by Selected State and Agency and Federal, 2019—*Continued*

(Number.)

State/agency	Number of incidents per bias motivation						Number of incidents per quarter				
	Race/ Ethnicity/ Ancestry	Religion	Sexual orientation	Disability	Gender	Gender Identity	1st quarter	2nd quarter	3rd quarter	4th quarter	Population[1]
Cities	7	1	2	0	0	0					
Bowman..	0	0	1	0	0	0	0	0	0	1	1,604
Fargo..	1	1	0	0	0	0	0	0	1	1	127,423
Grand Forks..	1	0	0	0	0	0	0	0	1	0	57,459
Mandan..	2	0	0	0	0	0	1	1	0	0	23,012
Valley City..	1	0	0	0	0	0	0	0	1	0	6,351
Williston...	2	0	1	0	0	0	0	2	0	1	28,966
Universities and Colleges	1	0	0	0	0	0					
University of North Dakota......................	1	0	0	0	0	0	0	1	0	0	17,646
Metropolitan Counties	4	0	0	0	0	0					
Burleigh..	1	0	0	0	0	0	0	0	1	0	
Grand Forks..	3	0	0	0	0	0	1	1	1	0	
Nonmetropolitan Counties.....................	2	0	1	0	0	0					
McLean...	1	0	0	0	0	0	0	1	0	0	
Mountrail..	1	0	0	0	0	0	0	0	1	0	
Sargent...	0	0	1	0	0	0	0	0	1	0	
OHIO											
Total	216	30	60	55	7	23					
Cities	189	23	52	46	7	18					
Akron..	1	0	0	2	0	0	2	0	1	0	197,882
Alliance...	1	0	0	0	0	0	1	0	0	0	21,536
Archbold...	0	0	1	0	0	0	0	0	1	0	4,320
Ashland...	0	0	1	0	0	0	0	0	0	1	20,410
Barberton	1	0	0	2	0	0	1	0	2	0	26,015
Bath Township, Summit County................	0	0	0	2	0	0	0	2	0	0	9,659
Bay Village..	0	0	0	1	0	0	0	0	1	0	15,235
Beachwood..	1	0	0	0	0	0	1	0	0	0	11,612
Bexley...	0	1	0	0	0	0	0	0	1	0	13,956
Blanchester...	1	0	0	0	0	0	1	0	0	0	4,251
Blue Ash..	1	0	0	0	0	0	0	0	0	1	12,307
Butler Township.....................................	0	0	0	1	0	0	1	0	0	0	7,819
Chillicothe...	8	0	0	0	0	0	1	2	3	2	21,670
Cincinnati..	24	1	4	3	0	0	6	9	10	7	303,335
Circleville..	3	0	0	0	0	0	2	1	0	0	14,025
Cleveland..	20	7	7	4	4	3	5	2	10	28	381,829
Colerain Township..................................	2	0	0	0	0	0	0	0	2	0	59,479
Columbiana...	0	0	1	0	0	0	0	1	0	0	6,209
Columbus..	35	6	12	5	0	8	11	12	26	17	906,120
Copley Township	0	0	1	1	0	0	0	1	1	0	17,309
Dayton..	6	0	1	0	0	0	3	2	1	1	140,427
Defiance..	1	0	0	0	0	3	0	1	1	2	16,601
Delaware...	1	0	1	0	0	0	1	0	1	0	40,616
Delhi Township......................................	1	0	0	0	0	0	1	0	0	0	29,811
East Liverpool..	1	0	0	0	0	0	0	1	0	0	10,653
Eaton..	0	0	0	0	1	0	0	0	1	0	8,136
Elyria..	3	0	1	0	0	0	0	0	2	2	53,806
Englewood...	0	0	0	1	0	0	0	0	1	0	13,478
Fairfax...	1	0	0	0	0	0	0	0	0	1	1,710
Franklin...	1	0	0	0	0	0	1	0	0	0	11,675
Gahanna..	3	0	0	0	0	0	1	1	1	0	35,847
Germantown..	1	0	0	0	0	0	1	0	0	0	5,500
Grafton..	0	0	0	0	1	0	0	1	0	0	5,808
Grandview Heights..................................	0	1	0	0	0	0	0	0	1	0	8,581
Green Township......................................	4	0	0	0	0	0	2	1	0	1	59,273
Greenville..	1	0	0	0	0	0	0	1	0	0	12,629
Grove City...	0	0	1	0	0	0	1	0	0	0	42,423
Hamilton..	3	0	0	0	0	1	2	0	2	0	62,155
Heath..	1	0	2	0	0	0	0	1	0	2	10,933
Hilliard..	3	0	0	0	0	0	3	0	0	0	37,578
Huber Heights..	2	1	0	2	0	0	0	1	3	1	38,183
Hudson..	1	0	0	1	0	0	1	1	0	0	22,286
Jackson Township, Stark County...............	2	0	0	0	0	0	0	1	1	0	40,347
Lancaster...	1	0	0	0	0	0	1	0	0	0	40,622

Table 13. Hate Crime Incidents Per Bias Motivation and Quarter, by Selected State and Agency and Federal, 2019—*Continued*

(Number.)

State/agency	Number of incidents per bias motivation						Number of incidents per quarter				Population[1]
	Race/ Ethnicity/ Ancestry	Religion	Sexual orientation	Disability	Gender	Gender Identity	1st quarter	2nd quarter	3rd quarter	4th quarter	
Lebanon	0	0	0	0	0	1	1	0	0	0	20,806
Lithopolis	0	0	1	0	0	0	0	0	1	0	1,777
Lockland	1	0	0	0	0	0	0	0	0	1	3,455
Logan	0	1	0	0	0	0	0	0	0	1	7,039
Lorain	1	0	0	0	0	0	0	0	1	0	64,022
Louisville	0	0	0	1	0	0	0	1	0	0	9,329
Lyndhurst	0	0	0	1	0	0	0	1	0	0	13,407
Madison Township, Franklin County	0	0	0	3	0	0	1	2	0	0	19,682
Madison Township, Lake County	1	0	0	0	0	0	0	1	0	0	15,646
Mansfield	2	0	1	0	0	0	0	1	1	1	46,418
Mason	1	0	0	0	0	0	0	1	0	0	33,939
Maumee	1	0	0	0	0	0	0	1	0	0	13,656
Mayfield Heights	0	0	1	0	0	0	0	0	0	1	18,519
Mentor-on-the-Lake	1	0	0	1	0	0	1	0	1	0	7,400
Miami Township, Montgomery County	0	0	1	0	0	0	0	0	1	0	29,188
Miamisburg	2	0	0	0	0	0	0	0	1	1	19,913
Middletown	7	1	3	3	0	0	3	3	6	2	48,878
Moraine	2	0	0	0	0	0	1	1	0	0	6,455
Mount Vernon	1	0	0	0	0	0	0	0	1	0	16,663
Napoleon	2	0	0	0	0	0	1	0	1	0	8,188
Nelsonville	1	0	0	0	0	0	0	1	0	0	5,158
New Albany	0	1	0	0	0	0	0	0	1	0	11,332
New Boston	1	0	0	0	0	0	1	0	0	0	2,093
New Franklin	0	0	0	1	0	0	0	0	1	0	14,162
New Knoxville	1	0	0	0	0	0	0	1	0	0	863
New Philadelphia	2	0	0	0	0	0	2	0	0	0	17,434
North Baltimore	1	0	0	0	0	0	0	1	0	0	3,557
North Canton	1	1	0	0	0	0	0	2	0	0	17,251
Norton	0	0	1	0	0	0	0	1	0	0	12,007
Norwood	0	0	0	0	0	1	0	1	0		19,922
Orrville	1	0	0	0	0	0	0	0	1	0	8,461
Portsmouth	0	0	2	0	0	0	1	1			20,353
Reading	1	0	0	0	0	0	1	0	0	0	10,995
Riverside	0	0	0	1	0	0	0	0	1	0	25,148
Rocky River	0	0	0	1	0	0	1	0	0	0	20,105
Salem	0	0	0	2	0	0	1	0	1	0	11,644
Shawnee Township	1	0	0	0	0	0	0	0	1	0	12,056
Shelby	0	0	0	1	0	0	1	0	0	0	8,997
Springfield Township, Hamilton County	2	0	0	0	0	0	0	0	2	0	36,696
Streetsboro	0	0	0	1	0	0	0	0	0	1	16,561
Toledo	2	0	2	0	0	0	2	1	0	1	273,505
Trotwood	2	0	0	0	0	1	0	0	2	1	24,435
Upper Arlington	1	1	0	0	0	0	1	1	0	0	35,754
Urbana	1	0	0	1	0	0	0	1	1	0	11,309
Van Wert	1	0	0	0	0	0	0	1	0	0	10,662
Wadsworth	0	0	2	0	0	0	1	0	1	0	24,058
Wapakoneta	1	0	0	0	0	0	0	0	1	0	9,717
Warren	1	0	0	0	0	0	0	0	1	0	38,012
Waverly	0	1	0	0	0	0	0	0	0	1	4,253
Weathersfield	0	0	0	1	0	0	0	1	0	0	8,017
West Carrollton	1	0	0	0	0	0	0	0	0	1	12,886
Whitehall	1	0	0	0	0	0	0	0	0	1	19,121
Wilmington	3	0	0	0	0	0	2	0	0	1	12,391
Wooster	1	0	0	2	0	0	0	1	1	1	26,615
Worthington	1	0	0	0	1	0	1	1	0	0	14,875
Youngstown	1	0	1	0	0	0	0	2	0	0	64,722
Zanesville	3	0	4	1	0	0	0	2	3	3	25,346
Universities and Colleges	2	1	1	0	0	0					
Ohio State University, Columbus	2	1	0	0	0	0	0	0	0	3	64,924
Otterbein University	0	0	1	0	0	0	1	0	0	0	3,258
Metropolitan Counties	13	1	2	0	0	2					
Clermont	0	1	0	0	0	0	0	0	1	0	
Cuyahoga	1	0	0	0	0	0	1	0	0		
Franklin	1	0	0	0	0	0	1	0	0	0	
Geauga	1	0	0	0	0	0	0	0	1	0	

Table 13. Hate Crime Incidents Per Bias Motivation and Quarter, by Selected State and Agency and Federal, 2019—Continued

(Number.)

State/agency	Number of incidents per bias motivation						Number of incidents per quarter				Population[1]
	Race/Ethnicity/Ancestry	Religion	Sexual orientation	Disability	Gender	Gender Identity	1st quarter	2nd quarter	3rd quarter	4th quarter	
Lawrence	0	0	1	0	0	0	0	1	0	0	
Lorain	0	0	0	0	0	1	0	0	1	0	
Lucas	3	0	0	0	0	0	0	0	1	2	
Medina	1	0	0	0	0	0	0	0	0	1	
Miami	1	0	0	0	0	0	0	1	0	0	
Montgomery	3	0	0	0	0	1	2	1	1	0	
Summit	1	0	1	0	0	0	1	0	1	0	
Union	1	0	0	0	0	0	0	1	0	0	
Nonmetropolitan Counties	11	5	3	8	0	1					
Champaign	1	0	0	2	0	0	1	0	0	2	
Columbiana	0	0	0	4	0	0	0	3	1	0	
Coshocton	1	1	0	0	0	0	0	1	0	1	
Defiance	0	0	1	0	0	0	0	0	1	0	
Hancock	0	1	0	0	0	0	0	0	0	1	
Hardin	0	1	0	1	0	0	2	0	0	0	
Highland	0	0	1	0	0	0	0	0	1	0	
Knox	2	1	0	0	0	0	1	0	1	1	
Logan	0	0	1	0	0	0	0	1	0	0	
Morgan	1	0	0	0	0	0	1	0	0	0	
Ross	2	0	0	0	0	0	1	0	1	0	
Tuscarawas	1	1	0	0	0	1	0	0	2	1	
Vinton	1	0	0	0	0	0	1	0	0	0	
Washington	0	0	0	1	0	0	0	0	0	1	
Wayne	2	0	0	0	0	0	0	0	2	0	
State Police Agencies	0	0	0	1	0	0					
Ohio State Highway Patrol	0	0	0	1	0	0	0	1	0	0	
Other Agencies	1	0	2	0	0	2					
Cleveland Metropolitan Park District	1	0	0	0	0	1	0	2	0	0	
Greater Cleveland Regional Transit Authority	0	0	0	0	0	1	0	1	0	0	
Ohio Department of Natural Resources	0	0	2	0	0	0	0	1	1	0	
OKLAHOMA											
Total	14	5	8	1	0	0					
Cities	10	3	5	0	0	0					
Chickasha	0	0	1	0	0	0	1	0	0	0	16,395
Collinsville	0	0	1	0	0	0	0	0	0	1	7,271
Cushing	1	0	0	0	0	0	0	1	0	0	7,639
McAlester	0	1	0	0	0	0	0	0	1	0	17,840
Noble	0	1	0	0	0	0	1	0	0	0	6,922
Norman	1	1	0	0	0	0	1	0	1	0	125,076
Oklahoma City	3	0	0	0	0	0	2	0	1	0	657,890
Pawnee	1	0	0	0	0	0	1	0	0	0	2,107
Sallisaw	1	0	0	0	0	0	0	0	1	0	8,391
Sulphur	0	0	1	0	0	0	1	0	0	0	5,028
Tulsa	1	0	2	0	0	0	1	0	2	0	401,700
West Siloam Springs	1	0	0	0	0	0	0	0	1	0	870
Wewoka	1	0	0	0	0	0	1	0	0	0	3,252
Universities and Colleges	0	0	1	0	0	0					
Northeastern Oklahoma A&M College	0	0	1	0	0	0	0	0	0	1	2,663
Metropolitan Counties	2	1	1	0	0	0					
Creek	0	1	0	0	0	0	0	0	1	0	
Logan	2	0	0	0	0	0	0	1	1	0	
Wagoner	0	0	1	0	0	0	0	0	0	1	
Nonmetropolitan Counties	2	1	1	1	0	0					
Craig	0	0	0	1	0	0	0	0	1	0	
Garvin	1	0	0	0	0	0	0	1	0	0	
Major	0	1	0	0	0	0	0	1	0	0	
Roger Mills	1	0	0	0	0	0	0	0	0	1	
Washita	0	0	1	0	0	0	0	1	0	0	

Table 13. Hate Crime Incidents Per Bias Motivation and Quarter, by Selected State and Agency and Federal, 2019—*Continued*

(Number.)

State/agency	Number of incidents per bias motivation						Number of incidents per quarter				
	Race/ Ethnicity/ Ancestry	Religion	Sexual orientation	Disability	Gender	Gender Identity	1st quarter	2nd quarter	3rd quarter	4th quarter	Population[1]
OREGON											
Total	116	29	27	2	2	6					
Cities	96	24	22	2	2	6					
Astoria..............................	1	0	0	0	0	0	0	0	1	0	10,040
Baker City..........................	1	0	0	0	0	0	1	0	0	0	9,750
Beaverton[2]........................	1	1	1	0	0	0	1	0	0	1	100,130
Bend..................................	4	4	0	0	0	0	2	2	3	1	100,588
Canby................................	1	0	1	0	0	0	0	0	1	1	17,962
Central Point......................	1	1	0	0	0	0	1	0	0	1	18,753
Coos Bay............................	3	0	0	0	0	0	2	0	0	1	16,471
Corvallis.............................	1	0	0	0	0	0	0	1	0	0	59,196
Cottage Grove....................	0	0	1	0	0	0	0	0	1	0	10,437
Eugene...............................	28	10	2	0	1	1	4	13	13	12	173,183
Forest Grove.......................	1	0	1	0	0	0	0	0	1	1	25,063
Gladstone...........................	2	0	1	0	0	0	0	1	1	1	12,340
Gresham.............................	1	0	0	0	0	0	0	0	1	0	110,692
Hermiston...........................	1	1	0	0	0	0	0	1	0	1	17,780
Hillsboro[2].........................	5	0	5	0	0	1	3	2	2	2	110,549
Hood River..........................	1	0	0	0	0	0	1	0	0	0	7,876
Klamath Falls......................	1	0	0	0	0	0	0	0	1	0	22,447
La Grande..........................	0	0	1	0	0	0	1	0	0	0	13,294
Lake Oswego......................	1	0	0	0	0	0	0	1	0	0	39,888
Madras...............................	1	0	0	0	0	0	0	0	0	1	7,028
McMinnville........................	1	0	0	0	0	0	0	0	0	1	34,935
Medford.............................	1	0	0	0	0	0	1	0	0	0	83,316
Milwaukie...........................	0	0	1	0	0	0	0	1	0	0	21,075
Myrtle Creek.......................	0	1	0	0	0	0	0	0	0	1	3,508
North Bend.........................	1	1	1	1	0	0	1	1	1	1	9,775
Ontario..............................	1	0	0	0	0	0	0	0	0	1	11,044
Oregon City........................	3	0	0	0	0	0	2	0	1	0	37,723
Portland[2]..........................	23	4	5	0	1	3	6	6	10	11	662,114
Redmond............................	1	0	0	0	0	0	0	0	0	1	31,558
Salem.................................	1	0	0	1	0	1	0	0	0	3	175,867
Sherwood...........................	1	0	0	0	0	0	0	0	0	1	19,865
Springfield..........................	1	0	0	0	0	0	1	0	0	0	63,438
St. Helens...........................	1	0	0	0	0	0	0	0	1	0	13,900
Tigard.................................	3	1	2	0	0	0	1	3	0	2	55,621
Tualatin..............................	2	0	0	0	0	0	0	0	1	1	27,788
West Linn...........................	1	0	0	0	0	0	0	1	0	0	26,962
Universities and Colleges	1	2	0	0	0	0					
Portland State University	1	0	0	0	0	0	0	1	0		35,257
University of Oregon..................	0	2	0	0	0	0	2	0			25,640
Metropolitan Counties	12	2	2	0	0	0					
Clackamas[2]........................	9	2	1	0	0	0	2	5	2	2	
Jackson..............................	1	0	0	0	0	0	0	0	1	0	
Washington........................	2	0	1	0	0	0	0	0	2	1	
Nonmetropolitan Counties........	7	1	2	0	0	0					
Coos..................................	6	0	1	0	0	0	4	2	0	1	
Jefferson............................	1	0	0	0	0	0	0	0	0	1	
Lincoln...............................	0	1	0	0	0	0	0	0	1	0	
Umatilla.............................	0	0	1	0	0	0	1	0	0	0	
State Police Agencies	0	0	1	0	0	0					
State Police, Marion County............	0	0	1	0	0	0	1	0	0	0	
PENNSYLVANIA											
Total	28	9	4	0	0	0					
Cities	22	8	4	0	0	0					
East Pennsboro Township	0	1	0	0	0	0	0	1	0		21,549
Forest City	1	0	0	0	0	0		0	1	0	1,741
Hampden Township..................	1	0	0	0	0	0	0	1	0		30,861
Johnstown.............................	2	0	0	0	0	0		0	2	0	20,663

Table 13. Hate Crime Incidents Per Bias Motivation and Quarter, by Selected State and Agency and Federal, 2019—Continued

(Number.)

State/agency	Number of incidents per bias motivation						Number of incidents per quarter				
	Race/ Ethnicity/ Ancestry	Religion	Sexual orientation	Disability	Gender	Gender Identity	1st quarter	2nd quarter	3rd quarter	4th quarter	Population[1]
Kenhorst	2	0	0	0	0	0		0	0	2	2,888
Philadelphia	7	4	1	0	0	0	1	7	2	2	1,589,014
Pittsburgh	5	2	3	0	0	0	0	3	5	2	300,548
Reading	3	0	0	0	0	0		0	3		88,549
Rush Township	1	0	0	0	0	0	0	1			3,254
Westtown-East Goshen Regional	0	1	0	0	0	0		0	1	0	32,366
Universities and Colleges	4	0	0	0	0	0					
Pennsylvania State University, University Park	2	0	0	0	0	0	0	0	2		50,426
Shippensburg University	2	0	0	0	0	0		0	2	0	7,345
State Police Agencies	2	1	0	0	0	0					
Bradford County	0	1	0	0	0	0		0	1	0	
Chester County	1	0	0	0	0	0		0	1		
Venango County	1	0	0	0	0	0		0	1	0	
RHODE ISLAND											
Total	4	5	8	0	0	0					
Cities	4	5	4	0	0	0					
Barrington	1	0	0	0	0	0	0	1	0	0	16,090
Central Falls	0	0	1	0	0	0	0	0	1	0	19,423
Cranston	0	1	0	0	0	0	0	0	0	1	81,471
Cumberland	1	0	0	0	0	0	0	0	1	0	35,206
East Greenwich	0	1	0	0	0	0	0	1	0	0	13,119
East Providence	0	1	0	0	0	0	0	1	0	0	47,590
Johnston	1	0	0	0	0	0	0	0	1	0	29,424
Pawtucket	0	0	2	0	0	0	1	1	0	0	72,030
Providence	1	2	1	0	0	0	1	3	0	0	179,762
Universities and Colleges	0	0	4	0	0	0					
Brown University	0	0	4	0	0	0	1	0	0	3	10,694
SOUTH CAROLINA											
Total	36	20	7	1	3	1					
Cities	20	4	5	1	2	0					
Bluffton	1	1	0	0	0	0	0	1	0	1	24,812
Calhoun Falls	1	0	0	0	0	0	1	0	0	0	1,912
Charleston	1	1	2	0	0	0	2	2	0	0	138,254
Clio	1	0	0	0	0	0	0	0	1	0	660
Darlington	0	0	1	0	0	0	1	0	0	0	5,886
Florence	2	0	0	0	0	0	1	0	1	0	37,640
Gaffney	1	0	0	0	0	0	0	1	0	0	12,528
Greenville	1	0	1	0	0	0	0	0	1	1	69,830
Hartsville	0	0	0	0	1	0	0	0	0	1	7,524
Inman	1	0	0	0	0	0	0	0	1	0	2,404
Lake View	1	0	0	0	0	0	0	0	1		755
McColl	0	0	0	0	1	0	0	1	0	0	1,981
Myrtle Beach	1	0	0	0	0	0	1	0	0	0	34,860
North Myrtle Beach	1	1	0	0	0	0	0	0	2	0	16,942
Pamplico	1	0	0	0	0	0	1	0	0	0	1,221
Rock Hill	2	0	1	1	0	0	2	0	0	2	75,342
Springdale	1	0	0	0	0	0	0	0	0	1	2,753
St. Matthews	1	0	0	0	0	0	0	1	0	0	1,900
Summerville	1	1	0	0	0	0	1	0	1	0	52,886
Williston	1	0	0	0	0	0	1	0	0	0	2,907
York	1	0	0	0	0	0	1	0	0	0	8,294
Universities and Colleges	1	0	0	0	1	0					
Medical University of South Carolina	1	0	0	0	0	0	0	1	0	0	3,421
The Citadel	0	0	0	0	1	0	0	0	0	1	4,305
Metropolitan Counties	9	13	1	0	0	1					
Beaufort	1	0	0	0	0	1	1	0	0	1	
Berkeley	2	9	0	0	0	0	0	1	1	9	
Charleston	1	1	0	0	0	0	0	0	1	1	

Table 13. Hate Crime Incidents Per Bias Motivation and Quarter, by Selected State and Agency and Federal, 2019—*Continued*

(Number.)

State/agency	Race/ Ethnicity/ Ancestry	Religion	Sexual orientation	Disability	Gender	Gender Identity	1st quarter	2nd quarter	3rd quarter	4th quarter	Population[1]
Greenville	1	0	0	0	0	0	0	0	1	0	
Lexington	0	0	1	0	0	0	1	0	0	0	
Pickens	1	0	0	0	0	0	0	0	1	0	
Spartanburg	3	3	0	0	0	0	2	1	1	2	
Nonmetropolitan Counties	6	3	1	0	0	0					
Bamberg	0	2	0	0	0	0	0	0	1	1	
Colleton	2	0	1	0	0	0	0	2	0	1	
Dillon	1	0	0	0	0	0	0	0	1	0	
Greenwood	0	1	0	0	0	0	1	0	0	0	
Marlboro	1	0	0	0	0	0	0	0	1	0	
Orangeburg	2	0	0	0	0	0	0	0	0	2	
SOUTH DAKOTA											
Total	13	3	4	0	0	0					
Cities	9	3	3	0	0	0					
Box Elder	1	0	0	0	0	0	1	0	0	0	10,077
Flandreau	0	1	0	0	0	0	0	0	1	0	2,323
Huron	1	0	0	0	0	0	1	0	0	0	13,840
Martin	1	0	0	0	0	0	0	0	0	1	1,071
Mitchell	0	0	1	0	0	0	0	1	0	0	15,733
Rapid City	1	0	0	0	0	0	0	1	0	0	76,343
Sioux Falls	3	2	2	0	0	0	1	1	2	3	185,628
Tea	1	0	0	0	0	0	0	0	0	1	5,898
Watertown	1	0	0	0	0	0	0	1	0	0	22,233
Metropolitan Counties	1	0	1	0	0	0					
Pennington	1	0	1	0	0	0	1	1	0	0	
Nonmetropolitan Counties	3	0	0	0	0	0					
Brown	1	0	0	0	0	0	0	1	0	0	
Stanley	1	0	0	0	0	0	0	0	1	0	
Walworth	1	0	0	0	0	0	0	0	1	0	
TENNESSEE											
Total	91	12	10	1	2	1					
Cities	38	8	6	1	1	0					
Centerville	1	0	0	0	0	0	0	0	1	0	3,564
Cleveland	7	0	0	0	0	0	2	2	2	1	45,453
Collierville	1	0	0	0	0	0	0	0	0	1	51,273
Cookeville	0	0	0	0	1	0	0	1	0	0	34,373
Covington	1	0	0	1	0	0	0	0	2	0	8,755
Goodlettsville	1	0	0	0	0	0	0	0	0	1	16,976
Greeneville	1	0	0	0	0	0	0	0	1	0	14,881
Kingsport	0	1	1	0	0	0	0	0	0	2	54,218
Knoxville	3	2	2	0	0	0	0	3	1	3	188,666
Lebanon	4	0	0	0	0	0	0	2	1	1	36,337
Livingston	0	1	0	0	0	0	0	1	0	0	4,014
Maryville	1	0	0	0	0	0	0	0	1	0	29,415
Memphis	4	0	1	0	0	0	0	2	1	2	650,410
Metropolitan Nashville Police Department	3	2	1	0	0	0	2	2	2	0	687,361
Milan	1	0	0	0	0	0	0	0	0	1	7,613
Morristown	2	0	0	0	0	0	0	0	2	0	30,044
Mountain City	1	0	0	0	0	0	0	1	0	0	2,407
Munford	0	1	0	0	0	0	1	0	0	0	6,083
Murfreesboro	0	0	1	0	0	0	0	1	0	0	145,929
Newbern	1	0	0	0	0	0	0	0	1	0	3,312
Pigeon Forge	2	0	0	0	0	0	0	1	1	0	6,383
Spring Hill	2	0	0	0	0	0	0	1	0	1	43,303
Springfield	1	1	0	0	0	0	0	2	0	0	17,022
White House	1	0	0	0	0	0	1	0	0	0	12,822
Universities and Colleges	0	0	1	0	0	0					
Tennessee Technological University	0	0	1	0	0	0	0	1	0	0	11,451

(Number.)

State/agency	Race/ Ethnicity/ Ancestry	Religion	Sexual orientation	Disability	Gender	Gender Identity	1st quarter	2nd quarter	3rd quarter	4th quarter	Population[1]
Metropolitan Counties	17	3	2	0	0	1					
Anderson..................................	0	0	1	0	0	0	0	0	1	0	
Blount.....................................	3	1	0	0	0	1	2	0	2	1	
Bradley	2	0	1	0	0	0	0	3	0	0	
Dickson...................................	1	0	0	0	0	0	0	1	0	0	
Knox..	3	0	0	0	0	0	0	0	0	3	
Montgomery............................	1	0	0	0	0	0	1	0	0	0	
Roane......................................	1	0	0	0	0	0	0	1	0	0	
Sullivan...................................	1	2	0	0	0	0	0	0	1	2	
Washington..............................	5	0	0	0	0	0	0	3	1	1	
Nonmetropolitan Counties............	5	1	0	0	0	0					
DeKalb.....................................	1	0	0	0	0	0	0	1	0	0	
Dyer..	0	1	0	0	0	0	0	0	1	0	
Henderson................................	1	0	0	0	0	0	0	0	0	1	
McMinn...................................	1	0	0	0	0	0	0	1	0	0	
Monroe....................................	1	0	0	0	0	0	0	0	0	1	
Warren.....................................	1	0	0	0	0	0	0	0	0	1	
State Police Agencies...................	30	0	1	0	1	0					
Department of Safety...................	30	0	1	0	1	0	7	12	10	3	
Other Agencies	1	0	0	0	0	0					
Tennessee Bureau of Investigation	1	0	0	0	0	0	0	0	1	0	
TEXAS											
Total	300	44	71	19	7	18					
Cities	227	33	64	14	5	14					
Abilene....................................	0	0	3	0	0	0	1	2	0	0	123,665
Addison...................................	1	0	0	0	0	0	0	0	0	1	16,339
Alamo......................................	3	1	0	0	0	0	1	0	0	3	19,903
Amarillo...................................	1	0	0	0	0	0	0	1	0	0	201,036
Angleton..................................	1	0	1	0	0	0	1	1	0	0	19,660
Arlington..................................	14	0	2	0	0	0	2	2	8	4	402,304
Austin......................................	5	2	3	0	0	0	3	2	3	2	986,062
Balch Springs............................	2	0	0	0	0	0	1	0	0	1	25,511
Beaumont................................	2	0	0	0	0	2	1	0	1	2	118,562
Blue Mound..............................	1	0	0	0	0	0	0	0	0	1	2,485
Boerne.....................................	1	0	0	0	0	0	1	0	0	0	18,135
Borger	1	0	0	0	0	0	0	0	0	1	12,536
Brady	1	0	0	0	0	0	1	0	0	0	5,288
Breckenridge............................	1	0	0	0	0	0	0	1	0	0	5,453
Brenham..................................	2	1	0	0	0	0	1	1	1	0	17,375
Brownwood..............................	1	0	0	0	0	0	0	0	1	0	18,646
Burkburnett..............................	0	1	0	0	0	0	0	0	1	0	11,305
Burleson..................................	2	0	1	0	0	0	0	2	1	0	48,743
Carrollton................................	1	0	0	0	0	0	0	1			139,179
Cedar Park................................	2	1	1	1	0	0	1	2	0	2	80,170
Cleburne...................................	1	0	0	0	0	0	0	0	0	1	30,860
College Station	1	0	0	0	0	0	1	0	0	0	119,246
Commerce................................	4	0	0	0	0	0	2	1	1		9,467
Converse..................................	0	0	1	0	0	0	0	0	0	1	28,598
Corpus Christi............................	1	0	0	0	0	0	0	0	1	0	329,320
Corrigan...................................	1	2	0	0	0	0	0	2	1	0	1,605
Dallas......................................	13	3	13	0	0	1	2	6	10	12	1,363,295
Decatur....................................	1	0	0	1	0	0	1	0	1	0	7,116
Denton.....................................	3	1	0	0	1	0	4	1	0	0	141,492
DeSoto.....................................	1	1	1	1	0	0	1	1	0	2	54,026
Dickinson.................................	1	0	0	0	0	0	0	0	0	1	21,101
Dumas.....................................	2	0	0	0	0	0	0	0	2	0	14,290
Edcouch...................................	18	0	0	0	0	0	11	7			3,378
El Campo..................................	1	0	0	0	0	0	0	0	0	1	11,615
Elgin..	3	0	0	0	0	0	0	1	1	1	10,475
El Paso.....................................	3	0	0	0	0	0	1	0	2	0	686,793
Ennis.......................................	0	1	0	0	0	1	0	0	1	1	20,096
Fate...	0	0	1	0	0	0	0	0	1	0	15,378

Table 13. Hate Crime Incidents Per Bias Motivation and Quarter, by Selected State and Agency and Federal, 2019—*Continued*

(Number.)

State/agency	Number of incidents per bias motivation						Number of incidents per quarter				Population[1]
	Race/Ethnicity/Ancestry	Religion	Sexual orientation	Disability	Gender	Gender Identity	1st quarter	2nd quarter	3rd quarter	4th quarter	
Ferris	1	0	0	0	0	0	0	0	0	1	2,876
Floresville	3	0	0	0	0	0	2	0	1	0	7,970
Fort Worth[2]	8	2	5	0	0	0	2	2	5	5	915,237
Frisco	1	1	0	0	0	0	1	0	1	0	199,445
Gainesville	1	0	0	0	0	0	0	0	0	1	16,688
Garland	2	0	0	0	0	0	0	0	1	1	244,277
Gatesville	0	1	0	0	0	0	0	0	0	1	12,311
Georgetown	1	0	0	0	0	0	0	0	1	0	78,332
Giddings	1	0	0	0	0	0	0	0	1	0	5,124
Gladewater	4	0	1	0	0	0	2	1	1	1	6,349
Glenn Heights	1	0	0	0	0	0	0	0	0	1	13,520
Granbury	0	1	0	0	0	0	0	0	0	1	10,752
Grapeland	0	0	0	1	0	0	0	1	0	0	1,421
Greenville	1	0	0	0	0	0	0	0	1	0	28,613
Hamilton	0	1	0	0	0	1	1	0	0	0	3,008
Harker Heights	0	0	0	0	1	0	0	0	0	1	32,527
Harlingen	0	1	1	0	0	0	0	1	1	0	65,481
Henderson	2	0	0	0	0	0	0	1	0	1	13,226
Hillsboro	1	0	0	0	0	0	0	1	0	0	8,476
Hollywood Park	1	0	1	0	0	0	0	1	0	1	3,406
Houston	13	2	9	2	0	3	5	6	9	9	2,355,606
Hurst	0	0	2	0	0	0	0	0	0	2	39,196
Iowa Park	1	0	0	0	0	0	1	0	0	0	6,369
Itasca	1	0	0	0	0	0	0	0	1	0	1,736
Jacksonville	1	0	0	0	0	1	0	2	0	0	14,969
Jarrell	1	0	0	0	0	0	0	1	0	0	1,800
Kennedale	1	0	0	0	0	0	0	0	0	1	8,792
Kingsville	0	0	0	0	1	0	0	0	1	0	25,401
Kyle	0	0	1	0	0	0	0	0	0	1	49,855
Lacy-Lakeview	1	0	0	0	0	0	1	0	0	0	6,720
La Grange	0	1	0	0	0	0	0	0	0	1	4,630
Lake Dallas	0	1	0	0	0	0	0	0	0	1	8,052
Lampasas	2	0	0	0	0	0	0	1	0	1	8,067
La Porte	0	0	1	1	0	0	0	0	0	2	35,622
Laredo	1	0	0	3	1	0	1	0	0	4	264,916
League City	0	0	1	0	0	0	0	0	1	0	109,401
Levelland	1	0	0	0	0	0	1	0	0	0	13,530
Lewisville	1	0	1	0	0	0	0	0	0	2	108,000
Livingston	0	0	1	0	0	0	0	1	0	0	5,112
Longview	2	1	0	0	0	0	1	1	1	0	81,783
Lubbock	1	0	2	0	0	0	0	0	2	1	259,208
Mansfield	1	0	0	0	0	0	0	0	0	1	72,979
Marble Falls	0	0	1	0	0	0	0	1	0	0	7,047
McKinney	2	0	0	0	0	0	0	2	0	0	200,615
Mesquite	3	0	0	0	0	0	2	0	1	0	143,078
Nederland	1	0	0	0	0	0	0	0	0	1	17,557
New Braunfels	5	0	1	0	1	1	0	1	4	3	88,706
North Richland Hills	4	0	0	0	0	0	0	1	1	2	71,816
Odessa[2]	3	0	2	1	0	0	2	0	3	0	123,468
Overton	1	1	0	0	0	0	1	0	0	1	2,510
Palestine	4	0	0	0	0	1	1	3	1	0	18,062
Pasadena	4	0	0	2	0	0	3	1	0	2	153,689
Pearland	1	0	0	0	0	0	0	1	0	0	126,206
Pflugerville	1	0	0	0	0	1	0	1	0	1	66,729
Pleasanton	2	0	0	0	0	0	0	0	0	2	10,911
Port Arthur	2	0	0	0	0	0	0	0	0	2	55,084
Port Isabel	2	0	0	0	0	0	0	1	1	0	5,058
Port Neches	0	0	0	0	0	1	0	0	1	0	12,808
Richardson	0	0	1	0	0	0	0	0	0	1	123,893
Rio Grande City	0	1	0	0	0	0	0	0	1	0	14,607
Rockdale	2	0	0	0	0	0	0	1	1	0	5,665
Rockwall	3	1	0	0	0	0	0	1	1	2	46,096
Roma	1	0	0	0	0	0	0	1	0	0	11,527
Rosenberg	1	1	0	0	0	0	1	0	0	1	38,936
Rowlett	1	0	0	0	0	0	1	0	0	0	67,604
San Antonio	5	0	4	0	0	0	3	3	2	1	1,559,166
San Juan	1	0	1	0	0	0	1	0	0	1	37,542

Table 13. Hate Crime Incidents Per Bias Motivation and Quarter, by Selected State and Agency and Federal, 2019—*Continued*

(Number.)

State/agency	Number of incidents per bias motivation						Number of incidents per quarter				Population[1]
	Race/ Ethnicity/ Ancestry	Religion	Sexual orientation	Disability	Gender	Gender Identity	1st quarter	2nd quarter	3rd quarter	4th quarter	
Santa Fe	0	0	1	0	0	0	0	0	0	1	13,657
Schulenburg	1	0	0	0	0	0	0	1	0	0	2,929
Silsbee	1	0	0	0	0	0	0	1	0	0	6,650
South Padre Island	0	1	0	0	0	0	0	1	0	0	2,805
Spur	2	0	0	0	0	0	0	0	0	2	1,207
Stafford	0	1	0	0	0	0	0	0	0	1	18,380
Sunset Valley	1	0	0	0	0	0	0	1	0	0	683
Sweeny	2	0	0	0	0	0	0	0	1	1	3,745
Sweetwater	1	0	0	0	0	0	0	0	1	0	10,467
Tahoka	0	0	0	1	0	0	0	0	1	0	2,624
Tool	1	0	0	0	0	0	0	1	0	0	2,337
Tyler	0	0	0	0	0	1	0	0	0	1	106,851
University Park	1	0	0	0	0	0	1	0	0	0	25,434
Vernon	4	0	0	0	0	0	1	0	0	3	10,312
Victoria	1	0	0	0	0	0	0	0	0	1	67,581
Vidor	2	0	0	0	0	0	0	0	1	1	10,499
Waco	4	1	0	0	0	0	2	1	0	2	139,870
Wallis	1	0	0	0	0	0	0	0	0	1	1,322
Wichita Falls	1	0	0	0	0	0	0	0	1	0	104,551
Willow Park	2	0	0	0	0	0	0	0	1	1	5,808
Winters	1	0	0	0	0	0	1	0	0	0	2,448
Universities and Colleges	8	2	1	0	0	0					
Houston Community College	1	0	0	0	0	0	0	0	1	0	82,166
Texas State University, San Marcos	2	0	0	0	0	0	0	0	2	0	42,924
Texas Woman's University	0	0	1	0	0	0	0	0	0	1	18,773
Tyler Junior College	2	0	0	0	0	0	0	0	0	2	15,992
University of Texas											
Austin	2	2	0	0	0	0	0	2	1	1	55,097
Houston	1	0	0	0	0	0	0	0	1	0	6,948
Metropolitan Counties	39	6	4	2	2	1					
Brazoria	1	0	0	0	0	0	0	0	0	1	
Chambers	1	0	0	0	0	0	1	0	0	0	
El Paso	1	0	0	0	0	0	0	0	1	0	
Fort Bend	2	0	0	0	0	0	1	1	0	0	
Galveston	0	0	0	1	0	0	1	0			
Harris	13	2	1	0	2	1	2	5	6	6	
Hudspeth	10	1	0	0	0	0	11	0	0	0	
Johnson	2	0	0	0	0	0	0	1	1	0	
Montgomery	1	1	0	0	0	0	2	0	0	0	
Randall	0	0	1	0	0	0	0	0	0	1	
Tarrant	3	0	0	0	0	0	0	0	1	2	
Travis	2	0	0	0	0	0	0	0	0	2	
Williamson	3	2	2	1	0	0	2	4	1	1	
Nonmetropolitan Counties	15	2	1	1	0	3					
Bailey	0	1	0	0	0	1	0	1	0	1	
Bee	0	0	0	1	0	0	0	0	0	1	
Cherokee	1	0	0	0	0	0	0	0	0	1	
Crockett	1	0	0	0	0	0	0	0	1	0	
Duval	1	0	0	0	0	0	0	1	0	0	
Floyd	1	0	0	0	0	0	0	0	0	1	
Houston	2	1	0	0	0	1	1	1	2	0	
Kerr	1	0	0	0	0	0	1	0	0	0	
Leon	2	0	0	0	0	0	0	0	1	1	
Llano	0	0	0	0	0	1	0	0	0	1	
McCulloch	1	0	0	0	0	0	0	0	1	0	
Nacogdoches	0	0	1	0	0	0	0	0	0	1	
Ward	4	0	0	0	0	0	1	2	1	0	
Washington	1	0	0	0	0	0	0	0	1	0	
Other Agencies	11	1	1	2	0	0					
Dallas-Fort Worth International Airport[2]	1	1	0	0	0	0	0	0	0	1	
Independent School District											
Austin	1	0	0	0	0	0	0	0	1	0	
Bay City	1	0	0	0	0	0	1	0	0	0	

(Number.)

State/agency	Number of incidents per bias motivation						Number of incidents per quarter				
	Race/ Ethnicity/ Ancestry	Religion	Sexual orientation	Disability	Gender	Gender Identity	1st quarter	2nd quarter	3rd quarter	4th quarter	Population[1]
Brazosport	1	0	0	0	0	0	0	1	0	0	
Houston	4	0	0	1	0	0	2	0	1	2	
Hutto	0	0	0	1	0	0	1	0	0	0	
Roma	2	0	0	0	0	0	0	1	1	0	
Spring Branch	1	0	1	0	0	0	1	0	1	0	
UTAH											
Total	12	3	3	0	0	0					
Cities	11	2	3	0	0	0					
Farmington	3	0	0	0	0	0	0	1	1	1	25,409
Kaysville	1	0	0	0	0	0	0	0	1	0	32,691
Layton	1	0	0	0	0	0	0	0	1	0	78,585
Moab	0	0	1	0	0	0	0	0	1	0	5,349
North Salt Lake	1	0	0	0	0	0	0	0	0	1	21,501
Ogden	1	0	0	0	0	0	0	0	0	1	87,875
Roy	0	1	1	0	0	0	0	2	0	0	39,001
Salt Lake City	1	0	0	0	0	0	1	0	0	0	202,426
Sandy	1	0	0	0	0	0	0	1	0	0	97,797
South Jordan	1	0	0	0	0	0	0	0	0	1	77,645
South Ogden	1	0	1	0	0	0	0	0	1	1	17,215
West Valley	0	1	0	0	0	0	0	1	0	0	137,269
Metropolitan Counties	0	1	0	0	0	0					
Washington	0	1	0	0	0	0	1	0	0	0	
Nonmetropolitan Counties	1	0	0	0	0	0					
Duchesne	1	0	0	0	0	0	0	1	0	0	
VERMONT											
Total	18	4	9	1	0	1					
Cities	15	3	7	0	0	1					
Barre	1	0	0	0	0	0	0	1	0	0	8,551
Bennington	3	1	1	0	0	0	5	0	0	0	14,912
Berlin	1	0	0	0	0	0	0	0	0	1	2,789
Brandon	0	0	1	0	0	0	0	0	0	1	3,744
Brattleboro	0	0	0	0	0	1	0	0	1	0	11,401
Burlington	1	1	1	0	0	0	0	1	1	1	42,958
Hartford	0	0	1	0	0	0	0	0	1	0	9,654
Milton	2	0	1	0	0	0	0	0	2	1	11,064
Montpelier	2	0	0	0	0	0	0	0	1	1	7,386
Newport	1	0	1	0	0	0	0	0	1	1	4,216
Rutland	2	0	1	0	0	0	1	0	2	0	15,191
South Burlington	0	1	0	0	0	0	1	0	0	0	19,687
St. Albans	1	0	0	0	0	0	0	0	1	0	6,800
Windsor	1	0	0	0	0	0	0	0	1	0	3,324
Universities and Colleges	2	1	2	0	0	0					
University of Vermont	2	1	2	0	0	0	0	0	5	0	15,629
State Police Agencies	1	0	0	1	0	0					
State Police											
Middlesex	1	0	0	0	0	0	1	0	0	0	
St. Albans	0	0	0	1	0	0	1	0	0	0	
VIRGINIA											
Total	102	27	27	3	1	3					
Cities	21	6	11	0	0	2					
Alexandria	2	1	2	0	0	0	2	2	0	1	162,258
Charlottesville	2	0	1	0	0	0	1	0	1	1	48,453
Chesapeake	2	0	0	0	0	0	0	1	0	1	243,726
Colonial Beach	0	1	0	0	0	0	0	0	0	1	3,593
Dayton	0	1	0	0	0	0	1	0	0	0	1,636
Glade Spring	0	1	0	0	0	1	0	0	0	2	1,426
Hampton	2	0	0	0	0	0	0	2	0	0	133,173

Table 13. Hate Crime Incidents Per Bias Motivation and Quarter, by Selected State and Agency and Federal, 2019—*Continued*

(Number.)

State/agency	Race/ Ethnicity/ Ancestry	Religion	Sexual orientation	Disability	Gender	Gender Identity	1st quarter	2nd quarter	3rd quarter	4th quarter	Population[1]
Harrisonburg	1	0	0	0	0	0	0	1	0	0	54,387
Leesburg	2	1	1	0	0	0	2	1	1	0	55,461
Lynchburg	1	0	0	0	0	0	0	0	0	1	82,512
Newport News	1	0	3	0	0	0	1	0	0	3	177,319
Purcellville	1	0	0	0	0	0	1	0	0	0	10,346
Richlands	1	0	0	0	0	0	0	1	0	0	5,198
Richmond	3	0	2	0	0	0	1	4	0	0	230,721
Roanoke	1	0	0	0	0	0	0	1	0	0	99,752
Suffolk	0	0	1	0	0	0	0	0	0	1	91,486
Vienna	0	0	1	0	0	0	0	0	0	1	16,660
Virginia Beach	1	1	0	0	0	0	1	0	1	0	449,038
Winchester	0	0	0	0	0	1	0	0	0	1	28,201
Woodstock	1	0	0	0	0	0	0	1	0	0	5,267
Universities and Colleges	2	1	4	0	0	0					
Hampton University	0	0	1	0	0	0	1	0	0	0	4,698
James Madison University	0	1	1	0	0	0	1	0	1	0	24,133
Longwood University	1	0	0	0	0	0	0	1	0	0	5,909
University of Mary Washington	1	0	1	0	0	0	0	1	0	1	5,373
University of Virginia	0	0	1	0	0	0	0	1	0	0	28,244
Metropolitan Counties	71	20	10	2	1	1					
Albemarle County Police Department	1	0	0	0	0	0	0	0	0	1	
Amelia	0	0	1	0	0	0	0	0	0	1	
Amherst	2	0	0	0	0	0	0	0	1	1	
Arlington County Police Department	8	4	1	0	0	0	6	6	1	0	
Bedford	1	1	0	0	0	0	0	0	2	0	
Campbell	1	0	0	0	0	0	0	1	0	0	
Chesterfield County Police Department	2	1	0	0	0	0	0	0	2	1	
Dinwiddie	0	2	0	0	0	0	0	1	0	1	
Fairfax County Police Department	27	8	2	0	0	0	9	12	7	9	
Fluvanna	1	0	1	0	0	0	0	0	0	2	
Franklin	2	0	0	0	0	0	1	0	1	0	
Giles	0	0	1	0	0	0	0	0	1	0	
Hanover	1	0	0	0	0	0	1	0	0	0	
Henrico County Police Department	1	0	0	0	0	0	1	0	0	0	
James City County Police Department	1	0	0	0	0	0	0	0	1	0	
Loudoun	12	2	2	1	1	1	9	6	2	2	
Nelson	0	0	1	0	0	0	1	0	0	0	
Prince George County Police Department	2	0	0	0	0	0	0	0	2	0	
Prince William County Police Department	3	1	0	0	0	0	0	2	2	0	
Roanoke County Police Department	0	1	1	0	0	0	0	1	1	0	
Spotsylvania	1	0	0	1	0	0	0	1	1	0	
Stafford	4	0	0	0	0	0	0	0	1	3	
Washington	1	0	0	0	0	0	0	1	0	0	
Nonmetropolitan Counties	5	0	2	0	0	0					
Accomack	1	0	0	0	0	0	0	0	1	0	
Charlotte	2	0	0	0	0	0	0	0	2	0	
Northampton	2	0	0	0	0	0	0	1	0	1	
Page	0	0	1	0	0	0	1	0	0	0	
Pittsylvania	0	0	1	0	0	0	0	1	0	0	
State Police Agencies	3	0	0	1	0	0					
State Police											
Dinwiddie County	1	0	0	0	0	0	0	0	1	0	
Fairfax County	0	0	0	1	0	0	0	1	0	0	
Prince William County	1	0	0	0	0	0	0	1	0	0	
Richmond	1	0	0	0	0	0	0	0	0	1	
WASHINGTON											
Total	331	76	116	8	8	17					
Cities	290	58	109	6	5	17					
Aberdeen	3	0	0	0	0	0	1	0	1	1	16,627
Auburn	1	1	1	1	0	0	0	1	0	3	83,468
Bainbridge Island	0	1	0	0	0	0	0	0	0	1	25,080

Table 13. Hate Crime Incidents Per Bias Motivation and Quarter, by Selected State and Agency and Federal, 2019—*Continued*

(Number.)

State/agency	Number of incidents per bias motivation						Number of incidents per quarter				Population[1]
	Race/ Ethnicity/ Ancestry	Religion	Sexual orientation	Disability	Gender	Gender Identity	1st quarter	2nd quarter	3rd quarter	4th quarter	
Bellevue	5	3	2	0	0	0	1	3	2	4	150,200
Bellingham	5	0	1	0	0	0	1	2	0	3	91,906
Blaine	0	0	1	0	0	0		0	1	0	5,534
Bonney Lake	1	0	0	0	0	0	0	0	0	1	21,574
Bothell	2	0	0	0	0	1	1	1	0	1	47,565
Bremerton	1	0	0	0	0	0	0	0	1	0	41,675
Brier	1	2	0	0	0	0	1	1	1	0	7,070
Burien	3	1	2	0	0	0	1	2	2	1	52,388
Chehalis	1	0	0	0	0	0	1	0	0	0	7,682
Covington	2	0	0	0	0	0	1	0	1	0	21,698
Des Moines	3	1	0	0	0	0	1	0	2	1	32,708
Ellensburg	1	0	0	0	0	0	1	0	0	0	21,324
Everett	5	2	1	0	0	0	2	3	0	3	112,302
Federal Way	1	0	0	0	0	0	0	1	0	0	98,025
Index	0	1	0	0	0	0	0	0	1	0	214
Issaquah	1	1	1	0	0	0	1	0	2	0	40,651
Kent	10	4	2	0	0	0	4	6	3	3	131,003
Lake Stevens	1	0	0	0	0	0	1	0	0	0	34,081
Longview	0	0	2	1	0	0	1	0	1	1	38,282
Maple Valley	1	0	0	0	0	0	0	0	0	1	27,705
Marysville	1	0	0	0	0	0	1	0	0	0	71,081
Mercer Island	1	2	0	0	0	0	2	1	0	0	26,408
Monroe	1	0	0	0	0	0	0	1	0	0	19,630
Montesano	1	0	0	0	0	0	1	0	0	0	4,033
Moses Lake	9	0	0	0	0	0	4	4	1	0	24,490
Mount Vernon	3	0	0	0	0	0	0	3	0	0	36,274
Mukilteo	1	1	0	0	0	0	0	1	0	1	21,704
Normandy Park	1	0	0	0	0	0	1	0	0	0	6,699
Oak Harbor	1	0	0	0	0	0	1	0	0	0	23,554
Olympia	1	1	1	0	0	1	4	0	0	0	53,286
Oroville	0	1	0	0	0	0	1	0		0	1,678
Port Angeles	1	0	2	0	1	0	3	0	0	1	20,207
Pullman	2	0	1	0	0	0	0	0	1	2	34,585
Puyallup	1	0	0	0	0	0	0	0	0	1	42,509
Redmond	1	0	0	0	0	0	1	0	0	0	69,501
Renton	4	2	1	1	0	0	2	3	3	0	103,452
Richland	0	1	0	0	0	0	0	0	0	1	58,514
Ruston	1	0	0	0	0	0	0	0	1	0	855
Sammamish[2]	2	0	2	0	0	0	2	0	1	0	66,820
SeaTac	3	0	1	0	0	0	1	0	1	2	29,533
Seattle[2]	178	26	80	3	4	13	50	76	98	68	763,706
Shoreline	0	1	1	0	0	0	0	0	2	0	57,216
South Bend	0	0	0	0	0	1	0	0	0	1	1,680
Spokane	4	2	3	0	0	0	2	3	3	1	220,432
Spokane Valley	5	0	2	0	0	0	1	2	2	2	100,983
Steilacoom	2	0	0	0	0	0	0	1	1	0	6,423
Sunnyside	1	0	0	0	0	0	0	0	1	0	16,839
Tacoma	6	1	0	0	0	0	2	2	1	2	218,650
Tukwila	0	1	0	0	0	0	0	0	0	1	20,439
Vancouver	6	2	2	0	0	1	1	7	2	1	185,034
Walla Walla	1	0	0	0	0	0	0	1	0	0	33,047
West Richland	1	0	0	0	0	0	0	1	0	0	15,343
Yakima	2	0	0	0	0	0	0	0	1	1	94,168
Zillah	1	0	0	0	0	0			1	0	3,164
Universities and Colleges	3	10	0	1	1	0					
Eastern Washington University	1	6	0	0	1	0	0	5	1	2	16,208
Evergreen State College	0	3	0	0	0	0	1	0	1	1	4,587
University of Washington	1	0	0	0	0	0	0	0	1	0	55,508
Western Washington University[2]	1	1	0	1	0	0	1	1	0	0	17,782
Metropolitan Counties	34	7	7	1	2	0					
Chelan	1	1	0	0	0	0	2	0	0	0	
Clark	1	0	1	0	0	0	1	1	0	0	
Cowlitz	0	0	0	1	0	0	0	0	1	0	
King	17	2	4	0	2	0	7	5	10	3	
Kitsap	1	0	0	0	0	0	0	0	1	0	

Table 13. Hate Crime Incidents Per Bias Motivation and Quarter, by Selected State and Agency and Federal, 2019—*Continued*

(Number.)

State/agency	Race/ Ethnicity/ Ancestry	Religion	Sexual orientation	Disability	Gender	Gender Identity	1st quarter	2nd quarter	3rd quarter	4th quarter	Population[1]
Pierce....................................	1	1	0	0	0	0	0	1	1	0	
Skagit....................................	2	0	0	0	0	0	0	1	0	1	
Snohomish..............................	3	1	1	0	0	0	0	0	4	1	
Spokane.................................	4	1	0	0	0	0	0	0	2	3	
Stevens..................................	0	0	1	0	0	0	0	0	0	1	
Whatcom................................	1	1	0	0	0	0	0	0	1	1	
Yakima...................................	3	0	0	0	0	0	0	1	1	1	
Nonmetropolitan Counties....................................	4	0	0	0	0	0					
Clallam..................................	2	0	0	0	0	0	1	0	1	0	
Island....................................	1	0	0	0	0	0	0	0	0	1	
Lewis.....................................	1	0	0	0	0	0	0	0	0	1	
Other Agencies	0	1	0	0	0	0					
Port of Seattle.........................	0	1	0	0	0	0	0	0	0	1	
WEST VIRGINIA											
Total	18	6	3	2	1	1					
Cities	8	1	2	1	0	0					
Huntington.............................	2	0	1	0	0	0	1	2	0	0	45,675
Morgantown............................	2	0	0	0	0	0	1	0	1	0	31,281
Moundsville............................	1	0	0	0	0	0	0	1	0	0	8,323
St. Albans...............................	0	0	0	1	0	0	1	0	0	0	9,956
Wheeling................................	3	1	0	0	0	0	2	1	1	0	26,562
White Sulphur Springs	0	0	1	0	0	0	0	1	0	0	2,395
Metropolitan Counties	4	1	0	1	0	0					
Hancock.................................	2	0	0	1	0	0	0	1	1	1	
Kanawha................................	0	1	0	0	0	0	1	0	0	0	
Monongalia.............................	1	0	0	0	0	0	0	0	0	1	
Putnam..................................	1	0	0	0	0	0	0	0	1	0	
Nonmetropolitan Counties....................................	5	1	0	0	1	0					
Hardy....................................	0	0	0	0	1	0	0	0	0	1	
Lewis.....................................	2	1	0	0	0	0	2	1	0	0	
Mason....................................	3	0	0	0	0	0	0	1	1	1	
State Police Agencies	1	3	0	0	0	1					
State Police											
Bridgeport.............................	0	1	0	0	0	0	0	0	0	1	
Hamlin..................................	0	0	0	0	0	1	0	1	0	0	
Morgantown...........................	1	0	0	0	0	0	0	0	0	1	
Wayne	0	2	0	0	0	0	0	1	0	1	
Other Agencies	0	0	1	0	0	0					
Metropolitan Drug Enforcement Network Team........	0	0	1	0	0	0	1	0	0	0	
WISCONSIN											
Total	39	18	5	4	2	6					
Cities	29	14	4	4	2	5					
Appleton	2	0	0	2	0	0	0	1	3	0	74,757
Barron	1	0	0	0	0	0	0	0	1	0	3,306
Beloit....................................	0	1	0	0	0	0	0	0	0	1	37,025
Campbell Township	0	1	0	0	0	0	0	1	0	0	4,337
Chippewa Falls........................	0	0	0	0	1	0	0	1	0	0	14,237
Ellsworth................................	1	0	0	0	0	0	0	0	1	0	3,306
Fond du Lac............................	0	2	0	0	0	0	1	1	0	0	42,954
Green Bay...............................	1	1	0	0	0	0	0	1	1	0	104,992
Hudson..................................	0	0	1	0	0	0	0	0	0	1	14,074
Janesville...............................	2	1	0	1	0	3	1	2	3	1	64,687
Jefferson................................	1	0	0	0	0	0	0	0	0	1	8,042
Juneau..................................	1	0	0	0	0	0	1	0	0	0	2,639
La Crosse...............................	0	1	0	0	1	0	0	0	1	1	51,591
Lake Delton............................	1	0	0	0	0	0	0	0	0	1	3,005
Madison.................................	3	1	3	0	0	0	1	0	4	2	261,270

Table 13. Hate Crime Incidents Per Bias Motivation and Quarter, by Selected State and Agency and Federal, 2019—Continued

(Number.)

State/agency	Number of incidents per bias motivation						Number of incidents per quarter				
	Race/ Ethnicity/ Ancestry	Religion	Sexual orientation	Disability	Gender	Gender Identity	1st quarter	2nd quarter	3rd quarter	4th quarter	Population[1]
Mayville	2	0	0	0	0	0	0	2	0	0	4,859
Menasha	1	0	0	0	0	0	0	1	0	0	17,809
Milwaukee	2	0	0	0	0	0	0	1	1	0	590,923
Monroe	4	0	0	0	0	0	1	0	3	0	10,537
Neenah	1	0	0	0	0	0	0	0	0	1	26,133
New London	0	1	0	0	0	0	0	0	1	0	7,118
North Fond du Lac	0	0	0	1	0	0	0	0	1	0	5,098
Oshkosh	0	2	0	0	0	0	1	0	0	1	66,797
Platteville	1	0	0	0	0	0	0	0	0	1	12,115
Port Washington	1	0	0	0	0	0	0	0	0	1	11,908
Rice Lake	1	0	0	0	0	2	0	0	3	0	8,369
Ripon	0	1	0	0	0	0	0	0	1	0	7,820
Sheboygan	1	0	0	0	0	0	1	0	0	0	48,035
Town of Madison	1	0	0	0	0	0	0	0	1	0	6,934
Wauwatosa	0	1	0	0	0	0	0	1	0	0	48,562
Winneconne	0	1	0	0	0	0	0	0	1	0	2,506
Wisconsin Rapids	1	0	0	0	0	0	1	0	0	0	17,613
Metropolitan Counties	4	4	0	0	0	0					
Columbia	0	2	0	0	0	0	1	1	0	0	
Dane	1	0	0	0	0	0	0	0	0	1	
Douglas	1	0	0	0	0	0	0	0	1	0	
Iowa	1	0	0	0	0	0	0	0	1	0	
Outagamie	0	1	0	0	0	0	0	1	0	0	
Rock	1	1	0	0	0	0	1	1	0	0	
Nonmetropolitan Counties	6	0	1	0	0	1					
Dodge	2	0	1	0	0	0	1	0	2	0	
Manitowoc	1	0	0	0	0	0	0	1	0	0	
Monroe	1	0	0	0	0	0	0	0	0	1	
Oneida	1	0	0	0	0	0	0	0	0	1	
Sauk	1	0	0	0	0	1	1	0	1	0	
WYOMING											
Total	4	0	1	0	0	0					
Cities	3	0	1	0	0	0					
Cody	1	0	0	0	0	0	0	1	0	0	9,865
Evanston	1	0	0	0	0	0	0	0	1	0	11,624
Laramie	0	0	1	0	0	0	0	0	1	0	32,669
Sheridan	1	0	0	0	0	0	1	0	0	0	17,895
Universities and Colleges	1	0	0	0	0	0					
University of Wyoming	1	0	0	0	0	0	0	0	1	0	13,963
FEDERAL											
Federal Agencies	63	47	19	0	0	3					
Federal Bureau of Investigation Field Offices											
Albany, NY	1	0	0	0	0	0			1		
Anchorage, AK	1	2	1	0	0	0		2		2	
Atlanta, GA[2]	4	1	0	0	0	0	1	1		2	
Baltimore, MD	2	2	0	0	0	0	1	1	1	1	
Birmingham, AL[2]	0	1	1	0	0	0		1			
Boston, MA	1	2	1	0	0	0	2	2			
Charlotte, NC	1	0	0	0	0	0			1		
Chicago, IL	1	1	0	0	0	0		1		1	
Cincinnati, OH	1	0	0	0	0	0		1			
Cleveland, OH	1	0	0	0	0	0		1			
Columbia, SC	1	0	0	0	0	0			1		
Dallas, TX	1	1	1	0	0	1	1	1	1	1	
Denver, CO	0	1	1	0	0	1		1	1	1	
Detroit, MI	3	1	2	0	0	0		3	2	1	
El Paso, TX	2	4	0	0	0	0		4	1	1	
Houston, TX	1	0	0	0	0	0	1				
Jacksonville, FL	1	0	0	0	0	0		1			
Kansas City, MO	3	0	1	0	0	0	2	1	1		
Las Vegas, NV	0	1	0	0	0	0	1				

Table 13. Hate Crime Incidents Per Bias Motivation and Quarter, by Selected State and Agency and Federal, 2019—Continued

(Number.)

State/agency	Number of incidents per bias motivation						Number of incidents per quarter				Population[1]
	Race/ Ethnicity/ Ancestry	Religion	Sexual orientation	Disability	Gender	Gender Identity	1st quarter	2nd quarter	3rd quarter	4th quarter	
Los Angeles, CA	0	1	1	0	0	0		1	1		
Memphis, TN	0	3	0	0	0	0		3			
Miami, FL	1	2	0	0	0	0			2	1	
Milwaukee, WI	1	0	0	0	0	0				1	
Minneapolis, MN	0	3	0	0	0	0	1		1	1	
Mobile, AL[2]	3	0	1	0	0	0			1	2	
New Haven, CT	0	1	0	0	0	0		1			
New Orleans, LA[2]	4	3	0	0	0	0		3		1	
New York, NY	1	5	0	0	0	0	2		2	2	
Newark, NJ	1	0	0	0	0	0				1	
Norfolk, VA	3	0	0	0	0	0	1			2	
Oklahoma City, OK	1	1	1	0	0	0	1	1	1		
Omaha, NE	2	1	0	0	0	0		3			
Philadelphia, PA	2	0	0	0	0	0		1	1		
Pittsburgh, PA	1	0	0	0	0	0				1	
Portland, OR	1	0	0	0	0	0				1	
Richmond, VA	1	0	0	0	0	0	1				
Sacramento, CA[2]	2	1	1	0	0	0		1	2		
Salt Lake City, UT[2]	4	1	1	0	0	0	2		1	2	
San Antonio, TX	0	1	0	0	0	0		1			
San Diego, CA	0	2	1	0	0	0	1	1		1	
Seattle, WA	0	0	1	0	0	0		1			
Springfield, IL	1	0	0	0	0	0			1		
St. Louis, MO	3	0	2	0	0	0	1	3		1	
Tampa, FL	1	0	0	0	0	1			2		
Washington, DC	1	4	1	0	0	0	1	3	2		
Pentagon Force Protection Agency	0	0	1	0	0	0	1	0	0		
U.S. Navy Law Enforcement	4	0	0	0	0	0	0	0	2	2	
United States Army	0	1	0	0	0	0	0	1	0	0	

[1]Population figures are published only for the cities. The figures listed for the universities and colleges are student enrollment and were provided by the United States Department of Education for the 2018 school year, the most recent available. The enrollment figures include full-time and part-time students.
[2]The figures shown include one incident reported with more than one bias motivation.
[3]Student enrollment figures were not available.

Table 14. Participation Table, Number of Participating Agencies and Population Covered, by Population Group and Federal, 2019

(Number.)

Population group	Number of participating agencies	Population covered
Total	15,588	305,284,239
Group I (cities 250,000 and over)	88	64,003,500
Group II (cities 100,000-249,999)	220	32,129,155
Group III (cities 50,000-99,999)	481	33,572,735
Group IV (cities 25,000-49,999)	872	30,181,113
Group V (cities 10,000-24,999)	1,774	28,305,204
Group VI1 (cities under 10,000)	7,875	22,762,154
Metropolitan counties[1]	1,924	71,500,130
Nonmetropolitan counties[1]	2,304	22,830,248
Federal[2]	50	

[1]The figures shown include universities and colleges, state police agencies, and/or other agencies to which no population is attributed.
[2]Population estimates are not attributed to the federal agencies.

METHODOLOGY

HATE CRIMES

The Federal Bureau of Investigation (FBI) began the procedures for implementing, collecting, and managing hate crime data after Congress passed the Hate Crime Statistics Act in 1990. This act required the collection of data "about crimes that manifest evidence of prejudice based on race, religion, sexual orientation, or ethnicity." Beginning in 2013, law enforcement agencies could submit hate crime data in accordance with a number of program modifications. In 1994, the Hate Crime Statistics Act was amended to include bias against persons with disabilities. The Church Arson Prevention Act, which was signed into law in July 1996, removed the sunset clause from the original statute and mandated that the collection of hate crime data become a permanent part of the UCR program. In 2009, Congress further amended the Hate Crime Statistics Act by passing the Matthew Shepard and James Byrd, Jr., Hate Crime Prevention Act. The amendment includes the collection of data for crimes motivated by bias against a particular gender and gender identity, as well as for crimes committed by, and crimes directed against, juveniles. In response to the Shepard/Byrd Act, the FBI modified its data collection so that reporting agencies could indicate whether hate crimes were committed by, or directed against, juveniles.

Definitions

Hate crimes include any crime motivated by bias against race, religion, sexual orientation, ethnicity/national origin, and/or disability. Because motivation is subjective, it is sometimes difficult to know with certainty whether a crime resulted from the offender's bias. Moreover, the presence of bias alone does not necessarily mean that a crime can be considered a hate crime. Only when law enforcement investigation reveals sufficient evidence to lead a reasonable and prudent person to conclude that the offender's actions were motivated, in whole or in part, by his or her bias should an incident be reported as a hate crime.

Data Collection

The UCR (Uniform Crime Reporting) program collects data about both single-bias and multiple-bias hate crimes. A single-bias incident is defined as an incident in which one or more offense types are motivated by the same bias. A multiple-bias incident is defined as an incident in which more than one offense type occurs and at least two offense types are motivated by different biases.

A table enumerating selected places in the United States that did not report hate crimes in 2019 is available at https://ucr.fbi.gov/hate-crime/2019/topic-pages/tables/participation.xls.

Important Note: Rape Data

In 2013, the UCR Program initiated the collection of rape data under a revised definition and removed the term "forcible" from the offense name. The UCR Program now defines rape as follows:

Rape (revised definition): Penetration, no matter how slight, of the vagina or anus with any body part or object, or oral penetration by a sex organ of another person, without the consent of the victim. (This includes the offenses of rape, sodomy, and sexual assault with an object as converted from data submitted via the National Incident-Based Reporting System.)

Rape (legacy definition): The carnal knowledge of a female forcibly and against her will. For tables within this publication that present data for 2018 only or provide a 2-year trend, the rape figures are an aggregate total of the data submitted based on both the legacy and revised UCR definitions. For 5- and 10-year trend tables, the rape figures for the previous year (2014 or 2009) are based on the legacy definition and the 2018 rape figures are an aggregate total based on both the legacy and revised definitions. For this reason, a percent change is not provided.

In 2016, the FBI Director approved the recommendation to discontinue the reporting of rape data using the UCR legacy definition beginning in 2017.

The offenses of fondling, incest, and statutory rape are included in the crimes against persons, *other* category.

Crimes Against Persons, Property, or Society

The UCR program's data collection guidelines stipulate that a hate crime may involve multiple offenses, victims, and offenders within one incident; therefore, the Hate Crime Statistics program is incident-based. According to UCR counting guidelines:

- One offense is counted for each victim in *crimes against persons*

- One offense is counted for each offense type in *crimes against property*

- One offense is counted for each offense type in *crimes against society*

Victims

In the UCR program, the victim of a hate crime may be an individual, a business, an institution, or society as a whole.

Offenders

According to the UCR program, the term *known offender* does not imply that the suspect's identity is known; rather, the term indicates that some aspect of the suspect was identified, thus distinguishing the suspect from an unknown offender. Law enforcement agencies specify the number of offenders, and when possible, the race of the offender or offenders as a group.

Race/Ethnicity

The UCR program uses the following racial designations in its Hate Crime Statistics program: White; Black; American Indian or Alaskan Native; Asian; Native Hawaiian or Other Pacific Islander; and Multiple Races, Group. In addition, the UCR program uses the ethnic designations of Hispanic or Latino and Not Hispanic or Latino.

The law enforcement agencies that voluntarily participate in the Hate Crime Statistics program collect details about an offender's bias motivation associated with 11 offense types already being reported to the UCR program: murder and nonnegligent manslaughter, rape, aggravated assault, simple assault, and intimidation (crimes against persons); and robbery, burglary, larceny-theft, motor vehicle theft, arson, and destruction/damage/vandalism (crimes against property). The law enforcement agencies that participate in the UCR program via the National Incident-Based Reporting System (NIBRS) collect data about additional offenses for *crimes against persons* and *crimes against property*. These data appear in the category of other. These agencies also collect hate crime data for the category called *crimes against society*, which includes drug or narcotic offenses, gambling offenses, prostitution offenses, and weapon law violations.

National Volume and Percent Distribution

In 2019, 2,172 law enforcement agencies (out of 15,588 participating agencies) reported 7,314 hate crime incidents involving 8,559 offenses. Of these, 7,103 were single-bias offenses. An analysis of the single-bias incidents revealed that 55.8 percent were racially/ethnically/ancestrally motivated, 21.4 percent were motivated by religious bias, 16.8 percent resulted from sexual orientation bias, 3.8 percent were motivated by gender and gender-identity bias, and 2.2 percent were prompted by a disability bias.

The majority of the 4,784 hate crime offenses that were racially motivated resulted from an anti-Black or African American bias (48.4 percent) followed by an anti-White basis (15.8 percent). Bias against people of more than one race accounted for 3.6 percent of offenses, while anti-Asian bias accounted

for 4.3 percent of racially motivated offenses, anti-Arab bias accounted for 2.6 percent of these offenses, anti–Native Hawaiian and Other Pacific Islander accounted for 0.5 percent of these offenses, and anti–American Indian or Alaska Native bias accounted for 2.6 percent of these offenses. Approximately 14.1 percent of crimes were classified as an anti-Hispanic or Latino bias.

Hate crimes motivated by religious bias accounted for 1,650 offenses reported by law enforcement. A breakdown of these offenses revealed 60.3 percent were motivated by anti-Jewish bias, 13.3 percent by anti-Islamic (Muslim) bias, 2.5 percent were anti–multiple religions or groups, 4.0 percent had an anti-Catholic bias, 1.5 percent were anti-Protestant, 2.8 percent were anti—Eastern Orthodox (Russian, Greek, or other), 3.6 percent were anti—other Christian, 0.4 percent were anti-atheism/agnosticism/etc., 0.8 percent were anti-Mormon, 0.4 percent were anti-Hindu, 0.4 percent were anti—Jehovah's Witness, 0.3 percent were anti-Buddhist, 3.0 percent were anti-Sikh, and the remainder, 6.5 percent, of offenses were based on a bias against other religions—those not specified.

In 2019, 1,395 offenses were committed on the basis of sexual orientation bias. Of the offenses based on sexual orientation, 24.5 percent were classified as having an anti–lesbian, gay, bisexual, or transgender (mixed group) bias; 62.2 percent were classified as having an anti–gay bias; 10.2 percent had an anti–lesbian basis; 1.9 percent had an anti-bisexual bias; and 1.2 percent had an anti-heterosexual bias.

Hate crime offenses committed based on disability totaled 169 offenses. The majority (68.6 percent) were classified as anti-mental disability, with the rest (32.49 percent) classified as anti–physical disability.

Of the 224 gender identity bias offenses reported, 173 (77.2 percent) were anti-transgender and 51 were anti–gender nonconforming. Of the 80 gender bias offenses reported, 62 were anti-female and 18 were anti-male.

Crimes Against Persons

Law enforcement agencies reported 5,512 hate crime offenses against persons in 2019. Approximately 40.0 percent involved intimidation, 36.7 percent involved simple assault, and 21.0 percent involved aggravated assault. There were 51 murders and 30 rapes.

Crimes Against Property

In 2019, hate crime offences against property totaled 2,811. Approximately 76.6 percent of offenses involved destruction/damage or vandalism. The remaining 23.4 percent of crimes against property consisted of robbery, burglary, larceny-theft, motor vehicle theft, arson, and other crimes.

PART 6

Indicators of School Crime and Safety, 2019

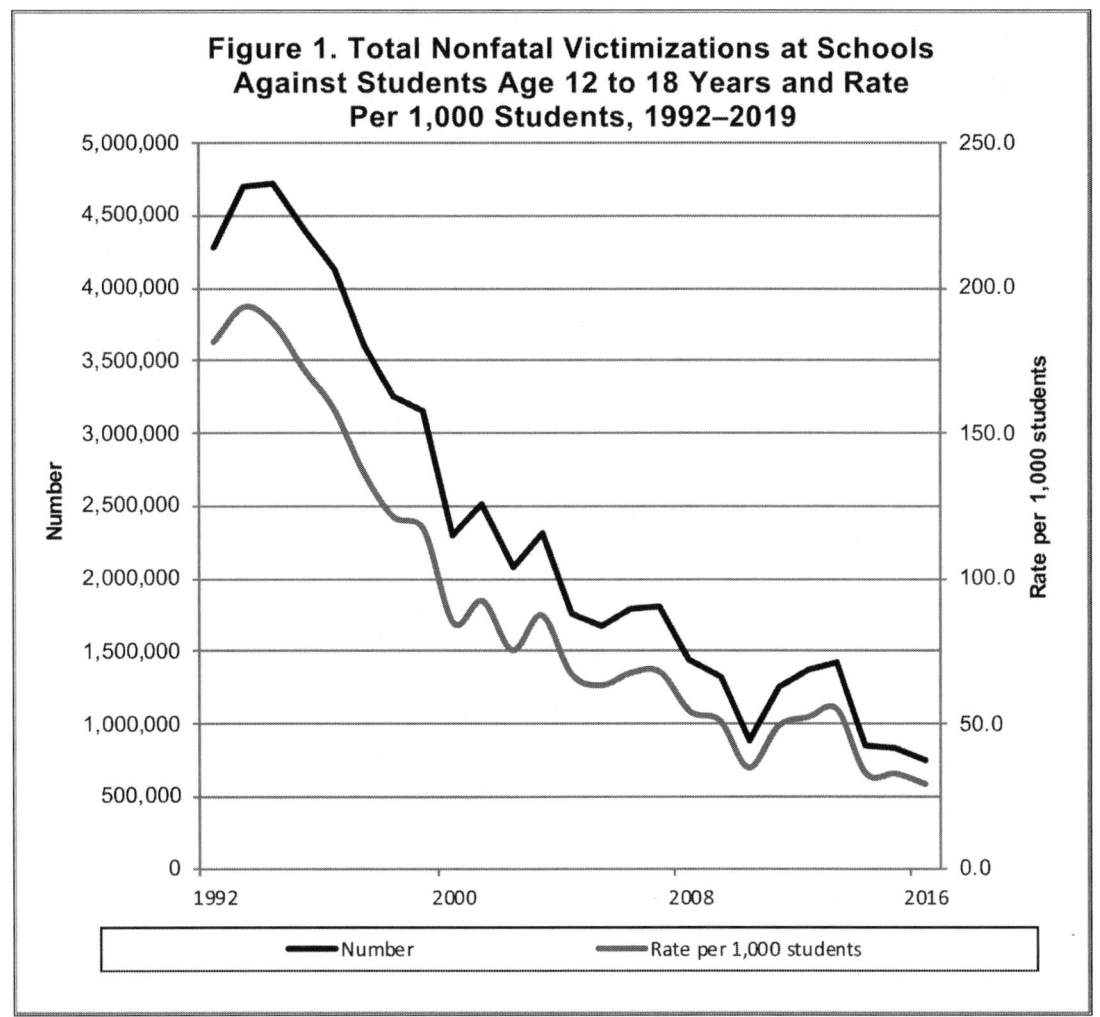

Figure 1. Total Nonfatal Victimizations at Schools Against Students Age 12 to 18 Years and Rate Per 1,000 Students, 1992–2019

- Approximately 764,600 nonfatal victimization incidents occurred at school in 2019 for students between 12 and 18 years of age, and approximately 509,300 incidents occurred away from school.

- Between 2001 and 2019, the percentage of students ages 12 to 18 who reported that gangs were present at their school during the school year showed an overall decrease (from approximately 20 percent to approximately 9 percent).

- In 2019, about 6.4 percent of students ages 12 to 18 reported being called hate-related words at school during the school year, representing a decrease from 13.3 percent in 2001. This percentage also decreased between 2001 and 2017 for male and female students and for White, Black, Asian, and Hispanic students. In 2019, about 23 percent of students reported seeing hate-related graffiti at school during the school year, representing a decrease from approximately 36 percent in 2001.

- The percentage of students in grades 9 through 12 who reported that illegal drugs were made available to them on school property in the last 12 months decreased from about 28.5 percent in 2001 to 21.8 percent in 2019.

- Approximately 22.2 percent of students age 12 to 18 years reported being bullied at school in 2019; only one percentage point differentiated public (22.7 percent) and private schools (21.7 percent); in public schools, 14.9 percent reported cyberbullying among students.

Table 1. School-Associated Violent Deaths of All Persons, Homicides and Suicides of Youth Ages 5 to 18 Years at School, and Total Homicides and Suicides of Youth Ages 5 to 18 Years, by Type of Violent Death: 1992–1993 to 2017–2018

(Number.)

Year	School-associated violent deaths[1] of all persons (includes students, staff, and other nonstudents)						Homicides of youth age 5 to 18 years		Suicides of youth age 5 to 18 years	
	Total	Homicides	Suicides	Legal interventions	Unintentional firearm-related deaths	Undetermined violent deaths	Homicides at school[2]	Total homicides	Suicides at school[2]	Total suicides[3]
1992–1993	57	47	10	0	0	0	34	3,003	6	1,657
1993–1994	48	38	10	0	0	0	29	3,253	7	1,779
1994–1995	48	39	8	0	1	0	28	3,001	7	1,704
1995–1996	53	46	6	1	0	0	32	2,791	6	1,691
1996–1997	48	45	2	1	0	0	28	2,430	1	1,584
1997–1998	57	47	9	1	0	0	34	2,231	6	1,681
1998–1999	47	38	6	2	1	0	33	1,923	4	1,480
1999–2000	37[4]	26[4]	11[4]	0[4]	0[4]	0[4]	14[4]	1,694	8[4]	1,420
2000–2001	34[4]	26[4]	7[4]	1[4]	0[4]	0[4]	14[4]	1,636	6[4]	1,451
2001–2002	36[4]	27[4]	8[4]	1[4]	0[4]	0[4]	16[4]	1,593	5[4]	1,343
2002–2003	36[4]	25[4]	11[4]	0[4]	0[4]	0[4]	18[4]	1,658	10[4]	1,264
2003–2004	45[4]	37[4]	7[4]	1[4]	0[4]	0[4]	23[4]	1,620	5[4]	1,411
2004–2005	52[4]	40[4]	10[4]	2[4]	0[4]	0[4]	22[4]	1,720	8[4]	1,484
2005–2006	44[4]	37[4]	6[4]	1[4]	0[4]	0[4]	21[4]	1,859	3[4]	1,311
2006–2007	63[4]	48[4]	13[4]	2[4]	0[4]	0[4]	32[4]	1,906	9[4]	1,243
2007–2008	44[4]	39[4]	7[4]	2[4]	0[4]	0[4]	21[4]	1,858	5[4]	1,256
2008–2009	44[4]	29[4]	15[4]	0[4]	0[4]	0[4]	18[4]	1,720	7[4]	1,425
2009–2010	35[4]	27[4]	5[4]	3[4]	0[4]	0[4]	19[4]	1,551	2[4]	1,441
2010–2011	32[4]	26[4]	6[4]	0[4]	0[4]	0[4]	11[4]	1,436	3[4]	1,559
2011–2012	45[4]	26[4]	14	5[4]	0[4]	0[4]	15[4]	1,360	5[4]	1,541
2012–2013	53[4]	41[4]	11[4]	1[4]	0[4]	0[4]	31[4]	1,310	6[4]	1,608
2013–2014	48[4]	26[4]	20[4]	1[4]	0[4]	0[4]	12[4]	1,160	8[4]	1,638
2014–2015	47[4]	28[4]	17[4]	2[4]	0[4]	0[4]	20[4]	1,273	9[4]	1,882
2015–2016	38[4]	30[4]	7[4]	1[4]	0[4]	0[4]	18[4]	1,478	3[4]	1,941
2016–2017	42[4]	28[4]	13[4]	1[4]	0[4]	0[4]	18[4]	1,587	6[4]	2,186
2017–2018	56[4]	46[4]	9[4]	1[4]	0[4]	0[4]	35[4]	1,502	8[4]	2,408

NOTE: Unless otherwise noted, data are reported for the school year, defined as July 1 through June 30. Some data have been revised from previously published figures. Violent deaths for which the manner was undetermined; that is, the information pointing to one manner of death was no more compelling than the information pointing to one or more other competing manners of death when all available information was considered.
[1] A school-associated violent death is defined as "a homicide, suicide, or legal intervention (involving a law enforcement officer), in which the fatal injury occurred on the campus of a functioning elementary or secondary school in the United States," while the victim was on the way to or from regular sessions at school, or while the victim was attending or traveling to or from an official school-sponsored event.
[2] "At school" includes on the property of a functioning elementary or secondary school, on the way to or from regular sessions at school, and while attending or traveling to or from a school-sponsored event.
[3] Excludes self-inflicted deaths among 5- to 9-year-olds. The number of self-inflicted deaths among 5- to 9-year-olds was generally less than 7 per year during the period covered by this table.
[4] Data from 1999-2000 onward are subject to change until law enforcement reports have been obtained and interviews with school and law enforcement officials have been completed. The details learned during the interviews can occasionally change the classification of a case.

Table 2. Number of Nonfatal Victimizations Against Students Ages 12 to 18 Years and Rate of Victimization Per 1,000 Students, by Type of Victimization and Location, 1992–2019

(Number; rate per 1,000 students.)

Location and year	Number of nonfatal victimizations		Violent		Rate of victimization per 1,000 students		Violent	
	Total	Theft	All violent	Violent excluding simple assault[1]	Total	Theft	All violent	Violent excluding simple assault[1]
At School[2]								
1992	4,281,200	2,679,400	1,601,800	197,600	181.5	113.6	67.9	8.4
1993	4,692,800	2,477,100	2,215,700	535,500	193.5	102.1	91.4	22.1
1994	4,721,000	2,474,100	2,246,900	459,100	187.7	98.4	89.3	18.3
1995	4,400,700	2,468,400	1,932,200	294,500	172.2	96.6	75.6	11.5
1996	4,130,400	2,205,200	1,925,300	371,900	158.4	84.5	73.8	14.3
1997	3,610,900	1,975,000	1,635,900	376,200	136.6	74.7	61.9	14.2
1998	3,247,300	1,635,100	1,612,200	314,500	121.3	61.1	60.2	11.7
1999	3,152,400	1,752,200	1,400,200	281,100	117.0	65.1	52.0	10.4
2000	2,301,000	1,331,500	969,500	214,200	84.9	49.1	35.8	7.9
2001	2,521,300	1,348,500	1,172,700	259,400	92.3	49.4	42.9	9.5
2002	2,082,600	1,088,800	993,800	173,500	75.4	39.4	36.0	6.3
2003	2,308,800	1,270,500	1,038,300	188,400	87.4	48.1	39.3	7.1
2004	1,762,200	1,065,400	696,800	107,300	67.2	40.6	26.6	4.1
2005	1,678,600	875,900	802,600	140,300	63.2	33.0	30.2	5.3
2006[3]	1,799,900	859,000	940,900	249,900	67.5	32.2	35.3	9.4
2007	1,801,200	896,700	904,400	116,100	67.8	33.7	34.0	4.4
2008	1,435,500	648,000	787,500	128,700	54.3	24.5	29.8	4.9
2009	1,322,800	594,500	728,300	233,700	51.0	22.9	28.1	9.0
2010	892,000	469,800	422,300	155,000	34.9	18.4	16.5	6.1
2011	1,246,200	647,700	598,600	89,500	49.3	25.6	23.7	3.5
2012	1,364,900	615,600	749,200	89,000	52.4	23.6	28.8	3.4
2013	1,420,900	454,900	966,000	125,500	55.0	17.6	37.4	4.9
2014	850,100	363,700	486,400	93,800	33.0	14.1	18.9	3.6
2015	841,100	309,100	531,900	99,000	32.9	12.1	20.8	3.9
2016[4]	NA	NA	NA	NA	NA	NA	NA	NA
2017	827,000	306,500	520,500	110,600	32.7	12.1	20.6	4.4
2018	836,100	225,600	610,500	152,400	32.9	8.9	24.0	6.0
2019	764,600	239,400	523,300	125,600	30.0	9.4	20.6	4.9
Away from School								
1992	4,084,100	1,857,600	2,226,500	1,025,100	173.1	78.7	94.4	43.5
1993	3,835,900	1,731,100	2,104,800	1,004,300	158.2	71.4	86.8	41.4
1994	4,147,100	1,713,900	2,433,200	1,074,900	164.9	68.1	96.7	42.7
1995	3,626,600	1,604,800	2,021,800	829,700	141.9	62.8	79.1	32.5
1996	3,483,200	1,572,700	1,910,600	870,000	133.5	60.3	73.3	33.4
1997	3,717,600	1,710,700	2,006,900	853,300	140.7	64.7	75.9	32.3
1998	3,047,800	1,408,000	1,639,800	684,900	113.8	52.6	61.3	25.6
1999	2,713,800	1,129,200	1,584,500	675,400	100.8	41.9	58.8	25.1
2000	2,303,600	1,228,900	1,074,800	402,100	85.0	45.3	39.6	14.8
2001	1,780,300	961,400	819,000	314,800	65.2	35.2	30.0	11.5
2002	1,619,500	820,100	799,400	341,200	58.6	29.7	28.9	12.4
2003	1,824,100	780,900	1,043,200	412,800	69.1	29.6	39.5	15.6
2004	1,371,800	718,000	653,700	272,500	52.3	27.4	24.9	10.4
2005	1,429,000	637,700	791,300	257,100	53.8	24.0	29.8	9.7
2006[3]	1,413,100	714,200	698,900	263,600	53.0	26.8	26.2	9.9
2007	1,371,700	614,300	757,400	337,700	51.6	23.1	28.5	12.7
2008	1,132,600	498,500	634,100	258,600	42.8	18.9	24.0	9.8
2009	857,200	484,200	372,900	176,800	33.1	18.7	14.4	6.8
2010	689,900	378,800	311,200	167,300	27.0	14.8	12.2	6.5
2011	966,100	541,900	424,300	137,600	38.2	21.4	16.8	5.4
2012	991,200	470,800	520,400	169,900	38.0	18.1	20.0	6.5
2013	778,500	403,000	375,500	151,200	30.1	15.6	14.5	5.8
2014	621,300	288,900	332,400	165,000	24.1	11.2	12.9	6.4
2015	545,100	263,100	281,900	110,900	21.3	10.3	11.0	4.3
2016[4]	NA	NA	NA	NA	NA	NA	NA	NA
2017	503,800	188,600	315,200	145,300	19.9	7.4	12.4	5.7
2018	410,200	158,500	251,400	117,500	16.1	6.3	9.9	4.6
2019	509,300	160,500	348,800	138,000	20.0	6.3	13.7	5.4

Note: "All violent" victimization includes the crimes of rape, sexual assault, robbery, aggravated assault, and simple assault. "Theft" includes attempted and completed purse-snatching, completed pickpocketing, and all attempted and completed thefts, with the exception of motor vehicle thefts. Theft does not include robbery, which involves the threat or use of force and is classified as a violent crime. "Total victimization" includes theft and violent crimes. Data in this table are from the National Crime Victimization Survey (NCVS); due to differences in time coverage and administration between the NCVS and the School Crime Supplement (SCS) to the NCVS, data in this table cannot be compared with data in tables that are based on the SCS. Detail may not sum to totals because of rounding.
NA = Not available.
[1] In previous versions of the table, "violent excluding simple assault" was labeled as "serious violent" victimization.
[2] "At school" includes in the school building, on school property, on a school bus, and going to or from school.
[3] Every 10 years, the survey sample is redesigned to reflect changes in the population. Due to the sample redesign and other methodological changes implemented in 2006, use caution when comparing 2006 estimates to other years.
[4] Every 10 years, the survey sample is redesigned to reflect changes in the population. Due to a sample increase and redesign in 2016, victimization estimates among youth in 2016 were not comparable to estimates for other years.

Table 3. Number of Nonfatal Victimizations Against Students Ages 12 to 18 Years and Rate of Victimization Per 1,000 Students, by Type of Victimization, Location, and Selected Student Characteristics, 2019

(Number; rate per 1,000 students.)

Location and year	Number of nonfatal victimizations				Rate of victimization per 1,000 students			
			Violent				Violent	
	Total	Theft	All violent	Violent excluding simple assault[1]	Total	Theft	All violent	Violent excluding simple assault[1]
At School[2]								
Total.........................	764,600	239,400	525,300	125,600	30.0	9.4	20.6	4.9
Sex								
Male	522,400	142,800	379,700	113,500	39.8	10.9	28.9	8.7
Female....................	242,200	96,600	145,600	12,000 !	19.5	7.8	11.7	1.0 !
Age								
12 to 14 years........	450,100	118,200	331,900	34,400	35.8	9.4	26.4	2.7
15 to 18 years........	314,500	121,200	193,300	91,200	24.3	9.3	14.9	7.0
Race/ethnicity[3]								
White......................	410,900	132,300	278,500	33,300 !	31.1	10.0	21.1	2.5 !
Black.......................	91,600	27,500	64,200	2,900 !	26.8	8.0	18.8	0.9 !
Hispanic..................	208,100	64,200	143,900	79,300 !	32.9	10.1	22.7	12.5 !
Other......................	54,100	15,400 !	38,700	10,100 !	21.1	6.0 !	15.1	3.9 !
Urbanicity[4]								
Urban......................	316,800	99,700	217,100	23,600 !	41.1	12.9	28.2	3.1 !
Suburban	331,600	101,100	230,500	82,200 !	23.1	7.1	16.1	5.7 !
Rural	116,200	38,600	77,600	19,700 !	33.3	11.1	22.3	5.7 !
Household income[5]								
Less than $25,000....	118,600	39,000	79,700	1,000 !	32.7	10.7	22.0	0.3 !
$25,000 to $49,999..	156,500	33,000	123,500	14,700 !	25.7	5.4	20.3	2.4 !
$50,000 to $99,999..	212,800	79,800	133,000	37,200 !	26.1	9.8	16.3	4.6 !
$100,000 or more....	276,800	87,700	189,100	72,700 !	36.2	11.5	24.7	9.5 !
Away from School								
Total........................	509,300	160,500	348,800	138,000	20.0	6.3	13.7	5.4
Sex								
Male	205,900	99,100	106,900	44,900	15.7	7.6	8.1	3.4
Female....................	303,400	61,500	241,900	93,200	24.4	5.0	19.5	7.5
Age								
12 to 14 years........	149,200	61,900	87,300	25,200	11.9	4.9	6.9	2.0
15 to 18 years........	360,100	98,600	261,500	112,900	27.8	7.6	20.2	8.7
Race/ethnicity[3]								
White......................	332,800	78,500	254,300	91,500	25.2	5.9	19.2	6.9
Black.......................	47,600	20,100	27,500 !	12,600 !	13.9	5.9	8.0 !	3.7 !
Hispanic..................	69,300	35,400	33,900	19,700 !	10.9	5.6	5.4	3.1 !
Other......................	59,600	26,500	33,100 !	14,300 !	23.3	10.3	12.9 !	5.6 !
Urbanicity[4]								
Urban......................	141,000	73,600	67,400	23,500 !	18.3	9.5	8.7	3.1 !
Suburban	278,900	44,100	234,800	98,500	19.5	3.1	16.4	6.9
Rural	89,400	42,900	46,500	16,000 !	25.6	12.3	13.4	4.6 !
Household income[5]								
Less than $25,000....	111,100	55,700	55,400	15,800 !	30.6	15.4	15.3	4.4 !
$25,000 to $49,999..	130,600	43,800	86,800	69,600	21.5	7.2	14.3	11.4
$50,000 to $99,999..	97,100	30,900	66,200	31,300	11.9	3.8	8.1	3.8
$100,000 or more....	170,400	30,100	140,400	21,400 !	22.3	3.9	18.3	2.8

NOTE: "All violent" victimization includes the crimes of rape, sexual assault, robbery, aggravated assault, and simple assault. "Theft" includes attempted and completed purse-snatching, completed pickpocketing, and all attempted and completed thefts, with the exception of motor vehicle thefts. Theft does not include robbery, which involves the threat or use of force and is classified as a violent crime. "Total victimization" includes theft and violent crimes. Data in this table are from the National Crime Victimization Survey (NCVS) and are reported in accordance with Bureau of Justice Statistics standards. Detail may not sum to totals because of rounding. The population size for students ages 12-18 was 25,528,100 in 2019.

! =Interpret data with caution. Estimate based on 10 or fewer sample cases, or the coefficient of variation is greater than 50 percent.
[1] In previous versions of the table, "violent excluding simple assault" was labeled as "serious violent" victimization.
[2] "At school" includes in the school building, on school property, on a school bus, and going to or from school.
[3] Race categories exclude persons of Hispanic ethnicity. "Other" includes Asian, Pacific Islander, American Indian/Alaska Native, and two or more races.
[4] Refers to the Standard Metropolitan Statistical Area (MSA) status of the respondent's household as defined by the U.S. Census Bureau. Categories include "central city of an MSA (Urban)," "in MSA but not in central city (Suburban)," and "not MSA (Rural)."
[5] Income data for 2019 were imputed. For more information, see Criminal Victimization, 2019, available at https://www.bjs.gov/content/pub/pdf/cv19.pdf.

Table 4. Percentage of Students Ages 12 to 18 Years Who Reported Criminal Victimization at School During the Previous 6 Months, by Type of Victimization and Selected Student and School Characteristics, Selected Years, 1995–2019

(Percent.)

Characteristic	1995	2001	2003	2005	2007	2009	2011	2013	2015	2017	2019
Total..............................	9.1	5.5	5.1	4.3	4.3	3.9	3.5	3.0	2.7	2.2	2.5
Sex											
Male	9.6	6.1	5.3	4.6	4.5	4.6	3.7	3.2	2.6	2.6	3.1
Female	8.5	4.9	4.8	3.9	3.9	3.2	3.4	2.8	2.8	1.8	1.9
Race/ethnicity[1]											
White........................	9.4	5.7	5.4	4.6	4.2	3.9	3.6	3.0	2.9	2.2	2.5
Black........................	9.6	6.1	5.1	3.9	4.3	4.4	4.6	3.2	2.2 !	2.6	3.0 !
Hispanic....................	7.1	4.6	3.9	3.9	3.6	3.9	2.9	3.2	2.3	2.0	1.8
Asian/Pacific Islander	8.3	3.7	3.2	1.4. !	3.4 !	*	2.3 !	2.4 !	*	2.1 !	*
Asian....................	NA	NA	3.3 !	1.5 !	3.6 !	*	2.5 !	2.6 !	*	2.1 !	*
Pacific Islander	NA	NA	*	*	*	*	*	*	*	*	*
American Indian/ Alaska Native	9.6 !	*	*	*	*	*	*	*	*	11.1 !	*
Two or more races	NA	NA	9.8	*	10.1	*	4.9 !	3.0 !	6.5 !	*	6.5 !
Grade											
6th............................	8.8	5.9	3.8	4.6	3.9	3.7	3.8	4.1	3.1	3.1	3.1
7th............................	10.6	5.8	6.3	5.4	4.7	3.4	3.1	2.5	3.4	2.6	2.9
8th............................	10.1	4.3	5.2	3.6	4.4	3.8	3.8	2.3	2.3	1.8	2.1
9th............................	11.4	7.9	6.3	4.7	5.3	5.3	5.1	4.1	3.0	2.7	2.6
10th..........................	8.7	6.5	4.7	4.3	4.4	4.2	3.0	3.3	1.6	2.7	3.3
11th..........................	7.0	4.8	5.0	3.6	4.0	4.7	3.1	3.3	4.4	1.4	2.4
12th..........................	5.8	2.9	3.6	3.7	2.7	2.0	2.9	2.0 !	1.3 !	1.4	1.1 !
School locale[2]											
Urban........................	NA	NA	NA	NA	NA	NA	NA	NA	3.1	2.5	3.3
Suburban	NA	NA	NA	NA	NA	NA	NA	NA	3.2	1.9	2.1
Rural	NA	NA	NA	NA	NA	NA	NA	NA	1.3 !	2.3	2.8 !
Town	NA	NA	NA	NA	NA	NA	NA	NA	2.2	2.0	2.4
Control of school[2,3]											
Public........................	9.3	5.7	5.1	4.4	4.5	4.1	3.7	3.1	2.8	2.2	2.7
Private........................	6.2	3.4	4.9	2.7	1.1 !	1.8 !	1.9 !	2.8 !	*	*	*
Theft.............................	7.0	4.2	4.0	3.1	3.0	2.8	2.6	1.9	1.9	1.5	1.5
Sex											
Male	7.0	4.5	3.9	3.1	3.0	3.4	2.6	2.0	1.7	1.6	1.6
Female	7.0	3.8	4.1	3.2	3.0	2.1	2.6	1.8	2.0	1.3	1.4
Race/ethnicity[1]											
White........................	7.3	4.1	4.3	3.4	3.1	2.9	2.5	1.6	2.0	1.3	1.6
Black........................	6.9	5.0	3.8	2.7	3.1	2.5	3.7	2.7	1.3 !	1.8	1.7 !
Hispanic....................	5.7	3.7	3.0	3.1	2.2	3.0	2.0	1.8	1.6	1.4	1.2
Asian/Pacific Islander	6.4	3.5	3.2	*	3.0 !	*	2.3 !	2.4 !	*	2.1 !	*
Asian....................	NA	NA	3.3 !	*	3.2 !	*	2.5 !	2.6 !	*	2.1 !	*
Pacific Islander	NA	NA	*	*	*	*	*	*	*	*	*
American Indian/ Alaska Native	7.2 !	*	*	*	*	*	*	*	*	7.2 !	*
Two or more races	NA	NA	8.3 !	*	5.3 !	*	3.7 !	*	4.3 !	*	*
Grade											
6th............................	5.4	4.0	2.2	2.8	2.6	1.3	2.7	1.4 !	1.6 !	1.0 !	1.4 !
7th............................	8.1	3.4	4.8	2.9	2.7	2.1	1.9	1.4	1.6 !	1.3 !	1.5 !
8th............................	7.8	3.3	4.1	2.4	2.5	2.0	2.0	1.0 !	1.8	1.1 !	1.1 !
9th............................	8.8	6.2	5.2	3.7	4.6	4.9	4.4	2.7	2.1	2.4	1.7
10th..........................	7.6	5.7	3.7	3.8	3.6	3.5	2.1	2.6	1.4 !	2.1	2.1
11th..........................	5.4	3.8	4.1	2.8	2.6	3.3	2.7	2.3	3.4	1.1 !	1.7 !
12th..........................	4.5	2.3	3.1	3.4	1.9	1.5	2.4	1.6 !	1.0 !	1.2 !	0.9!
School locale[2]											
Urban........................	NA	NA	NA	NA	NA	NA	NA	NA	2.3	1.6	2.0
Suburban	NA	NA	NA	NA	NA	NA	NA	NA	1.8	1.4	1.1
Rural	NA	NA	NA	NA	NA	NA	NA	NA	1.1 !	1.0 !	1.9 !
Town	NA	NA	NA	NA	NA	NA	NA	NA	1.6	1.4	1.5
Control of school[2,3]											
Public........................	7.2	4.4	4.0	3.3	3.2	2.9	2.7	1.9	1.9	1.5	1.7
Private........................	4.9	2.4	4.0	1.3 !	1.1 !	*	1.2 !	2.0 !	*	*	*
All Violent..............................	2.5	1.8	1.3	1.2	1.6	1.4	1.1	1.2	0.9	0.7	1.1
Sex											
Male	3.0	2.1	1.7	1.6	1.7	1.6	1.2	1.3	1.0	1.0	1.6
Female	2.0	1.4	0.9	0.8	1.4	1.1	0.9	1.1	0.9	0.5	0.5

Table 4. Percentage of Students Ages 12 to 18 Years Who Reported Criminal Victimization at School During the Previous 6 Months, by Type of Victimization and Selected Student and School Characteristics, Selected Years, 1995–2019—Continued

(Percent.)

Characteristic	1995	2001	2003	2005	2007	2009	2011	2013	2015	2017	2019
Race/ethnicity[1]											
White.............................	2.5	2.0	1.4	1.3	1.5	1.2	1.2	1.5	1.0	0.9	1.1
Black.............................	3.0	1.3 !	1.5	1.3 !	1.6 !	2.3	1.1 !	*	0.9 !	0.8 !	1.4 !
Hispanic........................	2.0	1.5	1.1	0.9	1.4	1.3 !	1.0	1.5	0.6 !	0.5 !	0.6 !
Asian/Pacific Islander	2.2 !	*	*	*	*	*	*	*	*	*	*
Asian...........................	NA	NA	*	*	*	*	*	*	*	*	*
Pacific Islander........................	NA	NA	*	*	*	*	*	*	*	*	*
American Indian/ Alaska Native	*	*	*	*	*	*	*	*	*	*	*
Two or more races	NA	NA	*	*	5.3 !	*	*	*	3.6	*	3.2 !
Grade											
6th................................	4.3	2.6	1.9	1.9	1.5 !	2.6	1.3 !	2.7	1.6 ~	2.1	1.7 !
7th................................	3.1	2.6	1.7	2.6	2.4	1.2	1.2 !	1.2 !	1.9	1.4 !	1.7
8th................................	2.7	1.3	1.4	1.4	2.1	2.0	2.1	1.4	0.6 !	0.7 !	1.0!
9th................................	2.9	2.4	1.5	1.0	1.2 !	0.9	1.1 !	1.4 !	0.8 !	*	1.1 !
10th...............................	1.8	1.2	1.3	0.5 !	1.2 !	1.0	0.9 !	1.0 !	*	0.7 !	1.2 !
11th...............................	1.6	1.6	0.9 !	0.7 !	1.5	1.5	*	1.0 !	1.3 !	*	0.8 !
12th...............................	1.6	0.9 !	0.5 !	*	0.8 !	*	*	*	*	*	*
School locale[2]											
Urban.............................	NA	NA	NA	NA	NA	NA	NA	NA	0.8 !	1.0	1.3
Suburban	NA	NA	NA	NA	NA	NA	NA	NA	1.5	0.5 !	1.0
Rural	NA	NA	NA	NA	NA	NA	NA	NA	*	1.3 !	1.2 !
Town	NA	NA	NA	NA	NA	NA	NA	NA	0.6 !	0.5. !	1.2 !
Control of school[2,3]											
Public.............................	2.6	1.8	1.4	1.2	1.7	1.4	1.1	1.2	1.0	0.8	1.2
Private............................	1.6	1.0 !	0.9 !	1.4 !	*	*	*	*	*	*	*
Violent Excluding Simple Assault[4]	0.5	0.4	0.2	0.3	0.4	0.3	0.1	0.2	0.2	0.2	0.3
Sex											
Male	0.7	0.5	0.3 !	0.3 !	0.5 !	0.6	0.2!	0.2!	0.2!	0.2!	0.4 !
Female	0.3	0.4 !	*	0.3	0.2 !	*	*	0.2	*	0.2!	*
Race/ethnicity[1]											
White.............................	0.5	0.4	0.2	0.3 !	0.2 !	0.3	0.2!	0.2!	0.3 !	0.3 !	0.2!
Black.............................	0.8 !	0.5 !	*	*	*	*	*	*	*	*	*
Hispanic........................	0.4 !	0.8 !	0.4 !	0.4 !	0.8 !	*	*	0.4 !	*	*	*
Asian/Pacific Islander	*	*	*	*	*	*	*	*	*	*	*
Asian...........................	NA	NA	*	*	*	*	*	*	*	*	*
Pacific Islander........................	NA	NA	*	*	*	*	*	*	*	*	*
American Indian/ Alaska Native	*	*	*	*	*	*	*	*	*	*	*
Two or more races	NA	NA	*	*	*	*	*	*	*	*	*
Grade											
6th................................	1.2!	*	*	*	*	*	*	0.8 !	*	*	*
7th................................	0.5 !	0.6 !	*	*	0.4 !	*	0.5	*	*	*	*
8th................................	0.6 !	0.3 !	*	*	*	*	#	*	*	*	*
9th................................	0.5 !	0.8 !	0.6 !	*	*	*	*	*	*	*	*
10th...............................	0.2 !	0.4 !	*	*	*	*	#	*	*	*	*
11th...............................	0.3 !	*	*	*	0.6 !	*	#	*	*	*	*
12th...............................	*	*	*	*	*	*	#	*	*	*	*
School locale[2]											
Urban.............................	NA	NA	NA	NA	NA	NA	NA	NA	*	*	0.3 !
Suburban	NA	NA	NA	NA	NA	NA	NA	NA	0.5 !	*	*
Rural	NA	NA	NA	NA	NA	NA	NA	NA	*	*	*
Town	NA	NA	NA	NA	NA	NA	NA	NA	*	*	*
Control of school[2,3]											
Public.............................	0.5	0.5	0.2	0.3	0.4	0.4	0.1!	0.2!	0.2!	0.2!	0.3 !
Private............................	*	*	*	*	*	*	*	*	*	*	*

NOTE: "Total victimization" includes theft and violent victimization. A single student could report more than one type of victimization. In the total victimization section, students who reported both theft and violent victimization are counted only once. "Theft" includes attempted and completed purse-snatching, completed pickpocketing, and all attempted and completed thefts, with the exception of motor vehicle thefts. Theft does not include robbery, which involves the threat or use of force and is classified as a violent crime. "All violent" victimization includes the crimes of rape, sexual assault, robbery, aggravated assault, and simple assault. "At school" includes in the school building, on school property, on a school bus, and, from 2001 onward, going to and from school. Some data have been revised from previously published figures.
NA = Not available.
* = Rounds to zero.
! = Interpret data with caution. The coefficient of variation (CV) for this estimate is between 30 and 50 percent.
^ = Reporting standards not met. Either there are too few cases for a reliable estimate or the coefficient of variation (CV) is 50 percent or greater.
[1]Race categories exclude persons of Hispanic ethnicity. Prior to 2003, separate data for Asian students, Pacific Islander students, and students of Two or more races were not collected.
[2]Excludes students with missing information about the school characteristic.
[3]Data for 2013 and prior years were based on school information provided by the respondent. Beginning in 2015, data were based on school information collected in the Common Core of Data and the Private School Universe Survey, which was appended to the School Crime Supplement data file; therefore, these data may not be entirely comparable with figures for earlier years.
[4]In previous versions of this table, "violent excluding simple assault" was labeled as "serious violent" victimization. This category includes all types of violent victimization with the exception of simple assault.

Table 5. Number and Percentage of Public School Teachers Who Reported That They Were Threatened with Injury or Physically Attacked by a Student from School During the Previous 12 Months, by Selected Teacher and School Characteristics, Selected Years, 1993–1994 Through 2015–2016

(Number; percent.)

Incident and year	Total	Sex		Race/ethnicity				Instructional level[1]	
		Male	Female	White	Black	Hispanic	Other[2]	Elementary	Secondary
				Number of teachers					
Threatened with Injury									
1993–1994	326,800	111,200	215,600	281,300	23,400	15,100	6,900	128,000	198,800
1999–2000	287,400	89,600	197,800	237,100	27,200	16,300	6,700	138,000	149,300
2003–2004	242,100	75,300	166,800	189,800	31,900	11,800	8,600	108,800	133,300
2007–2008	276,600	85,200	191,500	223,200	27,600	17,400	8,400	123,800	152,800
2011–2012	338,400	79,800	258,600	266,800	33,400	26,600	11,600	184,000	154,400
2015–2016	327,900	80,700	247,200	262,800	26,200	24,400	14,600	182,100	145,800
Physically Attacked									
1993–1994	112,400	28,700	83,700	96,300	7,600	5,900	2,600	71,600	40,700
1999–2000	125,000	29,100	95,900	103,100	11,000	8,400	2,500	94,400	30,600
2003–2004	121,400	21,700	99,700	95,500	14,800	6,400	4,700	85,100	36,300
2007–2008	146,400	33,400	113,000	124,100	11,600	7,800	2,800!	109,100	37,300
2011–2012	197,400	29,500	167,900	160,700	18,000	11,300	7,400	153,800	43,600
2015–2016	192,500	30,200	162,300	155,600	12,700	14,200	10,000	153,700	38,800
				Percent of teachers					
Threatened with Injury									
1993–1994	12.8	16.0	11.5	12.7	12.4	13.9	14.5	9.6	16.2
1999–2000	9.6	11.9	8.8	9.4	11.9	9.7	9.1	8.6	10.7
2003–2004	7.4	9.3	6.8	7.0	12.4	5.8	9.6	6.3	8.7
2007–2008	8.1	10.4	7.4	7.9	11.5	7.3	8.7	7.2	9.1
2011–2012	10.0	10.0	10.0	9.6	14.5	10.1	9.9	10.7	9.3
2015–2016	9.8	10.4	9.6	9.8	11.7	8.4	10.3	10.8	8.8
Physically Attacked									
1993–1994	4.4	4.1	4.5	4.3	4.0	5.4	5.4	5.4	3.3
1999–2000	4.2	3.9	4.3	4.1	4.8	5.0	3.4	5.9	2.2
2003–2004	3.7	2.7	4.1	3.5	5.8	3.2	5.3	5.0	2.4
2007–2008	4.3	4.1	4.4	4.4	4.9	3.3	3.0!	6.3	2.2
2011–2012	5.8	3.7	6.5	5.8	7.8	4.3	6.3	8.9	2.6
2015–2016	5.7	3.9	6.3	5.8	5.7	4.9	7.1	9.1	2.3

NOTE: Teachers who taught only prekindergarten students are excluded. Includes teachers in both traditional public schools and public charter schools. Race categories exclude persons of Hispanic ethnicity. Detail may not sum to totals because of rounding. Some data have been revised from previously published figures.
! = Interpret data with caution. The coefficient of variation (CV) for this estimate is between 30 and 50 percent.
[1]Instructional level divides teachers into elementary or secondary based on a combination of grades taught, main teaching assignment, and structure of teachers' class(es), rather than the level of school in which teachers taught. Teachers with only ungraded classes were classified based on their main teaching assignment and the structure of their class(es). Among teachers with regularly graded classes, elementary teachers generally include those teaching prekindergarten through grade 6 and those teaching multiple grades, with a preponderance of grades taught being kindergarten through grade 6. In general, secondary teachers include those teaching any of grades 7 through 12 and those teaching multiple grades, with a preponderance of grades taught being grades 7 through 12 and usually with no grade taught being lower than grade 5.
[2]Includes American Indian/Alaska Native, Asian, and Pacific Islander; for 2003-04 and later years, also includes two or more races.

Table 6. Percentage of Public Schools Recording Incidents of Crime at School and Reporting Incidents to Police, Number of Incidents, and Rate Per 1,000 Students, by Type of Crime, Selected Years, 1999–2000 Through 2017–2018

(Percent; number; rate per 1,000 students.)

Type of crime recorded or reported to police	Percent of schools						2015–2016		2017–2018	
	1999–2000	2003–2004	2005–2006	2007–2008	2009–2010	2013–2014[1]	Percent of schools	Number of incidents	Percent of schools	Number of incidents
Recorded Incidents										
Total	86.4	88.5	85.7	85.5	85.0	NA	78.9	1,381,200	79.8	1,438,500
Violent Incidents	71.4	81.4	77.7	75.5	73.8	65.0	68.9	864,900	70.7	962,300
Serious violent incidents	19.7	18.3	17.1	17.2	16.4	13.1	15.5	40,800	21.3	54,400
Rape or attempted rape	0.7	0.8	0.3	0.8	0.5	0.2!	0.9	1,100	0.9	1,100
Sexual assault other than rape[2]	2.5	3.0	2.8	2.5	2.3	1.7	3.4	6,100	5.2	7,100
Physical attack or fight with a weapon	5.2	4.0	3.0	3.0	3.9	1.8	2.6	5,300	3.0	10,500
Threat of physical attack with a weapon	11.1	8.6	8.8	9.3	7.7	8.7	8.5	18,300	13.2	26,700
Robbery with a weapon	0.5!	0.6	0.4	0.4!	0.2	‡	0.5 !	600	0.4	500
Robbery without a weapon	5.3	6.3	6.4	5.2	4.4	2.5	2.7	9,500	3.5	8,500
Physical attack or fight without a weapon	63.7	76.7	74.3	72.7	70.5	57.5	64.9	567,000	65.7	597,300
Threat of physical attack without a weapon	52.2	53.0	52.2	47.8	46.4	47.1	39.4	257,000	41.4	310,700
Theft/Larceny[3]	45.6	46.0	46.0	47.3	44.1	NA	38.7	166,000	33.4	132,500
Other Incidents[4]	72.7	64.0	68.2	67.4	68.1	NA	58.5	350,400	59.8	343,700
Possession of a firearm/explosive device	5.5	6.1	7.2	4.7	4.7	NA	4.0	10,500	3.3	3,600
Possession of a knife or sharp object	42.6	NA	42.8	40.6	39.7	NA	38.4	70,600	38.2	69,100
Distribution of illegal drugs[5]	12.3	12.9	NA	NA	NA	NA	NA	NA	NA	NA
Possession or use of alcohol or illegal drugs[5]	26.6	29.3	NA	NA	NA	NA	NA	NA	NA	NA
Distribution, possession, or use of illegal drugs[6]	NA	NA	25.9	23.2	24.6	NA	24.9	112,100	24.9	120,300
Inappropriate distribution, possession, or use of prescription drugs[7]	NA	NA	NA	NA	12.1	NA	9.5	20,100	9.7	21,100
Distribution, possession, or use of alcohol[6]	NA	NA	16.2	14.9	14.1	NA	13.3	29,900	13.4	29,000
Sexual harassment	36.3	NA	NA	NA	NA	NA	NA	NA	NA	NA
Vandalism	51.4	51.4	50.5	49.3	45.8	NA	33.4	107,200	33.1	100,600
Reported Incidents to Police										
Total	62.5	65.2	60.9	62.0	60.0	NA	47.4	448,900	46.9	422,800
Violent Incidents	36.0	43.6	37.7	37.8	39.9	NA	32.7	195,600	32.5	192,100
Serious violent incidents	14.8	13.3	12.6	12.6	10.4	NA	10.0	20,000	14.9	26,100
Rape or attempted rape	0.6	0.8	0.3	0.8	0.5	NA	0.7	900	0.8	1,000
Sexual assault other than rape[2]	2.3	2.6	2.6	2.1	1.4	NA	2.7	3,600	4.3	5,600
Physical attack or fight with a weapon	3.9	2.8	2.2	2.1	2.2	NA	1.3	2,500 !	1.5	2,400
Threat of physical attack with a weapon	8.5	6.0	5.9	5.7	4.5	NA	5.3	7,500	9.0	12,400
Robbery with a weapon	0.3!	0.6	0.4	0.4	0.2	NA	0.3 !	400 !	0.3	400
Robbery without a weapon	3.4	4.2	4.9	4.1	3.5	NA	1.9	5,000	2.4	4,300
Physical attack or fight without a weapon	25.8	35.6	29.2	28.2	34.3	NA	25.1	121,500	21.7	107,600
Threat of physical attack without a weapon	18.9	21.0	19.7	19.5	15.2	NA	12.9	54,200	14.3	58,400
Theft/larceny[3]	28.5	30.5	27.9	31.0	25.4	NA	18.1	71,600	14.9	53,900
Other Incidents[4]	52.0	50.0	50.6	48.7	46.3	NA	33.5	181,700	35.1	176,900
Possession of a firearm/explosive device	4.5	4.9	5.5	3.6	3.1	NA	1.9	7,500 !	2.1	2,300
Possession of a knife or sharp object	23.0	NA	25.0	23.3	20.0	NA	15.8	27,700	18.0	30,500
Distribution of illegal drugs[5]	11.4	12.4	NA	NA	NA	NA	NA	NA	NA	NA
Possession or use of alcohol or illegal drugs[5]	22.2	26.0	NA	NA	NA	NA	NA	NA	NA	NA
Distribution, possession, or use of illegal drugs[6]	NA	NA	22.8	20.7	21.4	NA	19.9	82,200	19.9	84,800
Inappropriate distribution, possession, or use of prescription drugs[7]	NA	NA	NA	NA	9.6	NA	7.4	15,100	7.1	15,100
Distribution, possession, or use of alcohol[6]	NA	NA	11.6	10.6	10.0	NA	8.6	17,800	8.0	16,900
Sexual harassment	14.7	NA	NA	NA	NA	NA	NA	NA	NA	NA
Vandalism	32.7	34.3	31.9	30.8	26.8	NA	12.9	31,600	12.0	27,300

NOTE: Responses were provided by the principal or the person most knowledgeable about crime and safety issues at the school. "At school" was defined to include activities that happen in school buildings, on school grounds, on school buses, and at places that hold school-sponsored events or activities. Respondents were instructed to include incidents that occurred before, during, and after normal school hours or when school activities or events were in session. Detail may not sum to totals because of rounding and because schools that recorded or reported more than one type of crime incident were counted only once in the total percentage of schools recording or reporting incidents.
NA = Not available.
! = Interpret data with caution. The coefficient of variation (CV) for this estimate is between 30 and 50 percent.
[1]Data for 2013-14 were collected using the Fast Response Survey System (FRSS), while data for all other years were collected using the School Survey on Crime and Safety (SSOCS). The 2013-14 FRSS survey was designed to allow comparisons with SSOCS data. However, all respondents to the 2013-14 survey could choose either to complete the survey on paper (and mail it back) or to complete the survey online, whereas all respondents to SSOCS had only the option of completing a paper survey prior to 2017-18, when SSOCS experimented with offering an online option to some respondents. The 2013-14 FRSS survey also relied on a smaller sample than SSOCS. The FRSS survey's smaller sample size and difference in survey administration may have impacted the 2013-14 results.
[2]Prior to 2015–2016, the wording of the survey item was "sexual battery other than rape."
[3]Theft/larceny is taking things worth over $10 without personal confrontation.
[4]Caution should be used when making direct comparisons of "Other incidents" between years because the survey questions about alcohol and drugs changed, as outlined in footnotes 5, 6, and 7, and because sexual harrassment was only included in 1999-2000.
[5]The survey items "Distribution of illegal drugs" and "Possession or use of alcohol or illegal drugs" appear only on the 1999-2000 and 2003-04 questionnaires. Different alcohol- and drug-related survey items were used on the SSOCS questionnaires for later years.
[6]The survey items "Distribution, possession, or use of illegal drugs" and "Distribution, possession, or use of alcohol" appear only on the SSOCS questionnaires for 2005-06 and later years.
[7]The survey item "Inappropriate distribution, possession, or use of prescription drugs" appears only on the SSOCS questionnaires for 2009-10 and later years.

Table 7. Percentage of Students Ages 12 to 18 Years Who Reported That Gangs Were Present at School During the School Year, by Sex, Race/Ethnicity, and Urbanicity, Selected Years, 2001–2019

(Percent.)

Student or school characteristic	2001[1]	2003[1]	2005[1]	2007	2009	2011	2013	2015	2017	2019[2]
Total	20.3	21.0	24.2	23.2	20.4	17.5	12.4	10.7	8.6	9.0
Sex										
Male	21.5	22.4	25.3	25.1	20.9	17.5	12.9	10.9	7.9	9.5
Female	18.9	19.6	22.9	21.3	19.9	17.5	12.0	10.4	9.3	8.5
Race/ethnicity[3]										
White	15.5	14.2	16.7	16.0	14.1	11.1	7.4	7.4	5.3	6.3
Black..	28.8	29.7	37.5	37.5	31.4	32.7	18.6	17.1	16.6	14.7
Hispanic..	32.3	37.3	38.9	36.1	33.0	26.4	20.1	15.3	12.3	12.5
Asian/Pacific Islander................................	23.3	21.8	21.3	18.1	16.9	10.1	9.8	5.0 !	2.4 !	5.3
Asian	NA	21.2	20.3	17.4	17.2	9.9	9.4	4.1 !	2.0 !	4.5
Pacific Islander	NA	^	^	^	^	^	^	^	^	^
American Indian/ Alaska Native.................	13.2 !	24.8 !	^	17.2 !	^	^	18.3	^	^	15.8 !
Two or more races....................................	NA	22.3	23.6	28.3	18.0	10.3	13.3	13.5	9.7	9.1
Grade										
6th...	11.3	10.9	12.1	15.3	11.0	8.2	5.0	5.7	4.8	5.8
7th...	15.8	16.4	17.3	17.4	14.8	10.2	7.7	6.8	5.4	5.5
8th...	17.4	17.9	19.1	20.6	15.9	11.3	7.8	7.2	6.6	5.9
9th...	24.3	26.2	28.3	28.0	24.9	21.7	13.9	13.3	10.9	11.6
10th...	23.8	26.6	32.6	28.1	27.7	23.0	17.7	13.3	11.4	12.1
11th...	24.2	23.5	28.0	25.9	22.6	23.2	17.1	13.3	9.7	9.9
12th...	21.2	22.4	27.9	24.4	21.9	21.3	14.6	13.1	9.8	11.0
School locale[4]										
Urban...	NA	NA	NA	NA	NA	NA	NA	15.4	12.3	13.5
Suburban..	NA	NA	NA	NA	NA	NA	NA	11.0	7.4	7.9
Rural..	NA	NA	NA	NA	NA	NA	NA	8.3	9.1	8.9
Town..	NA	NA	NA	NA	NA	NA	NA	4.9	5.6	6.0
Control of school[4,5]										
Public...	21.7	22.6	25.8	24.9	22.0	18.9	13.3	11.4	9.2	9.8
Private..	5.0	3.9	4.2	5.2	2.3 !	1.9 !	2.3 !	2.0 !	^	^

NOTE: "At school" includes in the school building, on school property, on a school bus, and going to and from school. Some data have been revised from previously published figures.

NA = Not available.

! = Interpret data with caution. The coefficient of variation (CV) for this estimate is between 30 and 50 percent.

^ = Reporting standards not met. Either there are too few cases for a reliable estimate or the coefficient of variation (CV) is 50 percent or greater.

[1]In 2005 and prior years, the period covered by the survey question was "during the last 6 months," but this was changed to "during this school year" beginning in 2007. Cognitive testing suggested that modifications to the reference period would not have a substantial impact on the survey responses.

[2]The 2019 survey included a split sample design to test alternate introductions for the section assessing the presence of gangs at school. Approximately 60 percent of the sample received the version of the questionnaire that was consistent with prior years, where the section introduction included the definition "All gangs, whether or not they are involved in violent or illegal activity, are included." The remaining 40 percent of the sample received the alternate questionnaire, which excluded the definition. Estimates in this table include all respondents, regardless of which version of the questionnaire they received. For more information about the 2019 survey collection and experiment, see Methodology Report: Split-Half Administration of the 2019 School Crime Supplement to the National Crime Victimization Survey (NCES 2021-016).

[3]Race categories exclude persons of Hispanic ethnicity. In 2001, separate data for Asian students, Pacific Islander students, and students of two or more races were not collected.

[4]Excludes students with missing information about the school characteristic.

[5]Data for 2013 and prior years were based on school information provided by the respondent. Beginning in 2015, data were based on school information collected in the Common Core of Data and the Private School Universe Survey, which was appended to the School Crime Supplement data file; therefore, these data may not be entirely comparable with figures for earlier years.

Table 8. Percentage of Students in Grades 9 to 12 Who Reported That Illegal Drugs Were Made Available to Them on School Property During the Previous 12 Months, by Selected Student Characteristics, Selected Years, 1993–2019

(Percent.)

Student characteristic	1993	1999	2001	2003	2005	2007	2009	2011	2013	2015	2017	2019
Total	24.0	30.2	28.5	28.7	25.4	22.3	22.7	25.6	22.1	21.7	19.8	21.8
Sex												
Male	28.5	34.7	34.6	31.9	28.8	25.7	25.9	29.2	24.5	24.2	20.9	22.8
Female	19.1	25.7	22.7	25.0	21.8	18.7	19.3	21.7	19.7	19.1	18.7	20.8
Race/Ethnicity												
White	24.1	28.8	28.3	27.5	23.6	20.8	19.8	22.7	20.4	19.8	17.7	19.8
Black	17.5	25.3	21.9	23.1	23.9	19.2	22.2	22.8	18.6	20.6	18.9	21.5
Hispanic	34.1	36.9	34.2	36.5	33.5	29.1	31.2	33.2	27.4	27.2	25.4	26.7
Asian[1]	NA	25.7	25.7	22.5	15.9	21.0	18.3	23.3	22.6	15.3	17.7	14.5
Pacific Islander[1]	NA	46.9	50.2	34.7	41.3	38.5	27.6	38.9	27.7	30.1 !	25.7	17.0 !
American Indian/Alaska Native	20.9	30.6	34.5	31.3	24.4	25.1	34.0	40.5	25.5	19.8	17.1	24.2
Two or more races[1]	NA	36.0	34.5	36.6	31.6	24.6	26.9	33.3	26.4	24.7	19.2	27.8
Sexual Identity[2]												
Heterosexual	NA	NA	NA	NA	NA	NA	NA	NA	NA	20.8	18.9	20.8
Gay, lesbian, or bisexual	NA	NA	NA	NA	NA	NA	NA	NA	NA	29.3	28.2	30.3
Not sure	NA	NA	NA	NA	NA	NA	NA	NA	NA	28.4	19.6	23.6
Grade												
9th	21.8	27.6	29.0	29.5	24.0	21.2	22.0	23.7	22.4	21.6	18.9	21.6
10th	23.7	32.1	29.0	29.2	27.5	25.3	23.7	27.8	23.2	21.9	20.3	23.7
11th	27.5	31.1	28.7	29.9	24.9	22.8	24.3	27.0	23.2	22.7	20.0	22.0
12th	23.0	30.5	26.9	24.9	24.9	19.6	20.6	23.8	18.8	20.3	19.6	19.6

NOTE: Students were asked if anyone offered, sold, or gave them an illegal drug on school property during the previous 12 months. "On school property" was not defined for respondents. Race categories exclude persons of Hispanic ethnicity.
NA = Not available.
! = Interpret data with caution. The coefficient of variation (CV) for this estimate is between 30 and 50 percent.
[1]Before 1999, Asian students and Pacific Islander students were not categorized separately, and students could not be classified as two or more races. Because the response categories changed in 1999, caution should be used in comparing data on race from 1993 with data from later years.
[2]Students were asked which of the following ("heterosexual (straight)," "gay or lesbian," "bisexual," or "not sure") best described them.

Table 9. Percentage of Students Age 12 to 18 Years Who Reported Being the Target of Hate-Related Words and Seeing Hate-Related Graffiti at School During the School Year, by Selected Student and School Characteristics and Location, Selected Years, 1999–2019

(Percent.)

Student/school characteristic	1999[1]	2001[1]	2003[1]	2005[1]	2007	2009	2011	2013	2015	2017	2019
Hate-Related Words											
Total	13.3	12.3	11.8	11.2	9.7	8.7	9.1	6.6	7.2	6.4	6.7
Sex											
Male	12.4	12.9	12.1	11.7	9.9	8.5	9.0	6.6	7.8	6.0	6.0
Female	14.4	11.8	11.4	10.7	9.6	8.9	9.1	6.7	6.7	6.9	7.5
Race/Ethnicity[2]											
White	12.6	12.0	11.0	10.4	8.9	7.2	8.3	5.3	6.3	6.1	5.6
Black	16.6	14.1	14.3	15.0	11.4	11.1	10.7	7.8	9.4	7.4	8.6
Hispanic	12.1	11.1	11.4	10.5	10.6	11.2	9.8	7.4	6.5	6.3	6.5
Asian/Pacific Islander	13.9	13.0	11.4	10.7	10.5	10.9	9.6	9.8	11.2	4.7	7.7
Asian	NA	NA	11.4	11.0	11.1	10.7	9.0	10.3	10.8	4.8	7.2
Pacific Islander	NA	NA	^	^	^	^	^	^	^	^	^
American Indian/Alaska Native	28.5	17.4 !	18.6 !	^	^	^	^	^	^	^	^
Two or more races	NA	NA	19.4	10.6	11.7	9.8	11.1	13.5	8.5	11.4	16.5
Grade											
6th	13.1	12.2	11.9	11.1	12.1	8.3	9.0	6.7	10.1	6.7	7.7
7th	15.8	14.2	12.5	13.1	10.7	9.6	9.9	7.5	7.0	7.3	8.1
8th	16.1	13.0	12.9	11.2	11.0	10.9	8.4	7.4	9.2	7.0	8.6
9th	13.3	12.2	13.5	12.8	10.9	8.0	10.2	6.6	7.4	8.2	6.7
10th	11.9	13.2	11.7	10.9	9.0	9.7	9.6	6.4	6.5	6.3	5.3
11th	10.6	12.7	8.3	9.0	8.6	8.4	8.7	7.5	6.0	4.7	6.8
12th	11.8	8.0	10.9	9.7	6.0	5.8	7.5	4.1	5.4	4.6	4.2
School Locale[3]											
City	NA	NA	NA	NA	NA	NA	NA	NA	7.4	6.7	7.9
Suburban	NA	NA	NA	NA	NA	NA	NA	NA	8.2	5.9	6.5
Town	NA	NA	NA	NA	NA	NA	NA	NA	5.5	7.5	5.8
Rural	NA	NA	NA	NA	NA	NA	NA	NA	6.3	6.7	6.8
Control of School[3,4]											
Public	13.9	12.7	11.9	11.6	10.1	8.9	9.3	6.6	7.5	6.7	7.1
Private	8.2	8.2	9.8	6.8	6.1	6.6	6.9	6.7	3.4 !	3.3	2.5 !
Hate-Related Graffiti											
Total	36.6	36.0	36.9	38.4	35.0	29.2	28.4	24.6	27.2	23.2	22.6
Sex											
Male	34.0	35.4	35.6	37.7	34.5	29.0	28.6	24.1	26.3	22.6	22.0
Female	39.3	36.6	38.2	39.1	35.5	29.3	28.1	25.1	28.1	23.8	23.1
Race/Ethnicity[2]											
White	36.8	36.5	35.8	38.5	35.6	28.3	28.2	23.7	28.6	24.0	22.9
Black	38.0	34.0	38.7	37.9	33.7	29.0	28.1	26.3	24.9	24.8	21.7
Hispanic	35.8	35.6	40.9	38.0	34.9	32.2	29.1	25.6	26.7	21.0	23.2
Asian/Pacific Islander	30.9	33.5	27.7	34.5	28.5	29.9	29.8	20.8	19.5	15.2	17.0
Asian	NA	NA	26.8	34.7	28.2	31.2	29.9	20.8	17.5	14.6	16.8
Pacific Islander	NA	NA	^	^	^	^	^	^	^	^	^
American Indian/Alaska Native	47.1	31.5	35.9	^	27.3	^	16.8 !	22.0 !	^	27.8 !	30.6 !
Two or more races	NA	NA	40.8	47.7	41.9	30.3	27.4	31.1	29.1	35.0	24.4
Grade											
6th	30.7	35.2	36.1	34.0	35.6	28.1	25.9	21.9	30.0	20.6	20.3
7th	35.1	35.5	37.6	37.0	32.4	27.9	26.0	21.7	24.7	21.2	22.5
8th	35.9	37.2	35.1	35.7	33.5	30.8	25.9	24.0	27.2	22.4	22.3
9th	39.5	36.1	37.6	41.6	34.6	28.1	28.7	27.2	28.2	25.2	25.2
10th	39.3	36.8	41.4	40.7	36.5	31.0	33.3	26.0	28.6	27.0	23.7
11th	37.3	36.5	37.2	40.2	35.4	27.4	32.1	25.8	26.2	22.6	22.0
12th	35.8	33.5	32.6	37.8	37.7	30.4	25.7	24.2	26.1	22.2	20.6
School Locale[3]											
City	NA	NA	NA	NA	NA	NA	NA	NA	27.9	24.3	24.3
Suburban	NA	NA	NA	NA	NA	NA	NA	NA	27.9	23.0	22.4
Town	NA	NA	NA	NA	NA	NA	NA	NA	35.6	28.9	22.3
Rural	NA	NA	NA	NA	NA	NA	NA	NA	22.3	21.4	24.1
Control of School[3,4]											
Public	38.3	37.8	38.5	40.0	36.5	30.7	29.7	25.6	28.6	25.1	24.2
Private	20.8	17.3	19.8	18.6	18.5	11.8	13.4	12.6	13.9	4.1	8.6

NOTE: "At school" includes in the school building, on school property, on a school bus, and, from 2001 onward, going to and from school. "Hate-related" refers to derogatory terms used by others in reference to students' personal characteristics. Some data have been revised from previously published figures.

NA = Not available.

! = Interpret data with caution. The coefficient of variation (CV) for this estimate is between 30 and 50 percent.

^ = Reporting standards not met. Either there are too few cases for a reliable estimate or the coefficient of variation (CV) is 50 percent or greater.

[1] In 2005 and prior years, the period covered by the survey question was "during the last 6 months," but this was changed to "during this school year" beginning in 2007. Cognitive testing suggested that modifications to the reference period would not have a substantial impact on the survey responses.

[2] Race categories exclude persons of Hispanic ethnicity. Prior to 2003, separate data for Asian students, Pacific Islander students, and students of two or more races were not collected.

[3] Excludes students with missing information about the school characteristic.

[4] Data for 2013 and prior years were based on school information provided by the respondent. Beginning in 2015, data were based on school information collected in the Common Core of Data and the Private School Universe Survey, which was appended to the School Crime Supplement data file; therefore, these data may not be entirely comparable with figures for earlier years.

Table 10. Percentage of Students Age 12 to 18 Years Who Reported Being Bullied at School During the School Year, by Type of Bullying and Selected Student and School Characteristics, Selected Years, 2005–2019

(Percent.)

Student/school characteristic	2005[1]	2007	2009	2011	2013	2015[2]	2017	2019[3]
Total	28.5	31.7	28.0	27.8	21.5	20.8	20.2	22.2
Sex								
Male	27.5	30.3	26.6	24.5	19.5	18.8	16.7	19.1
Female...................................	29.7	33.2	29.5	31.4	23.7	22.8	23.8	25.5
Race/Ethnicity								
White	30.3	34.1	29.3	31.5	23.7	21.6	22.8	24.6
Black......................................	29.2	30.4	29.1	27.2	20.3	24.7	22.9	22.2
Hispanic.................................	22.3	27.3	25.5	21.9	19.2	17.2	15.7	18.0
Asian/Pacific Islander	20.8	17.2	17.8	13.8	9.3	19.4	7.3	13.7
Asian..................................	20.9	18.1	17.3	14.9	9.2	15.6	7.3	13.5
Pacific Islander.....................	^	^	^	^	^	^	^	^
American Indian/Alaska Native	^	29.8	^	21.1 !	24.3 !	^	27.2	^
Two or more races......................	34.6	38.2	27.3	26.9	27.6	17.7	23.2	37.1
Grade								
6th	37.0	42.7	39.4	37.0	27.8	31.0	29.5	28.1
7th	35.1	35.6	33.1	30.3	26.4	25.1	24.4	28.0
8th	31.3	36.9	31.7	30.7	21.7	22.2	25.3	26.7
9th	28.3	30.6	28.0	26.5	23.0	19.0	19.3	18.9
10th	25.1	27.7	26.6	28.0	19.5	21.2	18.9	18.7
11th	23.5	28.5	21.1	23.8	20.0	15.8	14.7	21.7
12th	20.8	23.0	20.4	22.0	14.1	14.9	12.2	15.8
School Locale[4]								
City.......................................	NA	NA	NA	NA	NA	21.3	19.9	22.4
Suburban.................................	NA	NA	NA	NA	NA	21.3	18.1	20.5
Town......................................	NA	NA	NA	NA	NA	20.3	26.9	21.7
Rural......................................	NA	NA	NA	NA	NA	20.0	23.8	27.7
Control of School[4,5]								
Public.....................................	29.0	32.0	28.8	28.4	21.5	21.3	21.1	22.7
Private	23.3	29.1	18.9	21.5	22.4	15.3	15.0	21.7

NOTE: "At school" includes in the school building, on school property, on a school bus, and going to and from school. Race categories exclude persons of Hispanic ethnicity. Some data have been revised from previously published figures.
NA = Not available.
! = Interpret data with caution. The coefficient of variation (CV) for this estimate is between 30 and 50 percent.
^ =Reporting standards not met. Either there are too few cases for a reliable estimate or the coefficient of variation (CV) is 50 percent or greater.
[1]In 2005 and prior years, the period covered by the survey question was "during the last 6 months," but this was changed to "during this school year" beginning in 2007. Cognitive testing suggested that modifications to the reference period would not have a substantial impact on the survey responses.
[2]The 2015 survey included a split sample design to compare two versions of an updated questionnaire on bullying that would provide data on repetition and power imbalance aligned with the Centers for Disease Control and Prevention's uniform definition of bullying. Half the sample received version 1, and the other half received version 2. Estimates in this table are based on the 50 percent of the sample who received version 1 of the questionnaire. For more information, see Split-Half Administration of the 2015 School Crime Supplement to the National Crime Victimization Survey Methodology Report (NCES 2017-004).
[3]The 2019 survey included a split sample design to compare two versions of an updated questionnaire on bullying. Approximately 60 percent of the sample received version 1, which was consistent with prior years; the remaining 40 percent received version 2, which included changes such as removing the word "bullying." Estimates in this table are based on the 60 percent of the sample who received version 1 of the questionnaire. For more information, see Methodology Report: Split-Half Administration of the 2019 School Crime Supplement to the National Crime Victimization Survey (NCES 2021-016).
[4]Excludes students with missing information about the school characteristic.
[5]Data for 2013 and prior years were based on school information provided by the respondent. Beginning in 2015, data were based on school information collected in the Common Core of Data and the Private School Universe Survey, which was appended to the School Crime Supplement data file; therefore, these data may not be entirely comparable with figures for earlier years.

Table 11. Percentage of Public Schools Reporting Selected Types of Cyberbullying Problems Occurring at School or Away from School at Least Once a Week, by Selected School Characteristics, 2017–2018

(Percent.)

School characteristic	Cyberbullying among students	School environment is affected by cyberbullying	Staff resources are used to deal with cyberbullying
All Public Schools	14.9	8.8	8.1
School level[1]			
Primary	4.5	2.3	2.0
Middle	33.1	21.2	19.5
High school	30.2	18.0	18.9
Combined	20.2	10.2	5.3 !
Enrollment size			
Less than 300	10.9	5.8	4.4
300 to 499	10.9	6.2	4.6
500 to 999	15.5	9.1	9.5
1,000 or more	31.6	20.5	19.9
Locale			
City	12.7	7.4	7.4
Suburban	14.1	9.0	8.7
Town	20.2	10.3	9.4
Rural	15.8	9.3	7.4
Percent minority enrollment[2]			
0 to 25 percent	17.4	10.2	8.8
26 to 50 percent	14.2	8.7	8.1
51 to 75 percent	18.2	10.7	9.6
76 to 100 percent	10.2	5.8	6.1
Percent of students eligible for free or reduced-price lunch			
0 to 25 percent	12.9	6.8	7.2
26 to 50 percent	18.4	11.2	9.7
51 to 75 percent	16.5	10.1	8.1
76 to 100 percent	12.2	7.1	7.3
Prevalence of violent incidents at school during school year[3]			
No violent incidents	3.4	2.4 !	2.4 !
Any violent incidents	19.7	11.4	10.4

NOTE: Includes schools reporting that cyberbullying happens either "daily" or "at least once a week." "Cyberbullying" was defined for respondents as occurring "when willful and repeated harm is inflicted through the use of computers, cell phones, or other electronic devices." Responses were provided by the principal or the person most knowledgeable about crime and safety issues at the school. Respondents were instructed to include cyberbullying "problems that can occur anywhere (both at your school and away from school)."
! = Interpret data with caution. The coefficient of variation (CV) for this estimate is between 30 and 50 percent.
[1]Primary schools are defined as schools in which the lowest grade is not higher than grade 3 and the highest grade is not higher than grade 8. Middle schools are defined as schools in which the lowest grade is not lower than grade 4 and the highest grade is not higher than grade 9. High schools are defined as schools in which the lowest grade is not lower than grade 9. Combined schools include all other combinations of grades, including K–12 schools.
[2]Percent combined enrollment of Black, Hispanic, Asian, Pacific Islander, and American Indian/Alaska Native students, and students of two or more races.
[3]"Violent incidents" include rape or attempted rape, sexual assault other than rape, physical attack or fight with or without a weapon, threat of physical attack or fight with or without a weapon, and robbery with or without a weapon. Respondents were instructed to include violent incidents that occurred before, during, or after normal school hours or when school activities or events were in session.

Table 12. On-Campus Hate Crimes at Degree-Granting Postsecondary Institutions, by Level and Control of Institution, Type of Crime, and Category of Bias Motivating the Crime, Selected Years, 2010–2018

(Number.)

Type of crime and category of bias motivating the crime[1]	Total, 2010	Total, 2013	Total, 2014	Total, 2015	Total, 2016	2017 Total	2017 4-year Public	2017 4-year For profit	2017 4-year Non-profit	2017 2-year Public	2017 2-year For profit	2017 2-year Non-profit	2018 Total	2018 4-year Public	2018 4-year For profit	2018 4-year Non-profit	2018 2-year Public	2018 2-year For profit	2018 2-year Non-profit
All On-Campus Hate Crimes	928	778	794	859	1,071	973	418	420	1	134	0	0	814	362	320	7	121	0	4
Murder[2]	0	0	0	0	0	1	1	0	0	0	0	0	0	0	0	0	0	0	0
Sex offenses: forcible[3]	7	7	4	7	8	6	1	3	0	2	0	0	8	3	2	0	3	0	0
Race	0	2	1	0	1	0	0	0	0	0	0	0	1	1	0	0	0	0	0
Ethnicity	0	0	0	0	0	0	0	0	0	0	0	0	0	0	0	0	0	0	0
Religion	0	0	0	1	0	0	0	0	0	0	0	0	0	0	0	0	0	0	0
Sexual orientation	4	1	1	3	1	0	0	0	0	0	0	0	2	1	1	0	0	0	0
Gender	3	4	2	1	5	4	1	1	0	2	0	0	4	0	1	0	3	0	0
Gender identity	NA	NA	0	2	1	2	0	2	0	0	0	0	1	1	0	0	0	0	0
Disability	0	0	0	0	0	0	0	0	0	0	0	0	0	0	0	0	0	0	0
Sex offenses: non-forcible[4]	0	0	0	0	0	0	0	0	0	0	0	0	0	0	0	0	0	0	0
Robbery[5]	2	1	2	3	2	2	1	1	0	0	0	0	3	1	2	0	0	0	0
Aggravated assault[6]	17	7	18	18	35	15	6	3	0	6	0	0	26	14	9	0	2	0	1
Race	6	5	5	5	8	6	2	3	0	1	0	0	16	7	8	0	1	0	0
Ethnicity	1	1	4	4	15	5	1	0	0	4	0	0	3	3	0	0	0	0	0
Religion	1	0	1	0	1	1	1	0	0	0	0	0	0	0	0	0	0	0	0
Sexual orientation	9	1	7	7	8	2	2	0	0	0	0	0	5	4	1	0	0	0	0
Gender	0	0	1	1	1	0	0	0	0	0	0	0	1	0	0	0	0	0	1
Gender identity	NA	NA	0	1	2	0	0	0	0	0	0	0	1	0	0	0	1	0	0
Disability	0	0	0	0	0	1	0	0	0	1	0	0	0	0	0	0	0	0	0
Burglary[7]	11	4	28	4	6	3	0	2	0	1	0	0	7	0	7	0	0	0	0
Race	7	1	24	0	1	1	0	1	0	0	0	0	4	0	4	0	0	0	0
Ethnicity	0	0	0	0	0	1	0	0	0	1	0	0	0	0	0	0	0	0	0
Religion	0	1	3	0	0	0	0	0	0	0	0	0	2	0	2	0	0	0	0
Sexual orientation	2	0	1	0	2	0	0	0	0	0	0	0	0	0	0	0	0	0	0
Gender	1	2	0	0	3	1	0	1	0	0	0	0	0	0	0	0	0	0	0
Gender identity	NA	NA	0	4	0	0	0	0	0	0	0	0	1	0	1	0	0	0	0
Disability	1	0	0	0	0	0	0	0	0	0	0	0	0	0	0	0	0	0	0
Motor vehicle theft[8]	0	0	0	1	0	1	0	1	0	0	0	0	0	0	0	0	0	0	0
Arson[9]	0	0	1	2	2	1	1	0	0	0	0	0	0	0	0	0	0	0	0
Simple assault[10]	67	91	63	80	98	84	41	24	0	19	0	0	75	37	26	0	11	0	1
Race	25	36	14	36	42	41	18	16	0	7	0	0	28	16	8	0	4	0	0
Ethnicity	5	5	11	9	14	8	3	1	0	4	0	0	8	2	5	0	0	0	1
Religion	4	6	2	9	12	9	7	2	0	0	0	0	10	5	3	0	2	0	0
Sexual orientation	23	27	23	18	16	18	9	3	0	6	0	0	22	12	7	0	3	0	0
Gender	9	17	9	2	11	3	1	0	0	2	0	0	4	1	1	0	2	0	0
Gender identity	NA	NA	3	5	2	5	3	2	0	0	0	0	3	1	2	0	0	0	0
Disability	1	0	1	1	1	0	0	0	0	0	0	0	0	0	0	0	0	0	0
Larceny[11]	9	15	17	25	33	25	4	20	0	1	0	0	13	4	6	1	2	0	0
Race	1	5	5	1	12	7	1	6	0	0	0	0	2	1	0	0	1	0	0
Ethnicity	3	2	1	0	4	3	2	1	0	0	0	0	0	0	0	0	0	0	0
Religion	1	3	3	19	5	1	0	1	0	0	0	0	4	0	4	0	0	0	0
Sexual orientation	1	3	1	1	5	6	1	4	0	1	0	0	5	3	2	0	0	0	0
Gender	3	2	7	3	3	7	0	7	0	0	0	0	2	0	0	1	1	0	0
Gender identity	NA	NA	0	1	3	1	0	1	0	0	0	0	0	0	0	0	0	0	0
Disability	0	0	0	0	1	0	0	0	0	0	0	0	0	0	0	0	0	0	0
Intimidation[12]	260	296	339	355	426	397	194	155	0	48	0	0	337	145	142	3	46	0	1
Race	79	111	111	141	171	179	92	70	0	17	0	0	159	61	76	3	19	0	0
Ethnicity	17	49	32	37	48	47	21	19	0	7	0	0	37	17	17	0	3	0	0
Religion	38	25	35	48	67	49	27	18	0	4	0	0	42	20	13	0	8	0	1
Sexual orientation	87	68	78	77	83	67	30	25	0	12	0	0	66	39	19	0	8	0	0
Gender	37	37	63	34	28	26	11	12	0	3	0	0	18	4	9	0	5	0	0
Gender identity	NA	NA	13	11	20	20	9	7	0	4	0	0	13	3	7	0	3	0	0
Disability	2	6	7	7	9	9	4	4	0	1	0	0	2	1	1	0	0	0	0

Table 12. On-Campus Hate Crimes at Degree-Granting Postsecondary Institutions, by Level and Control of Institution, Type of Crime, and Category of Bias Motivating the Crime, Selected Years, 2010–2018—*Continued*

(Number.)

Type of crime and category of bias motivating the crime[1]	Total, 2010	Total, 2013	Total, 2014	Total, 2015	Total, 2016	2017 Total	2017 4-year Public	2017 4-year For profit	2017 4-year Non-profit	2017 2-year Public	2017 2-year For profit	2017 2-year Non-profit	2018 Total	2018 4-year Public	2018 4-year For profit	2018 4-year Non-profit	2018 2-year Public	2018 2-year For profit	2018 2-year Non-profit
Destruction, damage, and vandalism[13]	555	357	322	364	461	438	169	211	1	57	0	0	345	158	126	3	57	0	1
Race	257	147	116	151	174	185	79	79	0	27	0	0	135	66	46	1	21	0	1
Ethnicity	43	38	29	25	30	34	16	16	0	2	0	0	39	13	18	0	8	0	0
Religion	103	48	67	108	133	111	34	61	1	15	0	0	70	28	30	1	11	0	0
Sexual orientation	135	108	89	61	67	62	30	22	0	10	0	0	76	39	23	1	13	0	0
Gender	17	14	13	10	35	20	3	16	0	1	0	0	10	4	3	0	3	0	0
Gender identity	NA	NA	6	8	22	26	7	17	0	2	0	0	14	8	5	0	1	0	0
Disability	0	2	2	1	0	0	0	0	0	0	0	0	1	0	1	0	0	0	0

NOTE: Data are for degree-granting institutions, which are institutions that grant associate's or higher degrees and participate in Title IV federal financial aid programs. Some institutions that report Clery data--specifically, non-degree-granting institutions and institutions outside of the 50 states and the District of Columbia--are excluded from this table. A hate crime is a criminal offense that is motivated, in whole or in part, by the perpetrator's bias against a group of people based on their race, ethnicity, religion, sexual orientation, gender, gender identity, or disability. Includes on-campus incidents involving students, staff, and on-campus guests. Excludes off-campus crimes and arrests even if they involve college students or staff. Some data have been revised from previously published figures.

NA = Not available.

[1]Bias categories correspond to characteristics against which the bias is directed (i.e., race, ethnicity, religion, sexual orientation, gender, gender identity, or disability).

[2]Excludes suicides, fetal deaths, traffic fatalities, accidental deaths, and justifiable homicide (such as the killing of a felon by a law enforcement officer in the line of duty).

[3]Any sexual act directed against another person forcibly and/or against that person's will.

[4]Includes only statutory rape or incest.

[5]Taking or attempting to take anything of value using actual or threatened force or violence.

[6]Attack upon a person for the purpose of inflicting severe or aggravated bodily injury.

[7]Unlawful entry of a structure to commit a felony or theft.

[8]Theft or attempted theft of a motor vehicle.

[9]Willful or malicious burning or attempt to burn a dwelling house, public building, motor vehicle, or personal property of another.

[10]A physical attack by one person upon another where neither the offender displays a weapon, nor the victim suffers obvious severe or aggravated bodily injury involving apparent broken bones, loss of teeth, possible internal injury, severe laceration, or loss of consciousness.

[11]The unlawful taking, carrying, leading, or riding away of property from the possession of another.

[12]Placing another person in reasonable fear of bodily harm through the use of threatening words and/or other conduct, but without displaying a weapon or subjecting the victim to actual physical attack.

[13]Willfully or maliciously destroying, damaging, defacing, or otherwise injuring real or personal property without the consent of the owner or the person having custody or control of it.

METHODOLOGY

This annual report, a joint effort by the Bureau of Justice Statistics and the National Center for Education Statistics (NCES), provides the most current statistical information on the nature of crime in schools. It presents data on crime and safety at school from the perspectives of students, teachers, and principals. This report contains 23 indicators of crime and safety at school from a number of sources, including the National Crime Victimization Survey (NCVS), the School Crime Supplement to the NCVS, the Youth Risk Behavior Survey, the School Survey on Crime and Safety, and the School and Staffing Survey. Topics covered include victimization at school, teacher injury, bullying and cyber-bullying, school conditions, fights, weapons, availability and student use of drugs and alcohol, student perceptions of personal safety at school, and crime at postsecondary institutions. For more information or to access the full report, please see https://nces.ed.gov/programs/crimeindicators/index.asp>.

The indicators in this report are based on information drawn from a variety of independent data sources, including national and international surveys of students, teachers, principals, and postsecondary institutions and universe data collections from federal departments and agencies and international organizations. These sources include the Bureau of Justice Statistics, the National Center for Education Statistics, the Centers for Disease Control and Prevention, the Office of Postsecondary Education, the Center for Homeland Defense and Security of the U.S. Department of Defense, and the Organization for Economic Cooperation and Development. Each data source has an independent sample design, data collection method, and questionnaire design or is the result of a universe data collection. Universe data collections include a census of all known entities in a specific universe (e.g., all deaths occurring on school property). Readers should be cautious when comparing data from different sources. Differences in sampling procedures, populations, time periods, and question phrasing can all affect the comparability of results. For example, some questions from different surveys may appear the same, but were asked of different populations of students (e.g., students ages 12–18 or students in grades 9–12); in different years; about experiences that occurred within different periods of time (e.g., in the past 30 days or during the past 12 months); or at different locations (e.g., in school or anywhere).

Data

The Bureau of Justice Statistics' (BJS) **National Crime Victimization Survey (NCVS)** is the nation's primary source of information on criminal victimization. The survey has undergone several recent revisions and redesigns; information is available in the *Criminal Victimization chapter* and at <https://www.bjs.gov/index.cfm?ty=pbdetail&iid=6166>.

The accuracy of any statistic is determined by the joint effects of nonsampling and sampling errors. Both types of error affect the estimates presented in this report. Several sources can contribute to nonsampling errors. For example, members of the population of interest are inadvertently excluded from the sampling frame; sampled members refuse to answer some of the survey questions (item nonresponse) or all of the survey questions (questionnaire nonresponse); mistakes are made during data editing, coding, or entry; the responses that respondents provide differ from the "true" responses; or measurement instruments such as tests or questionnaires fail to measure the characteristics they are intended to measure. Although nonsampling errors due to questionnaire and item nonresponse can be reduced somewhat by the adjustment of sample weights and imputation procedures, correcting nonsampling errors or gauging the effects of these errors is usually difficult.

Sampling errors occur because observations are made on samples rather than on entire populations. Surveys of population universes are not subject to sampling errors. Estimates based on a sample will differ somewhat from those that would have been obtained by a complete census of the relevant population using the same survey instruments, instructions, and procedures. The standard error of a statistic is a measure of the variation due to sampling; it indicates the precision of the statistic obtained in a particular sample. In addition, the standard errors for two sample statistics can be used to estimate the precision of the difference between the two statistics and to help determine whether the difference based on the sample is large enough so that it represents the population difference.

Most of the data used in this report were obtained from complex sampling designs rather than a simple random design. The features of complex sampling require different techniques to calculate standard errors than are used for data collected using a simple random sampling. Therefore, calculation of standard errors requires procedures that are markedly different from the ones used when the data are from a simple random sample.

The Taylor series approximation technique or the balanced repeated replication (BRR) method was used to estimate most of the statistics and their standard errors in this report.

Standard error calculation for data from the School Crime Supplement was based on the Taylor series approximation method using PSU and strata variables available from each dataset. For statistics based on all years of NCVS data, standard errors were derived from a formula developed by the U.S. Census Bureau, which consists of three generalized variance function (gvf) constant parameters that represent the curve fitted to the individual standard errors calculated using the Balanced Repeated Replication (BRR) technique.

The coefficient of variation (CV) represents the ratio of the standard error to the mean. As an attribute of a distribution, the CV is an important measure of the reliability and accuracy of an estimate. With the exception of _Indicator 2_, the CV was calculated for all estimates in this report, and in cases where the CV was between 30 and 50 percent the estimates were noted with an "!" symbol (interpret data with caution). In _Indicator 2_, the "!" symbol cautions the reader that estimates marked indicate that the reported statistic was based on fewer than 10 cases or the CV was greater than 50 percent. With the exception of _Indicator 2_, in cases where the CV was 50 percent or greater, the estimate was determined not to meet reporting standards and was suppressed.

The **School-Associated Violent Deaths Study (SAVD)** is an epidemiological study developed by the Centers for Disease Control and Prevention in conjunction with the U.S. Department of Education and the U.S. Department of Justice. SAVD seeks to describe the epidemiology of school-associated violent deaths, identify common features of these deaths, estimate the rate of school-associated violent deaths in the United States, and identify potential risk factors for these deaths. The study includes descriptive data on all school-associated violent deaths in the United States, including all homicides, suicides, or legal intervention deaths in which the fatal injury occurred on the campus of a functioning elementary or secondary school; while the victim was on the way to or from regular sessions at such a school; or while attending or on the way to or from an official school-sponsored event. Victims of such incidents include nonstudents, as well as students and staff members. SAVD includes descriptive information about the school, event, victim(s), and offender(s). The SAVD study has collected data from July 1, 1992, through the present.

SAVD uses a four-step process to identify and collect data on school-associated violent deaths. Cases are initially identified through a search of the LexisNexis newspaper and media database. Then law enforcement officials from the office that investigated the deaths are contacted to confirm the details of the case and to determine if the event meets the case definition. Once a case is confirmed, a law enforcement official and a school official are interviewed regarding details about the school, event, victim(s), and offender(s). A copy of the full law enforcement report is also sought for each case. The information obtained on schools includes school demographics, attendance/absentee rates, suspensions/expulsions and mobility, school history of weapon-carrying incidents, security measures, violence

prevention activities, school response to the event, and school policies about weapon carrying. Event information includes the location of injury, the context of injury (while classes were being held, during break, etc.), motives for injury, method of injury, and school and community events happening around the time period. Information obtained on victim(s) and offender(s) includes demographics, circumstances of the event (date/time, alcohol or drug use, number of persons involved), types and origins of weapons, criminal history, psychological risk factors, school-related problems, extracurricular activities, and family history, including structure and stressors.

For some recent data, the interviews with school and law enforcement officials to verify case details have not been completed. The details learned during the interviews can occasionally change the classification of a case. Also, new cases may be identified because of the expansion of the scope of the media files used for case identification. Sometimes other cases not identified during earlier data years using the independent case finding efforts (which focus on nonmedia sources of information) will be discovered. Also, other cases may occasionally be identified while the law enforcement and school interviews are being conducted to verify known cases.

Created as a supplement to the NCVS and co-designed by the National Center for Education Statistics and Bureau of Justice Statistics, the School Crime Supplement (SCS) survey has been conducted in 1989, 1995, and biennially since 1999 to collect additional information about school-related victimizations on a national level. This report includes data from the 1995, 1999, 2001, 2003, 2005, 2007, 2009, 2011, 2013, 2015, and 2017 collections. The 1989 data are not included in this report as a result of methodological changes to the NCVS and SCS. The SCS was designed to assist policymakers, as well as academic researchers and practitioners at federal, state, and local levels, to make informed decisions concerning crime in schools. The survey asks students a number of key questions about their experiences with and perceptions of crime and violence that occurred inside their school, on school grounds, on the school bus, or on the way to or from school. Students are asked additional questions about security measures used by their school, students' participation in after-school activities, students' perceptions of school rules, the presence of weapons and gangs in school, the presence of hate-related words and graffiti in school, student reports of bullying and reports of rejection at school, and the availability of drugs and alcohol in school. Students are also asked attitudinal questions relating to fear of victimization and avoidance behavior at school.

The SCS survey was conducted for a 6-month period from January through June in all households selected for the NCVS (see discussion above for information about the NCVS sampling design and changes to the race/ethnicity variable beginning in 2003). Within these households, the eligible respondents for the SCS were those household members who had attended school at any time during the 6 months preceding the interview, were enrolled in grades 6–12, and were not homeschooled. In 2007, the questionnaire was changed and household members who attended school sometime during the school year of the interview were included. The age range of students covered in this report is 12–18 years of age. Eligible respondents were asked the supplemental questions in the SCS only after completing their entire NCVS interview. It should be noted that the first or unbounded NCVS interview has always been included in analysis of the SCS data and may result in the reporting of events outside of the requested reference period.

The **Youth Risk Behavior Surveillance System (YRBSS)** is an epidemiological surveillance system developed by the Centers for Disease Control and Prevention (CDC) to monitor the prevalence of youth behaviors that most influence health. The YRBSS focuses on priority health-risk behaviors established during youth that result in the most significant mortality, morbidity, disability, and social problems during both youth and adulthood. The YRBSS includes a national school-based Youth Risk Behavior Survey (YRBS) as well as surveys conducted in states and large urban school districts. This report uses 1993, 1995, 1997, 1999, 2001, 2003, 2005, 2007, 2009, 2011, 2013, 2015, and 2017 YRBSS data.

The national YRBS uses a three-stage cluster sampling design to produce a nationally representative sample of students in grades 9–12 in the United States. The target population consisted of all public and private school students in grades 9–12 in the 50 states and the District of Columbia. The first-stage sampling frame included selecting primary sampling units (PSUs) from strata formed on the basis of urbanization and the relative percentage of Black and Hispanic students in the PSU. These PSUs are either counties; subareas of large counties; or groups of smaller, adjacent counties. At the second stage, schools were selected with probability proportional to school enrollment size.

The final stage of sampling consisted of randomly selecting, in each chosen school and in each of grades 9–12, one or two classrooms from either a required subject, such as English or social studies, or a required period, such as homeroom or second period. All students in selected classes were eligible to participate. In surveys conducted before 2013, three strategies were used to oversample Black and Hispanic students: (1) larger sampling rates were used to select PSUs that are in high-Black and high- Hispanic strata; (2) a modified measure of size was used that increased the probability of selecting schools with a disproportionately high minority enrollment; and (3) two classes per grade, rather than one, were selected in schools with a high percentage of combined Black, Hispanic, Asian/ Pacific Islander, or American Indian/Alaska Native enrollment. In 2013, only selection of two classes per grade was needed to achieve an adequate precision with minimum variance.

The **School Survey on Crime and Safety (SSOCS)** is managed by the National Center for Education Statistics (NCES) on behalf of the U.S. Department of Education. SSOCS collects extensive crime and safety data from principals and school administrators of U.S. public schools. Data from this collection can be used to examine the relationship between school characteristics and violent and serious violent crimes in primary schools, middle schools, high schools, and combined schools. In addition, data from SSOCS can be used to assess what crime prevention programs, practices, and policies are used by schools.

Definitions

General Terms

Crime Any violation of a statute or regulation or any act that the government has determined is injurious to the public, including felonies and misdemeanors. Such violation may or may not involve violence, and it may affect individuals or property.

Incident A specific criminal act or offense involving one or more victims and one or more offenders.

Multistage sampling A survey sampling technique in which there is more than one wave of sampling. That is, one sample of units is drawn, and then another sample is drawn within that sample. For example, at the first stage, a number of Census blocks may be sampled out of all the Census blocks in the United States. At the second stage, households are sampled within the previously sampled Census blocks.

Prevalence The percentage of the population directly affected by crime in a given period. This rate is based upon specific information elicited directly from the respondent regarding crimes committed against his or her person, against his or her property, or against an individual bearing a unique relationship to him or her. It is not based upon perceptions and beliefs about, or reactions to, criminal acts.

School An education institution consisting of one or more of grades K–12.

School crime Any criminal activity that is committed on school property.

School year The 12-month period of time denoting the beginning and ending dates for school accounting purposes, usually from July 1 through June 30.

Stratification A survey sampling technique in which the target population is divided into mutually exclusive groups or strata based on some variable or variables (e.g., metropolitan area) and sampling of units occurs separately within each stratum.

Unequal probabilities A survey sampling technique in which sampled units do not have the same probability of selection into the sample. For example, the investigator may oversample rural students in order to increase the sample sizes of rural students. Rural students would then be more likely than other students to be sampled.

Specific Terms Used in Various Surveys

School-Associated Violent Deaths Study (SAVD)

Homicide An act involving a killing of one person by another resulting from interpersonal violence.

Legal intervention death An act involving the killing of one person by a law enforcement agent in the course of arresting or attempting to arrest a lawbreaker, suppressing a disturbance, maintaining order, or engaging in another legal action.

School-associated violent death A homicide or suicide in which the fatal injury occurred on the campus of a functioning elementary or secondary school in the United States, while the victim was on the way to or from regular sessions at such a school, or while the victim was attending or traveling to or from an official school-sponsored event. Victims included non-students as well as students and staff members.

Suicide An act of taking one's own life voluntarily and intentionally.

National Crime Victimization Survey (NCVS)

Aggravated assault Attack or attempted attack with a weapon, regardless of whether or not an injury occurs, and attack without a weapon when serious injury results.

At school (students) Inside the school building, on school property (school parking area, play area, school bus, etc.), or on the way to or from school.

Metropolitan Statistical Areas (MSAs) Geographic entities defined by the U.S. Office of Management and Budget (OMB) for use by federal statistical agencies in collecting, tabulating, and publishing federal statistics.

Rape Forced sexual intercourse including both psychological coercion as well as physical force. Forced sexual intercourse means vaginal, anal, or oral penetration by the offender(s). Includes attempts and verbal threats of rape. This category also includes incidents where the penetration is from a foreign object, such as a bottle.

Robbery Completed or attempted theft, directly from a person, of property or cash by force or threat of force, with or without a weapon, and with or without injury.

Serious violent victimization Rape, sexual assault, robbery, or aggravated assault.

Sexual assault A wide range of victimizations, separate from rape or attempted rape. These crimes include attacks or attempted attacks generally involving unwanted sexual contact between the victim and offender. Sexual assault may or may not involve force and includes such things as grabbing or fondling. Sexual assault also includes verbal threats.

Simple assault Attack without a weapon resulting either in no injury, minor injury, or an undetermined injury requiring less than 2 days of hospitalization. Also includes attempted assault without a weapon.

Theft Completed or attempted theft of property or cash without personal contact.

Victimization A crime as it affects one individual person or household. For personal crimes, the number of victimizations is equal to the number of victims involved. The number of victimizations may be greater than the number of incidents because more than one person may be victimized during an incident.

Victimization rate A measure of the occurrence of victimizations among a specific population group. For personal crimes, the number of victimizations is equal to the number of victims involved. Each victimization that is reported by the respondents is counted, so there may be one incident with two victims, which would be counted as two victimizations. The number of victimizations may be greater than the number of incidents because more than one person may be victimized during an incident.

Violent victimization Includes serious violent victimization, rape, sexual assault, robbery, aggravated assault, or simple assault.

School Crime Supplement (SCS)

At school In the school building, on school property, on a school bus, or going to or from school.

Bullied Students were asked if any student had bullied them at school in one or more ways during the school year. Specifically, students were asked if another student had made fun of them, called them names, or insulted them; spread rumors about them; threatened them with harm; pushed, shoved, tripped, or spit on them; tried to make them to do something they did not want to do; excluded them from activities on purpose; or destroyed their property on purpose.

Gang Street gangs, fighting gangs, crews, or something else. Gangs may use common names, signs, symbols, or colors. All gangs, whether or not they are involved in violent or illegal activity, are included.

Hate-related graffiti Hate-related words or symbols written in school classrooms, school bathrooms, school hallways, or on the outside of the school building.

Hate-related words Students were asked if anyone called them an insulting or bad name at school having to do with their race, religion, ethnic background or national origin, disability, gender, or sexual orientation.

Serious violent victimization Rape, sexual assault, robbery, or aggravated assault.

Total victimization Combination of violent victimization and theft. If a student reported an incident of either type, he or she is counted as having experienced any victimization. If the student reported having experienced both, he or she is counted once under "total victimization."

Violent victimization Includes serious violent victimization, rape, sexual assault, robbery, aggravated assault, or simple assault.

Youth Risk Behavior Survey (YRBS)

On school property On school property is included in the question wording, but was not defined for respondents.

Rural school A school located outside a Metropolitan Statistical Area (MSA).

Suburban school A school located inside an MSA, but outside the "central city."

Urban school A school located inside an MSA and inside the "central city."

Weapon Examples of weapons appearing in the questionnaire include guns, knives, and clubs.

School Survey on Crime and Safety (SSOCS)

Gang An ongoing loosely organized association of three or more persons, whether formal or informal, that has a common name, signs, symbols, or colors, whose members engage, either individually or collectively, in violent or other forms of illegal behavior.

Hate crime A criminal offense or threat against a person, property, or society that is motivated, in whole or in part, by the offender's bias against a race, color, national origin, ethnicity, gender, religion, disability, or sexual orientation.

Intimidation To frighten, compel, or deter by actual or implied threats. It includes bullying and sexual harassment. (Intimidation was not defined in the front of the questionnaire in 2005–06.)

Physical attack or fight An actual and intentional touching or striking of another person against his or her will, or the intentional causing of bodily harm to an individual.

Rape Forced sexual intercourse (vaginal, anal, or oral penetration). Includes penetration from a foreign object.

Robbery The taking or attempting to take anything of value that is owned by another person or organization, under confrontational circumstances by force or threat of force or violence and/or by putting the victim in fear. A key difference between robbery and theft/larceny is that a threat or battery is involved in robbery.

Serious violent incidents Include rape, sexual battery other than rape, physical attacks or fights with a weapon, threats of physical attack with a weapon, and robbery with or without a weapon.

Sexual battery An incident that includes threatened rape, fondling, indecent liberties, child molestation, or sodomy. Principals were instructed that classification of these incidents should take into consideration the age and developmentally appropriate behavior of the offenders.

Sexual harassment Unsolicited, offensive behavior that inappropriately asserts sexuality over another person. The behavior may be verbal or nonverbal.

Theft/larceny Taking things valued at over $10 without personal confrontation. Specifically, the unlawful taking of another person's property without personal confrontation, threat, violence, or bodily harm. Included are pocket picking, stealing purse or backpack (if left unattended or no force was used to take it from owner), theft from a building, theft from a motor vehicle or motor vehicle parts or accessories, theft of bicycles, theft from vending machines, and all other types of thefts.

Vandalism The willful damage or destruction of school property, including bombing, arson, graffiti, and other acts that cause property damage. Includes damage caused by computer hacking.

Violent incidents Include rape, sexual battery other than rape, physical attacks or fights with or without a weapon, threats of physical attack with or without a weapon, and robbery with or without a weapon.

Weapon Any instrument or object used with the intent to threaten, injure, or kill. Includes look-alikes if they are used to threaten others.

PART 7

Jail Inmates in 2019

HIGHLIGHTS

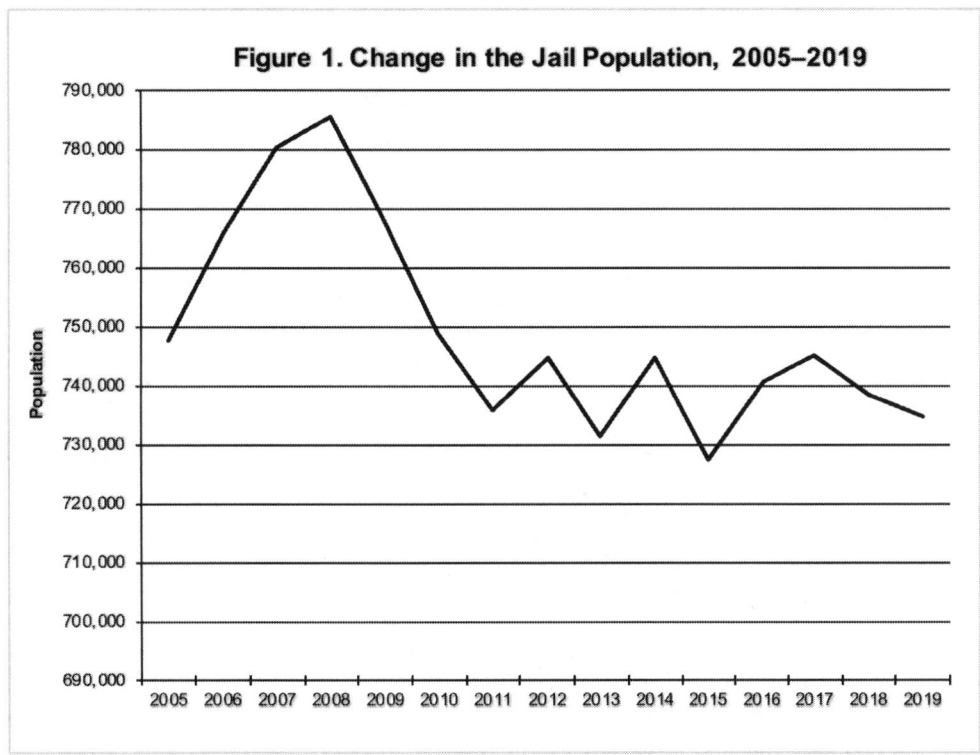

Figure 1. Change in the Jail Population, 2005–2019

- The number of inmates confined in county and city jails was an estimated 734,500 at midyear 2019, lower than the peak of 785,500 inmates on an average day at midyear 2008.

- At midyear 2019, the jail incarceration rate had decreased approximately 13 percent from midyear 2008, declining from a peak of 258 per 100,000 U.S. residents at midyear to about 224 per 100,000 population.

- Approximately 10.3 million admissions to jail occurred in 2019, continuing the trend of steady decline that has been experienced since 2008.

- Fewer than 3,000 juveniles age 17 years or younger were held in local jails at midyear 2019; this was significantly below the peak of about 7,600 in 2000 and 2010.

- Approximately 81 percent of jail beds were occupied in 2019, down from 95 percent in 2007, while 15 percent of jails were operating at or above 100 percent of their operating capacity.

- At yearend 2019, Blacks (600 per 100,000 Black residents) were incarcerated in jail at a rate 3.5 times that of Whites (184 per 100,000 White residents).

Table 1. Inmates Confined at Midyear, Average Daily Population and Incarceration Rates, 2005–2019

(Number; percent.)

Year	Confined inmates[1]	Average daily population[2]	Annual admissions[3]	Jail incarceration rate[4]
2005[5]	747,500	733,400	12,100,000	253
2006	765,800 B	755,300 B	12,200,000	256 B
2007	780,200 B	773,100 B	13,100,000 B	259 B
2008	785,500 B	776,600 B	13,600,000 B	258 B
2009	767,400 B	768,100 B	12,800,000 B	250 B
2010	748,700 B	748,600 B	12,900,000 B	242 B
2011	735,600	735,600	11,800,000 B	236 B
2012	744,500	737,400	11,600,000 B	237 B
2013	731,200	731,400	11,700,000 B	231 B
2014	744,600	739,000	11,400,000 B	234 B
2015	727,400	719,500 B	10,700,000 B	227
2016	740,700	731,300	10,600,000 B	229 B
2017	745,200	745,600	10,600,000	229 B
2018	738,400	737,900	10,700,000 B	226
2019	734,500	741,900	10,300,000	224
Average Annual Percent Change				
2005–2019	-1.7	1.2	-14.9	-11.5
2018–2019	-0.5	0.5	-3.7	-0.9

NOTE: Data are rounded to the nearest 100 for confined inmates and for average daily population (ADP), and to the nearest 100,000 for annual admissions. Results may differ from previous reports in the series due to data updates from jail authorities.
* = Comparison year.
B = Difference with comparison year is significant at the 95% confidence level.
[1]Number of inmates held on the last weekday in June.
[2]The ADP is the sum of all inmates in jail each day for one year, divided by the number of days in the year. The ADP for 2015 and 2016 was calculated for the calendar year ending on December 31. The ADP for all other years was calculated for the 12-month period ending on June 30.
[3]Annual admissions in 2005 and 2007 to 2014 were estimated based on admissions during a one-week period in June. The 2006, 2015, and 2016 annual admissions were for the calendar year ending on December 31. The 2017 to 2019 annual admissions were for the 12-month period ending on June 30.
[4]Number of confined inmates in local jails at midyear per 100,000 U.S. residents.
[5]Differences between 2005 and 2019 were not tested because the statistics for these two years are based on complete enumerations of jails.

Table 2. Jail Incarceration Rates, by Sex, Race, and Ethnicity, Midyear 2005, 2008, and 2010–2019

(Rate.)

Characteristic	2005[1]	2008	2010	2011	2012	2013	2014	2015[2]	2016[2]	2017	2018	2019*
Total	253	258 B	242 B	236 B	237 B	231 B	233 B	227	229 B	229 B	226	224
Adults[3]	334	338 B	315 B	307 B	308 B	299 B	302 B	293 B	296 B	295 B	290	287
Sex												
Male	448	457 B	431 B	419 B	418 B	404 B	405 B	395 B	398 B	395 B	387	386
Female	63	65	59 B	59 B	62 B	64 B	67	64 B	66	69 B	69 B	66
Race/Ethnicity												
White[4]	167	167 B	167 B	167 B	173 B	174 B	178 B	178 B	180	187	187	184
Black[4]	803	825 B	745 B	721 B	709 B	668 B	667 B	640 B	633 B	616	593	600
Hispanic	263	273 B	235 B	219 B	212 B	199 B	200 B	184	196 B	185 B	183	176
American Indian/Alaska Native[4]	339	386	426	410	401	437	443	378	379	366	401	420
Asian[4]	40	37 B	31 B	32 B	30 B	28 B	32 B	30 B	30 B	26	26	25
Other[4,5]	34	37 B	26 B	26 B	34	33	24 B	36	40	39	50	33

Note: Rates are based on the number of confined inmates at midyear in local jails per 100,000 U.S. residents (for total) or per 100,000 U.S. residents of a given demographic group. Data are based on the inmate population confined on the last weekday in June and include both adults and juveniles, unless otherwise specified. Results may differ from previous reports in the series due to data updates from jail authorities.
* = Comparison year.
B = Difference with comparison year is significant at the 95% confidence level.
[1]Differences between 2005 and 2019 were not tested because the statistics for these two years are based on complete enumerations of jails.
[2]In 2015 and 2016, the Annual Survey of Jails collected demographic data on inmate population at year-end instead of midyear. Because jails typically hold fewer inmates at year-end than at midyear, the 2015 and 2016 inmate populations were adjusted for seasonal variation.
[3]Excludes persons under age 18.
[4]Excludes persons of Hispanic/Latino origin (e.g., White refers to non-Hispanic Whites and Black refers to non-Hispanic Blacks).
[5]Includes Native Hawaiians, Other Pacific Islanders, and persons of two or more races.

Table 3. Number of Confined Inmates in Local Jails, by Characteristics, 2005, 2008, 2010, and 2015–2019

(Number; percent.)

Characteristic	2005[1]	2008	2010	2015[2]	2016[2]	2017	2018	2019*	Change from 2008 to 2019 Count	Change from 2008 to 2019 Percent
Total	747,500	785,500[B]	748,700[B]	727,400	740,700	745,200	738,400	734,500	-51,000	-6.5
Sex										
Male...	653,000	685,900[B]	656,400[B]	623,600	633,100	631,500	623,400	623,700	-62,200	-9.1
Female..	94,600	99,700[B]	92,400[B]	103,800[B]	107,600[B]	113,700[B]	115,100[B]	110,700	11,000	11
Adult	740,800	777,800[B]	741,200	723,800	736,800	741,600	735,000	731,600	-46,200	-5.9
Male...	646,800	678,700[B]	649,300[B]	620,300	629,700	628,200	620,500	621,100	-57,600	-8.5
Female..	94,000	99,200[B]	91,900[B]	103,500[B]	107,100[B]	113,400[B]	114,500[B]	110,500	11,300	11.4
Juvenile[3]	6,800	7,700[B]	7,600[B]	3,600[B]	3,900[B]	3,600[B]	3,400[B]	2,900	-4,800	-62.3
Held as adult[4]	5,800	6,400[B]	5,600[B]	3,200[B]	3,200[B]	3,200[B]	2,700[B]	2,200	-4,200	-65.6
Held as juvenile...........................	1,000	1,300[B]	1,900[B]	400[B]	700	300	700	700	-600	-46.2
Race/Ethnicity										
White[5]	331,000	333,300[B]	331,600[B]	351,600[B]	356,100	370,100	368,500	362,900	29,600	8.9
Black[5]	290,500	308,000[B]	283,200[B]	255,200[B]	254,600[B]	250,100	242,300	247,100	-60,900	-19.8
Hispanic.......................................	111,900	128,500[B]	118,100[B]	103,900	112,700[B]	108,400	109,300	106,900	-21,600	-16.8
American Indian/Alaska Native[5]........................	7,600	9,000	9,900	9,000	9,000	8,800	9,700	10,200	1,200	13.3
Asian[5]	4,900	5,000[B]	4,400[B]	5,200[B]	5,200[B]	4,800	4,800	4,700	-300	-6
Other[5,6]	1,500	1,800[B]	1,500[B]	2,500	2,900	2,900	3,900	2,600	800	44.4
Conviction Status										
Convicted......................................	284,400	291,300[B]	291,300[B]	273,000[B]	258,500	263,200[B]	248,500	253,700	-37,600	-12.9
Unconvicted..................................	463,200	494,300[B]	457,400[B]	454,400[B]	482,100	482,000	490,000	480,700	-13,600	-2.8
Most Serious Type of Offense										
Felony...	NC	NC	NC	494,100[B]	516,400	516,800	504,900	513,900	NC	NC
Misdemeanor.................................	NC	NC	NC	193100[B]	188,000[B]	194,700[B]	192,000[B]	170,300	NC	NC
Other[7]..	NC	NC	NC	40,200[B]	36,300[B]	33,600[B]	41,600[B]	50,300	NC	NC

NOTE: Data are based on the inmate population confined on the last weekday in June, unless specified. Data are adjusted for non-response and rounded to the nearest 100. Details may not sum to totals due to rounding. Results may differ from previous reports in the series due to data updates from jail authorities.
* = Comparison year.
B = Difference with comparison year is significant at the 95% confidence level.
NC = Not collected. The Annual Survey of Jails (ASJ) began collecting inmate counts by offense severity in 2015.
[1]In 2015 and 2016, the Annual Survey of Jails collected demographic data on the inmate population at year-end instead of midyear. Jails typically hold fewer inmates at year-end than at midyear. The 2015 and 2016 inmate populations were adjusted for seasonal variation and represent estimated midyear counts.
[2]Differences between 2005 and 2019 were not tested because the statistics for these two years are based on complete enumerations of jails.
[3]Persons age 17 or younger.
[4]Includes juveniles who were tried or awaiting trial as adults.
[5]Excludes persons of Hispanic/Latino origin (e.g., White refers to non-Hispanic Whites and Black refers to non-Hispanic Blacks).
[6]Includes Native Hawaiians, Other Pacific Islanders, and persons of two or more races.
[7]Includes civil infractions and unknown offenses.

Table 3A. Percent of Confined Inmates in Local Jails, of Confined Inmates in Local Jails, by Characteristics, 2005, 2008, 2010, and 2015–2019

(Percent.)

Characteristic	2005[1]	2008	2010	2015[2]	2016[2]	2017	2018	2019*
Sex								
Male	87.3	87.3[B]	87.7[B]	85.7[B]	85.5[B]	84.7	84.4[B]	84.9
Female	12.7	12.7[B]	12.3[B]	14.3[B]	14.5[B]	15.3	15.6[B]	15.1
Adult	99.1	99.0[B]	99.0[B]	99.5[B]	99.5[B]	99.5[B]	99.5[B]	99.6
Male	86.5	86.4[B]	86.7[B]	85.3[B]	85.0[B]	84.3[B]	84.0[B]	84.6
Female	12.6	12.6[B]	12.3[B]	14.2[B]	14.5[B]	15.2	15.5[B]	15.0
Juvenile[3]	0.9	1.0[B]	1.0[B]	0.5[B]	0.5[B]	0.5[B]	0.5[B]	0.4
Held as adult[4]	0.8	0.8[B]	0.8[B]	0.4[B]	0.4[B]	0.4[B]	0.4[B]	0.3
Held as juvenile	0.1	0.2[B]	0.3[B]	0.1[B]	0.1	<0.05	0.1	0.1
Race/Ethnicity								
White[5]	44.3	42.4[B]	44.3[B]	48.3[B]	48.1[B]	49.7	49.9	49.4
Black[5]	38.9	39.2[B]	37.8[B]	35.1[B]	34.4	33.6	32.8	33.6
Hispanic	15.0	16.4[B]	15.8[B]	14.3	15.2[B]	14.5	14.8	14.6
American Indian/Alaska Native[5]	1.0	1.1[B]	1.3	1.2	1.2	1.2[B]	1.3	1.4
Asian[5]	0.7	0.6[B]	0.6[B]	0.7[B]	0.7[B]	0.6	0.7	0.6
Other[5,6]	0.2	0.2[B]	0.2[B]	0.3	0.4	0.4	0.5	0.4
Conviction Status								
Convicted	38.0	37.1[B]	38.9[B]	37.5[B]	34.9	35.3	33.6	34.5
Unconvicted	62.0	62.9[B]	61.1[B]	62.5[B]	65.1	64.7	66.4	65.5
Most Serious Type of Offense								
Felony	NC	NC	NC	67.8[B]	69.7	69.4	68.4[B]	70.0
Misdemeanor	NC	NC	NC	26.5[B]	25.4[B]	26.1[B]	26.0[B]	23.2
Other[7]	NC	NC	NC	5.5[B]	4.9[B]	4.5[B]	5.6[B]	6.8

NOTE: Data are based on the inmate population confined on the last weekday in June, unless specified. Data are adjusted for non-response and rounded to the nearest 100. Details may not sum to totals due to rounding. Results may differ from previous reports in the series due to data updates from jail authorities.
* = Comparison year.
B = Difference with comparison year is significant at the 95% confidence level.
NC = Not collected. The Annual Survey of Jails (ASJ) began collecting inmate counts by offense severity in 2015.
[1]In 2015 and 2016, the Annual Survey of Jails collected demographic data on the inmate population at year-end instead of midyear. Jails typically hold fewer inmates at year-end than at midyear. The 2015 and 2016 inmate populations were adjusted for seasonal variation and represent estimated midyear counts.
[2]Differences between 2005 and 2019 were not tested because the statistics for these two years are based on complete enumerations of jails.
[3]Persons age 17 or younger.
[4]Includes juveniles who were tried or awaiting trial as adults.
[5]Excludes persons of Hispanic/Latino origin (e.g., White refers to non-Hispanic Whites and Black refers to non-Hispanic Blacks).
[6]Includes Native Hawaiians, Other Pacific Islanders, and persons of two or more races.
[7]Includes civil infractions and unknown offenses.

Table 4. Average Daily Jail Population, by Size of Jurisdiction, 2019

(Number; percent.)

Jail jurisdiction size	Jail jurisdictions		Total average daily population		Mean average daily population
	Number	Percent	Number	Percent	
Total	2,850	100.0	741,900	100.0	261
49 or fewer............................	991	34.8	19,700	2.7	20
50 to 99	504	17.7	36,500	4.9	72
100 to 249	642	22.5	101,000	13.6	160
250 to 499	348	12.2	120,400	16.2	349
500 to 999	215	7.5	151,100	20.4	706
1,000 to 2,499	123	4.3	178,900	24.1	1,445
2,500 and over	27	0.9	134,400	18.1	5,039

NOTE: The average daily population (ADP) is the sum of all inmates in jail each day for the 12-month period ending on June 30, divided by the number of days in the 12-month period. The ADP is rounded to the nearest 100. Jail jurisdiction size is based on the ADP. Details may not sum to totals due to rounding. Standard errors were not calculated because these data represent a complete enumeration based on the 2019 Census of Jails.

Table 5. Jail Capacity, Midyear Population, and Percent of Capacity Occupied in Local Jails, 2005–2019

(Number; percent.)

Year	Jail capacity[1]	Midyear population[2]	Percent of capacity occupied[3]
2005[4]	787,000	747,500	95.0
2006..	795,000 [B]	765,800 [B]	96.3 [B]
2007..	810,500 [B]	780,200 [B]	96.3 [B]
2008..	828,700 [B]	785,500 [B]	94.8 [B]
2009..	849,900 [B]	767,400 [B]	90.2 [B]
2010..	857,900 [B]	748,700 [B]	87.3 [B]
2011..	870,400 [B]	735,600	84.5 [B]
2012..	877,400 [B]	744,500	84.9 [B]
2013..	872,900 [B]	731,200	83.8 [B]
2014..	890,500	744,600	83.6 [B]
2015..	901,400	727,400	80.7
2016..	915,400	740,700	80.9
2017..	915,100	745,200	81.4
2018..	907,000	738,400	81.4
2019*..	907,000	734,500	80.9

NOTE: Data are rounded to the nearest 100 for jail capacity and midyear population. Results may differ from previous reports in the series due to data updates from jail authorities.
* = Comparison year.
B = Difference with comparison group is significant at the 95% confidence level.
[1]Maximum number of beds or inmates assigned by a rating official to a facility, excluding separate temporary holding areas.
[2]The number of inmates held on the last weekday in June.
[3]The midyear inmate population divided by the rated capacity.
[4]Differences between 2005 and 2019 were not tested because the statistics for these two years are based on complete enumerations of jails.

Table 6. Percent of Jail Capacity Occupied at Midyear, by Size of Jurisdiction, 2019

(Number; percent.)

Jail jurisdiction size (ADP)	Midyear population[1]	Rated capacity[2]	Percent of capacity occupied at midyear[3]	Percent of jail jurisdictions operating at more than 100% of rated capacity at midyear
Total	734,500	907,700	80.9	15.0
49 or fewer............................	19,300	33,700	57.2	5.4
50 to 99	35,500	49,200	72.0	12.9
100 to 249	100,100	122,100	82.0	22.6
250 to 499	118,700	138,400	85.8	24.4
500 to 999	150,400	180,100	83.5	25.2
1,000 to 2,499	178,400	219,800	81.2	16.5
2,500 or more	132,200	164,400	80.4	19.3

NOTE:Jail jurisdiction size is based on the average daily population (ADP). Data are rounded to the nearest 100 for midyear population and rated capacity. Details may not sum to totals due to rounding. Standard errors were not calculated because these data represent a complete enumeration based on the 2019 Census of Jails.
[1]The number of inmates held on the last weekday in June.
[2]Maximum number of beds or inmates assigned by a rating official to a facility, excluding separate temporary holding areas.
[3]The midyear population divided by the rated capacity.

Table 7. Inmate Turnover Rate and Expected Average Length of Stay, by Size of Jurisdiction, 2019

(Number; percent.)

Jail jurisdiction size (ADP)	Average daily population[1]	Annual admissions	Weekly inmate turnover rate[2]	Expected average time in jail (days)[3]
Total	741,900	10,322,600	53.1	26.2
49 or fewer..........................	19,700	712,800	138.0	10.1
50 to 99	36,500	713,100	74.2	18.7
100 to 249	101,000	1,670,000	61.9	22.1
250 to 499	120,400	1,696,500	53.9	25.9
500 to 999	151,100	1,910,500	48.2	28.9
1,000 to 2,499	178,900	2,254,100	48.3	29.0
2,500 or more	134,400	1,365,600	39.3	35.9

NOTE: Jail jurisdiction size is based on the average daily population (ADP). Data are rounded to the nearest 100 for the ADP. Details may not sum to totals due to rounding. Standard errors were not calculated because these data represent a complete enumeration based on the 2019 Census of Jails.
[1]The sum of all inmates in jail each day for the 12-month period ending on June 30, divided by the number of days in the 12-month period.
[2]The sum of weekly admissions and releases, divided by the ADP. Weekly admissions and releases are calculated as the annual admissions and releases, divided by the number of weeks in the 12-month period.
[3]The ADP divided by the number of annual admissions, then multiplied by the number of days in a year.

Table 8. Persons Under Jail Supervision, by Confinement Status, 2005–2019

(Number; percent.)

Year	Persons under jail supervision at midyear[1]					Persons serving weekend-only sentences on the weekend before midyear[5]	
	Total[2]	Held in jail[3]		Supervised outside of a jail facility[4]			
		Number	Percent	Number	Percent	Number	Percent
2005[6]	805,300	747,500	92.8	57,800	7.2	14,100	1.8
2006....................................	814,600[B]	765,800[B]	94.0[B]	48,800[B]	6.0[B]	11,400[B]	1.4[B]
2007....................................	838,000[B]	780,200[B]	93.1[B]	57,800[B]	6.9[B]	10,500[B]	1.3[B]
2008....................................	846,000[B]	785,500[B]	92.8[B]	60,500[B]	7.2[B]	12,300[B]	1.5[B]
2009....................................	826,400[B]	767,400[B]	92.9[B]	59,000[B]	7.1[B]	11,200[B]	1.4[B]
2010....................................	799,500[B]	748,700[B]	93.6[B]	50,800[B]	6.4[B]	9,900[B]	1.2[B]
2011....................................	787,000[B]	735,600	93.5[B]	51,400[B]	6.5[B]	11,400[B]	1.4[B]
2012....................................	798,200[B]	744,500	93.3[B]	53,700[B]	6.7[B]	10,400[B]	1.3[B]
2013....................................	779,700	731,200	93.8[B]	48,500[B]	6.2[B]	11,000[B]	1.4[B]
2014....................................	798,400[B]	744,600	93.3[B]	53,800[B]	6.7[B]	9,700[B]	1.2[B]
2015....................................	774,500	727,400	93.9[B]	47,100[B]	6.1[B]	7,800[B]	1.0[B]
2016....................................	789,400[B]	740,700	93.8[B]	48,700[B]	6.2[B]	5,500[B]	0.7[B]
2017....................................	794,300[B]	745,200	93.8[B]	49,100[B]	6.2[B]	6,800	0.9
2018....................................	790,400[B]	738,400	93.4[B]	52,000[B]	6.6[B]	5,900	0.7[B]
2019*..................................	773,200	734,500	95.0	38,700	5.0	6,500	0.8

NOTE: Data are based on the number of inmates supervised on the last weekday in June, unless specified. Data are rounded to the nearest 100. Details may not sum to totals due to rounding.
* = Comparison year.
B = Difference with comparison year is significant at the 95% confidence level.
[1]Confined inmates in local jails and persons supervised outside of jail.
[2]The total population under jail supervision differs from past reports because persons serving weekend-only sentences are listed separately in this report instead of being included in the population supervised outside of jail.
[3]Inmates held on the last weekday in June.
[4]Includes unconfined persons under jail supervision in programs outside of jail, including electronic monitoring, home detention, day reporting, community service, alcohol or drug treatment programs, and other pre-trial supervision and work programs. Excludes persons supervised by a probation or parole agency. In 2015 and 2016, data on the population supervised outside of jail were collected at December 31. For all other years, data were collected on the last weekday in June.
[5]Persons who served their sentences of confinement on weekends only (i.e., Friday to Sunday) on the weekend before the last weekday in June. In 2015 and 2016, the number of weekenders was collected for the weekend before December 31.
[6]Differences between 2005 and 2019 were not tested because the statistics for these two years are based on complete enumerations of jails.

Table 9. Staff Employed in Local Jails, by Sex, 2013 and 2015–2019

(Number; percent; ratio.)

Job function	Number						Percent of all staff					
	2013[1,2]	2015[2]	2016[2]	2017	2018	2019*	2013[1,2]	2015[2]	2016[2]	2017	2018	2019*
Job Function												
Total..	220,000	213,000[B]	226,300[B]	225,700[B]	221,600[B]	237,500	100.0	100.0	100.0	100.0	100.0	100.0
Correctional Officers[3]............................	173,900	169,300[B]	178,800	179,500	174,500[B]	184,100	79.0	79.5[B]	79.0[B]	79.3[B]	78.7[B]	77.5
Male	123,400	117,300[B]	124,300	123,200	119,900[B]	127,300	56.1	55.1[B]	54.9[B]	55.0[B]	54.1	53.6
Female	50,500	51,900[B]	54,500	56,300	54,600	56,800	23.0	24.4	24.1	24.4	24.6[B]	23.9
Inmate-to-correctional-officer ratio........................	4.2	4.1[B]	3.9	4.2[B]	4.2[B]	4.0						
All Other Staff[4].................................	46,100	43,700[B]	47,500[B]	46,200[B]	47,100[B]	53,400	21.0	20.5[B]	21.0[B]	20.6[B]	21.3[B]	22.5
Male	20,800	19,700[B]	21,000[B]	20,300[B]	20,600[B]	25,400	9.5	9.3[B]	9.3[B]	9.4[B]	9.3[B]	10.7
Female	25,200	24,000[B]	26,500[B]	25,900[B]	26,500[B]	28,000	11.5	11.3[B]	11.7	11.3[B]	12.0	11.8

NOTE: Data are based on the number of staff employed on the last weekday in June, unless specified. Data are rounded to the nearest 100 for the number of employed staff. Details may not sum to totals due to rounding. Results may differ from previous reports in the series due to data updates from jail authorities.
* = Comparison year.
B = Difference with comparison year is significant at the 95% confidence level.
[1]Differences between 2013 and 2019 were not tested because the statistics for these two years are based on complete enumerations of jails.
[2]In 2013, 2015, and 2016, data on jail staff were collected at year-end instead of midyear.
[3]Includes deputies, monitors, and other custody staff who spend more than 50% of their time with the incarcerated population.
[4]Includes administrators, clerical and maintenance staff, educational staff, professional and technical staff, and other unspecified staff who spend more than 50% of their time in the facility.

Table 10. Jail Incarceration Rates at Midyear, by Race or Ethnicity, 2005–2019

(Number.)

Year	Total	White[1]	Black[1]	Hispanic	Native[1]	Asian[1]
2005...	253	167	803	263	339	40
2006...	256	169	810	271	370	36
2007...	259	170	817	276	373	37
2008...	258	167	825	273	386	37
2009...	250	163	797	256	398	35
2010...	242	167	745	235	426	31
2011...	236	167	721	219	410	32
2012...	237	173	709	212	401	30
2013...	231	174	668	199	437	28
2014...	233	178	667	200	443	32
2015...	227	178	640	184	378	30
2016[1]..	229	180	633	196	379	30
2017[1]..	229	187	617	185	366	26
2018...	226	187	593	183	401	26
2019...	224	184	600	176	420	25

NOTE: Rates are based on the number of inmates held on the last weekday in June. Results may differ from previous reports in the series due to data updates from jail authorities. In 2015 and 2016, the Annual Survey of Jails collected inmate counts by race or ethnicity at year-end. Because jails typically hold fewer inmates at year-end than at midyear, the 2015 and 2016 incarceration rates were adjusted for seasonal variation and represent estimated midyear rates.
[1]Excludes persons of Hispanic origin (e.g., White refers to non-Hispanic Whites and Black refers to non-Hispanic Blacks).

METHODOLOGY

Findings in this report are based on the 2005, 2013, and 2019 Census of Jails (COJ) and the 2006 to 2018 Annual Survey of Jails (ASJ). The Bureau of Justice Statistics (BJS) periodically conducts the COJ, collecting a complete enumeration of local jail facilities and Federal Bureau of Prisons (BOP) detention facilities. The 2019 COJ was the eleventh collection in the series since 1970. In the years between complete enumerations of jails, BJS conducts the ASJ, a national survey administered to a sample of approximately 900 jails (BOP detention facilities are excluded from the ASJ), to provide nationwide statistics on the number and characteristics of local jail inmates.

In 2013, BJS conducted both the COJ and ASJ. The 2013 ASJ collected jail population data at midyear, and the 2013 COJ collected jail population and facility data at year-end. Statistics for 2013 in the *Jail Inmates* series are based on the 2013 ASJ midyear data, except for statistics on staff employed in local jails (see table 10 of this report), which are based on the 2013 COJ year-end data. COJ and ASJ collections are currently conducted through Web-based surveys. RTI International is the data collection agent for the COJ and ASJ.

The Universe of the Census of Jails and the Annual Survey of Jails

The COJ and ASJ gather data from jails that hold inmates beyond arraignment, usually for a period exceeding 72 hours. Jail facilities are intended to hold adults, but some also hold juveniles (persons age 17 or younger). The universe of the COJ consists of all local jail jurisdictions (including county, city, regional, and privately operated jail facilities) and BOP detention facilities that function as jails. The universe of the ASJ includes all local jail jurisdictions but excludes BOP detention facilities. For consistency of historical comparisons, data from BOP detention facilities are excluded from BJS's *Jail Inmates* series, including this report.

The universe of the COJ and ASJ excludes separate temporary holding facilities (such as drunk tanks and police lockups) that do not hold persons after they have been formally charged in court. However, temporary holding facilities that are operated as part of a local jail are included. Also excluded are combined jail and prison systems in Alaska, Connecticut, Delaware, Hawaii, Rhode Island, and Vermont. These combined systems are operated by state departments of corrections and included in BJS's National Prisoner Statistics program. However, there are 15 independently operated jails in Alaska that are included in the universe of the COJ and ASJ.

Jail Jurisdictions and Facilities

A jail jurisdiction is a legal entity that has responsibility for managing jail facilities. Jail jurisdictions typically operate at the county level, with a sheriff 's office or jail administrator managing the local facilities. Most jail jurisdictions have one facility each, but some jail jurisdictions have multiple facilities under a central authority. Based on the 2019 COJ, 6.7 percent of jail jurisdictions had more than one facility, while 15 percent of all jail facilities were part of a multi-facility jurisdiction. As of June 28, 2019 (the reference date of the 2019 COJ), there were 2,850 active jail jurisdictions in the country operating a total of 3,119 county (2,708), city (299), regional (78), and private (34) jail facilities.

Adjusting for Seasonal Variation in the Jail Population

Prior to 2015, the ASJ asked jails to report total and detailed inmate counts on the last weekday in June (the midyear reference date). In 2015 and 2016, the ASJ collected the total confined population at midyear, but detailed inmate counts by characteristic (i.e., sex, race or ethnicity, age category, conviction status, and most serious type of offense) on December 31 (the year-end reference date). Starting with the 2017 collection, the ASJ reverted back to the midyear reference. Comparisons of year-end data with midyear data need to consider seasonal variations, as jails typically hold fewer inmates at year-end than at midyear.

To adjust for seasonal variation, the numbers of inmates by characteristics for 2015 and 2016 in table 3 were multiplied by the ratio of the midyear confined population to the year-end confined population of the corresponding year.

Item Non-Response Rates and Imputation

Item response rates ranged from 90% to 100% in the 2019 COJ. Key population items (including one-day counts of the confined population, population by sex and juvenile status, population by race or ethnicity, admissions by sex, ADP by sex, and rated capacity) had item response rates of more than 95 percent. For responding jail jurisdictions that were unable to provide some requested items, a last observation carried forward (LOCF) procedure was used to replace missing values with the most recent (2016, 2017, or 2018) ASJ or MCI data from the same jail jurisdictions, adjusted for year-to-year difference in the total confined population. For cases with no prior-year data, a weighted sequential hot-deck procedure was implemented to impute missing data, where the donor for each missing item was randomly selected from a set of similar jails, sorted by related auxiliary population values. Donor pools, also referred to as imputation classes, were formed by state, ADP category, and regional jail indicators. Within each imputation class, jails were sorted by confined jail population at midyear 2019.

Terms and Definitions

Admissions: Persons who are officially booked and housed in jails by formal legal document and the authority of the courts or some other official agency. Jail admissions include persons sentenced to weekend programs and those who are booked into the facility for the first time. Excluded from jail admissions are inmates re-entering the facility after an escape, work release, medical appointment or treatment facility appointment, and bail and court appearances. BJS collects jail admissions for the last 7 days in June.

Average daily population (ADP): The average is derived by the sum of inmates in jail each day for a year, divided by the number of days in the year.

Average annual change: The mean average change across a 12-month time period.

Calculating annual admissions: Annual jail admissions are calculated by multiplying weekly admissions by the sum of 365 days divided by 7 days.

Calculating weekly jail turnover rate: This rate is calculated by adding admissions and releases and dividing by the average daily population.

Inmates confined: The number of inmates held in custody.

Jail incarceration rate: The number of inmates held in the custody of local jails, per 100,000 U.S. residents.

Percent of capacity occupied: This percentage is calculated by taking the number of inmates, dividing by the rated capacity, and multiplying by 100.

Rated capacity: The number of beds or inmates assigned by a rating official to a facility, excluding separate temporary holding areas.

Releases: Persons released after a period of confinement (e.g., sentence completion, bail or bond releases, other pretrial releases, transfers to other jurisdictions, and deaths). Releases include those persons who have completed their weekend program and who are leaving the facility for the last time. Excluded from jail releases are temporary discharges including work release, medical appointment or treatment center, court appearance, furlough, day reporting, and transfers to other facilities within the jail's jurisdiction.

Standard errors and tests of significance: As with any survey, the ASJ estimates are subject to error arising from sampling rather than using a complete enumeration of the jail population. A common way to express this sampling variability is to construct a 95 percent confidence interval around each survey estimate. Typically, multiplying the standard error by 1.96 and then adding or subtracting the result from the estimate produces the confidence interval. This interval expresses the range of values that could result among 95 percent of the different samples that could be drawn.

Under jail supervision but not confined: This classification includes all persons in community-based programs operated by a jail facility. These programs include electronic monitoring, house arrest, community service, day reporting, and work programs. The classification excludes persons on pretrial release and who are not in a community-based program run by the jail, as well as persons under supervision of probation, parole, or other agencies; inmates on weekend programs; and inmates who participate in work release programs and return to the jail at night.

Weekend programs: Offenders in these programs are allowed to serve their sentences of confinement only on weekends (i.e., Friday to Sunday).

PART 8

Law Enforcement Officers Killed and Assaulted, 2019

HIGHLIGHTS

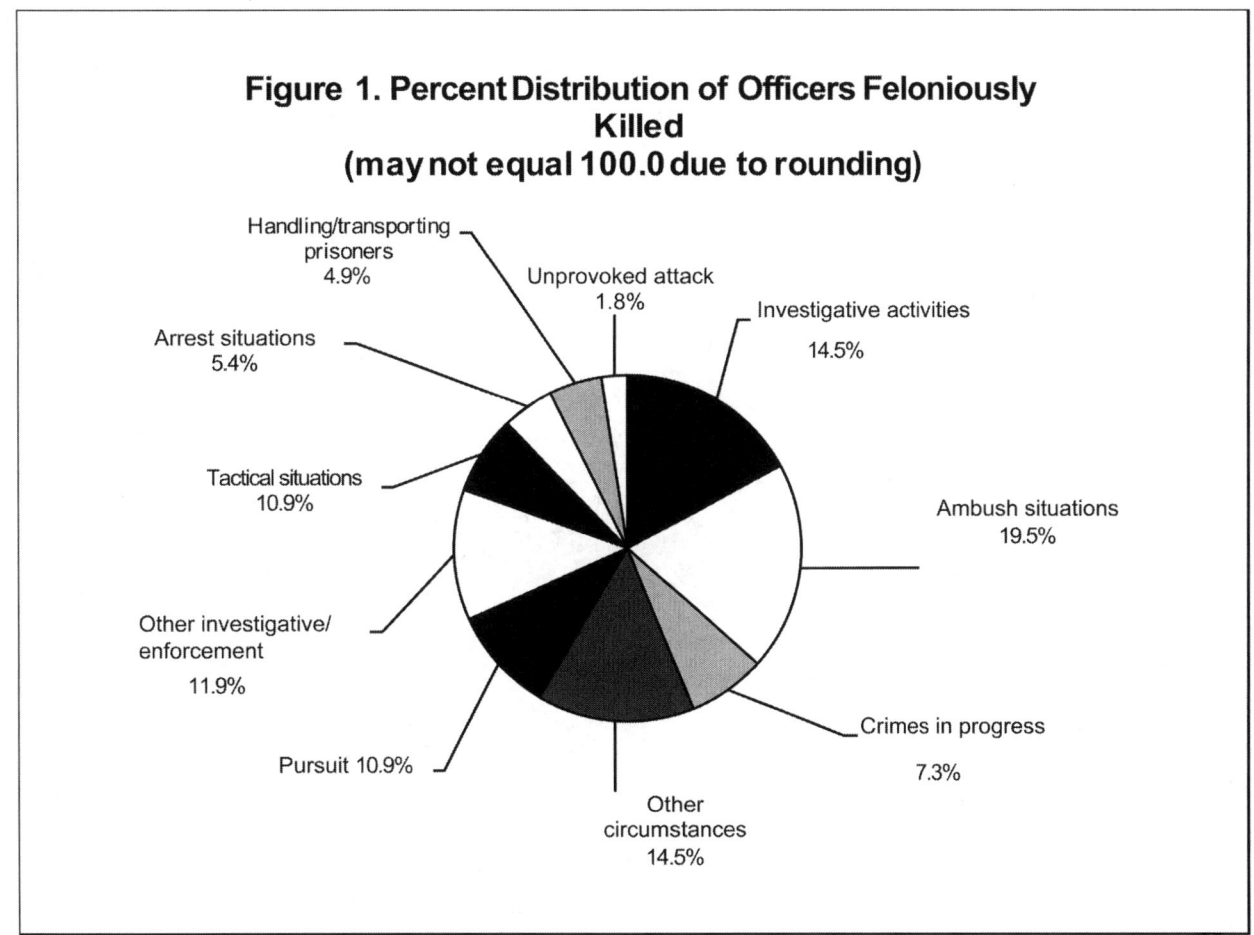

**Figure 1. Percent Distribution of Officers Feloniously Killed
(may not equal 100.0 due to rounding)**

Handling/transporting prisoners 4.9%

Unprovoked attack 1.8%

Investigative activities 14.5%

Arrest situations 5.4%

Ambush situations 19.5%

Tactical situations 10.9%

Other investigative/ enforcement 11.9%

Crimes in progress 7.3%

Pursuit 10.9%

Other circumstances 14.5%

- In 2019, 48 law enforcement officers died from injuries incurred in the line of duty during felonious incidents. Of the officers feloniously killed, 25 were employed by city police departments, including 7 who were members of law enforcement agencies in cities with 100,000 to 249,99 or more inhabitants.

- Line-of-duty deaths in 2019 occurred in 19 states and Puerto Rico. By region, 27 officers were feloniously killed in the South, 9 officers in the Midwest, 92 officers in the West, 1 officer in the Northeast, and 2 officers in Puerto Rico.

- The average age of the officers who died in 2019 was 40 years old. The slain officers' average length of law enforcement service was 13 years. Of these officers, 45 were male and 3 were female.

- In 2019, 41 law enforcement officers died as the result of accidents that occurred in the line of duty. Accidental line-of-duty deaths of law enforcement officers occurred in 23 states.

- Participating federal law enforcement agencies reported that 17,188 officers were injured but nonfatally assaulted while performing their duties in 2019.

- No federal law enforcement officers were feloniously killed in 2018. Of the 2,136 reported assaulted, 372 were reported as injured.

Table 1. Law Enforcement Officers Feloniously Killed, by Region, Geographic Division, and State/Territory, 2010–2019

(Number.)

Area	Total	2010	2011	2012	2013	2014	2015	2016	2017	2018	2019
Number of Victim Officers.................	511	55	72	49	27	51	41	66	46	56	48
Northeast..	45	3	10	6	2	8	4	4	3	4	1
New England...................................	9	1	0	2	1	1	0	1	0	3	0
Connecticut.................................	0	0	0	0	0	0	0	0	0	0	0
Maine...	1	0	0	0	0	0	0	0	0	1	0
Massachusetts..............................	6	1	0	1	1	0	0	1	0	2	0
New Hampshire............................	2	0	0	1	0	1	0	0	0	0	0
Rhode Island................................	0	0	0	0	0	0	0	0	0	0	0
Vermont......................................	0	0	0	0	0	0	0	0	0	0	0
Middle Atlantic..............................	36	2	10	4	1	7	4	3	3	1	1
New Jersey..................................	4	0	2	0	0	1	0	0	0	0	1
New York....................................	18	0	4	2	1	5	2	1	2	1	0
Pennsylvania................................	14	2	4	2	0	1	2	2	1	0	0
Midwest...	99	10	21	6	4	8	5	13	11	12	9
East North Central..........................	63	8	12	2	3	5	3	6	8	8	8
Illinois..	14	4	1	0	1	0	1	0	2	2	3
Indiana.......................................	10	0	2	0	1	3	0	1	1	2	0
Michigan.....................................	15	3	4	1	1	0	0	2	2	1	1
Ohio...	16	1	4	1	0	1	1	2	2	2	2
Wisconsin....................................	8	0	1	0	0	1	1	1	1	1	2
West North Central........................	36	2	9	4	1	3	2	7	3	4	1
Iowa...	5	0	1	0	1	0	0	2	1	0	0
Kansas..	9	0	1	2	0	1	0	2	0	3	0
Minnesota...................................	6	2	1	1	0	1	1	0	0	0	0
Missouri......................................	10	0	3	1	0	1	0	2	1	1	1
Nebraska.....................................	1	0	0	0	0	0	1	0	0	0	0
North Dakota...............................	3	0	1	0	0	0	0	1	1	0	0
South Dakota...............................	2	0	2	0	0	0	0	0	0	0	0
South...	231	22	29	22	15	17	19	30	24	26	27
South Atlantic................................	100	11	18	10	5	10	3	13	8	15	7
Delaware.....................................	3	0	1	0	0	0	0	0	2	0	0
District of Columbia.....................	0	0	0	0	0	0	0	0	0	0	0
Florida..	26	4	6	2	2	4	1	0	3	4	0
Georgia.......................................	28	5	3	1	0	2	1	7	1	5	3
Maryland.....................................	8	1	0	0	1	0	0	2	1	2	1
North Carolina.............................	11	1	2	3	0	2	0	1	0	1	1
South Carolina.............................	9	0	2	1	0	1	1	1	0	3	0
Virginia.......................................	10	0	3	0	1	1	0	2	1	0	2
West Virginia................................	5	0	1	3	1	0	0	0	0	0	0
East South Central.........................	43	4	6	5	3	0	5	4	1	6	9
Alabama......................................	11	1	1	2	0	0	0	0	0	1	6
Kentucky.....................................	6	0	0	1	1	0	2	0	0	2	0
Mississippi...................................	15	3	1	1	2	0	2	1	1	2	2
Tennessee....................................	11	0	4	1	0	0	1	3	0	1	1
West South Central........................	88	7	5	7	7	7	11	13	15	5	11
Arkansas......................................	10	2	1	0	0	1	1	1	2	0	2
Louisiana.....................................	23	3	0	2	1	1	6	4	4	1	1
Oklahoma....................................	3	0	0	0	0	0	0	0	2	1	0
Texas..	52	2	4	5	6	5	4	8	7	3	8
West...	110	17	10	9	6	14	9	17	6	13	9
Mountain.......................................	54	10	5	5	1	7	7	8	4	6	1
Arizona.......................................	18	4	3	2	0	3	0	2	1	3	0
Colorado.....................................	11	1	2	1	0	0	2	2	1	2	0
Idaho...	1	0	0	0	0	0	1	0	0	0	0
Montana......................................	4	2	0	0	0	1	0	0	1	0	0
Nevada.......................................	6	1	0	1	0	2	1	0	1	0	0
New Mexico.................................	5	0	0	0	0	0	3	2	0	0	0
Utah...	9	2	0	1	1	1	0	2	0	1	1
Wyoming.....................................	0	0	0	0	0	0	0	0	0	0	0
Pacific...	56	7	5	4	5	7	2	9	2	7	8
Alaska...	5	2	0	0	0	2	0	1	0	0	0
California.....................................	41	5	3	2	5	5	2	6	2	5	6
Hawaii...	1	0	0	0	0	0	0	0	0	1	0
Oregon..	3	0	2	0	0	0	0	1	0	0	0
Washington..................................	6	0	0	2	0	0	0	1	0	1	2
Puerto Rico and other outlying areas.....	26	3	2	6	0	4	4	2	2	1	2
American Samoa............................	0	0	0	0	0	0	0	0	0	0	0
Guam...	0	0	0	0	0	0	0	0	0	0	0
Mariana Islands.............................	0	0	0	0	0	0	0	0	0	0	0
Puerto Rico...................................	25	3	2	5	0	4	4	2	2	1	2
U.S. Virgin Islands..........................	1	0	0	1	0	0	0	0	0	0	0

Table 2. Law Enforcement Officers Feloniously Killed, by Population Group/Agency Type, 2010–2019

(Number.)

Population group/agency type	Total	2010	2011	2012	2013	2014	2015	2016	2017	2018	2019
Number of Victim Officers	511	55	72	49	27	51	41	66	46	56	48
Group I (cities 250,000 and over)	86	12	13	6	4	8	10	12	8	7	6
Group II (cities 100,000–249,999)	45	3	9	4	2	6	2	8	2	2	7
Group III (cities 50,000–99,999)	34	3	9	2	2	2	1	2	4	4	5
Group IV (25,000–49,999)	36	6	4	2	3	2	4	6	2	4	3
Group V (cities 10,000–24,999)	34	2	5	3	2	4	2	5	2	7	2
Group VI (cities under 10,000)	54	5	10	4	3	5	5	8	8	4	2
Metropolitan counties	111	9	14	11	6	11	5	15	7	21	12
Nonmetropolitan counties	38	6	4	5	3	4	2	3	5	2	4
State agencies	35	5	0	5	2	4	4	4	4	3	4
Federal agencies	12	1	2	1	0	1	2	1	2	1	1
Puerto Rico and other outlying areas	26	3	2	6	0	4	4	2	2	1	2

Table 3. Law Enforcement Officers Feloniously Killed, by Time of Incident, 2010–2019

(Number.)

Time of day	Total	2010	2011	2012	2013	2014	2015	2016	2017	2018	2019
Number of Victim Officers.....................	511	55	72	49	27	51	41	66	46	56	48
Total A.M. hours...	215	23	36	24	13	20	22	28	17	19	13
12:01 a.m.–2 a.m....................................	51	7	7	5	3	4	4	7	4	4	6
2:01 a.m.–4 a.m....................................	38	4	9	3	3	6	6	3	2	1	1
4:01 a.m.–6 a.m....................................	21	3	2	3	3	3	1	1	1	3	1
6:01 a.m.–8 a.m....................................	22	2	5	3	0	1	1	1	5	3	1
8:01 a.m.–10 a.m..................................	34	1	3	4	1	0	8	10	2	2	3
10:01 a.m.–noon	49	6	10	6	3	6	2	6	3	6	1
Total P.M. hours...	291	32	36	23	14	31	18	37	29	37	34
12:01 p.m.–2 p.m.	40	2	5	2	3	7	1	10	2	5	3
2:01 p.m.–4 p.m....................................	50	4	6	3	3	9	2	8	5	8	2
4:01 p.m.–6 p.m....................................	44	4	8	3	1	6	2	3	5	8	4
6:01 p.m.–8 p.m....................................	42	4	5	6	2	1	5	2	3	7	7
8:01 p.m.–10 p.m.	61	10	3	6	2	4	7	9	5	2	13
10:01 p.m.–midnight	54	8	9	3	3	4	1	5	9	7	5
Not reported...	5	0	0	2	0	0	1	1	0	0	1

Table 3A. Law Enforcement Officers Feloniously Killed, by Lighting and Weather/Environmental Conditions by Location of Incident, 2015–2019[1]

(Number.)

Characteristic	Total	Commercial			Government		
		Inside of structure	Outside	Location not reported	Inside of structure	Outside	Location not reported
Number of Victim Officers...................................	257	18	24	0	6	7	0
Lighting							
Artificial	59	14	9	0	5	4	0
Dark...................................	62	1	5	0	0	0	0
Dawn.....................................	6	0	2	0	0	0	0
Daylight.................................	104	3	7	0	1	3	0
Dusk......................................	15	0	1	0	0	0	0
Not reported	11	0	0	0	0	0	0
Weather/environmental							
Blizzard	0	0	0	0	0	0	0
Blowing dirt/sand/soil	0	0	0	0	0	0	0
Clear......................................	156	0	20	0	0	6	0
Cloudy/partly cloudy........................	17	0	3	0	0	0	0
Earthquake.................................	0	0	0	0	0	0	0
Fire/fog/smog/smoke	3	0	0	0	0	0	0
Flooding...................................	0	0	0	0	0	0	0
Freezing rain/hail/sleet......................	0	0	0	0	0	0	0
Hurricane..................................	0	0	0	0	0	0	0
Indoors (no adverse conditions)	52	18	0	0	6	0	0
Rain	11	0	0	0	0	0	0
Severe crosswinds/high winds.................	0	0	0	0	0	0	0
Snow	2	0	1	0	0	0	0
Tornado	0	0	0	0	0	0	0
Other	1	0	0	0	0	0	0
Unknown..................................	4	0	0	0	0	1	0
Not reported	11	0	0	0	0	0	0

Table 3A. Law Enforcement Officers Feloniously Killed, by Lighting and Weather/Environmental Conditions by Location of Incident, 2015–2019[1] —*Continued*

(Number.)

Characteristic	Public space[2]			Residential			Other		
	Inside of structure	Outside	Location not reported	Inside of structure	Outside	Location not reported	Inside of structure	Outside	Location not reported
Number of Victim Officers	1	110	0	27	62	0	0	2	0
Lighting									
Artificial	0	15	0	6	6	0	0	0	0
Dark	0	33	0	7	15	0	0	1	0
Dawn	0	1	0	0	3	0	0	0	0
Daylight	1	46	0	9	33	0	0	1	0
Dusk	0	11	0	0	3	0	0	0	0
Not reported	0	4	0	5	2	0	0	0	0
Weather/environmental									
Blizzard	0	0	0	0	0	0	0	0	0
Blowing dirt/sand/soil	0	0	0	0	0	0	0	0	0
Clear	0	79	0	0	49	0	0	2	0
Cloudy/partly cloudy	0	9	0	0	5	0	0	0	0
Earthquake	0	0	0	0	0	0	0	0	0
Fire/fog/smog/smoke	0	3	0	0	0	0	0	0	0
Flooding	0	0	0	0	0	0	0	0	0
Freezing rain/hail/sleet	0	0	0	0	0	0	0	0	0
Hurricane	0	0	0	0	0	0	0	0	0
Indoors (no adverse conditions)	1	0	0	27	0	0	0	0	0
Rain	0	7	0	0	4	0	0	0	0
Severe crosswinds/high winds	0	0	0	0	0	0	0	0	0
Snow	0	0	0	0	1	0	0	0	0
Tornado	0	0	0	0	0	0	0	0	0
Other	0	0	0	0	1	0	0	0	0
Unknown	0	3	0	0	0	0	0	0	0
Not reported	0	9	0	0	2	0	0	0	0

[1]Ten years of data for the topics presented in this table are not available at this time. A 10-year table is expected to be available for the publication of 2020 data.
[2]Examples of public space include, but are not limited to, alleys, highways, lakes, parks, rivers, roads, and sidewalks.

Table 4. Law Enforcement Officers Feloniously Killed, by Day of Incident, 2010–2019

(Number.)

Day of the week	Total	2010	2011	2012	2013	2014	2015	2016	2017	2018	2019
Number of Victim Officers......	511	55	72	49	27	51	41	66	46	56	48
Sunday	72	5	13	7	2	9	5	13	8	4	6
Monday............	62	5	12	5	3	7	6	4	8	7	5
Tuesday............	70	11	11	10	5	5	6	6	3	7	6
Wednesday............	82	12	8	5	3	4	9	15	7	14	5
Thursday............	75	11	9	9	6	7	3	12	6	7	5
Friday............	69	6	11	5	5	8	4	7	9	8	6
Saturday	81	5	8	8	3	11	8	9	5	9	15

Table 5. Law Enforcement Officers Feloniously Killed, by Month of Incident, 2010–2019

(Number.)

Month	Total	2010	2011	2012	2013	2014	2015	2016	2017	2018	2019
Number of Victim Officers......	511	55	72	49	27	51	41	66	46	56	48
January............	37	4	9	6	2	2	0	2	4	4	4
February............	41	4	3	4	5	1	0	9	2	8	5
March............	49	5	9	1	1	8	6	5	4	7	3
April............	31	1	9	4	3	1	0	1	4	6	2
May............	52	7	3	3	1	9	10	3	7	4	5
June............	36	4	6	4	2	4	3	3	2	3	5
July............	46	7	8	2	1	4	1	10	4	6	3
August............	43	4	7	8	2	3	6	5	5	0	3
September............	35	1	1	5	4	6	4	3	2	6	3
October	38	4	5	1	1	4	4	9	5	4	1
November............	49	6	2	4	0	5	4	13	5	4	6
December............	54	8	10	7	5	4	3	3	2	4	8

Table 6. Law Enforcement Officers Feloniously Killed, by Age Group of Victim Officer, 2010–2019

(Number; years.)

Age group	Total	2010	2011	2012	2013	2014	2015	2016	2017	2018	2019
Number of Victim Officers............	511	55	72	49	27	51	41	66	46	56	48
Under 25 years	21	3	2	2	0	5	2	2	1	1	3
25–30 years............	91	12	17	8	2	3	5	10	11	16	7
31–35 years............	110	12	11	12	9	11	9	15	8	14	9
36–40 years............	74	9	12	8	7	7	2	8	7	7	7
41–45 years............	85	7	10	8	4	12	9	12	9	8	6
46–50 years............	67	5	13	6	1	9	10	9	6	2	6
51–55 years............	36	1	4	5	2	3	2	8	2	6	3
56–60 years............	15	4	3	0	1	0	1	0	2	0	4
Over 60 years............	11	2	0	0	1	1	1	2	0	2	2
Not reported............	1	0	0	0	0	0	0	0	0	0	1
Average age (years)............	39	38	38	38	39	39	40	40	38	37	40

Table 7. Law Enforcement Officers Feloniously Killed, by Years of Service of Victim Officer, 2010–2019

(Number.)

Years of service	Total	2010	2011	2012	2013	2014	2015	2016	2017	2018	2018
Number of Victim Officers	511	55	72	49	27	51	41	66	46	56	48
Less than 1	18	1	0	2	0	2	4	2	1	3	3
1–5	127	22	17	12	4	11	8	13	14	14	12
6–10	127	13	24	13	10	8	11	13	10	18	7
11–15	79	5	8	5	8	11	4	13	7	10	8
16–20	80	9	8	10	1	13	5	13	9	4	8
21–25	38	1	12	1	1	5	6	4	2	2	4
26–30	28	1	1	4	2	0	2	8	2	3	5
More than 30	10	3	2	1	1	1	0	0	0	1	1
Not reported	4	0	0	1	0	0	1	0	1	1	0
Average years of service	12	10	12	12	13	13	12	13	11	10	13

Table 8. Law Enforcement Officers Feloniously Killed, by Profile of Victim Officer, Average Demographics, 2000–2019

(Number.)

Average	2019	5-year averages		10-year averages	
		2010–2014	2015–2019	2000–2009	2010–2019
Age	40	38	39	38	39
Years of service	13	12	12	10	12
Height	5'11"	5'11"	5'10"	5'11"	5'10"
Weight	203	204	203	199	203

Note: The deaths of the 72 law enforcement officers that resulted from the events of September 11, 2001, are not included in this table.

Table 9. Law Enforcement Officers Feloniously Killed, by Race, Ethnicity, and Sex of Victim Officer, 2010–2019

(Number.)

Characteristic	Total	2010	2011	2012	2013	2014	2015	2016	2017	2018	2019
Number of Victim Officers	511	55	72	49	27	51	41	66	46	56	48
Race											
White	442	47	68	43	25	47	29	61	35	47	40
Black/African American	55	7	3	6	2	2	8	4	9	7	7
American Indian/Alaska Native	5	0	1	0	0	0	2	0	2	0	0
Asian/Native Hawaiian/Other Pacific Islander[1]	1	1	NA	NA	NA	NA	NA	NA	NA	NA	NA
Asian[1]	6	NA	0	0	0	2	2	1	0	0	1
Native Hawaiian/Other Pacific Islander[1]	2	NA	0	0	0	0	0	0	0	2	0
Ethnicity[2]											
Hispanic or Latino	62	NA	7	9	2	11	4	7	6	5	11
Not Hispanic or Latino	377	NA	65	35	24	39	36	57	37	51	33
Not reported	72	55	0	5	1	1	1	2	3	0	4
Sex											
Male	485	53	69	44	25	51	38	64	43	53	45
Female	26	2	3	5	2	0	3	2	3	3	3

NA = Not available.
[1] Prior to 2011, the race categories "Asian" and "Native Hawaiian/Other Pacific Islander" were combined.
[2] Beginning in 2011, ethnicity was added to the data collection.

Table 10. Law Enforcement Officers Feloniously Killed, by Use of Firearm by Victim Officer, Assisting Officer, and Offender During Incident, 2010–2019

(Number; percent.)

Characteristic	Total	2010	2011	2012	2013	2014	2015	2016	2017	2018	2019
Number of victim officers.................	511	55	72	49	27	51	41	66	46	56	48
Average number of rounds fired by victim officers.................	1.4	1.9	2.1	0.7	0.9	1.0	1.7	1.2	1.0	1.4	1.8
Average number of rounds fired by assisting officers[1].................	11.6	6.7	10.4	7.8	2.8	12.8	8.2	13.8	9.4	20.2	16.8
Average number of rounds fired by offenders[2].................	6.4	4.3	4.9	6.6	5.0	4.7	5.8	8.0	5.7	5.7	14.3
Number of victim officers who fired own weapon................	107	16	18	6	5	5	6	15	10	16	10
Average number of rounds fired by victim officers who fired own weapon.................	7.3	7.5	9.7	6.0	5.8	9.6	11.2	6.1	4.4	4.8	9.4
Average number of victim officer's rounds that struck offenders.................	1.3	1.3	0.8	1.5	0.7	4.0	0.7	0.3	1.5	1.7	1.9
Percentage hit rate of victim officers' rounds striking offenders.................	18.3	19.6	6.3	40.0	13.3	41.7	6.0	1.5	32.4	35.3	19.7
Average number of rounds fired by assisting officers.................	7.0	3.2	8.0	14.7	2.7	2.5	2.0	6.0	6.0	7.4	11.4
Average number of rounds fired by offenders ..	7.2	7.3	9.5	7.8	6.7	4.3	10.0	3.4	8.4	6.3	8.1
Number of victim officers who attempted to (but did not) use own firearm(s)	70	7	11	2	3	8	7	11	10	5	6
Average number of rounds fired by assisting officers.................	18.5	12.4	5.8	0.0	1.0	15.2	23.0	40.0	15.7	33.5	2.5
Average number of rounds fired by offenders ..	5.4	3.3	3.2	2.0	2.3	8.2	3.4	11.2	3.1	15.0	3.3
Number of victim officers who did not use and did not attempt to use own firearm(s)	301	20	40	38	18	34	26	39	24	30	32
Average number of rounds fired by assisting officers[1].................	13.0	7.2	12.4	6.0	3.0	12.5	3.4	18.2	8.1	24.7	21.0
Average number of rounds fired by offenders ..	6.6	3.9	4.2	5.0	5.3	4.3	5.9	9.8	5.6	5.3	18.9
Number of victim officers who did not use own firearm(s), but attempt to use own firearm(s) information was not reported........	18	12	1	0	0	2	0	1	0	2	0
Average number of rounds fired by assisting officers[3].................	10.0	4.8		0.0	0.0	41.0	0.0		0.0		0.0
Average number of rounds fired by offenders[4].................	3.5	4.0		0.0	0.0	2.0	0.0	3.0	0.0	1.0	0.0
Number of victim officers in which victim officer's use of firearm(s) was unknown or not reported	15	0	2	3	1	2	2	0	2	3	0

NOTE: When calculating the averages presented in this table, the FBI's Law Enforcement Officers Killed and Assaulted Program used all available data for each incident. For example, in a specific incident, if the number of rounds fired by the victim officer is known, but the number of rounds fired by the offender is not known, the known number was included in the calculation for the average number of rounds fired by victim officers.
[1]The number of rounds fired (1,100) during an incident in 2013 was excluded when calculating the average number of rounds fired by assisting officers to provide more accurate statistics.
[2]The number of rounds fired (1,046) during an incident in 2017 was excluded when calculating the average number of rounds fired by offenders to provide more accurate statistics.
[3]For 2011, 2016, and 2018, the victim officers were alone at the time of the incident; therefore, the number of rounds fired by assisting officers is not relevant.
[4]For 2011, number of rounds data were not available for inclusion in these averages.

Table 11. Law Enforcement Officers Feloniously Killed, by Victim Officer Killed with Own Weapon, Disarmed[1] of Weapon, and Weapon Stolen[2] by Offender, 2010–2019

(Number.)

Characteristic	Total	2010	2011	2012	2013	2014	2015	2016	2017	2018	2019
Number of victim officers	511	55	72	49	27	51	41	66	46	56	48
Killed with own weapon	20	5	3	1	1	1	4	0	1	4	0
Disarmed of weapon/weapon taken from victim officer	20	5	3	1	1	1	4	0	1	4	0
Weapon stolen[2]	11	4	1	0	0	0	3	0	1	2	0
Weapon not stolen	9	1	2	1	1	1	1	0	0	2	0
Weapon stolen information not reported	0	0	0	0	0	0	0	0	0	0	0
Not disarmed of weapon/weapon not taken from victim officer	0	0	0	0	0	0	0	0	0	0	0
Weapon stolen	0	0	0	0	0	0	0	0	0	0	0
Weapon not stolen	0	0	0	0	0	0	0	0	0	0	0
Weapon stolen information not reported	0	0	0	0	0	0	0	0	0	0	0
Disarmed of weapon/weapon taken information not reported	0	0	0	0	0	0	0	0	0	0	0
Weapon stolen	0	0	0	0	0	0	0	0	0	0	0
Weapon not stolen	0	0	0	0	0	0	0	0	0	0	0
Weapon stolen information not reported	0	0	0	0	0	0	0	0	0	0	0
Killed with weapon other than own	491	50	69	48	26	50	37	66	45	52	48
Disarmed of weapon/weapon taken from victim officer	37	3	9	5	3	7	5	3	0	2	0
Weapon stolen	22	1	4	3	2	6	2	2	0	2	0
Weapon not stolen	15	2	5	2	1	1	3	1	0	0	0
Weapon stolen information not reported	0	0	0	0	0	0	0	0	0	0	0
Not disarmed of weapon/weapon not taken from victim officer	453	47	59	43	23	43	32	63	45	50	48
Weapon stolen	3	2	0	0	0	0	0	0	1	0	0
Weapon not stolen	449	44	59	43	23	43	32	63	44	50	48
Weapon stolen information not reported	1	1	0	0	0	0	0	0	0	0	0
Disarmed of weapon/weapon taken information not reported	1	0	1	0	0	0	0	0	0	0	0
Weapon stolen	0	0	0	0	0	0	0	0	0	0	0
Weapon not stolen	1	0	1	0	0	0	0	0	0	0	0
Weapon stolen information not reported	0	0	0	0	0	0	0	0	0	0	0

NOTE: The term "weapon" includes all weapon types that may be issued to a law enforcement officer.

[1] The term "disarmed" indicates the victim officer was physically disarmed of one or more of his or her weapons by the offender(s) during the incident.

[2] The term "stolen" indicates a weapon issued to the victim officer was taken from the scene of the incident by the offender(s).

Table 12. Law Enforcement Officers Feloniously Killed with Own Weapons, by Victim Officer's Type of Weapon, 2010–2019

(Number.)

Type of weapon	Total	2010	2011	2012	2013	2014	2015	2016	2017	2018	2019
Number of Victim Officers Killed with Own Weapon.	20	5	3	1	1	1	4	0	1	4	0
Total, handgun.................................	19	5	3	1	1	1	3	0	1	4	0
.38 caliber...............................	1	0	1	0	0	0	0	0	0	0	0
.40 caliber...............................	8	1	2	0	0	1	1	0	1	2	0
.45 caliber...............................	1	1	0	0	0	0	0	0	0	0	0
9 millimeter.............................	7	3	0	0	1	0	1	0	0	2	0
Not reported.............................	2	0	0	1	0	0	1	0	0	0	0
Rifle, total...................................	0	0	0	0	0	0	0	0	0	0	0
Shotgun, total.............................	0	0	0	0	0	0	0	0	0	0	0
Other..	1	0	0	0	0	0	1	0	0	0	0

Table 13. Law Enforcement Officers Feloniously Killed, Time of Incident, by Type of Assignment, 2019

(Number.)

Characteristic and time	Total	2-officer patrol	1-officer patrol		Court/prisoner security		Investigative/detective		Plainclothes assignment	
			Alone	Assisted	Alone	Assisted	Alone	Assisted	Alone	Assisted
Number of Victim Officers............	48	3	13	14	0	0	2	1	0	0
Total A.M. hours.............................	13	1	2	3	0	0	1	0	0	0
12:01 a.m.–2 a.m..........................	6	1	2	1	0	0	0	0	0	0
2:01 a.m.–4 a.m............................	1	0	0	0	0	0	0	0	0	0
4:01 a.m.–6 a.m............................	1	0	0	0	0	0	0	0	0	0
6:01 a.m.–8 a.m............................	1	0	0	1	0	0	0	0	0	0
8:01 a.m.–10 a.m...........................	3	0	0	1	0	0	0	0	0	0
10:01 a.m.–noon	1	0	0	0	0	0	1	0	0	0
Total P.M. hours.............................	34	2	10	11	0	0	1	1	0	0
12:01 p.m.–2 p.m	3	0	1	1	0	0	0	0	0	0
2:01 p.m.–4 p.m............................	2	0	0	1	0	0	0	0	0	0
4:01 p.m.–6 p.m............................	4	0	2	1	0	0	0	0	0	0
6:01 p.m.–8 p.m............................	7	1	1	3	0	0	1	0	0	0
8:01 p.m.–10 p.m...........................	13	0	3	4	0	0	0	1	0	0
10:01 p.m.–midnight	5	1	3	1	0	0	0	0	0	0
Not reported.................................	1	0	1	0	0	0	0	0	0	0

Table 13. Law Enforcement Officers Feloniously Killed, Time of Incident, by Type of Assignment, 2019—*Continued*

(Number.)

Characteristic and time	Special assignment		Tactical assignment (uniformed)		Undercover		Other[1]		Off duty
	Alone	Assisted	Alone	Assisted	Alone	Assisted	Alone	Assisted	
Number of Victim Officers............	1	3	0	3	1	1	0	1	5
Total A.M. hours.............................	0	1	0	2	0	0	0	0	3
12:01 a.m.–2 a.m..........................	0	0	0	0	0	0	0	0	2
2:01 a.m.–4 a.m............................	0	0	0	0	0	0	0	0	1
4:01 a.m.–6 a.m............................	0	0	0	1	0	0	0	0	0
6:01 a.m.–8 a.m............................	0	0	0	0	0	0	0	0	0
8:01 a.m.–10 a.m...........................	0	1	0	1	0	0	0	0	0
10:01 a.m.–noon	0	0	0	0	0	0	0	0	0
Total P.M. hours	1	2	0	1	1	1	0	1	2
12:01 p.m.–2 p.m.	0	0	0	0	0	0	0	1	0
2:01 p.m.–4 p.m............................	1	0	0	0	0	0	0	0	0
4:01 p.m.–6 p.m............................	0	1	0	0	0	0	0	0	0
6:01 p.m.–8 p.m.	0	0	0	0	0	1	0	0	0
8:01 p.m.–10 p.m...........................	0	1	0	1	1	0	0	0	2
10:01 p.m.–midnight	0	0	0	0	0	0	0	0	0
Not reported.................................	0	0	0	0	0	0	0	0	0

[1]Includes officers on overtime/extra duty activities and other types of assignments not listed.

Table 14. Law Enforcement Officers Feloniously Killed, by Circumstance Encountered by Victim Officer Upon Arrival at Scene of Incident, 2015–2019[1]

(Number.)

Circumstance	Total	2015	2016	2017	2018	2019
Number of victim officers	257	41	66	46	56	48
Administrative assignment	4	1	0	1	2	0
Prisoner transport	4	1	0	1	2	0
Other administrative assignment	0	0	0	0	0	0
Ambush (entrapment/premeditation)	44	7	19	5	11	2
Arrest situation	15	2	4	4	2	3
Attempting to restrain/control/handcuff offender(s)	8	2	0	1	2	3
Attempting to restrain/control/handcuff other individual[2]	0	NA	NA	NA	NA	0
Maintaining custody of prisoner (in vehicle, precinct, etc.)[2]	0	NA	NA	NA	NA	0
Verbal advisement only	7	0	4	3	0	0
Assisting another law enforcement officer	13	2	4	2	2	3
Foot pursuit	4	1	0	0	2	1
High-risk traffic stop[2]	0	NA	NA	NA	NA	0
Officer down (requiring emergency assistance)	0	0	0	0	0	0
Officer requiring emergency assistance (not pursuit)	1	0	1	0	0	0
Providing/deploying flares, traffic cones, etc.	3	1	1	1	0	0
Providing/deploying spike strips/stop sticks[2]	0	NA	NA	NA	NA	0
Traffic control (crash scene, directing traffic, etc.)[2]	0	NA	NA	NA	NA	0
Vehicular pursuit	4	0	1	1	0	2
Other emergency circumstance	1	0	1	0	0	0
Other nonemergency circumstance	0	0	0	0	0	0
Assisting motorist	1	1	0	0	0	0
Citizen complaint	0	0	0	0	0	0
Animal bite	0	0	0	0	0	0
Animal disturbance (barking dog, unleashed dog, etc.)	0	0	0	0	0	0
Business check	0	0	0	0	0	0
Check on welfare of citizen	0	0	0	0	0	0
Drug complaint	0	0	0	0	0	0
Traffic complaint	0	0	0	0	0	0
Trespassing[2]	0	NA	NA	NA	NA	0
Verbal complaint of noncriminal violation	0	0	0	0	0	0
Other citizen complaint[2]	0	NA	NA	NA	NA	0
Crime in progress	13	1	2	2	4	4
Active shooter[2]	0	NA	NA	NA	NA	0
Assault	0	0	0	0	0	0
Burglary	3	0	1	0	2	0
Larceny-theft	1	0	0	0	0	1
Mass casualty[2]	0	NA	NA	NA	NA	0
Motor vehicle theft	0	0	0	0	0	0
Person with firearm (no shots fired)	1	0	0	0	1	0
Robbery	4	0	1	1	0	2
Shooting/shots being fired (not "active shooter" situation)	2	1	0	1	0	0
Tampering with vehicle	0	0	0	0	0	0
Other crime against person	0	0	0	0	0	0
Other crime against property	2	0	0	0	1	1
Disorder/disturbance	10	1	2	1	3	3
Civil disorder (mass disobedience, riot, etc.)	0	0	0	0	0	0
Disturbance (disorderly subject, fight, etc.)	5	0	1	0	2	2
Domestic disturbance (family quarrel, no assault)	2	0	1	1	0	0
Domestic violence	3	1	0	0	1	1
Encounter/assist an emotionally disturbed person	1	0	0	1	0	0
Investigative/enforcement	105	17	28	21	24	15
Active shooter[2]	0	NA	NA	NA	NA	0
Animal cruelty[2]	0	NA	NA	NA	NA	0
Drug-related matter (drug bust, buy, etc.)	4	0	1	1	0	2
Handling person with mental illness	3	2	0	0	1	0
High-risk traffic stop[3]	1	0	0	1	0	0
Investigative activity	21	1	6	2	8	4
Mass casualty[2]	0	NA	NA	NA	NA	0
Motor vehicle crash	1	0	0	1	0	0

Table 14. Law Enforcement Officers Feloniously Killed, by Circumstance Encountered by Victim Officer Upon Arrival at Scene of Incident, 2015–2019[1]—*Continued*

(Number.)

Circumstance	Total	2015	2016	2017	2018	2019
Official contact (not an arrest situation)[2]	0	NA	NA	NA	NA	0
Possible DUI/DWI suspect (operating a vehicle)	0	0	0	0	0	0
Serving/attempting to serve search warrant (non-tactical)[2]	0	NA	NA	NA	NA	0
Surveillance activity[2]	0	NA	NA	NA	NA	0
Suspicious package[2]	0	NA	NA	NA	NA	0
Suspicious person/circumstance	26	5	11	6	3	1
Tactical situation[4]	24	4	7	6	7	NA
Traffic violation stop	16	4	1	3	2	6
Undercover situation	0	0	0	0	0	0
Wanted person	9	1	2	1	3	2
Out of service (court, dining, etc.)[3]	0	NA	NA	NA	NA	0
Providing/deploying equipment (flares, traffic cones, etc.)[3]	0	NA	NA	NA	NA	0
Pursuit	23	4	4	6	6	3
Foot	13	2	4	3	4	0
Vehicular (anything other than foot)	10	2	0	3	2	3
Report of crime	0	0	0	0	0	0
Active shooter[2]	0	NA	NA	NA	NA	0
Assault	0	0	0	0	0	0
Burglary	0	0	0	0	0	0
Homicide	0	0	0	0	0	0
Larceny-theft	0	0	0	0	0	0
Mass casualty[2]	0	NA	NA	NA	NA	0
Motor vehicle theft	0	0	0	0	0	0
Person with firearm (no shots fired)	0	0	0	0	0	0
Robbery	0	0	0	0	0	0
Shooting/shots fired (not "active shooter" situation)	0	0	0	0	0	0
Tampering with vehicle	0	0	0	0	0	0
Other crime against person	0	0	0	0	0	0
Other crime against property	0	0	0	0	0	0
Respond to alarm (audible/silent)	0	0	0	0	0	0
Burglary	0	0	0	0	0	0
Fire[2]	0	NA	NA	NA	NA	0
Medical emergency[2]	0	NA	NA	NA	NA	0
Robbery	0	0	0	0	0	0
Serving/attempting to serve court order (eviction notice, subpoena, etc.)[3]	1	NA	NA	NA	NA	1
Tactical situation[4]	9	NA	NA	NA	NA	9
Active shooter[2]	0	NA	NA	NA	NA	0
Barricaded/hostage situation[2]	3	NA	NA	NA	NA	3
Mass casualty[2]	0	NA	NA	NA	NA	0
Serving/attempting to serve arrest warrant[2]	2	NA	NA	NA	NA	2
Serving/attempting to serve search warrant[2]	3	NA	NA	NA	NA	3
Other tactical situation[2]	1	NA	NA	NA	NA	1
Traffic control (crash scene, directing traffic, etc.)	2	1	0	0	1	0
Unprovoked attack	15	3	3	3	1	5
Other	1	1	0	0	0	0
Not applicable[3]	0	NA	NA	NA	NA	0

NA = Not available.

[1] Ten years of data for the topics presented in this table are not available at this time. A 10-year table is expected to be available for the publication of 2020 data.
[2] Beginning in 2019, this category/subcategory was added as an option to the list of circumstances.
[3] Prior to 2019, the circumstance "High-risk traffic stop" was collected as "Traffic stop (felony traffic stop)."
[4] Prior to 2019, the circumstance "Tactical situation" was collected under the category of "Investigative/enforcement" and did not include subcategories.

Table 15. Law Enforcement Officers Feloniously Killed, by Specific Activity Being Performed by Victim Officer at Time of Attack, 2015–2019[1]

(Number.)

Circumstance	Total	2015	2016	2017	2018	2019
Number of victim officers..	257	41	66	46	56	48
Administrative assignment	7	4	0	1	2	0
Prisoner transport..	4	1	0	1	2	0
Other administrative assignment	3	3	0	0	0	0
Arrest situation	40	5	7	9	12	7
Attempting to restrain/control/handcuff offender(s).....	29	5	4	5	9	6
Attempting to restrain/control/handcuff other individual [2]	0	NA	NA	NA	NA	0
Maintaining custody of prisoner (in vehicle, precinct, etc.) [2]	0	NA	NA	NA	NA	0
Verbal advisement only	11	0	3	4	3	1
Assisting another law enforcement officer	9	1	2	2	1	3
Foot pursuit..	2	0	0	0	1	1
High-risk traffic stop [2]	0	NA	NA	NA	NA	0
Officer down (requiring emergency assistance).........	0	0	0	0	0	0
Officer requiring emergency assistance (not pursuit).....	0	0	0	0	0	0
Providing/deploying flares, traffic cones, etc.	3	1	1	1	0	0
Providing/deploying spike strips/stop sticks [2]	0	NA	NA	NA	NA	0
Traffic control (crash scene, directing traffic, etc.) [2]	0	NA	NA	NA	NA	0
Vehicular pursuit	2	0	0	0	0	2
Other emergency circumstance	1	0	1	0	0	0
Other nonemergency circumstance	1	0	0	1	0	0
Assisting motorist	2	1	0	1	0	0
Citizen complaint	4	1	0	0	2	1
Animal bite	0	0	0	0	0	0
Animal disturbance (barking dog, unleashed dog, etc.).....	0	0	0	0	0	0
Business check	0	0	0	0	0	0
Check on welfare of citizen	3	1	0	0	2	0
Drug complaint	0	0	0	0	0	0
Traffic complaint	1	0	0	0	0	1
Trespassing[2]	0	NA	NA	NA	NA	0
Verbal complaint of noncriminal violation................	0	0	0	0	0	0
Other citizen complaint [2]	0	NA	NA	NA	NA	0
Crime in progress	14	2	3	3	4	2
Active shooter [2]	0	NA	NA	NA	NA	0
Assault	0	0	0	0	0	0
Burglary	3	0	1	0	2	0
Larceny-theft...	1	0	0	0	0	1
Mass casualty [2]	0	NA	NA	NA	NA	0
Motor vehicle theft..	0	0	0	0	0	0
Person with firearm (no shots fired)	2	1	0	0	1	0
Robbery	3	1	1	1	0	0
Shooting/shots being fired (not "active shooter" situation).....	4	0	1	2	1	0
Tampering with vehicle	0	0	0	0	0	0
Other crime against person	0	0	0	0	0	0
Other crime against property...................................	1	0	0	0	0	1
Disorder/disturbance	12	1	4	0	2	5
Civil disorder (mass disobedience, riot, etc.).............	0	0	0	0	0	0
Disturbance (disorderly subject, fight, etc.)	4	0	1	0	1	2
Domestic disturbance (family quarrel, no assault).....	3	0	1	0	0	2
Domestic violence	5	1	2	0	1	1
Encounter/assist an emotionally disturbed person........	0	0	0	0	0	0
Investigative/enforcement	112	18	33	22	25	14
Active shooter [2]	0	NA	NA	NA	NA	0
Animal cruelty [2]	0	NA	NA	NA	NA	0
Drug-related matter (drug bust, buy, etc.)	1	0	1	0	0	0
Handling person with mental illness	2	1	0	0	1	0
High-risk traffic stop [3]..	2	0	1	0	1	0
Investigative activity..	21	1	6	5	6	3
Mass casualty [2]	0	NA	NA	NA	NA	0
Motor vehicle crash...	2	0	0	1	0	1
Official contact (not an arrest situation) [2]	2	NA	NA	NA	NA	2
Possible DUI/DWI suspect (operating a vehicle)	1	0	1	0	0	0

Table 15. Law Enforcement Officers Feloniously Killed, by Specific Activity Being Performed by Victim Officer at Time of Attack, 2015–2019[1]—*Continued*

(Number.)

Circumstance	Total	2015	2016	2017	2018	2019
Serving/attempting to serve search warrant (non-tactical) [2]	0	NA	NA	NA	NA	0
Surveillance activity [2]	0	NA	NA	NA	NA	0
Suspicious package [2]	0	NA	NA	NA	NA	0
Suspicious person/circumstance	28	6	12	5	4	1
Tactical situation[4]	33	6	9	7	11	NA
Traffic violation stop	17	3	3	4	2	5
Undercover situation	0	0	0	0	0	0
Wanted person	3	1	0	0	0	2
Out of service (court, dining, etc.)[3]	0	NA	NA	NA	NA	0
Providing/deploying equipment (flares, traffic cones, etc.)[3]	0	NA	NA	NA	NA	0
Pursuit	22	2	8	5	5	2
Foot	17	1	7	4	4	1
Vehicular (anything other than foot)	5	1	1	1	1	1
Report of crime	0	0	0	0	0	0
Active shooter [2]	0	NA	NA	NA	NA	0
Assault	0	0	0	0	0	0
Burglary	0	0	0	0	0	0
Homicide	0	0	0	0	0	0
Larceny-theft	0	0	0	0	0	0
Mass casualty [2]	0	NA	NA	NA	NA	0
Motor vehicle theft	0	0	0	0	0	0
Person with firearm (no shots fired)	0	0	0	0	0	0
Robbery	0	0	0	0	0	0
Shooting/shots fired (not "active shooter" situation)	0	0	0	0	0	0
Tampering with vehicle	0	0	0	0	0	0
Other crime against person	0	0	0	0	0	0
Other crime against property	0	0	0	0	0	0
Respond to alarm (audible/silent)	0	0	0	0	0	0
Burglary	0	0	0	0	0	0
Fire [2]	0	NA	NA	NA	NA	0
Medical emergency [2]	0	NA	NA	NA	NA	0
Robbery	0	0	0	0	0	0
Serving/attempting to serve court order (eviction notice, subpoena, etc.)[3]	1	NA	NA	NA	NA	1
Tactical situation[4]	10	NA	NA	NA	NA	10
Active shooter [2]	0	NA	NA	NA	NA	0
Barricaded/hostage situation [2]	3	NA	NA	NA	NA	3
Mass casualty [2]	0	NA	NA	NA	NA	0
Serving/attempting to serve arrest warrant [2]	2	NA	NA	NA	NA	2
Serving/attempting to serve search warrant [2]	4	NA	NA	NA	NA	4
Other tactical situation [2]	1	NA	NA	NA	NA	1
Traffic control (crash scene, directing traffic, etc.)	6	1	4	0	1	0
Other	18	5	5	3	2	3

[1] Ten years of data for the topics presented in this table are not available at this time. A 10-year table is expected to be available for the publication of 2020 data.
[2] Beginning in 2019, this category/subcategory was added as an option to the list of circumstances.
[3] Prior to 2019, the circumstance "High-risk traffic stop" was collected as "Traffic stop (felony traffic stop)."
[4] Prior to 2019, the circumstance "Tactical situation" was collected under the category of "Investigative/enforcement" and did not include subcategories.

Table 16. Law Enforcement Officers Feloniously Killed During Traffic-Related Incidents,[1] by Circumstance at Scene of Incident, by Type of Assignment, 2015–2019[2]

(Number.)

Location of offender	Total	Approaching offender(s)	Approaching suspect vehicle		Returning to victim officer's vehicle	Seated in victim officer's vehicle	
			On driver's side	On passenger's side		Prior to approaching suspect vehicle	After obtaining contact with offenders
Number of Victim Officers Killed During Traffic-Related Incidents	34	3	5	2	2	4	1
Prone...............	0	0	0	0	0	0	0
On ground...............	0	0	0	0	0	0	0
On vehicle/object...............	0	0	0	0	0	0	0
Seated	15	1	4	1	0	2	1
In suspect's vehicle...............	15	1	4	1	0	2	1
In victim officer's vehicle...............	0	0	0	0	0	0	0
Outside in vicinity of suspect's vehicle...............	0	0	0	0	0	0	0
Outside in vicinity of victim officer's vehicle	0	0	0	0	0	0	0
Standing	10	0	1	1	1	2	0
In vicinity of suspect's vehicle...............	9	0	1	1	1	1	0
In vicinity of victim officer's vehicle...............	1	0	0	0	0	1	0
Unrestricted Movement	3	1	0	0	1	0	0
Outside of suspect's vehicle...............	2	1	0	0	1	0	0
Outside of victim officer's vehicle	1	0	0	0	0	0	0
Other...............	5	0	0	0	0	0	0
Multiple locations due to multiple offenders...............	0	0	0	0	0	0	0
Unknown...............	1	1	0	0	0	0	0
Not reported...............	0	0	0	0	0	0	0

NOTE: For 2015 through 2019, 26 of the 34 victim officers who were feloniously killed during traffic-related incidents contacted radio dispatchers prior to or during the attack.
[1] Traffic-related incidents include traffic stops (high-risk traffic stops and traffic violation stops), investigating possible DUI/DWI suspects, and assisting motorists.
[2] Ten years of data for the topics presented in this table are not available at this time. A 10-year table is expected to be available for the publication of 2020 data.

Table 16. Law Enforcement Officers Feloniously Killed During Traffic-Related Incidents,[1] by Circumstance at Scene of Incident, by Type of Assignment, 2015–2019[2]—*Continued*

(Number.)

Location of offender	Standing in vicinity of suspect's vehicle		Standing in vicinity of victim officer's vehicle		Other	Unknown	Not reported
	On driver's side	On passenger's side	On driver's side	On passenger's side			
Number of Victim Officers Killed During Traffic-Related Incidents	8	1	3	0	5	0	0
Prone	0	0	0	0	0	0	0
On ground	0	0	0	0	0	0	0
On vehicle/object	0	0	0	0	0	0	0
Seated	5	0	0	0	1	0	0
In suspect's vehicle	5	0	0	0	1	0	0
In victim officer's vehicle	0	0	0	0	0	0	0
Outside in vicinity of suspect's vehicle	0	0	0	0	0	0	0
Outside in vicinity of victim officer's vehicle	0	0	0	0	0	0	0
Standing	2	1	2	0	0	0	0
In vicinity of suspect's vehicle	2	1	2	0	0	0	0
In vicinity of victim officer's vehicle	0	0	0	0	0	0	0
Unrestricted Movement	0	0	1	0	0	0	0
Outside of suspect's vehicle	0	0	0	0	0	0	0
Outside of victim officer's vehicle	0	0	1	0	0	0	0
Other	1	0	0	0	4	0	0
Multiple locations due to multiple offenders	0	0	0	0	0	0	0
Unknown	0	0	0	0	0	0	0
Not reported	0	0	0	0	0	0	0

NOTE: For 2015 through 2019, 26 of the 34 victim officers who were feloniously killed during traffic-related incidents contacted radio dispatchers prior to or during the attack.
[1] Traffic-related incidents include traffic stops (high-risk traffic stops and traffic violation stops), investigating possible DUI/DWI suspects, and assisting motorists.
[2] Ten years of data for the topics presented in this table are not available at this time. A 10-year table is expected to be available for the publication of 2020 data.

Table 17. Law Enforcement Officers Feloniously Killed, by Type of Weapon, 2010–2019

(Number.)

Type of weapon	Total	2010	2011	2012	2013	2014	2015	2016	2017	2018	2019
Number of Victim Officers.........................	511	55	72	49	27	51	41	66	46	56	48
Total firearms	471	54	63	44	26	46	38	62	42	52	44
Handgun...	343	38	49	34	18	33	29	37	32	39	34
Rifle	100	15	7	7	5	10	7	23	9	10	7
Shotgun..	22	1	6	3	3	3	1	1	1	2	1
Multiple firearms used by offender(s), unable to determine which caused fatal injury[1]	2	NA	1	0	0	0	0	1	0	0	0
Type of firearm unknown...........................	2	0	0	0	0	0	1	0	0	0	1
Type of firearm not reported	2	0	0	0	0	0	0	0	0	1	1
Knife or other cutting instrument[2].................	0	0	NA	NA	NA	NA	NA	NA	NA	NA	NA
Knife[2]..	3	NA	1	1	0	0	0	0	1	0	0
Other cutting instrument[2]...........................	0	NA	0	0	0	0	0	0	0	0	0
Blunt instrument...	0	0	0	0	0	0	0	0	0	0	0
Bomb..	0	0	0	0	0	0	0	0	0	0	0
Personal weapons (hands, feet, fists, etc.)	5	0	2	2	0	1	0	0	0	0	0
Vehicle...	32	1	6	2	1	4	3	4	3	4	4
Other..	0	0	0	0	0	0	0	0	0	0	0
Number of Victim Officers Who Had Prior Knowledge That a Weapon Might Be Involved in the Incident............................	167	20	25	6	8	15	17	26	11	24	15

NA = Not available.
[1] Beginning in 2011, a new option was added: "Multiple firearms used by offender(s), unable to determine which caused fatal injury."
[2] For 2010, the type of weapon categories "Knife" and "Other cutting instrument" were combined.

Table 18. Law Enforcement Officers Feloniously Killed, by Number of Victim Officers Wearing Uniform, Body Armor, or Holster, 2010–2019

(Number.)

Characteristic	Total	2010	2011	2012	2013	2014	2015	2016	2017	2018	2019
Number of Victim Officers........................	511	55	72	49	27	51	41	66	46	56	48
Wearing body armor.....................................	365	37	52	25	19	40	30	51	35	46	30
In uniform..	344	34	47	25	18	40	28	50	33	40	29
Not in uniform	21	3	5	0	1	0	2	1	2	6	1
Wearing holster	480	52	69	43	27	48	37	65	44	52	43
In uniform..	422	45	61	38	20	43	35	59	39	45	37
Not in uniform	50	7	8	2	7	5	2	4	5	6	4
Wearing uniform not reported	8	0	0	3	0	0	0	2	0	1	2

Table 19. Law Enforcement Officers Feloniously Killed, Age Group of Known Offender, 2010–2019

(Number.)

Age group	Total	2010	2011	2012	2013	2014	2015	2016	2017	2018	2019
Number of Known Offenders	537	80	76	51	28	60	37	56	44	56	49
Under 18	17	1	5	1	0	3	0	3	1	1	2
18–24	125	24	20	14	9	13	4	12	3	14	12
25–30	137	23	19	15	7	18	14	6	10	14	11
31–35	90	12	9	6	6	10	10	10	12	10	5
36–40	51	8	7	4	2	9	1	6	5	5	4
41–45	37	6	3	5	0	1	1	5	6	4	6
46–50	30	0	5	2	3	3	2	6	3	1	5
51–55	19	3	4	1	1	1	3	2	1	3	0
56–60	14	2	4	0	0	2	2	3	0	1	0
Over 60	9	1	0	1	0	0	0	1	3	3	0
Not reported	8	0	0	2	0	0	0	2	0	0	4
Average age	32	31	32	31	31	31	34	35	36	33	31

Table 20. Law Enforcement Officers Feloniously Killed, by Profile of Known Offender, Average Demographics, 2000–2019

(Number.)

Characteristic	2019	5-year averages		10-year averages	
		2010–2014	2015–2019	2000–2009	2010–2019
Age	31	31	34	30	32
Height	5'10"	5'10"	5'10"	5'10"	5'10"
Weight	181	181	186	177	183

NOTE: The 14 known offenders involved in the events of September 11, 2001, are not included in this table.

Table 21. Law Enforcement Officers Feloniously Killed, by Race, Ethnicity, and Sex of Known Offender, 2010–2019

(Number.)

Characteristic	Total	2010	2011	2012	2013	2014	2015	2016	2017	2018	2019
Number of Known Offenders	537	80	76	51	28	60	37	56	44	56	49
Race											
White	303	32	44	32	15	43	18	33	26	32	28
Black/African American	199	39	28	17	12	14	18	17	16	23	15
American Indian/Alaska Native	12	4	2	1	0	2	1	1	1	0	0
Asian/Native Hawaiian/Other Pacific Islander[1]	2	2	NA	NA	NA	NA	NA	NA	NA	NA	NA
Asian[1]	3	NA	1	0	0	1	0	0	1	0	0
Native Hawaiian/Other Pacific Islander[1]	3	NA	0	1	0	0	0	0	0	1	1
Not reported	15	3	1	0	1	0	0	5	0	0	5
Ethnicity[2]											
Hispanic or Latino	77	NA	7	7	3	19	3	9	5	10	14
Not Hispanic or Latino	354	NA	68	41	23	39	33	41	38	45	26
Not reported	106	80	1	3	2	2	1	6	1	1	9
Sex											
Male	523	78	74	50	27	55	37	56	44	54	48
Female	14	2	2	1	1	5	0	0	0	2	1

NA = Not available.
[1] Prior to 2011, the race categories "Asian" and "Native Hawaiian/Other Pacific Islander" were combined.
[2] Beginning in 2011, ethnicity was added to the data collection.

Table 22. Law Enforcement Officers Feloniously Killed, by Status of Known Offender at Time of Incident, 2010–2019

(Number.)

Characteristic	Total	2010	2011	2012	2013	2014	2015	2016	2017	2018	2019
Number of Known Offenders	537	80	76	51	28	60	37	56	44	56	49
Under Judicial Supervision	144	19	19	12	6	12	11	15	18	20	12
Conditional release, pending criminal prosecution	27	1	5	2	2	1	3	1	3	6	3
Escapee from mental institution[1]	0	NA	NA	NA	NA	NA	NA	NA	NA	NA	0
Escapee from penal institution	2	1	0	0	0	0	0	0	0	1	0
Halfway house	2	0	1	0	0	0	0	0	1	0	0
Home confinement/house arrest[1]	0	NA	NA	NA	NA	NA	NA	NA	NA	NA	0
Parole	43	8	4	4	2	5	3	3	5	3	6
Patient in mental institution[1]	0	NA	NA	NA	NA	NA	NA	NA	NA	NA	0
Probation	58	9	7	5	2	5	4	10	5	8	3
Serving time in penal institution[2]	1	NA	0	0	0	0	0	0	1	0	0
Other judicial supervision[2]	10	NA	2	1	0	1	1	1	3	1	0
Multiple forms of judicial supervision	1	0	0	0	0	0	0	0	0	1	0
Known to Agency as:											
Anti-government/political[3]	0	NA	NA	NA	NA	NA	NA	NA	NA	NA	0
Anti-law enforcement[3]	1	NA	NA	NA	NA	NA	NA	NA	NA	NA	1
Controlled substance dealer	64	7	9	6	4	12	2	4	2	10	8
Controlled substance possessor	64	12	9	5	2	10	2	9	1	10	4
Controlled substance user	81	19	13	6	3	8	2	12	4	10	4
Domestic terrorist[4]	0	NA	NA	NA	NA	NA	NA	NA	NA	NA	0
Gang member/affiliated with gang member(s)[5]	36	NA	8	4	2	7	4	7	0	2	2
Having history of assaulting/threatening law enforcement officer(s)[3]	2	NA	NA	NA	NA	NA	NA	NA	NA	NA	2
International terrorist[4]	0	NA	NA	NA	NA	NA	NA	NA	NA	NA	0
Known or suspected terrorist (domestic or international)[4,5]	2	NA	1	0	0	0	0	0	1	0	NA
Militia member[3]	0	NA	NA	NA	NA	NA	NA	NA	NA	NA	0
Sovereign citizen[3]	0	NA	NA	NA	NA	NA	NA	NA	NA	NA	0
Survivalist[3]	0	NA	NA	NA	NA	NA	NA	NA	NA	NA	0
Violent offender[3]	4	NA	NA	NA	NA	NA	NA	NA	NA	NA	4
Other[5]	84	NA	11	2	7	6	7	12	15	24	0
Use of Alcohol and/or Controlled Substance											
Under influence	119	17	12	13	4	13	13	16	6	16	9
Alcohol	28	6	4	3	3	2	3	1	1	2	3
Controlled substance[6]	10	10	NA	NA	NA	NA	NA	NA	NA	NA	NA
Amphetamines/methamphetamines	14	NA	0	0	1	3	0	4	1	2	3
Barbiturates	1	NA	0	0	0	1	0	0	0	0	0
Cocaine (all forms except Crack)	1	NA	0	1	0	0	0	0	0	0	0
Crack/cocaine	1	NA	0	0	0	1	0	0	0	0	0
Hashish/hash oil	0	NA	0	0	0	0	0	0	0	0	0
Heroin	2	NA	0	0	0	0	2	0	0	0	0
Lysergic Acid Diethylamide (a.k.a. LSD)	0	NA	0	0	0	0	0	0	0	0	0
Marijuana	22	NA	2	2	0	3	2	4	2	7	0
Morphine	0	NA	0	0	0	0	0	0	0	0	0
Opium/opiate	0	NA	0	0	0	0	0	0	0	0	0
Phencyclidine (a.k.a. PCP)	1	NA	0	0	0	1	0	0	0	0	0
Synthetic cathinones (a.k.a. Bath salts)[7]	0	NA	NA	NA	NA	NA	NA	NA	NA	NA	0
Other drug/substance	3	NA	1	0	0	0	0	1	0	1	0
Multiple forms of substances	35	1	5	7	0	2	6	6	2	4	2
Type of drug/substance not reported	1	0	0	0	0	0	0	0	0	0	1
Not under influence	47	10	11	3	3	4	2	3	3	4	4
Use of alcohol/controlled substance unknown	330	48	48	28	20	42	19	31	35	33	26
Use of alcohol/controlled substance not reported	41	5	5	7	1	1	3	6	0	3	10
Known to Agency as Having Prior Mental Disorders	26	2	7	2	2	1	3	2	2	5	0
Relationship Between Victim Officer and Offender											
Prior relationship through law enforcement (arrest, investigation, etc.)	51	8	11	4	3	3	4	10	3	5	0
Prior relationship through non-law enforcement (acquaintance, neighbor, relative, etc.)	5	1	0	0	2	0	0	0	0	1	1
No known relationship	473	66	65	47	23	57	33	45	40	50	47
Not reported	8	5	0	0	0	0	0	1	1	0	1

[1] Beginning in 2019, new options were added, including: "Escapee from mental institution," "Home confinement/house arrest," and "Patient in mental institution."
[2] Beginning in 2011, new options were added, including: "Serving time in penal institution" and "Other judicial supervision."
[3] Beginning in 2019, new options were added, including: "Anti-government/political," "Anti-law enforcement," "Having history of assaulting/threatening law enforcement officer(s)," "Militia member," "Sovereign citizen," "Survivalist," and "Violent offender."
[4] From 2011 through 2018, "Domestic terrorist" and "International terrorist" were combined.
[5] Beginning in 2011, new options were added, including: "Gang member/affiliated with gang member(s)," "Known or suspected terrorist (domestic or international)," and "Other."
[6] Beginning in 2011, new options were added to indicate the type of controlled substance the offender had used at the time of the incident.
[7] Beginning in 2019, a new option was added to the list of controlled substances: "Synthetic cathinones (a.k.a. Bath salts)."

Table 23. Law Enforcement Officers Feloniously Killed, by Judicial History of Known Offender Prior to Incident, 2010–2019

(Number.)

Judicial history prior to incident	Total	2010	2011	2012	2013	2014	2015	2016	2017	2018	2019
Number of Known Offenders	537	80	76	51	28	60	37	56	44	56	49
Previously arrested	454	71	64	42	20	51	32	47	40	51	36
Convicted on prior criminal charge[1]	55	55	NA	NA	NA	NA	NA	NA	NA	NA	NA
Conviction as adult[2]	296	NA	48	29	13	35	29	39	34	39	30
Conviction as juvenile	107	10	18	6	2	10	9	14	12	15	11
Halfway house[3]	9	NA	1	1	0	2	0	1	2	2	0
House arrest[3]	0	NA	0	0	0	0	0	0	0	0	0
Incarceration in penal institution[3]	92	NA	19	4	4	9	10	11	13	22	NA
Parole or probation[4]	41	41	NA	NA	NA	NA	NA	NA	NA	NA	NA
Parole[4]	91	NA	14	7	3	12	12	13	11	9	10
Probation[4]	212	NA	37	17	8	26	18	31	22	32	21
Prior arrest for:											
Aggravated assault (excluding officers)	11	NA	NA	NA	NA	NA	NA	NA	NA	NA	11
Assault on law enforcement officer/resisting arrest	20	20	NA	NA	NA	NA	NA	NA	NA	NA	NA
Assault on law enforcement officer (aggravated or simple)	53	NA	10	1	1	7	5	7	7	5	10
Crime of violence (includes arrests for aggravated assault, murder, rape, and robbery)	44	44	NA	NA	NA	NA	NA	NA	NA	NA	NA
Domestic violence	8	NA	NA	NA	NA	NA	NA	NA	NA	NA	8
Drug law violation	247	39	27	20	8	34	15	27	22	33	22
Murder	24	7	1	2	0	1	3	4	2	2	2
Other crime of violence (includes arrests for aggravated assault, rape, and robbery)	210	NA	38	19	12	22	24	35	30	30	NA
Resisting arrest	107	NA	19	9	3	15	11	14	13	13	10
Robbery	8	NA	NA	NA	NA	NA	NA	NA	NA	NA	8
Sex offense	0	NA	NA	NA	NA	NA	NA	NA	NA	NA	0
Threats against law enforcement	1	NA	NA	NA	NA	NA	NA	NA	NA	NA	1
Weapons violation	213	40	32	15	7	26	19	21	16	20	17
None of the above	5	NA	NA	NA	NA	NA	NA	NA	NA	NA	5

NA = Not available.

[1] For 2010, adult and juvenile convictions were combined into one category, "Convicted on prior criminal charge."
[2] In 2011, "Conviction as adult" was added as an option for judicial history.
[3] In 2011, new options for judicial history were added, including: "Halfway house," "House arrest," and "Incarceration in penal institution."
[4] In 2019, counts for "Incarceration in penal institution" stopped being collected.

Table 24. Law Enforcement Officers Feloniously Killed, by Disposition of Known Offender, 2008–2017

(Number.)

Disposition	2008–2012	2013–2017	2008–2017
Number of Known Offenders	294	225	519
Fugitive	1	0	1
Arrested and Charged	187	136	323
Guilty of murder	126	88	214
Received death sentence	18	12	30
Received life imprisonment	75	53	128
Received prison term (ranging from 8.75 years to 999 years)	32	22	54
Sentence unknown	1	1	2
Guilty of lesser offense related to murder	18	3	21
Guilty of crime other than murder	11	6	17
Acquitted/dismissed/nolle prosequi	16	6	22
Indeterminate charge and sentence	1	0	1
Committed to psychiatric institution	6	8	14
Case pending/disposition unknown	7	24	31
Died in custody prior to sentencing	2	1	3
Not Arrested	170	144	314
Justifiably killed	64	57	121
by victim officer	21	9	30
by person(s) other than victim officer[1]	22	NA	22
by assisting officer(s)[1]	15	29	44
by officer(s) responding to scene of incident[1]	0	4	4
by officer(s) at other scene of incident[1]	6	15	21
Committed suicide	36	25	61
Killed by civilian(s)	2	0	2
Died under other circumstance	3	3	6
Died by unknown cause	0	1	1
Other	1	1	2
Not Reported	0	2	2

NOTE: Due to delays in court proceedings, this table runs two years behind the publication year.
[1] Beginning in 2011, new options were added to identify the other persons who justifiably killed the offender(s).

Table 25. Law Enforcement Officers Accidentally Killed, by Region, Geographic Division, and State/Territory, 2010–2019

(Number.)

Area	Total	2010	2011	2012	2013	2014	2015	2016	2017	2018	2019
Number of Victim Officers.................	503	72	53	48	49	45	45	52	48	50	41
Northeast..	62	8	8	9	5	8	5	5	6	5	3
New England.....................................	14	3	2	4	0	1	0	1	1	1	1
Connecticut...................................	3	2	0	0	0	0	0	0	0	1	0
Maine..	3	0	1	0	0	0	0	0	1	0	1
Massachusetts.............................	7	1	1	3	0	1	0	1	0	0	0
New Hampshire...........................	0	0	0	0	0	0	0	0	0	0	0
Rhode Island................................	1	0	0	1	0	0	0	0	0	0	0
Vermont..	0	0	0	0	0	0	0	0	0	0	0
Middle Atlantic................................	48	5	6	5	5	7	5	4	5	4	2
New Jersey...................................	16	4	1	1	0	2	3	2	1	2	0
New York......................................	22	1	5	2	3	3	0	2	3	1	2
Pennsylvania................................	10	0	0	2	2	2	2	0	1	1	0
Midwest..	78	14	7	3	4	4	6	12	9	11	8
East North Central...........................	51	7	3	3	4	3	4	8	6	8	5
Illinois..	18	3	0	1	2	1	1	2	2	3	3
Indiana...	5	2	0	0	0	1	0	0	0	1	1
Michigan......................................	11	0	1	0	1	1	2	2	2	2	0
Ohio...	11	1	2	1	1	0	0	3	1	1	1
Wisconsin.....................................	6	1	0	1	0	0	1	1	1	1	0
West North Central..........................	27	7	4	0	0	1	2	4	3	3	3
Iowa...	5	0	1	0	0	0	0	3	0	0	1
Kansas..	3	2	0	0	0	0	0	1	0	0	0
Minnesota....................................	2	0	0	0	0	0	0	0	1	0	1
Missouri.......................................	13	4	3	0	0	1	2	0	1	2	0
Nebraska......................................	2	0	0	0	0	0	0	0	1	0	1
North Dakota................................	1	0	0	0	0	0	0	0	0	1	0
South Dakota................................	1	1	0	0	0	0	0	0	0	0	0
South..	273	39	27	28	31	19	29	24	27	27	22
South Atlantic..................................	112	16	16	14	9	4	12	8	14	13	6
Delaware.......................................	0	0	0	0	0	0	0	0	0	0	0
District of Columbia.....................	1	1	0	0	0	0	0	0	0	0	0
Florida..	25	4	1	2	1	1	1	4	4	4	3
Georgia..	27	3	6	4	2	1	5	2	2	1	1
Maryland......................................	12	3	2	3	0	0	3	1	0	0	0
North Carolina.............................	16	0	4	2	1	1	0	1	0	6	1
South Carolina.............................	13	2	1	0	2	0	2	0	4	1	1
Virginia...	17	3	2	3	3	1	1	0	3	1	0
West Virginia................................	1	0	0	0	0	0	0	0	1	0	0
East South Central...........................	54	6	3	3	7	7	9	1	5	5	8
Alabama.......................................	13	0	2	1	3	2	2	0	1	1	1
Kentucky......................................	7	1	0	1	0	0	2	0	1	2	0
Mississippi....................................	15	2	0	0	4	2	2	0	1	2	2
Tennessee.....................................	19	3	1	1	0	3	3	1	2	0	5
West South Central..........................	107	17	8	11	15	8	8	15	8	9	8
Arkansas.......................................	6	0	0	0	4	0	0	1	1	0	0
Louisiana......................................	24	3	3	2	3	1	2	5	1	3	1
Oklahoma....................................	12	1	0	2	2	2	1	0	2	1	1
Texas..	65	13	5	7	6	5	5	9	4	5	6
West..	85	11	10	8	9	13	5	9	6	6	8
Mountain..	37	4	4	6	4	4	2	5	2	1	5
Arizona...	12	1	2	1	2	2	0	2	0	0	2
Colorado......................................	11	0	0	4	0	1	2	1	0	1	2
Idaho..	0	0	0	0	0	0	0	0	0	0	0
Montana.......................................	2	0	1	0	0	0	0	0	0	0	1
Nevada...	2	0	0	0	1	0	0	0	1	0	0
New Mexico..................................	5	1	0	0	1	1	0	1	1	0	0
Utah..	4	2	0	1	0	0	0	1	0	0	0
Wyoming......................................	1	0	1	0	0	0	0	0	0	0	0
Pacific...	48	7	6	2	5	9	3	4	4	5	3
Alaska...	1	0	0	0	1	0	0	0	0	0	0
California......................................	38	6	5	0	3	9	2	4	4	4	1
Hawaii..	3	0	1	2	0	0	0	0	0	0	0
Oregon...	1	0	0	0	0	0	1	0	0	0	0
Washington..................................	5	1	0	0	1	0	0	0	0	1	2
Puerto Rico and other outlying areas.....	5	0	1	0	0	1	0	2	0	1	0
American Samoa...............................	0	0	0	0	0	0	0	0	0	0	0
Guam..	0	0	0	0	0	0	0	0	0	0	0
Mariana Islands................................	0	0	0	0	0	0	0	0	0	0	0
Puerto Rico.......................................	5	0	1	0	0	1	0	2	0	1	0
U.S. Virgin Islands.............................	0	0	0	0	0	0	0	0	0	0	0

Table 26. Law Enforcement Officers Accidentally Killed, by Population Group/Agency Type, 2010–2019

(Number.)

Area	Total	2010	2011	2012	2013	2014	2015	2016	2017	2018	2019
Number of Victim Officers........................	503	72	53	48	49	45	45	52	48	50	41
Group I (cities 250,000 and over)................	60	9	5	9	5	6	4	4	4	10	4
Group II (cities 100,000–249,999)...............	31	3	3	3	4	1	3	3	2	5	4
Group III (cities 50,000–99,999)..................	25	2	5	1	5	2	3	2	0	3	2
Group IV (25,000–49,999).........................	26	6	3	6	1	2	1	1	1	5	0
Group V (cities 10,000–24,999)...................	17	2	0	1	3	2	1	1	4	1	2
Group VI (cities under 10,000)....................	59	4	7	2	6	7	7	10	7	7	2
Metropolitan counties................................	102	13	11	12	10	10	10	12	9	9	6
Nonmetropolitan counties..........................	55	9	3	4	5	7	4	4	8	3	8
State agencies...	99	19	12	6	8	5	12	9	13	3	12
Federal agencies	24	5	3	4	2	2	0	4	0	3	1
Puerto Rico and other outlying areas...........	5	0	1	0	0	1	0	2	0	1	0

Table 27. Law Enforcement Officers Accidentally Killed, by Time of Incident, 2010–2019

(Number.)

Time of day	Total	2010	2011	2012	2013	2014	2015	2016	2017	2018	2019
Number of Victim Officers........................	503	72	53	48	49	45	45	52	48	50	41
Total A.M. hours......................................	234	39	22	25	16	26	17	25	25	22	17
12:01 a.m.–2 a.m....................................	49	10	5	6	3	6	2	6	4	4	3
2:01 a.m.–4 a.m......................................	50	8	9	5	5	4	4	5	3	3	4
4:01 a.m.–6 a.m......................................	26	4	3	4	1	1	2	3	4	3	1
6:01 a.m.–8 a.m......................................	51	5	3	5	3	7	4	5	7	7	5
8:01 a.m.–10 a.m....................................	25	4	1	4	2	3	2	1	3	3	2
10:01 a.m.–noon	33	8	1	1	2	5	3	5	4	2	2
Total P.M. hours	257	32	31	23	30	19	27	24	22	25	24
12:01 p.m.–2 p.m.	38	4	6	3	3	4	4	6	2	3	3
2:01 p.m.–4 p.m.	38	5	6	5	4	4	4	3	3	1	3
4:01 p.m.–6 p.m.	39	3	7	2	4	3	5	5	4	4	2
6:01 p.m.–8 p.m.	43	5	4	2	3	2	2	3	5	9	8
8:01 p.m.–10 p.m.	46	6	3	5	10	2	5	4	5	4	2
10:01 p.m.–midnight	53	9	5	6	6	4	7	3	3	4	6
Not reported..	12	1	0	0	3	0	1	3	1	3	0

Table 28. Law Enforcement Officers Accidentally Killed, by Day and Time of Incident, 2019

(Number.)

Time of day	Total	Sunday	Monday	Tuesday	Wednesday	Thursday	Friday	Saturday
Number of Victim Officers	41	2	4	8	4	5	10	8
Total A.M. hours	17	2	1	3	2	4	3	2
12:01 a.m.–2 a.m.	3	1	0	2	0	0	0	0
2:01 a.m.–4 a.m.	4	1	0	0	0	1	0	2
4:01 a.m.–6 a.m.	1	0	0	0	0	0	1	0
6:01 a.m.–8 a.m.	5	0	1	1	1	1	1	0
8:01 a.m.–10 a.m.	2	0	0	0	0	2	0	0
10:01 a.m.–noon	2	0	0	0	1	0	1	0
Total P.M. hours	24	0	3	5	2	1	7	6
12:01 p.m.–2 p.m.	3	0	0	1	0	1	1	0
2:01 p.m.–4 p.m.	3	0	1	0	0	0	2	0
4:01 p.m.–6 p.m.	2	0	0	0	0	0	0	2
6:01 p.m.–8 p.m.	8	0	1	4	0	0	1	2
8:01 p.m.–10 p.m.	2	0	0	0	0	0	1	1
10:01 p.m.–midnight	6	0	1	0	2	0	2	1

Table 29. Law Enforcement Officers Accidentally Killed, by Day of Incident, 2010–2019

(Number.)

Day of the week	Total	2010	2011	2012	2013	2014	2015	2016	2017	2018	2019
Number of Victim Officers	503	72	53	48	49	45	45	52	48	50	41
Sunday	72	11	7	6	6	9	6	10	7	8	2
Monday	65	8	7	7	6	5	12	7	3	6	4
Tuesday	70	7	10	5	7	9	3	6	11	4	8
Wednesday	49	8	2	2	6	4	5	7	5	6	4
Thursday	67	10	10	8	4	5	6	7	5	7	5
Friday	93	17	7	8	12	8	4	8	9	10	10
Saturday	87	11	10	12	8	5	9	7	8	9	8

Table 30. Law Enforcement Officers Accidentally Killed, by Month of Incident, 2010–2019

(Number.)

Month	Total	2010	2011	2012	2013	2014	2015	2016	2017	2018	2019
Number of Victim Officers	503	72	53	48	49	45	45	52	48	50	41
January	43	8	4	4	1	6	6	2	6	2	4
February	33	9	4	1	0	2	1	1	6	4	5
March	49	3	8	3	5	2	5	9	3	6	5
April	38	6	1	3	5	5	5	1	5	4	3
May	51	4	8	4	9	6	2	3	6	6	3
June	49	15	5	4	2	1	5	5	4	4	4
July	38	3	5	8	6	1	3	4	3	2	3
August	34	4	3	2	3	1	5	5	6	3	2
September	45	6	4	6	3	5	3	9	4	3	2
October	45	10	2	4	5	6	2	7	2	4	3
November	34	1	3	5	3	4	5	4	1	5	3
December	44	3	6	4	7	6	3	2	2	7	4

Table 31. Law Enforcement Officers Accidentally Killed, by Age Group of Victim Officer, 2010–2019

(Number.)

Age group	Total	2010	2011	2012	2013	2014	2015	2016	2017	2018	2019
Number of Victim Officers......................	503	72	53	48	49	45	45	52	48	50	41
Under 25	35	2	3	2	1	4	7	2	1	11	2
25–30..	91	15	9	6	6	7	10	12	11	6	9
31–35..	88	15	3	9	5	9	4	12	11	10	10
36–40..	77	13	11	6	11	8	7	6	6	4	5
41–45..	69	5	8	13	11	5	7	5	5	8	2
46–50..	56	8	9	8	5	3	2	7	4	7	3
51–55..	41	6	5	3	8	5	3	4	1	2	4
56–60..	22	5	2	1	2	2	3	1	5	0	1
Over 60	20	2	3	0	0	2	1	2	4	2	4
Unknown...	1	1	0	0	0	0	0	0	0	0	0
Not reported..	3	0	0	0	0	0	1	1	0	0	1
Average age (years)...................................	39	39	41	40	41	39	37	38	40	36	40

Table 32. Law Enforcement Officers Accidentally Killed, by Years of Service of Victim Officer, 2010–2019

(Number; years.)

Years of service	Total	2010	2011	2012	2013	2014	2015	2016	2017	2018	2019
Number of Victim Officers......................	503	72	53	48	49	45	45	52	48	50	41
Less than 1	36	4	2	2	2	5	4	6	3	5	3
1–5...	151	24	13	9	9	14	18	14	16	17	17
6–10...	104	18	13	14	12	13	3	9	10	8	4
11–15..	70	8	7	9	8	3	7	8	7	7	6
16–20..	57	8	6	8	7	3	9	5	3	6	2
21–25..	28	2	5	3	5	0	2	2	3	3	3
26–30..	29	4	3	3	3	5	2	5	1	0	3
More than 30	22	4	4	0	2	2	0	2	5	1	2
Not reported..	6	0	0	0	1	0	0	1	0	3	1
Average years of service............................	11	11	13	12	13	10	9	11	12	9	11

Table 33. Law Enforcement Officers Accidentally Killed, by Profile of Victim Officer, Average Demographics, 2000–2019

(Number.)

Characteristic	2019	5-year averages		10-year averages	
		2010–2014	2015–2019	2000–2009	2010–2019
Age	40	40	38	38	39
Years of service..	11	12	11	10	10
Height	5'11"	5'11"	5'11"	5'11"	5'11"
Weight	199	210	209	198	209

Table 34. Law Enforcement Officers Accidentally Killed, by Race, Ethnicity, and Sex of Victim Officer, 2010–2019

(Number.)

Characteristic	Total	2010	2011	2012	2013	2014	2015	2016	2017	2018	2019
Number of Victim Officers	503	72	53	48	49	45	45	52	48	50	41
Race											
White	419	60	45	36	43	43	33	40	42	38	39
Black/African American	61	8	7	10	6	0	9	9	3	7	2
American Indian/Alaska Native	10	2	0	0	0	0	0	2	2	4	0
Asian/Native Hawaiian/Other Pacific Islander[1]	1	1	NA	NA	NA	NA	NA	NA	NA	NA	NA
Asian[1]	6	NA	0	2	0	2	0	0	1	1	0
Native Hawaiian/Other Pacific Islander[1]	2	NA	1	0	0	0	1	0	0	0	0
Not reported	4	1	0	0	0	0	2	1	0	0	0
Ethnicity[2]											
Hispanic or Latino	39	NA	4	6	2	7	3	7	3	5	2
Not Hispanic or Latino	381	NA	46	40	47	38	40	43	44	45	38
Not reported	83	72	3	2	0	0	2	2	1	0	1
Sex											
Male	475	67	50	46	49	42	41	50	46	46	38
Female	28	5	3	2	0	3	4	2	2	4	3

NA = Not available.
[1]Prior to 2011, the race categories "Asian" and "Native Hawaiian/Other Pacific Islander" were combined.
[2]Beginning in 2011, ethnicity was added to the data collection.

Table 35. Law Enforcement Officers Accidentally Killed, Time of Incident, by Type of Assignment, 2019

(Number.)

Characteristic and time	Total	2-officer patrol	1-officer patrol		Investigative/detective		Tactical assignment (uniformed)		Plainclothes assignment	
			Alone	Assisted	Alone	Assisted	Alone	Assisted	Alone	Assisted
Number of Victim Officers	41	4	20	6	0	1	0	0	0	0
Total A.M. hours	17	3	11	0	0	0	0	0	0	0
12:01 a.m.–2 a.m.	3	1	1	0	0	0	0	0	0	0
2:01 a.m.–4 a.m.	4	0	4	0	0	0	0	0	0	0
4:01 a.m.–6 a.m.	1	0	1	0	0	0	0	0	0	0
6:01 a.m.–8 a.m.	5	1	3	0	0	0	0	0	0	0
8:01 a.m.–10 a.m.	2	1	1	0	0	0	0	0	0	0
10:01 a.m.–noon	2	0	1	0	0	0	0	0	0	0
Total P.M. hours	24	1	9	6	0	1	0	0	0	0
12:01 p.m.–2 p.m.	3	0	0	1	0	0	0	0	0	0
2:01 p.m.–4 p.m.	3	0	2	0	0	0	0	0	0	0
4:01 p.m.–6 p.m.	2	0	2	0	0	0	0	0	0	0
6:01 p.m.–8 p.m.	8	1	1	2	0	1	0	0	0	0
8:01 p.m.–10 p.m.	2	0	0	1	0	0	0	0	0	0
10:01 p.m.–midnight	6	0	4	2	0	0	0	0	0	0
Not reported	0	0	0	0	0	0	0	0	0	0

[1]Includes officers on overtime/extra duty activities and other types of assignments not listed.

Table 35. Law Enforcement Officers Accidentally Killed, Time of Incident, by Type of Assignment, 2019 —Continued

(Number.)

Characteristic and time	Special assignment		Undercover		Court/prisoner security		Other[1]		Off duty
	Alone	Assisted	Alone	Assisted	Alone	Assisted	Alone	Assisted	
Number of Victim Officers......................	3	4	0	1	0	0	2	0	0
Total A.M. hours...	1	1	0	0	0	0	1	0	0
12:01 a.m.–2 a.m..................................	0	1	0	0	0	0	0	0	0
2:01 a.m.–4 a.m....................................	0	0	0	0	0	0	0	0	0
4:01 a.m.–6 a.m....................................	0	0	0	0	0	0	0	0	0
6:01 a.m.–8 a.m....................................	1	0	0	0	0	0	0	0	0
8:01 a.m.–10 a.m..................................	0	0	0	0	0	0	0	0	0
10:01 a.m.–noon..................................	0	0	0	0	0	0	1	0	0
Total P.M. hours...	2	3	0	1	0	0	1	0	0
12:01 p.m.–2 p.m.	1	0	0	0	0	0	1	0	0
2:01 p.m.–4 p.m.	0	1	0	0	0	0	0	0	0
4:01 p.m.–6 p.m.	0	0	0	0	0	0	0	0	0
6:01 p.m.–8 p.m.	1	1	0	1	0	0	0	0	0
8:01 p.m.–10 p.m.	0	1	0	0	0	0	0	0	0
10:01 p.m.–midnight	0	0	0	0	0	0	0	0	0
Not reported..	0	0	0	0	0	0	0	0	0

[1] Includes officers on overtime/extra duty activities and other types of assignments not listed.

Table 36. Law Enforcement Officers Accidentally Killed, by Lighting and Weather/Environmental Conditions by Location of Incident, 2019

(Number.)

Characteristic	Total	Aircraft accident	Drowning	Fall	Firearm-related incident	Motor vehicle crash	Pedestrian officer struck by vehicle	Other
Number of Victim Officers..	41	0	2	0	3	19	16	1
Lighting	10	0	0	0	2	5	3	0
Artificial	10	0	1	0	1	5	3	0
Dark..	1	0	0	0	0	1	0	0
Dawn...	15	0	0	0	0	7	7	1
Daylight	4	0	1	0	0	0	3	0
Dusk..	1	0	0	0	0	1	0	0
Not reported	19	0	0	0	1	13	3	2
Weather/environmental								
Blizzard	2	0	0	0	0	0	2	0
Blowing dirt/sand/soil...	0	0	0	0	0	0	0	0
Clear..	25	0	1	0	2	14	8	0
Cloudy/partly cloudy...	2	0	0	0	0	2	0	0
Earthquake...	0	0	0	0	0	0	0	0
Fire/fog/smog/smoke...	0	0	0	0	0	0	0	0
Flooding..	0	0	0	0	0	0	0	0
Freezing rain/hail/sleet..	0	0	0	0	0	0	0	0
Hurricane	0	0	0	0	0	0	0	0
Indoors (no adverse conditions)	0	0	0	0	0	0	0	0
Rain...	4	0	0	0	0	1	3	0
Severe crosswinds/high winds...............................	0	0	0	0	0	0	0	0
Snow	3	0	0	0	1	0	1	1
Tornado...	0	0	0	0	0	0	0	0
Other	0	0	0	0	0	0	0	0
Not reported..	5	0	1	0	0	2	2	0

Table 37. Federal Law Enforcement Officers Killed and Assaulted, Department and Agency, by Number of Victim Officers and Known Offenders, 2018–2019

(Number.)

Department and agency	Victim officers		Known offenders	
	2018	2019	2018	2019
Number of Victim Officers/Known Offenders	1,768	2,136	1,049	1,469
Amtrak (National Railroad Passenger Corporation)	0	0	0	0
Office of Inspector General	0	0	0	0
Architect of the Capitol[1]	0		0	
Office of Inspector General	0		0	
Corporation for National and Community Service	0	0	0	0
Office of Inspector General	0	0	0	0
Federal Deposit Insurance Corporation	0	0	0	0
Office of Inspector General	0	0	0	0
Federal Housing Finance Agency[2]		0		0
Office of Inspector General		0		0
Library of Congress	0	0	0	0
Office of Inspector General	0	0	0	0
National Aeronautics and Space Administration	0	0	0	0
Office of Inspector General, Office of Investigations	0	0	0	0
National Science Foundation[2]		0		0
Office of Inspector General		0		0
Pension Benefit Guaranty Corporation	0	0	0	0
Office of Inspector General	0	0	0	0
Smithsonian Institution	0	0	0	0
Office of Inspector General[2]		0		0
Office of Protection Services[1]	0		0	
Tennessee Valley Authority	0	0	0	0
Office of Inspector General[2]		0		0
Tennessee Valley Authority Police	0	0	0	0
U.S. Agency for International Development[1]	0		0	
Office of Inspector General, Office of Investigations	0		0	
U.S. Capitol Police[2]	18		12	
U.S. Department of Agriculture	8	4	8	4
U.S. Forest Service, Law Enforcement and Investigations	8	4	8	4
Office of Inspector General[1]	0		0	
U.S. Department of Commerce	0	0	0	0
Bureau Industry and Security, Office Export Enforcement[2]		0		0
National Oceanic and Atmospheric Administration[2]		0		0
Office of Inspector General[1]	0		0	
Office of the Secretary, Executive Protection Unit[2]		0		0
Office of Security	0	0	0	0
U.S. Department of Defense	16	47	13	37
Defense Criminal Investigative Service	0	0	0	0
Defense Intelligence Agency Police	0	0	0	0
Defense Logistics Agency	0	0	0	0
National Security Agency[1]	1		1	
Pentagon Force Protection Agency[1]	1		1	
U.S. Department of the Air Force[3]	0	0	0	0
Office of Special Investigations		0		0
U.S. Department of the Army	12	0	9	0
U.S. Department of the Navy	2	0	2	0
Commander, Navy Installations Command[1]	2		2	
Naval Criminal Investigative Service	0	0	0	0
U.S. Marine Corps[2]		47		37
U.S. Department of Education[2]		0		0
Office of Inspector General		0		0

Table 37. Federal Law Enforcement Officers Killed and Assaulted, Department and Agency, by Number of Victim Officers and Known Offenders, 2018–2019—*Continued*

(Number.)

Department and agency	Victim officers		Known offenders	
	2018	2019	2018	2019
U.S. Department of Health and Human Services..	3	0	2	0
Food and Drug Administration[2]		0		0
National Institutes of Health Police	3	0	2	0
Office of Inspector General..	0	0	0	0
U.S. Department of Homeland Security	751	733	403	420
Federal Emergency Management Agency, Mount Weather Police	0	0	0	0
Federal Protective Service	22	3	17	3
Office of Inspector General...	0	0	0	0
Transportation Security Administration, Office of Law Enforcement/Federal Air Marshal Service	0	0	0	0
U.S. Coast Guard	0	0	0	0
U.S. Customs and Border Protection (CBP).......................................	634	609	315	335
CBP, Air and Marine Operations...	30	13	6	2
CBP, Office of Field Operations..	75	135	55	88
CBP, U.S. Border Patrol..	529	461	254	245
U.S. Immigration and Customs Enforcement	75	94	54	54
U.S. Secret Service...	20	27	17	28
U.S. Department of the Interior..	689	978	414	777
Bureau of Indian Affairs...	511	765	408	764
Bureau of Land Management...	6	4	3	4
National Park Service (NPS)[4,5]..	167	206		6
NPS Rangers[6]..		170		
NPS, U.S. Park Police...		36		6
Office of Inspector General[2]		0		0
U.S. Fish and Wildlife Service (FWS)	5	3	3	3
FWS, Division of Refuge Law Enforcement	5	3	3	3
FWS, Office of Law Enforcement...	0	0	0	0
U.S. Department of Justice..	271	369	191	227
Bureau of Alcohol, Tobacco, Firearms and Explosives...........................	13	16	17	4
Federal Bureau of Investigation..	15	17	10	18
Office of Inspector General[2]		0		0
U.S. Drug Enforcement Administration	16	8	14	11
U.S. Marshals Service...	227	328	150	194
U.S. Department of Labor	0		0	
Office of the Assistant Secretary for Administration and Management, Division of Protective Operations[1]	0		0	
U.S. Department of State	0	0	0	0
Office of Inspector General...	0	0	0	0
U.S. Department of Transportation	0	0	0	0
National Highway Traffic Safety Administration, Office of Odometer Fraud Investigations...	0	0	0	0
Office of Inspector General[1]	0		0	
U.S. Department of the Treasury	1	0	1	0
Bureau of Engraving and Printing Police	0	0	0	0
Office of Special Inspector General for the Troubled Asset Relief Program	0	0	0	0
Office of Inspector General[1]	0		0	
Treasury Inspector General for Tax Administration	0	0	0	0
U.S. Mint Police[1]...	1		1	
U.S. Department of Veterans Affairs...	0		0	
Office of Inspector General[1]	0		0	
U.S. Environmental Protection Agency	0	0	0	0
Criminal Investigation Division...	0	0	0	0
Office of Inspector General, Office of Investigations	0	0	0	0
U.S. General Services Administration..	0	0	0	0
Office of Inspector General, Office of Investigations	0	0	0	0
U.S. Government Publishing Office...	0	0	0	0
Uniformed Police Branch..	0	0	0	0

Table 37. Federal Law Enforcement Officers Killed and Assaulted, Department and Agency, by Number of Victim Officers and Known Offenders, 2018–2019—*Continued*

(Number.)

Department and agency	Victim officers		Known offenders	
	2018	2019	2018	2019
U.S. National Archives and Records Administration	0	0	0	0
Office of Inspector General...	0	0	0	0
U.S. Nuclear Regulatory Commission²..		0		0
Office of Inspector General...		0		0
U.S. Office of Personnel Management...	0	0	0	0
Office of Inspector General...	0	0	0	0
U.S. Peace Corps²..		0		0
Office of Inspector General...		0		0
U.S. Postal Service...	11	5	5	4
Office of Inspector General...	0	1	0	1
U.S. Postal Inspection Service (including the U.S. Postal Police).............................	11	4	5	3
U.S. Securities and Exchange Commission²...		0		0
Office of Inspector General...		0		0

¹For 2019, data were not reported by these departments, agencies, or offices.
²For 2018, data were not reported by these departments, agencies, or offices.
³For 2018, data reported by the U.S. Department of the Air Force were aggregated and not submitted separately.
⁴For 2018, data reported by the National Park Service were aggregated and not submitted separately.
⁵For 2018, known offender data were not reported by the National Park Service.
⁶For 2019, known offender data were not reported by the National Park Service Rangers.

Table 38. Federal Law Enforcement Officers Killed and Assaulted, Department and Agency, by Number of Victim Officers Killed and Injured, 2019[1]

(Number.)

Department and agency	Killed		Injured	
	Firearms	Other weapons	Firearms	Other weapons
Number of Victim Officers..................................	0	0	20	352
U.S. Department of Agriculture..............................	0	0	0	1
U.S. Forest Service, Law Enforcement and Investigations...	0	0	0	1
U.S. Department of Defense	0	0	0	1
U.S. Marine Corps...	0	0	0	1
U.S. Department of Homeland Security	0	0	17	223
Federal Protective Service	0	0	0	3
U.S. Customs and Border Protection (CBP)...........	0	0	2	175
CBP, Air and Marine Operations	0	0	1	0
CBP, Office of Field Operations........................	0	0	0	61
CBP, U.S. Border Patrol..................................	0	0	1	114
U.S. Immigration and Customs Enforcement	0	0	15	42
U.S. Secret Service...	0	0	0	3
U.S. Department of the Interior.............................	0	0	1	106
Bureau of Indian Affairs....................................	0	0	1	74
Bureau of Land Management.............................	0	0	0	0
National Park Service	0	0	0	31
NPS Rangers	0	0	0	19
NPS, U.S. Park Police.....................................	0	0	0	12
U.S. Fish and Wildlife Service, Division of Refuge Law Enforcement	0	0	0	1
U.S. Department of Justice....................................	0	0	2	17
Bureau of Alcohol, Tobacco, Firearms and Explosives...........................	0	0	1	0
Federal Bureau of Investigation..........................	0	0	1	3
U.S. Drug Enforcement Administration	0	0	0	1
U.S. Marshals Service.......................................	0	0	0	13
U.S. Postal Service...	0	0	0	4
U.S. Postal Inspection Service (including the U.S. Postal Police)............................	0	0	0	4

[1]This table includes federal agencies that indicated one or more of their law enforcement officers were killed or assaulted.

Table 39. Federal Law Enforcement Officers Killed and Assaulted, Department and Agency, by Extent of Injury of Victim Officer, 2015–2019[1]

(Number.)

Department and agency	2015 Killed	2015 Injured	2015 Not injured	2016 Killed	2016 Injured	2016 Not injured	2017 Killed	2017 Injured	2017 Not injured	2018 Killed	2018 Injured	2018 Not injured	2019 Killed	2019 Injured	2019 Not injured
Number of Victim Officers	1	176	814	1	324	1,122	0	426	1,358	2	374	1,392	0	372	1,764
U.S. Capitol Police[3]	0	5	8	0	4	21	0	9	7	0	3	15			
U.S. Department of Agriculture[3]										0	0	8	0	1	3
U.S. Forest Service, Law Enforcement and Investigations										0	0	8	0	1	3
U.S. Department of Defense[4]							0	2	21	0	5	11	0	1	46
National Security Agency[2]							0	0	0	0	1	0			
Pentagon Force Protection Agency[2]							0	0	0	0	0	1			
U.S. Department of the Army							0	0	0	0	3	9	0	0	0
U.S. Department of the Navy[5]							0	2	21	0	1	1			
Commander, Navy Installations Command[2]										0	1	1			
U.S. Marine Corps[6]													0	1	46
U.S. Department of Health and Human Services[3]										0	3	0	0	0	0
National Institutes of Health Police										0	3	0	0	0	0
U.S. Department of Homeland Security	0	36	103	0	146	357	0	225	462	0	219	532	0	240	493
Federal Protective Service[3]										0	20	2	0	3	0
U.S. Customs and Border Protection (CBP)	0	24	81	0	139	345	0	137	369	0	162	472	0	177	432
CBP, Air and Marine Operations	0	0	19	0	0	19	0	5	7	0	3	27	0	1	12
CBP, Office of Field Operations	0	24	62	0	7	61	0	29	33	0	24	51	0	61	74
CBP, U.S. Border Patrol[7]				0	132	265	0	103	329	0	135	394	0	115	346
U.S. Immigration and Customs Enforcement[8]	0	4	4	0	0	0	0	76	83	0	30	45	0	57	37
U.S. Secret Service	0	8	18	0	7	12	0	12	10	0	7	13	0	3	24
U.S. Department of the Interior	0	85	485	0	117	504	0	124	600	0	83	606	0	107	871
Bureau of Indian Affairs	0	74	431	0	86	418	0	105	504	0	72	439	0	75	690
Bureau of Land Management	0	1	2	0	0	4	0	0	4	0	3	3	0	0	4
National Park Service (NPS)[9]	0	7	47	0	31	76	0	15	83	0	8	159	0	31	175
NPS Rangers													0	19	151
NPS, U.S. Park Police													0	12	24
U.S. Fish and Wildlife Service, Division of Refuge Law Enforcement	0	3	5	0	0	6	0	4	9	0	0	5	0	1	2
U.S. Department of Justice	1	49	214	1	57	240	0	66	267	2	52	217	0	19	350
Bureau of Alcohol, Tobacco, Firearms and Explosives	0	1	10	0	0	11	0	0	18	0	2	11	0	1	15
Federal Bureau of Investigation	0	9	17	0	5	11	0	4	12	0	7	8	0	4	13
U.S. Drug Enforcement Administration	0	1	10	0	2	3	0	1	9	0	4	12	0	1	7
U.S. Marshals Service	1	38	177	1	50	215	0	61	228	2	39	186	0	13	315
U.S. Department of the Treasury	0	0	1	0	0	0	0	0	1	0	0	1	0	0	0
Internal Revenue Service[10]	0	0	0	0	0	0	0	0	1						
Treasury Inspector General for Tax Administration	0	0	1	0	0	0	0	0	0	0	0	0	0	0	0
U.S. Mint Police[2,3]										0	0	1			
U.S. Postal Service	0	1	3	0	0	0	0	0	0	0	9	2	0	4	1
Office of Inspector General[3]										0	0	0	0	0	1
U.S. Postal Inspection Service (including the U.S. Postal Police)	0	1	3	0	0	0	0	0	0	0	9	2	0	4	0

[1] This table includes federal agencies that indicated one or more of their law enforcement officers were killed or assaulted.
[2] For 2019, data were not reported by these departments, agencies, or offices.
[3] For 2015, 2016, and 2017, data were not reported by these departments, agencies, or offices.
[4] For 2015 and 2016, data were not reported by the U.S. Department of Defense.
[5] For 2017, data reported by the U.S. Department of the Navy were aggregated and not submitted separately.
[6] For 2017 and 2018, data were not reported by the U.S. Marine Corps.
[7] For 2015, extent of injury data for 349 victim officers were not reported by the CBP, U.S. Border Patrol.
[8] For 2015 and 2016, data requests to the U.S. Immigration and Customs Enforcement (ICE) were inadvertently received and addressed by entities within ICE that did not possess the appropriate resources to provide comprehensive and complete data; therefore, caution must be taken when comparing 2015 and 2016 data to 2017, 2018, and 2019 data.
[9] For 2015, 2016, 2017, and 2018, data reported by the National Park Service were aggregated and not submitted separately.
[10] For 2018 and 2019, data were not reported by the Internal Revenue Service.

Table 40. Federal Law Enforcement Officers Killed and Assaulted, by Region, Geographic Division, and State/Territory, 2019

(Number.)

Area	Total	Firearm	Knife or other cutting instrument	Bomb	Blunt instrument	Personal weapons	Vehicle	Other
Number of Victim Officers..................................	2,136	180	23	0	24	1,117	216	576
Northeast..	95	7	2	0	1	60	13	12
New England..	38	1	0	0	1	29	0	7
Connecticut..	21	0	0	0	0	18	0	3
Maine...	3	0	0	0	1	0	0	2
Massachusetts	3	0	0	0	0	3	0	0
New Hampshire	6	1	0	0	0	5	0	0
Rhode Island...	2	0	0	0	0	0	0	2
Vermont...	3	0	0	0	0	3	0	0
Middle Atlantic..	57	6	2	0	0	31	13	5
New Jersey	7	2	0	0	0	5	0	0
New York	40	4	0	0	0	20	13	3
Pennsylvania	10	0	2	0	0	6	0	2
Midwest	272	18	3	0	0	49	6	196
East North Central...	42	5	0	0	0	20	1	16
Illinois...	11	2	0	0	0	9	0	0
Indiana	0	0	0	0	0	0	0	0
Michigan..	24	2	0	0	0	7	0	15
Ohio..	5	1	0	0	0	2	1	1
Wisconsin	2	0	0	0	0	2	0	0
West North Central	230	13	3	0	0	29	5	180
Iowa..	0	0	0	0	0	0	0	0
Kansas...	12	0	1	0	0	7	4	0
Minnesota	5	0	0	0	0	5	0	0
Missouri...	12	8	0	0	0	3	1	0
Nebraska	0	0	0	0	0	0	0	0
North Dakota..	83	0	1	0	0	4	0	78
South Dakota	118	5	1	0	0	10	0	102
South..	565	67	7	0	7	289	46	149
South Atlantic	179	15	2	0	1	87	8	66
Delaware..	0	0	0	0	0	0	0	0
District of Columbia...................................	81	3	0	0	1	24	0	53
Florida	37	3	2	0	0	20	3	9
Georgia	17	1	0	0	0	16	0	0
Maryland	2	0	0	0	0	0	0	2
North Carolina...	16	3	0	0	0	13	0	0
South Carolina...	3	0	0	0	0	2	0	1
Virginia..	19	2	0	0	0	12	4	1
West Virginia	4	3	0	0	0	0	1	0
East South Central..	47	14	1	0	0	19	2	11
Alabama	7	7	0	0	0	0	0	0
Kentucky	7	0	0	0	0	7	0	0
Mississippi	10	0	0	0	0	3	0	7
Tennessee..	23	7	1	0	0	9	2	4
West South Central	339	38	4	0	6	183	36	72
Arkansas..	2	0	0	0	0	1	1	0
Louisiana	10	0	0	0	0	2	4	4
Oklahoma	10	1	2	0	0	4	1	2
Texas	317	37	2	0	6	176	30	66
West...	1,003	60	8	0	15	595	139	186
Mountain..	627	32	6	0	10	438	97	44
Arizona..	180	13	2	0	1	127	14	23
Colorado	25	1	0	0	0	14	2	8
Idaho...	270	1	3	0	0	196	70	0
Montana	33	1	1	0	0	28	3	0
Nevada	5	1	0	0	0	3	1	0
New Mexico	106	13	0	0	9	65	6	13
Utah..	4	0	0	0	0	3	1	0
Wyoming	4	2	0	0	0	2	0	0
Pacific	376	28	2	0	5	157	42	142
Alaska	3	0	0	0	0	0	2	1
California..	260	20	2	0	3	95	28	112
Hawaii	0	0	0	0	0	0	0	0
Oregon	21	0	0	0	0	5	9	7
Washington	92	8	0	0	2	57	3	22

Table 40. Federal Law Enforcement Officers Killed and Assaulted, by Region, Geographic Division, and State/Territory, 2019—*Continued*

(Number.)

Area	Total	Firearm	Knife or other cutting instrument	Bomb	Blunt instrument	Personal weapons	Vehicle	Other
Puerto Rico and other outlying areas........................	9	3	0	0	0	4	0	2
American Samoa...	0	0	0	0	0	0	0	0
Guam...	0	0	0	0	0	0	0	0
Mariana Islands..	0	0	0	0	0	0	0	0
Puerto Rico...	5	1	0	0	0	2	0	2
U.S. Virgin Islands..	4	2	0	0	0	2	0	0
Foreign	22	0	0	0	0	19	0	3
Ecuador..	1	0	0	0	0	0	0	1
Okinawa, Japan..	15	0	0	0	0	15	0	0
Iwakuni, Japan..	4	0	0	0	0	4	0	0
Mexico..	2	0	0	0	0	0	0	2
Location not reported[1]	170	25	3	0	1	101	12	28

[1]Location data for 170 victim officers were not provided by the National Park Service Rangers.

METHODOLOGY

Officers Killed

When an officer is killed in the line of duty, the FBI gathers data about circumstances pertaining to the death. The data come from various sources:

- City, university and college, county, state, tribal, and federal law enforcement agencies participating in the Uniform Crime Reporting Program may report line-of-duty deaths that occur in their jurisdictions

- FBI field offices report line-of-duty deaths of law enforcement officers that occur in the United States and its outlying areas

- Several nonprofit organizations, such as the Concerns of Police Survivors and the National Law Enforcement Officers Memorial Fund, which provide various services to the families of fallen officers, also furnish information about line-of-duty deaths

When the FBI receives notification of a line-of-duty death, the Law Enforcement Officers Killed and Assaulted (LEOKA) Program's staff works with FBI field offices to contact the fallen officer's employing agency and request additional details about the fatal incident. The LEOKA staff also obtains criminal history data from the FBI's Interstate Identification Index about individuals who are identified in connection with line-of-duty felonious deaths.

Officers Assaulted

The Uniform Crime Reporting (UCR) Program collects information monthly about assaults on duly sworn city, university and college, county, state, and tribal law enforcement officers. The agencies that employ these officers collect and submit data either through their state UCR Programs or, for non-Program states, directly to the FBI. For assault data to be included in this publication, law enforcement agencies must have submitted information for all 12 months of 2019 regarding their sworn officers who were assaulted as well as the number of officers and civilians their agencies employed full time for the reporting year.

Law enforcement agencies report to the UCR Program the number of assaults resulting in injuries to their officers or instances in which an offender used a weapon that could have caused injury or death. Law enforcement agencies report other assaults (i.e., those not causing injury) if they involved more than verbal abuse or minor resistance to an arrest.

The data in this report pertain to felonious deaths, accidental deaths, and assaults of duly sworn law enforcement officers who, at the time of the incident, met the following criteria. These law enforcement officers:

- Wore/carried a badge (ordinarily).

- Carried a firearm (ordinarily).

- Were duly sworn and had full arrest powers.

- Were members of a law enforcement agency.

- Were acting in an official capacity, whether on or off duty, at the time of incident.

- If killed, the deaths were directly related to the injuries received during the incident.

An exception to the above criteria includes individuals who were killed or assaulted while acting in a law enforcement capacity at the request of a law enforcement agency whose officers meet the LEOKA criteria. (See below for further explanation in reference to this exception.)

Exclusions from the LEOKA Program's Data Collection

Deaths resulting from the following are not included in the LEOKA Program's statistics:

- Natural causes, such as, heart attack, stroke, aneurism, etc.

- On duty, but death is attributed to their own personal situation, such as, domestic violence, neighbor conflict, etc.

- Suicide

Examples of job positions not typically included in the LEOKA Program's statistics (unless they meet the above exception):

- Corrections/correctional officers

- Bailiffs

- Probation/parole officers

- Federal judges

- U.S. and Assistant U.S. Attorneys

- Bureau of Prison Officers

- Private Security Officers

In September 2014, the LEOKA Program expanded its collection criteria to include the data of individuals who are killed or assaulted while temporarily serving as a law enforcement officer at the request of a law enforcement agency whose officers meet the general current collection criteria. These individuals must be under the supervision of a certified law enforcement officer from the requesting agency at the time of the incident, but they are not required to be in the physical presence of the supervisory officer while they are working an assigned duty. Example of permitted exception: An unpaid reserve officer responded to a structure fire along with a law enforcement officer. As the reserve officer exited the patrol unit, he was immediately confronted in an ambush-style attack and was fatally shot by the offender.

Example of permitted exception: A correctional officer was fatally shot while assisting local law enforcement agencies who were tracking a man wanted for murdering his parents. The officer was a canine handler at a local correctional facility and was asked to assist during the incident based on the need for the canine. (If the correctional officer was working in his/her normal capacity as a correctional officer when killed, that correctional officer would not be counted in the LEOKA Program's statistics.)

Federal Law Enforcement Officers Killed and Assaulted

Data published by the FBI concerning federal officers who were killed or assaulted in the line of duty are provided by the following six federal departments:

- U.S. Capitol Police

- U.S. Department of Defense

- U.S. Department of Homeland Security

- U.S. Department of the Interior

- U.S. Department of Justice

- U.S. Department of the Treasury

- U.S. Postal Inspection Service

Within these departments are the agencies, bureaus, and services that employ most of the personnel who are responsible for protecting government officials and enforcing and investigating violations of federal law. Every year, the FBI contacts these agencies and requests information about the officers who were killed or assaulted in the line of duty.

The information concerning federal officers differs slightly from the data regarding assaults on city, university and college, county, state, and tribal law enforcement officers. First, the data regarding federal officers include all reports of assaults regardless of the extent (or the absence) of personal injury. Second, the circumstance categories are tailored to represent the unique duties of federal law enforcement personnel.

Data Considerations

When reviewing the tables, charts, and summaries presented in this publication, readers should be aware of certain features of the LEOKA data collection process that could affect their interpretation of the information.

- The data in the tables and charts reflect the number of victim officers, not the number of incidents or weapons used.

- The UCR Program considers any parts of the body that can be used as weapons (such as hands, fists, or feet) to be personal weapons and designates them as such in its data.

- Law enforcement agencies use a different methodology for collecting and reporting data about officers who were killed than the methodology used for those who were assaulted. As a result, information about officers killed and information about officers assaulted reside in two separate databases, and the data are not comparable.

- Because the information in the tables of this publication is updated each year, the FBI cautions readers against making comparisons between the data in this publication and those in prior editions.

Caution Against Comparisons with Data from Other Organizations

The FBI's LEOKA Program is one of a number of entities that report information concerning line-of-duty deaths and/or assaults of law enforcement officers in the United States. Each organization has its own purpose and may use different methods to collect and report information or focus on somewhat different aspects of these important topics. Therefore, care should be taken not to compare LEOKA data to data provided by other entities, such as the Officer Down Memorial Page, National Law Enforcement Officers Memorial Fund, and others.

History

Beginning in 1937, the FBI's UCR Program collected and published statistics on law enforcement officers killed in the line of duty in its annual publication, *Crime in the United States*. Statistics regarding assaults on officers were added in 1960. In June 1971, executives from the law enforcement conference, "Prevention of Police Killings," called for an increase in the FBI's involvement in preventing and investigating officers' deaths. In response to this directive, the UCR Program expanded its collection of data to include more details about the incidents in which law enforcement officers were killed and assaulted.

Using this comprehensive set of data, the FBI began in 1972 to produce two reports annually, the *Law Enforcement Officers Killed Summary* and the *Analysis of Assaults on Federal Officers*. These two reports were combined in 1982 to create the annual publication, *Law Enforcement Officers Killed and Assaulted*.

Definitions

Type of Incident

Feloniously Killed – Incident type in which an officer, while engaged in or on account of the performance of their official duties, was fatally injured as a direct result of a willful and intentional act by an offender.

Accidentally Killed – Incident type in which an officer was fatally injured as a result of an accident or negligence that occurred while the officer was acting in an official capacity. Due to the hazardous nature of the law enforcement profession, deaths of law enforcement officers are considered accidental if the act causing the death is found not to be willful and intentional.

Assaulted – An unlawful attack by one person upon another for the purpose of inflicting severe or aggravated bodily injury. This type of assault is accompanied by the use of a weapon or by a means likely to produce death or great bodily injury.

Detailed Assault Data – The detailed data collection is limited to officers who are assaulted and injured with firearms or knives/other cutting instruments. – Incident type in which an officer, while engaged in or on account of the performance of their official duties, received nonfatal injuries as a direct result of a willful and intentional act by an offender.

Race

White – A person having origins in any of the original peoples of Europe, the Middle East, or North Africa.

Black/African American – A person having origins in any of the black racial groups of Africa. Terms such as "Haitian" or "Negro" can be used in addition to "Black or African American."

Asian – Included within "Asian/Pacific Islander" in LEOKA publication tables referring to Race – A person having origins in any of the original peoples of the Far East, Southeast Asia, or the Indian subcontinent, including, for example, Cambodia, China, India, Japan, Korea, Malaysia, Pakistan, the Philippine Islands, Thailand, and Vietnam.

Native Hawaiian/Other Pacific Islands – Included within "Asian/Pacific Islander" in LEOKA publication tables referring to Race – A person having origins in any of the original peoples of Hawaii, Guam, Samoa, or other Pacific Islands, e.g., individuals who are Carolinian, Fijian, Kosraean, Melanesian, Micronesian, Northern Mariana Islander, Palauan, Papua New Guinean, Ponapean (Pohnpelan), Polynesian, Solomon Islander, Tahitian, Tarawa Islander, Tokelauan, Tongan, Trukese (Chuukese), and Yapese. (NOTE: The term "Native Hawaiian" does not include individuals who are native to the state of Hawaii simply by virtue of being born there.)

American Indian/Alaska Native – A person having origins in any of the original peoples of North and South America (including Central America), and who maintains tribal affiliation or community attachment.

Type of Assignment

2-Officer vehicle – An assignment where the officer is on patrol and is accompanied by another law enforcement officer(s) in the agency's marked patrol vehicle.

1-Officer vehicle – An assignment where the officer is on patrol and is not accompanied by another officer in the agency's marked patrol vehicle.

Foot patrol – An assignment where the officer is patrolling a designated route on foot.

Administrative – Included within "Other" in LEOKA publication tables referring to Type of Assignment – An assignment in which an officer is working management, performance, or executive duties of the local, state, or federal jurisdiction. Examples include, but are not limited to:

- handling, transporting, or maintaining custody of persons who are in the custodial care of a law enforcement agency subsequent to an arrest and/or while dealing with persons who are being detained in accordance with the law;

- attending community meetings, crime preventive programs, or other organized functions as an official representative of a law enforcement agency;

- performing duties and recreational activities associated with agency sanctioned programs such as D.A.R.E., Boys and Girls Clubs, or other youth programs; or

- serving of writs, notices, summonses, subpoenas, hearing notices, notifications, and other civil processes; and transporting of papers, equipment, or persons associated with official agency sanctioned activities, functions, and programs.

Investigative/detective – Included within "Other" in LEOKA publication tables referring to Type of Assignment – An officer whose occupation is mainly to investigate and solve crimes.

Plainclothes assignment – Included within "Other" in LEOKA publication tables referring to Type of Assignment – A non-uniformed assignment where the officer's role and identity as a sworn law enforcement officer is not intended to be confidential or clandestine.

Tactical assignment (uniformed) – Included within "Other" in LEOKA publication tables referring to Type of Assignment – A uniformed assignment where an officer is strategically deployed in order to achieve a specific goal or objective. These are typically high-risk assignments.

Undercover – Included within "Other" in LEOKA publication tables referring to Type of Assignment – A non-uniformed assignment where the officer requires anonymity or blending into a group or environment to gather evidence or intelligence. The disclosure of the officer's identity would pose a significant safety risk.

Off duty – An officer who is off duty at the time of incident, but is acting in such a way which is sanctioned by, recognized by, or derived from authority.

Circumstances at Scene of Incident

Disturbance (bar fight, person with firearm, etc.) – A breach of the peace type of circumstance resulting in a call for law enforcement to respond. Examples include, but are not limited to: curfew violations, disorderly persons, drinking in public, fights, fireworks violations, gambling in public space, persons under the influence, landlord/tenant disputes, loitering, loud noise of any type (excluding animal disturbance complaints by a citizen), littering, nuisance complaints, prostitution offenses, trespassing or unwanted guests, vagrancy violations, and verbal altercations.

Domestic disturbance (family quarrel, etc.) – A breach of the peace or crime against a person occurring within a family, families, or other relatives or members of the household. Examples include, but are not limited to: family disputes, family intimidations, family arguments, and assisting citizens with the removal of legally owned possessions at locations where prior domestic disturbances or other related offenses have occurred. (Family includes a current or former spouse, parent, or guardian of the victim; a person with whom the victim shares a child in common; a person who is or has been in a social relationship of a romantic or intimate nature with the victim; a person who is cohabiting with or has cohabited with the victim as a spouse, parent, or guardian; or by a person who is or has been similarly situated to a spouse, parent, or guardian of the victim.)

Domestic violence – Included within "Domestic disturbance (family quarrels, etc.)" in LEOKA publication tables referring to Circumstance at Scene of Incident – The use, attempted use, or threatened use of physical force, or a weapon; or the use of coercion or intimidation; or committing a crime against property by a current or former spouse, parent, or guardian of the victim; a person with whom the victim shares a child in common; a person who is or has been in a social relationship of a romantic or intimate nature with the victim; a person who is cohabiting with or has cohabited with the victim as a spouse, parent, or guardian; or by a person who is or has been similarly situated to a spouse, parent, or guardian of the victim.

Burglary – The unlawful entry of a structure with the intent to commit a felony or a theft.

Burglary in progress/pursuing burglary suspect – Situation where an officer is pursuing, arresting, or attempting to arrest an offender involved in a burglary.

Robbery – The taking, or attempting to take, anything of value under confrontational circumstances from the care, custody, or control of a person by force, threat of force, or violence and/or by putting the victim in fear of immediate harm.

Robbery in progress/pursuing robbery suspect – Situation where an officer is pursuing, arresting, or attempting to arrest an offender involved in a robbery.

Drug-related matter – Situation where an officer is pursuing, arresting, or attempting to arrest an offender involved in a drug-related matter, such as, drug busts, buys, etc.

Drug complaint – Included within "Drug-related matter" in LEOKA publication tables referring to Circumstance at Scene of Incident – Incident where a citizen reports the use or presence of illegal drugs or drug paraphernalia. Examples include, but are not limited to, the possession, buying, or selling of illegal drugs or drug paraphernalia.

Attempting other arrest – Situation where an officer is arresting or attempting to arrest an offender either through verbal advisement or through physical contact, such as, attempting to restrain, control, or handcuff the offender.

Civil disorder (mass disobedience, riot, etc.) – An activity where an officer is to control, disperse, or terminate a riot or mass disobedience.

Handling, transporting, custody of prisoner – Situation where an officer is handling, transporting, or maintaining custody of persons who are in the custodial care of a law enforcement agency subsequent to an arrest and/or while dealing with persons who are being detained in accordance with the law.

Investigating suspicious person/circumstance – An activity where an officer's intent is to investigate an unusual occurrence, an out-of-the-ordinary condition, or a suspicious person or circumstance.

Ambush – Situation where an officer is assaulted, unexpectedly, as the result of premeditated design by the perpetrator.

Ambush (entrapment/premeditation) – Situation where an unsuspecting officer was targeted or lured into danger as the result of conscious consideration and planning by the offender.

Unprovoked attack – An attack on an officer not prompted by official contact at the time of the incident between the officer and the offender.

Investigative activity (surveillance, search, interview, etc.) – An activity where an officer is making official inquiries relating to prior criminal offenses and/or perpetrators. Examples include, but are not limited to, obtaining follow-up information or additional information relating to any crime (excluding drug offense complaints) or interviewing a citizen relating to any criminal matter (excluding drug offenses).

Handling person with mental illness – Situation where an officer is handling a person who is known or suspected to be suffering from a mental illness that impairs judgment, behavior, perceptions of reality, or their ability to cope with the ordinary demands of life. Examples include, but are not limited to: mental patients, suicidal persons, service of commitment orders, and calls to investigate persons or activities where it is suspected that a person is suffering from a mental illness.

Felony vehicle stop – A vehicle stop made by an officer that is considered to be high-risk in nature.

Traffic violation stop – A vehicle stop made by an officer due to a motorist's violation of traffic rules and regulations.

Tactical situation (barricaded offender, hostage taking, high-risk entry, etc.) – Situation where an officer is strategically deployed in order to achieve a specific goal or objective. Examples include, but are not limited to: serving search warrants, hostage situations, barricaded offenders, search warrants for drug violations, and any other situations that could be deemed "high-risk," such as, serving an arrest warrant on a known armed felon.

PART 9

Probation and Parole, 2017–2018

HIGHLIGHTS

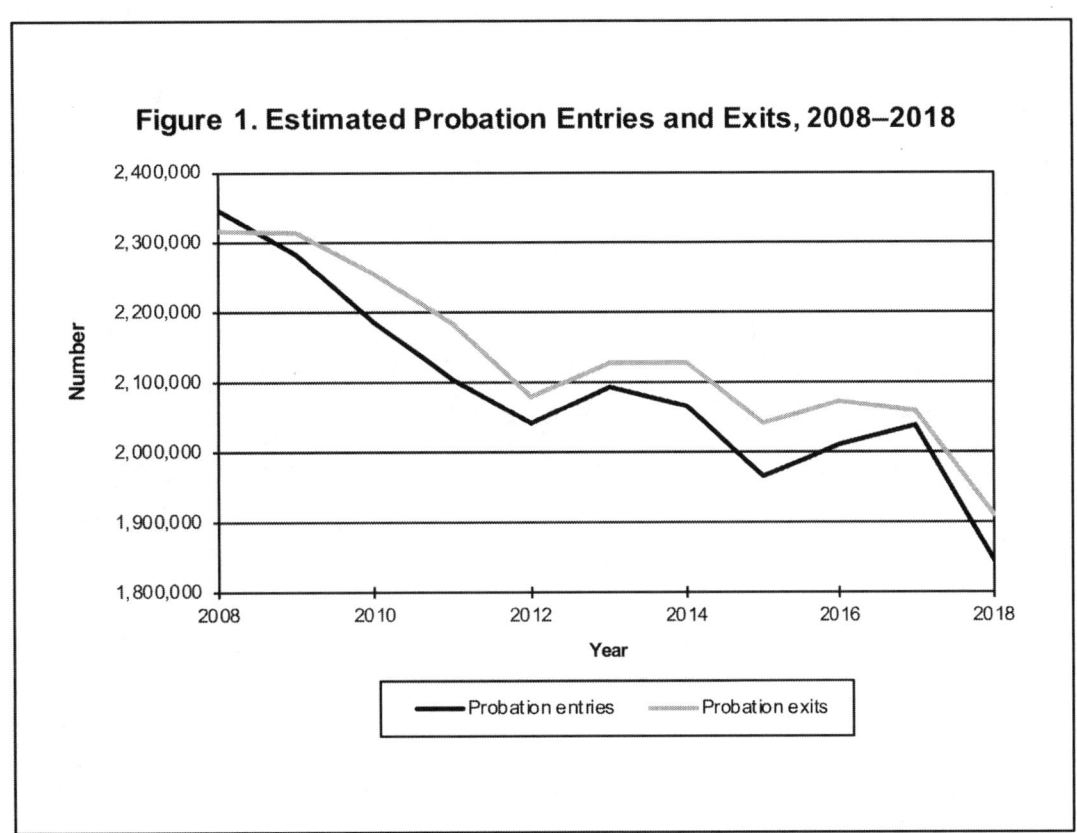

Figure 1. Estimated Probation Entries and Exits, 2008–2018

- At yearend 2018, an estimated 4,399,000 adults were under community supervision, down by about 109,900 offenders (2.4 percent) from yearend 2017; the total community supervision population in 2018 was at its lowest level since 1998.

- Approximately 1 in 58 adults in the United States was under community supervision at yearend 2018, down from 1 in 45 in 2008.

- Between yearend 2017 and yearend 2018, the adult probation population declined by approximately 3 percent (about 52,500 offenders), a 17 percent decline since 2008.

- The adult parole population increased by 0.3 percent between yearend 2017 and yearend 2018 and 6 percent from 2008 to 2018.

- Probation exits in 2018 outpaced entries, the 10th consecutive year of this trend, while parole exits in 2017 exceeded entries for the first time since 2009.

Table 1. Adults Under Community Supervision on Probation or Parole, 2008–2018

(Number; percent.)

Year	Total[1]	Probation	Parole
2008	5,093,400	4,271,200	826,100
2009	5,019,900	4,199,800	824,600
2010	4,888,500	4,055,900	840,800
2011	4,818,300	3,973,800	855,500
2012	4,790,700	3,944,900	858,400
2013	4,749,800	3,912,900	849,500
2014	4,713,200	3,868,400	857,700
2015	4,650,900	3,789,800	870,500
2016	4,537,100	3,673,100	874,800
2017	4,508,900	3,647,200	875,000
2018	4,399,000	3,540,000	878,000
Percent change, December 31			
2008–2018	-13.6	-17.1	6.3
2016–2018	-3.0	-3.6	0.4
2016–2017	-0.6	-0.7	<0.05
2017–2018	-2.4	-2.9	0.3

NOTE: Counts are rounded to the nearest 100. Details may not sum to totals due to rounding. Counts are for December 31 of each year. Percent change is the difference in populations on December 31.
[1]Details may not sum to totals because community-supervision counts were adjusted to exclude parolees who were also on probation.

Table 2. Rates of U.S. Adult Residents on Community Supervision, Probation, and Parole, 2008–2018

(Number; rate.)

Year	Number per 100,000 U.S. adult residents			U.S. adult residents on:		
	Community supervision[1,2]	Probation	Parole	Community supervision[1]	Probation	Parole
2008	2,202	1,847	357	1 in 45	1 in 54	1 in 280
2009	2,148	1,797	353	1 in 47	1 in 56	1 in 283
2010	2,067	1,715	356	1 in 48	1 in 58	1 in 281
2011	2,017	1,663	358	1 in 50	1 in 60	1 in 279
2012	1,984	1,634	356	1 in 50	1 in 61	1 in 281
2013	1,946	1,603	348	1 in 51	1 in 62	1 in 287
2014	1,911	1,568	348	1 in 52	1 in 64	1 in 288
2015	1,872	1,526	350	1 in 53	1 in 66	1 in 285
2016	1,811	1,466	349	1 in 55	1 in 68	1 in 287
2017	1,784	1,443	346	1 in 56	1 in 69	1 in 289
2018	1,726	1,389	344	1 in 58	1 in 72	1 in 290

NOTE: Counts for 2016 and earlier may have been revised based on updated reporting and may differ from numbers in past reports. Rates are based on the total community-supervision, probation, and parole population counts as of December 31 of the reporting year and were calculated using U.S. Census Bureau estimates of the U.S. resident population of persons age 18 or older for January 1 of the following year.
[1]Includes adults on probation and adults on parole.
[2]Details may not sum to totals because community-supervision counts were adjusted to exclude parolees who were also on probation.

Table 3. Parolees on Probation Excluded from the January 1 and December 31 Community Supervision Populations, 2007–2018

(Number.)

Year	January 1[1]	December 31
2007	NA	3,562
2008	3,562	3,905
2009	3,905	4,959
2010	8,259	8,259
2011	8,259	10,958
2012	10,958	12,672
2013	12,672	12,511
2014	12,511	12,919
2015	12,919	9,375
2016	9,375	10,822
2017	10,822	13,302
2018	13,302	18,878

NOTE: Counts for 2016 and earlier may have been revised based on updated reporting and may differ from numbers in past reports. The community-supervision counts were adjusted to exclude parolees who were also on probation.
NA = Not available.
[1]For 2011 through 2018, data are based on the December 31 count of the prior reporting year. For 2010, the December 31, 2010 count was used as a proxy because additional states reported these data in 2010.

Table 4. One-Day Difference Based on Reporting Changes for Probation and Parole, 2008–2017

(Number.)

Year	Probation population difference from December 31 to January 1 of the following year	Parole population difference from December 31 to January 1 of the following year
2008	-33,670	1,390
2009	-73,120	13,700
2010	-2,400	-80
2011	9,770	-2,830
2012	2,960	-23,640
2013	20,980	540
2014	9,750	170
2015	-64,150	130
2016	5,030	2,200
2017	-45,010	-1,240

NOTE: Counts are calculated as the difference between December 31 of the year displayed and January 1 of the following year and are rounded to the nearest 10.

Table 5. Estimated Total Probation Movements, Entries, and Exits, 2008–2018

(Number.)

Year	Total movements	Probation entries	Probation exits
2008	4,663,500	2,346,600	2,316,900
2009	4,597,000	2,283,300	2,313,700
2010	4,442,300	2,185,500	2,256,800
2011	4,287,600	2,104,800	2,182,800
2012	4,122,900	2,042,900	2,080,000
2013	4,220,200	2,093,600	2,126,600
2014	4,194,900	2,065,800	2,129,100
2015	4,009,300	1,966,100	2,043,200
2016	4,083,600	2,012,200	2,071,400
2017	4,100,300	2,039,500	2,060,800
2018	3,755,700	1,845,200	1,910,500

NOTE: Counts for 2016 and earlier may have been revised based on updated reporting and may differ from numbers in past reports. Counts are rounded to the nearest 100. Counts are based on movements from January 1 to December 31 each year.

Table 6. Estimated Total Parole Movements, Entries, and Exits, 2008–2018

(Number.)

Year	Total movements	Parole entries	Parole exits
2008	1,141,900	575,500	566,400
2009	1,144,000	570,700	573,300
2010	1,128,300	565,500	562,800
2011	1,080,900	546,300	534,600
2012	997,700	500,900	496,800
2013	921,100	467,200	453,900
2014	913,900	461,100	452,800
2015	938,900	475,200	463,700
2016	913,100	457,100	456,000
2017	887,700	442,000	445,700
2018	901,100	447,200	453,900

NOTE: Counts for 2016 and earlier may have been revised based on updated reporting and may differ from numbers in past reports. Counts are rounded to the nearest 100. Counts are based on movements from January 1 to December 31 each year.

Table 7. Adults Under Community Supervision, 2018

(Number; percent; rate.)

Jurisdiction	Community supervision population, January 1, 2018[1]	Entries Reported	Entries Estimated[2]	Exits Reported	Exits Estimated[2]	Community supervision population, December 31, 2018[1]	Change, 2018 Number	Change, 2018 Percent	Number under community supervision per 100,000 adult residents, 12/31/18[3]
U.S. Total............................	4,462,600	2,022,200	2,292,400	2,299,400	2,364,400	4,399,000	-63,600	-1.4	1,726
Federal	128,200	50,600	50,600	58,000	58,000	122,800	-5,400	-4.2	48
State....................................	4,334,400	1,971,500	2,241,700	2,241,500	2,306,400	4,276,200	-58,200	-1.3	1,678
Alabama..............................	61,000	18,500	18,500	18,500	18,500	60,900	-100	-0.2	1,599
Alaska[4]	4,100	900	1,400	1,300	2,100	3,400	-600	-15.6	618
Arizona................................	84,600	34,900	34,900	35,100	35,100	84,300	-300	-0.3	1,509
Arkansas..............................	52,000	24,100	24,100	20,100	20,100	53,800	1,800	3.4	2,323
California[4].........................	328,200	168,000	168,000	186,800	186,800	312,400	-15,800	-4.8	1,018
Colorado	91,400	64,700	64,700	64,000	64,400	91,300	-100	-0.1	2,042
Connecticut[4]	43,900	25,200	25,200	25,100	25,100	43,100	-700	-1.7	1,518
Delaware	15,400	10,700	10,700	11,500	11,500	14,500	-900	-5.5	1,890
District of Columbia..............	9,000	5,400	5,400	5,800	5,800	8,600	-400	-4.7	1,483
Florida[4]	214,100	139,200	150,300	149,300	154,800	209,400	-4,800	-2.2	1,216
Georgia[4]	437,000	49,100	255,400	259,200	259,200	433,200	-3,800	-0.9	5,369
Hawaii	21,500	5,600	5,600	5,000	5,000	21,900	400	1.7	1,958
Idaho	38,100	18,400	18,400	16,800	16,800	39,700	1,600	4.1	2,996
Illinois	115,300	81,700	81,700	90,600	90,600	116,100	800	0.7	1,175
Indiana	118,200	93,000	93,000	92,800	92,800	118,400	200	0.1	2,303
Iowa	35,400	19,400	19,400	19,200	19,200	35,600	200	0.6	1,462
Kansas	22,200	25,600	25,600	25,900	25,900	21,900	-300	-1.3	991
Kentucky	60,800	29,500	29,500	27,500	27,500	62,800	2,000	3.3	1,812
Louisiana	70,900	29,800	29,800	36,500	36,500	62,300	-8,500	-12.1	1,749
Maine	6,700	3,300	3,300	3,000	3,000	6,800	<50	0.5	620
Maryland	81,700	36,000	36,000	37,100	37,100	80,600	-1,100	-1.4	1,710
Massachusetts[4]	58,700	63,500	63,500	68,500	68,500	53,700	-5,000	-8.5	966
Michigan[4]	169,100	96,800	101,300	100,800	105,300	164,800	-4,300	-2.5	2,099
Minnesota	105,800	56,300	56,300	54,600	54,600	107,500	1,700	1.6	2,482
Mississippi...........................	37,200	15,700	15,700	15,700	15,700	37,200	-100	-0.1	1,628
Missouri[4]............................	60,100	40,300	40,400	37,600	37,600	63,100	3,000	4.9	1,326
Montana[4]	10,600	5,500	5,700	4,700	4,900	11,400	700	7.5	1,358
Nebraska	15,200	12,300	12,300	12,100	12,100	15,900	600	4.6	1,087
Nevada	18,700	9,900	9,900	8,800	8,800	19,800	1,100	5.9	832
New Hampshire	6,400	3,500	3,500	3,600	3,600	6,300	-100	-1.1	570
New Jersey...........................	154,500	27,600	27,600	35,800	35,800	146,300	-8,200	-5.3	2,099
New Mexico[4]	15,100	8,000	8,000	8,100	8,100	13,700	-1,300	-8.7	850
New York	143,300	44,500	44,500	48,000	48,000	139,700	-3,500	-2.5	903
North Carolina	96,000	62,900	62,900	64,600	64,600	94,100	-1,900	-2.0	1,155
North Dakota.......................	7,200	5,000	5,000	5,200	5,200	7,000	-200	-2.8	1,201
Ohio[4]..................................	254,300	138,500	147,700	140,000	147,100	253,900	-400	-0.2	2,785
Oklahoma............................	43,800	11,700	11,700	12,200	12,200	43,300	-500	-1.1	1,448
Oregon................................	63,500	32,200	32,200	35,800	35,800	59,900	-3,600	-5.6	1,794
Pennsylvania[4]......................	292,100	138,200	138,200	142,300	142,300	288,000	-4,100	-1.4	2,831
Rhode Island[4]......................	22,400	300	4,600	200	6,000	20,900	-1,400	-6.4	2,453
South Carolina.....................	37,000	17,100	17,100	17,500	17,500	36,700	-300	-0.9	916
South Dakota.......................	8,600	6,000	6,000	5,400	5,400	9,200	600	6.9	1,375
Tennessee............................	71,800	23,700	23,700	25,600	25,600	72,100	300	0.5	1,362
Texas..................................	477,800	167,700	167,700	170,800	170,800	474,600	-3,200	-0.7	2,209
Utah	16,300	9,400	9,400	9,100	9,100	16,600	300	1.9	736
Vermont[4]............................	5,000	U	2,800	U	3,000	4,800	-200	-3.9	940
Virginia	64,200	32,400	32,400	31,600	31,600	65,000	800	1.3	973
Washington.........................	88,000	48,500	51,500	41,500	50,300	88,900	900	1.0	1,501
West Virginia	9,900	8,000	8,000	7,000	7,000	10,900	1,000	10.1	756
Wisconsin[4,5]	64,600	U	28,400	300	29,100	63,900	-700	-1.1	1,404
Wyoming	6,000	3,400	3,400	3,100	3,100	6,300	300	5.3	1,426

NOTE: Counts are rounded to the nearest 100. Details may not sum to totals due to rounding. Data quality may vary across jurisdictions for counts of entries and exits. Therefore, the population on December 31, 2018 does not equal the population on January 1, 2018, plus entries, minus exits. Rates are based on the total community-supervision, probation, and parole population counts as of December 31 of the reporting year and were calculated using U.S. Census Bureau estimates of the U.S. resident population of persons age 18 or older for January 1 of the following year.
U = Not known.
[1]The January 1 population excludes 13,302 persons. The December 31 population excludes 18,878 parolees who were also on probation to avoid double counting.
[2]Reported data will equal estimated data in cases where no imputation was required.
[3]Rates were calculated using the estimated U.S. adult resident population in each jurisdiction on January 1, 2019.
[4]See Methodology for more detail.
[5]The only exits reported were deaths.

Table 8. Adults on Probation, 2018

(Number; percent; rate.)

Jurisdiction	Probation population, January 1, 2018	Entries Reported	Entries Estimated[1]	Exits Reported	Exits Estimated[1]	Probation population, December 31, 2018	Change, 2018 Number	Change, 2018 Percent	Number on probation per 100,000 adult residents, 12/31/18[2]
U.S. Total...............	3,602,213	1,582,751	1,845,200	1,853,462	1,910,500	3,539,950	-62,263	-1.7	1,389
Federal...............	16,314	7,111	7,111	8,363	8,363	14,943	-1,371	-8.4	6
State...............	3,585,899	1,575,640	1,838,100	1,845,099	1,902,100	3,525,007	-60,892	-1.7	1,383
Alabama...............	51,961	14,424	14,424	15,340	15,340	50,997	-964	-1.9	1,339
Alaska[3]...............	2,491	888	888	1,305	1,305	2,074	-417	-16.7	375
Arizona...............	77,129	23,118	23,118	23,403	23,403	76,844	-285	-0.4	1,375
Arkansas...............	33,622	13,250	13,250	10,216	10,216	36,719	3,097	9.2	1,584
California...............	233,046	119,639	119,639	136,629	136,629	209,765	-23,281	-10.0	684
Colorado...............	81,125	56,096	56,096	55,904	56,300	80,537	-588	-0.7	1,801
Connecticut...............	40,307	21,748	21,748	22,601	22,601	38,668	-1,639	-4.1	1,362
Delaware...............	15,010	10,528	10,528	11,362	11,362	14,176	-834	-5.6	1,844
District of Columbia............	5,684	4,245	4,245	4,365	4,365	5,564	-120	-2.1	964
Florida[3]...............	209,714	132,944	144,000	142,984	148,500	205,033	-4,681	-2.2	1,191
Georgia[3]...............	419,993	38,881	245,200	248,384	248,384	416,771	-3,222	-0.8	5,166
Hawaii...............	19,830	4,443	4,443	4,077	4,077	20,196	366	1.8	1,808
Idaho...............	33,002	15,530	15,530	14,139	14,139	34,392	1,390	4.2	2,598
Illinois...............	86,538	59,813	59,813	67,136	67,136	88,927	2,389	2.8	900
Indiana...............	111,156	87,651	87,651	86,821	86,821	111,986	830	0.7	2,178
Iowa...............	29,152	15,332	15,332	15,347	15,347	29,137	-15	-0.1	1,198
Kansas...............	16,909	21,151	21,151	21,605	21,605	16,455	-454	-2.7	745
Kentucky...............	44,480	18,557	18,557	16,070	16,070	46,967	2,487	5.6	1,354
Louisiana...............	38,822	13,565	13,565	17,362	17,362	35,025	-3,797	-9.8	983
Maine...............	6,709	3,308	3,308	2,954	2,954	6,742	33	0.5	618
Maryland...............	71,352	31,931	31,931	33,035	33,035	70,248	-1,104	-1.5	1,490
Massachusetts...............	57,261	61,204	61,204	66,237	66,237	52,228	-5,033	-8.8	940
Michigan[3]...............	153,345	87,589	92,000	90,356	94,900	150,338	-3,007	-2.0	1,915
Minnesota...............	98,746	49,385	49,385	48,055	48,055	100,076	1,330	1.3	2,312
Mississippi...............	27,820	9,162	9,162	9,688	9,688	27,294	-526	-1.9	1,196
Missouri[3]...............	42,526	25,266	25,300	24,083	24,100	43,871	1,345	3.2	921
Montana[3]...............	9,358	4,559	4,800	4,000	4,200	9,917	559	6.0	1,184
Nebraska...............	14,255	11,117	11,117	10,920	10,920	14,894	639	4.5	1,021
Nevada...............	13,625	4,518	4,518	4,883	4,883	13,260	-365	-2.7	559
New Hampshire...............	3,914	2,307	2,307	2,324	2,324	3,916	2	0.1	355
New Jersey...............	139,498	22,857	22,857	31,008	31,008	131,347	-8,151	-5.8	1,885
New Mexico[3]...............	12,352	5,737	5,700	6,131	6,100	12,090	-262	-2.1	747
New York...............	98,685	23,987	23,987	28,130	28,130	94,542	-4,143	-4.2	611
North Carolina...............	82,199	47,683	47,683	49,814	49,814	80,068	-2,131	-2.6	983
North Dakota...............	6,297	3,850	3,850	4,051	4,051	6,096	-201	-3.2	1,046
Ohio[3]...............	233,580	127,277	136,400	129,210	136,300	232,741	-839	-0.4	2,553
Oklahoma...............	42,052	11,349	11,349	11,839	11,839	41,562	-490	-1.2	1,388
Oregon...............	38,936	23,350	23,350	26,554	26,554	35,732	-3,204	-8.2	1,070
Pennsylvania...............	180,901	88,090	88,090	90,261	90,261	178,730	-2,171	-1.2	1,757
Rhode Island[3]...............	21,927	U	4,300	U	5,800	20,402	-1,525	-7.0	2,390
South Carolina...............	32,697	14,069	14,069	14,791	14,791	31,975	-722	-2.2	797
South Dakota...............	5,631	3,653	3,653	3,295	3,295	5,989	358	6.4	896
Tennessee...............	60,622	20,670	20,670	21,999	21,999	61,253	631	1.0	1,157
Texas...............	371,361	132,070	132,070	135,264	135,264	368,167	-3,194	-0.9	1,714
Utah...............	12,514	6,508	6,508	6,330	6,330	12,692	178	1.4	563
Vermont[3]...............	4,138	U	2,400	U	2,600	3,936	-202	-4.9	770
Virginia...............	62,443	31,631	31,631	30,963	30,963	63,111	668	1.1	945
Washington[3]...............	76,349	42,334	45,300	36,036	44,800	76,672	323	0.4	1,295
West Virginia...............	6,196	5,605	5605	5,208	5,208	6,593	397	6.4	458
Wisconsin[3,4]...............	43,542	U	21,600	145	22,300	42,909	-633	-1.5	943
Wyoming...............	5,097	2,771	2,771	2,485	2,485	5,383	286	5.6	1,215

NOTE: Data quality may vary across jurisdictions for counts of entries and exits. Therefore, the population on December 31, 2018 does not equal the population on January 1, 2018, plus entries, minus exits. Counts may not be actual as reporting agencies may provide estimates on some or all detailed data. Rates are based on the probation population counts as of December 31 of the reporting year and were calculated using U.S. Census Bureau estimates of the U.S. resident population of persons age 18 or older for January 1 of the following year.
U = Not known.
[1]Reported data will equal estimated data in cases where no imputation was required.
[2]Rates were calculated using the estimated U.S. adult resident population in each jurisdiction on January 1, 2019.
[3]See Probation: Explanatory Notes in Methodology for more detail.
[4]The only exits reported were deaths.

Table 9. Adults Exiting Probation, by Type of Exit, 2018

(Number.)

Jurisdiction	Total reported	Completion	Incarcerated With new sentence	Incarcerated Under current sentence	Incarcerated To receive treatment	Incarcerated Other/ unknown	Absconder	Discharged to warrant or detainer	Other unsatisfactory[1]	Death	Other[2]	Unknown or not reported
U.S. Total....................................	1,853,462	1,075,808	70,008	135,565	4,880	83,902	61,452	11,979	46,009	13,978	53,560	296,321
Federal	8,363	6,992	0	772	0	0	0	0	82	85	0	432
State...	1,845,099	1,068,816	70,008	134,793	4,880	83,902	61,452	11,979	45,927	13,893	53,560	295,889
Alabama*......................................	15,340	11,971	1,749	581	20	U	U	9	U	334	U	676
Alaska*..	1,305	1,163	650	X	X	X	210	X	X	7	24	-749
Arizona*......................................	23,403	16,735	U	5,608	X	567	U	U	X	342	151	0
Arkansas*....................................	10,216	5,543	593	3,118	703	0	0	8	0	238	13	0
California*...................................	136,629	71,868	0	46,479	0	18,282	0	0	0	0	0	0
Colorado*....................................	55,904	33,101	196	887	0	8,515	6,008	0	324	459	5,178	1,236
Connecticut*...............................	22,601	18,891	U	U	0	0	289	2,635	0	U	786	0
Delaware*....................................	11,362	6,946	308	848	U	U	U	U	1,469	126	1,665	0
District of Columbia....................	4,365	3,344	0	0	0	794	0	0	109	49	69	0
Florida*.......................................	142,984	80,725	14,033	21,559	24	1	243	4,923	2,698	1,101	2,083	15,594
Georgia*......................................	248,384	240,099	2,845	1,377	U	U	3,219	U	U	844	U	0
Hawaii*.......................................	4,077	2,866	184	638	U	340	U	U	U	43	6	0
Idaho*...	14,139	2,947	1,883	U	2,258	X	2	U	U	68	0	6,981
Illinois*.......................................	67,136	39,113	X	X	X	517	6,373	X	6,729	X	14,404	0
Indiana*......................................	86,821	49,623	9,704	10,545	0	0	9,211	0	0	0	7,738	0
Iowa	15,347	10,072	1,448	395	0	0	0	0	3,297	117	18	0
Kansas*.......................................	21,605	13,092	..	156	U	U	2,623	U	2,947	U	2,787	0
Kentucky*....................................	16,070	8,536	1,317	3,571	0	0	2,237	U	8	321	80	0
Louisiana*...................................	17,362	11,951	1,461	2,474	X	1	X	X	1,211	201	63	0
Maine*...	2,954	2,709	U	U	U	245	U	U	U	U	U	0
Maryland.....................................	33,035	21,211	2,798	2,127	U	X	U	U	4,242	641	1,488	528
Massachusetts*............................	66,237	U	U	U	U	U	U	U	U	U	U	66,237
Michigan*....................................	90,356	42,856	1,123	2,209	96	49	292	811	1,452	531	206	40,731
Minnesota...................................	48,055	U	U	U	U	U	U	U	U	U	U	48,055
Mississippi...................................	9,688	6,110	795	1,715	X	436	X	X	U	57	542	33
Missouri*.....................................	24,083	9,975	849	3,403	692	220	8,539	U	0	405	U	0
Montana*.....................................	4,000	1,708	351	583	3	33	10	0	0	85	33	1,194
Nebraska*....................................	10,920	7,277	1,982	101	0	130	0	0	1,369	61	0	0
Nevada..	4,883	2,625	U	U	U	X	28	U	1,916	314	U	0
New Hampshire	2,324	2,168	U	137	X	X	U	U	X	19	U	0
New Jersey...................................	31,008	U	U	U	U	U	7	U	U	13	U	30,988
New Mexico..................................	6,131	3,081	U	U	U	0	2,794	2	U	73	3	178
New York	28,130	16,241	U	U	U	U	U	U	U	437	U	11,452
North Carolina	49,814	25,133	3,088	1,889	X	X	7,772	X	9,359	779	X	1,794
North Dakota...............................	4,051	2,046	517	519	U	0	565	U	59	42	303	0
Ohio*..	129,210	52,767	4,219	8,174	934	2,699	8,623	2,196	4,850	1,139	1,855	41,754
Oklahoma*...................................	11,839	9,051	723	1,047	U	U	U	U	89	138	U	791
Oregon..	26,554	6,791	561	3,692	X	X	304	X	86	164	1,679	13,277
Pennsylvania*..............................	90,261	68,557	10,107	3,110	0	0	1,042	14	540	1,042	5,849	0
Rhode Island...............................	U	U	U	U	U	U	U	U	U	U	U	U
South Carolina............................	14,791	12,349	413	1,753	0	0	0	0	0	276	0	0
South Dakota*.............................	3,295	863	U	U	U	761	U	U	U	U	U	1,671
Tennessee*..................................	21,999	14,549	2,605	3,885	0	0	423	0	9	500	15	13
Texas*...	135,264	87,046	U	U	U	42,951	U	U	X	1,743	3,524	0
Utah...	6,330	2,382	547	473	0	0	38	0	1,645	106	1,139	0
Vermont......................................	U	U	U	U	U	U	U	U	U	U	U	U
Virginia	30,963	22,503	U	U	U	7,206	U	U	U	663	415	176
Washington*................................	36,036	17,017	935	582	21	155	2	1,381	1,398	178	1,088	13,279
West Virginia	5,208	1,767	1,876	611	129	X	319	X	79	71	356	0
Wisconsin....................................	145	U	U	U	U	U	X	U	U	145	U	U
Wyoming	2,485	1,448	148	547	0	0	279	0	42	21	0	0

Note: Based on reported data only. Counts may not be actual as reporting agencies may provide estimates on some or all detailed data.
* = Some or all data were estimates.
U = Not known.
X = Not applicable.
[1]Includes probationers discharged from supervision when they did not complete the conditions of probation or fulfill obligations.
[2]Includes 15,213 probationers who transferred to another jurisdiction and 38,347 probationers who exited supervision for other reasons.

Table 10. Characteristics of Adults on Probation, 2008 and 2018

(Percent.)

Characteristic	2008	2018
Total	100.0	100.0
Sex	76.0	75.0
Male	24.0	25.0
Female	100.0	100.0
Race/ethnicity	56.0	55.0
White[1]	29.0	30.0
Black[1]	13.0	13.0
Hispanic	1.0	1.0
American Indian/Alaska Native[1]	1.0	1.0
Asian/Native Hawaiian/Other Pacific Islander[1]	<1	<1
Two or more races[1]	1.0	<1
Status of supervision	100.0	100.0
Active	71.0	68.0
Residential/other treatment program	1.0	1.0
Financial conditions remaining...........................	2.0	3.0
Inactive	8.0	6.0
Absconder...	8.0	9.0
Supervised out of jurisdiction...........................	3.0	3.0
Warrant status	6.0	5.0
Other	2.0	5.0
Type of offense..	100.0	100.0
Felony	50.0	62.0
Misdemeanor	48.0	36.0
Other infractions	2.0	2.0
Most serious offense..	100.0	100.0
Violent	19.0	22.0
Domestic violence..	4.0	4.0
Sex offense..	3.0	4.0
Other violent offense	12.0	14.0
Property	25.0	25.0
Drug	28.0	26.0
Public order..	17.0	14.0
DWI/DUI	14.0	12.0
Other traffic offense	4.0	2.0
Other[2]	10.0	12.0

NOTE: Details may not sum to totals due to rounding. Estimates for 2008 may have been revised based on updated reporting and may differ from numbers in past reports. Characteristics are based on probationers with a known status.
[1]Excludes persons of Hispanic origin (e.g., White refers to non-Hispanic Whites and Black refers to non-Hispanic Blacks).
[2]Includes other offenses, such as public intoxication, disorderly conduct, false statement, insufficient funds, and other miscellaneous charges.

Table 11. Adults on Parole, 2018

(Number; percent; rate.)

Jurisdiction	Parole population, January 1, 2018	Entries		Exits		Parole population, December 31, 2018	Change, 2018[2]		Number on parole per 100,000 adult residents, 12/31/18[2]
		Reported	Estimated[1]	Reported	Estimated[1]		Number	Percent	
U.S. Total......................	873,712	439,399	447,200	445,961	453,900	877,953	4,241	0.5	344
Federal	111,883	43,537	43,537	49,606	49,606	107,872	-4,011	-3.6	42
State................................	761,829	395,862	403,600	396,355	404,300	770,081	8,252	1.1	302
Alabama...........................	9,358	4,094	4,094	3,186	3,186	10,266	908	9.7	270
Alaska[3]	1,563	U	500	..	700	1,348	-215	-13.8	244
Arizona............................	7,537	11,732	11,732	11,733	11,733	7,536	0	0	135
Arkansas...........................	23,782	10,814	10,814	9,841	9,841	24,698	916	3.9	1,066
California[3,4]....................	95,148	48,327	48,327	50,162	50,162	102,586	7,438	7.8	334
Colorado	10,237	8,598	8,598	8,076	8,076	10,759	522	5.1	241
Connecticut[3]...................	3,548	3,446	3,446	2,542	2,542	4,452	904	25.5	157
Delaware	368	125	125	143	143	350	-18	-4.9	46
District of Columbia..........	3,476	1,141	1,141	1,453	1,453	3,164	-312	-9	548
Florida	4,419	6,257	6,257	6,331	6,331	4,345	-74	-1.7	25
Georgia	21,067	10,200	10,200	10,841	10,841	20,426	-641	-3	253
Hawaii	1,666	1,146	1,146	876	876	1,673	7	0.4	150
Idaho...............................	5,102	2,826	2,826	2,661	2,661	5,267	165	3.2	398
Illinois.............................	28,794	21,871	21,871	23,480	23,480	27,185	-1,609	-5.6	275
Indiana	7,073	5,333	5,333	6,007	6,007	6,399	-674	-9.5	124
Iowa	6,414	4,073	4,073	3,835	3,835	6,652	238	3.7	274
Kansas	5,282	4,492	4,492	4,336	4,336	5,438	156	3	246
Kentucky	16,338	10,944	10,944	11,401	11,401	15,881	-457	-2.8	458
Louisiana	32,196	16,240	16,240	19,115	19,115	29,321	-2,875	-8.9	823
Maine	20	1	1	1	1	20	0	0	2
Maryland	10,338	4,083	4,083	4,083	4,083	10,338	0	0	219
Massachusetts[3]................	1,423	2,279	2,279	2,261	2,261	1,441	18	1.3	26
Michigan	15,722	9,209	9,209	10,452	10,452	14,479	-1,243	-7.9	184
Minnesota	7,048	6,875	6,875	6,542	6,542	7,381	333	4.7	171
Mississippi........................	9,392	6,515	6,515	6,041	6,041	9,866	474	5	432
Missouri...........................	17,623	15,071	15,071	13,472	13,472	19,251	1,628	9.2	404
Montana[3]	1,276	916	916	731	731	1,461	185	14.5	174
Nebraska	985	1,152	1,152	1,179	1,179	958	-27	-2.7	66
Nevada.............................	5,033	5,343	5,343	3,884	3,884	6,492	1,459	29	273
New Hampshire	2,436	1,218	1,218	1,284	1,284	2,367	-69	-2.8	215
New Jersey........................	15,005	4,756	4,756	4,794	4,794	14,967	-38	-0.3	215
New Mexico.......................	2,708	2,246	2,246	1,951	1,951	2,805	97	3.6	173
New York	44,572	20,467	20,467	19,847	19,847	45,192	620	1.4	292
North Carolina	13,802	15,185	15,185	14,772	14,772	14,215	413	3	175
North Dakota....................	904	1,153	1,153	1,151	1,151	906	2	0.2	155
Ohio................................	20,703	11,214	11,214	10,804	10,804	21,113	410	2	232
Oklahoma.........................	1,781	395	395	396	396	1,780		-0.1	59
Oregon.............................	24,539	8,851	8,851	9,207	9,207	24,183	-356	-1.5	724
Pennsylvania[3]..................	111,185	50,096	50,096	52,034	52,034	109,247	-1,938	-1.7	1,074
Rhode Island.....................	451	283	283	199	199	535	84	18.6	63
South Carolina..................	4,565	3,077	3,077	2,662	2,662	4,980	415	9.1	124
South Dakota....................	2,968	2,336	2,336	2,103	2,103	3,201	233	7.9	479
Tennessee.........................	11,132	3,038	3,038	3,572	3,572	10,842	-290	-2.6	205
Texas	109,151	35,585	35,585	35,523	35,523	109,213	62	0.1	508
Utah	3,781	2,882	2,882	2,749	2,749	3,914	133	3.5	174
Vermont[3]........................	861	U	400	U	400	870	9	1	170
Virginia	1,709	742	742	591	591	1,860	151	8.8	28
Washington.......................	11,663	6,162	6,162	5,485	5,485	12,222	559	4.8	206
West Virginia	3,690	2,422	2,422	1,825	1,825	4,287	597	16.2	298
Wisconsin[5]......................	21,095	U	6,800	124	6,900	21,015	-80	-0.4	462
Wyoming	900	651	651	617	617	934	34	3.8	211

NOTE: Data quality may vary across jurisdictions for counts of entries and exits. Therefore, the population on December 31, 2018 does not equal the population on January 1, 2018, plus entries, minus exits. Counts may not be actual as reporting agencies may provide estimates on some or all detailed data. Rates are based on the parole population counts as of December 31 of the reporting year and were calculated using U.S. Census Bureau estimates of the U.S. resident population of persons age 18 or older for January 1 of the following year.
U = Not known.
[1]Reported data will equal estimated data in cases where no imputation was required.
[2]Rates were calculated using the estimated U.S. adult resident population in each jurisdiction on January 1, 2019.
[3]See Methodology for more details.
[4]Includes Post-Release Community Supervision and Mandatory Supervision parolees: 45,899 on January 1, 2018 and 55,216 on December 31, 2018, with 28,324 parole entries and 31,699 parole exits.
[5]The only exits reported were deaths.

Table 12. Adults Entering Parole, by Type of Entry, 2018

(Number.)

Jurisdiction	Total reported	Discretionary[1]	Mandatory[2]	Reinstatement[3]	Term of supervised release[4]	Other	Unknown or not reported
U.S. Total...	439,399	192,296	89,915	15,634	85,899	5,965	49,690
Federal..	43,537	281	0	0	43,256	0	0
State...	395,862	192,015	89,915	15,634	42,643	5,965	49,690
Alabama*...	4,094	2,594	255	1,245	X	0	0
Alaska...	U	U	U	U	U	U	U
Arizona..	11,732	9,856	49	50	41	1,736	0
Arkansas*..	10,814	8,878	38	0	1,898	0	0
California*..	48,327	U	U	U	U	U	48,327
Colorado*..	8,598	3,649	3,588	1,235	0	126	0
Connecticut*......................................	3,446	1,210	U	605	1,631	0	0
Delaware*..	125	U	U	U	U	0	125
District of Columbia..........................	1,141	176	0	0	965	0	0
Florida...	6,257	54	5,242	0	939	22	0
Georgia*..	10,200	10,200	0	0	0	0	0
Hawaii*..	1,146	852	0	294	X	0	0
Idaho*..	2,826	1,907	U	818	U	6	95
Illinois..	21,871	15	20,179	38	X	583	1,056
Indiana...	5,333	0	5,333	0	0	0	0
Iowa	4,073	4,073	0	0	0	0	0
Kansas..	4,492	0	2	198	4,292	0	0
Kentucky..	10,944	6,058	4,549	0	337	0	0
Louisiana..	16,240	808	14,927	439	47	19	0
Maine...	1	0	0	1	0	0	0
Maryland*..	4,083	1,841	2,242	U	U	0	0
Massachusetts....................................	2,279	2,139	0	138	0	2	0
Michigan*..	9,209	8,412	490	307	0	0	0
Minnesota*...	6,875	0	19	0	6,340	516	0
Mississippi*..	6,515	4,668	X	1,053	X	794	0
Missouri*..	15,071	11,315	787	1,286	1,683	0	0
Montana...	916	916	0	0	0	0	0
Nebraska*..	1,152	909	X	243	X	0	0
Nevada*...	5,343	4,717	564	62	X	0	0
New Hampshire*................................	1,218	641	0	490	X	87	0
New Jersey..	4,756	2,690	2,066	X	0	0	0
New Mexico*......................................	2,246	U	U	3	1,983	260	0
New York..	20,467	6,587	5,365	X	7,603	912	0
North Carolina*..................................	15,185	41	298	X	14,846	0	0
North Dakota*....................................	1,153	1,153	X	U	X	0	0
Ohio...	11,214	127	8,653	2,434	X	0	0
Oklahoma*...	395	395	X	X	X	0	0
Oregon*...	8,851	2,540	6,240	6	6	59	0
Pennsylvania*.....................................	50,096	46,713	0	3,383	0	0	0
Rhode Island*....................................	283	283	X	X	X	0	0
South Carolina...................................	3,077	1,474	1,603	0	0	0	0
South Dakota*....................................	2,336	656	1,360	U	32	288	0
Tennessee..	3,038	2,949	4	83	0	2	0
Texas..	35,585	34,283	281	525	X	409	87
Utah...	2,882	2,694	0	44	0	144	0
Vermont...	U	U	U	U	U	U	U
Virginia	742	447	295	0	0	0	0
Washington..	6,162	192	5,389	581	0	0	0
West Virginia	2,422	2,325	97	0	0	0	0
Wisconsin...	U	U	U	U	U	U	U
Wyoming	651	578	0	73	0	0	0

NOTE: Based on reported data only. For imputed entries to parole, see appendix table 5. Counts may not be actual as reporting agencies may provide estimates on some or all detailed data.
* = Some or all data were estimates.
U = Not known.
X = Not applicable.
[1]Includes persons entering due to a parole board decision.
[2]Includes persons whose release from prison was not decided by a parole board and persons entering due to determinate sentencing, good-time provisions, or emergency releases.
[3]Includes persons returned to parole after serving time in a prison due to a parole violation. Depending on the reporting jurisdiction, reinstatement entries may include only parolees who were originally released from prison through a discretionary release, mandatory release, or a combination of both types. May also include those originally released through a term of supervised release.
[4]Includes persons sentenced by a judge to a fixed period of incarceration based on a determinate statute immediately followed by a period of supervised release in the community.

Table 13. Adults Exiting Parole, by Type of Exit, 2018

(Number.)

Jurisdiction	Total reported	Completion	Returned to incarceration				Absconder	Other unsatisfactory[1]	Death	Other[2]	Unknown or not reported
			With new sentence	With revocation	To receive treatment	Other/ unknown					
U.S. Total...............	445,961	240,542	31,029	70,224	2,026	8,372	8,927	5,168	6,712	13,880	59,081
Federal...................	49,606	29,108	1	12,069	0	0	0	293	814	0	7,321
State.....................	396,355	211,434	31,028	58,155	2,026	8,372	8,927	4,875	5,898	13,880	51,760
Alabama*..................	3,186	2,226	717	120	X	X	X	X	100	23	0
Alaska......................	U	U	U	U	U	U	U	U	U	U	U
Arizona....................	11,733	8,166	19	2,535	0	0	39	865	59	50	0
Arkansas*.................	9,841	4,313	567	4,736	0	0	0	0	192	33	0
California*................	50,162	U	U	U	U	U	U	U	U	U	50,162
Colorado..................	8,076	4,142	1,200	2,558	0	0	0	0	111	65	0
Connecticut*............	2,542	1,591	U	U	U	915	X	36	U	X	0
Delaware*................	143	26	1	1	U	U	U	0	3	112	0
District of Columbia..	1,453	576	0	0	0	565	0	124	64	124	0
Florida.....................	6,331	3,985	331	735	0	0	0	0	2	1,062	216
Georgia*..................	10,841	8,081	271	30	U	2,282	0	X	127	0	50
Hawaii*....................	876	211	2	352	U	U	176	0	10	125	0
Idaho*.....................	2,661	834	392	682	6	U	501	U	49	197	0
Illinois*...................	23,480	13,853	1,247	7,110	X	X	67	9	330	864	0
Indiana....................	6,007	3,301	363	1,778	0	0	372	0	43	150	0
Iowa.......................	3,835	1,920	715	998	0	0	1	159	42	0	0
Kansas....................	4,336	2,492	184	961	0	0	448	0	54	197	0
Kentucky.................	11,401	6,548	343	1,172	0	104	3,046	0	188	0	0
Louisiana*...............	19,115	11,233	1,809	777	X	1,375	X	818	287	2,816	0
Maine......................	1	0	0	0	0	0	0	0	1	0	0
Maryland..................	4,083	2,505	413	240	U	X	U	606	161	71	87
Massachusetts..........	2,261	1,497	64	453	0	0	0	219	21	7	0
Michigan*................	10,452	7,661	985	1,596	0	X	0	X	210	0	0
Minnesota*..............	6,542	3,526	381	2,591	0	0	0	0	44	0	0
Mississippi..............	6,041	3,784	709	1,208	X	X	X	U	53	69	218
Missouri...................	13,472	5,427	970	3,112	367	1,964	1,379	X	235	X	18
Montana*.................	731	404	29	3	0	243	0	0	18	0	34
Nebraska.................	1,179	764	X	393	X	X	X	0	5	17	0
Nevada*...................	3,884	2,726	356	356	X	325	40	X	81	X	0
New Hampshire........	1,284	635	U	649	X	X	U	X	U	U	0
New Jersey...............	4,794	2,899	105	1,492	X	0	X	0	129	169	0
New Mexico*............	1,951	586	41	1,160	U	33	U	94	32	5	0
New York.................	19,847	10,792	1,327	5,783	1,648	0	0	X	297	X	0
North Carolina.........	14,772	9,789	1,161	312	X	X	2,035	501	149	X	825
North Dakota...........	1,151	814	142	106	U	0	57	X	13	19	0
Ohio.......................	10,804	6,111	2,242	2,451	X	0	U	U	U	0	0
Oklahoma*...............	396	366	X	X	X	X	X	X	27	3	0
Oregon*...................	9,207	5,069	942	1,695	5	X	2	1,000	159	188	147
Pennsylvania*...........	52,034	33,223	5,395	4,497	0	0	593	290	760	7,276	0
Rhode Island............	199	143	15	36	0	0	0	0	5	0	0
South Carolina.........	2,662	2,375	24	159	0	0	0	39	65	0	0
South Dakota*..........	2,103	907	178	721	X	58	0	X	21	218	0
Tennessee...............	3,572	2,053	719	686	0	0	0	0	114	0	0
Texas*.....................	35,523	27,321	5,149	1,216	X	508	X	0	1,326	3	0
Utah.......................	2,749	617	500	1,464	0	0	0	108	45	15	0
Vermont...................	U	U	U	U	U	U	U	U	U	U	U
Virginia...................	591	419	124	40	0	0	0	0	3	2	3
Washington..............	5,485	3,749	853	805	0	0	0	0	78	0	0
West Virginia............	1,825	1,384	13	232	0	0	140	0	56	0	0
Wisconsin................	124	U	U	U	U	U	X	U	124	U	X
Wyoming.................	617	390	30	154	0	0	31	7	5	0	0

NOTE: Based on reported data only. Counts may not be actual as reporting agencies may provide estimates on some or all detailed data.
* = Some or all data were estimates.
U = Not known.
X = Not applicable.
[1]Includes persons discharged because they were released to special sentence. Also includes closure due to deportation, pending parole institutional hearing, other revocations, other unsuccessful discharges, and early terminations.
[2]Includes 1,642 parolees who were transferred to another state and 12,238 parolees who exited for other reasons.

Table 14. Characteristics of Adults on Parole, 2008 and 2018

(Percent.)

Characteristic	2008	2018
Total	100.0	100.0
Sex	100.0	100.0
Male	88.0	87.0
Female	12.0	13.0
Race/ethnicity	100.0	100.0
White[1]..	41.0	46.0
Black[1]...	38.0	37.0
Hispanic	19.0	15.0
American Indian/Alaska Native[1]	1.0	1.0
Asian[1]	1.0	1.0
Native Hawaiian/Other Pacific Islander[1].........	<1	<1
Two or more races[1]	<1	<1
Status of supervision	100.0	100.0
Active	85.0	82.0
Inactive	3.0	5.0
Absconder..	6.0	8.0
Supervised out of state...........................	4.0	4.0
Financial conditions remaining....................	<1	0.0
Other	2.0	2.0
Maximum sentence to incarceration...................	100.0	100.0
Less than 1 year	6.0	6.0
1 year or more	94.0	94.0
Most serious offense....................................	100.0	100.0
Violent	26.0	31.0
Sex offense...................................	NA	8.0
Other violent offense	NA	23.0
Property	24.0	20.0
Drug	37.0	30.0
Weapons...	3.0	5.0
Other[2]..	11.0	13.0

NOTE: Details may not sum to totals due to rounding. Estimates for 2008 may have been revised based on updated reporting and may differ from numbers in past reports. Characteristics are based on parolees with a known status.
NA = Not available.
[1]Excludes persons of Hispanic origin (e.g., White refers to non-Hispanic Whites and Black refers to non-Hispanic Blacks).
[2]Includes public order offenses.

METHODOLOGY

About the Data

The Bureau of Justice Statistics' (BJS) Annual Probation Survey and Annual Parole Survey began in 1980 and collect data from probation and parole agencies in the United States that supervise adults. In these data, adults are persons subject to the jurisdiction of an adult court or correctional agency. Juveniles prosecuted as adults in a criminal court are considered adults. Juveniles under the jurisdiction of a juvenile court or correctional agency are excluded from these data.

The National Criminal Justice Information and Statistics Service of the Law Enforcement Assistance Administration, BJS's predecessor agency, began a statistical series on parole in 1976 and on probation in 1979. The two surveys collect data on the total number of adults supervised in the community on January 1 and December 31 each year, the number of entries and exits to supervision during the reporting year, and characteristics of the population at yearend.

Both surveys cover all 50 states, the District of Columbia, and the federal system. BJS depends on the voluntary participation of state central reporters and separate state, county, and court agencies for these data.

Probation

The 2018 Annual Probation Survey was sent to 454 agencies, one less than the 2017 survey due to the closure of one agency in Ohio. The 454 respondents included 40 central state agencies and the District of Columbia; 415 separate state, county, or court agencies; and the U.S. federal system. States with multiple state agencies included Alabama (3), Colorado (8), Florida (41), Georgia (2), Idaho (2), Kentucky (2), Michigan (129), Missouri (2), Montana (4), New Mexico (2), Ohio (182), Oklahoma (3), Pennsylvania (2), Tennessee (3), and Washington (32). Georgia and Pennsylvania are both included as central state agencies, but each provides data from two departments within the state government. Of the 454 agencies in the population frame, 4 in Florida, 13 in Michigan, 1 in Montana, 1 in New Mexico, 13 in Ohio, and 4 in Washington provided no data for the 2018 collection. The final response rate for the 2018 Annual Probation Survey was 92.1 percent.

Of the 455 agencies in the population frame in 2017, 1 in Alabama, 1 in Alaska, 9 in Florida, 1 in Kentucky, 10 in Michigan, 1 in New Mexico, 20 in Ohio, and 4 in Washington provided no data for the 2017 collection. The final response rate for the 2017 Annual Probation Survey was 89.7 percent.

Probation: Explanatory Notes, 2018

Probation agencies vary in their ability to provide counts consistent with Bureau of Justice Statistics (BJS) definitions on an annual basis. Some agencies report the number of cases, while others report the number of individuals they supervise. Because an individual can have multiple probation sentences, counting cases can artificially inflate probation totals. BJS requests that agencies report the number of individuals under supervision, and each year some agencies make the conversion, resulting in what appears to be a large decrease from previous years' data. BJS documents these and other reporting anomalies below:

Alaska— The state supervises probation and parole in a combined program. The state agency was unable to report probation and parole data separately, so both populations were reported in the probation survey. The January 1, 2018 and December 31, 2018 probation population counts were derived based on the difference between the reported probation and imputed parole count (imputed using the December 31, 2017 parole population count).

Florida— Non-reporting agencies in 2018—four local agencies did not report data. The December 31, 2017 population count was used to estimate January 1, 2018 and December 31, 2018 counts for these agencies. Four other agencies did not report the number of entries to probation, and three did not report the number of exits from probation.

Georgia— Non-reporting agencies in 2018—one state agency did not report the number of entries to probation.

Michigan— Reporting changes from 2017 to 2018—one agency reported that changes in state laws, specifically the legalization of marijuana and the reduction of a Minor in Possession violation from a criminal misdemeanor to a civil infraction for the first offense, have dramatically reduced the agency's numbers. Non-reporting agencies in 2018—13 local agencies did not report data. For the non-reporting agencies, December 31, 2017 population counts were used to estimate January 1, 2018 and December 31, 2018 populations. Other agencies did not report the number of entries to or exits from probation.

Missouri— Non-reporting agencies in 2018—one local agency did not report the number of entries to or exits from probation.

Montana—Non-reporting agencies in 2018—one local agency did not report data. December 31, 2017 population counts were used to estimate January 1, 2018 and December 31, 2018 populations.

New Mexico—Non-reporting agencies in 2018—one local agency did not report data. For the non-reporting agency, December 31, 2017 population counts were used to estimate January 1, 2018 and December 31, 2018 populations.

Ohio— Non-reporting agencies in 2018—13 local agencies did not report data. For the non-reporting agencies, the December 31, 2017 population count was used to estimate January 1, 2018 and December 31, 2018 populations. One agency did not report the January 1, 2018 population total. Other agencies did not report data on entries to or exits from probation.

Rhode Island—Non-reporting agencies in 2018—the state agency did not report data on entries to or exits from probation.

Vermont—Non-reporting agencies in 2018—the state agency did not report data on entries to or exits from probation.

Washington— Non-reporting agencies in 2018—four local agencies did not report data. For the non-reporting agencies, December 31, 2017 population counts were used to estimate January 1, 2018 and December 31, 2018 populations. Other agencies did not report the number of entries to or exits from probation.

Wisconsin— The state probation agency, overseeing the entire state probation population, was able to report the number of probationers who died or absconded but not the total number of entries to or exits from probation during 2018. Total entries and exits were imputed for 2018.

The number of probation agencies included in the survey expanded in 1998 and continued to expand through 1999 to include misdemeanor probation agencies in a few states that fell within the scope of this survey. For a discussion of this expansion, see *Probation and Parole in the United States, 2010* (NCJ 236019, BJS web, November 2011).

Probation: Explanatory Notes, 2017

Alabama—Non-reporting agencies in 2017—one local agency did not report data. For the non-reporting agency, December 31, 2016 population counts were used to estimate January 1, 2017 and December 31, 2017 populations.

Alaska—Non-reporting agencies in 2017—the state agency was able to report a probation population on January 1, 2017 and entries to probation in 2017 but did not provide any additional data. January 1, 2017 was used to estimate the probation population on December 31, 2017 and exits from probation.

Colorado—Non-reporting agencies in 2017—one local agency did not report data on exits from probation.

Florida—Non-reporting agencies in 2017—nine local agencies did not report data. For the non-reporting agencies, the most

recently available December 31 population count was used to estimate January 1, 2017 and December 31, 2017 counts.

Georgia— Reporting changes from 2016 to 2017—a change in Georgia law, effective in 2017, allows the Department of Community Supervision to move a probationer to unsupervised status after 2 years and may be applied retroactively, provided that any restitution ordered be paid in full prior to allowing someone to be moved to unsupervised status. The other changes in status from prior years are due to a more accurate breakdown of cases not calculated in previous surveys. Non-reporting agencies in 2017—one state agency did not report the number of probation entries.

Kentucky—Non-reporting agencies in 2017—one local agency did not report data. For the non-reporting agency, December 31, 2016 population counts were used to estimate January 1, 2017 and December 31, 2017 populations.**

Michigan—Non-reporting agencies in 2017—10 local agencies did not report data. For the non-reporting agencies, December 31, 2016 population counts were used to estimate January 1, 2017 and December 31, 2017 populations. One agency did not report the January 1, 2017 population total. Other agencies did not report the number of entries to or exits from parole.

Montana—Non-reporting agencies in 2017—one local agency did not report data on entries to probation.

New Mexico—Non-reporting agencies in 2017—one local agency did not report data. For the non-reporting agency, December 31, 2016 population counts were used to estimate January 1, 2017 and December 31, 2017 populations.

North Dakota—Non-reporting agencies in 2017— the state agency did not report data on entries to probation.

Ohio— Reporting changes from 2016 to 2017—many agencies have been undergoing a change to their case management systems per statewide guidance. Agencies either struggled to report data in 2017 due to the change or reported that data were not comparable to previous years due to the change. Non-reporting agencies in 2017—20 local agencies did not report data. For the non-reporting agencies, the most recently available December 31 population count was used to estimate January 1, 2017 and December 31, 2017 populations. Other agencies did not report data on entries to or exits from probation.

Oklahoma—Reporting changes from 2016 to 2017—a municipal court was able to obtain more accurate information from its system starting in 2017. This change resulted in an increase of 9,000 probationers in 2017.

Rhode Island—Non-reporting agencies in 2017—the state agency did not report data on entries to or exits from probation.

Vermont—Non-reporting agencies in 2017—the state agency did not report data on entries to or exits from probation.

Washington—Non-reporting agencies in 2017—four local agencies did not report data. For the non-reporting agencies, December 31, 2016 population counts were used to estimate January 1, 2017 and December 31, 2017 populations. Other agencies did not report the number of entries to or exits from probation.

Wisconsin—The state probation agency, overseeing the entire state probation population, was able to report the number of probationers who died or absconded but not the total number of exits or entries to probation during 2017. Total entries and exits were imputed for 2017.

Parole

The 2017 and 2018 Annual Parole Survey was sent to 52 agencies: 50 central state reporters, the District of Columbia, and the U.S. federal system. In this report, federal parole includes a term of supervised release from prison, mandatory release, parole, military parole, and special parole. At sentencing, a federal judge orders a term of supervised release, which is served after release from a federal prison sentence. In the case of Alaska, probationers and parolees were supervised under a common program, and the state's data-provider was unable to report probation and parole counts separately. The state reported combined probationer and parolee counts through the probation questionnaire. January 1, 2018 and December 31, 2018 parolee counts were imputed for Alaska (see Imputing the January 1 parole population and Imputing the December 31 parole population, below), and these figures were deducted from the combined reported totals for calculating the state's January 1 and December 31 probationer counts. The final response rate for the 2018 Annual Parole Survey was 100 percent.

Alaska did not report parole populations for the 2017 collection year. (See Imputing the January 1 parole population.) The final response rate for the 2017 Annual Parole Survey was 98.1 percent.

Parole: Explanatory Notes, 2018

Each year, changes in legislation or o ender management systems require states to alter previously submitted data or the data they can currently submit. The Bureau of Justice Statistics documents these changes as reported by the data respondents:

Alaska—Alaska supervises probation and parole in a combined program. The state agency was unable to report probation and parole data separately, so both populations were reported in the probation survey. The January 1, 2018 and December

31, 2018 parole population counts were imputed based on the December 31, 2017 parole population count.

California—Parole data included Post-Release Community Supervision and Mandatory Supervision populations of 45,899 on January 1, 2018 and 55,216 on December 31, 2018, with 28,324 entries to and 31,699 exits from parole.

Connecticut—Reporting changes from 2017 to 2018—the Board of Pardons & Paroles reported that while the supervised population increased because the incarcerated population decreased in 2018, data sources were also different from prior years, which would lead to minor differences in data reported.

Massachusetts—Reporting changes from 2017 to 2018—the state reported only adult parolees committed to a Massachusetts institution and supervised in one of the nine regional parole offices or under the Warrant and Apprehension Unit of the Field Services Division. The caseload reported for the 2017 survey included interstate compact cases supervised by a Massachusetts jurisdiction for another state and adult parolees supervised by a Massachusetts jurisdiction but legally the responsibility of another jurisdiction.

Montana—Reporting changes from 2017 to 2018—the state converted all offender location data from one system to another in November 2018. Therefore, the population reported in 2019 for January 1, 2018 differed from the population reported in 2018 for December 31, 2017.

Ohio—The total parole population included a small, undetermined number of persons under concurrent parole and local probation supervision, temporary jail detention pending a revocation hearing, and temporary prison custody pending a revocation hearing.

Pennsylvania—The Pennsylvania Department of Corrections reported that 7 of the 65 participating county probation departments did not respond to the survey and that these counties' populations were estimated based on the prior year's caseload.

Vermont— Reporting changes from 2017 to 2018—the Vermont Department of Corrections improved its data analysis techniques to ensure a correct count of persons on parole. The state was unable to report the number of entries to or exits from parole.

Parole: Explanatory Notes, 2017

Alaska—Non-reporting agency in 2017—the state did not provide parole data for 2017. All 2017 populations were estimated.

California—Parole data included Post-Release Community Supervision and Mandatory Supervision populations of 44,998

on January 1, 2017 and 45,899 on December 31, 2017, with 26,418 entries to and 25,517 exits from parole.

Georgia—Updates to state law allow the State Board of Pardons and Paroles to consider commuting sentences of parolees serving a split sentence for a non-violent property or drug offense after the satisfactory completion of parole supervision.

Indiana—Reporting changes from 2016 to 2017—the Indiana Department of Corrections experienced a significant change in its parole population due to changes in state law concerning who is eligible to come to state prison. The state completely rewrote its criminal code, which affects prisoners admitted since July 2014, provides different sentences for every offense, and adds new "theft levels" and jurisdictions. As a result, the state agency went from having 20,000 to 11,000 prison admissions in 2017. These changes shifted many persons from state to county jurisdiction, and the lowest level of felony was no longer eligible for state prison.

Vermont—Reporting changes from 2016 to 2017—the Vermont Department of Corrections improved its data analysis techniques to ensure a correct count of persons on parole. These updates accounted for the decrease in the number of parolees. Vermont was unable to report the number of entries to or exits from parole.

Imputing for Non-Reporting Agencies

BJS used the following methods to impute missing probation and parole data for key items, including the January 1 population, entries, and exits and the December 31 population.

Imputing the January 1 probation population

When the January 1 probation population was missing, the December 31 probation population from the last reported year going back to 2010 was carried forward. This method was used to estimate the January 1, 2018 probation population in 38 non-reporting counties and district agencies in Florida, Michigan, Montana, New Mexico, Ohio, and Washington. The January 1, 2018 population was imputed for 0.8 percent of the total probation population. This method was used to estimate the January 1, 2017 probation population in 45 non-reporting counties and district agencies in Alabama, Florida, Kentucky, Michigan, New Mexico, Ohio, and Washington. The January 1, 2017 population was imputed for 1.4 percent of the total probation population.

Imputing the December 31 probation population

When counts were missing for the December 31 probation population, the missing values were imputed by assuming no

intra-year growth and setting the missing value to the January 1 population size.

This method was used to estimate the December 31, 2018 probation population in 37 non-reporting counties and district agencies in Florida, Kentucky, Michigan, Montana, New Mexico, Ohio, and Washington. The December 31, 2018 population was imputed for 0.9 percent of the total probation population. This method was used to estimate the December 31, 2017 probation population in 48 non-reporting counties and district agencies in Alabama, Alaska, Florida, Kentucky, Michigan, New Mexico, Ohio, and Washington. The December 31, 2017 population was imputed for 1.7 percent of the total probation population.

Imputing the January 1 parole population

When the January 1 parole population was missing, the December 31 probation population from the prior year was carried forward. This method was used to estimate the January 1 parole population in both 2018 and 2017 for Alaska, which represented 0.2 percent of the total parole population.

Imputing the December 31 parole population

When counts were missing for the December 31 parole population, the missing values were imputed by adding to (or subtracting from) the January 1 parole population to estimate population change based on what was observed in the prior year. The intra-year change in population from January 1 to December 31 of the prior year was multiplied by the January 1 reporting-year count to estimate the reporting-year population change. This method was used to estimate the December 31 parole population for Alaska, which represented 0.2 percent of the total parole population in 2018 and 2017.

Imputing parole entries

To estimate parole entries for agencies that did not report these data in the reporting year but did report in the prior year, BJS calculated the ratio of entries in the prior year to the agency's parole population on January 1 of the prior year and applied that ratio to the agency's January 1 population of the reporting year. This method was used to estimate parole entries in Alaska, Vermont, and Wisconsin. Total entries were imputed for 1.7 percent of the entering parole population in 2018 and 1.9 percent in 2017.

Imputing probation and parole exits

A single method was used to estimate exits from probation that were not imputed with the first method noted above and for all parole agencies. For both probation and parole, BJS added each agency's estimated entries to that agency's population on January 1 and subtracted that estimate from the population on December 31.

For probation, this method was used for 46 non-reporting agencies in Colorado, Florida, Michigan, Ohio, Rhode Island, Vermont, Washington, and Wisconsin in 2018 and totaled 2.1 percent of the exiting probation population. In 2017, this method was used for 24 non-reporting agencies in Alaska, Colorado, Florida, Michigan, Ohio, Rhode Island, Vermont, Washington, and Wisconsin, totaling 2.3 percent of the exiting probation population.

For parole, this method was used in Alaska, Vermont, and Wisconsin. Total exits were imputed for 1.8 percent of the exiting parole population in 2018 and 2.0 percent in 2017.

Estimating change in population counts

Technically, the change in the probation and parole populations from the beginning of the year to the end of the year should equal the difference between entries and exits during the year. However, those numbers may not be equal. Some probation and parole information systems track the number of cases that enter and exit community supervision, not the number of offenders. This means that entries and exits may include case counts as opposed to counts of individuals, while the beginning and yearend population counts represent individuals. Some individuals are being supervised for more than one charge or case simultaneously. Additionally, all of the data on entries and exits may not have been logged into the information systems, or the information systems may not have fully processed all of the data before the data were submitted to BJS.

Jurisdiction counts reported for January 1 may differ from December 31 counts reported in the previous year. As a result, the direction of change based on year-end data could be in the opposite direction of the within-year change.

Types of Federal Offenders Under Community Supervision

Since the Sentencing Reform Act of 1984 was enacted on November 1, 1987, offenders sentenced to federal prison are no longer eligible for parole but are required to serve a term of supervised release following release from prison. Those sentenced to prison prior to November 1, 1987, continue to be eligible for parole, as do persons violating laws of the District of Columbia, military offenders, and foreign treaty transfer offenders. (See http://www.uscourts.gov/news/TheThirdBranch/11-05-01/Parole_in_the_Federal_Probation_System.aspx.)

In 2008, the Annual Parole Survey included a new type of entry-to-parole category—term of supervised release—to better classify the large majority of entries to parole reported by the federal system. It is a fixed period of release to the community that follows a fixed period of incarceration based on a determinate sentencing statute. Both are determined by a judge at the time of sentencing. For details about estimating methods used to analyze national trends for all types of entry to parole, see *Probation and Parole in the United States, 2010* (NCJ 236019, BJS web, November 2011).

The Sentencing Reform Act also required the adoption and use of sentencing guidelines, which took effect on the same day. Many offenses for which probation had been the typical sentence prior to this date, particularly property and regulatory offenses, subsequently resulted in sentences to prison. Changes in how federal o enders are supervised in the community were first described in the BJS report *Federal Offenders Under Community Supervision, 1987-96* (NCJ 168636, BJS web, August 1998) and updated in *Federal Criminal Case Processing, 2002: With Trends 1982-2002, Reconciled Data* (NCJ 207447, BJS web, January 2005).

PART 10

Update on Prisoner Recidivism: A 9-Year Follow-Up Period (2005–2014)

HIGHLIGHTS

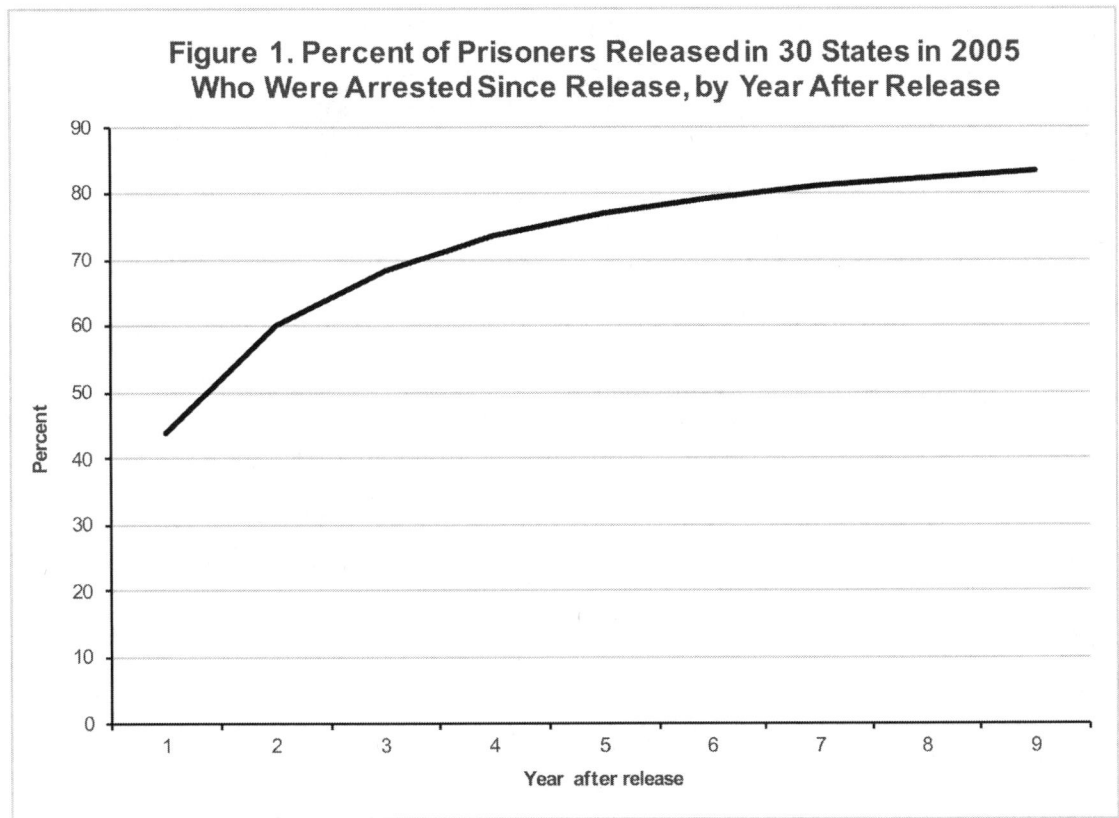

Figure 1. Percent of Prisoners Released in 30 States in 2005 Who Were Arrested Since Release, by Year After Release

- At yearend 2018, an estimated 4,399,000 adults were under community supervision, down by about 109,900 offenders (2.4 percent) from yearend 2017; the total community supervision population in 2018 was at its lowest level since 1998.

- Approximately 1 in 58 adults in the United States was under community supervision at yearend 2018, down from 1 in 45 in 2008.

- Between yearend 2017 and yearend 2018, the adult probation population declined by approximately 3 percent (about 52,500 offenders), a 17 percent decline since 2008.

- The adult parole population increased by 0.3 percent between yearend 2017 and yearend 2018 and 6 percent from 2008 to 2018.

- Probation exits in 2018 outpaced entries, the 10th consecutive year of this trend, while parole exits in 2017 exceeded entries for the first time since 2009.

Table 1. Characteristics of Prisoners Released in 30 States in 2005

(Percent; number.)

Characteristic	Percent	Most serious commitment offense		
		Rape/sexual assault	Assault	Other than rape/sexual assault
Total	100.0	100.0	100.0	100.0
Sex				
Male	89.3	98.4	93.0	88.8
Female	10.7	1.6	7.0	11.2
Race/Hispanic origin				
White[1]	39.7	52.1	36.1	39.1
Black/African American[1]	40.1	27.2	38.0	40.8
Hispanic/Latino	17.7	17.2	22.5	17.7
Other[1,2]	2.4	3.5	3.4	2.4
Age at release				
24 or younger	17.7	12.3	19.4	18.0
25–29	19.4	15.9	21.3	19.6
30–34	16.0	14.1	17.1	16.1
35–39	15.7	14.0	14.9	15.8
40 or older	31.2	43.8	27.3	30.6
Median (years)	34	38	32	34
Mean	35.0	38.8	34.0	34.8
Type of release				
Conditional	74.1	67.9	75.3	74.4
Unconditional	25.9	32.1	24.7	25.6
Maximum sentence length[3]				
1–2 years	19.2	10.5	12.9	19.6
2–5 years	44.7	34.2	56.3	45.3
5–10 years	22.1	28.0	20.4	21.8
10 years or more	14.0	27.3	10.4	13.3
Median (months)	36	60	36	36
Number of prior arrests per released prisoner[4]				
4 or fewer	24.8	52.4	25.0	23.4
5–9	30.3	26.6	30.2	30.5
10 or more	44.9	21.0	44.8	46.2
Median (arrests)	9	4	9	9
Mean	11.0	6.3	10.8	11.3
At least one prior arrest for:				
Drug offense	70.7	30.5	57.9	72.8
Property offense	81.3	55.8	78.0	82.6
Number of released prisoners	401,288	20,195	38,468	381,093

Note: Persons could have been in prison for more than one offense, the most serious of which is reported. Percentages exclude missing data. Data on prisoners' age at release were reported for 100% of cases; race/Hispanic origin, for 99.86%; type of prison release, for 98.19%; and maximum sentence length, for 99.72%. Details may not sum to totals due to rounding.
[1]Excludes persons of Hispanic/Latino origin (e.g., White refers to non-Hispanic Whites and Black refers to non-Hispanic Blacks).
[2]Includes Asians, Native Hawaiians, and Other Pacific Islanders; American Indians and Alaska Natives; and persons of two or more races.
[3]Based on the released prisoners' total maximum sentence length for all commitment offenses. Study excludes prisoners sentenced to less than one year.
[4]Includes arrests for any type of crime prior to the prisoners' date of release in 2005.

Table 2. Prisoners Released in 30 States in 2005 Who Were Arrested Within 9 Years Following Release, by Most Serious Commitment Offense and Types of Post-Release Arrest Charges

(Percent.)

Most serious commitment offense	Any offense	Violent post-release arrest offense					Other post-release arrest offense		
		Total violent[1]	Homicide	Rape/sexual assault	Robbery	Assault	Property	Drug	Public order
All prisoners....................	83.3	39.1	1.2	2.6	7.8	31.3	48.0	48.0	68.4
Violent[1].......................	78.1	43.4	1.4	4.0	9.2	34.1	39.6	36.7	65.0
Homicide....................	60.0	29.5	2.7	1.9	4.3	23.1	24.4	26.1	45.8
Rape/sexual assault............	66.9	28.1	0.2	7.7	3.8	18.7	24.2	18.5	58.9
Robbery	84.1	47.2	1.5	3.4	16.8	34.3	47.7	45.3	67.1
Assault	82.9	50.7	1.4	2.8	7.7	44.2	44.3	43.2	69.6
Property....................	87.8	40.3	1.0	2.5	9.1	31.9	63.5	48.4	72.4
Drug	83.7	34.0	1.1	1.6	5.8	28.0	42.4	60.4	66.9
Public order	81.8	39.8	1.3	2.4	6.7	32.5	42.5	38.8	70.1
Rape/sexual assault*...........	66.9	28.1	0.2	7.7	3.8	18.7	24.2	18.5	58.9
Offense other than rape/sexual assault[2].....	84.1 B	39.6 B	1.2 B	2.3 B	8.0 B	31.9 B	49.2 B	49.6 B	68.9 B

Note: Detail may not sum to total due to rounding. The numerator for each percentage is the number of persons arrested for that offense during the 9-year follow-up period, and the denominator is the number released after serving time for each type of commitment offense. Persons could have been in prison for more than one offense, the most serious of which is reported. Details may not sum to totals because a person may be arrested more than once for different types of offenses and each arrest may involve more than one offense.
* = Comparison group.
B = Difference with comparison group (rape/sexual assault) is significant at the 95% confidence level.
[1] Includes other miscellaneous violent offenses that are not shown separately.
[2] Includes the 381,093 prisoners whose most serious commitment offense was an offense other than rape or sexual assault.

Table 3. Cumulative Percent of Prisoners Released in 30 States in 2005 Who Were Arrested Following Release, by Year Following Release and Most Serious Commitment Offense

(Percent.)

Year after release	All prisoners		Most serious commitment offense					
			Rape/sexual assault		Assault		Offense other than rape/sexual assault	
	Year of first arrest	Cumulative arrest percentage	Year of first arrest	Cumulative arrest percentage	Year of first arrest	Cumulative arrest percentage	Year of first arrest	Cumulative arrest percentage
1...........................	43.8	43.8	29.0	29.0	43.2	43.2	44.5	44.5
2...........................	16.2	60.0	12.9	41.9	16.2	59.4	16.4	60.9
3...........................	8.3	68.3	7.0	48.9	8.5	67.9	8.4	69.3
4...........................	5.1	73.4	4.9	53.8	5.6	73.5	5.2	74.4
5...........................	3.5	76.9	4.4	58.2	4.1	77.5	3.5	77.9
6...........................	2.3	79.3	3.6	61.8	2.1	79.6	2.3	80.2
7...........................	1.7	80.9	2.0	63.8	1.5	81.2	1.7	81.8
8...........................	1.3	82.3	1.9	65.7	1.1	82.3	1.3	83.1
9...........................	1.0	83.3	1.2	66.9	0.7	82.9	1.0	84.1

Note: Persons could have been in prison for more than one offense, the most serious of which is reported.

Table 4. Cumulative Percent of Prisoners Released in 29 States in 2005 After Serving a Sentence for Rape/Sexual Assault or Assault Who Had an Arrest That Led to a Conviction After Release

(Percent.)

Year after release	All prisoners	Most serious commitment offense	
		Rape/sexual assault	Assault
1....................	25.4	12.8	22.4
2....................	39.6	22.3	37.7
3....................	49.0	28.4	46.4
4....................	55.3	34.2	53.5
5....................	59.8	38.5	58.3
6....................	63.1	42.2	62.1
7....................	65.7	45.2	65.1
8....................	67.8	48.1	67.7
9....................	69.2	49.6	68.8

Note: Estimates based on time from release to first arrest that led to a conviction among prisoners released in 29 of the study's 30 states (all but Louisiana). Persons could have been in prison for more than one offense, the most serious of which is reported.

Table 5. Cumulative Percent of Prisoners Released in 30 States in 2005 After Serving a Sentence for Rape/Sexual Assault Who Were Arrested for Rape/Sexual Assault After Release, by Age and Year After Release

(Percent.)

Most serious commitment offense	Year 1	Year 2	Year 3	Year 4	Year 5	Year 6	Year 7	Year 8	Year 9
All prisoners	0.5	0.9	1.2	1.5	1.8	2.0	2.2	2.4	2.6
Prisoners released after serving a sentence for rape/sexual assault...	1.9	3.5	4.4	5.1	5.9	6.3	6.9	7.6	7.7
Age at release									
24 or younger...................................	2.5	7.1	9.4	9.7	10.3	10.5	11.2	11.7	11.8
25–39...	2.8	3.8	4.3	4.9	6.3	6.8	7.5	8.2	8.4
40 or older	0.8	2.2	3.0	3.9	4.2	4.5	5.0	5.8	5.9
Race/Hispanic origin									
White[1]	1.6	2.6	3.2	3.9	4.6	5.1	5.5	5.8	6.2
Black/African American[1]...................	1.7	4.4	4.6	6.0	6.5	6.8	7.7	9.7	9.7
Hispanic/Latino	3.3	4.9	7.5	7.5	8.1	8.1	8.6	8.6	8.6
Other[1,2]...	1.0	2.6	3.8	4.1	4.5	4.7	6.7	6.7	6.9

Note: Persons could have been in prison for more than one offense, the most serious of which is reported. Data on prisoners' sex and age at release were known for 100% of cases, and race/Hispanic origin was known for 99.86%. Details may not sum to total due to rounding.
[1]Excludes persons of Hispanic/Latino origin (e.g., White refers to non-Hispanic Whites and Black refers to non-Hispanic Blacks).
[2]Includes Asians, Native Hawaiians, and Other Pacific Islanders; American Indians and Alaska Natives; and persons of two or more races.

Table 6. Cumulative Percent of Prisoners Released in 30 States in 2005 After Serving a Sentence for Rape/Sexual Assault or Assault Who Were Arrested Outside Their State of Release, by Year of Release

(Percent.)

Year after release	All prisoners	Most serious commitment offense	
		Rape/sexual assault	Assault
1..	3.3	2.1	3.6
2..	5.7	3.4	6.4
3..	7.7	5.2	8.4
4..	9.3	6.7	10.2
5	10.8	8.2	11.9
6..	12.1	9.4	13.1
7..	13.3	10.1	14.4
8..	14.4	10.6	15.6
9..	15.4	11.4	16.7

Note: Persons could have been in prison for more than one offense, the most serious of which is reported.

Table 7. Annual Arrest Percentage of Prisoners Released in 30 States in 2005 After Serving a Sentence for Rape/Sexual Assault or Assault, by Prisoner Characteristics

(Number; percent.)

Characteristic	Number of released prisoners	Total arrested within 9 years	Year 1	Year 2	Year 3	Year 4	Year 5	Year 6	Year 7	Year 8	Year 9
All prisoners	401,288	83.3	43.8	37.6	34.2	31.9	30.0	27.9	27.2	25.9	24.0
Prisoners released after serving a sentence for rape/sexual assault	20,195	66.9	29.0	26.6	24.2	19.3	20.2	19.5	17.6	17.3	16.1
Age at release											
24 or younger..........................	2,486	83.8	42.9	37.5	29.7	21.2	26.9	21.9	25.5	27.5	18.7
25–39....................................	8,867	72.0	32.7	30.4	27.5	21.7	23.1	22.5	19.3	17.5	17.5
40 or older	8,842	57.1	21.3	19.7	19.2	16.3	15.3	15.7	13.7	14.3	14.0
Race/Hispanic origin											
White[1].................................	10,499	61.3	23.8	22.0	20.1	16.7	16.4	17.2	14.0	15.9	12.8
Black/African American[1]..........	5,482	78.6	35.0	34.1	30.1	24.8	27.4	21.6	26.0	25.3	25.7
Hispanic/Latino	3,459	64.9	34.9	26.6	27.1	16.4	20.9	22.4	15.1	9.2	11.2
Other[1,2]................................	713	66.9	25.4	31.7	19.7	24.3	11.6	17.2	13.6	11.5	9.8
Prisoners released after serving a sentence for assault	38,468	82.9	43.2	38.1	34.0	32.4	31.3	29.0	29.0	28.4	24.8
Age at release											
24 or younger..........................	7,468	87.3	50.9	43.5	35.4	31.0	35.5	29.1	25.8	29.1	27.4
25–39....................................	20,511	85.2	44.1	39.1	36.1	33.8	32.2	30.0	32.1	30.8	26.7
40 or older	10,489	75.4	35.9	32.4	28.9	30.7	26.5	27.1	25.3	23.4	19.2
Race/Hispanic origin											
White[1].................................	13,841	80.3	38.8	34.5	32.5	29.7	30.9	29.7	27.5	26.6	23.1
Black/African American[1]..........	14,562	86.4	45.2	41.4	35.7	35.0	31.2	30.3	29.9	28.9	25.6
Hispanic/Latino	8,629	80.6	46.0	37.5	32.8	33.0	31.7	24.9	28.8	28.7	25.4
Other[1,2]................................	1,312	85.0	47.0	44.6	34.6	29.5	34.0	32.6	33.1	37.6	24.8

Note: Persons could have been in prison for more than one offense, the most serious of which is reported. Percentages exclude missing data. Data on prisoners' age at release were reported for 100% of cases, and race/Hispanic origin was known for 99.86%.
[1]Excludes persons of Hispanic/Latino origin (e.g., White refers to non-Hispanic Whites and Black refers to non-Hispanic Blacks).
[2]Includes Asians, Native Hawaiians, and Other Pacific Islanders; American Indians and Alaska Natives; and persons of two or more races.

Table 8. Annual Arrest Percentage of Prisoners Released in 30 States in 2005 After Serving a Sentence for Rape/Sexual Assault or Assault, by Types of Post-Release Arrest Offenses

(Percent.)

Most serious commitment offense and type	Number of released prisoners	Year 1	Year 2	Year 3	Year 4	Year 5	Year 6	Year 7	Year 8	Year 9
Commitment offense: rape or sexual assault										
Post-release arrest offense										
Violent..	28.1	6.6	6.4	5.3	5.4	5.3	3.7	4.1	3.0	2.6
Property......................................	24.2	5.7	5.7	4.7	4.0	4.7	3.8	4.2	4.5	3.1
Drug	18.5	4.2	4.5	3.8	1.9	3.3	3.0	3.1	3.1	3.3
Public order................................	58.9	23.4	20.9	19.5	15.3	14.7	14.7	13.9	13.4	13.0
Commitment offense: rape or sexual assault										
Post-release arrest offense										
Violent..	50.7	12.9	13.1	10.4	11.1	11.6	8.1	8.6	8.6	7.5
Property......................................	44.3	12.5	10.7	11.1	8.8	7.9	8.0	8.7	8.9	8.3
Drug	43.2	11.5	12.1	7.8	9.2	8.7	8.1	8.7	9.0	8.0
Public order................................	69.6	30.9	25.1	23.2	22.4	20.0	19.3	19.2	19.6	16.3

Note: Persons could have been in prison for more than one offense, the most serious of which is reported.

Table 9. Types of Offenses for Which Prisoners Were Arrested Within 9 Years Following Release in 30 States in 2005, by Most Serious Commitment Offense

(Number; percent.)

Post-release arrest offense	Number of post-release arrest offenses	Most serious commitment offense							
		Violent							
		Homicide	Rape/sexual assault	Robbery	Assault	Other violent	Year 7	Year 8	Year 9
Any arrest after release									
All released prisoners	43.9	37.7	34.3	31.9	30.1	28.0	27.4	25.9	24.0
Violent*	38.9	33.7	30.4	28.1	27.2	25.0	25.2	24.1	21.4
Property	50.8 A	41.6 A	38.3 A	36.5 A	33.2 A	31.3 A	30.6 A	29.3 A	27.6 A
Drug	42.8 A	38.5 A	34.9 A	31.8 A	30.2 A	37.6 A	26.7 A	25.0	23.4 A
Public order	40.5	34.3	31.2	28.9	28.0	27.0 A	25.8	23.8	22.5
Violent arrest after release									
All released prisoners	9.0	8.3	7.6	7.6	7.2	6.5	6.6	6.0	5.2
Violent*	11.0	10.2	8.4	8.8	8.9	6.8	6.9	6.5	5.8
Property	9.3 A	7.8 A	7.7	7.8 A	6.9 A	7.1	7.2	6.2	5.7
Drug	6.8 A	7.2 A	6.7 A	6.2 A	6.2 A	5.3 A	5.7 A	5.4 A	4.4 A
Public order	9.7	8.6 A	8.3	8.1	7.3 A	7.2	6.6	6.4	5.3
Arrest after release for same type as most serious commitment offense[1]									
All released prisoners	21.0	18.0	15.6	14.5	13.7	12.2	11.8	11.5	10.6
Violent	11.0	10.2	8.4	8.8	8.9	6.8	6.9	6.5	5.8
Property	25.0	20.6	17.6	16.9	15.6	14.2	14.1	13.9	12.6
Drug	22.0	19.6	17.2	15.0	13.8	12.2	11.5	11.4	11.0
Public order	29.2	23.8	21.1	19.2	18.4	18.2	17.0	16.0	14.5
Arrest after release for different type as most serious commitment offense[2]									
All released prisoners	36.1	30.9	28.0	26.3	24.6	23.1	22.8	21.5	20.0
Violent	35.2	30.4	27.6	25.1	23.9	22.7	22.8	22.0	19.5
Property	42.4	34.4	31.6	30.6	27.6	26.0	25.6	24.1	23.0
Drug	34.8	31.3	27.9	26.0	24.6	22.7	22.2	20.7	19.1
Public order	26.3	22.6	20.7	19.8	18.7	17.9	18.0	16.6	16.0

Note: Persons could have been in prison for more than one offense; the most serious one is reported in this table. Each arrest may include more than one type of offense. "Type of offense" refers to the categories of violent, property, drug, and public order. Public order includes 0.8% of cases in which prisoners' most serious offense was unspecified.
* = Comparison group.
A = Difference with comparison group is significant at the 95% confidence level.
[1,2] Percentages in these two categories do not sum to the "any arrest after release" category because categories overlap.

Table 10. Characteristics of Male Prisoners Released in 30 States in 2005, by Most Serious Commitment Offense

(Number; percent.)

Characteristic	All male prisoners	Most serious commitment offense		
		Rape/sexual assault	Assault	Other than rape/sexual assault
Total	100.0	100.0	100.0	100.0
Race/Hispanic origin				
White[1]..	38.4	51.7	36.1	37.6
Black/African American[1]	40.9	27.4	37.2	41.7
Hispanic/Latino..............................	18.4	17.3	23.2	18.4
Other[1,2]	2.4	3.6	3.4	2.3
Age at release				
24 or younger	18.3	12.3	19.6	18.7
25–29	19.7	15.9	21.7	20.0
30–34	15.9	14.0	17.1	16.0
35–39	15.2	13.9	14.7	15.3
40 or older	30.8	44.0	26.9	30.1
Median (years)...............................	34	38	32	34
Mean	34.9	38.9	34.0	34.6
Type of prison release				
Conditional	74.3	68.0	76.0	74.7
Unconditional...............................	25.7	32.0	24.0	25.3
Maximum sentence length[3]				
1–2 years	18.1	10.4	12.4	18.6
2–5 years	44.6	34.4	56.4	45.2
5–10 years	22.5	27.8	20.5	22.2
10 years or more	14.7	27.4	10.7	14.0
Median (months)...........................	39	60	36	36
Number of prior arrests per released prisoner[4]				
4 or fewer	24.5	52.0	24.2	22.8
5–9	30.4	26.8	30.2	30.6
10 or more	45.2	21.2	45.6	46.6
Median (arrests)	9	4	9	9
Mean	11.0	6.4	10.9	11.3
At least one prior arrest for:				
Drug offense.................................	70.5	30.6	58.5	72.9
Property offense............................	81.2	56.1	78.6	82.7
Number of released prisoners......................	358,398	19,871	35,771	338,527

Note: Persons could have been in prison for more than one offense, the most serious of which is reported. Percentages exclude missing data. Data on male prisoners' age at release were reported for 100% of cases; race/Hispanic origin, for 99.85%; type of prison release, for 98.21%; and maximum sentence length, for 99.72%.
[1]Excludes persons of Hispanic/Latino origin (e.g., White refers to non-Hispanic Whites and Black refers to non-Hispanic Blacks).
[2]Includes Asians, Native Hawaiians, and Other Pacific Islanders; American Indians and Alaska Natives; and persons of two or more races.
[3]Based on the released prisoners' total maximum sentence length for all commitment offenses. Study excludes prisoners sentenced to less than one year.
[4]Includes arrests for any type of crime prior to the prisoners' date of release in 2005.

Table 11. Characteristics of Female Prisoners Released in 30 States in 2005, by Most Serious Commitment Offense

(Number; percent.)

Characteristic	All female prisoners	Most serious commitment offense	
		Rape/sexual assault	Assault
Total	100.0	100.0	100.0
Race/Hispanic origin			
White[1]..	51.0	75.9	35.5
Black/African American[1]	33.9	14.3	47.9
Hispanic/Latino	12.3	8.6	13.0
Other[1,2]	2.9	1.2	3.6
Age at release			
24 or younger	12.0	15.0	17.2
25–29	16.6	15.9	16.0
30–34	17.1	20.1	17.4
35–39	19.7	16.1	17.6
40 or older	34.6	32.8	31.8
Median (years)..	36	34	35
Mean	36.0	35.7	34.8
Type of prison release			
Conditional	71.9	62.7	66.8
Unconditional..	28.1	37.3	33.2
Maximum sentence length[3]			
1–2 years	27.8	17.8	19.8
2–5 years	45.8	21.6	55.2
5–10 years	18.3	36.6	18.3
10 years or more	8.1	24.0	6.7
Median (months)..	36	60	36
Number of prior arrests per released prisoner[4]			
4 or fewer	28.0	78.9	35.5
5–9	29.3	12.6	30.7
10 or more..	42.7	8.5	33.8
Median (arrests)	8	2	6
Mean	10.8	3.8	9.0
At least one prior arrest for:			
Drug offense..	72.0	27.4	49.8
Property offense..	81.8	36.4	69.8
Number of released prisoners...........................	42,890	324	2,697

Note: Persons could have been in prison for more than one offense, the most serious of which is reported. Percentages exclude missing data. Data on female prisoners' age at release were reported for 100% of cases; race/Hispanic origin, for 99.97%; and maximum sentence length, for 99.68%.
[1]Excludes persons of Hispanic/Latino origin (e.g., White refers to non-Hispanic Whites and Black refers to non-Hispanic Blacks).
[2]Includes Asians, Native Hawaiians, and Other Pacific Islanders; American Indians and Alaska Natives; and persons of two or more races.
[3]Based on the released prisoners' total maximum sentence length for all commitment offenses. Study excludes prisoners sentenced to less than one year.
[4]Includes arrests for any type of crime prior to the prisoners' date of release in 2005.

Table 12. Cumulative Arrest Percentage of Male Prisoners Released in 30 States in 2005 After Serving a Sentence for Rape/Sexual Assault or Assault Who Were Arrested After Release, by Year of Release

(Percent.)

| Year after release | All male prisoners | Most serious commitment offense | |
		Rape/sexual assault	Assault
1...	44.8	29.0	44.1
2...	61.1	42.0	60.3
3...	69.4	49.1	68.9
4...	74.4	53.9	74.5
5...	77.9	58.4	78.5
6...	80.2	62.0	80.6
7...	81.8	64.0	82.1
8...	83.1	65.9	83.1
9...	84.0	67.1	83.8

Note: Persons could have been in prison for more than one offense, the most serious of which is reported.

Table 13. Cumulative Arrest Percentage of Female Prisoners Released in 30 States in 2005 After Serving a Sentence for Rape/Sexual Assault or Assault Who Were Arrested After Release, by Year of Release

(Percent.)

| Year after release | All female prisoners | Most serious commitment offense | |
		Rape/sexual assault	Assault
1...	35.1	28.8	31.5
2...	50.8	38.1	47.0
3...	59.2	40.7	54.9
4...	64.7	44.6	60.3
5...	68.9	47.0	64.4
6...	71.4	50.0	67.1
7...	73.6	53.8	69.0
8...	75.3	53.8	70.9
9...	76.7	54.4	71.7

Note: Persons could have been in prison for more than one offense, the most serious of which is reported.

METHODOLOGY

Measuring Recidivism

Recidivism measures require three characteristics:

1. a starting event, such as a release from prison

2. a measure of failure following the starting event, such as a subsequent arrest, conviction, or return to prison

3. an observation or follow-up period that generally extends from the date of the starting event to a predefined end date (e.g., 6 months, 1 year, 3 years, 5 years, or 9 years).

This study used four outcome measures to examine the recidivism patterns of former state prisoners. Arrest data were used because they provided the offense details needed to produce these four measures for prisoners from all 30 states in the study.

1. Cumulative arrest percentage is the percentage of prisoners who had been arrested at least once at various points in the follow-up period. For example, the cumulative arrest percentage for year-5 is the percentage of all released prisoners who had at least one arrest during the 5-year period. BJS previously examined the cumulative percentage of prisoners who had a subsequent conviction or returned to prison within 5 years following release. The return-to-prison analysis for the 5-year follow-up study was limited to 23 of the study's 30 states with the data needed to identify returns to prison during the entire observation period.

2. Annual percentage of first arrests is the percentage of prisoners who had their first arrest following release during a specific year in the follow-up period. The denominator for each annual first-arrest percentage from years 1 through 9 is the total number of prisoners released in the 30 states during 2005. The numerators are the number of prisoners arrested for the first time during each of those years (i.e., they had not been arrested during a prior year in the follow-up period). The sum of the annual first-arrest percentages during a follow-up period equals the cumulative arrest percentage for the same period.

3. Annual arrest percentage of released prisoners includes those who were arrested at least once during a particular year within the follow-up period. The denominator for each percentage from years 1 through 9 is the total number of prisoners released in the 30 states during 2005. The numerators are the number of prisoners arrested during the particular year, regardless of whether they had been arrested during a prior year.

4. Annual volume of arrests is the total number of arrests of released prisoners during a particular year in the follow-up period. The total volume of arrests is the sum of each annual volume of arrests during the entire follow-up period. A prisoner may have had multiple arrests during a year or in the follow-up period, and a single arrest may have involved charges for more than one crime.

Measuring Desistance

Desistance is measured as the percentage of prisoners who, after a particular year, had no subsequent arrests during the remainder of the 9-year follow-up period. For example, if a prisoner was arrested during year-3 but was not arrested during years 4 through 9, the prisoner would be classified as having desisted during year-3. While recidivism is a measure of arrest at any point during the follow-up period, desistance is a measure of the absence of arrest between a particular point within the follow-up period and the end of the follow-up period.

Importance of Recidivism and Desistance Measures

Measures of recidivism and desistance provide information relevant to a deeper understanding of criminal behavior and the administration of justice in a wide range of policy areas. For example, law enforcement officials interested in the amount of crime committed by released prisoners can turn to statistics on the annual volume of arrests. Parole and probation agencies interested in the involvement of various types of former prisoners in criminal activities after release may focus on variations in cumulative arrest percentages. Treatment providers looking for measures of program effectiveness will be interested in desistance patterns. Additionally, task forces and policymakers examining the movement of criminals across state borders will be interested in the types of released prisoners most likely to commit new crimes (i.e., recidivate) in other states.

Sampling

This study estimates the recidivism patterns of persons released in 2005 from state prisons in 30 states. States were included in this study if the state departments of corrections could provide the prisoner records and the FBI or state identification numbers on persons released from prison during 2005. The fingerprint-based identification numbers were required to obtain the criminal history records on released prisoners. The prisoner records—obtained from the state departments of corrections through the Bureau of Justice Statistics' (BJS) National Corrections Reporting Program (NCRP)—also included each prisoner's sex, race, Hispanic origin, date of birth, confinement offenses, sentence length, type of prison release, and date of release. The 30 states whose departments of corrections submitted the NCRP data on prisoners released in 2005 included Alaska, Arkansas, California, Colorado, Florida, Georgia, Hawaii, Iowa, Louisiana, Maryland, Michigan, Minnesota, Missouri, Nebraska, Nevada, New Jersey, New York, North Carolina, North Dakota, Ohio, Oklahoma, Oregon, Pennsylvania, South Carolina, South Dakota, Texas, Utah, Virginia, Washington, and West Virginia.

Across the 30 states in 2005, a total of 412,731 prisoners were released and were eligible for this study. That number excludes 131,997 prisoners (for a total of 544,728) who were sentenced to less than one year, transferred to the custody of another authority, died in prison, were released on bond, were released to seek or participate in an appeal of a case, or escaped from prison or were absent without official leave. The first release during 2005 was used for those prisoners released multiple times during the year.

From the universe of persons released from prison in the 30 states in 2005 in this study, all males and females who were in prison for homicide were selected with certainty into the study. Analyses were done to determine the number of non-homicide prisoners that would be needed from each state's universe of released prisoners to yield a statistically sound estimate of that state's recidivism and desistance rates. As a result, states contributed different numbers of records to the final sample. To achieve the desired state-level samples, lists of all males and females imprisoned for a non-homicide offense were sorted separately by the county in which the sentence was imposed, race, Hispanic origin, age, and most serious commitment offense. The within-state sampling rate for female prisoners was double that of males to improve the precision of female recidivism and desistance estimates. The combined number of persons in the 30 state samples totaled 70,878 individuals who were representative of all state prisoners released in those states during 2005. (This number dropped to 67,966 after accounting for those who died during the subsequent 9 years, lacked criminal history records, or had invalid release records.) Each prisoner in the sample was assigned a weight based on the probability of selection within the state.

Collecting and Processing Criminal Records for Recidivism Research

In 2008, BJS entered into a data-sharing agreement with the FBI's Criminal Justice Information Services Division and the International Justice and Public Safety Network (Nlets) to allow BJS access to criminal history records through the FBI's Interstate Identification Index (III). Additionally, a data

security agreement was executed between BJS, the FBI, and Nlets to de ne the operational and technical practices used to protect the confidentiality and integrity of the criminal history data during data exchange, processing, and storage.

The FBI's III is an automated pointer system that allows authorized agencies to determine whether any state repository has criminal history records on an individual. Nlets is a computer-based network that is responsible for interstate transmissions of federal and state criminal history records. It allows authorized users to query III and send requests to states holding criminal history records on an individual. The FBI also maintains criminal history records for which it has sole responsibility for disseminating, such as information on federal arrests. The identification bureaus that operate the central repositories in each state respond automatically to requests over the Nlets network with an individual's criminal history record. Put together, these requests represent the individual's national criminal history record.

Once BJS received approval from the FBI's Institutional Review Board to conduct this recidivism study on prisoners released in 2005, Nlets transmitted the state and FBI identification numbers on the sampled prisoners to the FBI's III system to collect the criminal history records on behalf of BJS. e criminal history records include information from the state of release and all other states in which the sampled prisoners had been arrested both prior to the release in 2005 and afterward.

Nlets parsed the fields from individual criminal history records into a relational database consisting of state- and federal-specific numeric codes and text descriptions (e.g., criminal statutes and case outcome information) into a uniform record layout. NORC at the University of Chicago assisted BJS with standardizing the content of the relational database into a uniform coding structure to support national-level recidivism research.

BJS conducted a series of data-quality checks on the criminal history records to assess the accuracy and completeness of the information, including an examination of the response messages and the identification numbers that failed to match a record in III. To ensure that the correct records were received on the released prisoners using their fingerprint-based identification numbers, BJS compared other individual identifiers in the NCRP data to those reported in the criminal history records. For 98 percent of cases, a released prisoner's date of birth in the NCRP data exactly matched the prisoner's birthdate in the criminal history records. Nearly 100 percent (99.9 percent) of the NCRP and criminal history records matched prisoner sex, race, and Hispanic origin.

BJS reviewed the criminal history records for differences and inconsistencies in reporting practices and noticed some variations across states. During data processing and analysis, steps were taken to standardize the information and to minimize the impact these variations had on the overall recidivism and desistance estimates. For example, administrative (e.g., a criminal registration or the issuance of a warrant) and procedural (e.g., transferring a suspect to another jurisdiction) records embedded in the criminal history data that did not refer to an actual arrest were identified and removed. Traffic offenses (except for vehicular manslaughter, driving while intoxicated, and hit-and-run) were also excluded because the reporting of these events in the criminal history records varied widely by state.

Deaths During the Follow-Up Period

BJS documented that 2,173 of the 70,878 sampled prisoners died during the 9-year follow-up period, and BJS removed these cases from the recidivism and desistance analysis along with four additional cases that were determined to be invalid release records. The fingerprint-verified death notices obtained through the FBI's III system were used to identify some of the sampled prisoners who died within the 9 years following release in 2005. Additional deaths were identified through the Social Security Administration's (SSA) public Death Master File (DMF). While the public DMF provided a more complete source of death information than the FBI's III system, the public DMF provided death information only for the years 2005 to 2011. Therefore, the identification of those who died between 2012 and 2014 was limited to the FBI's III data, which included only fingerprint-verified deaths. The number of released prisoners who were identified as dead between 2005 and 2011 in the public DMF is an undercount of the actual number of deaths within the sample. Due to state disclosure laws, the public DMF does not include information on certain protected state death records received via SSA's contracts with the states. Beginning in 2011, the SSA removed more than 4 million state-reported death records from the public DMF and began adding fewer records to the public DMF. As a result, the public DMF contains an undercount of annual deaths.

The extent to which the public DMF undercounts the annual number of deaths is not exactly known. Analyses of deaths in the public DMF compared to those reported by the Centers for Disease Control and Prevention's (CDC) mortality counts suggest that the public DMF undercounted the overall number of deaths in the United States by about 10 percent in 2005. The undercount increased during succeeding years, and as of 2010, the public DMF contained less than half (45 percent) of the deaths reported by the CDC. If the number of released prisoners who died during the follow-up period and were removed from the recidivism and desistance analysis were adjusted to account for this undercount, the estimated cumulative recidivism rate would likely increase by about one percentage point.

Missing Criminal History Records

Among the 68,701 sampled prisoners not identified as deceased during the follow-up period, BJS did not receive criminal history records on 735 prisoners, either because the state departments of correction were unable to provide their FBI or state identification number or because the prisoner had an identification number that did not link to a criminal history record either in the FBI or state record repositories. To account for the missing criminal history records and to ensure the recidivism and desistance statistics were representative of all 68,701 prisoners in the analysis, BJS developed weighting class adjustments to account for those prisoners without criminal history information to reduce nonresponse bias.

To create the statistical adjustments, the 68,701 sampled prisoners were stratified into groups by crossing the two categories of sex (male or female), five categories of age at release (24 or younger, 25 to 29, 30 to 34, 35 to 39, or 40 or older), four categories of race/Hispanic origin (non-Hispanic White, non-Hispanic Black, Hispanic, or other race), and four categories of the most serious commitment offense (violent, property, drug, or public order). Within each of the subgroups, statistical weights were applied to the data of the 67,966 prisoners with criminal history information to allow their data to represent the 735 prisoners without criminal history information.

Conducting Tests of Statistical Significance

This study was based on a sample, not a complete enumeration, so the estimates are subject to sampling error. One measure of the sampling error associated with an estimate is the standard error. The standard error can vary from one estimate to the next. In general, an estimate with a smaller standard error provides a more reliable approximation of the true value than an estimate with a larger standard error. Estimates with relatively large standard errors should be interpreted with caution. BJS conducted tests to determine whether differences in the estimates were statistically significant once sampling error was taken into account.

All differences discussed in this report are statistically significant at the 95 percent confidence interval level. Standard errors were generated using Stata, a statistical so ware package that calculates sampling errors for data from complex sample surveys.

Offense Definitions

Violent offenses include homicide, rape or sexual assault, robbery, assault, and other miscellaneous or unspecified violent offenses.

Property offenses include burglary, fraud or forgery, larceny, motor vehicle theft, and other miscellaneous or unspecified property offenses.

Drug offenses include possession, trafficking, and other miscellaneous or unspecified drug offenses.

Public order offenses include violations of the peace or order of the community or threats to the public health or safety through unacceptable conduct, interference with a governmental authority, or the violation of civil rights or liberties. This category includes weapons offenses, driving under the influence, probation and parole violation, obstruction of justice, commercialized vice, disorderly conduct, and other miscellaneous or unspecified offenses.

Arrests for probation and parole violations

In this report, arrests for probation and parole violations were included as public order offenses. Excluding arrests for probation and parole violations from the analysis would have had only a small impact on the recidivism rates. Excluding probation and parole violations from the annual arrest percentages, 39.5 percent of prisoners released in 30 states in 2005 were arrested in year-1, 34.3 percent were arrested in year-2, 31.5 percent in year-3, 29.7 percent in year-4, 28.2 percent in year-5, 25.9 percent in year-6, 25.9 percent in year-7, 24.6 percent in year-8, and 23.0 percent in year-9. Overall, excluding probation and parole violations, 82.4 percent of prisoners released in 30 states in 2005 were arrested within 9 years. In other words, 99 percent of prisoners who were arrested during the 9-year follow-up period were arrested for an offense other than a probation or parole violation.

PART 11

Victims of Identity Theft, 2018

HIGHLIGHTS

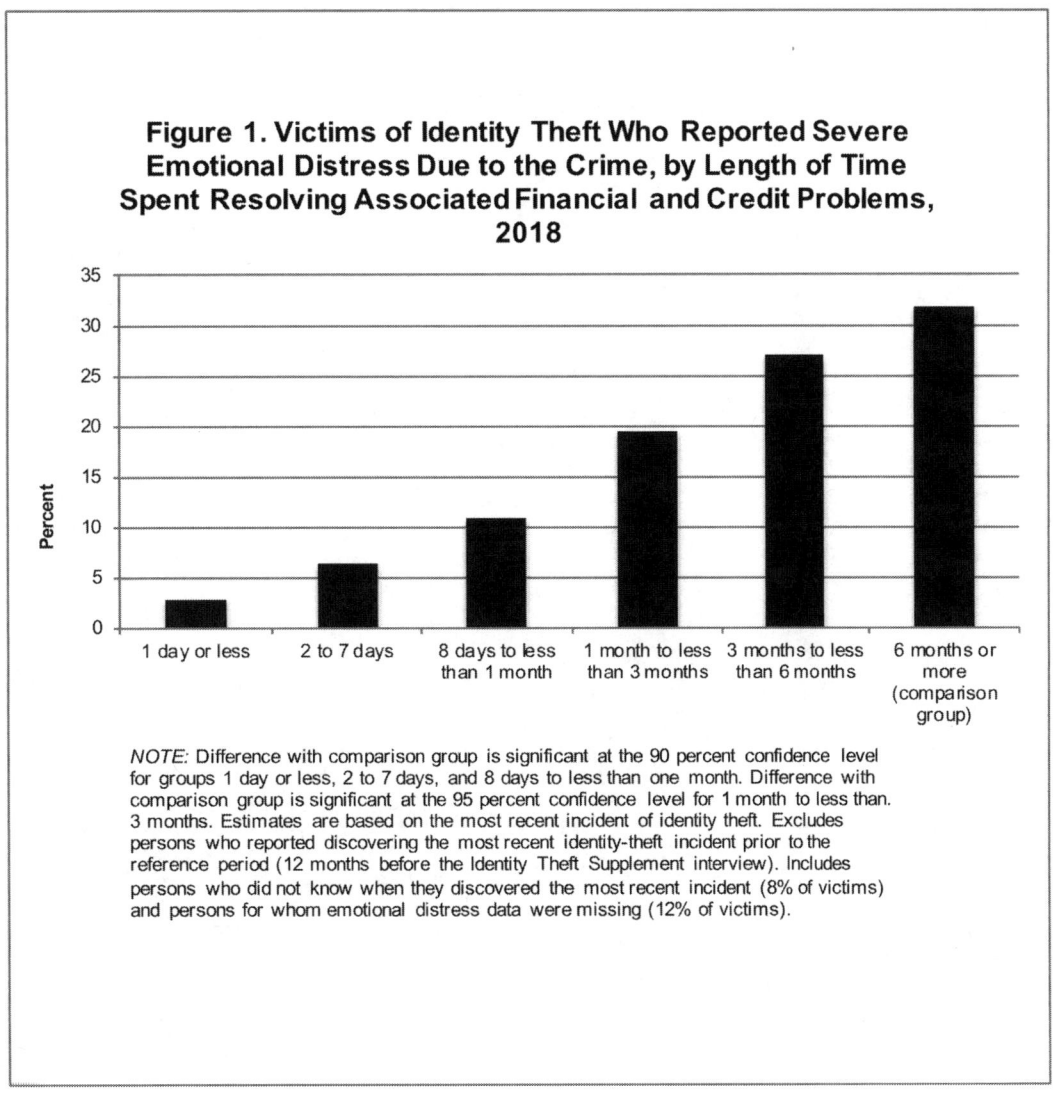

Figure 1. Victims of Identity Theft Who Reported Severe Emotional Distress Due to the Crime, by Length of Time Spent Resolving Associated Financial and Credit Problems, 2018

NOTE: Difference with comparison group is significant at the 90 percent confidence level for groups 1 day or less, 2 to 7 days, and 8 days to less than one month. Difference with comparison group is significant at the 95 percent confidence level for 1 month to less than 3 months. Estimates are based on the most recent incident of identity theft. Excludes persons who reported discovering the most recent identity-theft incident prior to the reference period (12 months before the Identity Theft Supplement interview). Includes persons who did not know when they discovered the most recent incident (8% of victims) and persons for whom emotional distress data were missing (12% of victims).

- In 2018, approximately 9 percent of persons age 16 or older had been victims of identity theft during the prior 12 months.

- For 90 percent of identity-theft victims, the most recent incident involved only the misuse or attempted misuse of at least one type of existing account, such as a credit card or bank account.

- More than half (55 percent) of all victims who resolved the financial and credit problems associated with identity theft did so in 1 day or less.

- Monetary losses across all identity theft incidents totaled approximately $15.1 billion.

- Half of all victims of identity theft (51 percent) lived in households with incomes of $75,000 or more.

Table 1. Percent of Respondents Who Reported Experiencing Identity Theft in the Past 12 Months, by Most Recent Incident's Discovery and Type of Theft, 2018

(Percent.)

Type of identity theft		Discovered within reference period		
	Total	Yes[1]	No[2]	Unknown[3]
Total	100.0	89.4	3.0	7.7
Misused only one type of existing account ..	100.0	89.8	2.5	7.7
Credit card...	100.0	89.1	2.2	8.7
Bank..	100.0	90.3	2.8	7.0
Other...	100.0	91.6	2.8	5.5
Opened new account only	100.0	88.5	3.3	8.2
Misused personal information only.............	100.0	77.9	12.9	9.2
Misused multiple types...............................	100.0	89.6	4.1	6.3
Existing account only[4]..............................	100.0	90.8	3.5	5.7
Other[5]...	100.0	87.0	5.4	7.5

NOTE: Details may not sum to totals due to rounding. Estimates are based on the most recent incident of identity theft and unweighted data. The reference period is 12 months before the Identity Theft Supplement interview.
[1]The most recent identity-theft incident was discovered during the reference period.
[2]The most recent identity-theft incident was discovered prior to the reference period.
[3]The most recent identity-theft incident was discovered on an unknown date.
[4]Includes victims who experienced two or more of the following: misuse of a credit card, bank account, or other existing account.
[5]Includes victims who experienced two or more of the following: misuse of an existing account, personal information to open a new account, or personal information for other fraudulent purposes.

Table 2. The Most Recent Incident of Identity Theft Based on All Reported Incidents and Restricted Data, by Type of Theft, 2018

(Number; percent.)

Type of identity theft	Number of victims		Percent of all persons age 16 years or older	
	Full data*	Restricted[1]	Full data*	Restricted[1]
Total	23,901,320	23,183,020	9.3	9.0
Misused only one type of existing account	20,204,030	19,663,220	7.8	7.6
Credit card..	9,871,670	9,650,050	3.8	3.7
Bank	8,725,600	8,467,070	3.4	3.3
Other	1,606,760	1,546,110	0.6	0.6
Opened new account only	1,032,410	996,000	0.4	0.4
Misused personal information only.................	717,060	634,780	0.3	0.2
Misused multiple types...............................	1,947,820	1,889,010	0.8	0.7
Existing account only[2]...............................	1,329,760	1,295,940	0.5	0.5
Other[3]...	618,060	593,070	0.2	0.2

NOTE: Details may not sum to totals due to rounding. Estimates are based on the most recent incident of identity theft. In 2018, there were 258 million persons age 16 or older living in noninstitutionalized, residential settings in the United States.
* = Comparison group.
[1]Excludes persons who reported discovering the most recent identity-theft incident prior to the reference period (12 months before the Identity Theft Supplement interview). Includes persons who did not know when they discovered the most recent incident (8% of victims).
[2]Includes victims who experienced two or more of the following: misuse of a credit card, bank account, or other existing account.
[3]Includes victims who experienced two or more of the following: misuse of an existing account, personal information to open a new account, or personal information for other fraudulent purposes.

Table 3. Victims of Identity Theft, by Type of Most Recent Incident of Theft, 2018

(Number; percent.)

Type of identity theft	Number of victims	Percent of all persons	Percent of all victims
Total	23,183,020	9.0	100.0
Only one type of existing account	19,663,220	7.6	84.8
Credit card*	9,650,050	3.7	41.6
Bank	9,650,050 [B]	3.3 [B]	36.5 [B]
Other	1,546,110 [B]	0.6 [B]	6.7 [B]
Opened new account only	996,000 [B]	0.4 [B]	4.3 [B]
Misused personal information only......................	634,780 [B]	0.2 [B]	2.7 [B]
Multiple types...	1,889,010 [B]	0.7 [B]	8.1 [B]
Existing account only[1]...................................	1,295,940 [B]	0.5 [B]	5.6 [B]
Other[2]...	593,070 [B]	0.2 [B]	2.6 [B]

NOTE: Details may not sum to totals due to rounding. Estimates are based on the most recent incident of identity theft. Excludes persons who reported discovering the most recent identity-theft incident prior to the reference period (12 months before the Identity Theft Supplement interview). Includes persons who did not know when they discovered the most recent incident (8% of victims). In 2018, there were 258 million persons age 16 or older living in noninstitutionalized, residential settings in the United States.
* = Comparison group.
B = Significant difference from comparison year at 95% confidence level.
[1]Includes victims who experienced two or more of the following: misuse of a credit card, bank account, or other existing account.
[2]Includes victims who experienced two or more of the following: misuse of an existing account, personal information to open a new account, or personal information for other fraudulent purposes.

Table 4. Demographic Characteristics of Victims of Identity Theft and the U.S. Residential Population Age 16 Years or Older, 2018

(Number; percent.)

Demographic characteristics	Victims of identity theft			U.S. residential population	
	Number of victims	Percent of U.S. residential population age 16 or older[1]	Percent of all victims	Number of persons age 16 or older	Percent of persons age 16 or older
Total	23,183,020	9.0	100.0	258,175,200	100.0
Sex					
Male*...	11,219,660	9.0	48.4	125,188,140	48.5
Female..	11,963,360 [B]	9.0	51.6 [B]	132,987,070	51.5
Race/Ethnicity					
White[2]*.....................................	16,560,830	10.1	71.4	163,585,560	63.4
Black[2]	2,100,740 [B]	6.8 [B]	9.1 [B]	30,846,330	11.9
Hispanic......................................	2,719,120 [B]	6.4 [B]	11.7 [B]	42,553,730	16.5
Asian[2].......................................	1,192,880 [B]	7.8 [B]	5.1 [B]	15,277,670	5.9
Other[2,3].....................................	609,440 [B]	10.3	2.6 [B]	5,911,910	2.3
Age					
16 to 17 years............................	99,310 [B]	1.2 [B]	0.4 [B]	7,979,760	3.1
18 to 24 years............................	1,759,310 [B]	5.9 [B]	7.6 [B]	29,916,270	11.6
25 to 34 years............................	4,410,270 [B]	9.8 [B]	19.0 [B]	44,892,670	17.4
35 to 49 years*..........................	6,772,500	11.0	29.2	61,627,990	23.9
50 to 64 years............................	6,478,060	10.3 [A]	27.9	62,994,100	24.4
65 years or older........................	3,661,570 [B]	7.2 [B]	15.8 [B]	50,764,410	19.7
Household income					
$24,999 or less..........................	2,847,190 [B]	6.0 [B]	12.3 [B]	47,499,520	18.4
$25,000 to $49,999	4,323,590 [B]	6.5 [B]	18.6 [B]	66,365,670	25.7
$50,000 to $74,999	4,211,840 [B]	8.8 [B]	18.2 [B]	47,790,700	18.5
$75,000 or more*	11,800,400	12.2	50.9	96,519,310	37.4

NOTE: Details may not sum to totals due to rounding. Estimates are based on the most recent incident of identity theft. Missing data for household income were imputed. Excludes persons who reported discovering the most recent identity-theft incident prior to the reference period (12 months before the Identity Theft Supplement interview). Includes persons who did not know when they discovered the most recent incident (8% of victims).
* = Comparison group.
A = Difference with comparison group is significant at the 90% confidence level.
B = Significant difference from comparison year at 95% confidence level.
[1]Estimates are based on the number of persons in each category. For example, the percentage for males is the number of male victims of identity theft divided by the total number of males age 16 or older multiplied by 100.
[2]Excludes persons of Hispanic origin (e.g., White refers to non-Hispanic Whites and Black refers to non-Hispanic Blacks).
[3]Includes Native Hawaiians, Other Pacific Islanders, American Indians, Alaska Natives, and persons of two or more races.

Table 5. Ways Victims Discovered Identity Theft, by Type of Theft, 2018

(Percent; number.)

Way victims discovered identity theft	Any identity theft	Misuse of exiating account only[1]*	Other identity theft[2]
Total	100.0	100.0	100.0
Contacted by financial institution about suspicious activity......	43.9	46.0	12.3[B]
Noticed fraudulent charges on account...................................	20.1	21.3	2.5[B!]
Noticed money missing from account	9.4	9.9	1.1 B[!]
Contacted financial institution to report a theft........................	6.6	6.9	2.4[B]
Credit card declined, check bounced, or account closed due to insufficient funds..................	3.4	3.5	1.0[B!]
Notified by company or agency..	5.1	3.6	27.6[B]
Received a bill or contacted about an unpaid bill.....................	3.3	2.5	15.4[B]
Problems with applying for a loan, applying for governmental benefits, or filing income taxes...........	1.1	0.4	11.5[B]
Discovered through credit report or credit monitoring service..	1.9	1.4	9.7[B]
Received merchandise or card that victim did not order or did not receive product the victim ordered........	0.6	0.4	4.1[B]
Notified by police...	0.3	0.1	3.1[B]
Another way[3]...	4.3	4.0	9.3[B]
Number of victims...	23,111,320	21,686,080	1,425,240

NOTE: Estimates are based on the most recent incident of identity theft. Excludes persons who reported discovering the most recent identity-theft incident prior to the reference period (12 months before the Identity Theft Supplement interview). Includes persons who did not know when they discovered the most recent incident (8% of victims).
! = Interpret with caution. Estimate is based on 10 or fewer sample cases, or coefficient of variation is greater than 50%.
* = Comparison group.
B = Significant difference from comparison year at 95% confidence level.
[1]Includes identity-theft incidents involving only the misuse of one type of existing account or the misuse of multiple types of existing accounts.
[2]Includes the following identity-theft incidents: the misuse of at least one type of existing account and the misuse of personal information to open a new account or for other fraudulent purposes; and the misuse of personal information to open a new account or for other fraudulent purposes.
[3]Includes noticing from suspicious contact, such as phishing; having problems logging into or accessing account; noticing account information was missing or stolen; someone else notifying the respondent; and discovery in other ways.

Table 6. Victims of Identity Theft Who Knew How the Offender Obtained Their Personal Information, by Method Offender Used and Type of Theft, 2018

(Dollars; percent.)

Type of identity theft	Number of victims who knew how the offender obtained their personal information	Method offender used to obtain personal information				
		Lost/stolen from place[1]	Purchase/transaction[2]*	Hacking computer/scam email or phone call	Stolen from files/misused by person with access[3]	Other
Total	5,821,510	15.7[B]	47.6	7.8[B]	21.7[B]	7.2[B]
Misused only one type of existing account	4,653,250	14.3[B]	53.8	7.4[B]	17.3[B]	7.2[B]
Credit card..	1,950,340	12.7[B]	56.8	6.9[B]	18.3[B]	5.2[B]
Bank...	2,358,870	16.7[B]	57.9	5.3[B]	14.1[B]	6.1[B]
Other..	344,050	6.5 !	9.1	24.8[B]	34.2[B]	25.4[B]
Opened new account only	299,170	19.9[B]	3.0[!]	10.6[B]	55.0[B]	11.6[B]
Misused personal information only.................	162,940	20.3[B]	<0.1 !	8.1[B]	63.5[B]	8.1[B]
Misused multiple types....................................	706,190	22.0[B]	36.8	9.4[B]	29.6[B]	5.0[B]

NOTE: Estimates are based on the most recent incident of identity theft and on the 5.8 million victims (25% of all victims) who knew how the offender obtained their information. Excludes persons who reported discovering the most recent identity-theft incident prior to the reference period (12 months before the Identity Theft Supplement interview). Includes persons who did not know when they discovered the most recent incident (8% of victims).
* = Comparison group.
! = Interpret with caution. Estimate is based on 10 or fewer sample cases, or coefficient of variation is greater than 50%.
B = Significant difference from comparison group at 95% confidence level.
[1]Includes lost information that someone found and information that was stolen from the mail or from a place where it was stored, including a wallet, a home, an office, or a car.
[2]Includes information that was stolen during in-person and online transactions, including by use of a skimmer or card reader.
[3]Includes information that was stolen from personnel files at a place of employment, stolen from an office or a company that had the victimís personal information in its files, or used without permission by someone with access to such files.

Table 7. Financial Loss from Victims' Most Recent Incident of Identity Theft, by Type of Loss and Theft, 2018

(Dollars; percent; number.)

Type of loss	Total identity theft	Misused only one type of existing account			Opened new account only	Misused personal information only*	Misused multiple types	
		Credit card	Bank	Other			Existing account only[1]	Other[2]
Any Loss[3]								
Mean...........................	$800	$610 [B]	$660 [B]	$490 [B]	$2,850	$3,560	$1,030 [B]	$3,060
Median........................	$200	$200	$200	$100	$800	$1,000	$300	$600
Percent experiencing a loss	69.3	72.1 [B]	75.0 [B]	48.2 [B]	38.1	32.4	77.8 [B]	69.2 [B]
Direct[4,5]								
Mean...........................	$800	$610 [B]	$660 [B]	$490 [B]	$3,000	$4,400	$1,010 [B]	$3,050
Median........................	$200	$200	$200	$100	$800	$2,000	$300	$600
Percent experiencing a loss	68.4	71.7 [B]	74.3 [B]	47.7 [B]	35.6 [B]	25.6	77.1 [B]	67.5 [B]
Indirect[6]								
Mean...........................	$160	$100 [A]	$120	$100 [A]	$260	$200	$300	$380
Median........................	$30	<$10	$30	$50	$50	$30	$100	$60
Percent experiencing a loss	4.8	3.1 [B]	5.1 [B]	2.6 [B]	7.4 [A]	12.8	7.5 [A]	14.8
Total Out of Pocket								
Mean...........................	$640	$440 [B]	$560 [A]	$320 [B]	$1,380	$1,290	$910	$1,150
Median........................	$100	$70	$100	$100	$200	$200	$200	$200
Percent experiencing a loss	12.1	7.9 [B]	13.9 [A]	13.8 [B]	11.6 [B]	19.7	20.8	24.2
Number of Victims	23,183,020	9,650,050	8,467,070	1,546,110	996,000	634,780	1,295,940	593,070

NOTE: stimates are based on the most recent incident of identity theft. Means and percentages were calculated using SPSS Complex Samples software. Excludes persons who reported discovering the most recent identity-theft incident prior to the reference period (12 months before the Identity Theft Supplement interview). Includes persons who did not know when they discovered the most recent incident (8% of victims).
* = Comparison group.
A = Significant difference from comparison year at 90% confidence level.
B = Significant difference from comparison year at 95% confidence level.
[1]Includes victims who experienced two or more of the following: misuse of a credit card, bank account, or other existing account.
[2]Includes victims who experienced two or more of the following: misuse of an existing account, personal information to open a new account, or personal information for other fraudulent purposes.
[3]Includes any direct or indirect loss of $1 or more.
[4]Includes victims who had a direct loss of $1 or more and no indirect loss and victims who had both direct and indirect losses of $1 or more.
[5]Mean amounts for direct losses could be greater than mean amounts of any loss due to top-coding, a procedure used to protect respondents with large loss amounts from the risk of disclosure.
[6]Includes victims who had an indirect loss of $1 or more and no direct loss and victims who had both direct and indirect losses of $1 or more.

Table 8. Financial Loss for All Incidents of Identity Theft, 2018

(Dollars; percent; number.)

Estimate	Financial loss
Total	$15,132,093,700
Mean..	$930
Median..	$300
Percent of victims experiencing a loss...	70.3
Number of victims..	23,183,020

NOTE: Means and percentages were calculated using SPSS Complex Samples software. Financial loss includes any financial loss of $1 or more. Excludes persons who reported discovering the most recent identity-theft incident prior to the reference period (12months before the Identity Theft Supplement interview). Includes persons who did not know when they discovered the most recent incident (8% of victims).

Table 9. Victims of Identity Who Had Experienced Emotional Distress, by Type of Theft, 2018

(Percent.)

Type of identity theft	Total	None	Mild	Moderate	Severe
Total	100.0	20.5	48.1	22.9	8.4
Misused only one type of existing account	100.0	22.0 B	49.4 B	21.6	7.1 B
Credit card	100.0	23.7 B	52.5 B	19.5 B	4.3 B
Bank	100.0	19.7 B	46.5 B	23.6	10.2 B
Other	100.0	23.9 B	45.7 A	23.5	6.9 B
Opened new account only	100.0	12.3	36.9	35.5 A	15.3 B
Misused personal information only...................................	100.0	10.4	43.8	28.6	17.2 A
Misused multiple types...........................	100.0	13.3	42.6	27.9	16.2
Existing account only[1]*...................................	100.0	14.9 A	44.7	28.3	12.0 B
Other[2]	100.0	9.8	37.9	27.1	25.2

NOTE: Estimates are based on the most recent incident of identity theft. Excludes persons who reported discovering the most recent identity-theft incident prior to the reference period (12 months before the Identity Theft Supplement interview) and persons for whom emotional distress data were missing (less than 1% of victims). Includes persons who did not know when they discovered the most recent incident (8% of victims).
* = Comparison group.
A = Significant difference from comparison group at 90% confidence level.
B = Significant difference from comparison group at 95% confidence level.
[1]Includes victims who experienced two or more of the following: misuse of a credit card, bank account, or other existing account.
[2]Includes victims who experienced two or more of the following: misuse of an existing account, personal information to open a new account, or personal information for other fraudulent purposes.

Table 10. Percent of Victims of Identity Theft, by Type of Organization Contacted, 2018

(Percent; number.)

Type of organization contact	Percent of victims
Credit card company or bank..	88.1
Credit bureau	8.2
Credit-monitoring services	5.9
Document-issuing agency[1]........................	2.1
Consumer agency[2]........................	1.2
Federal Trade Commission	0.6
Victim services agency[3]	0.6
Attorney	0.3
Other........................	0.6
Number of Victims	23,183,020

NOTE: Details do not sum to totals because victims could contact multiple organizations. Estimates are based on the most recent incident of identity theft. Excludes persons who reported discovering the most recent identity-theft incident prior to the reference period (12 months before the Identity Theft Supplement interview). Includes persons who did not know when they discovered the most recent incident (8% of victims).
[1]Includes agencies that issue drivers' licenses or Social Security cards.
[2]Includes state or local consumer affairs agencies, such as the state attorney general's office, and consumer agencies, such as the Better Business Bureau.
[3]Includes agencies other than the police that deal with victims of crime.

Table 11. Actions Persons Age 16 Years or Older Took During the Past 12 Months to Reduce the Risk of Identity Theft, by Victims and Non-Victims of Past-Year Identity Theft, 2018

(Percent.)

Action taken	Total	Victims[1]	Non-victims[2]*
Any Action...	89.0	97.8 B	88.2
Checked bank or credit statements........................	81.9	94.6 B	80.7
Shredded or destroyed documents with personal information	74.2	82.6 B	73.3
Checked credit report	50.6	67.1 B	49.0
Changed passwords on financial accounts	45.3	69.9 B	42.9
Used identity-theft security program on computer	25.2	36.7 B	24.0
Purchased identity-theft insurance or credit-monitoring service	11.9	20.4 B	11.1
Purchased identity-theft protection	8.7	15.3 B	8.1

NOTE: Details do not sum to totals because respondents could take multiple actions.
* = Comparison group.
B = Significant difference from comparison group at 95% confidence level.
[1]Excludes persons who reported discovering the most recent identity-theft incident prior to the reference period (12 months before the Identity Theft Supplement interview). Includes persons who did not know when they discovered the most recent incident (8% of victims).
[2]Includes persons who reported discovering the most recent identity-theft incident prior to the reference period (12†months before the Identity Theft Supplement interview).

Table 12. Actions Victims of Identity Theft Took in the Past 12 Months to Reduce the Risk of Identity Theft, by Whether the Action Was Taken in Response to or Independent of Previous Identity Theft, 2018

(Percent.)

Type of action	Total	Action taken in response to identity theft	Action taken independent of identity theft	Unknown
Any. Action	100.0	91.1	6.7	2.2
Checked bank or credit statements................................	100.0	61.8	31.4	6.7
Shredded or destroyed documents with personal information..................	100.0	45.6 B	47.5 B	6.9
Checked credit report*	100.0	61.9	31.7	6.4
Changed passwords on financial accounts	100.0	61.9	31.8	6.3
Used identity-theft security program on computer	100.0	45.3 B	48.8 B	5.9
Purchased identity-theft insurance or credit monitoring service	100.0	49.3 B	44.8 B	5.9
Purchased identity-theft protection	100.0	55.4 B	39.8 B	4.8 B

NOTE: Details may not sum to totals due to rounding. Excludes persons who reported discovering the most recent identity-theft incident prior to the reference period (12 months before the Identity Theft Supplement interview). Includes persons who did not know when they discovered the most recent incident (8% of victims).
* = Comparison group.
* = Comparison group.
B = Significant difference from comparison group at 95% confidence level.

Table 13. Persons Age 16 or Older Who Experienced Identity Theft in Their Lifetime, by Type of Identity Theft Experienced Outside of the Past Year and Ongoing Problems from Identity Theft, 2018

(Number; percent.)

Identity theft during lifetime and outside past 12 months	Number of victims	Percent of all persons age years 16 or older	Percent of victims whose problems resulting from identity theft were unresolved[1]
At least one incident of identity theft during lifetime........................	48,097,440	18.6	6.5
At least one incident of identity theft outside of the past 12 months	29,569,340	11.5	4.3
Misused only one type of existing account	22,680,190 B	8.8 B	2.0 B
Credit card..	12,928,360 B	5.0 B	1.2 B
Bank	8,982,340 B	3.5 B	2.8 B
Other	769,490 B	0.3 B	5.5 B
Opened new account only	1,830,970 B	0.7 B	11.7 B
Misused personal information only...................................	2,498,610 B	1.0 B	11.3 B
Misused multiple types..	2,502,330	1.0	12.7
Existing account*[2]	1,144,130 B	0.4 B	4.3 B
Other[3]	1,358,200	0.5	19.8

NOTE: Details do not sum to totals due to a small number of victims who did not know the type of identity theft they experienced outside of the past 12 months. In 2018, there were 258 million persons age 16 or older living in noninstitutionalized, residential settings in the United States.
* = Comparison group.
B = Significant difference from comparison year at 95% confidence level.
[1]Based on the number of persons who experienced the type of identity theft. Problems include credit and financial problems, emotional distress, and relationship problems.
[2]Includes victims who experienced two or more of the following: misuse of a credit card, bank account, or other existing account.
[3]Includes victims who experienced two or more of the following: misuse of an existing account, personal information to open a new account, or personal information for other fraudulent purposes.

METHODOLOGY

The 2018 Identity Theft Supplement (ITS) was administered as a supplement to the National Crime Victimization Survey (NCVS), a collection by the Bureau of Justice Statistics (BJS). From January 1, 2018, to June 30, 2018, approximately 140,000 persons age 16 or older received the ITS at the end of their NCVS interview.

The NCVS sample was redesigned in 2016. (Please see *Criminal Victimization, 2016,* on the BJS Web site for more information.) From 2015 to 2016, the NCVS sample size increased by 41 percent (from 95,760 to 134,690 households interviewed) to facilitate the ability to produce state- and local-level victimization estimates for the largest 22 states. At the same time, the sample was adjusted to reflect the U.S. population counts in the U.S. Census Bureau's 2010 decennial census (rather than being based on the 2000 decennial census, as was the case from 2006 through 2015).

This report focuses primarily on the level and nature of identity theft in 2018 and is based on the full sample unless otherwise specified. Data users should use caution when comparing 2018 estimates to those from previous years.

Identity-theft victims are persons age 16 or older who experienced one or more of the following:

Misuse of an existing account—completed or attempted unauthorized use of one or more existing accounts, such as a credit card, debit card, checking, savings, telephone, mortgage, or insurance account.

Misuse of a new account—completed or attempted unauthorized use of personal information to open a new account, such as a credit card or debit card, checking, savings, telephone, online, mortgage, or insurance account.

Misuse of personal information—completed or attempted unauthorized use of personal information for fraudulent purposes, such as getting medical care, a job, or government benefits; renting an apartment or house; or providing false information to law enforcement when charged with a crime or traffic violation. This excludes the completed or attempted unauthorized use of personal information to open a new account or to misuse an existing account.

Data Collection

The Identity Theft Supplement (ITS) was administered as a supplement to the Bureau of Justice Statistics' National Crime Victimization Survey (NCVS). The NCVS collects data on crime reported and not reported to police against persons age 12 or older from a nationally representative sample of U.S. households. The sample includes persons living in group quarters (such as dormitories, rooming houses, and religious group dwellings). It excludes persons living in military barracks and institutional settings (such as correctional or hospital facilities) and persons who are homeless.

From January 1, 2018, to June 30, 2018, 140,000 persons age 16 or older in sampled NCVS households received the ITS at the end of the NCVS interview. Proxy respondents did not receive the ITS. If the NCVS interview was conducted in some language other than English, the ITS interview was allowed to be conducted in that language by either the interviewer or a reliable translator. All NCVS and ITS interviews were conducted using computer-assisted personal interviewing by telephone or personal visit. A final sample size of about 96,100 persons of the original NCVS-eligible respondents completed the ITS questionnaire, a person response rate of 77 percent.

The combined ITS response rate was about 54 percent. Because of the level of non-response, a bias analysis was conducted. The result of the non-response bias analysis suggested that there was little or no bias of substantive importance due to non-response in the ITS estimates.

The ITS collected individual data on the prevalence of and victim response to attempted or successful misuse of an existing account, misuse of personal information to open a new account, or misuse of personal information for other fraudulent purposes. Respondents were asked whether they experienced any of these types of misuse during the 12 months prior to the interview.

Persons who reported experiencing one or more incidents of identity theft over the prior 12 months were asked questions about the incident and their response to the incident, such as how they discovered the identity theft; financial, credit, and other problems resulting from the incident; time spent resolving associated problems; and reporting to police and credit bureaus. For most sections of the survey instrument, the ITS asked victims who experienced more than one incident during the 12-month reference period to describe only the most recent incident when answering questions about details of the identity-theft incident. It asked victims who experienced multiple incidents of identity theft during the year to provide details on the total financial losses they experienced as a result of all incidents. It also asked all respondents a series of questions about identity theft they experienced outside of the 12-month reference period and about measures they took to avoid or minimize the risk of becoming an identity-theft victim.

Changes in BJS Identity-Theft Statistics Over Time

In 2008, the Bureau of Justice Statistics (BJS) conducted the first ITS to the NCVS. Prior to that year, BJS reports on identity theft used household-level data from the core NCVS. Data were reported for the household as a whole rather than for individual respondents, and the questions were more limited, providing less detail on the characteristics of the incident and the victim response. For additional information, see *Identity Theft, 2005* (NCJ 219411, BJS web, November 2007); *Identity Theft Reported by Households, 2007 Statistical Tables* (NCJ 230742, BJS web, June 2010); and *Identity Theft Reported by Households, 2005-2010* (NCJ 236245, BJS web, November 2011).

The 2008 collection, like the 2018 ITS collection, gathered detailed information on victim experiences with identity theft from persons age 16 or older. For more information, see *Victims of Identity Theft, 2008* (NCJ 231680, BJS web, December 2010). Following the administration of the 2008 ITS, BJS made substantial changes to the survey instrument, making it difficult to compare estimates from the 2008 ITS to estimates from later iterations of the ITS. For details on these changes, see Victims of Identity Theft, 2012 (NCJ 243779, BJS web, December 2013).

In-Depth Defining of Identity Theft

As with many other crime types, there is no standard definition of identity theft used nationwide. The ITS was developed in conjunction with the Federal Trade Commission (FTC)—the U.S. government's consumer protection agency—in addition to a range of government and private experts from the criminal justice and financial fields. The definition used for the supplement follows from the FTC's general definition of identity theft: a fraud that is committed or attempted using a person's identifying information without authority. (Fair and Accurate Credit Transactions Act of 2003, P.L. 108-159.)

Many state legal codes use a similar definition of identity theft, though the codes vary from one state to the next in terms of how personal information is defined and the type of misuse that must occur. For example, the California Penal Code specifies that identity theft occurs when an individual "willfully obtains personal identifying information, as defined in subdivision (b) of Section 530.55, of another person, and uses that information for any unlawful purpose, including to obtain, or attempt to obtain, credit, goods, services, real property, or medical information without the consent of that person." The list of personal identifying information includes, "any name, address, telephone number, health insurance number, taxpayer identification number, school identification number, state or federal driver's license, or identification number, social security number, place of employment, employee identification number, professional or occupational number, mother's maiden name, demand deposit account number, savings account number, checking account number, PIN (personal identification number) or password, alien registration number, government passport number, date of birth, unique biometric data including fingerprint, facial scan identifiers, voiceprint, retina or iris image, or other unique physical representation, unique electronic data including information identification number assigned to the person, address or routing code, telecommunication identifying information or access device, information contained in a birth or death certificate, or credit card number of an individual person, or an equivalent form of identification." (California Penal Code Part 1. Title 13. Chapter 8. Section 530.5. and California Penal Code Part 1. Title 13. Chapter 8. Section 530.55.)

The Pennsylvania Code defines identifying information as "any document, photographic, pictorial or computer image of another person, or any fact used to establish identity, including, but not limited to, a name, birth date, Social Security number, driver's license number, non-driver governmental identification number, telephone number, checking account number, savings account number, student identification number, employee or payroll number or electronic signature." It specifies that identity theft occurs when a person "possesses or uses, through any means, identifying information of another person without the consent of that other person to further any unlawful purpose." (Pennsylvania Code Title 18. Section 4120.)

The primary categories of identity theft used in the ITS were modeled after a survey on identity theft conducted by the FTC in 2005 and 2006. The categories of identity theft identified in the initial FTC survey were the misuse of an existing credit card or credit card account, the misuse of an existing non-credit card account, and the misuse of personal information to open new accounts or to engage in types of fraud other than the misuse of existing or new financial accounts. The ITS splits the latter category into two separate groups.

Possible Overreporting of Losses from Jointly Held Accounts

Persons may have experienced the unauthorized use of a jointly held account. Joint accounts present a difficulty with counting financial harm or loss because of the potential for double-counting loss (e.g., both account holders report the same $500 loss). Because financial loss was not attributed to a particular type of identity theft, victims of multiple types of identity theft may have experienced some financial loss from a joint account and an independently held account. Therefore, it was not possible to correct for potential overreporting due to joint account-holders who may have been double-counted.

Standard Error Computations

When national estimates are derived from a sample, caution must be taken when comparing one estimate to another. Although one estimate may be larger than another, estimates based on a sample have some degree of sampling error. The sampling error of an estimate depends on several factors, including the amount of variation in the responses, the size of the sample, and the size of the subgroup for which the estimate is computed. When the sampling error around the estimates is taken into consideration, the estimates that appear different may not be statistically different.

One measure of the sampling error associated with an estimate is the standard error. The standard error may vary from one estimate to the next. In general, for a given metric, an estimate with a smaller standard error provides a more reliable approximation of the true value than an estimate with a larger standard error. Estimates with relatively large standard errors are associated with less precision and reliability and should be interpreted with caution.

The U.S. Census Bureau produces generalized variance function (GVF) parameters for BJS. The GVFs take into account aspects of the NCVS's complex sample design and represent the curve fitted to a selection of individual standard errors based on the Jackknife Repeated Replication technique. Except where otherwise noted, the GVF parameters were used to generate standard errors for each point estimate (e.g., numbers or percentages) in the report.

BJS conducted tests to determine whether differences in estimated numbers and percentages were statistically significant once sampling error was taken into account. Using statistical programs developed specifically for the NCVS, all comparisons in the text were tested for significance. The primary test procedure used was Student's t-statistic, which tests the difference between two sample estimates. The significance level was set at the 95 percent confidence level to ensure observed difference between estimates were larger than what was expected due to sampling variation.

Data users may employ estimates and standard errors of the estimates provided in this report to generate a confidence interval around the estimate as a measure of the margin of error. The following example illustrates how standard errors may be used to generate confidence intervals:

According to the ITS, in 2016 an estimated 10.2 percent of persons age 16 or older experienced identity theft. Using GVFs, BJS determined that the estimate has a standard error of 0.18. A confidence interval around the estimate was generated by multiplying the standard errors by ±1.96 (the t-score of a normal, two-tailed distribution that excludes 2.5 percent at either end of the distribution). Therefore, the confidence interval around the estimate is 10.2 ± (0.18 × 1.96) or 9.85 percent to 10.55 percent. In other words, if BJS used the same sampling method to select different samples and computed an interval estimate for each sample, the true population parameter (percent of identity-theft victims) would be expected to fall within the interval estimates 95 percent of the time.

BJS also calculated a coefficient of variation (CV) for all estimates, representing the ratio of the standard error to the estimate. CVs provide a measure of reliability and a means to compare the precision of estimates across measures with differing levels or metrics. In cases where the CV was greater than 50 percent, or the unweighted sample had 10 or fewer cases, the estimate was noted with a "!" symbol (interpret data with caution; estimate is based on 10 or fewer sample cases, or the CV exceeds 50 percent).

Many variables examined in this report may be related to one another and to other variables not included in the analyses. Complex relationships among variables were not fully explored and warrant more extensive analysis. Readers are cautioned not to draw causal inferences based on the results presented.

For more information, please see https://bjs.ojp.gov/content/pub/pdf/vit18.pdf

APPENDIX A: SOURCES FOR TABLES

Part 1. Capital Punishment, 2019

1	Bureau of Justice Statistics, National Prisoner Statistics program (NPS-8), 2019
2	Bureau of Justice Statistics, National Prisoner Statistics program (NPS-8), 2019
3	Bureau of Justice Statistics, National Prisoner Statistics program (NPS-8), 2019
4	Bureau of Justice Statistics, National Prisoner Statistics program (NPS-8), 2019
5	Bureau of Justice Statistics, National Prisoner Statistics program (NPS-8), 2019
6	Bureau of Justice Statistics, National Prisoner Statistics program (NPS-8), 2019
7	Bureau of Justice Statistics, National Prisoner Statistics program (NPS-8), 1930–2019
8	Bureau of Justice Statistics, National Prisoner Statistics program (NPS-8), 1953–2019
9	Bureau of Justice Statistics, National Prisoner Statistics program (NPS-8), 1973–2019
10	Bureau of Justice Statistics, National Prisoner Statistics program (NPS-8), 1968–2019
11	Bureau of Justice Statistics, National Prisoner Statistics program (NPS-8), 2019
12	Bureau of Justice Statistics, National Prisoner Statistics program (NPS-8), 2019
13	Bureau of Justice Statistics, National Prisoner Statistics program (NPS-8), 2019
14	Bureau of Justice Statistics, National Prisoner Statistics program (NPS-8), 2019
15	Bureau of Justice Statistics, National Prisoner Statistics data series (NPS-8), 2019

Part 2. Crime in the United States, 2019

1	Bureau of Justice Statistics, Census of Jails, 2019; and Annual Survey of Jails, 2020
2	United States Department of Justice, Federal Bureau of Investigation, Uniform Crime Reports, 2019
3	United States Department of Justice, Federal Bureau of Investigation, Uniform Crime Reports, 2019
4	United States Department of Justice, Federal Bureau of Investigation, Uniform Crime Reports, 2019
5	United States Department of Justice, Federal Bureau of Investigation, Uniform Crime Reports, 2019
6	United States Department of Justice, Federal Bureau of Investigation, Uniform Crime Reports, 2019
7	United States Department of Justice, Federal Bureau of Investigation, Uniform Crime Reports, 2019
8	United States Department of Justice, Federal Bureau of Investigation, Uniform Crime Reports, 2019
9	United States Department of Justice, Federal Bureau of Investigation, Uniform Crime Reports, 2019
10	United States Department of Justice, Federal Bureau of Investigation, Uniform Crime Reports, 2019
11	United States Department of Justice, Federal Bureau of Investigation, Uniform Crime Reports, 2019
12	United States Department of Justice, Federal Bureau of Investigation, Uniform Crime Reports, 2019
13	United States Department of Justice, Federal Bureau of Investigation, Uniform Crime Reports, 2019
14	United States Department of Justice, Federal Bureau of Investigation, Uniform Crime Reports, 2019
15	United States Department of Justice, Federal Bureau of Investigation, Uniform Crime Reports, 2019
16	United States Department of Justice, Federal Bureau of Investigation, Uniform Crime Reports, 2019
17	United States Department of Justice, Federal Bureau of Investigation, Uniform Crime Reports, 2019

18   United States Department of Justice, Federal Bureau of Investigation, Uniform Crime Reports, 2019

19   United States Department of Justice, Federal Bureau of Investigation, Uniform Crime Reports, 2019

20   United States Department of Justice, Federal Bureau of Investigation, Uniform Crime Reports, 2019

21   United States Department of Justice, Federal Bureau of Investigation, Uniform Crime Reports, 2019

22   United States Department of Justice, Federal Bureau of Investigation, Uniform Crime Reports, 2019

23   United States Department of Justice, Federal Bureau of Investigation, Uniform Crime Reports, 2019

24   United States Department of Justice, Federal Bureau of Investigation, Uniform Crime Reports, 2019

25   United States Department of Justice, Federal Bureau of Investigation, Uniform Crime Reports, 2019

26   United States Department of Justice, Federal Bureau of Investigation, Uniform Crime Reports, 2019

27   United States Department of Justice, Federal Bureau of Investigation, Uniform Crime Reports, 2019

28   United States Department of Justice, Federal Bureau of Investigation, Uniform Crime Reports, 2019

29   United States Department of Justice, Federal Bureau of Investigation, Uniform Crime Reports, 2019

30   United States Department of Justice, Federal Bureau of Investigation, Uniform Crime Reports, 2019

31   United States Department of Justice, Federal Bureau of Investigation, Uniform Crime Reports, 2019

32   United States Department of Justice, Federal Bureau of Investigation, Uniform Crime Reports, 2019

33   United States Department of Justice, Federal Bureau of Investigation, Uniform Crime Reports, 2019

34   United States Department of Justice, Federal Bureau of Investigation, Uniform Crime Reports, 2019

35   United States Department of Justice, Federal Bureau of Investigation, Uniform Crime Reports, 2019

36   United States Department of Justice, Federal Bureau of Investigation, Uniform Crime Reports, 2019

37   United States Department of Justice, Federal Bureau of Investigation, Uniform Crime Reports, 2019

38   United States Department of Justice, Federal Bureau of Investigation, Uniform Crime Reports, 2019

39   United States Department of Justice, Federal Bureau of Investigation, Uniform Crime Reports, 2019

40   United States Department of Justice, Federal Bureau of Investigation, Uniform Crime Reports, 2019

41   United States Department of Justice, Federal Bureau of Investigation, Uniform Crime Reports, 2019

41A   United States Department of Justice, Federal Bureau of Investigation, Uniform Crime Reports, 2019

42   United States Department of Justice, Federal Bureau of Investigation, Uniform Crime Reports, 2019

43   United States Department of Justice, Federal Bureau of Investigation, Uniform Crime Reports, 2019

44   United States Department of Justice, Federal Bureau of Investigation, Uniform Crime Reports, 2019

45   United States Department of Justice, Federal Bureau of Investigation, Uniform Crime Reports, 2019

46   United States Department of Justice, Federal Bureau of Investigation, Uniform Crime Reports, 2019

47   United States Department of Justice, Federal Bureau of Investigation, Uniform Crime Reports, 2019

48   United States Department of Justice, Federal Bureau of Investigation, Uniform Crime Reports, 2019

49   United States Department of Justice, Federal Bureau of Investigation, Uniform Crime Reports, 2019

50   United States Department of Justice, Federal Bureau of Investigation, Uniform Crime Reports, 2019

51   United States Department of Justice, Federal Bureau of Investigation, Uniform Crime Reports, 2019

52   United States Department of Justice, Federal Bureau of Investigation, Uniform Crime Reports, 2019

53   United States Department of Justice, Federal Bureau of Investigation, Uniform Crime Reports, 2019

54   United States Department of Justice, Federal Bureau of Investigation, Uniform Crime Reports, 2019

55   United States Department of Justice, Federal Bureau of Investigation, Uniform Crime Reports, 2019

56   United States Department of Justice, Federal Bureau of Investigation, Uniform Crime Reports, 2019

Part 3. Criminal Victimization, 2019

1   Bureau of Justice Statistics, National Crime Victimization Survey, 2015–2019

2   Bureau of Justice Statistics, National Crime Victimization Survey, 2015–2019

3   Bureau of Justice Statistics, National Crime Victimization Survey, 2018 and 2019

4   Bureau of Justice Statistics, National Crime Victimization Survey, 2015–2019

5   Bureau of Justice Statistics, National Crime Victimization Survey, 2018 and 2019; and Federal Bureau of Investigation, Crime in the United States, 2018, https://ucr.fbi.gov/crime-in-the-u.s/2018/crime-in-the-u.s.-2018/topic-pages/tables/table-1

6   Bureau of Justice Statistics, National Crime Victimization Survey, 2018 and 2019

7   Bureau of Justice Statistics, National Crime Victimization Survey, 2015–2019

8   Bureau of Justice Statistics, National Crime Victimization Survey, 2018 and 2019

9   Bureau of Justice Statistics, National Crime Victimization Survey, 2018 and 2019

10   Bureau of Justice Statistics, National Crime Victimization Survey, 2019

11   Bureau of Justice Statistics, National Crime Victimization Survey, 2018 and 2019

12   Bureau of Justice Statistics, National Crime Victimization Survey, 2019

Part 4. Federal Justice Statistics, 2017–2018

1   Bureau of Justice Statistics, based on data from the Administrative Office of the U.S. Courts, Probation and Pretrial Services Automated Case Tracking System; U.S. Marshals Service, Justice Detainee Information System; and Federal Bureau of Prisons, SENTRY database, fiscal year-end 2008, 2017, and 2018.

2   Bureau of Justice Statistics, based on data from the U.S. Marshals Service, Justice Detainee Information System, fiscal years 2017 and 2018.

3   Bureau of Justice Statistics, based on data from the Executive Office for U.S. Attorneys, National Legal Information Office Network System database, fiscal years 2008 and 2016-2018.

4   Bureau of Justice Statistics, based on data from the Executive Office for U.S. Attorneys, National Legal Information Office Network System database, fiscal year 2018.

5   Bureau of Justice Statistics, based on data from the Administrative Office of the U.S. Courts, Probation and Pretrial Services Automated Case Tracking System, fiscal year 2018.

6   Bureau of Justice Statistics, based on data from the Administrative Office of the U.S. Courts, Criminal Master File, fiscal year 2018.

7   Bureau of Justice Statistics, based on data from the Administrative Office of the U.S. Courts, Criminal Master File, fiscal year 2018.

8   Bureau of Justice Statistics, based on data from the Federal Bureau of Prisons, SENTRY database, fiscal year 2018.

9   Bureau of Justice Statistics, based on data from the Federal Bureau of Prisons, SENTRY database, fiscal year-end 2008 and 2018.

10   Bureau of Justice Statistics, based on data from the Administrative Office of the U.S. Courts, Probation and Pretrial Services Automated Case Tracking System, fiscal year-end 2018.

Part 5. Hate Crime Statistics, 2017

1   Federal Bureau of Investigation, Hate Crime Statistics, 2019

2   Federal Bureau of Investigation, Hate Crime Statistics, 2019

3   Federal Bureau of Investigation, Hate Crime Statistics, 2019

4   Federal Bureau of Investigation, Hate Crime Statistics, 2019

5   Federal Bureau of Investigation, Hate Crime Statistics, 2019

6   Federal Bureau of Investigation, Hate Crime Statistics, 2019

7   Federal Bureau of Investigation, Hate Crime Statistics, 2019

8   Federal Bureau of Investigation, Hate Crime Statistics, 2019

9   Federal Bureau of Investigation, Hate Crime Statistics, 2019

10   Federal Bureau of Investigation, Hate Crime Statistics, 2019

11   Federal Bureau of Investigation, Hate Crime Statistics, 2019

12   Federal Bureau of Investigation, Hate Crime Statistics, 2019

13   Federal Bureau of Investigation, Hate Crime Statistics, 2019

14   Federal Bureau of Investigation, Hate Crime Statistics, 2019

Part 6. Indicators of School Crime and Safety, 2018

1   Centers for Disease Control and Prevention (CDC), 1992-2018 School-Associated Violent Death Surveillance System (SAVD-SS) (partially funded by the U.S. Department of Education, Office of Safe and Healthy Students), previously unpublished tabulation; and CDC, National Center for Health Statistics, 1992-2018 National Vital Statistics System (NVSS), previously unpublished tabulation prepared by CDC's National Center for Injury Prevention and Control

2   U.S. Department of Justice, Bureau of Justice Statistics, National Crime Victimization Survey (NCVS), 1992 through 2019

3   U.S. Department of Justice, Bureau of Justice Statistics, National Crime Victimization Survey (NCVS), 2019

4   U.S. Department of Justice, Bureau of Justice Statistics, School Crime Supplement (SCS) to the National Crime Victimization Survey, 1995 through 2019

5   U.S. Department of Education, National Center for Education Statistics, Schools and Staffing Survey (SASS), "Public School Teacher Data File," 1993-94, 1999-2000, 2003-04, 2007-08, and 2011-12; "Charter School Teacher Data File," 1999-2000; and National Teacher and Principal Survey (NTPS), "Public School Teacher Data File," 2015-16

6   U.S. Department of Education, National Center for Education Statistics, 1999-2000, 2003-04, 2005-06, 2007-08, 2009-10, 2015-16, and 2017-18 School Survey on Crime and Safety (SSOCS), 2000, 2004, 2006, 2008, 2010, 2016, and 2018; and Fast Response Survey System (FRSS), "School Safety and Discipline: 2013-14," FRSS 106, 2014

7   U.S. Department of Justice, Bureau of Justice Statistics, School Crime Supplement (SCS) to the National Crime Victimization Survey, 1995 through 2019

8   Centers for Disease Control and Prevention, Division of Adolescent and School Health, Youth Risk Behavior Surveillance System (YRBSS), 1993 through 2019

9   U.S. Department of Justice, Bureau of Justice Statistics, School Crime Supplement (SCS) to the National Crime Victimization Survey, 1999 through 2019 U.S. Department of Justice, Bureau of Justice Statistics, School Crime Supplement (SCS) to the National Crime Victimization Survey, 1999 through 2019

10   U.S. Department of Justice, Bureau of Justice Statistics, School Crime Supplement (SCS) to the National Crime Victimization Survey, selected years, 2005 through 2019

11   U.S. Department of Education, National Center for Education Statistics, 2017-18 School Survey on Crime and Safety (SSOCS), 2018

12   U.S. Department of Education, Office of Postsecondary Education, Campus Safety and Security Reporting System, 2010 through 2018

Part 7. Jail Inmates in 2019

1   Bureau of Justice Statistics, Annual Survey of Jails, 2006-2018; Census of Jails, 2005 and 2019; Mortality in Correctional Institutions (formerly Deaths in Custody Reporting Program), 2006 (admissions only); and U.S. Census Bureau, Population Estimates by Age, Sex, Race, and Hispanic Origin for the United States: January 1, 2005 to January 1, 2019

2   Bureau of Justice Statistics, Annual Survey of Jails, 2008 and 2010-2018; and Census of Jails, 2005 and 2019

3   Bureau of Justice Statistics, Annual Survey of Jails, 2008 and 2010–2018; and Census of Jails, 2005 and 2019

3A   Bureau of Justice Statistics, Annual Survey of Jails, 2010–2018, and Census of Jails, 2005 and 2019

4   Bureau of Justice Statistics, Census of Jails, 2019

5   Bureau of Justice Statistics, Annual Survey of Jails, 2006–2018; and Census of Jails, 2005 and 2019

6   Bureau of Justice Statistics, Census of Jails, 2019

7   Bureau of Justice Statistics, Census of Jails, 2019

8   Bureau of Justice Statistics, Annual Survey of Jails, 2006–2018; and Census of Jails, 2005 and 2019

9   Bureau of Justice Statistics, Annual Survey of Jails, 2015–2018; and Census of Jails, 2013 and 2019

10   Bureau of Justice Statistics, Annual Survey of Jails, 2006–2018; and Census of Jails, 2005 and 2019

Part 8. Law Enforcement Officers Killed and Assaulted, 2019

1   United States Department of Justice, Federal Bureau of Investigation, Uniform Crime Reports, 2019

2   United States Department of Justice, Federal Bureau of Investigation, Uniform Crime Reports, 2019

3 and 3A   United States Department of Justice, Federal Bureau of Investigation, Uniform Crime Reports, 2019

4   United States Department of Justice, Federal Bureau of Investigation, Uniform Crime Reports, 2019

5   United States Department of Justice, Federal Bureau of Investigation, Uniform Crime Reports, 2019

6   United States Department of Justice, Federal Bureau of Investigation, Uniform Crime Reports, 2019

7   United States Department of Justice, Federal Bureau of Investigation, Uniform Crime Reports, 2019

8   United States Department of Justice, Federal Bureau of Investigation, Uniform Crime Reports, 2019

9   United States Department of Justice, Federal Bureau of Investigation, Uniform Crime Reports, 2019

10   United States Department of Justice, Federal Bureau of Investigation, Uniform Crime Reports, 2019

11   United States Department of Justice, Federal Bureau of Investigation, Uniform Crime Reports, 2019

12   United States Department of Justice, Federal Bureau of Investigation, Uniform Crime Reports, 2019

13   United States Department of Justice, Federal Bureau of Investigation, Uniform Crime Reports, 2019

14   United States Department of Justice, Federal Bureau of Investigation, Uniform Crime Reports, 2019

15   United States Department of Justice, Federal Bureau of Investigation, Uniform Crime Reports, 2019

16   United States Department of Justice, Federal Bureau of Investigation, Uniform Crime Reports, 2019

17   United States Department of Justice, Federal Bureau of Investigation, Uniform Crime Reports, 2019

18   United States Department of Justice, Federal Bureau of Investigation, Uniform Crime Reports, 2019

19   United States Department of Justice, Federal Bureau of Investigation, Uniform Crime Reports, 2019

20   United States Department of Justice, Federal Bureau of Investigation, Uniform Crime Reports, 2019

21   United States Department of Justice, Federal Bureau of Investigation, Uniform Crime Reports, 2019

22   United States Department of Justice, Federal Bureau of Investigation, Uniform Crime Reports, 2019

23   United States Department of Justice, Federal Bureau of Investigation, Uniform Crime Reports, 2019

24   United States Department of Justice, Federal Bureau of Investigation, Uniform Crime Reports, 2019

25	United States Department of Justice, Federal Bureau of Investigation, Uniform Crime Reports, 2019
26	United States Department of Justice, Federal Bureau of Investigation, Uniform Crime Reports, 2019
27	United States Department of Justice, Federal Bureau of Investigation, Uniform Crime Reports, 2019
28	United States Department of Justice, Federal Bureau of Investigation, Uniform Crime Reports, 2019
29	United States Department of Justice, Federal Bureau of Investigation, Uniform Crime Reports, 2019
30	United States Department of Justice, Federal Bureau of Investigation, Uniform Crime Reports, 2019
31	United States Department of Justice, Federal Bureau of Investigation, Uniform Crime Reports, 2019
32	United States Department of Justice, Federal Bureau of Investigation, Uniform Crime Reports, 2019
33	United States Department of Justice, Federal Bureau of Investigation, Uniform Crime Reports, 2019
34	United States Department of Justice, Federal Bureau of Investigation, Uniform Crime Reports, 2019
35	United States Department of Justice, Federal Bureau of Investigation, Uniform Crime Reports, 2019
36	United States Department of Justice, Federal Bureau of Investigation, Uniform Crime Reports, 2019
37	United States Department of Justice, Federal Bureau of Investigation, Uniform Crime Reports, 2019
38	United States Department of Justice, Federal Bureau of Investigation, Uniform Crime Reports, 2019
39	United States Department of Justice, Federal Bureau of Investigation, Uniform Crime Reports, 2019
40	United States Department of Justice, Federal Bureau of Investigation, Uniform Crime Reports, 2019

Part 9. Probation and Parole, 2017–2018

1	Bureau of Justice Statistics, Annual Probation Survey and Annual Parole Survey, 2008–2018
2	Bureau of Justice Statistics, Annual Probation Survey and Annual Parole Survey, 2008–2018; and U.S. Census Bureau, National Intercensal Estimates, 2009–2019
3	Bureau of Justice Statistics, Annual Probation Survey and Annual Parole Survey, 2008–2018
4	Bureau of Justice Statistics, Annual Probation Survey and Annual Parole Survey, 2008–2018
5	Bureau of Justice Statistics, Annual Probation Survey, 2008–2018
6	Bureau of Justice Statistics, Annual Parole Survey, 2008–2018
7	Bureau of Justice Statistics, Annual Probation Survey and Annual Parole Survey, 2018; and U.S. Census Bureau, National Intercensal Estimates, 2019
8	Bureau of Justice Statistics, Annual Probation Survey, 2018; and U.S. Census Bureau, National Intercensal Estimates, 2019
9	Bureau of Justice Statistics, Annual Probation Survey, 2018
10	Bureau of Justice Statistics, Annual Probation Survey, 2008 and 2018
11	Bureau of Justice Statistics, Annual Parole Survey, 2018; and U.S. Census Bureau, National Intercensal Estimates, 2019
12	Bureau of Justice Statistics, Annual Parole Survey, 2018
13	Bureau of Justice Statistics, Annual Parole Survey, 2018
14	Bureau of Justice Statistics, Annual Parole Survey, 2008 and 2018

Part 10. 2018 Update on Prisoner Recidivism: A 9-Year Follow-up Period (2005-2014)

| 1 | Bureau of Justice Statistics, Recidivism of State Prisoners Released in 2005 data collection, 2005–2014 |
| 2 | Bureau of Justice Statistics, Recidivism of State Prisoners Released in 2005 data collection, 2005–2014 |

3	Bureau of Justice Statistics, Recidivism of State Prisoners Released in 2005 data collection, 2005–2014
4	Bureau of Justice Statistics, Recidivism of State Prisoners Released in 2005 data collection, 2005–2014
5	Bureau of Justice Statistics, Recidivism of State Prisoners Released in 2005 data collection, 2005–2014
6	Bureau of Justice Statistics, Recidivism of State Prisoners Released in 2005 data collection, 2005–2014
7	Bureau of Justice Statistics, Recidivism of State Prisoners Released in 2005 data collection, 2005–2014
8	Bureau of Justice Statistics, Recidivism of State Prisoners Released in 2005 data collection, 2005–2014
9	Bureau of Justice Statistics, Recidivism of State Prisoners Released in 2005 data collection, 2005–2014
10	Bureau of Justice Statistics, Recidivism of State Prisoners Released in 2005 data collection, 2005–2014
11	Bureau of Justice Statistics, Recidivism of State Prisoners Released in 2005 data collection, 2005–2014
12	Bureau of Justice Statistics, Recidivism of State Prisoners Released in 2005 data collection, 2005–2014
13	Bureau of Justice Statistics, Recidivism of State Prisoners Released in 2005 data collection, 2005–2014

Part 11. Victims of Identity Theft, 2018

1	Bureau of Justice Statistics, National Crime Victimization Survey, Identity Theft Supplement, 2018
2	Bureau of Justice Statistics, National Crime Victimization Survey, Identity Theft Supplement, 2018
3	Bureau of Justice Statistics, National Crime Victimization Survey, Identity Theft Supplement, 2018
4	Bureau of Justice Statistics, National Crime Victimization Survey, Identity Theft Supplement, 2018
5	Bureau of Justice Statistics, National Crime Victimization Survey, Identity Theft Supplement, 2018
6	Bureau of Justice Statistics, National Crime Victimization Survey, Identity Theft Supplement, 2018
7	Bureau of Justice Statistics, National Crime Victimization Survey, Identity Theft Supplement, 2018
8	Bureau of Justice Statistics, National Crime Victimization Survey, Identity Theft Supplement, 2018
9	Bureau of Justice Statistics, National Crime Victimization Survey, Identity Theft Supplement, 2018
10	Bureau of Justice Statistics, National Crime Victimization Survey, Identity Theft Supplement, 2018
11	Bureau of Justice Statistics, National Crime Victimization Survey, Identity Theft Supplement, 2018
12	Bureau of Justice Statistics, National Crime Victimization Survey, Identity Theft Supplement, 2018
13	Bureau of Justice Statistics, National Crime Victimization Survey, Identity Theft Supplement, 2018

APPENDIX B. COVID-19: IMPACT OF COVID-19 ON THE LOCAL JAIL POPULATION, JANUARY-JUNE 2020

1	Bureau of Justice Statistics, Census of Jails, 2019, and Annual Survey of Jails, 2020
2	Bureau of Justice Statistics, Census of Jails, 2019, and Annual Survey of Jails, 2020
3	Bureau of Justice Statistics, Census of Jails, 2019; and Annual Survey of Jails, 2020
4	Bureau of Justice Statistics, Annual Survey of Jails, 2020
5	Bureau of Justice Statistics, Census of Jails, 2019; and Annual Survey of Jails, 2020
6	Bureau of Justice Statistics, Census of Jails, 2019; and Annual Survey of Jails, 2020

Table 1. Number Of Inmates Confined in Local Jails on the Last Weekday in June 2019 and the Last Weekday of Each Month, January–June 2020

(Number.)

Last weekday in:	Number
June 2019*	734,500
January 2020	711,900 [B]
February 2020	710,300 [B]
March 2020	585,900 [B]
April 2020	519,500 [B]
May 2020	536,600 [B]
June 2020	549,100 [B]

*Comparison month.
B = Difference with comparison month is significant at the 95% confidence level.

Table 2. Local Jail Population as a Percentage of the June 2019 Jail Population, by Region, January–June 2020

(Number.)

Region	June 2019*	January 2020	February 2020	March 2020	April 2020	May 2020	June 2020
U.S. Total	100.0	96.9 [B]	96.7 [B]	79.8 [B]	70.7 [B]	73.1 [B]	74.8 [B]
Northeast	100.0	103.4	102.7	75.8 [B]	66.2 [B]	70.2 [B]	75.5 [B]
Midwest	100.0	96.2 [B]	95.8 [B]	81.9 [B]	74.6 [B]	77.4 [B]	78.6 [B]
South	100.0	95.7	96.6	78.4 [B]	66.7 [B]	67.6 [B]	67.9 [B]
West	100.0	92.0	91.5	78.3 [B]	66.3 [B]	65.9 [B]	67.0 [B]

NOTE: Data are based on the inmate population confined on the last weekday of each month.
*Comparison month.
B = Difference with comparison month is significant at the 95% confidence level.

Table 3. Inmate Population Change and Inmate and Staff COVID-19 Testing and Cases in the 50 Largest Local Jail Jurisdictions, March–June 2020

(Number; percent.)

Location	Inmates in custody[1]			Inmate tests[2]				Staff tests[3]	
	Number in 2019	Number in 2020	Percent change	Total tests conducted	Percent of admissions that were tested	Number of positive tests	Percent of tests that were positive	Number who tested positive	Percent who tested positive
U.S. total[4]..	734,500	549,100	-25.2	215,360	9.0	24,550	11.4	10,850	4.7
50 largest local jail jurisdictions............................									
Estimated[4]..	180,700	134,200	-25.7	88,900	18.7	12,670	14.3	4,570	6.7
Reported...	173,966	125,949	NC	77,087	:	11,471		4,277	:
Los Angeles County, CA	17,385	12,045	-30.7	13,197	57.8	2,640	20.0	292	6.3
Harris County, TX..	8,883	8,517	-4.1	4,401	22.4	1,120	25.4	366	6.9
Maricopa County, AZ	7,873	4,501	-42.8	2,837	13.3	804	28.3	131	5.5
New York City, NY.....................................	7,341	3,927	-46.5	NR	NR	NR	NR	1,432	14.7
San Diego County, CA	5,959	3,650	-38.7	1,681	9.3	18	1.1	12	0.6
Cook County, IL...	5,666	4,617	-18.5	7,477	56.6	776	10.4	382	10.4
San Bernardino County, CA	5,623	4,553	-19.0	409	2.0	159	38.9	33	2.5
Orange County, CA	5,480	3,070	-44.0	2,113	18.4	403	19.1	30	2.0
Dallas County, TX.......................................	4,817	5,125	6.4	1,058	6.1	563	53.2	6	0.3
Shelby County, TN......................................	4,776	3,429	-28.2	1,504	17.5	280	18.6	153	12.3
Philadelphia City, PA	4,670	3,872	-17.1	4,540	76.6	229	5.0	199	10.1
Miami-Dade County, FL	4,302	3,271	-24.0	746	5.8	262	35.1	210	7.4
Tarrant County, TX.....................................	4,144	4,008	-3.3	565	3.8	215	38.1	67	7.0
Bexar County, TX..	3,963	3,620	-8.7	4,164	25.5	518	12.4	86	8.7
Riverside County, CA	3,796	3,140	-17.3	3,418	24.0	271	7.9	NR	NR
Broward County, FL	3,758	2,878	-23.4	294	3.5	56	19.0	13	0.9
Las Vegas, NV...	3,749	2,464	-34.3	5,227	26.1	93	1.8	36	2.9
Sacramento County, CA	3,546	2,515	-29.1	1,182	9.8	9	0.8	14	2.0
Hillsborough County, FL[5]..........................	3,302	NR	NR	NR	NR	NR	NR	NR	NR
Santa Clara County, CA	3,200	2,102	-34.3	2,036	33.5	40	2.0	16	1.6
Jacksonville City, FL...................................	3,199	2,791	-12.8	NR	NR	NR	NR	NR	NR
Fresno County, CA......................................	3,090	2,191	-29.1	1,948	26.6	598	30.7	42	7.1
Pinellas County, FL.....................................	3,019	2,144	-29.0	63	0.7	15	23.8	28	2.6
Fulton County, GA[5]....................................	2,945	NR	NR	NR	NR	NR	NR	NR	NR
Allegheny County, PA.................................	2,720	1,996	-26.6	205	6.0	46	22.4	17	2.1
Polk County, FL[5,6]......................................	NR	NR	NR	NR	NR	NR	NR	NR	NR
Gwinnett County, GA	2,603	1,872	-28.1	312	4.1	18	5.8	12	1.3
Orange County, FL......................................	2,530	2,149	-15.1	881	8.9	8	0.9	47	2.9
Alameda County, CA	2,458	1,733	-29.5	1,409	15.6	65	4.6	37	8.5
El Paso County, TX......................................	2,279	2,030	-10.9	215	2.6	79	36.7	13	2.0
Marion County, IN......................................	2,204	1,756	-20.3	755	10.8	177	23.4	11	1.4
Southwest Virginia Regional Jail Authority, VA..............	2,181	1,703	-21.9	0	0.0	0	NR	0	0.0
Cuyahoga County, OH.................................	2,179	1,161	-46.7	1,464	23.1	162	11.1	40	5.4
Davidson County, TN..................................	2,168	1,743	-19.6	981	12.8	218	22.2	40	5.1
Salt Lake County, UT..................................	2,153	1,179	-45.2	147	2.1	23	15.6	34	4.6
Franklin County, OH	2,124	1,673	-21.2	130	2.0	29	22.3	33	5.4
Travis County, TX.......................................	2,057	1,778	-13.6	340	3.9	9	2.6	29	2.8
Clayton County, GA....................................	2,055	1,998	-2.8	200	3.0	40	20.0	21	11.5
King County, WA[6]......................................	NR	1,312	NR	235	3.3	8	3.4	16	2.3
Palm Beach County, FL...............................	2,045	1,580	-22.7	207	2.6	58	28.0	36	4.1
Denver County, CO......................................	2,044	974	-52.3	4,692	65.9	648	13.8	58	8.2
Milwaukee County, WI................................	2,027	1,362	-32.8	1,761	22.0	139	7.9	15	2.6
Cobb County, GA[5]......................................	2,022	NR	NR	NR	NR	NR	NR	NR	NR
Essex County, NJ...	2,021	1,778	-12.0	2,422	48.2	499	20.6	102	15.0
El Paso County, CO......................................	2,020	1,316	-34.9	16	0.3	0	0.0	7	1.5
York County, PA..	2,013	1,214	-39.7	151	7.1	0	0.0	0	0.0
Dekalb County, GA[6]....................................	NR	1,217	NR	117	1.6	25	21.4	44	8.4
Kern County, CA..	1,892	1,769	-6.5	145	1.9	23	15.9	24	5.6
Chatham County, GA...................................	1,857	1,207	-35.0	370	11.0	4	1.1	4	1.0
Delaware County, PA...................................	1,828	1,019	-44.3	1,072	57.8	124	11.6	89	18.6

NOTE: Jail jurisdictions are listed in order of their confined inmate population at midyear 2019. Data were estimated for jail jurisdictions that did not respond in 2019. Most jail jurisdictions consist of a single facility, but some have multiple facilities, or multiple facility operators, called reporting units (RU). If at least one RU responded, the jail jurisdiction is counted as a responding jail jurisdiction and data were estimated for the non-responding RU in that jail jurisdiction. For 2020, data were estimated for one RU in Marion County, IN, Davidson County, TN, and Franklin County, OH, that did not report on the number of confined inmates at midyear 2020, the number of inmates tested for COVID-19 and positive tests, or the number of staff that tested positive for COVID-19. Data were estimated for one RU in Sacramento County, CA, that did not report on the number of staff that tested positive for COVID-19. For 2019, data were estimated for one RU in El Paso County, TX, Gwinnett County, GA, and Milwaukee County, WI, that did not report on the number of confined inmates at midyear 2019.
NC = Not calculated because the numerator and denominator are not based on the same jail jurisdictions.
NR = Not reported.
[1]Number of inmates confined on the last weekday in June.
[2]Inmates may be tested more than once and may account for multiple positive tests.
[3]Includes deputies, monitors, and other custody staff who spend more than 50% of their time with the incarcerated population, and administrators, clerical and maintenance staff, educational staff, professional and technical staff, and other unspecified staff who spend more than 50% of their time in the facility. Multiple positive results for the same employee were counted only once. The 2020 Annual Survey of Jails (ASJ) did not capture the number of staff who were tested for COVID-19, due to potential employee testing practices (i.e., tests conducted in jail versus employees who tested during their personal time).
[4]Data were adjusted for survey and item non-response.Imputed values were used to calculate aggregate statistics but are not displayed for individual jail jurisdictions in this table.
[5]Did not respond or provide complete data to the 2020 ASJ.
[6]Did not respond to the 2019 Census of Jails.

Table 4. COVID-19 Deaths Among Local Jail Inmates and Staff, March 1–June 30, 2020

(Number; percent.)

COVID-19 deaths in responding jails[2]	Inmates	Staff[1]
Total Deaths...	43	40
Confirmed[3]	33	32
Suspected[4]...	10	8
Deaths based on medical examiner's or coroner's evaluation.........	30	27
Inmate and staff population at midyear 2020 in jails that reported on COVID-19 deaths.....................................		
Number of inmates and staff	376,500	160,500
As percentage of inmate population and staff employed in all jails...	68.6	67.8

NOTE: Data are based on the inmate population confined on the last weekday of each month.
*Comparison month.
B = Difference with comparison month is significant at the 95% confidence level.

INDEX